OFFICIAL OVERSTREET® INDIAN ARROWHEADS IDENTIFICATION AND PRICE GUIDE

8TH EDITION

BY ROBERT M. OVERSTREET

SPECIAL CONTRIBUTORS TO THIS EDITION:
Richard Michael Gramly, PhD • Duncan Caldwell

SPECIAL ADVISORS TO THIS EDITION:
David Abbott • Mark Berreth • Tommy Beutell • John Byrd
Woodson Carter • Nick Cavallini • Jerry Chubbuck • John Cockrell
Gary Davis • Tom Davis • Gary Fogelman • Jacky Fuller • Richard
Michael Gramly, PhD • Ron L. Harris • Jim Hogue • Bill Jackson
Glen Kizzia • Glenn Leesman • Mike McCoy • Roy McKey
Randy McNeice • Bob McWilliams • Donald Meador
Roy Motley • Jack Myers • Lyle Nickel • Shawn Novack
John T. Pafford • Rodney Peck • Alan L. Phelps • Michael Redwine
Floyd Ritter • Dwain Rogers • Dick Savidge • Jerry Scott • Mike Speer
Ben E. Stermer • Art Tatum • Carlos Tatum • Jim Tatum, PhD
Jeb Taylor • Larry Troman • Greg Truesdell • Eric C. Wagner
Sam Williams • Warner Williams • Brian Wrage

HOUSE OF COLLECTIBLES **NEW YORK**
GEMSTONE PUBLISHING, INC.

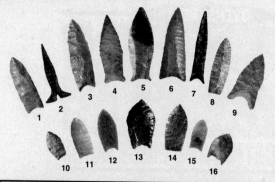

ABOUT THE FRONT COVER: The cover features 10,000 to 14,000 year old points from the Paleo period. These points were used as throwing spears and knives by early man in North America in hunting the big game & other animals such as Bison, Caribou, Mammoth and Mastodon. **Beginning at top left:** 1-Clovis from N.E OK; 2-Wheeler from Hardin Co. TN; 3-Black Rock Concave from Lake Co., OR; 4-Beaver Lake from Lauderdale Co., AL; 5-Cumberland from Jackson Co., AL; 6-Redstone from Hamilton Co., FL; 7-Wheeler from Mason Co., WVA; 8-Milnesand from W. TX; 9-Quad from Lauderdale Co., AL; 10-Milnesand from Otero Co., NM; 11-Midland from Andrews Co., TX; 12-Folsom from NM; 13-Crowfield from Cuyahoga Co., OH; 14-Milnesand from NW Mexico; 15-Folsom from CO; 16-Folsom from W. TX.

THE OFFICIAL OVERSTREET INDIAN ARROWHEADS IDENTIFICATION AND PRICE GUIDE. Copyright © 2003 by Gemstone Publishing, Inc. All rights reserved. No part of this book may be reproduced in any form or by any means, electronic or mechanical, including photocopying, recording, or by any information storage and retrieval system, without permission in writing from the publisher.

THE OFFICIAL OVERSTREET INDIAN ARROWHEADS IDENTIFICATION AND PRICE GUIDE is an original publication of Gemstone Publishing Inc. and House of Collectibles. Distributed by Random House Information Group, a division of Random House, Inc., New York, and simultaneously in Canada by Random House of Canada Limited, Toronto. This edition has never before appeared in book form.

HOUSE OF COLLECTIBLES
Random House Information Group
1745 Broadway
New York, NY 10019

www.houseofcollectibles.com

Overstreet is a registered trademark of Gemstone Publishing Inc.

House of Collectibles is a registered trademark and the H colophon is a trademark of Random House, Inc.

Published by arrangement with Gemstone Publishing Inc.

Printed in the United States of America

ISSN: 1073-8622

ISBN: 0-609-81053-7

10 9 8 7 6 5 4 3 2 1

Eighth Edition-September 2003

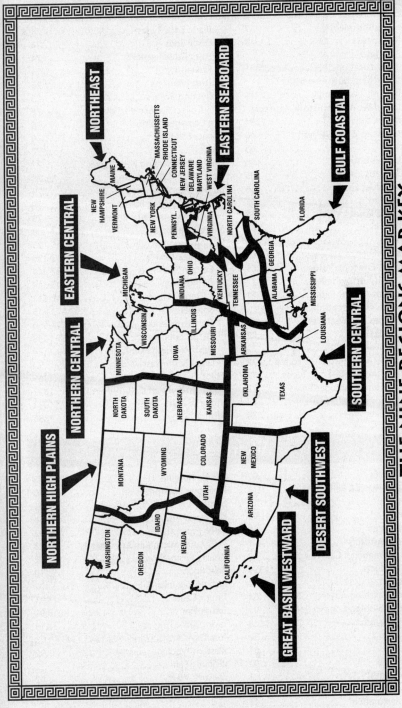

THE NINE REGIONS MAP KEY

NORTHEAST

EASTERN SEABOARD

GULF COASTAL

EASTERN CENTRAL

NORTHERN CENTRAL

SOUTHERN CENTRAL

NORTHERN HIGH PLAINS

DESERT SOUTHWEST

GREAT BASIN WESTWARD

NEW HAMPSHIRE
VERMONT
MAINE
MASSACHUSSETTS
RHODE ISLAND
CONNECTICUT
NEW JERSEY
DELAWARE
MARYLAND
WEST VIRGINIA
NEW YORK
PENNSYL.
VIRGINIA
NORTH CAROLINA
SOUTH CAROLINA
FLORIDA
GEORGIA
ALABAMA
MISSISSIPPI
LOUISIANA
ARKANSAS
TENNESSEE
KENTUCKY
INDIANA
OHIO
MICHIGAN
ILLINOIS
WISCONSIN
IOWA
MISSOURI
MINNESOTA
NORTH DAKOTA
SOUTH DAKOTA
NEBRASKA
KANSAS
OKLAHOMA
TEXAS
NEW MEXICO
COLORADO
WYOMING
MONTANA
UTAH
ARIZONA
IDAHO
NEVADA
WASHINGTON
OREGON
CALIFORNIA

This book is divided into nine regions and is set up starting with the Northeast and ending with the Great Basin Westward (east to west, right to left on this map). This is your key to the contents of this book, and versions of the map highlighting each individual section appear at the beginning of each regional section.

7

Table of Contents

Advertisers

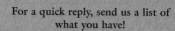

Acknowledgements

A very special thanks to Richard Michael Gramly, PhD for his well researched cover tie-end article specifically for this edition and for his contribution of photographs. Tremendous thanks is also given to my good friend Duncan Caldwell for his excellent article and price guide on "Collecting Old World Prehistoric Artifacts" and his contribution of many photographs as well.

My gratitude is also due the following people that so generously provided important data and or photographs used in this reference work: Leon Bain, Roger Barrett, Cedar Bear, Jerry Beckworth, Pete Bostrom, Bill & Tamara Breckinridge, Gilmer Brush, Larry Bumann, Tony Burnett, Nick Cavallini, Mark Corbitt, Joel Costanza, Darrin Dirksen, Alvin L. Downs, Terry M. Elliott, Daniel Fox, John Frump, Bill German, Brett & Amanda Gile, Dr. Michael Gramly, Jim Hall, Robert Hester, Rusty Holt, Raymond Jordan, Ben Kirkland, Toby Lowry, Mike Manis, Anthony Martinez, G. B. McNeice, Steve McDonald, Roy McKey, David Mega, Phil Mize, Patrick W. Mueller, Lyle Nickel, Tom Oryan, Alan L. Phelps, Allen Pierce, Dr. Jonathan R. Pilcher, MD, Eric Price, Michael Redwine, Jay & Teresa Rines, Jay Roach, Larry Roachelle, George Rodieck, Dwain Rogers, Jeff Schumacher, Tonisha Scott, Charles Smith, Art Tatum, Jim Tatum, Jeb Taylor, Harry B. Thomas, Eric C. Wagner, Steve Wallman, Daniel White and William C. Weathers, Sam Williams.

I am also in debt to Pete Bostrom and Dr. Michael Gramly for their valuable advice in keeping me up to date with changes in the archaeological arena.

This book also contains photos from the collections of Ray Acra, Tom Addis, Dick Agin, Ralph Allen, Chuck Andrew, Robert Beasley, Jerry Beaver, Jim Bergstrom, Tommy Beutell, Ken Bovat (photographer, N.Y.), John Byrd, Roland Callicutt, Phillip H. Cain, Jerry Chubbuck, Jim & Janice Cunningham, Leo Paul Davis, Kevin L. Dowdy, Tom Evans, Ted Filli, Gary Fogelman, Tom Fouts, Steven Fox, Jeff Galgoci, William German, Kenneth Hamilton, Scott Hanning, Jim Hill, Frank & Kathy Hindes, Bill Jackson, Mark L. Jewell, Glen Kizzia, Glenn Leesman, Mike Long, Skip Mabe, Edward Mason, Charles D. Meyer (deceased), Ron Miller, Sherri A. Monfee, Buzzy Parker, Floyd Ritter, George Roberts, Bob Roth, Arlene & Lori Rye, Richard Savidge, Charles Shewey, Mike Speer, Larry Allan Stanley, Scott Tickner, Brian K. Tilley, Kirk Trivalpiece, P.K. Veazey, R.S. Walker, Blake Warren, Warner Williams, Lyons D. Woody and John W. Young. We want to sincerely thank these people for making their collections available to us.

Gratitude is also due John Cockrell, Tom Davis, Gary Fogelman, Jacky Fuller, Don Meador, Roy Motley, Dwain Rogers and George E. Rodieck, Jr. who spent so much of their valuable time taking photographs for this edition; to Art Tatum and Alan Phelps for their many hours of expert help, photographs and points sent in for photographing.

Thanks is also given to Jim Hogue who spent countless hours photographing collections in his area for this edition as well as for his excellent research into previously published reports on types.

Very special credit is due my wife Caroline, who not only advises cover and layout designs, but is of tremendous help to me at the artifact shows handing out brochures and talking with collectors and dealers.

Thanks also to the staff of Gemstone Publishing--J. C. Vaughn (Executive Editor), Arnold T. Blumberg (Editor), Brenda Busick (Creative Director), Mark Huesman (Production Coordinator), and Jamie David (Administrative Assistant)--for their invaluable assistance in the production of this edition.

Our gratitude is given to all of our special advisors for their dedicated advice and input as well as help in typing, grading, and pricing; and to those who wish their names not to be listed and to all of advertisers in this edition.

PREDICTING THE LOCATION OF PALAEO-AMERICAN SITES IN NORTHERN NORTH AMERICA

Richard Michael Gramly, PhD
American Society for Amateur Archaeology

According to Webster's unabridged 20th century dictionary (1983: 1418), to predict means "to foretell; to prophesy; to prognosticate; to make known beforehand." And indeed, finding vestiges of Palaeo-Americans would appear to involve the personal magic of a seer or clairvoyant. The luck of being in the right place at the right time is another factor. Also, the assiduous collector who devotes a lot of time to searching plowed fields, lakeshores, and watercourses is more likely to encounter Palaeo sites – if there are any to be found in the region – than his less industrious brethren. Such is the proper reward for persistence!

Yet, it really should not be difficult to find Palaeo remains if we only knew the habits of these ancient folk and the behavior of animals who sustained them. In my opinion, the evidence is overwhelming that first Americans were preeminently hunters; the pursuit of red-blooded mammals, or the "chase," dictated their life and gave it meaning. No sound argument has ever been made for exclusive reliance upon plant foods by Palaeo-Americans; further, the evidence for fishing is weak (see Footnote 1) or non-existent. For cold, arctic-like regions inhabited by Palaeo-Americans it is doubtful if any band could have prospered solely upon a diet of plants and fish. Only meat and fat could have sustained inhabitants of a cold region, and only hides of caribou, deer, bear and fur-bearers could have kept them warm.

In deducing or predicting the location of Palaeo-American sites we must first agree what is meant by "Palaeo-American." The concept exists in opposition to "Neo-American," which implies recent or modern-day practices and behavior. In my opinion, ancient diet determines what cultural remains are Palaeo-American and what are not. Sometimes dietary evidence is difficult to obtain. Also, it is open to varying interpretation by different researchers.

Recognition of Palaeo-American Cultures through Diet

If there is evidence of actual predation (typically, a projectile point embedded in bone or lying where soft tissue must have been) of extinct or locally extirpated large mammals, then the presence of Palaeo-Americans can be inferred. Butchering marks or missing skeletal elements, such as ivory and long limb bones useful for manufacturing tools, are proof of human presence; however, in these cases the argument about the antiquity of the association is weaker or more circumstantial. Likewise, artifacts made from extinct or extirpated animal remains suggest, but do not necessarily prove, that Palaeo-Americans were on hand. Fossil mammoth ivory has been used throughout the centuries for carvings, and it still commands a high price per pound. It is not difficult to imagine that some bygone cultures of the New World scavenged body parts of long-dead animals for making artifacts.

Actual examples of ancient artifacts embedded in bone are among the rarest Palaeo-American vestiges. The Wacissa River in NW Florida has yielded the skull of a female *Bison antiquus* with a stone projectile point solidly lodged in its forehead. Radiocarbon dates of 10-11,000 years BP confirm the antiquity of this remarkable find (Webb *et al.* 1983). It is thought that the giant bison may have been ambushed at a waterhole. Unfortunately, the point fragment is too small to be culturally assignable.

Another example of an artifact that was found lodged within extinct animal bone – here, again, the object is too small to be culturally assignable – is the bone point from the Manis Mastodon site near Sequim, Washington (Gustafson *et al.* 1979). The point had penetrated two centimeters into the head of a rib. This injury had healed, and the animal was alive when it was lanced.

Much more common are skeletonized carcasses of extinct or extirpated animals with projectile points and butchering tools lying with them. Numerous examples from states and provinces extending

Hiscock site, Genesee County, NY. Springs still flow where this man-made pond now stands. An estimated 100 mastodons may have died here; many of their carcasses were scavenged by Palaeo-Americans. R.M. Gramly photo.

across the broad spectrum of Palaeo-American cultures can be offered. My favorites are: 1) John Cotter's original reports about the discovery of mammoth bones intimately associated with Clovis stone and bone tools at the Clovis type site near Blackwater Draw, New Mexico (see Footnote 2); 2) the often-reproduced, now classic, photograph of a Folsom point lying against an ancient *Bison* rib at the type site, Folsom, New Mexico; 3) The Olsen-Chubbuck site where an early form of *Bison* was driven into ambush (see Joe Ben Wheat's 1967 timeless article in *Scientific American* and also Wheat 1972); and 4) the Hiscock site in western New York State where Palaeo tools including recycled fluted (Clovis) projectile points have been unearthed intimately associated with mastodon bones (see Footnote 3).

Sites yielding stone projectiles with animal skeletons invariably have bones with butchering marks; yet, there are also presumed kill or scavenging sites yielding butchered remains but <u>no</u> stone tools or datable, assignable cultural remains. Good examples of the latter are the mastodon from Pleasant Lake, Michigan (Shipman *et al.* 1984) and the Adams Mastodon site, Harrison County, Kentucky (Walters 1988). At Adams, a disarticulated mastodon skeleton was interspersed with limestone slabs presumed to be stepping stones laid down for dry footing. A less convincing example of an extinct animal carcass that was handled by Palaeo-Americans is the Burning Tree mastodon, a well-preserved skeleton discovered in 1989 near Newark, Ohio. Here bones of one animal were found distributed among three clusters, perhaps representing meat caches; some of the bones had cut marks and gouges from being dragged about prior to caching (Fisher *et al.* 1994).

Hiscock site, Genesee County, NY. First fluted point discovered *in situ*, peat deposit resting upon boulder gravel. R.M. Gramly photo.

All doubt about the association of human beings and extinct or extirpated animals would be eliminated if a bone of a butchered animal were found that had been culturally modified at the actual butchering site! Such an artifact would be so rare that no archaeologist

Hiscock site, Genesee County, NY. This Clovis point of Pennsylvanian chert from Ohio/Indiana was used as a knife, perhaps by Palaeo-Americans who scavenged the site. R.M. Gramly photo.

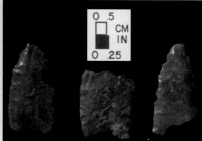

Hiscock site, Genesee County, NY. Three broken or reworked fluted points found in association with an Early Holocene fauna (mastodon, caribou, condor.) R.M. Gramly photo.

could ever hope to find it; however, such a discovery was indeed made at the Cooper site, North Canadian River, Oklahoma, in 1993 (Bement 1999). At this Folsom kill and butchering site, or "bonebed," a skull of *Bison antiquus* was unearthed with a lightning bolt painted in red ochre upon its forehead. In addition, many bison bones bore butchering marks, were piled about about in unnatural ways, and were intimately associated with flaked tools. The evidence that Palaeo-American diet included an extinct form of bison is indisputable at the Cooper site.

In many parts of North America, bones are seldom preserved in open-air sites; therefore, the diet of the site's ancient occupants is necessarily speculative. For these sites, if we take into account

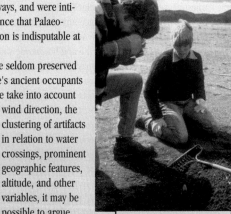

Moment of discovery of a complete fluted point at the Vail kill site, October, 1980. Photo by expedition member, J. Lothrop.

wind direction, the clustering of artifacts in relation to water crossings, prominent geographic features, altitude, and other variables, it may be possible to argue that extinct or extirpated animals were hunted and that a site is Palaeo-American in age.

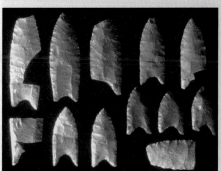

Vail Clovis site, NW Maine highlands. This aerial view at a time of low lake level shows the main habitation site along the ancient river and, on the opposite shore, the kill site that yielded 4 complete fluted points and 8 tip fragments. R.M. Gramly photo.

The 12 fluted points from the Vail kill site, Maine. Seven of the eight tip fragments have been conjoined to basal fragments discovered at the Vail encampment 600 feet away on the opposite shore of the river. R.M. Gramly photo.

An example of this line of reasoning is the Vail site of northwestern highland Maine (Gramly 1982, 1984, 1985). Although no bones whatsoever were unearthed at this repeatedly occupied site with its scores of fluted points (Clovis points) and thousands of other flaked tools, clusters of points at an associated site lying well upwind of the ancient habitations on the opposite side of an ancient river channel allow us to argue that caribou were taken. It was even possible to refit tip fragments of seven Clovis points found at the presumed kill site to bases discarded around the habitations!

In sum, recognizing the Palaeo-American presence through diet is sometimes an easy matter; however, in other more problematical cases it may require all the skills of a trained observer. We are hampered by our ignorance of the habits of some Palaeo-American prey, such as mastodons, mammoths, sloths, etc. Fortunately, bison (a species or race derived from *Bison antiquus*) and caribou survived into the modern era, affording us some idea of how their ancient cousins may have behaved.

Limits of Our Treatment

All the phases of the Fluted Point Tradition in northern North America, *i.e.* 1) Clovis, 2) Cumberland/ Barnes, and 3) Folsom/Crowfield, can be considered Palaeo-American based upon lines of evidence about diet. In radiocarbon years this archaeological tradition spans at least 700 years, from 11,100 until 10,400 years ago. In absolute or solar years, allowing for the correction to radiocarbon dates, the Fluted Point Tradition is 12-13,000 years old.

The enigmatic Goshen Complex, represented by the Mill Iron site in Montana (Frison 1996), is also Palaeo-American if we judge by the *Bison antiquus* and mammoth remains unearthed there. A series of radiocarbon dates from Mill Iron indicates that Plainview-like Goshen points are contemporary with the earliest phases of the Fluted Point Traditon.

Of lesser antiquity, but still Palaeo-American in focus, is the Lanceolate Point Tradition. Its earliest phase appears to be typified by the Agate Basin site on Wyoming's high plains (Frison and Stanford 1982). Projectile points from this kill and butchering site of *Bison antiquus* have excurvate bases, while forms later in the Tradition may all have had straight or incurvate bases. Considerable time must have elapsed during the evolution of the lanceolate point styles. Agate Basin points and derived forms are well known in northeastern North America, and they have been excavated from at least one strati-fied site east of the Mississippi River (the Olive Branch site – *cf.* Gramly 2002 for a discussion). At some time during the Lanceolate Point Tradition, between 9,900 and 10,600 radiocarbon years ago, the active floodplains of major rivers in the East began to be inhabited regularly. The traditional, peri-patetic lifestyle of Palaeo-Americans was set aside in favor of fishing, gathering of plant foods, and hunting a modern fauna. Across the High Plains, on the other hand, early forms of bison continued to be hunted in the ages-old manner. In northern North America too, caribou may still have been taken in regions pioneered by users of fluted points; however, here dietary evidence is slim and conjectural.

In the favored regions of the mid-continent's major waterways, a Neo-American, Archaic lifestyle seems to have appeared sometime during the 700-year prehistory of the Lanceolate Point Traditon. The mechanics of how this transition from old to new occurred have yet to be made known, and here is a fruitful field of research for future archaeologists.

It follows that the many archaeological cultures appearing on the heels of the Lanceolate Tradition are Neo-American. In most parts of northern North America, the bearers of the Dalton Tradition, for example, practiced an Archaic lifestyle. To be sure, hunting of relict populations of caribou, early bison and a few other species may have persisted in the Great Lakes, the Gaspé Peninsula, parts of the High Plains, peninsular Florida (as has been argued for users of Bolen notched projectile points) and elsewhere during the l0th millennium BP when the Dalton Tradition had its heyday. But the mammoth and mastodon had disappeared, and it becomes increasingly difficult to demonstrate adherence to the Palaeo-American diet.

If bearers of the Dalton Tradition (*ca.* 10,000-9200 BP), using a variety of projectile point styles (Beaver Lake, Meserve, Holland, Simpson) had Neo-American diets in most regions, then with few exceptions the cultures that came afterward were Neo-American. The most obvious exceptions are: 1) Eight to ten thousand year-old (radiocarbon) Cody Complex sites of the High Plains yielding *Bison antiquus* (*cf.* Frison and Todd 1987) – making Eden, Yuma, Scottsbluff, Firstview, etc, projectile points Palaeo-American forms; and 2) Equivalent-age cultural remains in the far Northeast, including the class of parallel-flaked Eastern Lanceolate points – these latter to be regarded as Palaeo-American point forms because caribou may have been the preferred quarry (see Footnote 4).

Along the waterways of middle North America during the era of the Cody Complex and Eastern Lanceolate cultures, we have the Hardin Tradition with its variety of elegant stemmed projectile points that may be divisible into several cultural phases representing hundreds of years. The Hardin Tradition is indubitably Neo-American and is equivalent to Archaic traditions of the Southeast (for example, Kirk). The centuries after Hardin, Cody and Eastern Lanceolates leading to the present day will not concern us here. Predicting the location of sites more recent than 8-9,000 years ago rightly belongs within the modern realm, when indeed, the present is the key to the past.

The Many Types of Palaeo-American Sites

In my opinion, evidence is inconclusive that northern North America harbors any cultural remains older than the Fluted Point Tradition. A possible exception is the Nenana Complex of Alaska, which has a flaked tool-kit not unlike the Clovis Phase of the Fluted Point Traditon. Fluted points appear to be lacking, however, and in their stead are very thin, triangular weapon tips resembling harpoon end-blades of arctic cultures of lesser antiquity. Radiocarbon dates for Nenana are just a little older (on the average) than the older dates for Clovis, which are in the neighborhood of 11,100-11,200 years BP.

Claims for artifacts of pre-Clovis age have been made at Meadowcroft Rockshelter in Pennsylvania, Cactus Hill in Virginia, Topper (Allendale) in South Carolina, among others. The evidence from these sites leads to questioning and is open to other interpretations; it is hardly "ironclad." Certainly, data are not on a par with the rich assemblages and associated features from bona-fide sites in the Old World. If pre-Clovis cultures exist in northern North America, then evidence that we can all accept will come to hand eventually. The search for more convincing data must continue; and hypotheses should not be accepted as facts.

In the meanwhile, I will confine my review of the types of Palaeo-American sites to the interval 11,200-8,500 years BP, that is to say, beginning with the Clovis Phase of the Fluted Point Tradition and ending with the Cody Complex and its eastern North America correlate – the Eastern Lanceolate group.

The outline below will direct our discussion and predictions of where Palaeo-American sites may be found:

I. Extractive Sites
        A. Quarries of flakable (knappable) stones
        B. Quarries of pigment
        C. Quarries of animal skeletons or "animal junkyards"
II. Caches or Deposits
        A. Of food/artifacts, within a structure
        B. Of artifacts, no evidence of a structure
        C. Of artifacts with human remains
III. Kill Sites
        A. Natural traps
        B. Water crossings
        C. Waterholes (springs, bogs, and the like)
IV. Habitation Sites
        A. In conjunction with extractive sites
        B. In conjunction with kill sites
        C. Within caves/rockshelters
        D. In the open, without (?) associations

I. Extractive Sites

Palaeo-Americans generated standardized weaponry and other tools, all of fine form and finish. Flaked tools were dynamic; that is to say, any implement could be transformed into another to satisfy the demands of the moment. An exhausted sidescraper might become a projectile point, a projectile point might serve as a chisel or wedge (*pièce esquillée*), a broken projectile could be altered into a drill, a sidescraper might be worked into an endscraper, an endscraper could be recycled into a graver – which, in turn, might be destined to end its useful life as a chisel bit! Resharpening flakes struck from broad, flat bifaces (themselves useful in butchering) might be converted into scrapers, cutters (utilized flakes), gravers, etc. A core biface itself, broken intentionally into pieces might become 2-3 fluted projectile points (see the insightful treatment of Anzick Clovis site bifaces by Wilke *et al.*, 1991).

Since stone tools must be transformable, Palaeo-Americans put a premium upon flawless flaking stone. They also preferred large-sized raw material for manufacturing big bifaces, and in regions devoid of superior toolstone, tools were carefully curated – nothing with a potential use being discarded. Knappers must have been on the alert for good stone wherever they traveled, always using the best a region had to offer. Being heirs to a million-year tradition of stone knapping, they knew what sediments and rock types were likely to contain superior raw material. Once they had identified such a source, they knew how to extract it under variable, perhaps extremely challenging, climatic conditions.

The various habits or external forms of raw material presented few problems to these canny petrologists. A layered, easily quarried and knapped chert was doubtless preferred, but Palaeo-American master knappers were also able to reduce chert (flint) locked within tough, spheroids or "cannonballs" (Gramly and Yahnig 1999). No modern knapper with a diamond saw could do it more easily or with greater economy!

It is possible that aesthetics played a part in the Palaeo-Americans' choice of raw materials, but I see no clear evidence of selecting specific colors or patterns of stone. On the contrary, we see a kaleidoscope of colors and patterns among flaked tools of a single implement cache, such as the one unearthed within an apple orchard in the Columbia River valley near East Wenatchee, Washington (Gramly 1993). On the face of it, any aphanitic stone of high purity was desirable to Palaeo-Americans, especially if it were available in large pieces.

Excavations within Feature 1 (the Richey Clovis Cache,) East Wenatchee Clovis site, Douglas Co., Washington, 1990. Two large Clovis points of colorful agate are shown *in situ* along with a sidescraper of yellow chalcedony (immediate foreground.) R.M. Gramly photo via Lithic Casting Lab (used by permission.)

A. Quarries of flakable stone

Palaeo-American quarries should be expected wherever excellent stone is found. Superficially, their workings are similar to the leavings of more recent groups, and cannot be segregated. To be certain of a Palaeo-American presence, a search for associated workshops must be made; workshops yield more clues about the age and cultural affiliation of ancient quarrymen. Flat, well-drained locations seem to have been preferred for workshops. Workshops may occur directly at the outcrop or as much as a kilometer away; easy access to water does not appear to have been a critical factor. Debris from the manufacture of fluted points and failed attempts at fluting should aid in recognition of early Palaeo-American stations; however, the presence of long flake-blades and cores capable of generating them should be taken as signs of Palaeo-American presence as well.

Workshops also will yield exhausted unifacial and bifacial tools purged from the Palaeo-American tool-kit when fresh replacements were made. Re-arming implies that considerable time may have been spent at some workshops; such places are perhaps better viewed as a short term habitation sites – see IV(A) below and also Footnote 5.

B. Quarries of pigment

Red ochre was employed to dress flaked tools during the Clovis Phase of the Fluted Point Tradition, as is shown by the much-discussed Anzick Cache, Wilsall, Montana (Lahren and Bonnichsen 1974). Human bones were directly associated with Clovis artifacts at this site. In all likelihood, painting burial objects with red ochre consigned them to a "realm of the dead" or "spirit world" situated to the West toward the setting sun. Such marking guarded against unknown persons who might violate burials, retrieving offerings to use in mundane tasks or everyday

Cal Sarver, discoverer of the Anzick Clovis Cache (and burial), Wilsall, Montana, points to cliff -- at the foot of which Clovis artifacts smeared with red ochre and human bones were uncovered by machinery. Photo courtesy of D. Simons

A complete fluted point made of agate, Anzick Clovis Cache, Wilsall, Montana. Note the residue of a red ochre dressing that escaped cleaning by the site's discoverers. Photo courtesy of D. Simons

Edge view of largest biface core ("platter-like biface"), Anzick Clovis Cache, Wilsall, Montana.. Photo courtesy of D. Simons

Basal half of a compositie (two-part) lance-head made of bone, Anzick Clovis Cache. Similar objects have been unearthed at the Blackwater Draw Clovis type site in New Mexico and elsewhere (Florida, Wyoming, etc.). Photo courtesy of D. Simons

work (see Footnote 6).

Red ochre crayons, grinding stones with traces of red pigment upon them, lumps of graphite that appear to have been rubbed for pigment, etc. have been noted at several Palaeo-American sites (see Gramly 2000: 42-43 for a discussion), but only during the Clovis Phase can we be certain that pigment was used in funerary rites.

The only quarry of pigment known to have been visited by Palaeo-Americans is the Sunrise Mine, Wyoming (Tankersley 2002: 136-149). Clovis points and other tools of similar antiquity have been discovered within pits (quarry pits?) at this locality. It is hard to believe that the Sunrise Mine is unique; similar occurrences should be sought. Occurrences of hematite and graphite should also be inspected for Palaeo-American vestiges.

C. Quarries of animal skeletons – the "junkyards" of the Palaeo-American era

While there is very good evidence from several geographic regions that Palaeo-Americans caused the death of some large proboscideans (mammoth and mastodon), most animals likely died because of sickness, old age, and starvation. In northern North America the time of greatest trial was likely late winter or earliest spring (March and April) as suggested by studies of tusk growth rings. The bodies of proboscideans and other megafauna such as *Bison antiquus* may have accumulated at their favorite haunts – waterholes and licks. Their carcasses could have been scavenged by many species as well as man. Meat might have been useful to dog and man alike, while the bones and tusks were the raw material of tools. Massive bone can be reduced much like stone, and keen-edged flake knives are derivable from bone "cores" (see Miller's report about Owl Cave, Idaho, for examples); while, by knocking off a few flakes, rude choppers can be manufactured from skeletal elements suitable for hefting (*cf.* Hannus 1989 for flaked mammoth bone from the Lange/Ferguson site, South Dakota). Tusk ivory was especially valuable for making long points with beveled hafting areas (slip-joints); over a hundred such artifacts have been discovered by divers in the rivers of Florida (see Footnote 7).

Core and flake of massive mammoth limb bone, Lange-Ferguson site, South Dakota. Photo used by permission of Lithic Casting Lab.

Among the scavenged carcasses of proboscideans and other animals that had lain down to die near them, one expects to find Palaeo-American butchering tools, or at least the marks of these tools. The Hiscock site, Genesee County, New York, has yielded bones representing at least a dozen mastodons plus contemporary caribou and condor (Laub *et al.* 1988); however, none of the fluted points found near (in some cases underneath) these bones appears to have been used to kill them! Unserviceable projectile points were recycled into knives, cutters and other instruments of help to persons scavenging carcasses.

The discoveries at Hiscock imply that anywhere extinct or extirpated animals died natural deaths and their carcasses accumulated in great number is a good place to discover Palaeo-American vestiges. For every stone artifact recovered there will be perhaps hundreds of bones and palaeo-botanical remains. Only a dedicated student of the past willing to shoulder the responsibility of conserving all animal remains should explore a skeleton "quarry" in search of artifacts. It is highly likely that some of the skeletal remains will have been modified by Palaeo-Americans on the spot as butchering tools; recognition of these impromptu tools is an art itself!

II. Caches or Deposits

Palaeo-American caches are an intriguing topic of study as they regularly occur in the "Clovis cultural system" (see Frison 1991: 331 for a perspective). They appear to be rare, however, after the end of the Fluted Point Tradition – yet see Butler and Fitzwater (1965) for a report of a possible cache of early Lanceolate point Tradition artifacts in Idaho. Predicting where a cache may be found seems to be more a matter of luck than informed deduction or guesswork. Nonetheless, before readers decline to search for Palaeo-American caches altogether, it is wise to review the many types and varieties.

A. Cache of food/artifacts within a structure

Human beings subsisting upon an animal diet are well aware that populations of prey rise and fall in response to predation, disease, changes in the animal's food supply, and other factors. Such are the uncertainties of hunting that when an opportunity to kill many animals is presented, it is wise to take advantage of it. Surplus food must be preserved against times of scarcity in well-constructed caches that exclude scavengers. In northern regions it is the bear, fox and especially the wolverine who are the boldest robbers of cached food supplies.

One of the best examples of a Palaeo-American cache structure made of massive stones is provided by the Adkins fluted point site in northern Maine (Gramly 1988). Very heavy rocks were slid into place around a shallow, oval pit and, in some unknown fashion, roofed over. A possible doorstone

Cache structure made of massive boulders surrounding a shallow, elliptical pit, Adkins fluted point (Clovis) site, Maine. Such a structure, when roofed, could have accommodated the meat of 10-15 caribou plus Palaeo-American artifacts. R.M. Gramly photo.

found by the chamber could have sealed in the (deboned?) carcasses of 11-15 caribou – enough to feed a family or hunting party for as many days.

Piles of mammoth bone at the Colby Clovis site in Wyoming's Bighorn Basin appear to be another type of food cache, one employing bones of the prey itself and perhaps hides in its construction (Frison and Todd 1986).

Fluted points and fluted point preform, broken during conversion into a projectile poiint, Adkins site, northern Maine. The cache structure lay only a few feet away from the habitation area that yielded these artifacts. R.M. Gramly photo.

Both the Adkins and Colby cache structures also might have stored personal property (clothing, tents, tools and implements) in addition to food. What these features actually contained, of course, will remain a matter for speculation. An oval pit (Feature 2) at the Vail fluted point site (Gramly 1982: 59-63) – an encampment located but a short distance away from Adkins – could have served as an in-ground storage chamber as well. How it was roofed over as a protection against scavengers remains a mystery. Worthy of note, a large, still useful, flaked tool (sidescraper) was unearthed lying against the pit wall where it may have been overlooked anciently. Many tools and much meat could have been stored within this capacious, flat-bottomed pit.

Another example of a pit that became a repository for Palaeo-American artifacts is the Richey Clovis Cache at the East Wenatchee site, central Washington state (Gramly 1990). An impressive toolkit useful in hunting and processing animals, some implements still harboring traces of blood belonging to ancient quarry, lay within a shallow, oval pit. I have argued that a sled placed within the pit may have served as a roof of a chamber. Nearby was a second, even larger, deeper pit. Two sizeable flaked arti-facts abandoned within it suggest that it too may have served as a store. These pits had been excavated on the perimeter of a Clovis habitation site of unknown extent.

The cache-pits or cache-piles of Adkins, Colby, Vail and East Wenatchee have counterparts at other fluted point habitation sites such as Debert in Nova Scotia (MacDonald 1968) and Gainey in Michigan (Simons *et al.* 1984). Later Palaeo-American manifestations, however, appear to lack such features, and some real behavioral differences are implied. Perhaps caches continued to be made during the decades after the Fluted Point Tradition, but storage was above-ground on platforms of poles and rocks?

B. Cache of artifacts, no evidence of a structure

Early Palaeo-American fluted point sites have also yielded tightly clustered groups of artifacts that were not secreted within commodious pits, but rather were placed in small hollows or just left upon the surface of the ground.

Examples of such caching are: 1) 39 flake tools discovered at the Udora Clovis site (see Footnote 8), southern Ontario Province (Storck and Tomenchuk 1990) and 2) 33 flake tools and rejected bifaces that had been left near an hearth at the Sugarloaf Clovis site, cen-tral Massachusetts (Gramly 1998). Falling within this catego-ry, as well, may be the group of 27 Clovis prismatic blade tools from a construction site in Navarro County, Texas (Collins 1999). Similar finds of prismatic

Group of 33 Clovis artifacts (scrapers, utilized flakes, point preform, and flut-ed points broken during fluting) that was buried in a small pit near a hearth, Sugarloaf site, S. Deerfield, central Massachusetts. R.M. Gramly photo.

blades and and/or cores across the mid-continent, all possibly of Palaeo-American (Clovis) origin, are reviewed by Collins.

The writer has investigated other finds of Palaeo-American flake tools showing evidence of use that once may have lain together in caches but apparently are not associated with habitations. These groups suffered disturbance by tractors and other heavy machinery; ultimately they became scattered by the plow. Two such groups, the first numbering about 200 pieces representing perhaps 100 whole imple-ments and the second much smaller (only 4 implements, although others may have been overlooked) came to light in central New York State (Whitney 1977: 9-10; Funk 1993: 174). The raw material of both caches was jasper (yellow-brown chert) that had been carried at least 200 km northward from southeastern Pennsylvania. The smaller cache contained a Paleo-American handaxe (Gramly 2000: 34), two sidescrapers, and the tip of a massive biface – likely a knife. Both caches came from opposite ends of a short valley connecting the Delaware and Susquehanna Rivers. There is little doubt in my mind that they were deposited by the same Palaeo-American (Clovis) group, who may have been pioneers of the region. The caches appear to be isolated and not associated with habitations.

Small cache of yellow-brown chert (jasper) tools, Fluted Point Tradition (likely Clovis Phase), found in Broome Co. (near Deposit), NY. R.M. Gramly photo.

Another type of implement cache belonging to the Fluted Point Tradition that is often found without pit or structural associations is the "biface group." Such groups consist primarily of 1) unfluted knives or celts, 2) completed fluted points (projectile and knives), and 3) preforms for fluted points. Some biface groups were deposited in the vicinity of ancient habitations; while, others are isolated occurrences. To a greater or lesser degree, these caches have all suffered disturbance, and their original positions within the earth (or on the surface) will forever remain in doubt.

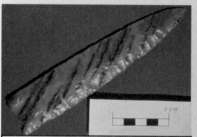

Large Clovis point of colorful chert, Simon cache, Big Camas Prairie, Idaho. 33 Palaeo-American flaked artifacts were unearthed by a road grader at this site. Photo courtesy of Lithic Casting Lab.

Five examples of "biface caches" command our attention. The first found (1963) is the Simon Cache on the Big Camas Prairie, south-central Idaho (Butler 1963). Thirty-three Clovis artifacts – 31 fluted and unfluted bifaces, an unworked spall, and a sidescraper – were exposed during road grading. None of the Simon artifacts, nor any belonging to the other four caches reviewed here, had been smeared with red ochre. Two sizes of completed fluted points were present (Woods and Titmus 1985).

Next to be discovered (1964), but only recently exhaustively reported (Morrow and Morrow 2002), is the

Colorful Clovis point discovered along with 12 others in 1968, Drake Clovis Cache, Colorado. Length = 3 1/2 inches. Lithic Casting Lab photo.

Excavations at the Lamb Clovis site, Genesee Co., western NY, 1986-90. This briefly occupied encampment is noteworthy for a cache of 18 Clovis points (projectiles and knives) and preforms. R.M. Gramly photo.

Selected fluted projectile points and knives and preforms found in cache at Lamb site, Genesee Co., NY. R.M. Gramly photo.

Chris Lamb, discoverer of Lamb site, holding base of large Clovis point from cache; the artifacts had been broken by farm machinery. R.M. Gramly photo.

Rummells-Maske Clovis Cache from southeastern Iowa. It consists of 20-22 fluted points (projectile tips and knives) plus a large sidescraper. Possibly a few more fluted points await discovery at the findspot, and it is likely that a habitation exists nearby. Fourteen years later, in 1968, Orville Drake and friends came upon a group of Clovis points between Sterling and Stoneham, eastern Colorado. A total of 13 points, many broken by farming machinery, a hammerstone and some small ivory fragments (perhaps representing a lancehead, billet or other implement) were retrieved

Findspot of the Trinity Cache of Cumberland points on the second terrace above the current floodplain of the Ohio River, northern Kentucky. This cluster of 11 points, badly disturbed by farm activity, is matched only by a find at the Thedford II site, Ontario Province. R. M. Gramly photo.

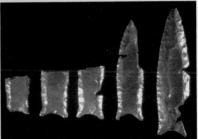

Five of 11 Cumberland fluted points in the Trinity Cache, Lewis Co., Kentucky. These five, badly broken by ploughing, are made of high-quality Indiana hornstone, which is found over 100 miles to the southwest. R. M. Gramly photo.

from the plow zone (Weinmeister 2002). No signs of Clovis habitations were noted at the Drake Cache findspot.

The fourth Clovis biface cache treated here was investigated in 1986-90 at the Lamb site, Genesee County, western New York State (Gramly 1999). Eighteen fluted knives and projectile points, fluted point preforms and two ovate knives were recovered in a small area that had suffered heavy disturbance by plowing. A few meters away were two habitation areas (locations of tents?) that yielded a wide array of Clovis unifacial and bifacial tools plus debitage.

Finally, we have the Trinity Cumberland Cache in Lewis County, northern Kentucky (Gramly *et al.* 1999 and 2000). Eleven fluted Cumberland points – one of which may be a knife and the other a drill – were found in isolation within a plowed and bull-dozed field. This find, a first within the borders of the United States, recalls a find of Cumberland/Barnes points and other artifacts recovered reported by Deller and Ellis (1992) from the Thedford II site, Ontario.

Cumberland/Barnes points, part of a cache found at the Thedford II site, Ontario Province. Photo courtesy of C. Ellis.

C. Cache of artifacts with human remains

Largest of the Cumberland points found in a cache on the edge of the Thedford II site, Ontario Province. Length is 4 1/8 inches (107 mm); raw meterial is Fossil Hill chert. R.M. Gramly photo.

Only one cache of artifacts, unquestionably belonging to the Fluted Point Tradition and closely associated with coeval human remains, has come to light in northern North America. This important find is the Anzick Clovis Cache at Wilsall, Montana (Taylor 1969; Lahren and Bonnichsen 1974; etc.). At the time of discovery the mass of fluted points, fluted point preforms, biface-cores, unifacial tools, and composite bone lance-tips – at least 110 artifacts, all told – was thickly coated with red ochre. Earnest attempts by the finders to scrub away the coating were not completely successful (Don Simons personal communication). The ochre dressing on the Anzick artifacts is much heavier than that reported for any other cached Clovis artifacts, and it is indubitably ceremonial.

Due to disturbance by machinery, the original attitudes of the Anzick artifacts and human remains will never be known. They may have lain together within a structure or perhaps just upon the ground surface; what is known is their position at the foot of a sheer rock face. Wyoming's Crook County Clovis Cache, unfortunately also impacted by heavy earth-moving equipment (Byrd 1997), lay against rimrock and within a deposit, perhaps natural, of red ochre (Tankersley 2000, 2002). No human bones were noted at this site; however, it would have been an easy matter to overlook them had they been as small-sized as the fragments found at Anzick.

A possible Clovis burial assemblage that is even more problematical is the "Fenn Cache." The 56 flaked tools, all purportedly from a single deposit discovered in a western state, bear traces of red ochre upon them (Frison and Bradley 1999). How thick this dressing once was cannot be known. Knowing nothing about its original context, the grouping must be accepted on faith. Since it was brought to the attention of researchers in the mid-1980s, many years before elaborate hoaxes involving "Palaeo-American" artifacts were perpetrated by notorious flintknappers, the Fenn Cache may be authentic.

A cache of the Fluted Point Tradition, also with a cloud of uncertainty hanging above it, is the Moosehorn fluted point discovery, northern Maine (Bonnichsen et al. 1983). Reputedly discovered underneath a small rock overhang not far from the St. Croix River, Calais, four fluted projectile points of the Cumberland/Barnes type, a broken biface and an unifacial "flake knife" are on record. Unfortunately, the whereabouts of only two of the fluted points are known. Neither had been dressed with red ochre.

A final assemblage of the Fluted Point Tradition to be discussed here is 4,500+ fragments derived from at least 200 flaked tools – nearly half of them bifaces and not fewer than 29 fluted projectile points – from the Crowfield site, near London, southern Ontario, (Deller and Ellis 1984). The cremat-

Two slightly damaged, completed Crowfield points from Feature 1, Crowfield type site. R.M. Gramly photo.

Feature 1 at the Crowfield site, southwestern Ontario Province. This ill-defined pit contained over 4,500 fragments of cremated, flaked tools, belonging to the Crowfield Phase, Fluted Point Tradition -- some are marked by wooden skewers. Photo courtesy of C. Ellis.

Some of the more than 4,500 cremated fragments representing over 200 whole flaked tools, found within Feature 1, Crowfield site. Crowfield is the concluding phase of the Palaeo-American Fluted Point Tradition. Photo courtesy of C. Ellis.

Selection of Crowfield points, all damaged by fire to some degree, from Feature 1, Crowfield site, Ontario. Photo courtesy of C. Ellis.

ed artifacts lay within a small, ill-defined pit beneath the surface of a plowed field; no contemporary habitation site is on record for the immediate vicinity. Even though human cremains were absent, and the Crowfield specimens had not been covered in red ochre, a mortuary association seems likely – why else the destruction of so much useful property? Cremation appears to have been carried out elsewhere, and perhaps some missing artifact fragments were left at the crematory.

The Folsom phase of the Fluted point Tradition as well as all Palaeo-American cultural phases following the Fluted point Tradition are virtually unrepresented by caches and associated human internments, however speculative. Rumors of such discoveries, however, abound. Apart from a very few witnessed finds, such as the Browns Valley, Minnesota, burial and its ripple-flaked points dating to the late 10th millennium BP (Anfinson 1997: 28-32), the scientific record is amazingly sparse. Rather than argue that inhumation with artifacts was seldom practiced during Folsom, Lanceolate Point, Cody, and Eastern Lanceolate times, it is more sensible to believe that such finds await us and have gone unrecognized.

Insofar as we may judge by the evidence above, Palaeo-American caches with human remains are not expectable near habitations. Their discovery is usually a matter of accident. In rocky regions, overhangs and the foot of sheer cliffs should be prospected; elsewhere, there is no formula to help in the search. Should a cache ever be deduced, it will he a vindication of archaeological science and a cause for wonder!

While the discovery of a Palaeo-American cache and burial seems to be a near-impossible challenge for me (and most readers?), caches without human remains are not so tall an order. Most will be found around Palaeo-American habitations and along well-traveled routes, where the distance to good sources of toolstone is great. Good places to cache implements will be at the entrance to interfluvial valleys. Trails, known to have been preferred by historic Indians, one expects, have ancient histories – perhaps even stretching back hundreds of generations to the most ancient Palaeo-American era (see Lantz 1984 for a discussion of the western Pennsylvania evidence).

III. Kill Sites

With no institutionalized buffers against want and populations that were too small to sustain craft specialization and trading, the attention of Palaeo-Americans was given over to food-getting and seeking toolstone for making tools used in food-getting. Places where animals and toolstone could be obtained dependably were foci of a band's annual round. Of course, there must have been many places where a chance encounters with animals resulted in a kill or where an isolated chunk of fine, knappable stone was discovered. Seldom would such events result in leavings for the archaeological record of use to future archaeologists.

Repeatedly visited kill sites or ones where a single kill of many animals was made command our attention.

A. Natural traps

George Frison in his landmark book, *Prehistoric Hunters of the High Plains* (1978), reviews the many types of natural traps used by bison hunters in the West during the Palaeo-America era and later. Among them are: 1) parabolic sand dunes as typified by the Casper site, Agate Basin/Lanceolate point Tradition (but see also the Haskett site and its associated dune field - Butler 1965), 2) arroyo traps - in use as early as the Folsom Phase of the Fluted Point Tradition (for an example see the Cooper bison hunting site described by Bement 1999), and 3) jumps like that of Bonfire Shelter, Val Verde County, Texas where an early form of bison was driven by Folsom and later Palaeo hunters along rimrock towards a concealed crevice and a lethal fall of 80-100 feet (Dibble and Lorrain 1968). Less spectacular jumps with a shorter fall may have been the norm, and the Hudson-Meng Alberta bison kill (dated around 10,000 year before present) is a good example (Agenbrod 1989).

To Frison's list above might be added ambushing places deep within gullies or canyons (ending in arroyos). The Domebo mammoth kill in Oklahoma immediately comes to mind (Leonhardy 1966). It would have been possible for Clovis hunters to have erected a barricade across the narrow Domebo branch of Tonkawa Creek, thereby penning the mammoth and affording spearmen a good target.

In the East, possible traps may have existed in the karstic limestone topography of the Aucilla River, western Florida where it is thought that mammoth, mastodon, and other extinct or extirpated species were waylaid by Clovis hunters (Dunbar *et al.* 1988). Animals descending into sinkholes to drink would have been easy to trap and kill. A near analogous situation may have existed at the foot of a cliff at the Kimmswick site. Here mastodon carcasses were excavated in close association with serviceable Clovis projectile points, debitage from tool resharpening, and a ground sloth hide – the latter perhaps serving as a platform above the mire (?) (Graham *et al.* 1981).

Other examples of entrapment, or at least, intercepting animals within ravines or gullies are hypothesized for the Sugarloaf Clovis site, central Massachusetts (Gramly 1998) and the Potts fluted point station, Oswego County, northcentral New York State (Gramly and Lothrop 1984). Caribou, it is felt, were the intended quarry.

B. Water crossings

The clearest example of how Palaeo-Americans sought an advantage by ambushing game at a stream crossing is furnished by the Vail site, northern Maine. There it is hypothesized (Gramly 1984) that caribou herds moving from the north and downwind traveled upon a flat plain of glacial outwash. Negotiating various water obstacles (ponds and springholes) and keeping a river channel on their left, the herds had to cross a short, steep-banked stream that was the outlet to a spring. As they emerged from the water, they were lanced. To date 12 fluted points have been discovered at this ambush; of the eight tip fragments found there it has been possible to restore seven to bases unearthed at the habitation site (Gramly 2003), downwind and on the opposite bank of the river (about 600 feet away).

The Vail kill site lies at a "kink" or S-bend of the Magalloway River valley (see Footnote 9). The slopes of the bordering hills are very steep here, and in some places there is sheer cliff or rock ledge. This difficult terrain forced caribou herds to travel the valley bottom and put them at the mercy of spear-wielding Clovis hunters.

Another site, which is regarded as an ambushing place where animals (bison or caribou) were taken at a river crossing, is Sinnock, in Manitoba (Buchner 1981). Points and other flaked tools belonging to the Lanceolate Tradition were retrieved from the surface of a flat, featureless bank of the Winnipeg River immediately north of Grand du Bonnet Falls. Bison approaching the river upwind and from the west sought to cross at narrows where hunters waited for them at the landings. At Sinnock it was possible to live at the very place where bison were slain, while in other places, as at the Vail site, camp was made well away from the killing ground.

Another type of water crossing that afforded good prospects to Palaeo-American hunters is a stream flowing into a lake. The strandlines of major lakes were natural highways for animals, and in southern Ontario the preferred quarry is thought to have been caribou (see Storck 1984 for a summary of discoveries made by researchers working in southern Ontario). Likewise, water crossings along ocean strandlines would seem excellent ambushing places for ancient fauna; however, discovery of such kill sites is no easy matter due to fluctuating sea levels of the post-Pleistocene.

Nonetheless, some coastal sections have remained stable in relation to the sea since the disappearance of glacial ice. These "hinge-points" where deep water is always close to shore and crustal rebound did not occur after the ice was "off-loaded" are good places to prospect for kill sites. One of the largest fluted point Palaeo-American (Clovis) sites known anywhere in North America is the Bull Brook site near Ipswich, eastern Massachusetts (Jordan 1960; Grimes 1979). It is located at such an "hinge-point". To date the kill site(s) that must have supported its many ancient occupants has not been discovered, but there are many water crossings that should be searched.

C. Waterholes (springs, bogs, and the like)

The earliest history of Palaeo-American studies involves the excavation of ponds and springs and recovery of extinct animal remains and associated artifacts. Sellards' 1952 book, *Early Man in America*, is an excellent starting point for exploring this topic in the West. His description of Evans' 1937 work at the Miami locality, Roberts County, Texas, where Clovis points and mammoth were found in a pond, 75 feet in diameter, is typical of early finds. The Blackwater Draw Clovis type site in New Mexico falls in this category as well, although it was a much more extensive topographic feature and had a stratified sequence of Palaeo-American utilization. The list of kills on the margin of ponds and bogs is very long, involving most Western states (*e.g.* The Lange-Ferguson site, South Dakota – Hannus 1989).

In the East, there are states with flat topography and small ponds scattered about the landscape that remind us of proven kill sites in the West. To be thorough, all such places should be inspected for remains. However, bone of extinct animals stands a poorer chance of survival in formerly forested regions, thus making kill sites harder to identify. Wherever Palaeo-American habitations are in close proximity to glacial kettle holes that would have provided rich fodder to browsing mastodon and mammoth, kill sites might be anticipated. Ponds and bogs in the neighborhood of the Paleo Crossing site (Brose 1994) and Nobles Pond site (Seeman *et al.* 1994) of northern Ohio are two occurrences that should be of interest to archaeologists.

Also in Ohio, we have the remarkable find of a Palaeo-American projectile point of the Hi-Lo or Transitional type still embedded within a beaver-chewed ash sapling (Gramly 1996). The point had been miscast, striking a tree on the edge of a pond or bog, and could not be withdrawn from the wood. What may have been the intended quarry of the ancient hunter is unknown. Perhaps it was giant beaver, caribou, or even mastodon? The area around Wapakoneta, northwestern Ohio, where the discovery was made is likely to have supported populations of all three species during the terminal Pleistocene/earliest Holocene.

As a general rule, ponds and springs seem to have been less critical to bison, caribou and other prey creatures of Palaeo-Americans than they were to proboscideans. Put another way, ponds and springs were the favored haunts of mammoth and mastodon; therefore, it was more likely that hunters should find and kill them there. Larger, shallower lakes in wide open landscapes (playas) seem to be a habitat preferred by bison, and not surprisingly kills were made there or on routes among lakes (*e.g.* the Stewart's Cattleguard Folsom site, Colorado (Jodry and Stanford 1992). Stewart's Cattleguard happens to be a rather high-altitude site (7600 feet above sea level).

Saline springs or "licks," on the other hand, appealed to the full spectrum of animals, and wherever they occur in North America a menagerie of Pleistocene/early Holocene species can be expected. A case in point is Big Bone Lick, northern Kentucky south of Cincinnati, Ohio. Visits of explorers and natural historians as early as the mid-18th century (Tankersley 2002) resulted in glowing reports about the abundance of ancient skeletons there. Only a few Palaeo-American artifacts, most being Clovis points, can be ascribed to palaeontological investigations at Big Bone. Recently, however, explorations by the American Society for Amateur Archaeology (Gramly and Vesper, no date) have revealed a Clovis habitation site on a hill above the saline springs. Similar discoveries might be expected near any lick or warm, mineral spring.

IV. Habitation Sites

One might argue that <u>every</u> Palaeo-American encampment exists in conjunction with either an extractive site or a kill site. In many cases they are one and the same, that is to say, hunters camped right where the kill was made or very near the actual outcrop where rock was extracted for toolmaking. In other cases, however, camp had to be established at considerable distance from where animals were waylaid or raw materials procured and processed. Disassociation may have resulted from a dearth of well-drained ground suitable for tenting (no small factor in a neo-arctic environment with perched watertables!) and an unfavorable wind direction, which might have carried the scent of waiting hunters to wary game.

Yet, there are Palaeo-American sites that appear unassociated with any critical natural resource (be it stone, plant, or animal). An archaeologist may be hard pressed for a reason why Palaeo-Americans selected a specific locale for living. Perhaps drawing upon previously cached stores of food enabled Palaeo-Americans to live for awhile in regions that could not nourish them or furnish important raw materials? Pioneers, new to a region and ignorant of its resources, and travelers on long journeys might have subsisted upon cached food and whatever unforseen bounty nature afforded them. Their camps would be predictably small and perhaps never reoccupied. Also, it can be anticipated, such camps would be a challenge to any archaeologist to detect and identify!

A. Habitation sites in conjunction with extractive sites

An example with which the writer is most familiar is the West Athens Hill quarry and workshop site in the Hudson River valley, south of Albany, New York. Excavations by the New York State Museum in 1966 (Ritchie and Funk 1973: 9-36) revealed Palaeo-

Archaeological excavations on the crest of West Athens Hill, Hudson River valley, New York State. This source of high-quality Normanskill chert was an active quarry (Figure straddles ancient quarry pit dug into shale) during the Clovis Phase of the Fluted Point Tradition. R.M. Gramly photo.

American quarry pits filled with rubble and artifacts and circular distributions of artifacts perhaps marking the outlines of tents or other shelters. These latter lay in the bottom of a gully just off the crest of West Athens Hill with its many quarry pits. These temporary structures, occupied while toolkits were being refitted, were well protected from wind gusts.

Habitation sites of similar character have been noted in central Ohio (Welling site – Prufer and Wright 1970), northern Maine (Munsungan Lake sites – Bonnichsen 1985), northern Virginia (the Flint Run Complex – Wilkison 1986), and western Kentucky (the Adams site – Sanders 1990), to name but a few. Most of the archaeologically investigated localities date to the Fluted Point Tradition, but examples dating to later phases of the Palaeo-American era can be offered, as well (*e.g.*, the Honey Run site in Ohio – Pi -Sunyer *et al.* 1975).

Ancient workshop of the Clovis Phase, Fluted Point Tradition concealed by heavy forest, Munsungan Lake lithic source, Piscataquis Co., northern Maine. Prospecting for Palaeo-American extractive sites may be arduous under current conditions. R.M. Gramly photo.

The sites of Flint Run, Virginia, serve as a model of the diversity one might observe where a valued raw material was extracted. Base camps featuring long-term occupation were even recognized at Flint Run – something that might be expected in a region where quality toolstone is concentrated in well-circumscribed districts but rare elsewhere (see Anderson and Sassaman 1996: 23-24 for a discussion of "lithic determinism" at Flint Run).

B. Habitation sites in conjunction with kill sites

For most Palaeo-American sites of the High Plains, habitation sites and kill sites are one in the same; that is to say, residence was right beside or very near to slain animals (proboscideans, bison, etc.). Such a "residential" strategy makes very good sense provided that killing is not performed over a protracted period. The strategy would be a poor one, however, if the principal quarry were small-sized and great numbers were needed, as in the case of caribou. A hunt for caribou might last weeks or even months. To camp right upon the killing ground would be to risk spooking the game.

On the High Plains one prospects for kill sites and invariably finds associated

Five fluted points found associated with a mammoth at the Naco kill and butchering site, Arizona. On the High Plains, Palaeo-American habitations were often located right beside kills. R.M. Gramly photo.

cultural remains by default, while in other regions where habitations were separated from kills, it is the habitation site (covering a larger area) that one finds first and the kill site afterward, if at all.

When no bones survive, as is often the case at Palaeo-American sites in the forested East, then kill sites may be impossible to locate. All that will remain are whole and

Possible shaft wrench of massive proboscidian bone, Murray Springs site, Arizona. Ancient Clovis hunters camped around a spring where they ambushed mammoth and bison coming to drink. Photo courtesy Lithic Casting Lab.

fragmentary projectile points and perhaps a few butchering tools (large bifaces, choppers, stone hammers, and the like). There must be excellent exposure of the ground surface for there to be even a "sporting chance" of making a discovery. Occasionally, hearths at an habitation site will yield scant, tantalizing remains of a species that were the Palaeo hunters' principal prey, although a kill site is nowhere to be found. A case in point is Fitting's description of the Holcombe site, Michigan, with its thousands of fluted points and other tools, flaked stone waste, and even hearths with calcined caribou bone (1975: 38-57). Somewhere along this beach of ancient Lake Algonquin (Lake Clinton) must be a place where caribou were intercepted by spear-wielding Holcombe hunters, but where?

At the Vail Clovis habitation site we located a kill site upwind and on the opposite shore of an ancient river channel (Gramly 1982). No bones survived at either the kill site or in a hearth at the habitations; yet it was possible to conjoin the tips of seven (7) fluted points at the kill site with matching bases abandoned at the tent loci. Hindsight tells us that because of the "kink" in the Magalloway River valley at this spot, we should have been searching all along for a kill site used by Palaeo-Americans. The truth is: The habitation site and its 13,000 artifacts were found first, then the kill site and its 12 tools long afterward!

C. Habitation sites within caves/rockshelters

Use of caves and rockshelters by Palaeo-Americans was infrequent, and even some of the evidence is equivocal – as, for example, the Palaeo projectile points (?) at Ventana Cave, Arizona (Haury 1943). The few bona-fide cases of Palaeo-American usage resulted in small assemblages of artifacts that represent brief visits. The much-described Palaeo-American Stratum IIa at the Meadowcroft Rockshelter, southwestern Pennsylvania, yielded fewer than 250 lithic items, most of them being debitage (Adovasio *et al.* 1987). Likewise, Charlie Lake Cave in British Columbia (Fladmark *et al.* 1988) with a component belonging to the Fluted Point Tradition only produced a few diagnostic artifacts. Such a dearth of cultural remains recalls the Dutchess Quarry Caves 1 and 8 (Funk *et al.* 1969; Funk and Steadman 1994). These two small caves in New York State's Hudson Lowland, however, did have bones of three extinct or extirpated species in addition to unquestionable Cumberland/Barnes points.

Dutchess Quarry Cave 8, Orange Co., NY. The basal zone of this small cave (just below where the figure is standing) yielded Cumberland/Barnes points and the bones of giant beaver, caribou and flat-headed peccary. Photo courtesy of D. Steadman and R.E. Funk.

Dutchess Quarry Cave 1, Orange Co., NY. The deepest cultural stratum produced caribou bones and a Cumberland/Barnes projectile point. R.E. Funk photo.

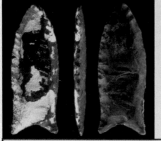

Cumberland/Barnes point discovered within deepest cultural zone of Dutchess Quarry Cave 1, New York State. Caribou bone associated with this point provided one of the earliest dates for a northern North American Palaeo-American site. Photo courtesy of Lithic Casting Lab.

The discredited Sandia Cave, New Mexico (Preston 1995), did yield Folsom points, and it is suggested that Palaeo-Americans came to Sandia Cave in order to quarry the thick deposits of limonite in its floor (Haynes and Agogino 1986). Actual Palaeo-American habitation remains (hearths, flaking "floors," etc.) were scarce.

A below-ground site that may have witnessed more intensive utilization by Palaeo-Americans is Sheriden cave, northwestern Ohio (Tankersley 2002). There several bone points of Upper Palaeolithic form and an Holcombe point belonging to the Fluted

Point Tradition have been unearthed intimately associated with extinct or extirpated species. Unfortunately the primary deposit that would have verified long-term residency, if it occurred at all, had been dug away by palaeontologists with no concern for the archaeological record.

The strongest case to be made for lengthy occupation of a cave or rockshelter by early Palaeo-Americans is the somewhat anomalous Bonfire Shelter, into which bison fell to their deaths. The butchering of bison at this "jump" took some time, and the excavators uncovered abundant traces of living by makers of Folsom points and later cultures (Dibble and Lorrain 1968). Apart from Bonfire Shelter, we do not observe intensive utilization of caves or fockshelters until the terminal Palaeo-American era when bearers of the Lanceolate Point Tradition (Windust Phase) moved about in the American Northwest. Then such living places were the norm, as evidenced by the many inhabited caves in lava formations (Rice 1972).

All in all, caves and rockshelters are poor places to discover Palaeo-American remains, although any finds that are made may prove interesting and datable both absolutely and by geo/faunal associations. Remembering the Anzick Cache in Montana, that lay at the foot of a cliff and less persuasive finds in similar locations (Crook County Cache and the Moosehorn, Maine find) there is always the possibility of an explorer chancing upon a spectacular cache of Palaeo-American artifacts underneath a rock overhang or deep with a cave. Such wishful thinking is hardly the stuff of everyday archaeological science, however.

D. Habitation sites in the open, without (?) associations

Palaeo-American sites in the open, discoveries have shown, are likely all linkable with extractive or kill sites nearby. The sole exceptions are 1) briefly occupied camps of travellers or fragmented bands subsisting upon caches and chance kills and 2) isolated artifact deposits representing burials or stores of implements for future use. A methodical search in the vicinity is sure to reveal a lithic source or killing ground if there has been no disruption by highways, quarrying or building construction. Also, being so old, many Palaeo-American sites have been lost to erosion – a fact that is often difficult to accept. Perhaps something deep within the human psyche makes us want to believe that landscapes trod upon by the first Americans have come down to us unscathed? In my experience it is seldom the case; the gulf between the present day and the most ancient past can be disturbingly profound.

Since clues in the modern landscape pinpointing kill and extractive sites – and by extension, associated Palaeo-American habitations – may have vanished, the wisest strategy for finding artifacts of the period is to cover <u>wide tracts of suitable ground</u>. In formerly glaciated North America "suitable" places to search are level stretches of warm, well-drained soils, which were created from glacial outwash and

the dune fields that developed upon it. Help in locating such promising places may be had from the Federal Aviation Administration's guidebook to airfields (see illustration). It is quite amazing how many airfields and Palaeo-American sites share a common outwash plain! Numerous examples can be offered, and I direct the skeptical reader to Spiess and Wilson's report (1987) about the Michaud fluted point (Clovis) site in southern Maine. The excavation was off the end of the Lewiston-Auburn airport runway. During this period a fatal airplane crash occurred, the debris being scattered about another (but still unexplored) Palaeo-American site a short distance away!

My advice to a would-be discover of Palaeo-American sites is to procure the FAA handbook and visit every airport within a specific district. I predict success within 1-3 days. It is highly likely that the new-found site will be a closed or single-component Palaeo-American encampment; sadly one may also learn that the encampment has been disturbed by airport con-

A useful publication for predicting the locations of Palaeo-American sites in formerly glaciated regions of northern North America.

33

struction.

A hint to all persons doing "blind searches" for Palaeo-American sites in the unglaciated areas eastern North America, is to inspect margins of all swamps and shallow lakes. A swath of ground extending backward several hundred meters from the immediate shore should be searched with no areas left unchecked. Animal trails bordered these locally important geographic features, and Palaeo-Americans surely made kills somewhere along them. A model for discovery is found in Joseph McAvoy's work on the southern interior Virginia coastal plain (1992). What might have been the quarry of Palaeo-Americans in coastal Virginia is conjectural, but it could have been proboscideans as well as lesser species, such as deer.

West of the Mississippi the problem of erasure of Palaeo-American kill and extractive sites by development is much less severe; however, in many areas associated large habitation sites, more typical of the East, are rarer. Of course, all badlands criss-crossed with ravines and arroyos must be scoured for kill sites under the assumption (sometimes erroneous) that places good for intercepting animals today were also good places in ancient times. A better strategy perhaps is to scout every playa or dip in the landscape that once may have held water. It has long been known that pluvial lake terraces are good places to discover Palaeo-American artifacts, and countless sites could be offered as examples (see Moratto 1984 for a review of the California evidence, which is widely applicable). What is less well understood, however, is the great depth of soil that may have accumulated around playas and lakes. One will have to test well below surface in some cases to discover Palaeo-American remains (read Agogino 1961 for examples of deeply buried sites near Albuquerque).

In sum

Although I do not enjoy a wide-ranging, labor-intensive, inductive or "shotgun" approach to discovering vestiges of Palaeo-Americans, I recognize that some workers enjoy being out of doors. The peace of mind that accompanies a protracted, undirected search is special. Still, in my opinion, deducing or predicting archaeological occurrences is the highest attainment to which a prehistorian may aspire. This method and the authoring of site reports are the true artforms of scientific archaeology. I do not turn aside from them willingly.

A deductive way of thinking becomes irresistibly alluring when there has been some history of success; (you believe) you begin to think as Palaeo-Americans did. Tracing the footsteps of these early Americans and your image of their thoughts are perhaps as close as anyone will ever be to those pioneers of a New World.

It is comforting to know that there are still untried opportunities to trace Palaeo-Americans and still good prospects of discovering sites, which reveal their manner of thinking. Do not believe the gloomy assessments of pundits who feel that every stone has been turned over in northern North America and that no surprises await the assiduous searcher! Every student of the past worth his salt knows that 1) the archaeological record is inexhaustible and 2) it was never complete to begin with. One has to make do with what has been inherited; however, every researcher knows of one or two highly promising places yet to be explored. There, one predicts, important finds stand to be made one day.

One of my favorite places for potential discovery is the southeastern corner of Lake Ontario in central New York State. Drawing upon everything I have been taught and being well aware of excellent fieldwork of my Canadian colleagues, B. Deller, C. Ellis, L. Jackson (1998) and P. Storck, at analogous locations along the shores of Lakes Huron and Ontario, I anticipate that the sandy plains bordering the many streams entering the lake there will yield sites. Who will scrutinize this under-explored part of New York State? I predict it harbors abundant traces of caribou-hunting, fluted point-using Palaeo-Americans.

Anticipating that a prediction might come true is almost as sweet as investigating the discovery itself.

FOOTNOTES

Footnote 1: The Shawnee Minisink site in Monroe Co., Pa. yielded some fish remains in a screened sample from a hearth within a fluted-point Palaeo-American horizon dated at *ca.* 10,900 years BP radiocarbon. See McNett (11985) and Kline (1996) for descriptions.

Footnote 2: For a review of the complex history of archaeological research at the Clovis type locality the reader is referred to James J. Hester's monograph, *Blackwater Locality No. 1: A Stratified Early man Site in Eastern New Mexico,* 1972, Fort Burgwin Research Center, Southern Methodist University. A more recent review of discoveries at Blackwater Draw is Anthony T. Boldurian and John L. Cotter's 1999 work Clovis Revisited, *University Museum Monograph* 103. University of Pennsylvania.

Footnote 3: Archaeological and palaeontological research at the large Hiscock site, near Batavia, western New York State began in the 1980s and is ongoing. The reader is referred to a group of essays about the site and its surroundings, which was edited by R. S. Laub, N. G. Miller, and D. W. Steadman (1988) and entitled, Late Pleistocene and Early Holocene Paleoecology and Archeology of the Eastern Great Lakes Region. It is *Bulletin of the Buffalo Society of Natural Sciences* 33. Buffalo, New York.

Dr. Richard S. Laub continues to publish about artifacts from the site. Most of his writings may be found in issues of *Current Research in the Pleistocene,* which is produced by the Center for the Study of the First Americans at Texas A and M University, College Station, Texas.

Footnote 4: Although there is an extensive literature about Eastern Lanceolate sites, radiocarbon dates are few or equivocal; dietary evidence is, likewise lacking or circumstantial. The reader is referred to 1) a well-written review by Richard Doyle *et al.* entitled "Late Paleo-Indian remains from Maine and their correlations in Northeastern prehistory" appearing in *Archaeology of Eastern North America* 13 (1985); 2) a recent (2000) study about the single-component Varney Farm site by James B. Petersen *et al.* within the same journal; and 3) an impressive volume devoted to Eastern Lanceolate point sites in Gaspé, Quebec Province by Jose Benmouyal (1987) entitled *Des Paleoindiens aux Iroquoiens en Gaspesie* – Dossier 63 in a series produced by Ministry of Cultural Affairs, Quebec, Canada.

Footnote 5: One of the most thorough, long-term studies of a Palaeo-American quarry and workshop complex is William Gardner and his students' work at Flint Run in Virginia's Shenandoah Valley. Reports are scattered in scholarly journals and many are out of print; data are also to be found in several PhD dissertations. The reader is directed to Gardner's 1974 summary report – The Flint Run Paleo-Indian Complex: A Preliminary Report of the 1971-73 Seasons, *Catholic University Archeology Laboratory, Occasional Publication* No. 1, Washington, D.C. Perspectives on discoveries at Flint Run may be found in Wittkofski and Reinhart (1989), Hranicky and McCary (1995), and Anderson and Sassaman (1996: 23-4).

Footnote 6: The reader is directed to David Sanger's excellent study of a "Red Paint" or Moorehead Complex cemetery, *ca.* 4-4,500 years BP, at the Cow Point site in eastern New Brunswick. In a departure from conventional thinking that usually viewed red ochre in burials as emblematic of blood and, therefore, life after death, Sanger argued for red ochre being the color of death and the spirit world.

Footnote 7: Since the 1950s, divers in Florida rivers have recovered scores of fragmentary and rarer complete artifacts made from proboscidean ivory. These slender objects are composite points made from straightened tusk segments, and when bound together, made lethal lanceheads useful against mammoths and mastodons themselves. Discovery of a lancehead juxtaposed with mammoth bones at the Clovis type site, Blackwater Draw (Cotter 1937; see also Jenks 1941) certainly suggests that it was an instrument of death; the point fragment embedded in a rib of the Manis mastodon at Sequim, Washington, may represent another lancehead (Gustafson *et al.* 1979).

Florida finds made in the last few decades are reported in back issue of the *Aucilla River Times* and the *Half Mile Rise Times* – both newsletters emanating from the University of Florida, Gainesville. One should also consult writings by James Dunbar and colleagues (1989, 1996) for artifact inventories and over-views.

Footnote 8: Among Canadian scholars and some researchers in the United States, the Clovis Phase of the Fluted Point Tradition is termed the "Gainey Phase". This concept of Palaeo-American studies stems from discoveries since 1980 at the Gainey site – an extensive encampment located in eastern Michigan. The Gainey assemblage has yet to be described exhaustively in the archaeological literature, nor has a full site report been published. For these reasons, and giving precedence to the time-honored type assemblage from the Blackwater Draw, New Mexico, type site, the writer eschews use of the term, "Gainey" in northern North America. Further, I consider all "Gainey points" to be so similar to points from the Clovis type site that continued use of the term is inadvisable.

An analogous typological problem is found with Cumberland points and their northern counter-parts – "Barnes points." Use of the term "Barnes" got its start in Ontario and Michigan (see Deller and Ellis (1992) for a review of the concept and W. B. Roosa's early work). The purported differences between these two point types has never been made clear, in my opinion. Adding confusion to the problem is the fact that the Cumberland River region itself has yet to furnish a type site! The term "Cumberland" is so well entrenched within the archaeological literature, however, that Barnes will never become a substitute for it. Recognizing this impasse, Robert E. Funk and I (1990) began to employ the term "Cumberland/Barnes". One hopes that this compromise will rise above provincial out-looks, forged in fires of regional pride?

Footnote 9: "Kinks" or S-bends in river valleys are fruitful places to search for Palaeo-American kill sites and should be carefully reconnoitred. In the Magalloway River valley, north of the Vail site, another such kink, termed "Wheeler Dam," was explored by the writer in the mid- 1980s. Two single-component Clovis habitation sites were discovered but to date no kill site. These sites, which are named Upper Wheeler Dam and Lower Wheeler Dam, await publication. Another northeastern North American fluted point (Clovis) habitation site that is located at a valley narrows or "kink" is Whipple, near Swanzey, southern New Hampshire (Curran 1987). The kill site that surely exists nearby awaits discovery.

References Cited

Adovasio, J. M., A. T. Boldurian and R. C. Carlisle
    1987   Who are those guys?: Early populations in eastern North America. Paper prepared for October 30-November 1 symposium, Baylor University, Texas. 22 pp.
Agenbrod, Larry D.
    1989   The Hudson-Meng Site: An Alberta Bison Kill in the Nebraska High Plains. Privately printed.
Agogino, George
    1961   A survey of Paleo-Indian sites along the middle Rio Grande drainage. Plains Anthropologist 6(11): 7-12.
Anderson, David G. and Kenneth E. Sassaman
    1996   Modeling Paleoindian and Early Archaic settlement in the Southeast: A historical perspective. Pp. 16-28 in Anderson and Sassaman (eds.) The Paleoindian and Early Achaic Southeast. University of Alabama Press. Tuscaloosa.
Anfinson, Scott F.
    1997   Southwestern Minnesota Archaeology. Minnesota Prehistoric Archaeology Series 14. Minnesota Historical Society. St. Paul.
Bement, Leland C.
    1999   Bison Hunting at the Cooper Site. University of Oklahoma Press. Norman.
Bonnichsen, Robson
    1985   Anatomy of an excavation. Explorations 1(2): 22-28. University of Maine, Orono.
Bonnichsen, Robson, Bruce Bourque, and David E. Young
    1983   The Moosehorn fluted point discovery, northern Maine. Archaeology of Eastern North America 11: 36-47.
Brose, David S.
    1994   Archaeological investigations at the Paleo Crossing site, a Paleoindian occupation in Medina County, Ohio. Pp. 61-76 in William S. Dancey (ed.) The First Discovery of America. Ohio Archaeological Council, Inc. Columbus.
Butler, B. Robert
    1963   An Early Man site at Big Camas Prairie, southcentral Idaho. Tebiwa 6(1): 22-33.
    1965   A report on investigations of an Early man site near Lake Channel, southern Idaho. Tebiwa 8(2): 1-20.
Butler, B. Robert and J. R. Fitzwater
    1965   A further note on the Clovis site at Big Camas Prairie, south-central Idaho. Tebiwa 8(1): 38-40.
Byrd, John
    1997   The Crook County Cache: A probable Clovis mortuary site in Wyoming. The Amateur Archaeologist 4(1): 19-23.
Collins, Michael B.
    1999   Clovis Blade Technology. University of Texas Press. Austin.
Cotter, John Lambert
    1937   The occurrence of flints and extinct animals in fluvial deposits near Clovis, New Mexico. Part IV: Report on the excavation at the gravel pit, 1936. Proceedings of the Academy of Natural Sciences of Philadelphia, Vol. LXXXXIX: 1-16.
Curran, Mary Lou

1987   The Spatial Organization of Paleoindian Populations in the Late Pleistocene of the Northeast. PhD dissertation. Department of Anthropology, University of Mass. Amherst.

Deller, D. Brian and Christoper J. Ellis
1984   Crowfield: A preliminary report on a probable Paleo-Indian cremation in southwestern Ontario. Archaeology of Eastern North America 12: 41-71.
1992   Thedford II: A Paleo-Indian Site in the Ausable River Watershed of Southwestern Ontario. Memoirs, Museum of Anthropology, University of Michigan 24. Ann Arbor.

Dibble, David S. and Dessamae Lorrain
1968   Bonfire Shelter: A Stratified Bison Kill Site, Val Verde County, TX. Texas Memorial Museum Miscellaneous Paper 1. University of Texas. Austin.

Dunbar, James S., Michael K. Faught, and S. David Webb
1988   Page/Ladson (8Je591): An underwater Paleo-Indian site in northwestern Florida. The Florida Anthropologist 41(3): 442-452.

Dunbar, James S., S. David Webb, and Dan Cring
1989   Culturally and naturally modified bones from a Paleoindian site in the Aucilla River, north Florida. Pp. 473-497 in Robson Bonnichsen and Marcella Sorg (eds.) Bone Modification. Center for the Study of the First Americans. Orono, Maine.

Dunbar, James S. and S. David Webb
1996   Bone and ivory tools from submerged Paleoindian sites in Florida. Pp. 331-353 in David G. Anderson and Kenneth E. Sassaman (eds.) The Paleoindian and Early Archaic Southeast. University of Alabama Press. Tuscaloosa.

Fisher, Daniel C., Bradley T. Lepper, and Paul E. Hooge
1994   Evidence for butchery of the Burning Tree mastodon. Pp. 43-60 in The First Discovery of America: Archaeological Evidence of the Early Inhabitants of the Ohio Area. The Ohio Archaeological Council. Columbus.

Fitting, James E.
1975   The Archaeology of Michigan. Cranbrook Institute of Science. Bloomfield Hills, Michigan.

Fladmark, Knut R., Jonathan C. Driver, and Diana Alexander
1988   The Paleoindian component at Charlie Lake Cave (HbRf39), British Columbia. American Antiquity 53(2): 371-384.

Frison, George C.
1978   Prehistoric Hunters of the High Plains. Academic Press. New York.
1991   The Clovis cultural complex: New data from caches of flaked stone and worked bone artifacts. Pp. 321-333 in Economies Among Prehistoric Hunter-Gatherers. University of Kansas Publications in Anthropology 19. Lawrence.
1996   (ed.) The Mill Iron Site. University of New Mexico Press.

Frison, George C. and Bruce Bradley
1999   The Fenn Cache: Clovis Weapons and Tools. One Horse Land and Cattle Company. Santa Fe, New Mexico.

Frison, George C. and Dennis J. Stanford
1982   The Agate Basin Site. Academic Press. New York.

Frison, George C. and Lawrence C. Todd
1986   The Colby Mammoth Site: Taphonomy and Archaeology of a Clovis kill in Northern Wyoming. University of New Mexico Pres. Albuquerque.
1987   (eds.) The Horner Site: The Type Site of the Cody Cultural Complex. Academic Press.

Funk, Robert E.
1993   Archaeological Investigations in the Upper Susquehanna Valley, New York State. Persimmon Press. Buffalo, New York.

Funk, R. E. and D. W. Steadman
1994   Archaeological and Paleoenvironmental Investigations in the Dutchess Quarry Caves.Persimmon Press. Buffalo, New York.

Funk, Robert E., George R. Walters, and William F. Ehlers, Jr.
1969   The archeology of Dutchess Quarry cave, Orange County, New York. Pennsylvania Archaeologist 39(1-4): 7-22.

Graham, Russell W., C. Vance Haynes, Donald Lee Johnson and Marvin Kay
1981   Kimmswick: A Clovis-mastodon association in eastern Missouri. Science 213: 1115-1117.

Gramly, Richard Michael
1982   The Vail Site: A Palaeo-Indian Encampment in Maine. Bulletin of the Buffalo Society of Natural Sciences 30. Buffalo, New York.
1984   Kill sites, killing ground and fluted points at the Vail site. Archaeology of Eastern North America 12: 110-121.
1985   Recherches archéologiques au site Paléoindien de Vail, dans le nord-ouest du Maine, 1980-1983. Recherches Amérindiennes au Québec 15(1-2): 57-118. University of Montreal.
1988   The Adkins Site: A Palaeo-Indian Habitation and Associated Stone Structure. Persimmon Press. Buffalo, New York.
1993   The Richey Clovis Cache: Earliest Americans Along the Columbia River. Persimmon Press. Buffalo, New York.
1996   An embedded projectile point found near Wapakoneta, Auglaize County, Ohio. Ohio Archaeologist 46(3): 5-9.
1998   The Sugarloaf Site: Palaeo-Americans on the Connecticut River. Persimmon Press. North Andover, Massachusetts.
1999   The Lamb Site: A Pioneering Clovis Encampment. Persimmon Press. North Andover, Massachusetts.
2000   Guide to the Palaeo-American Artifacts of North America (third edition). Persimmon Press. North Andover, Massachusetts.
2002   Olive Branch: A Very Early Archaic Site on the Mississippi River. American Society for Amateur Archaeology. North Andover, Massachusetts.
2003   More conjoined fluted projectile points from the Vail site, Maine. Current Research in the Pleistocene 20. In press.

Gramly, Richard Michael and Jonathan Lothrop
1984   Archaeological investigations of the Potts site, Oswego County, 1982 and 1983. Archaeology of Eastern North America 12: 122-158.

Gramly, Richard Michael, Dennis Vesper and Dave McCall
1999   A Cumberland point site near Trinity, Lewis County, northern Kentucky. The Amateur Archaeologist 6(1): 63-80.
2000   A Cumberland point site near Trinity, Lewis County, northern Kentucky. Current Research in the Pleistocene 17: 34-36.

Gramly, Richard Michael and Carl Yahnig
1991   The Adams Clovis site and the Little River, Christian County, Kentucky Workshop Complex. The Amateur Archaeologist 6(1): 39-62.

Grimes, John
1979   A new look at Bull Brook. Anthropology 3(1 and 2): 109-130.

Gustafson, Carl E., Delbert Gilbow, and Richard D. Daugherty
1979   The Manis Mastodon site: Early man on the Olympic Peninsula. Canadian Journal of Archaeology 3: 157-164.

Hannus, L. Adrien
1989   Flaked mammoth bone from the Lange/Ferguson site, White River Badlands area, South Dakota. Pp. 395-412 in Robson Bonnichsen and Marcella H. Sorg (eds.) Bone Modification. Center for the Study of the First Americans. Orono, Maine.

Haury, Emil W.
1943   The stratigraphy of Ventana Cave, Arizona. American Antiquity VIII(3): 218-223. Haynes, C. Vance, Jr. and George A. Agogino
1986   Geochronology of Sandia Cave. Smithsonian Contributions to Anthropology 32. Washington.

Hranicky, William Jack and Ben C. McCary
1995   Clovis Technology in Virginia. Archeological Society of Virginia Special Publication 31. Courtland, Virginia.

Jackson, Lawrence J.
1998   The Sandy Ridge and Halstead Paleo-Indian Sites. Memoirs, Museum of Anthropology, University of Michigan 32. Ann Arbor.

Jenks, Albert Ernest
1941   Beveled artifacts in Florida of the same type as artifacts found near Clovis, New Mexico. American Antiquity VI: 314-319.

Jodry, Margaret A. and Dennis J. Stanford
1992   Stewart's Cattle Guard site: An analysis of Bison remains in a Folsom kill-butchery campsite. Pp. 101-168 in Dennis J. Stanford and Jane S. Day (eds.), Ice Age Hunters of the Rockies. University Press of Colorado. Denver.

Jordan, Douglas Frederick

1960   The Bull Brook Site in Relation to "Fluted Point" Manifestations in Eastern North America. PhD dissertation. Department of Anthropology, Harvard University.

Kline, Donald E.
1996   Discovery of Shawnee Minisink: A Paleo-Indian site in the Delaware valley. The Amateur Archaeologist 3(1): 81-93.

Lahren, Larry and Robson Bonnichsen
1974   Bone foreshafts from a burial in southwestern Montana. Science 186: 147-150.

Lantz, Stanley W.
1984   Distribution of Paleo-Indian projectile points and tools from western Pennsylvania: Implications for regional differences. Archaeology of Eastern North America 12: 210-230.

Laub, Richard S., Mary F. DeRemer, Catherine A. Dufort, and William L. Parsons
1988   The Hiscock site: A rich Late Quaternary locality in western New York State. Bulletin of the Buffalo Society of Natural Science 33: 67-81.

Leonhardy, Frank C.
1966   Domebo: A Paleo-Indian Mammoth Kill in the Prairie-Plains. Contributions of the Museum of the Great Plains 1. Lawton, Oklahoma.

MacDonald, George F.
1968   Debert: A Palaeo-Indian Site in Central Nova Scotia. National Museum of Canada Anthropology Paper 16. Ottawa.

McAvoy, Joseph M.
1992   Nottoway River Survey, Part I: Clovis Settlement Patterns. Archeological Society of Virginia Special Publication 28. Courtland, Virginia.

McNett, Charles W., Jr. (ed.)
1985   Shawnee Minisink, Academic Press. Orlando.

Miller, Susanne J.
1989   Characteristics of mammoth bone reduction at Owl Cave, the Wadsen site, Idaho. Pp. 381-393 in Robson Bonnichsen and Marcella Sorg (eds.) Bone Modification. Center for the Study of the First Americans. Orono, Maine.

Moratto, Michael J.
1984   California Archaeology. Academic Press. New York.

Morrow, Juliet E. and Toby A. Morrow
2002   Rummells-Maske revisited: A fluted point cache from east central Iowa. Plains Anthropologist 47(183): 307-321.

Pi-Sunyer, Oriol, John Edward Blank, and Robert Williams
1975   The Honey Run site (33CO-3): A late Paleo-Indian locality in Coshocton County, Ohio. Pp. 230-251 in Olaf H. Prufer and Douglas H. McKenzie (eds.) Studies in Ohio Archaeology. Kent State University Press.

Preston, Douglas
1995   The mystery of Sandia Cave. The New Yorker (June 12 issue): 66-83.

Prufer, Olaf H. and Norman L. Wright
1970   The Welling site (33 Co-2): A fluted point workshop in Coshocton County, Ohio. Ohio Archaeologist 20(4): 259-268.

Rice, David G.
1972   The Windust Phase in Lower Snake River Region Prehistory. Washington State University Laboratory of Anthropology, Report of Investigations 50. Pullman.

Ritchie, William A. and Robert E. Funk
1973   Aboriginal Settlement Patterns in the Northeast. New York State Museum and Science Service Memoir 20. Albany.

Sanders, Thomas Nolan
1990   Adams: The Manufacturing of Flaked Stone Tools at a Paleoindian Site in Western Kentucky. Persimmon Press. Buffalo, New York.

Sanger, David
1973   Cow Point: An Archaic Cemetery in New Brunswick. Archaeological Survey of Canada Paper 12. Ottawa, Canada.

Seeman, Mark F., Garry Summers, Elaine Dowd, and Larry Morris
1994   Fluted point characteristics of three large sites: The implications for modeling Early Paleoindian settlement patterns in Ohio. Pp. 77-94 in William S. Dancey (ed.) The First Discovery of America. The Ohio Archaeological Council, Inc. Columbus.

Shipman, Pat, Daniel C. Fisher and Jennie J. Rose
1984   Mastodon butchery: Microscopic evidence of carcass processing and bone tool use. Paleobiology 10(3): 358-365.

Simons, Donald B., Michael J. Shott and Henry T. Wright
1984   The Gainey site: Variability in a Great Lakes artifact assemblage. Archaeology of Eastern North America 12: 12: 266-279.

Spiess, Arthur E. and Deborah Brush Wilson
1987   Michaud: A Paleoindian Site in the Central New England-Maritimes Region. Occasional Publications in Maine Archaeology 6. Maine Historic Preservation Commission. Augusta.

Storck, P. L.
1984   Glacial Lake Algonquin and Early Paleo-Indian settlement patterns in southcentral Ontario. Archaeology of Eastern North America 12: 286-298.

Storck, Peter L. and John Tomenchuk
1990   An Early Paleoindian cache of informal tools at the Udora site, Ontario. Research in Economic Anthropology (Supplement 5): 45-93.

Tankersley, Kenneth
2000   The Crook County Clovis Cache revisited. Current Research in the Pleistocene 17: 81-83.
2002   In Search of Ice Age Americans. Gibbs Smith, Publisher. Salt Lake City.

Taylor, Dee C.
1969   The Wilsall excavations: An exercise in frustration. Proceedings of the Montana Academy of Science 29: 147-150.

Walters, Matthew M.
1988   The Adams mastodon site, Harrison County, Kentucky. Pp. 43-46 in Charles D. Hockensmith, David Pollack and Thomas N. Sanders (eds.) Paleoindian and Archaic Research in Kentucky. Kentucky Heritage Council. Frankfort.

Webb, S. David, Jerald T. Milanich and Roger Alexan
1983   An extinct Bison kill site, Jefferson County, FL. The Florida Anthropologist 36(1-2): 81-2.

Weinmeister, Garry
2002   The Drake Clovis Cache. Indian Artifact Magazine 21(3): 50-52.

Wheat, Joe Ben
1967   A Paleo-Indian bison kill. Pp. 213-221 in E.B.W. Zubrow, Margaret C. Fritz, and John M. Fritz (eds.) New World Archaeology: Theoretical and Cultural Transformations. W.H. Freeman and Company. San Francisco.
1972   The Olsen-Chubbuck Site: A Paleo-Indian Bison Kill. Society for American Archaeology Memoir 26.

Whitney, Theodore
1977   Fluted points from the Chenango area. Bulletin, Chenango Chapter, New York State Archeological Association 17(1): 1-13 plus plates.

Wilke, Philip J., Jeffrey Flenniken and Terry L. Ozbun
1991   Clovis technology at the Anzick site, Montana. Journal of California and Great Basin Anthropology 13(2): 242-272.

Wilkison, Elizabeth M.
1986   A Complex of Palaeo-Indian Quarry-Workshop and Habitation Sites in the Flint Run Area of the Shenandoah Valley of Virginia. The Chesopiean 24(3): 1-36 (full number).

Wittkofski, J. Mark and Theodore R. Reinhart
1989   Paleoindian Research in Virginia: A Synthesis. Archeologial Society of Virginla, Special Publication 19. Courtland, Virginia.

Woods, James C. and Gene L. Titmus
1985   A review of the Simon Clovis Collection. Idaho Archaeologist 8(1): 3-8.

CLOVIS
14,000 B.P., CO,
agate

CLOVIS
14,000 B.P., KY,
burinated base,
Carter Cave chert

CLOVIS
14,000 B.P., OH,
Coshocton chert

CLOVIS
14,000 B.P., KY
Tyrone flint

CLOVIS
14,000 B.P., CO

SIMPSON
12,000 B.P., FL

PALEO SCRAPER
14,000 B.P., TX,
petrified wood

CUMBERLAND
12,000 B.P., KY,
Buffalo River chert

PALEO LANCET
14,000 B.P., OR,
obsidian

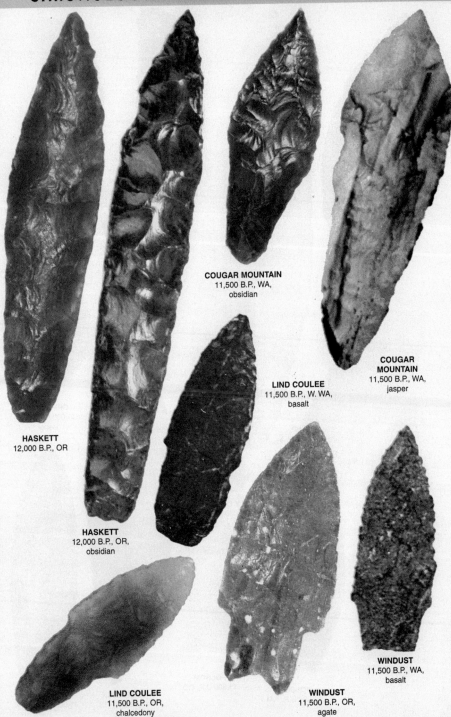

COUGAR MOUNTAIN
11,500 B.P., WA,
obsidian

**COUGAR
MOUNTAIN**
11,500 B.P., WA,
jasper

LIND COULEE
11,500 B.P., W. WA,
basalt

HASKETT
12,000 B.P., OR

HASKETT
12,000 B.P., OR,
obsidian

WINDUST
11,500 B.P., WA,
basalt

LIND COULEE
11,500 B.P., OR,
chalcedony

WINDUST
11,500 B.P., OR,
agate

CHRONOLOGICAL GALLERY OF POINT TYPES

BLACK ROCK CONCAVE
11,000 B.P., NV

CRESCENT
11,000 B.P., OR, obsidian

CRESCENT
11,000 B.P., OR, jasper

CRESCENT
11,000 B.P., OR, jasper

FOLSOM
11,000 B.P., CO

EARLY OVOID KNIFE
11,000 B.P., KY

CRESCENT
11,000 B.P., OR, jasper

FOLSOM
11,000 B.P., NM

FOLSOM
11,000 B.P., CO

KENNEWICK
11,000 B.P., OR, basalt

MILNESAND
11,000 B.P., W. TX

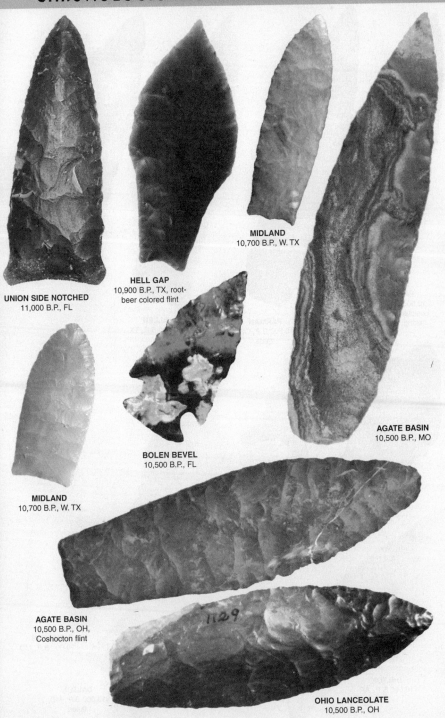

MIDLAND
10,700 B.P., W. TX

UNION SIDE NOTCHED
11,000 B.P., FL

HELL GAP
10,900 B.P., TX, root-
beer colored flint

AGATE BASIN
10,500 B.P., MO

BOLEN BEVEL
10,500 B.P., FL

MIDLAND
10,700 B.P., W. TX

AGATE BASIN
10,500 B.P., OH,
Coshocton flint

OHIO LANCEOLATE
10,500 B.P., OH

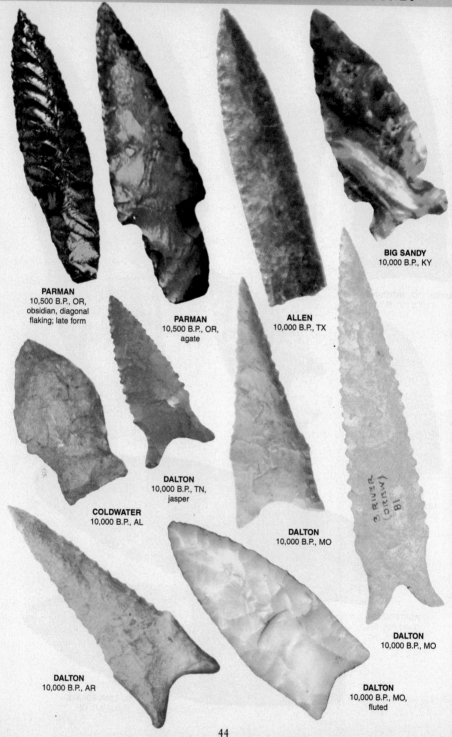

PARMAN
10,500 B.P., OR,
obsidian, diagonal
flaking; late form

PARMAN
10,500 B.P., OR,
agate

ALLEN
10,000 B.P., TX

BIG SANDY
10,000 B.P., KY

DALTON
10,000 B.P., TN,
jasper

COLDWATER
10,000 B.P., AL

DALTON
10,000 B.P., MO

DALTON
10,000 B.P., AR

DALTON
10,000 B.P., MO,
fluted

DALTON
10,000 B.P., MO

HI-LO
10,000 B.P., IN

JEFF
10,000 B.P., AL,
Horse Creek
chert

HOLLAND
10,000 B.P., AR

PIKE COUNTY
10,000 B.P., IL

QUAD
10,000 B.P., AL

PLAINVIEW
10,000 B.P., TX

SAN PATRICE-HOPE
10,000 B.P., TX,
petrified wood

SAN PATRICE-HOPE
10,000 B.P., AR

CHRONOLOGICAL GALLERY OF POINT TYPES

SAN PATRICE-ST. JOHN
10,000 B.P., TX,
petrified wood

SPEDIS
10,000 B.P., OR,
agate

SPEDIS
10,000 B.P., OR,
red agate

SPEDIS
10,000 B.P., WA,
pitchstone

SPEDIS
10,000 B.P., OR,
agate

SPEDIS
10,000 B.P., OR,
red agate

SPEDIS
10,000 B.P., OR

STANFIELD
10,000 B.P., AL,
type area

THEBES
10,000 B.P., IN

THEBES
10,000 B.P., OH

GREENBRIER
9,500 B.P., TN,
red jasper

GREENBRIER
9,500 B.P., KY,
red jasper

HARDAWAY
9,500 B.P., SC

46

HARDAWAY
9,500 B.P., NC,
quartz

OSCEOLA GREENBRIER
9,500 B.P., FL

OWL CAVE
9,500 B.P., WA,
basalt

SCOTTSBLUFF
9,500 B.P., OR,
jasper

SCOTTSBLUFF
9,500 B.P., TX

ST. CHARLES
9,500 B.P., IN

ST. CHARLES
9,500 B.P., IL

SANTA FE
9,500 B.P., FL

TALLAHASSEE
9,500 B.P., FL

SAINT CHARLES
9,500 B.P., IL

SAINT CHARLES
9,500 B.P., TN
hornstone

TALLAHASSEE
9,500 B.P., FL

BOLEN PLAIN
9,000 B.P., FL

COBBS TRIANGULAR
9,000 B.P., OH

DECATUR
9,000 B.P., KY

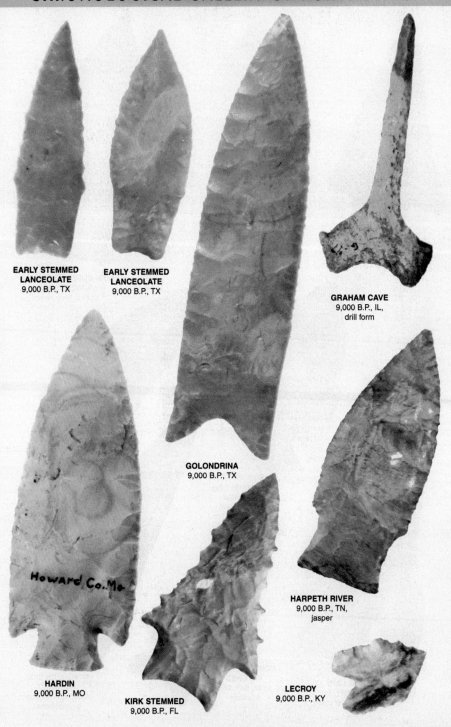

EARLY STEMMED LANCEOLATE
9,000 B.P., TX

EARLY STEMMED LANCEOLATE
9,000 B.P., TX

GRAHAM CAVE
9,000 B.P., IL,
drill form

GOLONDRINA
9,000 B.P., TX

HARPETH RIVER
9,000 B.P., TN,
jasper

Howard Co. Mo

HARDIN
9,000 B.P., MO

KIRK STEMMED
9,000 B.P., FL

LECROY
9,000 B.P., KY

KIRK STEMMED
9,000 B.P., KY

KIRK STEMMED
9,000 B.P., FL

KIRK CORNER NOTCHED
9,000 B.P., TN,
Buffalo River chert

**NORTHERN SIDE
NOTCHED**
9,000 B.P., OR,
obsidian

**NORTHERN SIDE
NOTCHED**
9,000 B.P., ID, obsidian

LOST LAKE
9,000 B.P., IN,
Buffalo River chert

**NORTHERN SIDE
NOTCHED**
9,000 B.P., OR,
obsidian

**NORTHERN SIDE
NOTCHED**
9,000 B.P., ID, fine
grained basalt

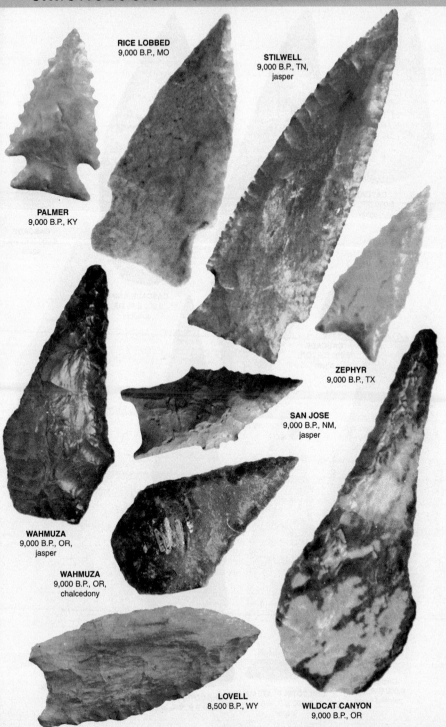

RICE LOBBED
9,000 B.P., MO

STILWELL
9,000 B.P., TN,
jasper

PALMER
9,000 B.P., KY

ZEPHYR
9,000 B.P., TX

SAN JOSE
9,000 B.P., NM,
jasper

WAHMUZA
9,000 B.P., OR,
jasper

WAHMUZA
9,000 B.P., OR,
chalcedony

LOVELL
8,500 B.P., WY

WILDCAT CANYON
9,000 B.P., OR

CASCADE
8,000 B.P., OR,
agate

CASCADE
8,000 B.P., OR,
agate

CASCADE KNIFE
8,000 B.P., OR,
obsidian

CASCADE
8,000 B.P., WA,
agate

CASCADE
8,000 B.P., OR,
obsidian, diago-
nal flaking

**CASCADE
DRILL**
8,000 B.P., OR,
chalcedony

CASCADE
8,000 B.P., OR,
petrified wood

CHILCOTIN PLATEAU
8,000 B.P., WA
jasper

CHILCOTIN PLATEAU
8,000 B.P., WA, jasper

EVA
8,000 B.P., TN

MACCORKLE
8,000 B.P., NY,
green slate

PINE TREE
8,000 B.P., TN

HAMILTON
8,000 B.P., FL

PINE TREE
8,000 B.P., KY

PINTO BASIN
8,000 B.P., NV,
jasper

**PINTO BASIN,
SLOPING
SHOULDER**
8,000 B.P., OR,
obsidian

STANLY
8,000 B.P., TN

WELLS
8,000 B.P., TX

BANDY
7,500 B.P., TX

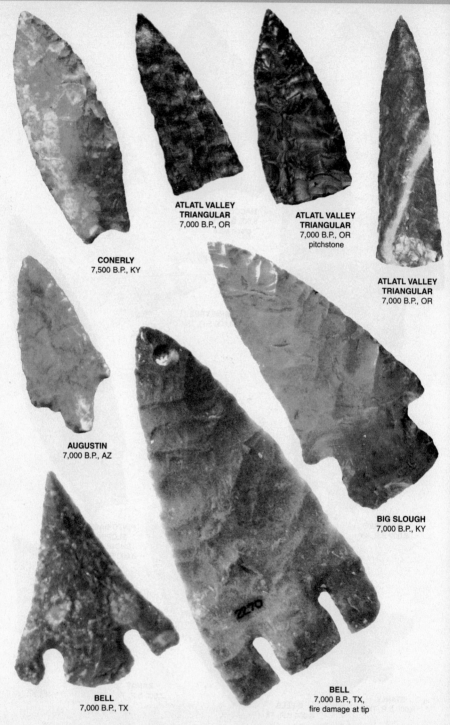

ATLATL VALLEY TRIANGULAR
7,000 B.P., OR

ATLATL VALLEY TRIANGULAR
7,000 B.P., OR
pitchstone

ATLATL VALLEY TRIANGULAR
7,000 B.P., OR

CONERLY
7,500 B.P., KY

AUGUSTIN
7,000 B.P., AZ

BIG SLOUGH
7,000 B.P., KY

BELL
7,000 B.P., TX

BELL
7,000 B.P., TX,
fire damage at tip

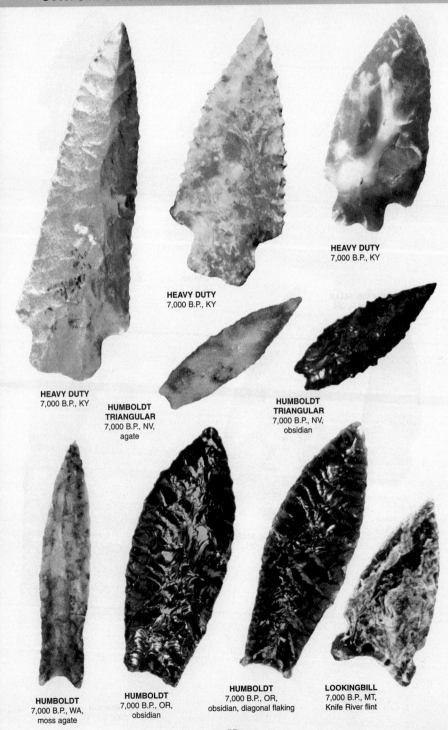

HEAVY DUTY
7,000 B.P., KY

HEAVY DUTY
7,000 B.P., KY

HEAVY DUTY
7,000 B.P., KY

**HUMBOLDT
TRIANGULAR**
7,000 B.P., NV,
agate

**HUMBOLDT
TRIANGULAR**
7,000 B.P., NV,
obsidian

HUMBOLDT
7,000 B.P., WA,
moss agate

HUMBOLDT
7,000 B.P., OR,
obsidian

HUMBOLDT
7,000 B.P., OR,
obsidian, diagonal flaking

LOOKINGBILL
7,000 B.P., MT,
Knife River flint

NEWTON FALLS
7,000 B.P., OH

NEWTON FALLS
7,000 B.P., OH

NEWNAN
7,000 B.P., FL

NIGHTFIRE
7,000 B.P., OR,
basalt

PENTAGONAL KNIFE
6,500 B.P., OH

ALMAGRE
6,000 B.P., TX

BENTON
6,000 B.P., TN

BUCK CREEK
6,000 B.P., KY

BUCK CREEK
6,000 B.P., KY

BUZZARD ROOST
6,000 B.P., TN

BUZZARD ROOST
6,000 B.P., TN
jasper

BENTON
6,000 B.P., TN,
Buffalo River chert

MARSHALL
6,000 B.P., TX

PAISANO
6,000 B.P., TX

PANDALE
6,000 B.P., TX

LEDBETTER
6,000 B.P., TN,
jasper

PEDERNALES
6,000 B.P., TX

PEDERNALES
6,000 B.P., TX

PICKWICK
6,000 B.P., TN,
jasper

PICKWICK
6,000 B.P., TN,
Horse Creek chert

PICKWICK
6,000 B.P., TN

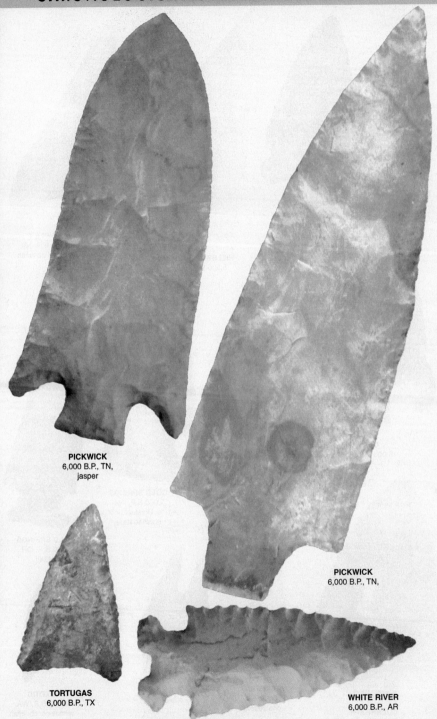

PICKWICK
6,000 B.P., TN,
jasper

PICKWICK
6,000 B.P., TN,

TORTUGAS
6,000 B.P., TX

WHITE RIVER
6,000 B.P., AR

MOUNT ALBION
5,800 B.P., AZ

OXBOW
5,500 B.P., ND,
Knife River Flint

HILLSBOROUGH
5,500 B.P., FL

TRIPLE T
5,500 B.P., NV,
banded obsidian

CLAY
5,000 B.P., FL

COLD SPRINGS
5,000 B.P., WA,
red basalt

COLD SPRINGS
5,000 B.P., WA,
agate. Unusual double
notched base

COLD SPRINGS
5,000 B.P., OR,
basalt

CULBREATH
5,000 B.P., FL

EXOTIC
5,000 B.P., OR,
chalcedony

EXOTIC DOUBLE TIP
5,000 B.P., OR,
obsidian

EXOTIC
5,000 B.P., OR,
chalcedony

EXOTIC
5,000 B.P., WA,
miniature, obsidian

GATECLIFF
5,000 B.P., OR,
jasper

GATECLIFF
5,000 B.P., CA,
obsidian

FRIO
5,000 B.P., TX,

GATECLIFF
5,000 B.P., OR,
agate

LANGTRY-
ARENOSA
5,000 B.P., TX

LEVY
5,000 B.P., FL

KINNEY
5,000 B.P., TX

LEVY
5,000 B.P., FL

GENESEE
5,000 B.P., PA,
Onondaga flint

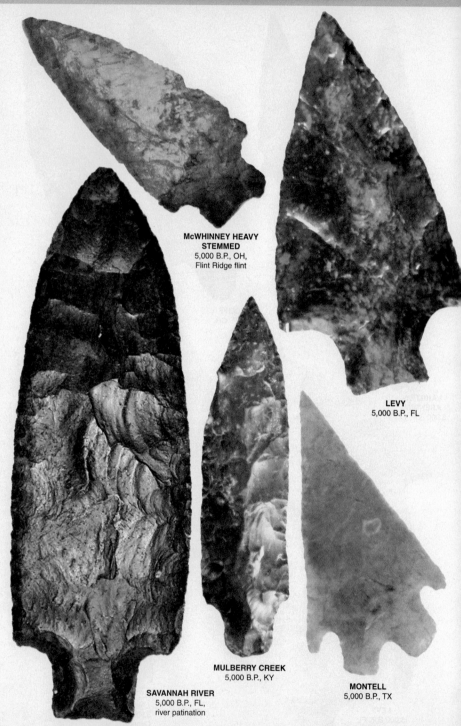

McWHINNEY HEAVY STEMMED
5,000 B.P., OH,
Flint Ridge flint

LEVY
5,000 B.P., FL

MULBERRY CREEK
5,000 B.P., KY

SAVANNAH RIVER
5,000 B.P., FL,
river patination

MONTELL
5,000 B.P., TX

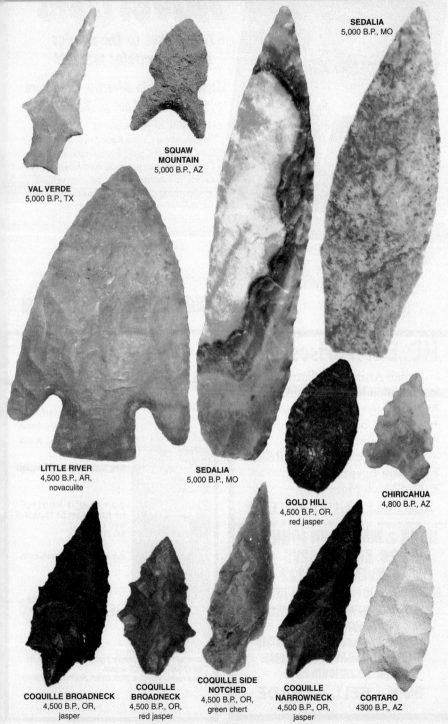

SEDALIA
5,000 B.P., MO

SQUAW MOUNTAIN
5,000 B.P., AZ

VAL VERDE
5,000 B.P., TX

LITTLE RIVER
4,500 B.P., AR,
novaculite

SEDALIA
5,000 B.P., MO

GOLD HILL
4,500 B.P., OR,
red jasper

CHIRICAHUA
4,800 B.P., AZ

COQUILLE BROADNECK
4,500 B.P., OR,
jasper

COQUILLE BROADNECK
4,500 B.P., OR,
red jasper

COQUILLE SIDE NOTCHED
4,500 B.P., OR,
green chert

COQUILLE NARROWNECK
4,500 B.P., OR,
jasper

CORTARO
4300 B.P., AZ

Introduction

Hunting arrowheads has been a popular pastime for many Americans over the past one hundred years. Even the Indians themselves cherished and collected rock crystals, gem stones, and points. In the past, large collections were put together with very little effort, since few people hunted and the supply of good artifacts was plentiful. Plowed fields along creeks and rivers, as well as river banks and dry lake beds, are the most popular places for hunting relics, as the early Indians built their villages and hunted game in such locations. The Indians' food supply, such as fish, game, mussels, etc. lived in or along rivers, creeks, springs, ponds, swamps and lakes. Early man preyed on this abundant food supply, migrating along these water routes, moving from place to place in search of better hunting grounds, as the game became depleted.

Fields are plowed in the Fall or Spring of each year. The most likely sites for hunting, of course, would be the large flat areas close to the original river or creek banks. Hunting in areas that may be large enough to support a small village and are on high ground, protected from a flooding river, are especially productive places. Village sites were usually built where a creek converged with a large river. Field hunting should be attempted after a hard rain. Heavy rains will create deep gullies and washed-out areas exposing the relics.

Here is where you can get lucky, especially if you are the first person in the field. All a collector has to do is walk along and pick up pieces of history. Be sure to ask permission before entering private property. Most farmers will give permission to enter their land if approached in a friendly manner.

Plowed fields next to springs and cave openings have also produced relics. Such a place is Castillian Springs, just above Nashville, Tennessee. Here, next to the spring, there are salt licks for animals. The Indians occupied and lived in this area for thousands of years from the Paleo to Woodland periods and later. The herd animals would always migrate here for salt and watering, providing the Indians with plentiful meat and nourishment right in their own backyard. Erosion around the spring has in the past produced many excellent artifacts. From fluted points to Doves, to Lost Lakes, to stemmed types, this area has been rich with many types of points.

Another similar site is Nickajack Cave and its surrounding fields, just below Chattanooga, Tennessee. Overhangs and rock shelters along rivers and creeks where early man lived, as well as river lands, have produced fine artifacts as well.

In the 1930s, the blow-outs, or dust storms, in the plains states produced many fine projectile points. The top layer of soil blew away, exposing relics left centuries ago by the Indians.

Sand bar hunting along the Tennessee River became possible after the Tennessee Valley Authority built their dams and began controlling the river level in the 1930's. During the development of the TVA system, hunting was excellent. Lake levels were dropped during the winter months, exposing the sand bars which were originally high areas in the now inundated fields along the river channel, where the early Indians built their villages and camp sites. As winter storms raged through the Tennessee Valley, the lake levels would rise and fall and the racing river would cut into the sand bars, exposing relics for anyone to merely come along and pick up.

Today most of the sand bars and plowed fields in many states have been "hunted out." But the energetic hunter can still find new relic-producing sites if he gathers his facts, follows all leads, studies maps of likely areas and hunts whenever he can. Sooner or later he will get lucky.

However, most collectors are neither energetic nor imaginative, and build their collections by systematically purchasing specimens one at a time. **Genuine** points can be found for sale at relic shows, and sometimes in local collections that come up for sale. **Warning:** fake relics (all recently made and aged) are being offered to the public everywhere as genuine prehistoric artifacts. Knowing the history or pedigree of a point is very important in the process of determining whether or not it is a genuine pre-Columbian piece. Before purchasing a relic from anyone, be sure the dealer will guarantee it to be a genuine, pre-Columbian artifact, and will give you your money back should you later discover otherwise. Many reputable dealers will give you a money back guarantee. Whenever possible, you should have an expert examine any and every piece for its authenticity before you buy.

HOW TO USE THIS BOOK

This book is set up by <u>regions of the country</u> to make it easy for you to classify your collection. All points in each region are arranged in alphabetical order. First turn to the region that applies to you. The book is set up beginning with the Northeast section, continuing westward to the Great Basin-Westward section. The nine regions are: Northeastern, Eastern Seaboard, Gulf Coastal, Eastern Central, Southern Central, Northern Central, Desert Southwest, Northern High Plains and Great Basin Westward.

CLASSIFICATION: Projectile points come in many shapes, colors and sizes. Their quality varies from thick, crude forms to very thin, beautifully flaked, symmetrical specimens. Over the past fifty years, hundreds of points have been classified and given names. The names of people, rivers, creeks, lakes, mountains, towns, etc. have been used in naming point types. Many of the types come from sites that were excavated from undisturbed stratigraphic layers where carbon dating was made. These forms of data are important in placing each type in time and showing the relationship of one type to another. You will soon see that most of the early types evolved into the later forms.

This book includes as many point types as possible with the idea of expanding to more types in future updated editions as the information becomes available to us. The point types are arranged in alphabetical order by section of the country. The archeological period and approximate dates of popular use are given for each point type. A general distribution area is given, along with a brief description of each type. There are several factors that determine a given type: **1**-Shape or form. **2**-Size. **3**-Style or flaking. **4**-Thickness or thinness. **5**-Kind of material

NEW ARROWHEADS LISTED

The field of Archaeology is an on-going science where sites are constantly being found and excavated. Occassionally, new types are discovered, named and reported in their published literature. As a result, the interrelationship of types, their age, as well as geographical dispersion is always changing. Due to this, the region boundaries may change in future editions. We are constantly on the outlook for photographs as well as the documentation of these types so they can be added to future volumes of this book. The author would appreciate receiving any photos and reports of this nature.

ARROWHEAD VALUES LISTED

Values listed in this book are for your information only. None of the points shown are for sale. Under each type, we have attempted to show a photographic spread of size, quality and variation of form (where available), from low to high grade, with corresponding prices. All values listed in this book are in U.S. currency and are wholesale/retail prices based on (but not limited to) reports from our extensive network of experienced advisors which include convention sales, mail order, auctions and unpublished personal sales. Overstreet, with several decades of market experience, has developed a unique and comprehensive system for gathering, documenting, averaging and pricing data on arrowheads. The end result is a true fair market value for your use. We have earned the reputation for our cautious, conservative approach to pricing arrowheads. You, the collector, can be assured that the prices listed in this volume are the most accurate and useful in print.

The low price is the wholesale price (the price dealers may pay for that point). **The high price** is the retail price (the price a collector may pay for that point). Each illustration also gives a brief description pointing out special features when applicable. The prices listed have been averaged from the highest and lowest prices we have seen, just prior to publication. We feel that this will give you a fair, realistic price value for each piece illustrated. If your point matches the illustrated example in both size, color, and quality, the listed value would then apply. **Warning:** The slightest dings or nicks can dramatically drop the grade and value of a point. Please see Grade vs. Value following this section.

HIGH PRICE- RETAIL PRICE, LOW PRICE - WHOLESALE PRICE

IMPORTANT NOTE: This book is not a dealer's price list, although some dealers may base their prices on the values listed. The true value of any arrowhead is what you are willing to pay. The top price listed is an indication of what collectors would pay while the lower price is what dealers would possibly pay. For one reason or another, these collectors might want a certain piece badly and will pay over the list price for comparable quality. This commonly occurs on many high grade, rare points.

DEALER'S POSITION

Dealers are not in a position to pay the full prices listed, but work on a percentage depending largely on the amount of investment required and the quality of material offered. What a dealer will pay depends on how long it will take him to sell the individual piece or collection after making the investment; the higher the demand and better the grade, the more the percentage. Most dealers are faced with expenses such as advertising, travel, telephone and mailing, rent, employee salaries, plus convention costs. These costs all go in before the relics are sold.

The high demand relics usually sell right away but the lower grades are difficult to sell due to their commonality and low demand. Sometimes a dealer will have cost tied up for several years before finally selling everything. Remember, his position is that of handling, demand, and overhead. Most dealers are victims of these economics.

How to Grade Points

B efore a point's true value can be assessed, its condition or state of preservation as well as quality must be determined. The better the quality and condition, and the larger the size, the more valuable the point. Perfect points that are classic for the type, thin, made of high quality materials with perfect symmetry and flaking are worth several times the price of common, but complete, low grade field points.

FACTORS THAT INFLUENCE THE GRADE AND VALUE OF POINTS:

Condition: Perfection is the rule. Nicks, chips, and breakage reduce value.

Size: Everything else being equal, a larger point will grade higher than a smaller point and larger points are worth more.

Form: The closer a point comes to being a classic for the type, the higher the grade and value.

Symmetry: Points with good balance and design are higher grade and worth more.

Flaking: Points with precision percussion and secondary flaking, a minimum of hinge fractures and problem areas are higher grade and worth more. Points with unusual flaking patterns, such as collateral or oblique transverse, enhance grade and value.

Thinness: The thinner the better.

After all the above steps have been considered, then the reader can begin to assign a grade to his point. Points are graded on a scale of 1 to10+, where a 10+ is the best and a 1 is the lowest grade for a complete point.

GRADING DEFINITIONS

Grade 10+: The exceptional perfect point. One of the few half dozen best known to exist. Perfect in every way, including thinness, flaking, material, symmetry and form. The best example you would ever expect to see of any given type. This grade is extremely rare, and applies to medium to large size points that normally occur in a given type.

Grade 10: A perfect point, including thinness, flaking, symmetry and form. This grade is extremely rare, and applies to all sizes of points that normally occur in a given type. A point does not have to be the largest known to qualify for this grade.

Grade 8 or 9: Near perfect but lacking just a little in size or material or thinness. It may have a small defect to keep it out of a 10 category. Still very rare, most high grade points would fall into this category.

Grade 6 or 7: Better than the average grade but not quite nice enough to get a high ranking. Flaking, size, and symmetry are just a little above the average. Points in this grade are still very hard to find in most states. A very collectible grade.

Grade 4 or 5: The average quality that is found. The flaking, thickness, and symmetry is average. 2 or 3 very minute nicks may be seen but none that would be considered serious.

Grade 1-3: Field grade points that have below average overall quality. Better points with more serious faults or dings would fall into this grade. The most common grade found and correspondingly, the least valuable.

Broken points: Usually little to no value. However, good high grade broken backs of popular type points have fetched good prices. Examples would be Paleo points and many of the rare Archaic beveled and notched types.

PRICING POINTS

After a point has been graded and assigned a grade number, it should be compared with similar points in the alphabetical listings. The prices listed will give the reader a guide as to the probable value of his point, but be careful, compare grade with grade. If your point has a little ear or tip broken, the value is affected drastically. Of course, state of perfection, thinness, rarity of type, quality of material and flaking, and size all enter into determining a value. Usually with everything being equal, the larger the size the higher the price.

Many factors affect value and should be considered when determining a price for your point. Besides those listed under Grading Points, the following should be considered:

FACTORS THAT INFLUENCE VALUE:

Provenance: When a point has been properly documented as to where and when it was found and by whom, the value increases. Points from key sites such as the Clovis site in New Mexico, the Quad site in Alabama, the Nuckolls site in Tennessee, the Hardaway site in North Carolina, etc. increases value. Well documented points from famous collections show increased value. Points that have been published show an increase in demand and makes them easier to sell (the wise investor should have all points checked before purchase, whether published or not, because many fakes have been published as genuine). Local points usually bring higher prices than imports from other states.

Material & Color: Most points are made of common local gray to brown cherts, but the type of material can enhance value. Points made from colorful or high quality material such as agate, petrified wood, agatized coral, quartz, crystal, flint, jasper, Horse Creek chert, Buffalo River chert, Flint Ridge chert, Carter Cave chert, Dover chert, etc. will increase value. Some materials became glassier and more colorful when heat treated by the Indians and would enhance the appearance. Certain local materials are more collectible in various states, such as rhyolite in North and South Carolina, Dover in Tennessee, Carter Cave chert or Kentucky hornstone in Kentucky, Flint Ridge chert in Ohio, Knife River flint in North and South Dakota, jasper in Pennsylvania, agatized coral in Florida or petrified wood in Arizona and New Mexico. Usually, points that are transparent or have pretty colors alone will sell for higher prices.

Symmetry: The left and right sides of points must be balanced to receive the highest grades. Value decreases as symmetry is lost.

Rarity: Obviously, some point types are scarcer and much harder to find than others. For instance, Clovis, which is found in most of North America, is more common than Folsom, which is rarely found in just a few western states. Paleo points are much more rare out west than in the east.

Popularity of Type: Market demand for certain point types can greatly influence the supply and value. The value of these points can vary with changing market demands and available supplies. Points with slight damage, such as a nick off the tip or wing, suffer a cut in value of about 60 percent. Medium damage, such as a missing wing, will cut the value about 90 percent. Field grade pieces and halves are usually sold at five dollars per gallon. The very best points have no top retail price and are always in very high demand. Local points are usually worth more in the area where they are found.

Grade and Its Effect on Value

Presented below are examples of the same point type in grades 10 through 3 and the effect on value. All are equal size and quality, except for the defects. These examples illustrate how value drops with grade. True number 10s are rare and the slightest dings or nicks can easily cause the value to drop dramatically.

When the novice grades points to determine value, it is a common mistake to grade his #5s and #6s as #9s and 10s. True 9s and 10s must be superb. They have to be perfect for 10s and near perfect for 9s, thin, symmetrical, and of high quality to reach this grade. Color, translucency and high quality material enhance value.

When dealers look at a collection to buy, they are faced with the economics of having to buy the whole collection to get the few points that they really want. For example, a virgin collection of 1000 complete points, all found by the owner, that is still intact and not picked over, would break down as follows: 92% (920 points) would be low grade, worth below $20 each with the remaining 8% worth $20 or more each. As you can see, most collections are loaded with low grade points making it very difficult for anyone to pay a large price just to get the few choice pieces.

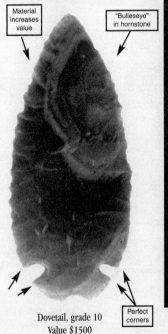

Material increases value

"Bulleseye" in hornstone

Perfect corners

Dovetail, grade 10
Value $1500

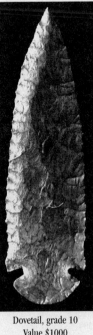

Dovetail, grade 10
Value $1000

Dovetail, grade 9
Value $600

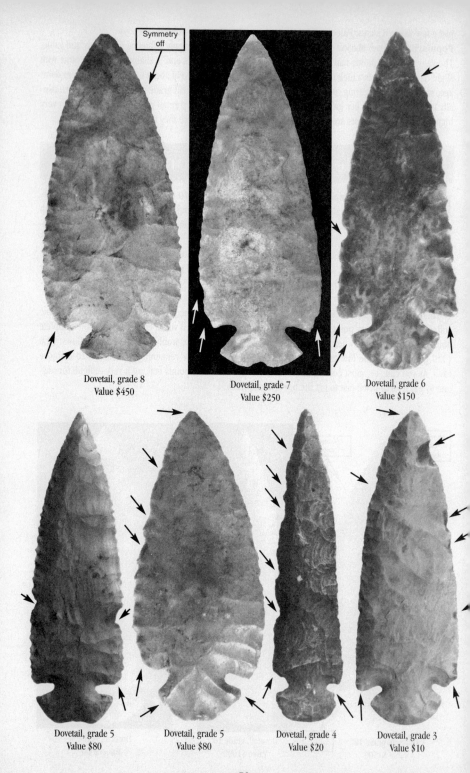

Symmetry off

Dovetail, grade 8
Value $450

Dovetail, grade 7
Value $250

Dovetail, grade 6
Value $150

Dovetail, grade 5
Value $80

Dovetail, grade 5
Value $80

Dovetail, grade 4
Value $20

Dovetail, grade 3
Value $10

How to Classify Arrowheads

It's as easy as **one, two, three** (well, seven actually) if you take the following steps. All arrowheads, according to their shape, have been divided into eight different forms listed below.

1. The country is divided into nine sections.

2. Decide which of the categories #1-8 listed below that your point belongs.

3. Go to the Thumbnail Guide at the beginning of the section that applies to your locale.

4. Match your arrowhead to one of the photos in that section.

5. Look up the name under the photo that matches your point in the alphabetical section.

6. Look at the numerous examples, actual size, and make a more detailed comparison.

7. If your point still does not match exactly, go back to the **Thumbnail Guide Section** and look for another match and start over with step four.

The 8 Forms of Arrowheads

1. **Auriculate.** These points have **ears** and a concave base.
   A. Auriculate Fluted. A fluted point is one that has a **channel flake** struck off one or both faces from the base.
   B. Auriculate Unfluted. All other eared forms are shown here.

2. **Lanceolate.** Points without **notches** or **shoulders** fall into this group. Bases are round, straight, concave or convex.

3. **Corner Notched.** The base-end has corner notches for **hafting**.

4. **Side Notched.** The base-end has side notches for **hafting**.

5. **Stemmed.** These points have a **stem** that is short or long, expanding or contracting. All stemmed points have **shoulders**.

6. **Stemmed-Bifurcated.** Since a number of stemmed points occur that have the base split into two **lobes**, they have been grouped together.

7. **Basal Notched.** This form has notches applied at the **base**.

8. **Arrow Points.** These points are generally small, thin triangle and other forms grouped for easy identification.

*See glossary for underlined words.

Identification/Classification

The following drawings illustrate point nomenclature used by collectors and professionals everywhere for point shapes and features.

Auriculate Forms

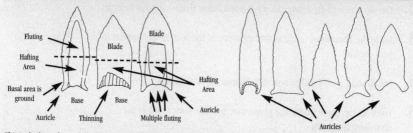

This is the basic form of the Paleo Period. Flaking tends to be parallel and the entire hafting area is usually ground.

Lanceolate Forms

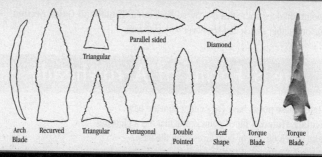

Basal, Corner & Side Notched Forms

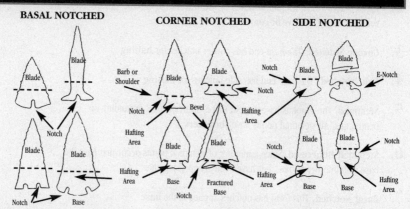

Basal notched forms appeared in the early Archaic Period and reappeared in the Woodland Period. Not a popular form of hafting since only a few types are known.

Corner notched forms appeared in the early Archaic Period and reappeared again in the Woodland Period and lasted to Historic times.

Side notched forms began in Transitional Paleo times and persisted through the Archaic Period, reappearing in Woodland times lasting into the Historic Period.

72

Stemmed Forms
(These drawings apply to points of all sizes)
Basal edge types   Shoulder types

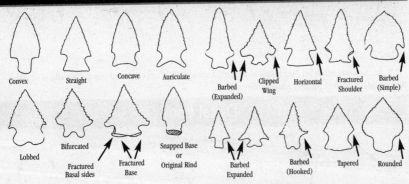

Convex | Straight | Concave | Auriculate | Barbed (Expanded) | Clipped Wing | Horizontal | Fractured Shoulder | Barbed (Simple)

Lobbed | Bifurcated | Fractured Basal sides | Fractured Base | Snapped Base or Original Rind | Barbed Expanded | Barbed (Hooked) | Tapered | Rounded

Note: The **Basal Edge** begins the hafting area of a point.

Note: The **shoulder** divides the blade from the hafting area.

Stemmed Forms
(Hafting Area Types)
(These drawings apply to points of all sizes)

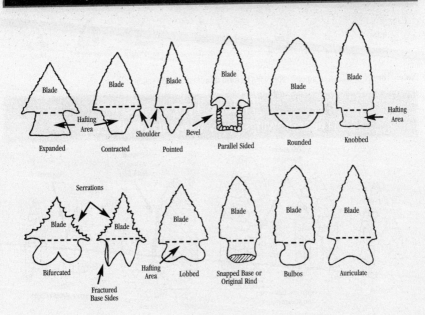

Blade — Hafting Area — Expanded | Blade — Hafting Area — Contracted | Blade — Shoulder — Pointed | Blade — Bevel — Parallel Sided | Blade — Rounded | Blade — Hafting Area — Knobbed

Serrations | Blade — Bifurcated | Blade — Fractured Base Sides | Blade — Hafting Area — Lobbed | Blade — Snapped Base or Original Rind | Blade — Bulbos | Blade — Auriculate

Note: Stemmed types began as early as the Paleo Period, but didn't really become popular until the Woodland Period. Consequently, this form has the most types and is the most difficult to classify.

Blade Beveling Types   # Blade Edge Types

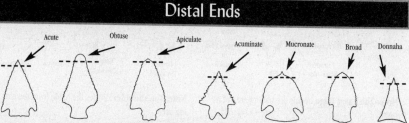

Left Hand   Right Hand   All Four Sides   No serrations   Fine serrations   Saw-Tooth serrations   Notched

Note: Alternate blade beveling began in the early Archaic Period and continued into the Woodland Period. Beveled points are very popular among collectors.

Distal Ends

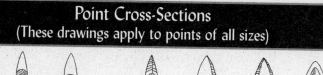

Acute   Obtuse   Apiculate   Acuminate   Mucronate   Broad   Donnaha

Note: The distal end of a point is located at the very tip and describes the shape of the penetrating part of the knife or projectile point.

Point Cross-Sections
(These drawings apply to points of all sizes)

Elliptical   Round   Uniface or Plano-convex   Median Ridged   Rhomboid   Flattened   Fluted

Note: The cross-section of a point represents its form if broken at mid-section.

Flaking Types
(These drawings apply to points of all sizes)

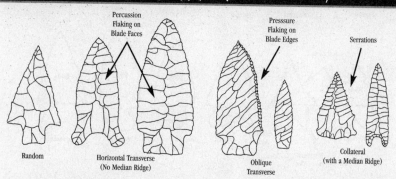

Percussion Flaking on Blade Faces   Presssure Flaking on Blade Edges   Serrations

Random   Horizontal Transverse (No Median Ridge)   Oblique Transverse   Collateral (with a Median Ridge)

Note: Points are rough shaped with an elk antler billet or hammer stone. Then fine pressure flaking is applied to the blade and stem edges with a sharp pointed antler. Billet and deer antler are alternated until the point is finally finished. During the flaking process, edges are lightly ground to prevent hinge fracturing on the blade edges.

The American Indian
Middle to Eastern U.S.

(Includes sections: Northeast, Eastern Seaboard, Gulf Coastal, Eastern Central, Southern Central and Northern Central)

Paleo	c. 14,000 - 11,000 B.P.
Late Paleo	c. 12,000 - 10,000 B.P.
Transitional Paleo	c. 11,000 - 9,000 B.P.
Early Archaic	c. 10,000 - 7,000 B.P.
Middle Archaic	c. 7,000 - 4,000 B.P.
Late Archaic	c. 4,000 - 3,000 B.P.
Woodland	c. 3,000 - 1,300 B.P.
Mississippian	c. 1,300 - 400 B.P.
Historic	c. 450 - 170 B.P.

Note: The dates given above are only approximations and should be used in a general context only. This data is constantly being revised as new information becomes available. **B.P. means "before present."** In 1998 new data was released to correct previously published dates acquired through carbon dating. All points are now older than first realized.

The American Indian West

(Includes sections: Desert Southwest, Northern High Plains and Great Basin-Westward)

Paleo	c. 14,000 - 8,000 B.P.
Early Archaic	c. 8,000 - 5,500 B.P.
Middle Archaic	c. 5,500 - 3,300 B.P.
Late Archaic	c. 3,500 - 2,300 B.P.

Desert Traditions:

Transitional	c. 2,300 - 1,600 B.P.
Developmental	c. 1,600 - 700 B.P.
Classic	700 - 400 B.P.
Historic	c. 400 - 170 B.P.

Note: The dates given above are only approximations and should be used in a general context only. This data is constantly being revised as new information becomes available. **B.P. means "before present."**

Collecting Points

WHY COLLECT PROJECTILE POINTS?

Whether you collect ancient Chinese cloisonné, Egyptian tomb pieces, or projectile points, there is a particular satisfaction in possessing a piece of history from the distant past--to hold in your hand an object that was made by someone thousands of years ago.

Projectile points may very well be the earliest evidence of man's ability to create, style, and manufacture objects of symmetry and beauty. If you ever have the privilege of seeing an exceptional piece, made of the finest material, and flaked to perfection, take a close look. You will soon realize that these early tools of man were made for two reasons: function and beauty. They represent a unique art form crafted by the world's earliest artists. Unique, because, like snowflakes, each specimen is an original and no two are exactly alike.

Many different materials were utilized in crafting these points. From crude slate, conglomerate or quartzite, to high quality flint, agate, jasper, chalcedony, petrified wood or volcanic obsidian, the list is endless. The Indians went to great lengths to obtain high quality material from the popular flint and chert quarries known to them, such as Dover in Northwest Tennessee, Flint Ridge in Ohio, and the many obsidian sources of the west. It is believed that extensive trade networks for flint and other objects were established in the earliest times and extended over vast areas from coast to coast.

The variations in shape and flaking style are clues to dating and identifying point types. The novice should study points from the different periods illustrated in this book and become familiar with the various styles produced. Generally speaking, the older Paleo and Archaic types are better made, exhibiting the finest flaking, thinness, edge work, and symmetry ever produced by man. The earliest points are mostly auriculate or eared. Some are grooved in the center or fluted. Later, these forms basically became side-notched, corner-notched, basal-notched or stemmed. With the introduction of the bow, most points became smaller and lighter with stemmed bases. However, during the Woodland period, Paleo auriculate and Archaic notched forms reappeared for a short period of time.

Some collectors specialize in a particular type, while others try to assemble a collection of many shapes and types. Most collectors are only interested in points from their immediate locale, and only if found by them. However, this author has learned after many years of hunting, that the only way to put together a quality collection is through intelligent buying. It's a rare occurrence today to find an outstanding piece for your collection by hunting in the field.

FIRE DAMAGED POINTS

Points made of flint, chert, chalcedony, and other materials are susceptible to damage when in close contact with fire and heat. This can occur when points shot at an animal are left in the butchered meat that is cooked over a fire. Fire damaged flint reflects a rather unique appearance, usually a circular pitted, or pock-marked look not unlike miniature moon craters.

There have been theories that the intense heat of fire actually brings about a molecular change or rearrangement of molecules. This undue stress or tension causes a change in the material which induces the pock-marks to form. This has been questioned and criticized by some geologists who flatly state that no such action takes place.

The acceptable and more logical explanation is that the change is purely physical. That is, the heat from the fire is applied and transferred in such a random and uneven manner that the coefficients of contraction and expansion cause the damage or pitting.

(Examples of fire damaged points) Note typical pitting damage to the surfaces.

The resultant conflict of expansion and non-expansion coefficients flake off the flint material due to tensions within itself. The resultant flake is quite different from a pressure or percussion flake in that it is circular and, of course, non-controllable. The examples illustrated show points with the typical pitting associated with fire damage.

IMPACT FRACTURES

When spear and arrow points are thrown or shot, they sometimes collide with hard objects such as bone in animals or rock or wood when the target is missed. If the angle at the point of impact is just right, the resulting blow will fracture the point, forming a flute or channel that runs from the tip toward the base. In other examples the fracturing will run up the side, or the tip of the point will simply snap off. Occasionally, these broken points with impact fluting are remade into new points with the flute channel still visible (see illustration). These should not be confused with real fluted Paleo points that were

Example of a repaired impact fracture. The point was retipped.

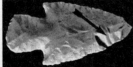

Impact fracture located at the tip

Left: Example of a long impact fracture that runs almost to the base.

found by later Indians and rechipped into a more recent point, also with the fluting still present. Points with well defined impact fractures are interesting additions to any collection and should not be overlooked when going through the junk boxes.

HAFTING

All finished arrow points and most knives were made to be inserted or tied onto a shaft or handle. To prevent movement, sinew, gut, and rawhide were used to tie the stone blades onto the shafts or handles. Fibers from hair and plants (grasses, tree bark, yucca, vines, etc.) were also employed for lashing.

Pitch, asphalt and resin were used as adhesives (when available) to glue the lashings to the stone and shaft. In some of the western states where climates are very dry, complete specimens of arrows and knives have been found preserved in caves. On rare occasions complete arrows and knives have been found with hafting completely intact. Of course, during the Indian wars out west in the 1800s, perfect hafted specimens were

Above: A complete knife with bone handle and flint blade recovered in eastern Colorado. Note drilled hole in handle

Above: A very rare example of an 9,000 year old Kirk Corner Notched point with original hafting petrified to the base. Reverse side shows a brown stain where hafting was.

collected and saved from the battlefields as well. Cane and many types of wood were employed for arrow shaft usage while bone, ivory and wooden handles were crafted for holding the knives.

DATING AND NAMING POINT TYPES

For decades, professional archaeologists and collectors have been interested in the age and classification of projectile points. Of course the best information has come from archaeologically controlled scientific excavations where exact locations, cultural association, and carbon dating of associated matter with point types was made.

Above: Rare examples of hafted arrow-points on wooden shafts. All were found in New Mexico or Nevada. The binding is fashioned of fibres from a local plant.

Above: A complete knife with bone handle and flint blade recovered 4 feet below the floor of a dry cave in Fort Rock desert in south central Oregon. Note the tally marks at the rear of the handle and the gut hafting and gum or asphaltum adhesive cementing the blade to the handle.

The carbon deposits from animal and vegetable remains are taken from these stratigraphic layers and dated through the carbon-14 process and other techniques. This gives an age for each layer and its associated artifacts. In 1997, it was reported that all previously published carbon-14 dates are now slightly older than realized. Adjustments should be made on a logarithmic scale with age. **Clovis** is now believed to be about 2,000 years earlier.

Many of these sites were occupied for thousands of years by various peoples who left projectile points around their campfires, buried for future discovery with thousands more lost through usage and breakage. The face of the land next to rivers where many of these sites are, is always changing due to flooding. Indian villages and campsites were either being eroded away or buried under silt deposited by the flooding river. Later, the sites that were destroyed would become occupied again, waiting for the next inundation. Over a period of thousands of years, these sites accumulated many stratified layers of silt, some of which contain evidence of human occupation. The most recent culture would be near the top with the oldest at the deepest levels.

Some of these excavated areas produce important point types which were named after the site from which they were found. Sometimes popular "type styles" such as **Clovis** are found all across the country while others are very localized and found only in a few counties. Some of the more famous type sites are **Cahokia** at St. Clair and Madison counties in Illinois, **Eva** and **Nuckolls** in northwest Tennessee, **Quad** and **Pine Tree** in northwest Alabama, **Black Rock Concave** in Black Rock Desert, Nevada, **Clovis** near Clovis, New Mexico, **Folsom** near Folsom, New Mexico, **Golondrina** in Val Verde Co., Texas, **Graham Cave** in Montgomery Co., Missouri, **Hardaway** in Stanly Co., North Carolina, **Hell Gap** from Hell Gap Valley in Wyoming, **LeCroy** in Hamilton Co., Tennessee, **Midland** near Midland, Texas, **Milnesand** in Milnesand, New Mexico, **Motley** in northeast Louisiana, **Plainview** near Plainview, Texas, **San Patrice** in DeSoto Co., Louisiana and **Sandia** from the Sandia Cave near Albuquerque, New Mexico. There are many more sites too numerous to list here.

These excavations have provided valuable information about point types and their cultural relationships. Papers published (by the archaeologists who worked the sites) about these excavations were the first attempt at typing or classifying projectile points. These papers and books are still important reference sources today and belong in every reference library.

How Points Were Made

Decades ago this author was spending his weekends hunting rivers, fields and streams for the elusive #9s and 10s but usually coming home with the average 3s and 4s. His hunting territory covered several states including dozens of private farms, rivers, creeks and lakes. The usual procedure when hunting on private land was always to ask permission. This required a short visit with the owner who would be sizing you up before allowing access to his land. Some of the farmers were very suspicious of strangers because of their hidden whiskey stills.

During these interesting visits, I would hear stories of how the farmers thought the Indians made arrowheads. A common tale was that the Indians would heat up a container of water. After getting it as hot as they could, they would take an eagle feather, dipping it in the scoulding water, then carefully releasing drops onto the flint causing an immediate fracturing to occur. Eventually they would end up with a finished arrowhead. Although this story was pretty common, I don't think any of the farmers ever tried it to see if it would really work.

Actually flint tools are made by the art of knapping flint. Hundreds of thousands of years ago, far away from this country, early homo erectines learned how to knap flint. The earliest forms from Africa have been dated to 2.2 million years ago. Secrets of the knappers art came with the first peoples to inhabit the Americas. Beginning with Paleo Man the best sources for quarrying flint and chert were soon found. The technique of exposing flint to heat to change its molecular structure making it more "glassy" and easier to flake was learned prior to Paleo times. Heat treating changes the color as well, sometimes making it difficult to match the altered stone with local sources.

Although small points were crafted from local materials such as small nodules that can be found along rivers and streams, the larger points were made from a large nodule. The flintknapper takes the nodule and knocks off a chunk forming a spall. He then strikes off long slivers that can be crafted into points. As the slivers are struck off, a circular core is formed. Eventually the core is discarded and the process starts over. Flint flakes can be removed easily in the direction of the force applied. Indians used hammer stones, elk billits, and other tools in rough shaping the stone through percussion blows. After a suitable form was achieved with the proper thickness, the final shaping was accomplished using tools such as the fine tips of antlers. This procedure is called "pressure flaking" and was carefully applied to all edges and was used to create the notches on side and corner notched points.

Examples of a group of spent cores made from spalls.

Buying Points

FINDING VERSUS BUYING POINTS

Why would a collector want to buy points instead of just finding his own? The answer to this question is very simple. Many people who collect just don't have the time to spend hunting in the field. In most cases, you can buy points cheaper than you can find them, when you consider travel, lodging, food, and the money you could be earning if you were at home. But the best reason for buying is to acquire quality pieces that are not available or found in your immediate area of hunting. Not all collectors are fortunate enough to live in an area that produces high quality material. Many collectors hunt in plowed fields that do sometimes produce high quality points, but unfortunately most are broken or chipped by the plow and cutting harrow.

One collector lived and hunted in central Alabama and Mississippi for ten years, keeping every piece that was found. Later, when he took a realistic look at his collection, it was only worth about $1,000.00 and the points in the collection looked very common. He began selling everything but the most perfect pieces. He used the money to finance hunting trips to other areas that were strong with quality points, and also began to buy nice pieces as they became available. His previous collection was basically all the same color. He soon found that points from other areas were more colorful, and within three years he had built a large collection that anyone would be proud to own. He kept up this style of collecting for several years and has owned many super quality pieces worth a substantial amount of money. If he had not ventured out into other hunting areas his collection today would still be worth little and of low quality. Try acquiring a quality item, whether it be stone, bone, pottery, or flint. After all, isn't this what collecting is all about?

HOW TO BUY AUTHENTIC RELICS

The best way to recognize an old point is by knowing how both river and field patination affect the type of flint from which the point is made. Each point type also has its own style of chipping that you should study and understand. A Paleo point never has random flaking, while Archaic and Woodland points do. You should understand that changes in patination along the edges or near the tip of an arrowhead are signs of rechipping. Hinge fractures are good indicators to the authenticity of a point. An old point will patinate underneath the hinge fractures while recently applied patina will only be on the surface. Hold the point up to a light source and look along the edges for restoration. You can also lightly tap the surface of a point with a steel knife blade to find a restored area. The restored spot will have a dull sound. Restored areas will also look different under a black light.

If you go to a show, flea market, or someone's house to buy relics, you should first size up the collection or inventory that is for sale. Look for any questionable pieces. If the relics past the test, then you must assess the seller. If he looks untrustworthy, you should probably not take the risk.

But if you are convinced the person is of good character and the piece you want really looks good and authentic, you could use the following guidelines to protect yourself. First, ask for a money back guarantee in writing. Some dealers will comply but may put a time limit on it. Also ask if the point has been restored or rechipped. Second, you could ask for a satisfaction guarantee. This means that if you do get a piece that becomes questionable later, you would be able to trade it for another item of equal value that you feel is a good authentic piece. This arrangement would help you feel more secure about what you are buying. Third, especially if a lot of money is at risk, you should tell the person that you want to send the relic to someone for authentication before the sale is final. If a lot of money is at risk, you may want to get more than one opinion. Ask around to find out who the best authenticators are for your area.

There is a lot of competition in the Indian relic market. Some people will condemn a competitor's piece to persuade you to buy from them. They will also try to buy a good item from you at a cheap price. Others may say a relic is bad just to convince you that they are experts. To be truly knowledgeable in Indian relics, this book will help, but you need to learn as much as you can. Study the flint types of your collecting area and how they look with natural patination. Learn to match flaking styles with types. Simply look at as many good authentic points as you can. Remember, the people who think they know more than everyone else are usually the ones who get burned.

Market Reports

Photographs of needed types have been pouring in from collectors over the past two years. It has been impressive how many individuals now have scanners and/or digital cameras and have been able to email pictures to me for inclusion in future editions of this book. If you have points worthy of inclusion, shoot or scan at 300 pixels/inch with a ruler along side and email to: (obob@gemstonepub.com). Be sure to send location, type, material, etc. with each picture.

The arrowhead market has continued to show growth in many areas with points from the Paleo period leading the way. Fluted points of all types continue to sell for record prices everywhere. Early Archaic beveled types have shown increased demand as have the smaller, true arrowpoints. Points made of exotic or colorful materials are in the most demand as are all higher grade examples of most types. Low, field grade points continue to languish with slow sales.

Certification has become more and more widely used. It is important before spending a large sum of money for a point that you have the benefit of an expert opinion, and it should be someone of your choice. There are quite a number of people papering points across the country. Be sure to check their reputation before choosing the right certifier to certify your points. On expensive points, it might be wise to have at least a couple of experts see the point before spending your money.

The following market reports were prepared by some of our advisors from around the country and are included here for your information.

Great Basin and Columbia River artifacts continue to be in extremely high demand regardless of the grade. Columbia River points should continue to rise in value over the next several years because there is literally no new material to be found. The main reason is because of the dams that were installed on the Columbia and Snake rivers in the '50s and '60s. Up to 98 percent of all relic sites are now under water. What few areas are not covered up are on Federal lands and off limits to collecting. About the only way you can obtain the treasured Columbia River gems now is to seek out and purchase Old Timers collections or buy them from people who have already done this and are willing to sell some of them.

Winged points like the Columbia Plateaus, Wallulas, Eastgates, Elkos and Hells Canyons are always in high demand. Translucent agate points and blades are the most highly sought relics followed by any agate material, petrified wood, jasper and then obsidian. As always, Paleo relics continue to be very scarce from this region and always in incredible demand.

G-9 & G-10 grade material continues to escalate

in price and justifiably so. G-10 Columbia Plateaus will now top $1000 each. I have been offered $1000 apiece for several of my Plateau points and have seen a frame of 35 Plateaus sell for nearly $600 each. True G-10s are extremely rare and the prices reflect that. A G-9 will easily go to 400 or 500 dollars if it has the wings and colors people are attracted to. Klickitat daggers in G-9 and G-10 condition seem to be underpriced and in great demand, however the lower grade Klicitats do not seem to be in the demand they were 4 or 5 years ago. I think the advent of the Internet has helped satisfy that demand. Medium and large knives are also in high demand.

Some undervalued sleeper points from the Columbia River would be the Early Stem (Shaniko point), Hell's Canyon, Pentagonal Knife, and Mule Ear Knife. Hell's Canyon points are extremely hard to obtain and do not fully reflect this in their pricing yet. The Shanikos are very underpriced and should see a good rise in value also as they are not easy to obtain and take the form of Cody Complex points. The Pentagonal knives are probably the most undervalued in my opinion.

Columbia River artifacts should continue rising in value because of the nonexistent new supply of relics, the high quality of workmanship and gem materials used. I believe some people are tired of watching their 401K statements plummet in value from the stock market, and some of these people are putting some money into relics.

Great Basin artifacts have really exploded in price the last 2 years and are continuing to be in extremely high demand. Large knives 5 inches and longer made of translucent Obsidian are almost impossible to keep in stock as are G-8 and higher Humboldts. Northern Side Notch points over 2 inches long are incredibly good sellers and once they go over 3 inches long in grade 9 or 10 can approach $1000 each. Cougar Mountain and Black Rock Concave points are extremely rare and if you have a chance to obtain one that is authentic you need to do it. Haskett points are also extremely hard to obtain and in great demand.

Some sleepers in the Great Basin area of collecting would be higher grade Eastgates, Rose Spring, Nightfire, Early Stemmed and Gatecliff points. I would look for some nice increases in value in these style points.

The overall demand for all Western points is still very high and I look for it to continue for many years because of the fact a lot of land out West is Federal land and off limits for collecting. There is a limited supply of available relics and a high demand for them.

The advent of the Internet has opened up the availability of obtaining relics for everyone. This is good! Along with the good also comes the bad though. Be sure you get a guarantee and return privilege of at least 14 days and preferably 30 days from whomever you buy a relic. Some people are not honest on the Internet and will sell fakes on purpose. There are a couple of good websites that can help you with questions about reputable artifact dealers also. The AACA (Authentic Artifact Collectors Association), and The Arrowpack website are a couple of them.

Artifact collecting is a very rewarding hobby and very interesting one also. Whether you collect field grade or high grade artifacts, there is a whole lot of history behind them. There are also many things to study regarding every point type! When you own an arrowpoint or blade, you own a piece of history! Good luck and good collecting.

John Byrd - Piedmont, SC
Northern Plains section

In the past two years our economy has taken a dramatic downturn but the values of artifacts have remained stable across the board. Though the overall prices have not risen considerably, it would have been much better to have your money in quality artifacts than in the stock market.

High quality items have always been a better investment than the common grades because there is a greater demand among collectors. Of course, Paleo-Indian projectile points are still the most eagerly sought after but almost any high grade specimen is a good commodity to have. For decades, artifacts from the Midwest, Central States and the extreme Southeast have been the focus of most collector attention. However, material from these regions has become so expensive that other areas have started to draw much more interest. As a result, Great Basin, Northern High Plains and Eastern artifacts have become more popular.

About the only areas of Indian art that have declined in demand are the Indian rugs and jewelry. Prices do not seem to have dropped but the desirability certainly has. At most of the major shows I have attended there have been very few sales of these items. Consequently, some of the dealers who have specialized in these items are changing their focus. I do not expect this trend to be long-term, but it is noteworthy at the moment.

For me, one of the most refreshing occurrences in the artifact market has been the influx of Neolithic arrowheads from the Sahara Desert in Northwest Africa. I am amazed at the quality of the artifacts from this region and consider them every bit as fine as the Columbia River Gem Points. Best of all, they are dirt cheap when compared to American Indian material. At the moment there are literally hundreds of thousands of these on the market but I can guarantee that the day will come when the sources for these will start to dry up. When that happens the prices will skyrocket. So, I think this is one of the best investments anywhere in today's artifact market.

The process of negative legislation continues to have a great impact on this hobby. Just recently, Georgia enacted new laws making it illegal to collect artifacts or relics of any kind from its waterways. So, the popular hobby of relic diving in the rivers has become illegal. If you plan on looking for artifacts along the riverbanks and sand bars on Kansas rivers you must have the written permission of land owners on both sides of the river. Many states allow collecting on private property but require written permission from the property owner. If you collect, make sure you are legal because it can be expensive if you don't. For example: an Oregon collector recently was fined 2.5 million dollars for illegal collecting in Nevada. Our hobby cannot stand this kind of adverse publicity.

In the past I have heard many complaints about the amount of fake artifacts encountered at most of the artifact shows. I agree that it is substantial and for this reason you need to purchase from reputable dealers who are willing to accept returns if an item is found to be bogus. A few dealers even offer a lifetime guarantee of authenticity. Don't just research the artifacts you wish to add to your collection, check out the reliability and reputation of those you buy from also. The Internet and online auctions are extremely popular but be very cautious. I continue to feel that about 75% of the artifacts offered there are questionable. Make sure you have full money back return privileges. Check to see if the Internet seller you are buying from is a member of AACA (Authentic Artifact Collectors Association). Members of this organization agree to high standards to protect not only you the purchaser but also their own integrity.

This is a great hobby and it is continuing to grow in popularity. I would recommend that you seek out the particular area that interests you most, purchase the best quality you can afford, and most of all just enjoy it.

Tom and David Davis - (Davis Artifacts, Inc.) Eastern Central section

The market for authentic relics seems to be stronger than ever. We used to discuss what would happen to the market if and when some of the huge oldtime collections were sold. This has happened in the past couple years. Relics from both the Clemmons Caldwell and Earl Townsend collections have become available to today's collectors. To purchase some of these pieces, many collectors have sold their artifacts to fund their purchases. This has been very healthy for the market and has made some pieces available that haven't been for sale for many years.

Birdstone, bannerstone, and top-end flint prices have exploded. When the stock market plunged, many people pulled their funds and invested in upper-end artifacts. These have traditionally been excellent investments that have yielded high returns. Relics can be handled and enjoyed much more than stocks!

Upper-end paleo points have continued to climb, but the lower grades seem to be fairly flat. The only other flat places in the market seem to be in lower-end flint and Texas flint. This will most likely change with time.

Internet sales are still on the increase, but it seems that some of these collectors still don't educate themselves on the detection of reproductions. This results in a large turnover of Internet based collectors because many of them move on to something else once they learn they have been taken. Some think the problem of reproductions is new while it is nearly as old as the hobby. Reproductions have been on the market since at least the late 1800s! The key to detecting them is education. Read all you can and talk to everyone who is willing to share their knowledge with you. You can also send your relics to one of the authenticators who will offer an opinion on your relics for a fee.

Despite the sagging stock market, and reports of a slow economy, Indian relics more than held their own at auctions, shows and sales throughout the year. The trend of recent past years continues, that is, the prices continue to rise, especially for caliber items.

At the low or beginning end, there's never much change, because, as always, there are lots of field grade and average quality material to go around. Dollar points are still dollar points and if sold in bulk bring even less. Endscrapers and flake tools still struggle for respectability, though there are some collectors who recognize and go after the Paleo form tools. A Paleo form endscaper of pretty, quality flint might get $5-15, but often will be bunched into a box lot. If a well known Paleo site is attached to such a piece, the price will go up to $25-35. This holds true for the host of Paleo form tools such as flake gravers, coronet gravers, limaces, endscapers, spokeshaves, etc.

Fluted points continue to be sought after by many. Small 1-2" points now fetch $250-500 or more. Points in the 3-4" range are rare anyway, but will command prices in the thousands of dollars. A 2-1/2" brown jasper point with a tip ding sold at auction for $700.

Early Archaic points are often well made and bring good value - types like Kirk's, St. Charles, Amos and Palmer. A small Amos, 1" or so, of red jasper, sold for $35. Dovetails are also often well made of pretty nice flints, and though not common certainly do occur, mostly in average sizes. A 3" dove of Flintridge white/gray chalcedony sold for $350.

Axes, celts, pestles and gouges have all held their values. As before, and as with all categories, the better quality and better documented items realize top value. Beater axes can be had for $10-25, sometimes less, as these are often thrown into box lots, along with all manner of broken stone tools, or rough and crude stone tools, or things like pitted stones and netweights. Average complete axes will bring $50-$250, while better and larger axes will be $300-750 and up.

Gouges usually sell well. They're kind of scarce and there's a cadre of collectors who specialize in obtaining them. A used up, average example will get $65-90. A good example - $200-300. A great

'celery stalk' specimen will go $500 and up.

Celts continue to be one of the harder stone tools to move, probably because there are so many of them. Average and used up specimens are often box lotted, or sell for $3-5 each. Good celts or even better celts can be had for $20-35. The rare large or exquisite celt can get to a couple of hundred dollars.

Pestles are usually an easy sell. Average pestles can go $50-150, while better, larger ones can see several hundred up to $1000 or more for a well executed three footer.

Points of the Archaic types, like Brewerton, or Bare Island and related types, sell grade or average for $3-10. Many of these are made of non-silicates or coarse silicates, like rhyolite, argillite, indurated shale, quartzite, etc., making for generally coarse products. Some of these are well made though, and if of a colorful quartzite or particularly well done, and of a type like Poplar Island or Piedmont, and of size, 4" or better, it'll go $500 and up.

Bifurcated type points are also generally good sellers, especially in the $5-10 range. There's quite a few of these around and most collectors have them. Really nice, large, or 'eccentric' specimens can go $50-100. The Broadpoints of the Northeast continue to be a main attraction for collectors. The Perkiomen Broadpoint always brings spirited bidding at auctions. Grade specimens, 1-2", of jasper, sell for $25-75, sometimes more. Slightly better and all of a sudden, hundreds of dollars will be offered. A specimen 4" or better will be in the thousands. The same holds true for some of the Atlantic Phase blades from Maine or Massachusetts for example. A 5-1/4" specimen of a stemmed Atlantic Phase type blade from Ontario sold for $2900.

Slate category artifacts are often scarce in the Northeast, especially the exotic forms like birdstones, bar amulets, boatstones, etc. Gorgets and pendants are common in the grade to average ranges, and sell for $50-150. Better quality items will be in the $300-800 range. Not many birds, bars or boats come along in any given year in the Northeast, but a bar bird from Massachusetts sold for $7000+, and a red slate bar bird from Pennsylvania sold for $6500. Bannerstones usually incite spirited bidding at auctions, even for so-so or average specimens, which will sell for $200-400. Good to better quality ones will go $750-

1500, and the rare, fine specimen $2500 and up.

Pottery is finally, after many years of languishing, realizing what it should be worth. It's rare, it's fragile. Prices in the $400-700 range are not uncommon for average, 6" in diameter let's say, vessels with 20-40% restoration. Complete vessels are going for $1000 and up.

Pipes are also a favorite category, and one where restoration is tolerated, if not desired. Plain or restored pipes, stone or clay, can bring $100-300. Effigy pipes can get to $5000-10,000, like the Micmac Frog Effigy pipe that went for $5500. And there's all ranges in between, depending on quality of work, culture, material, etc.

Historic items seem to show up less and less, things like brass items, glass beads, gun parts, etc. They have good value when they do appear, but some collectors are nervous about having materials that can be construed as burial items. Generally, what's on the market has a history, and would be 'grandfathered' under any new laws or regulations. Certainly no newly dug up burial items are coming on the market, and it's been this way for many, many years in the circles I travel in.

No surprise, beaded items and related things like catlinite pipes and southeast pottery continue to be the top sellers at most auctions and in private sales. Beaded moccasins average $500-800, pipe bags, $2000-4000. Catlinite pipes - $500-5000, those at the upper end will have an original wood stem and a long history. Pueblo and Anasazi pottery of colorful designs, and complete, will bring thousands of dollars. The market was strong throughout 2002 and it looks like more of the same to come. And rightly so. These ancient things should be valuable, and they should be available to the populace, most of whom will take better care of them anyway. This must not be construed as a criticism, but only reality. Most institutions have enough artifacts and have a hard time coming up with the funds and personnel to properly curate what they do have. Their goal should not necessarily be to have everything, but to strive to obtain the finest and best to concentrate preservation efforts on, and hold for the American people.

Ron Harris - Hickory, NC
North Carolina Piedmont Region

The current state of the economy has impacted the Indian artifact market to varying degrees in the Carolina Piedmont. However, the slump certainly hasn't in the least dampened the enthusiasm or growing interest in the hobby of collecting Indian arrowheads. In fact more and more hobbyists, collectors, investors, buyers, sellers, traders, dealers and interested citizens in general continue to attend, support, and sponsor artifact shows held periodically in the region.

Despite the economic situation, it is observed that the buying, selling and trading of arrowheads and Indian artifacts in general has been quite brisk. However, to insure the maximum value for their dollar, most everyone has become more conservative and judicious in the way they apply their money during artifact sales, trades or acquisitions.

Some individuals in the region were more adversely impacted by the economy slump than others due to layoffs, cutbacks, unemployment, etc. This resulted in some collectors having to resort to selling some or all of their artifact collection to make ends meet during these difficult times. Others, less drastically affected by the economy, were fortunate in being financially able to acquire artifacts and/or entire collections that otherwise would not have been available under different economic conditions.

Regardless of the economic situation, Paleo and early archaic projectile points continue to be the most coveted and desired artifacts in the Carolina Piedmont. Clovis, Hardaway-Dalton, Hardaway corner-notch, Palmer and Kirk Corner Notched points draw the most interest and command premium prices, especially those in the G-7 through G-10 category. Sales in this group are reported to range from several hundred dollars to several thousand dollars per piece depending on the size, shape, quality, color and provenience.

The next most desired point types in the region include: Kirk Stemmed, Lecroy, Stanly, Morrow Mountain, Guilford and Savannah River. Classic G-9 and G-10 examples in this group are highly desirable and reported sales average from $100 to $1,000 for top specimens.

The third most desired point groups in the region include: Yadkin, Yadkin Eared, Uwharrie, Pee Dee and Caraway. The Yadkin point seems to be the most desirable of this group and competition among collectors for the better examples is keen. Prices in this group are reported to range from $25 to several hundred dollars, depending on quality and desirability to the collector.

Ground stone tools such as axes and celts are also popular with collectors but not to the extent of arrowhead popularity. Reported sales of ground stone artifacts average from a low of $25 upward to $2500 for high grade grooved axes.

Prehistoric and protohistoric pottery or ceramics is popular among some of the collectors and reported sales have ranged from $100 to $2000 depending on the size, quality and location found.

Fakes continue to plague the market and frequently appear at relic shows despite the best efforts of show sponsors and promoters. A fake is defined as a modern made (knapped) point that is often artificially aged and represented to a potential buyer as an authentic prehistoric artifact. Many such fakes are being offered and sold on Internet auctions. It is "Buyer Beware" when dealing with such online auctions. Many have been "burned" by Internet auctions that advertised "authentic" artifacts with low "reserves" and in reality turned out to be modern made "fakes".

Reproduction points are modern knapped points offered by flint knappers who honestly represent them as modern made replications of ancient point styles and types. Reproductions make excellent study pieces and are becoming more popular to many individuals who collect, display, and represent them as objects of "art". This is also a way for one to own or have a reasonable facsimile or replication of the ancient artifact that they otherwise could not afford.

Many collectors have now changed their opinion about "restored" arrowheads in view of the high cost involved in acquiring upper grade arrowheads. In the past many collectors would not think of owning a restored piece but now, professional high-quality restoration is more and more accepted and desired. This is especially true for personally found "heartbreakers," arrowheads with broken points, barbs, stems or blades that can easily be restored to the original shape.

Restoration also provides an opportunity to own an exceptional "authentic" piece at an affordable price. Professionally restored artifacts make great show, educational and reference displays and provides a "true" representation of the ancient artifact if done properly.

Authentic high quality prehistoric arrowheads are less frequently found today for many reasons. Present day collectors often dream of the days past when it was not uncommon to find or to acquire pristine and classic specimens that are seen in some of the today's more prominent old time collections. In this regard, high quality casts of many of those old-time classic specimens are sometimes available from various sources. Casts are actually molded over the original artifact and then professionally tinted to an exacting color match. Museum quality artifact casts, although somewhat expensive, are becoming more popular today and make excellent study pieces for reference collections. Having a cast of the original authentic arrowhead sometimes is the only way to actually possess the "likeness" of those coveted artifacts found long ago. Casts in certain instances are displayed in private collections, museums and institutions throughout the nation and world in order to give many the benefit of viewing the likeness of the original artifact.

Bottom line, however, is the fact there is nothing better than finding or having the true authentic ancient arrowhead or artifact that makes up the majority of most serious collections and institutional displays. **The Overstreet Indian Arrowheads Identification and Price Guide** is the nationally recognized authority on arrowhead identification and pricing for all regions. It has proved invaluable for the novice, amateur and professional alike. This comprehensive publication is updated every two years and contains the very latest in information concerning arrowhead identification, classification, cultural sequences, and price evaluations for various types from all regions of the United States. Regional advisors provide timely information that enables the publication to keep its readers current on the latest findings and data from issue to issue.

As the interest in and value of arrowheads and artifacts increases, one has to be aware of the potential hazard of theft. There have been reports of break-ins both at private residences and public institutions where artifacts have been stolen, presumably for resale on the black market. One such case involved a local community college where someone, despite elaborate security measures, forced open display cases and removed a quantity of valuable and irreplaceable artifacts that were locally found and donated by an estate to the institution for permanent educational display. There are reports of private homes having been entered and artifact collections taken in the absence of the homeowner. If you have a valuable collection, it is imperative that you maintain a reliable security system and/or appropriate insurance coverage. One should have detailed inventory, evaluation, photos and any other means of documentation of the collection in the event of fire or theft.

The "next" generation of collectors is coming along and is noticeably interested and intrigued by the hobby of Indian arrowhead collecting. Present generation collectors provide encouragement and support for these youngsters and welcome the opportunity to assist and educate whenever possible.

The outlook for the artifact hobby is great and it is foreseen that the economy will certainly recover and the hobby will continue to grow in leaps and bounds. In addition to being an enjoyable hobby, it is a good investment for the future and at the same time serves to preserve our prehistory, provided adequate records and provenience is maintained.

Remember, the best way to educate yourself in the art of arrowhead collecting is to view other authentic collections, both private and at museums, especially in your own area. Also, talk with old time experienced collectors who can provide valuable information and tips to both novice and advanced collectors. Most old time collectors are eager to share information and provide timely advice that will assist you in areas of artifact authenticity, values and acquisition.

Happy hunting and collecting!

Bill and Donna Jackson · Mt. Sterling, KY
Great Basin & Northern Central sections

The artifact market continues to offer tremendous collecting pleasure as well as potentially lucrative financial rewards so long as one is knowledgeable on the subject and deals with honorable trustworthy individuals whose good reputations precede them.

The key to navigating in today's artifact market is learning to know with certainty whether or not an artifact has true antiquity. In just the past few years, many individuals have appointed themselves artifact authenticators. That is good…if, in fact, they issue certificates of authenticity with the benefit of the experience one needs to accurately judge whether a piece is old or was made last week by a clever faker who has utilized modern techniques to age his pieces. Not all authenticators use the same standards to arrive at their decisions, and as such, there are occasions where authenti-

cators will disagree. This can be very confusing for new collectors. We urge those who have made, or plan to make, a considerable investment in artifacts to do your "due diligence," and learn for yourselves the features that distinguish ancient from modern.

In this regard, the best advice we can offer is for you to invest in a microscope with built-in illumination and use it! Learn what makes a piece unquestionably old, how to tell if the patination is ancient or if it was chemically induced last week, and beware of "dealers" who offer no money-back guarantees of authenticity with their artifacts. Believe us, it is not rocket science. You can learn to determine the difference; it simply requires your effort. For those interested, we continue to offer classes teaching the methods we at Jackson Galleries employ to evaluate artifacts. Beyond ourselves, Gregory Perino, Tom Davis, John Berner, Dwain Rogers, Sam Williams, Carlos Tatum, Ben Stermer, Jeb Taylor, Roy Motley, and Jim Fisher are some additional seasoned industry veteran authenticators who can be of tremendous benefit in helping collectors learn.

That said, we have observed that the artifact market itself has changed dramatically over the last two years and these changes need to be seriously considered. More and more folks are using the Internet to buy and sell their artifacts. We see that prices are far more unstable right now than in recent years, which we believe is a direct result of the influx of so many new dealers and their inventories, some hobbyists and some professionals. In this period we have seen artifacts that in our opinion should command high prices sell very inexpensively while pieces that we know to be fairly average have brought some extreme prices. To gain the best understanding of pricing trends, the major dealers will publish catalogs and the prices they ask will likely represent fair market at that time. Subscribe to the catalogs, study, and begin to track your observations.

One constant we can point out with certainty is that 'perfect' artifacts continue to command higher and higher prices. Lesser grades will always have less appeal and will tend not to appreciate nearly as rapidly or steeply as the higher grade material. We not only offer North American artifacts, but also global antiquities from China, Egypt, Ancient Rome and Greece, and PreColumbian from Mesoamerica, and we have observed the same trends in these collecting arenas as well. No matter what you choose to collect in the ancient antiquities realm, to build your collection in today's market you can spend your time continuously searching for bargains on the Internet or elsewhere, and/or you can decide to collect from major dealers (the majority of whom advertise within the pages of this publication) and build a solid collection that is bound to appreciate. Either way, it can be tremendous fun. All else aside, remember to always make your collecting fun! The joy is in the chase, the history, and the electrifying connection with the past. Study, learn, hunt, and enjoy. Good luck and good collecting.

Donald E. Meador - Dallas, TX

Texas and the surrounding area have enjoyed a very good fifteen years of an increasing market interest which has driven current prices to exceptional levels on the higher quality pieces. This ongoing increase in relic prices has surely made investors take a second look at putting money into IRAs and the Stock Market.

Texas has nine excellent shows now that are drawing a lot of new people into the field. Buyers are being more particular and more conscious about quality due to the price differences. Most buyers are asking for authentication papers on high quality pieces now.

Some of my customers, who still have time to go out and hunt, have reported that there are less places to dig and hunt now. This is due to many factors such as urban expansion, depletion of sites due to exhaustive hunting, etc.

More old collections have become available the last six months due to the increased values. We are seeing a more diversified type of collector and dealer who are starting in the business now. There are a lot of type collectors coming to shows now looking for needed types or upgrades for their collections. Paleo points are still leading the market with top archaic pieces not far behind.

Examples of recent sales in grades 8.5 to 10 are: Alberta 4"+ $3,000 to $15,000; Allen 4"+ $2,000 to $5,000; Barber 4"+ $2,000 to $5,000; Base Tang Knives 4"+ $2,000 to $5,000; Castroville 5"+ $1,000 to $4,000; Clovis 5"+ $2,000 to $25,000; Corner Tang Knives 5"+ $3,000 to $6,000; Covington 5"+ $2,000 to $4,000; Delhi 4"+ $1,000 to $2,000; Eden 5"+ $3,000 to $15,000; Ensor 5"+ $2,000 to $4,000; Fairland 4"+ $2,000 to $5,000; Firstview 5"+ $2,000 to $20,000; Folsom 2"+ $2,000 to $20,000; Gahagan 5"+ $1,000 to $3,000; Golondrina 5"+ $2,000 to $5,000; Kinney 4"+ $200 to $1000; Marcos 5"+ $2,000 to $4,000; Marshall 5"+ $100 to $1500; Mid-Back Tang 4"+ $400 to $2500; Midland 3"+ $2,000 to $5,000; Milnesand 3"+ $1500 to $2500; Nolan 5"+ $100-$1500; Pelican 3"+ $300 to $2000; Plainview 5"+ $2,000 to $5,000; San Saba 5"+ $3,000 to $5,000; Scottsbluff 5"+ $3,000 to $15,000; Victoria 4"+ $2,000 to $5,000.

Excellent quality rootbeer, agate, alibates, Georgetown, petrified wood and Edwards Plateau material continue to be the most valuable here. I still believe that the hobby of collecting is the most exciting and healthy savings plan that a person can become involved in.

I recommend buying all the artifact books and price guides you can get that are available. Get a mentor to help you when you start in the artifact business and don't buy from your mentor.

Roy Motley
Northern Central section

The Indian artifact-collecting hobby has continued to grow in the Mid-West. The market for middle grade artifacts remains steady with large numbers of new collectors entering the market. Artifacts in the $50 to $250 range appeal to the newer collectors, with the large numbers of new collectors, the "online auctions" on the Internet help this price range remain very strong.

With the dropping stock market and 401Ks, more and more investors are leaving Wall Street behind and investing in artifacts. This has resulted in very active upper-end artifact sells. It also tends to bring the "Fakers" out trying to make a fast buck. With that said it is no wonder a growing trend in the artifact business is Authentication. Most sellers are seeing higher prices if their artifacts have been papered by one or more of the leading authenticators. And most of the higher end buyers will not buy unless an authenticator they trust has authenticated an artifact.

Authentic "bird points" seem to be one of the fastest growing styles of points that is being collected and sold, bringing prices anywhere from $25 to $300 and up depending on the type and material. Paleo and Archaic points still remain highly sought after and prices remain in the upper range. For example a 6-inch Agate Basin point made from Burlington chert recently sold for over $3000. Woodland and Mississippian points are still holding their values and appears as if they should rise more as collectors that may not be able to afford some of the Paleo points invest in points of this area.

In closing, the market for ancient points is stronger than ever, prices continue to climb, business is good, ancient points are still being found, old collections are being sold, and there are a lot of points to be collected.

Lyle Nickel
Southern Central section

The last two years have been a very interesting period for those active in the artifact scene. I have collected artifacts for over 35 years and have at times personally wondered how much influence a fluctuating economy had on artifact prices. Given the strong, sometimes almost emotional attachment to owning artifacts by most collectors, would an economic downturn be measurably reflected in the artifact market? Well my answer is "yes". You will not find an Arrowheads listing on the New York Stock Exchange but there is obvious relativity between the economy and the artifact market. We also found that in arrowhead collecting, just like stocks, some are blue chip stocks and some are speculative. What I am saying is a honestly graded, high quality, rare, authentic artifact will always be in demand and will have less volatility of its bottom market price. Some will continue to rise even through the economic decline. We always thought we knew that, well now I feel we really do.

We have also witnessed some changes in the environment of the artifact market with the spread of computer and website selling. A number of large, longtime collectors have recently sold or placed their artifacts for sale. Artifact shows and auctions seem to grow in numbers and popularity every year. All of these activities increase the availability of saleable artifacts by putting buyers and sellers in contact with each other. It's just happening on a more frequent basis now.

It appears medium to field grade points have been the most adversely affected. Highly recognized types such as Clovis, Folsom, Firstview,

Scottsbluff, Allen, Dalton, Montell, Andice/Calf Creek/Bell are always in demand and some examples have actually shown appreciation in value. The market still demands a premium price for high grade, rare flint. Four figure sums are regularly paid for superb large examples of rarity and five figure sales for individual pieces of superior quality are still out there.

Sometimes we have to look at why we collect and what we expect from the hobby in return. Artifact collecting is not all about the value of our collectables. It's about an appreciation of the past and a willingness to actively take part in saving it for the future. It's a lot about the learning process and the friends made in the fields, shows or wherever they may present themselves.

Good luck and good hunting.

John T. Pafford - Eva, Tennessee
Eastern Central section

There have been several changes in market trends over the past two years. In large part this has stemmed from the availability of a larger quantity of high grade material. The source(s) for such a large influx of high quality artifacts on the market has resulted from the dissemination of the Earl C. Townsend Jr. and J. Clemens Caldwell collections. Although private sales from the Caldwell collection have not directly affected many in the market, it has resulted in many collectors offering previously unobtainable artifacts on the market for the purposes of raising capital. The same has proven to be true for the Townsend collection. In the past, many have predicted that this sudden influx of G-10s on the market would prove to be a fatal blow to the high prices paid for top quality artifacts. However, this has not been the case with numerous new collectors appearing across the nation to take advantage of the sudden availability of such high quality material. This has had the effect of further escalating prices to unprecedented levels. The increase of available superior flint, bannerstones, birdstones, pipes, etc. has driven collectors into a buying frenzy, in an attempt to secure great pieces while they last.

Also, another reason for such aggressive buying habits in the market stems from the fact that most of the well-known artifacts being purchased have a rich quantity of documentation for the collector's peace of mind. It has been these select "famous" artifacts that have truly set all-time price records. For instance, an Indiana Hornstone dovetail from the Townsend collection, known as the "Boonville Spear", reportedly sold for $70,000! Also, a well-known Flint Ridge Dovetail from the Townsend Collection sold for $85,000! In past editions, many market analysts have pointed to fluted Paleo artifacts as the market leader. However, on the national scene it seems as though interest in high quality Archaic points such as Dovetails and Lost Lakes has foreshadowed the recognized "king" of the flint market. At several public auctions, G-10 Lost Lakes and Dovetails have sold in the $7500 range. This represents a huge increase in the value of these point types over the past couple of years. As previously mentioned, private sales for famous Archaic flints have far surpassed record fluted point prices. Whether this is a market trend or an anomaly remains to be seen. However, it is certain that the high prices being paid for these artifacts has had a trickle down effect in relation to grades 8 and 9. These grades are increasingly being priced at levels that were previously occupied by G-10s. Many collectors that in the past enjoyed collecting nice artifacts of this quality have actually been forced out of the market from the rapid increase in prices.

Tennessee point types that have experienced the most growth over the last couple of years include the stalwart Clovis, Cumberland, Dovetail, and Lost Lake point types. Although regional point types such as Motley, Copena, Quad, and Benton have shown increased desirability in recent years, their prices have remained relatively steady. Overall, with the increase of high tech reproductions on the market, the well-documented artifacts have proven to be the best sellers. Field grade artifacts have shown little, if any, increase in prices over the past two years. More and more, with turbulence in the stock market people are turning to artifacts not only as an enjoyable hobby, but also as a sound investment for the future.

Ben Stermer - Phoenix, AZ
(Western Typology Artifact Authentication Service)

Prices for top-quality artifacts continue to increase, as does demand. Artifacts from the western United States continue to be popular, and many previously unknown and/or unnamed types have been published since the last Edition, and some previously established types have been categorized and separated. This is of course very attractive to "type" collectors attempting to build a collection containing at least one fine example of each point from a certain area. It also makes identification much easier than it has been previously. Arrow points from the Columbia Plateau region and the Great Basin are highly sought, as are coastal California types and the fine arrow points found throughout the southwest. Many fine examples are in museums and private collections throughout the west, but equally fine specimens can still be purchased legally through legitimate dealers or private collectors. Through systematic and careful buying, one can put together a collection of fine examples from any period(s) they desire. Over the past few years I have had the pleasure of examining many of the finest examples of all point types, as well as some of the best fakes. It is wise to learn as much as you can about the type(s) of artifacts BEFORE you buy that first piece, if possible. When buying top dollar pieces, mistakes can get very expensive very quickly. Always require at least a 30 day return privilege. Any legitimate seller will honor this type of guarantee. If not, better to pass it up. I have learned, there will always be something better around the next turn. In addition, always buy what you can afford, as you can always upgrade later.

Jim and Carlos Tatum
Gulf Coastal section

Since the last edition of the **Overstreet Price Guide** in 2001, interest and activity in artifact collecting has increased in intensity in the Southeast. Interest in artifacts from the region, especially Florida, has grown nationwide, and fine Newnans and Hillsboroughs, are now in demand throughout the country on a par with Dovetails and Hardins. Check the inventory of just about any of the large dealers across the US and you will usually find a representation of Florida points.

One indicator of growing interest in artifacts is the increase in new archaeological societies and the greater number of shows in the region. Two new groups are the Tri State Archaeological Society (Alabama, Florida and Georgia) and the Sunshine State Archaeological Society (Florida chapter of the Central States Archaeological Society). Membership is strong in all the societies in the region. New collectors are emerging upon the scene, proudly showing their latest finds at the shows and new books are being published about our hobby. Of the latter, two fine additions are **The Best of the Best, Vol. 2**, by Kevin Dowdy (dealing specifically with Georgia, Florida and Alabama), and **The Anthropology of Florida Points and Blades**, by Lloyd Schroeder.

Although all the shows have been well attended, overall the weak economy has had its effect on buying and selling as well. Sales are somewhat slow for average to low end artifacts, but it seems that the finest items are always in strong demand, and there are still plenty of buyers with the means to purchase a choice, rare artifact when it becomes available on the market. Recent downward trends in the stock market have caused many investors to shy away from paper intangibles and put their money in things they can tread upon or grasp, such as land and artifacts. These involve high end top quality items, as in any type of collecting. Quality over quantity is always good advice.

As to popularity of artifact types, first and foremost we have high quality Hillsboroughs, followed closely by Newnans and Paleos. Two types currently in demand are Florida Hardins and Lost Lake type Bolens. Wallers and Edgefields continue to sell quickly at shows. A large collection sold recently in Florida which contained many Tick Island items, and a good portion of these are now on the market. These include shell gouges, celts, picks, and plummets, and also some exquisitely engraved bone items. Warning: for years there have been many Tick Island fakes. Know either the item or the dealer before purchasing.

Eric C. Wagner · AACA Vice President
Eastern Central section

During the past two years, authentic relics have proven to be a much better investment then the stock market. At times it has been a buyers market, but in most cases sellers are holding out for top dollar. Field grade points are selling on the Internet for 2-5 dollars each and remaining steady. As always, artifacts with COAs from respected authenticators bring a premium over nonpapered points on the Internet. The reason for this is that the relic is being sold by a picture and the buyer can't hold the relic in hand before purchasing it. Paleo points, other than very high end, have dropped somewhat in price over the

past year. A Clovis point that would have brought $1000-$1200 two years ago now fetches $700-$800 However, not many dealers are letting them go that cheap!

Recent prices noticed of sold relics are as follows: 3" Clovis @ $600, 4" Flintridge Adena G-9 Davis COA @ $365, 8" Woodland Knife G-8 Jackson @ $285, 5" Woodland Knife G-8 Davis COA @ $250, 2 7/8" Clovis G-9 Jackson COA @ $850, 3 1/8" Dovetail G-7 Perino COA @ $300, and 4" Snyders G-8 Perino COA @ $500.

Collecting online has grown by leaps and bounds over the past two years. A couple of online artifact related organizations have memberships approaching 2000, and many new websites have popped up. There are online auctions, and many dealers have websites with relics for sale. With a simple Internet search you can locate these sites and spend literally hours viewing artifacts for sale and learning valuable information about the hobby.

eBay has the most active artifact auction on the Net, however there are many questionable listings. It is highly advisable to buy from someone with a good return period, as you are buying from a picture and probably need to hold the artifact in your hand to determine if you like it. The AACA (Authentic Artifact Collectors Association) has set an Internet standard of a 14 day unconditional return period. Buying from AACA members is the safest way to collect online.

Over all, the market is slightly down because of a poor economy, and there is less money available to be spent on relics. Are prices down? Not really. If anything the trading volume is down. Collecting authentic relics is a great hobby and a good place to invest your money.

Good luck with your collecting!

Warner Williams
Eastern Seaboard section

The demand for all types of top quality points in our region continues to climb, especially for the 9 and 10 category points. They are becoming more difficult to find or obtain. When a collector is willing to sell a quality point, the price escalates to what one is willing to pay regardless of the book value price. The lower grade points 5 and below have seemed to stabilize and continue to sell at Guide values or less due to the lack of demand.

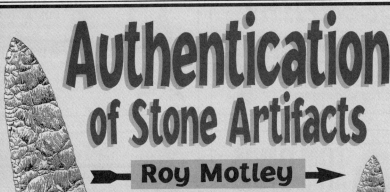

Authentication
of Stone Artifacts

→ **Roy Motley** →

▼ *Specializing in Midwestern Flint and Axes*
▼ *Appraisal Service*
▼ *Over 25 Years of Experience*

KRM CONSULTANTS
Karen and Roy Motley
29802 SE Moreland Sch Rd.
Blue Springs, MO 64014
(816)229-6025
E-Mail-Krmconsultants@aol.com

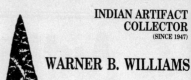

NORTHEASTERN SECTION:

This section includes point types from the following states: Connecticut, Delaware, Maine, Maryland, Massachusetts, New Hampshire, New Jersey, New York, Pennsylvania, Vermont.

The points in this section are arranged in alphabetical order and are shown **actual size**. All types are listed that were available for photographing. Any missing types will be added to future editions as photographs become available. We are always interested in receiving sharp, black and white or color glossy photos or color slides of your collection. Be sure and include a ruler in the photograph so that proper scale can be determined.

Lithics: Materials employed in the manufacture of projectile points from this region are: argillite, Coshocton chert, Coxsackie chert, crystal quartz, dolomite, felsite, Helderberg cherts, jasper, Ledge Ridge chert, milky quartz, Onondaga chert, quartzite, rhyolite, shale, siltstone, slate, vein quartz.

Important sites: Bull Brook (Paleo, Ipswich, Mass.), Burwell-Karako (Conn.), John's Bridge (Early Archaic, Conn.), Neville (Early Archaic, Manchester, NH), Plenge (Paleo, NJ), Shoop (Paleo, Dauphin Co., PA), Vail (Paleo, Maine), Titicut (Early Archaic, Bridgewater, MA), Wapanucket (Middleboro, MA).

Regional Consultant:
Gary Fogelman

Special Advisors:
Dr. Richard Michael Gramly
Richard Savidge

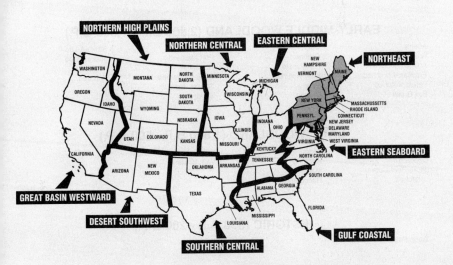

NORTHEASTERN POINT TYPES
(Archaeological Periods)

PALEO (14,000 B.P - 8,000 B.P.)

Agate Basin	Crowfield	Haw River	Ohio Lanceolate
Amos	Cumberland (Barnes)	Holcomb	Redstone
Beaver Lake	Debert	Northumberland Fluted	Scraper
Clovis	Graver	Knife	

EARLY ARCHAIC (10,000 B.P - 6,500 B.P.)

Angostura	Kanawha	MacCorkle	St. Charles
Arden	Kessel	Muncy Bifurcate	Scottsbluff
Brodhead Side-Notched	Kirk Corner Notched	Neville	Stanly
Charleston Pine Tree	Kirk Stemmed	Palmer	Stark
Dalton Classic	Kline	Penn's Creek Series	Strike-A-Lite I
Dalton Nuckolls	Lake Erie	Penn's Creek Bifurcate	Susquehanna Bifurcate
Decatur	LeCroy	St. Albans	Taunton Riv. Bif.
Hardaway	Lost Lake	St. Anne	Thebes

MID-LATE ARCHAIC (6,000 B.P - 4,000 B.P.)

Atlantic Phase Blade	Drill	Morrow Mountain	Swatara-Long
Bare Island	Duncan's Island	Newmanstown	Taconic Stemmed
Bone/Antler	Eshback	Otter Creek	Vestal Notched
Brewerton Corner	Genesee	Patuxent	Virginsville
Notched	Ground Slate	Pentagonal Knife	Vosburg
Brewerton Eared	Guilford	Piedmont, Northern	Wading River
Triangular	Hoover's Island	Piney Island	Wapanucket
Brewerton Side Notched	Kittatiny	Poplar Island	
Burwell	Lacawaxan	Savannah River	
Chillesquaque	Lamoka	Snook Kill	
Crooked Creek	Lycoming County	Squibnocket Stemmed	
Dewart Stemmed	Merrimack Stemmed	Squibnocket Triangular	

TERMINAL ARCHAIC (3,800 B.P - 3,000 B.P.)

Ashtabula	Frost Island	Meadowood	Schuylkill
Conodoquinet/Canfield	Koens Crispin	Normanskill	Susquehanna Broad
Drill	Lehigh	Orient	Wayland Notched
Drybrook Fishtail	Mansion Inn Blade	Perkiomen	

EARLY-MIDDLE WOODLAND (2,800 B.P - 1,500 B.P.)

Adena	Garver's Ferry	Piscataway	Strike-A-Lite II
Adena Blade	Greene	Port Maitland	Tocks Island
Adena (Robbins)	Hellgramite	Randolph	Vernon
Erb Basal Notched	Kiski Notched	Sandhill Stemmed	Waratan
Forest Notched	Oley	Shark's Tooth	
Fox Creek	Ovates	Snyders	

LATE WOODLAND (1,500 B.P - 500 B.P.)

Erie Triangle	Jacks Reef Pentagonal	Susquehannock Triangle
Goddard	Levanna	Web Blade
Jacks Reef Corner	Madison	
Notched	Raccoon Notched	

HISTORIC (350 B.P - 200 B.P.)

Trade Points

NORTHEASTERN UNITED STATES
THUMBNAIL GUIDE SECTION

The following references are provided to aid the collector in easier and quicker identification of point types. All photos are exactly 30% of actual size and are proportional to each other. Each point pictured in this section represents a classic form for the type. When a match is found, go to the alphabetical location of that type for more examples in true actual size.

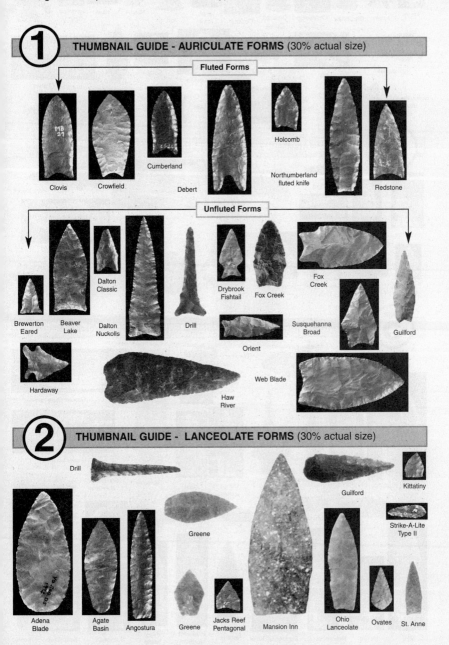

1 THUMBNAIL GUIDE - AURICULATE FORMS (30% actual size)

Fluted Forms

Clovis

Crowfield

Cumberland

Debert

Holcomb

Northumberland fluted knife

Redstone

Unfluted Forms

Brewerton Eared

Beaver Lake

Dalton Classic

Dalton Nuckolls

Drill

Drybrook Fishtail

Fox Creek

Fox Creek

Orient

Susquehanna Broad

Guilford

Hardaway

Haw River

Web Blade

2 THUMBNAIL GUIDE - LANCEOLATE FORMS (30% actual size)

Drill

Greene

Guilford

Kittatiny

Strike-A-Lite Type II

Adena Blade

Agate Basin

Angostura

Greene

Jacks Reef Pentagonal

Mansion Inn

Ohio Lanceolate

Ovates

St. Anne

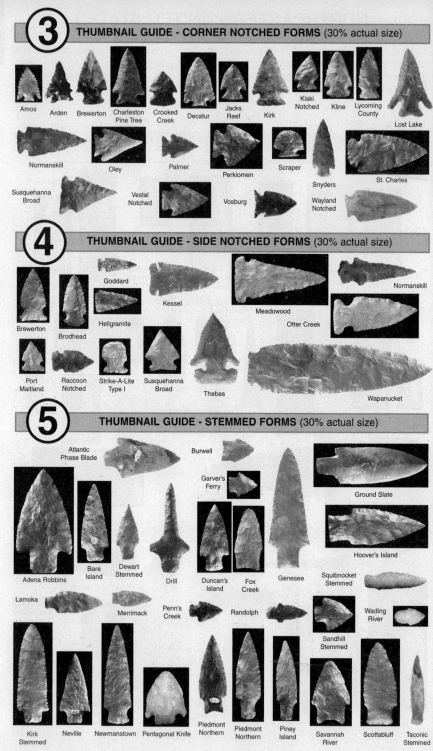

3 THUMBNAIL GUIDE - CORNER NOTCHED FORMS (30% actual size)

Amos
Arden
Brewerton
Charleston Pine Tree
Crooked Creek
Decatur
Jacks Reef
Kirk
Kiski Notched
Kline
Lycoming County
Lost Lake

Normanskill
Oley
Palmer
Perkiomen
Scraper
Snyders
St. Charles

Susquehanna Broad
Vestal Notched
Vosburg
Wayland Notched

4 THUMBNAIL GUIDE - SIDE NOTCHED FORMS (30% actual size)

Goddard
Kessel
Meadowood
Normanskill
Otter Creek

Brewerton
Brodhead
Hellgramite

Port Maitland
Raccoon Notched
Strike-A-Lite Type I
Susquehanna Broad
Thebes
Wapanucket

5 THUMBNAIL GUIDE - STEMMED FORMS (30% actual size)

Atlantic Phase Blade
Burwell
Garver's Ferry
Ground Slate
Hoover's Island

Adena Robbins
Bare Island
Dewart Stemmed
Drill
Duncan's Island
Fox Creek
Genesee
Squibnocket Stemmed

Lamoka
Merrimack
Penn's Creek
Randolph
Wading River
Sandhill Stemmed

Kirk Stemmed
Neville
Newmanstown
Pentagonal Knife
Piedmont Northern
Piedmont Northern
Piney Island
Savannah River
Scottsbluff
Taconic Stemmed

96

Contracting Stems

Conodoquinet
Canfield

Piscataway

Adena

Atlantic
Phase Blade

Koens
Crispin

Lehigh

Mansion Inn

Morrow
Mountain

Swatara-Long

Poplar Island

Schuylkill

Snook
Kill

Stark

Virginsville

Expanding Stems

Chillesquaque

Drybrook
Fishtail

Forest
Notched

Frost
Island

Susquehanna
Broad

Vernon

Perkiomen

Ashtabula

Lackawaxen

Normanskill

Orient

Patuxent

Piedmont

Perkiomen

Susquehanna
Broad

Tocks
Island

Waratan

⑥ THUMBNAIL GUIDE - STEMMED-BIFURCATED FORMS (30% actual size)

Lake Erie

Muncy
Bifurcated

St. Albans

Kanawha

Kirk
Stemmed

LeCroy

MacCorkle

Penn's
Creek

Stanly

Susquehanna
Bifurcate

Taunton
River
Bifurcate

⑦ BASAL NOTCHED FORMS

⑧ TRIANGLES

Erb Basal

Eshback

Erie
Triangle

Levanna

Madison

Squibnocket
Triangle

Susquehannock
Triangle

ADENA - Late Archaic to late Woodland, 3000 - 1200 B.P.

(Also see Adena Blade, Koens Crispin, Lehigh, Neville, Piney Island, Turkeytail)

G6, $12-$20
PA

G7, $35-$50
W. PA

LOCATION: Northeastern to Southeastern states. **DESCRIPTION:** A medium to large, thin, narrow, triangular blade with a medium to long, narrow to broad rounded "beaver tail" stem. Most examples are from average to excellent quality. Bases can be ground. Has been found with *Nolichucky, Camp Creek, Candy Creek, Ebenezer* and *Greenville* points (Rankin site, Cocke Co., TN). **I.D. KEY:** Rounded base, woodland flaking.

G7, $40-$70
Columbia Co., PA

ADENA BLADE - Late Archaic to Woodland, 3000 - 1200 B.P.

(Also see Adena, Turkeytail)

LOCATION: Southeastern to Northeastern states. **DESCRIPTION:** A large size, thin, broad, ovate blade with a rounded base and is usually found in caches. **I.D. KEY:** Woodland flaking, large direct strikes.

G5, $15-$25
PA

98

Flintridge flint

G5, $15-$30
PA

G9, $250-$450
Bridgewater, MA

G8, $80-$150
York Co., PA

ADENA - ROBBINS - Late Archaic to Woodland, 3000 - 1800 B.P.
(Also see Duncan's Island, Genesee, Neville and Piedmont)

Quartzite

G8, $150-$250
Montgomery Co.,
PA

Colorful
Flintridge
flint

G9, $300-$500
Beaver Co., PA

LOCATION: Eastern to Southeastern states. **DESCRIPTION:** A large, broad, triangular point that is thin and well made with a long, wide, rounded to square stem that is parallel sided. The blade has convex sides and square to slightly barbed shoulders. Many examples show excellent secondary flaking on blade edges. **I.D. KEY:** Square base, heavy secondary flaking.

AGATE BASIN - Transitional Paleo to early Archaic, 10,500 - 8000 B.P.
(Also see Angostura, Eden and Greene)

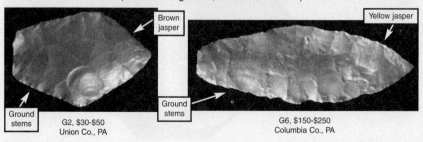

Brown
jasper

Yellow jasper

Ground
stems

Ground
stems

G2, $30-$50
Union Co., PA

G6, $150-$250
Columbia Co., PA

100

AGATE BASIN (continued)

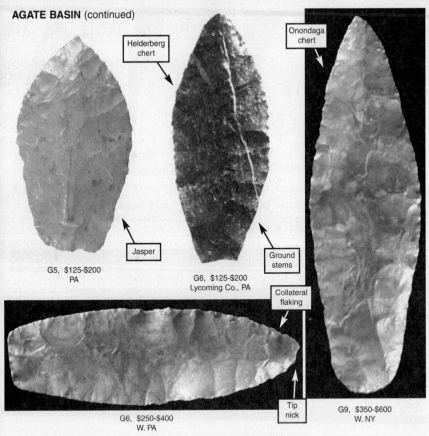

Helderberg chert

Onondaga chert

Jasper

G5, $125-$200
PA

Ground stems

G6, $125-$200
Lycoming Co., PA

Collateral flaking

G6, $250-$400
W. PA

Tip nick

G9, $350-$600
W. NY

LOCATION: Midwestern to Northeastern states. **DESCRIPTION:** A medium to large size lanceolate blade, usually of high quality. Bases are either convex, concave or straight, and are usually ground. Some examples are median ridged and have random to parallel flaking. **I.D. KEY:** Basal form and flaking style.

AMOS - Early Archaic, 10,000 - 9000 B.P.

(Also see Charleston Pine Tree, Kirk Corner Notched, Palmer)

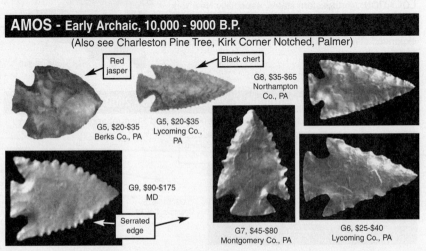

Red jasper

Black chert

G8, $35-$65
Northampton Co., PA

G5, $20-$35
Berks Co., PA

G5, $20-$35
Lycoming Co., PA

G9, $90-$175
MD

Serrated edge

G7, $45-$80
Montgomery Co., PA

G6, $25-$40
Lycoming Co., PA

AMOS (continued)

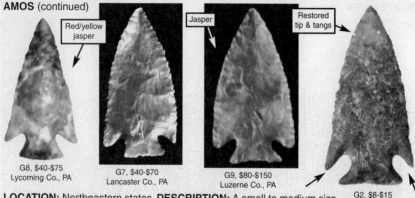

Red/yellow jasper

Jasper

Restored tip & tangs

G8, $40-$75
Lycoming Co., PA

G7, $40-$70
Lancaster Co., PA

G9, $80-$150
Luzerne Co., PA

G2, $8-$15
Lycoming Co., PA

LOCATION: Northeastern states. **DESCRIPTION:** A small to medium size corner notched point with serrated edges and barbed shoulders. The base is straight to convex. **I.D. KEY:** Edgework.

ANGOSTURA - Early Archaic, 10,000 - 8000 B.P.

(Also see Agate Basin, Clovis-unfluted, Eden, Greene, Guilford and Plainview)

Note parallel diagonal flaking

G8, $250-$400
Barry, Mass.

LOCATION: Eastern states. **DESCRIPTION:** A medium to large size lanceolate blade with a contracting, concave base. Both broad and narrow forms occur. Flaking can be parallel oblique to random. Bases are not usually ground but are thinned. **I.D. KEY:** Basal form, early flaking on blade.

ARDEN - Early Archaic, 9000 - 8000 B.P.

(Also see Charleston Pine Tree)

LOCATION: Northeastern states, especially New York. **DESCRIPTION:** A small to medium size, serrated, corner notched point with barbed shoulders and an expanded stem. **I.D. KEY:** Basal form, one barb round and the other stronger.

G4, $5-$10
NY

ASHTABULA - Late Archaic to Woodland, 4000 - 2500 B.P.

(Also see Koens Crispin, Lehigh, Perkiomen and Susquehanna Broad)

Banded shale

G3, $15-$25
Columbia Co., PA

IMPORTANT:
This Ashtabula is shown full size

ASHTABULA (continued)

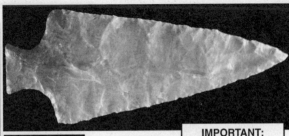

G10, $800-$1400
Broome Co., NY

G8, $400-$750
Union Co., PA

G3, $12-$20
Lycoming Co., PA

IMPORTANT:
These Ashtabulas
are shown half size

LOCATION: Northeastern states, especially Northeastern Ohio and Western Penn. **DESCRIPTION:** A medium to large size, broad, thick, expanded stem point with tapered shoulders. **I.D. KEY:** Basal form, one barb round and the other stronger.

ATLANTIC PHASE BLADE - Late-Terminal Archaic, 4300 - 3700 B.P.
(Also see Koens Crispin, Savannah River, Schuylkill and Snook Kill)

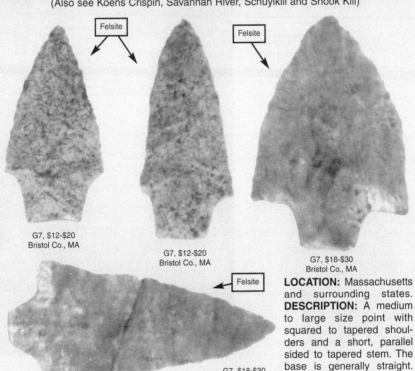

Felsite

Felsite

Felsite

G7, $12-$20
Bristol Co., MA

G7, $12-$20
Bristol Co., MA

G7, $18-$30
Bristol Co., MA

G7, $18-$30
Plymouth Co., MA

LOCATION: Massachusetts and surrounding states. **DESCRIPTION:** A medium to large size point with squared to tapered shoulders and a short, parallel sided to tapered stem. The base is generally straight. **I.D. KEY:** Base form.

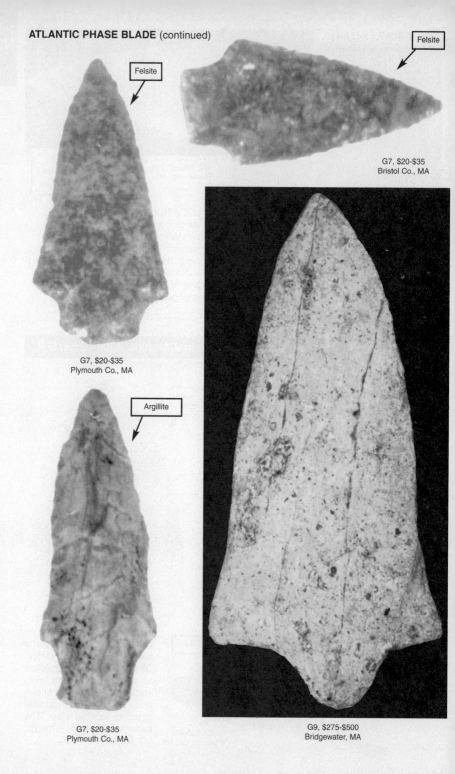

Felsite

Felsite

G7, $20-$35
Bristol Co., MA

G7, $20-$35
Plymouth Co., MA

Argillite

G7, $20-$35
Plymouth Co., MA

G9, $275-$500
Bridgewater, MA

(Also see Duncan's Island, Lackawaxen, Lamoka, Neville, Newmanstown, Piedmont, Piney Island, Poplar Island, Snook Kill)

Quartzite

Quartzite

Quartzite

Quartzite

G3, $5-$10
York Co., PA

G5, $15-$25
Cecil Co., MD

G6, $15-$30
Lancaster Co., PA

G8, $25-$40
Montgomery Co., PA

Quartzite

G7, $30-$55
Northumberland Co., PA

Argillite

G8, $35-$60
Northumberland Co., PA

LOCATION: Northeastern states. **DESCRIPTION:** A medium to large size, narrow, thick stemmed point with tapered shoulders. One shoulder is higher than the other and the blade is convex to straight. The stem is parallel to expanding. Similar to *Little Bear Creek* in the Southeast. **I.D. KEY:** Narrow stemmed point.

BARE ISLAND (continued)

Argillite

G8, $35-$60
Northumberland Co., PA

BEAVER LAKE - Paleo, 12,000 - 8000 B.P.

(Also see Clovis Unfluted, Cumberland and Orient)

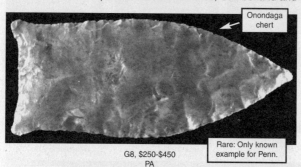

Onondaga chert

Rare: Only known example for Penn.

G8, $250-$450
PA

LOCATION: South eastern to Northeastern states. **DESCRIPTION:** A medium to large size lanceolate blade with flaring ears. Associated with *Cumberland*, but thinner than unfluted *Cumberlands*. Bases are ground and blade edges are recurved. **I.D. KEY:** Paleo flaking, shoulder area.

BONE/ANTLER - Mid-Archaic to Historic, 4500 - 100 B.P.

(Also see Trade Points)

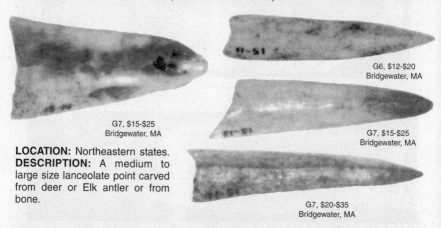

G6, $12-$20
Bridgewater, MA

G7, $15-$25
Bridgewater, MA

G7, $15-$25
Bridgewater, MA

G7, $20-$35
Bridgewater, MA

LOCATION: Northeastern states. **DESCRIPTION:** A medium to large size lanceolate point carved from deer or Elk antler or from bone.

BREWERTON CORNER NOTCHED - Middle to Late Archaic, 6000 - 4000 B.P.

(Also see Crooked Creek, Jacks Reef, Kirk, Kiski, Lycoming County, Normanskill, Palmer & Snyders)

BREWERTON CORNER NOTCHED (continued)

Jasper

Black flint

Onondaga chert

G5, $6-$12
Monroe Co., PA

G5, $5-$10
Luzurne Co., PA

G6, $6-$12
Lycoming Co., PA

G6, $6-$12
Lycoming Co., PA

G8, $12-$20
Columbia Co., NY

Onondaga chert

Black chert

G10, $25-$40
Columbia Co., NY

G7, $15-$25
Columbia Co., NY

G7, $15-$30
Columbia Co., NY

G9, $30-$50
Lycoming Co., PA

LOCATION: Eastern to midwestern states. **DESCRIPTION:** A small to medium size, thick, triangular point with faint corner notches and a concave, straight or convex base. Called *Freeheley* in Michigan. **I.D. KEY:** Width, thickness.

BREWERTON EARED-TRIANGULAR - Middle to Late Archaic, 6000 - 4000 B.P.

(Also see Fox Creek, Steubenville & Yadkin)

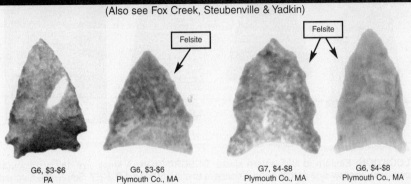

Felsite

Felsite

G6, $3-$6
PA

G6, $3-$6
Plymouth Co., MA

G7, $4-$8
Plymouth Co., MA

G6, $4-$8
Plymouth Co., MA

BREWERTON EARED-TRIANGULAR (continued)

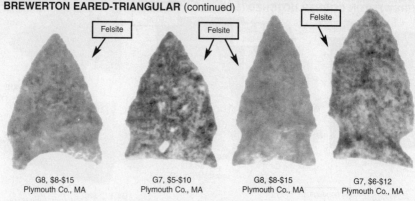

Felsite

Felsite

Felsite

G8, $8-$15
Plymouth Co., MA

G7, $5-$10
Plymouth Co., MA

G8, $8-$15
Plymouth Co., MA

G7, $6-$12
Plymouth Co., MA

LOCATION: Eastern to midwestern states. **DESCRIPTION:** A small size, triangular, eared point with a concave base. **I.D. KEY:** Small basal ears.

BREWERTON SIDE-NOTCHED - Late Archaic, 6000 - 4000 B.P.

(Also see Meadowood, Otter Creek, Perkiomen, Susquehanna Broad)

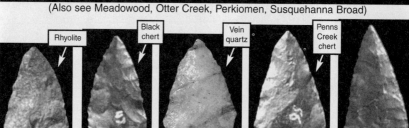

Rhyolite

Black chert

Vein quartz

Penns Creek chert

G4, $3-$6
Lycoming Co., PA

G6, $8-$15
Union Co., PA

G4, $4-$8
Bres, CT

G7, $8-$15
Monroe Co., PA

G7, $8-$15
Lycoming Co., PA

Felsite

G7, $8-$15
Plymouth Co., MA

G8, $8-$15
Luzerne Co., PA

G6, $5-$10
Bres, CT

G8, $15-$25
Luzerne Co., PA

LOCATION: Eastern to midwestern states. **DESCRIPTION:** A small size, thick, triangular point with shallow side notches and a concave to straight base. **I.D. KEY**. Small side notched point.

BREWERTON SIDE-NOTCHED (continued)

G6, $15-$30
NY

BRODHEAD SIDE-NOTCHED - Early Archaic , 9000 - 7000 B.P.

(Also see Bennington Quail Tail, Brewerton, Crooked Creek, Dovetail, Kiski, Lycoming Co.)

G5, $5-$10
Lycoming Co., PA

G7, $12-$20
Lancaster Co., PA

Gray chert

G7, $12-$20
Lycoming Co., PA

G6, $8-$15
Lycoming Co., PA

G7, $15-$25
Lycoming Co., PA

LOCATION: Northeastern states. **DESCRIPTION:** A medium size, side to corner notched point with an expanded, convex base. The notching occurs near the base and are wide. **I.D. KEY:** Wide notches, convex base.

BURWELL - Late Archaic, 5000 - 4000 B.P.

LOCATION: Northeastern states. **DESCRIPTION:** A small size, parallel stemmed point with weak, tapered shoulders and a short blade. The base is concave. **I.D. KEY:** Broad, parallel stem, tapered shoulders.

G6, $4-$8
Washingtonboro, PA

CHARLESTON PINE TREE - Early Archaic, 10,000 - 7000 B.P.

(Also see Arden, Kirk Corner Notched, Lycoming Co., Oley, Palmer, Vestal Notched, Vosburg)

CHARLESTON PINETREE (continued)

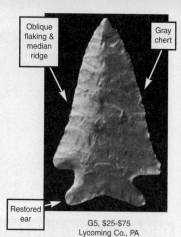

Oblique flaking & median ridge

Gray chert

Restored ear

G3, $5-$10
Lycoming Co., PA

G9, $35-$65
NY

G5, $25-$75
Lycoming Co., PA

LOCATION: Eastern to Southeastern states. The St. Albans site is in West Virginia. Points here were dated to 9,900 B.P. **DESCRIPTION:** A medium to large size, corner notched, usually serrated point with parallel flaking to the center of the blade forming a median ridge. The bases are ground and can be concave, convex, straight, bifurcated or auriculate. Called *Pine Tree* in the Southeast. **I.D. KEY:** Archaic flaking with long flakes to the center of the blade.

CHILLESQUAQUE SERIES - Mid Archaic, 6,000 - 5,000 B.P.
(Also see Lycoming County Series and Penn's Creek Series)

LOCATION: Northeastern states. **DESCRIPTION:** A small size, corner to side notched to expanded stem point. Shoulders can be strong to tapered. **I.D. KEY.** Wide side to corner notches.

G5, $5-$10
Lancaster Co., PA

CLOVIS - Early Paleo, 14,000 - 11,000 B.P.
(Also see Crowfield, Cumberland, Debert, Holcomb & Redstone)

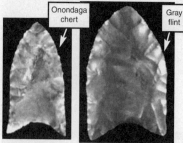

Onondaga chert

Gray flint

LOCATION: All of North America. **DESCRIPTION:** A medium to large size, auriculate, fluted, lanceolate point with convex sides and a concave base that is ground. Most examples are fluted on both sides about 1/3 the way up from the base. The flaking can be random to parallel. The oldest point type in the hemisphere. Materials used in this area are: Argillite, black flint, chalcedony, conglomerate, coshocton, coxsackie, jasper, Onondaga, quartz crystal, quartzite, rhyolite, shale & upper Mercer black chert. **I.D. KEY:** Auricles and fluting.

G3 $125-$200
Lycoming Co., PA

G5, $200-$350
Lycoming Co., PA

Onondaga chert

White flint

Chalcedony

G6, $250-$400
Lycoming Co., PA

G6, $275-$500
Lehigh Co., PA

G6, $350-$600
Lancaster Co., PA

G6, $350-$600
Chester Co., PA

Black flint

Milky quartz

G6, $275-$500
PA

G6, $450-$750
Lancaster Co., PA

Onondaga chert

Black chert

G7, $650-$1000
Lycoming Co., PA

G6, $275-$500
Columbia Co., PA

Onondaga chert

G8, $900-$1500
Lycoming Co.,
PA

Black flint

Yellow jasper

G8, $400-$700
Lehigh Co., PA

G10, $1500-$2500
Lancaster Co., PA

CLOVIS (continued)

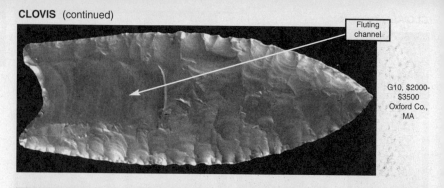

Fluting channel

G10, $2000-$3500 Oxford Co., MA

CONODOQUINET/CANFIELD - Late Archaic, 4000 - 3500 B.P.

(Also see Dewart Stemmed, Duncan's Island, Lehigh, Lamoka, Morrow Mountain, Neville, Piscataway, Sandhill Stemmed)

G3, $3-$5
Lycoming Co., PA

Argillite

G3, $4-$8
Lycoming Co., PA

Gray chert

Black chert

LOCATION: Northeastern states. **DESCRIPTION:** A medium size, narrow, contracted stem point with sloping shoulders. Base is rounded to pointed. **I.D. KEY:** Base form.

G6, $5-$10
Lycoming Co., PA

Tip damage

Chert

G4, $4-$8
Lycoming Co., PA

G6, $5-$10
NY

CROOKED CREEK SERIES - Archaic, 6000 - 4000 B.P.

(Also see Brewerton, Decatur, Dovetail, Kiski, Lycoming County and Palmer)

Black chert

LOCATION: Northeastern states. **DESCRIPTION:** A small to medium size, short, corner to side notched point with a broad base that has rounded to squared corners. Shoulders are barbed to rounded. **I.D. KEY:** Short, notched point with a large base.

G5, $5-$15
Lycoming Co., PA

CROWFIELD - Late Paleo, 11,000 - 10,000 B.P.

(Also see Clovis, Cumberland, Debert, Holcomb, Parallel Lanceolate, Plainview)

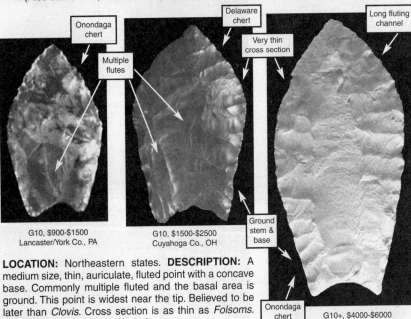

Onondaga chert

Multiple flutes

Delaware chert

Very thin cross section

Long fluting channel

Ground stem & base

Onondaga chert

G10, $900-$1500
Lancaster/York Co., PA

G10, $1500-$2500
Cuyahoga Co., OH

G10+, $4000-$6000
Chautauqua Co., NY

LOCATION: Northeastern states. **DESCRIPTION:** A medium size, thin, auriculate, fluted point with a concave base. Commonly multiple fluted and the basal area is ground. This point is widest near the tip. Believed to be later than *Clovis*. Cross section is as thin as *Folsoms*. **I.D. KEY:** Multiple flutes, blade form.

CUMBERLAND (Barnes) - Paleo, 11,000 - 10,000 B.P.

(Also see Beaver Lake, Clovis, Crowfield, Debert, Holcomb, Plainview, Redstone)

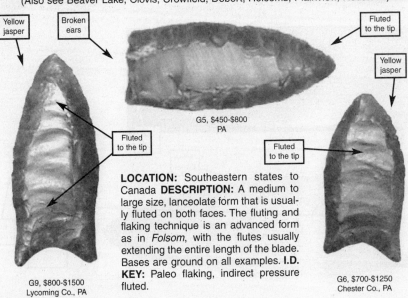

Yellow jasper

Broken ears

Fluted to the tip

Yellow jasper

G5, $450-$800
PA

Fluted to the tip

Fluted to the tip

LOCATION: Southeastern states to Canada **DESCRIPTION:** A medium to large size, lanceolate form that is usually fluted on both faces. The fluting and flaking technique is an advanced form as in *Folsom*, with the flutes usually extending the entire length of the blade. Bases are ground on all examples. **I.D. KEY:** Paleo flaking, indirect pressure fluted.

G9, $800-$1500
Lycoming Co., PA

G6, $700-$1250
Chester Co., PA

113

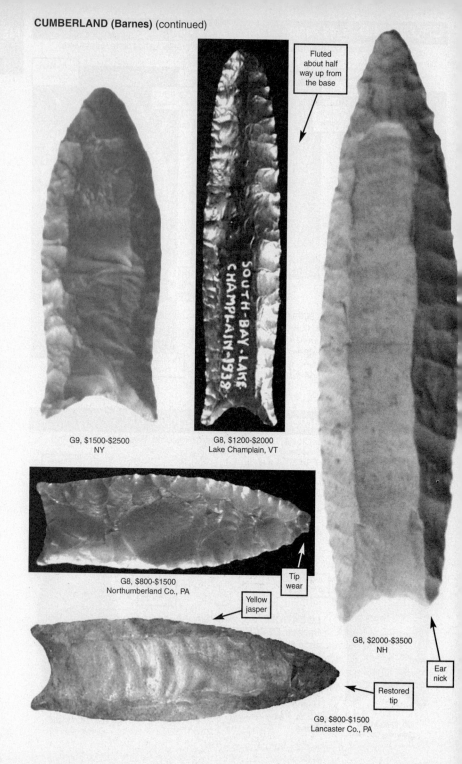

Fluted about half way up from the base

SOUTH-BAY-LAKE CHAMPLAIN-1938

G9, $1500-$2500
NY

G8, $1200-$2000
Lake Champlain, VT

G8, $800-$1500
Northumberland Co., PA

Tip wear

Yellow jasper

G8, $2000-$3500
NH

Ear nick

Restored tip

G9, $800-$1500
Lancaster Co., PA

CUMBERLAND (Barnes) (continued)

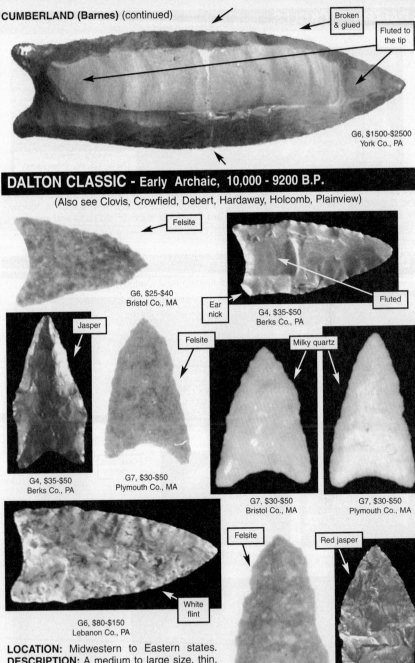

Broken & glued

Fluted to the tip

G6, $1500-$2500
York Co., PA

DALTON CLASSIC - Early Archaic, 10,000 - 9200 B.P.

(Also see Clovis, Crowfield, Debert, Hardaway, Holcomb, Plainview)

Felsite

G6, $25-$40
Bristol Co., MA

Ear nick

Fluted

G4, $35-$50
Berks Co., PA

Jasper

Felsite

Milky quartz

G4, $35-$50
Berks Co., PA

G7, $30-$50
Plymouth Co., MA

G7, $30-$50
Bristol Co., MA

G7, $30-$50
Plymouth Co., MA

White flint

G6, $80-$150
Lebanon Co., PA

Felsite

Red jasper

G4, $25-$40
Bristol Co., MA

G4, $40-$75
Jefferson Co., PA

LOCATION: Midwestern to Eastern states.
DESCRIPTION: A medium to large size, thin, auriculate, fishtailed point. Usually finely serrated and sometimes fluted. Beveling may occur on one side of each face but is usually on the right side. All bases are ground. **I.D. KEY:** Basal form and flaking style.

DALTON-NUCKOLLS - Early Archaic, 10,000 - 9200 B.P.

(Also see Angostura, Dalton Classic, Plainview)

G10, $1200-$2000
Chester Co., PA, Yellow Jasper.

LOCATION: Midwestern to Northeastern states. Type site is in Humphreys Co., TN.
DESCRIPTION: A medium to large size variant form, probably occuring from resharpening the *Greenbrier Dalton*. Bases are squared to lobbed to eared, and have a shallow concavity. Bases are ground and some examples are fluted. **I.D. KEY:** Broad base and shoulders, flaking on blade.

DEBERT - Paleo, 11,000 - 9500 B. P.

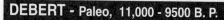

(Also see Clovis, Crowfield, Cumberland, Dalton, Holcomb)

Jasper

Impact
fracture

Broken
& glued

G6, $600-$1000
Vail Debert site, ME, Photo courtesy Dr. R.M. Gramly.

Both pieces found
at diff. times separated from kill and
camp site. Note
patination variation.

Onondaga
chert

G6, $300-$500
Lycoming Co., PA

G4, $150-$250
Lycoming Co., PA

G6, $550-$1000
Montgomery Co., PA

G9, $900-$1500
Oxford Co., MA

116

DEBERT (continued)

LOCATION: Northeastern states. Type site is the Vail site in Maine. **DESCRIPTION:** A medium to large size, thin, auriculate point that evolved from *Clovis*. Most examples are fluted twice on each face resulting in a deep basal concavity. The second flute usually removed traces of the first fluting. A very rare form of late *Clovis*. **I.D. KEY:** Deep basal notch.

G5, $350-$600
Vail site, ME. Photo by Dr. Gramly

Classic form

Fluting channel

Note deeply indented bases

G9, $2500-$4000
Snyder Co., PA. Yellow Jasper.

DECATUR - Early Archaic, 9000 - 3000 B.P.

(Also see Charleston Pine Tree, Dovetail, Kirk, Kiski, Lost Lake, Palmer)

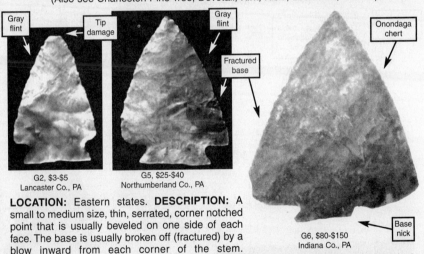

Gray flint

Tip damage

Gray flint

Fractured base

Onondaga chert

G2, $3-$5
Lancaster Co., PA

G5, $25-$40
Northumberland Co., PA

Base nick

G6, $80-$150
Indiana Co., PA

LOCATION: Eastern states. **DESCRIPTION:** A small to medium size, thin, serrated, corner notched point that is usually beveled on one side of each face. The base is usually broken off (fractured) by a blow inward from each corner of the stem. Sometimes the sides of the stem and backs of the tangs are also fractured, and rarely the tip may be fractured by a blow on each side directed towards the base. Bases are usually ground and flaking is of high quality. **I.D. KEY:** Squared base, one barb shoulder.

DEWART STEMMED - Late Archaic, 5000 - 2500 B.P.

(Also see Bare Island, Duncan's Island, Garver's Ferry, Lamoka, Merrimack, Neville, Piney Island)

DEWART STEMMED (continued)

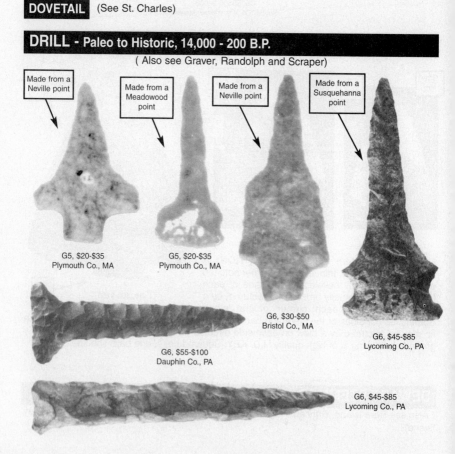

Vein quartz

G4, $4-$8
Peach Bottom, PA

G4, $4-$8
Northumberland Co., PA

G6, $5-$10
Northumberland Co., PA

G6, $5-$10
Lycoming Co., PA

LOCATION: Northeastern states. **DESCRIPTION:** A medium size, narrow, stemmed point with strong shoulders. Tips are sharp and the stem is parallel to contracting. The base is normally unfinished. **I.D. KEY:** Unfinished base.

DOVETAIL (See St. Charles)

DRILL - Paleo to Historic, 14,000 - 200 B.P.
(Also see Graver, Randolph and Scraper)

Made from a Neville point

Made from a Meadowood point

Made from a Neville point

Made from a Susquehanna point

G5, $20-$35
Plymouth Co., MA

G5, $20-$35
Plymouth Co., MA

G6, $30-$50
Bristol Co., MA

G6, $45-$85
Lycoming Co., PA

G6, $55-$100
Dauphin Co., PA

G6, $45-$85
Lycoming Co., PA

DRILL (continued)

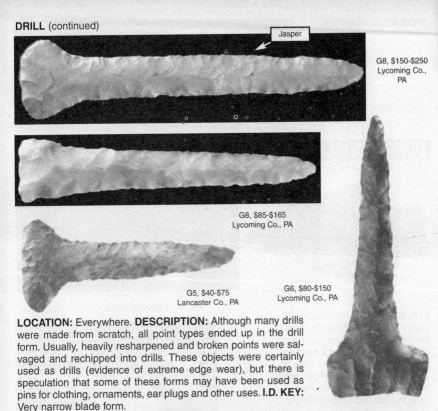

Jasper

G8, $150-$250
Lycoming Co.,
PA

G8, $85-$165
Lycoming Co., PA

G5, $40-$75
Lancaster Co., PA

G6, $80-$150
Lycoming Co., PA

LOCATION: Everywhere. **DESCRIPTION:** Although many drills were made from scratch, all point types ended up in the drill form. Usually, heavily resharpened and broken points were salvaged and rechipped into drills. These objects were certainly used as drills (evidence of extreme edge wear), but there is speculation that some of these forms may have been used as pins for clothing, ornaments, ear plugs and other uses. **I.D. KEY:** Very narrow blade form.

DRYBROOK FISHTAIL - Late Archaic to Woodland, 3500 - 2500 B.P.

(Also see Forest Notched, Frost Island, Orient, Patuxent, Perkiomen, Susquehanna Broad)

G5, $12-$20
Luzerne Co., PA

G6, $15-$25
Lycoming Co., PA

G6, $15-$25
Centre Co., PA

LOCATION: Northeastern states. **DESCRIPTION:** A medium size, narrow, triangular point that expands towards the base. Shoulders are rounded and taper into an expanded base. The base is straight to concave. Some examples have basal ears that are rounded to pointed. **I.D. KEY:** Basal form, rounded shoulders.

G7, $30-$50
Luzerne Co., PA

DRYBROOK FISHTAIL
(continued)

G8, $40-$70
Lancaster Co., PA

DUNCAN'S ISLAND - Mid to Late Archaic, 6000 - 4000 B. P.
(Also see Bare Island, Dewart Stemmed, Neville, Newmanstown, Piedmont, Piney Island)

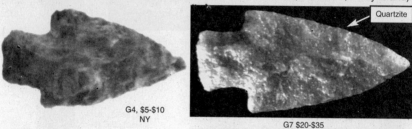

Quartzite

G4, $5-$10
NY

G7 $20-$35
Montgomery Co., PA

Quartzite

LOCATION: Northeastern states. **DESCRIPTION:** A medium to large size stemmed point with convex sides and a medium length square stem. The base is usually straight to slightly convex. Shoulders are straight to tapered. **I.D. KEY:** Square stem.

G5, $18-$30
Lancaster Co., PA

G4, $12-$20
PA

Broken tang

Argillite

G6, $40-$75
PA

G8, $30-$50
PA

G8, $30-$55
PA

G6, $25-$40
PA

ERB BASAL NOTCHED - Mid-Woodland, 2000 - 1200 B.P.

(Also see Eshback, Oley)

G4, $5-$10
PA

G7, $25-$40
Union Co., PA

G7, $25-$40
Union Co., PA

G7, $25-$40
Centre Co., PA

G6, $15-$30
Union Co., PA

G8, $30-$50
Luzurne Co., PA

121

ERB BASAL NOTCHED (continued)

LOCATION: Northeastern states. **DESCRIPTION:** A small to medium size, broad, basal notched point. Tangs can drop even with or below the base. **I.D. KEY:** Basal form.

ERIE TRIANGLE - Late Woodland, 1500 - 200 B.P.

(Also see Levanna, Madison, Susquehannock Triangle, Yadkin)

LOCATION: Northeastern states. **DESCRIPTION:** A small size, thin, triangular point with sharp basal corners and a straight to concave base. **I.D. KEY:** Triangular form.

G5, $3-$8
Lycoming Co., PA

ESHBACK - Late Archaic, 5500 - 3500 B.P.

(Also see Erb Basal Notched, Oley)

G3, $8-$15
Monroe Co., PA

G3, $12-$20
Lycoming Co., PA

G4, $15-$25
Lycoming Co., PA

G7, $25-$40
Northampton Co., PA

 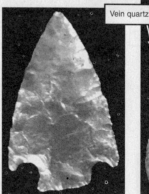 

Vein quartz

G7, $20-$35
Northampton Co., PA

G7, $20-$35
Lycoming Co., PA

G9, $40-$70
Montgomery Co., PA

LOCATION: Northeastern states. **DESCRIPTION:** A small to medium size, broad, basal notched point. Tangs can extend beyond the base. Bases are straight, concave or convex. Similar to *Eva* points found in the Southeast. **I.D. KEY:** Basal form.

FOREST NOTCHED - Early Woodland, 3000 - 2000 B.P.

(Also see Drybrook, Frost Island, Orient, Patuxent, Perkiomen and Susquehanna Broad, Table Rock)

FOREST NOTCHED (continued)

LOCATION: Northeastern. **DESCRIPTION:** A medium size, narrow point with very wide side notches. The basal area is relatively long and expands. The base is straight. Shoulders are rounded. **I.D. KEY:** Base form and rounded shoulders.

G6, $5-$15
Clinton Co., PA

FOX CREEK - Woodland, 2500 - 1200 B.P.

(Also see Dalton and Savannah River)

G4, $6-$12
Monroe Co., PA

G3, $8-$15
Plymouth Co., MA

G3, $8-$15
Lycoming Co., PA

G3, $5-$15
Monroe Co., PA

G5, $8-$15
Luzerne Co., PA

G7, $25-$40
Luzerne Co., PA

G7, $30-$50
Luzerne Co., PA

LOCATION: Northeastern. **DESCRIPTION:** A medium size blade with a squared to tapered hafting area and a straight to concave base. Shoulders, when present are very weak and tapered. **I.D. KEY:** Basal form.

FOX CREEK (continued)

Purple argillite

G4, $8-$15
Union Co., PA

Yellow Jasper

G8, $90-$165
Dauphin Co., PA

LOCATION: Northeastern. **DESCRIPTION:** A medium size blade with a squared to tapered hafting area and a straight to concave base. Shoulders, when present are very weak and tapered. **I.D. KEY:** Basal form.

FROST ISLAND - Late Archaic -Early Woodland, 3200 - 2500 B.P.

(Also see Drybrook, Forest Notched, Orient, Patuxent, Perkiomen, Susquehanna Broad)

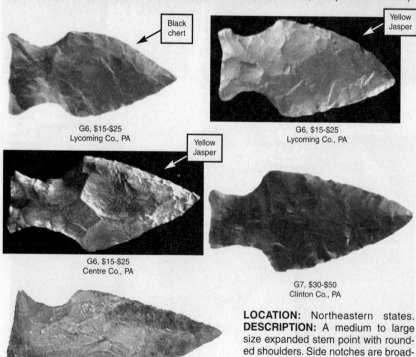

Black chert

G6, $15-$25
Lycoming Co., PA

Yellow Jasper

G6, $15-$25
Lycoming Co., PA

Yellow Jasper

G6, $15-$25
Centre Co., PA

G7, $30-$50
Clinton Co., PA

G6, $15-$30
Lycoming Co., PA

LOCATION: Northeastern states. **DESCRIPTION:** A medium to large size expanded stem point with rounded shoulders. Side notches are broader than the *Forest Notched* type. **I.D. KEY:** Long expanded base, rounded shoulders.

124

GARVER'S FERRY - Late Woodland, 1800 - 1300 B.P.

(Also see Crooked Creek, Dewart Stemmed, Lamoka, Merrimack, Neville, Wading River)

LOCATION: Northeastern states. **DESCRIPTION:** A small size dart point with a short stem that is slightly expanding. The base is straight. Some examples are corner notched. **I.D. KEY:** Basal form, early flaking. **I.D. KEY:** Expanded stem, small size.

G6, $5-$10
Lycoming Co., PA.
Red Jasper.

GENESEE - Late Archaic, 5000 - 4000 B.P.

(Also see Bare Island, Neville, Newmanstown, and Piedmont)

G5, $15-$25
Centre Co., PA

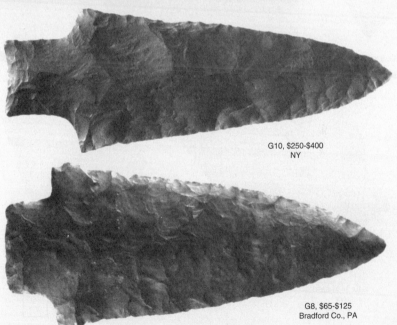

G10, $250-$400
NY

G8, $65-$125
Bradford Co., PA

LOCATION: Northeastern states. Named for the Genesee Valley located in New York state. **DESCRIPTION:** A medium to large size point with prominent shoulders, a thick cross section and a squarish base. Shoulders can be straight to tapered to slightly barbed. Basal area can be ground. **I.D. KEY:** Expanded base, usually thin.

125

Onondaga chert

G9, $200-$350
W. PA

G10, $450-$850
NY

Edge nick

G5, $30-$50
NY

GODDARD - Mississippian, 1000 - 800 B.P.

(Also see Jacks Reef & Raccoon Notched)

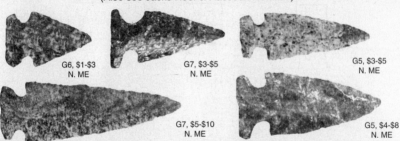

G6, $1-$3
N. ME

G7, $3-$5
N. ME

G5, $3-$5
N. ME

G7, $5-$10
N. ME

G5, $4-$8
N. ME

LOCATION: Northeastern states. Type site is located at Penobscot Bay, Maine.
DESCRIPTION: A small to medium side, thin, narrow, side to corner notched point with a straight to convex base. Similar in style to *Jacks Reef Corner Notched* and *Raccoon Creek* points. Also similar to *Knight Island* points of the Southeast. A late Ceramic Period point. Some examples in the type area are made of high grade, colorful material that would be worth more. **I.D. KEY:** Thin, side notched point.

GRAVER - Paleo to Archaic, 14,000 - 4000 B.P.

(Also see Drill & Scraper)

Graver tips

Graver tips

G8, $20-$40

Graver tips

G7, $15-$30

G8, $20-$40

All from the Shoop site, Dauphin Co.,
PA. Onondaga chert.

LOCATION: Paleo and Archaic sites everywhere **DESCRIPTION:** An irregular shaped uniface tool with sharp, pointed projections used for puncturing, incising, tattooing, etc. Some examples served a dual purpose for scraping as well. In later times, *Perforators* took the place of *Gravers*.

GREENE - Middle to late Woodland, 1700 - 1200 B.P.

(Also see Agate Basin, Angostura, Eden & Mansion Inn)

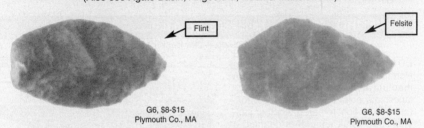

Flint

Felsite

G6, $8-$15
Plymouth Co., MA

G6, $8-$15
Plymouth Co., MA

LOCATION: New York into Massachusetts and Connecticut. **DESCRIPTION:** A medium size, fairly broad lanceolate point with a tapering basal area and a straight base. Some examples form a pentagonal shape. **I.D. KEY:** Ovate to pentagonal form.

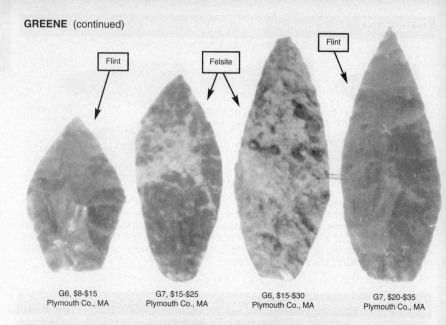

G6, $8-$15	G7, $15-$25	G6, $15-$30	G7, $20-$35
Plymouth Co., MA	Plymouth Co., MA	Plymouth Co., MA	Plymouth Co., MA

GROUND SLATE - Archaic, 6000 - 4500 B.P.

(Also see Bare Island)

G6, $125-$200
New England

LOCATION: Northeastern states. **DESCRIPTION:** A large size stemmed point completely ground from slate. Bases vary from expanding to contracting. Often found with notches in the stem. Examples of facial grinding of flaked Paleo and Archaic points have been found in the Eastern U.S.

GUILFORD - Middle Archaic, 6500 - 5000 B.P.

(Also see Agate Basin)

LOCATION: Eastern seaboard to Northeastern states. **DESCRIPTION:** A medium to large size, thick, narrow lanceolate point. The base varies from round to straight to eared. Another variation has weak shoulders defining a stemmed area. **I.D. KEY:** Thickness, early parallel flaking.

Guilford Yuma form

G6, $15-$25
MD

GUILFORD (continued)

Round base form

G7, $8-$15
NY

HARDAWAY - Early Archaic 9500 - 8000 B.P.

(Also see Dalton-Greenbrier and Palmer)

LOCATION: Eastern states. Type site is in Stanly Co., NC, Yadkin River. Very rare in Northeast. **DESCRIPTION:** A small to medium size point with shallow side notches and expanded auricles forming a wide, deeply concave base. Ears and base are usually ground. This type evolved from the *Dalton* point. **I.D. KEY:** Eared form, heavy grinding in shoulders, paleo parallel flaking.

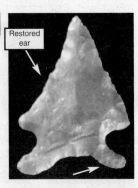

Restored ear

G5, $25-$40
Lycoming Co., PA.
Yellow Jasper.

HAW RIVER - Transitional Paleo, 11,000 - 8000 B.P.

G8, $40-$75
NY

IMPORTANT: Shown 85% of actual size

LOCATION: Eastern seaboard to Northeastern states. **DESCRIPTION:** A medium to large size, broad, elliptical blade with a basal notch and usually rounded tangs that turn inward. **I.D. KEY:** Notched base.

HELLGRAMITE - Early Woodland, 3000 - 2500 B.P.

(Also see Brewerton, Kessel, Kirk, Meadowood)

Onondaga chert

G3, $5-$10
Lycoming Co., PA.
Chert.

G3, $5-$10
Lancaster Co., PA

129

HELGRAMITE(continued)

LOCATION: Northeastern states. **DESCRIPTION:** A small to medium size triangular point with very weak side notches. The blade edges are finely serrated and the base is straight to convex. **I.D. KEY:** Weak notches, serrated edges.

HOLCOMB- Paleo, 11,000 - 10,000 B.P.

(Also see Clovis, Crowfield, Cumberland, Dalton, Debert, Plainview)

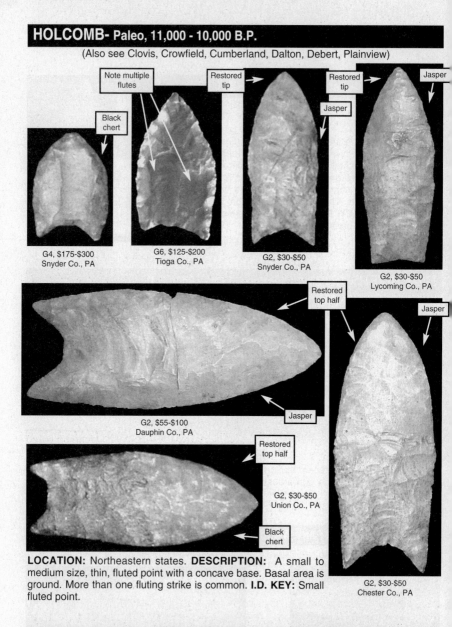

Note multiple flutes

Black chert

Restored tip

Jasper

Restored tip

Jasper

G4, $175-$300
Snyder Co., PA

G6, $125-$200
Tioga Co., PA

G2, $30-$50
Snyder Co., PA

G2, $30-$50
Lycoming Co., PA

Restored top half

Jasper

Jasper

G2, $55-$100
Dauphin Co., PA

Restored top half

G2, $30-$50
Union Co., PA

Black chert

LOCATION: Northeastern states. **DESCRIPTION:** A small to medium size, thin, fluted point with a concave base. Basal area is ground. More than one fluting strike is common. **I.D. KEY:** Small fluted point.

G2, $30-$50
Chester Co., PA

HOOVER'S ISLAND- Archaic, 6000 - 4000 B.P.

(Also see Bare Island, Duncan's Island, Genesee, Lackawaxen, Newmanstown, Patuxent, Piedmont, Piney Island)

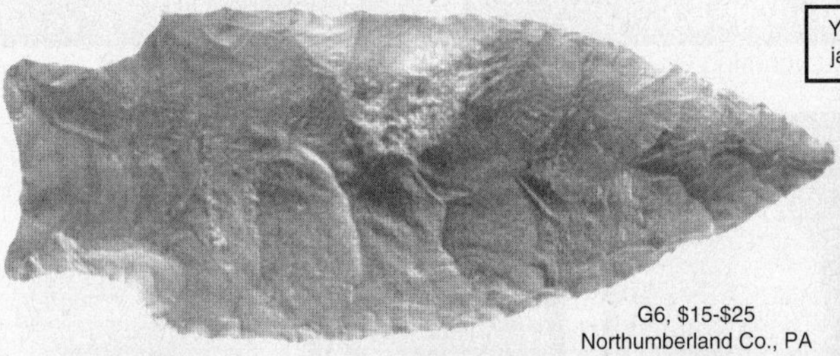

G6, $15-$25
Northumberland Co., PA

Yellow jasper

Classic form

G6, $25-$40
Northumberland Co., PA

Argillite

G8, $35-$65
Northumberland Co., PA

G7, $25-$45
York Co., PA

G9, $90-$175
York Co., PA

LOCATION: Pennsylvania to northern Maryland. **DESCRIPTION:** A medium to large size, broad, expanded to parallel stemmed point. Bases are straight to concave. Basal corners are sharp. Shoulders are tapered to rounded. **I.D. KEY:** Sharp basal corners, tapered shoulders. Belongs to the Piedmont series and is also known as *Southern Piedmont*.

JACKS REEF CORNER NOTCHED - Late Woodland to Mississippian, 1500 - 1000 B.P.

(Also see Kiski, Lycoming Co., Oley, Palmer, Raccoon Notched, Vosburg)

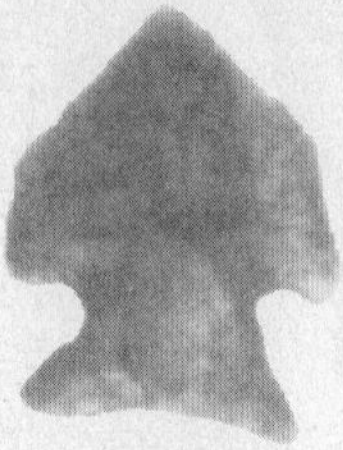

G5, $12-$20
Plymouth Co., MA

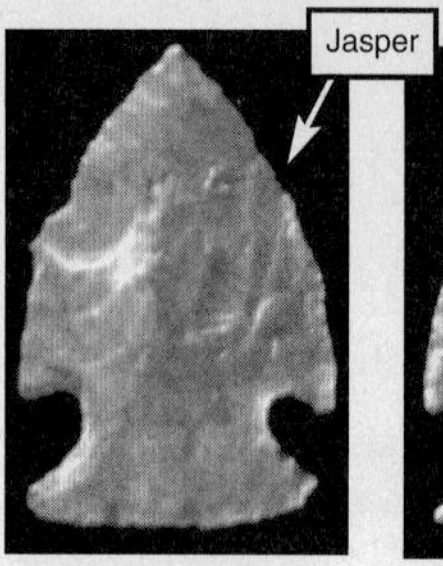

Jasper

G6, $30-$55
Lycoming Co., PA

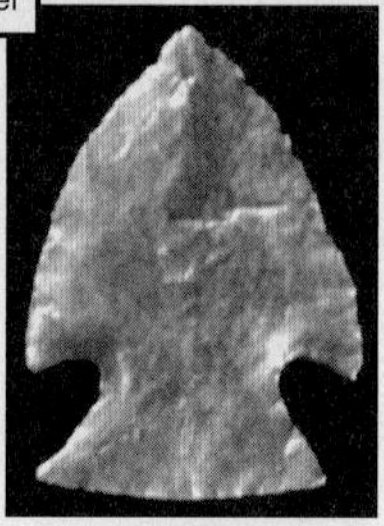

G8, $30-$50
Eastern Shore, MD

G8, $25-$45
NY

G7, $20-$35
Lycoming Co., PA

G6, $20-$30
Lycoming Co.,PA

Hornfels

G6, $30-$50
Lycoming Co., PA

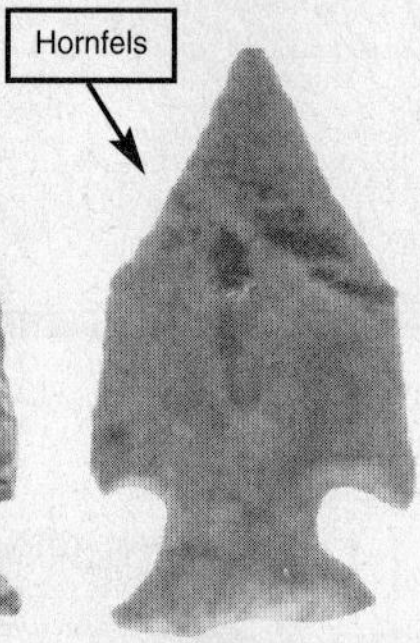

G6, $20-$35
Plymouth Co., MA

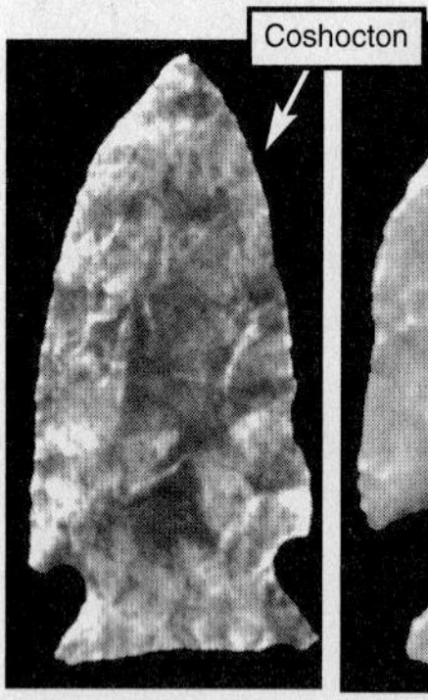

Coshocton

Jasper

G6, $15-$25
Northumberland Co., PA

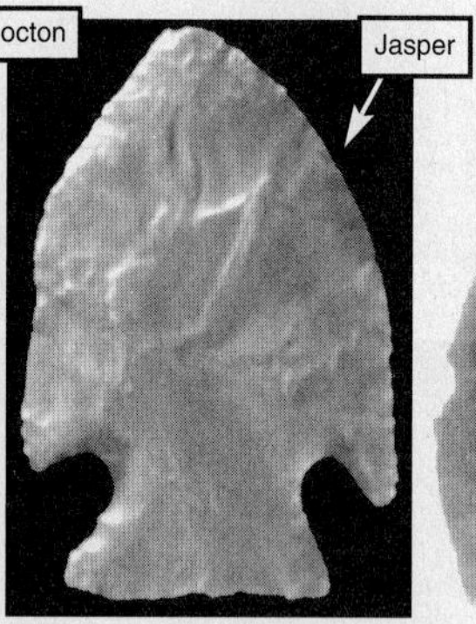

G6, $35-$65
Lycoming Co., PA

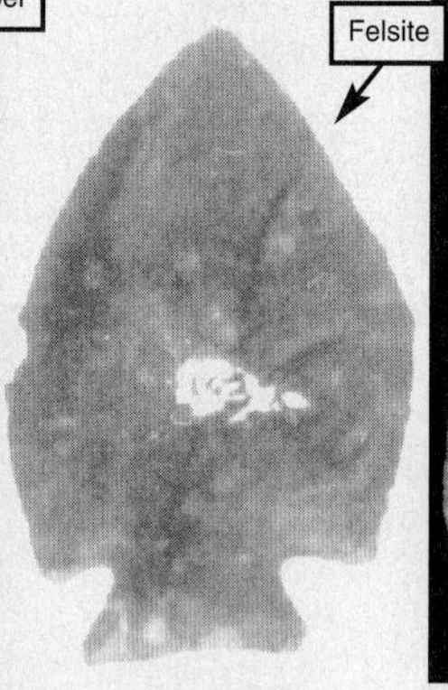

Felsite

Jasper

G7, $35-$60
Plymouth Co., MA

G7, $25-$45
Lycoming Co., PA

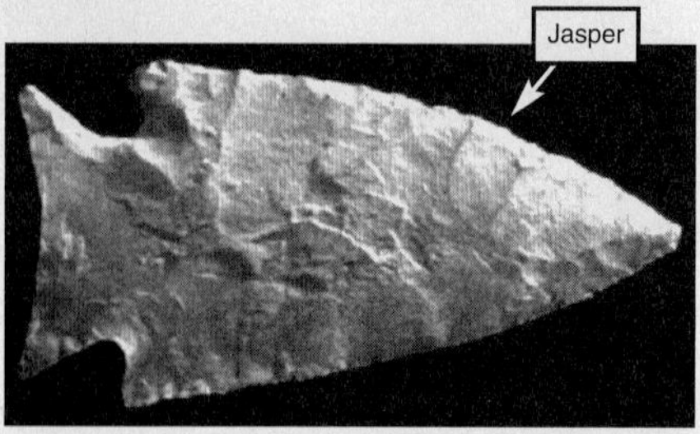

Jasper

G8, $75-$140
Lycoming Co., PA

132

JACKS REEF CORNER NOTCHED (continued)

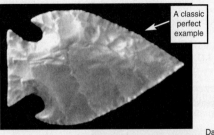

A classic perfect example

LOCATION: Southeastern to Northeastern states. **DESCRIPTION:** A small to medium size, very thin, corner notched point that is well made. The blade is convex to pentagonal. Some examples are widely corner notched and appear to be expanded stem points with barbed shoulders. **I.D. KEY:** Thinness, sharp corners.

G10, $150-$250
Dauphin Co., PA. **Yellow Jasper.**
Classic form. Excellent quality.

JACKS REEF PENTAGONAL - Late Woodland to Mississippian, 1500 - 1000 B.P.

(Also see Erie Triangle, Levanna, Madison, Susquehannock Triangle)

Onondaga chert

G2, $.50-$1
CT

G3, $.50-$1
CT

G3, $.50-$1
CT

G3, $1-$2
CT

G4, $5-$10
Lycoming Co., PA

G6, $25-$45
Lycoming Co., PA

G5, $6-$12
Union Co., PA

LOCATION: Southeastern to Northeastern states. **DESCRIPTION:** A small to large size, very thin, five sided point with a sharp tip. The hafting area is usually contracted with a slightly concave to straight base. This type is called *Pee Dee* in North and South Carolina. **I.D. KEY:** Pentagonal form.

KANAWHA - Early Archaic, 9000 - 5000 B.P.

(Also see Kirk Serrated, Lake Erie, LeCroy, MacCorkle, St. Albans, Stanly, Susquehanna Birfurcate)

G5, $12-$20
Union Co., PA

G6, $18-$30
Chester Co., PA

KANAWHA (continued)

LOCATION: Southeastern to Northeastern states. Type site is in Kanawha Co., WVA.
DESCRIPTION: A small to medium size, fairly thick, shallowly bifurcated stemmed point.
The basal lobes are usually rounded and the shoulders are tapered. Believed to be the
ancestor to the *Stanly* type. Very similar to the *Fox Valley* point found in Illinois. Shoulders
can be clipped wing, turning towards the tip. **I.D. KEY:** Archaic flaking, weak basal lobes.

KESSEL- Early Archaic, 10,000 - 8000 B.P.

(Also see Cache River, Goddard, Hellgramite, Meadowood, Raccoon Notched)

G7, $60-$100
Burlington Co., NJ

Black
chert

LOCATION: Northeastern states.
DESCRIPTION: A medium to large
size, thin, triangular side notched
point. Notches are close to the
base, are very narrow and angle in
from the sides. The base is concave. Almost identical in form and
age to the *Cache River* type from
Arkansas. **I.D. KEY:** Basal notches, thinness.

G8, $35-$65
W. PA

KIRK CORNER NOTCHED - Early to Mid-Archaic, 9000 - 6000 B.P.

(Also see Amos, Brewerton, Charleston Pine Tree, Crooked Creek, Kline & Palmer)

Coxsackie
chert

G4, $15-$25
Lycoming Co., PA

G8, $150-$250
NY

LOCATION: Southeastern to Northeastern states. **DESCRIPTION:** A medium to large
size, corner notched point. Blade edges can be convex to recurved and are finely serrated
on many examples. The base can be convex, concave, straight, bifurcated or auriculate.
Points that are beveled on one side of each face would fall under the *Lost Lake* or *Hardin*
type. **I.D. KEY:** Secondary edgework.

KIRK CORNER NOTCHED (continued)

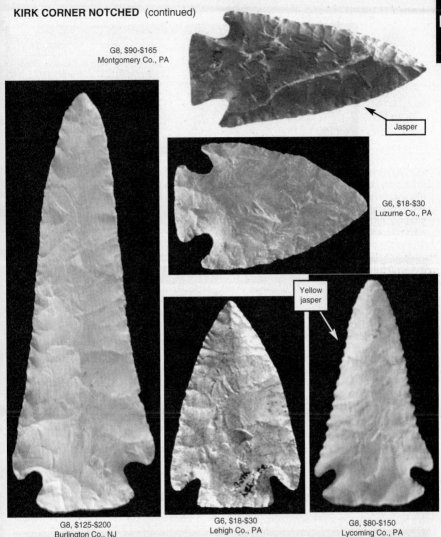

G8, $90-$165
Montgomery Co., PA

Jasper

G6, $18-$30
Luzurne Co., PA

Yellow
jasper

G8, $125-$200
Burlington Co., NJ

G6, $18-$30
Lehigh Co., PA

G8, $80-$150
Lycoming Co., PA

KIRK STEMMED - Early to Mid-Archaic, 9000 - 6000 B.P.

(Also see Bare Island, Duncan's Island, Fountain Creek, Genesee, Heavy Duty, Lackawaxen, Neville, Newmanstown)

Jasper

G3, $4-$8
Luzurne Co., PA

Chert

G6, $8-$15
Montour Co., PA

KIRK STEMMED (continued)

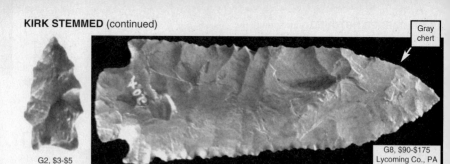

Gray chert

G2, $3-$5
Lycoming Co., PA

G8, $90-$175
Lycoming Co., PA

LOCATION: Eastern states. **DESCRIPTION:** A medium to large size, barbed, stemmed point with deep notches or fine serrations along the blade edges. The stem is parallel, contracting or expanding. The stem sides may be steeply beveled on opposite faces. The base can be concave, convex or straight, and can be very short. The shoulders are usually strongly barbed. This form is believed to have evolved into *Stanly* and other types. **I.D. KEY:** Serrations.

KISKI NOTCHED - LATE WOODLAND, 2000 - 1400 B.P.

(Also see Brewerton, Crooked Creek, Jacks Reef, Lycoming Co., Palmer)

LOCATION: Northeastern states. **DESCRIPTION:** A small size side or corner notched point. **I.D. KEY:** Notching and size.

G4, $5-$10
Lycoming Co., PA

KITTATINY - Middle Archaic, 6000 - 5000 B.P.

(Also see Brewerton Eared, Jacks Reef Pentagonal, Levanna)

LOCATION: Northeastern states. **DESCRIPTION:** A small size lanceolate blade with recurved side edges. The base is straight, with the corners forming tiny ears. The stem is square to expanding. The *Nolichucky* type found in the Southeast is similar in outline. **I.D. KEY:** Triangular and basal form.

G5, $5-$10, Lycoming Co., PA, **Yellow Jasper.**

KLINE - Early Archaic, 9000 - 7000 B.P.

(Also see Brodhead Side Notched, Kirk, Lycoming Co., St. Charles, Susquehanna Broad)

Restored tip

Note early archaic parallel flaking

G3, $8-$15
Lycoming Co., PA

G5, $25-$40
Lycoming Co., PA

LOCATION: Northeastern states. **DESCRIPTION:** A medium to large size corner notched point with a convex base that is ground. Shoulders are strong and are horizontal to slightly barbed. Basal corners are rounded. **I.D. KEY:** Corner notching, early flaking.

KOENS CRISPIN - Late Archaic, 4000 - 3000 B.P.

(Also see Adena, Atlantic Phase Blade, Lehigh, Morrow Mountain, Poplar Island, Schuylkill, Virginsville)

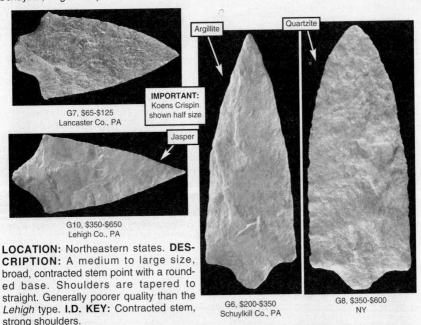

G7, $65-$125
Lancaster Co., PA

Argillite

Quartzite

IMPORTANT: Koens Crispin shown half size

Jasper

G10, $350-$650
Lehigh Co., PA

G6, $200-$350
Schuylkill Co., PA

G8, $350-$600
NY

LOCATION: Northeastern states. **DESCRIPTION:** A medium to large size, broad, contracted stem point with a rounded base. Shoulders are tapered to straight. Generally poorer quality than the *Lehigh* type. **I.D. KEY:** Contracted stem, strong shoulders.

LACKAWAXEN - Archaic, 6000 - 4000 B.P.

(Also see Bare Island, Duncan's Island, Neville, Piedmont, Tocks Island)

G6, $65-$125
Northampton Co., PA

Minor tip damage

G5, $15-$25
Northampton Co., PA

LOCATION: Northeastern states. **DESCRIPTION:** A medium to large size, narrow, expanded to contracting to parallel stemmed point with strong, tapered shoulders. **I.D. KEY:** Long, narrow stemmed point.

LAKE ERIE - Early to Mid-Archaic, 9000 - 5000 B.P.

(Also see Erie Triangle, Fox Valley, Kirk-Bifurcated, LeCroy, MacCorkle, Penn's Creek, St. Albans, Stanly, Susquehanna Bifurcate)

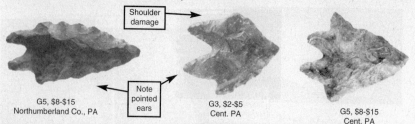

Shoulder damage

Note pointed ears

G5, $8-$15
Northumberland Co., PA

G3, $2-$5
Cent. PA

G5, $8-$15
Cent. PA

LOCATION: Northeastern states. **DESCRIPTION:** A small to medium size, thin, deeply notched or bifurcated stemmed point. The basal lobes are parallel with a tendency to turn inward and are pointed. The outward sides of the basal lobes are usually fractured from the base towards the tip and can be ground. **I.D. KEY:** Pointed basal lobes.

LAMOKA - Middle Archaic, 5500 - 4500 B.P.

(Also see Dewart Stemmed, Duncan's Island, Garver's Ferry, Merrimack, Neville, Piney Island, Randolph, Sandhill Stemmed, Wading River)

Black chert

G4, $1-$3
Lycoming Co. PA

G4, $1-$3
Lycoming Co. PA

G6, $6-$12
PA

G6, $6-$12
Lycoming Co. PA

G6, $5-$10
Lycoming Co. PA

G6, $8-$15
Lycoming Co. PA

G8, $12-$20
Lycoming Co. PA

G5 $8-$15
Columbia Co., NY

G5, $8-$15
Columbia Co., NY

G8, $8-$15
Lycoming Co. PA

G6, $8-$15
Columbia Co., NY

G8, $12-$20
Monroe Co., PA

G8, $8-$15
Lycoming Co. PA

LAMOKA (continued)

LOCATION: Northeastern states. **DESCRIPTION:** A small to medium size, narrow, thick, spike point. The shoulders are tapered and the stem is square to contracting to expanding. The base on some examples shows the natural rind of the native material used. Called *Bradley Spike* in the Southeast. **I.D. KEY:** Thin, spike point.

LECROY - Early to Mid-Archaic, 9000 - 5000 B.P.

(Also see Decatur, Kanawha, Kirk Serrated, Lake Erie, MacCorkle, Charleston Pine Tree, St. Albans, Stanly, Susquehanna Bifurcate & Taunton River Bifurcate)

Resharpened many times

Jasper

G5, $12-$20
Union Co., PA

G5, $12-$20
Lycoming Co., PA

G5, $12-$20
Union Co., PA

G3, $5-$10
Northumberland Co., PA

G6, $12-$20
Union Co., PA

Serrated edge

G7, $15-$25
Union Co., PA

Serrated edge

G7, $15-$25
Union Co., PA

Serrated edge

Milky quartz

G8, $15-$30
Lancaster Co., PA

G6, $12-$20
Berks Co., PA

G8, $15-$30
MD. Yellow Jasper.

G9, $25-$40
Lycoming Co., PA

LOCATION: Eastern states. Type site is in Hamilton Co., Tennessee. **DESCRIPTION:** A small to medium size, thin, bifurcated point with deeply notched or serrated blade edges. Basal ears can either droop or expand out. The base is usually large in comparison to the blade size. Bases can be ground. **I.D. KEY:** Basal form, thinness.

LEHIGH - Late Archaic, 4000 - 3000 B.P.

(Also see Adena, Koens Crispin, Morrow Mountain, Poplar Island, Schuylkill, Virginsville)

LOCATION: Northeastern states. **DESCRIPTION:** A medium to large size, broad, contracted to square stemmed point. Shoulders are horizontal to contracting. The base is straight to rounded. **I.D. KEY:** Broad, contracting stem.

Jasper

G5, $25-$40
Luzurne Co.,
PA

G4, $15-$30
Northampton Co., PA

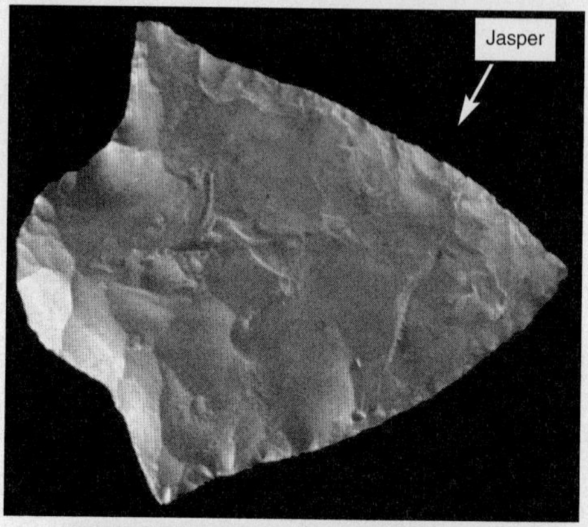

G7, $80-$150
Luzurne Co.,
PA

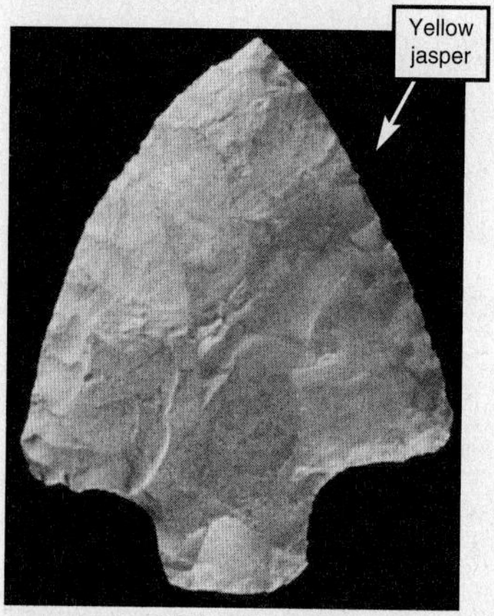

Jasper

Yellow
jasper

G5, $35-$60
Northampton Co., PA

Rhyolite

Yellow
jasper

G5, $25-$40
Northampton Co., PA

G8, $150-$250
Lancaster Co., PA

LEVANNA - Late Woodland to Mississippian, 1300 - 600 B.P.

(Also see Madison, Susquehannock Triangle)

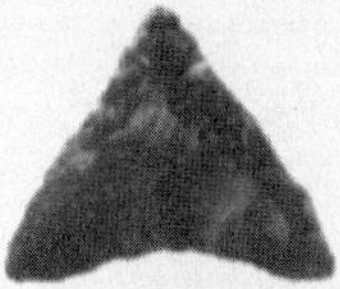

G3, $3-$6
Lycoming Co., PA

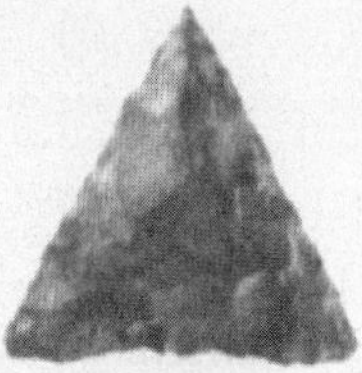

G5, $5-$10
Lycoming Co., PA

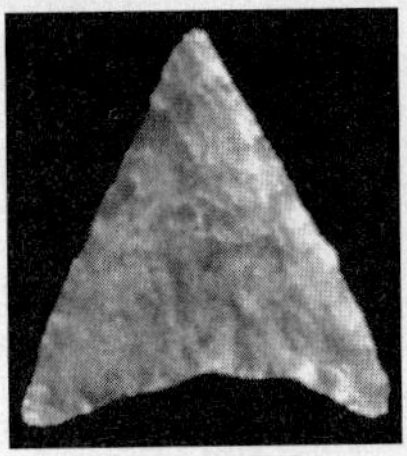

G6, $8-$15
Lycoming Co., PA

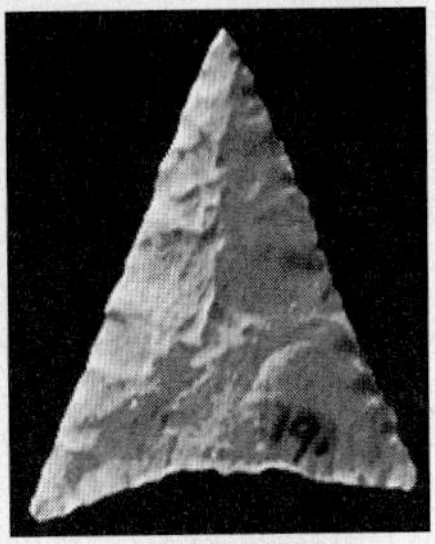

G6, $12-$20
Oswego Co., NY

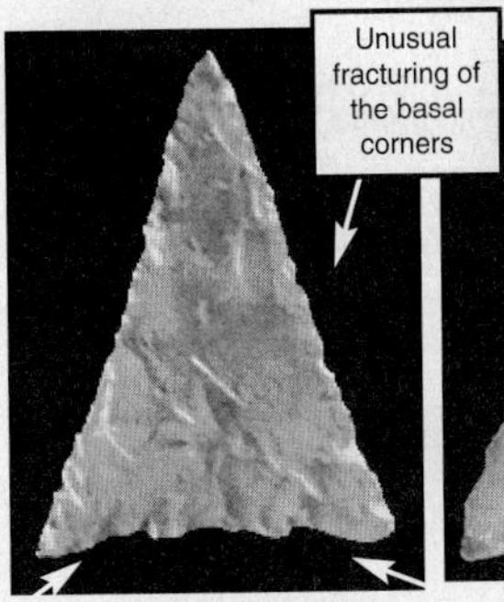

Unusual fracturing of the basal corners

G8, $25-$40
Oswego Co., NY

Vein quartz

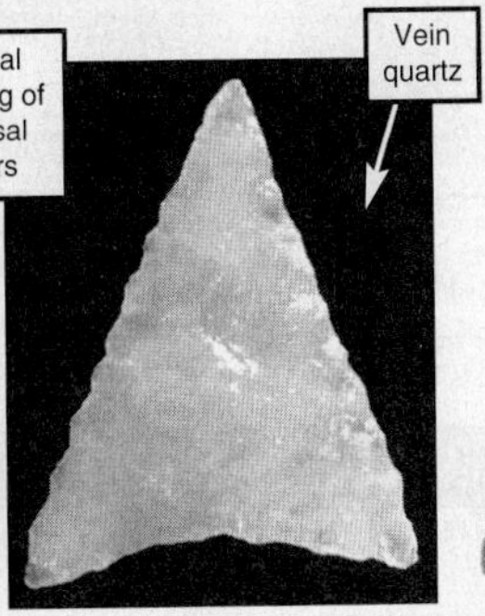

G8, $15-$30
PA

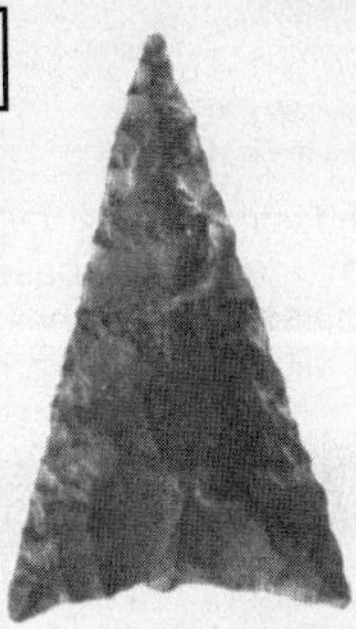

G8, $15-$30
PA

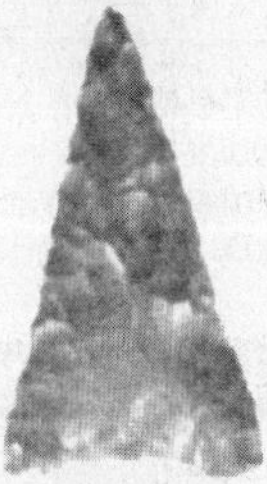

G6, $6-$12
PA

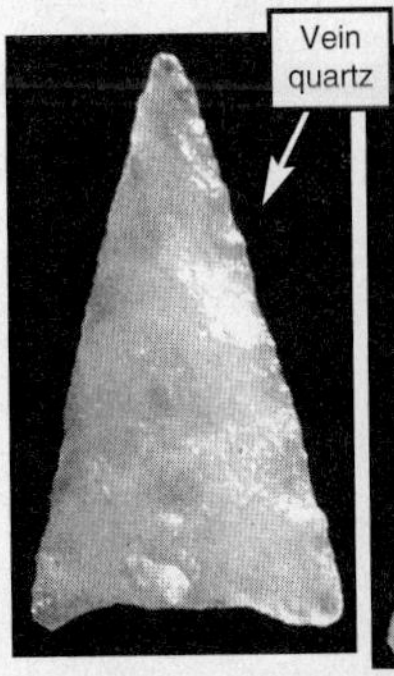

Vein quartz

G6, $15-$30
PA

Coxsackie chert

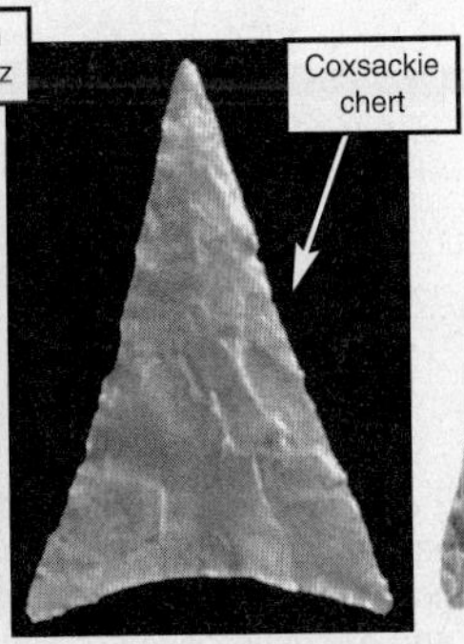

G8, $25-$40
Lycoming Co., PA

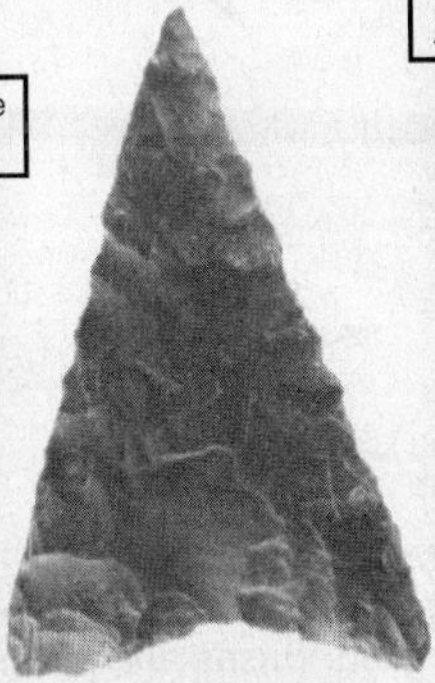

G8, $30-$50
PA

Yellow jasper

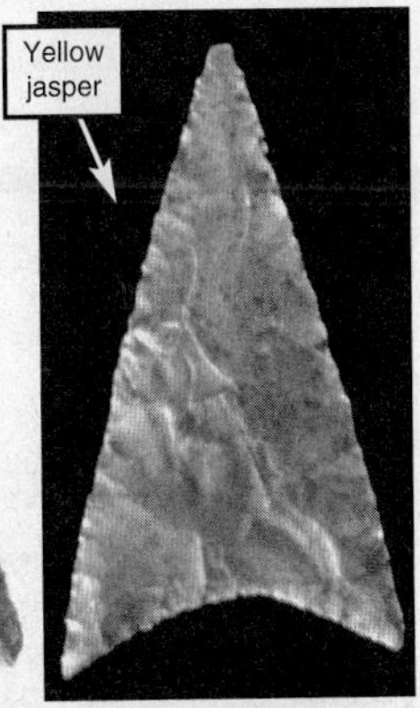

G9, $30-$50
Carbon Co., PA

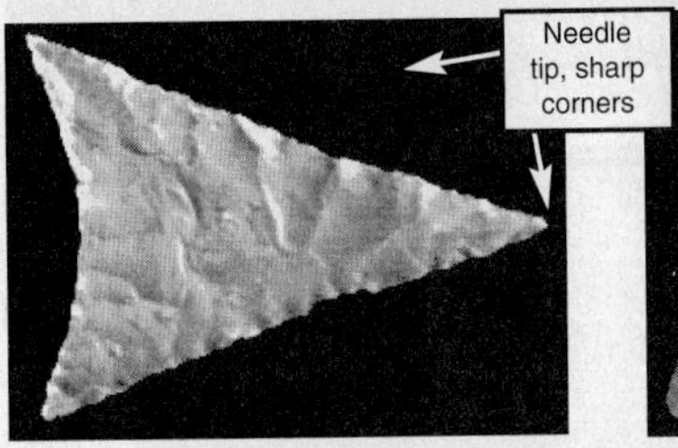

Needle tip, sharp corners

G10, $30-$50
Oswego Co., NY

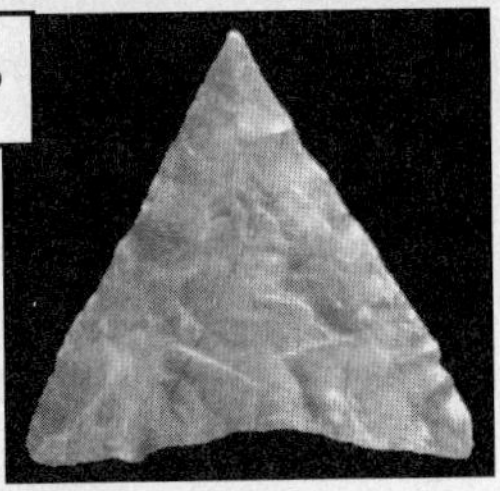

G6, $15-$30
Northumberland Co., PA

Vein quartz

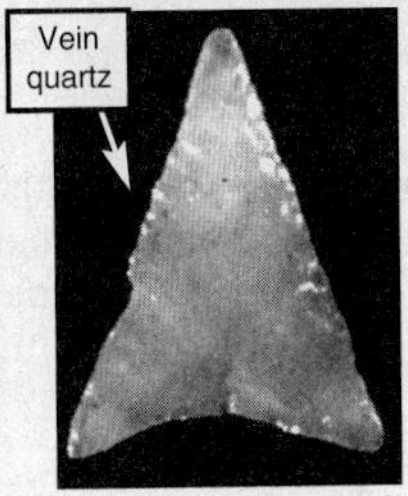

G6, $8-$15
Lancaster Co., PA

LEVANNA (continued)

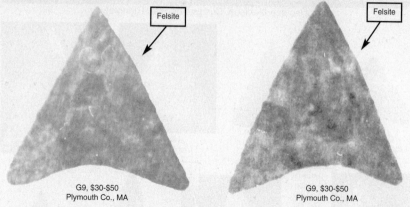

Felsite

Felsite

G9, $30-$50
Plymouth Co., MA

G9, $30-$50
Plymouth Co., MA

LOCATION: Northeastern states. **DESCRIPTION:** A small to medium size, thin, triangular point with a concave to straight base. Believed to be replaced by *Madison* points in later times. Some examples have the basal corners fractured. Called *Yadkin* in North Carolina. **I.D. KEY:** Medium thick cross section triangle.

LOST LAKE - Early Archaic, 9000 - 6000 B.P.

(Also see Charleston Pine Tree, Decatur, Kirk, St. Charles and Thebes)

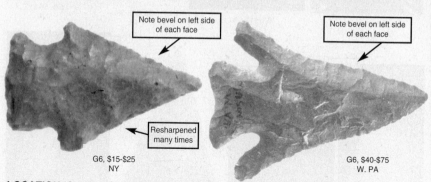

Note bevel on left side
of each face

Note bevel on left side
of each face

Resharpened
many times

G6, $15-$25
NY

G6, $40-$75
W. PA

LOCATION: Southeastern, Midwestern to Northeastern states. **DESCRIPTION:** A medium to large size, broad, corner notched point that is beveled on one side of each face. Some examples are finely serrated. Bases are ground. Unbeveled examples would fall into the *Kirk Corner Notched* type. **I.D. KEY:** Notching and opposite beveled blade edge.

LYCOMING COUNTY SERIES - Middle Archaic, 6000 - 4000 B.P.

(Also see Brewerton, Crooked Creek, Garver's Ferry, Otter Creek, Penn's Creek)

LOCATION: Pennsylvania. **DESCRIPTION:** A local variation of the Brewerton type. A small to medium size point with strong shoulders. The series occurs as side notched, corner notched and stemmed forms.

Tip nick

G3, $4-$8
Lycoming Co., PA. Jasper

MacCORKLE - Early Archaic, 8000 - 6000 B.P.

(Also see Kanawha, Kirk Serrated, Lake Erie, LeCroy, St. Albans, Stanly, Susquehanna Bifurcate)

Green slate

Coshocton flint

G4, $8-$15
Union Co., PA

G7, $25-$45
NY

G8, $60-$100
Union Co., OH

LOCATION: Midwestern to Eastern states. **DESCRIPTION:** A medium to large size, thin, usually serrated, widely corner notched point with large round ears and a deep notch in the center of the base. Bases are usually ground. Called *Nottoway River Bifurcate* in Virginia. **I.D. KEY:** Basal notching, early Archaic flaking.

MADISON - Mississippian, 1100 - 200 B.P.

(Also see Jacks Reef, Levanna, Squibnocket Triangle, Susquehannock triangle)

Gray flint

G2, $.50-$1
Lycoming Co., PA

G8, $5-$10
Union Co., PA

G3, $2-$4
Lycoming Co., PA

G2, $3-$5
Lycoming Co., PA

G5, $5-$10
Lycoming Co., PA

Black chert

G10, $8-$15
Lycoming Co., PA

G8, $5-$10
Lycoming Co., PA

G5, $5-$10
Lycoming Co., PA

LOCATION: Midwestern to Eastern states. Type site is in Madison Co., IL. Found at Cahokia Mounds (un-notched Cahokias). Used by the Kaskaskia tribe into the 1700s. **DESCRIPTION:** A small to medium size, thin, triangular point with usually straight sides and base. Some examples are notched on two to three sides. Many are of high quality and some are finely serrated. **I.D. KEY:** Thin triangle.

(Also see Koens Crispin, Greene, Lehigh, Morrow Mountain, Schuylkill, Virginsville, Wayland Notched & Web Blade)

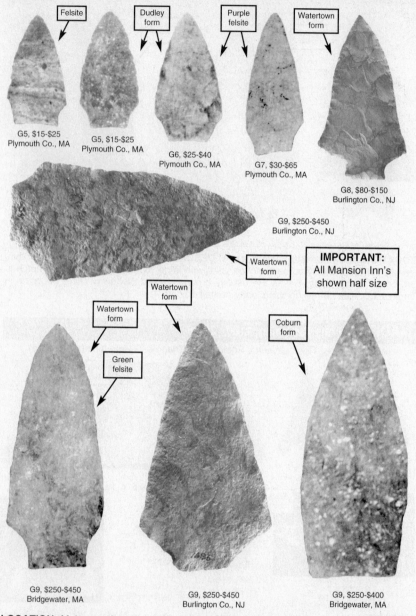

Felsite

G5, $15-$25
Plymouth Co., MA

G5, $15-$25
Plymouth Co., MA

Dudley form

G6, $25-$40
Plymouth Co., MA

Purple felsite

G7, $30-$65
Plymouth Co., MA

Watertown form

G8, $80-$150
Burlington Co., NJ

G9, $250-$450
Burlington Co., NJ

Watertown form

IMPORTANT:
All Mansion Inn's shown half size

Watertown form

Watertown form

Coburn form

Green felsite

G9, $250-$450
Bridgewater, MA

G9, $250-$450
Burlington Co., NJ

G9, $250-$400
Bridgewater, MA

LOCATION: Maine southward into New Jersey. Type site is in Massachusetts. **DESCRIPTION:** A medium to large size, broad, blade with a short, contracting stem. Believed to be preforms related to the *Perkiomen* and *Susquehanna* types. Three forms have been identified: Coburn, Dudley and Watertown. **I.D. KEY:** Size and base form.

Watertown form

Watertown form

G9, $250-$400
NJ

G6, $150-$250
Plymouth Co., MA

G9, $300-$500
Middlesboro, MA

MEADOWOOD - Late Archaic to early Woodland, 4000 - 2500 B.P.

(Also see Kessel, Otter Creek, Wapanucket)

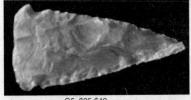

G5, $25-$40
NJ

G6, $30-$50
PA

G6, $35-$60
Luzerne Co., PA

G8, $60-$100
NY

MEADOWOOD (continued)

Preform for type

G6, $35-$60
NY

G8, $50-$80
NY

LOCATION: Northeastern states. **DESCRIPTION:** A medium to large size point with shallow side notches near the base. The base can be straight to slightly convex. Blade edges can be straight to slightly convex to recurved. Some specimens show a lot of reworking and may be used up and asymmetrical.

MERRIMACK STEMMED - Mid-Archaic, 6000 - 5000 B.P.

(Also see Dewart Stemmed, Lamoka, Taconic Stemmed, Wading River)

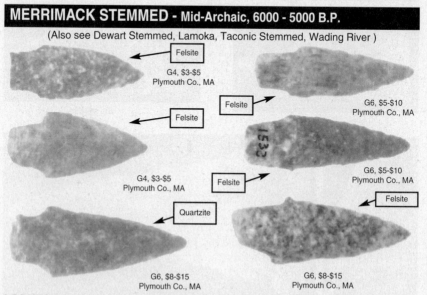

Felsite

G4, $3-$5
Plymouth Co., MA

Felsite

G6, $5-$10
Plymouth Co., MA

Felsite

Felsite

G4, $3-$5
Plymouth Co., MA

Felsite

G6, $5-$10
Plymouth Co., MA

Felsite

Quartzite

G6, $8-$15
Plymouth Co., MA

G6, $8-$15
Plymouth Co., MA

LOCATION: Pennsylvania into New York and Massachusetts. **DESCRIPTION:** A small to medium size, narrow, stemmed point with slight, tapered shoulders. The stem expands, contracts or is parallel sided. **I.D. KEY:** Base form.

(Also see Koens Crispin, Lehigh, Piscataway, Poplar Island, Stark, Swatara/Long, Virginsville)

G4, $8-$15
PA

G4, $12-$20
Carbon Co., PA

Quartzite

Quartzite

G6, $25-$40
Lancaster Co., PA

G5, $15-$30
Lancaster Co., PA

Quartzite

G4, $3-$10
PA

G6, $25-$40
Lancaster Co., PA

LOCATION: Northeastern states. **DESCRIPTION:** A medium to large size, broad, triangular point with a very short, contracting to rounded stem. Shoulders are usually weak but can be barbed. The blade edges on some examples are serrated with needle points. **I.D. KEY:** Contracted base and Archaic parallel flaking.

MUNCY BIFURCATE - Archaic, 8500 - 7000 B.P.

(Also see Fox Valley, Kanawha, Neville and Stanly)

LOCATION: North eastern states. **DESCRIPTION:** A small to medium point with prominent shoulders and a contracting to parallel sided stem. The Base has a shallow notch. Possibly related to *Neville*. **I.D. KEY:** Base form.

G6, $5-$10
Lycoming Co., PA

G4, $3-$6
Lycoming Co., PA

G5, $4-$8
Union Co., PA

NEVILLE - Archaic, 7000 - 6000 B.P.

(Also see Adena Robbins, Bare Island, Duncan's Island, Genesee, Merrimack, Muncy Bifurcate, Newmanstown, Snook Kill, Stark)

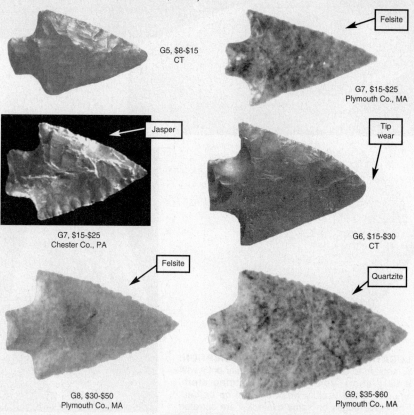

G5, $8-$15
CT

G7, $15-$25
Plymouth Co., MA

G7, $15-$25
Chester Co., PA

G6, $15-$30
CT

G8, $30-$50
Plymouth Co., MA

G9, $35-$60
Plymouth Co., MA

LOCATION: Northeastern states. **DESCRIPTION:** A medium size, triangular point with barbed to horizontal shoulders and a short, square to contracting stem. **I.D. KEY:** Stem form.

NEVILLE (continued)

Felsite

G8, $30-$50
Plymouth Co., MA

G9, $35-$60
Plymouth Co., MA

NEWMANSTOWN - Archaic, 7000 - 5000 B.P.

(Also see Bare Island, Duncan's Island, Lackawaxen, Neville, Piedmont, Taconic Stemmed, Tocks Island)

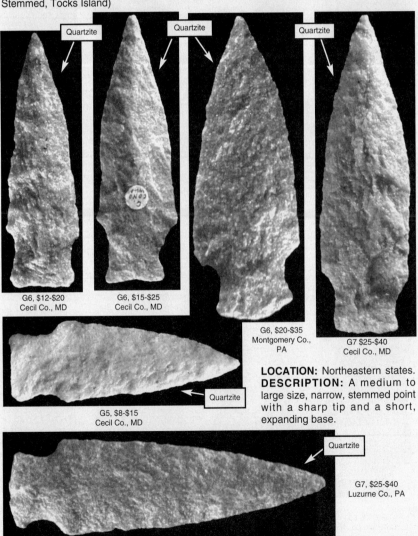

Quartzite

Quartzite

Quartzite

G6, $12-$20
Cecil Co., MD

G6, $15-$25
Cecil Co., MD

G6, $20-$35
Montgomery Co.,
PA

G7 $25-$40
Cecil Co., MD

Quartzite

G5, $8-$15
Cecil Co., MD

LOCATION: Northeastern states.
DESCRIPTION: A medium to large size, narrow, stemmed point with a sharp tip and a short, expanding base.

Quartzite

G7, $25-$40
Luzurne Co., PA

149

NORMANSKILL- Late Archaic to early Woodland, 4000 - 2500 B.P.

(Also see Brewerton Corner Notched, Drybrook, Meadowood, Orient, Susquehanna Broad, Tocks Island)

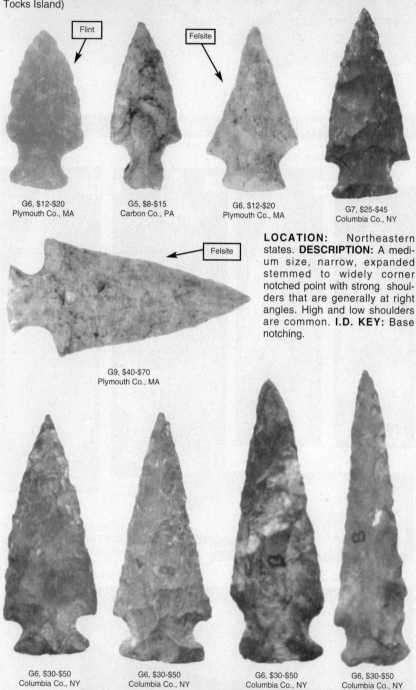

Flint

Felsite

G6, $12-$20
Plymouth Co., MA

G5, $8-$15
Carbon Co., PA

G6, $12-$20
Plymouth Co., MA

G7, $25-$45
Columbia Co., NY

Felsite

G9, $40-$70
Plymouth Co., MA

LOCATION: Northeastern states. **DESCRIPTION:** A medium size, narrow, expanded stemmed to widely corner notched point with strong shoulders that are generally at right angles. High and low shoulders are common. **I.D. KEY:** Base notching.

G6, $30-$50
Columbia Co., NY

G6, $30-$50
Columbia Co., NY

G6, $30-$50
Columbia Co., NY

G6, $30-$50
Columbia Co., NY

NORTHUMBERLAND FLUTED KNIFE - Paleo, 12,000 - 10,000 B. P.

NE

(Also see Clovis, Crowfield, Cumberland, Debert, Holcomb, Plainview, Redstone)

LOCATION: Northeastern states. **DESCRIPTION:** A medium to large size, lanceolate form that is usually fluted on both sides. Fluting can extend to the tip. A variant form of the *Barnes Cumberland*, but the base form is different. **I.D. KEY:** Paleo flaking, indirect pressure fluted.

G4, $300-$500
Lancaster Co., PA

Fluting channel

Yellow jasper

Yellow jasper

Short flute

G5, $900-$1500
Schuylkill Co., PA

Yellow jasper

Long flute channel

Note parallel flaking to the center

Yellow jasper

Short flute

G10, $2500-$4000
Northumberland Co., PA

G9, $2000-$3500
Montgomery Co., PA. Both faces shown. Fluted one side only.

Long flute channel

Black chert

Tip & edge wear

Yellow jasper

Jasper

G5, $800-$1500
PA

G5, $1200-$2000
Lycoming Co., PA

G5, $1500-$2500
Indiana Co., PA

Yellow jasper

Edge & tip wear

G5, $1500-$2500
Indiana Co., PA

Long fluting

G10, $7000-$10,000
PA

OHIO LANCEOLATE - Late Paleo, 10,500 - 7000 B.P.

(Also see Angostura, Beaver Lake, Clovis, Dalton, Cumberland & Parallel Lanceolate)

Side nick

G2, $80-$150
Western PA

LOCATION: Ohio into W. Pennsylvania. **DESCRIPTION:** A medium to large size lanceolate point with parallel to convex sides and a concave base that is ground. Flaking is early collateral to oblique transverse. Base has light grinding, not fluted or basally thinned. Thinner than *Clovis* or *Agate Basin*. **I.D. KEY:** Base form and parallel flaking.

OLEY - Woodland, 2200 - 1500 B. P.

(Also see Charleston Pine Tree, Erb Basal Notched, Eshbach, Vestal Notched)

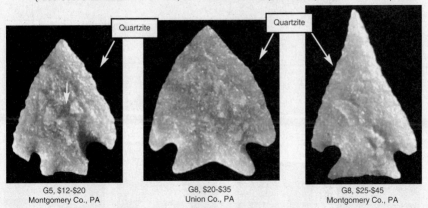

Quartzite   Quartzite

G5, $12-$20
Montgomery Co., PA

G8, $20-$35
Union Co., PA

G8, $25-$45
Montgomery Co., PA

LOCATION: Southeast Pennsylvania. **DESCRIPTION:** A small to medium size corner notched barbed point with an expanding base. Blade edges are concave to recurved. Base is concave. **I.D. KEY:** Base form and barbs.

ORIENT - Late Archaic to Woodland, 4000 - 2500 B. P.

(Also see Drybrook, Forest Notched, Frost Island, Susquehanna Broad, Perkiomen & Taconic Stemmed)

Felsite

Felsite

G3, $12-$20
Plymouth Co., MA

G5, $25-$45
Plymouth Co., MA

G5, $15-$25
Northampton Co.,
PA

G6, $25-$40
Northampton Co., PA

G6, $25-$45
Northampton Co., PA

Jasper

G5, $15-$25
Lancaster Co., PA

Jasper

G6, $25-$45
Lancaster Co., PA

Felsite

Black flint

G8, $35-$65
Lycoming Co., PA

Jasper

G8, $35-$65
Northampton Co.,
PA

G8, $30-$50
Northampton Co.,
PA

G8, $25-$45
Plymouth Co., MA

G8, $35-$65
Lancaster Co., PA

Jasper

G7, $30-$50
Burlington Co., NJ

G6, $25-$40
Lycoming Co., PA

G9, $45-$80
Montgomery Co., PA

G9, $50-$90
Lancaster Co., PA

LOCATION: Northeastern states. **DESCRIPTION:** A small to medium size point with broad side notches, rounded shoulders and an expanding base. The base on some examples form auricles. **I.D. KEY:** Base form and rounded shoulders.

154

Jasper

G10, $400-$750
Lycoming Co., PA

OTTER CREEK - Mid to Late Archaic, 5000 - 3500 B.P.

(Also see Brewerton Side Notched, Goddard, Perkiomen, Raccoon Notched, Susquehanna Broad)

Onondaga chert

G5, $8-$15
PA

G5, $15-$30
Columbia Co., NY

G5, $20-$35
PA

Black chert

Gray chert

G6, $25-$45
Union Co., PA

G6, $25-$40
PA

G6, $25-$40
Lycoming Co., PA

G78, $30-$50
PA

LOCATION: Northeastern states. **DESCRIPTION:** A medium to large size, side notched point with a straight, concave or convex base. Notching is prominent, shoulders are tapered to barbed. Bases are ground. **I.D. KEY:** Side notching.

155

OTTER CREEK (continued)

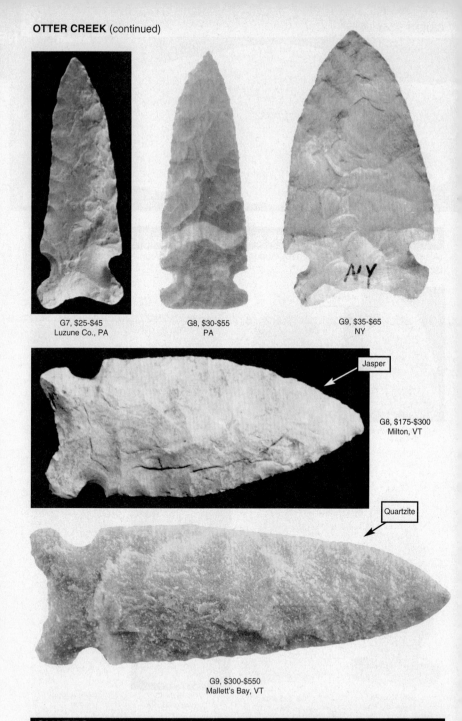

G7, $25-$45
Luzune Co., PA

G8, $30-$55
PA

G9, $35-$65
NY

Jasper

G8, $175-$300
Milton, VT

Quartzite

G9, $300-$550
Mallett's Bay, VT

OVATES - Woodland, 3000 - 2000 B.P.

(Also see Nodena (Arkansas), Strike-A-Lite Type II)

OVATES (continued)

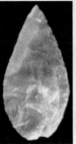

G5, $8-$15
Chester Co., PA

G6, $8-$15
Montgomery Co., PA

G5, $8-$15
Chester Co., PA

G5, $8-$15
Chester Co., PA

G6, $15-$25
Montgomery Co., PA

LOCATION: Northeastern states. **DESCRIPTION:** A small size tear-drop shaped point with rounded shoulders and base. **I.D. KEY:** Ovoid form.

PALMER - Early Archaic, 9000 - 8000 B.P.

(Also see Amos, Brewerton, Charleston Pine Tree, Kirk Corner Notched, Kiski, Kline)

Jasper

G6, $20-$35
Montour Co., PA

G6, $25-$40
Luzurne Co., PA

G5, $15-$25
Luzurne Co., PA

G5, $15-$25
Lycoming Co., PA

G4, $10-$20
Lycoming Co., PA

G6, $20-$35
Union Co., PA

LOCATION: Eastern states. **DESCRIPTION:** A small to medium size, corner-notched point with a ground concave, convex, or straight base. Shoulders are barbed to contracting. Many are serrated and large examples would fall under the *Charleston Pine Tree* or *Kirk* Type. **I.D. KEY:** Basal form and notching.

PATUXENT - Late Archaic, 4000 - 3000 B.P.

(Also see Bare Island, Duncan's Island, Frost Island, Orient, Piedmont)

LOCATION: Southeastern PA., MD., VA. **DESCRIPTION:** A small to medium size point with weak, tapered shoulders and an expanding base. The base is concave forming ears. **I.D. KEY:** Basal form and weak shoulders.

G6, $15-$30
Montgomery
Co., PA

Quartzite

PENN'S CREEK BIFURCATE- Early Archaic, 9000 - 7000 B.P.

(Also see Culpepper, Kirk Stemmed, LeCroy, MacCorkle, St. Albans, Susquehanna Bifurcate)

LOCATION: Pennsylvania. **DESCRIPTION:** A small size bifurcated point with Archaic flaking. Shoulders are weakly barbed and the base expands to ears. **I.D. KEY:** Basal form and early flaking.

G4, $12-$20
Northumberland Co., PA

PENN'S CREEK SERIES - Early Archaic, 9000 - 7000 B.P.

(Also see Lycoming County Series)

G4, $4-$8
Peach Bottom, PA

LOCATION: Central Pennsylvania. **DESCRIPTION:** A small size point that is stemmed, corner or side notched.

PENTAGONAL KNIFE - Mid-Archaic, 6500 - 4000 B.P.

(Also see Jacks Reef Corner Notched)

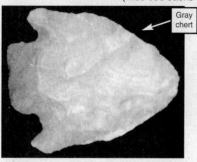

Gray chert

G6, $15-$25
Crawford Co., PA

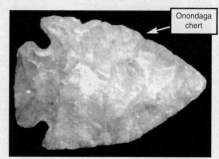

Onondaga chert

G6, $30-$50
Crawford Co.,, PA

LOCATION: Pennsylvania into Ohio, Kentucky, Tennessee and Alabama. **DESCRIPTION:** A medium to large size pentagonal shaped point with a flaring or corner notched stem. Some examples are base notched. Similar to but older than the *Afton* point found in the Midwest. Similar to *Jacks Reef* but thicker. **I.D. KEY:** Blade form.

PERKIOMEN- Late Archaic to early Woodland, 4000 - 2500 B.P.

(Also see Ashtabula, Frost Island, Manson Inn, Susquehanna Broad, Waratan)

Yellow jasper

G4, $70-$135
Lancaster Co., PA

Rare variegated jasper

G8, $275-$500
PA

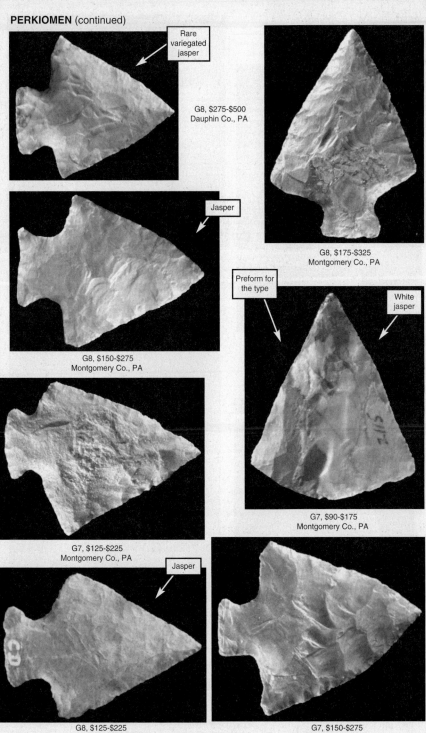

Rare variegated jasper

G8, $275-$500
Dauphin Co., PA

G8, $175-$325
Montgomery Co., PA

Jasper

G8, $150-$275
Montgomery Co., PA

Preform for the type

White jasper

G7, $90-$175
Montgomery Co., PA

G7, $125-$225
Montgomery Co., PA

Jasper

G8, $125-$225
Lancaster Co., PA

G7, $150-$275
Montgomery Co., PA

Variegated jasper

G8, $200-$350
PA

LOCATION: Northeastern states. **DESCRIPTION:** A medium to large size broad point with strong shoulders and a small, expanding base that is usually bulbous. Shoulders usually slope upwards. Blades can be asymmetrical. **I.D. KEY:** Broad shoulders and small base.

G9, $650-$1200
Montgomery Co., PA

Jasper

Jasper

G10, $800-$1500
Montgomery Co., PA

G10, $3000-$5000
Dauphin Co., PA

(Also see Bare Island, Duncan's Island, Genesee, Hoover's Island, Neville, Lackawaxen, Newmanstown, Patuxent, Piney Island, Tocks Island)

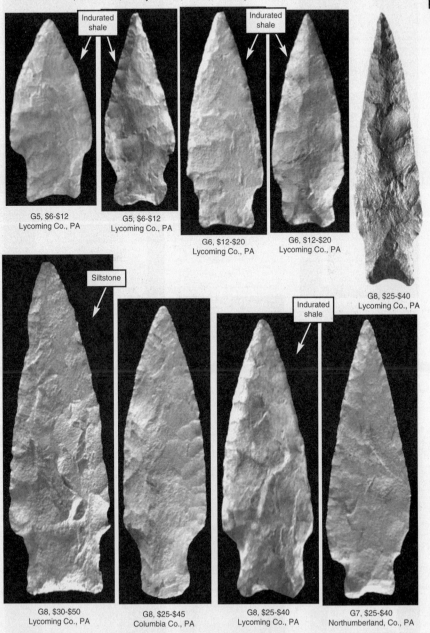

Indurated shale

Indurated shale

G5, $6-$12
Lycoming Co., PA

G5, $6-$12
Lycoming Co., PA

G6, $12-$20
Lycoming Co., PA

G6, $12-$20
Lycoming Co., PA

G8, $25-$40
Lycoming Co., PA

Siltstone

Indurated shale

G8, $30-$50
Lycoming Co., PA

G8, $25-$45
Columbia Co., PA

G8, $25-$40
Lycoming Co., PA

G7, $25-$40
Northumberland, Co., PA

LOCATION: Central Pennsylvania northward. **DESCRIPTION:** A medium to large size, narrow stemmed point. Base varies from straight to convex, from square to expanding or contracting. Shoulders are usually tapered. Named by Fogelman. Usually made of siltstone and indurated shale. **I.D. KEY:** Base form and narrow width.

G7, $25-$40
Columbia Co., NY

G7, $30-$50
Northumberton Co., PA

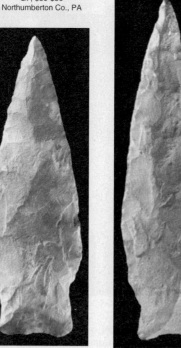

G8, $30-$50
Northumberton Co., PA

G8, $35-$60
Northumberton Co., PA

G10+, $550-$900
Lancaster Co., PA

162

PINEY ISLAND - Late Archaic, 6000 - 2000 B.P.

(Also see Bare Island, Duncan's Island, Lamoka, Patuxent, Piedmont, Squibnocket Stemmed)

G6, $20-$35
Northampton Co., PA

G5, $15-$25
Columbia Co., PA

G8, $25-$40
Columbia Co., PA

G8, $35-$60
Carbon Co., PA

LOCATION: Northeastern states. **DESCRIPTION:** A medium size, narrow, long stemmed point with tapered shoulders. **I.D. KEY:** Basal form and narrow width.

PISCATAWAY - Mid to late Woodland, 2500 - 500 B.P.

(Also see Morrow Mountain, Poplar Island, Schuylkill, Stark, Virginsville)

Quartzite

G7, $20-$35
Chester Co., PA

Milky quartz

Chalcedony

Jasper

Jasper

G5, $5-$10
Lancaster Co., PA

G5, $5-$10
Chester Co., PA

G7, $20-$35
Chester Co., PA

G5, $15-$25
Chester Co., PA

G6, $15-$25
Chester Co., PA

PISCATAWAY (continued)

LOCATION: Eastern to Northeastern states. **DESCRIPTION:** A small to medium size, very narrow triangular point with tapered shoulders and a short tapered stem. The base is pointed to rounded. **I.D. KEY:** Basal form and narrow width.

POPLAR ISLAND - Mid-Archaic, 6000 - 4000 B.P.

(Also see Koens Crispin, Morrow Mountain, Piscataway, Schuylkill, Stark, Virginsville)

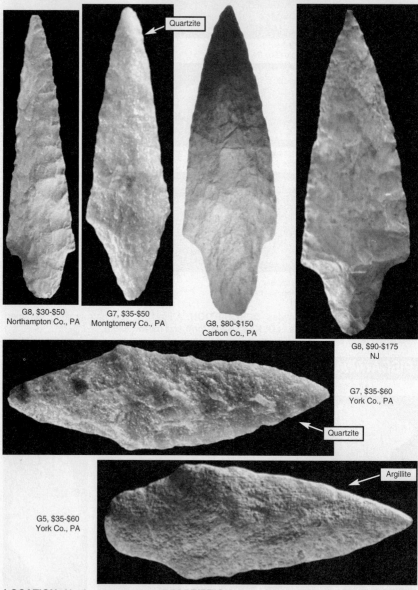

G8, $30-$50
Northampton Co., PA

G7, $35-$50
Montgtomery Co., PA

G8, $80-$150
Carbon Co., PA

G8, $90-$175
NJ

G7, $35-$60
York Co., PA

G5, $35-$60
York Co., PA

LOCATION: Northeastern states. **DESCRIPTION:** A medium to large size, narrow, triangular point with tapered shoulders and a long contracting base. The base can be pointed to rounded. **I.D. KEY:** Basal form and narrow width.

POPLAR ISLAND (continued)

Argillite

G67, $90-$175
Lancaster Co., PA

Quartzite

G9, $150-$250
Montgtomery Co., PA

G9, $150-$250
Carbon Co., PA

PORT MAITLAND - Mid Woodland, 2500 - 1400 B.P.

(Also see Brewerton, Goddard, Raccoon Notched)

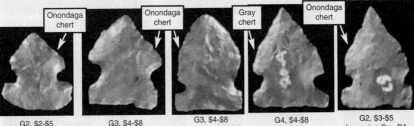

Onondaga chert

Onondaga chert

Gray chert

Onondaga chert

G2, $2-$5
Monroe Co., PA

G3, $4-$8
Union Co., PA

G3, $4-$8
Lycoming Co., PA

G4, $4-$8
Lycoming Co., PA

G2, $3-$5
Lycoming Co., PA

LOCATION: Northeastern states. **DESCRIPTION:** A small size side notched point with a straight to slightly concave base. Side notches form square corners at the base. **I.D. KEY:** Notching form and small size.

RACCOON NOTCHED - Late Woodland, 1500 - 1000 B.P.

(Also see Brewerton, Goddard, Jacks Reef, Port Maitland)

RACCOON NOTCHED (continued)

LOCATION: Northeastern states. **DESCRIPTION:**
A small to medium size, thin, side notched point.
Blade edges are convex to pentagonal shape.
Known as *Knight Island* in Southeast. **I.D. KEY:**
Side notching and thinness.

G5, $25-$40
Union Co., PA

Red jasper

RANDOLPH - Woodland to Historic, 2000 - 200 B.P.

(Also see Dewart Stemmed, Lamoka, Merrimack, Wading River)

G7, $5-$10
Union Co., PA

G5, $3-$7
Union Co., PA

LOCATION: Eastern to Northeastern states. **DESCRIPTION:** A medium size, narrow, thick, spike point with tapered shoulders and a short to medium, contracted, rounded stem. Many examples have exaggerated spikes along the blade edges. **I.D. KEY:** Blade form and spikes.

REDSTONE - Paleo, 13,000 - 9000 B.P.

(Also see Clovis, Crowfield, Cumberland, Debert, Holcomb)

LOCATION: Southeastern to Northeastern states. **DESCRIP-TION:** A small to large size, thin, auriculate, fluted point with convex sides expanding to a wide, deeply concave base. Fluting can extend most of the way down each face. Multiple flutes are usual. A very rare type. **I.D. KEY:** Batan fluted, edgework on the hafting area.

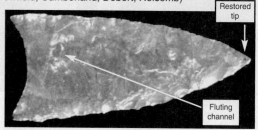

Restored tip

Fluting channel

G7, $350-$600
Lycoming Co., PA. Coshocton chert.

ST. ALBANS - Early to Mid-Archaic, 9000 - 5000 B.P.

(Also see Charleston Pine Tree, Decatur, Fox Valley, Kanawha, Kirk Serrated, Lake Erie, LeCroy, MacCorkle, Stanly & Susquehanna Bifurcate)

Milky quartz

G4, $8-$15
Lycoming Co., PA

G5, $15-$25
Lycoming Co., PA

G5, $15-$25
MD

G8, $25-$40
Lycoming Co., PA

ST. ALBANS (continued)

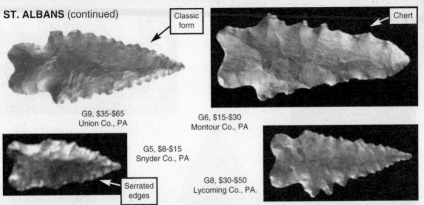

Classic form

Chert

G9, $35-$65
Union Co., PA

G6, $15-$30
Montour Co., PA

G5, $8-$15
Snyder Co., PA

Serrated edges

G8, $30-$50
Lycoming Co., PA.

LOCATION: Eastern to Northeastern states. Type site is in Kanawha Co., WVA. **DESCRIPTION:** A small to medium size, usually serrated, bifurcated point. Basal lobes usually flare outward, and are weakly bifurcated. **I.D. KEY:** Weak bifurcation, base more narrow than shoulders.

ST. ANNE - Early Archaic, 9000 - 8000 B.P.

(Also see Agate Basin, Angostura, Plainview and Scottsbluff)

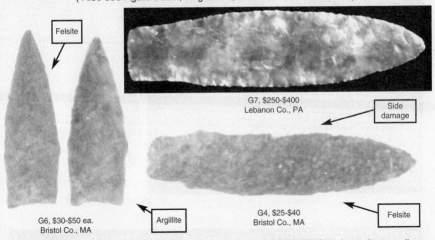

Felsite

G7, $250-$400
Lebanon Co., PA

Side damage

G6, $30-$50 ea.
Bristol Co., MA

Argillite

G4, $25-$40
Bristol Co., MA

Felsite

LOCATION: Northeastern states into eastern Canada. **DESCRIPTION:** A small to medium size, narrow, lanceolate point with very weak shoulders. The base is rectangular shaped and is ground. Similar to *Eden* points found further west. **I.D. KEY:** Weak shoulders, narrow blade.

ST. CHARLES - Early Archaic, 9500 - 8000 B.P.

(Also see Brodhead Side Notched, Decatur, Kirk, Kline, Lost Lake & Thebes)

LOCATION: Midwest to Eastern states. **DESCRIPTION:** Also known as *Dovetail*. A medium to large size, corner notched, dovetailed base point. The blade is beveled on one side of each face when resharpened. Bases are straight, convex or bifurcated and are ground and can be fractured from both corners of the base. **I.D. KEY:** Dovetailed base.

ST. CHARLES (continued)

Yellow jasper

G2, $12-$25
Lancaster Co., PA

Ground base

G4, $20-$35
NJ

G2, $15-$30
Lancaster Co., PA

G4, $25-$40
PA

G6, $65-$125
MD

G5, $65-$125
PA

SANDHILL STEMMED - Mid-Woodland, 2200 - 1700 B.P.

(Also see Dewart Stemmed, Garver's Ferry, Lamoka, Merrimack, Wading River)

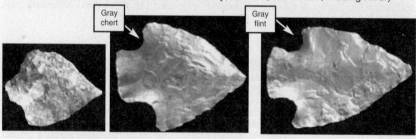

G7, $6-$12
PA

Gray chert

G7, $8-$15
Lycoming Co., PA

Gray flint

G3, $5-$10
Lycoming Co., PA

168

SANDHILL STEMMED (continued)

White chert

Red jasper

G5, $4-$8
Lycoming Co., PA

G7, $6-$12
Lycoming Co., PA

G5, $6-$12
Monroe Co., PA

G8, $8-$15
Lycoming Co., PA

LOCATION: Northeastern states. **DESCRIPTION:** A small point with a straight to contracting base. Shoulders are tapered to slightly barbed.

SAVANNAH RIVER - Mid Archaic to Woodland, 5000 - 2000 B.P.

(Also see Atlantic Phase Blades, Fox Creek, Genesee, Piedmont)

Tip nick

Quartzite

G4, $8-$15
Northumberland Co., PA

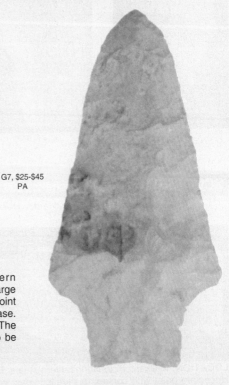

G7, $25-$45
PA

LOCATION: Southeastern to Eastern states. **DESCRIPTION:** A medium to large size, straight to contracting stemmed point with a concave, straight or bifurcated base. The shoulders are tapered to square. The stems are narrow to broad. Believed to be related to the earlier Stanly point.

SCHUYLKILL - Late Archaic, 4000 - 2000 B.P.

(Also see Adena, Atlantic Phase Blades, Condoquinet Canfield, Koens Crispin, Lehigh, Morrow Mountain, Piscataway, Poplar Island, Stark, Virginsville)

LOCATION: Northeastern states. **DESCRIPTION:** A medium to large size, narrow point with a long, tapered, rounded stem. Shoulders are usually at a sharper angle than Poplar Island. **I.D. KEY:** Sharp corners, narrow blade, long tapering stem.

G6, $30-$50
Carbon Co., PA

G7, $40-$75
PA

G4, $15-$25
York Co., PA

SCOTTSBLUFF - Early Archaic, 9500 - 7000 B.P.

(Also see Eden, Fox Creek, Hardin, Holland, St. Anne and Steubenville)

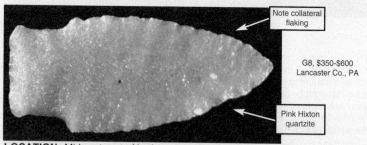

Note collateral flaking

G8, $350-$600
Lancaster Co., PA

Pink Hixton quartzite

LOCATION: Midwestern to Northeastern states. **DESCRIPTION:** A medium to large size, lanceolate point with convex to parallel sides, weak shoulders, and a broad parallel to expanding stem. The hafting area is ground. Most examples have horizontal to oblique parallel flaking and are of high quality and thinness. Also known as *Stringtown*.

SCRAPER - Paleo to Archaic, 14,000 - 5000 B.P.

(Also see Drill, Graver, Strike-A-Lite)

SCRAPER (continued)

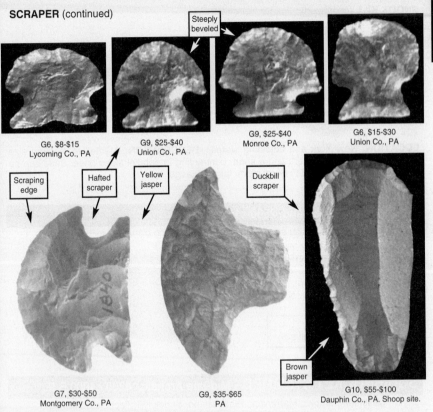

Steeply beveled

G6, $8-$15
Lycoming Co., PA

G9, $25-$40
Union Co., PA

G9, $25-$40
Monroe Co., PA

G6, $15-$30
Union Co., PA

Scraping edge

Hafted scraper

Yellow jasper

Duckbill scraper

Brown jasper

G7, $30-$50
Montgomery Co., PA

G9, $35-$65
PA

G10, $55-$100
Dauphin Co., PA. Shoop site.

LOCATION: Paleo to early Archaic sites everywhere. **DESCRIPTION:** Thumb, Duckbill, and Turtleback forms are small to medium size, thick, ovoid shaped, uniface, scraping tools that are steeply beveled, especially at the broadest end. Side scrapers are long hand-held uniface flakes with beveling on all blade edges of one face. Broken points are also utilized as scrapers.

SHARK'S TOOTH - Woodland to Historic, 2000 - 100 B.P.

(Also see Bone/Antler)

LOCATION: Coastal states from Maine to Florida. **DESCRIPTION:** Salvaged from Shark remains and as fossilized teeth found along the shoreline. Used as arrowpoints by Woodland Indians into historic times.

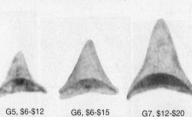

G5, $6-$12
Seaver farm, MA

G6, $6-$15
Seaver farm, MA

G7, $12-$20
Seaver farm, MA

G7, $15-$25
Seaver farm, MA

SNOOK KILL - Late Archaic, 4000 - 2000 B.P.

(Also see Atlantic Phase Blades, Dewart Stemmed, Koens Crispin, Lehigh, Merrimack, Sandhill Stemmed, Stark & Taconic Stemmed)

SNOOK KILL (continued)

G5, $15-$30
NY

Impact fracture

LOCATION: New York and adjoining states. **DESCRIPTION:** A small to medium size point with tapered shoulders and a short, contracting to parallel sided base. Base can be straight to convex. **I.D. KEY:** Short stem, tapered tangs.

SNYDERS - Woodland, 2500 - 1500 B.P.

(Also see Brewerton and Lycoming County)

LOCATION: West. New York eastward into Ohio. **DESCRIPTION:** A medium to large size, broad, thin, wide corner notched point. Made by the Hopewell culture. **I.D. KEY:** Size and broad corner notches.

IMPORTANT:
Snyders point shown half size

G7, $80-$150
W. NY

SQUIBNOCKET STEMMED - Mid-late Archaic, 4200 - 4000 B.P.

(Also see Lamoka, Merrimack, Piney Island, Snook Kill, Taconic Stemmed)

G4, $4-$8
CT

LOCATION: Conn., Massachusetts into New York. **DESCRIPTION:** A medium size, narrow, stemmed point with very weak shoulders and a rounded stem. **I.D. KEY:** Narrowness and weak shoulders.

SQUIBNOCKET TRIANGLE - Mid-late Archaic, 4500 - 4000 B.P.

(Also see Levanna, Madison and Susquehannock Triangle)

All quartz

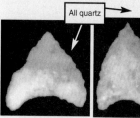    

| G4, $4-$8 | G4, $4-$8 | G5, $5-$10 | G5, $5-$10 | G5, $5-$10 |
| Plymouth Co., MA | Plymouth Co., MA | Plymouth Co., MA | Plymouth Co., MA | Plymouth Co., MA |

LOCATION: Conn., Massachusetts into New York. **DESCRIPTION:** A small size, broad, triangular point with excurvate sides and an incurvate base. Basal corners turn inward. **I.D. KEY:** Narrowness and weak shoulders.

172

STANLY - Early Archaic, 8000 - 5000 B.P.

(Also see Kanawha, Kirk-Bifurcated, LeCroy, Muncy, Savannah River)

G5, $20-$35
Union Co., PA

G9, $25-$40
NJ

Yellow jasper

G5, $15-$25
Lycoming Co., PA

G6, $20-$35
Lycoming Co., PA

G6, $20-$35
Union Co., PA

G6, $15-$25
MD

Called Stanly Narrow Blade in North Carolina

LOCATION: Southeastern to Northeastern states. **DESCRIPTION:** A small to medium size, broad shoulder point with a small birfucated stem. Some examples are serrated and show high quality flaking. The shoulders are very prominent and can be tapered, horizontal or barbed. **I.D. KEY:** Tiny bifurcated base.

STARK - Early Archaic, 7000 - 6500 B.P.

(Also see Adena, Koens Crispin, Lehigh, Morrow Mountain, Neville, Piscatawa, Poplar Island and Schuylkill)

Felsite

G5, $12-$20
Plymouth Co., MA

Felsite

G4, $5-$10
CT

Felsite

Felsite

G5, $12-$20
Plymouth Co., MA

Felsite

G5, $12-$20
Plymouth Co., MA

LOCATION: Conn., Mass. into New York. **DESCRIPTION:** A small to medium size, narrow, contracted stemmed point with tapering shoulders and a rounded to pointed stem. Similar to *Piscataway* and *Rossville* points found further south.

STARK (Continued)

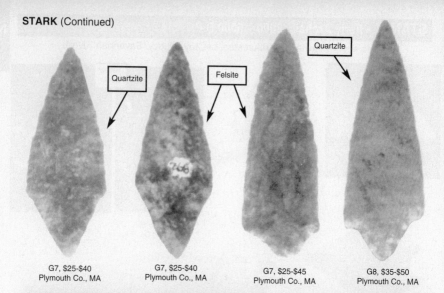

G7, $25-$40
Plymouth Co., MA

G7, $25-$40
Plymouth Co., MA

G7, $25-$45
Plymouth Co., MA

G8, $35-$50
Plymouth Co., MA

STRIKE-A-LITE, type I - Early to late Archaic, 9000 - 4000 B.P.

(Also see Drill, Scraper)

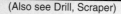

G5, $4-$8
Monroe Co., PA

G4, $5-$10
Lycoming Co., PA

G5, $5-$10
Lycoming Co., PA

G4, $5-$10
Lycoming Co., PA.

LOCATION: Northeastern states. **DESCRIPTION:** A small to medium size friction tool made either from scratch or from broken points. The blunt-end of these objects is beveled from both sides, to create an edge for striking a hard object to emit sparks for igniting combustible material for the creation of fire. These are unlike blunts or scrapers of similar form that are only beveled on one side of the face. The striking edge usually shows extreme wear.

STRIKE-A-LITE, type II - Woodland, 3000 - 1000 B.P.

(Also see Drill, Ovates)

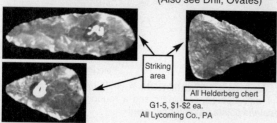

G1-5, $1-$2 ea.
All Lycoming Co., PA.

LOCATION: Northeastern states. **DESCRIPTION:** A small size, narrow, tear drop form created for striking a hard object to emit sparks for igniting combustible material for the creation of fire. The striking edge usually shows extreme wear.

174

(Also see Kanawha, Kirk Stemmed, Lake Erie, LeCroy, MacCorkle, Muncy, Penn's Creek, St. Albans, Stanly, and Taunton River Bifurcate)

G8, $15-$25
Lycoming Co., PA

G8, $15-$25
Union Co., PA

G8, $12-$20
Lycoming Co., PA

Jasper

Yellow jasper

G5, $12-$20
Lycoming Co., PA

G7, $20-$35
Carbon Co., PA

G7, $20-$35
Dauphin Co., PA

Chert

G7, $25-$40
Union Co., PA

G7, $25-$45
Union Co., PA

G8, $30-$50
Union Co., PA

LOCATION: Northeastern states. **DESCRIPTION:** A small to medium size bifurcated point with barbed shoulders and squared basal ears. **I.D. KEY:** Square basal ears.

(Also see Ashtabula, Drybrook, Frost Island, Orient, Patuxent, Perkiomen and Waratan)

Felsite

Felsite

Red shale

G4, $8-$15
Plymouth Co., MA

G4, $8-$15
Plymouth Co., MA

G4, $8-$15
Plymouth Co., MA

G5, $25-$40
Plymouth Co., MA

Yellow jasper

Yellow jasper

G6, $30-$50
Lancaster Co., PA

G4, $12-$20
Northampton Co., PA

G7, $45-$85
Lycoming Co., PA

Rhyolite

Yellow jasper

G5, $25-$40
Lycoming Co., PA

G5, $15-$30
Luzurne Co., PA

G7, $45-$85
Lancaster Co., PA

LOCATION: Northeastern states. **DESCRIPTION:** A medium to large size, broad, expanded stem point with tapered to clipped wing shoulders. The blade width varies from narrow to broad. Many examples are asymmetrical. Early forms have ground bases. An extremely popular type in the collecting area.

G9, $150-$250
NJ

Gray chert

G6, $30-$50
Lycoming Co., PA

Felsite

G6, $35-$50
Plymouth Co., MA

G8, $80-$150
Columbia Co., PA

G9, $300-$500
Bridgewater, MA

SUSQUEHANNOCK TRIANGLE - Late Woodland, 1500 - 400 B.P.

(Also see Erie Triangle, Levanna, Madison, Squibnocket Triangle, Yadkin)

LOCATION: Pennsylvania.
DESCRIPTION: A small to medium size triangle. Some examples can be serrated.
I.D. KEY: Triangle.

G6, $15-$25
Lycoming Co., PA

Yellow jasper

Serrated edge

Yellow jasper

G7, $25-$40
NJ

SWATARA-LONG - Archaic, 5000 - 4000 B.P.

(Also see Koens Crispin, Lehigh, Morrow Mountain, Poplar Island & Virginsville)

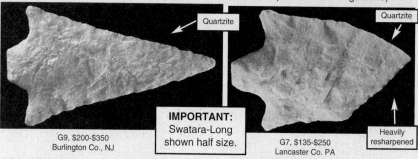

Quartzite

Quartzite

Heavily resharpened

G9, $200-$350
Burlington Co., NJ

IMPORTANT:
Swatara-Long shown half size.

G7, $135-$250
Lancaster Co. PA

LOCATION: Northeastern states. **DESCRIPTION:** A medium to large, broad, stemmed point with a straight to contracting stem. Shoulders are rounded, tapered or barbed.

TACONIC STEMMED - Mid-Archaic, 5000 - 4000 B.P.

(Also Drybrook, Lamoka, Merrimack, Newmanstown, Orient)

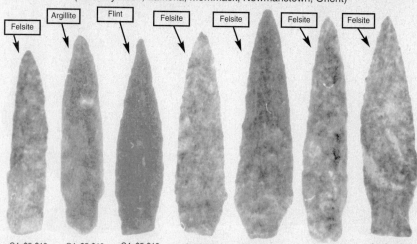

Felsite

Argillite

Flint

Felsite

Felsite

Felsite

Felsite

G4, $5-$10
Plymouth Co.,
MA

G4, $5-$10
Plymouth Co.,
MA

G4, $5-$10
Plymouth Co.,
MA

G5, $8-$15
Plymouth Co.,
MA

G7, $15-$25
Plymouth Co.,
MA

G6, $12-$20
Plymouth Co.,
MA

G7, $15-$25
Plymouth Co.,
MA

TACONIC STEMMED (Continued)

LOCATION: Easterm Penn. into New Jersey, New York and Mass. **DESCRIPTION:** A medium to large, narrow, stemmed point with a straight, or contracting or expanding stem. Shoulders are weak and are tapered.

TAUNTON RIVER BIFURCATE - Early Archaic, 9000 - 8000 B.P.

(Also see LeCroy, MacCorkle, Susquehanna Bifurcate)

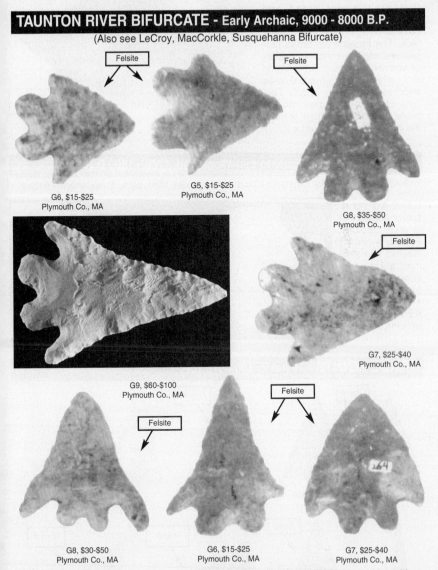

Felsite

Felsite

G6, $15-$25
Plymouth Co., MA

G5, $15-$25
Plymouth Co., MA

G8, $35-$50
Plymouth Co., MA

Felsite

G7, $25-$40
Plymouth Co., MA

G9, $60-$100
Plymouth Co., MA

Felsite

Felsite

G8, $30-$50
Plymouth Co., MA

G6, $15-$25
Plymouth Co., MA

G7, $25-$40
Plymouth Co., MA

LOCATION: New England states. **DESCRIPTION:** A medium size barbed point with an expanding bifurcated base. Lobes are parallel sided to expanding and rounded. **I.D. KEY:** Barbs, bifurcated base.

THEBES - Early Archaic, 10,000 - 8000 B.P.

(Also see Lost Lake and St. Charles)

THEBES (Continued)

LOCATION: New York eastward into Ohio. **DESCRIPTION:** A medium to large size, wide blade with deep, angled side notches that are parallel sided and squared. Resharpened examples have beveling on one side of each face. The bases have broad proportions and are concave, straight or convex and are ground. Some examples have unusual side notches called *Key notch*. This type of notch is angled into the blade to produce a high point in the center, forming the letter E.

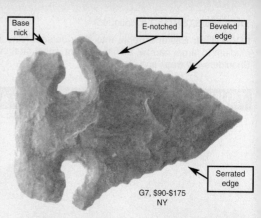

Base nick

E-notched

Beveled edge

Serrated edge

G7, $90-$175
NY

TOCKS ISLAND - Early to mid-Woodland, 1700 - 1500 B.P.

(Also see Bare Island, Duncan's Island, Lackawaxen, Merrimack, Susquehanna Broad)

LOCATION: Lower Hudson river area. **DESCRIPTION:** A small to medium size stemmed point with a small, expanding base. Shoulders are barbed. **I.D. KEY:** Short expanding stem.

White quartz

G5, $45-$80
Monmouth Co., NJ

TRADE POINTS - Historic, 400 - 170 B.P.

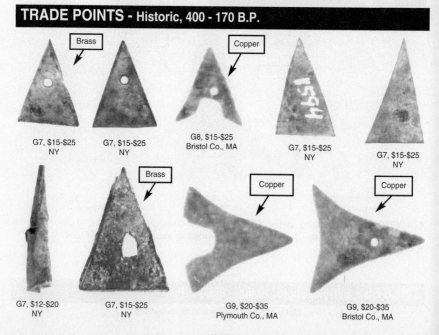

Brass

Copper

G7, $15-$25
NY

G7, $15-$25
NY

G8, $15-$25
Bristol Co., MA

G7, $15-$25
NY

G7, $15-$25
NY

Brass

Copper

Copper

G7, $12-$20
NY

G7, $15-$25
NY

G9, $20-$35
Plymouth Co., MA

G9, $20-$35
Bristol Co., MA

TRADE POINTS (Continued)

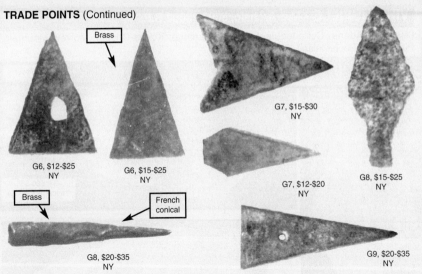

Brass

G6, $12-$25
NY

G6, $15-$25
NY

G7, $15-$30
NY

G7, $12-$20
NY

G8, $15-$25
NY

Brass

French conical

G8, $20-$35
NY

G9, $20-$35
NY

LOCATION: All States. These points were made of copper, iron and steel and were traded to the Indians by the French, British and others from the 1600s to the 1800s. Examples have been found all over the United States. Similar points were used against Custer at the battle of the Little Big Horn.

VERNON - Early Woodland, 2800 - 2500 B.P.

(Also see Brewerton, Kiski, Kline, Lycoming Co.)

LOCATION: Northeastern states.
DESCRIPTION: A small to medium size triangular point with a short, expanding stem. The base has rounded corners and the shoulders are usually barbed. **I.D. KEY:** Expanded base, barbed shoulders.

G4, $3-$6
Long Level, PA

VESTAL NOTCHED - Late Archaic, 4500 - 4000 B.P.

(Also see Brewerton, Kiski, Kline, Lycoming Co.)

G6, $5-$15
Luzurne Co., PA

G6, $5-$15
Luzurne Co., PA

LOCATION: Northeastern states. **DESCRIPTION:** A small to medium size triangular point with a short, expanding stem. The base has rounded corners and the shoulders are usually barbed. **I.D. KEY:** Expanded base, barbed shoulders.

VIRGINSVILLE - Mid-Archaic, 5000 - 3000 B.P.

(Also see Adena, Conodoquinet Canfield, Lehigh, Koens-Crispin, Morrow Mountain, Piscataway, Poplar Island, Schuylkill)

Quartzite

Rhyolite

G7, $20-$35
Lancaster Co., PA

Quartzite

G4, $12-$20
Montgomery Co., PA

G6, $15-$25
PA

Tip nick

Rhyolite

G7, $30-$50
Lancaster Co., PA

G7, $25-$40
Lancaster Co., PA

LOCATION: Northeastern states. **DESCRIPTION:** A medium to large size triangular point with contracting shoulders and base that is usually rounded. **I.D. KEY:** Diamond shape.

VIRGINSVILLE
(Continued)

G6, $15-$25
Lancaster Co., PA

VOSBURG - Archaic, 5000 - 4000 B.P.

(Also see Brewerton, Crooked Creek, Goddard, Jacks Reef, Kiski)

G7, $20-$35
Lycoming Co., PA

G5, $12-$20
Lycoming Co., PA

G4, $5-$10
Lycoming Co., PA

Tip
wear

G3, $5-$10
Lycoming Co., PA

G7, $20-$35
Lycoming Co., PA

G7, $20-$35
Lycoming Co., PA

LOCATION: Northeastern states. **DESCRIPTION:**
A small to medium size corner notched point with
a short, expanding base that is sometimes eared.
I.D. KEY: Broad expanding base.

Gray
chert

G5, $15-$25
Union Co., PA

G7, $20-$35
Union Co., PA

G5, $15-$25
Bainbridge, PA

G7, $20-$35
Northampton Co., PA

183

VOSBURG (Continued)

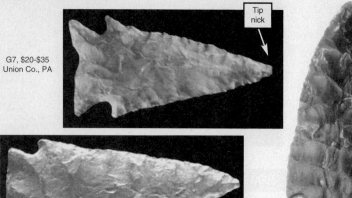

G7, $20-$35
Union Co., PA

Tip nick

G7, $25-$40
Centre Co., PA

G10, $150-$250
Columbia Co., NY

WADING RIVER - Archaic, 4200 - 4000 B.P.

(Also see Dewart Stemmed, Garver's Ferry, Lamoka, Merrimack, Sandhill Stemmed,)

Flint

G2, $1-$3
Plymouth Co.,
MA

Felsite

G3, $2-$4
Plymouth Co.,
MA

Quartz

G6, $5-$10
Plymouth Co.,
MA

Quartz

G6, $5-$10
Plymouth Co.,
MA

G6, $4-$8
Plymouth Co., MA

Felsite

G5, $4-$8
Plymouth Co., MA

Quartz

G6, $4-$8
Plymouth
Co., MA

Quartz

G6, $5-$10
Plymouth Co.,
MA

LOCATION: Massachusetts and surrounding states. **DESCRIPTION:** A small size, thick, stemmed point. Stem can be contracting, expanding or parallel sided. Base is straight to rounded. **I.D. KEY:** Small size and thick cross section.

WAPANUCKET - Mid-Archaic, 6000 - 4000 B.P.

(Also see Bare Island, Benton (Central East), Genesee, Lackawaxen, Meadowood, New-manstown, Piedmont, Tocks Island)

LOCATION: Northeastern states. **DESCRIPTION:** A medium to very large size short stemmed point. Bases can be corner or side notched, knobbed, bifurcated or expanded. Found in caches and closely resembles the *Benton* point found further south. **I.D. KEY:** Large size, notched blade.

WAPANUCKET (Continued)

IMPORTANT: All Wapanuckets shown half size

Jasper

G8, $200-$350
Monmouth Co., NJ

G7, $125-$200
Burlington Co., NJ

G10, $350-$600
MA

WARATAN Woodland, 3000 - 1000 B.P.

(Also see Drybrook, Perkiomen, Susquehanna Broad)

LOCATION: Eastern states. **DESCRIPTION:** A small to medium size point with usually broad, tapered shoulders, weak corner notches and a very short, broad, concave base. The base expands on some examples giving the appearance of ears or auricles. **I.D. KEY:** Short, broad, eared base.

Vein quartz

G6, $20-$35
Montgomery Co., PA

WAYLAND NOTCHED - Late Archaic, 3700 - 2700 B.P.

(Also see Ashtabula, Frost Island, Mansion Inn, Orient, Perkiomen, Susquehanna Broad)

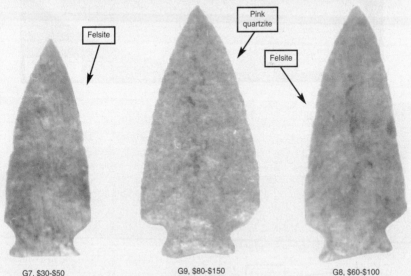

Felsite

Pink quartzite

Felsite

G7, $30-$50
Plymouth Co., MA

G9, $80-$150
Plymouth Co., MA

G8, $60-$100
Plymouth Co., MA

LOCATION: Maine southward into New Jersey. **DESCRIPTION:** A large size, broad, expanding stem point with tapered shoulders. Similar in form to the *Susquehanna Broad* point in which it is related. See *Mansion Inn* points which represent the preform for this type. **I.D. KEY:** Large size, broad, tapered shoulders.

G8, $300-$500
Bridgewater, MA

WEB BLADE - Woodland, 1500 - 500 B.P.

(Also see Adena Blade)

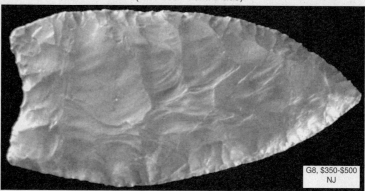

G8, $350-$500
NJ

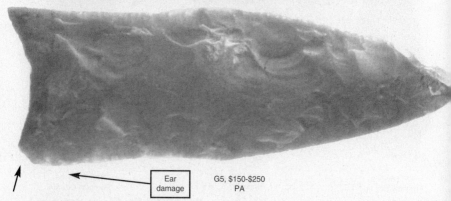

Ear
damage

G5, $150-$250
PA

LOCATION: Northeastern states. **DESCRIPTION:** A large size, lanceolate blade with a thin cross section. Bases can be concave to straight. Believed to be related to the Adena culture. **I.D. KEY:** Large, thin blade.

EASTERN SEABOARD SECTION:

This section includes point types from the following states: North Carolina, South Carolina, Virginia and West Virginia

The points in this section are arranged in alphabetical order and are shown **actual size**. All types are listed that were available for photographing. Any missing types will be added to future editions as photographs become available. We are always interested in receiving sharp, black and white or color glossy photos or color slides of your collection. Be sure to include a ruler in the photograph so that proper scale can be determined.

Lithics: Argillite, crystal, chalcedony, chert, flint, jasper, limestone, quartz, quartzite, rhyolite, shale, siltstone, slate, vein quartz.

Important sites: Baucom site, Union Co., N.C., Hardaway site in Stanly Co., NC., St. Albans site, Kanawha Co., WVA., Williamson site, Dinwiddie Co., VA.

Regional Consultants:
David Abbott
Ron L. Harris
Rodney Peck
Warner Williams

Special Advisors:
Tommy Beutell
Tom Davis

EASTERN SEABOARD POINT TYPES
(Archaeological Periods)

PALEO (14,000 B. P. - 10,000 B. P.)

Clovis
Clovis Unfluted

Drill
Redstone

LATE PALEO (12,000 B. P. - 10,000 B. P.)

Alamance

Quad

Simpson

EARLY ARCHAIC (10,000 B. P. - 7,000 B. P.)

Amos	Garth Slough	Kirk Corner Notched	St. Charles
Big Sandy	Guilford Yuma	Kirk Stemmed	Southampton
Bolen Bevel	Hardaway	Kirk Stemmed-Bifurcated	Stanly
Bolen Plain	Hardaway Blade	Lecroy	Stanly Narrow Stem
Decatur	Hardaway Dalton	Lost Lake	Taylor
Ecusta	Hardaway-Palmer	Palmer	Thebes
Edgefield Scraper	Hardin	Patrick Henry	Waller Knife
Fishspear	Jude	Rowan	
Fountain Creek	Kanawha Stemmed	St. Albans	

MIDDLE ARCHAIC (7,000 B. P. - 5,000 B. P.)

Appalachian	Guilford Round Base	Heavy Duty	Pickwick
Brewerton Eared	Guilford Stemmed	Morrow Mountain	
Brewerton Side Notched	Guilford Staright Base	Morrow Mountain Straight Base	
Buffalo Stemmed	Halifax	Otter Creek	

LATE ARCHAIC (5,000 B. P. - 3,000 B. P.)

Dismal Swamp
Exotic Forms
Holmes

Savannah River

EARLY WOODLAND (3,000 B. P. - 2,100 B. P.)

Adena	Fox Creek	Waratan	Yadkin Eared
Adena Robbins	Greeneville	Watered	
Armstrong	Gypsy	Will's Cove	
Dickson	Potts	Yadkin	

MIDDLE WOODLAND (2,100 B. P. - 1,500 B. P.)

Randolph

LATE WOODLAND (1,500 B. P. - 1,000 B. P.)

Jack's Reef Corner Notched
Pee Dee

Uwharrie

LATE PREHISTORIC (1,000 B. P. - 500 B. P.)

Badin
Caraway

Clarksville
Occaneechee

HISTORIC (450 B. P. - 170 B. P.)

Hillsboro

Trade Points

EASTERN SEABOARD
THUMBNAIL GUIDE SECTION

The following references are provided to aid the collector in easier and quicker identification of point types. All photos are exactly 30% of actual size and are proportional to each other. Each point pictured in this section represents a classic form for the type. When a match is found, go to the alphabetical location of that type for more examples in actual size.

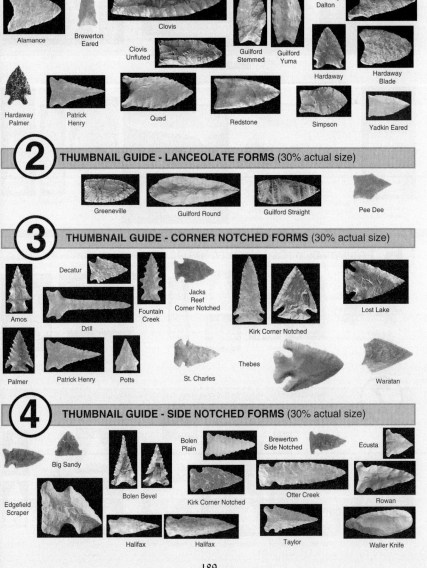

① THUMBNAIL GUIDE - AURICULATE FORMS (30% actual size)

Alamance · Brewerton Eared · Clovis · Clovis Unfluted · Guilford Stemmed · Guilford Yuma · Hardaway Dalton · Hardaway · Hardaway Blade · Hardaway Palmer · Patrick Henry · Quad · Redstone · Simpson · Yadkin Eared

② THUMBNAIL GUIDE - LANCEOLATE FORMS (30% actual size)

Greeneville · Guilford Round · Guilford Straight · Pee Dee

③ THUMBNAIL GUIDE - CORNER NOTCHED FORMS (30% actual size)

Decatur · Amos · Drill · Fountain Creek · Jacks Reef Corner Notched · Kirk Corner Notched · Lost Lake · Palmer · Patrick Henry · Potts · St. Charles · Thebes · Waratan

④ THUMBNAIL GUIDE - SIDE NOTCHED FORMS (30% actual size)

Big Sandy · Bolen Plain · Brewerton Side Notched · Ecusta · Edgefield Scraper · Bolen Bevel · Kirk Corner Notched · Otter Creek · Rowan · Halifax · Halifax · Taylor · Waller Knife

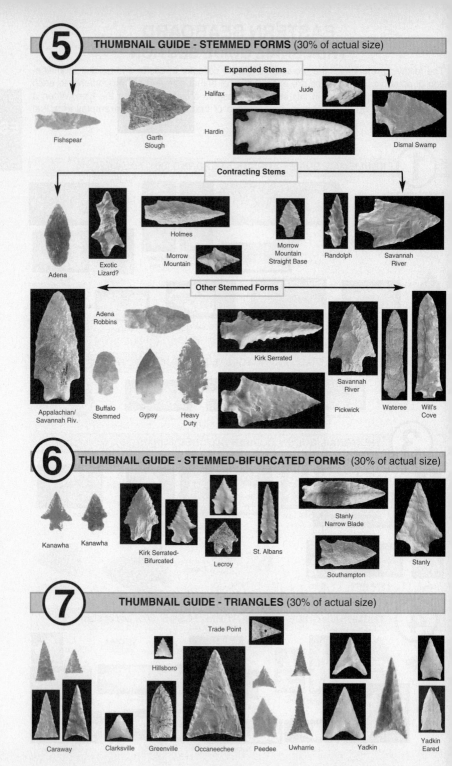

⑤ THUMBNAIL GUIDE - STEMMED FORMS (30% of actual size)

Expanded Stems

Fishspear

Garth Slough

Halifax

Hardin

Jude

Dismal Swamp

Contracting Stems

Adena

Exotic Lizard?

Holmes

Morrow Mountain

Morrow Mountain Straight Base

Randolph

Savannah River

Other Stemmed Forms

Appalachian/ Savannah Riv.

Adena Robbins

Buffalo Stemmed

Gypsy

Heavy Duty

Kirk Serrated

Savannah River

Pickwick

Wateree

Will's Cove

⑥ THUMBNAIL GUIDE - STEMMED-BIFURCATED FORMS (30% of actual size)

Kanawha

Kanawha

Kirk Serrated-Bifurcated

Lecroy

St. Albans

Stanly Narrow Blade

Southampton

Stanly

⑦ THUMBNAIL GUIDE - TRIANGLES (30% of actual size)

Trade Point

Hillsboro

Caraway

Clarksville

Greenville

Occaneechee

Peedee

Uwharrie

Yadkin

Yadkin Eared

ADENA - Late Archaic to early Woodland, 3000 - 1200 B. P.

(Also see Dickson)

ES

G4, $2-$4
Kanawha Co., WVA

G4, $2-$4
Kanawha Co., WVA

LOCATION: Tenn. into Ohio and West Virginia. **DESCRIPTION:** A medium to large, thin, narrow, triangular blade that is sometimes serrated, and with a medium to long, narrow to broad rounded "beaver tail" stem. Most examples are from average to excellent quality. Bases can be ground. **I.D. KEY:** Rounded base, woodland flaking.

ADENA-DICKSON (see Dickson)

ADENA ROBBINS - Late Archaic to early Woodland, 3000 - 1200 B. P.

(Also see Savannah River)

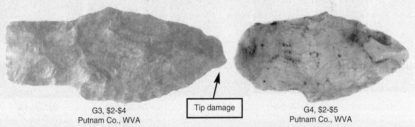

G3, $2-$4
Putnam Co., WVA

Tip damage

G4, $2-$5
Putnam Co., WVA

LOCATION: Tenn. into Ohio and West Virginia. **DESCRIPTION:** A medium to large, thin, narrow, triangular blade that is sometimes serrated, and with a medium to long, narrow to broad stem that is parallel sided. Base can be straight to rounded. Most examples are from average to excellent quality. Bases can be ground. **I.D. KEY:** Rounded base, woodland flaking.

ALAMANCE - Late Paleo, 10,000 - 8000 B. P.

(Also see Hardaway & Hardaway Dalton)

LOCATION: Coastal states from Virginia to Florida. **DESCRIPTION:** A broad, short, auriculate point with a deeply concave base. The broad basal area is usually ground and can be expanding to parallel sided. A variant form of the *Dalton-Greenbrier* evolving later into the *Hardaway* type. **I.D. KEY:** Width of base and strong shoulder form.

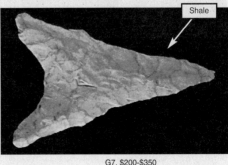

Shale

G7, $200-$350
Cent. NC

ALAMANCE (continued)

G8, $250-$450
Chesterfield Co., SC

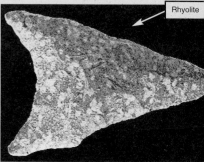

Rhyolite

G6, $200-$350
Johnson Co., NC

AMOS - Early Archaic, 9900 - 8900 B. P.

(Also see Decatur, Kirk Corner Notched and Palmer)

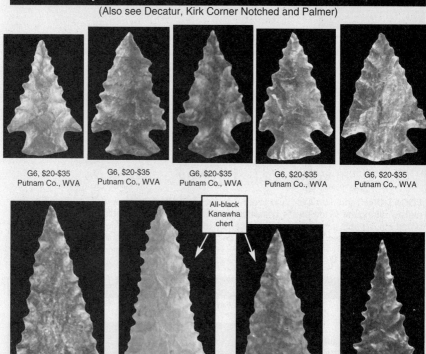

G6, $20-$35
Putnam Co., WVA

G6, $20-$35
Putnam Co., WVA

G6, $20-$35
Putnam Co., WVA

G6, $20-$35
Putnam Co., WVA

G6, $20-$35
Putnam Co., WVA

All-black
Kanawha
chert

G8, $65-$125
Putnam Co., WVA

G9, $90-$165
Putnam Co., WVA

G9, $55-$100
Putnam Co., WVA

G7, $35-$65
Putnam Co., WVA

LOCATION: West Virginia into Pennsylvania and New York. Type site is in Kanawha Co., WVA. **DESCRIPTION:** A medium size, serrated, corner notched point with an expanding stem. Bases are straight, concave or convex and are ground. Basal corners are sharp to rounded. **I.D. KEY:** Deep serrations and expanding stem.

AMOS (continued)

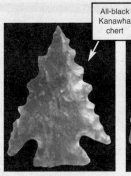

All-black Kanawha chert

ES

G7, $35-$60
Putnam Co., WVA

G8, $60-$100
Putnam Co., WVA

G6, $30-$50
Putnam Co., WVA

G7, $40-$70
Putnam Co., WVA

ANGELICO CORNER-NOTCHED (See Decatur)

APPALACHIAN - Middle Archaic, 6000 - 3000 B. P.

(Also see Rowan, Savannah River and Southampton)

Quartzite

G7, $65-$125
McDowell Co., NC

LOCATION: East Tennessee and Georgia into the Carolinas. **DESCRIPTION:** A medium to large size, rather crudely made stemmed point with a concave, straight or convex base. Most examples are made of quartzite. Shoulders are tapered and the base is usually ground. This point was named by Lewis & Kneberg for examples found in East Tenn. and Western North Carolina which were made of quartzite. However, this is the same type as *Savannah River.* **I.D. KEY:** Material Quartzite used.

ARMSTRONG - Woodland, 2450 - 1600 B. P.

(Also see Brewerton, Ecusta, Palmer, Patrick Henry and Potts)

LOCATION: West Virginia and neighboring states.
DESCRIPTION: A small, short, corner notched point with barbed shoulders. Base is straight to convex and expands.
I.D. KEY: Tangs and broad notches.

G4, $4-$8
Kanawha Co., WVA

BADIN - Late Prehistoric, 1000 - 800 B. P.

(Also see Caraway, Fox Creek, Guilford and Hillsboro)

LOCATION: Carolinas to Virginia. **DESCRIPTION:** A medium size triangular point that is larger and thicker than Hillsboro. Sides are convex with straight to slightly convex or concave bases. **I.D. KEY:** Thickness and crudeness.

G5, $6-$10
Montgomery Co., NC

BIG SANDY - Early to Late Archaic, 10,000 - 3000 B. P.

(Also see Bolen, Pine Tree, Rowan and Taylor)

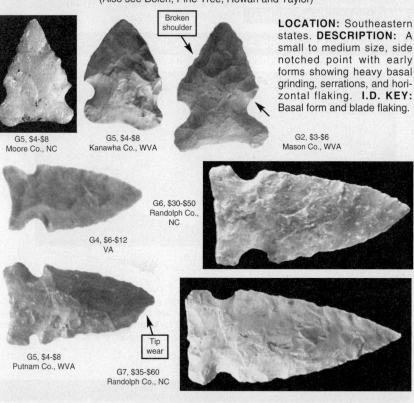

Broken shoulder

LOCATION: Southeastern states. **DESCRIPTION:** A small to medium size, side notched point with early forms showing heavy basal grinding, serrations, and horizontal flaking. **I.D. KEY:** Basal form and blade flaking.

G5, $4-$8
Moore Co., NC

G5, $4-$8
Kanawha Co., WVA

G2, $3-$6
Mason Co., WVA

G6, $30-$50
Randolph Co., NC

G4, $6-$12
VA

G5, $4-$8
Putnam Co., WVA

Tip wear

G7, $35-$60
Randolph Co., NC

BOLEN BEVEL - Early Archaic, 10,000 - 7000 B. P.

(Also see Big Sandy, Patrick Henry and Taylor)

LOCATION: Coastal states into South Carolina. **DESCRIPTION:** A small to medium size, side-notched point with early forms showing basal grinding, beveling on one side of each face, and serrations. Bases can be straight, concave or convex. The side notch is usually broader than in *Big Sandy* points. E-notched or expanded notching also occurs on early forms. **I.D. KEY:** Basal form and notching.

BOLEN BEVEL (continued)

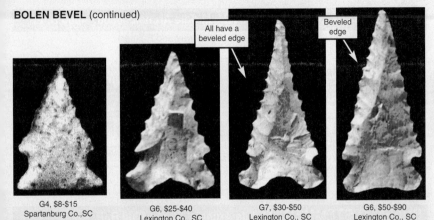

All have a beveled edge

Beveled edge

ES

G4, $8-$15
Spartanburg Co.,SC

G6, $25-$40
Lexington Co., SC

G7, $30-$50
Lexington Co., SC

G6, $50-$90
Lexington Co., SC

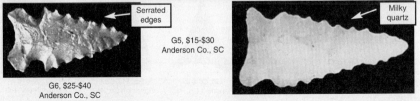

G6, $40-$70
SC

G6, $40-$70
Edgefield Co., SC

BOLEN PLAIN - Early Archaic, 9000 - 7000 B. P.

(Also see Big Sandy and Taylor)

Serrated edges

Milky quartz

G5, $15-$30
Anderson Co., SC

G6, $25-$40
Anderson Co., SC

LOCATION: Coastal states into South Carolina. **DESCRIPTION:** A small to medium size, side-notched point with early forms showing basal grinding and serrations. Bases are straight, concave or convex. The side notches are usually broader than in the *Big Sandy* type, and can be expanded to E-notched on some examples. **I.D. KEY:** Basal form and flaking on blade.

BREWERTON EARED - Middle Archaic, 6000 - 4000 B. P.

(Also see Hardaway, Yadkin Eared)

LOCATION: Eastern to midwestern states. **DESCRIPTION:** A small size, triangular, eared point with a concave base. Shoulders are weak and tapered. Ears are the widest part of the point. **I.D. KEY:** Small ears, weak shoulders.

G3, $3-$5
Kanawha Co., WVA

BREWERTON SIDE NOTCHED - Middle Archaic, 6000 - 4000 B. P.

(Also see Big Sandy, Hardaway and Palmer)

LOCATION: Eastern to midwestern states. **DESCRIPTION:** A small to medium size triangular point with broad side notches. Bases are straight to convex to concave. **I.D. KEY:** Thickness and width.

G4, $5-$9
Mason Co., WVA

G6, $8-$15
Mason Co., WVA

BUFFALO STEMMED - Middle Archaic, 6000 - 4000 B. P.

(Also see Holmes and Savannah River)

Altered to a scraper

LOCATION: West Virginia. **DESCRIPTION:** A medium size, broad, parallel stemmed point with tapered shoulders. **I.D. KEY:** Width, squared stem.

G4, $2-$5
Putnam Co., WVA

CARAWAY - Late Prehistoric, 1000 - 200 B. P.

(Also see Clarksville, Hillsboro, Uwharrie and Yadkin)

Serrated on one side only

G6, $12-$20
Randolph Co., NC

G5, $5-$15
Randolph Co., NC

G5, $8-$15
Randolph Co., NC

G6, $12-$20
Randolph Co., NC

G5, $8-$15
Randolph Co., NC

Serrated edge

Serrated edge

G6, $12-$20
Randolph Co., NC

G6, $12-$20
Randolph Co., NC

G8, $20-$35
Surry Co., NC

G7, $12-$20
Randolph Co., NC

G5, $12-$25
Randolph Co., NC

LOCATION: Coincides with the Mississippian culture in the Eastern states. **DESCRIPTION:** A small to medium size, thin, triangular point with usually straight sides and base, although concave bases are common. Some examples are notched on two to three sides. Many are of high quality and some are finely serrated. Similar to *Madison* found elsewhere.

CARAWAY (continued)

Serrated edge

G5, $8-$15
Rockingham Co., NC

G5, $12-$20
Randolph Co., NC

G5, $12-$20
Randolph Co., NC

G5, $12-$20
Randolph Co., NC

G7 $15-$30
Randolph Co., NC

G6, $15-$25
Randolph Co., NC

G7, $15-$30
Randolph Co., NC

G8, $20-$35
Randolph Co., NC

G8, $30-$50
Randolph Co., NC

CACTUS HILL (This small triangular point was dated approx. 15,000 B.P. in Virginia but verification is needed from other sites.)

CLARKSVILLE - Late Prehistoric, 1000 - 500 A. D.

(Also see Caraway, Hillsboro, Uwharrie and Yadkin)

G4, $4-$8
Randolph Co., NC

G4, $47-$8
Randolph Co., NC

G3, $4-$8
Randolph Co., NC

G6, $6-12
Randolph Co., NC

G6, $8-$15
Randolph Co., NC

LOCATION: Far Eastern states. **DESCRIPTION:** A small size triangular point with all three sides approximately the same width. The base is straight to slightly concave. Examples made from quartzite and quartz tend to be thick in cross section.

CLOVIS - Early Paleo, 14,000 - 9000 B. P.

(Also see Redstone, Quad and Simpson)

CLOVIS (continued)

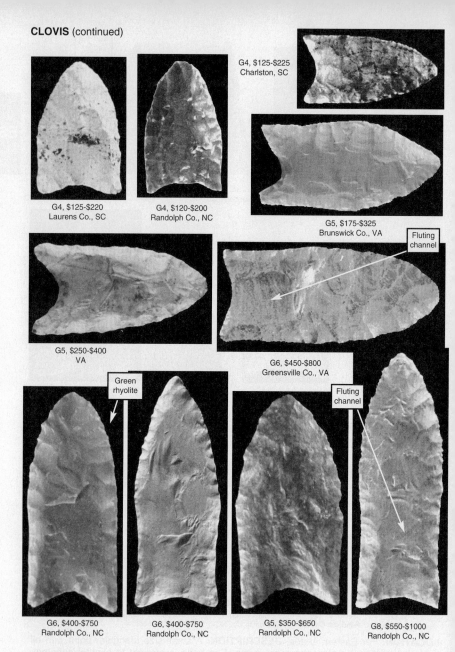

G4, $125-$225
Charlston, SC

G4, $125-$220
Laurens Co., SC

G4, $120-$200
Randolph Co., NC

G5, $175-$325
Brunswick Co., VA

Fluting channel

G5, $250-$400
VA

G6, $450-$800
Greensville Co., VA

Green rhyolite

Fluting channel

G6, $400-$750
Randolph Co., NC

G6, $400-$750
Randolph Co., NC

G5, $350-$650
Randolph Co., NC

G8, $550-$1000
Randolph Co., NC

LOCATION: All of North America. **DESCRIPTION:** A medium to large size, auriculate, fluted, lanceolate point with convex sides and a concave base that is ground. Most examples are fluted on both sides about 1/3 the way up from the base. The flaking can be random to parallel. *Clovis* is the earliest point type in the hemisphere. It is believed that this form was brought here from Siberia or Europe 14,000 years ago. Current theories place the origin of *Clovis* in the Eastern U.S. since more examples are found there. **I.D. KEY:** Paleo flaking, shoulders, baton or billet fluting instead of indirect style.

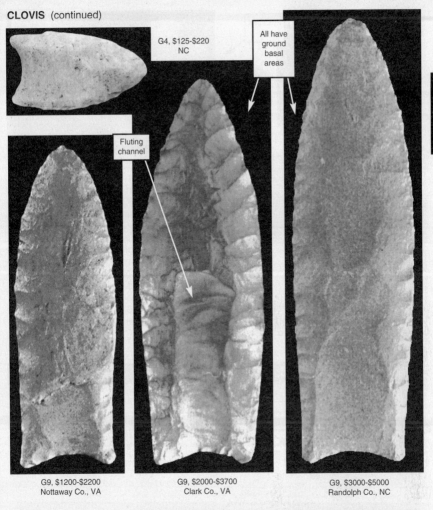

G4, $125-$220
NC

All have ground basal areas

Fluting channel

ES

G9, $1200-$2200
Nottaway Co., VA

G9, $2000-$3700
Clark Co., VA

G9, $3000-$5000
Randolph Co., NC

CLOVIS-UNFLUTED - Paleo, 14,000 - 9000 B. P.

(Also see Fox Creek and Simpson)

LOCATION: All of North America.
DESCRIPTION: A medium to large size, auriculate point identical to fluted *Clovis,* but not fluted. A very rare type.

G5, $125-$200
Sussex Co., VA.
Basal thinning.

DECATUR - Early Archaic, 9000 - 3000 B. P.

(Also see Amos, Ecusta, Palmer and St. Charles)

DECATUR (continued)

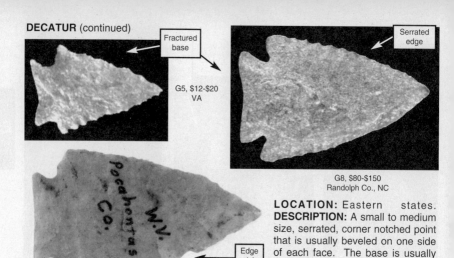

Fractured base

G5, $12-$20
VA

Serrated edge

G8, $80-$150
Randolph Co., NC

Edge nick

G6, $40-$70
Pocahantas Co., WVA

LOCATION: Eastern states. **DESCRIPTION:** A small to medium size, serrated, corner notched point that is usually beveled on one side of each face. The base is usually broken off (fractured) by a blow inward from each corner of the stem. Sometimes the side of the stem and backs of the tangs are also fractured, and rarely the tip may be fractured by a blow on each side directed towards the base. Bases are usually ground and flaking is high quality. Basal and shoulder fracturing also occurs in *Abbey, Dovetail, Eva, Kirk, Motley* and *Snyders*. Unfractured forms are called *Angelico Corner-Notched* in Virginia.

DICKSON - Woodland, 2500 - 1600 B. P.

(Also see Adena)

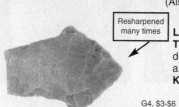

Resharpened many times

G4, $3-$6
Putnam Co., WVA

LOCATION: W.Virginia to Missouri. **DESCRIPTION:** A small to large size point with tapered shoulders and a contracting stem. High quality flaking and thinness is evident on most examples. **I.D. KEY:** Basal form.

DISMAL SWAMP - Late Archaic to early Woodland, 3500 - 2000 B. P.

(Also see Garth Slough, Savannah River and Waratan)

LOCATION: North Carolina to Virginia. Similar to *Perkiomen* found in Pennsylvania. **DESCRIPTION:** A medium to large size, broad point with strong shoulders and a small, expanding base that is usually bulbous, blades can be asymmetrical. **I.D. KEY:** Broad shoulders and small base.

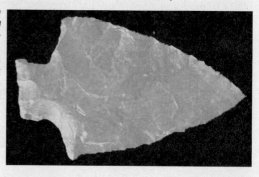

G6, $15-$30
Bethany, WVA

DRILL - Paleo to Historic, 14,000 - 200 B. P.

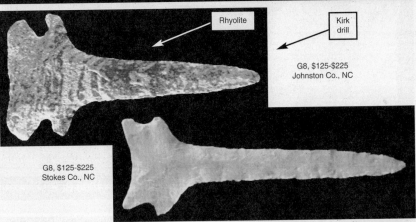

Rhyolite

Kirk drill

G8, $125-$225
Johnston Co., NC

ES

G8, $125-$225
Stokes Co., NC

LOCATION: All of North America. **DESCRIPTION:** Although many drills were made from scratch, all point types were made into the drill form. Usually, heavily resharpened and broken points were salvaged and rechipped into drills. These objects were certainly used as drills (evidence of extreme edge wear), but there is speculation that some of these forms may have been used as pins for clothing, ornaments, ear plugs and other uses.

ECUSTA - Early Archaic, 8000 - 5000 B. P.

(Also see Bolen Plain, Palmer and Potts)

G4, $8-$15
Bethany, WVA

G5, $10-$18
Bethany, WVA

G6, $10-$18
Bethany, WVA

G2, $2-$5
VA

LOCATION: Southeastern states. **DESCRIPTION:** A small size, serrated, side-notched point with usually one side of each face steeply beveled, although examples exist with all four sides beveled and flaked to a median ridge. The base and notches are ground. Very similar to *Autauga*, with the latter being corner-notched.

EDGEFIELD SCRAPER - Early Archaic, 9000 - 6000 B. P.

EDGEFIELD SCRAPER (continued)

Beveled edge. Back side is flat

LOCATION: Southern Atlantic coast states. **DESCRIPTION:** A medium to large size corner notched point that is asymmetrical. Many are uniface and usually steeply beveled along the diagonal side. The blade on all examples leans heavily to one side. Used as a hafted scraper.

G8, $45-$80
Edgefield Co., SC

EXOTIC FORMS - Woodland to Mississippian, 5000 - 1000 B. P.

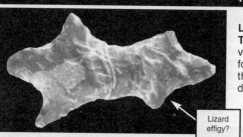

LOCATION: Everywhere. **DESCRIPTION:** The forms illustrated here are very rare. Some are definitely effigy forms while others may be no more than unfinished and unintentional doodles.

Lizard effigy?

G8, $45-$85
Randolph Co., NC

FISHSPEAR - Early to Mid-Archaic, 9000 - 6000 B.P.

(Also see Randolph)

G3, $8-$15
Kanawha Co., WVA

LOCATION: Northeastern states. **DESCRIPTION:** A medium to large size, narrow, thick, stemmed point with broad side notches to an expanding stem. Bases are usually ground and blade edges can be serrated. Named due to its appearance that resembles a fish. **I.D. KEY:** Narrowness, thickness and long stem.

FOUNTAIN CREEK - Early Archaic, 9000 - 7000 B. P.

(Also see Kirk Stemmed)

G6, $15-$25
Wayne Co., NC

G7, $30-$50
Nash Co., NC

FOUNTAIN CREEK (continued)

G4, $10-$18
Randolph
Co., NC

LOCATION: Eastern states. **DESCRIPTION:** A medium size, narrow corner notched to expanded stemmed point with notched blade edges and a short, rounded base which is ground. **I.D. KEY:** Edgework. **I.D. KEY:** Exaggerated barbs.

Tip nick

Note
strong
barbs

G9, $80-$150
Randolph Co., NC

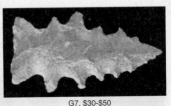

G7, $30-$50
Chatham Co., NC

FOX CREEK - Woodland, 2500 - 1200 B. P.

(Also see Badin, Clovis Unfluted and Guilford Stemmed)

LOCATION: Northeastern states. **DESCRIPTION:** A medium size blade with a squared to tapered hafting area and a straight to slightly concave base. Shoulders, when present are very weak and tapered.

G6, $12-$20
Bethany, WVA

FOX VALLEY (See Kanawha Stemmed; See N. Central section for Fox Valley points)

GARTH SLOUGH - Early Archaic, 9000 - 4000 B. P.

(Also see Fox Valley and Stanly)

LOCATION: Southeastern states. **DESCRIPTION:** A small size point with wide, expanded barbs and a small squared base. Rare examples have the tangs clipped (called clipped wing). The blade edges are convex with fine serrations. A similar type of a later time period, called *Catahoula*, is found in the Midwestern states. A bifurcated base would place it into the *Fox Valley* type. **I.D. KEY:** Expanded barbs, early flaking.

G6, $30-$50
Pearson Co., NC

GREENEVILLE - Woodland, 3000 - 1500 B.P.

(Also see Caraway, Clarksville, Madison)

GREENEVILLE (continued)

LOCATION: Southeast to eastern states.
DESCRIPTION: A small to medium size lanceolate point with convex sides becoming contracting to parallel at the base. The basal edge is slightly concave, convex or straight. This point is usually wider and thicker than *Guntersville*, and is believed to be related to *Camp Creek*, *Ebenezer* and *Nolichucky* points.

G8, $20-$35
Davidson Co., NC

GUILFORD-ROUND BASE - Middle Archaic, 6500 - 5000 B. P.

(Also see Cobbs and Lerma in other sections)

Milky quartz

Milky quartz

G6, $12-$20
Sussex Co., VA

G5, $8-$15
Randolph Co., NC

G6, $15-$30
Fairfield Co., SC

G6, $12-$20
Randolph Co., NC

G6, $15-$30
Randolph Co., NC

G8, $25-$45
Randolph Co., NC

G7, $15-$30
Randolph Co., NC

GUILFORD-ROUND BASE (continued)

G8, $40-$75
Randolph Co., NC

LOCATION: North Carolina and surrounding areas. **DESCRIPTION:** A medium to large size, thick, narrow, lanceolate point with a convex, contracting base. This type is usually made of Quartzite or other poor quality flaking material which results in a more crudely chipped form than *Lerma* (its ancestor). **I.D. KEY:** Thickness, archaic blade flaking.

GUILFORD-STEMMED - Middle Archaic, 6500 - 5000 B. P.

(Also see Stanly Narrow Stem, Waratan and Yadkin Eared)

G5, $6-$12
Stokes Co., NC

G5, $8-$15
Anderson Co., SC

G6, $20-$35
Orangeburg Co., SC

G4, $12-$20
Newberry Co., SC

LOCATION: Far Eastern states. **DESCRIPTION:** A medium size, thick, narrow, lanceolate point with a straight to concave, contracting base. All examples have weak, tapered shoulders. Some bases are ground. Called *Briar Creek* in Georgia.

GUILFORD-STRAIGHT BASE - Middle Archaic, 6500 - 5000 B. P.

(Also see Fox Creek)

G4, $3-$5
VA

G4, $4-$8
Newberry Co., SC

205

GUILFORD-STRAIGHT BASE (continued)

Vein quartz

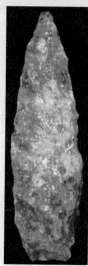

G6, $25-$40
Edgecombe Co., NC

G5, $8-$15
Rowan Co., NC

G6, $8-$15
Dinwiddie Co., VA

G5, $8-$15
Newberry Co., SC

G9, $45-$80
Pearson Co., NC

LOCATION: Far Eastern states. **DESCRIPTION:** A medium size, thick, narrow, lanceolate point with a contracting stem and a straight base. This point is similar to *Greene* points, a later period New York Woodland type.

GUILFORD-YUMA - Early Archaic, 7500 - 5000 B. P.

(Also see Clovis Unfluted and Yadkin Eared)

Milky quartz

G5, $6-$12
NC

G6, $12-$20
Randolph Co., NC

G6, $15-$25
Surry Co., NC

G6, $12-$20
Ashe Co., NC

206

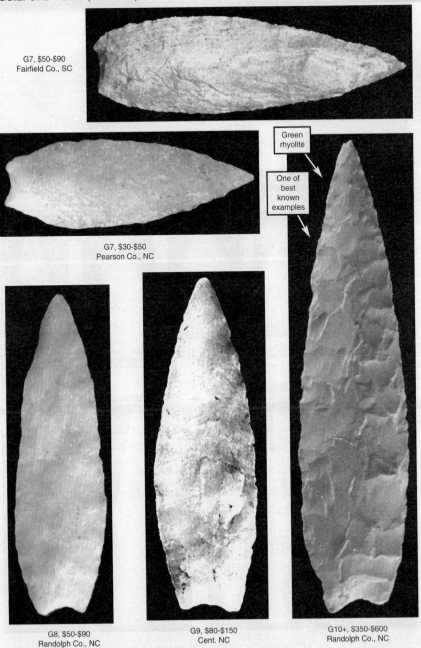

G7, $50-$90
Fairfield Co., SC

ES

G7, $30-$50
Pearson Co., NC

Green
rhyolite

One of
best
known
examples

G8, $50-$90
Randolph Co., NC

G9, $80-$150
Cent. NC

G10+, $350-$600
Randolph Co., NC

LOCATION: Far Eastern states. **DESCRIPTION:** A medium to slightly large size, thick, narrow, lanceolate point with a contracting stem and a concave base. Quality of flaking is governed by the type of material, usually quartzite, slate, rhyolite and shale. Bases can be ground. Believed to be an early form for the type and may be related to the *Conerly* type.

GYPSY - Woodland, 2500 - 1500 B. P.

(Also see St. Charles)

LOCATION: North Carolina. **DESCRIPTION:** A small to medium size triangular point with a bulbous stem. Shoulders are usually well defined and can be barbed. **I.D. KEY:** Bulbous base.

G8, $20-$35
Surry Co., NC

HALIFAX - Middle to Late Archaic, 6000 - 3000 B. P.

(Also see Holmes, Rowan and Southampton)

Milky quartz

Milky quartz

G2, $1-$2
Southampton Co., VA

G3, $2-$5
Southampton Co., VA

G3, $2-$5
Southampton Co., VA

G4, $4-$8
Sussex Co., VA

G6, $5-$10
Sussex Co., VA

Quartzite

Worn tip

Quartzite

G6, $15-$25
Sussex Co., VA

G8, $12-$20
Southampton Co., VA

G5, $8-$15
Prince George Co., VA

G5, $5-$10
Sussex Co., VA

LOCATION: Southeastern states. **DESCRIPTION:** A small to medium size, narrow, side notched to expanded stemmed point. Shoulders can be weak to strongly tapered. Typically one shoulder is higher than the other. North Carolina examples are made of quartz, rhyolite and shale.

HARDAWAY - Early Archaic, 9500 - 8000 B. P.

(Also see Alamance, Hardaway-Dalton, Patrick Henry and Taylor)

G6, $70-$130
Randolph Co., NC

G6, $65-$125
Southampton Co., VA

G5, $35-$65
NC

G6, $80-$150
Richmond Co., NC

Milky quartz

G7, $90-$175
Moore Co., NC

G7, $125-$200
SC

G5, $90-$175
Cent. NC

G7, $150-$250
Southampton Co., VA

G6, $250-$400
Randolph Co., NC

G7, $125-$225
Sussex Co., VA

G8, $150-$250
Chatham Co., NC

G7, $150-$275
Charles Co., VA

G7, $175-$300
Randolph Co., NC

G8, $175-$300
Moore Co., NC

HARDAWAY (continued)

G10, $275-$500
Randolph Co., NC

G6, $150-$300
Randolph Co., NC

G5, $125-$200
Chatham Co., NC.

G7, $200-$350
Randolph Co., NC

G6, $150-$250
Davidson Co., NC

G9, $250-$450
Rowan Co., NC

G6, $175-$300
Moorh Co., NC

G6, $250-$400
Cent. NC

G8, $350-$600
Cent. NC

LOCATION: Southeastern states, especially North Carolina. Type site is Stanly Co. NC, Yadkin River. **DESCRIPTION:** A small to medium size point with shallow side notches and expanded auricles forming a wide, deeply concave base. Wide specimens are called *Cow Head Hardaways* in North Carolina by some collectors. Ears and base are usually heavily ground. This type evolved from the *Dalton* point. **I.D. KEY:** Heavy grinding in shoulders, paleo flaking.

HARDAWAY BLADE - Early Archaic, 9500 - 9000 B. P.

(Also see Alamance)

LOCATION: North Carolina. **DESCRIPTION:** A small to medium size, thin, broad, blade with a concave base. The base usually is ground and has thinning strikes. A preform for the *Hardaway* point.

G4, $25-$40
Cent. NC

HARDAWAY-DALTON - Early Archaic, 9500 - 8000 B. P.

(Also see Alamance and Hardaway)

G6, $150-$250
Harnet Co., NC

Tip wear

G6, $90-$175
Central NC

G6, $125-$225
Cranville Co., NC

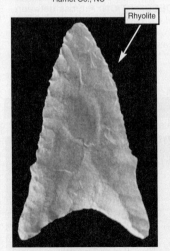

Rhyolite

G10, $400-$750
Randolph Co., NC

G6, $125-$200
Central NC

Speckled rhyolite

G5, $65-$125
VA

211

HARDAWAY-DALTON
(continued)

Speckled rhyolite

G7, $350-$600
Randolph Co., NC

G8, $250-$475
Montgtomery Co., NC

G9, $500-$900
Central NC

LOCATION: Southeastern states. **DESCRIPTION:** A small to medium size, serrated, auriculate point with a concave base. Basal fluting or thinning is common. Bases are ground. Ears turn outward or have parallel sides. A cross between *Hardaway* and *Dalton*. **I.D. KEY:** Width of base, location found.

HARDAWAY PALMER - Early Archaic, 9500 - 8000 B. P.

(Also see Hardaway and Palmer)

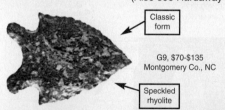

Classic form

G9, $70-$135
Montgomery Co., NC

Speckled rhyolite

LOCATION: Southeastern states. **DESCRIPTION:** A cross between *Hardaway* and *Palmer* with expanded auricles and a concave base that is ground.

HARDIN - Early Archaic, 9000 - 6000 B. P.

(Also see Kirk and Lost Lake)

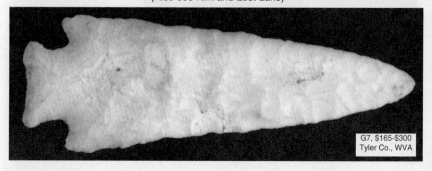

G7, $165-$300
Tyler Co., WVA

212

HARDIN (continued)

LOCATION: Midwestern to Eastern states. **DESCRIPTION:** A large size, well made triangular barbed point with an expanded base that is usually ground. Resharpened examples have one beveled edge on each face. This type is believed to have evolved from the *Scottsbluff* type. **I.D. KEY:** Notches and stem form.

ES

HEAVY DUTY - Early to Middle Archaic, 7000 - 5000 B. P.
(Also see Appalachian, Kirk Stemmed and Southampton)

LOCATION: Ohio into West Virginia. **DESCRIPTION:** A medium to large size, thick, serrated point with a parallel stem and straight to slightly concave base. A variant of *Kirk Serrated* found in the Southeast. **I.D. KEY:** Base, thickness, flaking.

G4, $12-$20
Bethany, WVA

HILLSBORO - Historic, 300 - 200 B. P.
(Also see Caraway and Clarksville)

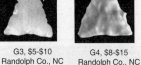

Milky quartz   Serrated edge   Milky quartz

G3, $5-$10   G4, $8-$15   G4, $7-$12   G5, $8-$15   G6, $8-$15
Randolph Co., NC   Randolph Co., NC   Randolph Co., NC   Randolph Co., NC   Randolph Co., NC

LOCATION: North Carolina. **DESCRIPTION:** A small size, thin, triangular, arrow point with a straight to concave base. Blade edges can be serrated. Smaller than Badin to very small size.

HOLMES - Late Archaic, 4000 - 3000 B. P.
(Also see Savannah River, Southampton and Stanly Narrow Blade)

Quartzite

LOCATION: Far Eastern states. **DESCRIPTION:** A medium size, narrow point with weak, tapered shoulders and a slight concave base.

G4, $8-$15
Sussex Co., VA

JACKS REEF CORNER NOTCHED - Late Woodland to Mississippian, 1500 - 1000 B. P.
(Also see Kirk Corner Notched and Peedee)

LOCATION: Southeastern states. **DESCRIPTION:** A small to medium size, very thin, corner notched point that is well made. The blade is convex to pentagonal. Some examples are widely corner notched and appear to be expanded stem points with barbed shoulders. Rarely, they are basal notched. **I.D. KEY:** Thinness, made by the birdpoint people.

JACKS REEF CORNER NOTCHED (continued)

Black flint

G4, $15-$25
Ashe Co., NC

G6, $25-$45
Ashe Co., NC

G4, $12-$20
Mason Co., WVA

G4, $12-$20
Mason Co., WVA

G6, $25-$45
Bethany, WVA

Tang nick

G6, $25-$45
Mason Co., WVA

JACKS REEF PENTAGONAL   (See Peedee)

JUDE - Early Archaic, 9000 - 6000 B. P.
(Also see Garth Slough and Halifax)

LOCATION: Southeastern states.
DESCRIPTION: A small size, short, barbed, expanded to parallel stemmed point. Stems can be as large as the blade. Rare in this area. **I.D. KEY**: Basal form and flaking.

G5, $8-$15
Montgomery Co., NC

KANAWHA STEMMED - Early Archaic, 8200 - 5000 B. P.
(Also see Kirk Stemmed-Bifurcated, LeCroy, St. Albans, Southampton and Stanly)

G3, $5-$12
Kanawha Co., WVA

G4, $8-$15
Chilhowie, VA

G5, $12-$20
Kanawha Co., WVA

G8, $25-$40
Putnam Co., WVA

214

KANAWHA STEMMED (continued)

LOCATION: Eastern to Southeastern states. Type site is in Kanawha Co., WVA. **DESCRIPTION:** A small to medium size, fairly thick, shallowly bifurcated stemmed point. The basal lobes are usually rounded and the shoulders tapered or clipped wing turning towards the tip. Believed to be the ancestor to the *Stanly* type. The St. Albans site dated *Kanawha* to 8,200 B.P. Identical to *Fox Valley* found in Illinois.

Black chert

G8, $25-$45
Mecklenburg Co., VA

KIRK CORNER NOTCHED - Early to Middle Archaic, 9000 - 6000 B. P.

(Also see Amos, Bolen, Hardin, Jacks Reef, Lost Lake, St. Charles, Taylor and Thebes)

Serrated edge

G6, $20-$35
Surry Co., NC

Broken tang

Speckled rhyolite

G3, $4-$8
NC

G6, $25-$40
Randolph Co., NC

G5, $30-$50
Richmond Co., NC

Serrated edges

G8, $55-$100
Ashe Co., NC

G8, $65-$125
Johnston Co., NC

LOCATION: Eastern states. **DESCRIPTION:** A medium to large size, corner notched point. Blade edges can be convex to recurved and are finely serrated on many examples. The base can be convex, concave, straight or auriculate. Points that are beveled on one side of each face would fall under the *Lost Lake* type. **I.D. KEY:** Secondary edgework.

Serrated edge

G8, $45-$80
Alleghany Co., NC

G6, $20-$35
Randolph Co., NC

G8, $55-$100
Randolph Co., NC

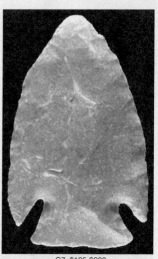

G8, $35-$60
Ashe Co., NC

G5, $25-$45
Ashe Co., NC

G7, $125-$200
Randolph Co., NC

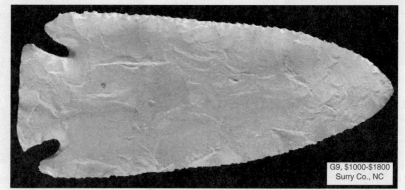

G9, $1000-$1800
Surry Co., NC

KIRK CORNER NOTCHED (continued)

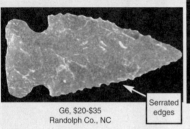

G6, $20-$35
Randolph Co., NC

Serrated edges

G8, $90-$165
Randolph Co., NC

KIRK STEMMED - Early to Middle Archaic, 9000 - 6000 B. P.

(Also see Bolen, Fountain Creek, Heavy Duty, and Stanly)

G2, $4-$8
Cent. NC

G4, $6-$10
Kanawha Co., WVA

G7, $8-$15
NC

Serrated edges

G7, $25-$40
Cent. NC

Rhyolite

G6, $12-$20
NC

G6, $25-$40
Cent. NC

G5, $15-$30
Ashe Co., NC

LOCATION: Southeastern to Eastern states. **DESCRIPTION:** A medium to large size, barbed, stemmed point with deep notches or fine serrations along the blade edges. The stem is parallel to expanding. The stem sides may be steeply beveled on opposite faces. Some examples also have a distinct bevel on the right side of each blade edge. The base can be concave, convex or straight, and can be very short. The shoulders are usually strongly barbed. Believed to have evolved into *Stanly* and other types. The St. Albans site dated this type from 8,850 to 8,980 B.P. **I.D. KEY:** Serrations.

217

KIRK STEMMED (continued)

Serrated edges

Rhyolite

Serrated edges

G6, $25-$40
Randolph Co., NC

G6, $25-$40
NC

G8, $125-$200
Randolph Co., NC

KIRK STEMMED-BIFURCATED - Early Archaic, 9000 - 7000 B. P.

(Also see Cave Spring, Fox Valley, LeCroy, St. Albans, Southhampton and Stanly)

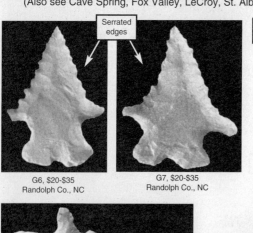

Serrated edges

Serrated edges

G6, $20-$35
Randolph Co., NC

G7, $20-$35
Randolph Co., NC

G7, $25-$40
Wilson Co., NC

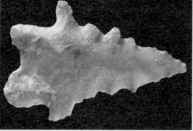

G5, $15-$30
Randolph Co., NC

G5, $5-$10
VA

LOCATION: Southeastern to Eastern states. **DESCRIPTION:** A medium to large point with deep notches or fine serrations along the blade edges. The stem is parallel sided to expanded and is bifurcated. Believed to be an early form for the type which later developed into *Stanly* and others. Some examples have a steep bevel on the right side of each blade edge.

ES

LECROY - Early to Middle Archaic, 9000 - 5000 B. P.

(Also see Decatur, Kanawha Stemmed, Kirk Stemmed-Bifurcated, St. Albans, Southampton and Stanly)

G4, $10-$20
Emporia Co., VA

G4, $10-$20
Stokes Co., NC

G6, $15-$30
Washington Co., VA

G8, $25-$40
Randolph Co., NC

Milky quartz

G7, $25-$40
Randolph Co., NC

G5, $15-$30
Montgomery Co., NC

G9, $30-$50
Randolph Co., NC

G6, $15-$30
Iredell Co., NC

Milky quartz

G6, $25-$40
Randolph Co., NC

Nice serrations

G8, $25-$45
Alleghany Co., NC

G8, $25-$45
Alleghany Co., NC

G8, $25-$40
Richmond Co., NC

LECROY (continued)

LOCATION: Southeastern into northeastern states. Type site-Hamilton Co., TN.
DESCRIPTION: A small to medium size, thin, usually broad point with deeply notched or serrated blade edges and a deeply bifurcated base. Basal ears can either droop or expand out. The stem is usually large in comparison to the blade size. Some stem sides are fractured in Northern examples *(Lake Erie)*. Bases are usually ground. St. Albans site dated *LeCroy* to 8,300 B.P. **I.D. KEY:** Basal form.

LOST LAKE - Early Archaic, 9000 - 6000 B. P.

(Also see Bolen, Decatur, Hardin, Kirk, Palmer, St. Charles, Taylor and Thebes)

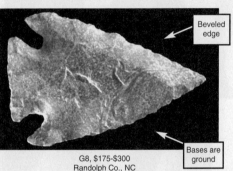

Beveled edge

Bases are ground

G8, $175-$300
Randolph Co., NC

LOCATION: Southeastern states.
DESCRIPTION: A medium to large size, broad, corner notched point that is beveled on one side of each face. The beveling continues when resharpened and creates a flat rhomboid cross section. Most examples are finely serrated and exhibit high quality flaking and symmetry. Also known as *Deep Notch*. **I.D. KEY:** Notching, secondary edgework is always opposite creating at least slight beveling.

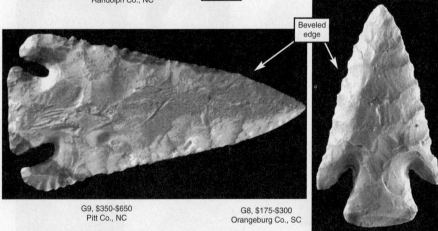

Beveled edge

Beveled edge

G9, $350-$650
Pitt Co., NC

G8, $175-$300
Orangeburg Co., SC

MORROW MOUNTAIN - Middle Archaic, 7000 - 5000 B. P.

(Also see Adena and Randolph)

G7, $12-$20
Randolph Co., NC, Type II

G7, $12-$20
Stokes Co., NC, Type II

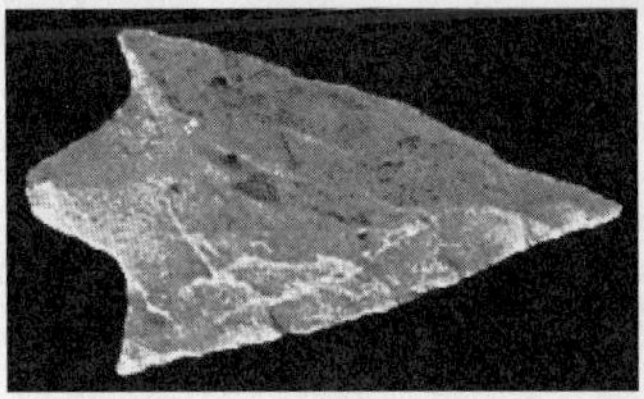

ES

G7, $8-$15
Caswell Co., NC, Type II

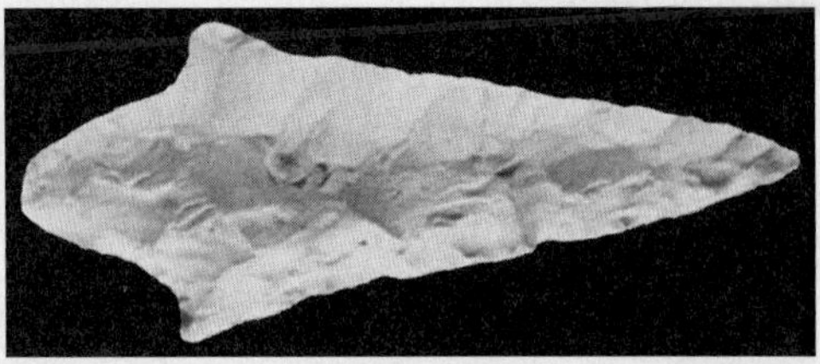

G8, $15-$30
Randolph Co., NC, Type II

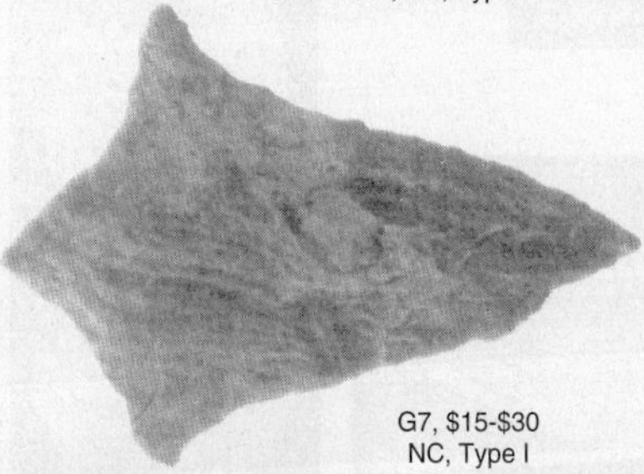

G7, $15-$30
NC, Type I

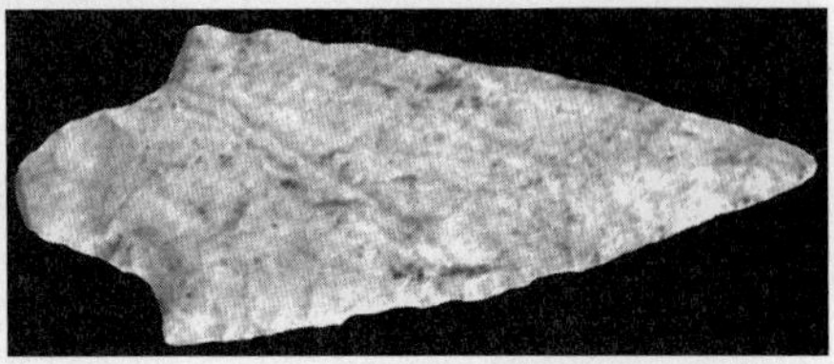

G7, $15-$25
Randolph Co., NC, Type II

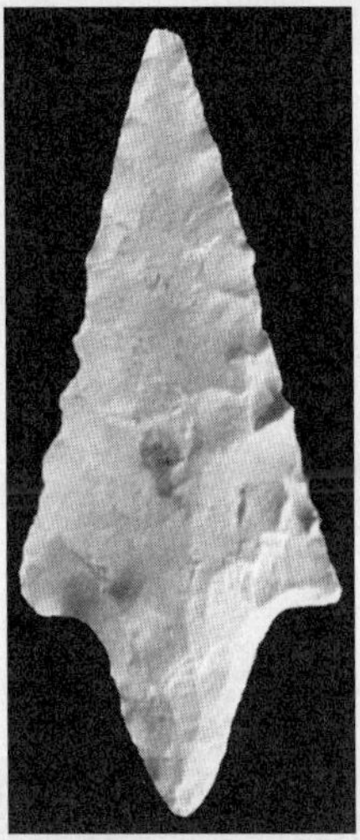

G7, $25-$45
Randolph Co., NC, Type II

G7, $35-$65
Randolph Co., NC, Type I

G6, $20-$35
NC, Type II

G7, $25-$40
Randolph Co., NC, Type II

LOCATION: Midwestern to Southeastern states. **DESCRIPTION:** A medium to large size, triangular point with a very short contracting to rounded stem. Shoulders are usually weak but can be barbed. The blade edges on some examples are serrated with needle points. **I.D. KEY:** Contracted base and Archaic parallel flaking.

G8, $30-$50
Randolph Co., NC, Type I

Quartzite

G9, $55-$100
Randolph Co., NC, Type II

G6, $25-$45
Randolph Co., NC, Type II

G8, $80-$150
SC, Type I

G8, $65-$125
Randolph Co., NC, Type II

ES

G6, $55-$100
Grandville Co., NC, Type II

MORROW MOUNTAIN STRAIGHT BASE - Middle Archaic, 7000 - 5000 B. P.

(Also see Adena and Savannah River)

Vein quartz

LOCATION: Southeastern states. **DESCRIPTION:** A medium size, thin, strongly barbed point with a contracting stem and a straight base. Some examples are serrated and have a needle tip. Look for Archaic parallel flaking.

G7, $8-$15
Bristol, VA

G7, $10-$18
Johnson Co., NC

OCCANEECHEE - Mississippian to Historic, 600 - 400 B. P.

(Also see Yadkin)

Tip damage

G5, $45-$75
Randolph Co., NC

LOCATION: North Carolina. **DESCRIPTION:** A large size triangular point with a concave base. Base corners can be sharp to rounded.

OTTER CREEK - Middle to Late Archaic, 6000 - 3500 B. P.

(Also see Big Sandy and Rowan)

G6, $25-$40
Bethany, WVA

G5, $15-$25
Bethany, WVA

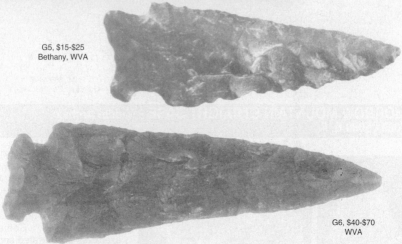

G6, $40-$70
WVA

LOCATION: Northeastern states. **DESCRIPTION:** A medium to large size, narrow side-notched point with a straight, concave or convex base. Notching is prominent, shoulders are tapered to barbed. Bases are ground. **I.D. KEY:** Side notching.

PALMER - Early Archaic, 9000 - 6000 B. P.

(Also see Amos, Ecusta, Hardaway-Palmer, Kirk Corner Notched and Taylor)

Crystal

Serrated edges

G4, $12-$20
Onslow Co., NC

Milky quartz

G6, $35-$60
Randolph Co., NC

G5, $12-$20
Ashe Co., NC

G7, $25-$40
Surry Co., NC

G5, $30-$40
Ashe Co., NC

LOCATION: Southeastern to Eastern states. **DESCRIPTION:** A small size, corner notched, triangular point with a ground concave, convex or straight base. Many are serrated and large examples would fall under the *Pine Tree* or *Kirk* type. This type developed from *Hardaway* in North Carolina where cross types are found.

PALMER (continued)

G8, $25-$45
Davidson Co., NC

G7, $30-$50
Randolph Co., NC

G7, $35-$60
Randolph Co., NC

G10+ $175-$300
Randolph Co., NC

G8, $60-$100
Randolph Co., NC

G5, $15-$25
Ashe Co., NC

G4, $15-$25
Ashe Co., NC

Serrated
edge

G8, $40-$75
Randolph Co., NC

G5, $15-$30
Ashe Co., NC

G7, $55-$100
Randolph Co., NC

G3, $8-$15
Randolph Co., NC

PATRICK HENRY - Early Archaic, 9500 - 8500 B. P.

(Also see Bolen, Decatur, Palmer and Taylor)

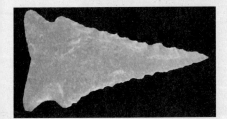

LOCATION: Eastern seaboard states.
DESCRIPTION: A medium size corner notched point with a fish-tailed base. Blade edges can be serrated and the basal area is ground.

G8, $60-$100
Randolph Co., NC

PEE DEE - Late Woodland to Mississippian, 1500 - 1000 B. P.

(Also see Caraway and Jacks Reef)

G3, $5-$10
Smyth Co., VA

G2, $4-$8
Yadkin Co., NC

G4, $5-$10
Rancolph Co., NC

G5, $15-$30
Randolph Co., NC

G6, $15-$25
Wilkes Co., NC

G7, $25-$45
SC

G4, $8-$15
Surry Co., NC

Note pentagonal form

G4, $15-$25
Yadkin Co., NC

G4, $8-$15
Surry Co., NC

G6, $15-$25
Rancolph Co., NC

G5, $15-$30
Randolph Co., NC

G5, $15-$30
Wilkes Co., NC

LOCATION: Eastern seaboard states. **DESCRIPTION:** A small to large size, very thin, five sided point with a sharp tip. The hafting area is usually contracted with a slightly concave to straight base. Called *Jacks Reef* elsewhere.

PICKWICK - Middle to Late Archaic, 6000 - 3500 B. P.

(Also see Savannah River and Stanly)

Recurved blade

G8, $100-$190
Jasper Co., SC

Note expanded barbs, typical for the type

226

G7, $50-$90
Iredell Co., NC

ES

LOCATION: Southeastern states into North and South Carolina. **DESCRIPTION:** A medium to large size, expanded shoulder, contracted to expanded stem point. Blade edges are recurved, and many examples show fine secondary flaking with serrations. Some are beveled on one side of each face. The bevel is steep and shallow. Shoulders are horizontal, tapered or barbed and form sharp angles. Some stems are snapped off or may show original rind. **I.D. KEY:** Barbs and blade form.

POTTS - Woodland, 3000 - 1000 B. P.

(Also see Ecusta and Waratan)

LOCATION: Far Eastern states. **DESCRIPTION:** A medium size triangular point with a short, straight base that has shallow corner notches.

G5, $8-$15
Rockingham Co., NC

QUAD - Late Paleo, 10,000 - 6000 B. P.

(Also see Simpson and Waratan)

G5, $125-$240
Myrtle Beach, SC

G7, $200-$375
Orangeburg Co., SC

LOCATION: Southeastern states. **DESCRIPTION:** A medium to large size lanceolate point with flaring "squared" auricles and a concave base which is ground. Most examples show basal thinning and some are fluted. **I.D. KEY:** Paleo flaking, squarish auricles.

RANDOLPH - Woodland to Historic, 2000 - 200 B. P.

(Also see Morrow Mountain)

RANDOLPH (continued)

G3, $4-$8
Randolph Co., NC

G4, $5-$10
Randolph Co., NC

G6, $8-$15
Randolph Co., NC

G3, $4-$8
Randolph Co., NC

G8, $20-$35
Randolph Co., NC

G5, $8-$15
Randolph Co., NC

G8, $12-$20
Randolph Co., NC

G5, $6-$12
Randolph Co., NC

G6, $15-$25
Randolph Co., NC

G8, $15-$25
Randolph Co., NC

G8, $25-$45
Randolph Co., NC

G8, $15-$25
Guilford Co., NC

G8, $20-$35
Randolph Co., NC

LOCATION: Far Eastern states. Type site is Randolph Co., NC. **DESCRIPTION:** A medium size, narrow, thick, spike point with tapered shoulders and a short to medium contracted, rounded stem. Many examples from North Carolina have exaggerated spikes along the blade edges.

REDSTONE - Paleo, 13,000 - 9000 B. P.

(Also see Clovis)

LOCATION: Southeastern states. **DESCRIPTION:** A medium to large size, thin, auriculate, fluted point with convex sides expanding to a wide, deeply concave base. The hafting area is ground. This point is widest at the base. Fluting can extend most of the way down each face. Multiple flutes are usual. (**Warning:** The most common resharpened *Clovis* point is often sold as this type. *Redstones* are extrememly rare and are almost never offered for sale.) **I.D. KEY:** Baton fluted, edgework on the hafting area.

Brown jasper

Multiple fluting channels

G7, $700-$1300
Randolph Co., NC

Note multiple fluting strikes, characteristic of this rare type

G8, $1200-$2000
Cooper River, SC

ES

ROWAN - Transitional Paleo, 9500 - 8000 B. P.

(Also see Big Sandy and Bolen)

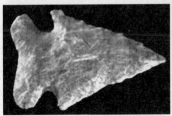

G5, $12-$20
Johnson Co., NC

G5, $12-$20
Moore Co., NC

G4, $4-$8
Ashe Co., NC

G6, $12-$20
Ashe Co., NC

LOCATION: Far Eastern states. Type site is Rowan Co., North Carolina. **DESCRIPTION:** A medium to large size, side-notched point that can be easily confused with the *Big Sandy* type. The basal area is usually wider than the blade. Some examples have expanded ears, and grinding commonly occurs around the basal area. Believed to be an intermediate form developing from *Dalton, Quad, Greenbrier* or *Hardaway* and changing into *Big Sandy* and other later side notched forms.

229

ROWAN (continued)

Rhyolite

G6, $20-$35
Moore Co., NC

G6, $15-$30
Randolph Co., NC

G5, $15-$25
Danville Co., NC

G7, $25-$40
Randolph Co., NC

G7, $30-$50
Randolph Co.,
NC

Rhyolite

G8, $35-$65
Randolph Co.,
NC

G9 $55-$100
Randolph Co., NC

G8, $65-$125
Iredell Co., NC

ST. ALBANS - Early to Middle Archaic, 9000 - 5000 B. P.

(Also see Decatur, Kanawha, Kirk Stemmed-Bifurcated, LeCroy, Southampton and Stanly)

LOCATION: Eastern states. Type site is in Kanawha Co., WVA. **DESCRIPTION:** A small to medium size, narrow, usually serrated, bifurcated point. Basal lobes usually flare outward and most examples are sharply barbed. The basal lobes are more shallow than in the *LeCroy* type, otherwise they are easily confused. St. Albans site dated this type to 8,850 B.P. **I.D. KEY:** Shallow basal lobes and narrowness.

230

ST. ALBANS (continued)

From the St. Albans type site. Black Kanawha chert

Serrated edges

First stage

Rhyolite

G6, $12-$20
Kanawha Co., WVA

G6, $25-$45
Randolph Co., NC

G7, $35-$65
Randolph Co., NC

G7, $35-$65
Randolph Co., NC

G8, $60-$100
Montgomery Co., NC

Rhyolite

G7, $65-$125
Randolph Co., NC

Extreme size for type

ST. CHARLES - Early Archaic, 9500 - 8000 B. P.

(Also see Bolen Beveled, Decatur, Lost Lake and Thebes)

LOCATION: Midwest into the southeast. **DESCRIPTION:** Also known as *Dovetail* and *Plevna*. A medium to large size, corner notched, dovetailed base point. The blade is beveled on one side of each face (usually the left side) on resharpened examples. Bases are always convex. Straight bases would place a point into the *Lost Lake* type. Bases are ground and can be fractured on both sides or center notched on some examples. **I.D. KEY:** Dovetailed base.

Beveled edge

Beveled edge

G4, $20-$35
Ashe Co., NC

G5, $25-$40
Ashe Co., NC

Beveled edge

G8, $175-$300
Randolph Co., NC

231

(Also see Appalachian, Kirk and Stanly)

G7, $15-$30
VA

Yellow
translucent
quartz

G9, $80-$150
Yancey Co., NC

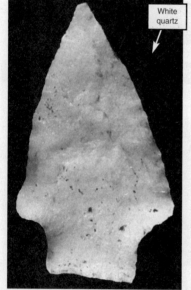

White
quartz

G6, $20-$35
Randolph Co., NC

G8, $45-$80
Randolph Co., NC

LOCATION: Southeastern to Eastern states.
DESCRIPTION: A medium to large size, straight to contracting stemmed point with a straight or concave to bifurcated base. The shoulders are tapered to square. The stems are narrow to broad. Believed to be related to the earlier *Stanly* point. Aka *Appalachian* points in East Tenn. & Western North Carolina.

ES

G7, $65-$125
Randolph Co., NC

G8, $125-$200
Randolph Co., NC

G9, $150-$250
Alleghany Co., NC

SIMPSON - Late Paleo, 12,000 - 8000 B. P.

(Also see Clovis-unfluted and Quad)

G4, $150-$250
Edgefield Co.,
SC

LOCATION: Southern Southeastern states. **DESCRIPTION:** A medium to large size lanceolate, auriculate blade with recurved sides, outward flaring ears and a concave base. The hafting area constriction is more narrow than in the *Suwannee* type. Fluting is absent.

SOUTHAMPTON - Early Archaic, 8000 - 6000 B. P.

(Also see Kanawha, St. Albans and Stanly)

Milky quartz

Quartzite

G4, $4-$8
Southampton Co., VA

G3, $3-$6
Sussex Co., VA

G4, $4-$8
Sussex Co., VA

G6, $5-$10
NC

Quartzite

G5, $6-$12
Sussex Co., VA

G6, $6-$12
Sussex Co., VA

G6, $6-$12
Southampton Co., VA

G6, $6-$12
Sussex Co., VA

LOCATION: Far Eastern states. **DESCRIPTION:** A medium to large size, narrow, thick, bifurcated stemmed point. The basal lobes can expand and the center notch is shallow. Bases are usually ground.

(Also see Garth Slough, Kanawha Stemmed, Kirk Stemmed-Bifurcated, Savannah River and Southampton)

G8, $35-$65
Sussex Co., VA

G5, $12-$20
Sussex Co., VA

G6, $35-$65
Sussex Co., VA

G8, $40-$75
Sussex Co., VA

G6, $30-$55
Sussex Co., VA

G8, $50-$90
Sussex Co., VA

LOCATION: Southeastern to Eastern states. Type site is Stanly Co., NC. **DESCRIPTION:** A small to medium size, broad shoulder point with a small bifurcated stem. Some examples are serrated and show high quality flaking. The shoulders are very prominent and can be tapered, horizontal or barbed. **I.D. KEY:** Small bifurcated base.

G7, $35-$60
Montgomery Co., NC

G8, $45-$80
Randolph Co., NC

STANLY NARROW STEM - Early Archaic, 8000 - 5000 B. P.

(Also see Kirk Stemmed-Bifurcated, St. Albans, Savannah River & Southampton)

G3, $4-$8
Alleghany Co., NC

G4, $12-$20
Stokes Co., NC

G5, $8-$15
Moore Co., NC

G6, $15-$25
Randolph Co., NC

G6, $12-$20
Sussex Co., VA

G9, $40-$75
Randolph Co., NC

ES

G9, $40-$75
Randolph Co., NC

G8, $35-$65
Randolph Co., NC

G6, $25-$40
Montgomery Co., NC

G7, $30-$50
Randolph Co., NC

G6, $25-$40
Randolph Co., NC

G7, $40-$75
Randolph Co., NC

G7, $40-$75
Davidson Co., NC

G8, $55-$100
Randolph Co., NC

LOCATION: Far Eastern states. **DESCRIPTION:** A medium size, narrow shoulder point with a parallel sided stem and a concave base. Believed to have evolved from *Kirk* points and later evolved into *Savannah River* points. Similar to *Northern Piedmont* in Penn.

G7, $40-$75
Montgomery Co., NC

G7, $55-$100
Randolph Co., NC

G8, $65-$125
Moore Co., NC

TAYLOR - Early Archaic, 9000 - 6000 B. P.

(Also see Big Sandy, Bolen, Ecusta, Hardaway, Kirk and Palmer)

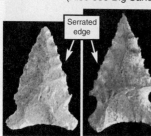

Serrated edge

Serrated edge

Vein quartz

G5, $15-$25
Wilkes Co., NC

G6, $25-$40
Stanly Co., NC

G6, $25-$45
Moore Co., NC

G2, $6-$10
Newberry Co., SC

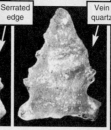

G6, $25-$45
Randolph Co., NC

G8, $25-$50
Randolph Co., NC

G8, $30-$50
Pearson Co., NC

TAYLOR (continued)

Beveled edge | Beveled edge

G8, $70-$135
Lexington Co., SC

Slate

G9, $90-$165
Richmond Co., NC

Serrated edge

G9, $100-$190
Kershaw Co., SC

ES

LOCATION: Far Eastern states. **DESCRIPTION:** A medium to large size, side notched to auriculate point with a concave base. Basal areas are ground. Blade edges can be serrated. A cross between *Hardaway* and *Palmer*. Called *Van Lott* in South Carolina.

THEBES - Early Archaic, 10,000 - 8000 B. P.

(Also see Big Sandy, Bolen, Kirk Corner Notched, Lost Lake and St. Charles)

LOCATION: Midwestern to Eastern states. **DESCRIPTION:** A medium to large size, wide, blade with deep, angled side notches that are parallel sided and squared. Resharpened examples have beveling on one side of each face. The bases of this type have broad proportions and are concave, straight or convex and are ground. Some examples have unusual side notches called Key Notches. This type of notch is angled into the blade to produce a high point in the center, forming the letter E.

Beveled edge

G8, $125-$225
WVA

TRADE POINTS - Historic, 400 - 170 B. P.

$12-$20
NC, Copper.

$15-$30
NC, Copper, circa 1800.

These points were made of copper, iron, and steel and were traded to the Indians by the French, British and others from the 1600s through the 1800s. Examples have been found all over the United States.

UWHARRIE - Late Woodland, 1600 - 1000 B. P.

(Also see Caraway, Clarksville, Hillsboro, Pee Dee and Yadkin)

UWHARRIE (continued)

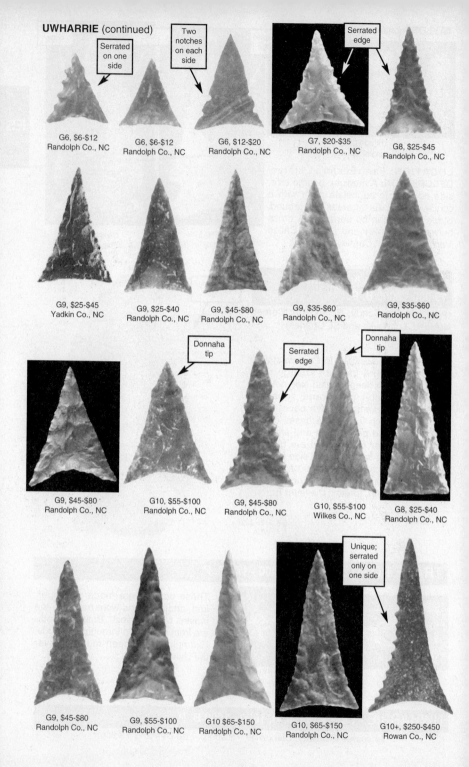

Serrated on one side

Two notches on each side

Serrated edge

Serrated edge

G6, $6-$12
Randolph Co., NC

G6, $6-$12
Randolph Co., NC

G6, $12-$20
Randolph Co., NC

G7, $20-$35
Randolph Co., NC

G8, $25-$45
Randolph Co., NC

G9, $25-$45
Yadkin Co., NC

G9, $25-$40
Randolph Co., NC

G9, $45-$80
Randolph Co., NC

G9, $35-$60
Randolph Co., NC

G9, $35-$60
Randolph Co., NC

Donnaha tip

Serrated edge

Donnaha tip

G9, $45-$80
Randolph Co., NC

G10, $55-$100
Randolph Co., NC

G9, $45-$80
Randolph Co., NC

G10, $55-$100
Wilkes Co., NC

G8, $25-$40
Randolph Co., NC

Unique; serrated only on one side

G9, $45-$80
Randolph Co., NC

G9, $55-$100
Randolph Co., NC

G10 $65-$150
Randolph Co., NC

G10, $65-$150
Randolph Co., NC

G10+, $250-$450
Rowan Co., NC

UWHARRIE (continued)

LOCATION: North and South Carolina. **DESCRIPTION:** A small to medium size, thin, triangular arrow point with concave sides and base. Tips and corners can be very sharp. Side edges are straight to concave. Called *Hamilton* in Tennessee. Some examples have special constricted tips called *Donnaha Tips.* Smaller than *Yadkin.*

WALLER KNIFE - Early Archaic, 9000 - 5000 B. P.

(Also see Edgefield Scraper)

G7, $25-$40
SC

LOCATION: Southern Southeastern states. **DESCRIPTION:** A medium size double uniface knife with a short, notched base, made from a flake. Only the cutting edges have been pressure flaked.

WARATAN - Woodland, 3000 - 1000 B. P.

(Also see Potts and Yadkin)

Quartzite

Vein quartz

G7, $20-$35
Davidson Co., NC

G6, $12-$20
Sussex Co., VA

G6, $12-$20
Southampton Co., VA

LOCATION: Far Eastern states. **DESCRIPTION:** A medium to large size point with usually broad, tapered shoulders, weak corner notches and a very short, broad, concave base. The base expands on some examples giving the appearance of ears or auricles.

WATEREE - Woodland, 3000 - 1500 B. P.

(Also see Will's Cove)

G6, $20-$35
Fairfield Co., SC

LOCATION: Far Eastern states. **DESCRIPTION:** A medium size, narrow point with a recurvate blade, horizontal shoulders and a very short stem. Similar to North Carolina's *Will's Cove.*

WILL'S COVE - Woodland, 3000 - 1000 B. P.

(Also see Wateree)

G6, $35-$60
Randolph Co., NC

Rhyolite

Green rhyolite

G6, $45-$80
Ashe Co., NC

G9, $60-$100
Randolph Co., NC

G8, $50-$90
Randolph Co., NC

G10, $175-$325
Randolph Co.,
NC. The best
known example.

LOCATION: Far Eastern states. **DESCRIPTION:** A medium size, very narrow point with horizontal shoulders and a short, narrow stem with parallel sides and a straight base.

YADKIN - Woodland to Mississippian, 2500 - 500 B. P.

(Also see Caraway, Clarksville, Hillsboro, Occaneechee, Peedee, Uwharrie and Yadkin)

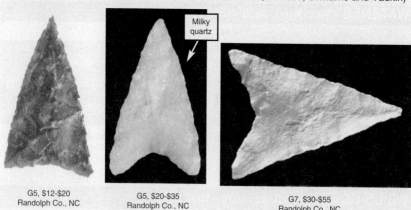

Milky
quartz

G5, $12-$20
Randolph Co., NC

G5, $20-$35
Randolph Co., NC

G7, $30-$55
Randolph Co., NC

YADKIN (continued)

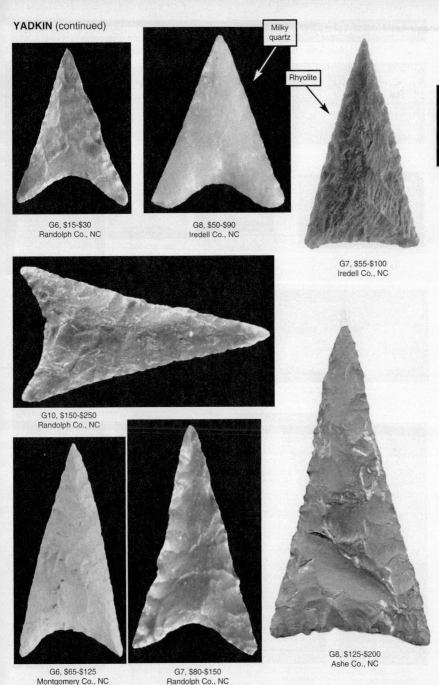

Milky
quartz

Rhyolite

ES

G6, $15-$30
Randolph Co., NC

G8, $50-$90
Iredell Co., NC

G7, $55-$100
Iredell Co., NC

G10, $150-$250
Randolph Co., NC

G6, $65-$125
Montgomery Co., NC

G7, $80-$150
Randolph Co., NC

G8, $125-$200
Ashe Co., NC

LOCATION: Southeastern and Eastern states. Type site is Yadkin River in central North Carolina. **DESCRIPTION:** A small to medium size, broad based, fairly thick, triangular point with a broad, concave base and straight to convex to recurved side edges. Called *Levanna* in New York.

243

YADKIN-EARED - Woodland to Mississippian, 2500 - 500 B. P.

(Also see Guilford-Yuma, Hardaway, Potts, and Waratan)

G4, $10-$18
Rowan Co., NC

G4, $10-$18
Montgomery Co., NC

G7, $30-$50
Guildord Co., NC

G8, $35-$65
Rowan Co., NC

G9, $50-$90
Iredell Co., NC

Quartzite

G6, $30-$50
Sussex Co., VA

G6, $30-$50
Iredell Co., NC

Quartzite

G9, $55-$100
Randolph Co., NC

G10, $75-$140
Allendale Co., SC

G7, $60-$115
Cent. NC

G6, $50-$90
Randolph Co., NC

LOCATION: Eastern Seaboard states, esp. North Carolina. **DESCRIPTION:** A small to medium size triangular, auriculate point with a concave base. The ears are produced by a shallow constriction or notching near the base. The notches are steeply beveled on one edge of each face on some examples.

GULF COASTAL SECTION:

This section includes point types from the following states:
Florida, S. Alabama, S. Georgia, S. Mississippi, S. South Carolina and S.E. Louisiana.

The points in this section are arranged in alphabetical order and are shown **actual size**. All types are listed that were available for photographing. Any missing types will be added to future editions as photographs become available. We are always interested in receiving sharp, black and white, color glossy photos or color slides of your collection. Be sure to include a ruler in the photograph so that proper scale can be determined.

Lithics: Agate, agatized coral, agite, chalcedony, chert, conglomerate, flint, Coastal Plain chert, crystal quartz, hematite, petrified palmwood, quartzite, Tallahatta quartzite and vein quartz.

Special note: Points that are clear, colorful, made of coral, fossilized palmwood or other exotic material will bring a premium price when offered for sale. Exotic materials are pointed out where known.

Regional Consultants:
Tommy Beutell, Gary Davis
Jacky Fuller, Shawn Novak
Jerry Scott, Carlos Tatum
Jim Tatum

GULF COASTAL
(Archaeological Periods)

PALEO (14,000 B. P. - 11,000 B. P.)

Bone Pin
Clovis
Drill

Redstone

LATE PALEO (12,000 B. P. - 10,000 B. P.)

Beaver Lake
Paleo Knife
Simpson
Simpson-Mustache
Suwannee

Union Side Notched

TRANSITIONAL PALEO (11,000 B. P. - 9,000 B. P.)

Cowhouse Slough
Marianna

Stanfield
Union Side Notched

Wheeler

EARLY ARCHAIC (10,500 B. P. - 7,000 B. P.)

Boggy Branch	Edgefield Scraper	Kirk Stemmed	Taylor Side Notched
Bolen Beveled	Gilchrist	Lost Lake	Thonotosassa
Bolen Plain	Hamilton	Osceola Greenbrier	Wacissa
Chipola	Hardaway	Santa Fe	Waller Knife
Cobbs	Hardin	Six Mile Creek	
Conerly	Kirk Corner Notched	Tallahassee	

MIDDLE ARCHAIC (7,000 B. P. - 4,000 B. P.)

Abbey	Culbreath	Marion	South Prong Creek
Alachua	Cypress Creek	Morrow Mountain	Scraper
Arredondo	Elora	Newnan	Sumter
Bascom	Hardee Beveled	Pickwick	Westo
Benton	Hillsborough	Putnam	
Clay	Ledbetter	Savannah River	
Cottonbridge	Levy	Seminole	

LATE ARCHAIC (4,000 B. P. - 3,000 B. P.)

Citrus
Evans

Hernando
Lafayette

WOODLAND (3,000 B. P. - 1,300 B. P.)

Adena	Copena	Oauchita	Taylor
Bradford	Durant's Bend	Ocala	Weeden Island
Broad River	Duval	O'leno	Yadkin
Broward	Jackson	Sarasota	
Columbia	Leon	Sting Ray Barb	

MISSISSIPPIAN (1300 B. P. - 400 B. P.)

Harahey
Itcheetucknee

Pinellas
Safety Harbor

Tampa
Trade

GULF COASTAL
THUMBNAIL GUIDE SECTION

The following references are provided to aid the collector in easier and quicker identification of point types. All photos are exactly 30% of actual size and are proportional to each other. Each point pictured in this section represents a classic form for the type. When a match is found, go to the alphabetical location of that type for more examples in actual size.

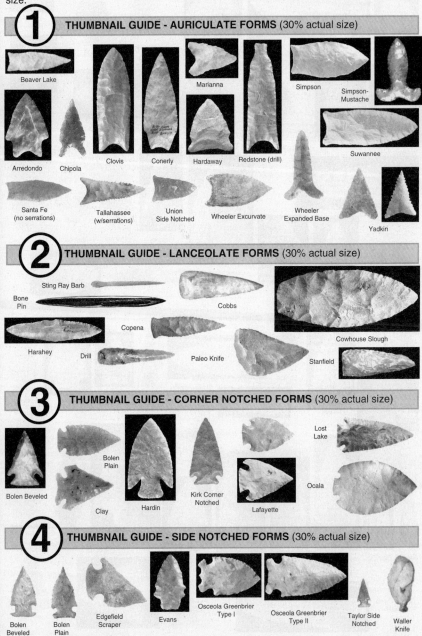

① THUMBNAIL GUIDE - AURICULATE FORMS (30% actual size)

Beaver Lake

Marianna

Simpson

Simpson-Mustache

GC

Arredondo   Chipola   Clovis   Conerly   Hardaway   Redstone (drill)   Suwannee

Santa Fe (no serrations)   Tallahassee (w/serrations)   Union Side Notched   Wheeler Excurvate   Wheeler Expanded Base   Yadkin

② THUMBNAIL GUIDE - LANCEOLATE FORMS (30% actual size)

Sting Ray Barb

Bone Pin

Cobbs

Copena

Cowhouse Slough

Harahey   Drill   Paleo Knife   Stanfield

③ THUMBNAIL GUIDE - CORNER NOTCHED FORMS (30% actual size)

Bolen Plain

Lost Lake

Bolen Beveled

Ocala

Clay   Hardin   Kirk Corner Notched   Lafayette

④ THUMBNAIL GUIDE - SIDE NOTCHED FORMS (30% actual size)

Bolen Beveled   Bolen Plain   Edgefield Scraper   Evans   Osceola Greenbrier Type I   Osceola Greenbrier Type II   Taylor Side Notched   Waller Knife

247

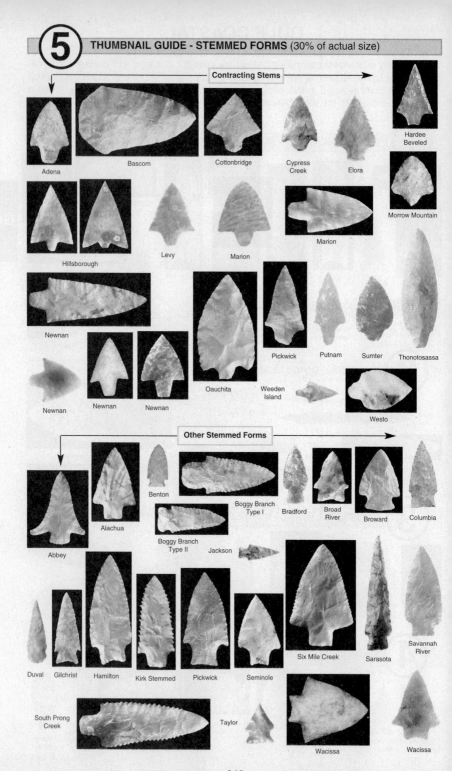

Contracting Stems

Adena

Bascom

Cottonbridge

Cypress Creek

Elora

Hardee Beveled

Morrow Mountain

Hillsborough

Levy

Marion

Marion

Newnan

Newnan

Newnan

Newnan

Oauchita

Pickwick

Putnam

Sumter

Thonotosassa

Weeden Island

Westo

Other Stemmed Forms

Abbey

Alachua

Benton

Boggy Branch Type I

Boggy Branch Type II

Jackson

Bradford

Broad River

Broward

Columbia

Duval

Gilchrist

Hamilton

Kirk Stemmed

Pickwick

Seminole

Six Mile Creek

Sarasota

Savannah River

South Prong Creek

Taylor

Wacissa

Wacissa

248

Citrus	Clay	Culbreath	Hernando	Lafayette

Durant's Bend	Ichetucknee	O'leno	Pinellas	Safety Harbor	Tampa

GC

ABBEY - Early to Middle Archaic, 6000 - 4000 B. P.

(Also see Alachua, Cottonbridge, Elora, Levy, Notchaway, Pickwick, Savannah River, Six Mile Creek, South Prong Creek and Wacissa)

Base nick

G5, $15-$25
Decatur Co., GA

G4, $15-$25
Decatur Co., GA

G6, $30-$50
Decatur Co., GA

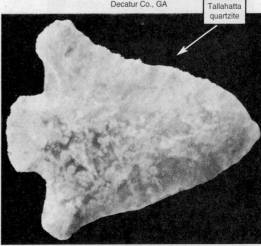

Tallahatta quartzite

G10, $175-$300
Sou. AL

249

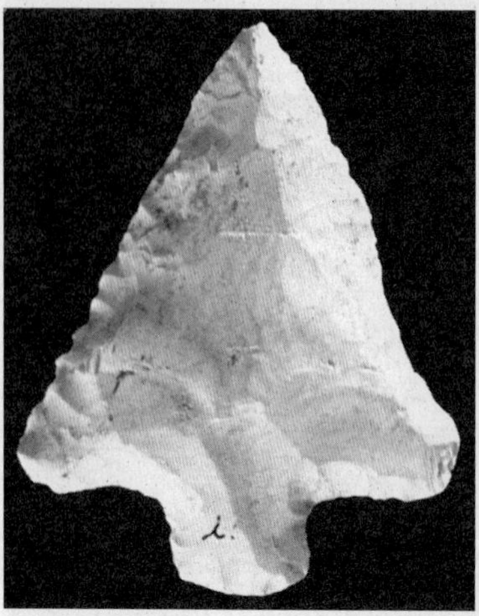

G6, $25-$40
Decatur Co., GA

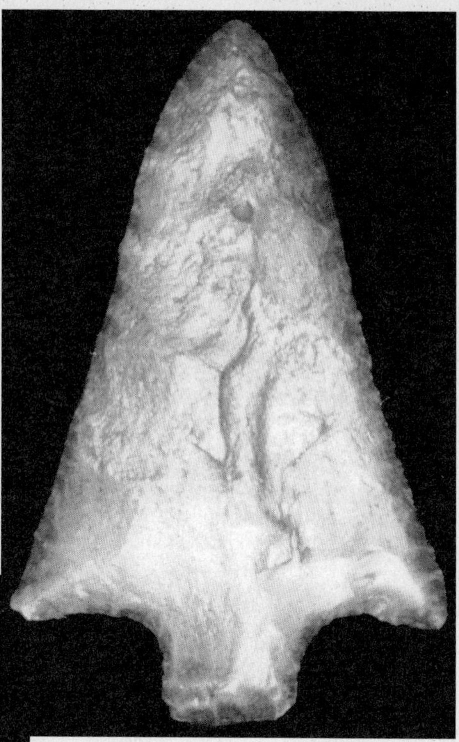

G10, $250-$400
Albany, GA

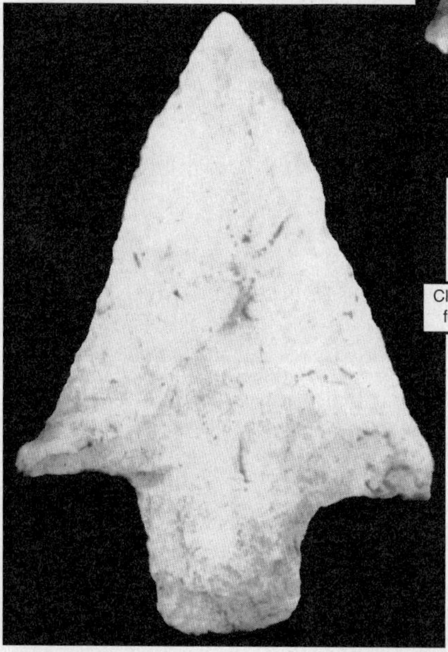

G7, $35-$60
GA

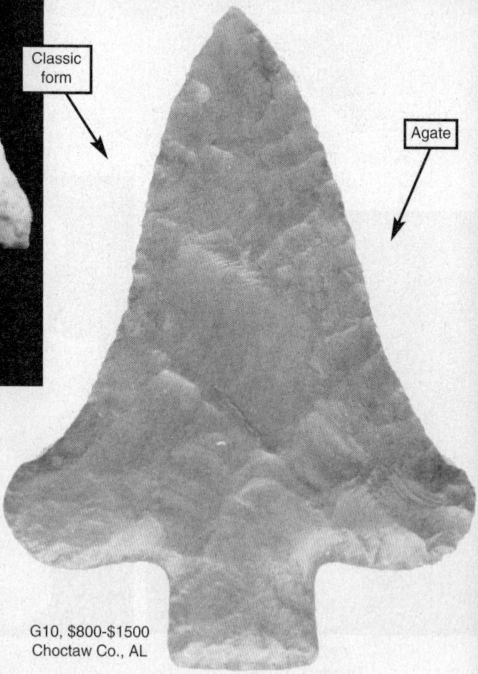

Classic
form

Agate

G10, $800-$1500
Choctaw Co., AL

LOCATION: GA, AL, FL. **DESCRIPTION:** A medium sized, broad, stemmed point that is fairly thick and is steeply beveled on all four sides of each face. Blade edges are concave to straight. Shoulders are broad and tapered. A relationship to *Elora, Maples* and *Pickwick* has been suggested. **I.D. KEY:** Expanded barbs & fine edgework.

250

ADENA - Late Archaic to late Woodland, 3000 - 1200 B. P.

(Also see Cypress Creek, Elora, Levy, Pickwick, Putnam, Sumter & Thonotosassa)

G5, $30-$50
Suwannee Co., FL

LOCATION: Eastern to Southeastern states. **DESCRIPTION:** A medium to large, thin, narrow, triangular blade that is sometimes serrated, and with a medium to long, narrow to broad rounded "beaver tail" stem. Most examples are from average to excellent quality. **I.D. KEY:** Rounded base, woodland flaking.

G9, $80-$150
Jackson Co., FL

ALACHUA - Middle Archaic, 5500 - 4000 B. P.

(Also see Abbey, Cypress Creek, Hardee Beveled, Levy, Marion, Morrow Mountain, Newnan, Putnam, Six Mile Creek)

Tallahatta quartzite

G9, $80-$150
Sou. AL

LOCATION: Gulf Coastal states. **DESCRIPTION:** A rare type. *Newnans* with straight horizontal shoulders and straight stems that don't contract as much. **I.D. KEY:** Squared base, one barb shoulder.

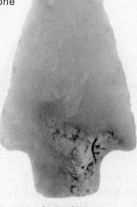

Clear

G7, $65-$125
FL

G7, $150-$250
Jackson Co., FL

G4, $8-$15
Hillsborough Co., FL

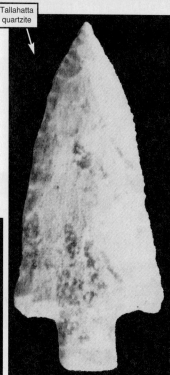

Tallahatta
quartzite

G6, $35-$60
Miller Co., GA

G10, $250-$550
Sou. AL

ARREDONDO - Middle to Late Archaic, 6000 - 3500 B. P.

(Also see Buzzard Roost Creek, Hamilton, Kirk Stemmed, Savannah River, Seminole and Wacissa)

G6, $30-$50
Jefferson Co., FL

G5, $15-$25
Marion Co., FL

G6, $30-$50
FL.

LOCATION: AL, GA, FL. **DESCRIPTION:** A thick, medium to large size point with a short, broad blade and a wide, concave to bifurcated base which can be thinned. Basal ears are rounded to pointed. Could be related to *Hamilton* points. **I.D. KEY:** Basal form and thickness.

ARREDONDO (continued)

G6, $35-$65
FL

Classic
example

G10 $150-$250
FL

G7, $150-$250
Hillsborough Co., FL

BASCOM - Middle to Late Archaic, 4500 - 3500 B. P.

(Also see Morrow Mountain and Savannah River)

G10, $175-$300
SC coast cache.

G10, $200-$350
SC coast cache.

IMPORTANT:
All Bascoms shown
half size.

G9, $65-$125
SC coast cache.

253

BASCOM (continued)

G8, $175-$300
AL

Tallahatta
quartzite

G6, $45-$85
Burke Co., GA

G10, $150-$275
Savannah, GA

G9, $225-$400
AL

G9, $80-$150
SC coast cache.

G9, $65-$125
SC coast cache.

LOCATION: AL, GA. & SC. **DESCRIPTION:** A large size, broad point with weak shoulders tapering to the base which is usually straight but can be convex. A preform for the *Savannah River* point. A cache of *Bascom* and *Savannah River* were found together. **I.D.KEY:** Basal form.

BEAVER LAKE - Paleo, 12,000 - 9500 B. P.

(Also see Simpson, Suwannee and Tallahassee)

Finely
serrated

G10+, $1500-$2200
Jackson Co., FL

LOCATION: Southeastern states. **DESCRIPTION:** A medium to large size lanceolate blade with flaring ears. Contemporaneous and associated with *Cumberland*, but thinner than unfluted *Cumberlands*. Basal areas are ground and blade edges are recurved. **I.D. KEY:** Paleo flaking, shoulder area.

BEAVER LAKE (continued)

Very thin in cross section

Clear with color

GC

G6, $50-$100
Columbia Co., FL

G10, $250-$400
FL

G9, $225-$400
Sumter Co., FL

G9, $200-$350
FL

G9, $350-$600
Sumter Co., FL

BENTON - Middle Archaic, 6000 - 4000 B. P.

(Also see Hamilton, Savannah River)

G7, $150-$250
Baker Co., GA

G7, $55-$100
Dougherty Co., GA

IMPORTANT:
All Bentons are shown half size

G8, $175-$300
Baker Co., GA

LOCATION: Southeastern states into southern Georgia. **DESCRIPTION:** A medium to large size, broad, stemmed point with straight to convex sides. Bases can be corner or side notched, double notched, knobbed, bifurcated or expanded. Some examples show parallel oblique flaking. All four sides are beveled and basal corners usually have tangs. **I.D. KEY:** Wide, squared, eared or notched base.

BOGGY BRANCH-TYPE I - Early to Middle Archaic, 9000 - 6000 B. P.

(Also see Kirk Stemmed and South Prong Creek)

G10, $800-$1500
Henry Co., AL

IMPORTANT:
This Boggy shown half size

LOCATION: Small area in SE AL & SW GA. **DESCRIPTION:** A medium to large size serrated point with weak shoulders and a large bulbous base which is usually ground. Blade flaking is similar to *Kirk Stemmed*. Most examples are made of coastal plain chert. Very rare in the small type area. **I.D. KEY:** Basal form and edgework.

255

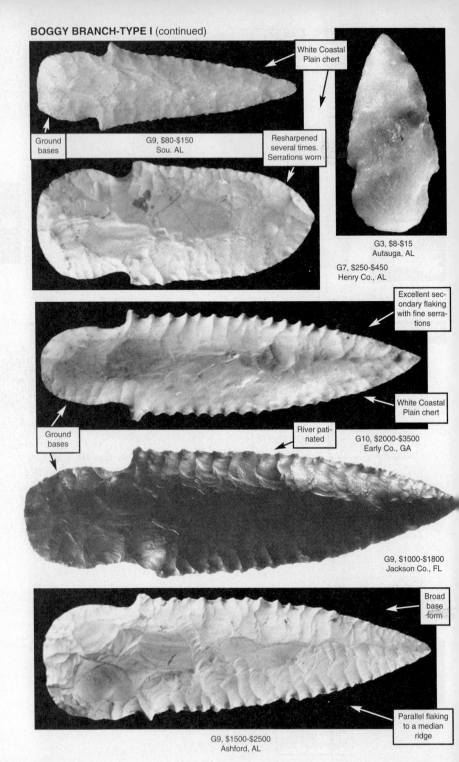

White Coastal Plain chert

Ground bases

G9, $80-$150
Sou. AL

Resharpened several times. Serrations worn

G3, $8-$15
Autauga, AL

G7, $250-$450
Henry Co., AL

Excellent secondary flaking with fine serrations

White Coastal Plain chert

Ground bases

River patinated

G10, $2000-$3500
Early Co., GA

G9, $1000-$1800
Jackson Co., FL

Broad base form

Parallel flaking to a median ridge

G9, $1500-$2500
Ashford, AL

BOGGY BRANCH-TYPE II - Early to Middle Archaic, 9000 - 6000 B. P.

(Also see Kirk Stemmed and South Prong Creek)

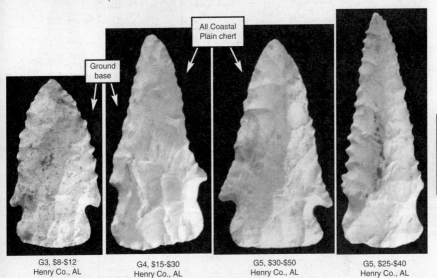

Ground base

All Coastal Plain chert

G3, $8-$12
Henry Co., AL

G4, $15-$30
Henry Co., AL

G5, $30-$50
Henry Co., AL

G5, $25-$40
Henry Co., AL

LOCATION: Southern Southeastern states. **DESCRIPTION:** A small to medium size serrated point with weak shoulders and a bulbous base which is usually ground. The base is shorter and smaller than in type I. **I.D. KEY:** Basal form and early flaking.

BOLEN BEVELED - Early Archaic, 10,500 - 8000 B. P.

(Also Clay, Lafayette, Lost Lake and Osceola Greenbriar)

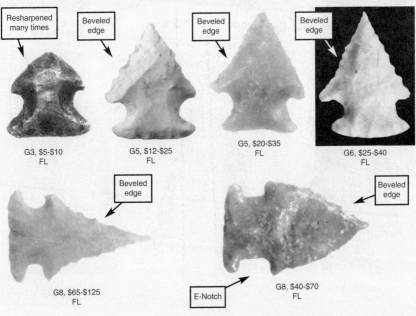

Resharpened many times

Beveled edge

Beveled edge

Beveled edge

G3, $5-$10
FL

G5, $12-$25
FL

G5, $20-$35
FL

G6, $25-$40
FL

Beveled edge

Beveled edge

G8, $65-$125
FL

E-Notch

G8, $40-$70
FL

BOLEN BEVELED (continued)

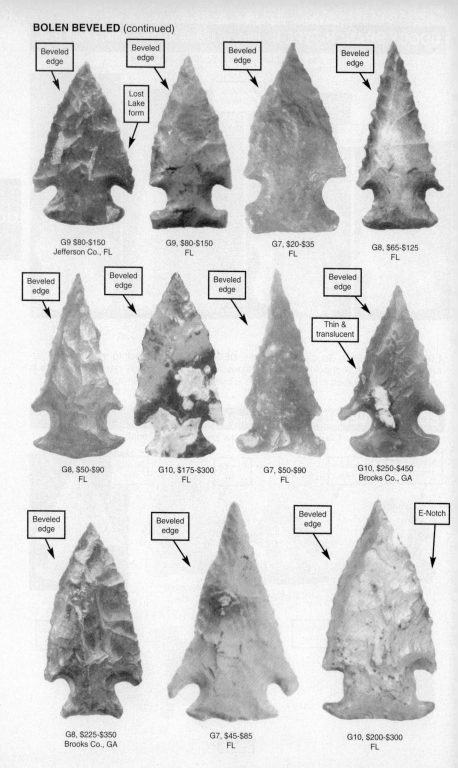

Beveled edge

Beveled edge

Lost Lake form

Beveled edge

Beveled edge

G9 $80-$150
Jefferson Co., FL

G9, $80-$150
FL

G7, $20-$35
FL

G8, $65-$125
FL

Beveled edge

Beveled edge

Beveled edge

Beveled edge

Thin & translucent

G8, $50-$90
FL

G10, $175-$300
FL

G7, $50-$90
FL

G10, $250-$450
Brooks Co., GA

Beveled edge

Beveled edge

Beveled edge

E-Notch

G8, $225-$350
Brooks Co., GA

G7, $45-$85
FL

G10, $200-$300
FL

BOLEN BEVELED (continued)

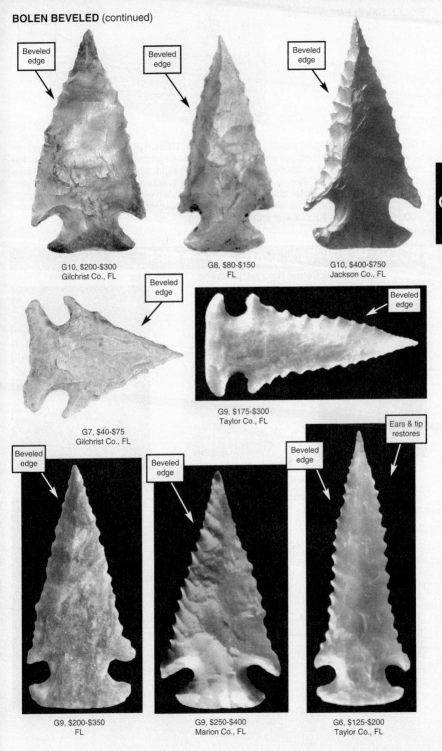

GC

Beveled edge

G10, $200-$300
Gilchrist Co., FL

Beveled edge

G8, $80-$150
FL

Beveled edge

G10, $400-$750
Jackson Co., FL

Beveled edge

Beveled edge

G7, $40-$75
Gilchrist Co., FL

G9, $175-$300
Taylor Co., FL

Beveled edge

Beveled edge

Beveled edge

Ears & tip restores

G9, $200-$350
FL

G9, $250-$400
Marion Co., FL

G6, $125-$200
Taylor Co., FL

259

BOLEN BEVELED (continued)

G9, $200-$350
Jefferson Co., FL

Beveled edge

LOCATION: Southeastern states including Florida. **DESCRIPTION:** A small to medium size, side to corner notched point with early forms showing basal grinding, beveling on one side of each face, and serrations. Bases can be straight, concave or convex. The side notch is usually broader than in *Big Sandy* points. E-notched or expanded notching also occurs on early forms. **Note:** *Bolens* have been found with horse remains in Florida indicating use in killing the horse which was probably hunted into extinction in the U.S. about 7,000 years ago. **I.D. KEY:** Basal form and notching.

BOLEN PLAIN - Early Archaic, 9000 - 7000 B. P.

(Also see Kirk Corner Notched, Lafayette, Osceola Greenbriar and Taylor)

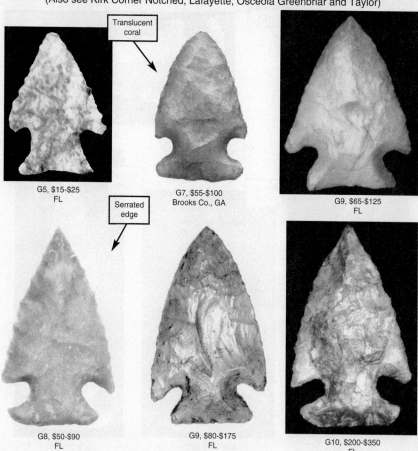

Translucent coral

G5, $15-$25
FL

G7, $55-$100
Brooks Co., GA

G9, $65-$125
FL

Serrated edge

G8, $50-$90
FL

G9, $80-$175
FL

G10, $200-$350
FL

260

BOLEN PLAIN (continued)

Oblique transverse flaking, very thin

E-Notch

E-Notch

Serrated edge

GC

G9 $300-$500
Brooks Co., GA

G9, $200-$350
Burke Co., GA

G8, $65-$125
FL

Petrified wood

G9, $80-$150
FL

G7, $150-$250
S.W. GA

G9, $150-$250
FL

G9, $200-$350
Columbia Co., FL

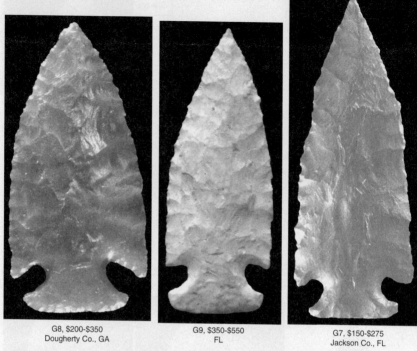

G8, $200-$350
Dougherty Co., GA

G9, $350-$550
FL

G7, $150-$275
Jackson Co., FL

LOCATION: Eastern states. **DESCRIPTION:** A small to medium size, side to corner notched point with early forms showing basal grinding and serrations. Bases are straight, concave or convex. The side notches are usually broader than in the *Big Sandy* type, and can be expanded to E-notched on some examples. **I.D. KEY:** Basal form and flaking on blade.

BONE PIN - Transitional Paleo to Historic, 12,000 - 200 B. P.

$12-$20
Hillsborough Co., FL

$12-$20
FL

$15-$30
FL

$15-$30
FL.

$40-$75
Jefferson Co., FL

LOCATION: Florida. **DESCRIPTION:** Medium to large size, slender, double pointed spear pins made from deer leg bone, some camel and rarely mammoth. Less than 1% are mammoth ivory. The bone is usually blackened with age.

BRADFORD - Woodland to Mississippian, 2000 - 800 B. P.

(Also see Broward, Columbia and Sarasota)

G3, $3-$6
Hillsborough Co., FL

G6, $15-$30
FL

LOCATION: Southern Southeastern states. **DESCRIPTION:** A medium size, narrow, expanded stem point with tapered to rounded shoulders. Basal corners can also be rounded. Bases are straight to slightly convex.

G8, $35-$60
Suwannee Co., FL

BROAD RIVER - Woodland, 3000 - 1500 B. P.

(Also see Broward, Columbia, Sarasota, Savannah River and Wacissa)

G5, $8-$12
Beaufort Co., SC

G6, $10-$15
Henry Co., AL

LOCATION: Southern Southeastern states. **DESCRIPTION:** A small size, thick point with small shoulder barbs, a parallel sided stem and a straight to concave base.

BROWARD - Woodland to Mississippian, 2000 - 800 B. P.

(Also see Bradford, Broad River, Columbia and Sarasota)

G5, $10-$15
Seminole Co., GA

G9, $25-$45
FL

BROWARD (continued)

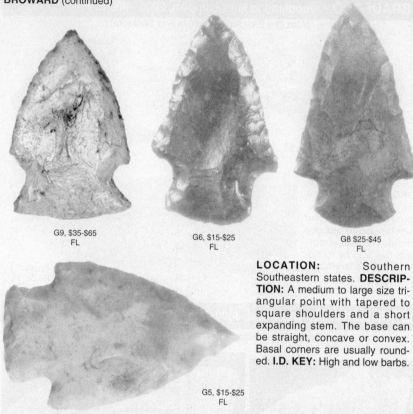

G9, $35-$65
FL

G6, $15-$25
FL

G8 $25-$45
FL

LOCATION: Southern Southeastern states. **DESCRIPTION:** A medium to large size triangular point with tapered to square shoulders and a short expanding stem. The base can be straight, concave or convex. Basal corners are usually rounded. **I.D. KEY:** High and low barbs.

G5, $15-$25
FL

CHIPOLA - Early Archaic, 10,000 - 8000 B. P.

(Also see Gilchrist and Hardaway)

Rare Chipola variant

G10, $500-$800
Pasco Co., FL

LOCATION: Southern Southeastern states. **DESCRIPTION:** A small to medium size triangular point with long, expanding auricles and a tapered shoulder. Bases are deeply concave and are thinned. A *Dalton* variant form. Similar to *San Patrice* points found in Louisiana and Texas. May be related to *Gilchrist*. Rare in type area.

CHIPOLA (continued)

Clear

G8, $200-$350
Chipola River, FL

G9, $350-$600
Hamilton Co., FL

CITRUS - Late Archaic to Woodland, 3500 - 2000 B. P.
(Also see Culbreath and Hernando)

GC

G9, $150-$250
FL

G9, $150-$250
FL

G9, $200-$350
FL

G9, $200-$350
Taylor Co., FL

G9, $400-$750
Columbia Co., FL

265

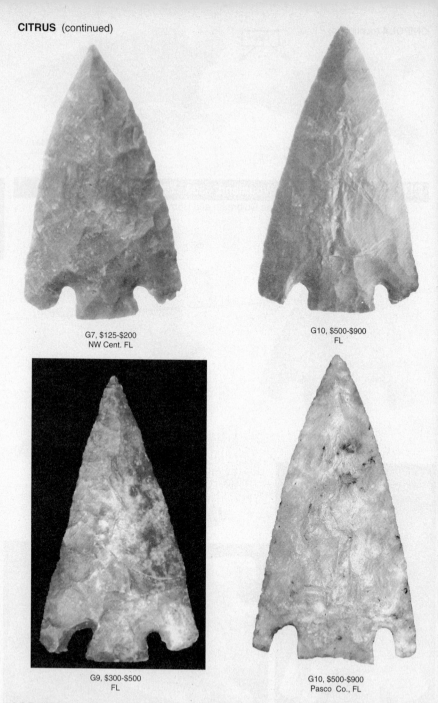

G7, $125-$200
NW Cent. FL

G10, $500-$900
FL

G9, $300-$500
FL

G10, $500-$900
Pasco Co., FL

LOCATION: Southern Southeastern states including Florida. **DESCRIPTION:** A medium to large size basal-notched point. The stem is wider than *Hernando*. The base and tangs usually forms an arc on most examples. **I.D. KEY:** Notches and random flaking on blade. *Citruses* usually have broader stems than *Hernandos*.

(Also see Kirk Corner Notched and Lafayette)

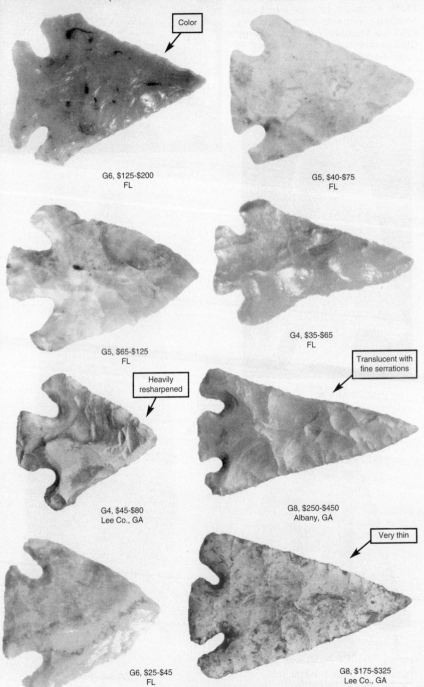

GC

Color

G6, $125-$200
FL

G5, $40-$75
FL

G5, $65-$125
FL

G4, $35-$65
FL

Heavily
resharpened

Translucent with
fine serrations

G4, $45-$80
Lee Co., GA

G8, $250-$450
Albany, GA

Very thin

G6, $25-$45
FL

G8, $175-$325
Lee Co., GA

CLAY (continued)

LOCATION: Southern Southeastern states including Florida. **DESCRIPTION:** A medium to large size basal-notched point with outward-flaring, squared shoulders (clipped wing). Blades are recurvate. Related to *Lafayette* points. **I.D. KEY:** Deep notches and squared barbs. Asymmetric with on squared and one pointed or rounded barb.

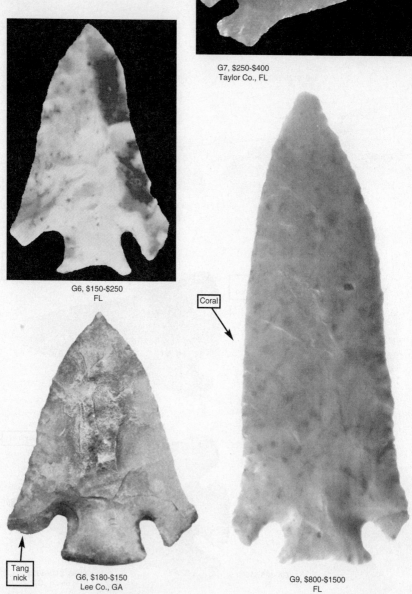

G7, $250-$400
Taylor Co., FL

G6, $150-$250
FL

Coral

Tang
nick

G6, $180-$150
Lee Co., GA

G9, $800-$1500
FL

CLOVIS - Early Paleo, 14,000 - 9000 B. P.

(Also see Chipola, Redstone, Simpson and Suwannee)

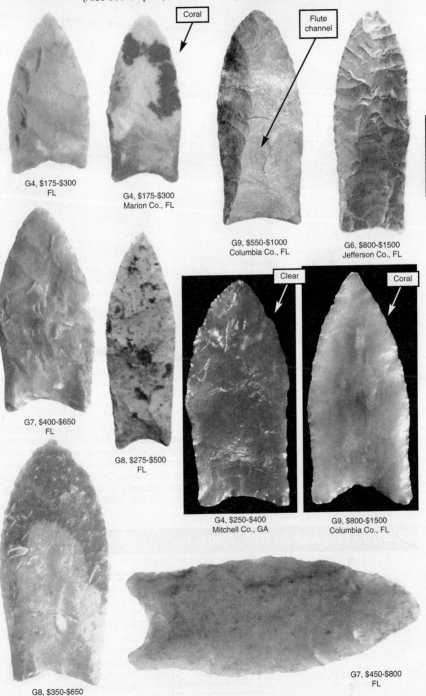

Coral

Flute channel

GC

G4, $175-$300
FL

G4, $175-$300
Marion Co., FL

G9, $550-$1000
Columbia Co., FL

G6, $800-$1500
Jefferson Co., FL

Clear

Coral

G7, $400-$650
FL

G8, $275-$500
FL

G4, $250-$400
Mitchell Co., GA

G9, $800-$1500
Columbia Co., FL

G8, $350-$650
FL

G7, $450-$800
FL

269

CLOVIS (continued)

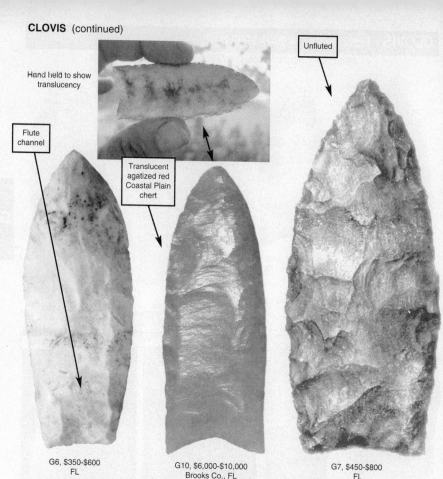

Hand held to show translucency

Unfluted

Flute channel

Translucent agatized red Coastal Plain chert

G6, $350-$600
FL

G10, $6,000-$10,000
Brooks Co., FL

G7, $450-$800
FL

LOCATION: All of North America. **DESCRIPTION:** A medium to large size, auriculate, fluted, lanceolate point with convex sides and a concave base that is ground. Most examples are fluted on both sides about 1/3 the way up from the base. The flaking can be random to parallel. *Clovis* is the earliest point type in the hemisphere. It is believed that this form was developed here after early man arrived from Russia and Europe 20,000 to 50,000 years ago. Current theories place the origin of *Clovis* in the Eastern U.S. since more examples are found from Florida to Pennsylvania than anywhere else. **I.D. KEY:** Paleo flaking, shoulders, batan fluting instead of indirect style.

COBBS - Early Archaic, 9000 - 5000 B. P.

(Also see Bolen Beveled and Lost Lake)

G10, $350-$600
Jackson Co., FL

IMPORTANT:
Cobbs shown half size

LOCATION: Southeastern states. **DESCRIPTION:** A medium to large size , lanceolate blade with a broad, rounded to square base. One side of each face is usually steeply beveled. These are un-notched preforms for early Archaic beveled types.

270

COLUMBIA - Woodland, 2000 - 1000 B. P.

(Also see Bradford, Hamilton, Ledbetter, Sarasota and Thonotosassa)

LOCATION: Southern South - eastern states. **DESCRIPTION:** A medium to large size stemmed point. Shoulders are tapered to horizontal and are weak. Stem is short and slightly expanding. Base is straight.

GC

Translucent

G8, $55-$100
Brooks Co., GA.

G9, $65-$125
FL

Tip nick

G5, $15-$25
FL

G7, $20-$35
FL

G9, $125-$200
Levy Co., FL

G9, $80-$150
FL

G9, $90-$175
FL

271

G9, $150-$250
FL

CONERLY - Middle Archaic, 7500 - 4500 B. P.

(Also see Beaver Lake, Simpson and Suwannee)

G8, $45-$80
Screven Co., GA

G9, $150-$250
Beaufort Co., SC

G5, $20-$35
Burke Co., GA

G10, $175-$300
Savannah River, GA

LOCATION: Southern Southeastern states, especially Tennessee, Georgia and Florida.
DESCRIPTION: A medium to large auriculate point with a contracting, concave base which can be ground. On some examples, the hafting area can be seen with the presence of very weak shoulders. The base is usually thinned. Believed to be related to the *Guilford* type.
I.D. KEY: Base concave, thickness, flaking.

COPENA - Woodland, 2500 - 1500 B. P.

(Also see Duval and Safety Harborl)

Serrated edge

G7, $65-$125
Brooks Co., GA

LOCATION: Southern Gulf states. **DESCRIPTION:** A medium size lanceolate point with recurved blade edges and a straight to slightly convex base. Florida Copenas are usually smaller than those found further north. **I.D. KEY:** Recurved blade edges.

COTTONBRIDGE - Middle Archaic, 6000 - 4000 B. P.

(Also see Abbey and Elora)

G7, $25-$45
FL

G7, $35-$60
Henry Co., AL

LOCATION: Southern Gulf states. **DESCRIPTION:** A medium size, broad, stemmed point that is fairly thick and beveled on all four sides. Shoulders are tapered and blade edges are straight. Base is small and rounded with contracting sides. **I.D. KEY:** Small, round base.

COWHOUSE SLOUGH - Transitional Paleo, 10,000 - 6000 B. P.

(Also see Stanfield)

G6, $80-$150
Hillsborough Co., FL

LOCATION: Gulf Coastal states. **DESCRIPTION:** A medium to large size, broad, lanceolate blade with a contracting, straight to slightly convex base which may be ground as well as fluted or thinned. **I.D. KEY:** Paleo flaking.

G8, $65-$125
Brooks Co., GA

G9, $650-$1200
Gilchrist Co., FL

Classic example

Beautiful random percussion flaking

G6, $100-$180
FL

CULBREATH - Late Archaic to Woodland, 5000 - 3000 B. P.

(Also see Citrus, Clay, Hernando, Kirk Corner Notched and Lafayette)

G9, $65-$125
FL

G9, $40-$75
FL

CULBREATH (continued)

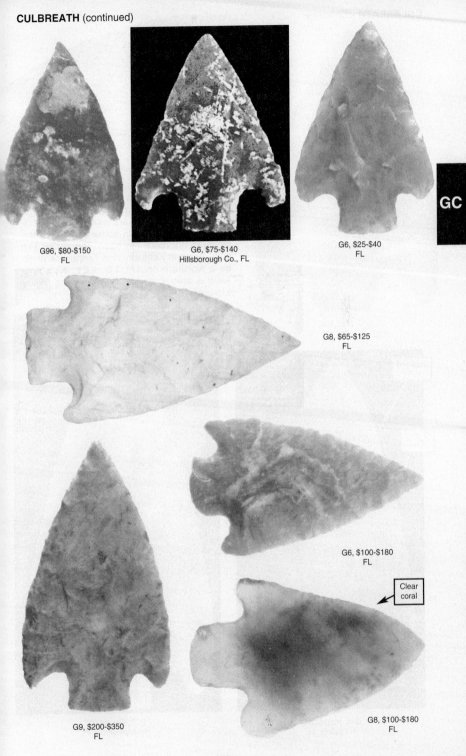

G96, $80-$150
FL

G6, $75-$140
Hillsborough Co., FL

G6, $25-$40
FL

G8, $65-$125
FL

G6, $100-$180
FL

Clear
coral

G9, $200-$350
FL

G8, $100-$180
FL

275

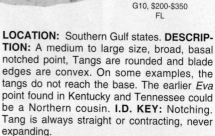

G10, $200-$350
FL

LOCATION: Southern Gulf states. **DESCRIPTION:** A medium to large size, broad, basal notched point, Tangs are rounded and blade edges are convex. On some examples, the tangs do not reach the base. The earlier *Eva* point found in Kentucky and Tennessee could be a Northern cousin. **I.D. KEY:** Notching. Tang is always straight or contracting, never expanding.

G10, $350-$650
FL

Agatized coral

Classic form

G10, $650-$1200
N.W. Cent. FL

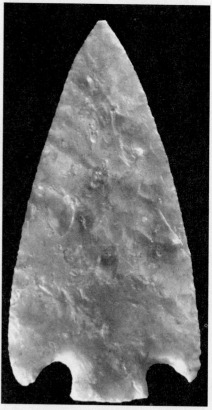

G10, $800-$1500
Hillsborough Co., FL

CYPRESS CREEK - Middle Archaic, 5500 - 3000 B. P.

(Also see Alachua, Hillsborough, Levy, Morrow Mountain, Putnam and Sumter)

G4, $5 -$10
FL

G6, $15-$25
FL

G7, $40-$75
Pasco Co., FL

LOCATION: Southern Southeastern states. **DESCRIPTION:** A medium size point with a short, pointed to rounded contracting base. Shoulders have short barbs and can be asymmetrical with one barbed and the other tapered.

G8, $35-$60
FL

G8, $65-$125
Pasco Co., FL

G7, $25-$40
FL

DRILL - Paleo to Historic, 14,000 - 200 B. P.

(Also see Edgefield Scraper)

Agate

G9, $45-$85
FL

G8, $45-$85
FL

Newnan
drill

G5, $8-$15
Marion Co., FL

Putnam
drill

G5, $8-$15
Marion Co., FL

Pin
drill

G8, $35-$65
FL

G8, $20-$35
FL

G8, $30-$55
FL

G9, $150-$250
FL

LOCATION: Everywhere. **DESCRIPTION:** Although many drills were made from scratch, all point types were made into the drill form. Usually, heavily resharpened and broken points were salvaged and rechipped into drills. These objects were certainly used as drills (evidence of extreme edge wear), but there is speculation that some of these forms may have been used as pins for clothing, ornaments, ear plugs and other uses.

DURANT'S BEND - Woodland-Mississippian, 1600 - 1000 B. P.

(Also see Pinellas)

G8, $12-$20 ea.
Dallas Co., AL

DURANT'S BEND (continued)

G7, $8-$15
Dallas Co., AL

G7, $8-$15
Dallas Co., AL

G9, $25-$40
Dallas Co., AL.

G10, $35-$65
Sou. AL

G8, $15-$30
Dallas Co., AL

G8, $15-$30
Dallas Co., AL

G10, $55-
$100
Dallas Co.,
AL

LOCATION: Southern Alabama. **DESCRIPTION:** A small size, narrow, triangular point with flaring ears and a serrated blade. Made from nodular black chert or milky quartz.

DUVAL - Late Woodland, 2000 - 1000 B. P.

(Also see Bradford, Copena, Jackson and Westo)

G5, $12-$20
FL

G6, $15-$25
Marion Co., FL

G5, $12-$20
Marion Co., FL

Coastal
Plain chert

G7, $15-$30
Jefferson Co., FL

G8, $25-$40
Marion Co., FL

G7, $30-$50
Marion Co., FL

G9, $35-$65
FL

G9, $40-$75
FL

LOCATION: Gulf states. **DESCRIPTION:** A small to medium size, narrow, spike point with shallow side notches, an expanding stem and a straight to concave base. The base can be slight to moderate. Similar to *Bradley Spike* points from Tennessee.

EDGEFIELD SCRAPER - Early Archaic, 10,500 - 8000 B. P.

LOCATION: Southern Atlantic coast states, especially South Carolina, Georgia, Alabama and Florida. **DESCRIPTION:** A medium to large size corner notched point that is asymmetrical. Many are uniface and usually steeply beveled along the diagonal side. The blade on all examples leans heavily to one side. Used as a hafted scraper.

279

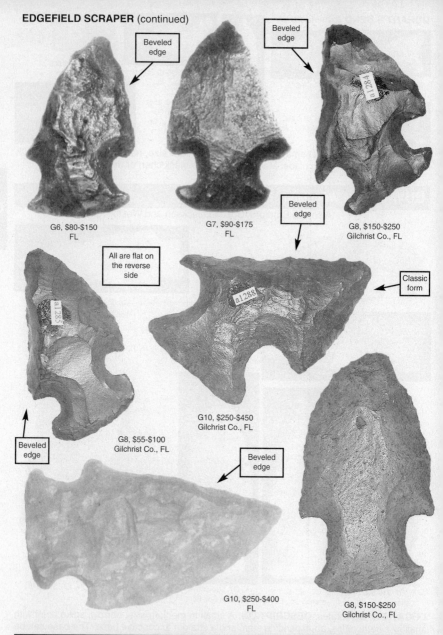

Beveled edge

G6, $80-$150
FL

Beveled edge

G7, $90-$175
FL

Beveled edge

G8, $150-$250
Gilchrist Co., FL

All are flat on the reverse side

Beveled edge

Classic form

Beveled edge

G8, $55-$100
Gilchrist Co., FL

G10, $250-$450
Gilchrist Co., FL

Beveled edge

G10, $250-$400
FL

G8, $150-$250
Gilchrist Co., FL

ELORA - Middle to Late Archaic, 6000 - 3000 B. P.

(Also see Abbey, Alachua, Cottonbridge, Kirk Stemmed, Levy, Newnan, Notchaway, Pickwick, Putnam, Savannah River, Six Mile Creek and South Prong Creek)

LOCATION: Southeastern states. **DESCRIPTION:** A medium size, broad, thick point with tapered shoulders and a short, contracting stem that is sometimes fractured or snapped off. However, some examples have finished bases. Early examples are serrated. **I.D. KEY:** One barb sharper, edgework.

ELORA (continued)

Serrated edge

Serrated edge

G6, $20-$35
FL

Base snapped off

G3, $8-$15
Decatur Co., GA

GC

G5, $8-$15
FL

G7, $30-$50
FL

EVANS - Late Archaic to Woodland, 4000 - 2000 B. P.

(Also see Merkle)

Translucent Coastal Plain chert

G6 $12-$20
Brooks Co., GA

G5, $15-$25
Natchez, MS

G6, $20-$35
Dixie Co., FL

G6, $20-$35
Natchez, MS

281

EVANS (continued)

LOCATION: Southeastern states into southern Alabama and Mississippi. **DESCRIPTION:** A medium to large size stemmed point that is notched on each side somewhere between the point and shoulder. **I.D. KEY:** Side notches with stem.

GILCHRIST - Early Archaic, 10,000 - 7000 B. P.

(Also see Chipola, Beaver Lake and Taylor)

IMPORTANT: THIS POINT SHOWN HALF SIZE

G8, $250-$350
Barbour Co., AL

G7, $20-$35
FL

G6, $15-$30
FL

G7, $15-$25
FL

G8, $80-$150
Marion Co., FL

Clear

Clear

Natural hole in material

G7, $300-$500
FL

Bifurcated, eared stem

G8, $275-$500
FL

G9, $450-$800
FL

GILCHRIST (continued)

LOCATION: Southern Southeastern states. **DESCRIPTION:** A small to medium size, broad point with a short stem that is square, bifurcated or auriculate. Shoulders are weak and can be tapered, horizontal or slightly barbed. The blade can be straight or concave and could be ground. Early forms may be related to *Suwannee*.

GREENBRIAR   (See Osceola Greenbriar)

HAMILTON - Early Archaic, 8000 - 5000 B. P.

(Also see Columbia, Kirk, Savannah River, Seminole and Thonotosassa)

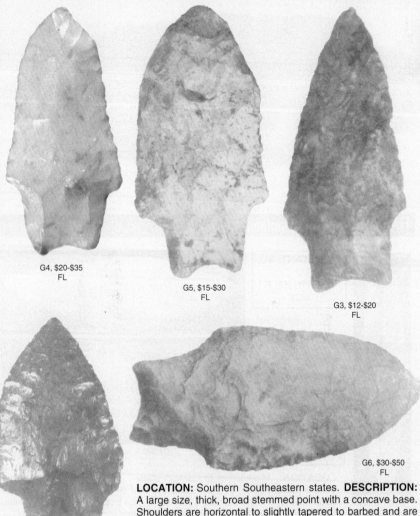

G4, $20-$35
FL

G5, $15-$30
FL

G3, $12-$20
FL

G6, $30-$50
FL

G6, $20-$35
FL

LOCATION: Southern Southeastern states. **DESCRIPTION:** A large size, thick, broad stemmed point with a concave base. Shoulders are horizontal to slightly tapered to barbed and are weaker than *Savannah River* points. Basal corners are slightly rounded **I.D. KEY:** Broad shoulders, basal form; i.e. short, wide tangs with a concave base. Confused with *Savannah Rivers* which have straight to concave bases, stronger shoulders and are not as old. Related to *Arredondo* points.

283

G8, $35-$60
FL

G7, $200-$350
FL

HARAHEY - Mississippian, 700 - 350 B. P.

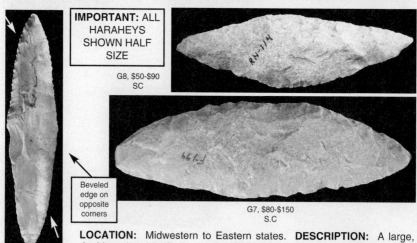

IMPORTANT: ALL HARAHEYS SHOWN HALF SIZE

G8, $50-$90
SC

G7, $80-$150
S.C

Beveled edge on opposite corners

G8, $175-$350
Early Co., GA

LOCATION: Midwestern to Eastern states. **DESCRIPTION:** A large, double pointed knife that is usually beveled on one or all four sides of each face. The cross section is rhomboid. The true buffalo skinning knife. **I.D. KEY:** Two and four beveled double pointed form.

HARDAWAY - Early Archaic, 9500 - 8000 B. P.

(Also see Chipola, Santa Fe, Tallahassee and Union Side Notched)

HARDAWAY (continued)

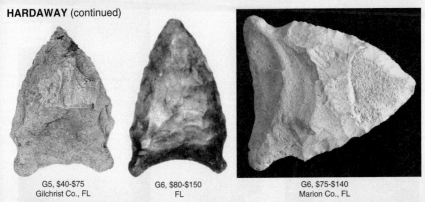

G5, $40-$75
Gilchrist Co., FL

G6, $80-$150
FL

G6, $75-$140
Marion Co., FL

LOCATION: The Carolinas into Florida. **DESCRIPTION:** A small to medium size point with shallow side notches and expanding auricles forming a wide, deeply concave base. Ears and base are usually heavily ground. This type evolved from the *Dalton* point. **I.D. KEY:** Heavy grinding in shoulders, paleo flaking.

HARDEE BEVELED - Middle Archaic, 5500 - 3000 B. P.

(Also see Alachua, Levy, Marion and Putnam)

Fine serrations

Fine serrations

Classic example

G9, $80-$150
Hillsborough Co., FL

G9, $125-$200
Pasco Co., FL

G6, $30-$50
FL

G10, $125-$200
FL

G8, $35-$65
FL

G7, $20-$35
FL

285

HARDEE BEVELED (continued)

Beveled edge

G7, $150-$250
FL.

G9, $55-$100
FL

Fine serrations

G9, $125-$200
FL

Fine serrations

G7, $80-$150
FL

Fine serrations

Talahatta quartzite

G10, $80-$150
FL

G9, $40-$70
FL

G10, $250-$450
Sou. AL

HARDEE BEVELED (continued)

LOCATION: Southern Southeastern states. **DESCRIPTION:** A small to medium size stemmed point that occurs in two forms. One has a distinct bevel on one side of each face. The other has the typical bifacial beveling. Shoulders are tapered to horizontal and are sharp. This type resembles the other Florida Archaic stemmed points (see above) except for the bevel and may be their ancestor. Found mostly in Tampa Bay vicinity. **I.D. KEY:** Beveling and sharp shoulders.

HARDIN - Early Archaic, 9000 - 6000 B. P.

(Also see Cypress Creek, Kirk Corner Notched, Lafayette and Ocala)

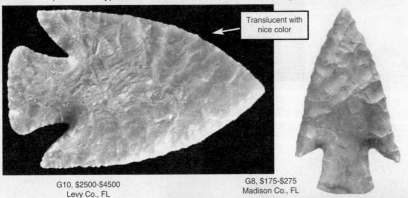

Translucent with nice color

G10, $2500-$4500
Levy Co., FL

G8, $175-$275
Madison Co., FL

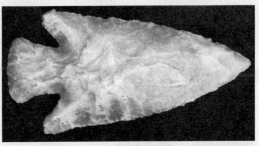

LOCATION: Midwestern to Eastern states. **DESCRIPTION:** A large, well made triangular barbed point with an expanded base that is usually ground. Resharpened examples have one beveled edge on each face. This type is believed to have evolved from the *Scottsbluff* type. **I.D. KEY:** Notches and stem form.

G8, $250-$400
Tampa, FL

HERNANDO - Late Archaic, 4000 - 2500 B. P.

(Also see Citrus and Culbreath)

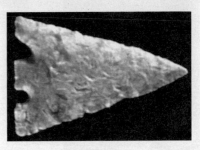

G10, $125-$250
FL

G9, $125-$250
Marion Co., FL

287

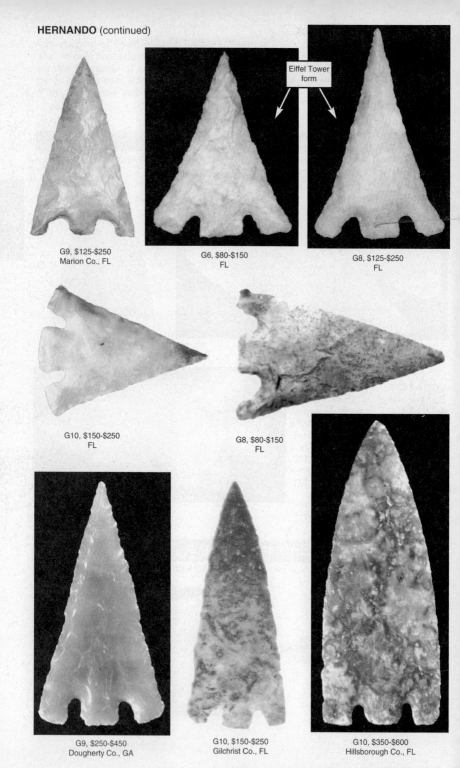

Eiffel Tower form

G9, $125-$250
Marion Co., FL

G6, $80-$150
FL

G8, $125-$250
FL

G10, $150-$250
FL

G8, $80-$150
FL

G9, $250-$450
Dougherty Co., GA

G10, $150-$250
Gilchrist Co., FL

G10, $350-$600
Hillsborough Co., FL

HERNANDO (continued)

LOCATION: Georgia, Alabama and Florida. **DESCRIPTION:** A medium to large size, basal notched, triangular point with wide flaring tangs that may extend beyond the base. Side edges are straight to concave. Similar in outline only to the much earlier *Eva* type. Has been found in same layer with a form (Copena?) resembling *Safety Harbor* points. **I.D. KEY:** Narrow stem.

HILLSBOROUGH - Middle Archaic, 5500 - 3000 B. P.

(Also see Marion and Newnan)

GC

G9, $125-$200
FL

G10, $175-$300
Marion Co., FL

G10, $275-$500
Hillsborough Co., FL

G8, $150-$250
FL

G9, $350-$600
FL

LOCATION: Florida only. **DESCRIPTION:** A medium to large size, broad, triangular point with a small contracting base. Shoulders are barbed and can expand beyond the base. **I.D. KEY:** Small base, barbed shoulders. **CAUTION:** Some very well made reproductions of this type are beging sold especially in states north of Floriida.

G10, $550-$1000
FL

289

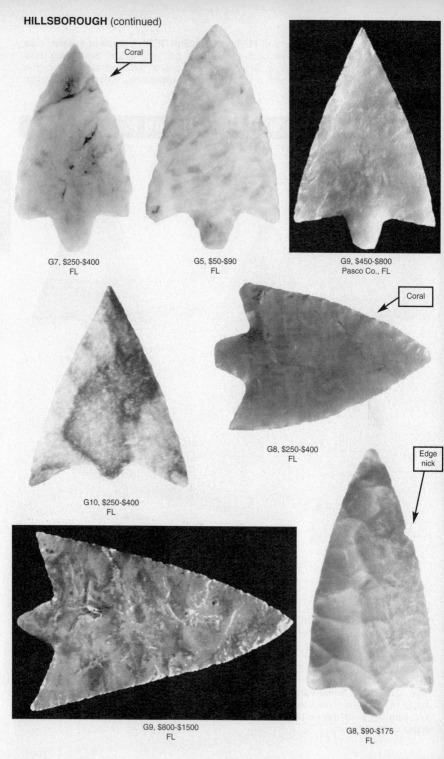

HILLSBOROUGH (continued)

Coral

G7, $250-$400
FL

G5, $50-$90
FL

G9, $450-$800
Pasco Co., FL

Coral

G8, $250-$400
FL

G10, $250-$400
FL

Edge nick

G9, $800-$1500
FL

G8, $90-$175
FL

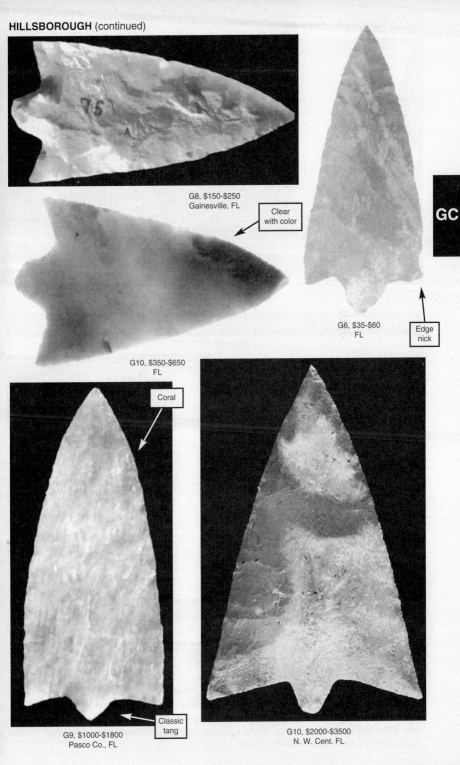

GC

G8, $150-$250
Gainesville, FL

Clear with color

G6, $35-$60
FL

Edge nick

G10, $350-$650
FL

Coral

G9, $1000-$1800
Pasco Co., FL

Classic tang

G10, $2000-$3500
N. W. Cent. FL

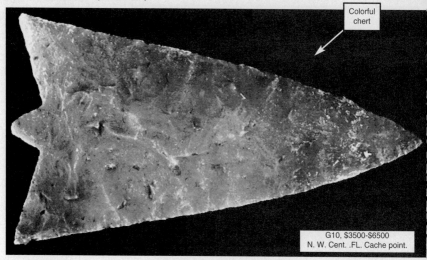

Colorful chert

G10, $3500-$6500
N. W. Cent. .FL. Cache point.

ICHETUCKNEE - Mississippian to Historic, 700 - 200 B. P.
(Also see Pinellas)

G7, $50-$75
Marion Co., FL

G6, $25-$40
FL

Color

LOCATION: Southeastern states. **DESCRIPTION:** A small to medium size, thin, narrow, lanceolate point with usually a straight base. Flaking quality is excellent. This point is called *Guntersville* to the north. **I.D. KEY:** Narrowness and blade expansion; blade edges curve inward at base.

G9, $45-$85
Lafayette Co., FL

JACKSON - Late Woodland to Mississippian, 2000 - 700 B. P.
(Also see Duval)

G10, $20-$35
FL

G10, $20-$35
FL

LOCATION: Coastal states. **DESCRIPTION:** A small size, thick, narrow, triangular point with wide, shallow side notches. Some examples have an unfinished rind or base. Called *Swan Lake* in upper Southeastern states

JACKSON (continued)

G5, $8-$15
FL.

KASKASKIA POINT (See Trade Points)

KIRK CORNER NOTCHED - Early to Middle Archaic, 9000 - 6000 B. P.

(Also see Bolen, Hardin, Lafayette and Ocala)

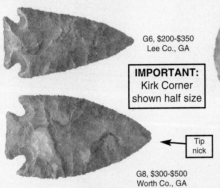

G6, $200-$350
Lee Co., GA

IMPORTANT:
Kirk Corner
shown half size

G5, $125-$200
Chattahoochee Co., GA

Tip
nick

G8, $300-$500
Worth Co., GA

LOCATION: Southeastern states. **DESCRIPTION:** A medium to large size, corner notched point. Blade edges can be convex to recurved and are finely serrated on many examples. The base can be concave, convex, straight or auriculate. **I.D. KEY:** Secondary edgework.

KIRK STEMMED - Early to Middle Archaic, 9000 - 6000 B. P.

(Also see Abbey, Arredondo, Boggy Branch, Bolen, Elora, Hamilton and Six Mile Creek)

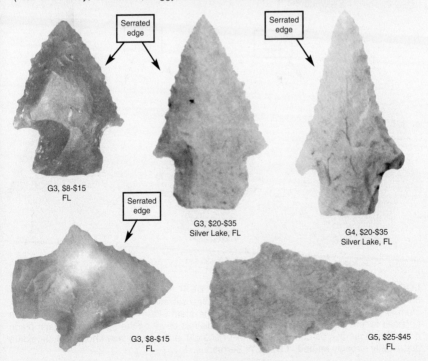

Serrated
edge

Serrated
edge

G3, $8-$15
FL

Serrated
edge

G3, $20-$35
Silver Lake, FL

G4, $20-$35
Silver Lake, FL

G3, $8-$15
FL

G5, $25-$45
FL

293

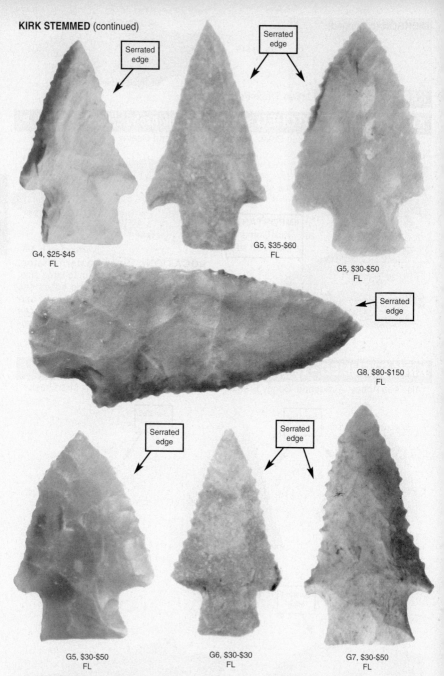

Serrated edge

Serrated edge

G4, $25-$45
FL

G5, $35-$60
FL

G5, $30-$50
FL

Serrated edge

G8, $80-$150
FL

Serrated edge

Serrated edge

G5, $30-$50
FL

G6, $30-$30
FL

G7, $30-$50
FL

LOCATION: Eastern to Gulf Coastal states. **DESCRIPTION:** A medium to large size, barbed, stemmed point with deep notches or fine serrations along the blade edges. The stem is parallel, contracting or expanding. The stem sides may be steeply beveled on opposite faces. Some examples also have a distinct bevel on the right side of each blade edge. The base can be concave, convex or straight, and can be very short. The shoulders are usually strongly barbed. **I.D. KEY:** Serrations.

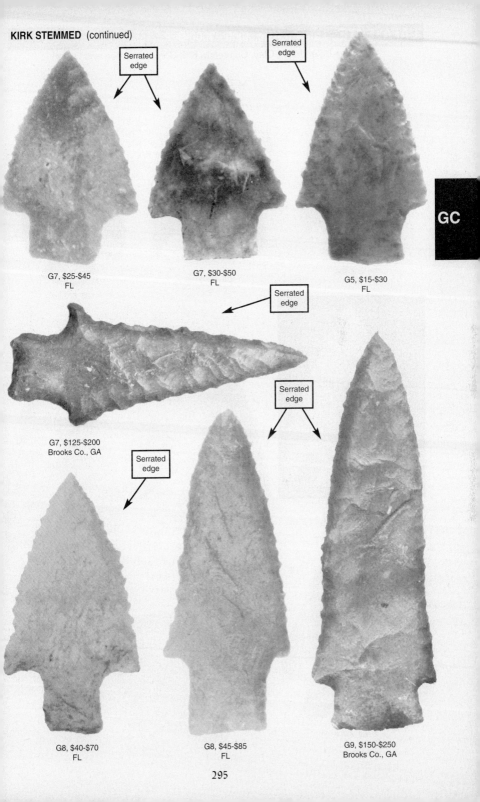

KIRK STEMMED (continued)

Serrated edge

Serrated edge

GC

G7, $25-$45
FL

G7, $30-$50
FL

G5, $15-$30
FL

Serrated edge

Serrated edge

G7, $125-$200
Brooks Co., GA

Serrated edge

G8, $40-$70
FL

G8, $45-$85
FL

G9, $150-$250
Brooks Co., GA

(Also see Bolen Plain, Clay, Culbreath, Kirk Corner Notched and Ocala)

G6, $35-$60
FL

G8, $55-$100
FL

G5, $25-$40
FL

G8, $80-$150
Marion Co., FL

G10, $150-$250
FL

G7, $65-$125
FL

G7, $55-$100
FL

G9, $80-$150
FL

LAFAYETTE (continued)

Tip
nick

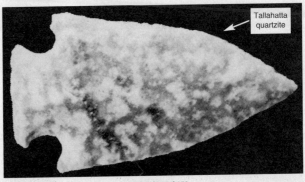

Tallahatta
quartzite

G10, $250-$450
Sou. AL

GC

LOCATION: Southern to Southeastern states. **DESCRIPTION:** A medium size, broad, corner-notched point with a straight to concave base. Tangs and basal corners are more rounded than pointed. Related to *Clay* points. Previously shown (in error) as *Ocala* points. Tangs expand.

G5, $18-$30
FL

G9, $170-$325
Marion Co., FL

G6, $350-$650
FL

297

LEDBETTER - Mid to late Archaic, 6,000 - 3500 B. P.

(Also see Pickwick and Levy)

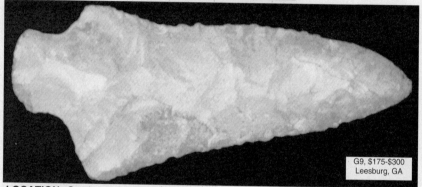

Note asymmetrical blade

G7, $80-$150
Marion Co., FL

G9, $175-$300
Leesburg, GA

LOCATION: Southeastern into the Gulf states. **DESCRIPTION:** A medium to large size *Pickwick* point that is asymmetrical with one side of the blade curving to the tip more than the other. Bases are contracting to expanding. Blade edges can be serrated. **I.D. KEY:** Asymmetrical blade.

LEON - Woodland - Mississippian, 1500 - 1000 B. P.

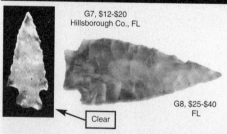

G7, $12-$20
Hillsborough Co., FL

G8, $25-$40
FL

Clear

LOCATION: Southern to Southeastern states. **DESCRIPTION:** A small size cone notched point. Blade edges are straight to convex. Bases expand with sharp to rounded basal corners. **I.D. KEY:** Size and corner notching.

LEVY - Late Archaic, 5000 - 3000 B. P.

(Also see Abbey, Alachua, Cypress Creek, Elora, Hardee Beveled, Ledbetter, Marion, Newnan, Oauchita, Putnam, Savannah River and Sumter)

LOCATION: Southern to Southeastern states. **DESCRIPTION:** A medium size, broad, contracted stemmed point with wide, tapered to slightly barbed shoulders. May have evolved from the earlier *Newnan* form. **I.D. KEY:** Edgework and one ear is stronger. *Levy* tangs have concave edges connecting base and tang corners.

298

LEVY (continued)

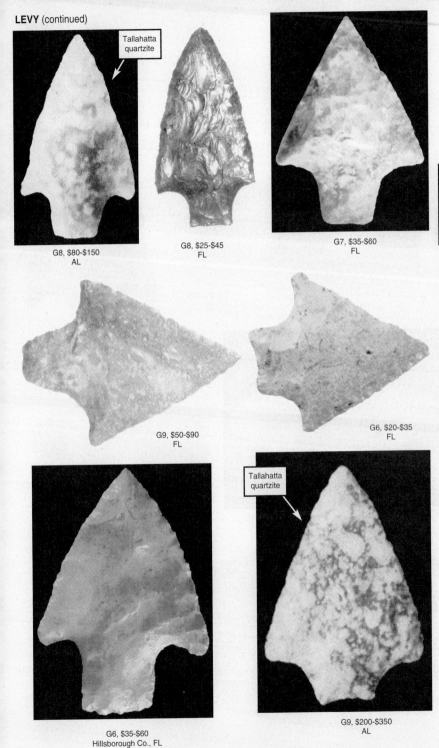

Tallahatta quartzite

G8, $80-$150
AL

G8, $25-$45
FL

G7, $35-$60
FL

GC

G9, $50-$90
FL

G6, $20-$35
FL

G6, $35-$60
Hillsborough Co., FL

Tallahatta quartzite

G9, $200-$350
AL

299

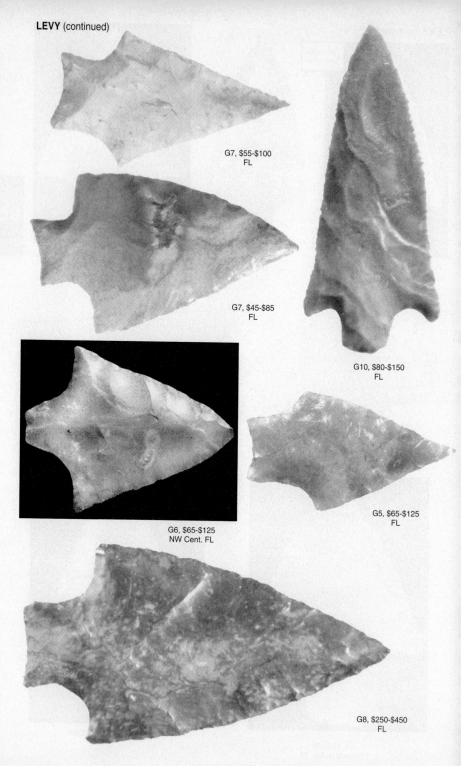

G7, $55-$100
FL

G7, $45-$85
FL

G10, $80-$150
FL

G6, $65-$125
NW Cent. FL

G5, $65-$125
FL

G8, $250-$450
FL

GC

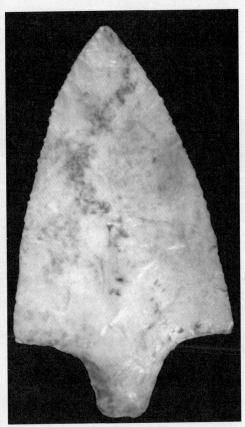

G10, $500-$900
FL

G10, $400-$750
Gilchrist Co., FL

LOST LAKE - Early Archaic, 9000 - 6000 B. P.
(Also see Bolen Beveled, Kirk Corner Notched)

Translucent

G10, $1200-$2000
Suwannee Co., FL

G8, $350-$600
Baker Co., GA

G8, $500-$800
Dougherty Co., GA

G9, $1200-$2000
Taylor Co., FL

IMPORTANT:
Lost Lakes are
all shown half
size

301

LOST LAKE (continued)

Fractured base

IMPORTANT:
These two Lost Lakes are shown half size

G10, $2500-$4000
Gilchrist Co., FL

G10, $2700-$5000
Taylor Co., FL

Beveled edge

G10, $800-$1500
Gilchrist Co., FL

Ear nick

Beveled edge

G8, $1200-$2000
Gilchrist Co., FL

LOCATION: Southeastern states. **DESCRIPTION:** A medium to large size, broad, corner notched point that is beveled on one side of each face. The beveling continues when resharpened which created a flat rhomboid cross section. Also known as Deep Notch. **I.D. KEY:** Notching, secondary edgework is always opposite creating at least slight beveling.

MARIANNA - Transitional Paleo, 10,000 - 8500 B. P.

(Also see Conerly)

LOCATION: Southern to Southeastern states. **DESCRIPTION:** A rare type. A medium size lanceolate point with a constricted, concave base. Look for parallel to oblique flaking.

G5, $8-$15
FL

(Also see Adena, Alachua, Cottonbridge, Cypress Creek, Hardee Beveled, Levy, Morrow Mountain, Newnan, Pickwick and Putnam)

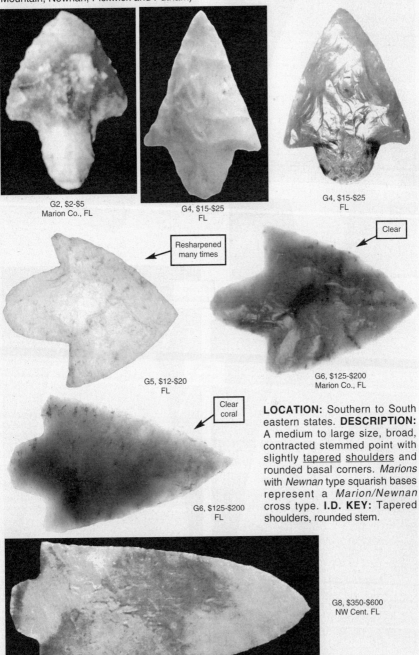

GC

G2, $2-$5
Marion Co., FL

G4, $15-$25
FL

G4, $15-$25
FL

Resharpened many times

Clear

G5, $12-$20
FL

G6, $125-$200
Marion Co., FL

Clear coral

G6, $125-$200
FL

LOCATION: Southern to South eastern states. **DESCRIPTION:** A medium to large size, broad, contracted stemmed point with slightly <u>tapered</u> <u>shoulders</u> and rounded basal corners. *Marions* with *Newnan* type squarish bases represent a *Marion/Newnan* cross type. **I.D. KEY:** Tapered shoulders, rounded stem.

G8, $350-$600
NW Cent. FL

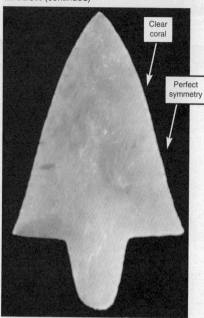

Clear coral

Perfect symmetry

G10, $1500-$2500
Hillsborough Co., FL

G8, $150-$250
Marion Co., FL

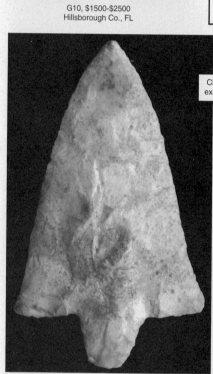

G8, $275-$500
FL

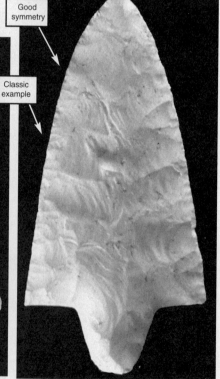

Good symmetry

Classic example

G9, $1000-$1800
Hillsborough Co., FL

Colorful coral

G9, $800-$1500
FL

GC

G10 $1200-$2000
Hillsborough Co., FL

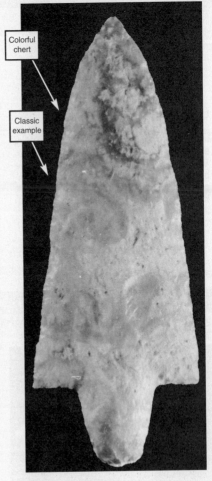

Colorful chert

Classic example

G10, $2000-$3500
Hillsborough Co., FL

MORROW MOUNTAIN - Middle Archaic, 7000 - 5000 B. P.

(Also see Bascom, Cypress Creek, Eva, Marion, Putnam and Thonotosassa)

Tallahatta quartzite

G4, $15-$30
Sou. AL

G7, $40-$80
Allendale Co., SC

Tallahatta quartzite

LOCATION: Midwestern to Southeastern states. **DESCRIPTION:** A medium to large size, triangular point with a very short contracting to rounded stem. Shoulders are usually weak, but can be barbed. The blade edges on some examples are serrated with needle points. **I.D. KEY:** Contracted base and Archaic parallel flaking.

G6, $250-$400
Sou. AL

NEWNAN - Middle Archaic, 7000 - 3000 B. P.

(Also see Adena, Alachua, Cypress Creek, Hardee Beveled, Hillsborough, Levy, Marion, Morrow Mountain, Oauchita and Putnam)

G4 $50-$90
Alachua Co., FL

LOCATION: Southern Southeastern states. **DESCRIPTION:** A medium to large size, broad, stemmed point with a short to long contracting base. Shoulders form a straight line and are horizontal to downward and outward sloping. Stems have contracted, straight sides and a straight to rounded base. *Newnans* with *Marion*-type rounded bases represent a *Newnan/Marion* cross type and would fall under *Marion* if the shoulders slope up.

306

NEWNAN (continued)

G10, $250-$450
Sou. AL

Tallahatta
quartzite

Agatized
coral

GC

G8, $350-$600
FL

Agatized
coral

G7, $250-$450
Marion Co., FL

G8, $400-$750
N.W. Cent. FL

G8, $150-$250
FL

G10, $650-$1200
Hillsborough Co., FL

G5, $90-$175
S. AL

Tallahatta
quartzite

G5, $55-$100
Marion Co., FL

G8, $200-$350
Hillsborough Co., FL

G9, $550-$1000
FL

G9, $650-$1200
FL

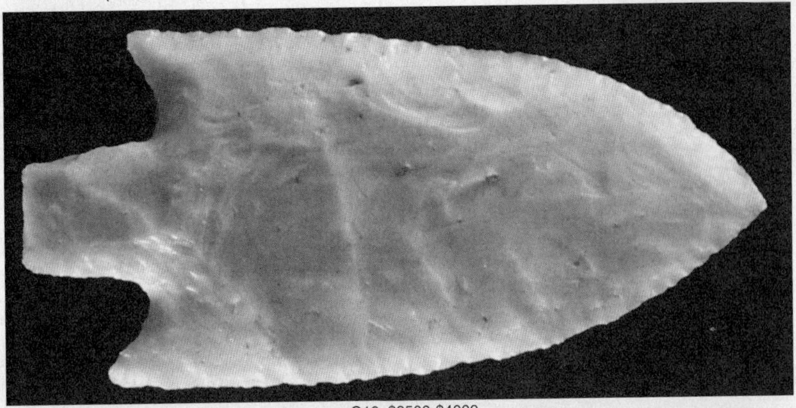

GC

G10, $2500-$4000
Flagler Co., FL

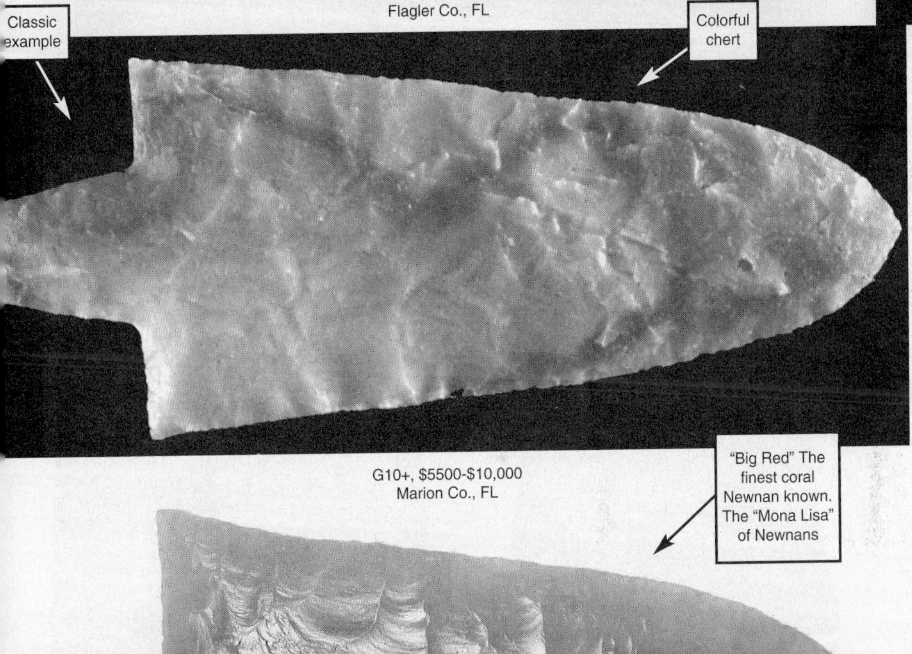

Classic example

Colorful chert

G10+, $5500-$10,000
Marion Co., FL

"Big Red" The finest coral Newnan known. The "Mona Lisa" of Newnans

Translucent red coral.

G10+, $12,000-$20,000
Hillsborough Co., FL

NEWNAN (continued)

Resharpened anciently

Classic example. Good symmetry

G9, $2500-$4000
Dixie Co., FL

G10+, $7000-$12,000
Dixie Co., FL

NOTCHAWAY (Same as Wacissa; see Wacissa)

OAUCHITA - Woodland, 3000 - 1500 B. P.

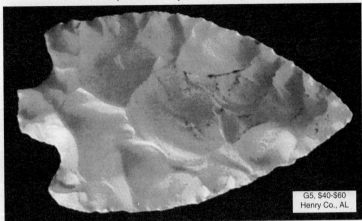

(Also see Levy and Newnan)

G5, $40-$60
Henry Co., AL

LOCATION: Southern Southeastern states. **DESCRIPTION:** A medium to large size, broad, point with a short contracted stem and drooping shoulders.

OCALA - Woodland, 2500 - 1500 B. P.

(Also see Bolen, Clay, Culbreath, Kirk Corner Notched & Lafayette)

Broken & glued

G7, $250-$400
Marion Co., AL

LOCATION: Gulf Coastal states. **DESCRIPTION:** A medium to large size broad corner-notched point with a straight to convex base. Tangs and basal corners are sharp to rounded. Tangs curve inward. Rare in Florida. According to Bullen this type is larger and better crafted than *Bolens* or *Lafayettes* and dates to 2500 B.P. **I.D. KEY:** Size and corner notching.

GC

G8, $35-$65
FL

O'LENO - Woodland, 2000 - 800 B. P.

(Also see Pinellas, Tampa and Yadkin)

RALPH ALLEN
AL: HENRY

G7, $20-$35
Henry Co., AL

G6, $15-$25
Marion Co., FL

G65, $15-$25
N.W. FL

LOCATION: Southern Southeastern states. **DESCRIPTION:** A medium size, broad, triangle point with a straight to slightly concave base.

OSCEOLA-GREENBRIAR - Early Archaic, 9500 - 6000 B. P.

(Also see Bolen)

G4, $12-$20, type II
FL

G2, $12-$20, type II
FL

G7, $80-$150, type II
FL

G7, $80-$150, type II
Marion Co., FL

LOCATION: Gulf Coastal states. **DESCRIPTION:** A medium to large size, broad, side-notched point with two base variations. The base is either concave or has two shallow notches creating a high point in the center. Bases and notches are usually ground. This type is found in the same layer with *Bolen* points in Florida.

G5, $20-$35, type II
FL

G7, $55-$100, type II
FL

G7, $35-$60, type II
FL

GC

G6, $30-$50, type II
FL

G6, $55-$100, type II
FL

G6, $40-$75, type II
Marion Co., FL

G5, $20-$35, type II
FL

G8, $90-$175, type I
FL

G7, $55-$100, type I
FL

G7, $30-$50, type II
FL

G4, $30-$50, type II
FL

G7, $50-$90, type II
FL

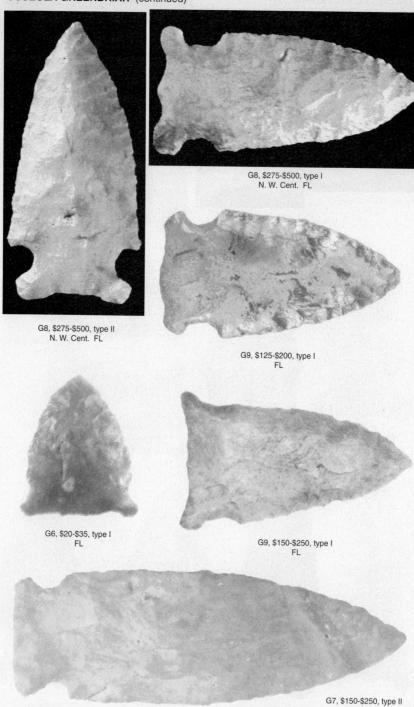

G8, $275-$500, type I
N. W. Cent. FL

G8, $275-$500, type II
N. W. Cent. FL

G9, $125-$200, type I
FL

G6, $20-$35, type I
FL

G9, $150-$250, type I
FL

G7, $150-$250, type II
FL

PALEO KNIFE - Paleo, 10,000 B. P.
(Also see Scraper)

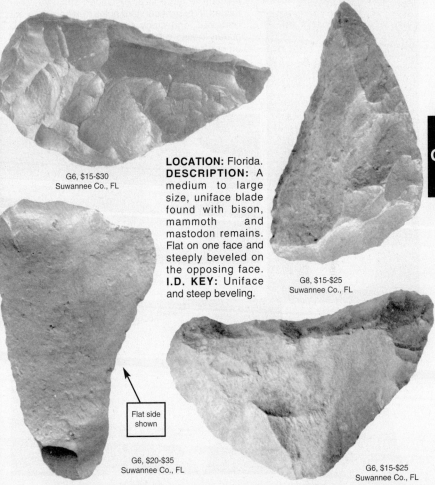

G6, $15-$30
Suwannee Co., FL

LOCATION: Florida.
DESCRIPTION: A medium to large size, uniface blade found with bison, mammoth and mastodon remains. Flat on one face and steeply beveled on the opposing face.
I.D. KEY: Uniface and steep beveling.

G8, $15-$25
Suwannee Co., FL

Flat side shown

G6, $20-$35
Suwannee Co., FL

G6, $15-$25
Suwannee Co., FL

PICKWICK - Middle to Late Archaic, 6000 - 3500 B. P.
(Also see Elora, Ledbetter and Savannah River)

G8, $80-$150
FL

315

PICKWICK (continued)

LOCATION: Found North of the Suwannee River into Georgia and Alabama. **DESCRIPTION:** A medium to large size, expanded shoulder, contracted to expanded stem point. Blade edges are recurved, and many examples show fine secondary flaking with serrations. Some are beveled on one side of each face. The bevel is steep and shallow. Shoulders are horizontal, tapered or barbed and form sharp angles. Some stems are snapped off or may show original rind.

Tallahatta quartzite

G9, $275-$500
Sou. AL

G6, $80-$150
Marion Co., FL

Tallahatta quartzite

G5, $30-$50
Sou. AL

Tallahatta quartzite

G8, $165-$300
FL

G5, $35-$60
Sou. AL

Tallahatta quartzite

GC

G3, $15-$30
FL

Restored tip

Agate

G9, $250-$450
Sou. AL

Fine secondary retouch

G9, $600-$1000
Madison Co., FL

G3, $80-$150
Choctaw, AL

317

PINELLAS - Mississippian, 800 - 400 B. P.

(Also see O'Leno, Safety Harbor, Tallahassee and Yadkin)

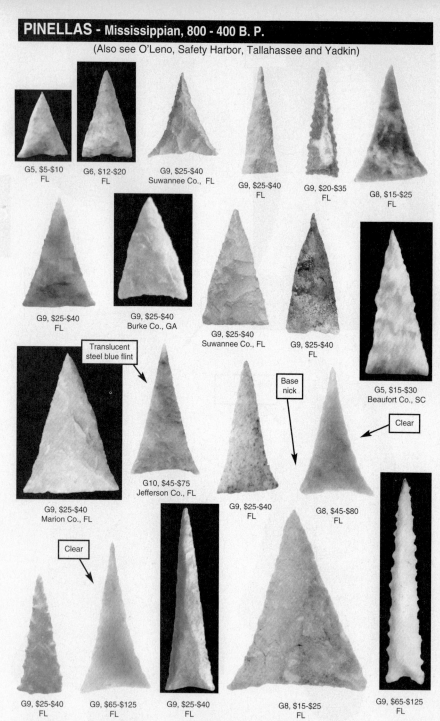

G5, $5-$10
FL

G6, $12-$20
FL

G9, $25-$40
Suwannee Co., FL

G9, $25-$40
FL

G9, $20-$35
FL

G8, $15-$25
FL

G9, $25-$40
FL

G9, $25-$40
Burke Co., GA

G9, $25-$40
Suwannee Co., FL

G9, $25-$40
FL

G5, $15-$30
Beaufort Co., SC

Translucent
steel blue flint

Base
nick

Clear

G10, $45-$75
Jefferson Co., FL

G9, $25-$40
Marion Co., FL

G9, $25-$40
FL

G8, $45-$80
FL

Clear

G9, $25-$40
FL

G9, $65-$125
FL

G9, $25-$40
FL

G8, $15-$25
FL

G9, $65-$125
FL

LOCATION: Gulf Coastal states. **DESCRIPTION:** A small, narrow, thick to thin, triangular point with a straight to slightly concave base. Blade edges can be serrated.

PUTNAM - Late Archaic, 5000 - 3000 B. P.

(Also see Cypress Creek, Hardee Beveled, Levy, Marion, Morrow Mountain, Newnan, Sumter and Thonotosassa)

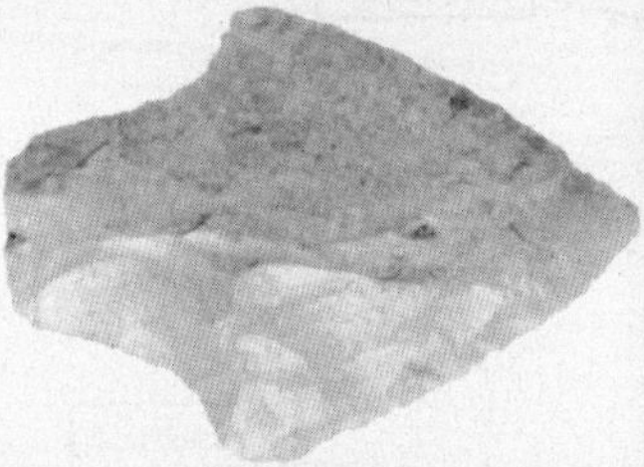

G2, $5-$10
FL

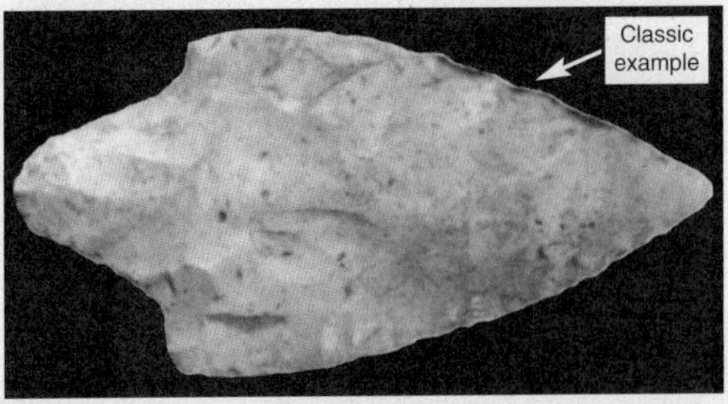

Classic
example

G7, $25-$40
FL

GC

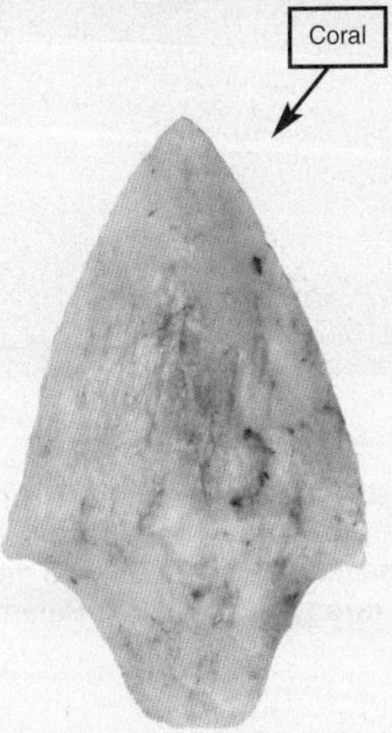

Coral

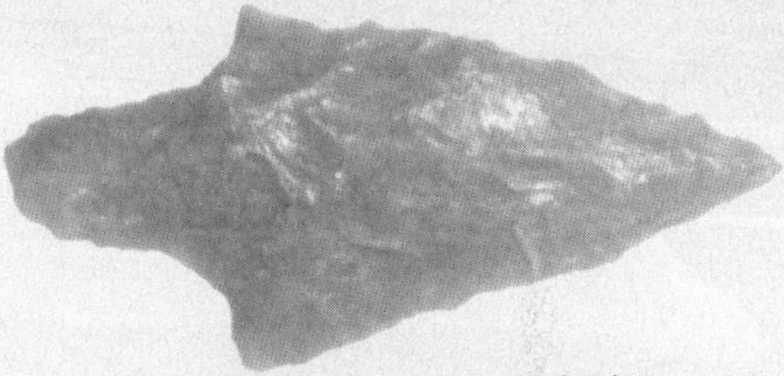

G5, $25-$40
FL

G5, $15-$25
FL

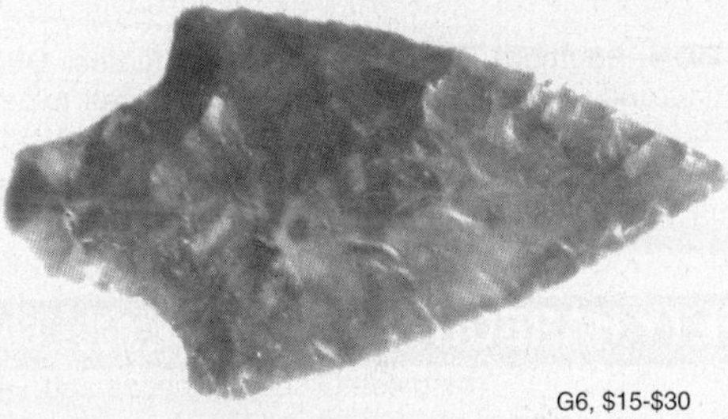

G6, $15-$30
FL

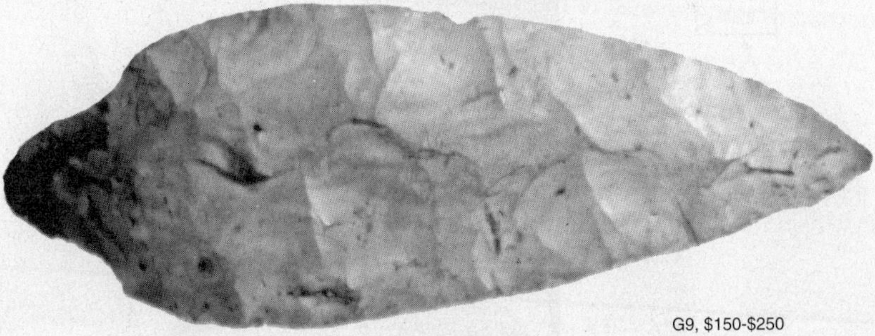

G9, $150-$250
FL

LOCATION: Southern Southeastern states. **DESCRIPTION:** A medium to large size, broad, contracted stemmed point with rounded shoulders. This type is usually a resharpened *Thonotosassa*. The stem is fairly long with a convex base. The shoulders are tapered and can be rounded. Believed to have evolved from the Marion type. **I.D. KEY:** Weak shoulders, rounded tangs formed by continuous recurved edges.

REDSTONE - Paleo, 13,500 - 11,000 B. P.

(Also see Clovis, Simpson and Suwannee)

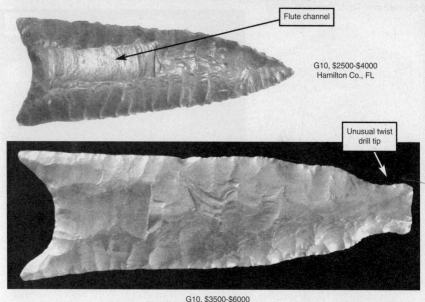

Flute channel

G10, $2500-$4000
Hamilton Co., FL

Unusual twist
drill tip

G10, $3500-$6000
Jackson Co., FL

LOCATION: Southern Southeastern to gulf states. **DESCRIPTION:** A medium to large size, thin auriculate fluted point with convex sides expanding to a wide, deeply concave base. The hafting area is ground. This point is widest at the base. Fluting can extend most of the way down each face. Multiple flutes are usual. A very rare type. **I.D. KEY:** Batan or billet fluted, edgework on the hafting area.

SAFETY HARBOR - Mississippian, 800 - 600 B. P.

(Also see O'Leno, Pinellas and Tallahassee)

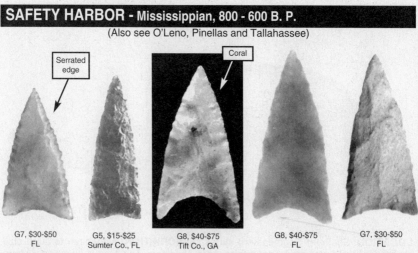

Serrated
edge

Coral

| G7, $30-$50 FL | G5, $15-$25 Sumter Co., FL | G8, $40-$75 Tift Co., GA | G8, $40-$75 FL | G7, $30-$50 FL |

LOCATION: Gulf Coastal states. Named in the 1960s by Jarl Malwin. **DESCRIPTION:** A medium size, narrow, thin, triangular point with a concave base. Basal corners are sharp. Blade edges can be serrated. These have been confused with *Santa Fe* and *Tallahassee* points which are much older. Basal edges of *Safety Harbor* points are not ground.

SAFETY HARBOR (continued)

G6, $20-$35
FL

G3, $12-$20
FL

G6, $30-$50
FL

Serrated edge

G9, $90-$175
Sumter Co., FL

GC

G9, $65-$125
FL

G10, $150-$275
Sumter Co., FL

SANTA FE - Early Archaic 9500 - 8000 B.P
(Also see Beaver Lake, Hardaway, Safety Harbor and Tallahassee)

G7, $55-$100
FL

G7, $55-$100
Beaufort Co., SC

G9, $80-$150
FL.

G7, $55-$100
FL

G8, $90-$175
FL

G7, $55-$100
FL

G8, $175-$300
FL

SANTA FE (continued)

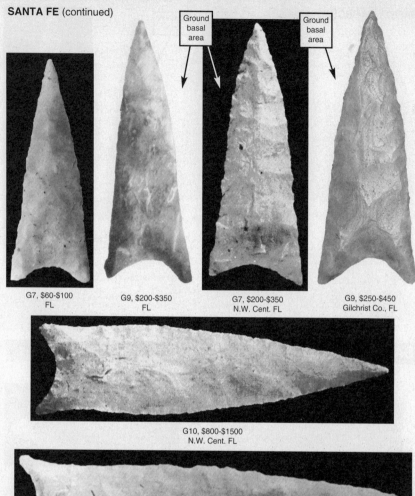

Ground basal area

Ground basal area

G7, $60-$100
FL

G9, $200-$350
FL

G7, $200-$350
N.W. Cent. FL

G9, $250-$450
Gilchrist Co., FL

G10, $800-$1500
N.W. Cent. FL

G10, $1200-$2200
N.W. Cent. FL

LOCATION: Gulf Coastal states. **DESCRIPTION:** A medium to large size auriculate point with expanding auricules and a concave base. Hafting area is not well defined and is always ground. Blade edges are not serrated as in *Tallahassee*. A *Dalton* culture variant. See Ripley Bullen (1975). **Note:** Bullen and the first Florida archaeologists classified this type as Early Archaic. Then, point type books published later (by authors who were not professional archaeologists) retained the names of these Dalton variants and applied them to similar, but much later, look-alike forms such as *Copena, Safety Harbor* and *Yadkin*. These later forms are generally smaller, long and narrow and unground. The *Dalton* forms are usually larger, wider and most are ground on the base. Our advisors are split on this issue, but we believe that Bullen had it right and strongly advise our readers to refer to his reference and use his recommendations for Florida point classifications. **I.D. KEY:** True Santa Fe points are always ground and have *Dalton* flaking.

SARASOTA - Woodland, 3000 - 1500 B. P.

(Also see Bradford, Columbia, Ledbetter and Pickwick)

LOCATION: Southern Southeastern states. **DESCRIPTION:** A medium to large size stemmed point with horizontal shoulders. The stem can be parallel sided to slightly expanding or contracting. Blade edges are slightly convex to recurved. Similar to the northern *Pickwick* type.

G5, $12-$20
FL

GC

G6, $45-$80
FL

SAVANNAH RIVER - Middle Archaic to Woodland, 5000 - 2000 B. P.

(Also see Abbey, Arredondo, Bascom, Elora, Hamilton, Kirk, Levy, Seminole, Thonotosassa and Wacissa)

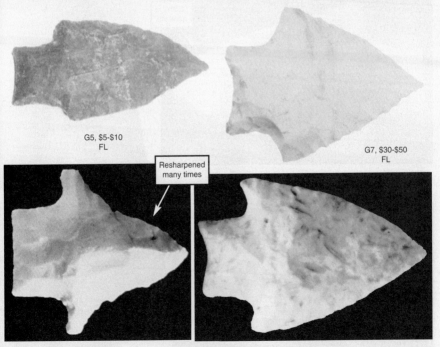

G5, $5-$10
FL

G7, $30-$50
FL

Resharpened many times

G4, $12-$20
Burke Co., GA

G9, $35-$65
FL

Tallahatta quartzite

G5, $35-$60
Sou. AL

G7, $40-$75
Marion Co., FL

G8, $65-$125
Dodge Co., GA

Tallahatta quartzite

G8, $125-$200
Sou. AL

Tallahatta quartzite

G7, $55-$100
Sou. AL

G5, $35-$60
FL

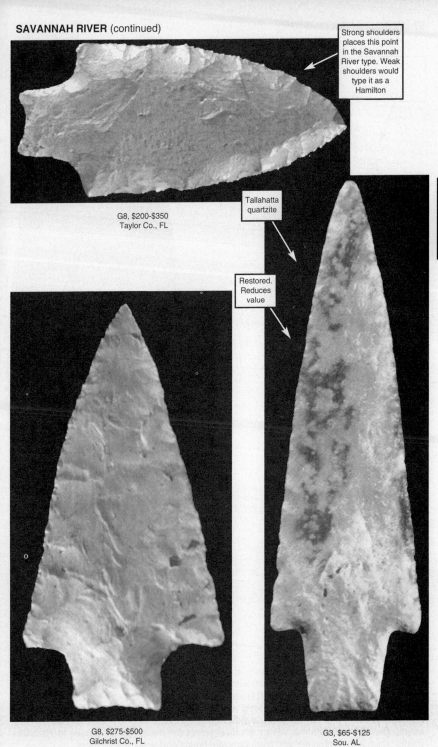

Strong shoulders places this point in the Savannah River type. Weak shoulders would type it as a Hamilton

GC

Tallahatta quartzite

Restored. Reduces value

G8, $200-$350
Taylor Co., FL

G8, $275-$500
Gilchrist Co., FL

G3, $65-$125
Sou. AL

Found with the cache of coastal SC Bascom points

Classic form

G9, $650-$1200
Coastal SC

G10, $1200-$2200
Gilchrist Co., FL

LOCATION: Southeastern to Eastern states. **DESCRIPTION:** A medium to large size, straight to contracting stemmed point with a straight to concave base. The shoulders are tapered to square and are strong. The stems are narrow to broad. Believed to be related to the earlier *Stanly* point. The preform is called *Bascom*. A large cache of *Bascom* and *Savannah River* points were found together in South Carolina. **KEY:** Stems have straight bases, shoulders are strong, *Savannah River* points are usually large. Similar to *Hamilton* points which are much older and have concave bases and weaker shoulders.

SCRAPER - Late Archaic, 5000 - 3500 B. P.

(Also see Abbey, Elora, Hamilton, Levy, Paleo Knife, Savannah River and Wacissa)

G6, $5-$10
Marion Co., FL

G8, $10-$20
Marion Co., FL

Steeply
beveled
edge

GC

LOCATION: Paleo to early Archaic sites throughout North America. **DESCRIPTION:** Thumb, Duckbill and Turtleback forms are small to medium size, thick, ovoid shaped, uniface, scraping tools that are steeply beveled, especially at the broadest end. Side scrapers are long hand-held uniface flakes with beveling on all blade edges of one face. Scraping was done primarily from the sides of these blades.

SEMINOLE - Late Archaic, 5000 - 3500 B. P.

(Also see Abbey, Elora, Hamilton, Levy, Savannah River and Wacissa)

G8, $80-$150
Burke Co., GA

G7, $40-$75
Decatur Co., GA

LOCATION: Gulf Coastal states. **DESCRIPTION:** A medium to large size, broad point with barbed shoulders and a concave base.

G8, $125-$200
Gadsden Co., FL

327

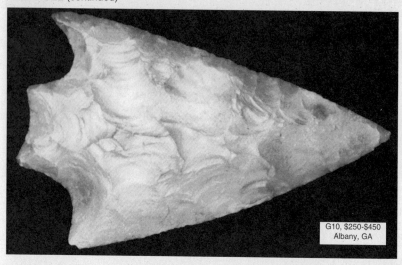

G10, $250-$450
Albany, GA

SIMPSON - Late Paleo, 12,000 - 8000 B. P.

(Also see Beaver Lake, Clovis, Conerly, Simpson-Mustache and Suwannee)

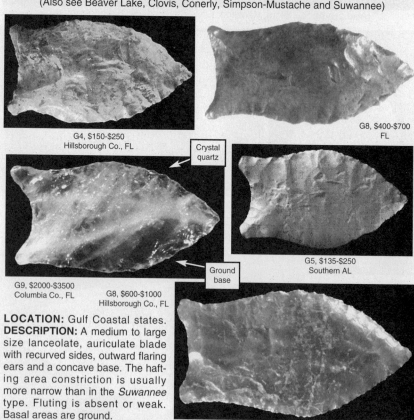

G4, $150-$250
Hillsborough Co., FL

G8, $400-$700
FL

Crystal quartz

Ground base

G5, $135-$250
Southern AL

G9, $2000-$3500
Columbia Co., FL

G8, $600-$1000
Hillsborough Co., FL

LOCATION: Gulf Coastal states.
DESCRIPTION: A medium to large size lanceolate, auriculate blade with recurved sides, outward flaring ears and a concave base. The hafting area constriction is usually more narrow than in the *Suwannee* type. Fluting is absent or weak. Basal areas are ground.

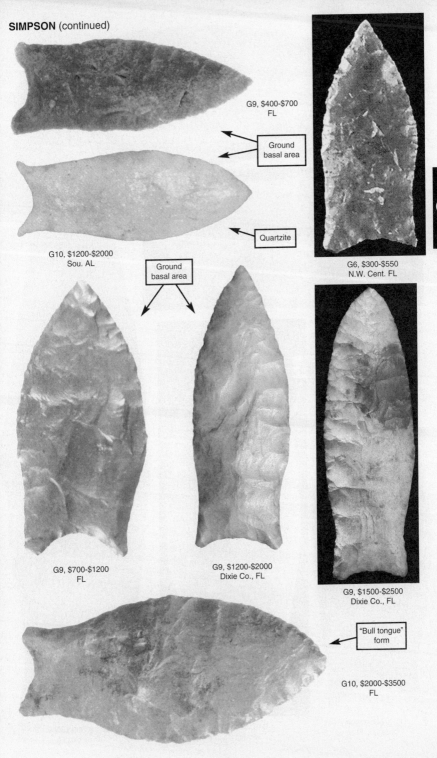

SIMPSON (continued)

G9, $400-$700
FL

Ground basal area

Quartzite

G10, $1200-$2000
Sou. AL

Ground basal area

GC

G6, $300-$550
N.W. Cent. FL

G9, $700-$1200
FL

G9, $1200-$2000
Dixie Co., FL

G9, $1500-$2500
Dixie Co., FL

"Bull tongue" form

G10, $2000-$3500
FL

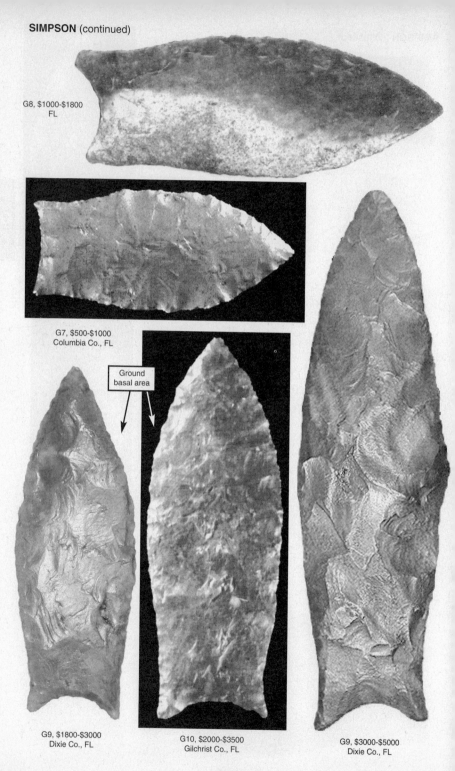

G8, $1000-$1800
FL

G7, $500-$1000
Columbia Co., FL

Ground
basal area

G9, $1800-$3000
Dixie Co., FL

G10, $2000-$3500
Gilchrist Co., FL

G9, $3000-$5000
Dixie Co., FL

Tip flake fracture

"Bull tongue" form

G7, $1800-$3000
Brooks Co., GA

GC

Semi-clear

G9, $2500-$4000
Jackson Co., FL

Ear nick

G7, $1200-$2000
Columbia Co., FL

G8, $2000-$3500
Citrus Co., FL

SIMPSON-MUSTACHE - Late Paleo, 12,000 - 8000 B. P.

(Also see Beaver Lake, Conerly, Suwannee and Wheeler Expanded Base)

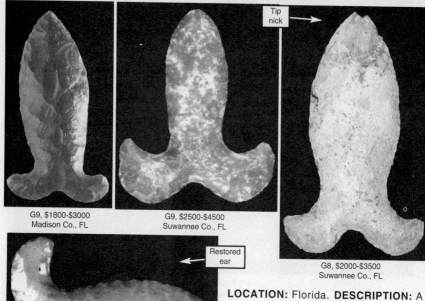

G9, $1800-$3000
Madison Co., FL

G9, $2500-$4500
Suwannee Co., FL

Tip nick

G8, $2000-$3500
Suwannee Co., FL

Restored ear

G6, $650-$1200
Suwannee Co., FL

LOCATION: Florida. **DESCRIPTION:** A small to medium size, narrow point with large up-turning ears and a convex base. Very rare in the type area. Fluting is absent. Only about a dozen including broken ones are known. A very rare type.

SIX MILE CREEK - Middle Archaic, 7500 - 5000 B. P.

(Also see Cottonbridge, Elora, Kirk Serrated and South Prong Creek)

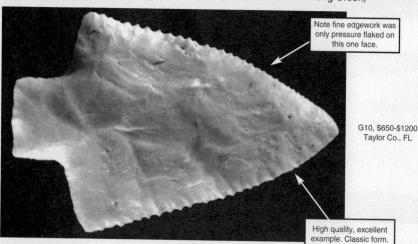

Note fine edgework was only pressure flaked on this one face.

G10, $650-$1200
Taylor Co., FL

High quality, excellent example. Classic form.

SIX MILE CREEK (continued)

Serrations were formed on this face only

G4, $25-$40
Decatur Co., GA

LOCATION: Gulf Coastal states. **DESCRIPTION:** A medium to large size, broad, stemmed, serrated point. The serrations are uniquely formed by careful pressure flaking applied from the side of only one face. Normal *Kirk* serrations are pressure flaked alternately from both faces. Believed to be a later *Kirk* variant.

GC

SOUTH PRONG CREEK - Late Archaic, 5000 - 3000 B. P.

*(Also see Abbey, Cottonbridge, Elora, Savannah River and Six Mile Creek)

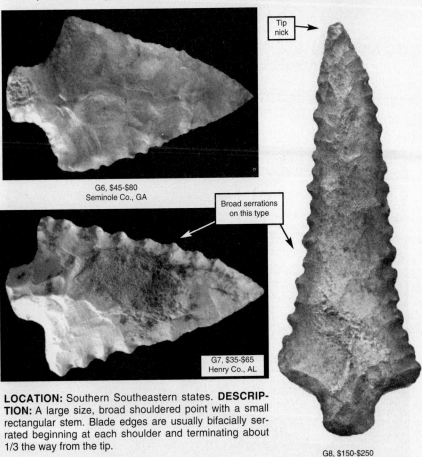

Tip nick

G6, $45-$80
Seminole Co., GA

Broad serrations on this type

G7, $35-$65
Henry Co., AL

G8, $150-$250
Albany, GA

LOCATION: Southern Southeastern states. **DESCRIPTION:** A large size, broad shouldered point with a small rectangular stem. Blade edges are usually bifacially serrated beginning at each shoulder and terminating about 1/3 the way from the tip.

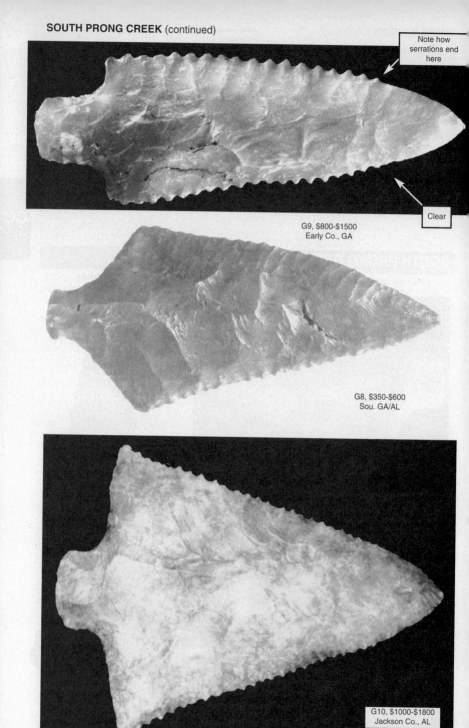

Note how serrations end here

Clear

G9, $800-$1500
Early Co., GA

G8, $350-$600
Sou. GA/AL

G10, $1000-$1800
Jackson Co., AL

334

STANFIELD - Transitional Paleo, 10,000 - 8000 B. P.

(Also see Cottonbridge, Elora, Kirk Serrated and South Prong Creek)

G10, $150-$250
FL

IMPORTANT:
Stanfields
shown half size

G7, $65-$125
FL

LOCATION: Southeast ern states. **DESCRIPTION:** A medium to large size, narrow, lanceolate point with parallel sides and a straight base. Some rare examples are fluted. Bases are ground.

STING RAY BARB - Woodland-Historic, 2500 - 400 B. P.

G5, $10-$20
FL

G8, $12-$25
FL

G9, $30-$50
FL

LOCATION: Florida. **DESCRIPTION:** Not only bone and wood were utilized as arrow points. These barbs taken from rays were hafted to shafts as well. Found on coastal occupation sites.

SUMTER - Middle Archaic, 7000 - 5000 B. P.

(Also see Adena, Elora, Kirk, Levy, Putnam, Thonotosassa & Westo)

G7, $45-$80
FL

G5, $25-$45
FL

G6, $30-$50
Marion Co., FL

G7, $30-$50
FL

LOCATION: Southern Southeastern states. **DESCRIPTION:** A medium to large size, broad, thick point with weak, tapered shoulders and a contracting stem. These may be small versions of the *Thonotosassa* type and are believed to be related.

SUWANNEE - Late Paleo, 12,000 - 10,500 B. P.

(Also see Beaver Lake, Clovis, Conerly, Simpson and Union Side Notched)

Slight
ear ding

G4, $45-$75
Taylor Co., FL

G7, $350-$600
FL

G3, $125-$200
FL

G7, $200-$375
Marion Co., FL

SUWANNEE (continued)

G8, $650-$1200
Columbia Co., FL

G6, $350-$600
Suwannee Co., FL

Agatized
coral

G9, $800-$1400
Marion Co., FL

GC

G9, $1800-$3000
N.W. Cent. FL

Agatized
coral

G8, $1200-$2000
N.W. Cent. FL

G10, $1800-$3200
Wakulla Co., FL

337

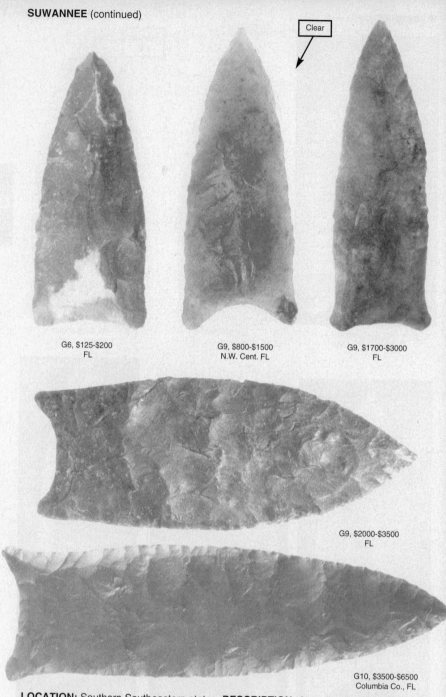

Clear

G6, $125-$200
FL

G9, $800-$1500
N.W. Cent. FL

G9, $1700-$3000
FL

G9, $2000-$3500
FL

G10, $3500-$6500
Columbia Co., FL

LOCATION: Southern Southeastern states. **DESCRIPTION:** A medium to large size, fairly thick, broad, auriculate point. The basal constriction is not as narrow as in *Simpson* points. Most examples have ground bases and are usually unfluted. **I.D. KEY:** Thickness and broad hafting area, expanding ears, less waisted than *Simpsons*.

(Also see Beaver Lake, Hardaway, Safety Harbor, Pinellas, Sante Fe and Yadkin)

GC

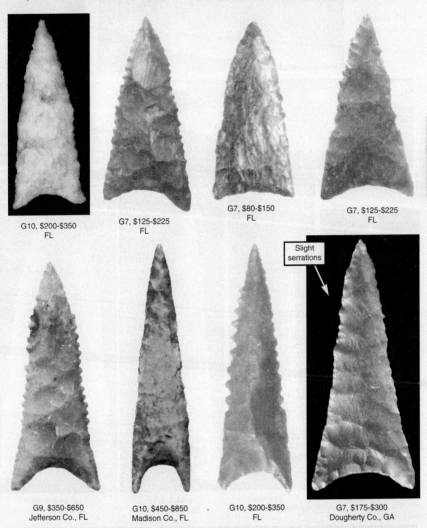

G10, $200-$350
FL

G7, $125-$225
FL

G7, $80-$150
FL

G7, $125-$225
FL

Slight
serrations

G9, $350-$650
Jefferson Co., FL

G10, $450-$850
Madison Co., FL

G10, $200-$350
FL

G7, $175-$300
Dougherty Co., GA

LOCATION: Gulf Coastal states. **DESCRIPTION:** A medium to large size auriculate, serrated triangular point with expanding auricules and a concave base. Hafting area is not well defined and is always ground. Blade edges are serrated (see Santa Fe) and are resharpened on each face rather than the usual *Dalton* procedure of beveling on opposite faces. A *Dalton* culture variant. See Ripley Bullen (1975). **Note:** Bullen and the first Florida archaeologists classified this type as Early Archaic. Then, point type books published later (by authors who were not professional archaeologists) retained the names of these *Dalton* variants and applied them to similar, but much later, look-alike forms such as *Copena, Safety Harbor* and *Yadkin*. These later forms are generally smaller, long and narrow and unground. The *Dalton* forms are usually larger, wider and most are ground on the base. Our advisors are split on this issue, but we believe that Bullen had it right and strongly advise our readers to refer to his reference and use his recommendations for Florida point classifications. **I.D. KEY:** True Tallahassees are always ground and have *Dalton* flaking.

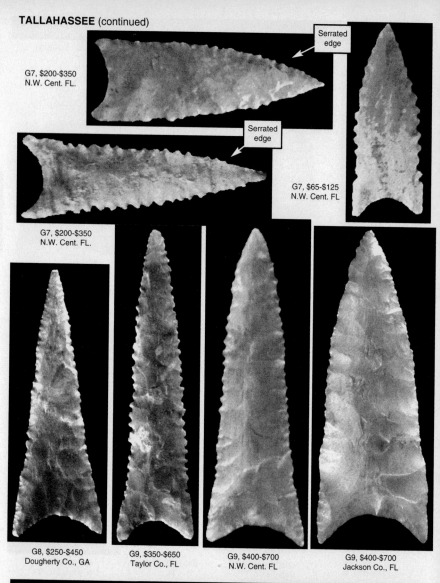

Serrated edge

Serrated edge

G7, $200-$350
N.W. Cent. FL.

G7, $200-$350
N.W. Cent. FL.

G7, $65-$125
N.W. Cent. FL

G8, $250-$450
Dougherty Co., GA

G9, $350-$650
Taylor Co., FL

G9, $400-$700
N.W. Cent. FL

G9, $400-$700
Jackson Co., FL

TAMPA - Mississippian, 800 - 400 B. P.

(Also see O'Leno and Pinellas)

G10, $90-$175
FL

G8, $30-$50
FL

LOCATION: Gulf Coastal states. **DESCRIPTION:** A small size, narrow to broad, tear drop shaped point with a rounded base. Similar to the *Nodena* type found further north and west. A rare point.

TAMPA (continued)

G6, $12-$20
FL

G9, $35-$65
FL

G10, $125-$200
Hernando Co., FL

G10, $80-$150
FL

G10, $150-$250
FL

G9, $65-$125
FL

TAYLOR - Woodland, 2500 - 2200 B. P.

(Also see Bolen Plain and Kirk)

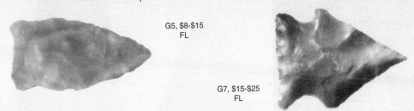

G5, $8-$15
FL

G7, $15-$25
FL

LOCATION: Gulf Coastal states. **DESCRIPTION:** A small to medium size, corner notched point with a straight to incurvate base. Basal areas are not ground. Blade edges are straight to excurvate and shoulders are weak.

TAYLOR SIDE-NOTCHED - Early Archaic, 9000 - 8000 B. P.

(Also see Bolen Beveled Plain and Osceola Greenbrier)

Translucent

Unbeveled

IMPORTANT:
Taylors shown
half size

G9, $250-$400
Baker Co., GA

G9, $550-$1000
Worth Co., GA

LOCATION: South Carolina into southern Georgia. **DESCRIPTION:** A medium size, side-notched point with a slightly concave base. Some examples are beveled and serrated. Base and notches are ground. Shoulders are pointed. Blade edges are straight to slightly concave or convex.

THONOTOSASSA - Early Archaic, 8000 - 5000 B. P.

(Also see Hamilton, Morrow Mountain, Putnam, Savannah River and Sumter)

341

G7, $25-$45
FL

G8, $80-$150
FL

G10, $400-$700
Six Mile Creek, FL

G9, $55-$100
FL

G7, $55-$100
FL

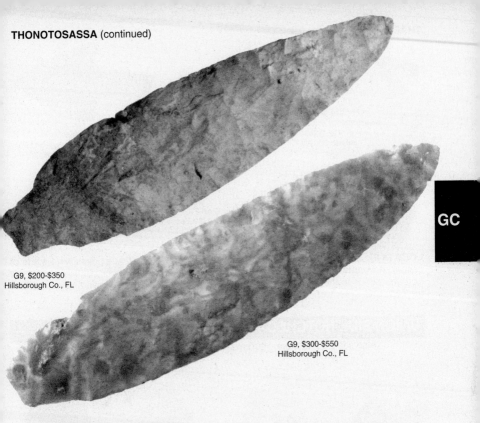

G9, $200-$350
Hillsborough Co., FL

G9, $300-$550
Hillsborough Co., FL

GC

LOCATION: Florida only. **DESCRIPTION:** A large size, narrow, usually heavy, crudely made blade with weak shoulders and a stem that can be parallel sided to contracting. The base can be straight to rounded. Believed to be related to the smaller *Sumter* type. Also believed to be the first Florida point with heated stone. Found almost exclusively in Central Florida.

TRADE POINTS - Historic, 400 - 170 B. P.

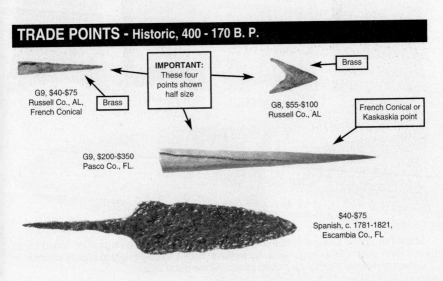

IMPORTANT: These four points shown half size

G9, $40-$75
Russell Co., AL,
French Conical

Brass

Brass

G8, $55-$100
Russell Co., AL

French Conical or
Kaskaskia point

G9, $200-$350
Pasco Co., FL.

$40-$75
Spanish, c. 1781-1821,
Escambia Co., FL

TRADE (continued)

$40-$75
French Conical or Kaskaskia,
c. 1702-1763,
Baldwin Co., AL

$8-$15
Bottle Glass, c.1750,
Creek, Monroe Co., AL

$35-$60
Red Stick Creek (cut brass) Fort Mims
Massacre (30 August 1813)
Baldwin Co., AL

$25-$40
Creek? (cut brass),
c. 1780, Escambia
Co., FL

LOCATION: All of United States and Canada. **DESCRIPTION:** Trade points were made of copper, iron and steel and were traded to the Indians by the French, British and others from the 1600s to the 1800s. The French Conical point (above) is known as Kaskaskia in the midwest.

UNION SIDE NOTCHED - Trans. Paleo, 11,000 - 10,000 B. P.

(Also see Beaver Lake, Hardaway, Osceola Greenbrier and Suwannee)

All have basal grinding

G7, $200-$350
FL

G8, $275-$500
FL

G8, $275-$500
FL

G8, $280-$525
FL

G6, $125-$200
FL

G9, $350-$600
Alachua Co., FL

LOCATION: Gulf Coastal states. **DESCRIPTION:** A medium to large size, broad blade with weak side notches expanding into auricles. Base can be straight to slightly concave or convex and is usually heavily ground all around the basal area.

WACISSA - Early Archaic, 9000 - 6000 B. P.

(Also see Abbey, Arredondo, Bolen, Elora, Hamilton, Kirk Stemmed, Savannah River and Seminole)

Serrated edge

G6, $35-$55
Mitchell Co., GA

G8, $30-$50
Allendale Co., SC

Clear

G9, $150-$250
FL

G5, $12-$20
Henry Co., AL

LOCATION: Gulf Coastal states. **DESCRIPTION:** A small to medium size, thick, short, broad stemmed point that is beveled on all four sides. Shoulders are moderate to weak and horizontal to slightly barbed. Some examples are serrated.

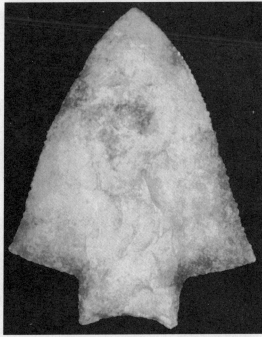

G10 $450-$800
Jackson Co., FL

WALLER KNIFE - Early Archaic, 9000 - 5000 B. P.

(Also see Edgefield Scraper)

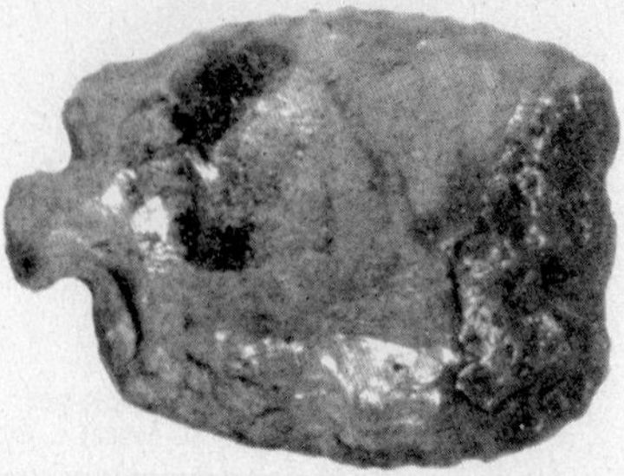

G6, $35-$65
FL

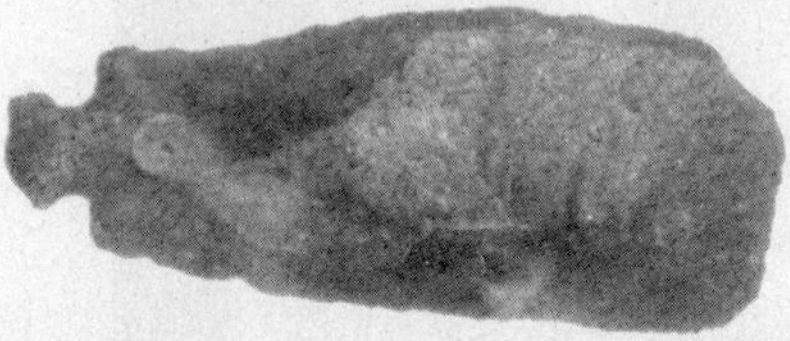

G8, $40-$70
FL

G8, $30-$50
FL

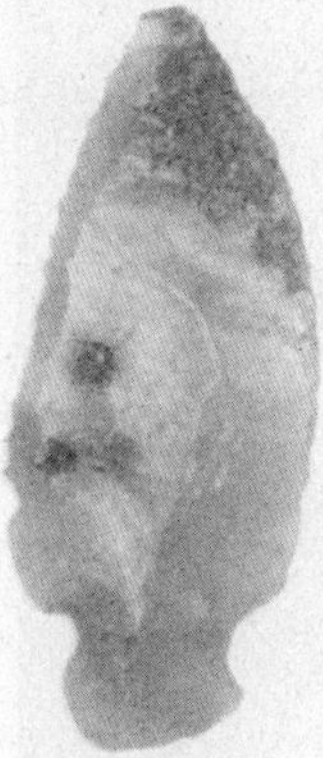

G8, $50-$85
Dixie Co., FL

G7, $30-$45
FL

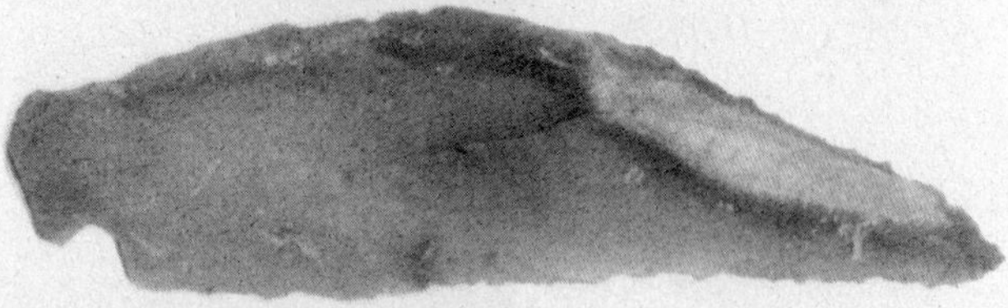

G7, $20-$35
FL

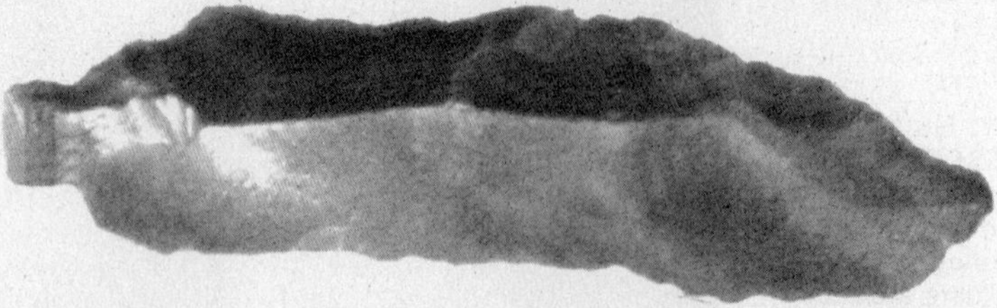

G8, $25-$45
FL

LOCATION: Gulf Coastal states. **DESCRIPTION:** A medium size double uniface knife with a short, notched base, made from a flake. Only the cutting edges have been pressure flaked. The classical Waller exhibits a dorsal ridge.

WEEDEN ISLAND - Woodland, 2500 - 1000 B. P.

(Also see Jackson)

Asymmetrical

Tip nick →

G8, $15-$30
FL

GC

G5, $3-$6
FL

G7, $4-$8
FL

G6, $5-$10
FL

G8, $10-$20
FL

G8, $10-$20
Marion Co., FL

G8 $8-$15
FL

LOCATION: Gulf Coastal states.
DESCRIPTION: A small size triangular point with a contracting stem. Shoulders can be tapered to barbed. Bases are straight to rounded.

G8, $15-$25
Marion Co., FL

WESTO - Archaic, 5000 - 4000 B. P.

(Also see Duval, Sumter)

G7, $30-$50
FL

G9, $50-$90
FL

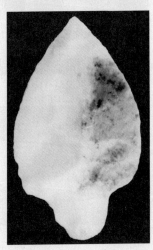

LOCATION: Northern Florida into Georgia. **DESCRIPTION:** A small to medium size, narrow to broad point with a straight to convex blade edge and a short, rounded stem. Shoulders are tapered and many examples are made of quartz and are relatively thick in cross section. **I.D. KEY:** Thickness & short, rounded stem.

347

WHEELER - Transitional Paleo, 10,000 - 8000 B. P.

(Also see Beaver Lake and Simpson-Mustache)

Expanded base form. Collateral flaking

Excurvate form

G10, $1500-$2500
Hamilton Co., FL

LOCATION: Southeastern states to Florida. **DESCRIPTION:** A small to medium size triangular, auriculate point with a concave base. The ears are produced by a shallow constriction or notching near the base. This form occurs in three forms: Excurvate, recurvate and expanded base. Excurvate and expanded base forms are shown. A very rare type in Florida.

G7, $250-$400
FL

YADKIN - Woodland to Mississippian, 2500 - 500 B. P.

(Also see Pinellas, Safety Harbor, Santa Fe and Tallahassee)

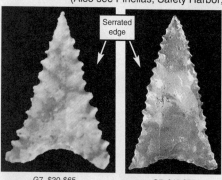

Serrated edge

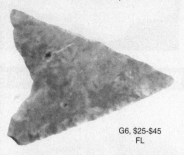

G6, $25-$45
FL

G7, $30-$65
Allendale Co., SC

G7, $40-$75
Tift Co., GA

LOCATION: Florida into the Carolinas & southern Georgia. **DESCRIPTION:** A small to medium size, broad based, sometimes serrated, triangular point with a broad, concave base and straight to convex to recurved side edges. Bases are not ground. **I.D. KEY:** Broadness of base tangs, lack of grinding.

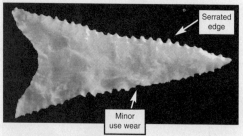

Serrated edge

Minor use wear

G9, $175-$300
Allendale Co., SC

EASTERN CENTRAL SECTION:

This section includes point types from the following states: Alabama, Georgia, Indiana, Kentucky, Michigan, Mississippi, Ohio and Tennessee.

The points in this section are arranged in alphabetical order and are shown **actual size**. All types are listed that were available for photographing. Any missing types will be added to future editions as photographs become available. We are always interested in receiving sharp, black and white or color glossy photos or color slides of your collection. Be sure to include a ruler in the photograph so that proper scale can be determined.

Lithics: Materials employed in the manufacture of projectile points from this region include: agate, chalcedony, chert, crystal, flint, limestone, quartz, quartzite and silicified sandstone.

Important Sites: Nuckolls, Humphreys Co., TN.; Cotaco, Cotaco Creek, Morgan Co., AL.; Cumberland, Cumberland River Valley, TN.; Damron, Lincoln Co., TN.; Elk River, Limestone Co., AL.; Eva, Benton Co., TN.; Quad, Limestone Co., AL.; Pine Tree, Limestone Co., AL.; Dover Flint, Humphreys Co., TN.; Redstone, Madison Co., AL.; Plevna (Dovetail), Madison Co., AL.; Stone Pipe, Wheeler Reservoir, Limestone Co., AL. for Wheeler and Decatur points.

EC

Regional Consultants:
Tom Davis, Woodson Carter
Roy McKey, John T. Pafford, Eric C. Wagner

EASTERN CENTRAL
(Archaeological Periods)

PALEO (14,000 B. P. - 11,000 B. P.)

Beaver Lake	Clovis-Hazel	Cumberland	Graver	Redstone
Clovis	Clovis Unfluted	Debert	Lancet	Scraper

TRANSITIONAL PALEO (11,000 B. P. - 9,000 B. P.)

Agate Basin	Hinds	Paint Rock Valley	Square Knife	Wheeler Recurvate
Early Ovoid Knife	Jeff	Pelican	Stanfield	Wheeler Triangular
Haw River	Marianna	Plainview	Wheeler Excurvate	
Hi-Lo	Ohio Lanceolate	Quad	Wheeler Expanded	

EARLY ARCHAIC (10,000 B. P. - 7,000 B. P.)

Alamance	Dalton Colbert	Greenbrier	Leighton	St. Charles
Alberta	Dalton Greenbrier	Hardaway	Lerma	St. Helena
Angostura	Dalton Hemphill	Hardaway Dalton	Limeton Bifurcate	St. Tammany
Autauga	Dalton Nuckolls	Hardin	Lost Lake	Stanly
Big Sandy	Damron	Harpeth River	MacCorkle	Steubenville
Big Sandy Broad Base	Decatur	Heavy Duty	Meserve	Stilwell
Big Sandt Contracted	Decatur Blade	Hidden Valley	Neuberger	Stringtown
Base	Eastern Stemmed	Holland	Newton Falls	Tennessee River
Big Sandy E-Notched	Lanceolate	Johnson	Palmer	Tennessee Saw
Big Sandy Leighton	Ecusta	Jude	Perforator	Thebes
Base	Elk River	Kanawha Stemmed	Pine Tree	Warrick
Cave Spring	Eva	Kirk Corner Notched	Pine Tree Corner	Watts Cave
Cobbs Triangular	Fishspear	Kirk Snapped Base	Notched	White Springs
Coldwater	Fountain Creek	Kirk Stemmed	Rice Lobbed	
Conerly	Frederick	Kirk Stemmed-Bifur.	Russel Cave	
Crawford Creek	Garth Slough	Lake Erie	San Patrice-Hope	
Dalton Classic	Graham Cave	Lecroy	St. Albans	

MIDDLE ARCHAIC (7,000 B. P. - 4,000 B. P.)

Appalachian	Brewerton Side Notched	Guilford Round Base	Morrow Mountain Round	Savage Cave
Benton	Brunswick	Halifax	Base	Savannah River
Benton Blade	Buck Creek	Kays	Morrow Mountain	Searcy
Benton Bottle Neck	Buggs Island	Ledbetter	Straight Base	Smith
Benton Double Notched	Buzzard Roost Creek	Limestone	Motley	Sykes
Benton Narrow Blade	Copena Auriculate	Maples	Mountain Fork	Tortugas
Big Slough	Cypress Creek	Matanzas	Mulberry Creek	Turkeytail Tupelo
Brewerton Corner	Elora	McIntire	Patrick	Wade
Notched	Epps	McWhinney Heavy	Pentagonal Knife	Warito
Brewerton Eared	Exotic Forms	Stemmed	Pickwick	
Triangular	Frazier	Morrow Mountain	Ramey Knife	

LATE ARCHAIC (4,000 B. P. - 3,000 B. P.)

Ashtabula	Dagger	Merom	Smithsonia	Turkeytail-Harrison
Bakers Creek	Etley	Mud Creek	Snake Creek	Turkeytail-Hebron
Beacon Island	Evans	Orient	Square-end Knife	
Bradley Spike	Flint Creek	Pontchartrain Type I & II	Sublet Ferry	
Copena Classic	Little Bear Creek	Rankin	Swan Lake	
Copena Round Base	Meadowood	Rheems Creek	Table Rock	
Copena Triangular	Merkle	Shoals Creek	Turkeytail-Fulton	

WOODLAND (3,000 B. P. - 1,300 B. P.)

Addison Micro-Drill	Chesser	Greeneville	Morse Knife	Spokeshave
Adena	Coosa	Hamilton	Mouse Creek	Tear Drop
Adena Blade	Cotaco Creek	Hamilton Stemmed	New Market	Vallina
Adena-Narrow Stem	Cotaco Creek Blade	Hopewell	Nolichucky	Washington
Adena-Notched Base	Cotaco-Wright	Intrusive Mound	North	Waubesa
Adena Robbins	Cresap	Jacks Reef Corner	Nova	Yadkin
Adena Vanishing Stem	Dickson	Notched	Ohio Double Notched	
Alba	Duval	Jacks Reef Pentagonal	Red Ochre	
Benjamin	Ebenezer	Knight Island	Ross	
Camp Creek	Fairland	Lowe	Sand Mountain	
Candy Creek	Gibson	Montgomery	Snyders	

MISSISSIPPIAN (1300 B. P. - 400 B. P.)

Duck River Sword	Harahey	Mace	Sun Disc
Fort Ancient	Keota	Madison	Washita
Fort Ancient Blade	Levanna	Nodena	
Guntersville	Lozenge	Pipe Creek	

HISTORIC (450 B. P. - 170 B. P.)

Trade Points

EASTERN CENTRAL
THUMBNAIL GUIDE SECTION

The following references are provided to aid the collector in easier and quicker identification of point types. All photos are exactly 30% of actual size and are proportional to each other. Each point pictured in this section represents a classic form for the type. When a match is found, go to the alphabetical location of that type for more examples in actual size.

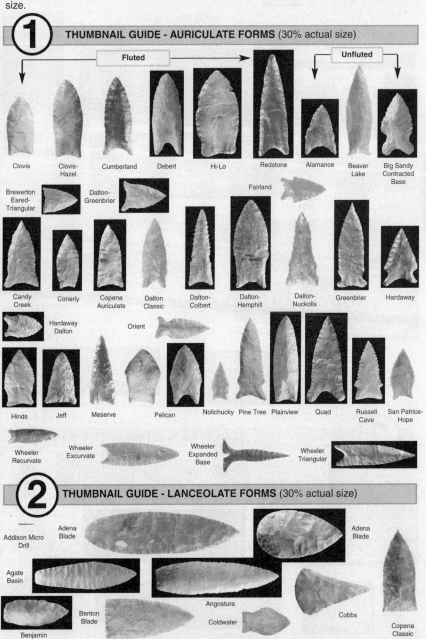

① THUMBNAIL GUIDE - AURICULATE FORMS (30% actual size)

Fluted → Unfluted

Clovis | Clovis-Hazel | Cumberland | Debert | Hi-Lo | Redstone | Alamance | Beaver Lake | Big Sandy Contracted Base

EC

Brewerton Eared-Triangular | Dalton-Greenbrier | Fairland | Candy Creek | Conerly | Copena Auriculate | Dalton Classic | Dalton-Colbert | Dalton-Hemphill | Dalton-Nuckolls | Greenbrier | Hardaway

Hardaway Dalton | Orient | Hinds | Jeff | Meserve | Pelican | Nolichucky | Pine Tree | Plainview | Quad | Russell Cave | San Patrice-Hope

Wheeler Recurvate | Wheeler Excurvate | Wheeler Expanded Base | Wheeler Triangular

② THUMBNAIL GUIDE - LANCEOLATE FORMS (30% actual size)

Addison Micro Drill | Adena Blade | Adena Blade | Agate Basin | Benton Blade | Angostura | Coldwater | Cobbs | Copena Classic | Benjamin

351

THUMBNAIL GUIDE - Lanceolate Forms (continued)

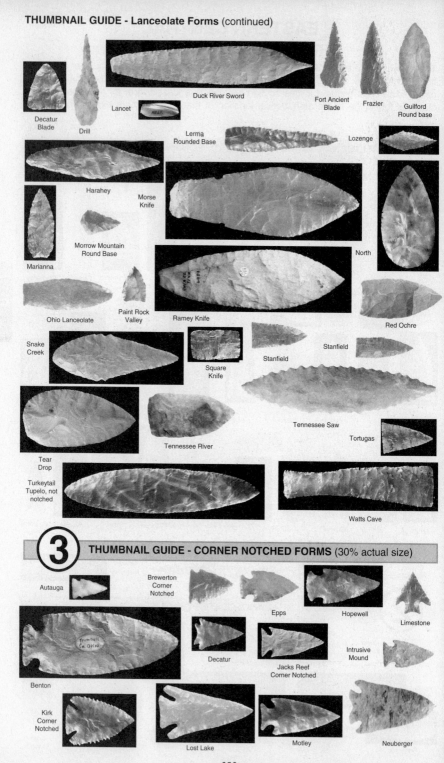

Decatur Blade

Drill

Lancet

Duck River Sword

Fort Ancient Blade

Frazier

Guilford Round base

Lerma Rounded Base

Lozenge

Harahey

Morse Knife

Morrow Mountain Round Base

North

Marianna

Ohio Lanceolate

Paint Rock Valley

Ramey Knife

Red Ochre

Snake Creek

Square Knife

Stanfield

Stanfield

Stanfield

Tennessee Saw

Tortugas

Tear Drop

Tennessee River

Turkeytail Tupelo, not notched

Watts Cave

③ THUMBNAIL GUIDE - CORNER NOTCHED FORMS (30% actual size)

Autauga

Brewerton Corner Notched

Epps

Hopewell

Limestone

Benton

Decatur

Jacks Reef Corner Notched

Intrusive Mound

Kirk Corner Notched

Lost Lake

Motley

Neuberger

THUMBNAIL GUIDE - Corner Notched Forms (continued)

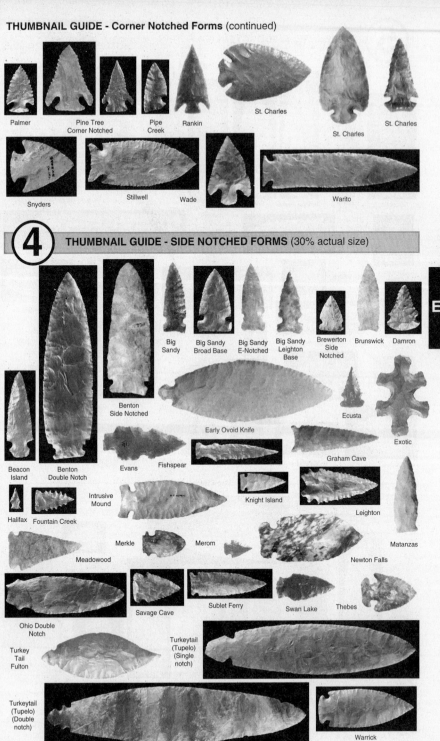

Palmer

Pine Tree
Corner Notched

Pipe
Creek

Rankin

St. Charles

St. Charles

St. Charles

Snyders

Stillwell

Wade

Warito

④ THUMBNAIL GUIDE - SIDE NOTCHED FORMS (30% actual size)

EC

Big
Sandy

Big Sandy
Broad Base

Big Sandy
E-Notched

Big Sandy
Leighton
Base

Brewerton
Side
Notched

Brunswick

Damron

Benton
Side Notched

Early Ovoid Knife

Ecusta

Exotic

Evans

Fishspear

Graham Cave

Beacon
Island

Benton
Double Notch

Intrusive
Mound

Knight Island

Leighton

Halifax

Fountain Creek

Merkle

Merom

Matanzas

Meadowood

Newton Falls

Ohio Double
Notch

Savage Cave

Sublet Ferry

Swan Lake

Thebes

Turkey
Tail
Fulton

Turkeytail
(Tupelo)
(Single
notch)

Turkeytail
(Tupelo)
(Double
notch)

Warrick

353

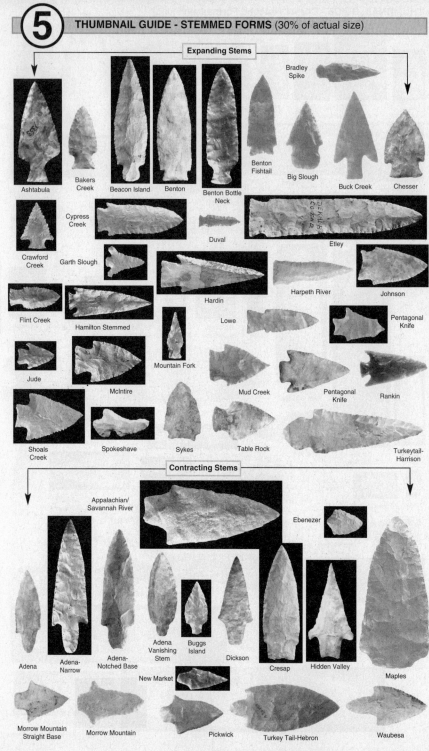

Expanding Stems

Bradley Spike

Ashtabula

Bakers Creek

Beacon Island

Benton

Benton Bottle Neck

Benton Fishtail

Big Slough

Buck Creek

Chesser

Crawford Creek

Garth Slough

Cypress Creek

Duval

Etley

Flint Creek

Hamilton Stemmed

Hardin

Harpeth River

Johnson

Jude

McIntire

Mountain Fork

Lowe

Mud Creek

Pentagonal Knife

Pentagonal Knife

Rankin

Shoals Creek

Spokeshave

Sykes

Table Rock

Turkeytail-Harrison

Contracting Stems

Appalachian/ Savannah River

Ebenezer

Adena

Adena-Narrow

Adena-Notched Base

Adena Vanishing Stem

Buggs Island

Dickson

Cresap

Hidden Valley

Maples

New Market

Morrow Mountain Straight Base

Morrow Mountain

Pickwick

Turkey Tail-Hebron

Waubesa

THUMBNAIL GUIDE - Stemmed Forms (continued)

Other Stemmed Forms

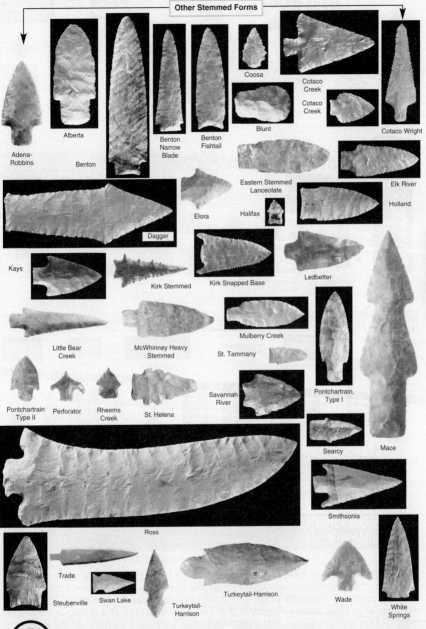

Adena-Robbins

Alberta

Benton

Benton Narrow Blade

Benton Fishtail

Coosa

Blunt

Cotaco Creek

Cotaco Creek

Cotaco Wright

Dagger

Eastern Stemmed Lanceolate

Elora

Halifax

Elk River

Holland

Kays

Kirk Stemmed

Kirk Snapped Base

Ledbetter

EC

Little Bear Creek

McWhinney Heavy Stemmed

Mulberry Creek

St. Tammany

Pontchartrain, Type I

Mace

Pontchartrain Type II

Perforator

Rheems Creek

St. Helena

Savannah River

Searcy

Ross

Smithsonia

Trade

Steubenville

Swan Lake

Turkeytail-Harrison

Turkeytail-Harrison

Wade

White Springs

⑥ THUMBNAIL GUIDE - STEMMED-BIFURCATED FORMS (30% of actual size)

Buzzard Roost Creek

Cave Spring

Fox Valley

Frederick

Haw River

355

THUMBNAIL GUIDE - Stemmed Bifurcated Forms (continued)

Heavy Duty · Kirk Stemmed-Bifurcated · Kanawha · Lake Erie · MacCorkle · LeCroy · Limeton · Neuberger · Patrick · Pine Tree · Rice Lobbed · St. Albans · Stanly

⑦ THUMBNAIL GUIDE - BASAL NOTCHED FORMS (30% of actual size)

Eva · Garth Slough · Buck Creek · Hamilton Stemmed · Rankin · Smith · Wade

⑧ THUMBNAIL GUIDE - ARROW POINTS (30% of actual size)

Greeneville · Guntersville · Knight Island · Keota · Montgomery · Alba · Camp Creek · Fort Ancient · Hamilton · Jacks Reef Corner Notched · Jacks Reef Pentagonal · Levanna · Madison · Mouse Creek · Nova · Sand Mountain · Valina · Washington · Washita · Yadkin · Nodena

ADDISON MICRO-DRILL - Late Woodland to Mississippian, 2000 - 1000 B. P.

(Also see Drill, Flint River Spike and Schild Spike)

LOCATION: Examples have been found in Alabama, Kentucky, Illinois, North Carolina, North Georgia and Tennessee. Named after the late Steve Addison who collected hundreds of examples. **DESCRIPTION:** Very small to medium size, narrow, slivers, flattened to rectangular in cross section. Theory is that this is the final form of a drilling process. The original form was flint slivers with sharp edges that were used as drills. As the sliver was turned in the drilling process, the opposite edges in the direction of movement began to flake off. As the drilling operation proceeded, the edges became steeper as more and more of each side was flaked. Eventually a thin, steeply flaked, rectangular drill form was left and discarded. Unique in that these micro artifacts are not made and then used, but are created by use, and discarded as the edges became eroded away by extremely fine flaking, thus reducing their effectiveness as a cutting edge.

ADDISON MICRO-DRILL (continued)

$4-$8 each
Shown actual size. All found in Bradley & Hamilton Co., TN.

ADENA - Late Archaic to Late Woodland, 3000 - 1200 B. P.

(Also see Adena Blade, Bakers Creek, Dickson, Kays, Little Bear Creek, Turkeytail and Waubesa)

Sonora flint

G5, $8-$15
KY

G6, $8-$15
AL

G6, $12-$20
Fentress Co., TN

G6, $20-$35
KY

G7, $20-$35
Hardin Co., TN

G7, $20-$35
TN

LOCATION: Eastern to Southeastern states. **DESCRIPTION:** A medium to large, thin, narrow, triangular blade that is sometimes serrated, and with a medium to long, narrow to broad rounded "beaver tail" stem. Most examples are from average to excellent quality. Bases can be ground. Has been found with *Nolichucky, Camp Creek, Candy Creek, Ebenezer* and *Greeneville* points (Rankin site, Cocke Co., TN). **I.D. KEY:** Rounded base, woodland flaking.

357

G9, $90-$175
OH

G7, $25-$45
KY

G9, $65-$125
KY

G9, $150-$250
KY

G9, $250-$550
KY

ADENA (continued)

G7, $165-$300
OH

EC

G7, $80-$150
KY

G9, $400-$750
KY

G9, $350-$600
KY

359

ADENA BLADE - Late Archaic to Woodland, 3000-1200 B. P.
(Also see Copena, North, Tear Drop and Tennessee River)

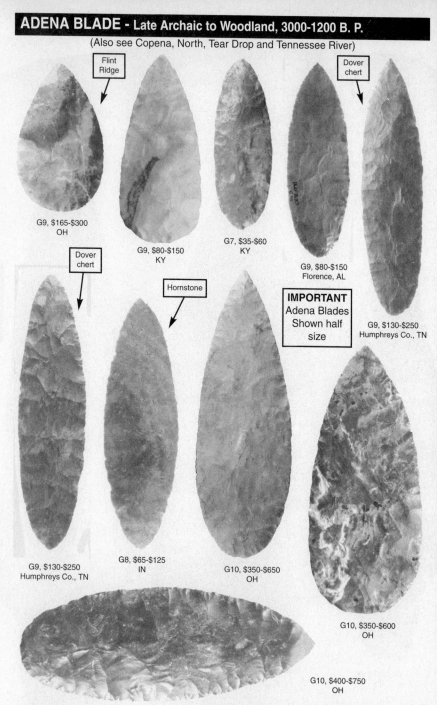

Flint Ridge

Dover chert

G9, $165-$300
OH

G9, $80-$150
KY

G7, $35-$60
KY

G9, $80-$150
Florence, AL

Dover chert

Hornstone

IMPORTANT
Adena Blades
Shown half
size

G9, $130-$250
Humphreys Co., TN

G9, $130-$250
Humphreys Co., TN

G8, $65-$125
IN

G10, $350-$650
OH

G10, $350-$600
OH

G10, $400-$750
OH

LOCATION: Midwestern to Eastern states. **DESCRIPTION:** A large size, thin, broad to narrow, ovate blade with a rounded to pointed base. Blade edgework can be very fine. Usually found in caches. **I.D. KEY:** Woodland flaking, large direct primary strikes.

ADENA-DICKSON (see Dickson)

ADENA-NARROW STEM - Late Archaic-Woodland, 3000 - 1200 B. P.

(Also see Little Bear Creek and Waubesa)

G7, $25-$40
Humphreys Co., TN

G6, $12-$20
OH

G6, $15-$25
KY

G7, $30-$50
Humphreys Co., TN

G6, $25-$40
TN

G9, $80-$150
TN

Serrated edge

Tan & purple chert

G9, $165-$300
Clifton, TN

EC

LOCATION: Eastern to Southeastern states. **DESCRIPTION:** A medium to large, thin, narrow triangular blade that is sometimes serrated, with a medium to long, narrow, rounded stem. Most examples are well made. **I.D. KEY:** Narrow rounded base with more secondary work than ordinary *Adena*.

ADENA-NOTCHED BASE - Late Archaic-Woodland, 3000 - 1200 B. P.

(Also see Adena and Little Bear Creek)

G7, $55-$100
OH

LOCATION: Southeastern states. **DESCRIPTION:** Identical to *Adena*, but with a notched or snapped-off concave base. **I.D. KEY:** Basal form different.

ADENA-ROBBINS - Late Archaic to Woodland, 3000 - 1800 B. P.

(See Alberta, Cresap, Dickson, Kays, Little Bear Creek, Mulberry Creek and Pontchartrain)

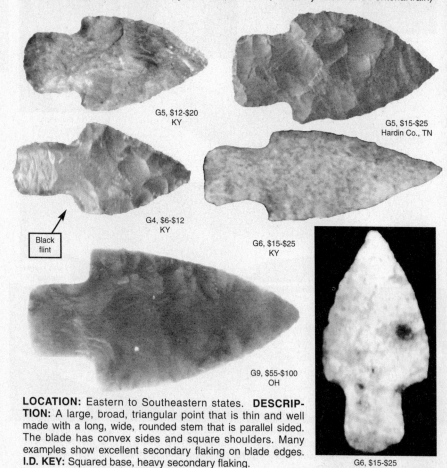

G5, $12-$20
KY

G5, $15-$25
Hardin Co., TN

G4, $6-$12
KY

Black flint

G6, $15-$25
KY

G9, $55-$100
OH

G6, $15-$25
KY

LOCATION: Eastern to Southeastern states. **DESCRIPTION:** A large, broad, triangular point that is thin and well made with a long, wide, rounded stem that is parallel sided. The blade has convex sides and square shoulders. Many examples show excellent secondary flaking on blade edges. **I.D. KEY:** Squared base, heavy secondary flaking.

362

Flintridge

G8, $125-$200
Morgan Co., OH

Red jasper

G9, $80-$150
KY

Hornstone

Dover flint

G9, $125-$200
OH

G9, $200-$350
OH

G9, $250-$450
Clark Co., KY

EC

ADENA-VANISHING STEM - Late Archaic to Woodland, 3000 - 1800 B. P.

(See Cresap, Dickson, Little Bear Creek, Mulberry Creek and Pontchartrain)

G6, $20-$35
KY

LOCATION: Eastern to Southeastern states. **DESCRIPTION:** A medium to large size point with a small, narrow, short stem that is rounded. **I.D. KEY:** Small stem.

G8, $35-$65
TN

ADENA-WAUBESA   (see Waubesa)

AFTON   (see Pentagonal Knife)

AGATE BASIN - Transitional Paleo to Early Archaic, 10,500 - 8000 B. P.

(Also see Angostura, Lerma, Ohio Lanceolate and Sedalia)

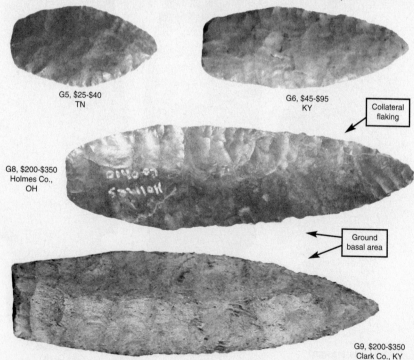

G5, $25-$40
TN

G6, $45-$95
KY

Collateral flaking

G8, $200-$350
Holmes Co.,
OH

Ground basal area

G9, $200-$350
Clark Co., KY

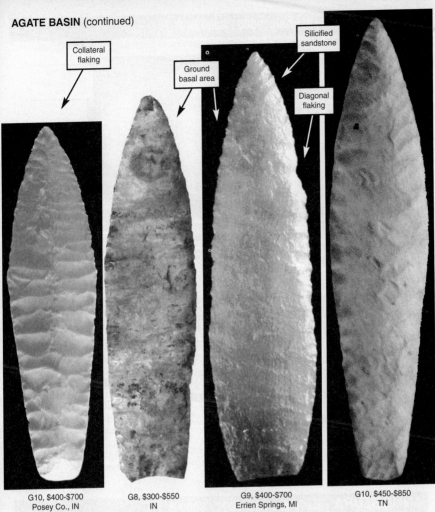

Collateral flaking

Ground basal area

Silicified sandstone

Diagonal flaking

G10, $400-$700
Posey Co., IN

G8, $300-$550
IN

G9, $400-$700
Errien Springs, MI

G10, $450-$850
TN

EC

LOCATION: Pennsylvania to Texas to Montana. **DESCRIPTION:** A medium to large size lanceolate blade of high quality. Bases are either convex, concave or straight and are usually ground. Some examples are median ridged and have random to parallel collateral flaking. Thicker than the *Ohio Lanceolate*. **I.D. KEY:** Basal form and flaking style.

ALAMANCE - Early Archaic, 10,000 - 8000 B. P.

(Also see Dalton, Hardaway and Haw River)

Minor blade nick

LOCATION: Coastal states from Virginia to Florida. **DESCRIPTION:** A broad, short, auriculate point with a deeply concave base. The broad basal area is usually ground and can be expanding to parallel sided. A variant form of the *Dalton-Greenbrier* evolving later into the *Hardaway* type. **ID. KEY:** Width of base and strong shoulder form.

G6, $40-$75
Autauga Co., AL

ALBERTA - Early Archaic, 9500 - 8000 B. P.

(Also see Eastern Stemmed Lanceolate, Holland and Scottsbluff and Stringtown)

Very rare
in the Eastern
U.S.

G6, $350-$600
MI

LOCATION: Northern states and Canada from Pennsylvania, Michigan to Montana.
DESCRIPTION: A medium to large size point with a broad, long, parallel stem and weak
shoulders. Believed to belong to the *Cody Complex* and is related to the *Scottsbluff* type.
I.D. KEY: Long stem, short blade.

ALBA - Woodland to Mississippian, 2000 - 400 B. P.

(Also see Agee, Bonham, Colbert, Cuney, Hayes, Homan, Keota, Perdiz, Scallorn and
Sequoyah)

G8, $30-$55
AL

G9, $50-$95
AL

G8, $50-$95
AL

LOCATION: Eastern Texas,
Arkansas and Louisiana.
DESCRIPTION: A small to
medium size, narrow, well
made point with prominent
tangs, a recurved blade and
a bulbous stem. Some examples are serrated. **I.D. KEY:**
Rounded base and expand-
ed barbs.

ANGOSTURA - Early Archaic, 9000 - 8000 B. P.

(Also see Browns Valley, Clovis-Unfluted, Paint Rock Valley, Plainview and Wheeler)

G9, $150-$250
Humphreys Co., TN

LOCATION: South Dakota southward to Texas and W. Tenn. **DESCRIPTION**: A medium
to large size lanceolate blade with a contracting, concave base. Both broad and narrow
forms occur. Flaking can be parallel oblique to random. Bases are not usually ground but
are thinned. **I.D. KEY:** Basal form, early flaking on blade.

ANGOSTURA (continued)

G9, $200-$350
Humphreys
Co., TN

APPALACHIAN - Mid-Archaic, 6000 - 3000 B. P.

(Also see Ashtabula, Hamilton and Savannah River)

Quartzite

G3, $20-$35
Polk Co., GA

G8, $125-$200
Norris Lake, TN

LOCATION: Southeastern states. **DESCRIPTION:** A medium to large size, rather crudely made stemmed point with a concave base. Most examples are made of quartzite. Shoulders are tapered and the base is usually ground. This form was named by Lewis & Kneberg for examples found in East Tenn. and Western North Carolina which were made of quartzite. However, this is the same type as *Savannah River*. **I.D. KEY:** Basal form.

ASHTABULA - Late Archaic, 4000 - 1500 B. P.

(Also see Appalachian and Table Rock)

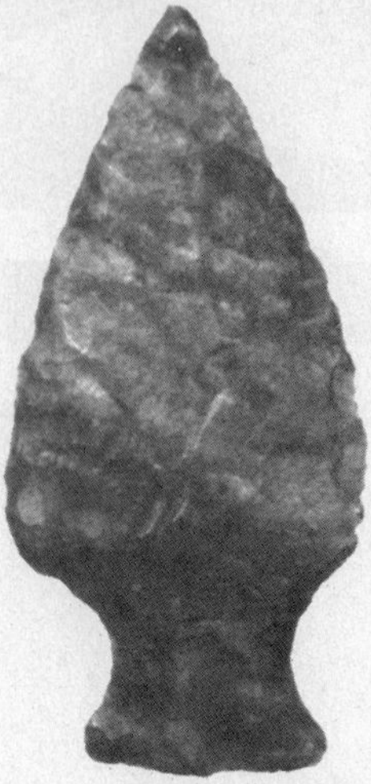

G8, $65-$125
OH

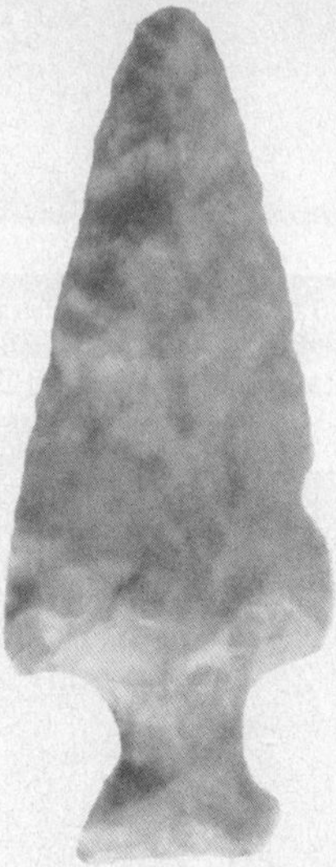

G4, $25-$45
OH

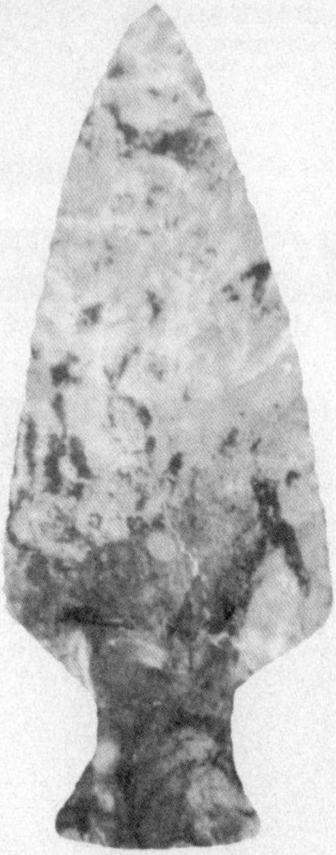

G9, $200-$350
OH

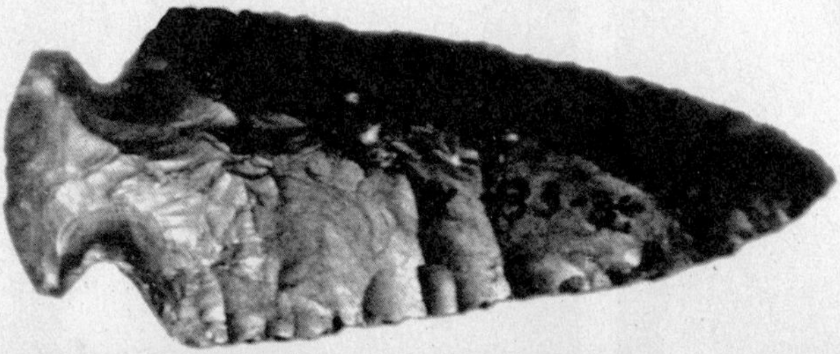

G8, $125-$225
OH

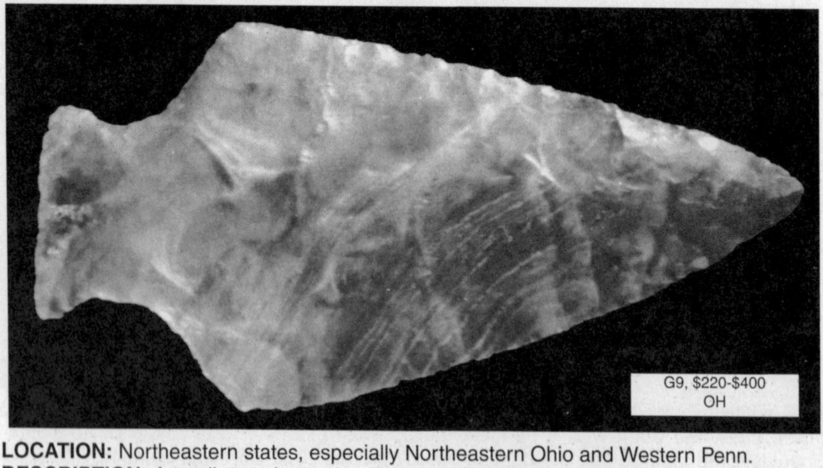

G9, $220-$400
OH

LOCATION: Northeastern states, especially Northeastern Ohio and Western Penn. **DESCRIPTION:** A medium to large size, broad, thick, expanded stem point with tapered shoulders. **I.D. KEY:** Basal form, one barb round and the other stronger.

AUTAUGA - Early Archaic, 9000 - 7000 B. P.

(Also see Brewerton, Ecusta and Palmer)

Milky quartz

G4, $4-$8
Madison Co., AL

G3, $4-$8
Monroe Co., MS

Milky quartz

G4, $5-$10
Autauga Co., AL

G4, $5-$10
Autauga Co., AL

Milky quartz

Classic form

Classic form

Classic form

G8, $12-$20
Autauga Co., AL

G8, $15-$25
Autauga Co., AL

G10, $35-$65
Humphreys Co., TN

G10, $35-$65
Tishimingo Co., MS

EC

LOCATION: Southeastern states. **DESCRIPTION:** A small, weakly corner notched point with a straight base, that is usually ground, and straight blade edges that are serrated. Blades can be beveled on one side of each face. **I.D. KEY:** Archaic flaking on blade.

BAKERS CREEK - Late Archaic to Woodland, 4000 - 1300 B. P.

(Also see Chesser, Copena, Harpeth River, Lowe, Mud Creek, Swan Lake & Table Rock)

Resharpened many times

Translucent flint

G4, $3-$6
S.E. TN

G4, $3-$6
Monroe Co., MS

G4, $3-$6
Bradley Co., TN

G5, $4-$8
MS

G4, $8-$15
KY

G5, $8-$15
S.E. TN

G7, $20-$35
KY

369

G8, $12-$20
S.E. TN

G6, $12-$20
Humphreys Co., TN

G6, $20-$35
Parsons, TN

G8, $35-$60
Humphreys Co., TN

G8, $80-$150
Colbert Co., AL

G5, $20-$35
KY

G8, $35-$60
TN

G6, $25-$40
TN

G10, $150-$275
TN

LOCATION: Southeastern states. **DESCRIPTION:** A small to large size expanded stem point with tapered or barbed shoulders. Bases are concave to convex to straight. Related to *Copena* (found with them in caches) and are called Stemmed *Copenas* by some collectors. Called *Lowe* and *Steuben* in Illinois. **I.D. KEY:** Expanded base, usually thin.

BAKERS CREEK (continued)

Dover chert

G8, $90-$165
Humphreys Co., TN

EC

G10, $150-$250
Lauderdale Co., AL

G9, $150-$250
Parsons, TN

G10, $250-$450
Humphreys Co., TN

BEACON ISLAND - Late Archaic, 4000 - 3000 B. P.
(Also see Big Slough and Flint Creek)

G3, $4-$8
Meigs Co., TN

G4, $5-$10
Lauderdale Co., AL

LOCATION: Southeastern states. **DESCRIPTION:** A small to large size triangular point with a bulbous stem. Shoulders are usually well defined and can be barbed. Similar to *Palmillas* in Texas. **I.D. KEY:** Bulbous base.

371

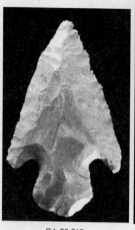

G4, $8-$15
Lauderdale Co., AL

G4, $12-$20
Lauderdale Co., AL

G6, $20-$35
Monroe Co., MS

G5 $20-$35
KY

G8, $40-$75
TN

Tip nick

G6, $35-$65
Humphreys Co., TN

G4, $15-$25
KY

G8, $55-$100
KY

372

(Also see Candy Creek, Cumberland, Dalton, Golondrina and Quad)

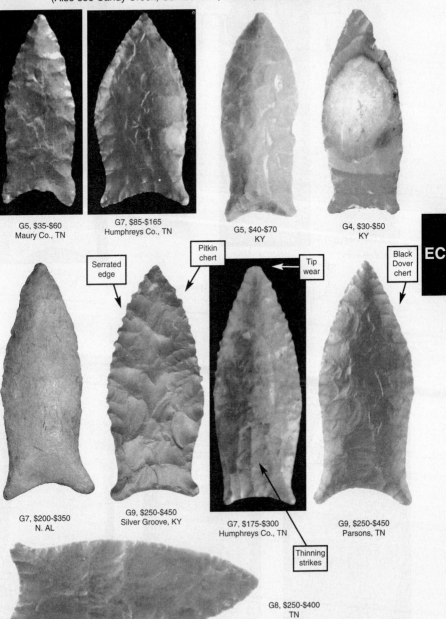

G5, $35-$60
Maury Co., TN

G7, $85-$165
Humphreys Co., TN

G5, $40-$70
KY

G4, $30-$50
KY

EC

Serrated edge

Pitkin chert

Tip wear

Black Dover chert

G7, $200-$350
N. AL

G9, $250-$450
Silver Groove, KY

G7, $175-$300
Humphreys Co., TN

Thinning strikes

G9, $250-$450
Parsons, TN

G8, $250-$400
TN

LOCATION: Southeastern states. **DESCRIPTION:** A medium to large size lanceolate blade with flaring ears and a concave base. Contemporaneous and associated with *Cumberland*, but thinner than unfluted *Cumberlands*. Bases are ground and blade edges are recurved. Has been found in deeper layers than *Dalton*. **I.D. KEY:** Paleo flaking, shoulder area.

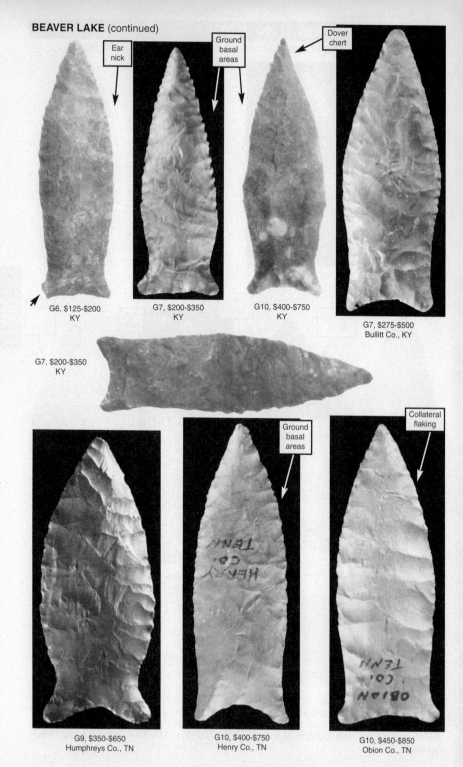

BEAVER LAKE (continued)

Ear nick

Ground basal areas

Dover chert

G6, $125-$200
KY

G7, $200-$350
KY

G10, $400-$750
KY

G7, $275-$500
Bullitt Co., KY

G7, $200-$350
KY

Ground basal areas

Collateral flaking

G9, $350-$650
Humphreys Co., TN

G10, $400-$750
Henry Co., TN

G10, $450-$850
Obion Co., TN

BEAVER LAKE (continued)

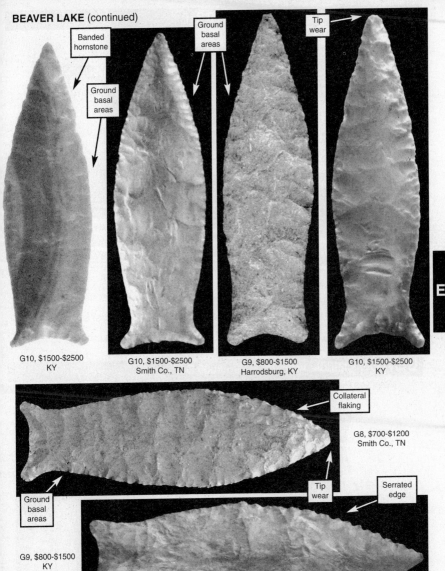

Banded hornstone

Ground basal areas

Ground basal areas

Tip wear

G10, $1500-$2500
KY

G10, $1500-$2500
Smith Co., TN

G9, $800-$1500
Harrodsburg, KY

G10, $1500-$2500
KY

EC

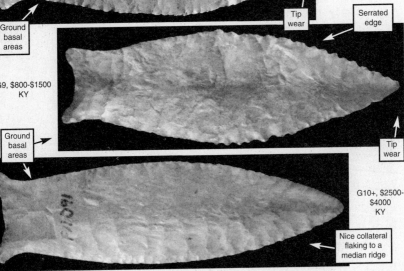

Collateral flaking

G8, $700-$1200
Smith Co., TN

Ground basal areas

Tip wear

Serrated edge

G9, $800-$1500
KY

Ground basal areas

Tip wear

G10+, $2500-$4000
KY

Nice collateral flaking to a median ridge

BENJAMIN - Woodland, 3000 - 1600 B. P.

(Also see Copena Round Base and Montgomery)

G5, $6-$10
Limestone Co., AL

G5, $8-$15
Morgan Co., AL

G7, $12-$20
TN

LOCATION: Southeastern states. **DESCRIPTION:** A medium to large size, thin, narrow, lanceolate point with random flaking and a rounded base. This point has been found in association with *Copena*.

BENTON - Middle Archaic, 6000 - 4000 B. P.

(Also see Buzzard Roost Creek, Cresap, Elk River, Sykes, Turkeytail and Warito)

G5, $15-$25
TN

G6, $20-$35
TN

G6, $25-$45
TN

G6, $30-$50
Lauderdale Co., AL

BENTON (continued)

From a cache

Fishtail form

From a cache

EC

G6, $35-$60
TN

G8, $45-$75
TN

G6, $35-$60
TN

Red, white & blue flint

G10, $550-$1000
Warren Co., TN

LOCATION: Southeastern to Midwestern states. **DESCRIPTION:** A medium to very large size, broad, stemmed point with straight to convex sides. Bases can be corner or side notched, double notched, knobbed, bifurcated or expanded. Some examples show parallel oblique flaking. All four sides are beveled and basal corners usually have tangs. Examples have been found in Arkansas with a steeply beveled edge on one side of each face (Transition form?). Found in caches with *Turkeytail* points in Mississippi on *Benton* sites. *Bentons* and *Turkeytails* as long as 16-3/4 inches were found together on this site and dated to about 4700 B.P. **I.D. KEY:** Wide squared, eared or notched base.

BENTON (continued)

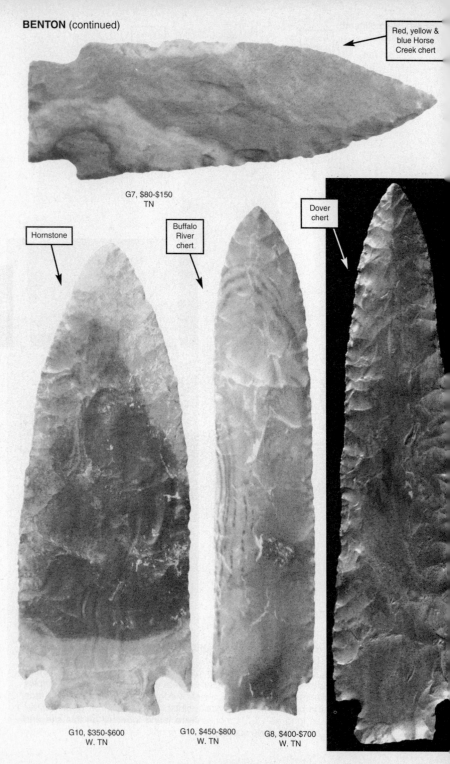

Red, yellow & blue Horse Creek chert

G7, $80-$150
TN

Hornstone

Buffalo River chert

Dover chert

G10, $350-$600
W. TN

G10, $450-$800
W. TN

G8, $400-$700
W. TN

BENTON (continued)

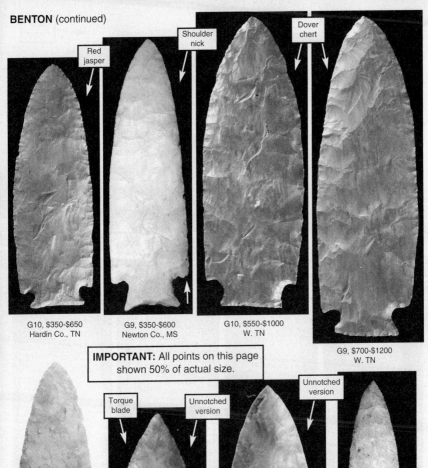

Red jasper

Shoulder nick

Dover chert

G10, $350-$650
Hardin Co., TN

G9, $350-$600
Newton Co., MS

G10, $550-$1000
W. TN

G9, $700-$1200
W. TN

EC

IMPORTANT: All points on this page shown 50% of actual size.

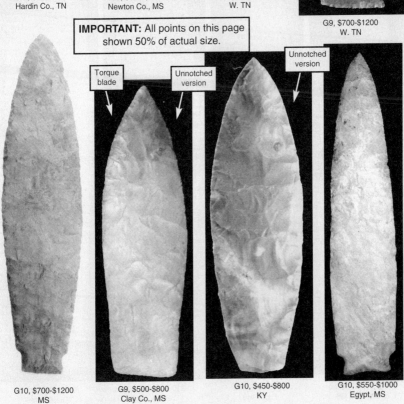

Torque blade

Unnotched version

Unnotched version

G10, $700-$1200
MS

G9, $500-$800
Clay Co., MS

G10, $450-$800
KY

G10, $550-$1000
Egypt, MS

379

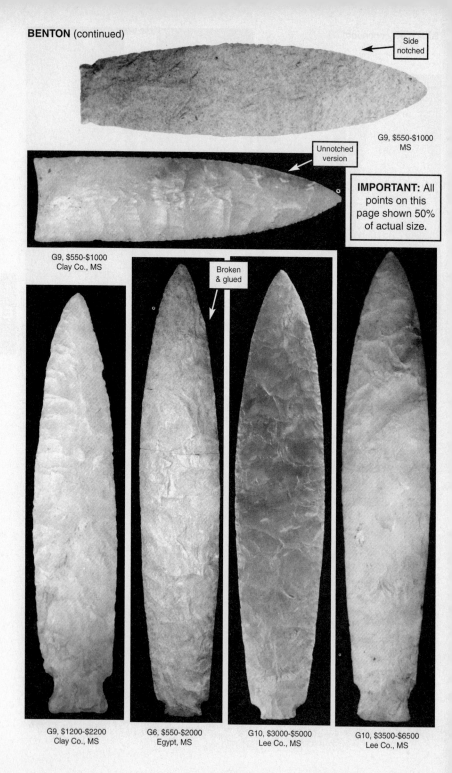

BENTON (continued)

Side notched

G9, $550-$1000
MS

Unnotched version

IMPORTANT: All points on this page shown 50% of actual size.

G9, $550-$1000
Clay Co., MS

Broken & glued

G9, $1200-$2200
Clay Co., MS

G6, $550-$2000
Egypt, MS

G10, $3000-$5000
Lee Co., MS

G10, $3500-$6500
Lee Co., MS

380

BENTON BLADE - Middle Archaic, 6000 - 4000 B. P.

(Also see Benton and Copena)

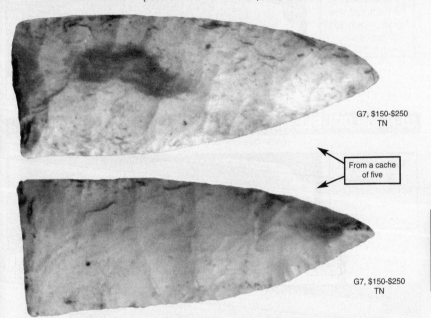

G7, $150-$250
TN

From a cache
of five

G7, $150-$250
TN

LOCATION: Southeastern to Midwestern states. **DESCRIPTION:** A medium to very large size, broad, finished blade used either as a knife or as a preform for later knapping into a *Benton* point. Usually found in caches. **I.D. KEY:** Archaic flaking similar to the *Benton* type.

BENTON-BOTTLE NECK - Middle Archaic, 6000 - 4000 B. P.

(Also see Benton and Table Rock)

G8, $200-350
TN

G7, $200-$350
KY

Sonora
flint

G7, $175-$300
Hardin Co., KY

IMPORTANT:
All Benton Bottle Necks shown
50% of actual size.

LOCATION: Southeastern to Midwestern states. **DESCRIPTION:** A medium to large size, narrow blade with tapered shoulders and an expanding stem that is usually convex. A variant form of the Benton cluster. **I.D. KEY:** Tapered shoulders, expanding stem.

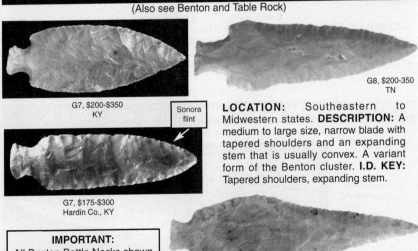

G10, $250-450
TN

EC

381

BENTON BOTTLE NECK (continued)

IMPORTANT:
All Benton Bottle
Necks shown 50%
of actual size.

G9, $800-$1500
Livingston Co., KY

Hornstone

Diagonal
flaking

BENTON DOUBLE-NOTCHED - Middle Archaic, 6000 - 4000 B. P.

(Also see Benton and Turkeytail)

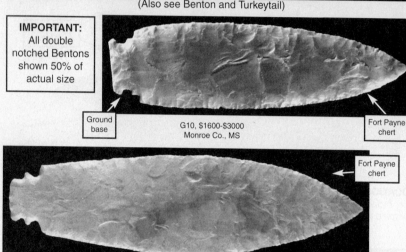

IMPORTANT:
All double
notched Bentons
shown 50% of
actual size

Ground
base

G10, $1600-$3000
Monroe Co., MS

Fort Payne
chert

Fort Payne
chert

G10, $2800-$4800
Lee Co., MS

LOCATION: Southeastern to Midwestern states. **DESCRIPTION:** A medium to very large size, broad, finished blade with double notches on each side of the blade at the base. Used as a knife and usually found in caches. Has been found associated with un-notched and double to triple-notched *Turkeytail* blades in Mississippi. Unique and rare. **I.D. KEY:** Multiple notching at base.

BENTON-NARROW BLADE - Middle Archaic, 6000 - 4000 B. P.

(Also see Elk River, Kays and Little Bear Creek)

G8, $250-$450
Hamilton Co. TN

LOCATION: Southeastern to Midwestern states. **DESCRIPTION:** A medium to large size, narrow, stemmed variant of the *Benton* form.

(Also see Cache River, Graham Cave, Newton Falls, Pine Tree and Savage Cave)

Vein quartz

Made into a blunt

G2, $2-$5
Macon Co., AL

G2, $2-$5
Fentress Co., TN

G6, $5-$10
TN

G7, $8-$15
KY

Flint

Ground base

G7, $8-$15
Sullivan Co., TN

G7, $8-$15
Polk Co., TN

G7, $12-$20
Dalton, GA

G7, $15-$25
Pikeville, TN

EC

Ground base

Ground base

G7, $15-$30
TN

G7, $20-$35
TN

G7, $25-$40
Jackson Co., AL

G7, $30-$50
Jackson Co., AL

G7, $30-$50
Jackson Co., AL

G7, $20-$35
KY

G6, $20-$35
Chattanooga, TN

LOCATION: Southeastern states. **DESCRIPTION:** A small to medium size, side-notched point with early forms showing heavy basal grinding, serrations, and horizontal flaking. This type may be associated with the *Frazier* point, being an unnotched form. Some examples have been carbon dated to 10,000 B.P., but most are associated with Mid-Archaic times. **I.D. KEY:** Basal form and blade flaking.

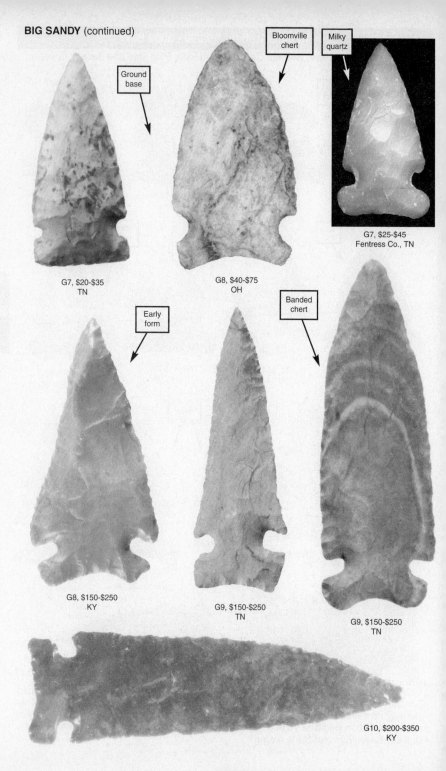

Ground base

Bloomville chert

Milky quartz

G7, $25-$45
Fentress Co., TN

G7, $20-$35
TN

G8, $40-$75
OH

Early form

Banded chert

G8, $150-$250
KY

G9, $150-$250
TN

G9, $150-$250
TN

G10, $200-$350
KY

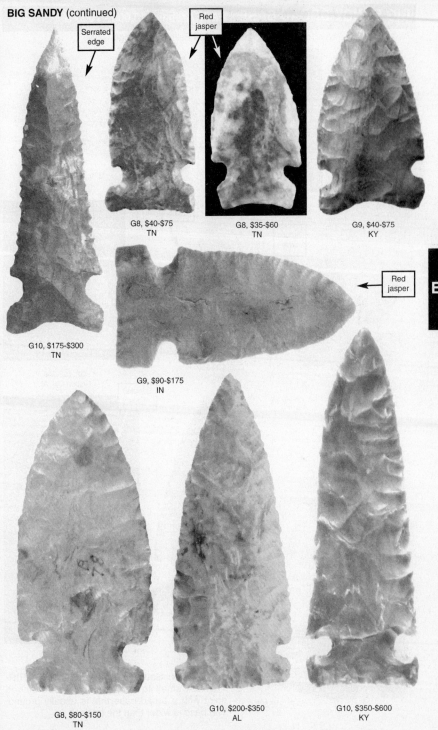

BIG SANDY (continued)

Serrated edge

Red jasper

Red jasper

EC

G8, $40-$75
TN

G8, $35-$60
TN

G9, $40-$75
KY

G10, $175-$300
TN

G9, $90-$175
IN

G8, $80-$150
TN

G10, $200-$350
AL

G10, $350-$600
KY

385

BIG SANDY-BROAD BASE - Early Archaic, 10,000 - 7000 B. P.

(Also see Cache River, Newton Falls and Savage Cave)

G6, $12-$20
TN

G6, $15-$30
Mid. TN

G10, $35-$60
KY

Ground
base

Resharpened
many times

G8, $20-$35
TN

G10, $30-$50
KY

G8, $25-$40
Colbert Co., AL

Serrated
edge

G6, $15-$25
OH

G6, $20-$35
KY

G8, $35-$60
S.W. KY

G7, $15-$25
TN

LOCATION: Southeastern states. **DESCRIPTION:** A small to medium size, side notched point with a broad base that is usually ground. The base is wider than the blade.

BIG SANDY-CONTRACTED BASE - Early Archaic, 10,000 - 7000 B. P.

(Also see MacCorkle, Pine Tree and Quad)

G4, $3-$6
Hamilton Co., TN

G5, $5-$10
Hamilton Co., TN

G5, $6-$12
OH

G3, $3-$6
Polk Co., TN

G4, $5-$10
Hamilton Co., TN

G6, $20-$35
S.E. TN

LOCATION: Southeastern states. **DESCRIPTION:** A small to medium size, side notched point with a deeply concave ground base, and drooping ears. Some examples exhibit nice parallel flaking.

G6, $25-$45
White Co., TN

G7, $20-$35
KY

EC

BIG SANDY E-NOTCHED - Early Archaic, 10,000 - 7000 B. P.

(Also see Leighton & Thebes)

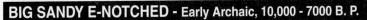

Resharpened into the notches

E-notched base

G5, $12-$20
Humphreys Co., TN

Purple & beige Buffalo River chert

G7, $55-$100
Humphreys Co., TN

G4, $5-$10
Humphreys Co., TN

Base nick

G9, $250-$450
Humphreys Co., TN

BIG SANDY E-NOTCH (continued)

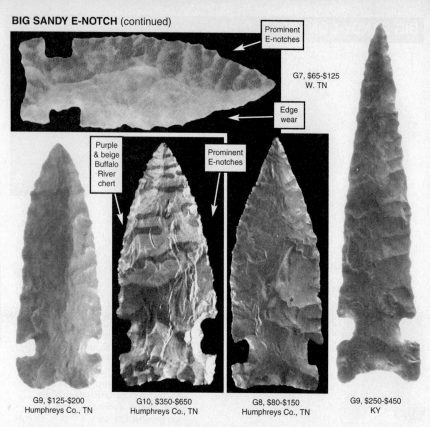

G7, $65-$125
W. TN

Prominent E-notches

Edge wear

Prominent E-notches

Purple & beige Buffalo River chert

G9, $125-$200
Humphreys Co., TN

G10, $350-$650
Humphreys Co., TN

G8, $80-$150
Humphreys Co., TN

G9, $250-$450
KY

LOCATION: Southeastern states. **DESCRIPTION:** A small to medium size expanded side-notched point. The notching is unique and quite rare for the type. This type of notch is angled into the blade to produce a high point or nipple in the center, forming the letter E. Also called key-notched. Rarely, the base is also E-notched. The same notching occurs in the *Bolen* and *Thebes* types. **I.D. KEY:** Two flake notching system.

BIG SANDY-LEIGHTON BASE - Early Archaic, 10,000 - 7000 B. P.

(Also see Leighton and Thebes)

Ear notch

Ear notches

Ear notch

G4, $6-$12
KY

G6, $25-$45
Jackson Co., AL

G6, $20-$35
Jackson Co., AL

LOCATION: Southeastern states. **DESCRIPTION:** A small to medium size side notched point with a small notch in one or both sides of the base (see *Leighton* points). The notch or notches were used to facilitate hafting. **I.D. KEY:** Basal side notching.

BIG SANDY-LEIGHTON BASE (continued)

Ear notches

G5, $12-$20
Warren Co., TN

Ear notches

G10, $175-$300
Coffee Lake, AL

BIG SLOUGH - Middle Archaic, 7000 - 4000 B. P.
(Also see Beacon Island and Elk River)

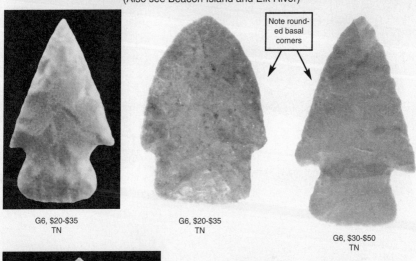

Note rounded basal corners

G6, $20-$35
TN

G6, $20-$35
TN

G6, $30-$50
TN

EC

G8, $65-$125
TN

G7, $35-$60
TN

LOCATION: Southeastern states. **DESCRIPTION:** A medium to large size, broad, stemmed point with a bulbous base. The blade is convex to recurved. The shoulders may show a weak to medium tang. **I.D. KEY:** Basal form and barbs.

389

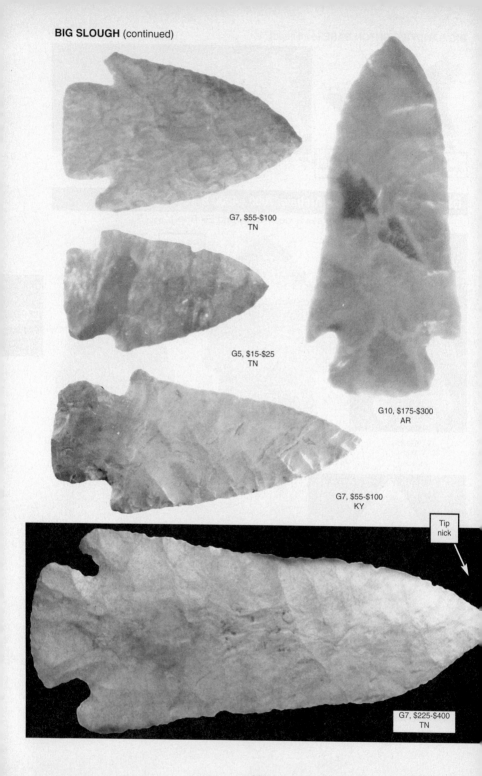

G7, $55-$100
TN

G5, $15-$25
TN

G10, $175-$300
AR

G7, $55-$100
KY

Tip
nick

G7, $225-$400
TN

BLUNT - Paleo to Woodland, 12,000 - 1000 B. P.

(Also see Drill, Perforator and Scraper)

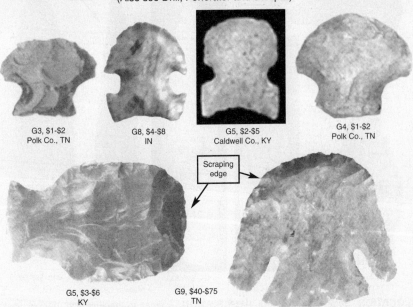

G3, $1-$2
Polk Co., TN

G8, $4-$8
IN

G5, $2-$5
Caldwell Co., KY

G4, $1-$2
Polk Co., TN

Scraping edge

G5, $3-$6
KY

G9, $40-$75
TN

EC

LOCATION: Throughout North America. **DESCRIPTION:** Blunts are usually made from broken points that are rechipped into this form, but can be made from scratch. All point types can occur as blunts. Some collectors call this form Stunners believing they were made to stun animals, not to kill. However, most archaeologists think they were used as knives and for scraping hides. Many blunts show excessive wear on the blunt edge proving their use as scrapers.

BRADLEY SPIKE - Late Archaic to Woodland, 4000 - 1800 B. P.

(Also see Buggs Island, Mountain Fork, New Market and Schild Spike)

G5, $2-$4
Polk Co., TN

G5, $1-$3
Polk Co., TN

G3, $1-$3
Polk Co., TN

G3, $1-$3
Polk Co., TN

G3, $1-$3
Polk Co., TN

G4, $2-$4
Polk Co., TN

G6, $3-$6
Bradley Co., TN

G6, $6-$12
Pikeville, TN

391

BRADLEY SPIKE (continued)

Black chert

G5, $4-$8
Dunlap, TN

G6, $6-$12
Fentress Co., TN

G9, $15-$25
Limestone Co., AL

G8, $20-$35
N.E. MS

Black chert

G10, $35-$60
Madison Co., AL

G10, $35-$60
N. AL

LOCATION: Southeastern states. **DESCRIPTION:** A small to medium size, narrow, thick, spike point. The shoulders are tapered and the stem contracts. The base on some examples shows the natural rind of the native material used.

BREWERTON CORNER NOTCHED - Middle to Late Archaic, 6000 - 4000 B. P.

(Also see Autauga)

G8, $15-$30
N. AL

G10, $35-$60
Humphreys Co., TN

LOCATION: Eastern to Midwestern states. **DESCRIPTION:** A small size, triangular point with faint corner notches and a straight to concave base. Called *Freeheley* in Michigan. **I.D. KEY:** Width, thickness.

G3, $2-$5
S.E. TN

BREWERTON EARED-TRIANGULAR - Mid-Archaic, 6000 - 4000 B. P.

(Also see Autauga, Camp Creek, Candy Creek, Nolichucky and Yadkin)

BREWERTON EARED TRIANGULAR (continued)

G3, $2-$4
Polk Co., TN

G5, $6-$12
TN

G3, $2-$5
Walker Co., AL

LOCATION: Eastern to Midwestern states. **DESCRIPTION:** A small size, triangular, eared point with a concave base. Shoulders are weak and tapered. Ears are widest part of point.

EC

BREWERTON SIDE NOTCHED - Mid-Archaic, 6000 - 4000 B. P.

(Also see Big Sandy, Brunswick, Hardaway and Matanzas)

G3, $1-$2
Trimble Co., KY

G4, $1-$3
Walker Co., GA

G4, $1-$3
Harrison Co. IN

G3, $1-$2
Dallas Isle, TN

G5, $2-$5
Harrison Co. IN

LOCATION: Eastern to Midwestern states. **DESCRIPTION:** A small to medium size, triangular point with shallow side notches and a concave to straight base.

BRUNSWICK - Middle Archaic, 5000 - 4500 B. P.

(Also see Brewerton, Greenbrier and Matanzas)

G7, $40-$75
KY

G6, $35-$65
KY

LOCATION: Kentucky, Indiana. **DESCRIPTION:** A medium sized point with weak side notches. The base can be slightly concave to straight. **I.D. KEY:** Weak notching.

BUCK CREEK - Middle to Late Archaic, 6000 - 3500 B. P.

(Also see Hamilton, Motley, Rankin, Smithsonia, Table Rock and Wade)

LOCATION: Kentucky and surrounding states. **DESCRIPTION:** A large, thin, broad, stemmed point with strong barbs and high quality flaking. Some have needle tips, blade edges are convex to recurved. Blade width can be narrow to broad. **I.D. KEY:** Barb expansion and notching.

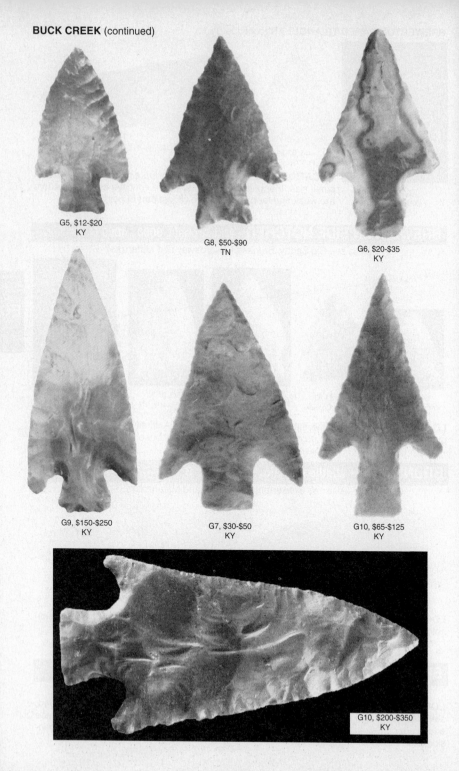

G5, $12-$20
KY

G8, $50-$90
TN

G6, $20-$35
KY

G9, $150-$250
KY

G7, $30-$50
KY

G10, $65-$125
KY

G10, $200-$350
KY

BUCK CREEK (continued)

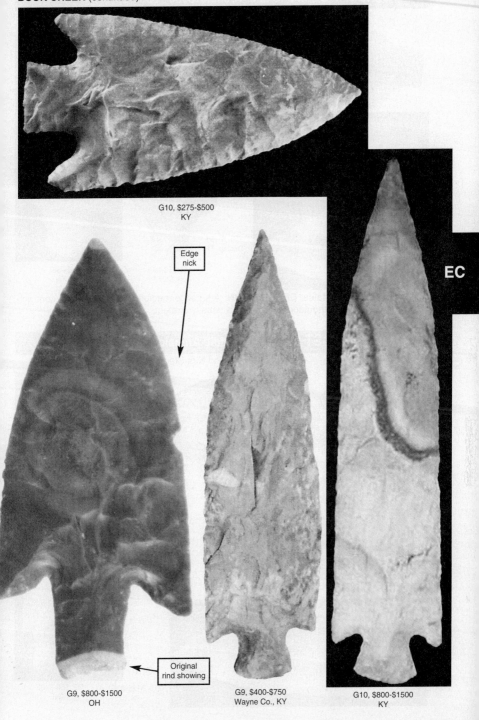

G10, $275-$500
KY

Edge nick

EC

Original rind showing

G9, $800-$1500
OH

G9, $400-$750
Wayne Co., KY

G10, $800-$1500
KY

BUGGS ISLAND - Mid to Late Archaic, 5500 - 3500 B. P.

(Also see Bradley Spike, Coosa, Ebenezer and New Market)

G3, $2-$4
S.E. TN

G4, $2-$4
Whitwell, TN

G5, $3-$6
Dunlap, TN

G4, $3-$6
Polk Co., TN

G5, $4-$8
S.E. TN

LOCATION: Eastern states. **DESCRIPTION:** A small to medium size point with a contracting stem and tapered shoulders. The base is usually straight.

BUZZARD ROOST CREEK - Middle Archaic, 6000 - 4000 B. P.

(Also see Benton and Kirk Stemmed)

G5, $8-$15
OH

G4, $3-$6
Marion Co., TN

G8, $30-$50
TN

G10, $125-$200
TN

G9, $55-$100
TN

G7, $25-$45
TN

Red
jasper

G8, $35-$65
TN

G7, $40-$75
TN

Colorful
chert

EC

G7, $40-$75
Colbert Co., AL

G10, $700-$1200
Marshall Co., AL

LOCATION: Southeastern states. **DESCRIPTION:** A medium to large size, stemmed point with a bifurcated base. Believed to be related to the *Benton* point. Found in Arkansas with the blade steeply beveled on one side of each face (transition form?). **I.D. KEY:** Bifurcated base and basal width. Found with *Benton* points. A notched base *Benton*.

397

CAMP CREEK - Woodland, 3000 - 1500 B. P.

(Also see Copena, Greeneville, Hamilton, Madison, Nolichucky and Yadkin)

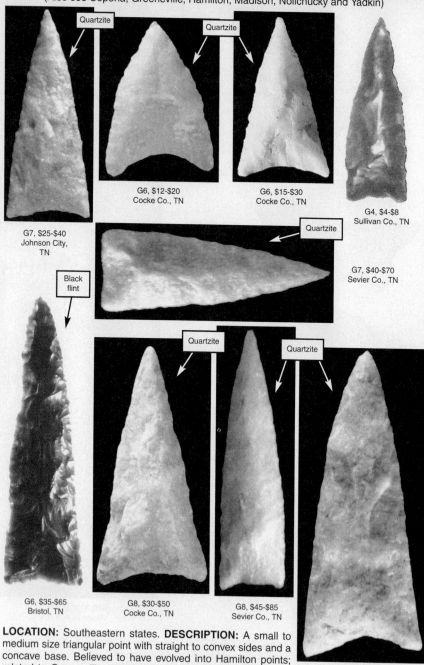

Quartzite

Quartzite

Quartzite

G6, $12-$20
Cocke Co., TN

G6, $15-$30
Cocke Co., TN

G4, $4-$8
Sullivan Co., TN

G7, $25-$40
Johnson City,
TN

Quartzite

G7, $40-$70
Sevier Co., TN

Black
flint

Quartzite

Quartzite

G6, $35-$65
Bristol, TN

G8, $30-$50
Cocke Co., TN

G8, $45-$85
Sevier Co., TN

LOCATION: Southeastern states. **DESCRIPTION:** A small to medium size triangular point with straight to convex sides and a concave base. Believed to have evolved into Hamilton points; related to Greeneville and Nolichucky points. Has been found with Adena stemmed in caches (Rankin site, Cocke Co.,TN).

G9, $90-$165
Dayton, TN

CANDY CREEK - Early Woodland, 3000 - 1500 B. P.

(Also see Beaver Lake, Brewerton, Camp Creek, Copena, Dalton, Nolichucky and Quad)

G2, $3-$6
Putnam Co., TN

G3, $4-$8
Dayton, TN

G7, $15-$50
Nickajack Lake, TN

G9, $80-$150
Dayton, TN

Basal areas
not ground

Paleo form,
but random
flaking

EC

G8, $80-$150
Dayton, TN

G8, $65-$125
Morgan Co., AL

LOCATION: Southeastern states. **DESCRIPTION:** A medium size, lanceolate, eared point with a concave base and recurved blade edges. Bases may be thinned or fluted and lightly ground. Flaking is of the random Woodland type and should not be confused with the earlier auriculate forms that have the parallel flaking. These points are similar to *Cumberland, Beaver Lake, Dalton* and *Quad,* but are shorter and of poorer quality. It is believed that Paleo people survived in East Tennessee to 3,000 B.P., and influenced the style of the *Candy Creek* point. Believed to be related to *Copena, Camp Creek, Ebenezer, Greenville* and *Nolichucky* points. **I.D. KEY:** Ears, thickness and Woodland flaking.

G8, $55-$100
Dayton, TN

G9, $65-$125
Bradley Co., TN

CAVE SPRING - Early Archaic, 9000 - 8000 B. P.

(Also see Frederick, Jude, LeCroy and Patrick)

Resharpened many times

Ground basal area

G2, $2-$5
Mason Co., WVA

G8, $15-$20
S.E. TN

G8, $12-$20
KY

G8, $15-$30
S.E. TN

G8, $15-$30
Colbert Co., AL

G8, $15-$30
Morgan Co., AL

Red jasper

Ground base

G10, $40-$75
Marion Co., AL

G7, $25-$40
Humphreys Co., TN

G7, $25-$40
Morgan Co., AL

LOCATION: Southeastern states. **DESCRIPTION**: A *Jude* with a bifurcated base. A small to medium size, stemmed point with a shallow bifurcated base. Blade edges are usually straight; shoulders are either tapered or barbed, and the stem usually expands with a tendency to turn inward at the base which is usually ground. **ID. KEY:** Early Archaic flaking.

CHESSER - Late Woodland-Miss., 1600 - 1200 B. P.

(Also see Bakers Creek, Lowe, McIntire, Mud Creek)

Coshocton chert

LOCATION: Ohio into Pennsylvania. **DESCRIPTION:** A medium size, broad point with a short, expanding stem. Bases are generally straight. Blade edges are convex to recurved and the shoulders are slightly barbed to tapered. **ID. KEY:** Broad, expanding stem.

G9, $80-$150
Hocking Co., OH

CLOVIS - Early Paleo, 14,000 - 9000 B. P.

(Also see Angostura, Browns Valley, Cumberland, Dalton, Folsom and Redstone)

All have ground basal area

Banded chert

G6, $150-$250
OH

G7, $150-$250
KY

G6, $125-$200
IN

G6, $150-$250
AL

EC

Flute channel

Edge wear

G6, $165-$300
KY

G7, $275-$500
OH

G5, $90-$175
KY

G8, $450-$800
TN

Flute channel

Ear nick

G7, $250-$400
IL

G8, $350-$600
Lauderdale Co., AL

G7, $350-$600
IN

G7, $275-$500
KY

CLOVIS (continued)

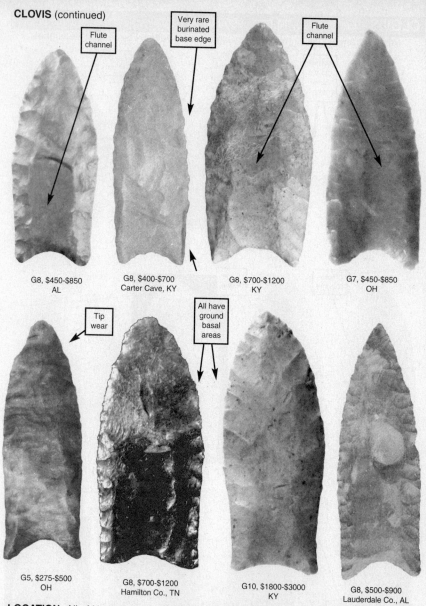

Flute channel

Very rare burinated base edge

Flute channel

G8, $450-$850
AL

G8, $400-$700
Carter Cave, KY

G8, $700-$1200
KY

G7, $450-$850
OH

Tip wear

All have ground basal areas

G5, $275-$500
OH

G8, $700-$1200
Hamilton Co., TN

G10, $1800-$3000
KY

G8, $500-$900
Lauderdale Co., AL

LOCATION: All of North America. **DESCRIPTION:** A medium to large size, auriculate, fluted, lanceolate point with convex sides and a concave base that is ground. Most examples are fluted on both sides about 1/3 the way up from the base. The flaking can be random to parallel. *Clovis* is the earliest point type in the hemisphere. It is believed that this form was brought here by early man from Siberia or Europe 14,000 years ago. *Clovis* technology more closely matches European Solutrean forms than anywhere else. There is no pre-*Clovis* evidence here (crude forms that would pre-date *Clovis*). The first *Clovis* find associated with Mastodons was in 1979 at Mastodon State Park, Jefferson Co., MO. in the Kimmswick bone bed dated to 12,000 B.P. carbon years. **I.D. KEY:** Paleo flaking, shoulders, baton or billet fluting instead of indirect style.

CLOVIS (continued)

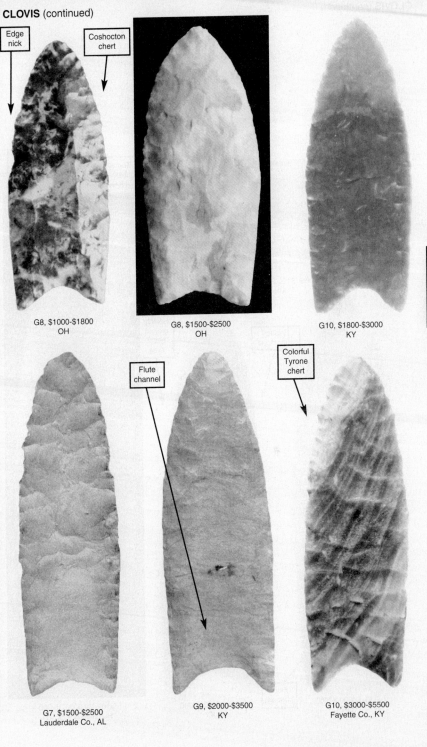

Edge nick

Coshocton chert

G8, $1000-$1800
OH

G8, $1500-$2500
OH

G10, $1800-$3000
KY

EC

Flute channel

Colorful Tyrone chert

G7, $1500-$2500
Lauderdale Co., AL

G9, $2000-$3500
KY

G10, $3000-$5500
Fayette Co., KY

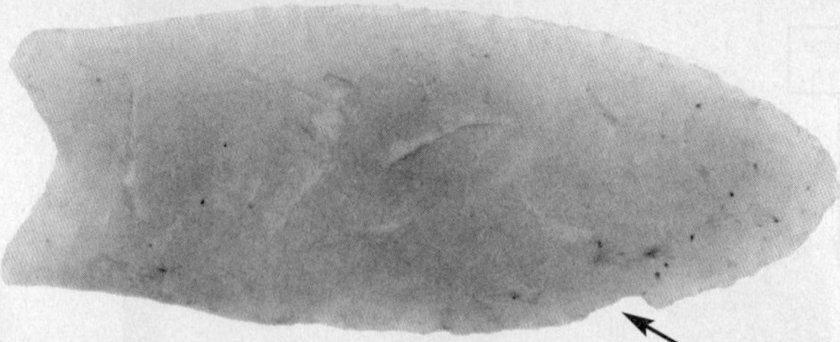

G8, $1200-$2200
TN

Translucent
chalcedony

Edge
nick

G9, $1200-$2000
OH

Buffalo
River
chert

Heavily
ground
basal
area

Silcified
sandstone

Flute
channel

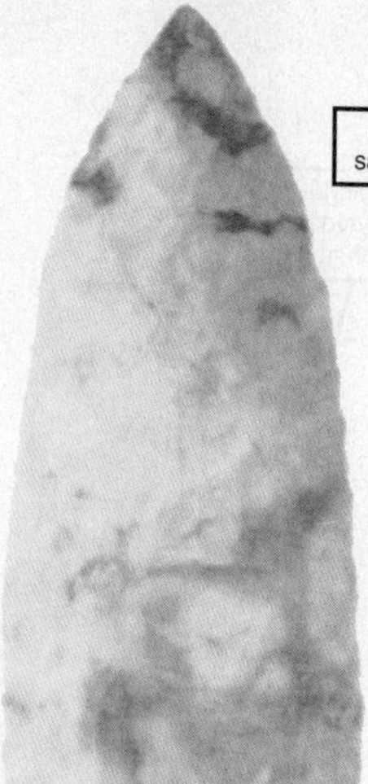

G10, $4000-$7000
OH

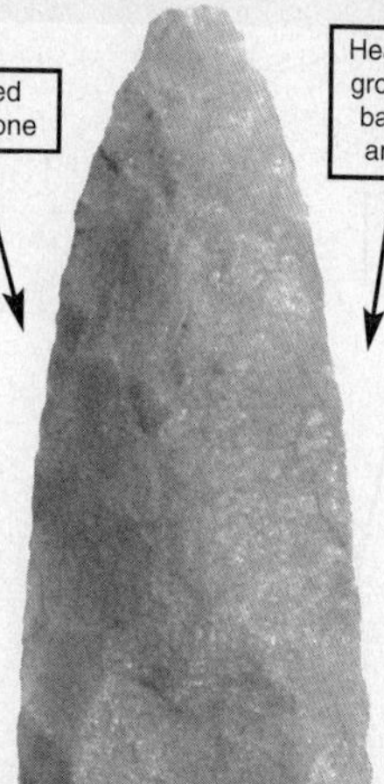

G9, $4000-$7500
KY

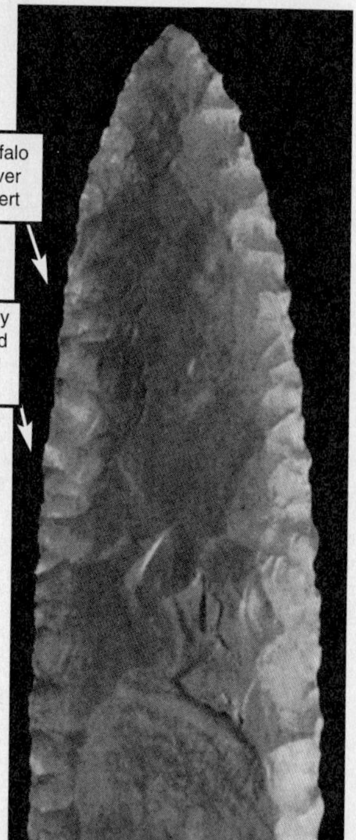

G10+, $8,000-$15,000
Humphreys Co., TN

G10, $4000-$7000
KY

Translucent high grade flint

Note long percussion flakes to the center

EC

G9, $8,000-$15,000
Clay Co., TN

G10, $15,000-$25,000+
Belgreen, AL

405

CLOVIS-HAZEL - Paleo, 14,000 - 9000 B. P.

(Also see Angostura, Beaver Lake, Candy Creek, Golondrina and Plainview)

Flute channel

G9, $700-$1200
Lewis Co., KY

G10, $1200-$2000
KY

G10, $1500-$2500
KY

G8, $800-$1500
KY

G7, $700-$1200
TN

Tip wear

LOCATION: Eastern U.S. from Florida, Alabama, Tennessee, Kentucky, Ohio westward. **DESCRIPTION:** A medium to large size, auriculate point that has similarities to the Ross County variety, but with a more fishtailed appearance and a longer hafting area.

CLOVIS-UNFLUTED - Paleo, 14,000 - 9000 B. P.

(Also see Angostura, Beaver Lake, Candy Creek, Golondrina and Plainview)

Knox chert

LOCATION: All of North America. **DESCRIPTION:** A medium to large size, auriculate point identical to fluted *Clovis,* but not fluted. A very rare type as most *Clovis* points are fluted in their finished form.

G8, $300-$550
Clark Co., KY

CLOVIS-UNFLUTED (continued)

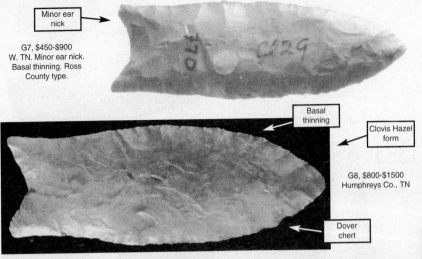

Minor ear nick →

G7, $450-$900
W. TN. Minor ear nick.
Basal thinning. Ross
County type.

Basal thinning

Clovis Hazel form

G8, $800-$1500
Humphreys Co., TN

Dover chert

COBBS TRIANGULAR - Early Archaic, 9000 - 5000 B. P.
(Also see Abasolo, Decatur, Lerma, Lost Lake and St. Charles)

Beveled edge

G7, $65-$125
KY

Beveled edge

G10, $200-$350
OH

LOCATION: Southeastern states. **DESCRIPTION:** A medium to large size, thin, lanceolate blade with a broad, rounded to square base. One side of each face is usually steeply beveled. These are un-notched preforms for early Archaic beveled types such as *Decatur, Dovetail, Lost Lake,* etc.

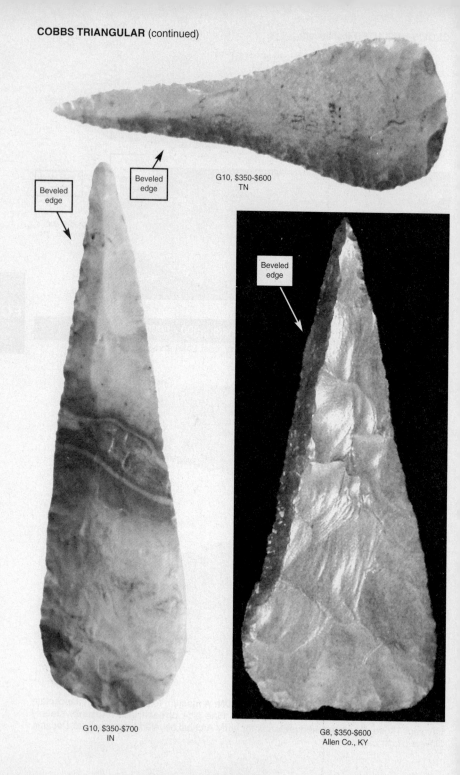

Beveled edge

Beveled edge

G10, $350-$600
TN

Beveled edge

G10, $350-$700
IN

G8, $350-$600
Allen Co., KY

COLDWATER - Trans. Paleo, 10,000 - 8000 B. P.

(Also see Hinds and Pelican)

LOCATION: East Texas into Arkansas, Louisiana & Tenn. **DESCRIPTION:** A medium size, Lanceolate point with a longer waist than *Pelican* and a straight to concave base which is ground. The blade expands up from the base.

G6, $150-$250
AL

Ground stem

CONERLY - Middle Archaic, 7500 - 4500 B. P.

(Also see Beaver Lake and Copena)

Fairly thick cross section

| G7, $25-$45 | G10, $65-$125 | G7, $30-$50 | G8, $35-$65 |
| Nickajack Lake, TN | Bradley Co., TN | TN | KY |

LOCATION: Southern Southeastern states, especially Tennessee, Georgia and Florida. **DESCRIPTION:** A medium to large auriculate point with a contracting, concave base which can be ground. On some examples, the hafting area can be seen with the presence of very weak shoulders. The base is usually thinned. Believed to be related to the *Guilford* type. **I.D. KEY:** Base concave, thickness, flaking.

COOSA - Woodland, 2000 - 1500 B. P.

(Also see Buggs Island and Crawford Creek)

 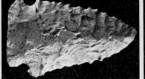 

G5, $1-$2
Nickajack Lake, TN

G5, $1-$3
Meigs Co., TN

G5, $1-$3
Jackson Co., AL

EC

409

COOSA (continued)

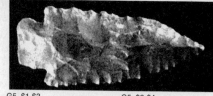

G5, $1-$3
Jackson Co., AL

G5, $2-$4
Jackson Co., AL

LOCATION: Southeastern states. **DESCRIPTION:** A medium size, usually serrated medium grade point with a short stem. Some examples are shallowly side-notched. Shoulders are roughly horizontal. **I.D. KEY:** Serrated blade edges, bulbous stem.

COPENA-AURICULATE - Middle Archaic-Woodland, 5000 - 2500 B. P.

(Also see Beaver Lake, Camp Creek, Candy Creek, Clovis, Quad and Yadkin)

Black chert

G4, $5-$10
Bradley Co., TN

G8, $12-$20
Nickajack Lake, TN

G8, $15-$25
Nickajack Lake, TN

G8, $15-$30
Decatur, AL

G9, $80-$150
Meigs Co., TN,
cache point.

G8, $90-$175
Meigs Co., TN,
cache point.

LOCATION: Southeastern states. **DESCRIPTION:** A medium to large size, lanceolate point with straight to recurved blade edges and a concave, auriculate base. Could be confused with *Beaver Lake, Candy Creek, Clovis, Cumberland* or other auriculate forms. Look for the random Woodland flaking on this type. Stems are not ground. **I.D. KEY:** Concave base.

COPENA-CLASSIC (Shield form) - Late Archaic to Woodland, 4000 - 1200 B. P.

(Also see Bakers Creek & Nolichucky)

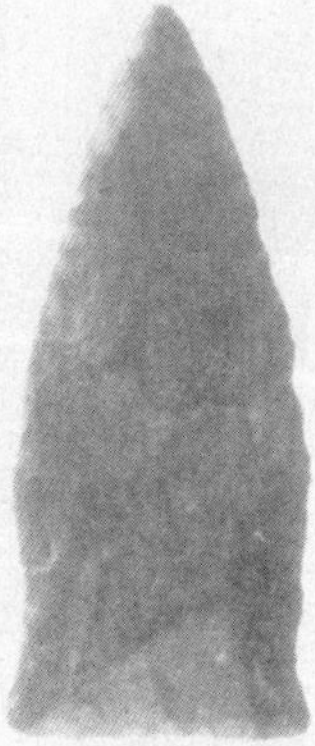

G5, $15-$25
TN

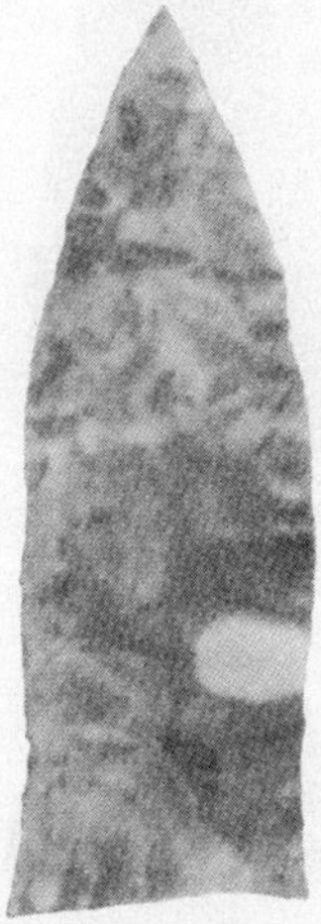

G6, $25-$40
TN

G5, $15-$25
TN

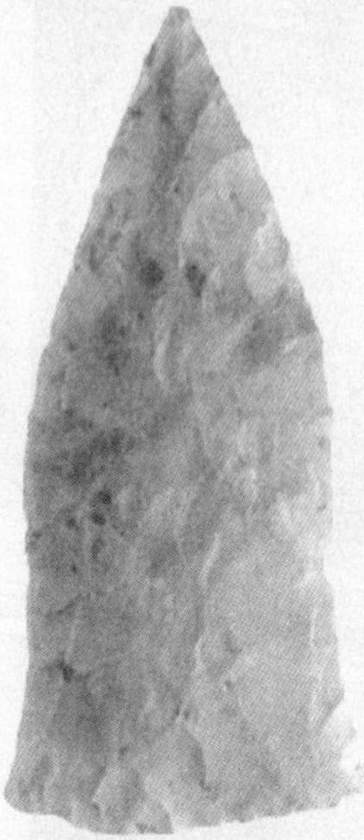

G7, $55-$100
Humphreys Co., TN

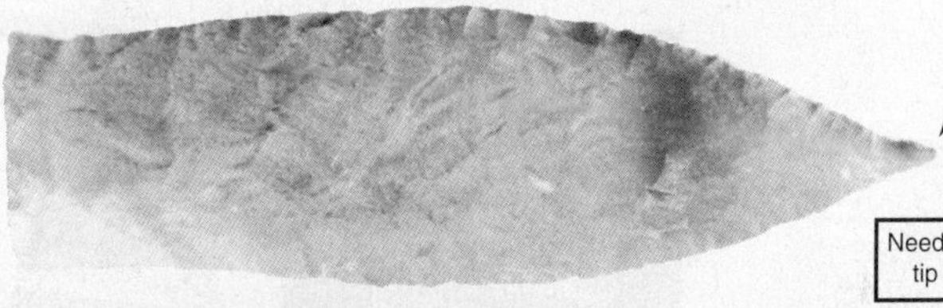
Needle
tip

G9, $125-$200
TN

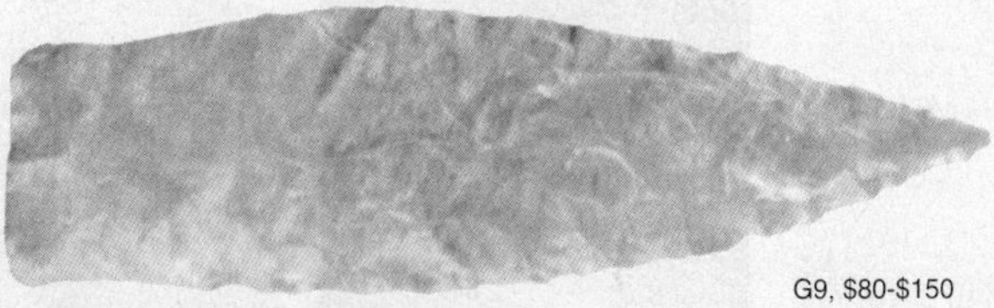

G9, $80-$150
TN

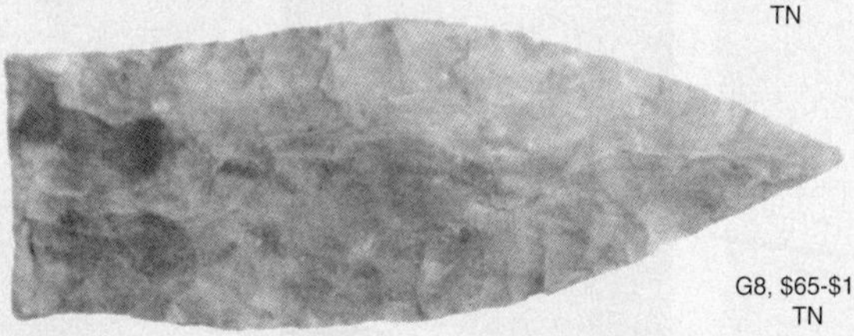

G8, $65-$125
TN

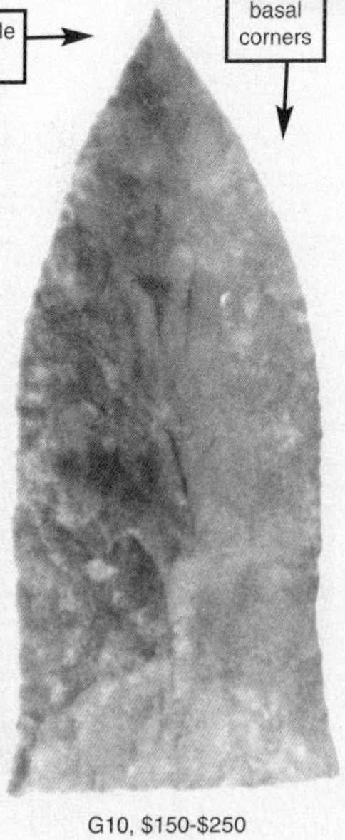
Needle
tip
Perfect
basal
corners

G10, $150-$250
TN

LOCATION: Southeastern states. **DESCRIPTION:** A medium to large size, lanceolate point with recurved blade edges and a straight to slightly convex base. This point usually occurs in Woodland burial mounds, but is also found in late Archaic sites in Tennessee. The Alabama and Tennessee forms are usually very thin with high quality primary and secondary flaking.

COPENA CLASSIC (continued)

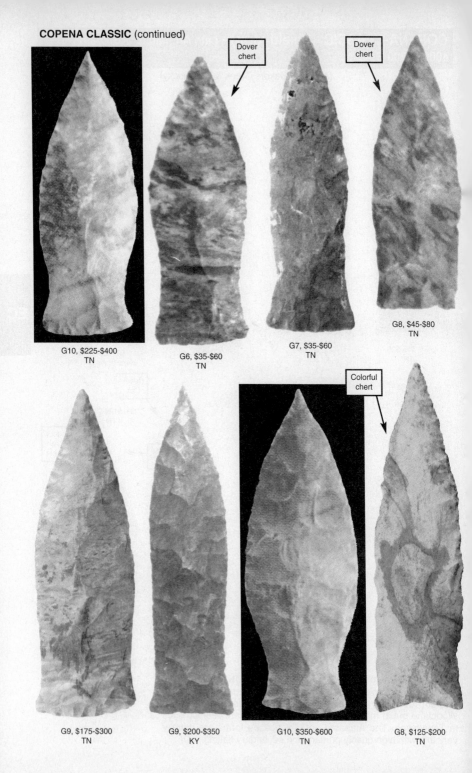

Dover chert

Dover chert

Colorful chert

G10, $225-$400
TN

G6, $35-$60
TN

G7, $35-$60
TN

G8, $45-$80
TN

G9, $175-$300
TN

G9, $200-$350
KY

G10, $350-$600
TN

G8, $125-$200
TN

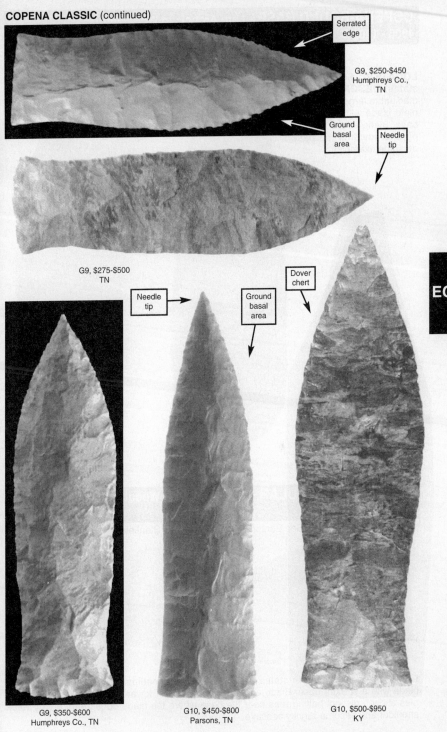

Serrated edge

G9, $250-$450
Humphreys Co., TN

Ground basal area

Needle tip

G9, $275-$500
TN

Needle tip

Ground basal area

Dover chert

EC

G9, $350-$600
Humphreys Co., TN

G10, $450-$800
Parsons, TN

G10, $500-$950
KY

413

COPENA-ROUND BASE - Late Archaic to Woodland, 4000 - 1200 B. P.

(Also see Frazier & Tennessee River)

LOCATION: Southeastern states. **DESCRIPTION:** A medium to large size lanceolate blade with a rounded base. Blade edges become parallel towards the base on some examples.

G6, $12-$20
Florence, AL

G8, $25-$45
TN

G8, $40-$75
KY

COPENA-TRIANGULAR - Late Archaic to Woodland, 4000 - 1800 B. P.

(See Benton Blade, Frazier and Stanfield)

← Sharp basal corners

G6, $15-$25
Parsons, TN

G8, $25-$45
Hardin Co., TN

LOCATION: Southeastern states. **DESCRIPTION:** A medium to large size lanceolate blade with a straight base. Blade edges become parallel towards the base. Some examples show a distinct hafting area near the base where the blade edges form a very weak shoulder and become slightly concave.

G8, $25-$40
W. KY

G5, $15-$25
TN

G8, $25-$40
Hardin Co., TN

G6, $25-$45
TN

EC

G8, $45-$80
TN

G10, $90-$175
Florence, AL

G10, $150-$250
TN, cache

G9, $125-$200
Decatur Co., TN

415

COPENA TRIANGULAR (continued)

G10+, $350-$600
AL

COTACO CREEK - Woodland, 2500 - 2000 B. P.

(Also see Flint Creek, Little Bear Creek, Smithsonia and Table Rock)

Serrated edge

Serrated edge

G6, $25-$40
Florence, AL

G8, $35-$65
Hickman Co., TN

G8, $35-$65
Florence, AL

Classic "blunt" tip

Pressure flaking extends all the way to tip

Classic form

G10, $300-$550
Florence, AL

G9, $80-$150
TN

G6, $15-$25
TN

Classic "blunt" tip

Needle tip

G10+, $700-$1200
W. TN, cache.

G6, $15-$25
TN

LOCATION: Southeastern states.
DESCRIPTION: A small to medium size, well made, broad, triangular stemmed point with wide rounded to square shoulders. Blade edges are usually finely serrated and some examples have blunt tips. **I.D. KEY:** Edgework and rounded shoulders.

EC

Classic "blunt" tip

Note serrations extend all around the tip

G10+, $500-$900
W. TN, cache.

G10+, $800-$1500
Ramar, TN

COTACO CREEK BLADE - Woodland, 2500 - 2000 B. P.

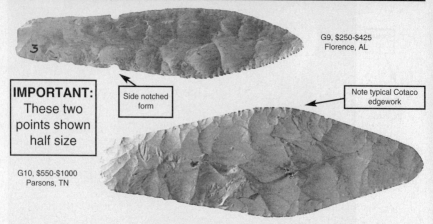

G9, $250-$425
Florence, AL

IMPORTANT: These two points shown half size

Side notched form

Note typical Cotaco edgework

G10, $550-$1000
Parsons, TN

LOCATION: Southeastern states. **DESCRIPTION:** A medium to large size lanceolate blade with a rounded base. Blade edges expand past mid-section. Some examples are side notched for hafting.

COTACO-WRIGHT - Woodland, 2500 - 1800 B. P.

(Also see Flint Creek and Little Bear Creek)

LOCATION: Southeastern states. **DESCRIPTION:** A small to medium size, well made, narrow, triangular stemmed point with rounded to square shoulders. Blade edges are usually finely serrated and some have blunt tips.

G7, $35-$50
Florence, AL

G7, $40-$70
Morgan Co., AL

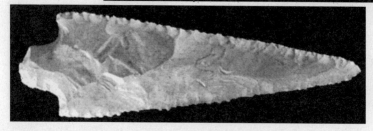

G9, $80-$150
Colbert Co., AL

CRAWFORD CREEK - Early Archaic, 8000 - 5000 B. P.

(Also see Coosa, Kirk Corner, Mud Creek and White Springs)

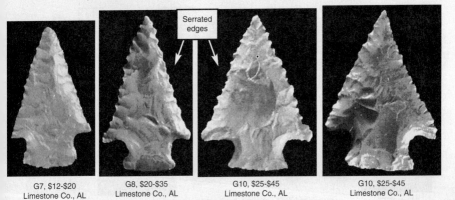

Serrated edges

G7, $12-$20
Limestone Co., AL

G8, $20-$35
Limestone Co., AL

G10, $25-$45
Limestone Co., AL

G10, $25-$45
Limestone Co., AL

LOCATION: Southeastern states. **DESCRIPTION:** A small to medium size point that is usually serrated with a short, straight to expanding stem. Shoulders are square to tapered. Blade edges are straight to convex. **I.D. KEY:** Early edgework.

CRESAP - Late Archaic to Woodland, 3000 - 2500 B. P.

(Also see Adena, Benton, Dickson)

G8, $65-$120, N. KY

Note fine edgework

G10, $350-$600
Trigg Co., KY

LOCATION: West Virginia into Kentucky. **DESCRIPTION:** A medium to large size point that has a medium-long contracting stem and slight shoulders. The base is usually straight. Stems can be ground. Associated with the early Adena culture. **I.D. KEY:** Long "squarish" tapered stem.

419

CUMBERLAND - Paleo, 12,000 - 8000 B. P.

(Also see Beaver Lake, Clovis, Copena Auriculate and Quad)

Fluted to tip

Tip nick. see pati- nation change

Tip nick

G5, $125-$200
Limestone Co., AL

G6, $250-$400
Limestone Co., AL

G5, $200-$350
Limestone Co., AL

G5, $200-$350
Limestone Co., AL

G6, $250-$450
Limestone Co., AL

Missing ear

Zaleski chert

Basal ears missing

Fluted to tip

G5, $150-$250
KY

G7, $400-$700
Franklin Co., OH

G5, $300-$550
KY

G6, $450-$800
Benton Co., TN

G5, $400-$750
Bedford Co., TN

Missing ear

LOCATION: Southeastern states to Canada. **DESCRIPTION:** A medium to large size, lanceolate, eared form that is usually fluted on both faces. The fluting and flaking technique is an advanced form as in *Folsom*, with the flutes usually extending the entire length of the blade. Bases are ground on all examples. An unfluted variant which is thicker than *Beaver Lake* has been found. This point is scarce everywhere and has been reproduced in large numbers. **I.D. KEY:** Paleo flaking, indirect pressure fluting.

CUMBERLAND (continued)

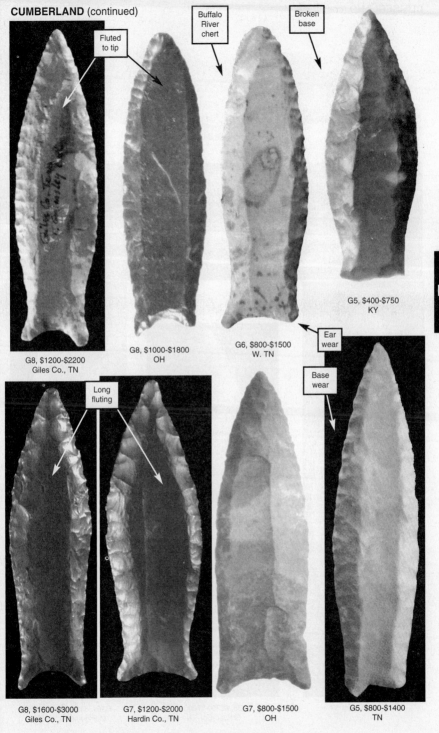

Fluted to tip

Buffalo River chert

Broken base

G5, $400-$750
KY

EC

G8, $1200-$2200
Giles Co., TN

G8, $1000-$1800
OH

G6, $800-$1500
W. TN

Ear wear

Base wear

Long fluting

G8, $1600-$3000
Giles Co., TN

G7, $1200-$2000
Hardin Co., TN

G7, $800-$1500
OH

G5, $800-$1400
TN

421

Fluted
to tip

G10+, $3000-$5000
KY

G10+, $3000-$5000
Colbert Co., AL

G7, $2700-$5000
KY

G8, $2700-$5000
Stewart Co., TN

G10+, $12,000-$20,000
Montgomery Co., TN

Fluted on one side only

G10, $8000-$15,000
Stewart Co., TN, Wells Creek.
Used in "Sun Circle & Human Hands."

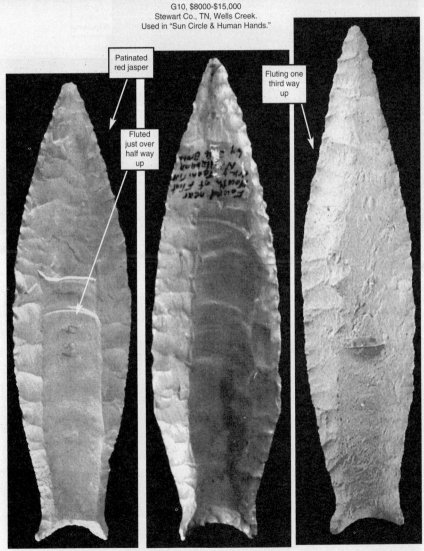

Patinated red jasper

Fluted just over half way up

Fluting one third way up

EC

G9, $15,000-$25,000
Nashville, TN

G9, $12,000-$20,000
Florence, AL, mouth of Flint Creek.

G9, $6500-$12,000
KY

423

CYPRESS CREEK - Middle to Late Archaic, 5000 - 3000 B. P.

(Also see Benton, Hardin, Kirk Corner Notched, Harpeth River and Lost Lake)

Dover chert

G8, $60-$100
Humphreys Co., TN

Classic drooping shoulders

G9, $650-$1200
Benton Co., TN

LOCATION: Southeastern states. **DESCRIPTION:** A medium to large size, broad stemmed point with an expanded base and drooping "umbrella" shoulder tangs. A cross between Lost Lake and Kirk Corner Notched. The blade is beveled on all four sides. **I.D. KEY:** Archaic flaking, shoulders droop.

DAGGER - Late Archaic to Woodland, 4000 - 1500 B. P.

(Also see Duck River Sword and Mace)

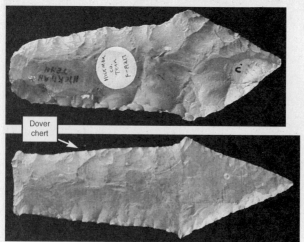

Dover chert

LOCATION: Southeastern states. **DESCRIPTION:** A large size knife with a handle fashioned for holding or for hafting. Most examples have a very thick cross section and are rare everywhere. Beware of counterfeits.

G8, $600-$1000
Hickman Co., TN

> **IMPORTANT:**
> Daggers shown half size

G8, $1000-$1800
Humphreys., TN

DAGGER (continued)

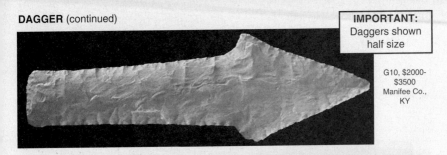

G10, $2000-
$3500
Manifee Co.,
KY

DALTON-CLASSIC - Early Archaic, 10,000 - 9200 B. P.

(Also see Clovis, Debert and Hardaway)

Flute
channel

Serrated
edge

Serrated
& beveled
edge

G6, $20-$35
KY

G9, $80-$150
TN

G6, $25-$40
AL

G6, $25-$40
Dubois Co., IN

Beveled
edge

G10, $200-$350
TN

Serrated
edge

G8, $90-$175
TN

G6, $30-$50
KY

EC

LOCATION: Midwestern to Southeastern states. **DESCRIPTION:** A medium to large size, thin, auriculate, fishtailed point. Many examples are finely serrated and exhibit excellent flaking. Beveling may occur on one side of each face but is usually on the right side. All have basal grinding. This early type spread over most of the Eastern and Midwestern U.S. and strongly influenced many other types to follow.

G7, $35-$65
TN

Serrated edge

G9, $90-$175
AL

G9, $150-$250
TN

Basal areas are ground

Serrated edge

G9, $200-$350
KY

G9, $350-$650
KY

G8, $200-$350
TN

DALTON-COLBERT - Early Archaic, 10,000 - 9200 B. P.

(Also see Beaver Lake, Dalton-Nuckolls, Plainview and Searcy)

G5, $20-$35
Hamilton Co., TN

Serrated edge

G5, $25-$40
Florence, AL

G7, $35-$50
TN

G8, $80-$150
Lauderdale Co., AL

G9, $175-$300
Stewart Co., TN

EC

LOCATION: Midwestern to Southeastern states. **DESCRIPTION:** A medium size, auriculate form with a squared base and a weakly defined hafting area which is ground. Some examples are serrated and exhibit parallel flaking of the highest quality. **I.D. KEY:** Squarish basal area.

DALTON-GREENBRIER - Early Archaic, 10,000 - 9200 B. P.

(Also see Beaver Lake, Greenbrier, Hardaway and Haw River)

Serrated edge

G6, $35-$60
Jamestown, TN

G6, $12-$20
TN

G6, $12-$20
Sullivan Co., TN

G2, $5-$10
Polk Co., TN

G6, $35-$60
Jackson Co., AL

G10, $80-$150
TN

427

Serrated edge

G7, $45-$80
Dayton, TN

G7, $45-$80
Walker Co., AL

G6, $35-$65, TN

G6, $40-$75
TN

G6, $35-$60
Hamilton Co., TN

G6, $25-$40
Huntsville, AL

G7, $125-$200
Humphreys Co., TN

LOCATION: Midwestern to Eastern states and Florida. **DESCRIPTION:** A medium to large size, auriculate form with a concave base and drooping to expanding auricles. Many examples are serrated, some are fluted on both sides, and all have basal grinding. Resharpened examples are usually beveled on the right side of each face although left side beveling does occur. Thinness and high quality flaking is evident on many examples. This early type spread over most the U.S. and strongly influenced many other types to follow. **I.D. KEY:** Expanded auricles.

DALTON-HEMPHILL - Early Archaic, 10,000 - 9200 B. P.

(Also see Cave Spring, Hardaway and Holland)

G8, $150-$250
KY

LOCATION: Midwestern to Eastern states. **DESCRIPTION:** A medium to large size point with expanded auricles and horizontal, tapered to weak shoulders. Blade edges are usually serrated and bases are ground. In later times, this variant developed into the *Hemphill* point. **I.D. KEY:** Straightened extended shoulders.

DALTON HEMPHILL (continued)

Dover chert

G8, $250-$400
Henry Co., TN

DALTON-NUCKOLLS - Early Archaic, 10,000 - 9200 B. P.

(Also see Dalton-Colbert and Hardaway)

EC

G6, $30-$50
Humphreys Co., TN

Made into a drill

G8, $45-$85
Humphreys Co., TN

G8, $45-$85
Humphreys Co., TN

Serrated edge

G8, $55-$100
Humphreys Co., TN

G9, $175-$300
Humphreys Co., TN

Serrated edge

LOCATION: Midwestern to Southeastern states. Type site is in Humphreys Co., TN. **DESCRIPTION:** A medium to large size variant form, probably occuring from resharpening the Greenbrier Dalton. Bases are squared to lobbed to eared, and have a shallow concavity. **I.D. KEY:** Broad base and shoulders, flaking on blade.

DAMRON - Early to Middle Archaic, 8000 - 4000 B. P.

(Also see Autauga, Ecusta, Gibson, Palmer and St. Charles)

G2, $1-$3
S.E. TN

G6, $8-$15
S.E. TN

G7, $15-$25
Limestone Co., AL

G7, $15-$25
Humphreys Co., TN

LOCATION: Southeastern states. **DESCRIPTION:** A small to medium size, triangular, side-notched point with a wide, prominent, convex to straight base. **I.D. KEY:** Basal form.

DEBERT- Paleo, 11,000 - 9500 B. P.

(Also see Clovis and Dalton)

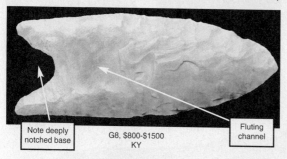

Note deeply notched base

G8, $800-$1500
KY

Fluting channel

LOCATION: Northeastern to Eastern states. **DESCRIPTION:** A medium to large size, thin, auriculate point that evolved from *Clovis*. Most examples are fluted twice on each face resulting in a deep basal concavity. The second flute usually removed traces of the first fluting. A very rare form of late *Clovis*. **I.D. KEY:** Deep basal notch.

DECATUR - Early Archaic, 9000 - 3000 B. P.

(Also see Cobbs Triangular, Ecusta, Hardin, Kirk, Lost Lake, Palmer and St. Charles)

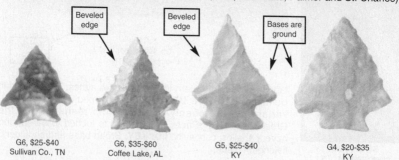

Beveled edge

Beveled edge

Bases are ground

G6, $25-$40
Sullivan Co., TN

G6, $35-$60
Coffee Lake, AL

G5, $25-$40
KY

G4, $20-$35
KY

DECATUR (continued)

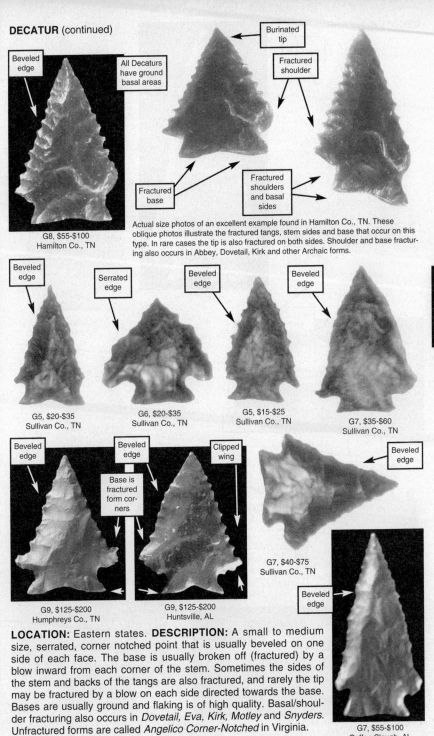

Burinated tip

Fractured shoulder

All Decaturs have ground basal areas

Beveled edge

Fractured base

Fractured shoulders and basal sides

G8, $55-$100
Hamilton Co., TN

Actual size photos of an excellent example found in Hamilton Co., TN. These oblique photos illustrate the fractured tangs, stem sides and base that occur on this type. In rare cases the tip is also fractured on both sides. Shoulder and base fracturing also occurs in Abbey, Dovetail, Kirk and other Archaic forms.

EC

Beveled edge

Serrated edge

Beveled edge

Beveled edge

G5, $20-$35
Sullivan Co., TN

G6, $20-$35
Sullivan Co., TN

G5, $15-$25
Sullivan Co., TN

G7, $35-$60
Sullivan Co., TN

Beveled edge

Beveled edge

Base is fractured form corners

Clipped wing

Beveled edge

G9, $125-$200
Humphreys Co., TN

G9, $125-$200
Huntsville, AL

G7, $40-$75
Sullivan Co., TN

Beveled edge

LOCATION: Eastern states. **DESCRIPTION:** A small to medium size, serrated, corner notched point that is usually beveled on one side of each face. The base is usually broken off (fractured) by a blow inward from each corner of the stem. Sometimes the sides of the stem and backs of the tangs are also fractured, and rarely the tip may be fractured by a blow on each side directed towards the base. Bases are usually ground and flaking is of high quality. Basal/shoulder fracturing also occurs in *Dovetail, Eva, Kirk, Motley* and *Snyders*. Unfractured forms are called *Angelico Corner-Notched* in Virginia.

G7, $55-$100
Coffee Slough, AL

431

DECATUR (continued)

Carter Cave flint

G9, $250-$450
KY

G6, $150-$250
KY

Base is fractured form corners

G9, $350-$650
Florence, AL

Serrated edge

G6, $80-$150
Coffee Lake, AL

Serrated edge

G9, $200-$350
Muhlenberg Co., KY

G7, $150-$250
KY

Base is fractured form corners

G10, $650-$1200
TN

432

DECATUR BLADE - Early Archaic, 9000 - 3000 B. P.

(Also see Hardaway Blade)

LOCATION: Eastern states. **DESCRIPTION:** A medium to large size, broad triangular blade with rounded corners and a straight base. A preform for *Decatur* points found on Decatur chipping sites.

G7, $5-$10
Morgan Co., AL. Found on a Decatur chipping site along with dozens of Decatur points.

DICKSON - Woodland, 2500 - 1500 B. P.

(Also see Adena, Cresap, Gary, Morrow Mountain and Waubesa)

EC

G6, $15-$30
KY

G6, $150-$250
Meigs Co., TN

G7, $30-$50
KY

G7, $20-$35
KY

G7, $25-$45
KY

LOCATION: Midwestern states. Type site: Fulton Co., MO., Dickson mounds, Don F. Dickson, 1927. **DESCRIPTION:** A medium to large size point with tapered shoulders and a contracting stem. High quality flaking and thinness is evident on most examples. **I.D. KEY:** Basal form.

433

DICKSON (continued)

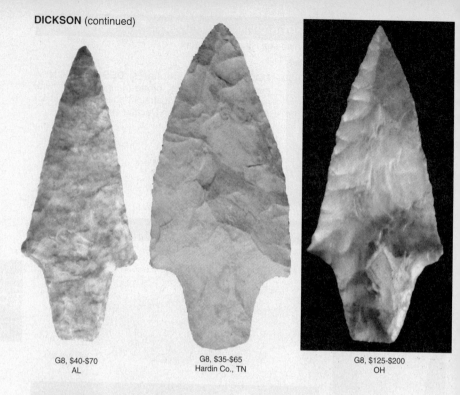

G8, $40-$70
AL

G8, $35-$65
Hardin Co., TN

G8, $125-$200
OH

DOVETAIL   (See St. Charles)

DRILL - Paleo to Historic, 14,000 - 200 B. P.

(Also see Addison Micro-Drill and Scraper)

Ground base

Wyandotte flint

St. Charles drill

Ground base

G4, $5-$10
Polk Co., TN

G4, $12-$20
Sou. IN

G6, $12-$20
KY

G4, $12-$20
Polk Co., TN

LOCATION: Everywhere. **DESCRIPTION:** Although many drills were made from scratch, all point types were made into the drill form. Usually, heavily resharpened and broken points were salvaged and rechipped into drills. These objects were certainly used as drills (evidence of extreme edge wear), but there is speculation that some of these forms may have been used as pins for clothing, ornaments, ear plugs and other uses.

DRILL (continued)

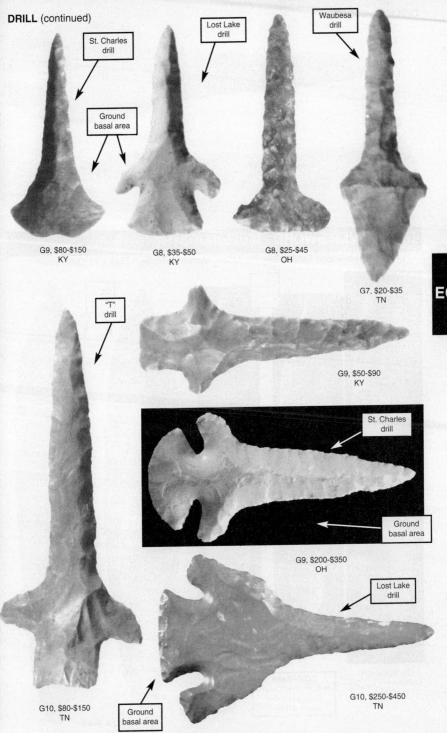

St. Charles drill

Ground basal area

Lost Lake drill

Waubesa drill

G9, $80-$150
KY

G8, $35-$50
KY

G8, $25-$45
OH

G7, $20-$35
TN

EC

"T" drill

G9, $50-$90
KY

St. Charles drill

Ground basal area

G9, $200-$350
OH

Lost Lake drill

G10, $80-$150
TN

Ground basal area

G10, $250-$450
TN

435

DRILL (continued)

G10, $150-$250
TN

G10, $150-$250
OH

DUCK RIVER SWORD - Mississippian, 1100 - 600 B. P.

(Also see Adena Blade, Dagger, Mace, Morse Knife, Sun Disk and Tear Drop)

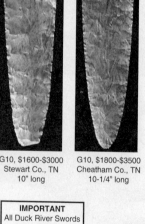

Dover chert

Dover chert

G8, $600-$1200
Montgomery Co., TN
13" long

G10, $1600-$3000
Stewart Co., TN
10" long

G10, $1800-$3500
Cheatham Co., TN
10-1/4" long

IMPORTANT
All Duck River Swords
above are shown
about 1/3 size.

G9, $2000-$2800
Stewart Co., TN

G10, $3000-$4800
TN

DUCK RIVER SWORD (continued)

LOCATION: Southeastern states. **DESCRIPTION:** A very large, narrow, double pointed ceremonial blade with a rounded base and a mucronate tip. Made by the Mississippians and used in their Eagle dances, as depicted on their shell gorgets, particularly at the Great Busk festival in the Fall. The famous Duck River cache of this type was found in the 1890s on the Duck River in Tennessee with lengths up to 30 inches. All are made of dover flint. Beware of reproductions.

DUVAL - Late Woodland, 2000 - 1000 B. P.

(Also see Bradley Spike, Fishspear & Mountain Fork)

G6, $20-$35
Bristol, TN

G6, $20-$35
Catoosa Co.,
GA

LOCATION: Southeastern states. **DESCRIPTION:** A small to medium size, narrow, spike point with shallow side notches and a straight to concave base. The base can be slight to moderate.

EARLY OVOID KNIFE - Trans. Paleo-early Archaic, 11,000 - 8000 B. P.

(Also see Turkeytail)

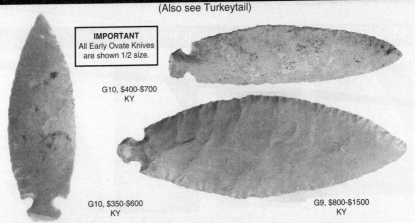

IMPORTANT
All Early Ovate Knives
are shown 1/2 size.

G10, $400-$700
KY

G10, $350-$600
KY

G9, $800-$1500
KY

LOCATION: Midwestern states from Kentucky, Arkansas north to Wisconsin and Michigan. **DESCRIPTION:** A medium to very large size, broad, thin blade that comes in two forms. It can be bi-pointed or it can have a small, rounded stem created by side notches. **I.D. KEY:** Stem size and blade form.

EASTERN STEMMED LANCEOLATE - Early Archaic, 9500 - 7000 B. P.

(Also see Alberta and Stringtown)

LOCATION: Pennsylvania, Ohio westward. **DESCRIPTION:** A medium to large size, broad stemmed point with convex to parallel sides and square shoulders. The stem is parallel sided to slightly expanding. The hafting area is ground. Most examples have horizontal to oblique parallel flaking and are of high quality and thinness. The Eastern form of the *Scottsbluff* type made by the Cody Complex people. The *Stringtown* is an eared version of this type. **I.D. KEY:** Base form and parallel flaking.

EASTERN STEMMED LANCEOLATE (continued)

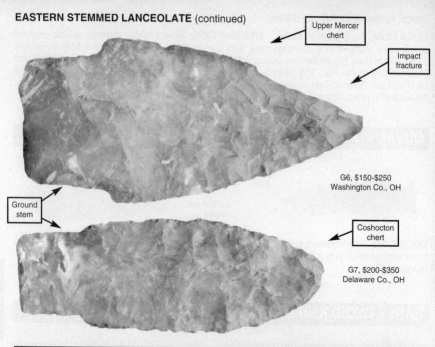

Upper Mercer chert

Impact fracture

Ground stem

G6, $150-$250
Washington Co., OH

Coshocton chert

G7, $200-$350
Delaware Co., OH

EBENEZER - Woodland, 2000 - 1500 B. P.

(Also see Buggs Island, Gary, Montgomery and Morrow Mountain)

Milky quartz

G4, $2-$4
Dallas Co., AL

G4, $2-$4
Dallas Co., AL

G4, $2-$4
Dallas Co., AL

G4, $2-$4
Polk Co., TN

G4, $3-$7
TN

LOCATION: Southeastern states. **DESCRIPTION:** A small size, broad, triangular point with a short, rounded stem. Some are round base triangles with no stem. Shoulders are tapered to square. Very similar to the earlier *Morrow Mountain Round Base* but with random Woodland chipping. Related to *Candy Creek, Camp Creek* and *Nolichucky*.

ECUSTA - Early Archaic, 8000 - 5000 B. P.

(Also see Autauga, Brewerton, Damron, Decatur and Palmer)

ECUSTA (continued)

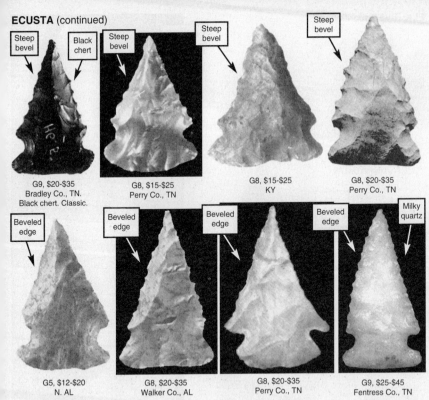

Steep bevel / Black chert
G9, $20-$35
Bradley Co., TN.
Black chert. Classic.

Steep bevel
G8, $15-$25
Perry Co., TN

Steep bevel
G8, $15-$25
KY

Steep bevel
G8, $20-$35
Perry Co., TN

Beveled edge
G5, $12-$20
N. AL

Beveled edge
G8, $20-$35
Walker Co., AL

Beveled edge
G8, $20-$35
Perry Co., TN

Beveled edge / Milky quartz
G9, $25-$45
Fentress Co., TN

EC

LOCATION: Southeastern states. **DESCRIPTION:** A small size, serrated, side-notched point with usually one side of each face steeply beveled. Although examples exist with all four sides beveled and flaked to a median ridge. The base and notches are ground. Very similar to *Autauga*, with the latter being corner-notched and not beveled.

ELK RIVER - Early Archaic, 8000 - 5000 B. P.

(Also see Benton and Buzzard Roost Creek)

G2, $5-$10
Meigs Co., TN

G4, $12-$20
Limestone Co., AL

G4, $8-$15
S.E. TN

G4, $12-$20
Meigs Co., TN

Diagonal flaking

G7, $35-$65
Colbert Co., AL

Thick cross section

Diagonal flaking

G7, $65-$125
Benton Co., TN

G7, $80-$150
Walker Co., AL

G9, $450-$850
Humphreys Co., TN

LOCATION: Southeastern states. **DESCRIPTION:** A medium to large size, narrow, stemmed blade with oblique parallel flaking. Shoulders are tapered, straight or barbed. Stems are parallel, contracting, expanding, bulbous or bifurcated. Believed to be related to *Benton* points. **I.D. KEY:** Squared base, diagonal parallel flaking.

ELK RIVER (continued)

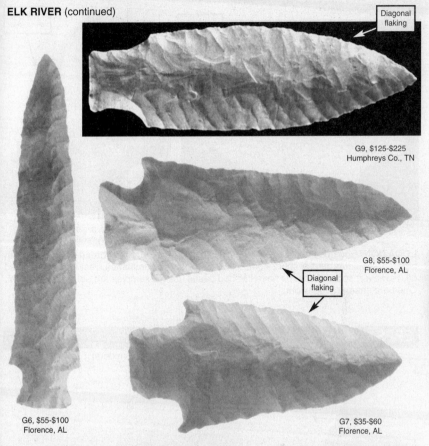

Diagonal flaking

G9, $125-$225
Humphreys Co., TN

G8, $55-$100
Florence, AL

Diagonal flaking

EC

G6, $55-$100
Florence, AL

G7, $35-$60
Florence, AL

ELORA - Middle to Late Archaic, 6000 - 3000 B. P.

(Also see Maples, Morrow Mountain, Pickwick, Savannah River and Shoals Creek)

Serrated edge

G4, $2-$5
Polk Co., TN

G7, $30-$50
Worth Co., GA

ELORA (continued)

Pink/white quartzite

Note fine serrations

G8, $35-$60
N. GA

G8, $25-$45
Fentress Co., TN

LOCATION: Southeastern states. **DESCRIPTION:** A medium size, broad, thick point with tapered shoulders and a short, contracting stem that is sometimes fractured or snapped off. However, some examples have finished bases. Early examples are serrated. **I.D. KEY:** One barb sharper, edgework.

EPPS - Late Archaic to Woodland, 4500 - 2500 B. P.

(Also see Buck Creek, Smithsonia, Motley, Snyders)

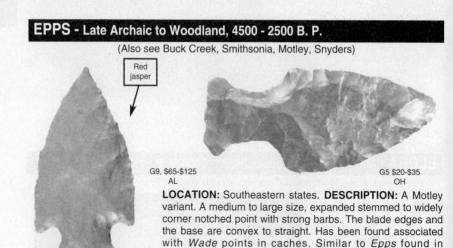

Red jasper

G9, $65-$125
AL

G5 $20-$35
OH

LOCATION: Southeastern states. **DESCRIPTION:** A Motley variant. A medium to large size, expanded stemmed to widely corner notched point with strong barbs. The blade edges and the base are convex to straight. Has been found associated with *Wade* points in caches. Similar to *Epps* found in Louisiana which has a straight base; *Motley*s are more barbed than *Epps*.

ETLEY - Late Archaic, 4000 - 2500 B. P.

(Also see Hardin, Mehlville, Pickwick and Stilwell)

IMPORTANT:
Etley shown half size

G8, $200-$350
Dekalb Co., IN

ETLEY (continued)

LOCATION: Midwestern states. **DESCRIPTION:** A large size, narrow point with barbed shoulders, recurved blade edges and an expanding stem. **I.D. KEY:** One barb sharper, edgework.

EVA - Early to Middle Archaic,   8000 - 5000 B. P.

(Also see Hamilton Stemmed and Wade)

G5, $15-$30
KY

G6, $25-$40
TN

G7, $35-$65
TN

G7, $25-$45
TN

G9, $80-$150
Giles Co., TN

G8, $65-$125
KY

G7, $35-$65
TN

EC

LOCATION: West Tennessee to SW Kentucky. Type site, Eva island in Humphreys Co., TN. **DESCRIPTION:** A medium to large size, triangular point with shallow basal notches, recurved sides and sometimes flaring tangs. Early examples show parallel flaking. **I.D. KEY:** Basal notches, Archaic flaking.
A large Eva cache was found that included a Pickwick point.

443

G9, $65-$125
TN

G8, $65-$125
TN

G7, $35-$65
TN

G10+, $1800-$3000
Humphreys Co., TN,
Eva Island cache.

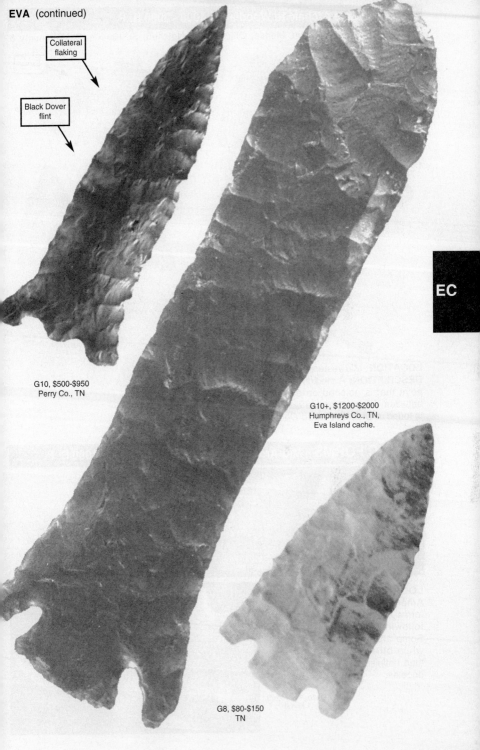

Collateral flaking

Black Dover flint

G10, $500-$950
Perry Co., TN

G10+, $1200-$2000
Humphreys Co., TN,
Eva Island cache.

EC

G8, $80-$150
TN

EVANS - Late Archaic to Woodland, 4000 - 2000 B. P.

(Also see Benton, Leighton, Merkle, Ohio Double-Notched, St. Helena, St. Tammany & Turkeytail)

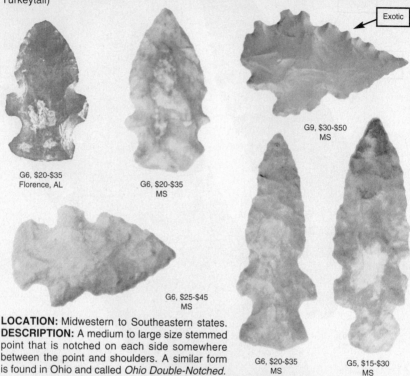

Exotic

G9, $30-$50
MS

G6, $20-$35
Florence, AL

G6, $20-$35
MS

G6, $25-$45
MS

LOCATION: Midwestern to Southeastern states.
DESCRIPTION: A medium to large size stemmed point that is notched on each side somewhere between the point and shoulders. A similar form is found in Ohio and called *Ohio Double-Notched*.

G6, $20-$35
MS

G5, $15-$30
MS

EXOTIC FORMS - Mid-Archaic to Mississippian, 5000 - 1000 B. P.

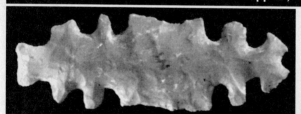

G9, $125-$225
N. TN

LOCATION: Throughout North America. **DESCRIPTION:** The forms illustrated on this and the following pages are very rare. Some are definitely effigy forms while others may be no more than unfinished and unintentional doodles.

G10, $125-$225
N. TN

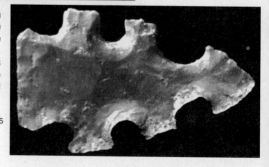

FAIRLAND - Woodland, 3000 - 1500 B. P.

(Also see Bakers Creek, Hardaway, Johnson, Limestone and Steubenville)

G6, $12-$20
MS

G6, $15-$25
Linden, TN

LOCATION: Texas, Arkansas, and Mississippi. **DESCRIPTION:** A small to medium size, thin, expanded stem point with a concave base that is usually thinned. Shoulders can be weak and tapered to slightly barbed. **I.D. KEY:** Basal form, systematic form of flaking.

FISHSPEAR - Early to Middle Archaic, 9000 - 4000 B. P.

(Also see Duval and Table Rock)

EC

G5, $12-$20
S.E. TN

G5, $12-$20
TN

G7, $30-$50
W. TN

G8, $35-$60
OH

G9, $80-$150
Parsons, TN

G9, $125-$200
West TN

LOCATION: Eastern states. **DESCRIPTION:** A medium to large size, narrow, thick, point with wide side notches. Bases are usually ground and blade edges can be serrated. Named due to its appearance that resembles a fish.

FLINT CREEK - Late Archaic to Woodland, 3500 - 1000 B. P.

(Also see Cotaco Creek, Elora, Kirk Stemmed, Mud Creek and Pontchartrain)

LOCATION: Southeastern and Gulf states. **DESCRIPTION:** A medium to large size, narrow, thick, serrated, expanded stem point. Shoulders can be horizontal, tapered or barbed. Base can be expanded, parallel sided or rounded. **I.D. KEY:** Thickness and flaking near point.

FLINT CREEK (continued)

Jaspr

G5, $5-$10
Fayette Co., AL

G5, $5-$10
Walker Co., AL

G5, $5-$10
Polk Co., TN

G6, $15-$25
TN

Serrated edge

G6, $15-$25
Linden, TN

G7 $20-$35
TN

Serrated edge

G6, $15-$25
TN

G8, $30-$55
TN

G9, $65-$125
Walker Co., AL

G9, $80-$150
W. TN

448

FLINT CREEK (continued)

G9, $65-$125
TN

FLINT RIVER SPIKE (see McWhinney Heavy Stemmed)

FORT ANCIENT - Mississippian to Historic, 800 - 400 B. P.

(Also see Hamilton, Madison and Sand Mountain)

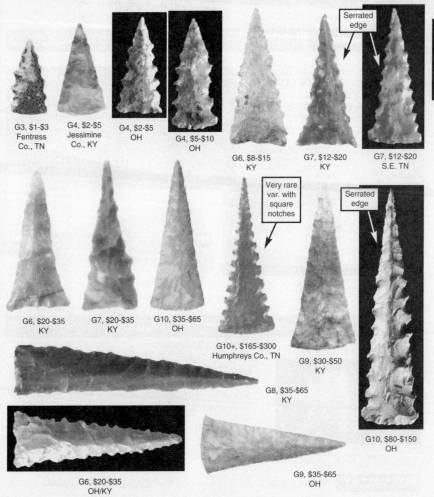

G3, $1-$3
Fentress
Co., TN

G4, $2-$5
Jessimine
Co., KY

G4, $2-$5
OH

G4, $5-$10
OH

G6, $8-$15
KY

G7, $12-$20
KY

Serrated edge

G7, $12-$20
S.E. TN

G6, $20-$35
KY

G7, $20-$35
KY

G10, $35-$65
OH

Very rare var. with square notches

G10+, $165-$300
Humphreys Co., TN

Serrated edge

G9, $30-$50
KY

G8, $35-$65
KY

G6, $20-$35
OH/KY

G9, $35-$65
OH

G10, $80-$150
OH

449

FORT ANCIENT (continued)

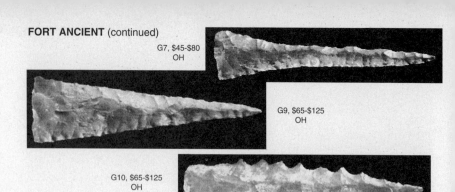

G7, $45-$80
OH

G9, $65-$125
OH

G10, $65-$125
OH

LOCATION: Southeastern states into Ohio. **DESCRIPTION:** A small to medium size, thin, narrow, long, triangular point with concave sides and a straight to slightly convex or concave base. Some examples are strongly serrated or notched. **I.D. KEY:** Edgework.

FORT ANCIENT BLADE - Mississippian to Historic, 800 - 400 B. P.

(Also see Copena)

LOCATION: Eastern to Southeastern states. **DESCRIPTION:** A medium size triangular blade with a squared base. Blade edges expand to meet the base **I.D. KEY:** Basal form.

Thin cross section

G8, $45-$85
Whitwell, TN

G5 $15-$30
N.E. AL

G8, $40-$75
Mason Co., KY

FOUNTAIN CREEK - Early Archaic, 9000 - 7000 B. P.

(Also see Kirk Stemmed)

LOCATION: North Carolina into east Tennessee. **DESCRIPTION:** A medium size, narrow point with notched blade edges and a short, rounded base which is ground. **I.D. KEY:** Edgework.

G10, $20-$35
Dayton, TN

Barbed edge

FOX VALLEY   (See Kanawha for a similar type found in Ky, TN, AL to WVA)

FRAZIER - Middle to Late Archaic, 7000 - 3000 B. P.

(Also see Big Sandy, Copena and Stanfield)

Black flint

G9, $25-$40
W. TN

LOCATION: Southeastern states. **DESCRIPTION:** A generally narrow, medium to large size lanceolate blade with a slightly concave to straight base. Flaking technique and shape is identical to that of *Big Sandy* points (minus the notches) and is found on *Big Sandy* sites. Could this type be unnotched *Big Sandy's*? **I.D. KEY:** Archaic flaking.

FREDERICK - Early to Middle Archaic, 9000 - 4000 B. P.

(Also see Cave Spring, Fox Valley, Garth Slough, Jude, Kanawha, Kirk, LeCroy, Rice Lobbed and Stanly)

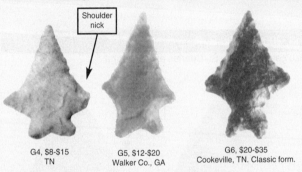

Shoulder nick

G4, $8-$15
TN

G5, $12-$20
Walker Co., GA

G6, $20-$35
Cookeville, TN. Classic form.

G7, $25-$45
S.E. TN. Classic form.

LOCATION: Southeastern states. **DESCRIPTION:** A small to medium size point with flaring shoulders and an extended narrow bifurcated base. A variation of the Fox Valley type. In the classic form, shoulders are almost bulbous and exaggerated.

GARTH SLOUGH - Early Archaic, 9000 - 4000 B. P.

(Also see Fox Valley, Frederick, Jude and Stanly)

G8, $25-$40
W. TN

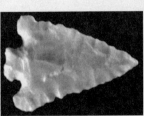

G8, $30-$50
Morgan Co., AL

G8, $25-$40
Morgan Co., AL

LOCATION: Southeastern states. **DESCRIPTION:** A small size point with wide, expanded barbs and a small squared base. Rare examples have the tangs clipped (called clipped wing). The blade edges are concave with fine serrations. A similar type of a later time period, called *Catahoula,* is found in the Midwestern states. A bifurcated base would place it into the *Fox Valley* type. **I.D. KEY:** Expanded barbs, early flaking.

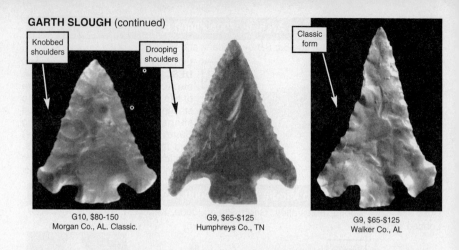

Knobbed shoulders

Drooping shoulders

Classic form

G10, $80-150
Morgan Co., AL. Classic.

G9, $65-$125
Humphreys Co., TN

G9, $65-$125
Walker Co., AL

GIBSON - Woodland, 2000 - 1500 B. P.

(Also see Hopewell, St. Charles and Snyders)

Hornstone with "bullesye" pattern

G7, $25-$45
KY

G7, $35-$65
KY

G7, $35-$65
OH

LOCATION: Midwestern to Eastern states. Type site is in Calhoun Co., Illinois. **DESCRIPTION:** A medium to large size side to corner notched point with a large, convex base. The base is typically broader than the blade. Made by the *Snyders* people. **I.D. KEY:** Short, broad base.

GRAHAM CAVE - Early to Mid-Archaic, 9000 - 5000 B. P.

(Also see Big Sandy, Newton Falls)

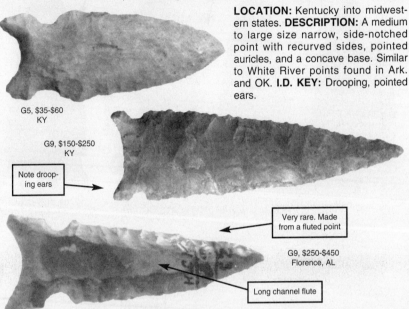

LOCATION: Kentucky into midwestern states. **DESCRIPTION:** A medium to large size narrow, side-notched point with recurved sides, pointed auricles, and a concave base. Similar to White River points found in Ark. and OK. **I.D. KEY:** Drooping, pointed ears.

G5, $35-$60
KY

G9, $150-$250
KY

Note drooping ears

Very rare. Made from a fluted point

G9, $250-$450
Florence, AL

Long channel flute

EC

GRAVER - Paleo to Archaic, 14,000 - 4000 B. P.

(Also see Perforator and Scraper)

G5, $8-$15
Humphreys Co., TN

Graver point

LOCATION: Found on Paleo and Archaic sites throughout North America. **DESCRIPTION:** An irregular shaped uniface tool with sharp, pointed projections used for puncturing, incising, tattooing, etc. Some examples served a dual purpose for scraping as well. In later times, *Perforators* took the place of *Gravers*.

GREENBRIER - Early Archaic, 9500 - 6000 B. P.

(Also see Brunswick, Dalton-Greenbrier, Hardaway and Pine Tree)

G4, $25-$45
TN

G9, $65-$125
KY

GREENBRIER (continued)

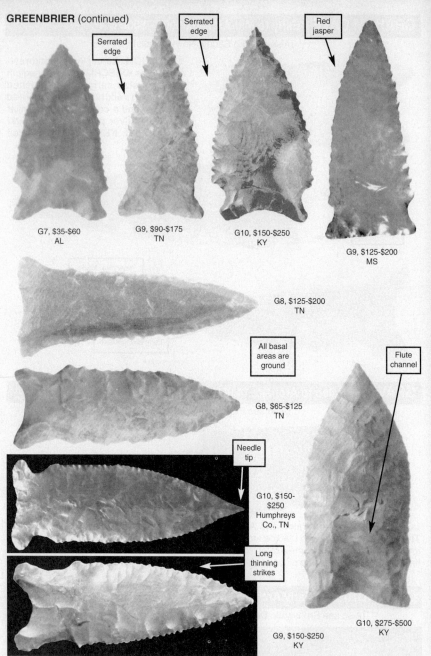

Serrated edge

Serrated edge

Red jasper

G7, $35-$60
AL

G9, $90-$175
TN

G10, $150-$250
KY

G9, $125-$200
MS

G8, $125-$200
TN

All basal areas are ground

G8, $65-$125
TN

Needle tip

Flute channel

G10, $150-$250
Humphreys Co., TN

Long thinning strikes

G9, $150-$250
KY

G10, $275-$500
KY

LOCATION: Southeastern states. **DESCRIPTION:** A medium to large size, auriculate point with tapered shoulders and broad, weak side notches. Blade edges are usually finely serrated. The base can be concave, lobbed, eared, straight or bifurcated and is ground. Early examples can be fluted. This type developed from the *Dalton* point and later evolved into other types such as the *Pine Tree* point. **I.D. KEY:** Heavy grinding in shoulders, good secondary edgework.

454

GREENBRIER (continued)

Needle tip & fine serrations

Serrated edge

G9, $125-$200
Coffee Lake, AL

G10, $125-$200
TN

G9, $150-$250
Florence, AL

EC

Dover chert

Serrated edge

G8, $150-$250
Humphreys Co., TN

Serrated edge

Serrated edge

G9, $150-$250
Humphreys Co., TN

G10, $150-$250
TN

G10, $250-$500
Humphreys Co., TN

G10, $350-$600
TN

455

GREENEVILLE - Woodland, 3000 - 1500 B. P.

(Also see Camp Creek, Guntersville, Madison and Nolichucky)

G6, $12-$20
E. KY

G6, $12-$20
Hamilton Co., TN

G8, $20-$35
Parsons, TN

G7, $15-$25
Humphreys Co., TN

G9, $40-$75
Humphreys Co., TN

LOCATION: Southeastern states. **DESCRIPTION:** A small to medium size lanceolate point with convex sides becoming contracting to parallel at the base. The basal edge is slightly concave, convex, or straight. This point is usually wider and thicker than *Guntersville*, and is believed to be related to *Camp Creek, Ebenezer* and *Nolichucky* points.

GUILFORD-ROUND BASE - Middle Archaic, 6500 - 5000 B. P.

(Also see Cobbs, Copena Round, Lerma & Morrow Mountain Round)

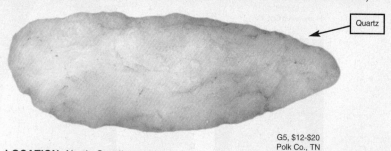

Quartz

G5, $12-$20
Polk Co., TN

G6, $20-$35
Polk Co., TN

LOCATION: North Carolina and surrounding areas into East Tennessee and Georgia. **DESCRIPTION:** A medium to large size, thick, narrow, lanceolate point with a convex, contracting base. This type is usually made of Quartzite or other poor quality flaking material which results in a more crudely chipped form than *Lerma* (its ancestor). **I.D. KEY:** Thickness, archaic blade flaking.

456

GUNTERSVILLE - Mississippian to Historic, 700 - 200 B. P.

(Also see Camp Creek, Greeneville, Madison and Nodena)

G5, $5-$10
Meigs Co.,
TN

G6, $15-$25
Meigs Co.,
TN

G6, $15-$25
Dayton, TN

G9, $15-$30
TN

G10, $25-$40
TN

G9, $25-$40
Jessimine
Co., KY

G10, $25-$45
KY

Banded
flint

G10, $35-$60
Hamilton Co.,
TN

G10, $25-$40
KY

Buffalo
River
chert

Perfect
"square"
base

EC

G6, $12-$20
KY

G8, $30-$50
Hamilton Co., TN

G10+, $55-$100
Cherokee Co.,
AL

G9, $30-$50
IN

G10, $40-$75
New Era, TN

G10+, $65-$125
TN

LOCATION: Southeastern states. **DESCRIPTION:** A small to medium size, thin, narrow, lanceolate point with usually a straight base. Flaking quality is excellent. Formerly called *Dallas* points. **I.D. KEY:** Narrowness & blade expansion.

HALIFAX - Middle to Late Archaic, 6000 - 3000 B. P.

(Also see Bakers Creek, Jude, Rheems Creek and Swan Lake)

457

HALIFAX (continued)

G5, $2-$3
Hinds Co., MS

G4, $2-$3
Hinds Co., MS

G5, $2-$3
Leflore Co., MS

G6, $5-$10
Walker Co., AL

LOCATION: Southeastern states. **DESCRIPTION:** A small to medium size, narrow, side notched to expanded stemmed point. Shoulders can be weak to strongly tapered. Typically one shoulder is higher than the other. North Carolina examples are made of quartz, rhyolite and shale.

HAMILTON - Woodland to Mississippian, 1600 - 1000 B. P.
(Also see Camp Creek, Fort Ancient, Madison and Sand Mountain)

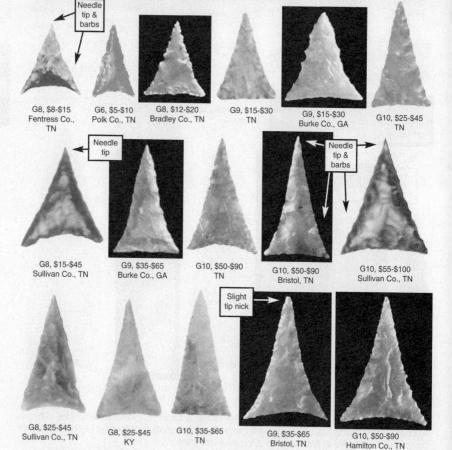

Needle tip & barbs

G8, $8-$15
Fentress Co., TN

G6, $5-$10
Polk Co., TN

G8, $12-$20
Bradley Co., TN

G9, $15-$30
TN

G9, $15-$30
Burke Co., GA

G10, $25-$45
TN

Needle tip

G8, $15-$45
Sullivan Co., TN

G9, $35-$65
Burke Co., GA

G10, $50-$90
TN

Needle tip & barbs

G10, $50-$90
Bristol, TN

G10, $55-$100
Sullivan Co., TN

G8, $25-$45
Sullivan Co., TN

G8, $25-$45
KY

G10, $35-$65
TN

Slight tip nick

G9, $35-$65
Bristol, TN

G10, $50-$90
Hamilton Co., TN

LOCATION: Southeastern states. **DESCRIPTION:** A small to medium size triangular point with concave sides and base. Many examples are very thin, of the highest quality, and with serrated edges. Side edges can also be straight. This type is believed to have evolved from *Camp Creek* points. Called *Uwharrie* in North Carolina. Some North Carolina and Tennessee examples have special constricted tips called *Donnaha Tips*.

HAMILTON (continued)

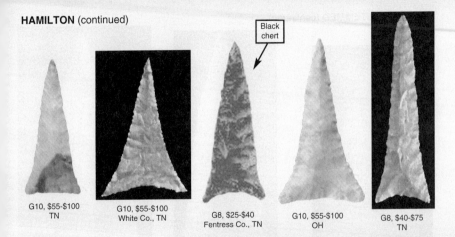

Black chert

G10, $55-$100
TN

G10, $55-$100
White Co., TN

G8, $25-$40
Fentress Co., TN

G10, $55-$100
OH

G8, $40-$75
TN

HAMILTON-STEMMED - Late Woodland to Mississippian, 3000 - 1000 B. P.

(Also see Buck Creek, Motley, Rankin, Smithsonia and Wade)

G4, $8-$15
Fentress Co., TN

G5, $20-$35
Putnam Co., TN

G8, $35-$60
Putnam Co., TN

G6, $30-$50
Fentress Co., TN

Hiwassee

G6, $25-$45
Hiwassee Isle, TN

G8, $35-$60
White Co., TN

LOCATION: Southeastern states. **DESCRIPTION:** A medium to large size, barbed, expanded stem point. Most examples have a sharp needle like point, and the blade edges are convex to recurved. Called *Rankin* in Northeast Tenn.

HAMILTON STEMMED (continued)

Classic

G6, $30-$50
Fentress Co., TN

G10, $90-$150
Dayton, TN

G10+, $200-$350
Meigs Co., TN

HARAHEY - Mississippian, 700 - 350 B. P.

(Also see Lerma, Ramey Knife and Snake Creek)

G10, $65-$125
TN

Quartz

G5, $20-$35
Fayatte Co., KY

G9, $125-$200
KY

HARAHEY (continued)

LOCATION: Kentucky to Texas, Arkansas and Missouri. **DESCRIPTION:** A large size, double pointed knife that is usually beveled on one side of each face. The cross section is rhomboid.

HARDAWAY - Early Archaic, 9500 - 8000 B. P.

(Also see Alamance, Dalton-Greenbrier, Haw River, Russel Cave, San Patrice and Wheeler)

G7, $30-$55
Fort Payne, AL

Ground basal area

G7, $125-$200
Lake Seminole, GA

G8, $25-$45
KY

Tip nick

G6, $80-$150
Sullivan Co., TN

EC

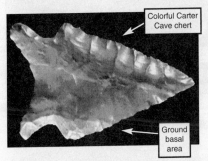

Colorful Carter Cave chert

Ground basal area

G8, $150-$275
Cent. KY

LOCATION: Southeastern states. **DESCRIPTION:** A small to medium size point with shallow side notches and expanded auricles forming a wide, deeply concave base. Wide specimens are called *Cow Head Hardaways* by some collectors in North Carolina. Ears and base are usually heavily ground. This type evolved from the *Dalton* point. **I.D. KEY:** Heavy grinding in shoulders, paleo flaking.

HARDAWAY-DALTON - Early Archaic, 9500 - 8000 B. P.

(Also see Alamance and Dalton)

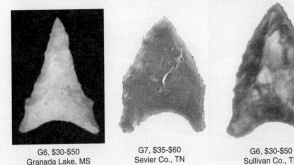
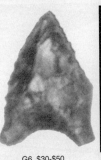

G6, $30-$50
Granada Lake, MS

G7, $35-$60
Sevier Co., TN

G6, $30-$50
Sullivan Co., TN

G6, $35-$60
Nickajack Lake, TN

LOCATION: Southeastern states. **DESCRIPTION:** A small to medium size, serrated, auriculate point with a concave base. Basal fluting or thinning is common. Bases are ground. Ears turn outward or have parallel sides. A cross between *Hardaway* and *Dalton*. **I.D. KEY:** Width of base, location found.

461

HARDAWAY DALTON (continued)

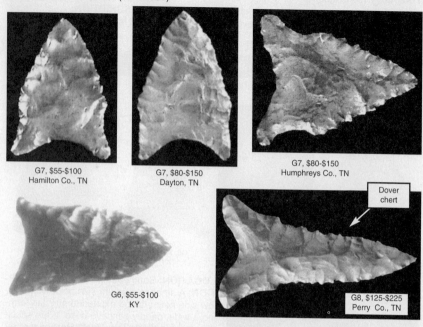

G7, $55-$100
Hamilton Co., TN

G7, $80-$150
Dayton, TN

G7, $80-$150
Humphreys Co., TN

Dover chert

G6, $55-$100
KY

G8, $125-$225
Perry Co., TN

HARDIN - Early Archaic, 9000 - 6000 B. P.

(Also see Buck Creek, Cypress Creek, Kirk, Lost Lake, Scottsbluff, St. Charles & Stilwell)

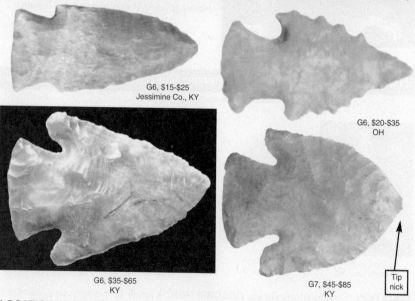

G6, $15-$25
Jessimine Co., KY

G6, $20-$35
OH

G6, $35-$65
KY

G7, $45-$85
KY

Tip nick

LOCATION: Midwestern to Eastern states. **DESCRIPTION:** A large size, well made triangular barbed point with an expanded base that is usually ground. Resharpened examples have one beveled edge on each face. This type is believed to have evolved from the *Scottsbluff* type. **I.D. KEY:** Notches and stem form.

HARDIN (continued)

Serrated edge

Ground basal area

G10, $250-$400
KY

G9, $65-$125
KY

G10, $350-$600
MS

EC

Beveled edge

Ground basal area

G6, $400-$750
OH

Colorful chert

G9, $1000-$1800
KY

463

HARDIN (continued)

Bischer chert

G8, $200-$350
IN

G6, $55-$100
Chickasaw Co., MS

"Knobbed" Hardin; one of the finest known

All basal areas are ground

G9, $450-$850
OH

G10+, $12,000-$22,000
Ohio Co., KY

464

HARPETH RIVER - Early Archaic, 9000 - 8000 B. P.

(Also see Bakers Cr., Cypress Cr., Dalton-Nuckolls, Mud Creek, Russell Cave and Searcy)

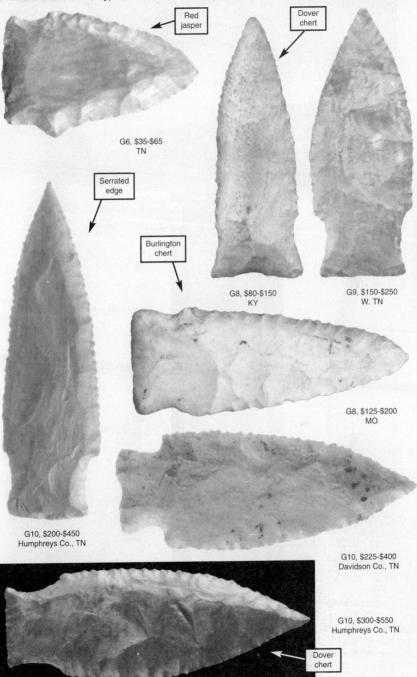

Red jasper

Dover chert

G6, $35-$65
TN

Serrated edge

Burlington chert

G8, $80-$150
KY

G9, $150-$250
W. TN

G8, $125-$200
MO

EC

G10, $200-$450
Humphreys Co., TN

G10, $225-$400
Davidson Co., TN

G10, $300-$550
Humphreys Co., TN

Dover chert

465

Ground stem

Dover chert

G9, $350-$600
Humphreys Co., TN

G7, $40-$75
W. TN

Serrated edge

Red/orange chert

Ground stem

G10, $350-$600
W. TN

G9, $650-$1200
Benton Co., TN

G10, $550-$1000
TN

LOCATION: Southwestern Kentucky into the Southeastern states. **DESCRIPTION:** A medium to large size, narrow, thick, serrated stemmed point that is steeply beveled on all four sides. The hafting area either has shallow side notches or an expanding stem. The base is usually thinned and ground. Rarely, the base is bifurcated. **I.D. KEY:** Weak notches, edgework.

HAW RIVER - Transitional Paleo, 11,000 - 8000 B. P.

(Also see Golondrina and Hardaway)

LOCATION: Southeastern states, especially North Carolina. **DESCRIPTION:** A medium to large size, thin, broad, elliptical blade with a basal notch and usually, rounded tangs that turn inward. Believed to be ancestor to the *Alamance* point. **I.D. KEY:** Notched base.

G5, $50-$150
Southeast, TN

HEAVY DUTY - Early to Middle Archaic, 7000 - 5000 B. P.

(Also see Harpeth River and Kirk Stemmed, McWhinney and Russell Cave)

Hornstone

Bufurcated base

Ground basal areas

G7, $25-$45
IN

G7, $25-$45
Hardin Co., KY

G7, $45-$85
KY

G8, $55-$100
KY

All have thick cross sections

Bufurcated base

G8, $65-$125
KY

G7, $35-$65
KY

LOCATION: Eastern states. **DESCRIPTION:** A medium to large size, thick, serrated point with a parallel stem and a straight to slightly concave base. Basal areas are ground. A variant of *Kirk Stemmed* found in the Southeast. **I.D. KEY:** Base, thickness, flaking.

467

Ground basal areas

G6, $20-$35
TN

G9, $45-$80
KY

G9, $55-$100
KY

Bufurcated base

Hornstone

G9, $65-$125
KY

G9, $150-$250
Coshocton Co., OH

Bufurcated base

G7, $45-$80
Preble Co., OH

Hornstone

G8, $90-$150
IN

468

HEAVY DUTY (continued)

Hornstone

G8, $175-$300
Rush Co., IN

G10, $350-$650
KY

G10, $300-$550
KY

EC

G10, $350-$650
OH

G9, $400-$750
KY

G10, $350-$650
KY

HI-LO - Transitional Paleo, 10,000 - 8000 B. P.

(Also see Angostura, Golondrina, Jeff, Johnson and Paint Rock Valley)

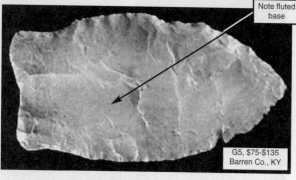

Note fluted base

G5, $75-$135
Barren Co., KY

G5, $50-$90
OH

G9, $150-$250
MI

G8, $125-$200
IN

LOCATION: Midwestern states. **DESCRIPTION:** A medium to large size, broad, eared, lanceolate point with a concave base. Believed to be related to *Plainview* and *Dalton* points.

HIDDEN VALLEY - Early to Middle Archaic, 8000 - 6000 B. P.

(also see Dickson and Morrow Mountain)

G10, $150-$250
TN

LOCATION: Arkansas, West Tennessee to Wisconsin. **DESCRIPTION:** A medium size point with square to tapered shoulders and a contracting base that can be pointed to straight. Flaking is earlier and more parallel than on *Gary* points. Called *Rice Contracted Stemmed* in Missouri.

HINDS - Transitional Paleo, 10,000 - 6000 B. P.

(Also see Pelican and Quad)

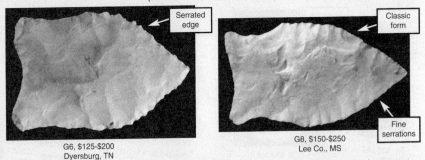

G6, $125-$200
Dyersburg, TN

G8, $150-$250
Lee Co., MS

LOCATION: Tennessee, N. Alabama, Mississippi, Louisiana and Arkansas. **DESCRIPTION:** A short, broad, auriculate point with basal grinding. Shoulders taper into a short expanding stem. Some examples are basally thinned or fluted. Related to *Pelican* and *Coldwater* points found in Texas.

HOLLAND - Early Archaic, 9500 - 7500 B. P.

EC

(Also see Dalton, Hardin and Scottsbluff)

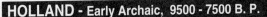

G8, $125-$200
West Memphis, TN

LOCATION: Midwestern states. **DESCRIPTION:** A medium to large size lanceolate blade that is very well made. Shoulders are weak to nonexistent. Bases can be knobbed to auriculate and are usually ground. Some examples have horizontal to oblique transverse flaking. **I.D. KEY:** Weak shoulders, early flaking.

G7, $65-$125
KY.

G8, $500-$900
Harrison Co., IN

HOPEWELL - Woodland, 2500 - 1500 B. P.

(Also see Dickson, Gibson, North, St. Charles and Snyders)

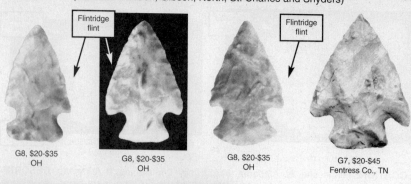

Flintridge flint

Flintridge flint

G8, $20-$35
OH

G8, $20-$35
OH

G8, $20-$35
OH

G7, $20-$45
Fentress Co., TN

G6, $35-$65
OH

Tip nick

G6, $35-$65
OH

G8, $125-$200
Livingston Co., KY

472

G5, $35-$65
KY

LOCATION: Midwestern to Eastern states. **DESCRIPTION:** A large size, broad, corner notched point that is similar to *Snyders.* Made by the Hopewell culture.

INTRUSIVE MOUND - Late Woodland-Miss., 1500 - 1000 B. P.

(also see Jacks Reef, Knight Island)

EC

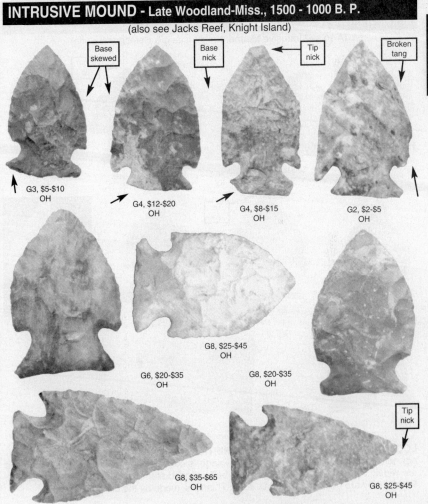

Base skewed

Base nick

Tip nick

Broken tang

G3, $5-$10
OH

G4, $12-$20
OH

G4, $8-$15
OH

G2, $2-$5
OH

G6, $20-$35
OH

G8, $25-$45
OH

G8, $20-$35
OH

G8, $35-$65
OH

Tip nick

G8, $25-$45
OH

473

INTRUSIVE MOUND (continued)

G9, $200-$350
Coshocton Co., OH

LOCATION: Ohio Valley area. **DESCRIPTION:** A very thin, narrow, medium size side to corner-notched point with a concave base and slightly barbed shoulders. Notching angles towards the tip. Contemporaneous with *Knight Island* & Jacks Reef points found in Kentucky, Tenn. and Alabama. **I.D. KEY:** Thinness of blade.

JACKS REEF CORNER NOTCHED - Late Woodland to Mississippian, 1500 - 1000 B. P.

(Also see Intrusive Mound, Knight Island & Pentagonal Knife)

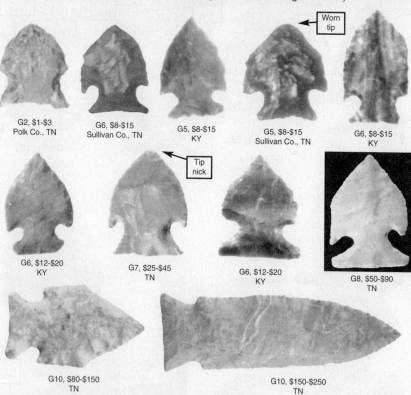

G2, $1-$3
Polk Co., TN

G6, $8-$15
Sullivan Co., TN

G5, $8-$15
KY

Worn tip

G5, $8-$15
Sullivan Co., TN

G6, $8-$15
KY

G6, $12-$20
KY

Tip nick

G7, $25-$45
TN

G6, $12-$20
KY

G8, $50-$90
TN

G10, $80-$150
TN

G10, $150-$250
TN

LOCATION: Southeastern states. **DESCRIPTION:** A small to medium size, very thin, corner notched point that is well made. The blade is convex to pentagonal. Some examples are widely corner notched and appear to be expanded stem points with barbed shoulders. Rarely, they are basal notched. **I.D. KEY:** Thinness, made by the birdpoint people.

JACKS REEF CORNER NOTCHED (continued)

Pentagonal form

Pentagonal form

G7, $20-$35
TN

G10, $125-$200
TN

G9, $90-$175
Clark Co., KY

G10, $90-$175
TN

G9, $65-$125
KY

EC

G8, $65-$125
TN

G10, $150-$250
OH

G8, $65-$125
TN

G10, $40-$75
TN

Beige chert

Very slight tip nick

G9, $125-$200
Savannah, TN

G8, $80-$150
TN

G9, $150-$250
Savannah, TN

G9, $50-$90
TN

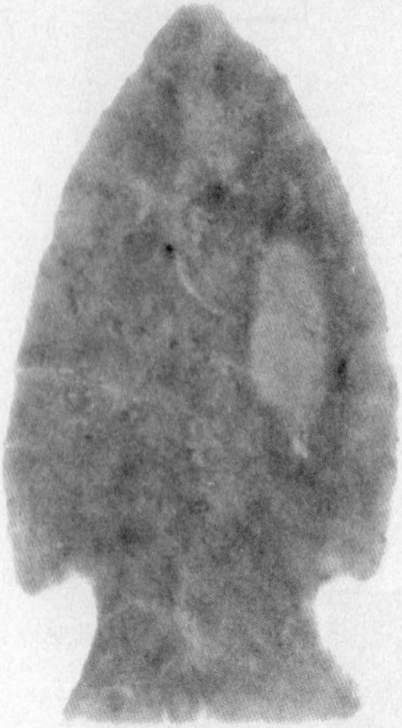

G6, $25-$45
KY

G8, $90-$175
TN

G8, $150-$250
TN

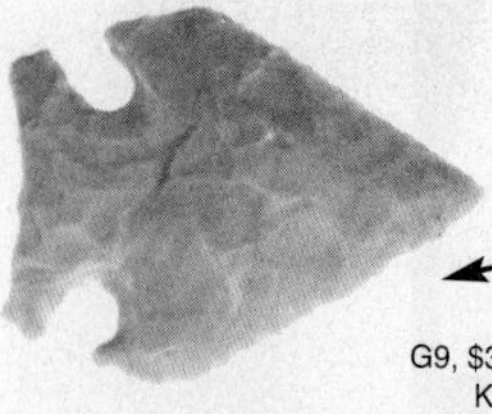

Pentagonal
form

G9, $30-$55
KY

G10, $200-$350
OH

G9, $200-$350
OH

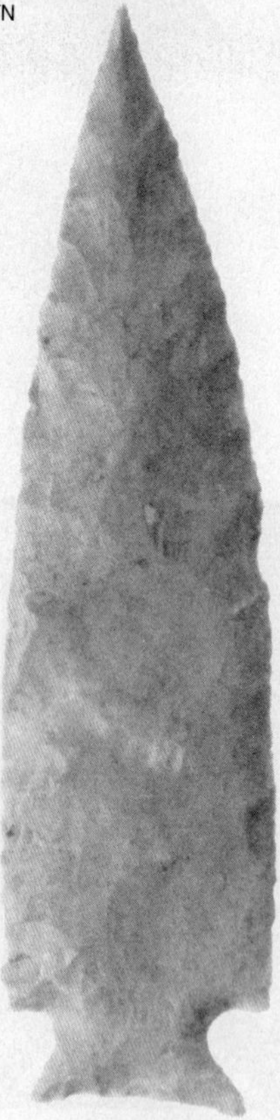

G10, $250-$450
TN

JACKS REEF PENTAGONAL - Late Woodland to Mississippian, 1500 - 1000 B. P.

(Also see Madison and Mouse Creek)

G2, $2-$4
Polk Co., TN

G3, $2-$5
Warren Co., TN

G5, $5-$10
Polk Co., TN

G6, $8-$15
Jessimine Co., KY

G6, $5-$10
AL

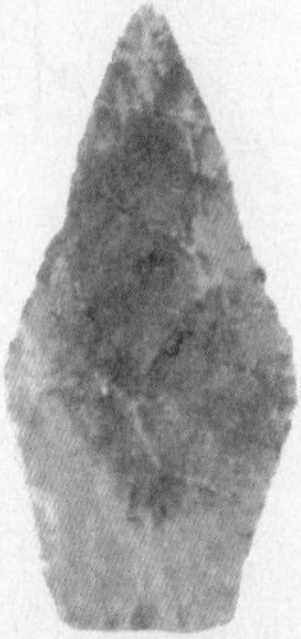

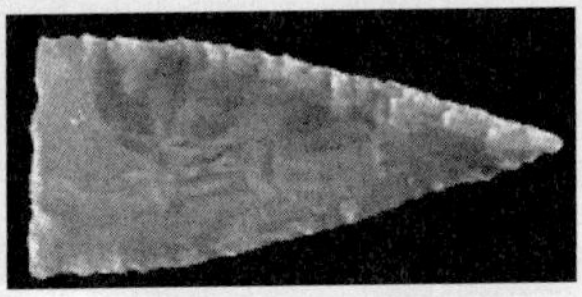

G7, $15-$25
Morgan Co., AL

G8, $20-$35
TN

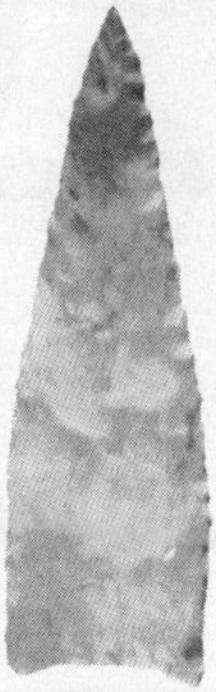

G10, $65-$150
TN

G9, $55-$100
TN

G10, $125-$200
Morgan Co., AL

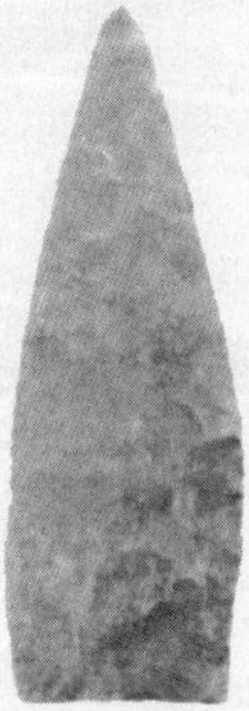

G10, $40-$75
TN

G10, $150-$250
TN

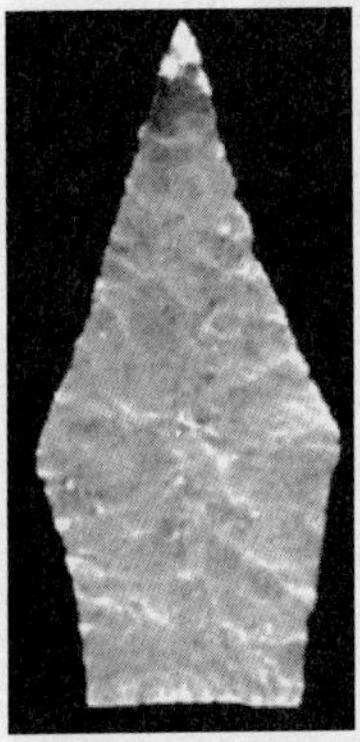

EC

G10+, $200-$350
Warren Co., TN

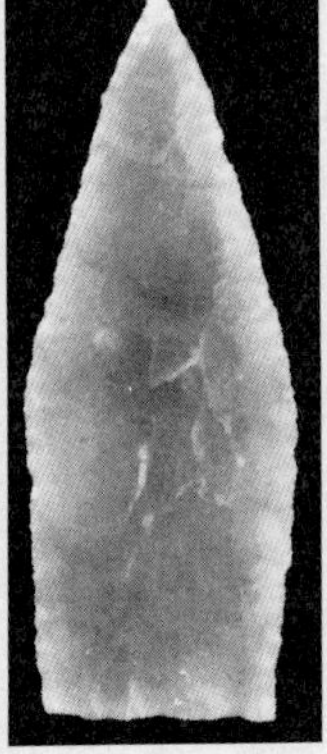

G10+, $200-$350
TN

G10, $65-$125
TN

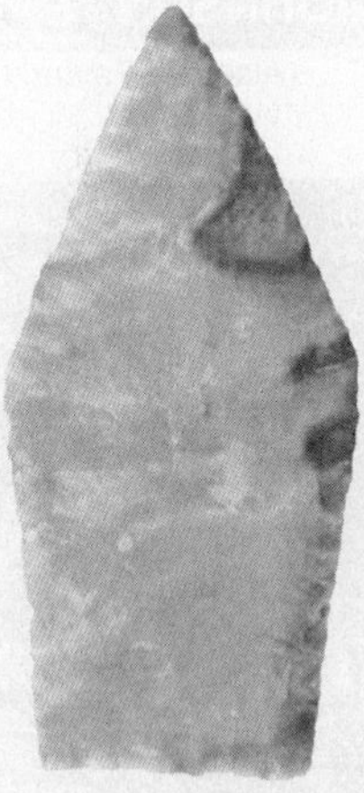

G10+, $300-$550
AL

LOCATION: Southeastern states. **DESCRIPTION:** A small to large size, very thin, five sided point with a sharp tip. The hafting area is usually contracted with a slightly concave to straight base. This type is called *Pee Dee* in North and South Carolina.

JEFF - Late Paleo, 10,000 - 8000 B. P.

(Also see Angostura, Browns Valley, Golondrina, Hi-Lo, Paint Rock Valley and Quad)

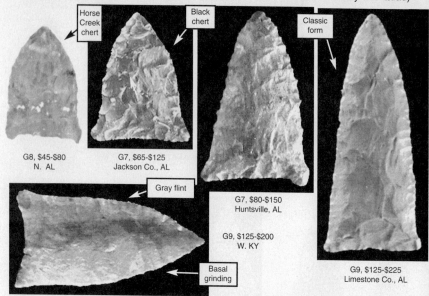

Horse Creek chert

Black chert

Classic form

Gray flint

Basal grinding

G8, $45-$80
N. AL

G7, $65-$125
Jackson Co., AL

G7, $80-$150
Huntsville, AL

G9, $125-$200
W. KY

G9, $125-$225
Limestone Co., AL

LOCATION: Southeastern states. **DESCRIPTION:** A medium sized, wide, lanceolate point with expanded auricles. The base is straight to slightly concave, is usually beveled or thinned, and may be ground. Auricles can either extend downward or out to the side. Some examples show fine pressure flaking on the blade edges. A rare type. **I.D. KEY:** One shoulder stronger.

JOHNSON - Early to Middle Archaic, 9000 - 5000 B. P.

(Also see Fairland, Hi-Lo, Limestone, McIntire, Savannah River and Steubenville)

G5, $15-$30
Natchez, MS

G5, $15-$30
N.E. AL

G6, $15-$30
TN

JOHNSON (continued)

LOCATION: Midwestern to Southeastern states. **DESCRIPTION:** A medium size, thick, well made, expanded stem point with a broad, concave base. Shoulders can be slightly barbed, straight or tapered. Basal corners are rounded to pointed to auriculate. Bases are thinned and ground. **I.D. KEY:** Pointed ears and thickness.

G8, $45-$85
Coffee Lake, AL

JUDE - Early Archaic, 9000 - 6000 B. P.

(Also see Cave Spring, Garth Slough, Halifax, Kanawha Stemmed, LeCroy, McIntire and Rheems Creek)

EC

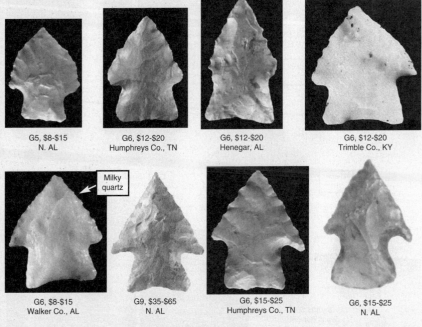

G5, $8-$15
N. AL

G6, $12-$20
Humphreys Co., TN

G6, $12-$20
Henegar, AL

G6, $12-$20
Trimble Co., KY

Milky quartz

G6, $8-$15
Walker Co., AL

G9, $35-$65
N. AL

G6, $15-$25
Humphreys Co., TN

G6, $15-$25
N. AL

LOCATION: Southeastern states. **DESCRIPTION:** A small size, short, barbed, expanded to parallel stemmed point with straight to convex blade edges. Stems are usually as large or larger than the blade. Bases are straight, concave, convex or bifurcated. Shoulders are either square, tapered or barbed. This is one of the earliest stemmed points along with *Pelican*. Some examples have serrated blade edges that may be beveled on one side of each face. **I.D. KEY:** Basal form and flaking.

KANAWHA STEMMED - Early Archaic, 8200 - 5000 B. P.

(Also see Frederick, Jude, Kirk Stemmed-Bifurcated, LeCroy, St. Albans and Stanly)

KANAWHA STEMMED (continued)

G5, $3-$5
Chattanooga, TN

G3, $1-$2
S.E. TN

G4, $3-$5
S.E. TN

G5, $3-$5
S.E. TN

G6, $4-$7
S.E. TN

G6, $8-$15
S.E. TN

G6, $8-$15
S.E. TN

G7, $30-$50
Warren Co., TN

G9, $45-$80
W. TN

Black chert

G6, $12-$25
Fentress Co., TN

G8, $15-$25
S.E. TN

G6, $8-$15
S.E. TN

Black chert

G6, $25-$40
OH

Note rounded lobes

G8, $35-$60
Watts Bar, TN

G9, $75-$125
KY

G10, $80-$150
Wayne Co., KY

G7, $55-$100
Monteray, TN

LOCATION: West Virginia into Southeastern states. First identified at the St. Albans site, Kanwaha Co., WVA. **DESCRIPTION:** A small to medium size, fairly thick, shallowly-bifurcated stemmed point. The basal lobes are usually rounded, expanding and the shoulders tapered to horizontal and can turn towards the tip. Believed to be the ancestor to the *Stanly* type.

KAYS - Middle Archaic to Woodland, 5000 - 2000 B. P.

(Also see Adena Robbins, Cresap, Little Bear Creek, McIntire and Pontchartrain)

G5, $8-$15
Morgan Co., AL

G5, $8-$15
Limestone Co., AL

G6, $12-$20
Florence, AL

G6, $12-$20
Limestone Co., AL

G7, $15-$25
Morgan Co., AL

G8, $20-$35
Decatur, AL

G10, $80-$150
AL

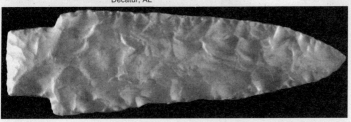

G9, $65-$125
Megis Co., TN.
Hiwassee River.

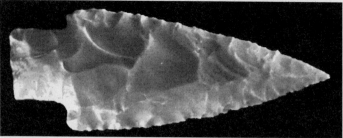

G8, $45-$85
Decatur, AL

LOCATION: Southeastern states. **DESCRIPTION:** A medium to large size, narrow, parallel sided stemmed point with a straight base. Shoulders are tapered to square. The blade is straight to convex. **I.D. KEY:** One barb is higher.

KEOTA - Mississippian, 800 - 600 B. P.

(Also see Merom)

G4, $1-$2
Meigs Co., TN

G4, $1-$2
Meigs Co., TN

G5, $5-$10
Wash. Co., AL

LOCATION: Okla, Ark, S.E. TN. & N. AL. **DESCRIPTION:** A small size, thin, triangular, side to corner-notched point with a rounded base.

KIRK CORNER NOTCHED - Early to Middle Archaic, 9000 - 6000 B. P.

(Also see Crawford Creek, Cypress Creek, Lost Lake, Neuberger, Pine Tree and St. Charles)

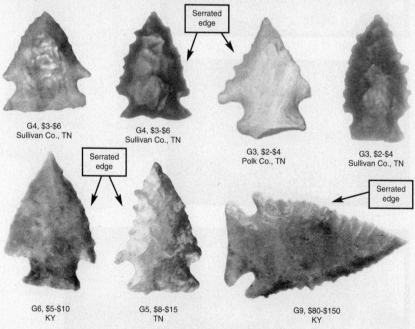

Serrated edge

G4, $3-$6
Sullivan Co., TN

G4, $3-$6
Sullivan Co., TN

G3, $2-$4
Polk Co., TN

G3, $2-$4
Sullivan Co., TN

Serrated edge

G6, $5-$10
KY

G5, $8-$15
TN

Serrated edge

G9, $80-$150
KY

KIRK CORNER NOTCHED (continued)

Serrated edge

G8, $35-$65
MS

G8, $25-$40
KY

G8, $30-$50
W. TN

All have ground basal areas

G8, $40-$75
KY

G5, $12-$20
KY

G5, $12-$20
Fentress Co., TN

Serrated edge

Serrated edge

If this point was beveled on opposite faces, it would be typed a Lost Lake

G8, $50-$90
OH

G7, $50-$90
KY

G9, $175-$300
Humphreys Co., TN

LOCATION: Southeastern states. **DESCRIPTION:** A medium to large size, corner notched point. Blade edges can be convex to recurved and are finely serrated on many examples. The base can be convex, concave, straight or auriculate. Points that are beveled on one side of each face would fall under the *Lost Lake* type. **I.D. KEY:** Secondary edgework.

483

KIRK CORNER NOTCHED (continued)

Bifurcated base form

G8, $55-$100
Spencer Co., OH

G7, $40-$75
KY

Serrated edge

G9, $80-$150
TN

G8, $80-$150
OH

If this point was beveled on opposite faces, it would be typed a Lost Lake

Serrated edge

Buffalo River chert

G10, $150-$250
TN

G9, $175-$300
KY

G9, $200-$350
Meade Co., KY

EC

G9, $250-$450
KY

Serrated edge

G9, $80-$150
Mt. Sterling, KY

If this point was beveled on opposite faces, it would be typed a Lost Lake

G8, $250-$400
KY

G8, $250-$400
TN

KIRK SNAPPED BASE - Early to Middle Archaic, 9000 - 6000 B. P.

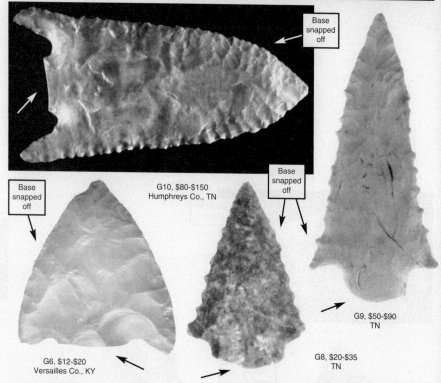

Base snapped off

Base snapped off

Base snapped off

G10, $80-$150
Humphreys Co., TN

G9, $50-$90
TN

G6, $12-$20
Versailles Co., KY

G8, $20-$35
TN

LOCATION: Southeastern to Eastern states. **DESCRIPTION:** A medium to large size, usually serrated, blade with long tangs and a base that has been snapped or fractured off. The shoulders are also fractured on some examples. This proves that the fracturing was intentional as in *Decatur* and other types.

KIRK STEMMED - Early to Middle Archaic, 9000 - 6000 B. P.

(Also see Elora, Flint Creek, Hamilton, Heavy Duty, St. Tammany and Stanly)

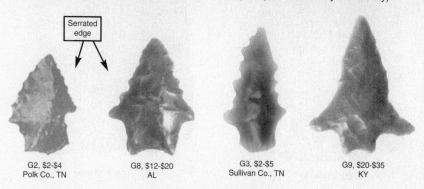

Serrated edge

G2, $2-$4
Polk Co., TN

G8, $12-$20
AL

G3, $2-$5
Sullivan Co., TN

G9, $20-$35
KY

KIRK STEMMED (continued)

Serrated edge

G7, $8-$15
AL

G9, $25-$45
Sullivan Co., TN

Serrated edge

G7, $15-$25
Jessimine Co., KY

G6, $15-$25
Sullivan Co., TN

EC

Serrated edge

Serrated edge

G5, $12-$20
KY

G7, $20-$35
KY

G7, $15-$25
OH

G6, $12-$20
KY

G7, $25-$45
KY

Dover chert

G9, $80-$150
Humphreys Co., TN

LOCATION: Southeastern to Eastern states. **DESCRIPTION:** A medium to large size, barbed, stemmed point with deep notches or fine serrations along the blade edges. The stem is parallel to expanding. The stem sides may be steeply beveled on opposite faces. Some examples also have a distinct bevel on the right side of each blade edge. The base can be concave, convex or straight, and can be very short. The shoulders are usually strongly barbed. Believed to have evolved into *Stanly* and other types. **I.D. KEY:** Serrations.

487

KIRK STEMMED (continued)

Serrated edge

Coshocton chert

G9, $40-$75
TN

G6, $20-$35
TN

G8, $45-$85
Marshall Co., KY

G8, $45-$85
OH

Serrated edge

G6, $25-$45
TN

G9, $45-$85
TN

G8, $35-$65
KY

G9, $350-$600
Franklin Co., AL

KIRK STEMMED (continued)

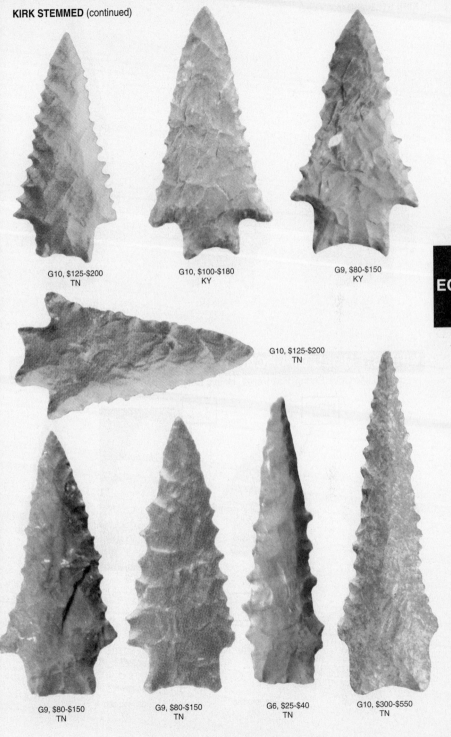

G10, $125-$200
TN

G10, $100-$180
KY

G9, $80-$150
KY

EC

G10, $125-$200
TN

G9, $80-$150
TN

G9, $80-$150
TN

G6, $25-$40
TN

G10, $300-$550
TN

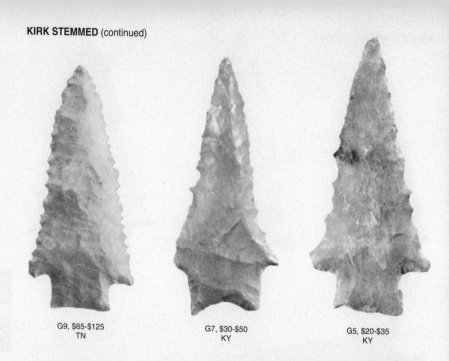

G9, $65-$125
TN

G7, $30-$50
KY

G5, $20-$35
KY

KIRK STEMMED-BIFURCATED - Early Archaic, 9000 - 7000 B. P.
(Also see Cave Spring, Fox Valley, Heavy Duty, LeCroy, St. Albans and Stanly)

Serrated
edge

Milky
Quartz

G4, $5-$10
KY

G6, $12-$20
S.E. TN

G6, $20-$35
N.E. TN

G6, $12-$20
KY

Serrated
edge

G7, $30-$50
OH

G6, $12-$20
KY

490

KIRK STEMMED BIFURCATED (continued)

G6, $25-$40
White Co., TN

Serrated
edge

G4, $6-$12
KY

Notched
edge

Serrated
edge

G6, $8-$15
TN

G9, $50-$90
KY

G6, $40-$75
Christian Co., KY

G6, $45-$80
KY

EC

LOCATION: Southeastern to Eastern states. **DESCRIPTION:** A medium to large size point with deep notches or fine serrations along the blade edges. The stem is parallel sided to expanded and is bifurcated. Believed to be an early form for the type which later developed into *Stanly* and other types. Some examples have a steep bevel on the right side of each blade edge.

KNIGHT ISLAND - Late Woodland, 1500 - 1000 B. P.

(Also see Cache River, Intrusive Mound and Jacks Reef)

G5, $20-$35
Humphreys Co., TN

G9, $80-$150
TN

Carter
Cave
chert

Shoulder
nick

G5, $12-$20
TN

G8, $35-$65
KY

G5, $20-$35
Humphreys Co., TN

G6, $30-$50
Humphreys Co., TN

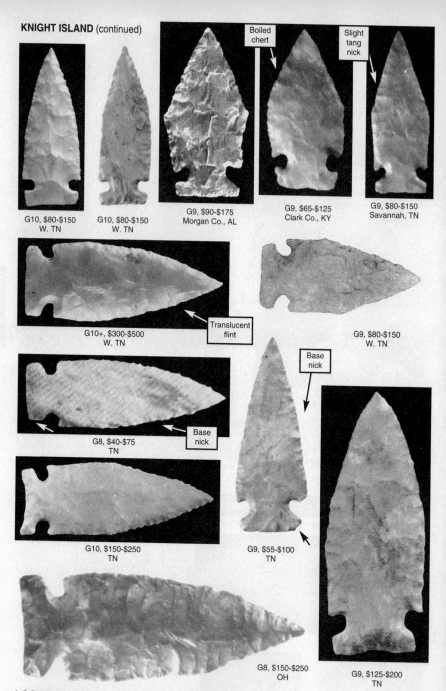

G10, $80-$150
W. TN

G10, $80-$150
W. TN

Boiled chert

G9, $90-$175
Morgan Co., AL

G9, $65-$125
Clark Co., KY

Slight tang nick

G9, $80-$150
Savannah, TN

Translucent flint

G10+, $300-$500
W. TN

G9, $80-$150
W. TN

G8, $40-$75
TN

Base nick

Base nick

G10, $150-$250
TN

G9, $55-$100
TN

G8, $150-$250
OH

G9, $125-$200
TN

LOCATION: Southeastern states. **DESCRIPTION:** A small to medium size, very thin, narrow, side-notched point with a straight base. Longer examples can have a pentagonal apperarance. Called *Raccoon Creek* in Ohio. A side-notched Jacks Reef. **I.D. KEY:** Thinness, basal form. Made by the bird point people.

LAKE ERIE - Early to Middle Archaic, 9000 - 5000 B. P.

(Also see Fox Valley, Jude, Kirk Stemmed-Bifurcated, LeCroy, MacCorkle, St. Albans and Stanly)

Ears are fractured

Basal sides are fractured

G5, $4-$8
Madison, IN

G5, $4-$8
Madison, IN

G5, $4-$8
Carroll, Co., OH

G9, $20-$35
Ross Co., OH. Classic

G7, $15-$25
OH

EC

G5, $4-$8
OH

G6, $8-$15
Cleveland, OH

Coshocton chert

Black chert

Coshocton chert

Coshocton chert

G9, $30-$50
Cleveland, OH

G7, $15-$25
OH

G8, $35-$65
Carroll Co., OH

G9, $65-$125
Cleveland, OH

G9, $65-$125
Cleveland, OH

LOCATION: Northeastern states. **DESCRIPTION:** A small to medium size, thin, deeply notched or serrated, bifurcated stemmed point. The basal lobes are parallel with a tendency to turn inward and are pointed. The outward sides of the basal lobes are usually fractured from the base towards the tip and can be ground.

LANCET - Paleo to Archaic, 14,000 - 5000 B. P.

(Also see Drill and Scraper)

493

LANCET (continued)

All are Flint Ridge flint

$3-$5 ea.
All from Flint Ridge, OH

LOCATION: Found on all early man sites. **DESCRIPTION:** A medium to large size sliver used as a knife for cutting. Recent experiments proved that these knives were sharper than a surgeon's scalpel. Similar to *Burins* which are fractured at one end to produce a sharp point.

LECROY - Early to Middle Archaic, 9000 - 5000 B. P.

(Also see Decatur, Fox Valley, Jude, Kanawha Stemmed, Kirk Stemmed-Bifurcated, Lake Erie, MacCorkle, Pine Tree, Rice Lobbed, St. Albans and Stanly)

Black Kanawha flint

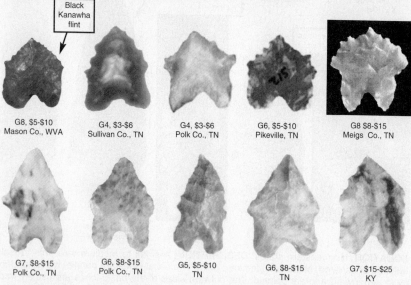

G8, $5-$10 Mason Co., WVA	G4, $3-$6 Sullivan Co., TN	G4, $3-$6 Polk Co., TN	G6, $5-$10 Pikeville, TN	G8 $8-$15 Meigs Co., TN
G7, $8-$15 Polk Co., TN	G6, $8-$15 Polk Co., TN	G5, $5-$10 TN	G6, $8-$15 TN	G7, $15-$25 KY

LOCATION: Southeastern states. Type site-Hamilton Co., TN. Named after Archie LeCroy. **DESCRIPTION:** A small to medium size, thin, usually broad point with deeply notched or serrated blade edges and a deeply bifurcated base. Basal ears can either droop or expand out. The stem is usually large in comparison to the blade size. Some stem sides are fractured in Northern examples *(Lake Erie)*. Bases are usually ground. **I.D. KEY:** Basal form.

LECROY (continued)

Worn tip

G3, $3-$6
Polk Co., TN

Ear wear

G3, $3-$6
TN

G6, $6-$12
S.E. TN

G6, $6-$12
TN

G10+, $40-$70
Dayton, TN

Shale

G7, $25-$40
S.E. TN

G9, $25-$40
Bradley Co., TN

G6, $12-$20
TN

EC

G7, $15-$25
KY

G9, $35-$60
KY

Serrated edge

G9, $25-$45
Hamilton Co., TN

Double uniface

G9, $35-$60
Cave City, KY

G9, $45-$85
Florence, AL

G10+, $55-$100
Dayton, TN

G10, $40-$75
OH

495

LEDBETTER - Middle to Late Archaic, 6000 - 3500 B. P.

(Also see Little Bear Creek, Mulberry Creek, Pickwick and Shoals Creek)

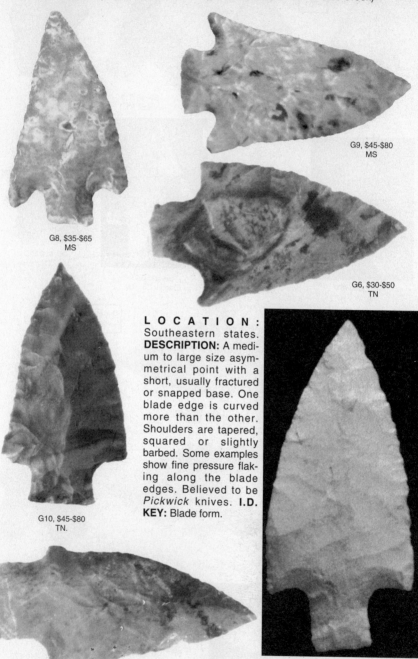

G9, $45-$80
MS

G8, $35-$65
MS

G6, $30-$50
TN

G10, $45-$80
TN.

LOCATION: Southeastern states. **DESCRIPTION:** A medium to large size asymmetrical point with a short, usually fractured or snapped base. One blade edge is curved more than the other. Shoulders are tapered, squared or slightly barbed. Some examples show fine pressure flaking along the blade edges. Believed to be *Pickwick* knives. **I.D. KEY:** Blade form.

G5, $20-$35
TN

G10, $55-$100
Benton Co., TN

496

LEDBETTER (continued)

Talahatta Quartite

G7, $80-$150
AL

LEIGHTON - Early Archaic, 8000 - 5000 B. P.

(Also see Benton, Big Sandy, Evans, Merkle, Ohio Double Notched and St. Helena)

G7, $30-$50
Florence, AL

G6, $15-$25
KY

Tip nick

G5, $20-$35
Dayton, TN

G9, $80-$150
Lauderdale Co., AL

LOCATION: Southeastern states. **DESCRIPTION:** A medium to large size, double side-notched point that is usually serrated and has a concave base that is ground. **I.D. KEY:** Basal notching, archaic flaking.

Dover chert

G7, $60-$100
Humphreys Co., TN

Note double notched base

G10, $275-$500
Colbert Co., AL

497

LERMA - Early to Mid-Archaic, 10,000 - 5000 B. P.

(Also see Adena Blade, Harahey, North, Paleo Knife, Snake Creek, Tear Drop & Tenn. Saw)

Resharpened several times

Very thin

G7, $30-$50
Meigs Co., TN

LOCATION: Siberia to Alaska, Canada, Mexico, South America, and across the U.S. **DESCRIPTION:** A large size, narrow, thick, lanceolate blade with a rounded base. Some Western examples are beveled on one side of each face. Flaking tends to be collateral and finer examples are thin in cross section.

G10, $250-$400
TN

G9, $250-$450
Humphreys Co., TN.

G9, $90-$175
TN

498

LERMA (continued)

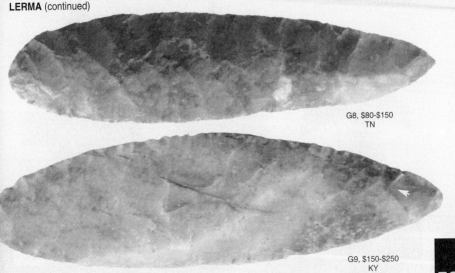

G8, $80-$150
TN

G9, $150-$250
KY

LEVANNA - Late Woodland to Mississippian, 1300 - 600 B. P.

(Also see Hamilton, Madison, Tortugas and Yadkin)

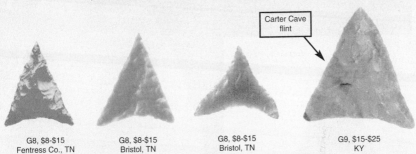

Carter Cave flint

G8, $8-$15
Fentress Co., TN

G8, $8-$15
Bristol, TN

G8, $8-$15
Bristol, TN

G9, $15-$25
KY

LOCATION: Southeastern to Northeastern states. **DESCRIPTION:** A small to medium size, thin, triangular point with a concave to straight base. Believed to be replaced by Madison points in later times. Called *Yadkin* in North Carolina. **I.D. KEY:** Medium thick cross section.

LIMESTONE - Late Archaic to Early Woodland, 5000 - 2000 B. P.

(Also see Fairland, Johnson, McIntire)

G4, $6-$12
Walker Co., AL

G5, $6-$12
AL

G5, $8-$15
KY

G9, $35-$60
Limestone Co., AL

G7, $20-$35
Madison Co., AL

G7, $35-$50
Limestone Co., AL

G10, $90-$175
Morgan Co., AL

Tang nick

G9, $45-$80
Colbert Co., AL

G7, $80-$150
Marion Co., AL

LOCATION: Southeastern states. **DESCRIPTION:** A small to medium size, triangular stemmed point with an expanded, concave base and barbed to tapered shoulders. Blade edges are concave, convex or straight. **I.D. KEY:** Concave base, one barb is higher.

LIMETON BIFURCATE - Early Archaic, 9000 - 6000 B. P.

(Also see Haw River)

LOCATION: Eastern states. **DESCRIPTION:** A medium size, crudely made, broad, lanceolate blade with a central notch in the base.

G6, $5-$10
Southeast, TN

LITTLE BEAR CREEK - Late Archaic to late Woodland, 4000 - 1500 B. P.

(Also see Adena, Kays, McWhinney, Mulberry Creek, Pickwick and Ponchartrain)

Yellow jasper

G5, $12-$20
N.E. MS

G3, $8-$15
Polk Co., TN

EC

LOCATION: Southeastern states. **DESCRIPTION:** A medium to large size, narrow point with a long parallel stem that may contract or expand slightly. Blade edges are slightly convex. Shoulders are usually squared, tapered or slightly barbed. The base can be fractured or snapped off. Blade edges can be beveled on one side of each face and finely serrated. Called *Sarasota* in Florida. **I.D. KEY:** Straight base, woodland flaking.

G5, $15-$25
Polk Co., TN

Gray flint

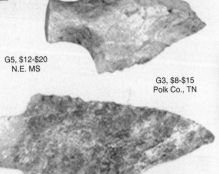

G6, $25-$45
Polk Co., TN

G6, $30-$50
Hardin Co., TN

G7, $55-$65
Florence, AL

G8, $55-$85
W. TN

501

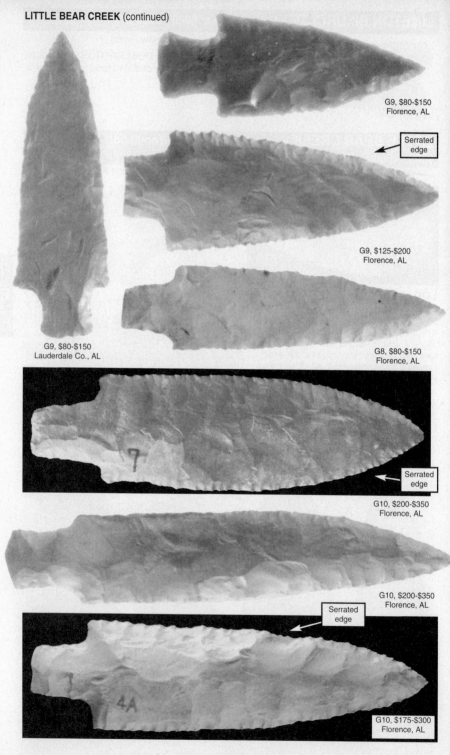

G9, $80-$150
Florence, AL

Serrated
edge

G9, $125-$200
Florence, AL

G9, $80-$150
Lauderdale Co., AL

G8, $80-$150
Florence, AL

Serrated
edge

G10, $200-$350
Florence, AL

G10, $200-$350
Florence, AL

Serrated
edge

G10, $175-$300
Florence, AL

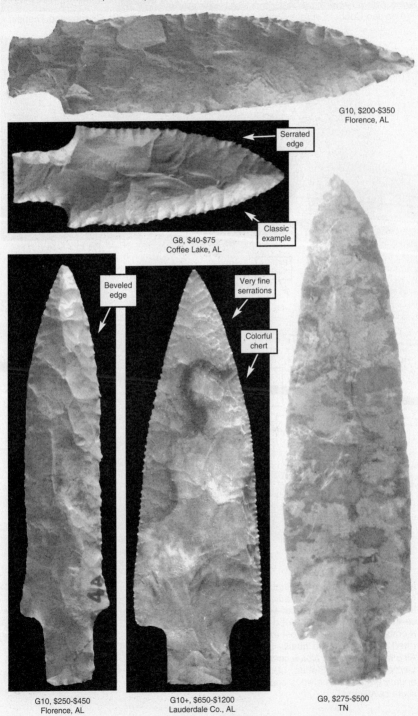

G10, $200-$350
Florence, AL

Serrated edge

Classic example

G8, $40-$75
Coffee Lake, AL

Beveled edge

Very fine serrations

Colorful chert

EC

G10, $250-$450
Florence, AL

G10+, $650-$1200
Lauderdale Co., AL

G9, $275-$500
TN

LOST LAKE - Early Archaic, 9000 - 6000 B. P.
(Also see Cobbs, Cypress Creek, Hardin, Kirk Corner Notched, St. Charles and Thebes)

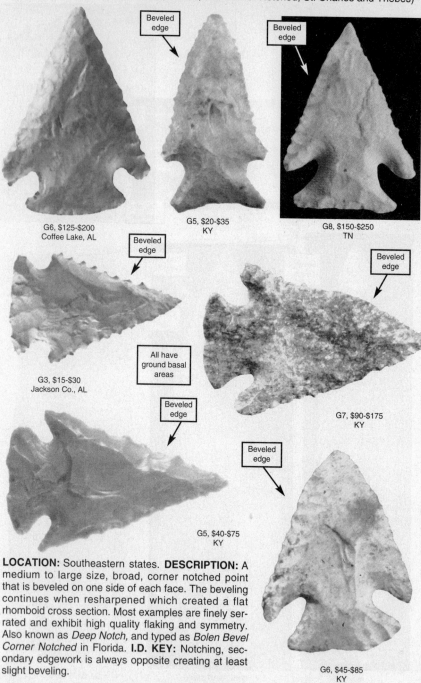

Beveled edge

Beveled edge

G6, $125-$200
Coffee Lake, AL

G5, $20-$35
KY

G8, $150-$250
TN

Beveled edge

Beveled edge

G3, $15-$30
Jackson Co., AL

All have ground basal areas

Beveled edge

G7, $90-$175
KY

Beveled edge

G5, $40-$75
KY

Beveled edge

G6, $45-$85
KY

LOCATION: Southeastern states. **DESCRIPTION:** A medium to large size, broad, corner notched point that is beveled on one side of each face. The beveling continues when resharpened which created a flat rhomboid cross section. Most examples are finely serrated and exhibit high quality flaking and symmetry. Also known as *Deep Notch,* and typed as *Bolen Bevel Corner Notched* in Florida. **I.D. KEY:** Notching, secondary edgework is always opposite creating at least slight beveling.

504

Beveled edge

Beveled edge

G8, $80-$150
OH

Beveled edge

Sunfish style

Beveled edge

G10, $250-$400
KY

EC

Beveled edge

All have ground basal areas

G9, $250-$450
KY

Beveled edge

Beveled edge

G8, $150-$250
KY

Beveled edge

G10, $200-$350
KY

G7, $200-$350
IN

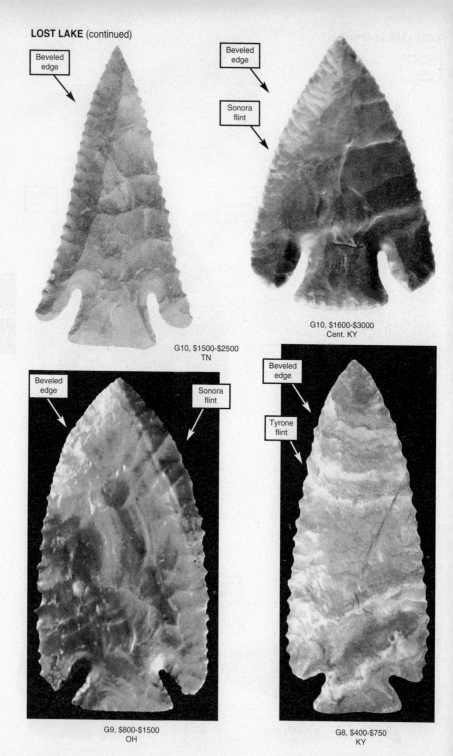

LOST LAKE (continued)

Beveled edge

Beveled edge

Sonora flint

G10, $1500-$2500
TN

G10, $1600-$3000
Cent. KY

Beveled edge

Sonora flint

Beveled edge

Tyrone flint

G9, $800-$1500
OH

G8, $400-$750
KY

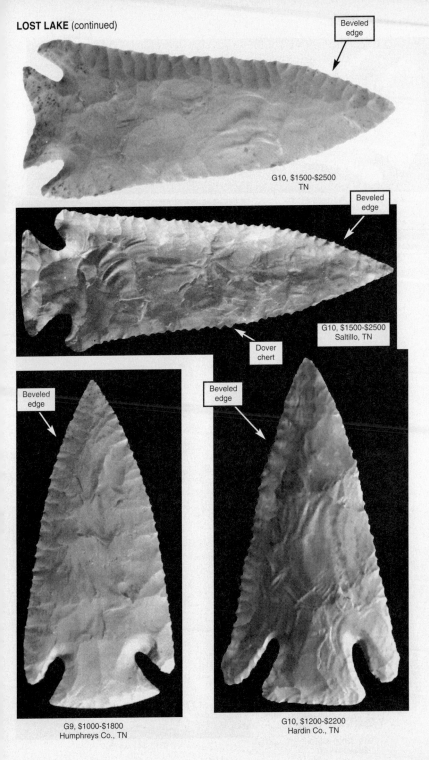

Beveled edge

G10, $1500-$2500
TN

Beveled edge

Dover chert

G10, $1500-$2500
Saltillo, TN

EC

Beveled edge

Beveled edge

G9, $1000-$1800
Humphreys Co., TN

G10, $1200-$2200
Hardin Co., TN

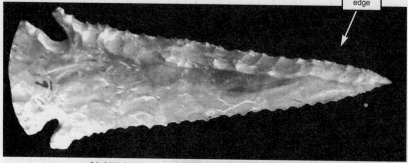

Beveled edge

G8, $550-$1000
Humphreys Co., TN

Beveled edge

G10, $3000-$5000
Ballard Co., KY

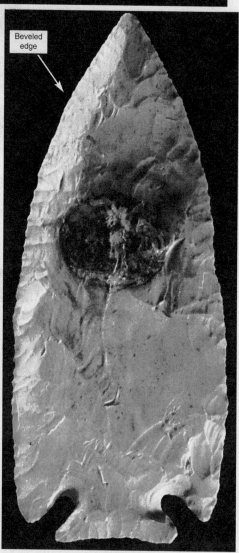

Beveled edge

G10, $4000-$7500
OH

LOWE - Mississippian, 1650 - 1450 B. P.

(Also see Bakers Creek, Chesser, McIntire, Mud Creek and Table Rock)

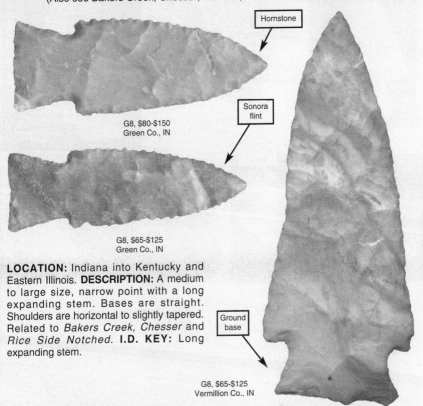

Hornstone

Sonora flint

G8, $80-$150
Green Co., IN

G8, $65-$125
Green Co., IN

Ground base

G8, $65-$125
Vermillion Co., IN

LOCATION: Indiana into Kentucky and Eastern Illinois. **DESCRIPTION:** A medium to large size, narrow point with a long expanding stem. Bases are straight. Shoulders are horizontal to slightly tapered. Related to *Bakers Creek, Chesser* and *Rice Side Notched.* **I.D. KEY:** Long expanding stem.

EC

LOZENGE - Mississippian, 1000 - 400 B. P.

(Also see Nodena)

LOCATION: Midwestern to Southeastern states. **DESCRIPTION:** A small size, narrow, thin, double pointed arrow point.

G8, $8-$15
KY

MACCORKLE - Early Archaic, 8000 - 6000 B. P.

(Also see Kanawha Stemmed, Kirk Stemmed-Bifurcated, LeCroy, Rice Lobbed and St. Albans)

LOCATION: Midwestern to Southeastern states. **DESCRIPTION:** A medium to large size, thin, usually serrated, widely corner notched point with large round ears and a deep notch in the center of the base. Bases are usually ground. The smaller examples can be easily confused with the *LeCroy* point. Shoulders and blade expand more towards the base than *LeCroy*, but only in some cases. Called *Nottoway River Bifurcate* in Virginia. **I.D. KEY:** Basal notching, early Archaic flaking.

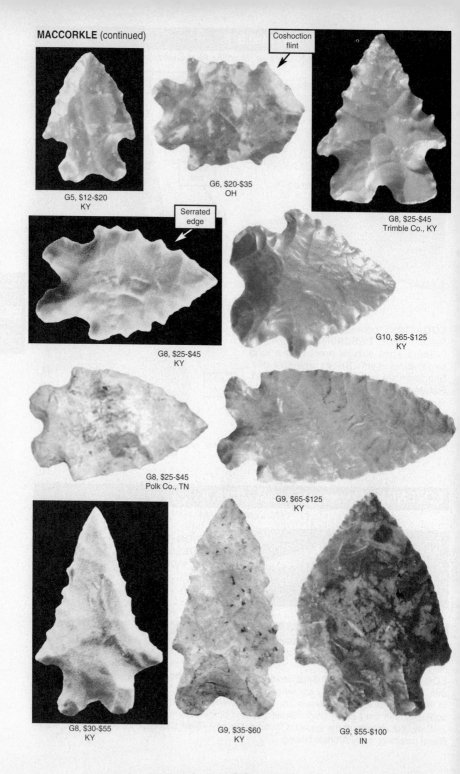

MACCORKLE (continued)

Coshoction flint

Serrated edge

G5, $12-$20
KY

G6, $20-$35
OH

G8, $25-$45
Trimble Co., KY

G8, $25-$45
KY

G10, $65-$125
KY

G8, $25-$45
Polk Co., TN

G9, $65-$125
KY

G8, $30-$55
KY

G9, $35-$60
KY

G9, $55-$100
IN

510

MACCORKLE (continued)

G8, $40-$75
Stark Co. OH

G10, $90-$175
KY

G9, $150-$250
KY

MACE - Mississippian, 1100 - 600 B. P.
(Also see Dagger and Sun Disc)

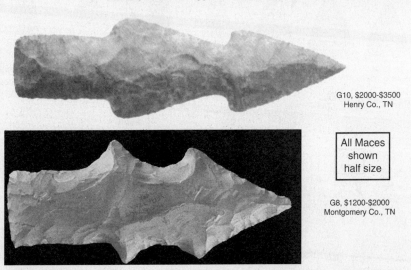

G10, $2000-$3500
Henry Co., TN

All Maces
shown
half size

G8, $1200-$2000
Montgomery Co., TN

LOCATION: Southeastern states. **DESCRIPTION:** A very large, thick, hand-held barbed dagger used in the Sun dance ceremony along with the Duck River Swords, Sun Discs and shell gorgets by the Mississippian culture. Such dances are depicted on the shell gorgets themselves. These objects are made from high grade flint and are flaked to perfection. **Warning:** Absolute provinence is needed to prove authenticity. Very rare, existing mostly in museum collections. **I.D. KEY:** Thickness, notching, flaking.

MACE (continued)

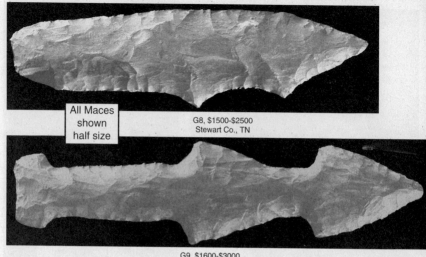

All Maces shown half size

G8, $1500-$2500
Stewart Co., TN

G9, $1600-$3000
Stewart Co., TN

MADISON - Mississippian, 1100 - 200 B. P.

(Also see Camp Creek, Fort Ancient, Guntersville, Hamilton, Levanna, Sand Mountain and Valina)

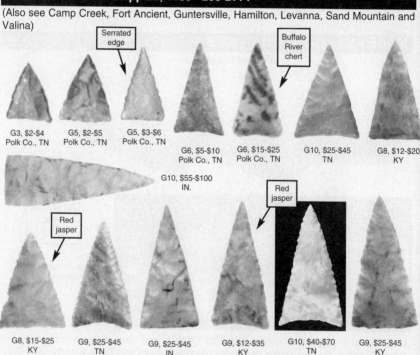

Serrated edge

Buffalo River chert

G3, $2-$4
Polk Co., TN

G5, $2-$5
Polk Co., TN

G5, $3-$6
Polk Co., TN

G6, $5-$10
Polk Co., TN

G6, $15-$25
Polk Co., TN

G10, $25-$45
TN

G8, $12-$20
KY

G10, $55-$100
IN.

Red jasper

Red jasper

G8, $15-$25
KY

G9, $25-$45
TN

G9, $25-$45
IN

G9, $12-$35
KY

G10, $40-$70
TN

G9, $25-$45
KY

LOCATION: Coincides with the Mississippian culture in the Eastern states. **DESCRIPTION:** A small to medium size, thin, triangular point with usually straight sides and base. Some examples are notched on two to three sides. Many are of high quality and some are finely serrated.

MADISON (continued)

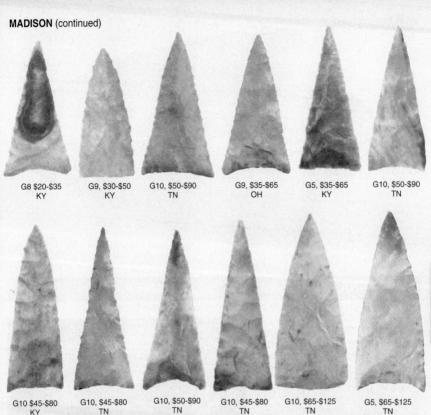

G8 $20-$35 KY	G9, $30-$50 KY	G10, $50-$90 TN	G9, $35-$65 OH	G5, $35-$65 KY	G10, $50-$90 TN

EC

G10 $45-$80 KY	G10, $45-$80 TN	G10, $50-$90 TN	G10, $45-$80 TN	G10, $65-$125 TN	G5, $65-$125 TN

MAPLES - Middle Archaic, 4500 - 3500 B. P.

(Also see Elora, Morrow Mountain and Savannah River)

G8, $80-$150
KY

LOCATION: Southeastern states. **DESCRIPTION:** A very large, broad, thick, short stemmed blade. Shoulders are tapered and the stem is contracting with a concave to straight base. Usually thick and crudely made, but fine quality examples have been found. Flaking is random and this type should not be confused with *Morrow Mountain* which has Archaic parallel flaking. **I.D. KEY:** Thickness, notching, flaking.

MAPLES (continued)

G9, $150-$250
AL

MARIANNA - Transitional Paleo, 10,000 - 8500 B. P.
(Also see Angostura, Browns Valley and Conerly)

LOCATION: Southern to South-eastern states. **DESCRIPTION:** A medium size lanceolate point with a constricted, concave base. Look for parallel to oblique flaking.

G7, $15-$25
Dayton, TN. Note diagonal flaking.

MATANZAS - Mid-Archaic to Woodland, 4500 - 2500 B. P.
(Also see Brewerton Side Notched, Brunswick and Swan Lake)

LOCATION: Ohio westward to Iowa. **DESCRIPTION:** A narrow, medium size point with broad side notches to an expanding stem.

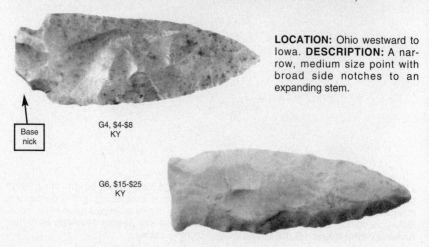

Base
nick

G4, $4-$8
KY

G6, $15-$25
KY

514

MCINTIRE - Middle to Late Archaic, 6000 - 4000 B. P.

(Also see Bakers Creek, Chesser, Kays, Limestone, Lowe, Mud Creek and Smithsonia)

G8, $30-$50
Humphreys Co., TN

G7, $20-$35
Limestone Co., AL

G8, $40-$75
TN

EC

LOCATION: Southeastern states. **DESCRIPTION:** A medium to large point with straight to convex blade edges and a broad parallel to expanding stem. Shoulders are square to slightly barbed and the base is usually straight.

MCWHINNEY HEAVY STEMMED - Mid-Late Archaic, 6000 - 3000 B. P.

(Also see Heavy Duty, Little Bear Creek, Mud Creek, Mulberry Creek and Pickwick)

G6, $25-$45
Sou IN

G7, $35-$65
S.W. OH

Flintridge
flint →

MCWHINNEY HEAVY STEMMED (continued)

LOCATION: Illinois, Ohio into Kentucky. **DESCRIPTION:** A medium size, fairly thick point with a short stem and squared shoulders. Stems can be bulbous, straight to expanding. On some examples side notches occur where the stem and shoulders intersect. Previously known as the *Flint River Spike* point.

MEADOWOOD - Late Archaic to Woodland, 4000 - 2000 B. P.

(Also see Big Sandy and Newton Falls)

G7, $40-$75
KY

G5, $65-$125
OH

G6, $25-$40
TN

LOCATION: Northeastern to Eastern states. **DESCRIPTION:** Medium to large size, thick, broad side notched point. Notches occur close to the base. This point is found from Indiana to New York.

G7, $150-$250
OH

516

MEADOWOOD (continued)

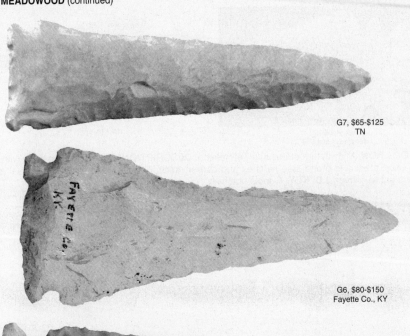

G7, $65-$125
TN

G6, $80-$150
Fayette Co., KY

G7, $150-$285
KY

MERKLE - Late Archaic to Woodland, 4000 - 2000 B. P.
(Also see Evans and Leighton)

G6, $25-$45
Hamilton Co., TN

G5, $8-$15
OH.

G6, $20-$35
KY

G6, $25-$45
Hamilton Co., TN

MERKLE (continued)

G5, $25-$40
Nickajack Lake, TN

G9, $35-$65
KY

LOCATION: Midwestern states into Tennessee. **DESCRIPTION:** A medium size point with a short stem and broad side notches and corner notches at the base. Bases are usually straight to convex. **I.D. KEY:** Double notching.

MEROM - Late Archaic, 4000 - 3000 B. P.

(Also see Keota)

G7, $3-$5
TN

G6, $3-$5
Polk Co., TN

G7, $4-$8
Polk Co., TN

G5, $1-$3
Meigs Co., TN

LOCATION: Illinois into Tenn. & Kent.. **DESCRIPTION:** A small size, triangular, point with wide side notches and a convex base. Some examples have fine serrations.

MESERVE - Early to Middle Archaic, 9500 - 4000 B. P.

(Also see Dalton)

G8, $60-$100
OH

LOCATION: Midwestern states, rarely into Ohio & Tennessee. **DESCRIPTION:** A medium size, auriculate form with a blade that is beveled on one side of each face. Beveling extends into the basal area. This type is related to *Dalton* points.

G9, $65-$125
TN

MONTGOMERY - Woodland, 2500 - 1000 B. P.

(Also see Benjamin, Ebenezer and Morrow Mountain)

LOCATION: Southeastern states. **DESCRIPTION:** A small, broad, tear-drop shaped point with a rounded base. Flaking is random. This type is similar to *Catan* found in Texas.

MONTGOMERY (continued)

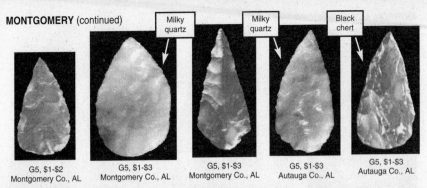

Milky quartz

Milky quartz

Black chert

G5, $1-$2
Montgomery Co., AL

G5, $1-$3
Montgomery Co., AL

G5, $1-$3
Montgomery Co., AL

G5, $1-$3
Autauga Co., AL

G5, $1-$3
Autauga Co., AL

MORROW MOUNTAIN - Middle Archaic, 7000 - 5000 B. P.

(Also see Buggs Island, Cypress Creek, Ebenezer, Elora, Eva and Maples)

EC

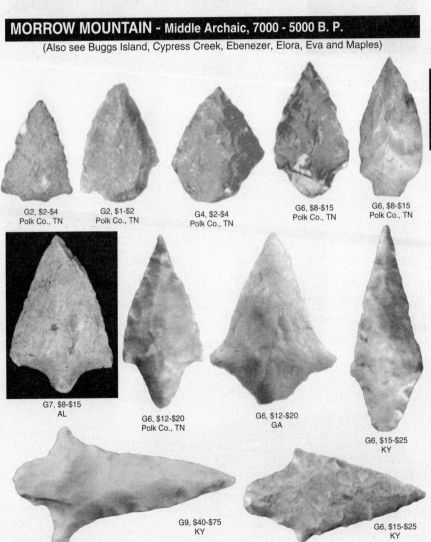

G2, $2-$4
Polk Co., TN

G2, $1-$2
Polk Co., TN

G4, $2-$4
Polk Co., TN

G6, $8-$15
Polk Co., TN

G6, $8-$15
Polk Co., TN

G7, $8-$15
AL

G6, $12-$20
Polk Co., TN

G6, $12-$20
GA

G6, $15-$25
KY

G9, $40-$75
KY

G6, $15-$25
KY

519

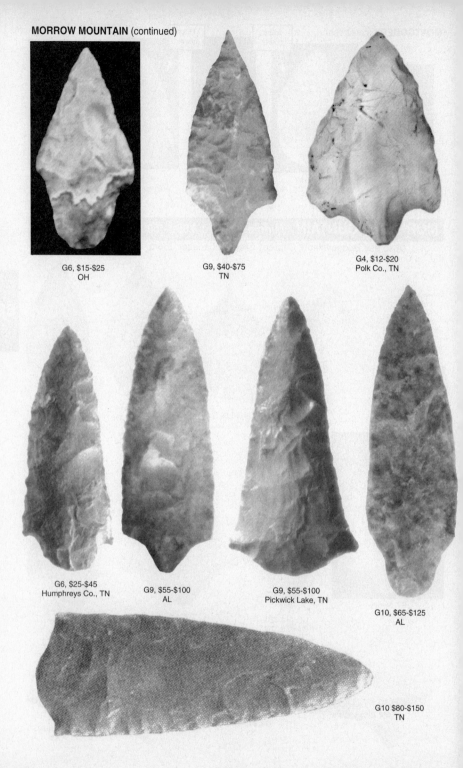

G6, $15-$25
OH

G9, $40-$75
TN

G4, $12-$20
Polk Co., TN

G6, $25-$45
Humphreys Co., TN

G9, $55-$100
AL

G9, $55-$100
Pickwick Lake, TN

G10, $65-$125
AL

G10 $80-$150
TN

MORROW MOUNTAIN (continued)

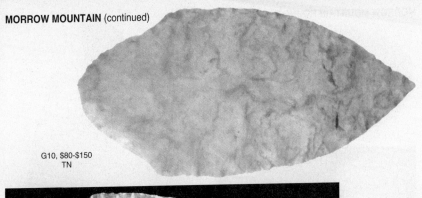

G10, $80-$150
TN

G10, $125-$200
N. AL

LOCATION: Midwestern to Southeastern states. **DESCRIPTION:** A medium to large size, triangular point with a very short contracting to rounded stem. Shoulders are usually weak but can be barbed. The blade edges on some examples are serrated with needle points. **I.D. KEY:** Contracted base and Archaic parallel flaking.

MORROW MOUNTAIN ROUNDED BASE -
Middle Archaic, 7000 - 5000 B. P.

(Also see Ebenezer, Guilford Round Base and Montgomery)

G3, $1-$2
Polk Co., TN

G4, $2-$4
Polk Co., TN

G5, $2-$4
Polk Co., TN

LOCATION: Midwestern to Southeastern states. **DESCRIPTION:** A small to medium size tear-drop point with a pronounced, short, rounded base and no shoulders. Some examples have a straight to slightly convex base. This type has similarities to Gypsum Cave points found in the Western states.

521

G5, $3-$6
Polk Co., TN

Agate

G8, $12-$20
Nickajack Lake, TN

G8, $12-$20
Polk Co., TN

MORROW MOUNTAIN STRAIGHT BASE -
Middle Archaic, 7000 - 5000 B. P.

(Also see Hidden Valley, Mud Creek)

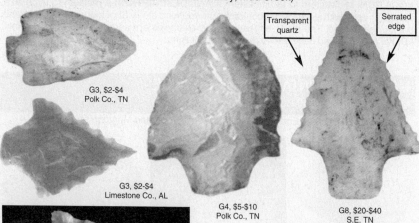

G3, $2-$4
Polk Co., TN

G3, $2-$4
Limestone Co., AL

G6, $12-$20
Decatur, AL

Transparent quartz

Serrated edge

G4, $5-$10
Polk Co., TN

G8, $20-$40
S.E. TN

LOCATION: Southeastern states. **DESCRIPTION:** A medium size, thin, strongly barbed point with a contracting stem and a straight base. Some examples are serrated and have a needle tip. Look for Archaic parallel flaking.

MORSE KNIFE - Woodland, 3000 - 1500 B. P.

(Also see Cotaco Creek, Duck River Sword, Ramey Knife and Snake Creek)

IMPORTANT:
Morse Knives are
shown half size

Hornstone

Broken
& glued

EC

G10, $350-$650
TN

G10, $450-$850
TN

G9, $400-$700
KY

G4, $200-$350
IN

LOCATION: Midwestern to Southeastern states. **DESCRIPTION:** A large lanceolate blade with a long contracting stem and a rounded base. The widest part of the blade is towards the tip.

MOTLEY - Late Archaic to Woodland, 4500 - 2500 B. P.

(Also see Buck Creek, Epps, Hamilton, Smithsonia, Snyders and Wade)

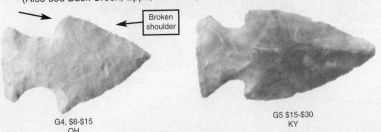

Broken
shoulder

G4, $8-$15
OH

G5 $15-$30
KY

LOCATION: Southeastern states. **DESCRIPTION:** A medium to large size, expanded stemmed to widely corner notched point with strong barbs. The blade edges and the base are convex to straight. Has been found associated with *Wade* points in caches. Similar to *Epps* found in Louisiana which has a straight base; *Motleys* are more barbed than *Epps*.

523

MOTLEY (continued)

Worn shoulder

Worn edge

G4, $12-$20, KY

G7, $25-$45
KY

G4, $15-$30
KY

G8, $45-$85
OH

G8, $150-$250
KY

Tang nick

G4, $55-$100
Dickson Cave, KY

G6, $25-$45
AL

G5, $25-$45
KY

G9, $80-$150
KY

G7, $65-$125
KY

G6, $20-$35
KY

524

Tang
nick

G4, $15-$25
AL

G6, $125-$200
Dickson Cave, KY

G7, $45-$75
MI

Dover
chert

EC

Dover
chert

G9, $400-$700
Dickson Co., TN

G8, $275-$500
Sumner Co., TN

G10+ $2000-$3500
Dickson Co., TN

MOUNTAIN FORK - Middle Archaic to Woodland, 6000 - 2000 B. P.

(Also see Bradley Spike, Duval and New Market)

G4, $8-$15
Decatur, AL

G6, $20-$35
Limestone Co., AL

LOCATION: Southeastern states. **DESCRIPTION:** A small to medium size, narrow, thick, stemmed point with tapered shoulders.

G4 $8-$15
Ft. Payne, AL

G6, $15-$25
S.E. TN

G6, $12-$20
W. TN

MOUSE CREEK - Woodland, 1500 - 1000 B. P.

(Also see Jacks Reef Pentagonal)

Tip
nick

G4, $8-$15
Bradley Co., TN

G7, $20-$35
Madison Co., AL

G6, $15-$25
S.E. TN

G9, $40-$70
Bradley Co., TN

G8, $35-$60
Morgan Co., TN

LOCATION: Southeastern states. **DESCRIPTION:** A small to medium size, thin, pentagonal point with prominent shoulders, a short pointed blade and a long, expanding stem. The base is concave with pointed ears. The hafting area is over half the length of the point. This type is **very rare** and could be related to Jacks Reef. A similar form is found in OK, TX, & LA called "Snow Lake."

Side
nick

G6, $35-$60
Dayton, TN.
Side nick

MUD CREEK - Late Archaic to Woodland, 4000 - 2000 B. P.

(Also see Bakers Creek, Beacon Island, Chesser, Flint Creek, Little Bear Creek, Lowe, McIntire, McWhinney and Mulberry Creek)

LOCATION: Southeastern states. **DESCRIPTION:** A medium size point with slightly recurved blade edges, a narrow, needle like tip, square to tapered shoulders and an expanded stem. Called *Patuxent* in Virginia. **I.D. KEY:** Thickness, point form, high barb.

526

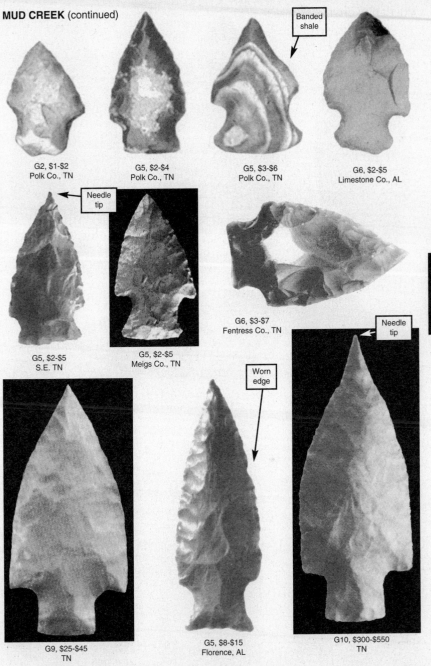

Banded shale

G2, $1-$2
Polk Co., TN

G5, $2-$4
Polk Co., TN

G5, $3-$6
Polk Co., TN

G6, $2-$5
Limestone Co., AL

Needle tip

EC

G5, $2-$5
S.E. TN

G5, $2-$5
Meigs Co., TN

G6, $3-$7
Fentress Co., TN

Needle tip

Worn edge

G9, $25-$45
TN

G5, $8-$15
Florence, AL

G10, $300-$550
TN

MULBERRY CREEK - Mid-Archaic to Woodland, 5000 - 3000 B. P.

(Also see Little Bear Creek, McWhinney and Pickwick)

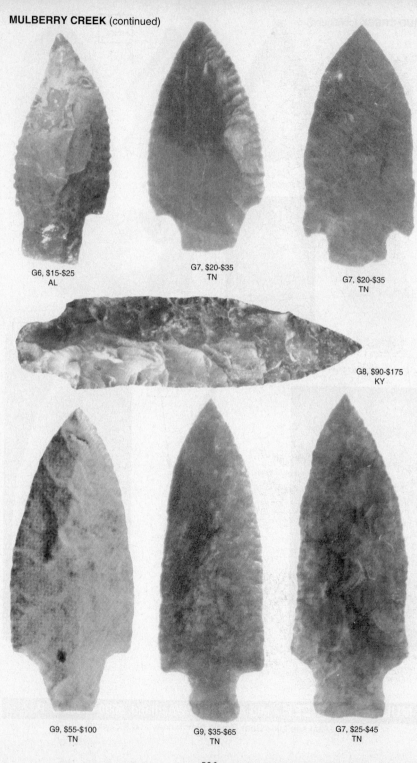

G6, $15-$25
AL

G7, $20-$35
TN

G7, $20-$35
TN

G8, $90-$175
KY

G9, $55-$100
TN

G9, $35-$65
TN

G7, $25-$45
TN

G9, $150-$275
Lauderdale Co., AL

LOCATION: Southeastern states. **DESCRIPTION:** A medium to large size, thick, stemmed point with recurved blade edges. Shoulders are usually tapered, but can be barbed. The blade is widest near the center of the point. Stems can be expanding, parallel or contracting. Bases are straight to convex.

EC

G7, $35-$65
TN

G9, $175-$300
Florence, AL

G9, $200-$375
TN

529

NEUBERGER - Early-Mid Archaic, 9000 - 6000 B. P.

(Also see Kirk Corner Notched and Pine Tree)

LOCATION: Tennessee, Kentucky, Ohio to Illinois. **DESCRIPTION:** A medium to large size, broad, corner notched point with a short, auriculated base. Blade edges are recurved and the base is indented. Shoulders curve in towards the base.

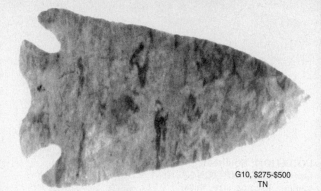

G10, $275-$500
TN

G10, $400-$750
KY

NEW MARKET - Woodland, 3000 - 1000 B. P.

(Also see Bradley Spike, Buggs Island, Duval, Flint River and Schild Spike)

G5, $6-$12
Limestone Co., AL

G6, $8-$15
Fort Payne, AL

G6, $8-$15
N. AL

G5, $8-$15
Humphreys Co., TN

G6, $15-$25
Hamilton Co., TN

NEW MARKET (continued)

Needle tip →

G7, $20-$35
Morgan Co., AL

G6, $15-$25
Limestone Co., AL

G7, $20-$35
Decatur, AL

G10, $65-$125
New Market, AL

G8, $20-$35
TN

LOCATION: Southeastern states. **DESCRIPTION:** A small to medium size point with tapered shoulders and an extended, rounded base. Shoulders are usually asymmetrical with one higher than the other.

EC

NEWTON FALLS - Early to Mid-Archaic, 7000 - 5000 B. P.

(Also see Benton, Big Sandy, Cache River, Graham Cave and Meadowood)

G5, $15-$25
Madison, IN

G8, $25-$45
OH

G8, $35-$65
Madison, IN

G8, $80-$150
OH

LOCATION: Ohio and surrounding states. **DESCRIPTION:** A medium to large size, narrow, side notched point with paralled sides on longer examples and a straight to concave base which could be ground. Similar to *Big Sandy, Godar, Hemphill* and *Osceola* found in other areas. **I.D. KEY:** Size and narrowness.

531

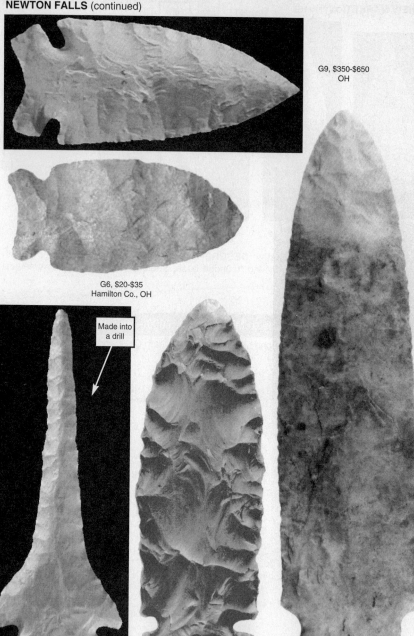

G9, $350-$650
OH

G6, $20-$35
Hamilton Co., OH

Made into
a drill

G8, $150-$350
OH

G7, $65-$125
Fentress Co., TN

G10, $700-$1200
OH

NODENA - Mississippian to Historic, 600 - 400 B. P.

(Also see Guntersville and Lozenge)

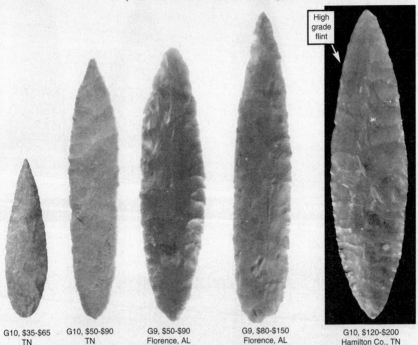

High grade flint

G10, $35-$65
TN

G10, $50-$90
TN

G9, $50-$90
Florence, AL

G9, $80-$150
Florence, AL

G10, $120-$200
Hamilton Co., TN

EC

LOCATION: Midwestern to Southeastern states. **DESCRIPTION:** A small to medium size, narrow, thin elliptical shaped arrow point with a pointed to rounded base. Some examples have oblique, parallel flaking. Called *Tampa* in Florida. Used by the Quapaw Indians.

NOLICHUCKY - Woodland, 3000 - 1500 B. P.

(Also see Camp Creek, Candy Creek, Copena Auriculate, Greeneville and Yadkin)

G6, $3-$6
S.E. TN

G8, $15-$25
Bristol, TN

G6, $12-$20
Bristol, TN

G6, $4-$8
Meigs Co., TN

G5, $3-$6
Meigs Co., TN

LOCATION: Southeastern states. **DESCRIPTION:** A small to medium size, triangular point with recurved blade edges and a straight to concave base. Most examples have small pointed ears at the basal corners. Bases could be ground. Believed to have evolved from *Candy Creek* points and later developed into *Camp Creek*, *Greeneville* and *Guntersville* points. Found with *Ebenezer*, *Camp Creek*, *Candy Creek* and *Greeneville* in caches (Rankin site, Cocke Co. TN.) **I.D. KEY:** Thickness and hafting area.

G9, $25-$45
Bradley Co., TN

G9, $25-$45
TN

G10, $80-$150
Bristol, TN

G10, $80-$150
Dunlap, TN

NORTH - Woodland, 2200 - 1600 B. P.

(Also see Adena Blade, Hopewell, Snyders and Tear Drop)

G8, $80-$150
Scioto Co., OH

LOCATION: Midwestern to Eastern states. **DESCRIPTION:** A large, thin, elliptical, broad, well made blade with a concave blade. This type is usually found in caches and is related to the Snyders point of the Hopewell culture. Believed to be unnotched Snyders points.

NOVA - Woodland to Mississippian, 1600 - 1000 B. P.

(Also see Durant's Bend and Washington)

LOCATION: Southeastern states. **DESCRIPTION:** A small point shaped like a five pointed star.

G8, $3-$5
Dallas Co., AL

G5, $1-$2
Dallas Co., AL

G6, $1-$3
Dallas Co., AL

G2, $1-$2
Dallas Co., AL

OHIO DOUBLE NOTCHED - Woodland, 3000 - 2000 B. P.

(Also see Benton, Evans, Leighton and St. Helena)

G7, $35-$60
KY

G8, $125-$200
Trimble Co., KY

LOCATION: Ohio and surrounding states. **DESCRIPTION:** A medium to large size, narrow, rather crude, point with side notches on both sides and a short base that is usually notched.

OHIO LANCEOLATE -Trans. Paleo-Early Archaic, 10,500 - 8000 B. P.

(Also see Agate Basin, Angostura, Browns Valley, Sedalia)

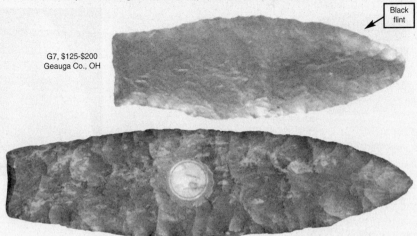

Black flint

G7, $125-$200
Geauga Co., OH

G10, $275-$500
Richland Co., OH

OHIO LANCEOLATE (continued)

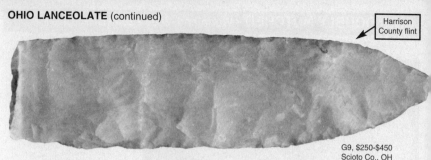

Harrison County flint

G9, $250-$450
Scioto Co., OH

LOCATION: Ohio and surrounding states. **DESCRIPTION:** A medium to large size lanceolate point with a straight base. Blade edges are slightly recurved becoming constricted at the basal hafting area. Thinner than *Clovis* or *Agate Basin*. Not fluted or basally thinned. Has light grinding at the stem.

ORIENT - Late Archaic to Woodland, 4000 - 2500 B. P.

(Also see Big Sandy Auriculate)

G6, $3-$5
Perry Co., TN

G7, $20-$35
Madison Co., AL

LOCATION: Midwestern to Eastern states. **DESCRIPTION:** A small to medium size point with broad side notches, rounded shoulders and an expanding base. The base on some examples form auricles. **I.D. KEY:** Base form and rounded shoulders.

PAINT ROCK VALLEY - Transitional Paleo, 10,000 - 6000 B. P.

(Also see Angostura, Browns Valley, Frazier, Hardaway Blade, Jeff and Tortugas)

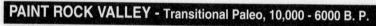

G7, $35-$65
Colbert Co., AL

G7, $35-$65
Warren Co., TN

G7, $35-$65
Madison Co., AL

G10, $200-$350
Lauderdale Co., AL

PAINT ROCK VALLEY (continued)

LOCATION: Southeastern states. **DESCRIPTION:** A medium size, wide, lanceolate point with a concave base. Flaking is usually parallel with fine secondary work on the blade edges. The bases may be multiple fluted, thinned or beveled.

PALMER - Early Archaic, 9000 - 6000 B. P.

(Also see Autauga, Decatur, Ecusta, Kirk Corner Notched and Pine Tree)

Black flint

G6, $5-$10
Polk Co., TN

G6, $5-$10
Polk Co., TN

G7, $8-$15
Sullivan Co., TN

G7, $8-$15
Polk Co., TN

EC

G7, $8-$15
Polk Co., TN

G7, $8-$15
Polk Co., TN

G6, $8-$15
Sullivan Co., TN

G7, $8-$15
Fentress Co., TN

G6, $8-$15
Jefferson Co., TN

Serrated edge

G4, $5-$10
Dayton, TN

G7, $10-$15
Jefferson Co., TN

G7, $8-$15
Polk Co., TN

G7, $8-$15
E. TN

G7, $8-$15
Jefferson Co., TN

Milky quartz

G7, $15-$25
Autauga Co., AL

Serrated edge

G7, $25-$45
KY

LOCATION: Southeastern to Eastern states. **DESCRIPTION:** A small size, corner notched, triangular point with a ground concave, convex or straight base. Many are serrated and large examples would fall under the *Pine Tree* or *Kirk* type. This type developed from *Hardaway* in North Carolina where cross types are found.

PALMER (continued)

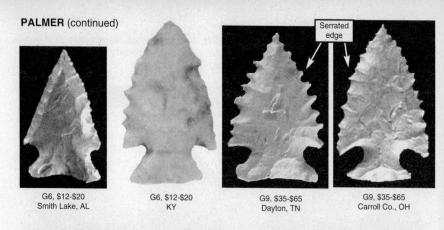

Serrated edge

G6, $12-$20
Smith Lake, AL

G6, $12-$20
KY

G9, $35-$65
Dayton, TN

G9, $35-$65
Carroll Co., OH

PATRICK - Mid-Archaic, 5000 - 3000 B. P.

(Also see Cave Spring, Fox Valley, Kanawha Stemmed, LeCroy, Stanly and Wheeler)

G5, $3-$6
Sequatchie Valley, TN

G5, $5-$10
KY

G7, $8-$15
Dunlap., TN

LOCATION: Eastern states. **DESCRIPTION:** A small to medium size, narrow point with very weak shoulders and a long, parallel sided, bifurcated stem.

PELICAN - Transitional Paleo, 10,000 - 6000 B. P.

(Also see Hinds and Arkabutla and Coldwater in SW Section)

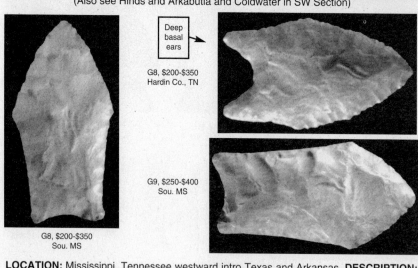

Deep basal ears

G8, $200-$350
Hardin Co., TN

G9, $250-$400
Sou. MS

G8, $200-$350
Sou. MS

LOCATION: Mississippi, Tennessee westward intro Texas and Arkansas. **DESCRIPTION:** A short, broad, usually auriculate point with basal grinding. Shoulders taper into a long contracting stem. Some examples are basally thinned or fluted. **I.D. KEY:** Basal contraction, small size.

PENTAGONAL KNIFE - Mid-Archaic, 6500 - 4000 B. P.

(Also see Jacks Reef Corner Notched)

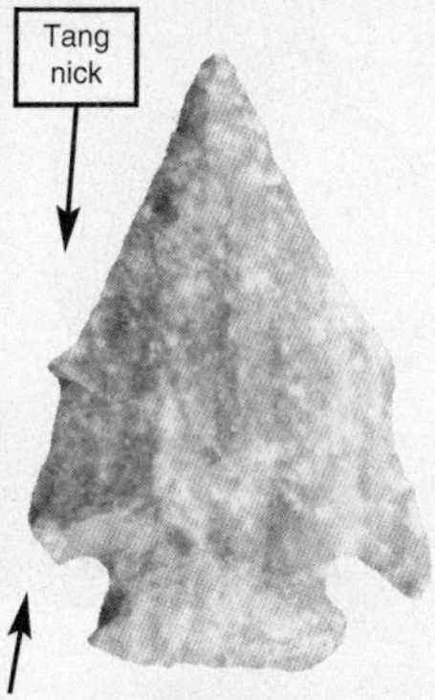
Tang
nick

G6, $25-$45
OH

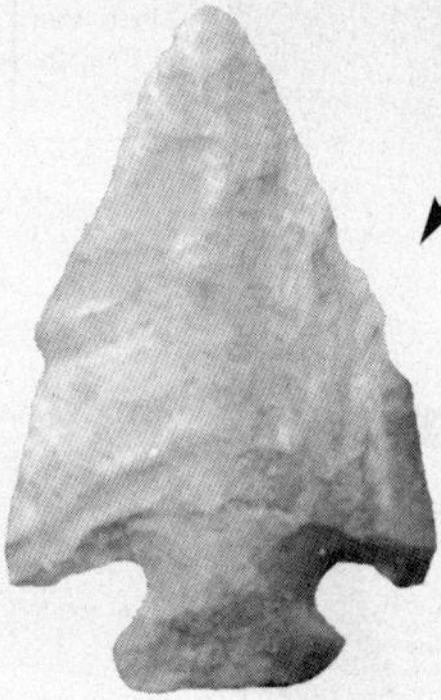

G7, $40-$75
OH

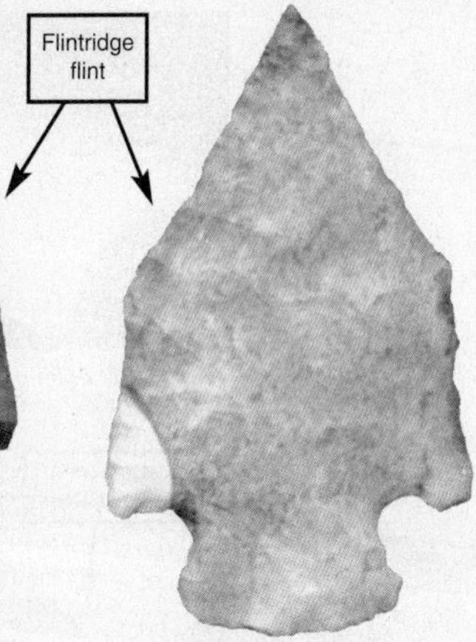
Flintridge
flint

G7, $65-$125
Coshocton Co., OH

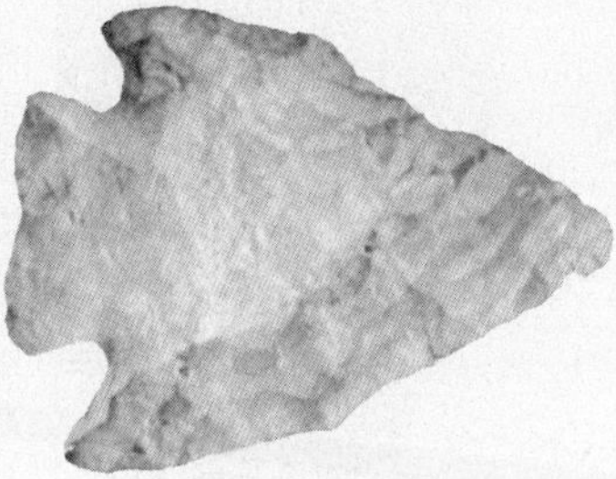

G7, $30-$50
Delaware Co., OH

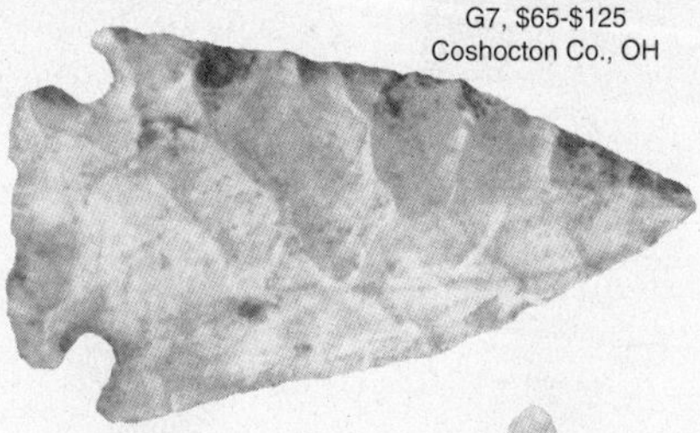

G8, $65-$125
OH

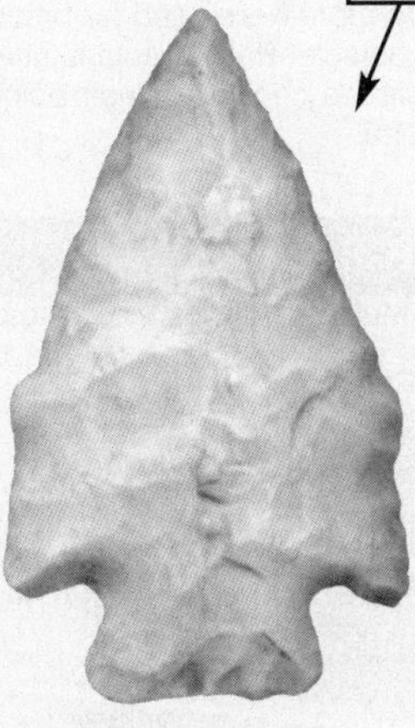

G8, $80-$150
Highland Co., OH

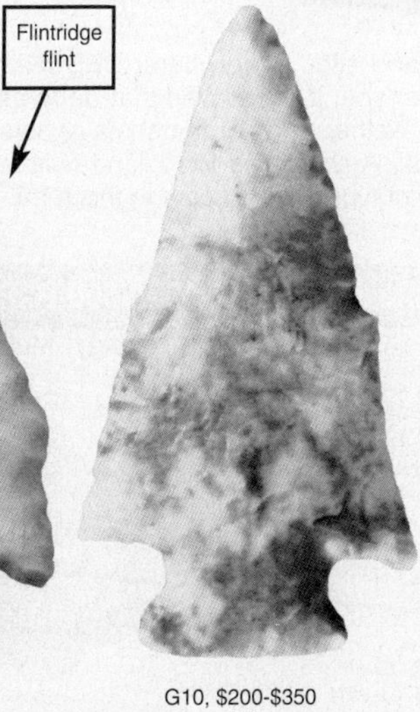
Flintridge
flint

G10, $200-$350
OH

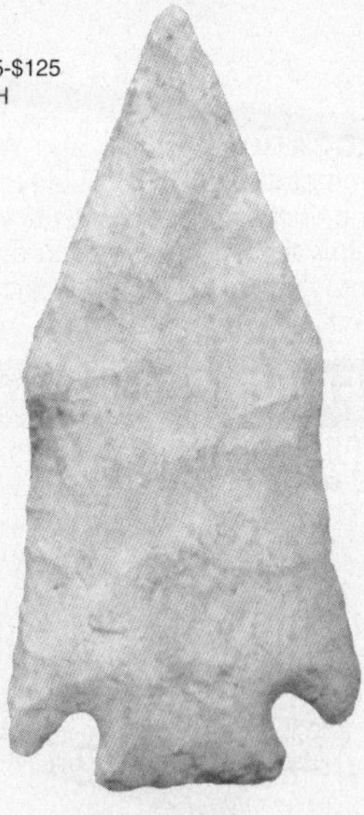

G10, $250-$450
Delaware Co., OH

LOCATION: Ohio into Kentucky, Tennessee and Alabama. **DESCRIPTION:** A medium to large size pentagonal shaped point with a flaring or corner notched stem. Some examples are base notched. Similar too but older than the *Afton* point found in the Midwest. Similar to *Jacks Reef* but thicker. **I.D. KEY:** Blade form.

EC

PERFORATOR - Archaic to Mississippian, 9000 - 400 B. P.

(Also see Drill, Graver and Lancet)

Made from
a Beacon
Island point →

G3, $.50-$1
Polk Co., TN

G8, $12-$20
KY

G8, $12-$20
Polk Co., TN

Made from a
Waubesa point →

G10, $40-$75
TN

G7, $20-$35
TN

G7, $20-$35
TN

LOCATION: Archaic and Woodland sites everywhere. **DESCRIPTION:** A jabbing projection at the tip would qualify for the type. It is believed that *perforators* were used for tattooing, incising or to punch holes in leather or other materials or objects. Paleo peoples used *Gravers* for the same purpose. All Archaic and Woodland cultures converted their points into this type. Therefore, most point types could occur in this form.

PICKWICK - Middle to Late Archaic, 6000 - 3500 B. P.

(Also see Elora, Ledbetter, Little Bear Creek, McWhinney, Mulberry Creek and Shoals Creek)

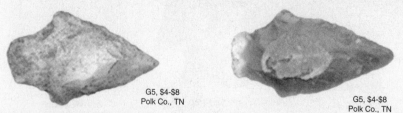

G5, $4-$8
Polk Co., TN

G5, $4-$8
Polk Co., TN

LOCATION: Southeastern states. **DESCRIPTION:** A medium to large size, expanded shoulder, contracted to expanded stem point. Blade edges are recurved, and many examples show fine secondary flaking with serrations. Some are beveled on one side of each face. The bevel is steep and shallow. Shoulders are horizontal, tapered or barbed and form sharp angles. Some stems are snapped off or may show original rind.

PICKWICK (continued)

G5, $4-$8
Polk Co., TN

G6, $15-$25
Polk Co., TN

G6, $15-$30
Florence, AL

G6, $25-$45
Florence, AL

EC

G5, $4-$8
Meigs Co., TN

G9, $35-$65
TN

G8, $55-$100
Florence, AL

G7, $25-$45
Meigs Co., TN

G9, $150-$250
Florence, AL

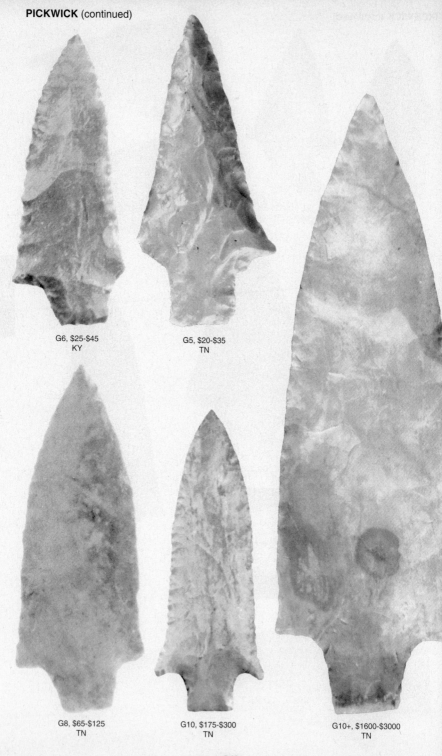

G6, $25-$45
KY

G5, $20-$35
TN

G8, $65-$125
TN

G10, $175-$300
TN

G10+, $1600-$3000
TN

Red, yellow & blue Horse Creek chert

G10, $250-$450
TN

Talahatta Quartzite

EC

G10, $350-$650
Marion Co., AL

G10+, $1600-$3000
Humphreys Co., TN

543

(Also see Big Sandy, Decatur, Greenbrier, Kirk and Palmer)

G6, $15-$25
Sullivan Co., TN

G9, $40-$75
Sullivan Co., TN

G6, $15-$25
Sullivan Co., TN

G6, $20-$35
KY

Bifurcated base

G9, $125-$200
KY

G6, $15-$25
Polk Co., TN

G9, $80-$150
AL

LOCATION: Southeastern states.
DESCRIPTION: A medium to large size, side notched, usually serrated point with parallel flaking to the center of the blade forming a median ridge. The bases are ground and can be concave, convex, straight, or auriculate. This type developed from the earlier *Greenbrier* point. Small examples would fall into the *Palmer* type.
I.D. KEY: Archaic flaking with long flakes to the center of the blade.

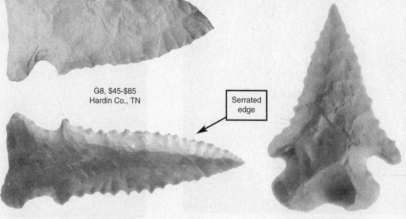

G8, $45-$85
Hardin Co., TN

Serrated edge

G9, $125-$200
Lauderdale Co., AL

G8, $125-$200
Barkley Lake, KY

PINE TREE (continued)

G10, $200-$350
Coffee Lake, AL

Note how pressure flak-ing goes to the center, typical of the type

G9, $250-$400
Florence, AL

Dover chert

G9, $80-$150
Stewart Co., TN

EC

Needle tip

Buffalo River chert

G10+, $700-$1200
Giles Co., TN

G10, $450-$800
Humphreys Co., TN

G10, $800-$1500
Trigg Co., KY

PINE TREE CORNER NOTCHED - Early Archaic, 8000 - 5000 B. P.

(Also see Kirk, Neuberger and Palmer)

Serrated edge

G6, $25-$45
KY

G8, $65-$125
Dayton, TN

G8, $90-$175
IN

G8, $90-$175
TN

G8, $90-$175
Humphreys Co., TN

G8, $80-$150
KY

G9, $150-$250
KY

G8, $65-$125
KY

G10, $275-$500
TN

EC

Serrated edge

G9, $150-$250
TN

G7, $65-$125
KY

G10, $200-$350
KY

Serrated edge

Serrated edge

G9, $150-$250
Monroe Co., KY

G10, $175-$300
Cent. KY

G10, $200-$375
OH

Serrated edge

G9, $150-$250
KY

G7, $55-$100
OH

LOCATION: Southeastern States. **DESCRIPTION:** A small to medium size, thin, corner notched point with a concave, convex, straight, bifurcated or auriculate base. Blade edges are usually serrated and flaking is parallel to the center of the blade. The shoulders expand and are barbed. The base is ground. Small examples would fall under the *Palmer* type. **I.D. KEY:** Archaic flaking to the center of each blade.

547

PINE TREE CRONER NOTCHED (continued)

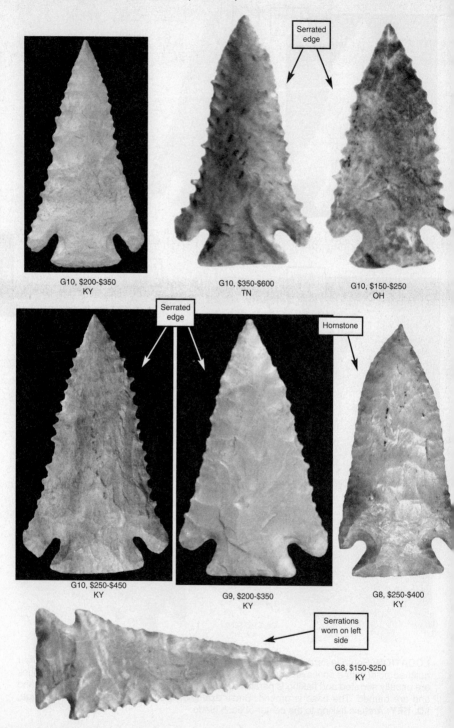

Serrated edge

G10, $200-$350
KY

G10, $350-$600
TN

G10, $150-$250
OH

Serrated edge

Hornstone

G10, $250-$450
KY

G9, $200-$350
KY

G8, $250-$400
KY

Serrations worn on left side

G8, $150-$250
KY

PINE TREE CORNER NOTCHED
(continued)

Serrated edge

Red jasper

Serrated edge

EC

G9, $250-$450
TN

G10, $350-$650
TN

G10, $450-$800
TN

Serrated edge

G10, $450-$950
TN

PIPE CREEK - Mississippian, 1200 - 1000 B. P.

G7, $15-$25
Portland Lake, TN

G8, $20-$35
W. TN

G9, $25-$40
W. TN

549

PIPE CREEK (continued)

G8, $30-$50
W. TN

G6, $15-$30
TN

G6, $20-$35
Burke Co., GA

G6, $25-$40
W.TN

LOCATION: Texas to Southeastern states. **DESCRIPTION:** An unusual knife form having a single corner notch at one basal corner. The base is straight to slightly convex and can be lopsided. Perino and others speculate that this tool was used by early arrow makers in preparing feathers for use on arrow shafts.

PLAINVIEW- Late Paleo, 10,000 - 7000 B. P.

(Also see Angostura, Browns Valley, Clovis and Dalton)

LOCATION: DESCRIPTION: A medium size, thin, lanceolate point with usually parallel sides and a concave base that is ground. Some examples are thinned or fluted and are believed to be related to the earlier *Clovis* and contemporary *Dalton* type. Flaking is of high quality and can be collateral to oblique transverse.

G5, $90-$175
TN

G6, $125-$200
W,. Memphis, TN

PLAINVIEW (continued)

G9, $700-$1200
Central OH

Basal thinning

PLEVNA   (See St. Charles)

PONTCHARTRAIN (Type I) - Late Archaic-Woodland, 4000 - 2000 B. P.

(Also see Kays, Little Bear Creek and Mulberry Creek)

EC

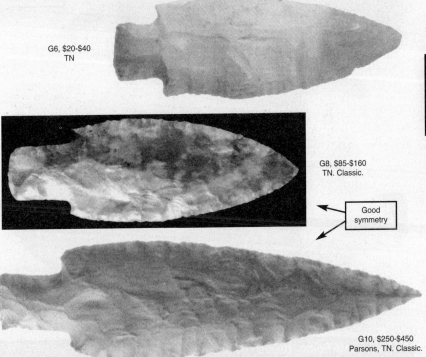

G6, $20-$40
TN

G8, $85-$160
TN. Classic.

Good symmetry

G10, $250-$450
Parsons, TN. Classic.

LOCATION: Mid-southeastern states. **DESCRIPTION:** A medium to large size, thick, narrow, stemmed point with weak, tapered or barbed shoulders. The stem is parallel sided with a concave base. Some examples are finely serrated and are related and similar to the *Flint Creek* type.

PONTCHARTRAIN (Type II) - Woodland, 3400 - 2000 B. P.

(Also see Buck Creek, Hardin and Hamilton Stemmed)

LOCATION: Mid-southeastern states. **DESCRIPTION:** A medium to large size, broad, stemmed point with barbed shoulders. The stem is parallel to slightly contracting and the base is straight to convex.

PONTCHARTRAIN II (continued)

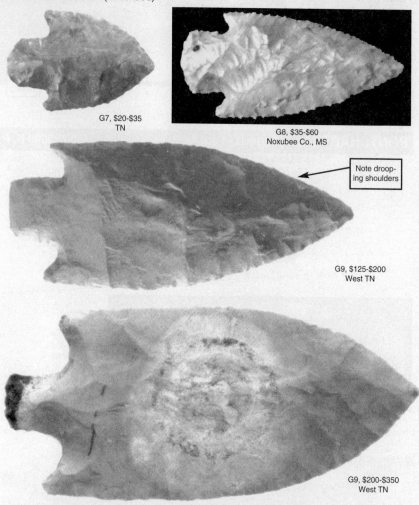

G7, $20-$35
TN

G8, $35-$60
Noxubee Co., MS

Note drooping shoulders

G9, $125-$200
West TN

G9, $200-$350
West TN

QUAD - Late Paleo, 10,000 - 6000 B. P.
(Also see Beaver Lake, Candy Creek, Cumberland, Golondrina and Hinds)

G6, $40-$75
KY

G6, $65-$125
KY

LOCATION: Southeastern states. **DESCRIPTION:** A medium to large size lanceolate point with flaring "squared" auricles and a concave base which is ground. Most examples show basal thinning and some are fluted. Believed to be related to the earlier *Cumberland* point. **I.D. KEY:** Paleo flaking, squarish auricles.

552

QUAD (continued)

G6, $65-$125
KY

G6, $65-$125
KY

G7, $80-$150
TN

G8, $65-$125
TN

Impact fracture

G6, $80-$150
KY

EC

G3, $40-$75
Coffee Lake, AL

G8, $150-$250
KY

G8, $150-$250
TN

G8, $200-$350
Lauderdale Co., AL

G7, $125-$200
KY

G8, $350-$600
Wayne Co., KY

G8, $350-$600
KY

G10, $1200-$2000
Valley Cooper, KY

G7, $275-$500
Butler Co., OH

Blade edge wear

All basal areas are ground

Note thinning strikes from base

G10, $600-$1000
Preble Co., KY

G10, $600-$1000
Lauderdale Co., AL

G10, $700-$1200
TN/AL

554

QUAD (continued)

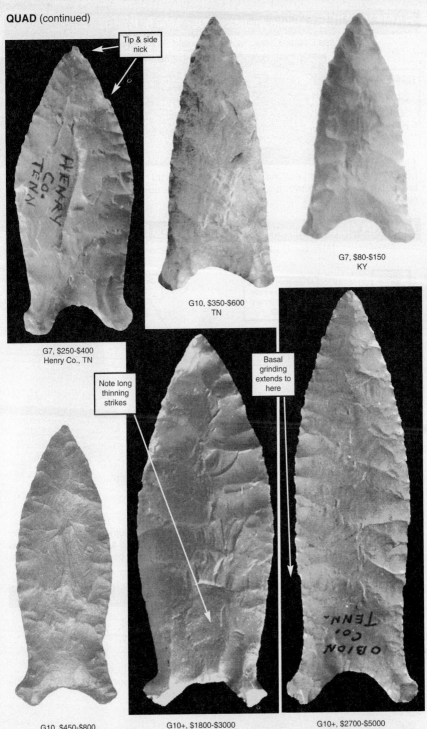

Tip & side nick

G7, $250-$400
Henry Co., TN

G10, $350-$600
TN

G7, $80-$150
KY

EC

Note long thinning strikes

Basal grinding extends to here

G10, $450-$800
Gerrard Co., KY

G10+, $1800-$3000
Montgomery Co., TN

G10+, $2700-$5000
Obion Co., TN

RAMEY KNIFE - Middle Archaic, 5000 - 4000 B. P.

(Also see Cotaco Creek, Morse Knife and Snake Creek)

IMPORTANT: Shown 50% actual size.

G8, $450-$800
KY

Note side notches

LOCATION: Type site is at the Cahokia Mounds in IL. **DESCRIPTION:** A large size broad, lanceolate blade with a rounded base and high quality flaking. The Tenn. form is similar to the Illinois form.

RANKIN - Late Archaic-Woodland, 4000 - 2500 B. P.

(Also see Buck Creek, Hamilton Stemmed and Wade)

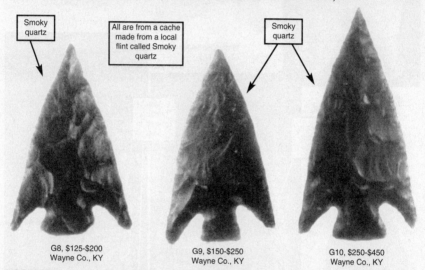

Smoky quartz

All are from a cache made from a local flint called Smoky quartz

Smoky quartz

G8, $125-$200
Wayne Co., KY

G9, $150-$250
Wayne Co., KY

G10, $250-$450
Wayne Co., KY

LOCATION: Tennessee into Kentucky. **DESCRIPTION:** A medium size, thin, well made barbed dart point with a short, expanding stem. Barbs are pointed and can extend beyond the base. Blade is recurved with a needle tip. **I.D. KEY:** Drooping barbs, short base.

RED OCHRE - Woodland, 3000 - 1500 B. P.

G8, $125-$200
KY

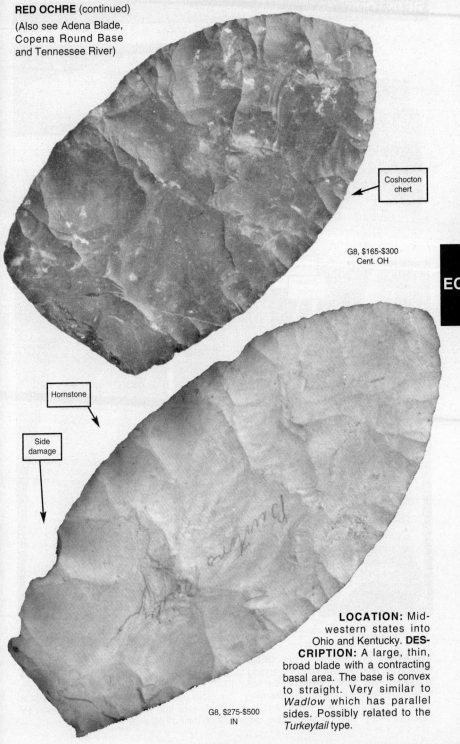

RED OCHRE (continued)

(Also see Adena Blade, Copena Round Base and Tennessee River)

Coshocton chert

G8, $165-$300
Cent. OH

EC

Hornstone

Side damage

G8, $275-$500
IN

LOCATION: Midwestern states into Ohio and Kentucky. **DESCRIPTION:** A large, thin, broad blade with a contracting basal area. The base is convex to straight. Very similar to *Wadlow* which has parallel sides. Possibly related to the *Turkeytail* type.

557

(Also see Clovis and Cumberland)

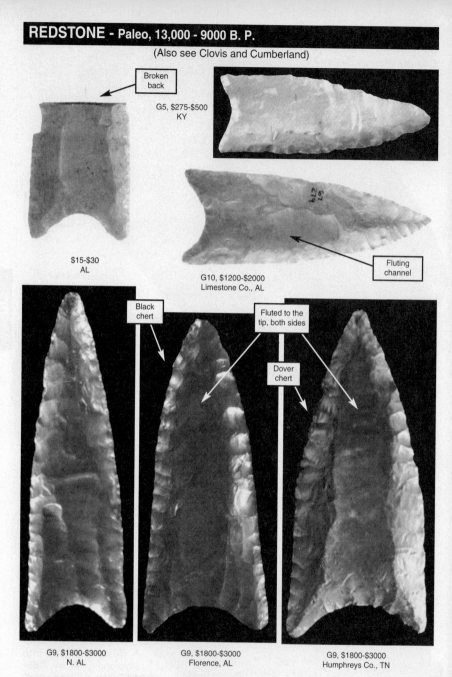

Broken back

G5, $275-$500
KY

$15-$30
AL

Fluting channel

G10, $1200-$2000
Limestone Co., AL

Black chert

Fluted to the tip, both sides

Dover chert

G9, $1800-$3000
N. AL

G9, $1800-$3000
Florence, AL

G9, $1800-$3000
Humphreys Co., TN

LOCATION: Southeastern states. **DESCRIPTION:** A medium to large size, thin, auriculate, fluted point with convex sides expanding to a wide, deeply concave base. The hafting area is ground. This point is widest at the base. Fluting can extend most of the way down each face. Multiple flutes are usual. (**Warning:** The more common resharpened *Clovis* point is often sold as this type. *Redstones* are extremely rare and are almost never offered for sale.) **I.D. KEY:** Baton or billet fluted, edgework on the hafting area.

REDSTONE (continued)

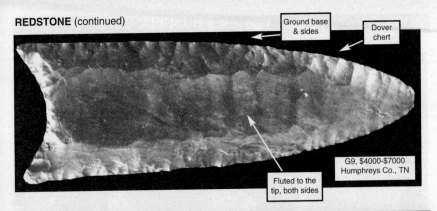

Ground base & sides

Dover chert

Fluted to the tip, both sides

G9, $4000-$7000
Humphreys Co., TN

RHEEMS CREEK - Late Archaic to Woodland, 4000 - 2000 B. P.

(Also see Halifax and Jude)

Base nick

EC

G2, $1-$2
Meigs Co., TN

G2, $1-$2
N. AL

G3, $2-$4
Huntsville, AL

G5, $3-$6
Meigs Co., TN

LOCATION: Southeastern states. **DESCRIPTION:** A small size, stubby, parallel sided, stemmed point with straight shoulders. Similar to *Halifax* which expands at the base.

RICE LOBBED - Early Archaic, 9000 - 5000 B. P.

(Also see Fox Valley, LeCroy, MacCorkle and Pine Tree)

G8, $60-$100
OH

LOCATION: Midwestern to Northeastern states. **DESCRIPTION:** A medium to large size bifurcated to lobbed base point with serrated blade edges. The base has a shallow indentation compared to the other bifurcated types. Shoulders are sharp and prominent. Called *Culpepper Bifurcate* in Virginia.

G5, $20-$35
OH

ROSS - Woodland, 2500 - 1500 B. P.
(Also see Hopewell, North & Snyders)

RUSSELL CAVE - Early Archaic, 9000 - 7000 B. P.
(Also see Hardaway, Harpeth River, Heavy Duty, Pine Tree and Searcy)

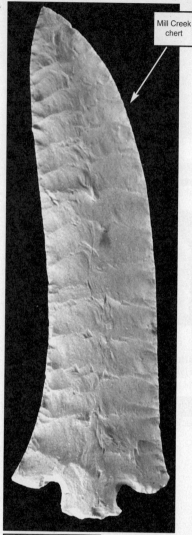

Mill Creek chert

G10, $7,000-$10,000
Tell City, IN

IMPORTANT: Shown 50% of actual size.

Bifurcated base

G5, $12-$20
S.E. TN

G6, $20-$35
Davidson Co., TN

Bifurcated base

G6, $20-$35
Clarksville, TN

G6, $20-$35
W. TN

Note fine serrations

G9, $45-$90
Huntsville, AL

G9, $70-$135
Camden, TN

LOCATION: Midwestern to Eastern states. **DESCRIPTION:** A very large size ceremonial blade with an expanded, rounded base. Some examples have a contracting "V" shaped base. **I.D. KEY:** Size, base form.

560

RUSSELL CAVE (continued)

LOCATION: Southeastern states.
DESCRIPTION: A medium size, triangular point with weak shoulders and an expanding to auriculate base. The stem appears to be an extension of the blade edges, expanding to the base. Most examples are serrated and beveled on one side of each face, although some examples are beveled on all four sides. The base is straight, concave, bifurcated or auriculate. **I.D. KEY:** Notched base and edgework.

G8, $45-$80
Humphreys Co., TN

ST. ALBANS - Early to Middle Archaic, 8900 - 8000 B. P.

(Also see Decatur, Fox Valley, Jude, Kanawha Stemmed, Kirk Stemmed-Bifurcated, Lake Erie, LeCroy, MacCorkle, Pine Tree, Rice Lobbed and Stanly)

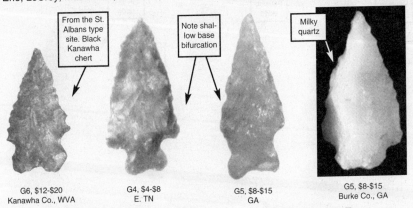

G6, $12-$20
Kanawha Co., WVA

G4, $4-$8
E. TN

G5, $8-$15
GA

G5, $8-$15
Burke Co., GA

LOCATION: A West Virginia type that extends into Pennsylvania, Virginia, Tennessee and the Carolinas. **DESCRIPTION:** Called *St. Albans Side Notched* in type site report. A small to medium size, usually serrated, narrow, bifurcated point. Basal lobes usually flare outwards. Weak shoulders are formed by slight side notches producing basal lobes or ears. The basal lobes are more shallow than in the *LeCroy* type, otherwise they are easily confused. **I.D. KEY:** Shallow basal lobes.

ST. CHARLES - Early Archaic, 9500 - 8000 B. P.

(Also see Decatur, Gibson, Kirk Corner Notched, Thebes and Warrick)

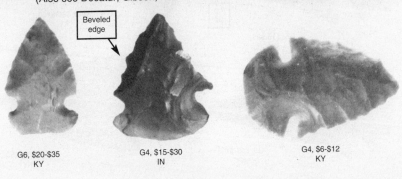

G6, $20-$35
KY

G4, $15-$30
IN

G4, $6-$12
KY

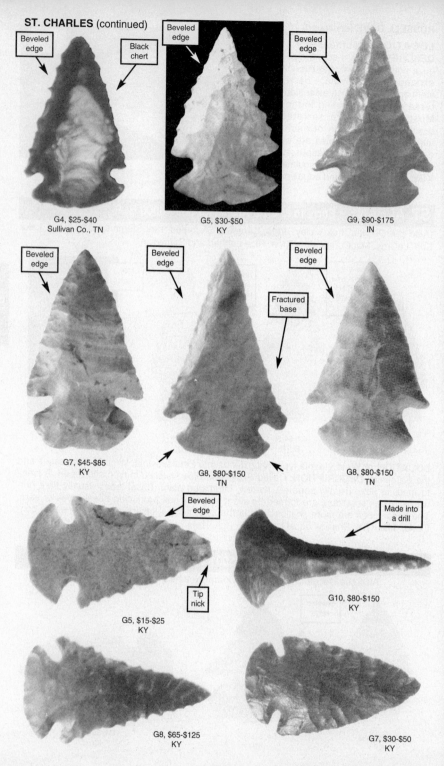

ST. CHARLES (continued)

Beveled edge

Black chert

G4, $25-$40
Sullivan Co., TN

Beveled edge

G5, $30-$50
KY

Beveled edge

G9, $90-$175
IN

Beveled edge

G7, $45-$85
KY

Beveled edge

Fractured base

G8, $80-$150
TN

Beveled edge

G8, $80-$150
TN

Beveled edge

Tip nick

G5, $15-$25
KY

Made into a drill

G10, $80-$150
KY

G8, $65-$125
KY

G7, $30-$50
KY

562

ST. CHARLES (continued)

Beveled edge

Beveled edge

Ground base and notches

Quartz

G8, $80-$150
Meade Co., KY

G10, $200-$350
KY

G9, $175-$300
OH

EC

Base nick

Hornstone

G6, $125-$200
Cynthianna, KY

G8, $175-$300
Mason Co., KY

G7, $200-$350
Clark Co., KY

LOCATION: Midwestern to Eastern states. **DESCRIPTION:** A medium to large size, broad, thin, elliptical, corner notched point with a dovetail base. First stage forms are not beveled. Beveling on opposite sides of each face occurs during the resharpening process. The base is convex and most examples exhibit high quality flaking. There is a rare variant that has the barbs clipped (clipped wing) as in the *Decatur* type. There are many variations on base style from bifurcated to eared, rounded or squared. Base size varies from small to very large. Contemporary with the *Hardin* and *Decatur* points. Formally called *Dovetail* and *Plevna* which were the resharpened (beveled) forms. It was previously reported in error that the unbeveled forms were from the late Archaic when actually all are the same type from the early Archaic period. **I.D. KEY:** Dovetail base.

563

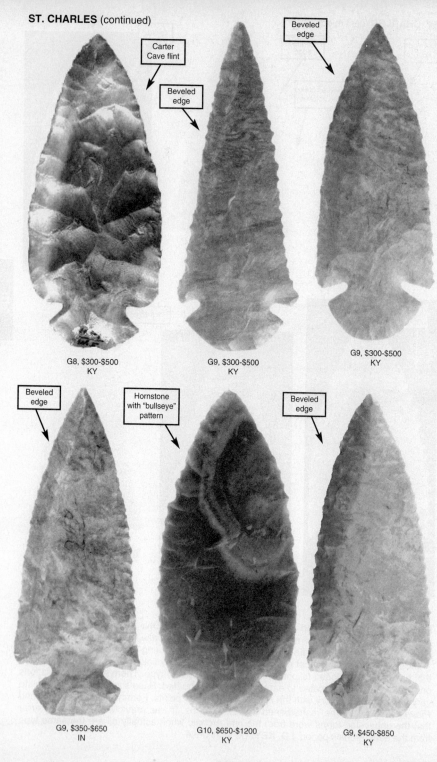

Carter Cave flint

Beveled edge

Beveled edge

G8, $300-$500
KY

G9, $300-$500
KY

G9, $300-$500
KY

Beveled edge

Hornstone with "bullseye" pattern

Beveled edge

G9, $350-$650
IN

G10, $650-$1200
KY

G9, $450-$850
KY

564

ST. CHARLES (continued)

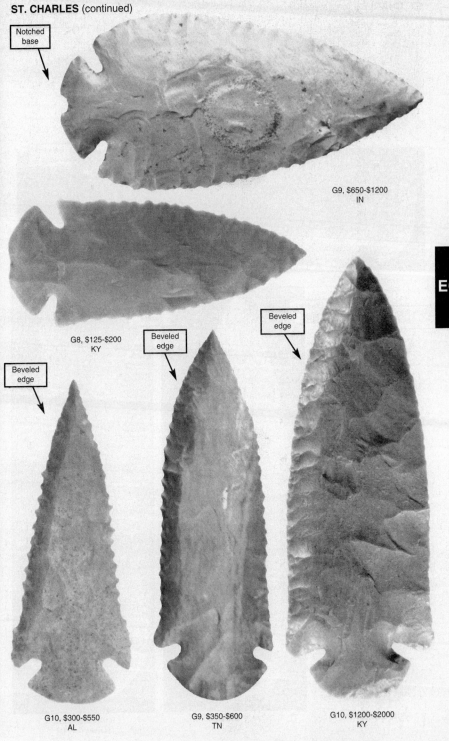

Notched base

G9, $650-$1200
IN

G8, $125-$200
KY

Beveled edge

Beveled edge

Beveled edge

G10, $300-$550
AL

G9, $350-$600
TN

G10, $1200-$2000
KY

EC

565

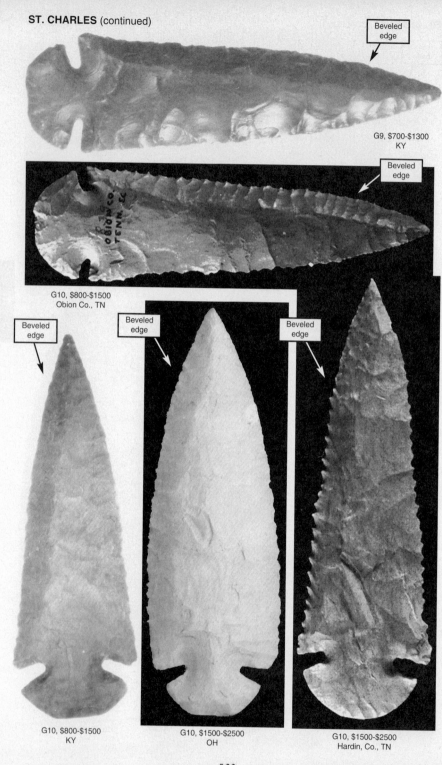

Beveled edge

G9, $700-$1300
KY

Beveled edge

G10, $800-$1500
Obion Co., TN

Beveled edge

Beveled edge

Beveled edge

G10, $800-$1500
KY

G10, $1500-$2500
OH

G10, $1500-$2500
Hardin, Co., TN

ST. HELENA - Early to Mid-Archaic, 8000 - 5000 B. P.

(Also see Benton, Evans, Leighton and Ohio Double Notched)

Unusual chisel tip

G7, $20-$35
Jefferson Co., MS

Multiple notching

Unusual chisel tip

G9, $25-$40
Jefferson Co., MS

G9, $30-$50
Jefferson Co., MS

LOCATION: Mississippi into LA. **DESCRIPTION:** A medium size, broad point with multiple side notches, a chisel tip and an expanding stem. Until now, the chisel tip technology was only known in the Northwest making this eastern U.S. occurrence even more unique. **I.D. KEY:** Chisel tip and Multiple notches.

ST. TAMMANY - Early to Mid-Archaic, 8000 - 5000 B. P.

(Also see Evans, Kirk Stemmed and St. Helena)

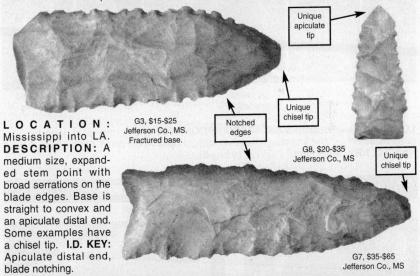

Unique apiculate tip

Unique chisel tip

Notched edges

G3, $15-$25
Jefferson Co., MS.
Fractured base.

LOCATION: Mississippi into LA. **DESCRIPTION:** A medium size, expanded stem point with broad serrations on the blade edges. Base is straight to convex and an apiculate distal end. Some examples have a chisel tip. **I.D. KEY:** Apiculate distal end, blade notching.

G8, $20-$35
Jefferson Co., MS

Unique chisel tip

G7, $35-$65
Jefferson Co., MS

SAN PATRICE-HOPE VARIETY - Early Archaic, 10,000 - 8000 B. P.

(Also see Coldwater, Dalton, Hinds, Palmer, Pelican)

LOCATION: W. Alabama to Louisiana into Oklahoma. **DESCRIPTION:** A small size, thin, auriculate point with a concave base. Some examples are thinned from the base. Basal area is longer than the "St. Johns" variety and is usually ground. **I.D. KEY:** Extended auriculate base and small size.

567

SAN PATRICE-HOPE (continued)

G9, $150-$250
N. AL

G9, $175-$300
Sou. MS

G9, $175-$300
Sou. MS

G8, $150-$250
Sou. MS

SAND MOUNTAIN - Late Woodland to Mississippian, 1500 - 400 B. P.
(Also see Durant's Bend, Fort Ancient and Madison)

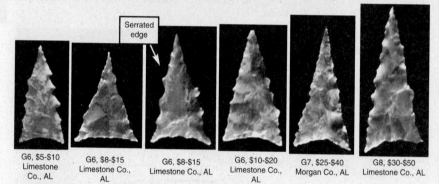

Serrated edge

G6, $5-$10
Limestone
Co., AL

G6, $8-$15
Limestone Co.,
AL

G6, $8-$15
Limestone Co., AL

G6, $10-$20
Limestone Co.,
AL

G7, $25-$40
Morgan Co., AL

G8, $30-$50
Limestone Co., AL

LOCATION: Southeastern states. **DESCRIPTION:** A small size, triangular point with serrated blade edges and a concave base. A straight base would place it in the *Fort Ancient* type. **I.D. KEY:** Basal corners are not symmetrical.

SAVAGE CAVE - Early to Middle Archaic, 7000 - 4000 B. P.
(Also see Big Sandy and Newton Falls)

G5, $8-$15
Meigs Co., TN

G6, $10-$20
Henry Co., AL

568

SAVAGE CAVE (continued)

LOCATION: Kentucky and surrounding states. **DESCRIPTION:** A medium to large size, broad, side notched point that is usually serrated. Bases are generally straight but can be slightly concave or convex.

SAVANNAH RIVER - Middle Archaic to Woodland, 5000 - 2000 B. P.

(Also see Appalachian, Elora, Hamilton, Johnson, Kirk, Maples and Stanly)

G3, $2-$4
Polk Co., TN

G3, $2-$5
Polk Co., TN

G6, $5-$10
Polk Co., TN

EC

Petrified peat bog

Quartzite

Ground stem

G6, $15-$25
GA

Quartz

G5 $6-$12
Polk Co., TN

G9, $150-$250
TN

LOCATION: Southeastern to Eastern states. **DESCRIPTION:** A medium to large size, straight to contracting stemmed point with a straight, concave or bifurcated base. The shoulders are tapered to square. The stems are narrow to broad. Believed to be related to the earlier *Stanly* point.

SCRAPER - Paleo to Archaic, 14,000 - 5000 B. P.

(Also see Drill, Graver, Lancet and Spokeshave)

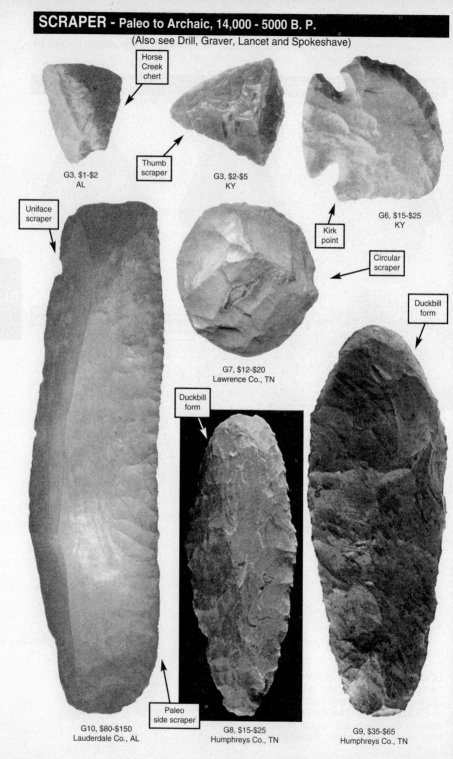

Horse Creek chert

G3, $1-$2
AL

Thumb scraper

G3, $2-$5
KY

Kirk point

G6, $15-$25
KY

Uniface scraper

Circular scraper

G7, $12-$20
Lawrence Co., TN

Duckbill form

Duckbill form

Paleo side scraper

G10, $80-$150
Lauderdale Co., AL

G8, $15-$25
Humphreys Co., TN

G9, $35-$65
Humphreys Co., TN

SCRAPER (continued)

LOCATION: Paleo to early Archaic sites throughout North America. **DESCRIPTION:** Thumb, duckbill and turtleback forms are small to medium size, thick, ovoid shaped, uniface, scraping tools that are steeply beveled, especially at the broadest end. Side scrapers are long hand-held uniface flakes with beveling on all blade edges of one face. Scraping was done primarily from the sides of these blades.

SEARCY - Early to Middle Archaic, 7000 - 5000 B. P.

(Also see Dalton-Colbert, Harpeth River, Kirk Stemmed and Russell Cave)

G5, $15-$25
Meigs Co., TN

G6, $15-$25
W. TN

LOCATION: Midwestern states. **DESCRIPTION:** A small to medium size, thin, lanceolate point with a squared hafting area that (usually) has concave sides and base which is ground. Many examples are serrated.

SHOALS CREEK - Late Archaic to Woodland, 4000 - 2000 B. P.

(Also see Elora, Kirk Stemmed, Ledbetter, Little Bear Creek, Pickwick and Smithsonia)

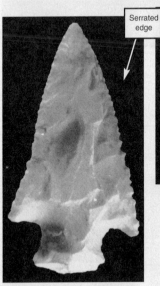

Serrated edge

G6, $18-$30
Lawrence Co., AL

G6, $20-$35
Lawrence Co., AL

Serrated edge

G7, $20-$35
Lawrence Co., AL

LOCATION: Southeastern states. **DESCRIPTION:** A medium to large size point with serrated edges, an expanded base and sharp barbs.

571

SMITH - Middle Archaic, 7000 - 4000 B. P.

(Also see Eva, Hamilton, Rankin and Wade)

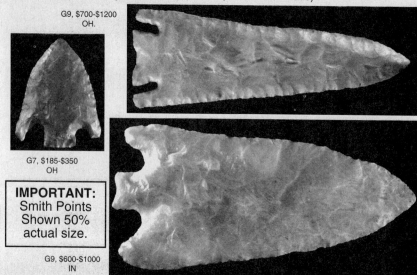

G9, $700-$1200
OH.

G7, $185-$350
OH

IMPORTANT:
Smith Points
Shown 50%
actual size.

G9, $600-$1000
IN

LOCATION: Midwestern states into Ohio. **DESCRIPTION:** A very large size, broad, point with long parallel shoulders and a squared to slightly expanding base. Some examples may appear to be basally notched due to the long barbs.

SMITHSONIA - Late Archaic to Woodland, 4000 - 1500 B. P.

(See Buck Creek, Cotaco Cr., Hamilton, Motley, Shoals Creek, Table Rock and Wade)

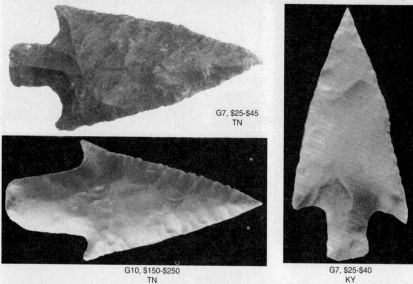

G7, $25-$45
TN

G10, $150-$250
TN

G7, $25-$40
KY

LOCATION: Southeastern states. **DESCRIPTION:** A medium size, triangular point with tapered to barbed shoulders and a parallel sided stem with a straight base. Many examples have finely serrated blade edges which are usually straight. **I.D. KEY:** High barb on one side and fine edgework.

572

Fine serrations

EC

G7, $55-$100
Colbert Co., AL

G8, $80-$150
Colbert Co., AL

G8, $90-$175
Humphreys Co., TN

LOCATION: Southeastern states. **DESCRIPTION:** A medium size, triangular point with tapered to barbed shoulders and a parallel sided stem with a straight base. Many examples have finely serrated blade edges which are usually straight. **I.D. KEY:** High barb on one side and fine edgework.

SNAKE CREEK - Late Archaic, 4000 - 3000 B. P.

(Also see Harahey, Lerma, Morse, Ramey Knife and Tear Drop)

Double and single side notches

G9, $350-$600
Hardin Co., TN. Snake Creek.

LOCATION: Tennessee and Kentucky **DESCRIPTION:** A large size, broad, ovoid blade with shallow side notches about 30 to 40% of the way between the base and tip. Double side notches are common. The stem contracts to a rounded base.

SNAKE CREEK (continued)

Single side notches

Double side notches

G10, $300-$500
Humphreys Co., TN

G9, $350-$600
Hardin Co., TN. Snake Creek.

SNYDERS (Hopewell) - Woodland, 2500 - 1500 B. P.

(Also see Buck Creek, Hopewell, Motley and North)

G5, $15-$25
KY

G8, $20-$35
OH

574

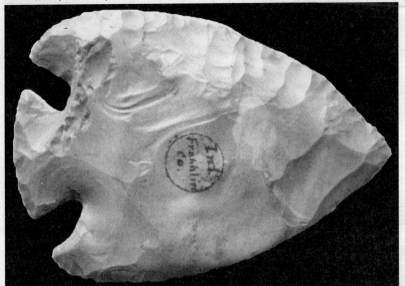

G9, $300-$500
Franklin Co., IN

EC

Snyders "Mackinaw"
variety with narrow
notches

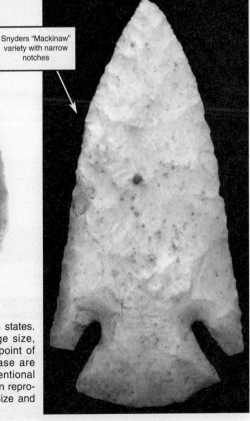

G5, $55-$100
OH

LOCATION: Midwestern to Eastern states.
DESCRIPTION: A medium to large size,
broad, thin, wide corner notched point of
high quality. Blade edges and base are
convex. Many examples have intentional
fractured bases. This point has been reproduced in recent years. **I.D. KEY:** Size and
broad corner notches.

G9, $250-$450
OH

575

SPOKESHAVE - Woodland, 3000 -1500 B. P.

G8, $25-$40
OH

G8, $25-$45
IN

LOCATION: Kentucky, Ohio into Indiana. **DESCRIPTION:** A medium to large size stemmed tool used for scraping. The blade is asymmetrical with one edge convex and the other concave.

SQUARE-END KNIFE - Late Archaic to Historic, 3500 - 400 B. P.

(Also see Angostura, Fort Ancient Blade, Frazier and Watts Cave Knife)

G8, $80-$150
TN

G7, $65-$125
Humphreys Co.,
TN

LOCATION: Midwestern states. **DESCRIPTION:** A medium to large size rectangular blade. Edges are generally straight to slightly convex.

G7, $80-$150
TN

STANFIELD - Transitional Paleo, 10,000 - 8000 B. P.

(Also see Angostura, Copena, Fort Ancient Blade, Frazier and Tennessee River)

G6, $15-$30
Colbert Co., AL

STANFIELD (continued)

Ground basal area

Basal thinning

G8, $20-$35
Colbert Co., AL

Ground basal area

G6, $12-$20
Lauderdale Co., AL

G8, $20-$35
Colbert Co., AL

G6, $12-$20
Colbert Co., AL.

G6, $20-$35
Colbert Co., AL.

Ground base

G5 $25-$45
Humphreys Co., TN

EC

LOCATION: Southeastern states. Type site is in Colbert Co., AL. **DESCRIPTION:** A medium size, narrow, lanceolate point with parallel sides and a straight base. Some rare examples are fluted. Bases are usually ground and flattened. Flaking is to the center of the blade. This point has been confused with the *Tennessee River* point which is simply a preform for early non-beveled Archaic types. This type is smaller, narrowerer and is flaked to the center of the blade and is much rarer than the type with which it is often confused.

STANLY - Early Archaic, 8000 - 5000 B. P.

(Also see Fox Valley, Frederick, Garth Slough, Kanawha Stemmed, Kirk Stemmed - Bifurcated and Savannah River)

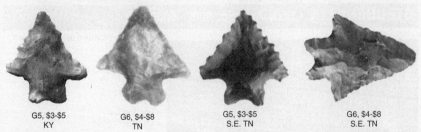

G5, $3-$5
KY

G6, $4-$8
TN

G5, $3-$5
S.E. TN

G6, $4-$8
S.E. TN

LOCATION: Southeastern to Eastern states. Type site is Stanly Co., N.C. **DESCRIPTION:** A small to medium size, broad shoulder point with a small bifurcated stem. Some examples are serrated and show high quality flaking. The shoulders are very prominent and can be tapered, horizontal or barbed. **I.D. KEY:** Tiny bifurcated base.

STANLY (continued)

Tip wear →

G4, $1-$3
Polk Co., TN

G4, $1-$3
Polk Co., TN

G5, $4-$8
KY

G5, $8-$15
OH

G8, $25-$45
TN

G8 $12-$20
Cumberland Co., KY

Base nick →

G5, $4-$8
Polk Co., TN

Side nick ←

G6, $15-$30
OH

G5, $12-$20
TN

STEUBENVILLE - Early Archaic, 9000 - 6000 B. P.

(Also see Holland and Johnson)

G6, $35-$65
OH

STEUBENVILLE (continued)

LOCATION: Ohio into the Northeast. **DESCRIPTION:** A medium to large size, broad, triangular point with weak tapered shoulders, a wide parallel sided stem and a concave base. The basal area is ground. Believed to be developed from the *Scottsbluff* type.

G7, $60-$100
OH

STILWELL - Early Archaic, 9000 - 7000 B. P.
(Also see Kirk Corner Notched, Neuberger and Pine Tree)

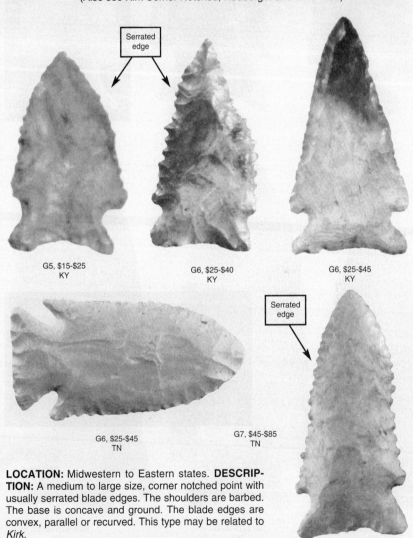

Serrated edge

G5, $15-$25
KY

G6, $25-$40
KY

G6, $25-$45
KY

G6, $25-$45
TN

Serrated edge

G7, $45-$85
TN

LOCATION: Midwestern to Eastern states. **DESCRIPTION:** A medium to large size, corner notched point with usually serrated blade edges. The shoulders are barbed. The base is concave and ground. The blade edges are convex, parallel or recurved. This type may be related to *Kirk*.

579

Serrated edge

G8, $90-$175
OH

G7, $45-$85
KY

G6, $25-$45
TN

G7, $80-$150
IN

G8, $175-$300
TN

G10, $250-$450
KY

STILWELL (continued)

Serrated edge

G10, $1200-$2000
Benton Co., TN

Ground base
and notches

Serrated edge

EC

G10, $200-$350
TN

G9, $450-$850
Posey Co., IN

G9, $800-$1500
IN

581

STRINGTOWN - Early Archaic, 9500 - 7000 B. P.

(Also see Alberta and Eastern Stemmed Lanceolate)

Coshocton chert

Jasper

G6, $125-$200 OH

Note eared base

Flintridge flint

G5, $80-$150 OH

Base nick

G7, $250-$450 OH

Flintridge flint

G8, $750-$1200 Licking Co., OH

LOCATION: Pennsylvania, Ohio westward. **DESCRIPTION:** A medium to large size, broad stemmed point with convex to parallel sides and square shoulders. The stem is parallel sided to slightly expanding. The base is eared and the hafting area is ground. Most examples have horizontal to oblique parallel flaking and are of high quality and thinness. The Eastern form of the *Scottsbluff* type made by the Cody Complex people. The Eastern Stemmed Lanceolate is a variation of this form. **I.D.KEY:** Base form and parallel flaking.

SUBLET FERRY - Late Archaic to Woodland, 4000 - 2000 B. P.

(Also see Big Sandy, Brewerton Side Notched, Coosa and Meadowood)

G4, $4-$8 Hamilton Co., TN

G5, $8-$15 Jackson Co., AL

LOCATION: Southeastern states. **DESCRIPTION:** A small to medium size point with side notches that are very close to the base. The base is straight to slightly convex. Blade edges are straight to convex and may be serrated.

G6, $12-$20 Florence, AL

582

SUBLET FERRY (continued)

G9, $40-$70
TN

Notching occurs close to the base

G8, $18-$30
Humphreys Co., TN

G9, $45-$80
Humphreys Co., TN

EC

SUN DISC - Mississippian, 1100 - 600 B. P.

(Also see Duck River Sword and Mace)

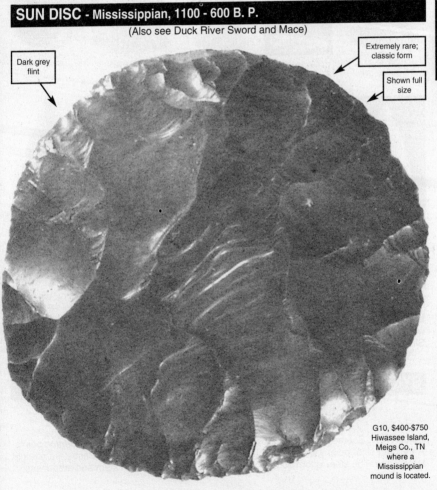

Dark grey flint

Extremely rare; classic form

Shown full size

G10, $400-$750
Hiwassee Island, Meigs Co., TN where a Mississippian mound is located.

SUN DISC (continued)

LOCATION: Southeastern states. **DESCRIPTION:** A large size, disc shaped object used in the Sun dance ceremony along with the Duck River Swords and shell gorgets by the Mississippian culture. Such dances are depicted on the shell gorgets themselves. These objects are made from high grade flint and are flaked to a sharp edge. **Warning:** Absolute provinence is needed to prove authenticity. Very rare, existing mostly in museum collections.

SWAN LAKE - Late Archaic to Woodland, 3500 - 2000 B. P.

(Also see Bakers Creek, Brewerton, Durst, Halifax and Matanzas)

G3, $1-$2
Dunlap, TN

G7, $12-$20
Dayton, TN

G7, $12-$20
Fentress Co., TN

G8, $15-$25
Dunlap, TN

G8, $15-$25
TN

G7, $12-$25
Fentress Co., TN

G7, $12-$20
Dunlap, TN

G6, $12-$20
Pikeville, TN

G8, $20-$35
Fentress Co., TN

G8, $20-$35
Dunlap, TN

LOCATION: Southeastern to Eastern states. **DESCRIPTION:** A small size, thick, triangular point with wide, shallow side notches. Some examples have an unfinished rind or base. Similar to the side-notched *Lamoka* in New York. Called *Jackson* in Florida.

SYKES - Early to Late Archaic, 6000 - 5000 B. P.

(Also see Benton)

LOCATION: Southeastern states. **DESCRIPTION:** Believed to be related to *Benton* points. A medium size, point with a broad blade and a very short, broad stem. Bases are straight to concave. The stem is formed by corner notches. **I.D. KEY:** Short stem and broadness.

SYKES (continued)

G6, $15-$25
KY

G4, $5-$10
AL

G8, $15-$25
Limestone Co., AL

Shown full size

G7, $25-$45
TN

TABLE ROCK - Late Archaic, 4000 - 3000 B. P.

(Also see Bakers Creek, Buck Creek, Cotaco Creek, Fishspear, Motley and Smithsonia)

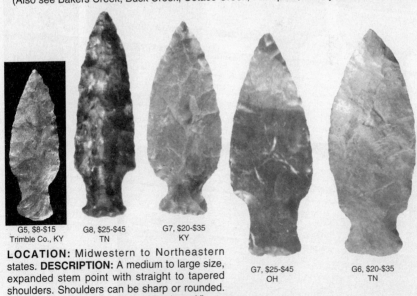

G5, $8-$15
Trimble Co., KY

G8, $25-$45
TN

G7, $20-$35
KY

G7, $25-$45
OH

G6, $20-$35
TN

LOCATION: Midwestern to Northeastern states. **DESCRIPTION:** A medium to large size, expanded stem point with straight to tapered shoulders. Shoulders can be sharp or rounded. This point type is also know as "Bottleneck".

585

G6, $20-$35
KY

G7, $30-$50
OH

G7, $25-$45
OH

G7, $25-$45
KY

G6, $20-$35
OH

G7, $25-$40
OH

G9, $150-$250
TN

G7, $25-$45
Decatur, AL

G7, $50-$90
KY

586

TEAR DROP - Woodland, 2000 - 1000 B. P.

(Also see Adena Blade and Red Ochre)

G8, $250-$400
OH

Made from
white chert

G10, $700-$1200
Humphreys Co., TN
Cache blade

G10, $800-$1500
TN

IMPORTANT:
Tear Drop points
shown half size.

EC

LOCATION: Southeastern states. **DESCRIPTION:** A large size, broad, thin, ellipitcal blade with a rounded to straight base. Usually found in caches and are believed to be a little later than the *Adena* blades. Usually made from a special white chert. Some examples have been found stained with red ochre.

TENNESSEE RIVER - Early Archaic, 9000 - 6000 B. P.

(Also see Adena Blade, Cobbs Triangular, Kirk, Red Ochre and Stanfield)

G7, $40-$75
KY

LOCATION: Southeastern states. **DESCRIPTION:** These are unnotched preforms for early Archaic types such as *Kirk, Eva*, etc. and would have the same description as that type without the notches. Bases can be straight, concave or convex. **I.D. KEY:** Archaic style edgework. **NOTE:** This type has been confused with the *Stanfield* point which is a medium size, narrow, thicker point. A beveled edge would place your point under the *Cobbs Triangular* type

G6, $30-$50
Florence, AL

587

G8, $80-$150
TN

Resharpened
many times

G8, $45-$85
KY

G8, $65-$125
KY

G6, $150-$250
TN

EC

G10, $350-$650
OH

G10, $400-$700
OH

TENNESSEE SAW - Early Archaic, 8000 -6000 B. P.

(Also see Lerma)

IMPORTANT: THIS POINT SHOWN HALF SIZE

G10, $600-$1000
TN

LOCATION: Tennessee and Kentucky. **DESCRIPTION:** A very large by-pointed, serrated blade that was probably used as a knife. Very rare in collecting area. **I.D. KEY:** Size and serrations.

TENNESSEE SWORD   (See Duck River Sword)

THEBES - Early Archaic, 10,000 - 8000 B. P.

(Also see Big Sandy E-Notched, Lost Lake and St. Charles)

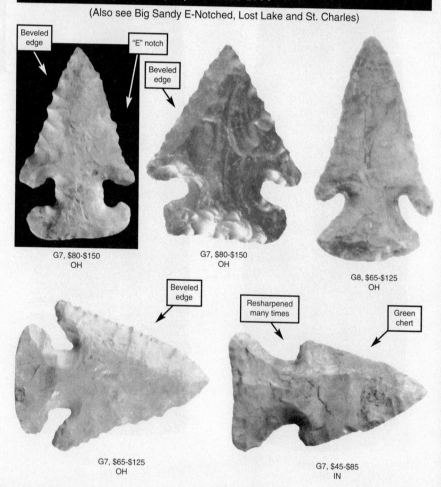

Beveled edge

"E" notch

Beveled edge

G7, $80-$150
OH

G7, $80-$150
OH

G8, $65-$125
OH

Beveled edge

Resharpened many times

Green chert

G7, $65-$125
OH

G7, $45-$85
IN

590

THEBES (continued)

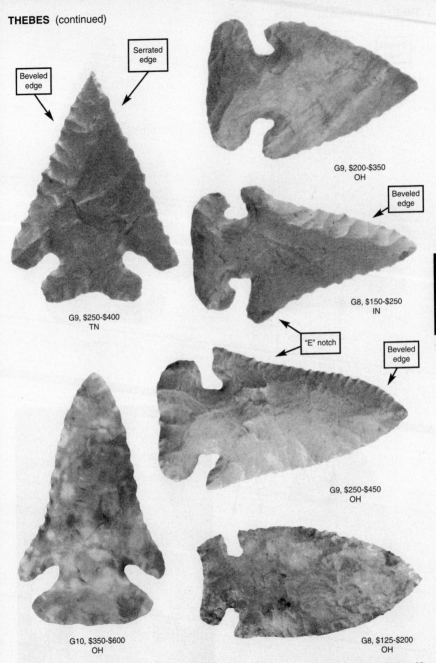

Beveled edge

Serrated edge

G9, $200-$350
OH

Beveled edge

G9, $250-$400
TN

G8, $150-$250
IN

"E" notch

Beveled edge

G9, $250-$450
OH

G10, $350-$600
OH

G8, $125-$200
OH

EC

LOCATION: Midwestern states. **DESCRIPTION:** A medium to large size, wide, blade with deep, angled side notches that are parallel sided and squared. Resharpened examples have beveling on one side of each face. The bases of this type have broad proportions and are concave, straight or convex and are ground. Some examples have unusual side notches called Key notch. This type of notch is angled into the blade to produce a high point in the center, forming the letter E. See *Big Sandy E-Notched*.

THEBES (continued)

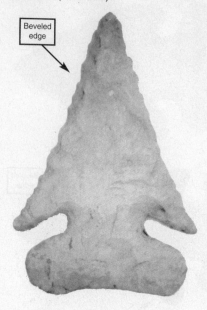

Beveled edge

G10, $300-$500
OH

G10, $300-$550
OH

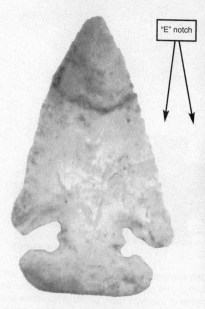

"E" notch

G9, $650-$1200
OH

G9, $275-$500
Sou. IN

592

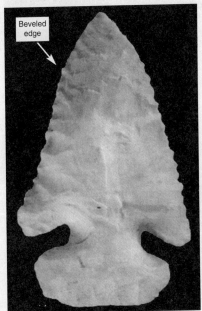

Beveled edge

G10, $275-$500
OH

Beveled edge

G10, $300-$500
OH

EC

Beveled edge

Coshocton chert

G9, $350-$600
OH

G8, $350-$650
IN

TORTUGAS - Middle Archaic to Woodland, 6000 - 1000 B. P.

(Also see Frazier, Levanna and Paint Rock Valley)

G3, $2-$4
Fentress Co., TN

G5, $2-$5
Fentress Co., TN

G5, $4-$8
Tishomingo Co., MS

G5, $4-$8
Decatur, AL

Dover chert

G8, $20-$35
Parsons, TN

G9, $25-$45
Camden, TN

LOCATION: Typically found in northern Mexico into southern Texas. Similar points (shown here) are also found in Mississippi, Alabama and western Tenn. **DESCRIPTION:** A medium size, fairly thick, triangular point with straight to convex sides and base. Some examples are beveled on one side of each face. Bases are usually thinned. This type is much thicker than *Madison* points and are more triangular than *Frazier* points.

TRADE POINTS - Historic, 400 - 170 B. P.

$10-$20
Tellico
Plains, TN
Cherokee

$65-$125, Tn, Cherokee
c. 1810-1830 (cut sheet iron)

$15-$25, Tn, Cherokee
c. 1810-1830 (cut sheet iron)

$20-$40, French conical (Kaskaskia)
Elmore Co., AL. Circa 1700-1763

These points were made of copper, iron, and steel and were traded to the Indians by the French, British and others from the 1600s to the 1800s. Examples have been found all over the United States.

$75-$150
Eastern U.S.

594

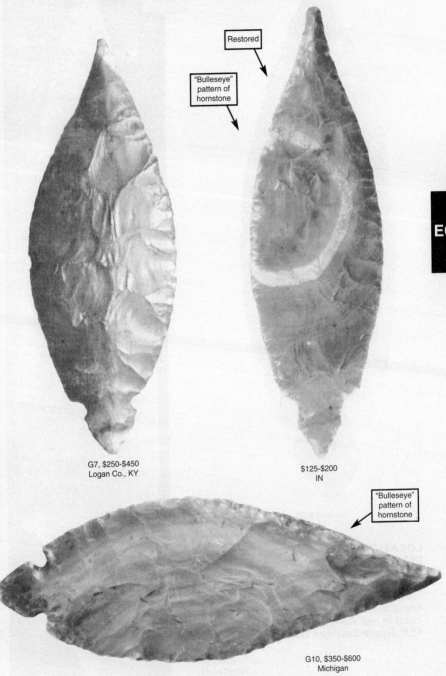

Restored

"Bulleseye" pattern of hornstone

EC

G7, $250-$450
Logan Co., KY

$125-$200
IN

"Bulleseye" pattern of hornstone

G10, $350-$600
Michigan

G8, $350-$650
IN

One of the finest known

LOCATION: Midwestern to Eastern states.
DESCRIPTION: A medium to large size, wide, thin, elliptical blade with shallow notches very close to the base. This type is usually found in caches and has been reproduced in recent years. Made by the Adena culture. A similar form, but much earlier, is found in late *Benton* caches in Mississippi. **I.D. KEY:** Smaller base than the Harrison Var.

G10+, $3500-$6500
Butler Co., KY

596

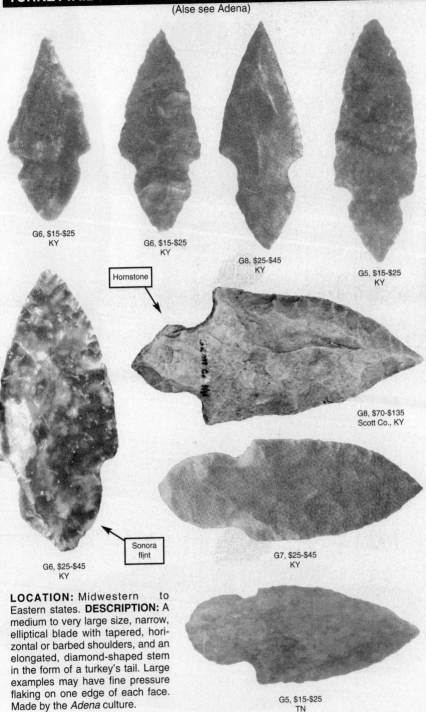

G6, $15-$25
KY

G6, $15-$25
KY

G8, $25-$45
KY

G5, $15-$25
KY

EC

Hornstone

G8, $70-$135
Scott Co., KY

Sonora flint

G6, $25-$45
KY

G7, $25-$45
KY

G5, $15-$25
TN

LOCATION: Midwestern to Eastern states. **DESCRIPTION:** A medium to very large size, narrow, elliptical blade with tapered, horizontal or barbed shoulders, and an elongated, diamond-shaped stem in the form of a turkey's tail. Large examples may have fine pressure flaking on one edge of each face. Made by the *Adena* culture.

597

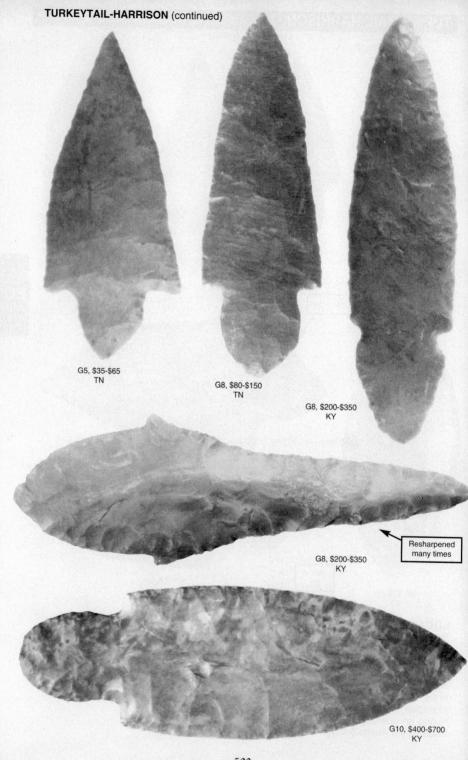

G5, $35-$65
TN

G8, $80-$150
TN

G8, $200-$350
KY

Resharpened
many times

G8, $200-$350
KY

G10, $400-$700
KY

G8, $65-$125
Hickman Co., TN

EC

G8, $80-$150
TN

G10, $450-$800
KY

G10, $1200-$2000
IN

TURKEYTAIL-HEBRON - Late Archaic to Woodland, 3500 - 2500 B. P.
(Also see Waubesa)

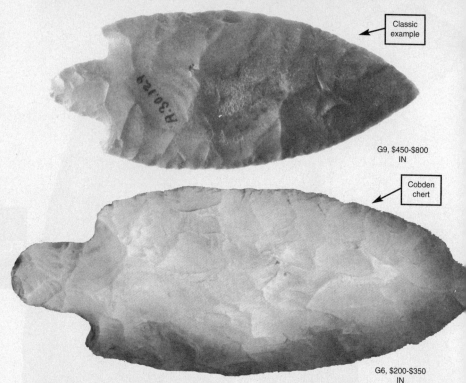

Classic example

G9, $450-$800
IN

Cobden chert

G6, $200-$350
IN

LOCATION: Great Lakes area from Wisconsin to New York. **DESCRIPTION:** A medium to large size blade with barbed shoulders, and a narrow contracting stem with a convex base. Made by the *Adena* culture. A rare type.

TURKEYTAIL-TUPELO - Late Archaic, 4750 - 3900 B. P.
(Also see Benton and Warito)

IMPORTANT
All Tupelo points on this page are shown 1/2 size

Double notched form

Broken & glued

G3, $650-$1200
Monroe Co., MS

Double notched form

G10+, $3000-$5000
Lee Co., MS

TURKEYTAIL-TUPELO (continued)

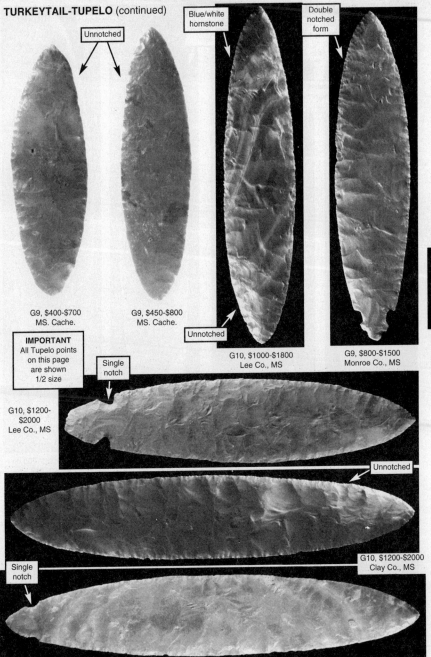

Unnotched

Blue/white hornstone

Double notched form

Unnotched

EC

G9, $400-$700
MS. Cache.

G9, $450-$800
MS. Cache.

IMPORTANT
All Tupelo points
on this page
are shown
1/2 size

G10, $1000-$1800
Lee Co., MS

G9, $800-$1500
Monroe Co., MS

Single notch

G10, $1200-
$2000
Lee Co., MS

Unnotched

G10, $1200-$2000
Clay Co., MS

Single notch

G10, $1500-$2800
Lee Co., MS

LOCATION: Mississippi, Alabama and Tennessee. **DESCRIPTION:** A large size, thin, well-made blade that is found in caches with large *Benton* and *Warito* points. Some are not notched, but most have single, double or triple notches. Polishing occurs on the edges and surfaces of a few examples, possibly used as dance blades. These are unique and 1000 years older than the northern type.

601

TURKEYTAIL-TUPELO (continued)

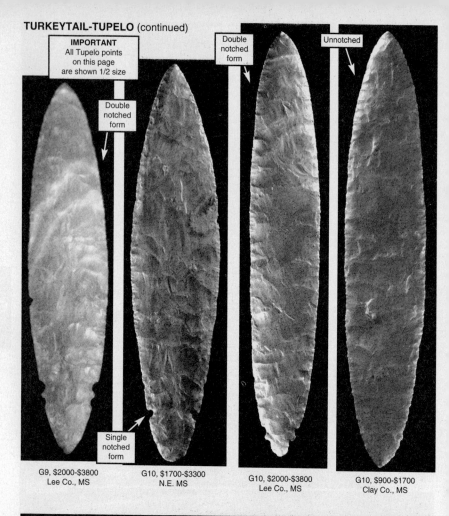

IMPORTANT
All Tupelo points
on this page
are shown 1/2 size

Double
notched
form

Single
notched
form

Double
notched
form

Unnotched

G9, $2000-$3800
Lee Co., MS

G10, $1700-$3300
N.E. MS

G10, $2000-$3800
Lee Co., MS

G10, $900-$1700
Clay Co., MS

VALINA - Woodland, 2500 - 1000 B. P.

(Also see Madison and Morrow Mountain)

G5, $1-$2
Sequatchie Valley, TN

G5, $1-$2
Meigs Co., TN

G7, $1-$3
Meigs Co., TN

LOCATION: Eastern states. **DESCRIPTION:** A small size, broad triangle with rounded basal corners and a convex base.

WADE - Late Archaic to Woodland, 4500 - 2500 B. P.

(Also see Buck Creek, Eva, Hamilton Stemmed, Motley, Rankin, Smith and Smithsonia)

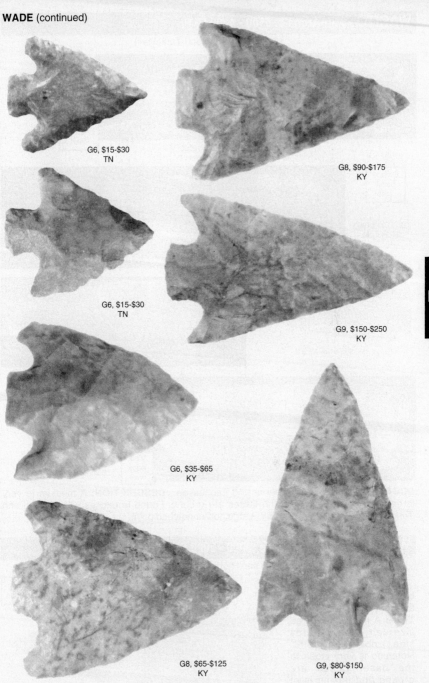

G6, $15-$30
TN

G8, $90-$175
KY

G6, $15-$30
TN

G9, $150-$250
KY

EC

G6, $35-$65
KY

G8, $65-$125
KY

G9, $80-$150
KY

LOCATION: Southern states. **DESCRIPTION:** A medium to large size, broad, well barbed, stemmed point. Some examples appear to basal notched. The blade is straight to convex. The stem is straight to expanding or contracting. On some examples, the barbs almost reach the base and are rounded to pointed. Has been found with *Motley* points in caches.

WARITO - Mid-Archaic, 5500 - 4500 B. P.

(Also see Benton and Turkeytail)

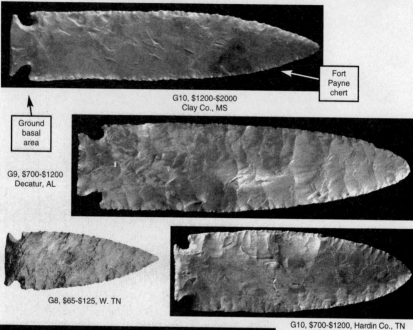

Fort Payne chert

G10, $1200-$2000
Clay Co., MS

Ground basal area

G9, $700-$1200
Decatur, AL

G8, $65-$125, W. TN

G10, $700-$1200, Hardin Co., TN

IMPORTANT
Warito points are shown 1/2 size

Minor edge wear

G6, $350-$600,
Sumner Co., TN

LOCATION: Mississippi, Alabama and Tennessee. **DESCRIPTION:** A medium to very large size corner notched point. Bases are ground. Found in caches with *Benton* and *Turkeytail Tupelo* points. **I.D. KEY:** Large corner notched point.

WARRICK - Early Archaic, 9000 - 5000 B. P.

(Also see Hardin and St. Charles)

LOCATION: Ohio and adjacent states. **DESCRIPTION:** A medium to large size, fairly thick, sturdy side notched point. Notching is very close to the base. Bases are ground and flaking is of high quality.

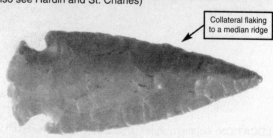

Collateral flaking to a median ridge

G9, $135-$250
IN

604

WARRICK (continued)

G5, $35-$50
IN

G8, $55-$100
IN

G9, $150-$250
KY

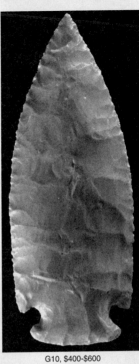

G10, $400-$600
Harrison Co.,IN

EC

WASHINGTON - Woodland, 3000 - 1500 B. P.

(Also see Durant's Bend and Nova)

G5, $8-$15
Dallas Co., AL. Classic.

LOCATION: Southeastern states. **DESCRIPTION:** A small size, serrated, corner to side notched point with a concave, expanded base.

WASHITA - Mississippian, 800 -400 B. P.

(Also see Keota)

G2, $.50-$1
S.E. TN

G2, $.50-$1
Hiwassee Isle, TN

G3, $1-$2
S.E. TN

G8, $8-$15
Lauderdale Co., AL

LOCATION: Midwestern states into Tenn. and Ala **DESCRIPTION:** A small size, thin, triangular side notched arrow point with a concave base. Basal area is usually large in proportion to the blade size. A Mississippian point probably transported between the Mississippian sites.

WATTS CAVE - Trans. Paleo to Early Archaic, 10,000 - 8000 B. P.

(Also see Square End Knife)

605

WATTS CAVE (continued)

Finely serrated edge ←

IMPORTANT
This knife
shown
1/2 size

G10, $350-$600
Dickson Cave, KY

LOCATION: Tennessee into Kentucky and Ohio. **DESCRIPTION:** A large size, serrated, knife form with squared corners and the blade expanding towards both ends. First recognized as a type from Watts Cave in Kentucky. Some examples are fluted.

WAUBESA - Woodland, 2500 - 1500 B. P.
(Also see Adena, Dickson and Turkeytail-Hebron)

Resharpened many times

Made into a perforator

G9, $35-$60
TN

G7, $20-$35
TN

G9, $40-$75
TN

G9, $35-$60
TN

G6, $15-$30
Fentress Co., TN

G10, $125-$200
TN

G9, $65-$125
TN

G6, $15-$30
KY

WAUBESA (continued)

Dover chert

G9, $35-$65
TN

G8, $30-$50
KY

G10, $150-$250
TN

G10, $150-$250
TN

EC

G10, $300-$550
TN

Hornstone

G8, $35-$60
KY

G6, $30-$55
TN

G7, $40-$75
TN

607

G8, $80-$150
KY

G8, $55-$100
MS

G8, $125-$200
KY

G10, $350-$600
TN

G10, $350-$600
TN

G9, $250-$400
Humphreys Co., TN

G10, $400-$750
Parsons, TN

WHEELER EXCURVATE - Transitional Paleo, 10,000 - 8000 B. P.

(Also see Angostura)

G6, $80-$150
Limestone Co., AL

G6, $125-$200
Limestone Co., AL

Rare fluted form

Thin, with collateral flaking

G9, $450-$800
Limestone Co., AL

G10, $350-$600
Colbert Co., AL

G10, $350-$600
N. AL

EC

G8, $450-$800
Hardin Co., TN

G7, $150-$250
Decatur, AL

G7, $80-$150
Madison Co., AL

Broken & glued

Rare fluted form

Fort Payne chert

G8, $375-$700
Hardin Co., TN

G8, $600-$1000
Limestone Co., AL

G2, $30-$50
TN

LOCATION: Southeastern states. **DESCRIPTION:** A small to medium size, lanceolate point with a deep concave base that is steeply beveled. Some examples are fluted, others are finely serrated and show excellent quality collateral flaking. Most bases are deeply notched but some examples have a more shallow concavity. Basal grinding does occur but is usually absent. The ears on some examples turn inward. Blade edges are excurvate. **I.D. KEY:** Base form and flaking style.

WHEELER EXPANDED BASE - Transitional Paleo, 10,000 - 8000 B. P.

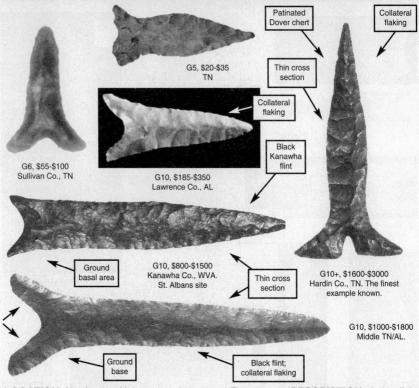

Patinated Dover chert

Collateral flaking

Thin cross section

Collateral flaking

Black Kanawha flint

G5, $20-$35
TN

G6, $55-$100
Sullivan Co., TN

G10, $185-$350
Lawrence Co., AL

Ground basal area

G10, $800-$1500
Kanawha Co., WVA.
St. Albans site

Thin cross section

G10+, $1600-$3000
Hardin Co., TN. The finest example known.

G10, $1000-$1800
Middle TN/AL.

Ground base

Black flint; collateral flaking

LOCATION: Northwest Alabama and southern Tennessee. **DESCRIPTION:** A small to medium size, very narrow, thin, lanceolate point with expanding, squared ears forming a "Y" at the base which is "V" notched. Most examples have high quality collateral flaking. This very rare type has been found on *Wheeler* sites in the type area. Scarcity of this type suggests that it was not in use but for a short period of time. **I.D. KEY:** Notch and ears.

WHEELER RECURVATE - Transitional Paleo 10,000 - 8000 B. P.

(Also see Patrick)

G8, $65-$125
AL

G8, $65-$125
Hamilton Co., TN

G8, $65-$125
Hamilton Co., TN

G8, $150-$250
AL

LOCATION: Southeastern states. **DESCRIPTION:** A small to medium size, lanceolate point with recurved blade edges and a deep concave base that is steeply beveled. The blade edges taper towards the base, forming the hafting area. Basal grinding is absent. Rare examples are fluted.

WHEELER RECURVATE (continued)

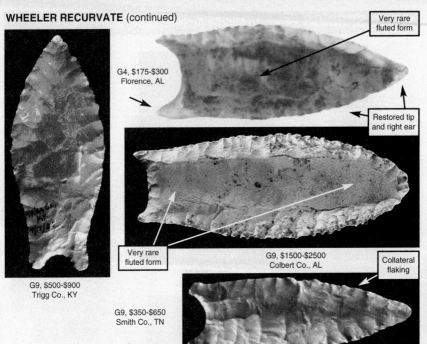

Very rare fluted form

G4, $175-$300
Florence, AL

Restored tip and right ear

Very rare fluted form

G9, $1500-$2500
Colbert Co., AL

Collateral flaking

G9, $500-$900
Trigg Co., KY

G9, $350-$650
Smith Co., TN

EC

WHEELER TRIANGULAR - Transitional Paleo 10,000 - 8000 B. P.

(Also see Camp Creek, Copena, Madison and Sand Mountain)

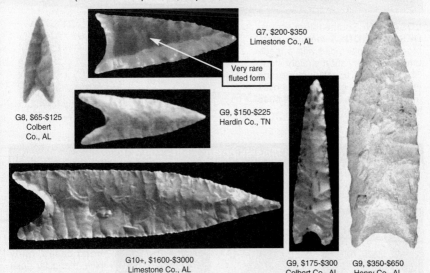

G7, $200-$350
Limestone Co., AL

Very rare fluted form

G8, $65-$125
Colbert Co., AL

G9, $150-$225
Hardin Co., TN

G10+, $1600-$3000
Limestone Co., AL

G9, $175-$300
Colbert Co., AL

G9, $350-$650
Henry Co., AL

LOCATION: Southeastern states. **DESCRIPTION:** A small to medium size, lanceolate point with straight sides and a deep concave base that is steeply beveled. On some examples, the ears point inward toward the base. This is a rare form and few examples exist. **I.D. KEY:** Beveled base and Paleo flaking.

611

WHITE SPRINGS - Early to Middle Archaic, 8000 - 6000 B. P.

(Also see Benton)

G7, $12-$20
Florence, AL

G8, $15-$30
Limestone Co., AL

G7, $35-$65
KY

Early parallel flaking

G10, $50-$90
Colbert Co., AL

G5, $2-$5
Limestone Co., AL

LOCATION: Southeastern states. **DESCRIPTION:** A medium size, broad, triangular point with a medium to wide very short straight stem. Shoulders are usually square and the base is straight, slightly convex or concave. **I.D. KEY:** Short base and early flaking.

YADKIN - Woodland to Mississippian, 2500 - 500 B. P.

(Also see Camp Creek, Hamilton, Levanna and Nolichucky)

Black flint

G6, $5-$10
Bristol, TN

G6, $5-$10
Bristol, TN

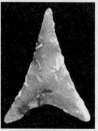

G7, $8-$15
Bristol, TN

LOCATION: Southeastern and Eastern states. **DESCRIPTION:** A small to medium size, broad based, fairly thick, triangular point with a broad, concave base and straight to convex to recurved side edges.

612

SOUTHERN CENTRAL SECTION:

This section includes point types from the following states:
Arkansas, Louisiana, Oklahoma, Texas

The points in this section are arranged in alphabetical order and are shown **actual size**. All types are listed that were available for photographing. Any missing types will be added to future editions as photographs become available. We are always interested in receiving sharp, black and white or color glossy photos or color slides of your collection. Be sure and include a ruler in the photograph so that proper scale can be determined.

Lithics: Materials employed in the manufacture of projectile points from this region are: basalt, chalcedony, chert, conglomerate, crystal, flint, novaculite, obsidian, quartz, quartzite with lesser amounts of agate, jasper, and petrified wood.

Regional Consultant:
Dwain Rogers

Special Advisors:
Nick Cavallini, Tom Davis, Glen Kizzia, Bob McWilliams, Donald Meador,
Bob Miller, Jack Myers, Lyle Nickel, Michael Redwine,
Michael Speer, Art Tatum, Sam Williams

SC

613

SOUTHERN CENTRAL
(Archaeological Periods)

PALEO (14,000 B.P. - 11,000 B.P.)

Chopper	Clovis	Graver	Scraper

LATE PALEO (12,000 B.P. - 10,000 B.P.)

Agate Basin	Folsom	Goshen

TRANSITIONAL PALEO (11,000 B.P. - 9,000 B.P.)

Agate Basin	Barber	Golondrina	Milnesand	Victoria
Allen	Browns Valley	Hell Gap	Paleo Knife	
Archaic Knife	Coldwater	Mahaffey	Pelican	
Arkabutla	Crescent Knife	Midland	Plainview	

EARLY ARCHAIC (10,000 B.P. - 7,000 B.P.)

Albany Knife	Dalton Classic	Firstview	Lerma Pointed	San Patrice-Hope Var.
Alberta	Dalton Colbert	Frederick	Lerma Rounded	San Patrice-Keithville Var.
Andice	Dalton Greenbrier	Gower	Martindale	
Angostura	Dalton Hemphill	Graham Cave	Meserve	San Patrice-St. Johns Var.
Baker	Dalton Hempstead	Hardin	Perforator	
Bandy	Darl Stemmed	Hidden Valley	Pike County	Scottsbluff I & II
Big Sandy	Dovetail	Holland	Red River Knife	Wells
Cache River	Early Stemmed	Hoxie	Rice Lobbed	Zella
Calf Creek	Early Stemmed	Jakie Stemmed	Rio Grande	Zephyr
Cosotat River	Lanceolate	Jetta	Rodgers Side Hollowed	
Dalton Breckenridge	Early Triangular	Johnson	San Patrice-Geneill	

MIDDLE ARCHAIC (7,000 B.P. - 4,000 B.P.)

Abasolo	Coryell	Lange	Nolan	Travis
Afton	Dawson	Langtry	Paisano	Uvalde
Almagre	Exotic	Langtry-Arenosa	Palmillas	Val Verde
Axtel	Frio	Little River	Pandale	White River
Bell	Hemphill	Marshall	Pedernales	Williams
Brewerton Eared	Hickory Ridge	Matanzas	San Jacinto	Zorra
Brewerton Side Notched	Kerrville Knife	McKean	Savage Cave	
Bulverde	Kings	Merkle	Savannah River	
Carrizo	Kinney	Montell	Searcy	
Carrolton	La Jita	Motley	Tortugas	

LATE ARCHAIC (4,000 B.P. - 3,000 B.P.)

Base Tang Knife	Delhi	Gahagan	Refugio
Big Creek	Desmuke	Gary	Sabine
Castroville	Elam	Hale	Smith
Catan	Ellis	Marshall	Table Rock
Coahuila	Ensor	Marcos	Trinity
Conejo	Ensor Split-Base	Mid-Back Tang	Turkeytail
Corner Tang Knife	Epps	Morhiss	
Covington	Evans	Pandora	
Dallas	Friday	Pontchartrain I, II	

WOODLAND (3,000 B.P. - 1,300 B.P.)

Adena Blade	Dickson	Gibson	Peisker Diamond	Shumla
Adena-Robbins	Duran	Godley	Pogo	Sinner
Burkett	Edgewood	Grand	Reed	Spokeshave
Charcos	Edwards	Hare Biface	Rice Shallow Side	Steuben
Cupp	Fairland	Knight Island	Notched	Yarbrough
Darl	Figueroa	Matamoros	Rockwall	
Darl Blade	Friley	Morill	San Gabriel	
Deadman's	Gar Scale	Oauchita	San Saba	

MISSISSIPPIAN (1300 B.P. - 400 B.P.)

Agee	Catahoula	Haskell	LeFlore Blade	Perdiz	Steiner
Alba	Cliffton	Hayes	Livermore	Round-End Knife	Talco
Antler	Colbert	Homan	Lott	Sabinal	Toyah
Bassett	Dardanelle	Howard	Maud	Sallisaw	Turner
Blevins	Fresno	Huffaker	Mineral Springs	Scallorn	Washita
Bonham	Garza	Hughes	Moran	Schustorm	Washita-Peno
Caddoan Blade	Harahey	Kay Blade	Morris	Sequoyah	Young
Caracara	Harrell	Keota	Nodena	Starr	

HISTORIC (450 B.P. - 170 B.P.)

Cuney	Guerrero	Trade Points

SOUTHERN CENTRAL
THUMBNAIL GUIDE SECTION

The following references are provided to aid the collector in easier and quicker identification of point types. All photos are exactly 30% of actual size and are proportional to each other. Each point pictured in this section represents a classic form for the type. When a match is found, go to the alphabetical location of that type for more examples in true actual size.

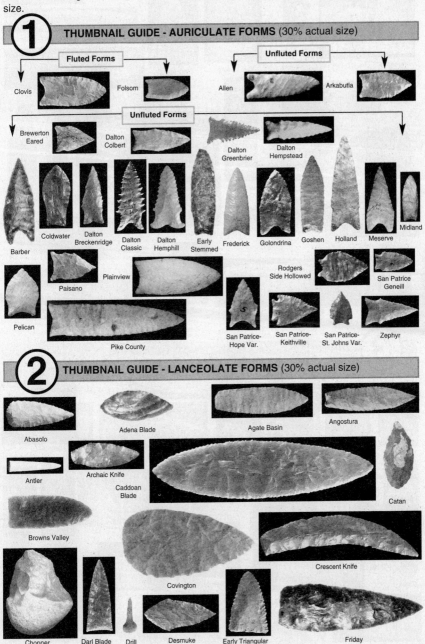

1 THUMBNAIL GUIDE - AURICULATE FORMS (30% actual size)

Fluted Forms

Clovis

Folsom

Unfluted Forms

Allen

Arkabutla

Unfluted Forms

Brewerton Eared

Dalton Colbert

Dalton Greenbrier

Dalton Hempstead

Barber

Coldwater

Dalton Breckenridge

Dalton Classic

Dalton Hemphill

Early Stemmed

Frederick

Golondrina

Goshen

Holland

Meserve

Midland

Paisano

Plainview

Rodgers Side Hollowed

San Patrice Geneill

Pelican

San Patrice- Hope Var.

San Patrice- Keithville

San Patrice- St. Johns Var.

Zephyr

Pike County

SC

2 THUMBNAIL GUIDE - LANCEOLATE FORMS (30% actual size)

Abasolo

Adena Blade

Agate Basin

Angostura

Antler

Archaic Knife

Caddoan Blade

Catan

Browns Valley

Covington

Crescent Knife

Chopper

Darl Blade

Drill

Desmuke

Early Triangular

Friday

615

THUMBNAIL GUIDE - Lanceolate Forms (continued)

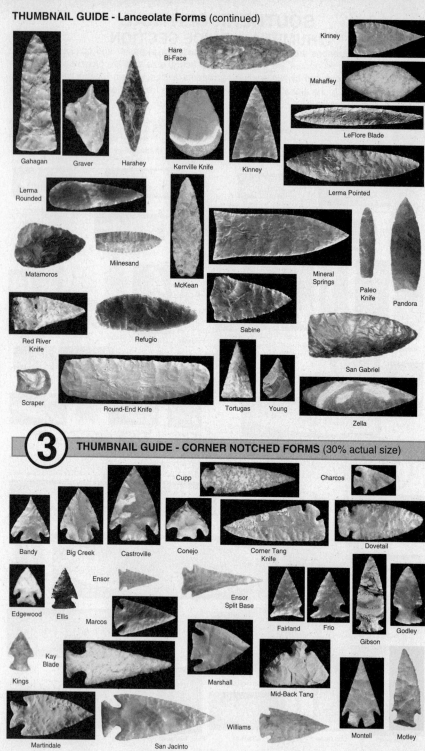

Kinney

Hare Bi-Face

Mahaffey

LeFlore Blade

Gahagan   Graver   Harahey

Kerrville Knife   Kinney

Lerma Pointed

Lerma Rounded

Milnesand

Matamoros

McKean

Mineral Springs

Paleo Knife   Pandora

Red River Knife

Refugio

Sabine

San Gabriel

Scraper

Round-End Knife

Tortugas   Young

Zella

③ THUMBNAIL GUIDE - CORNER NOTCHED FORMS (30% actual size)

Cupp

Charcos

Bandy   Big Creek   Castroville   Conejo

Corner Tang Knife

Dovetail

Edgewood   Ellis

Ensor

Marcos

Ensor Split Base

Fairland   Frio

Gibson

Godley

Kings

Kay Blade

Marshall

Mid-Back Tang

Montell   Motley

Martindale

San Jacinto

Williams

616

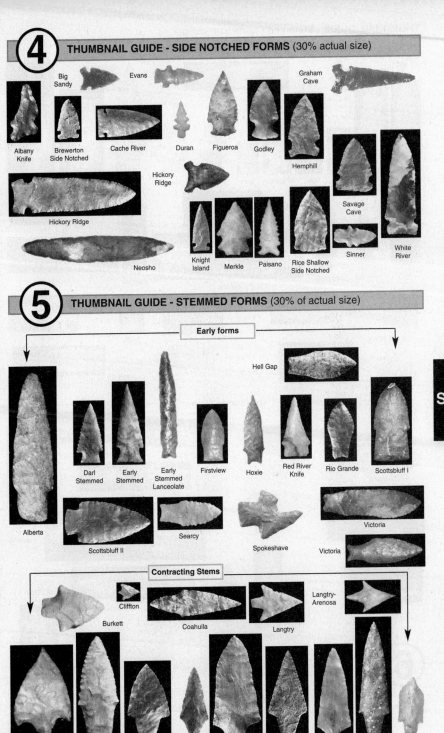

Big Sandy

Evans

Graham Cave

Albany Knife

Brewerton Side Notched

Cache River

Duran

Figueroa

Godley

Hemphill

Hickory Ridge

Hickory Ridge

Savage Cave

Knight Island

Merkle

Paisano

Rice Shallow Side Notched

Sinner

White River

Neosho

⑤ THUMBNAIL GUIDE - STEMMED FORMS (30% of actual size)

Early forms

Hell Gap

SC.

Alberta

Darl Stemmed

Early Stemmed

Early Stemmed Lanceolate

Firstview

Hoxie

Red River Knife

Rio Grande

Scottsbluff I

Scottsbluff II

Searcy

Spokeshave

Victoria

Victoria

Contracting Stems

Cliffton

Burkett

Coahuila

Langtry

Langtry-Arenosa

Almagre

Coryell

Dickson

Gary

Hale

Hidden Valley

Peisker Diamond

Pogo

Pontchartrain II

617

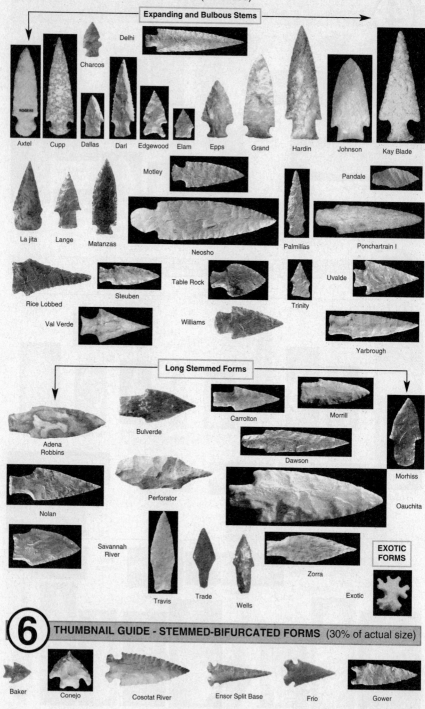

Expanding and Bulbous Stems

Axtel | Cupp | Charcos | Dallas | Darl | Delhi | Edgewood | Elam | Epps | Grand | Hardin | Johnson | Kay Blade

La jita | Lange | Matanzas | Motley | Neosho | Palmillas | Pandale | Ponchartrain I

Rice Lobbed | Steuben | Table Rock | Trinity | Uvalde | Val Verde | Williams | Yarbrough

Long Stemmed Forms

Adena Robbins | Bulverde | Carrolton | Morrill | Dawson | Morhiss

Nolan | Perforator | Oauchita

Savannah River | Travis | Trade | Wells | Zorra | Exotic

EXOTIC FORMS

⑥ THUMBNAIL GUIDE - STEMMED-BIFURCATED FORMS (30% of actual size)

Baker | Conejo | Cosotat River | Ensor Split Base | Frio | Gower

THUMBNAIL GUIDE - Stemmed-Bifurcated Forms (continued)

Jakie Stemmed

Jetta

Montell

Pedernales

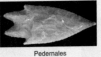

Uvalde

⑦ THUMBNAIL GUIDE - BASAL NOTCHED FORMS (30% of actual size)

Andice

Base Tang

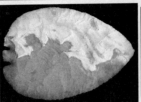
Base Tang

Bell

Calf Creek

Carrizo

Little River

Oauchita

San Saba

Shumla

Smith

Smith

SC

⑧ THUMBNAIL GUIDE - ARROW POINTS (30% of actual size)

Colbert

Deadman's

Agee

Alba

Basset

Blevins

Bonham

Caracara

Catahoula

Cuney

Dardanelle   Edwards

Fresno

Friley

Garza

Guerrero

Harrell

Haskell

Hayes

Homan   Howard

Huffaker

Hughes

Keota

Knight Island

Livermore

Lott

Maud

Moran

Morris

Nodena

Perdiz

Reed

Rockwall

Sabinal

Sallisaw

Scallorn

Schustorm

Sequoyah

Starr

Steiner

Talco

Toyah

Turner

Washita

Washita-Peno

ABASOLO - Early to Middle Archaic, 7000 - 5000 B. P.

(Also see Catan and Matamoros)

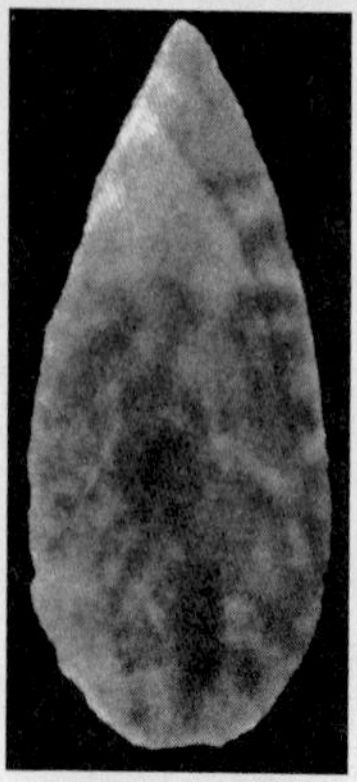

G7, $12-$20
TX

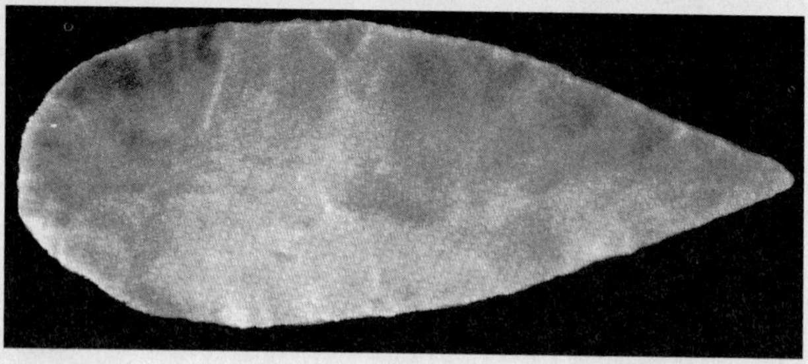

G10, $45-$80
TX

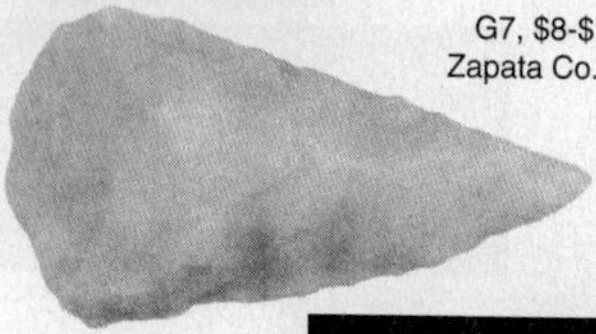

G7, $8-$15
Zapata Co., TX

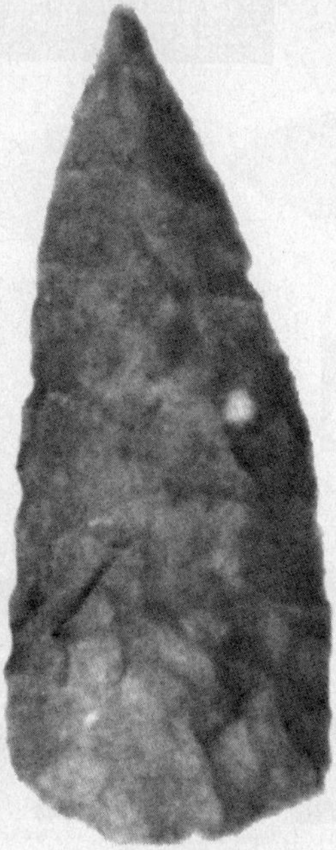

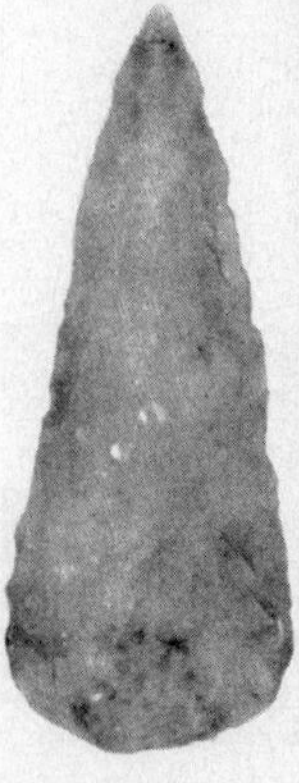

G7, $12-$20
Zapata Co., TX

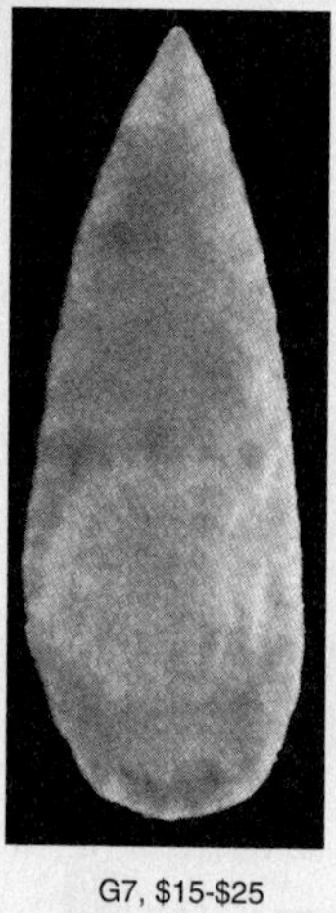

G7, $15-$25
TX

G5, $15-$25
TX

G7, $30-$50
TX

LOCATION: Southern Midwestern states and Mexico. **DESCRIPTION:** A medium to large size, broad, lanceolate point with a rounded base. The blade can be beveled on one side of each face and the base can be thinned. **I.D. KEY:** Early form of flaking on blade with good secondary edgework and rounded base.

ADENA BLADE - Late Archaic to Late Woodland, 3000 - 1200 B. P.

(Also see Harahey, Lerma, Pandora)

LOCATION: Arkansas eastward. **DESCRIPTION:** A large size, thin, broad, ovate blade with a rounded to pointed base and is usually found in caches. **I.D. KEY:** Woodland flaking, large direct strikes.

ADENA BLADE (continued)

G7, $20-$35
AR

ADENA-DICKSON (See Dickson)

ADENA-ROBBINS - Late Archaic to Woodland, 3000 - 1800 B. P.
(Also see Bulverde, Carrolton and Wells)

G4, $8-$15
AR

G3, $5-$10
AR

LOCATION: Arkansas eastward. **DESCRIPTION:** A large, broad, triangular point that is thin and well made with a long, wide, rounded stem that is parallel sided. The blade has convex sides and square shoulders. Many examples show excellent secondary flaking on blade edges. **I.D. KEY:** Squared base, heavy secondary flaking.

SC

G5, $25-$45
AR

AFTON - Middle Archaic to early Woodland, 5000 - 2000 B. P.
(Also see Apple Creek, Ferry and Helton)

LOCATION: Midwestern states and is rarely found in some Eastern and Southeastern states. **DESCRIPTION:** A medium to large size pentagonal shaped point with a flaring or corner notched stem. Some examples are base notched and some are stemmed. **I.D. KEY:** Blade form.

G4, $15-$25
N.E. OK

AFTON (continued)

Kay County chert

G9, $275-$500
N.E. OK

AGATE BASIN - Transitional Paleo to Early Archaic, 10,500 - 8000 B. P.

(Also see Allen, Angostura, Hell Gap, Lerma, Mahaffey and Sedalia)

Basal area is ground

G4, $125-$225
Tulsa Co., OK

G4, $125-$225
Tulsa Co., OK

G6, $125-$225
Osage Co., OK

G5, $130-$250
Tulsa Co., OK

G8, $165-$300
TX

LOCATION: New Mexico to Montana eastward to Pennsylvania. **DESCRIPTION:** A medium to large size lanceolate blade of usually high quality. Bases are either convex, concave or straight, and are normally ground. Some examples are median ridged and have random to parallel flaking. **I.D. KEY:** Basal form and flaking style.

AGATE BASIN (continued)

G4, $35-$65
N.E. OK

The Wagoner Co. Agate Basin laying *in situ* (as found).

G8, $200-$350
Wagoner Co., OK

SC

Collateral flaking

Collateral flaking

G5, $80-$150
Williamson Co., TX

G7, $200-$350
Union Parrish, LA

G6, $125-$200
Burnet Co., TX

G8, $250-$400
N. OK

623

AGEE - Mississippian, 1200 - 700 B. P.

(Also see Alba, Dardanelle, Hayes, Homan and Keota)

G5, $25-$40
AR

Tip
nick

Drooping
tangs

G2, $30-$50
AR

G8, $80-$150
AR

G6, $90-$175
AR

G8, $150-$275
AR

G9, $200-$380
AR

G7, $100-$180
AR. Novaculite

G7, $80-$140
AR. Black flint.

$30-$50, AR. glued.

G7, $80-$150
AR

G8, $150-$250
Pike Co., AR

Black
flint

Tang
nick

G9, $175-$325
AR

G9, $80-$150
AR. Gray chert.

G7, $45-$85
AR

G8, $125-$225
AR. Grey chert.

G10, $275-$500
Pike Co., AR

G5, $50-$90
AR. Brown flint.

G6, $90-$175
Pike Co., AR.
Brown chert.

G8, $165-$300
Little Riv. Co., AR

Glued

Novaculite

Glued

Glued

Novaculite

G7, $225-$400
AR

G10, $450-$850
AR. Crenshaw Site.

G10, $600-$1000
AR. Kid Site.

G7, $500-$900
Pike Co., AR

G9, $600-$1000
Pike Co., AR

LOCATION: Arkansas Caddo sites. **DESCRIPTION:** The finest, most exquisite arrow point made in the United States. A small to medium size, narrow, very thin, expanded barbed, corner notched point. Tips are needle sharp. Some examples are double notched at the base. A rare type that has only been found on a few sites. Total estimated known examples are 1100 to 1200. **I.D. KEY:** Basal form and barb expansion.

ALBA - Woodland to Mississippian, 1100 - 800 B. P.

(Also see Agee, Bonham, Colbert, Cuney, Hayes, Homan, Keota, Perdiz, Scallorn and Sequoyah)

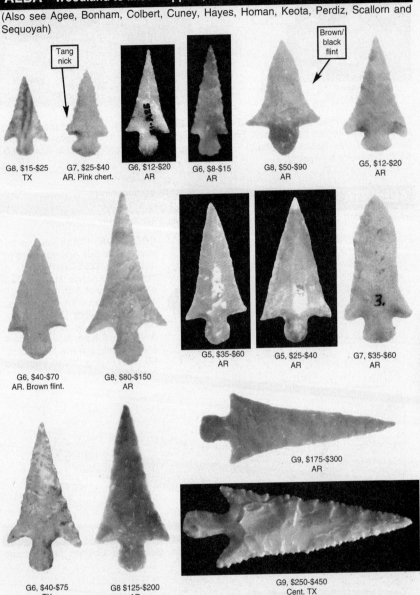

Tang nick

Brown/black flint

G8, $15-$25
TX

G7, $25-$40
AR. Pink chert.

G6, $12-$20
AR

G6, $8-$15
AR

G8, $50-$90
AR

G5, $12-$20
AR

G6, $40-$70
AR. Brown flint.

G8, $80-$150
AR

G5, $35-$60
AR

G5, $25-$40
AR

G7, $35-$60
AR

SC

G9, $175-$300
AR

G6, $40-$75
TX

G8 $125-$200
AR

G9, $250-$450
Cent. TX

LOCATION: Eastern Texas, Arkansas and Louisiana. **DESCRIPTION:** A small to medium size, narrow, well made point with prominent tangs, a recurved blade and a bulbous stem. Some examples are serrated. **I.D. KEY:** Rounded base and expanded barbs.

ALBANY KNIFE - Early Archaic 10,000 - 8000 B. P.

(Also see Red River Knife and San Patrice)

ALBANY KNIFE (continued)

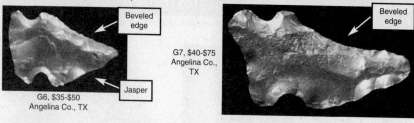

Beveled edge

Jasper

G6, $35-$50
Angelina Co., TX

G7, $40-$75
Angelina Co.,
TX

Beveled edge

LOCATION: Louisiana, E. Texas and Arkansas. **DESCRIPTION:** A small to medium size knife form of the *San Patrice* point. Form is asymmetrical with a steeply beveled edge on the diagonal side. Bases are ground. Similar to the <u>Edgefield</u> <u>Scraper</u> found in Florida. **I.D. KEY:** Symmetry & beveling.

ALBERTA - Early Archaic, 9500 - 7500 B. P.

(Also see Angostura, Brown's Valley, Clovis, Plainview and Scottsbluff)

G7, $200-$350
N. OK

LOCATION: Oklahoma northward to Canada and eastward to Michigan. **DESCRIPTION:** A medium to large size, broad stemmed point with weak, horizontal to tapered shoulders. Made by the Cody Complex people who made *Scottsbluff* points. A very rare type. Basal corners are rounded and the tip is blunt. **I.D. KEY:** Long, broad stem and blunted tip.

G7, $200-$350
N.E. OK

ALLEN - Transitional Paleo to Early Archaic, 10,000 - 7500 B. P.

(Also see Angostura, Barber, Brown's Valley, Clovis, Golondrina, Goshen, McKean and Plainview)

G9, $700-$1250
N.E. OK

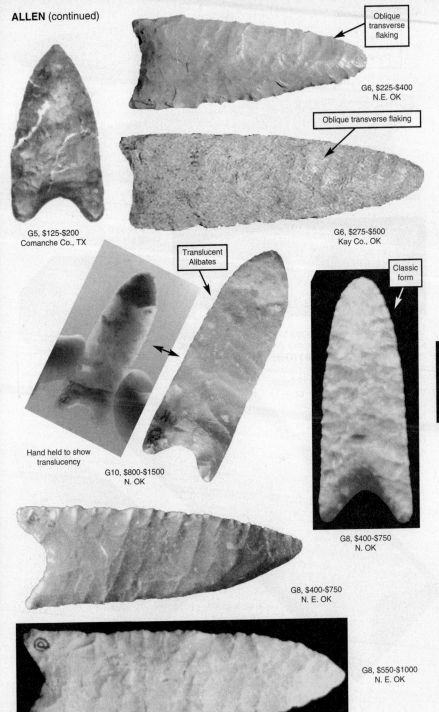

ALLEN (continued)

Oblique transverse flaking

G6, $225-$400
N.E. OK

Oblique transverse flaking

G6, $275-$500
Kay Co., OK

G5, $125-$200
Comanche Co., TX

Translucent
Alibates

Classic
form

SC

Hand held to show
translucency

G10, $800-$1500
N. OK

G8, $400-$750
N. OK

G8, $400-$750
N. E. OK

G8, $550-$1000
N. E. OK

627

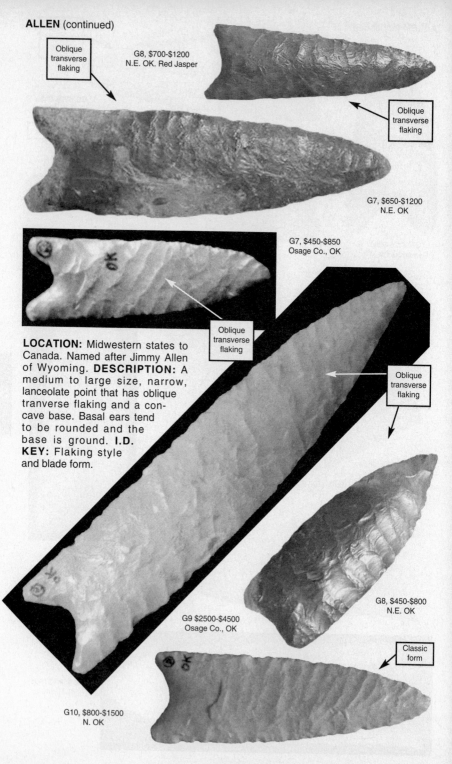

ALLEN (continued)

Oblique transverse flaking

G8, $700-$1200
N.E. OK. Red Jasper

Oblique transverse flaking

G7, $650-$1200
N.E. OK

G7, $450-$850
Osage Co., OK

Oblique transverse flaking

Oblique transverse flaking

LOCATION: Midwestern states to Canada. Named after Jimmy Allen of Wyoming. **DESCRIPTION:** A medium to large size, narrow, lanceolate point that has oblique tranverse flaking and a concave base. Basal ears tend to be rounded and the base is ground. **I.D. KEY:** Flaking style and blade form.

G8, $450-$800
N.E. OK

Classic form

G9 $2500-$4500
Osage Co., OK

G10, $800-$1500
N. OK

628

ALMAGRE - Early Archaic, 6000 - 4500 B. P.

(Also see Gary, Hidden Valley, Langtry-Arenosa and Morrow Mountain)

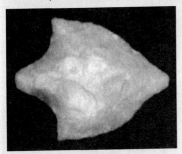

G4, $8-$15
S.W. TX

G4, $8-$15
Val Verde Co., TX

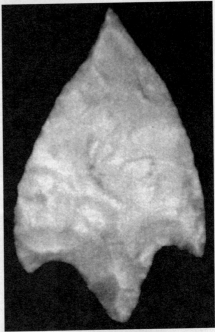

G8, $40-$70
Uvalde Co., TX

SC

LOCATION: Midwestern states. **DESCRIPTION:** A broad, triangular point with pointed barbs and a long contracted pointed to rounded base. This point could be a preform for the *Langtry-Arenosa* type.

ANDICE - Early Archaic, 8000 - 5000 B. P.

(Also see Bell, Calf Creek and Little River)

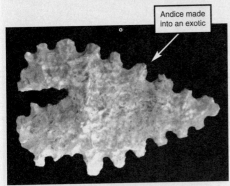

Andice made into an exotic

G7, $175-$300
Bandera Co., TX

LOCATION: Southern to Central Texas, Oklahoma and Kansas. **DESCRIPTION:** A broad, thin, large, triangular point with very deep, parallel basal notches. Larger than *Bell* or *Calf Creek* Points. Tangs reach the base. Because of the deep notches, tangs were easily broken off making complete, unbroken specimens rare. Found in a cave hafted to a wooden handle with pitch adhesive; used as a knife. **I.D. KEY:** Location and deep parallel basal notches.

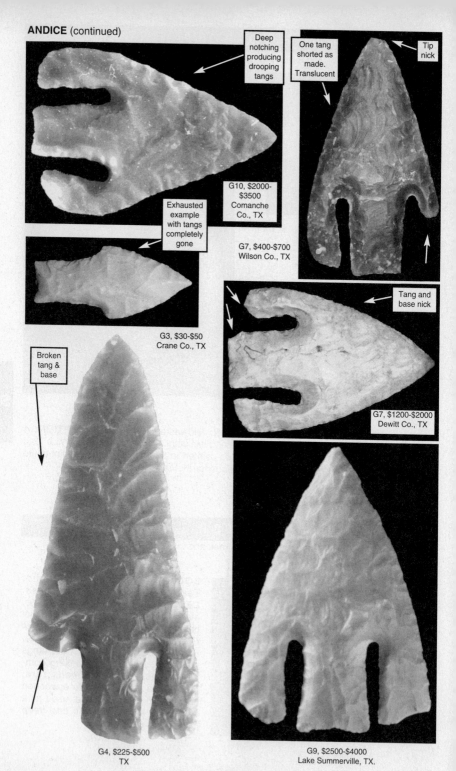

Deep notching producing drooping tangs

One tang shorted as made. Translucent

Tip nick

G10, $2000-$3500 Comanche Co., TX

Exhausted example with tangs completely gone

G7, $400-$700 Wilson Co., TX

G3, $30-$50 Crane Co., TX

Tang and base nick

G7, $1200-$2000 Dewitt Co., TX

Broken tang & base

G4, $225-$500 TX

G9, $2500-$4000 Lake Summerville, TX.

ANGOSTURA - Early Archaic, 10,000 - 8000 B. P.

(Also see Agate Basin, Allen, Archaic Knife, Hell Gap, Lerma, Midland, Milnesand, Plainview, Victoria & Zella)

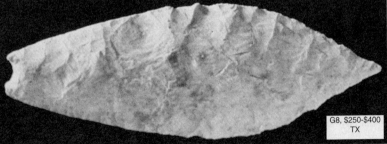

G8, $165-$300
N. OK

G5, $65-$125
Crane Co., TX

Resharpened many times

Made into a drill

G6, $55-$100
Crane Co., TX

Beveled edge

G6, $80-$150
Crane Co., TX

G9, $250-$400
Bell Co., TX

SC

G8, $250-$400
Bell Co., TX

G8, $250-$400
TX

LOCATION: Midwest to Western states. **DESCRIPTION:** A medium to large size, lanceolate blade with a contracting, concave, straight or convex base. Both broad and narrow forms occur. Flaking can be parallel oblique to random. Blades are commonly steeply beveled on one side of each face; some are serrated and most have basal grinding. Formerly called Long points. **I.D. KEY:** Basal form, flaking on blade which can be beveled.

ANTLER - Mississippian, 1300 - 400 B. P.

(Also see Angostura, Golondrina, Midland, Pelican and Plainview)

G4, $5-$10
Saline Co., AR

View from the base

G7, $12-$20
Saline Co., AR

LOCATION: Most of United States. **DESCRIPTION:** A medium size, conical shaped point made from deer antler.

ARCHAIC KNIFE - Transitional Paleo, 10,000 - 5000 B. P.

(Also see Angostura, Darl Stemmed, Early Stemmed and Victoria)

LOCATION: Texas, Oklahoma and Arkansas. **DESCRIPTION:** A medium to large size, lanceolate point with a contracting basal area. Shoulders are weakly tapered to non-existant.

G6, $15-$25
Comal Co., TX

G6, $15-$30
Comal Co., TX

ARENOSA (See Langtry-Arenosa)

ARKABUTLA - Transitional Paleo, 10,000 - 8000 B. P.

(Also see Angostura, Coldwater, Golondrina, Midland, Pelican, Plainview, Rodgers Dide Hollowed and San Patrice)

G7, $125-$225
Mineola, TX

G8, $150-$275
Cent. TX

LOCATION: Texas and New Mexico. **DESCRIPTION:** A small to medium size, broad, thin, lanceolate point with expanded auricles. Blade edges recurve into the base which is concave. **I.D. KEY:** Eared basal form.

AXTEL - Early-mid Archaic 7,000 - 3500 B. P.

(Also see Godley, Lajita, Palmillas and Williams)

AXTEL (continued)

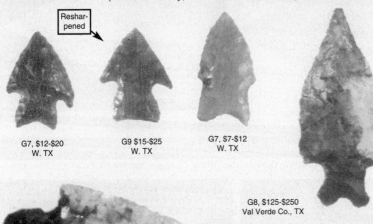

G2, $3-$5
Bell Co., TX

Edge damage

Ground stems

ROGERS

LOCATION: Central Texas. **DESCRIPTION:** A medium size, narrow point with barbed shoulders and a bulbous stem. Called "Penny Points" by local collectors. Stem edges are usually ground. **I.D. KEY:** Bulbous stem that is ground. See Prewitt, p.90, Tex. Arc. Society 66, 1995 and *Field Guide to Stone Artifacts of Texas*, Turner & Hester, p.75, 1993

G8, $35-$50
Coryell Co., TX

BAKER - Early Archaic, 7500 - 6000 B. P.

(Also see Bandy, Pedernales and Uvalde)

Resharpened

G7, $12-$20
W. TX

G9 $15-$25
W. TX

G7, $7-$12
W. TX

G8, $125-$250
Val Verde Co., TX

SC

G9, $200-$375
Val Verde Co., TX

LOCATION: W. Texas into New Mexico. **DESCRIPTION:** A small size, thin dart point with a short to long expanding stem that is bifurcated to concave. Tips are sharp and shoulders are barbed. Some basal areas can be ground. **I.D. KEY:** Base extended and bifurcated, early flaking.

BANDY - Early Archaic, 7500 - 5000 B. P.

(Also see Baker, Marcos, Marshall and Martindale)

LOCATION: Southern Texas. **DESCRIPTION:** A small sized *Martindale* more commonly found in southern Texas. A corner notched to expanded stemmed point. The base is usually ormed by two curves meeting at the center but can be straight to concave. **I.D. KEY:** Basal form, early flaking.

633

BANDY (continued)

G8, $60-$100
Comanche Co., TX

G8, $60-$100
Comanche Co., TX

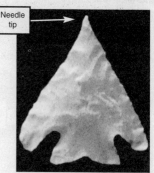

Needle tip

G9, $80-$150
Austin, TX

G10, $150-$250
TX

G7, $150-$275
Val Verde Co., TX

BARBER - Transitional Paleo, 10,000 - 7000 B. P.

(Also see Allen, Angostura, Clovis, Golondrina, Goshen, Kinney, McKean and Plainview)

G5, $150-$250
Llano Co., TX

G7, $200-$350
Llano Co., TX

G8, $450-$800
Williamson Co., TX

634

BARBER (continued)

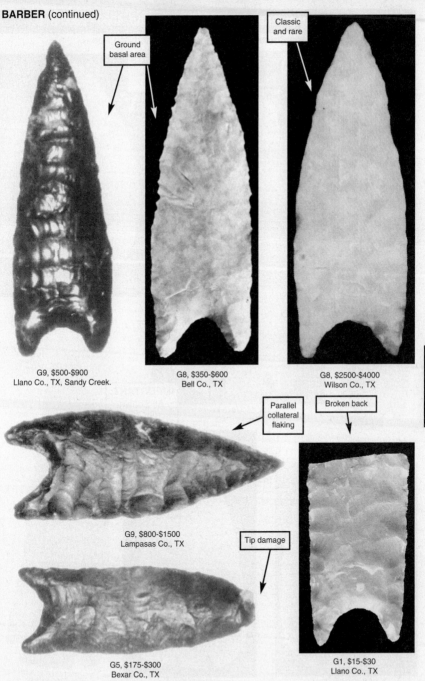

Ground basal area

Classic and rare

G9, $500-$900
Llano Co., TX, Sandy Creek.

G8, $350-$600
Bell Co., TX

G8, $2500-$4000
Wilson Co., TX

Parallel collateral flaking

Broken back

G9, $800-$1500
Lampasas Co., TX

Tip damage

G5, $175-$300
Bexar Co., TX

G1, $15-$30
Llano Co., TX

LOCATION: Central Texas. **DESCRIPTION:** A small to medium size, lanceolate point with a deeply concave base and pointed ears that tend to turn inward. Similar to *Wheeler* points found in the Southeast. Basal area is usually ground. Flaking is early parallel. **I.D. KEY:** Deep basal concavity, parallel flaking. **NOTE:** A rare type.

BASE TANG KNIFE - Late Archaic to Woodland, 4000 - 2000 B. P.

(Also see Corner Tang, Mid-Back Tang and San Saba)

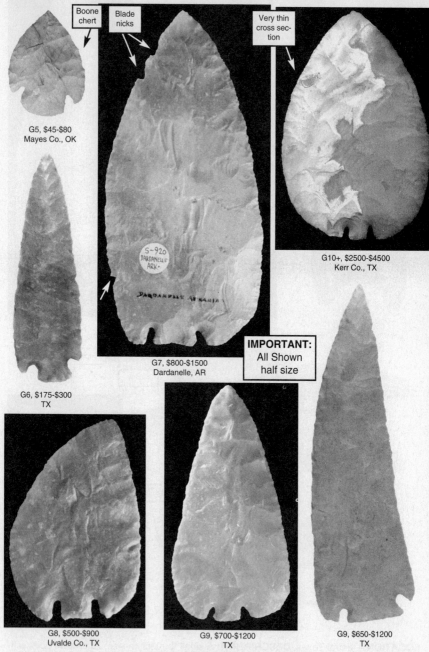

Boone chert

Blade nicks

Very thin cross section

G5, $45-$80
Mayes Co., OK

G10+, $2500-$4500
Kerr Co., TX

S-920
DARDANELLE
ARK·

DARDANELLE ARKANSA

G7, $800-$1500
Dardanelle, AR

IMPORTANT:
All Shown
half size

G6, $175-$300
TX

G8, $500-$900
Uvalde Co., TX

G9, $700-$1200
TX

G9, $650-$1200
TX

LOCATION: Central Texas. **DESCRIPTION:** A large size, broad, blade with small basal notches and a concave base. Most examples curve more on one side and are believed to have been used as knives. **I.D. KEY:** Large size, small basal notches.

636

BASSETT - Mississippian, 800 - 400 B. P.

(Also see Cliffton, Perdiz, Rockwall and Steiner)

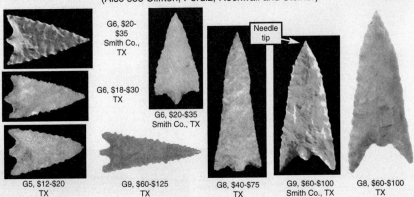

G6, $20-$35 Smith Co., TX

G6, $18-$30 TX

G6, $20-$35 Smith Co., TX

Needle tip

G5, $12-$20 TX

G9, $60-$125 TX

G8, $40-$75 TX

G9, $60-$100 Smith Co., TX

G8, $60-$100 TX

LOCATION: Midwestern states. **DESCRIPTION:** A small size, thin, triangular point with pointed tangs and a small pointed base. High quality flaking is evident on most examples. **I.D. KEY:** Small pointed base.

BAYOGOULA (A Louisian type; see North Central section for example found at Cahokia Mounds).

BELL - Middle Archaic, 7000 - 5000 B. P.

(Also see Andice and Calf Creek).

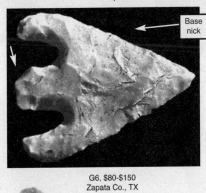

Base nick

G6, $80-$150 Zapata Co., TX

G8, $200-$350 TX

G8, $800-$1500 Val Verde Co., TX

637

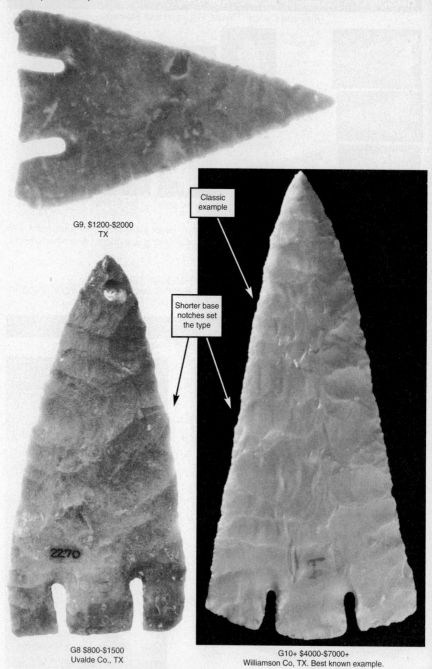

G9, $1200-$2000
TX

Classic
example

Shorter base
notches set
the type

G8 $800-$1500
Uvalde Co., TX

G10+ $4000-$7000+
Williamson Co, TX. Best known example.

LOCATION: Central Texas. **DESCRIPTION:** A small to medium size point with medium-deep parallel basal notches, but not as deep as in *Andice*. Larger examples usually would fall under *Andice*. Found primarily in Texas. Tangs can turn inward at the base. **I.D. KEY:** Shorter tangs and notching.

BIG CREEK - Late Archaic to early Woodland, 3500 - 2500 B. P.
(Also see Ellis, Grand, Kings, Marcos and Williams)

G5, $8-$15
Saline Co., AR

G7, $30-$50
AR

G6, $12-$20
AR

G8, $25-$40
Saline Co., AR

LOCATION: Arkansas and surrounding states. **DESCRIPTION:** A small to medium size, short, broad, corner notched point with a bulbous base. Believed to be related to *Marcos* points. The tips are needle sharp on some examples, similar to *Mud Creek* points from Alabama. Tangs can be weak to very long. Small *Big Sloughs* of the Southeast would be indistinguishable to this type. **I.D. KEY:** Rounded base and barbs drop.

SC

BIG SANDY - Early to Late Archaic, 10,000 - 3000 B. P.
(Also see Cache River, Ensor, Frio, Hickory Ridge and Savage Cave)

G5, $6-$10
Brewster Co., TX

G5, $6-$10
Val Verde Co., TX

G8, $150-$250
Travis Co., TX

G6, $12-$20
Athens, TX

G7, $20-$35
Saline Co., AR

639

BIG SANDY (continued)

LOCATION: Eastern Texas eastward. **DESCRIPTION:** A small to medium size, side notched point with early forms showing basal grinding, serrations and horizontal flaking. Bases are straight to concave. Deeply concave bases form ears. **I.D. KEY:** Basal form.

G7, $55-$100
AR

BLEVINS - Mississippian, 1200 - 600 B. P.

(Also see Hayes, Howard and Sequoyah)

LOCATION: Midwestern states. **DESCRIPTION:** A small size, narrow spike point with two or more notches on each blade side. The base is diamond shaped. A cross between *Hayes* and *Howard*. **I.D. KEY:** Diamond shaped base.

G8, $35-$60
W. AR.

BONHAM - Woodland to Mississippian, 1200 - 600 B. P.

(Also see Alba, Bulbar Stemmed, Cuney, Hayes, Moran, Perdiz, Rockwall & Sabinal)

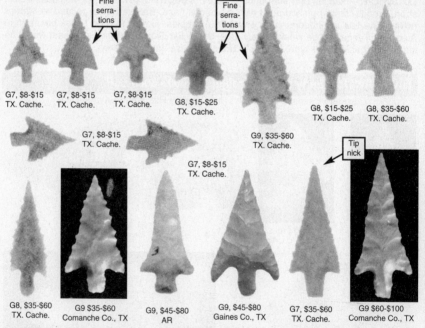

Fine serrations

Fine serrations

Tip nick

G7, $8-$15 TX. Cache.
G7, $8-$15 TX. Cache.
G7, $8-$15 TX. Cache.
G8, $15-$25 TX. Cache.
G8, $15-$25 TX. Cache.
G8, $35-$60 TX. Cache.
G7, $8-$15 TX. Cache.
G9, $35-$60 TX. Cache.
G7, $8-$15 TX. Cache.
G8, $35-$60 TX. Cache.
G9 $35-$60 Comanche Co., TX
G9, $45-$80 AR
G9, $45-$80 Gaines Co., TX
G7, $35-$60 TX. Cache.
G9 $60-$100 Comanche Co., TX

LOCATION: Texas and Oklahoma. **DESCRIPTION:** A small to medium size, thin, well made triangular point with a short to long squared or rounded, narrow stem. Many examples are finely serrated. Blade edges are straight, concave, or convex or recurved. Shoulders are squared to barbed. **I.D. KEY:** Long straight base, expanded barbs.

640

Bonham (continued)

G5, $15-$25
AR

G9, $65-$125
TX

Needle barbs

G9, $90-$175
Cent. TX

G10, $100-$190
TX

Fine serrations

G10, $275-$500
Comanche Co., TX

G10, $150-$250
TX

Blade found with Bonham points.

BRAZOS (See Darl Stemmed)

SC

BREWERTON EARED - Middle to Late Archaic, 6000 - 4000 B. P.

(Also see Rice Shallow Side Notched)

LOCATION: Northeast Texas eastward. **DESCRIPTION:** A small size, triangular point with shallow side notches and a concave base.

G4, $1-$2
Saline Co., AR

G7, $3-$5
AR

BREWERTON SIDE NOTCHED - Middle to Late Archaic, 6000 - 4000 B. P.

(Also see Big Sandy)

G2, $1-$2
Friendship Co., AR

G6, $2-$3
Waco, TX

LOCATION: Northeast Texas eastward. **DESCRIPTION:** A small size, triangular point with shallow side notches and a concave base.

641

BROWNS VALLEY - Transitional Paleo, 10,000 - 8000 B. P.

(Also see Agate Basin, Allen, Angostura, Barber, Clovis, Firstview, Midland and Plainview)

Knife River flint

G9, $1000-$1800
N.E. AR. Translucent pati-
nated Knife River flint.
Classic example.

Note oblique flaking

Orange/red jasper

Note oblique flaking

Ground basal area

G10, $500-$900
Terry Co., TX

Found far from known type area, but a classic example.

LOCATION: A Minnesota type that has been found in Arkansas and W. Texas. **DESCRIPTION:** A medium to large, thin, lanceolate blade with usually oblique to horizontal transverse flaking and a concave to straight base which can be ground. A very rare type. **I.D. KEY:** Paleo transverse flaking.

BULVERDE - Middle Archaic to Woodland, 5000 - 1000 B. P.

(Also see Carrolton, Delhi and Wells)

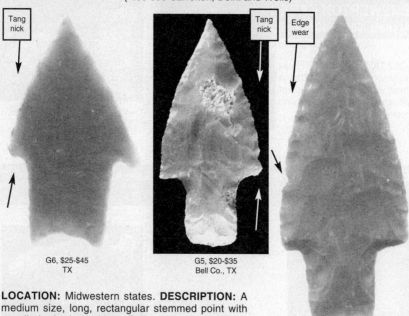

Tang nick

Tang nick

Edge wear

G6, $25-$45
TX

G5, $20-$35
Bell Co., TX

G7, $25-$40
TX

LOCATION: Midwestern states. **DESCRIPTION:** A medium size, long, rectangular stemmed point with usually barbed shoulders. Believed to be related to Carrolton. **I.D. KEY:** Long, squared base and barbed shoulders.

BULVERDE (continued)

G8, $35-$60
TX

Tip nick

G8, $45-$80
Kimble Co., TX

Classic example

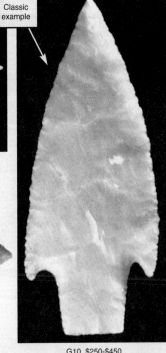

G10, $250-$450
Val Verde Co., TX

SC

G8, $45-$80
TX

BURKETT - Woodland, 2300 - 2000 B. P.

(Also see Dickson and Gary)

LOCATION: Arkansas into Missouri. **DESCRIPTION:** A broad, medium size point with a contracting to parallel sided stem and barbed to horizontal shoulders.

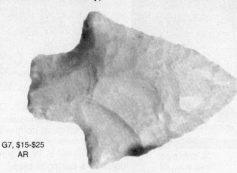

G7, $15-$25
AR

643

BURKETT (continued)

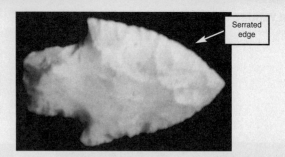

G6, $8-$15
Saline Co., AR

Serrated edge

CACHE RIVER - Early to Late Archaic, 10,000 - 5000 B. P.
(Also see Big Sandy, Hickory Ridge, Knight Island and White River)

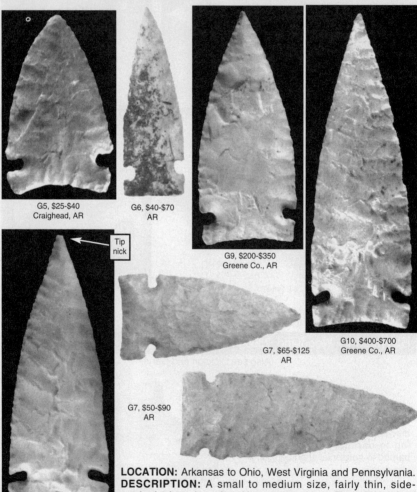

G5, $25-$40
Craighead, AR

G6, $40-$70
AR

Tip nick

G9, $200-$350
Greene Co., AR

G7, $65-$125
AR

G10, $400-$700
Greene Co., AR

G7, $50-$90
AR

G8, $275-$500
Greene Co., AR

LOCATION: Arkansas to Ohio, West Virginia and Pennsylvania. **DESCRIPTION:** A small to medium size, fairly thin, side-notched, triangular point with a concave base. Blade flaking is of the early parallel type. Could be related to *Big Sandy* points. Called *Kessell* in West Virginia. **I.D. KEY:** Base form, narrow notched & flaking of blade.

CADDOAN BLADE - Mississippian, 800 - 600 B. P.

(Also see Adena Blade)

IMPORTANT:
Caddoan Blades
shown 1/2 size

G5, $450-$800
AR

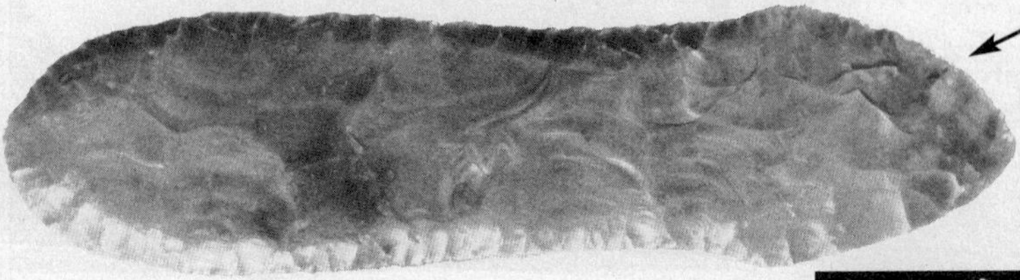
Minor
restoration

G7, $500-$950
TX

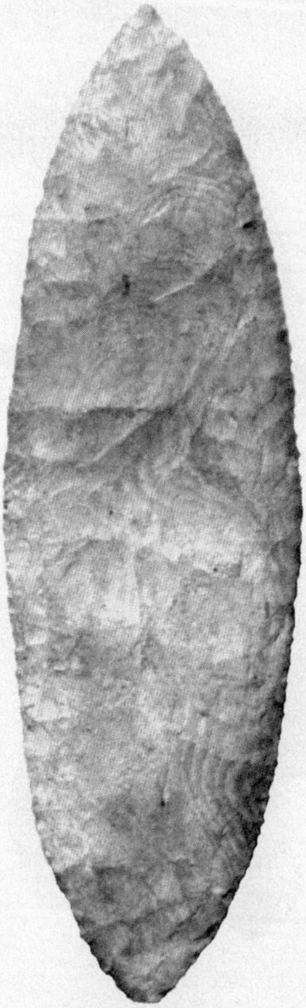

G9, $1000-$1800
AR

Kay
flint

G9, $800-$1500
AR

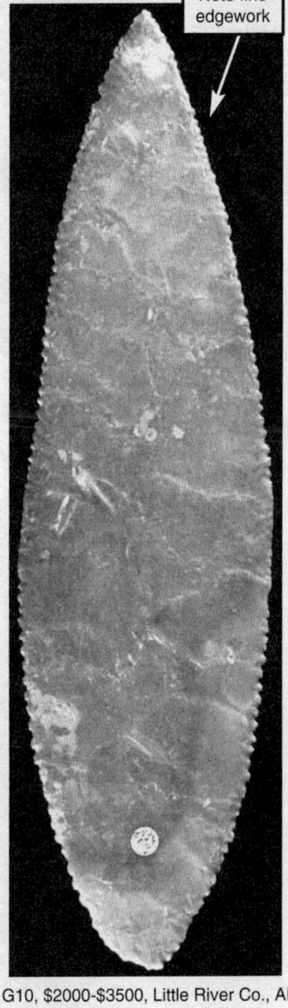
Note fine
edgework

G10, $2000-$3500, Little River Co., AR

LOCATION: Texas and Arkansas on Caddo culture sites. **DESCRIPTION:** A large size, thin, double pointed, elliptical, ceremonial blade with serrated edges. Examples with basal side notches have been found in Texas. Beware of fakes. **I.D. KEY:** Edgework, flaking style on blade.

CALF CREEK - Early to Middle Archaic, 8000 - 5000 B. P.

(Also see Andice and Bell)

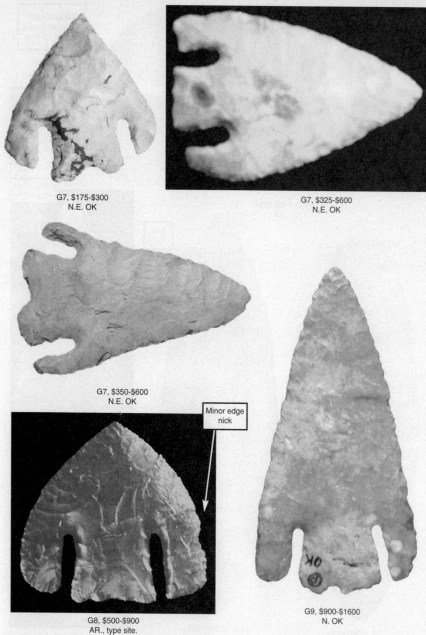

G7, $175-$300
N.E. OK

G7, $325-$600
N.E. OK

G7, $350-$600
N.E. OK

Minor edge
nick

G8, $500-$900
AR., type site.

G9, $900-$1600
N. OK

LOCATION: N.E. Texas, Western Arkansas, Missouri and eastern Oklahoma. **DESCRIPTION:** A medium to large size thin, triangular point with very deep parallel basal notches. *Andice* and *Bell* points, similar in form, are found in N.E. Texas. Very rare in type area. **I.D. KEY:** Notches almost straight up.

CALF CREEK (continued)

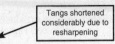

Tangs shortened considerably due to resharpening

G6, $150-$250
N.E. OK

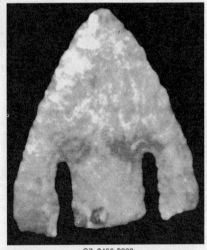

G7, $450-$800
N. OK

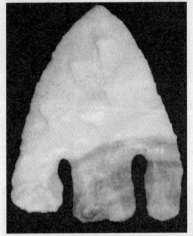

G7, $450-$800
N. E. OK

SC

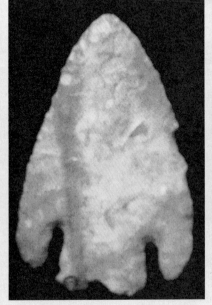

G7, $450-$800
OK

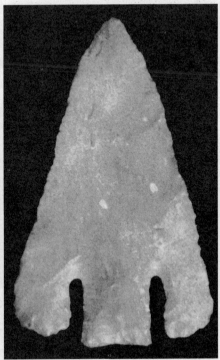

G9, $1700-$3000
N.E. OK

CARACARA - Mississippian to Historic, 600 - 400 B. P.

(Also see Huffaker, Reed and Washita)

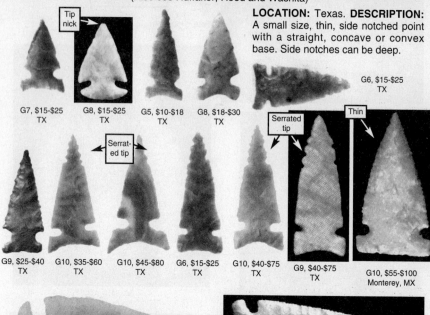

Tip nick

LOCATION: Texas. DESCRIPTION: A small size, thin, side notched point with a straight, concave or convex base. Side notches can be deep.

G6, $15-$25
TX

G7, $15-$25
TX

G8, $15-$25
TX

G5, $10-$18
TX

G8, $18-$30
TX

Serrated tip

Thin

Serrated tip

G9, $25-$40
TX

G10, $35-$60
TX

G10, $45-$80
TX

G6, $15-$25
TX

G10, $40-$75
TX

G9, $40-$75
TX

G10, $55-$100
Monterey, MX

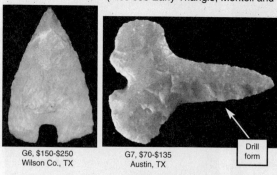

G10, $80-$150
TX

G10, $175-$300
Zapata Co., TX

CARRIZO - Middle Archaic, 7000 - 4000 B. P.

(Also see Early Triangle, Montell and Tortugas)

G6, $150-$250
Wilson Co., TX

G7, $70-$135
Austin, TX

Drill form

LOCATION: Texas to Colorado. DESCRIPTION: A small to medium size, triangular point with a deep single notch or a concave indention in the center of the base. Flaking is parallel to random. Blade edges are rarely serconfused with resharpened *Montells*. I.D. KEY: Basal notch.

G10, $275-$500
Wilson Co., TX

CARRIZO (continued)

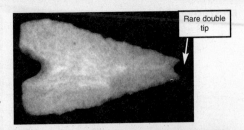

G8, $200-$350
Val Verde Co., TX, Devils River.

Rare double tip

CARROLTON - Middle to Late Archaic, 5000 - 3000 B. P.

(Also see Adena, Bulverde, Dallas, Morrill and Wells)

Tip nick

G2, $1-$2
Cent. TX

SC

G6, $12-$20
Comanche Co., TX

G6, $12-$20
Bell Co., TX

G7, $25-$40
Central TX

LOCATION: North Texas. **DESCRIPTION:** A medium to large size, long parallel stemmed point with a square base. Shoulders are usually tapered. Workmanship is crude to medium grade. Believed to be related to *Bulverde* points.

CASTROVILLE - Late Archaic to Woodland, 4000 - 1500 B. P.

(Also see Lange, Marcos, Marshall and San Jacinto)

G6, $15-$25
TX

G7, $125-$200
TX

CASTROVILLE (continued)

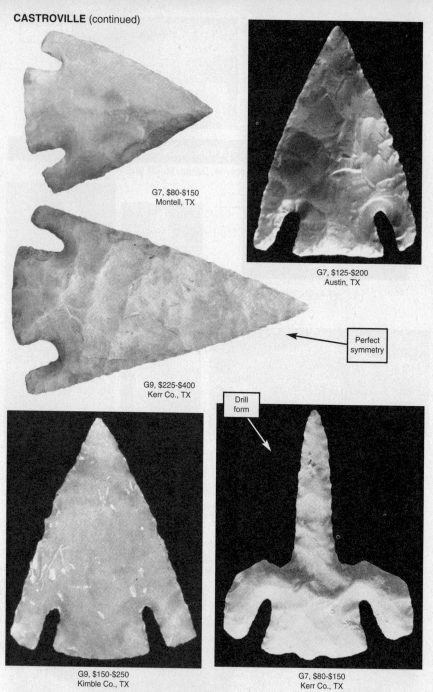

G7, $80-$150
Montell, TX

G7, $125-$200
Austin, TX

Perfect symmetry

G9, $225-$400
Kerr Co., TX

Drill form

G9, $150-$250
Kimble Co., TX

G7, $80-$150
Kerr Co., TX

LOCATION: Texas to Colorado. **DESCRIPTION:** A medium to large size, broad, corner notched point with an expanding base and prominent tangs that can reach the basal edge. The base can be straight to convex and is usually broader than in *Lange* and *Marshall*. **I.D. KEY:** Broad base, corner notches.

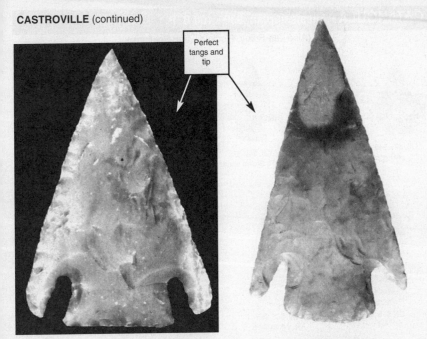

Perfect tangs and tip

G9, $300-$550
Kimble Co., TX

G9 $200-$350
TX

SC

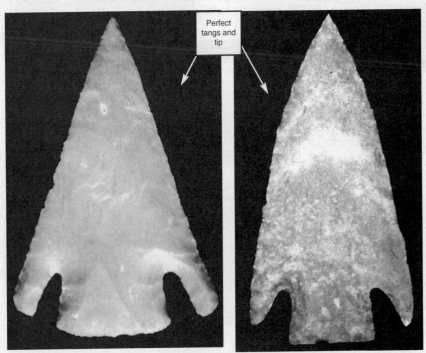

Perfect tangs and tip

G9, $275-$500
Kendall Co., TX

G9, $225-$400
Kimble Co., TX

CATAHOULA - Mississippian, 800 - 400 B. P.

(Also see Friley, Rockwall and Scallorn)

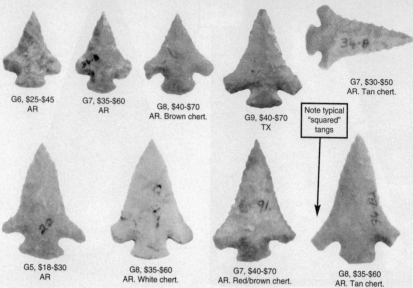

G6, $25-$45
AR

G7, $35-$60
AR

G8, $40-$70
AR. Brown chert.

G9, $40-$70
TX

G7, $30-$50
AR. Tan chert.

Note typical "squared" tangs

G5, $18-$30
AR

G8, $35-$60
AR. White chert.

G7, $40-$70
AR. Red/brown chert.

G8, $35-$60
AR. Tan chert.

LOCATION: East Texas, Louisiana to Arkansas. **DESCRIPTION**: A small size, thin, point with broad, flaring, squared tangs. The stem is parallel sided to expanding. The base is straight to concave. **I.D. KEY:** Expanded barbs.

CATAN - Late Archaic to Mississippian, 4000 - 300 B. P.

(Also see Abasolo, Matamoros and Young)

G6, $3-$7
TX

G5, $2-$5
AR

G5, $3-$7
TX

G5, $2-$5
W. TX

G5, $5-$10
TX

G6, $8-$15
TX

LOCATION: Southern Texas and New Mexico. **DESCRIPTION**: A small, thin, lanceolate point with a rounded base. Large examples would fall under the *Abasolo* type.

CHARCOS - Woodland, 3000 - 2000 B. P.

(Also see Duran, Evans and Sinner)

G5 $15-$20
MX

G8, $65-$125
TX

G9, $80-$150
TX

G8, $40-$75
TX

G7 $15-$25
MX

G10, $150-$250
TX

G80, $45-$80
TX

LOCATION: Northern Mexico into south Texas & Colorado. **DESCRIPTION:** A small size, thin, single barbed point with a notch near the opposite shoulder. Stem is rectangular. **I.D. KEY:** Asymmetrical form. Some are double notched. Beware of resharpened *Shumla* points with notches added in modern times to look like *Charcos*.

CHOPPER - Paleo to Archaic, 14,000 - 6000 B. P.

(Also see Kerrville Knife)

LOCATION: Paleo sites everywhere. **DESCRIPTION:** A medium to large size, thick, ovoid hand axe made from local creek or river stones. Used in the butchering process. Also known as Butted knife.

Chopper shown
half size

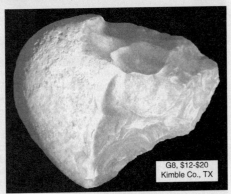

G8, $12-$20
Kimble Co., TX

CLIFFTON - Mississippian, 1200 - 500 B. P.

(Also see Bassett)

653

CLIFFTON (continued)

G9, $5-$10
TX

G6, $1-$2
TX

G1, $.50-$1
Waco, TX

G6, $4-$8
TX

LOCATION: Central Texas. **DESCRIPTION:** A small size, crude point that is usually made from a flake and is uniface. The base is sharply contracting to pointed. Preforms for *Perdiz*?

CLOVIS - Early Paleo, 14,000 - 9000 B. P.

(Also see Allen, Angostura, Barber, Browns Valley, Dalton, Golondrina and Plainview)

G6, $80-$150
AR

G5, $175-$250
LA

G5, $350-$600
Bell/Williamson Co., TX

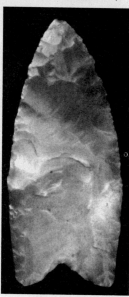

G6, $400-$700
Childress Co., TX

G7, $550-$1000
Wilson Co., TX

LOCATION: All of North America. **DESCRIPTION:** A medium to large size, auriculate, fluted, lanceolate point with convex sides and a concave base that is ground. Most examples are fluted on both sides about 1/3 the way up from the base. The flaking can be random to parallel. *Clovis* is the earliest point type in the hemisphere. It is believed that this form was developed elsewhere and brought here by early man from Siberia or Europe 14,000 years ago, just before the land bridge disappeared due to the melting of the glaciers. There is no pre-*Clovis* evidence here in the U.S. (no crude forms that pre-date *Clovis*). *Clovis*-like fluted points have been reported found in China dating to 11-12,000 B.P. *Clovis* has also been found in Alaska and southern Chile in South America. **I.D. KEY:** Paleo flaking, shoulders, batan fluting instead of indirect style. Basal form and fluting.

654

CLOVIS (continued)

All have ground basal areas

G8, $250-$450
TX

Fluting channel

G7, $400-$700
Comanche Co., TX

Red/yellow jasper

G8, $800-$1500
N.E. OK

SC

Fluting channel

G6, $450-$800
TX

G8, $700-$1200
Dawson, TX

G10, $8000-$15000+
Bexar Co., TX

Fluting channel

G7, $1200-$2000
TX

G7, $265-$500
Comanche Co., TX

Tip nick

Channel flute

Banded chert

G10, $1800-$3500
Bexar Co., TX

G8, $1500-$2400
Bastrop Co., TX

G8, $1800-$3000
TX

COAHUILA - Late Archaic to Woodland, 4000 - 2000 B. P.

(Also see Adena, Gary, Hidden Valley and Langtry)

G5, $12-$20
Comanche Co., TX

G7, $25-$40
Val Verde Co., TX

G9, $35-$60
TX

G8, $40-$75
Comanche Co., TX

LOCATION: Central Texas. **DESCRIPTION:** A medium to large size, narrow point with tapered shoulders and a long, pointed, contracting stem. A scarce type. **I.D. KEY:** Long, pointed stem. Rare type. Also known as *Jora* points.

SC

CODY KNIFE (See Red River Knife)

COLBERT - Mississippian, 1000 - 400 B. P.

(Also see Alba, Homa, Hughes and Keotal)

Serrated edges

G7, $25-$40
TX

G5, $2-$4
Ellis Co., TX

G8, $12-$20
TX

G5, $3-$6
Ellis Co., TX

Green chert

G6, $30-$50
AR

LOCATION: Northeast Texas, AR. & LA. **DESCRIPTION:** A small size, arrow point with barbs and a short, bulbous basal area & a straight base.

COLDWATER - Trans. Paleo, 10,000 - 8000 B. P.

(Also see Arkabutla, Pelican and San Patrice)

LOCATION: East Texas into Arkansas & Louisiana. **DESCRIPTION:** A medium size, Lanceolate point with a longer waist than *Pelican* and a straight to concave base which is ground. The blade expands up from the base.

COLDWATER (continued)

Petrified wood

G10, $200-$350
San Augustine Co., TX

CONEJO - Late Archaic, 4000 - 3000 B. P.

(Also see Bandy, Ellis, Fairland and Marshall)

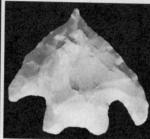

LOCATION: Texas and New Mexico **DESCRIPTION:** A medium size, corner notched point with an expanding, concave base and shoulder tangs that turn towards the base.

G4, $3-$5
Comanche Co., TX

G5, $8-$15
Schleicher Co., TX

CORNER TANG KNIFE - Late Archaic to Woodland, 4000 - 2000 B. P.

(Also see Base Tang, Crescent Knife and Mid-Back Tang Knife)

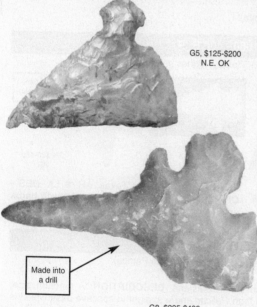

G5, $125-$200
N.E. OK

Made into a drill

G8, $225-$400
Kerr Co., TX

G6, $275-$425
Wilson Co., TX

658

CORNER TANG (continued)

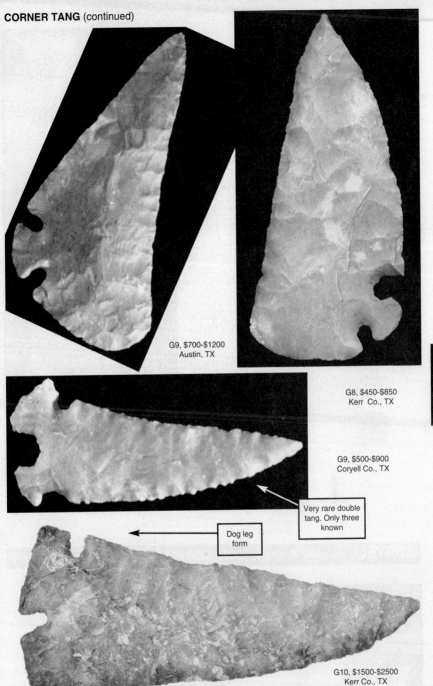

G9, $700-$1200
Austin, TX

G8, $450-$850
Kerr Co., TX

G9, $500-$900
Coryell Co., TX

Very rare double tang. Only three known

Dog leg form

G10, $1500-$2500
Kerr Co., TX

LOCATION: Texas to Oklahoma. **DESCRIPTION:** This knife is notched producing a tang at a corner for hafting to a handle. Tang knives are very rare and have been reproduced in recent years. **I.D. KEY:** Angle of hafting.

659

CORNER TANG (continued)

Dog leg form

G9, $800-$1500
Kerr Co., TX

G9, $1500-$2500
Coryell Co., TX

CORYELL - Middle Archaic, 7000 - 5000 B. P.
(Also see Searcy and Wells)

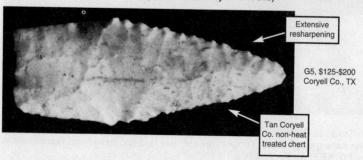

Extensive resharpening

G5, $125-$200
Coryell Co., TX

Tan Coryell Co. non-heat treated chert

Heat treated gray Coryell Co. chert

Ground stem

Heat treated brown Coryell Co. chert

G8, $200-$350
Coryell Co., TX

First stage form; Coryell Co. non-heat treated chert

Serrated edge

G7, $175-$300
Coryell Co., TX

First stage form; Heiner Lake tan Coryell Co. heat treated chert

ROGERS

SC

G10, $300-$500
Coryell Co., TX

G8, $250-$450
Coryell Co., TX

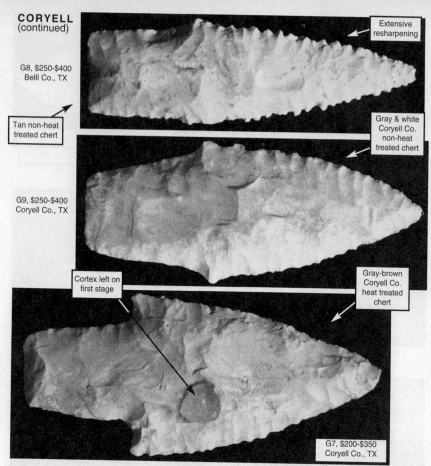

CORYELL
(continued)

G8, $250-$400
Belll Co., TX

Tan non-heat
treated chert

Extensive
resharpening

Gray & white
Coryell Co.
non-heat
treated chert

G9, $250-$400
Coryell Co., TX

Gray-brown
Coryell Co.
heat treated
chert

Cortex left on
first stage

G7, $200-$350
Coryell Co., TX

LOCATION: Eastern Texas with type area in Coryell Co.. **DESCRIPTION:** A medium to large size, serrated stemmed point with a large stem that usually tapers towards the base. Stems are usually ground. Serrations are not a product of resharpening. Shoulders are tapered to horizontal. Formerly known as "large stem Wells." This type has been found (in some camps) with Early Triangles in Coryell & Bell Co. with both types made from heat treated "Heiner Lake" tan chert. Similar to the *Searcy* point from Arkansas. **I.D. KEY:** Long stem and serrated blade edges. **NOTE:** Named **"Texas Kirk"** in Perino's book.

COSOTAT RIVER - Early Archaic, 9500 - 8000 B.°P.
(Also see Ensor Split Base and Frio)

G8, $150-$250
AR

662

COSOTAT RIVER (continued)

LOCATION: Texas into Oklahoma, Arkansas and Missouri. **DESCRIPTION:** A medium to large size, thin, usually serrated, widely corner notched point with large round to square ears and a shallow to deep notch in the center of the base. Bases are usually ground. **I.D. KEY:** Basal notching and early Archaic flaking.

G8, $175-$300
McIntosh Co., OK

COVINGTON - Late Archaic, 4000 - 3000 B. P.

(Also see Crescent Knife, Friday, Gahagan, Sabine, San Saba and San Gabriel)

SC

G6, $20-$35
TX

IMPORTANT: All Covingtons Shown 50% actual size.

G6, $25-$45
TX

G7 $45-$80
Travis Co., TX

G8 $65-$125
Williamson Co., TX

G6 $65-$125
Kimble Co., TX

G9, $80-$150
TX

G9, $65-$125
TX

LOCATION: Texas into Oklahoma. **DESCRIPTION:** A medium to large size, thin, lanceolate blade with a broad, rounded base.

G7, $25-$45
TX

G6, $45-$80
Kerr Co., TX

663

COVINGTON (continued)

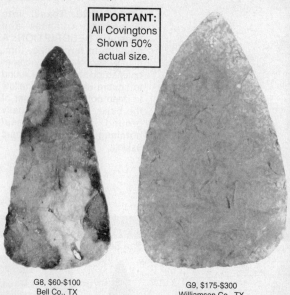

IMPORTANT:
All Covingtons
Shown 50%
actual size.

G8, $60-$100
Bell Co., TX

G9, $175-$300
Williamson Co., TX

G9, $225-$400
Kimble Co., TX

CRESCENT KNIFE - Early Archaic, 10,200 - 8000 B. P.
(Also see Base Tang, Corner Tang, Covington)

G8 $65-$125
Wilson Co., TX

Leon River
chert

IMPORTANT:
Shown 50% actual size.

G9 $125-$200
Llano Co., TX

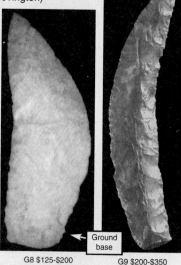

Ground
base

G8 $125-$200
Comal Co., TX

G9 $200-$350
Austin, TX

LOCATION: Texas. **DESCRIPTION:** A large
size, crescent shaped knife with a square to
rounded stem. The basal area is usually ground.
Found below and older than *Angostura* (10,000
B.P.) in Texas.

CUNEY - Historic, 400 - 200 B. P.
(Also see Bonham, Edwards, Morris, Perdiz, Rockwall and Scallorn)

LOCATION: Midwestern states. **DESCRIPTION:** A small size, well made, barbed, triangular point with a very short, small base that is bifurcated.

CUNEY (continued)

G5 $15-$20
Comache Co., TX

G9 $30-$50
TX

G6 $18-$30
AR

G9 $40-$75
Comache Co., TX

G7 $30-$50
Comache Co., TX

G10 $60-$100
AR. Tan chert.

CUPP - Late Woodland to Mississippian, 1500 - 600 B. P.

(Also see Epps, Gibson, Grand and Motley)

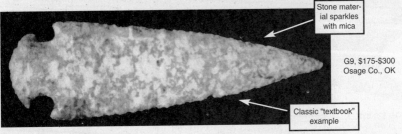

Stone material sparkles with mica

G9, $175-$300
Osage Co., OK

Classic "textbook" example

LOCATION: Northern Texas, Arkansas and Oklahoma. **DESCRIPTION:** A medium to large size, narrow barbed point with a short, expanding stem, broad corner notches and a convex base. Basal corners can be asymmetrical. Similar to *Motley*, but the base stem is shorter. *Epps* has square to tapered shoulders, otherwise is identical to *Motley*.

SC

DALLAS - Late Archaic to Woodland, 4000 - 1500 B. P.

(Also see Carrolton, Dawson, Elam, Travis and Wells)

G3, $1-$2
Hill Co., TX

G4, $1-$2
Waco, TX

G4, $2-$4
Waco, TX

G5, $3-$6
Comanche Co., TX

G5, $3-$5
Comanche Co., TX

G3, $1-$2
Waco, TX

LOCATION: Texas to Oklahoma. **DESCRIPTION:** A small to medium size point with a short blade, weak shoulders, and a long squared stem. Stem can be half the length of the point. Basal area can be ground. **I.D. KEY:** Size, squared stem.

665

DALTON-BRECKENRIDGE - Early Archaic, 10,000 - 9200 B. P.

(Also see Dalton Classic and Meserve)

LOCATION: Midwestern states, **DESCRIPTION:** A medium to large size, auriculate point with an obvious bevel extending the entire length of the point from tip to base. Similar in form to the *Dalton-Greenbrier*. Basal area is usually ground.

G4, $20-$35
AR

DALTON CLASSIC - Early Archaic, 10,000 - 9200 B. P.

(Also see Angostura, Barber, Clovis, Golondrina, Meserve, Plainview and San Patrice)

G5, $20-$35
AR

Almost exhausted point

Serrated edge. Needle tip

G6, $65-$125
N.E. AR

Flute channel

G5, $25-$40
AR

G5, $25-$40
AR

G6, $65-$100
TX

Resharpened several times. Serrated edge

G8, $60-$100
AR

Resharpened several times. Serrated edge

G9, $150-$275
AR

G9, $150-$250
AR

Serrated edge

G9, $175-$300
Greene Co., AR

Note "bulleseye" in hornstone

Petrified wood

G8, $175-$300
Greene Co., AR

G6, $60-$100
TX

G8, $225-$400
AR

G9, $175-$300
AR

Beveled edge

Exaggerated serrations

SC

G7, $80-$150
Titus Co., TX

G8, $250-$400
Greene Co., AR

G7, $200-$350
Greene Co., AR

G8, $250-$450
N.E. OK

LOCATION: Midwestern to Southeastern states. First recognized in Missouri. **DESCRIPTION:** A small to large size, thin, auriculate, fishtailed point. Many examples are finely serrated and exhibit excellent flaking. Some are fluted. Beveling may occur on one side of each face but is usually on the right side. All have basal grinding. This early type spread over most of the Eastern and Midwestern U.S. and strongly influenced many other types to follow.

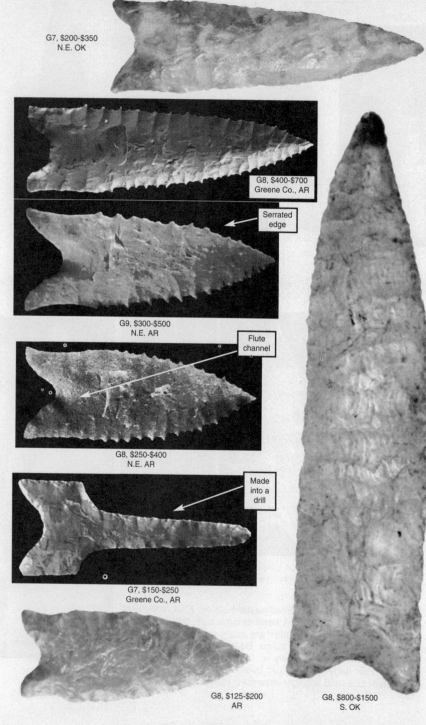

G7, $200-$350
N.E. OK

G8, $400-$700
Greene Co., AR

Serrated
edge

G9, $300-$500
N.E. AR

Flute
channel

G8, $250-$400
N.E. AR

Made
into a
drill

G7, $150-$250
Greene Co., AR

G8, $125-$200
AR

G8, $800-$1500
S. OK

668

DALTON-COLBERT - Early Archaic, 10,000 - 9200 B. P.

(Also see Beaver Lake, Dalton-Nuckolls, Plainview and Searcy)

G6, $40-$75
AR

LOCATION: Midwestern to Southeastern states. **DESCRIPTION:** A medium size, auriculate form with a squared base and a weakly defined hafting area which is ground. Some examples are serrated and exhibit parallel flaking of the highest quality. **I.D. KEY:** Squarish basal area.

G7, $35-$60
AR

DALTON-GREENBRIER - Early Archaic, 10,000 - 9200 B. P.

(Also see Dalton Breckenridge, Golondrina, Meserve, Pelican and Plainview)

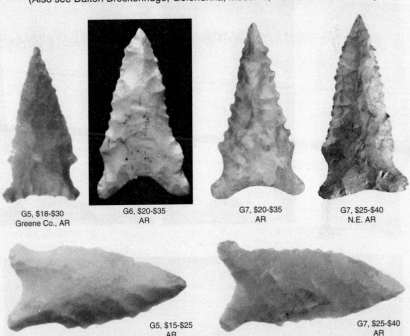

G5, $18-$30
Greene Co., AR

G6, $20-$35
AR

G7, $20-$35
AR

G7, $25-$40
N.E. AR

G5, $15-$25
AR

G7, $25-$40
AR

LOCATION: Midwestern to Eastern states and Florida. **DESCRIPTION:** A medium to large size, auriculate form with a concave base and drooping to expanding auricles. Many examples are serrated, some are fluted on both sides, and all have basal grinding. Resharpened examples are usually beveled on the right side of each face although left side beveling does occur. Thinness and high quality flaking is evident on many examples. This early variation developed in the Arkansas/Kentucky/Tennessee area. **I.D. KEY:** Expanded auricles.

DALTON-HEMPHILL - Early Archaic, 10,000 - 9200 B. P.

(Also see Firstview, Hardin, Holland and Scottsbluff)

Fluting channel

G7, $60-$100
Greene Co. AR

G7, $125-$225
Stone Co., AR

G8, $400-$750
Ozark Co., AR

G7, $300-$550
S.E. OK

G9, $400-$750
Little Rock, AR

LOCATION: Midwestern to Eastern states. **DESCRIPTION:** A medium to large size point with expanded auricles and horizontal, tapered to weak shoulders. Blade edges are usually serrated and bases are ground. In later times, this variant developed into the *Hemphill* point. **I.D. KEY:** Straightened extended shoulders.

DALTON-HEMPSTEAD - Early Archaic, 10,000 - 9200 B. P.

(Also see Dalton Breckenridge and Meserve)

G8, $125-$200
Saline Co., AR

LOCATION: Arkansas. **DESCRIPTION:** A medium size, narrow, auriculate, fishtailed point with wide side notches and a hafting area that is shorter than the classic *Dalton*. The base is concave and is ground. Blade edges can be serrated.

DARDANELLE - Mississippian, 600 - 400 B. P.

(Also see Agee, Keota and Nodena)

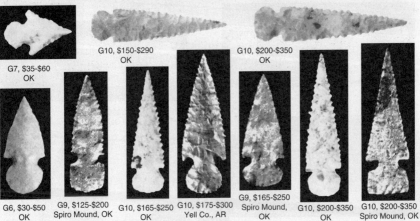

G7, $35-$60
OK

G10, $150-$290
OK

G10, $200-$350
OK

G6, $30-$50
OK

G9, $125-$200
Spiro Mound, OK

G10, $165-$250
OK

G10, $175-$300
Yell Co., AR

G9, $165-$250
Spiro Mound,
OK

G10, $200-$350
OK

G10, $200-$350
Spiro Mound, OK

SC

LOCATION: Arkansas to Oklahoma. **DESCRIPTION:** A small to medium size, narrow, thin, serrated, corner or side notched arrow point. Bases can be rounded or square. A *Nodena* variant form with basal notches. This type has been found in caches from the Spiro mound in Oklahoma and from Arkansas. **I.D. KEY:** Basal form.

DARL - Woodland, 2500 - 1000 B. P.

(Also see Darl Stemmed, Dawson, Hoxie & Zephyr)

Petrified
wood

LOCATION: Texas to Oklahoma. **DESCRIPTION:** A small to medium size, slender, triangular, expanded to parallel stemmed point. Some have a distinct bevel on one side (right) of each face. Shoulders are tapered to weakly barbed. **I.D. KEY:** Basal form. Bases expand.

G3, $3-$5
TX

G4, $6-$12
Hill Co., TX

G5, $12-$20
Austin, TX

G4, $12-$20
Ellis Co., TX

DARL (continued)

Serrated edge

G8, $20-$40
Hill Co., TX

G6, $15-$25
Hill Co., TX

G7, $25-$30
Hill Co., TX

G9 $30-$50
Hill Co., TX

G8, $25-$45
Hill Co., TX

G8, $30-$50
Hill Co., TX

Serrated edge

G8, $30-$50
Hill Co., TX

G8, $35-$60
Belton, TX

G8, $40-$75
TX

G8, $70-$125
Austin, TX

G9, $125-$200
Lufkin, TX

DARL BLADE - Woodland, 2500 - 1000 B. P.

(Also see Covington, Friday, Gahagan and Kinney)

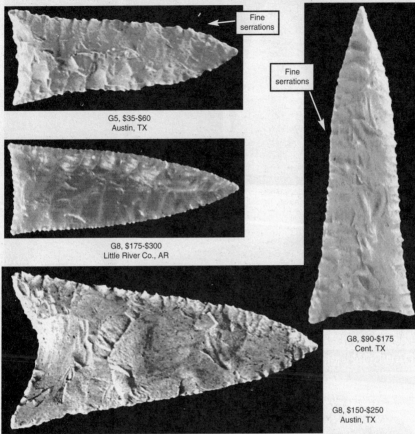

Fine serrations

G5, $35-$60
Austin, TX

G8, $175-$300
Little River Co., AR

Fine serrations

G8, $90-$175
Cent. TX

G8, $150-$250
Austin, TX

LOCATION: Texas to Oklahoma. **DESCRIPTION:** A medium to large size, thin, lanceolate blade with typical Darl flaking, fine edgework and a concave to straight base. **I.D. KEY:** Cross section thinness and fine secondary flaking on blade edges.

DARL STEMMED - Early Archaic, 8000 - 5000 B. P.

(Formerly Brazos; also see Darl, Hoxie and Zephyr)

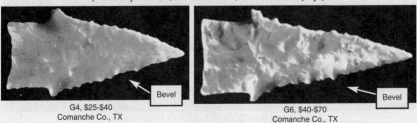

Bevel

G4, $25-$40
Comanche Co., TX

Bevel

G6, $40-$70
Comanche Co., TX

LOCATION: Central Texas. **DESCRIPTION:** A medium to large size, narrow point with horizontally barbed shoulders and an expanding to square stem. The blades on most examples are steeply beveled on one side of each face. Flaking is early parallel and is of much higher quality than *Darl*. **I.D. KEY:** Early flaking, straight base.

673

DARL STEMMED (continued)

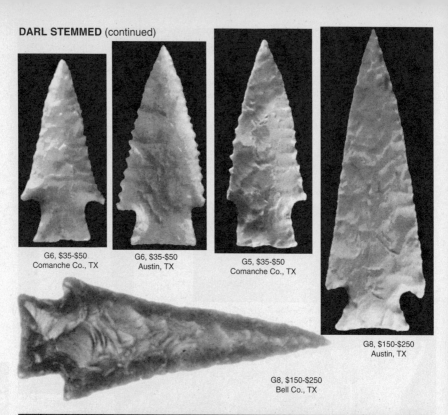

G6, $35-$50
Comanche Co., TX

G6, $35-$50
Austin, TX

G5, $35-$50
Comanche Co., TX

G8, $150-$250
Austin, TX

G8, $150-$250
Bell Co., TX

DAWSON - Middle Archaic, 7000 - 4000 B. P.

(Also see Adena, Carrolton, Darl and Wells)

G8, $60-$100
N.E. OK

G8, $70-
$125
Austin, TX

LOCATION: Texas. **DESCRIPTION:** A medium size, narrow, stemmed point with strong, tapered shoulders. The base is rounded to square.

DEADMAN'S - Desert Traditions-Developmental Phase, 1600 - 1300 B. P.

(Also see Gila Butte, Perdiz and Rose Springs)

LOCATION: Southeastern Arizona, southern New Mexico and western Texas. **DESCRIPTION:** A small arrow point with very deep basal notches creating a long, straight to slightly bulbous stem with a rounded basal edge. The blade is triangular. **I.D. KEY:** Long stem and barbs.

DEADMAN'S (continued)

G8, $50-$90
TX

G8, $50-$90
TX

G9, $70-$120
TX

G9, $70-$120
TX

G9, $70-$120
TX

G10, $80-$150
TX

DELHI - Late Archaic, 3500 - 2000 B. P.

(Also see Darl, Pogo and Pontchartrain)

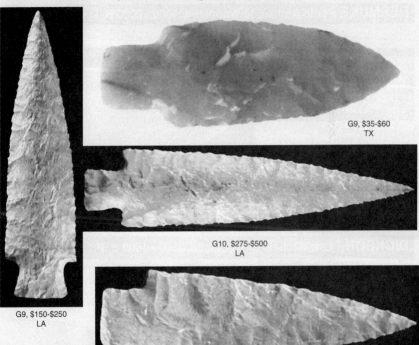

SC

G9, $35-$60
TX

G10, $275-$500
LA

G9, $150-$250
LA

G8, $80-$150
Comanche Co., TX

G7, $150-$250
E. TX

LOCATION: Louisiana into E. Texas. **DESCRIPTION:** A medium to large size, narrow, stemmed point with strong, barbed shoulders. The stem can be square or expands and the base is straight to slightly convex.

675

DELHI (continued)

G7, $80-$150
Bell Co., TX

DESMUKE - Late Archaic to Woodland, 4000 - 2000 B. P.

(Also see Lerma)

G5, $4-$8
Val Verde Co., TX

Petrified wood

G9, $20-$35
Austin, TX

LOCATION: Central to southern Texas. **DESCRIPTION:** A medium size lanceolate point with a recurved to convex blade and a contracting stem that is usually rounded. **I.D. KEY:** Stem form.

DICKSON - Late Archaic to Woodland, 2500 - 1600 B. P.

(Also see Burkett, Gary, Hidden Valley and Morrow Mountain)

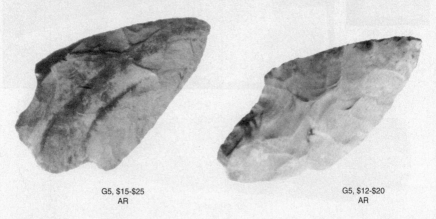

G5, $15-$25
AR

G5, $12-$20
AR

LOCATION: Midwestern states. **DESCRIPTION:** A medium to large size point with tapered shoulders and a contracting stem. High quality flaking and thinness is evident on most examples. **I.D. KEY:** Basal form.

676

DICKSON (continued)

G6, $15-$25
AR

G9, $60-$100
AR

G9, $80-$150
N. OK

G7, $75-$125
N.E. OK

DOUBLE TIP (Occurs in Carrizo and Pedernales types)

DOVETAIL - Early Archaic, 9500 - 8000 B. P.
(Also see Gibson and Thebes)

G6, $350-$600
Cherokee Co., TX

LOCATION: East Texas Eastward.
DESCRIPTION: Also known as *St. Charles*. A medium to large size, corner notched, dovetailed base point. The blade is beveled on one side of each face on resharpened examples. Bases are ground and can be fractured on both sides or center notched on some examples as found in Ohio. **I.D. KEY:** Dovetailed base, early flaking.

677

DOVETAIL (continued)

Rarity in area increases value

G9, $800-$1500
Cass Co., TX

G9, $450-$800
Taylor Co., TX

DRILL - Paleo to Historic, 14,000 - 200 B. P.

(Also see Perforator and Scraper)

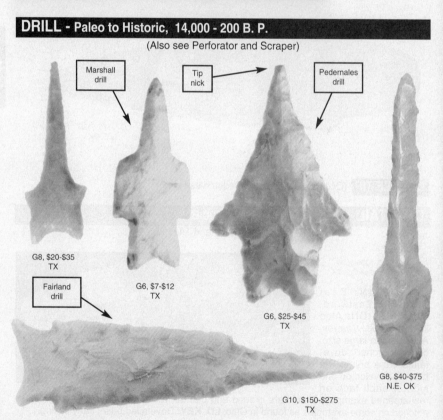

Marshall drill

Tip nick

Pedernales drill

G8, $20-$35
TX

G6, $7-$12
TX

Fairland drill

G6, $25-$45
TX

G8, $40-$75
N.E. OK

G10, $150-$275
TX

678

DRILL (continued)

G5 $5-$10
TX

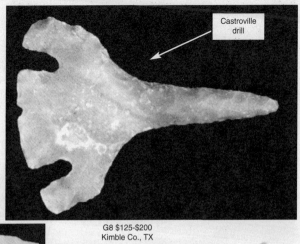

Castroville
drill

G8 $125-$200
Kimble Co., TX

Collection of drills from Bell & Coryell Co. Texas. Includes Castroville, Corner Tang, Fairland, Knife, Marcos, Marshall, San Saba

Pencil
drill

G10 $150-$250
TX

G8 $125-$200
Bell Co., TX

DRILL (continued)

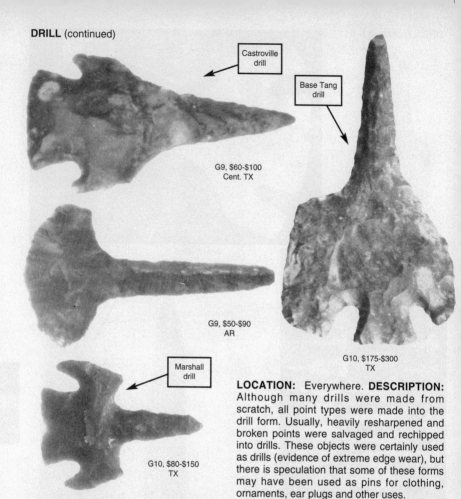

Castroville drill

Base Tang drill

G9, $60-$100
Cent. TX

G9, $50-$90
AR

G10, $175-$300
TX

Marshall drill

G10, $80-$150
TX

LOCATION: Everywhere. **DESCRIPTION:** Although many drills were made from scratch, all point types were made into the drill form. Usually, heavily resharpened and broken points were salvaged and rechipped into drills. These objects were certainly used as drills (evidence of extreme edge wear), but there is speculation that some of these forms may have been used as pins for clothing, ornaments, ear plugs and other uses.

DURAN - Woodland, 3000 - 2000 B. P.
(Also see Charcos, Evans and Sinner)

G9, $12-$20
TX

Translucent

G10, $40-$75
TX

G10, $40-$75
TX

G10, $45-$85
TX

G10, $20-$35
TX

G10, $50-$90
Val Verde Co., TX

G9, $35-$60
TX

LOCATION: Texas. **DESCRIPTION:** A small size, narrow, stemmed point with double notches on each side. Base can be parallel sided to tapered. **I.D. KEY:** Double notches.

DURAN (continued)

G9, $35-$70
TX

G5, $8-$15
TX

Tang nick

G10, $45-$85
TX

Tip nick

G8, $35-$50
TX

G5, $12-$20
Caedereyta, MX

G5, $12-$20
Caedereyta, MX

G10, $50-$90
Zapata Co., TX

G7, $35-$50
W. TX

EARLY STEMMED - Early Archaic, 9000 - 7000 B. P.

(Also see Castroville, Darl Stemmed, King, Lange, Scottsbluff and Zephyr)

SC

Side damage

G4, $20-$35
W. TX

G3, $12-$20
N.E. AR

G7, $60-$100
Angelina Co., TX

G5, $30-$50
N.E. AR

G9, $125-$200
Wilson Co., TX

LOCATION: Texas to Oklahoma. **DESCRIPTION:** A medium to large size, broad point with a medium to long expanded stem and shoulder barbs. Stems are ground. Often confused with *Lange* points which do not have ground stems. Also known as *Wilson* points from the Wilson-Leonard site in Bell Co.

EARLY STEMMED LANCEOLATE - Early Archaic, 9000 - 7000 B. P.

(Also see Angostura, Archaic Knife, Castroville, Darl Stemmed, Pontchartrain, Rio Grande, Victoria & Zephyr)

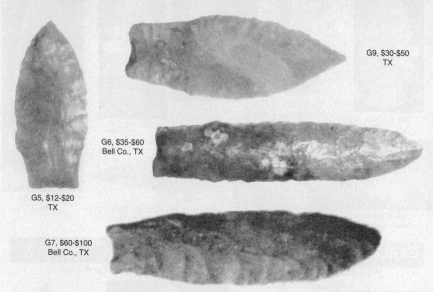

G9, $30-$50
TX

G6, $35-$60
Bell Co., TX

G5, $12-$20
TX

G7, $60-$100
Bell Co., TX

LOCATION: Texas to Oklahoma. **DESCRIPTION:** A medium to large size, narrow lanceolate stemmed point with weak, tapered shoulders.

EARLY TRIANGULAR - Early Archaic, 9000 - 7000 B. P.

(Also see Angostura, Carrizo, Clovis, Kinney and Tortugas)

Long thinning strikes from base

Long, parallel strikes across blade

G6, $20-$35
TX

G6, $25-$40
Comanche Co., TX

G3, $12-$20
TX

LOCATION: Texas. **DESCRIPTION:** A medium to large size, broad, triangle that is usually serrated. The base is either fluted or has long thinning strikes. Quality is excellent with early oblique transverse flaking and possible right hand beveling. **I.D. KEY:** Basal thinning and edgework.

EARLY TRIANGULAR (continued)

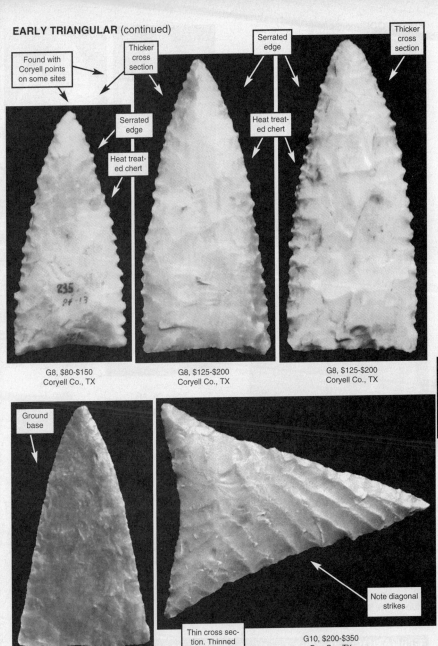

Found with Coryell points on some sites

Thicker cross section

Serrated edge

Thicker cross section

Serrated edge

Heat treated chert

Serrated edge

Heat treated chert

G8, $80-$150
Coryell Co., TX

G8, $125-$200
Coryell Co., TX

G8, $125-$200
Coryell Co., TX

SC

Ground base

Note diagonal strikes

Thin cross section. Thinned from the base.

G8, $95-$185
Bee Co., TX

G10, $200-$350
Bee Co., TX

ECCENTRIC (See Exotic Forms)

EDGEWOOD - Woodland, 3000 - 1500 B. P.
(Also see Ellis and Fairland)

EDGEWOOD (continued)

G4, $1-$3
McCulloch Co., TX

G4, $3-$5
Concho Co., TX

G4, $3-$5
McCulloch Co., TX

G4, $3-$5
Saline Co., AR

G4, $3-$5
Saline Co., AR

G6, $12-$20
Saline Co., AR

G4, $5-$8
Killeen, TX

G6, $8-$15
Comanche Co., TX

G7, $18-$30
McIntosh Co., OK

G6, $12-$20
McCulloch Co., TX

LOCATION: Texas to Oklahoma. **DESCRIPTION:** A small to medium size, expanded stem point with a concave base. Shoulders are barbed to tapered and the base is usually as wide as the shoulders.

EDWARDS - Woodland to Mississippian, 2000 - 1000 B. P.

(Also see Cuney, Haskell and Sallisaw)

Tip nick

G9, $20-$35
TX

G10, $325-$600
Comanche Co., TX

684

EDWARDS (continued)

G9, $18-$30
TX

G10, $20-$35
TX

G6, $7-$12
TX

G5, $15-$25
TX

G8, $65-$125
Spiro Mound, OK

G7, $25-$45
Spiro Mound, OK

LOCATION: Texas to Oklahoma. **DESCRIPTION:** A small size, thin, barbed arrow point with long, flaring ears at the base. Some examples are finely serrated. **I.D. KEY:** Basal form and flaking.

ELAM - Late Archaic to Woodland, 4000 - 2000 B. P.

(Also see Dallas, Darl and Ellis)

LOCATION: Texas. **DESCRIPTION:** A small size stubby point with a squared base and weak shoulders.

G6, $3-$5
Comanche Co., TX

G4, $3-$5
Comanche Co., TX

G4, $3-$5
Waco, TX

SC

ELLIS - Late Archaic, 4000 - 2000 B. P.

(Also see Edgewood, Ensor, Godley, Marcos and Scallorn)

G4, $3-$5
TX

G7, $3-$10
TX

G8, $12-$15
TX

G10, $12-$20
TX

G4, $3-$5
Comanche Co., TX

G5, $5-$10
TX

G5, $6-$10
Comanche Co., TX

Owl
Creek
Black
chert

LOCATION: Texas, Arkansas to Oklahoma. **DESCRIPTION:** A small to medium size, expanded stemmed to corner notched point with tapered to barbed shoulders. Bases are convex to straight.

685

ENSOR - Late Archaic to Early Woodland, 4000 - 1500 B. P.

(Also see Ellis, Frio, Marcos, Marshall and San Jacintol)

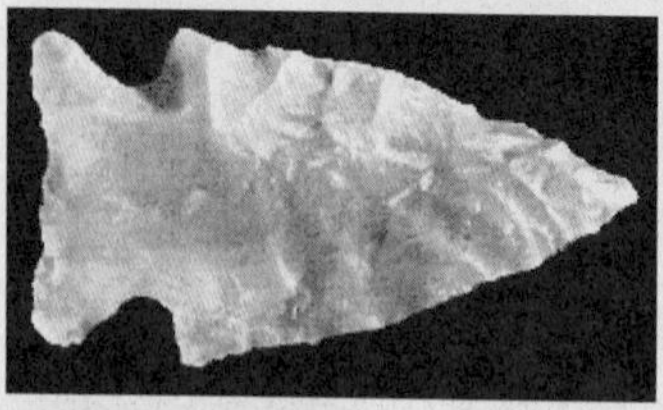

G5, $8-$15
Cent. TX

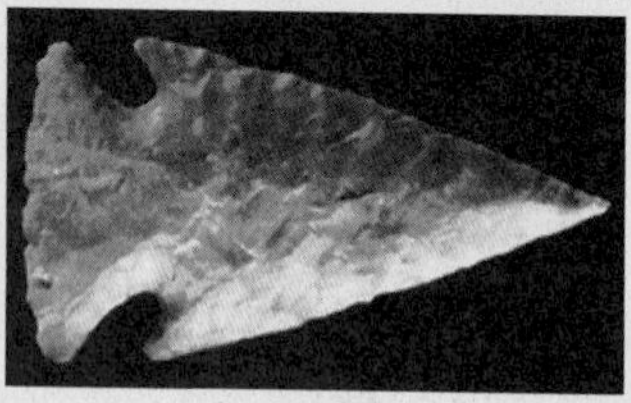

G6, $25-$40
Austin, TX

G5, $8-$15
Cent. TX

G5, $25-$40
Austin, TX

G8, $35-$60
Austin, TX

G8, $65-$125
TX

G8, $80-$150
Austin, TX

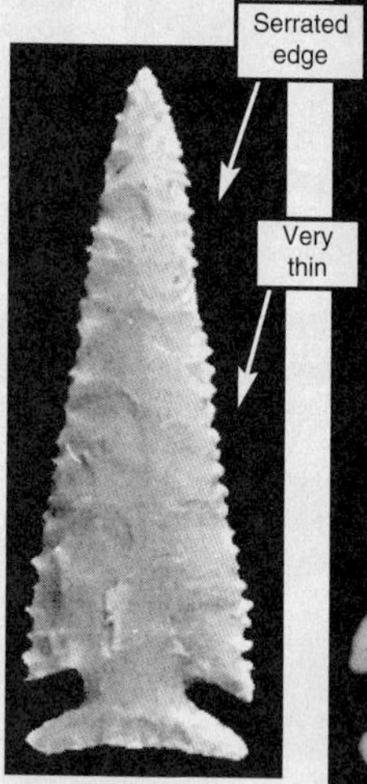

Serrated edge

Very thin

G9, $80-$150
Cent. TX

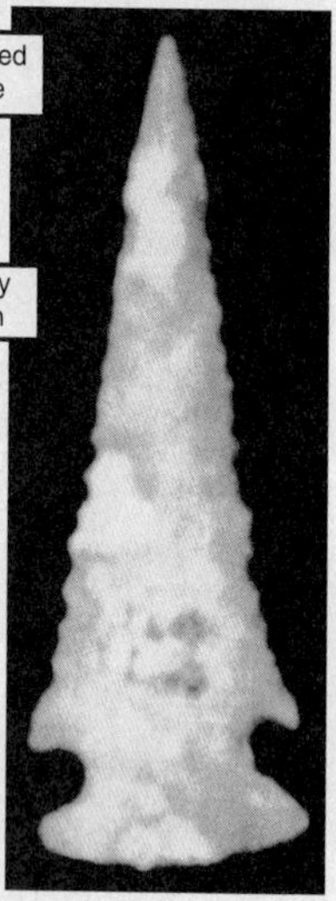

G9, $90-$175
N. OK

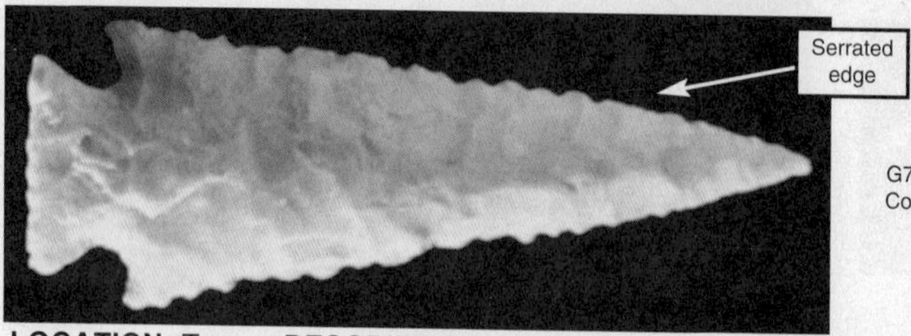

Serrated edge

G7, $150-$250
Coryell Co., TX

LOCATION: Texas. **DESCRIPTION:** A medium to large size, thin, well made corner-notched point with a concave, convex or straight base. Some examples are serrated and sharply barbed and tipped. **I.D. KEY:** Thinness, sharp barbs and edgework.

ENSOR (continued)

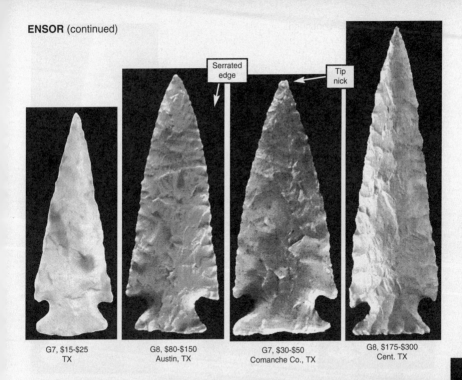

Serrated edge

Tip nick

G7, $15-$25
TX

G8, $80-$150
Austin, TX

G7, $30-$50
Comanche Co., TX

G8, $175-$300
Cent. TX

ENSOR SPLIT-BASE - Late Archaic to Early Woodland, 4000 - 1500 B. P.

(Also see Cosotat River, Edgewood, Frio and Martindale)

SC

G5, $25-$40
TX

G5, $35-$50
Gillespie Co., TX

G6, $35-$65
Austin, TX

G10, $175-$300
Kerr Co., TX

ENSOR-SPLIT BASE (continued)

G8, $125-$200
Comanche Co., TX

G7, $90-$175
Coryell Co., TX

G8, $150-$250
Bell Co., TX

LOCATION: Texas. **DESCRIPTION:** Identical to *Ensor* except for the bifurcated base. Look for *Ensor* flaking style. A cross type linking *Frio* with *Ensor*. **I.D. KEY:** Sharp barbs, thinness, edgework and split base.

EPPS - Late Archaic to Woodland, 3500 - 2000 B. P.

(Also see Cupp, Grand, Kay Blade & Motley)

G4, $5-$10
AR

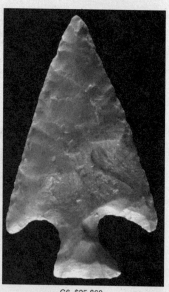

LOCATION: Eastern Texas to Louisiana. **DESCRIPTION:** A medium to large size point with wide corner notches, square to tapered shoulders and a straight base. *Cupp* has barbed shoulders. **I.D. KEY:** Square/tapered shoulders. **NOTE:** *Motley* has a curved base.

G6, $35-$60
LA

EVANS - Late Archaic To Woodland, 4000 - 2000 B. P.

(Also see Charcos, Duran and Sinner)

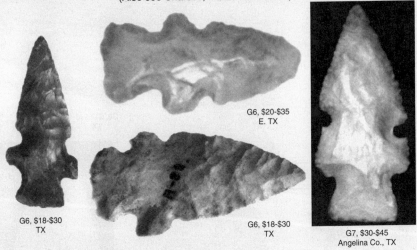

G6, $20-$35
E. TX

G6, $18-$30
TX

G6, $18-$30
TX

G7, $30-$45
Angelina Co., TX

LOCATION: Eastern Texas Eastward to Tennessee. **DESCRIPTION:** A medium to large size stemmed double notched point. The notching occurs somewhere between the tip and shoulders. **I.D. KEY:** Expanding stem and side notches.

EXOTIC FORMS - Mid Archaic to Mississippian, 5000 - 1000 B. P.

(Also see Double Tip)

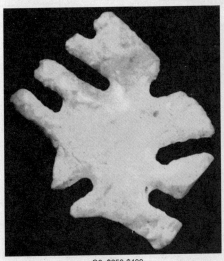

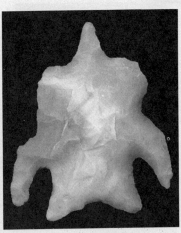

G9, $250-$400
N. OK

G7, 25-$40
Georgetown Co., TX

LOCATION: Everywhere **DESCRIPTION:** The forms illustrated here are very rare. Some are definitely effigy forms while others may be no more than the result of practicing how to notch, or unfinished and unintentional doodles.

FAIRLAND - Woodland, 3000 - 1500 B. P.

(Also see Edgewood, Ellis, Marcos and Marshall)

G5, $3-$5
TX

G6, $12-$20
TX

G6, $12-$20
TX

Perforator tip

G6, $45-$80
Killeen, TX

G6, $45-$80
Travis Co., TX

G7, $45-$80
Killeen, TX

G7, $35-$60
Bell Co., TX

G8, $90-$175
Bell Co., TX

Excellent quality

G10, $600-$1000
TX

FAIRLAND (continued)

The best known example

G10+, $1800-$3000+
Comanche Co., TX

LOCATION: Texas, Arkansas to Oklahoma. **DESCRIPTION:** A small to medium size, thin, expanded stem point with a concave base that is usually thinned. Shoulders can be weak and tapered to slightly barbed. The base is broad. **I.D. KEY:** Basal form, systematic form of flaking.

FIGUEROA - Woodland, 3000 - 1500 B. P.

(Also see Big Sandy, Brewerton, Ensor and Gibson)

G4, $5-$10
Sou. TX

G7, $15-$25
Comanche Co., TX

G9, $20-$35
Val Verde Co., TX

G6, $8-$15
Comanche Co., TX

SC

LOCATION: Texas. **DESCRIPTION:** A small to medium size side notched to expanded base point with a convex base. Basal corners are the widest part of the point. **I.D. KEY:** Basal form, wide notches.

FIRSTVIEW - Early Archaic, 8700 - 7000 B. P.

(Also see Alberta, Dalton, Eden, Red River and Scottsbluff)

Ground basal area

Resharpened many times

G5, $150-$275
Reeves Co., TX

LOCATION: Texas to Colorado. **DESCRIPTION:** A medium to large size lanceolate blade with early paleo flaking and very weak shoulders. A variant of the *Scottsbluff* type made by the Cody Complex people. Bases are straight and stem sides are parallel. Many examples are median ridged with collateral, parallel flaking. **I.D. KEY:** Broad base, weak shoulders.

691

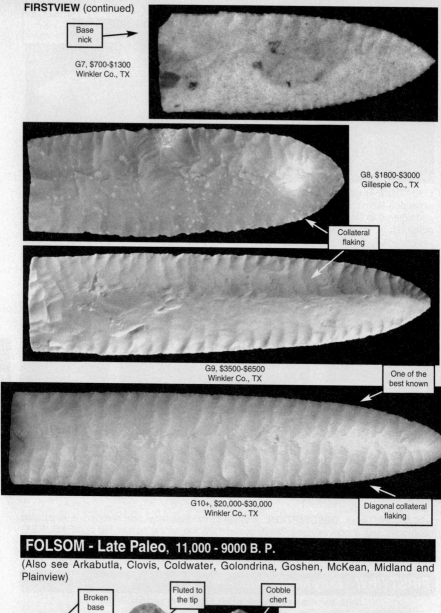

Base nick →

G7, $700-$1300
Winkler Co., TX

G8, $1800-$3000
Gillespie Co., TX

Collateral flaking

G9, $3500-$6500
Winkler Co., TX

One of the best known

G10+, $20,000-$30,000
Winkler Co., TX

Diagonal collateral flaking

FOLSOM - Late Paleo, 11,000 - 9000 B. P.

(Also see Arkabutla, Clovis, Coldwater, Golondrina, Goshen, McKean, Midland and Plainview)

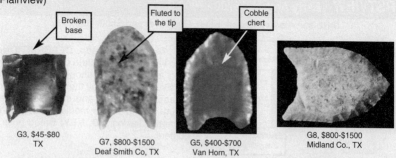

Broken base

Fluted to the tip

Cobble chert

G3, $45-$80
TX

G7, $800-$1500
Deaf Smith Co, TX

G5, $400-$700
Van Horn, TX

G8, $800-$1500
Midland Co., TX

FOLSOM (continued)

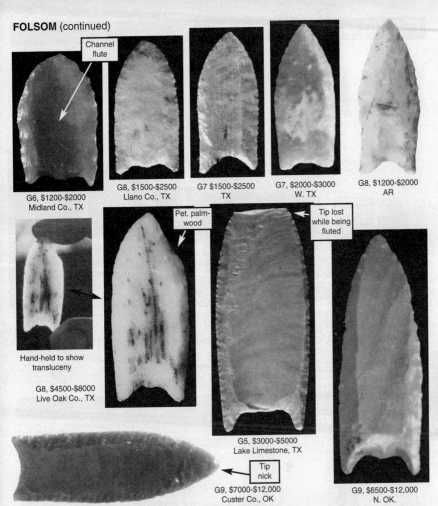

G6, $1200-$2000
Midland Co., TX

Channel flute

G8, $1500-$2500
Llano Co., TX

G7 $1500-$2500
TX

G7, $2000-$3000
W. TX

G8, $1200-$2000
AR

Hand-held to show
transluceny

G8, $4500-$8000
Live Oak Co., TX

Pet. palm-wood

Tip lost
while being
fluted

G5, $3000-$5000
Lake Limestone, TX

Tip nick

G9, $7000-$12,000
Custer Co., OK

G9, $6500-$12,000
N. OK.

SC

LOCATION: Texas to Montana to Canada. **DESCRIPTION:** A small to medium size, very thin, high quality, fluted point with contracted, pointed auricles and a concave base. Fluting usually extends the entire length of each face. Blade flaking is extremely fine. The hafting area is ground. A very rare type, even in area of highest incidence. Modern reproductions have been made and extreme caution should be exercised in acquiring an original specimen. Usually found in association with extinct bison fossil remains. **I.D. KEY:** Flaking style (Excessive secondary flaking)

FREDERICK - Late Paleo-Early Archaic, 8500 - 8000 B. P.

(Also see Angostura, Clovis, Dalton, Golondrina, and Plainview)

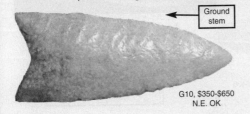

Ground stem

G10, $350-$650
N.E. OK

LOCATION: Texas, Oklahoma, Montana, Nebraska and Kansas. **DESCRIPTION:** A medium size, thin, lanceolate blade with early diagonal to collateral flaking and a concave base. Basal area is ground. **I.D. KEY:** Broad base, deep concavity.

693

FRESNO - Mississippian, 1200 - 250 B. P.

(Also see Bassett, Friley, Huffaker, Maud and Talco)

G8, $12-$20
TX

G4, $8-$15
Ellis Co., TX

G7, $5-$8
Nuevo Leon, MX

Alibates flint

G4, $8-$15
Washita Co., OK

G4, $8-$15
Odessa, TX

White chert

G4, $8-$15
Mays Co., OK

Alibates flint

Agalala flint

G7, $12-$20
Coleman Co., TX

G7, $12-$20
Custer Co., OK

G7, $12-$20
S.W. OK

G7, $5-$10
W. OK

G10, $60-$100
Nueces Co., TX

G10, $80-$150
Nueces Co., TX

LOCATION: Texas, Arkansas, Oklahoma and New Mexico. **DESCRIPTION:** A small, thin, triangular point with convex to straight sides and a concave to straight base. Many examples are deeply serrated and some are side notched.

FRIDAY - Woodland, 4000 - 1500 B. P.

(Also see Covington, Gahagan, Pandora, Sabine and San Gabriel)

G7, $125-$200
Waco, TX

G7, $18-$30
TX

G7, $25-$40
TX

G7, $50-$80
Coryell Co., TX

G10, $450-$800
Kimble Co., TX

G9, $225-$400
TX

IMPORTANT:
All Fridays shown
half size

694

FRIDAY (continued)

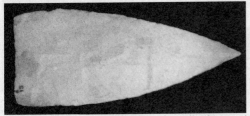

G7, $275-$500
Bell Co., TX

LOCATION: Texas to Oklahoma. **DESCRIPTION:** A medium to large, thin, lanceolate blade with recurved to straight sides, sharp corners and a straight base. Flaking quality is excellent. Many examples have a long triangular form.

IMPORTANT:
All Fridays
shown half size

G8, $225-$400
Jonestown, TX

G9, $400-$700
Williamson Co., TX

G10, $700-$1250
Kerr Co., TX

SC

FRILEY - **Late Woodland, 1500 - 1000 B. P.**

(Also see Edwards, Fresno, Morris and Steiner)

G6, $4-$8
TX

G5, $5-$10
Comanche Co., TX

G8, $25-$40
AR

G8, $30-$50
AR

G9, $35-$60
AR

G9, $80-$140
AR

LOCATION: East Texas, Arkansas to Louisiana. **DESCRIPTION:** A small size, thin, triangular point with exaggerated shoulders that flare outward and towards the tip. The base can be rounded to eared.

FRIO - Middle Archaic to Woodland, 5000 - 1500 B. P.

(Also see Big Sandy, Cosotat River, Ensor Split-Base, Fairland, Montell and Uvalde)

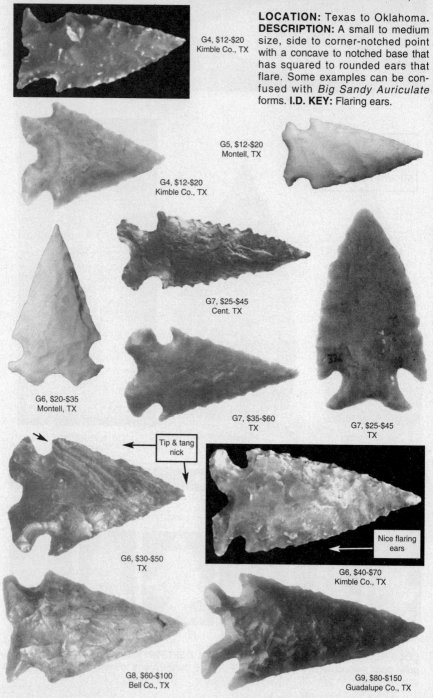

LOCATION: Texas to Oklahoma.
DESCRIPTION: A small to medium size, side to corner-notched point with a concave to notched base that has squared to rounded ears that flare. Some examples can be confused with *Big Sandy Auriculate* forms. **I.D. KEY:** Flaring ears.

G4, $12-$20
Kimble Co., TX

G5, $12-$20
Montell, TX

G4, $12-$20
Kimble Co., TX

G7, $25-$45
Cent. TX

G6, $20-$35
Montell, TX

G7, $35-$60
TX

G7, $25-$45
TX

Tip & tang nick

G6, $30-$50
TX

Nice flaring ears

G6, $40-$70
Kimble Co., TX

G8, $60-$100
Bell Co., TX

G9, $80-$150
Guadalupe Co., TX

696

FRIO (continued)

Black Leon
River chert

Leon
River
chert

Shoulder
nick

G4, $8-$15
Montell, TX

G6, $25-$40
TX

G7, $35-$60
Comanche Co., TX

G9 $150-$250
Tom Green Co., TX

G9 $175-$300
Comanche Co., TX

GAHAGAN - Woodland, 4000 - 1500 B. P.

SC

(Also see Covington, Darl Blade, Friday, Kinney, Mineral Springs, Sabine and San Gabriel)

IMPORTANT:
Gahagans
shown half size

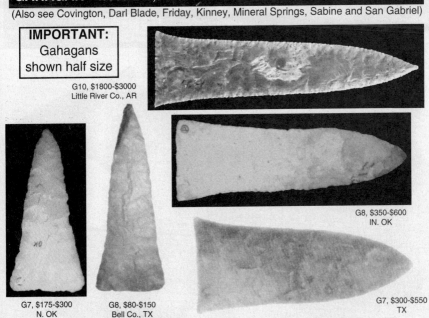

G10, $1800-$3000
Little River Co., AR

G8, $350-$600
IN. OK

G7, $175-$300
N. OK

G8, $80-$150
Bell Co., TX

G7, $300-$550
TX

LOCATION: Texas. **DESCRIPTION:** A large size, broad, thin, triangular blade with recurved sides and a straight base.

GAR SCALE - Late Woodland to Mississippian, 1800 - 400 B. P.

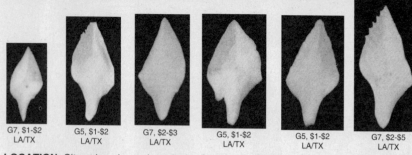

G7, $1-$2
LA/TX

G5, $1-$2
LA/TX

G7, $2-$3
LA/TX

G5, $1-$2
LA/TX

G5, $1-$2
LA/TX

G7, $2-$5
LA/TX

LOCATION: Sites along large rivers in the Southeast such as the Tennessee River and the Mississippi. **DESCRIPTION:** Scales from Garfish were utilized as arrow points. These scales are hard and are naturally bipointed which was easily adapted as tips for arrows. Some examples altered into more symmetrical forms by the Indians.

GARY - Late Archaic to early Woodland, 3200 - 1000 B. P.

(Also see Adena, Almagre, Burkett, Dickson, Hidden Valley, Langtry, Morrow Mountain and Waubesa)

Petrified wood

G4, $5-$10
Hill Co., TX

G6, $4-$8
Hill Co., TX

G7, $20-$35
TX

G5, $5-$10
LA

G9, $30-$50
TX

G6 $15-$25
AR

G5, $15-$25
N.E. OK

698

GARY (continued)

G7, $20-$35
Tulsa, OK

G9, $35-$60
N.E. OK

G9, $35-$60
N.E. OK

SC

LOCATION: Mississippi to Oklahoma. **DESCRIPTION:** A medium size, triangular point with a medium to long, contracted, pointed to rounded stem. Rarely, the base is straight. Shoulders are usually tapered. **I.D. KEY:** Similar to *Adena,* but thinned more. Another similar form, *Morrow Mountain* has earlier parallel flaking. **I.D. KEY:** Long contracted stem.

G7, $20-$35
McIntosh Co., OK

G7, $18-$30
AR

G9, $65-$125
Pike Co., AR

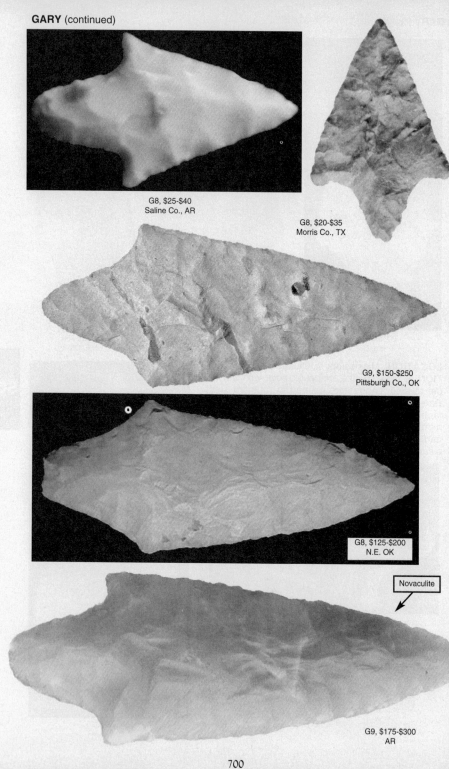

G8, $25-$40
Saline Co., AR

G8, $20-$35
Morris Co., TX

G9, $150-$250
Pittsburgh Co., OK

G8, $125-$200
N.E. OK

Novaculite

G9, $175-$300
AR

GARZA - Mississippian to Historic, 500 - 300 B. P.

(Also see Harrell, Lott, Starr and Toyah)

Tip nick

Chalcedony

Needle tip; side-notches

G10, $30-$50
TX

G5, $15-$20
TX

G7, $15-$30
TX

G10, $80-$150
TX

G7, $15-$30
MX

G9, $20-$35
TX

G9, $125-$200
TX

G10, $125-$200
TX

G9, $35-$60
TX

Side notches

LOCATION: Northern Mexico to Oklahoma. **DESCRIPTION:** A small size, thin, triangular point with concave to convex sides and base that has a single notch in the center. Many examples are serrated. See *Soto* in SW Section.

GIBSON - Mid to Late Woodland, 2000 - 1500 B. P.

(Also see Cupp, Dovetail, Epps, Grand and Motley)

LOCATION: Midwestern to Eastern states. **DESCRIPTION:** A medium to large size side to corner notched point with a large, convex base.

G8, $50-$90
AR

SC

GODLEY - Woodland, 2500 - 1500 B. P.

(Also see Ellis and Palmillas)

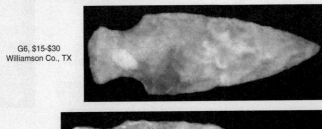

G6, $15-$30
Williamson Co., TX

G6, $15-$30
Williamson
Co., TX

G5, $12-$20
Williamson Co., TX

LOCATION: Texas. **DESCRIPTION:** A small to medium size point with broad, expanding side-notches, tapered shoulders and a convex base. Basal area can be ground. Many specimens show unique beveling at the stem, usually from the same side.

GOLONDRINA - Transitional Paleo, 9000 - 7000 B. P.

(Also see Angostura, Arkabutla, Dalton, Midland, Pelican, Plainview & San Patrice)

G6, $65-$125
Coryell Co., TX

G67, $80-$175
TX

G7, $150-$250
Zapata Co., TX

G7, $200-$350
Wilson Co., TX

G5, $80-$150
TX

G7, $150-$275
Webb Co., TX

G7, $150-$250
Webb Co., TX

G8, $275-$500
Wilson Co., TX

G7, $250-$450
Comanche Co., TX

LOCATION: Texas, Arkansas to Oklahoma. **DESCRIPTION:** A medium to large size auriculate unfluted point with rounded ears that flare and a deeply concave base. Basal areas are ground. Believed to be related to Dalton. **I.D. KEY:** Expanded ears, paleo flaking.

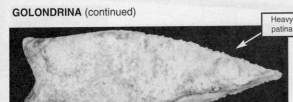

Heavy patina

G8, $250-$450
Wilson Co., TX

G8, $250-$450
TX

G8, $300-$550
Dyersburg, TN

G10, $700-$1200
TX

SC

GOSHEN - Paleo, 11,500 - 10,000 B. P.

(Also see Clovis, Midland, Milnesand)

G6, $200-$350
TX

G9, $1200-$2000
N. OK

GOSHEN (continued)

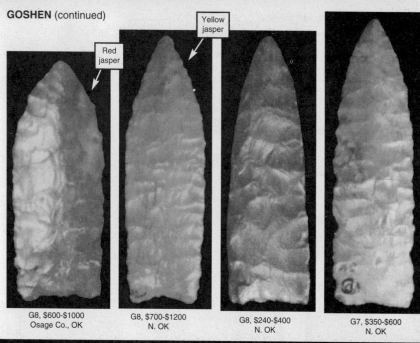

Red jasper

Yellow jasper

G8, $600-$1000
Osage Co., OK

G8, $700-$1200
N. OK

G8, $240-$400
N. OK

G7, $350-$600
N. OK

G10, $3000-$5000
Comanche Co., TX

LOCATION: Oklahoma to Montana. **DESCRIPTION:** A small to medium size, very thin, auriculate point with a concave base. Basal corners slope inward and are rounded. Flaking is oblique to horizontal transverse. A rare type. **I.D. KEY:** Thinness, auricles.

GOWER - Early Archaic, 8000 - 5000 B. P.

(Also see Barber, Jetta, Pedernales and Uvalde)

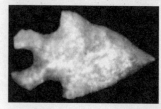

G7, $15-$25
Cent. TX

G5, $12-$20
Comanche Co., TX

LOCATION: Texas. **DESCRIPTION:** A medium size, narrow point with weak shoulders and a long, deeply bifurcated stem. One or both basal ears turn inward on some examples or flare outward on others. **I.D. KEY:** Narrowness, base form.

GOWER (continued)

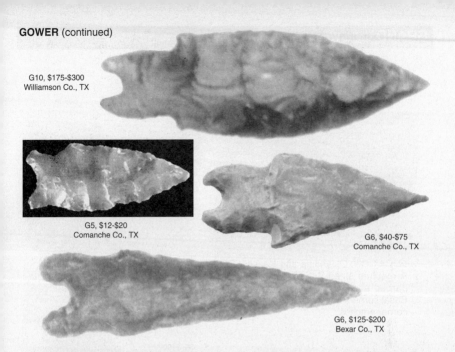

G10, $175-$300
Williamson Co., TX

G5, $12-$20
Comanche Co., TX

G6, $40-$75
Comanche Co., TX

G6, $125-$200
Bexar Co., TX

GRAHAM CAVE - Early to Middle Archaic, 9000 - 5000 B. P.
(Also see Big Sandy, Hickory Ridge and White River)

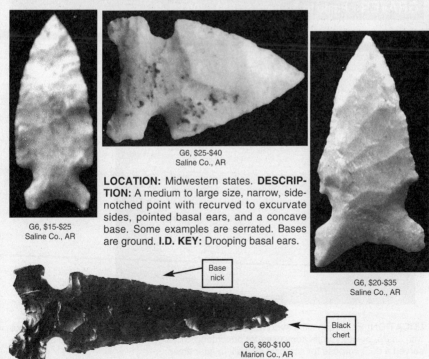

G6, $25-$40
Saline Co., AR

LOCATION: Midwestern states. **DESCRIPTION:** A medium to large size, narrow, side-notched point with recurved to excurvate sides, pointed basal ears, and a concave base. Some examples are serrated. Bases are ground. **I.D. KEY:** Drooping basal ears.

G6, $15-$25
Saline Co., AR

G6, $20-$35
Saline Co., AR

Base nick

Black chert

G6, $60-$100
Marion Co., AR

705

GRAND - Mid-Woodland, 1800 - 1600 B. P.

(Also see Big Creek, Cupp, Epps, Gibson and Motley)

G6, $30-$50
N.E. OK

LOCATION: Oklahoma into Kansas. **DESCRIPTION:** A medium sized, broad, corner notched point with barbed shoulders and an expanding, convex base. Basal corners can be sharp. **I.D. KEY:** Width of blade, corner notches.

G9, $150-$250
Cherokee Co., OK

GRAVER - Paleo to Archaic, 14,000 - 4000 B. P.

(Also see Drill, Perforator and Scraper)

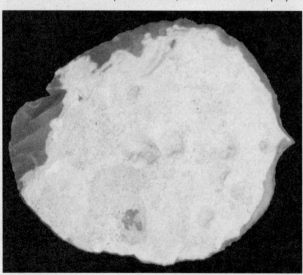

G8, $15-$30
Kimble Co., TX

LOCATION: Early man sites everywhere. **DESCRIPTION:** An irregular shaped uniface tool with sharp, pointed projections used for puncturing, incising, tattooing, etc. Some examples served a dual purpose for scraping as well. In later times.

GRAVER (continued)

G4, $2-$5
Kimble Co., TX

Graver tip

GUERRERO - Historic, 300 - 100 B. P.

(Also see Maud and Nodena)

G6, $8-$15
Montell, TX

G6, $40-$75
TX

LOCATION: Texas. **DESCRIPTION:** A small to medium size, narrow, thin, lanceolate point with a straight base. Similar to the Eastern *Guntersville* point. The last stone arrowhead in Texas. Also called "Mission point."

G3, $3-$6
TX

G2, $2-$5
TX

G3, $4-$8
TX

G3, $5-$10
TX

G6, $50-$90
TX

G7, $65-$125
TX

G8, $80-$150
TX

G7, $65-$125
TX

G6, $50-$90
TX

G6, $50-$90
TX

G6, $50-$90
TX

G9, $150-$250
Coke Co., TX

HALE (Bascom) - Late Archaic, 4000 - 3500 B. P.

(Also see Peisker Diamond)

G7, $25-$40
AR

LOCATION: Arkansas into Mississippi. **DESCRIPTION:** A large size, broad point with shoulders tapering to the base which is straight to rounded. Similar to the *Bascom* form found in Alabama and Georgia.

HARAHEY - Mississippian, 700 - 400 B. P.

(Also see Covington, Friday, Lerma and Refugio)

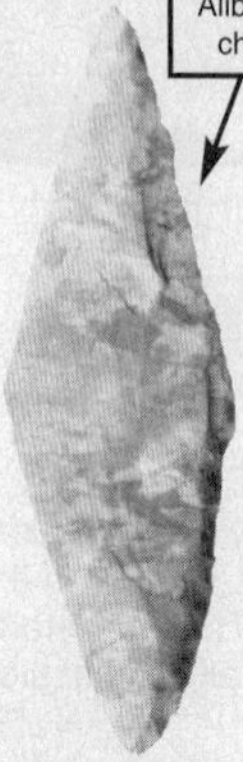

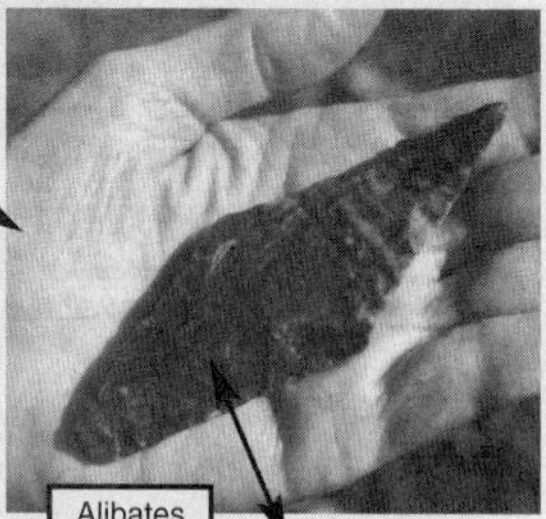

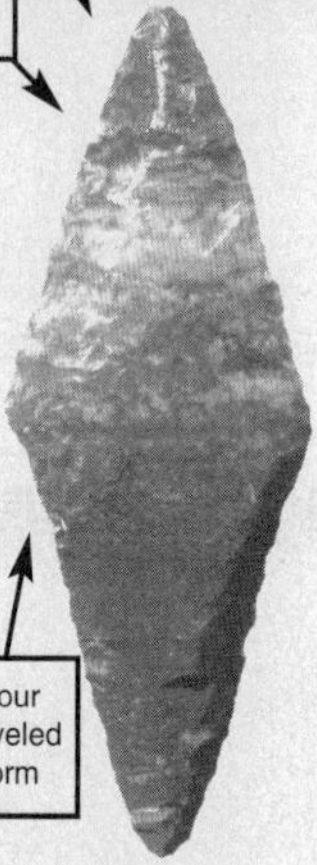

Alibates chert

G8, $150-$250
AR

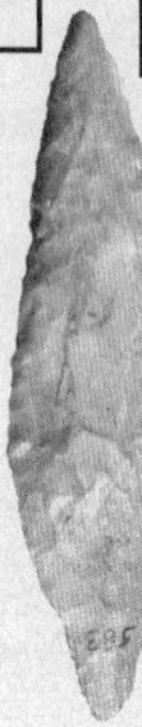

G7, $80-$150
Cent. TX

Four beveled form

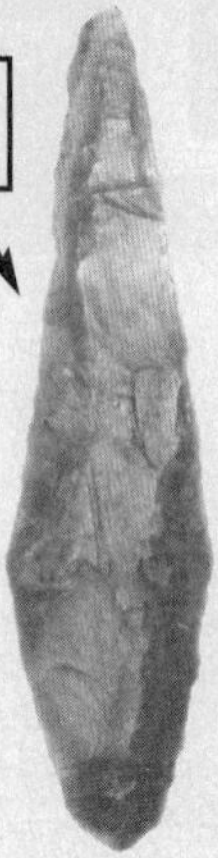

G7, $60-$100
Hamilton Co., TX

Hand held to show size comparison

IMPORTANT: All Haraheys shown 50% actual size

Alibates chert
Four beveled form

G8, $250-$450
Carson Co., TX

Alibates chert

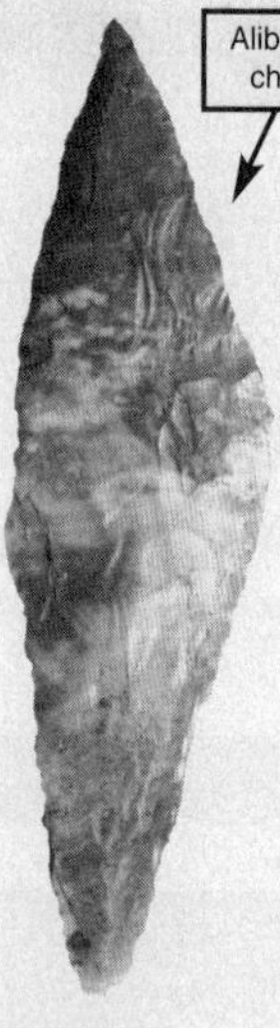

G7, $250-$400
Morrow Co., TX

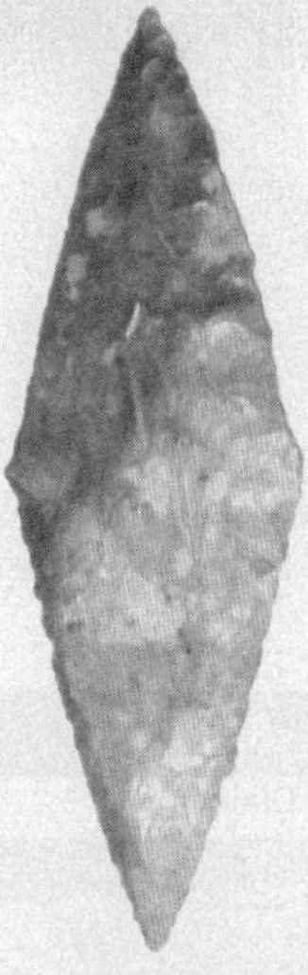

G9, $275-$500
Bell Co., TX

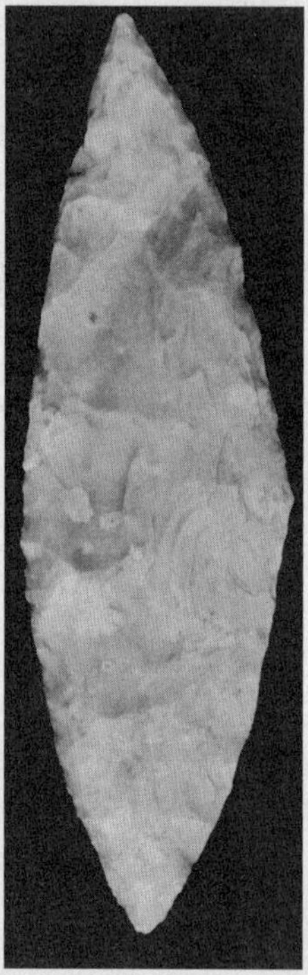

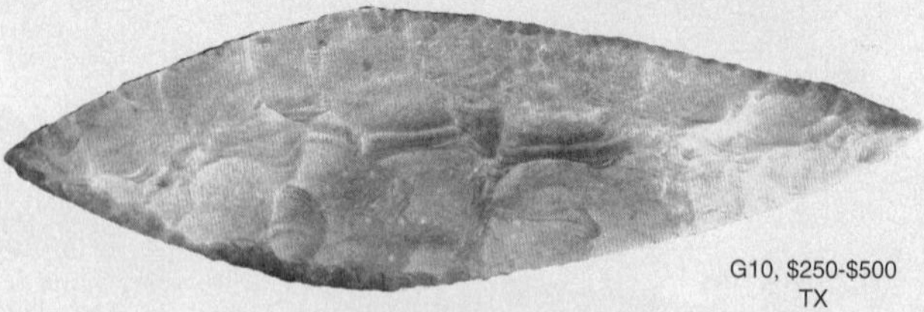

G9, $350-$600
Coryell Co., TX

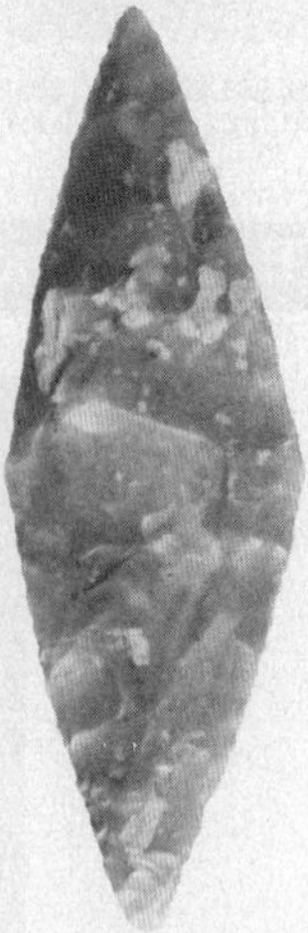

G8, $225-$400
Garza Co., TX

G10, $250-$500
TX

LOCATION: Texas to Colorado. **DESCRIPTION:** A large size, double pointed knife that is usually beveled on one or all four sides of each face. The cross section is rhomboid. The true buffalo skinning knife. Found associated with small arrow points in Texas. **I.D. KEY:** Two and four beveled double pointed form.

HARDIN - Early Archaic, 9000 - 6000 B. P.

(Also see Alberta, Dovetail, Kirk and Scottsbluff)

G4, $8-$15
AR

Petrified
wood

G9, $400-$800
Angelina Co., TX

G7, $60-$100
Coryell Co., TX

G7, $150-$250
Hamilton Co., TX

SC

G7, $80-$150
AR

G6, $20-$35
AR

G8, $125-$200
Greene Co., AR

LOCATION: Midwestern to Eastern states. **DESCRIPTION:** A large size, well made triangular barbed point with an expanded base that is usually ground. Resharpened examples have one beveled edge on each face. *Hardin* points are believed to have evolved from the *Scottsbluff* type. **I.D. KEY:** Notches and stem form.

HARDIN (continued)

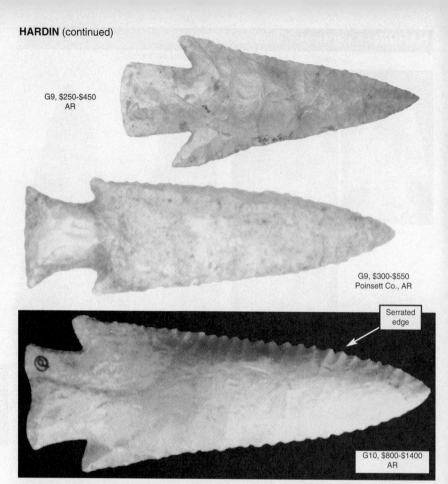

G9, $250-$450
AR

G9, $300-$550
Poinsett Co., AR

Serrated
edge

G10, $800-$1400
AR

HARE BIFACE - Late Archaic to Woodland, 3000 - 2000 B. P.

(Also see Covington, Friday, Pandora and San Gabriel)

LOCATION: Texas. **DESCRIPTION:** A medium to large size knife with excurvate sides and a rounded base.

G6, $20-$35
TX

G6, $80-$150
Bell Co., TX

HARRELL - Mississippian to Historic, 900 - 500 B. P.

(Also see Toyah and Washita)

Alibates flint — G5, $15-$30 Custer Co., OK

Alibates flint — G6, $25-$40 Custer Co., OK

G5, $20-$35 Custer Co., OK

Gray flint — G10, $65-$125 AR

Alibates flint — G7, $30-$50 Washita Co., OK

Alibates flint — G9, $60-$100 S.W. OK

Alibates flint — G7, $25-$40 S.W. OK

G9, $60-$100 Spiro Mound, OK

G6, $30-$50 AR

G9, $60-$100 Spiro Mound, OK

Alibates flint — G9, $80-$150 Taylor Co., TX

G10, $90-$175 S.W. OK

G9, $80-$150 Spiro Mound, OK

LOCATION: Texas to Oklahoma. **DESCRIPTION:** A small size, thin, triangular arrow point with side and a basal notch. Basal lobes are squared.

SC

HASKELL - Mississippian to Historic, 800 - 600 B. P.

(Also see Edwards, Huffaker, Reed, Toyah and Washita)

G4, $8-$15 AR

G4, $8-$15 AR

G3, $5-$10 AR

G4, $3-$5 Comanche Co., TX

G4, $8-$15 AR

G7, $25-$40 Cent. TX

G4, $12-$20 AR

G5, $8-$15 Odessa, TX

G5, $12-$20 Odessa, TX

G5, $25-$45 AR

G9, $115-$200 Pike Co., AR.

Black chert

G9, $125-$225 Spiro Mound, OK

G9, $45-$80 TX

LOCATION: Oklahoma to Arkansas. **DESCRIPTION:** A small size, thin, narrow, triangular, side notched point with a concave base. Rarely, basal tangs are notched.

711

HAYES - Mississippian, 1200 - 600 B. P.

(Also see Alba, Blevins, Homan, Howard, Perdiz, Sequoya and Turner)

G6, $18-$30
AR

G5, $8-$15
AR

Red chert

G8, $50-$90
AR

G8, $45-$80
AR

Red flint

G8, $50-$90
AR

G10, $80-$150
AR

Brown flint

G7, $30-$50
AR

Black flint

G10, $65-$125
AR

Black flint

G8, $50-$90
AR

Brown flint

G8, $50-$90
AR

Red chert

G10 $80-$150
AR

Incup tip

G9, $50-$90
AR

G9, $135-$250
AR

G7, $50-$90
AR

Serrated edges

Red chert

G10, $135-$250
AR

Incup tip

G6, $35-$60
AR

G10, $50-$90
AR

Gray, red flint

Incup tip

Red chert

G10, $65-$125
AR

G7, $35-$60
AR

Red, black, gray chert

G10, $135-$250
AR

LOCATION: Louisiana to Oklahoma. **DESCRIPTION:** A small to medium size, narrow, expanded tang arrow point with a turkeytail base. Blade edges are usually strongly recurved forming sharp pointed tangs. Base is pointed and can be double notched. Some examples are serrated. Has been found in caches. **I.D. KEY:** Diamond shaped base and flaking style.

HAYES (continued)

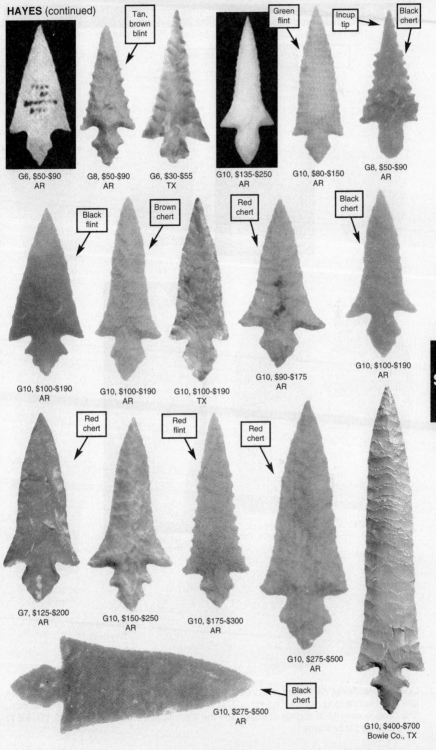

Tan, brown blint

Green flint

Incup tip

Black chert

G6, $50-$90
AR

G8, $50-$90
AR

G6, $30-$55
TX

G10, $135-$250
AR

G10, $80-$150
AR

G8, $50-$90
AR

Black flint

Brown chert

Red chert

Black chert

G10, $100-$190
AR

G10, $100-$190
AR

G10, $100-$190
TX

G10, $90-$175
AR

G10, $100-$190
AR

SC

Red chert

Red flint

Red chert

G7, $125-$200
AR

G10, $150-$250
AR

G10, $175-$300
AR

G10, $275-$500
AR

Black chert

G10, $275-$500
AR

G10, $400-$700
Bowie Co., TX

713

HELL GAP - Transitional Paleo, 10,900 - 9000 B. P.

(Also see Agate Basin, Angostura, Midland, Pelican and Rio Grande)

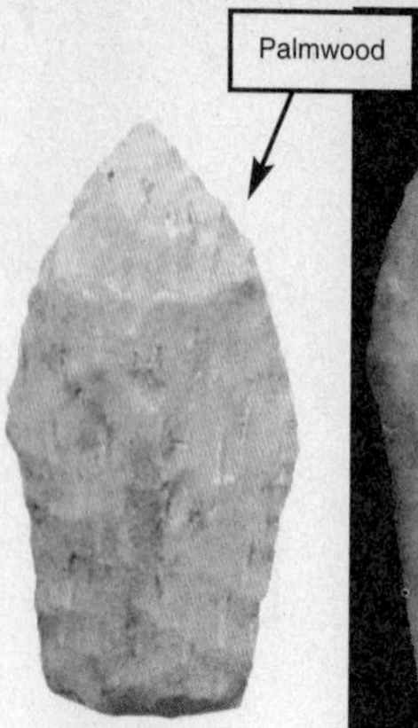
Palmwood

G6, $80-$150
TX

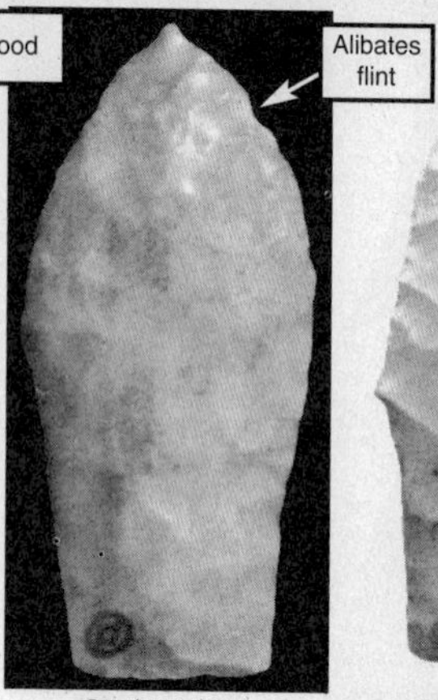
Alibates
flint

G7, $150-$275
N. OK

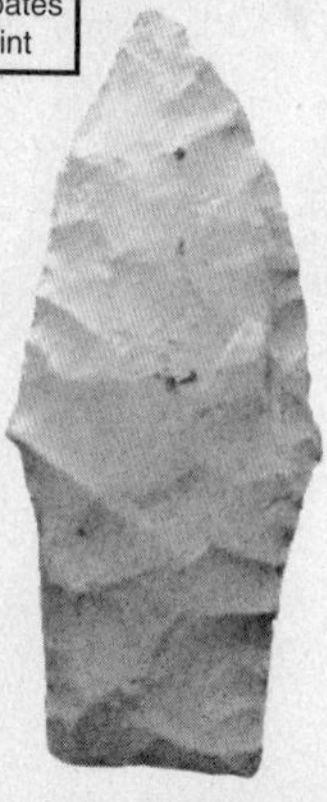

G7, $150-$275
TX

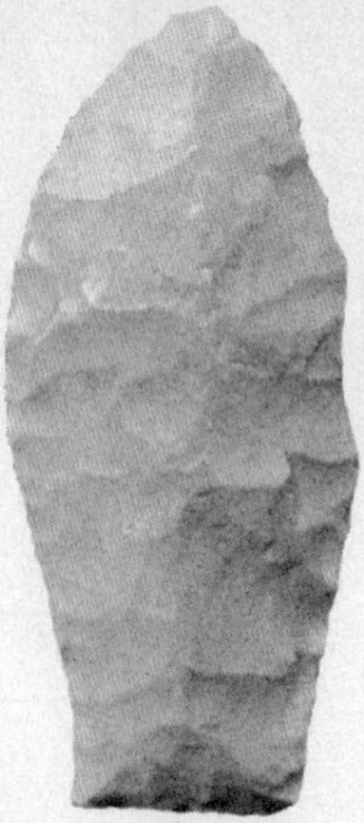

G5, $65-$125
Osage Co., OK

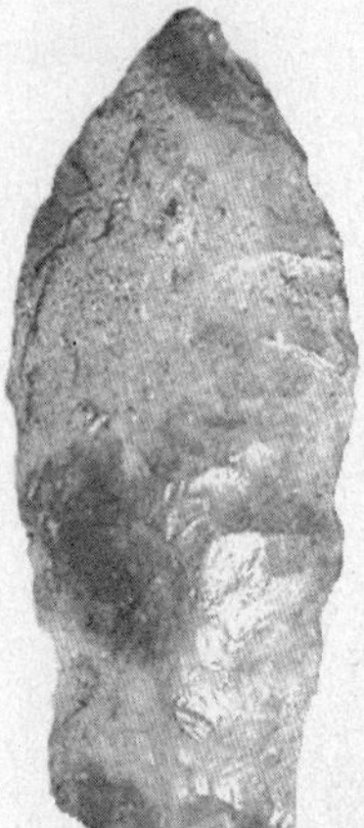

G3, $35-$60
Osage Co., OK

G5, $80-$150
Osage Co., OK

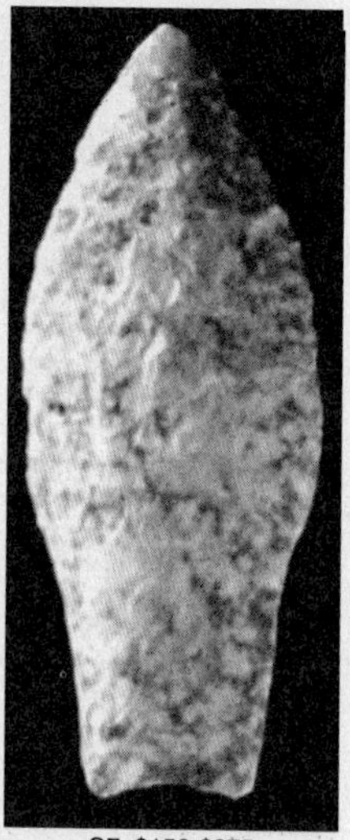

G7, $150-$275
Midland Co., TX

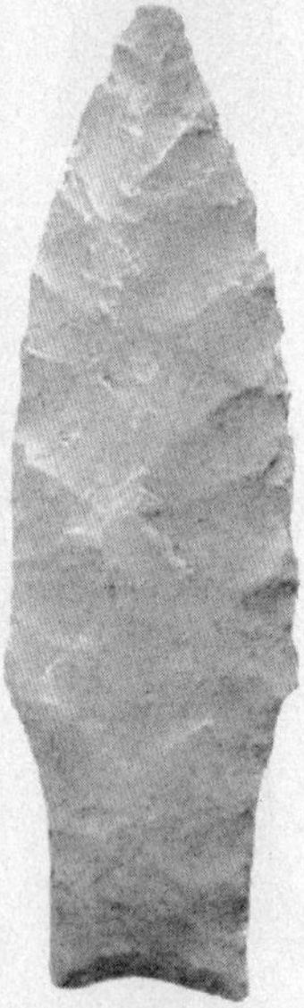

G8, $160-$300
Wise Co., TX

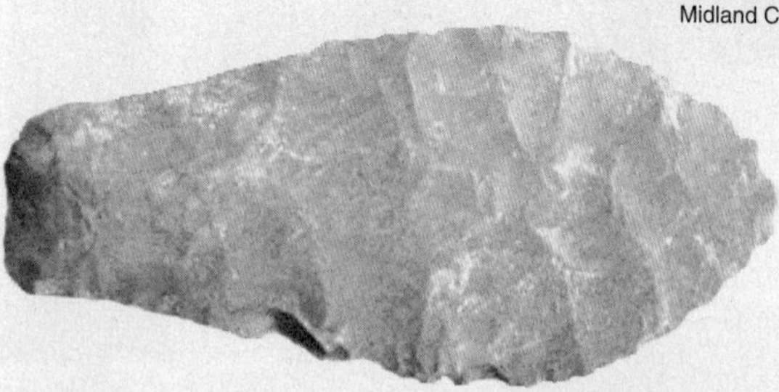

G5, $125-$200
Wilson Co., TX

LOCATION: Texas northward to Canada. **DESCRIPTION:** A medium to large size, lanceolate point with a long, contracting stem. The widest part of the blade is above mid-section. The base is straight to slightly concave and the stem edges are usually ground. **I.D. KEY:** Very high up blade stems.

G7, \$125-\$200
Tom Greene Co., TX

G8, \$150-\$250
Muscogee Co., OK

G10, \$250-\$400
TX

G7, \$175-\$300
N. OK

SC

G6, \$80-\$150
Osage Co., OK

Diagonal flaking

G6, \$125-\$200
Wilson Co., TX

Base nick

HEMPHILL - Middle Archaic, 7000 - 4000 B. P.

(Also see Big Sandy, Dalton-Hemphill, Graham Cave, Hemphill and Hickory Ridge)

LOCATION: Missouri, Illinois into Wisconsin. **DESCRIPTION:** A medium to large size side-notched point with a concave base and parallel to convex sides. These points are usually thinner and of higher quality than the similar *Osceola* type found in Wisconsin.

G4, \$15-\$30
Jonesboro, AR

715

HICKORY RIDGE - Middle Archaic, 7000 - 4000 B. P.

(Also see Big Sandy, Cache River and Hemphill)

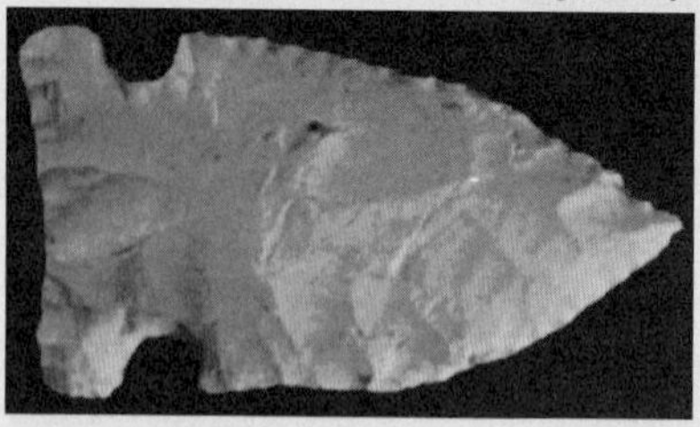

G6, $12-$20
Jonesboro, AR

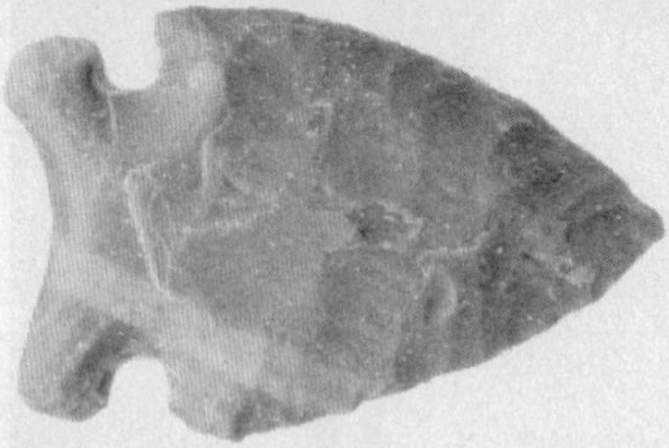

G6, $25-$40
Howard Co., AR

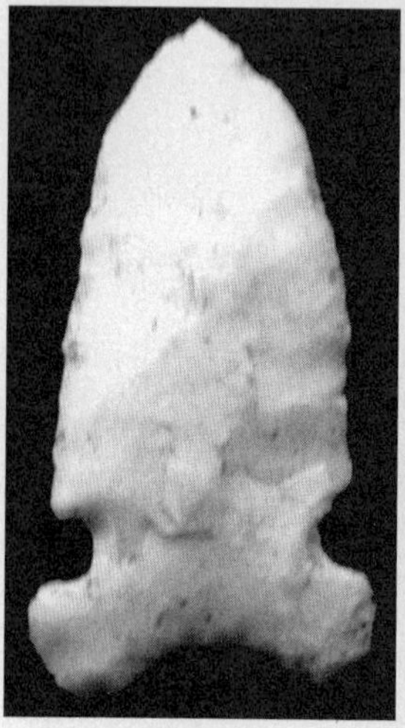

G5, $12-$20
Saline Co., AR

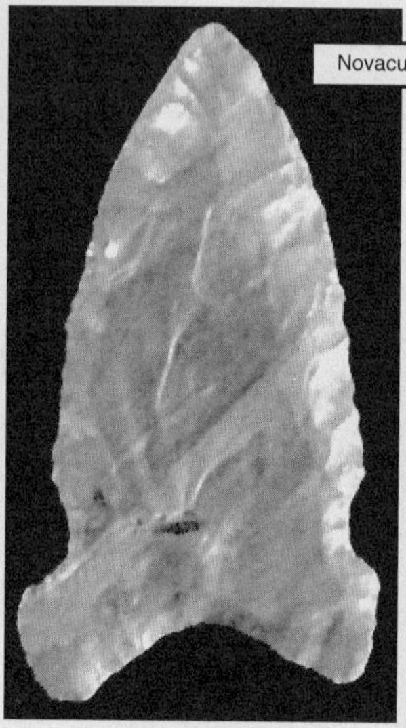

G6, $35-$60
Jonesboro, AR

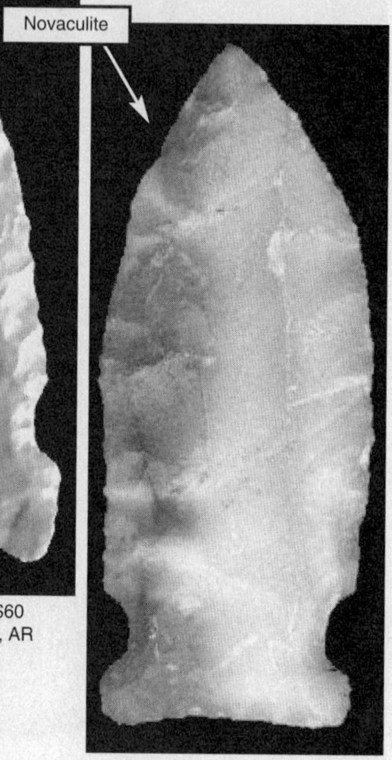
Novaculite

G7, $90-$175
Pike Co., AR

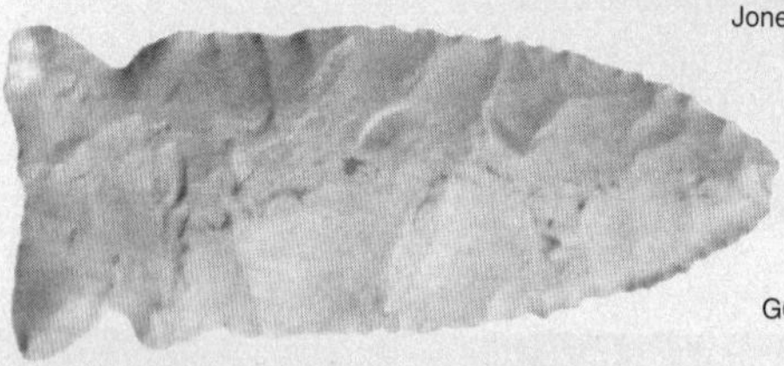

G6, $20-$35
AR

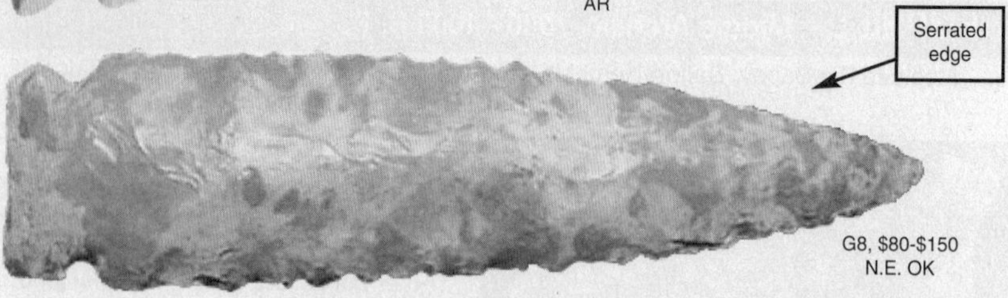
Serrated edge

G8, $80-$150
N.E. OK

LOCATION: Arkansas. **DESCRIPTION:** A medium to large size side-notched point. The base is straight to concave and early forms are ground. Basal corners are rounded to square. Side notches are usually wide. **I.D. KEY:** Broad, large side notched point.

HIDDEN VALLEY - Early to Middle Archaic, 8000 - 6000 B. P.

(Also see Burkett, Dickson, Gary, Langtry and Morrow Mountain)

G7, $35-$60
Craighead, AR

G6, $45-$80
Craighead, AR

G6, $45-$80
Craighead, AR

LOCATION: Arkansas to Wisconsin. **DESCRIPTION:** A medium size point with square to tapered shoulders and a contracting base that can be pointed to straight. Flaking is earlier and more parallel than on *Gary* points. Called *Rice Contracted Stemmed* in Missouri.

HOLLAND - Early Archaic, 10,000 - 7500 B. P.

(Also see Alberta, Dalton, Eden, Hardin and Scottsbluff)

G9, $350-$600
N. OK

G8, $325-$600
AR

HOLLAND (continued)

G6, $125-$225
N. OK

G8, $200-$350
Bowie Co., TX

G9, $350-$600
N. OK

Exotic form

G8, $300-$500
AR/MO

LOCATION: Midwestern to Northeastern states. **DESCRIPTION:** A medium to large size broad stemmed point of high quality. Shoulders are weak to nonexistant. Bases can be knobbed to auriculate and are usually ground. Some examples have horizontal to oblique transverse flaking. **I.D. KEY:** Weak shoulders, concave base.

HOMAN - Mississippian, 1000 - 700 B. P.

(Also see Agee, Alba, Colbert, Hayes, Hughes, Keota, Perdiz and Scallorn)

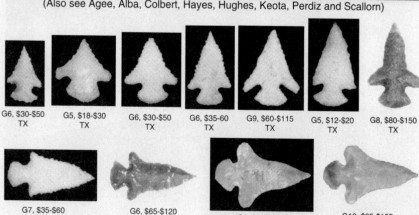

G6, $30-$50
TX

G5, $18-$30
TX

G6, $30-$50
TX

G6, $35-60
TX

G9, $60-$115
TX

G5, $12-$20
TX

G8, $80-$150
TX

G7, $35-$60
TX

G6, $65-$120
TX

G9, $100-$190
TX

G10, $65-$125
AR

718

HOMAN (continued)

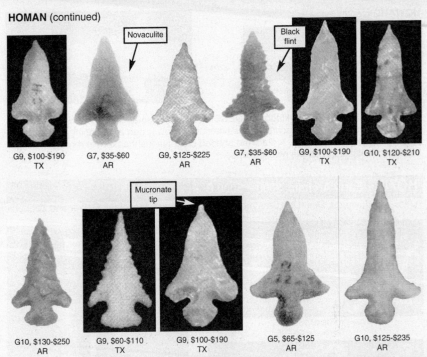

Novaculite

Black flint

G9, $100-$190
TX

G7, $35-$60
AR

G9, $125-$225
AR

G7, $35-$60
AR

G9, $100-$190
TX

G10, $120-$210
TX

Mucronate tip

G10, $130-$250
AR

G9, $60-$110
TX

G9, $100-$190
TX

G5, $65-$125
AR

G10, $125-$235
AR

LOCATION: Oklahoma to Arkansas. **DESCRIPTION:** A small size expanded barbed arrow point with a bulbous stem. Some tips are mucronate or apiculate. **I.D. KEY:** Bulbous stem.

SC

HOWARD - Mississippian, 700 - 500 B. P.

(Also see Blevins, Hayes and Sequoyah)

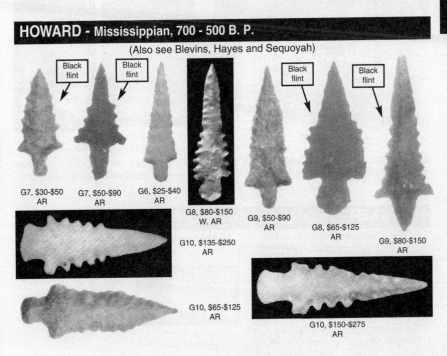

Black flint

Black flint

Black flint

Black flint

G7, $30-$50
AR

G7, $50-$90
AR

G6, $25-$40
AR

G8, $80-$150
W. AR

G9, $50-$90
AR

G8, $65-$125
AR

G9, $80-$150
AR

G10, $135-$250
AR

G10, $65-$125
AR

G10, $150-$275
AR

719

HOWARD (continued)

G9, $175-$325
W. AR

G10, $135-$250
AR

LOCATION: Louisiana to Oklahoma. **DESCRIPTION:** A small size, narrow, spike point with two or more barbs on each side, restricted to the lower part of the point and a parallel to expanding, rounded stem. A diamond shaped base places the point in the *Blevins* type. **I.D. KEY:** Multiple serrations near the base.

HOXIE - Early Archaic, 8000 - 5000 B. P.

(Also see Bulverde, Darl, Darl Stemmed, Early Stemmed Lanceolate, Gower and Zephyr)

G6, $15-$25
Comanche Co., TX

G7, $12-$20
Comanche Co., TX

Translucent

Beveled edge

G8, $60-$100
Austin, TX

G8, $35-$65
Austin, TX

G7, $20-$35
Comanche Co., TX

LOCATION: Texas. **DESCRIPTION:** A medium to large size, narrow point with weak shoulders and a parallel sided, concave base that is ground. Believed to be an early form of *Darl*.

HUFFAKER - Mississippian, 1000 - 500 B. P.

(Also see Duran, Evans, Fresno, Harrell, Haskell, Sinner and Washita)

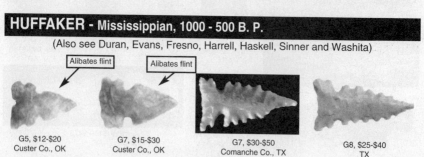

Alibates flint

Alibates flint

G5, $12-$20
Custer Co., OK

G7, $15-$30
Custer Co., OK

G7, $30-$50
Comanche Co., TX

G8, $25-$40
TX

720

HUFFAKER (continued)

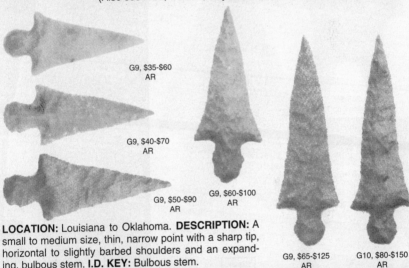

G8 $35-$60
TX

G7, $25-$45
TX

G8, $35-$60
S.W. OK

G9, $35-$60
S.W. OK

G8, $30-$50
S.W. OK

G8, $30-$50
S.W. OK

G7, $25-$40
S.W. OK

G7, $15-$30
S.W. OK

LOCATION: Texas northward to Canada. **DESCRIPTION:** A small size triangular point with a straight to concave base and double side notches. Blade edges can be heavily barbed. Bases can have a single notch. **I.D. KEY:** Double notches.

HUGHES - Mississippian, 1200 - 600 B. P.

(Also see Alba, Colbert, Hayes, Homan, Keota)

G9, $35-$60
AR

G9, $40-$70
AR

G9, $50-$90
AR

G9, $60-$100
AR

SC

LOCATION: Louisiana to Oklahoma. **DESCRIPTION:** A small to medium size, thin, narrow point with a sharp tip, horizontal to slightly barbed shoulders and an expanding, bulbous stem. **I.D. KEY:** Bulbous stem.

G9, $65-$125
AR

G10, $80-$150
AR

JAKIE STEMMED - Early Archaic, 8000 - 5000 B. P.

(Also see Cosatot River, Gower, Pedernales and Uvalde)

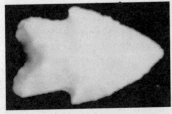

G7, $15-$30
Saline Co., AR

G8, $20-$35
Saline Co., AR

JAKIE STEMMED (continued)

LOCATION: Oklahoma, Ark., MO.
DESCRIPTION: A medium size point with an expanded to parallel sided, auriculate to bifurcated stem. Blade edges are serrated and the base is ground with rounded lobes.

G7, $25-$40
Saline Co., AR

JETTA - Early Archaic, 8000 - 5000 B. P.

(Also see Gower, Pedernales and Uvalde)

Classic basal form

Classic basal form

G5, $45-$85
Williamson Co., TX

G9, $150-$250
TX

Classic basal form

G6, $60-$100
McCullough Co., TX

G10, $500-$900
Three Rivers, TX

LOCATION: Texas to Oklahoma. **DESCRIPTION:** A medium to large size point with tapered, horizontal or short pointed shoulders and a deeply notched base. Basal tangs are rounded and the stem is more squared and wider than *Pedernalis*. A very rare type.

JOHNSON - Early to Middle Archaic, 9000 - 5000 B. P.

(Also see Bulverde and Savannah River)

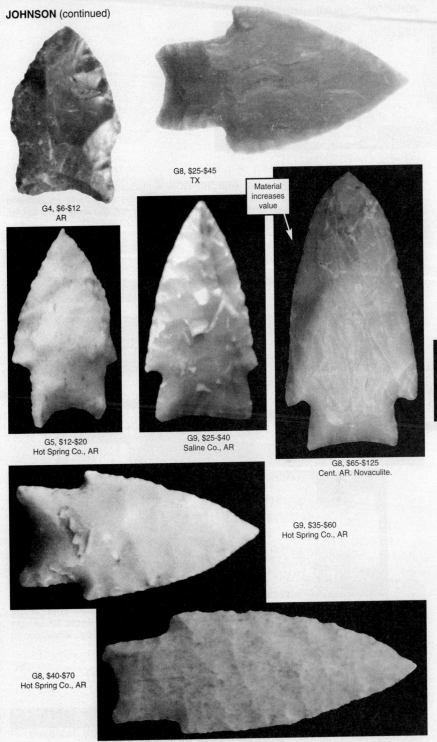

G4, $6-$12
AR

G8, $25-$45
TX

Material
increases
value

G5, $12-$20
Hot Spring Co., AR

G9, $25-$40
Saline Co., AR

G8, $65-$125
Cent. AR. Novaculite.

SC

G9, $35-$60
Hot Spring Co., AR

G8, $40-$70
Hot Spring Co., AR

JOHNSON(continued)

G5, $15-$30
AR

G6, $12-$20
Hot Spring Co., AR

LOCATION: Mississippi to Oklahoma. **DESCRIPTION:** A medium size, thick, well made, expanded stem point with a broad, short, concave base. Bases are usually thinned and grinding appears on some specimens. Shoulders can be slight and are roughly horizontal. **I.D. KEY:** Broad stem that is thinned.

JORA (see Coahuila)

KAY BLADE - Mississippian, 1000 - 600 B. P.

(Also see Cupp, Epps, Motley)

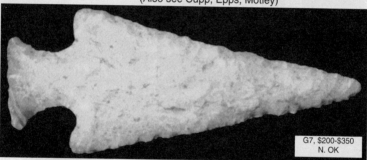

G7, $200-$350
N. OK

G7, $200-$350
N. OK

LOCATION: Oklahoma into mid-western states. **DESCRIPTION:** A medium to large size corner notched point with a long expanding stem and barbed shoulders. Bases are straight to almost convex. Used by the Mississippian, Caddoan people. **I.D. KEY:** Broad corner notches.

KEITHVILLE (See San Patrice - Keithville)

KEOTA - Mississippian, 800 - 600 B. P.

(Also see Agee, Alba, Colbert, Dardanelle, Hayes, Homan, Hughes and Sequoyah)

KEOTA (continued)

G3, $5-$10
Comanche
Co., TX

G9, $80-$140
TX

LOCATION: Texas, Arkansas to Oklahoma. **DESCRIPTION:** A small size, thin, triangular, side to corner-notched point with a rounded, bulbous base. The basal area is large on some specimens. **I.D. KEY:** Large bulbous base.

G8, $35-$125
Spiro Mound, OK

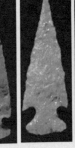

G9, $90-$175 ea.
Spiro Mound, OK

KERRVILLE KNIFE - Middle to Late Archaic, 5000 - 3000 B. P.

(Also see Chopper and Scraper)

SC

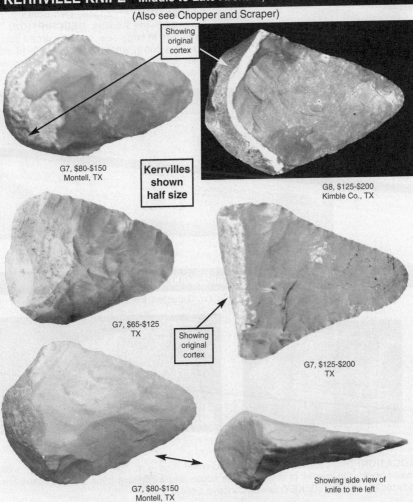

Showing original cortex

G7, $80-$150
Montell, TX

Kerrvilles shown half size

G8, $125-$200
Kimble Co., TX

G7, $65-$125
TX

Showing original cortex

G7, $125-$200
TX

G7, $80-$150
Montell, TX

Showing side view of knife to the left

725

KERRVILLE KNIFE (continued)

LOCATION: Midwestern states. **DESCRIPTION:** A large size, thick, triangular cutting or chopping tool with straight to slightly convex edges. The original rind occurs at the base. Also called fist axes.

Showing original cortex

Kerrvilles shown half size

G10, $90-$175
TX

KINGS - Middle Archaic, 5000 - 2000 B. P.

(Also see Big Creek, Cupp, Epps and Motley)

G3, $12-$20
TX

LOCATION: Arkansas, Oklahoma into Missouri and Kansas. **DESCRIPTION:** A medium to large size, corner notched point with strong, sharp shoulders and an expanding base. Bases are straight, concave or convex.

G9, $125-$225
N.E. OK

KINNEY - Middle Archaic-Woodland, 5000 - 2000 B. P.

(Also see Darl Blade, Early Triangular, Gahagan, Pandora and Tortugas)

G3, $6-$12
Comanche Co., TX

G3, $8-$15
Comanche Co., TX

LOCATION: Texas. **DESCRIPTION:** A medium to large size, thin, broad, lanceolate, well made blade with convex to straight blade edges and a concave base. Basal corners are pointed to rounded. **I.D. KEY:** Broad, concave base.

726

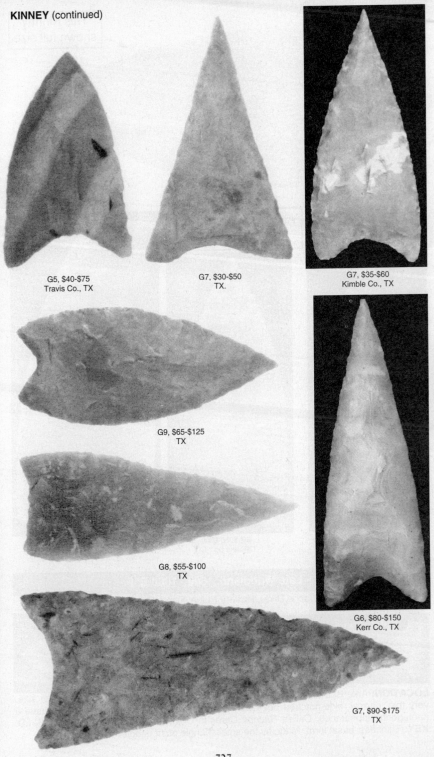

G5, $40-$75
Travis Co., TX

G7, $30-$50
TX.

G7, $35-$60
Kimble Co., TX

G9, $65-$125
TX

G8, $55-$100
TX

SC

G6, $80-$150
Kerr Co., TX

G7, $90-$175
TX

727

KINNEY (continued)

This Kinney shown full size

G8, $250-$400
Big Bend, TX

All Kinneys below are shown half size

G9, $275-$500
Coryell Co., TX

G9, $350-$600
Gillespie Co., TX

G9, $450-$900
Williamson Co., TX

KNIGHT ISLAND - Late Woodland, 1500 - 1000 B. P.

(Also see Brewerton, Cache River, Hickory Ridge, Reed, Schustorm and White River)

G10, $125-$200
N.E. AR

G7, $30-$50
N.E., AR

LOCATION: Arkansas to Southeastern states. **DESCRIPTION:** A small to medium size, very thin, narrow, side-notched point with a straight base. Longer examples can have a pentagonal appearance. Called *Racoon Creek* in Ohio. A side-notched Jacks Reef. **I.D. KEY:** Thinness, basal form. Made by the small triangle point people.

LA JITA - Middle Archaic, 7000 - 4000 B. P.

(Also see Axtel, Palmillas and Williams)

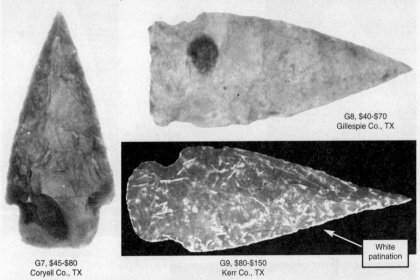

G8, $40-$70
Gillespie Co., TX

G7, $45-$80
Coryell Co., TX

G9, $80-$150
Kerr Co., TX

White patination

LOCATION: Texas. **DESCRIPTION:** A medium to large size, broad point with weak shoulders and a broad, bulbous base that expands and has rounded basal corners. **I.D. KEY:** Large bulbous base.

SC

LAMPASAS (See Zephyr)

LANGE - Middle Archaic to Woodland, 6000 - 1000 B. P.

(Also see Bulverde, Castorville, Morrill, Nolan and Travis)

G4, $5-$10
AR

G5, $8-$15
Comanche Co., TX

G6, $20-$35
Austin, TX

LOCATION: Louisiana to Texas to Oklahoma. **DESCRIPTION:** A medium to large size, narrow, expanded stem dart point with tapered to horizontal, barbed shoulders and a straight to convex base. **I.D. KEY:** Expanding base, tapered to horizontal shoulders.

729

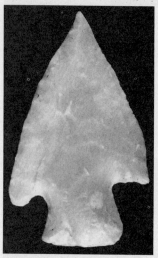

G7, $35-$50
Comal Co., TX

G8, $35-$65
Bexar Co., TX

G6, $35-$65
Bexar Co., TX

G7, $20-$35
Comanche Co., TX

Worn tip

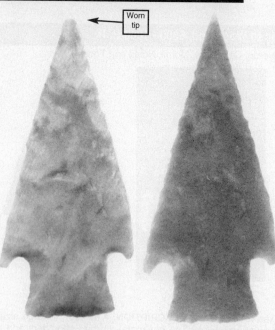

G7, $35-$65
TX

G9, $80-$150
TX

G9, $100-$180
TX

LANGTRY - Middle Archaic to Woodland, 5000 - 2000 B. P.

(Also see Almagre, Gary, Hidden Valley, Morrow Mountain and Val Verde)

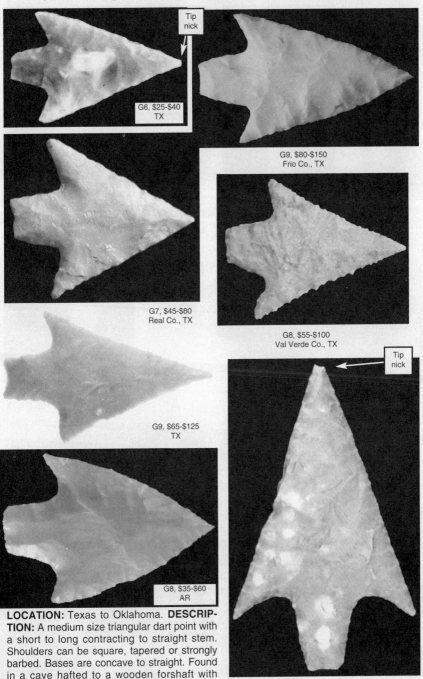

Tip nick

G6, $25-$40
TX

G9, $80-$150
Frio Co., TX

G7, $45-$80
Real Co., TX

G8, $55-$100
Val Verde Co., TX

SC

G9, $65-$125
TX

Tip nick

G8, $35-$60
AR

LOCATION: Texas to Oklahoma. **DESCRIPTION:** A medium size triangular dart point with a short to long contracting to straight stem. Shoulders can be square, tapered or strongly barbed. Bases are concave to straight. Found in a cave hafted to a wooden forshaft with pitch. **I.D. KEY:** Strong barbs, tapered stem.

G8, $80-$150
Kimble Co., TX

731

LANGTRY-ARENOSA - Middle Archaic to Woodland, 5000 - 2000 B. P.

(Also see Coahuila)

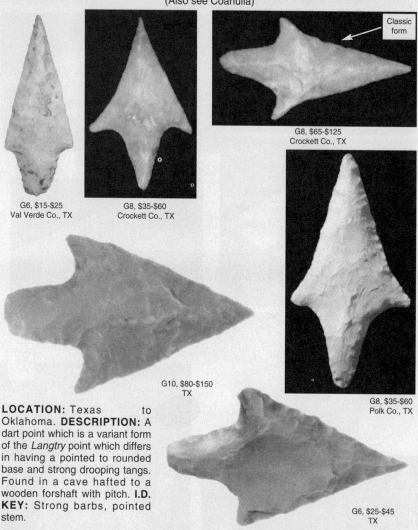

Classic form

G6, $15-$25
Val Verde Co., TX

G8, $35-$60
Crockett Co., TX

G8, $65-$125
Crockett Co., TX

G10, $80-$150
TX

G8, $35-$60
Polk Co., TX

G6, $25-$45
TX

LOCATION: Texas to Oklahoma. **DESCRIPTION:** A dart point which is a variant form of the *Langtry* point which differs in having a pointed to rounded base and strong drooping tangs. Found in a cave hafted to a wooden forshaft with pitch. **I.D. KEY:** Strong barbs, pointed stem.

LEFLORE BLADE - Mississippian-Historic, 500 - 250 B. P.

(Also see Agate Basin, Lerma)

G8, $175-$300
McIntosh Co., OK

LEFLORE BLADE (continued)

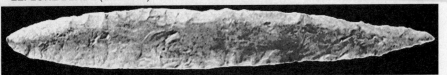

G8, $150-$275
McIntosh Co., OK

LOCATION: Oklahoma to N. Texas and Kansas. **DESCRIPTION:** A large size, narrow lanceolate, bi-pointed blade. Blade edges are usually smoothed. Much more narrow than *Lerma* points. **I.D. KEY:** Narrow width in relation to length.

LERMA POINTED BASE - Early Archaic, 9000 - 8000 B. P.

(Also see Agate Basin, Angostura, Desmuke, Harahey & LeFlore Blade)

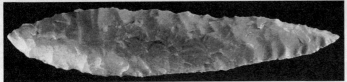

G8, $70-$135
Austin, TX

G6, $80-$150
TX

G8, $150-$250
Comanche Co., TX

G10, $175-$325
Wilson Co., TX

LOCATION: Siberia to Alaska, Canada, Mexico, South America and across the U.S. **DESCRIPTION:** A large size, narrow, lanceolate blade with a pointed base. Most are fairly thick in cross section but finer examples can be thin. Flaking tends to be collateral. Basal areas can be ground. Western forms are beveled on one side of each face. Similar forms have been found in Europe and Africa dating back to 20,000 - 40,000 B.P., but didn't enter the U.S. until after the advent of *Clovis*. **NOTE:** Lerma may be much older.

733

LERMA ROUNDED BASE - Early Archaic, 9000 - 8000 B. P.

(Also see Agate Basin, Angostura, Covington and Harahey)

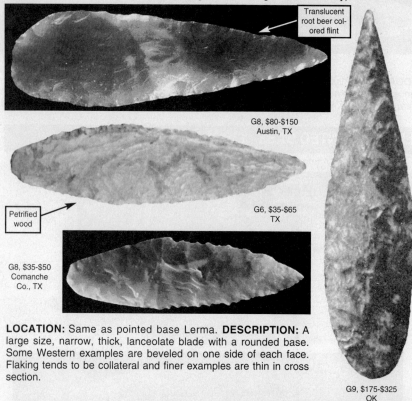

Translucent root beer colored flint

G8, $80-$150
Austin, TX

Petrified wood

G6, $35-$65
TX

G8, $35-$50
Comanche Co., TX

G9, $175-$325
OK

LOCATION: Same as pointed base Lerma. **DESCRIPTION:** A large size, narrow, thick, lanceolate blade with a rounded base. Some Western examples are beveled on one side of each face. Flaking tends to be collateral and finer examples are thin in cross section.

LITTLE RIVER - Mid to Late Archaic, 5000 -3000 B. P.

(Also see Smith)

Novaculite

G10, $125-$225
AR

LOCATION: NW Louisiana to Eastern Oklahoma. **DESCRIPTION:** A large size, broad point with an expanding to parallel sided stem. Shoulders are sharp to rounded and can extend almost to the base. The base is straight to slightly convex or concave. **I.D. KEY:** Base form.

734

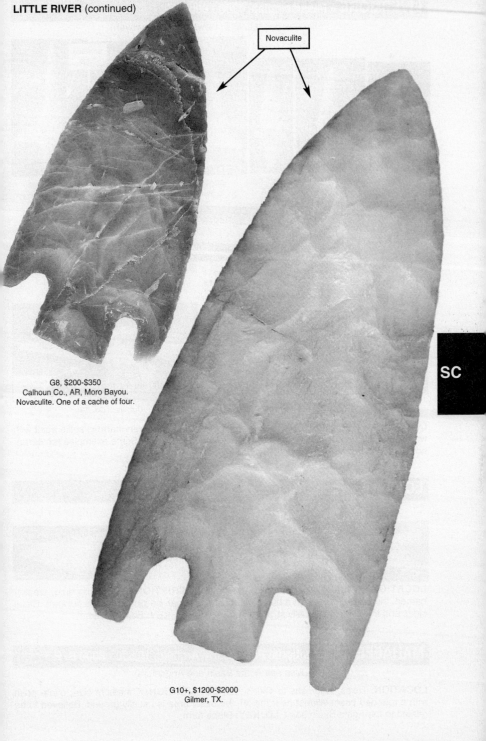

Novaculite

G8, $200-$350
Calhoun Co., AR, Moro Bayou.
Novaculite. One of a cache of four.

SC

G10+, $1200-$2000
Gilmer, TX.

LIVERMORE - Mississippian, 1200 - 600 B. P.

(Also see Bassett, Drill, Howard and Sequoyah)

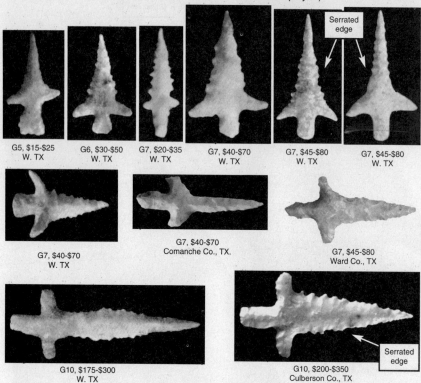

Serrated edge

G5, $15-$25
W. TX

G6, $30-$50
W. TX

G7, $20-$35
W. TX

G7, $40-$70
W. TX

G7, $45-$80
W. TX

G7, $45-$80
W. TX

G7, $40-$70
W. TX

G7, $40-$70
Comanche Co., TX.

G7, $45-$80
Ward Co., TX

G10, $175-$300
W. TX

G10, $200-$350
Culberson Co., TX

Serrated edge

LOCATION: Texas. **DESCRIPTION:** A small to medium size, very narrow, spike point with wide flaring barbs and a narrow stem that can be short to long. Some examples are serrated. **I.D. KEY:** Extreme narrowness of blade.

LOTT - Mississippian to Historic, 500 - 300 B. P.

(Also see Garza and Harrell)

G10, $90-$175
Garza Co., TX

G9, $55-$100
Garza Co., TX

LOCATION: Texas to Arizona. A rare type. **DESCRIPTION:** A medium size, weakly barbed, thin, arrow point with a bifurcated base. Ears can be long and flare outward. Basal sides and the base are usually straight. A rare type. **I.D. KEY:** Form of ears.

MAHAFFEY - Transitional Paleo-Early Archaic, 10,500 - 8000 B. P.

(Also see Agate Basin and Angostura)

LOCATION: Texas, Arkansas to Oklahoma. **DESCRIPTION:** A medium size, ovate point with a rounded base. Widest near the tip, the basal area is usually ground. Believed to be related to the Agate Basin point. **I.D. KEY:** Blade form.

MAHAFFEY (continued)

G8, $40-$70
Saline Co., AR

G8, $55-$100
N.E. OK

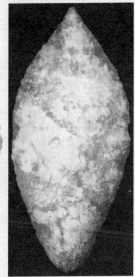

SC

G8, $65-$125
N.E. OK

G8, $200-$350
Wilson Co., TX

G9, $200-$350
TX

G8, $150-$250
Amarillo, TX

MARCOS - Late Archaic to Woodland, 3500 - 1800 B. P.

(Also see Castroville, Ensor, Fairland, Marshall and San Jacinto)

G7, $30-$50
Montell, TX

G10, $80-$150
TX

G10, $65-$125
TX

737

MARCOS (continued)

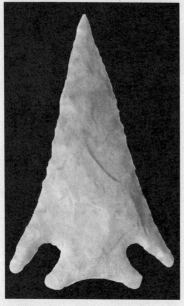

G10, $250-$450
TX

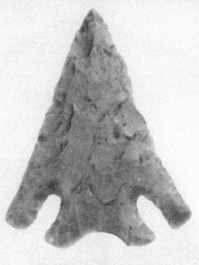

G6, $35-$65
TX

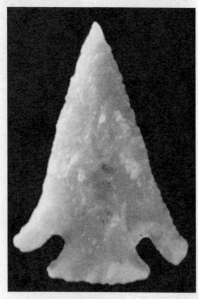

G9, $200-$350
TX

G10, $400-$750
Coryell Co., TX

LOCATION: Texas to Oklahoma. **DESCRIPTION:** A small to medium size, broad, corner notched point with an expanded stem. The blade edges are straight to recurved. Many examples have long barbs and a sharp pointed tip. Bases are convex, straight or concave. **I.D. KEY:** Angle of corner notches.

MARSHALL - Middle Archaic to Woodland, 6000 - 2000 B. P.

(Also see Castroville, Ensor, Marcos and San Jacinto)

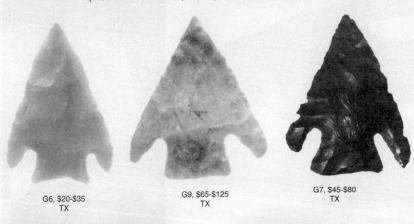

G6, $20-$35
TX

G9, $65-$125
TX

G7, $45-$80
TX

G7, $45-$80
Kimble Co., TX

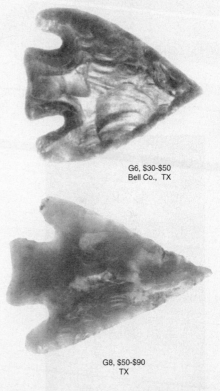

G6, $30-$50
Bell Co., TX

G8, $50-$90
TX

SC

G7, $55-$100
Kimble Co., TX

LOCATION: Texas to Colorado. **DESCRIPTION:** A medium to large size, broad, high quality, corner to basal notched point with long barbs that turn inward towards the base. Notching is less angled than in *Marcos*. Bases are straight to concave to bifurcated. **I.D. KEY:** Drooping tangs.

739

G9, $150-$250
Kimble Co., TX

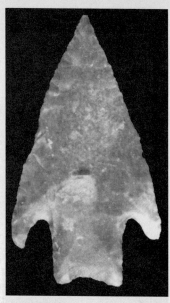

G8, $125-$200
Comal Co., TX

G7, $80-$150
TX

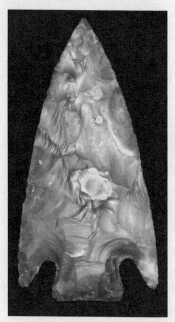

G9, $275-$450
Kerr Co., TX

G8, $165-$300
Belton, TX

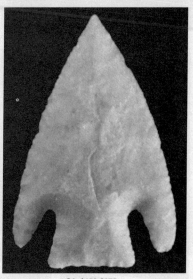

G9, $150-$275
Uvalde Co., TX

SC

G9, $200-$350
Austin, TX

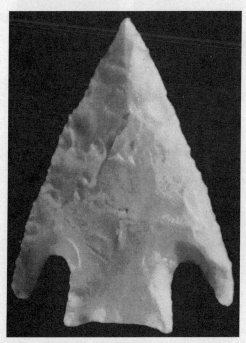

G8, $165-$300
Austin, TX

G8, $250-$450
Bell Co., TX

MARTINDALE - Early Archaic, 8000 - 5000 B. P.

(Also see Bandy, Marcos and Marshall)

LOCATION: Texas to Oklahoma. **DESCRIPTION:** A medium size corner notched to expanded stem point. The base is unique in that it is formed by two curves meeting at the center. Called *Bandy* in southern Texas. **I.D. KEY:** Basal form, early flaking.

G6, $25-$40
Comanche Co, TX

Caliche on surface

Black chert

Note typical "fishtailed" base

Minor side and tang damage

G7, $80-$150
Austin, TX

G8, $150-$250
Williamson Co., TX

G10, $275-$400
Austin, TX

MATAMOROS - Late Archaic to Mississippian, 3000 - 300 B. P.

(Also see Abasolo, Catan and Tortugas)

G8, $15-$25
TX

G7, $8-$15
TX

G6, $8-$15
TX

LOCATION: Texas. **DESCRIPTION:** A small to medium size, broad, triangular point with concave, straight, or convex base. On some examples, beveling occurs on one side of each face as in *Tortugas* points. Larger points would fall under the *Tortugas* type.

MATAMOROS (continued)

Petrified wood

Petrified wood

G7, $8-$15
TX

G8, $25-$45
TX

G8, $25-$45
TX

G8, $20-$35
TX

MATANZAS - Mid-Archaic to Mississippian, 4500 - 3000 B. P.

(Also see Palmillas)

LOCATION: Arkansas to Missouri. **DESCRIPTION:** A medium size, narrow, side notched dart point with an expanding stem and a straight base.

G7, $30-$50
AR

SC

MAUD - Mississippian, 800 - 500 B. P.

(Also see Fresno, Starr and Talco)

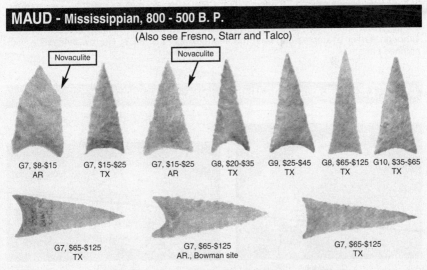

Novaculite

Novaculite

G7, $8-$15
AR

G7, $15-$25
TX

G7, $15-$25
AR

G8, $20-$35
TX

G9, $25-$45
TX

G8, $65-$125
TX

G10, $35-$65
TX

G7, $65-$125
TX

G7, $65-$125
AR., Bowman site

G7, $65-$125
TX

LOCATION: Texas, Arkansas to Oklahoma. **DESCRIPTION:** A small size, thin, triangular arrow point with straight to convex sides and a concave base. Basal corners are sharp. Associated with the Caddo culture in the Midwest. Blades are usually very finely serrated. **I.D. KEY:** Convex sides, sharp basal corners.

743

MAUD (continued)

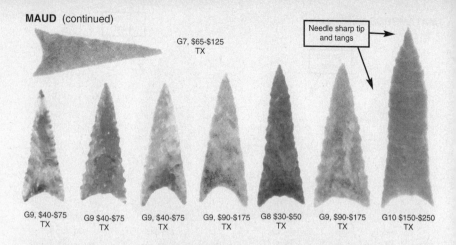

G7, $65-$125
TX

Needle sharp tip
and tangs →

G9, $40-$75
TX

G9 $40-$75
TX

G9, $40-$75
TX

G9, $90-$175
TX

G8 $30-$50
TX

G9, $90-$175
TX

G10 $150-$250
TX

MCKEAN - Middle to Late Archaic, 4500 - 2500 B. P.

(Also see Angostura, Folsom, Goshen)

G9, $250-$450
N. OK

LOCATION: N. Plains into Oklahoma. **DESCRIPTION:** A small to medium size, narrow, basal notched point. No basal grinding is evident. Similar to the much earlier *Wheeler* points of the Southeast. Basal ears are rounded to pointed. Flaking is more random although earlier examples can have parallel flaking. **I.D. KEY:** Narrow lanceolate with notched base.

MERKLE - Mid-Archaic to Mississippian, 4500 - 3000 B. P.

(Also see Duran, Evans, Sinner)

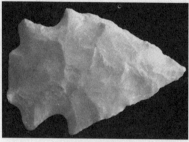

G6, $25-$50
Saline Co., AR

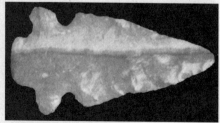

G7, $35-$60
N. OK

LOCATION: Arkansas to Missouri. **DESCRIPTION:** A medium size, side notched dart point with a short stem formed by corner notches. The base is straight. **I.D. KEY:** Straight base and double notches.

744

MERKLE (continued)

G5, $12-$20
Saline Co., AR

G7, $20-$35
AR

MESERVE - Early Archaic, 9500 - 4000 B. P.

(Also see Angostura, Dalton and Plainview)

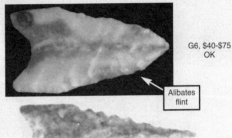

G6, $40-$75
OK

Alibates flint

G5, $25-$40
TX

G5, $35-$60
Amarillo, TX

G5, $60-$100
Abilene, TX

SC

G5, $35-$60
Abilene, TX

G8, $80-$150
Osage Co., OK

G6, $80-$150
Austin, TX

G6, $150-$250
N.E. OK

G8, $125-$200
Kay Co., OK

G7, $65-$125
Bell Co., TX

745

MESERVE (continued)

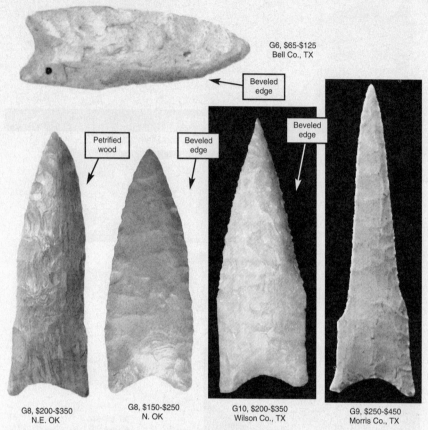

G6, $65-$125
Bell Co., TX

Beveled edge

Petrified wood

Beveled edge

Beveled edge

Beveled edge

G8, $200-$350
N.E. OK

G8, $150-$250
N. OK

G10, $200-$350
Wilson Co., TX

G9, $250-$450
Morris Co., TX

LOCATION: Texas westward to Arizona and northward to Montana. **DESCRIPTION:** A medium size, auriculate point with a blade that is beveled on one side of each face. Beveling extends into the basal area. This type is the western form of *Dalton* points.

MID-BACK TANG - Late Archaic to Woodland, 4000 - 2000 B. P.

(Also see Base Tang Knife and Corner Tang)

Leon River chert

G7, $250-$475
Coryell Co., TX.

746

MID-BACK TANG (continued)

LOCATION: Texas. **DESCRIPTION:** A variation of the corner tang knife with the hafting area occuring near the center of one side of the blade. A very rare type.

Classic form

G6, $200-$350
Coleman Co., TX

MIDLAND - Transitional Paleo, 10,700 - 9000 B. P.

(Also see Angostura, Arkabutla, Clovis, Folsom, Goshen, Milnesand and Plainview)

SC

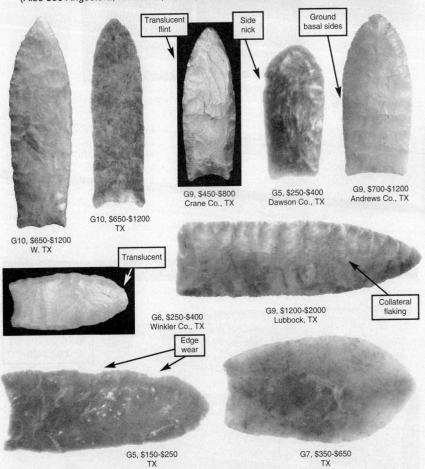

Translucent flint

Side nick

Ground basal sides

G9, $450-$800
Crane Co., TX

G5, $250-$400
Dawson Co., TX

G9, $700-$1200
Andrews Co., TX

G10, $650-$1200
TX

G10, $650-$1200
W. TX

Translucent

G6, $250-$400
Winkler Co., TX

G9, $1200-$2000
Lubbock, TX

Collateral flaking

Edge wear

G5, $150-$250
TX

G7, $350-$650
TX

LOCATION: Texas northward to Canada. **DESCRIPTION:** An unfluted *Folsom*. A small to medium size, thin, unfluted lanceolate point with parallel to convex sides. Basal thinning is weak and the blades exhibit fine micro edgework. Bases usually have a shallow concavity and are ground most of the way to the tip.

747

MILNESAND - Transitional Paleo, 11,000 - 8000 B. P.

(Also see Agate Basin, Angostura, Browns Valley, Firstview, Hell Gap and Rio Grande)

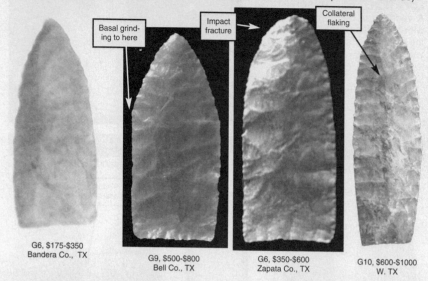

Basal grinding to here

Impact fracture

Collateral flaking

G6, $175-$350
Bandera Co., TX

G9, $500-$800
Bell Co., TX

G6, $350-$600
Zapata Co., TX

G10, $600-$1000
W. TX

G6, $250-$450
Cent. TX

LOCATION: Texas, New Mexico, northward to Canada and Alaska. **DESCRIPTION:** A medium size unfluted lanceolate point that becomes thicker and wider towards the tip. The base is basically square and ground. Thicker than *Midland*. **I.D. KEY:** Square base and Paleo flaking.

MINERAL SPRINGS - Mississippian, 1300 - 1000 B. P.

(Also see Gahagan)

IMPORTANT:
Both Mineral Springs shown half size

G9, $575-$1100
TX

G10+, $2500-$4000
Little River Co., AR.
Outstanding quality.

MINERAL SPRINGS (continued)

LOCATION: Texas, Oklahoma, Arkansas and Louisiana. **DESCRIPTION:** A broad, large size knife with recurved sides, sharp basal corners and a concave base. Some examples have notches at the basal corners.

MONTELL - Mid-Archaic to late Woodland, 5000 - 1000 B. P.

(Also see Ensor Split-Base and Uvalde)

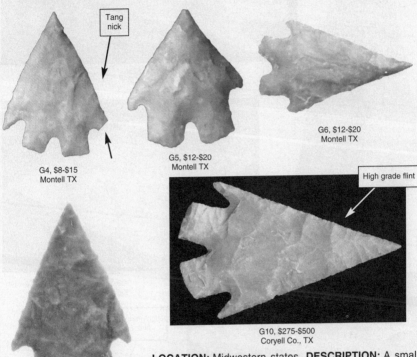

Tang nick

G4, $8-$15
Montell TX

G5, $12-$20
Montell TX

G6, $12-$20
Montell TX

High grade flint

G10, $275-$500
Coryell Co., TX

G6, $20-$35
TX

SC

LOCATION: Midwestern states. **DESCRIPTION:** A small to medium size, bifurcated point with barbed shoulders. The ears are usually squared and some examples are beveled on one side of each face and are serrated. The deep basal notch "buck tooth" form is the preferred style. **I.D. KEY:** Square basal lobes.

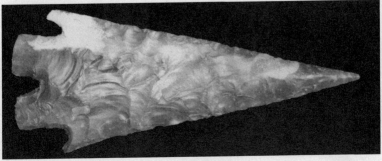

G10, $350-$600
Kerr Co., TX

749

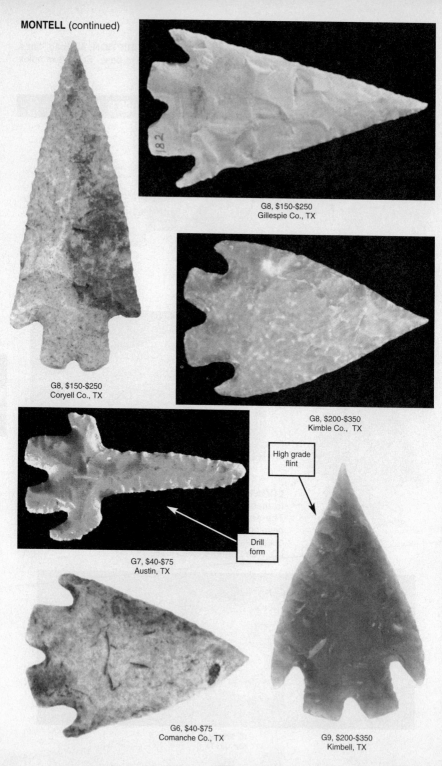

MONTELL (continued)

G8, $150-$250
Gillespie Co., TX

G8, $150-$250)
Coryell Co., TX

G8, $200-$350
Kimble Co., TX

Drill form

G7, $40-$75
Austin, TX

High grade flint

G6, $40-$75
Comanche Co., TX

G9, $200-$350
Kimbell, TX

750

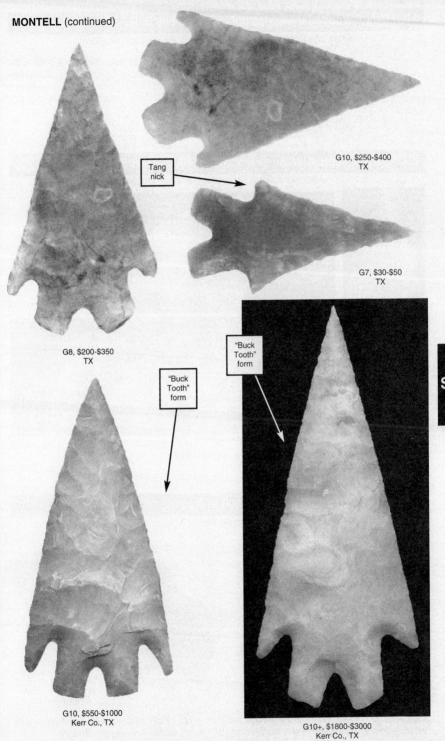

Tang nick

G10, $250-$400
TX

G7, $30-$50
TX

G8, $200-$350
TX

"Buck Tooth" form

"Buck Tooth" form

SC

G10, $550-$1000
Kerr Co., TX

G10+, $1800-$3000
Kerr Co., TX

MORAN - Woodland-Mississippian, 1200 - 600 B. P.

(Also see Bonham, Colbert, Rockwall, Sabinal and Scallorn)

G9, $60-$100
TX

LOCATION: Central Texas. **DESCRIPTION:** A small, thin, barbed arrow point with a narrow, rectangular base. Shoulders barbs are usually sharp. Very limited distributional area.

MORHISS - Late Archaic to Woodland, 4000 - 1000 B. P.

(Also see Adena, Bulverde, Carrolton and Morrill)

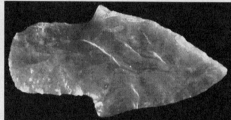

G5, $20-$35
Comanche Co., TX

G3, $2-$4
Hill Co., TX

G5, $25-$40
Victoria Co., TX

LOCATION: Texas to Oklahoma. **DESCRIPTION:** A medium to large size, thick, long stemmed point with weak shoulders and a convex base.

MORRILL - Woodland, 3000 - 1000 B. P.

(Also see Carrolton, Lange, Morhiss, Pontchartrain, Wells and Yarbrough)

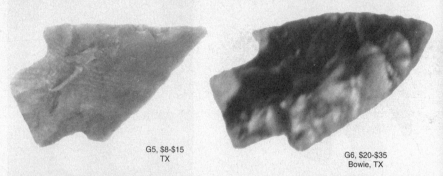

G5, $8-$15
TX

G6, $20-$35
Bowie, TX

LOCATION: Texas. **DESCRIPTION:** A medium size, thick, narrow, triangular point with weak, squared shoulders and a long rectangular stem. Bases are usually straight.

MORRILL (continued)

G6, $30-$50
Saline Co., AR

G7, $35-$60
Llano Co., TX

G8, $65-$125
Bell Co., TX

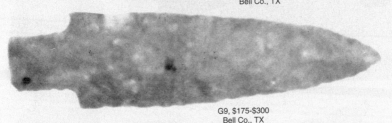

G9, $175-$300
Bell Co., TX

MORRIS - Mississippian, 1200 - 400 B. P.

(Also see Cuney, Friley and Sallisaw)

G4, $6-$12
TX

G4, $15-$30
AR

G5, $25-$40
Spiro Mound,
OK

G6 $35-$50
AR

Crystal quartz

G8, $150-$250
AR

G6, $30-$50
Comanche Co.,
TX

G6, $25-$40
Spiro Mound,
OK

LOCATION: Texas to Oklahoma. **DES-CRIPTION:** A small size, thin, barbed point with a bifurcated base and rounded ears. Blade edges can be serrated. **I.D. KEY:** Rounded basal ears.

G5, $65-$125
Spiro Mound, OK

753

MORROW MOUNTAIN (See Hale and Peisker Diamond)

MOTLEY - Middle Archaic to Woodland, 4500 - 2500 B. P.

(Also see Cupp, Epps, Gibson, Grand and Kings)

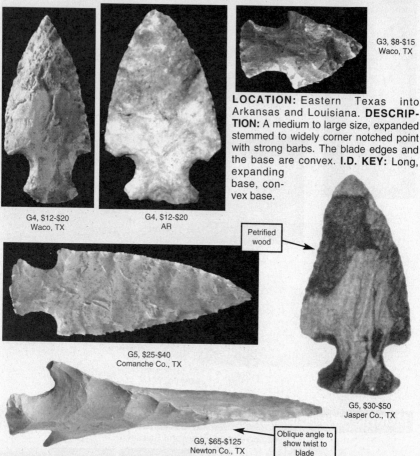

G3, $8-$15
Waco, TX

LOCATION: Eastern Texas into Arkansas and Louisiana. **DESCRIPTION:** A medium to large size, expanded stemmed to widely corner notched point with strong barbs. The blade edges and the base are convex. **I.D. KEY:** Long, expanding base, convex base.

G4, $12-$20
Waco, TX

G4, $12-$20
AR

Petrified wood

G5, $25-$40
Comanche Co., TX

G5, $30-$50
Jasper Co., TX

G9, $65-$125
Newton Co., TX

Oblique angle to show twist to blade

NEOSHO - Late Archaic, 400 - 250 B. P.

(Also see Palmillas)

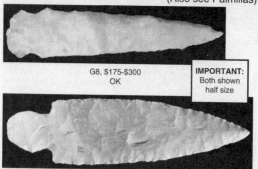

G8, $175-$300
OK

IMPORTANT: Both shown half size

LOCATION: Texas, Colorado, Oklahoma, into Arkansas & Missouri. **DESCRIPTION:** A large size, narrow knife form with broad to narrow side notches and a short, convex to a long tapered stem that can be pointed to rounded. Related to the *Harahey* Knife.

G7, $165-$300
Cache Riv., AR
Harrison form.

754

NEOSHO (continued)

IMPORTANT:
Shown half size

G7, $350-$600
S.W. TX

NODENA - Mississippian to Historic, 600 - 400 B. P.

(Also see Dardanelle, Guerrero and Guntersville)

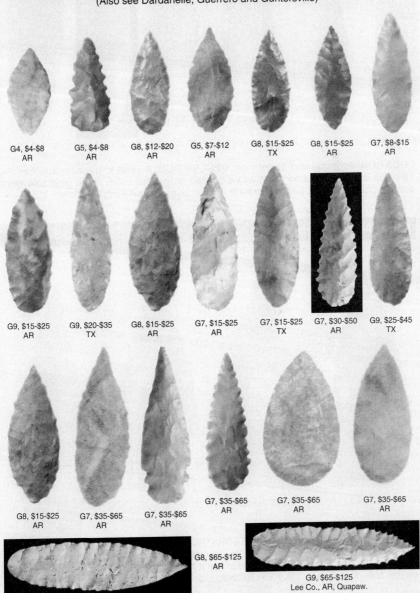

G4, $4-$8
AR

G5, $4-$8
AR

G8, $12-$20
AR

G5, $7-12
AR

G8, $15-$25
TX

G8, $15-$25
AR

G7, $8-$15
AR

G9, $15-$25
AR

G9, $20-$35
TX

G8, $15-$25
AR

G7, $15-$25
AR

G7, $15-$25
TX

G7, $30-$50
AR

G9, $25-$45
TX

G8, $15-$25
AR

G7, $35-$65
AR

G7, $35-$65
AR

G7, $35-$65
AR

G7, $35-$65
AR

G7, $35-$65
AR

G8, $65-$125
AR

G9, $65-$125
Lee Co., AR, Quapaw.

SC

755

NODENA (continued)

G9, $80-$150
AR

G8, $15-$25
AR

G7, $35-$65
AR

G7, $40-$70
TX

G9, $25-$45
TX

G9, $80-$150
AR

G7, $40-$70
Lufkin, TX

LOCATION: Arkansas and Tennessee. **DESCRIPTION:** A small to medium size, narrow, thin, elliptical shaped arrow point with a pointed to rounded base. Some examples have oblique, parallel flaking. Called *Tampa* in Florida. Used by the Quapaw Indians.

NOLAN - Mid-Archaic, 6000 - 4000 B. P.

(Also see Bulverde, Lange, Travis and Zorra)

G4, $8-$15
TX

G5, $12-$20
TX

G7, $15-$25
TX

G7, $65-$125
TX

LOCATION: Texas to Oklahoma. **DESCRIPTION:** A medium to large size, stemmed point with a needle like point. Shoulders are tapered to rounded. The stem is unique in that it is steeply beveled on one side of each face. **I.D. KEY:** Beveled stem.

NOLAN (continued)

Beveled stem on opposite faces

G7, $60-$100
Llano Co., TX

G8, $65-$125
Killeen, TX

G5, $35-$60
Comanche Co., TX

Unusual "eared" base

G7, $80-$150
Williamson Co., TX.

SC

Beveled stem on opposite faces

G9, $165-$300
Bell Co., TX

Beveled stem on opposite faces

G9, $150-$250
Austin, TX

Beveled stem on opposite faces

G7, $80-$150
Burnet Co., TX

757

NOLAN (continued)

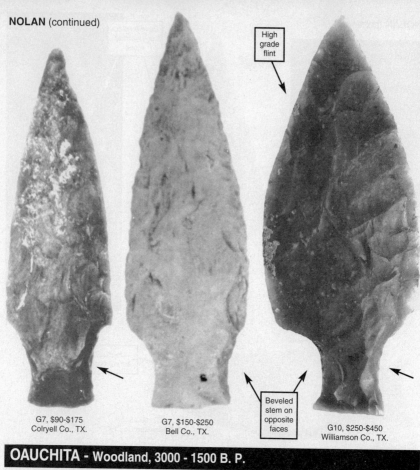

High grade flint

Beveled stem on opposite faces

G7, $90-$175
Colryell Co., TX.

G7, $150-$250
Bell Co., TX.

G10, $250-$450
Williamson Co., TX.

OAUCHITA - Woodland, 3000 - 1500 B. P.

(Also see Base Tang and Pontchartrain)

LOCATION: Texas.
DESCRIPTION: A large, broad, point with a short parallel stem and drooping shoulders.

G10, $700-$1200
Red River Co., TX

IMPORTANT: All Oauchitas shown half size

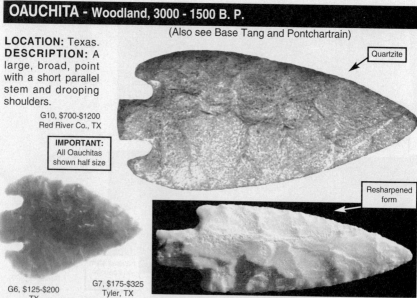

Quartzite

Resharpened form

G6, $125-$200
TX

G7, $175-$325
Tyler, TX

OAUCHITA (continued)

G9, $700-$1200
Tyler, TX

PAISANO - Mid-Archaic, 6000 - 5000 B. P.

(Also see Big Sandy, Dalton, San Patrice)

LOCATION: Texas. **DESCRIPTION:** A medium size point with broad side notches forming a squared to auriculate base that is concave. Some examples have notched/serrated edges.

SC

G8, $60-$100
McIntosh Co., OK

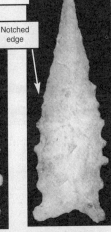

Needle tip

Notched edge

G5, $12-$20
Pecos Co., TX

G6, $18-$30
Val Verde Co., TX

G8, $80-$150
Reeves Co., TX

G9, $150-$250
Val Verde Co., TX

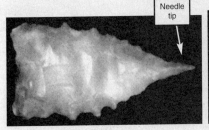

Needle tip

G6, $15-$30
Reeves Co., TX

G6, $25-$40
Comanche Co., TX

759

PAISANO (continued)

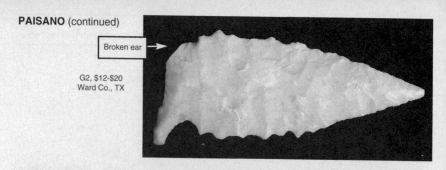

Broken ear →

G2, $12-$20
Ward Co., TX

PALEO KNIFE - Transitional Paleo, 10,000 - 8000 B. P.
(Also see Scraper, Round-End Knife and Square Knife)

Resharpened
Scottsbluff

Red agate

G7, $850-$1500
Amarillo,

OK.

G7, $350-$550
Cherokee Co., OK

Note collateral
flaking to center

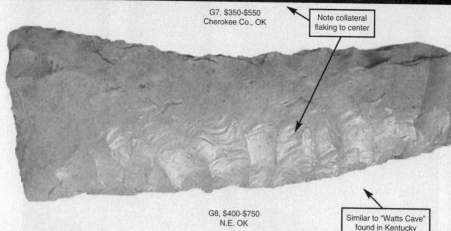

G8, $400-$750
N.E. OK

Similar to "Watts Cave"
found in Kentucky

LOCATION: All of North America. **DESCRIPTION:** A large size lanceolate blade finished with broad parallel flakes. These are found on Paleo sites and were probably used as knives.

PALMILLAS - Middle to Late Archaic, 6000 - 3000 B. P.

(Also see Axtel, Godley and Williams)

G3, $6-$12
Comanche Co., TX

G3, $5-$10
Comanche Co., TX

G3, $5-$10
Comanche Co., TX

G5, $5-$15
Comanche Co., TX

G7, $15-$25
Comanche Co., TX

G7, $12-$20
Comanche Co., TX.

G6, $12-$20
AR

G7, $15-$25
Comanche
Co., TX

SC

G8, $30-$50
Bell Co., TX

G6, $30-$50
Bell Co., TX

LOCATION: Texas to Oklahoma. **DESCRIPTION:** A small to medium size triangular point with a bulbous stem. Shoulders are prominent and can be horizontal to barbed or weak and tapered. Stems expand and are rounded. **I.D. KEY:** Bulbous stem.

PANDALE - Middle Archaic, 6000 - 3000 B. P.

(Also see Darl and Travis)

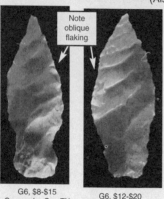

Note oblique flaking

G6, $8-$15
Comanche Co., TX

G6, $12-$20
Comanche Co., TX

G6, $35-$50
Val Verde Co., TX

G6, $35-$50
Val Verde Co., TX

LOCATION: Texas. **DESCRIPTION:** A medium size, narrow, stemmed point or spike with a steepy beveled or torque blade. Some examples show oblique parallel flaking.

G7, $35-$60
Lynn Co., TX

PANDORA - Late Archaic to Woodland, 4000 - 1000 B. P.

(Also see Adena Blade, Friday, Kinney and Refugio)

LOCATION: Central Texas southward. **DESCRIPTION:** A medium to large size, lanceolate blade with basically a straight base. Blade edges can be parallel to convex.

G5, $12-$20
Val Verde Co., TX

Classic form

G9, $35-$60
Comache Co., TX

G8, $65-$125
Cent. TX

762

PEDERNALES - Middle Archaic to Woodland, 6000 - 2000 B. P.

(Also see Hoxie, Jetta, Langtry, Montell, Uvalde and Val Verde)

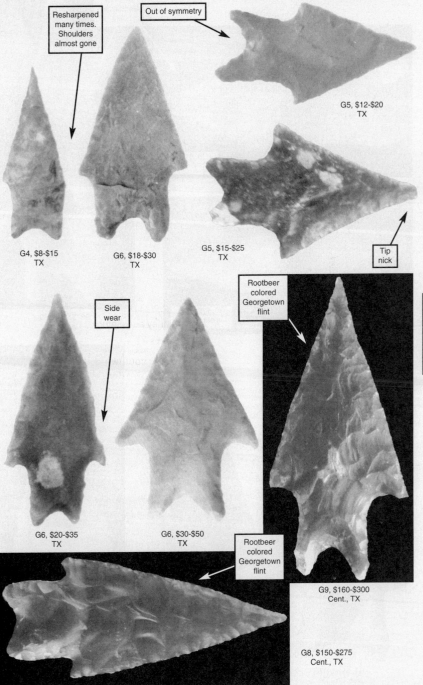

Resharpened many times. Shoulders almost gone

Out of symmetry

G5, $12-$20
TX

Tip nick

G4, $8-$15
TX

G6, $18-$30
TX

G5, $15-$25
TX

Side wear

Rootbeer colored Georgetown flint

SC

G6, $20-$35
TX

G6, $30-$50
TX

Rootbeer colored Georgetown flint

G9, $160-$300
Cent., TX

G8, $150-$275
Cent., TX

763

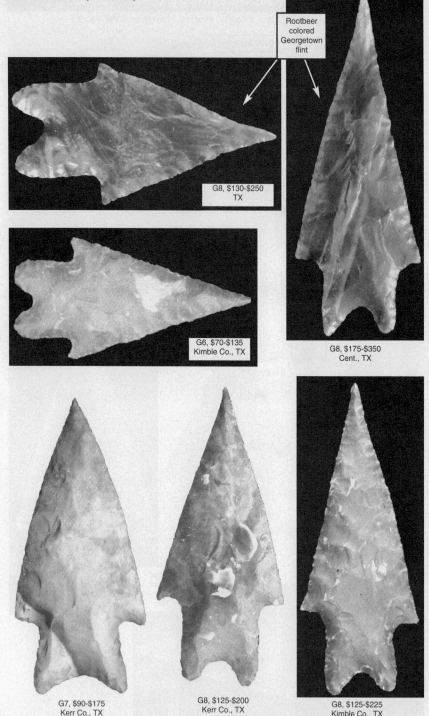

Rootbeer colored Georgetown flint

G8, $130-$250
TX

G6, $70-$135
Kimble Co., TX

G8, $175-$350
Cent., TX

G7, $90-$175
Kerr Co., TX

G8, $125-$200
Kerr Co., TX

G8, $125-$225
Kimble Co., TX

PEDERNALES (continued)

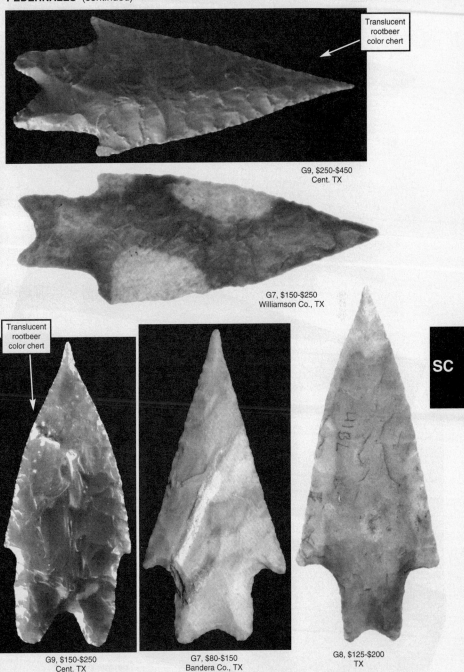

Translucent rootbeer color chert

G9, $250-$450
Cent. TX

G7, $150-$250
Williamson Co., TX

Translucent rootbeer color chert

SC

G9, $150-$250
Cent. TX

G7, $80-$150
Bandera Co., TX

G8, $125-$200
TX

LOCATION: Texas. **DESCRIPTION:** A medium to large size, thin, usually barbed, point with a broad, long, bifurcated stem. Tangs and tips are very sharp. Blade edges are convex, concave to recurved. These points are of high quality. **I.D. KEY:** Long bifurcated stem.

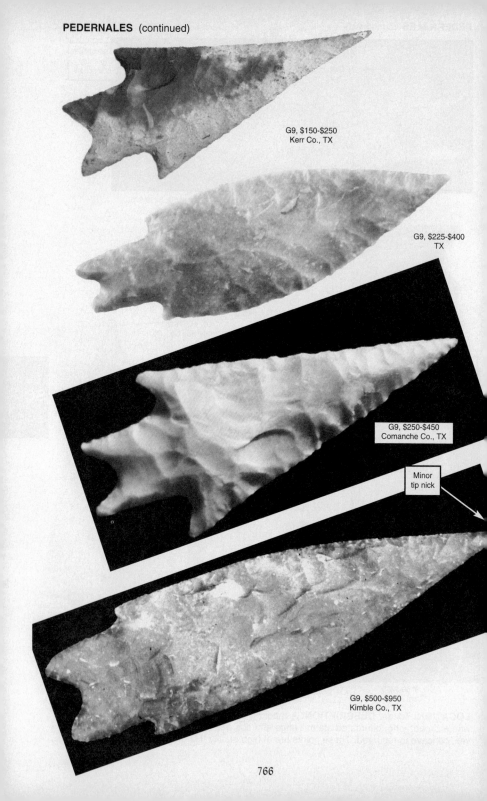

PEDERNALES (continued)

G9, $150-$250
Kerr Co., TX

G9, $225-$400
TX

G9, $250-$450
Comanche Co., TX

Minor
tip nick

G9, $500-$950
Kimble Co., TX

PEISKER DIAMOND - Woodland, 2500 - 2000 B. P.

(Also see Gary and Hale)

Translucent novaculite

G7, $25-$40
Howard Co., AR

LOCATION: Illinois, Missouri, Arkansas, Kansas into Iowa. **DESCRIPTION:** A large, broad blade with sharp shoulders and a short to moderate contracting base that comes to a point. Blade edges are recurved, convex or straight. Similar in form to the *Morrow Mountain* point found in the Southeast, but not as old. **I.D.KEY:** Contracted "v" base.

PELICAN - Transitional Paleo, 10,000 - 6000 B. P.

(Also see Arkabutla, Coldwater, Golondrina, Hell Gap, Midland, Rio Grande and San Patrice)

Petrified wood

G4, $45-$80
AR

G5, $50-$90
Cass Co., TX

G8, $80-$150
Lufkin, TX

G8, $125-$200
Jasper Co., TX

Chert

G8, $90-$175
TX

G8, $125-$225
N.W. LA

G9, $110-$200
AR

LOCATION: West Tennessee to Texas. **DESCRIPTION:** A short, broad, usually auriculate point with basal grinding. Shoulders taper into a long contracting stem. Some examples are basally thinned or fluted. **I.D. KEY:** Basal contraction, small size.

PELICAN (continued)

Petrified wood

Stem sides and base are ground

G9, $125-$225
Sabine Parrish, LA

G7, $150-$250
Smith Co., TX

G7, $125-$200
AR

G7, $125-$200
TX

G8, $175-$300
AR

G8, $250-$450
AR

PERDIZ - Mississippian, 1000 - 500 B. P.

(Also see Alba, Bassett, Bonham, Cliffton, Cuney, Hayes, Homan and Keota)

G5, $6-$10
Hill Co., TX

G4, $12-$20
TX

G7, $25-$40
TX

G7, $15-$30
Val Verde Co., TX

G5, $30-$50
Comanche Co., TX

G6, $35-$65
Comanche Co., TX

LOCATION: Texas to Oklahoma. **DESCRIPTION:** A small to medium size, thin, narrow, triangular arrow point with pointed barbs and a long, pointed to near pointed stem. Some examples are serrated. Tangs and tips are sharp. **I.D. KEY:** Long pointed stem and barbs.

PERDIZ (continued)

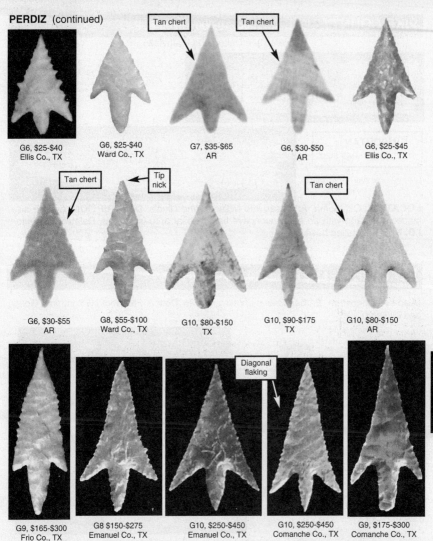

G6, $25-$40
Ellis Co., TX

G6, $25-$40
Ward Co., TX

Tan chert
G7, $35-$65
AR

Tan chert
G6, $30-$50
AR

G6, $25-$45
Ellis Co., TX

Tan chert
G6, $30-$55
AR

Tip nick
G8, $55-$100
Ward Co., TX

G10, $80-$150
TX

Tan chert
G10, $90-$175
TX

G10, $80-$150
AR

SC

G9, $165-$300
Frio Co., TX

G8 $150-$275
Emanuel Co., TX

G10, $250-$450
Emanuel Co., TX

Diagonal flaking
G10, $250-$450
Comanche Co., TX

G9, $175-$300
Comanche Co., TX

PERFORATOR - Archaic to Mississippian, 9000 - 400 B. P.

(Also see Drill, Graver and Scraper)

LOCATION: Archaic and Woodland sites everywhere. **DESCRIPTION:** A jabbing projection at the tip would qualify for the type. It is believed that *perforators* were used for tattooing, incising or to punch holes in leather or other materials or objects. Paleo peoples used *Gravers* for the same purpose. All Archaic and Woodland cultures converted their points into this type. Therefore, most point types could occur in this form.

G5, $5-$10
Comanche Co., TX.

769

PIKE COUNTY - Early Archaic, 10,000 - 9200 B. P.

(Also see Dalton and Plainview)

G10, $800-$1500
AR

Classic form

IMPORTANT:
Both shown half size

G9+, $1700-$3000
McIntosh Co., OK

LOCATION: Oklahoma, Arkansas into Missouri and Illinois. **DESCRIPTION:** A large size, lanceolate blade with an eared, concave base. Basal area is ground. Related To *Dalton*. **I.D. KEY:** Fishtailed base.

PLAINVIEW - Late Paleo, 10,000 - 7000 B. P.

(Also see Angostura, Barber, Brown's Valley, Clovis, Dalton, Frederick, Golondrina, Gosen and Midland)

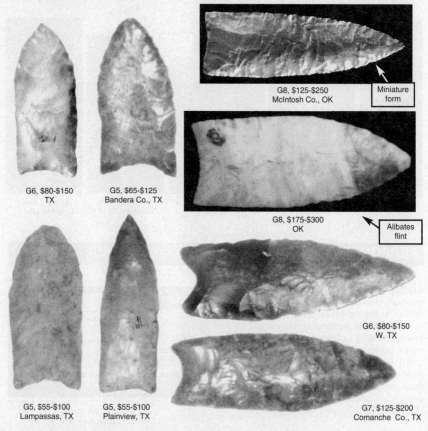

G8, $125-$250
McIntosh Co., OK

Miniature form

G6, $80-$150
TX

G5, $65-$125
Bandera Co., TX

G8, $175-$300
OK

Alibates flint

G6, $80-$150
W. TX

G5, $55-$100
Lampassas, TX

G5, $55-$100
Plainview, TX

G7, $125-$200
Comanche Co., TX

PLAINVIEW (continued)

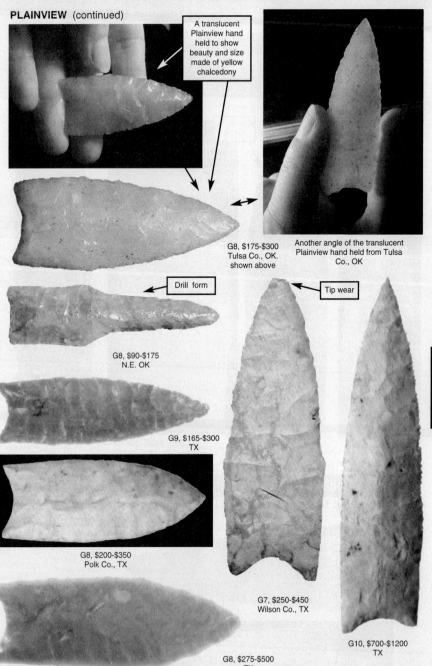

A translucent Plainview hand held to show beauty and size made of yellow chalcedony

SC

G8, $175-$300
Tulsa Co., OK.
shown above

Another angle of the translucent Plainview hand held from Tulsa Co., OK

Drill form

G8, $90-$175
N.E. OK

Tip wear

G9, $165-$300
TX

G8, $200-$350
Polk Co., TX

G7, $250-$450
Wilson Co., TX

G10, $700-$1200
TX

G8, $275-$500
TX

LOCATION: Mexico northward to Canada and Alaska. **DESCRIPTION:** A medium size, thin, lanceolate point with usually parallel sides and a concave base that is ground. Some examples are thinned or fluted and is believed to be related to the earlier *Clovis* and contemporary *Dalton* type. Flaking is of high quality and can be collateral to oblique transverse.

771

PLAINVIEW (continued)

Diagonal flaking

G10, $1200-$2000
Irion Co., TX

Collateral flaking

G7, $165-$300
Lee Co., TX

G7, $190-$350
Cole Co., OK

G7, $225-$400
Llano Co., TX

G9, $700-$1300
N. OK

POGO - Woodland to Mississippian, 2000 - 500 B. P.

(Also see Darl, Dickson, Hidden Valley, Lange, Morhiss, Pontchartrain and Travis)

G9, $90-$175
Montgomery Co., TX

G10, $200-$350
Trinity Co., TX

POGO (continued)

LOCATION: Texas. **DESCRIPTION:** A medium to large size contracted stem point with small, tapered shoulders. The base is usually straight. Also known as *Morhiss*.

PONTCHARTRAIN (Type I) - Late Archaic to Woodland, 3400 - 2000 B. P.

(Also see Lange, Morrill, Morhiss, Pogo and Travis)

G7, $15-$30
E. TX

G9, $60-$100
E. TX

LOCATION: Alabama to Texas. **DESCRIPTION:** A medium to large size, thick, narrow, stemmed point with weak, tapered or barbed shoulders. The stem is parallel sided with a convex to straight base. Some examples are finely serrated and are related and similar to the *Flint Creek* type.

SC

PONTCHARTRAIN (Type II) - Late Archaic to Woodland, 3400 - 2000 B. P.

(Also see Lange, Morrill and Morhiss)

LOCATION: Alabama to Texas. **DESCRIPTION:** A medium to large size, thick, broad, stemmed point with barbed shoulders. The stem is parallel sided to tapered with a convex to straight base.

G5, $15-$30
E. TX

RED RIVER KNIFE - Early Archaic, 9500 - 7000 B. P.

(Also see Albany Knife, Alberta, Eden, Firstview and Scottsbluff)

LOCATION: Texas to Colorado. **DESCRIPTION:** A medium size, asymmetrical blade with weak shoulders and a short, expanding stem. Bases are straight to slightly convex. It has been reported that these knifes were made by the Cody Complex people from *Scottsbluff* points. Look for early parallel flaking and stem grinding.

773

RED RIVER KNIFE (continued)

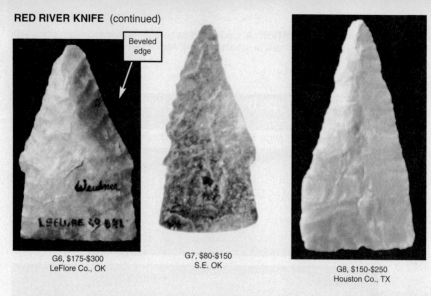

Beveled edge

G6, $175-$300
LeFlore Co., OK

G7, $80-$150
S.E. OK

G8, $150-$250
Houston Co., TX

REED - Woodland to Mississippian, 1500 - 500 B. P.

(Also see Haskell, Knight Island, Schustorm and Washita)

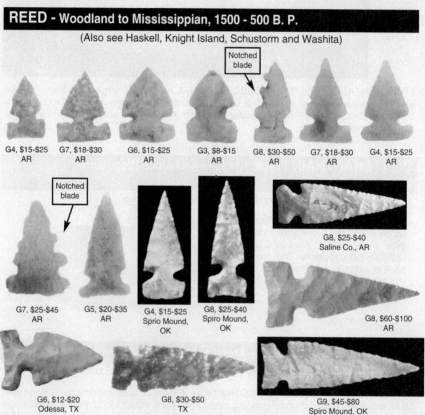

Notched blade

G4, $15-$25
AR

G7, $18-$30
AR

G6, $15-$25
AR

G3, $8-$15
AR

G8, $30-$50
AR

G7, $18-$30
AR

G4, $15-$25
AR

Notched blade

G7, $25-$45
AR

G5, $20-$35
AR

G4, $15-$25
Sprio Mound, OK

G8, $25-$40
Spiro Mound, OK

G8, $25-$40
Saline Co., AR

G8, $60-$100
AR

G6, $12-$20
Odessa, TX

G8, $30-$50
TX

G9, $45-$80
Spiro Mound, OK

LOCATION: Oklahoma to Arkansas. **DESCRIPTION:** A small size, thin, triangular, side notched point with a straight to concave base. Rarely, serrations occur.

REFUGIO - Late Archaic, 4000 - 2000 B. P.

(Also see Gahagan, Pandora and Sabine)

G6, $40-$75
Comanche Co.,
TX

LOCATION: S.W. to central Texas. **DESCRIPTION:** A medium to large size, narrow, lanceolate blade with a rounded base.

RICE CONTRACTED STEM (See Hidden Valley)

RICE LOBBED - Early Archaic, 9000 - 5000 B. P.

(Also see Uvalde)

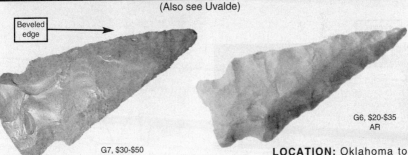

Beveled edge

SC

G6, $20-$35
AR

G7, $30-$50
N.E. OK

Note early parallel flaking

LOCATION: Oklahoma to Missouri. **DESCRIPTION:** A medium to large size bifurcated to lobed base point with serrated blade edges. The base has a shallow indentation compared to the other bifurcated types. Shoulders are sharp and prominent. Called *Culpepper Bifurcate* in Virginia.

G6 $15-$30
Newton Co., AR

RICE SHALLOW SIDE NOTCHED - Woodland, 1600 - 1400 B. P.

(Also see Brewerton Eared & Jakie Stemmed)

G4, $6-$10
Saline Co., AR

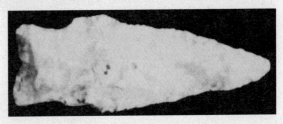

RICE SHALLOW SIDE NOTCHED
(continued)

LOCATION: Oklahoma to Missouri.
DESCRIPTION: A medium size, broad point with shallow side notches and a convex base.

G4, $6-$10
Saline Co., AR

RIO GRANDE - Early Archaic, 7500 - 6000 B. P.

(Also see Agate Basin, Angostura, Hell Gap and Pelican)

LOCATION: New Mexico, Texas to Colorado. **DESCRIPTION:** A medium to large size, lanceolate point with tapered shoulders and a long parallel sided to contracting stem. The base can be straight, concave or convex. **I.D. KEY:** Long contracting stem.

Rootbeer colored flint

Ground basal area

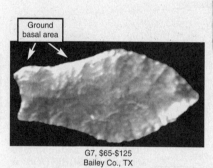

G7, $65-$125
Bailey Co., TX

G7, $55-$100
Uvalde, TX

Ground basal area

G8, $150-$275
W. TX

ROCKWALL - Late Woodland, 1400 - 1000 B. P.

(Also see Alba, Colbert, Moran, Sabinal, Scallorn and Shumla)

G2 $1-$3
Lonoke Co.,
AR

G2 $3-$5
Cent. AR

G3 $3-$6
TX

G7 $12-$20
TX

G5 $12-$20
Hill Co., TX

G6 $12-$20
TX

G7, $12-$20
Hill Co., TX

G2 $3-$5
Comanche
Co., TX

G9 $35-$60
TX

G4 $5-$10
Saline Co.,
AR

LOCATION: Louisiana to Oklahoma. **DESCRIPTION:** A small, thin, triangular arrow point with corner notches. Shoulders are barbed and usually extend almost to the base. Many examples are serrated. Tips and tangs are sharp. **I.D. KEY:** Broad corner notches

776

G5,$8-$15
Saline Co., AR

G6, $12-$20
Hill Co., TX

G7, $25-$40
Comanche
Co., TX

G9, $35-$65
Spiro Mound, OK

G8, $65-$125
Comanche
Co., TX

G8, $35-$65
TX

RODGERS SIDE HOLLOWED - Early Archaic, 10,000 - 8000 B. P.

(Also see Arkabutla, Dalton, Golondrina, Pelican and San Patrice)

Alibates flint

Fluted

Patinated Alibates flint

SC

G8, $275-$500
Kay Co., OK

G7, $165-$300
Collin Co., TX

G6, $80-$150
Llano Co., TX

G10, $250-$450
Lampasas Co., TX. Excellent
quality and classic example.

LOCATION: Texas. **DESCRIPTION:** A medium size, broad, unfluted auriculate point which is a variant form of the *San Patrice* type. Also known as *Brazos Fishtail*. Base is concave and is ground. Some examples are fluted. **I.D. KEY:** Expanding auricles.

Impact fracture

G6, $125-$200
Austin, TX

G8, $65-$125
TX

G7, $175-$300
Comanche, TX

777

ROUND-END KNIFE - Historic 1000 - 300 B. P.

(Also see Archaic Knife, Paleo Knife and Square-End Knife)

G7, $60-$100
Victoria, TX

LOCATION: Texas. **DESCRIPTION:** A large, narrow knife form with rounded ends. This form was hafted along one side leaving a cutting edge on the opposite side.

IMPORTANT:
Shown half size

G9, $600-$1000
Travis Co., TX

SABINAL - Mississippian, 1000 - 700 B. P.

(Also see Bonham & Rockwall)

G5, $5-$10
Bandera Co., TX

Serrated edge

G8, $45-$80
Comanche Co., TX

G5, $15-$30
Comanche Co., TX

G7, $45-$80
TX

G9, $55-$110
TX

G5, $25-$45
Uvalde Co., TX

G8, $25-$45
TX

LOCATION: Texas. **DESCRIPTION:** A small size, thin basal notched point with shoulders that flare outward and a short expanding to parallel sided stem.

SABINE - Late Archaic to Woodland, 4000 - 2000 B. P.

(Also see Covington, Friday, Gahagan, Refugio and San Gabriel)

LOCATION: Midwestern states. **DESCRIPTION:** A medium to large size, thin, lanceolate blade with a contracting, rounded to "V" base. Blade edges can be serrated.

G4, $12-$20
Comanche Co., TX

SALLISAW - Mississippian, 800 - 600 B. P.

(Also see Edwards, Haskell and Morris)

G6, $45-$80
Spiro Mound, OK

G10, $450-$800
Comanche Co., TX. very thin and
excellent quality.

LOCATION: Oklahoma to Arkansas and Texas. **DESCRIPTION:** A small size, thin, serrated, barbed point with long drooping basal tangs and a deeply concave base. A very rare type. **I.D. KEY:** Long drooping ears.

SAN GABRIEL - Woodland 2000 - 1500 B. P.

(Also see Covington, Friday, Gahagan, Kinney and Sabine)

SC

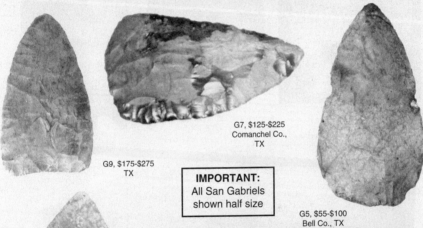

G9, $175-$275
TX

G7, $125-$225
Comanchel Co.,
TX

IMPORTANT:
All San Gabriels
shown half size

G5, $55-$100
Bell Co., TX

G9, $275-$500
TX

G10, $600-1000
Coryell Co., TX

LOCATION: Central Texas. **DESCRIPTION:** A large size, broad blade with a straight to slightly convex base.

779

SAN JACINTO - Mid-Archaic, 6000 - 4000 B. P.
(Also see Castroville, Ensor, Marcos and Marshall)

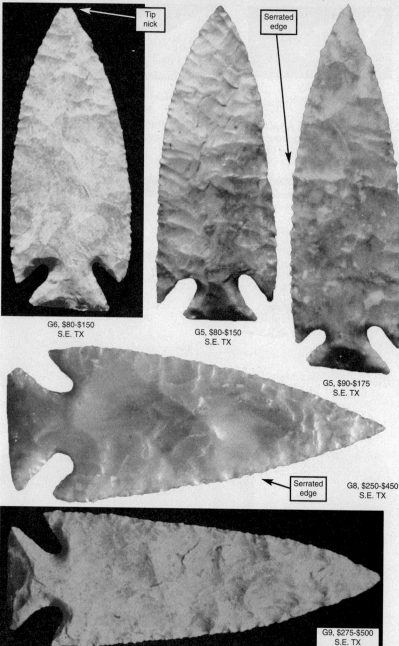

Tip nick

Serrated edge

G6, $80-$150
S.E. TX

G5, $80-$150
S.E. TX

G5, $90-$175
S.E. TX

Serrated edge

G8, $250-$450
S.E. TX

G9, $275-$500
S.E. TX

LOCATION: Texas S.E. Gulf Coast and Coastal. Plain areas. **DESCRIPTION:** A medium to large size, thin, corner notched knife with a straight base. Notches are deep and angular creating a broad expanding stem. Base width is less than shoulder width. Some examples are finely serrated. **I.D. KEY:** Deep corner notches. Named by Dwain Rogers.

780

SAN PATRICE-GENEILL - Early Archaic, 10,000 - 8000 B. P.
(Also see Dalton, Palmer, Pelican and Rodgers Side Hollowed)

Red chert

G5, $60-$100
AR

LOCATION: Louisiana to Oklahoma. **DESCRIPTION:** A scarce, small size, thin, stemmed point with a short, expanding concave base that forms small ears. Shoulders can be strong and sharp. Some examples are thinned from the base. Basal area is usually ground. **I.D. KEY:** Extended auriculate base and small size.

SAN PATRICE-HOPE VARIETY - Early Archaic, 10,000 - 8000 B. P.
(Also see Coldwater, Dalton, Hinds, Palmer, Pelican, Rodgers Side Hollowed and Zephyr)

Jasper

Petrified wood

Chert

G7, $55-$100
Bowie Co., TX

G9, $70-$125
TX

G8, $80-$150
San Augustine Co., TX

G7, $80-$150
Sabine Co., TX

SC

G9, $150-$275
N.E. TX

Petrified wood

G8, $90-$175
LA

G8, $125-$200
Liberty Co., TX

G10, $200-$350
Angelina Co., TX

LOCATION: Louisiana to Oklahoma. **DESCRIPTION:** A small size, thin, auriculate point with a concave base. Some examples are thinned from the base. Basal area is longer than the "St. Johns" variety and is usually ground. **I.D. KEY:** Extended auriculate base and small size.

781

SAN PATRICE-KEITHVILLE - Early Archaic, 10,000 - 8000 B. P.

(Also see Albany Knife, Dalton, Palmer, Pelican and Rodgers Side Hollowed)

Sugar quartz

G5, $30-$50
Titus Co., TX

G7, $80-$150
Lufkin, TX

G8, $65-$125
Bowie Co., TX

G6, $60-$100
Newton Co., TX

G7, $80-$150
N.E. OK

G6, $50-$100
Newton Co., TX

G9, $200-$350
Harris Co., TX

G7, $65-$125
Angelina Co., TX

LOCATION: Louisiana to Oklahoma. **DESCRIPTION:** A small size, thin, auriculate to side notched point forming a lobed base. Basal area is usually ground. Blade edges can be serrated. **I.D. KEY:** Lobbed base.

SAN PATRICE-ST. JOHNS VARIETY - Early Archaic, 10,000 - 8000 B. P.

(Also see Dalton, Palmer, Pelican and Rodgers Side Hollowed)

Palmwood

G5, $35-$60
San Augustine Co., TX

G5, $25-$45
E. TX

G5, $35-$60
E. TX

G4, $25-$45
E. TX

LOCATION: Louisiana to Oklahoma. **DESCRIPTION:** A small size, thin, auriculate to side notched point with a short, concave base. Some examples are fluted, others are thinned from the base. Basal area is usually ground. Blade edges can be serrated. **I.D. KEY:** Short auriculate base and small size.

SAN PATRICE-ST. JOHNS (continued)

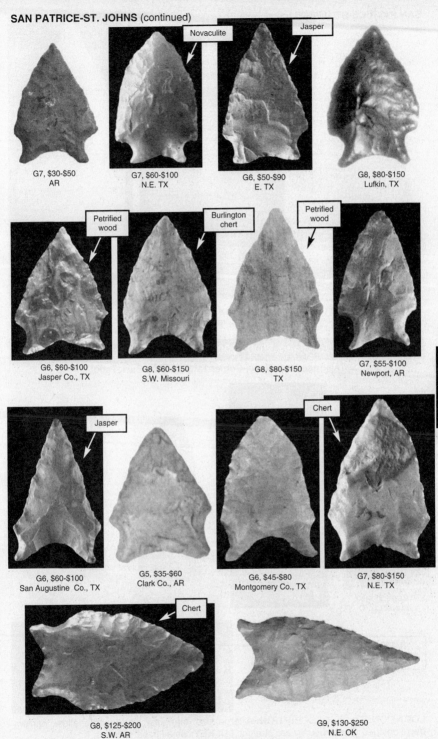

Novaculite

Jasper

G7, $30-$50
AR

G7, $60-$100
N.E. TX

G6, $50-$90
E. TX

G8, $80-$150
Lufkin, TX

Petrified wood

Burlington chert

Petrified wood

G6, $60-$100
Jasper Co., TX

G8, $60-$150
S.W. Missouri

G8, $80-$150
TX

G7, $55-$100
Newport, AR

SC

Jasper

Chert

G6, $60-$100
San Augustine Co., TX

G5, $35-$60
Clark Co., AR

G6, $45-$80
Montgomery Co., TX

G7, $80-$150
N.E. TX

Chert

G8, $125-$200
S.W. AR

G9, $130-$250
N.E. OK

783

SAN PATRICE-ST. JOHNS (continued)

Silcified sand-stone

G10, $125-$225
LA

G9, $175-$300
Craighead, AR

G10, $350-$600
AR

SAN SABA - Woodland, 3000 - 2000 B. P.

(Also see Base Tang, Corner Tang and Mid-Back Tang)

G9, $250-$450
Coryell Co., TX

G10, $400-$750
Comanche Co., TX

G8, $130-$250
Austin, TX

G8, $250-$400
TX

> **IMPORTANT:** All San Sabas shown half size

G9, $250-$450
Cent. TX

LOCATION: Texas. **DESCRIPTION:** A large size, triangular blade with shallow, narrow, basal notches. Bases usually are straight. **I.D. KEY:** Small basal notches.

SAVAGE CAVE - Early to Middle Archaic, 7000 - 4000 B. P.

(Also see Big Sandy, Cache River, Hemphill, Hickory Ridge and White River)

LOCATION: Kentucky, Tennessee to Arkansas.
DESCRIPTION: A medium to large size, broad, side notched point that is usually serrated. Bases are generally straight but can be slightly concave or convex.

G3, $3-$6
N.E. AR

G7, $15-$25
N.E. AR

G6, $8-$15
Jonesboro, AR

SAVANNAH RIVER - Middle Archaic to Woodland, 5000 - 2000 B. P.

(Also see Johnson)

G6, $18-$30
Greene Co., AR

G5, $20-$35
Jonesboro, AR

G5, $12-$20
Jonesboro, AR

LOCATION: Arkansas to Eastern states. **DESCRIPTION:** A medium to large size, straight to contracting stemmed point with a Straight or concave to bifurcated base. The shoulders are tapered to square. The stems are narrow to broad. Believed to be related to the earlier *Stanly* point. **I.D. KEY:** Broad, concave base.

SCALLORN - Woodland to Mississippian, 1300 - 500 B. P.

(Also see Alba, Catahoula, Cuney, Ellis, Homan, Keota, Rockwall, Sequoyah and Steiner)

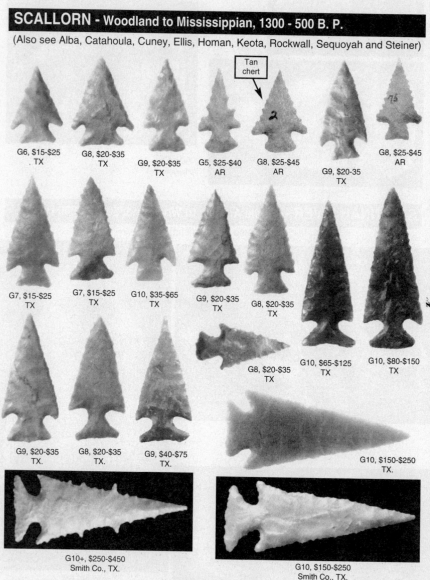

Tan chert

G6, $15-$25
. TX

G8, $20-$35
TX

G9, $20-$35
TX

G5, $25-$40
AR

G8, $25-$45
AR

G9, $20-35
TX

G8, $25-$45
AR

G7, $15-$25
TX

G7, $15-$25
TX

G10, $35-$65
TX

G9, $20-$35
TX

G8, $20-$35
TX

G8, $20-$35
TX

G10, $65-$125
TX

G10, $80-$150
TX

G9, $20-$35
TX.

G8, $20-$35
TX.

G9, $40-$75
TX.

G10, $150-$250
TX.

G10+, $250-$450
Smith Co., TX.

G10, $150-$250
Smith Co., TX.

LOCATION: Texas, Oklahoma. **DESCRIPTION:** A small size, corner notched arrow point with a flaring stem. Bases and blade edges are straight, concave or convex and many examples are serrated. Not to be confused with *Sequoyah* not found in Texas. **I.D. KEY:** Small corner notched point with sharp tangs and tip.

SCHUSTORM - Mississippian, 1200 - 600 B. P.

(Also see Knight Island, Reed and Washita)

LOCATION: Arkansas into Texas. **DESCRIPTION:** A small size, thin, triangular arrow point with small, weak side notches high up from the base. The base is concave **I.D. KEY:** Weak notches.

G9, $60-$100
AR., Bowman site.

SCOTTSBLUFF I - Early Archaic, 9500 - 7000 B. P.

(Also see Alberta, Cody Knife, Eden, Hardin, Holland and Red River)

G7, $150-$275
Angelina Co., TX

Ground basal area

G3, $50-$100
Lufkin, TX

G3, $55-$100
N.E. OK

Ground basal area

G4, $80-$150
N.E. OK

G6, $250-$400
Angelina Co., TX

G6, $150-$250
Angelina Co., TX

G6, $150-$250
TX

Ground basal area

G5, $150-$250
San Patricio Co., TX

Base nick

G7, $225-$400
Bexar Co., TX

SC

787

Base nick

Base nick

G5, $325-$600
Sabine Co., TX

G5, $250-$400
Wood Co., TX

G7, $200-$375
Childress Co., TX

G6, $175-$300
Bexar Co., TX

Petrified wood

Ground basal area

Edge wear

G9, $400-$700
Wilson Co., TX

G6, $225-$400
Upshur Co., TX

G8, $500-$900
N.E. OK

SCOTTSBLUFF I (continued)

G9, $900-$1600
Angelina Co., TX

LOCATION: Louisiana to New Mexico to Canada and the Northwest coast. **DESCRIPTION:** A medium to large size, broad stemmed point with convex to parallel sides and weak shoulders. The stem is parallel to expanding. The basal area is ground. Most examples have horizontal to oblique parallel flaking and are of high quality and thinness. Made by the Cody Complex people. Believed to have evolved into *Hardin* in later times. **I.D. KEY:** Broad stem, weak shoulders, collateral flaking.

SC

G8, $800-$1500
N.E. OK

G10, $2500-$4000+
Liberty Co., TX

G9, $3500-$6000+
TX

Base nick

G4, $150-$275
Angelina Co., TX.

G3, $65-$125
Athens, TX

G5, $90-$175
Cass Co., TX

Shoulder nick

G6, $150-$350
Angelina Co., TX

Base nick

G3, $40-$75
N.E. OK

G6, $150-$250
Haskle Co., OK

G4, $40-$75
Osage Co., OK

G8, $450-$800
AR

SCOTTSBLUFF II (continued)

LOCATION: Louisiana to New Mexico to Canada to the Northwest coast. **DESCRIPTION:** A medium to large size, broad stemmed point with convex to parallel sides and stronger shoulders than type I. The stem is parallel sided to slightly expanding. The hafting area is ground. Most examples have horizontal to oblique parallel flaking and are of high quality and thinness. Made by the Cody Complex people. **I.D. KEY:** Stronger shoulders.

G8, $300-$550
TX

SCRAPER - Paleo to Archaic, 14,000 - 5000 B. P.

(Also see Drill, Graver, Perforator and Paleo Knife)

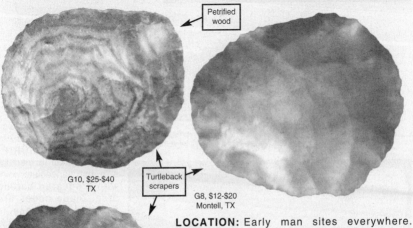

Petrified wood

SC

G10, $25-$40
TX

Turtleback scrapers

G8, $12-$20
Montell, TX

LOCATION: Early man sites everywhere. **DESCRIPTION:** Thumb, duckbill and turtleback forms are small to medium size, thick, ovoid shaped, uniface, scraping tools that are steeply beveled, especially at the broadest end. Side scrapers are long hand-held uniface flakes with beveling on all blade edges of one face. Scraping was done primarily from the sides of these blades. Many of these tools were hafted. Found hafted to wooden handles with pitch in caves.

G6, $25-$40
Lufkin, TX. Made from a
Pelican point.

G7, $8-$15
Montell, TX

SEARCY - Early to Middle Archaic, 7000 - 5000 B. P.

(Also see Coryell, Dalton, Early Stemmed, Hoxie, Rio Grande, Victoria & Wells)

SEARCY (continued)

Classic example from type county

G7, $45-$80
Searcy Co., AR

Classic example

G8, $80-$150
Morris Co., TX

G10, $150-$250
Benton Co., AR

G8, $80-$150
AR

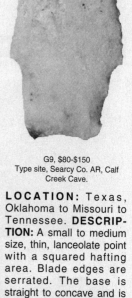

G9, $80-$150
Type site, Searcy Co. AR, Calf Creek Cave.

LOCATION: Texas, Oklahoma to Missouri to Tennessee. **DESCRIPTION:** A small to medium size, thin, lanceolate point with a squared hafting area. Blade edges are serrated. The base is straight to concave and is usually ground. **I.D. KEY:** Long squared stem, serrations.

SEQUOYAH - Mississippian, 1000 - 600 B. P.

(Also see Alba, Blevins, Hayes, Homan, Livermore, Scallorn and Steiner)

G5, $8-$15
Red River Co., TX

G5, $8-$15
Red River Co., TX

G5, $8-$15
Red River Co., TX

G5, $8-$15
Spiro Mound, OK

G5, $8-$15
Red River Co., TX

G4, $5-$10
Red River Co., TX

G5, $8-$15
Red River Co., TX

LOCATION: IL, OK, AR, MO. **DESCRIPTION:** A small size, thin, narrow point with coarse serrations and an expanded, bulbous stem. Believed to have been made by Caddo and other people. Named after the famous Cherokee of the same name. **I.D. KEY:** Bulbous base, coarse serrations.

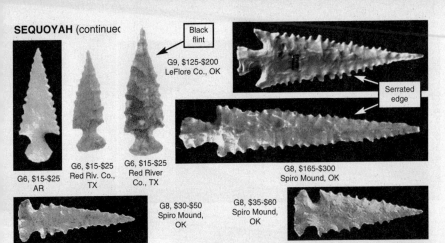

SEQUOYAH (continued)

Black flint

G9, $125-$200
LeFlore Co., OK

Serrated edge

G6, $15-$25
AR

G6, $15-$25
Red Riv. Co.,
TX

G6, $15-$25
Red River
Co., TX

G8, $165-$300
Spiro Mound, OK

G8, $30-$50
Spiro Mound,
OK

G8, $35-$60
Spiro Mound,
OK

SHUMLA - Woodland, 3000 - 1000 B. P.

(Also see Bell, Calf Creek, Marshall and Rockwall)

SC

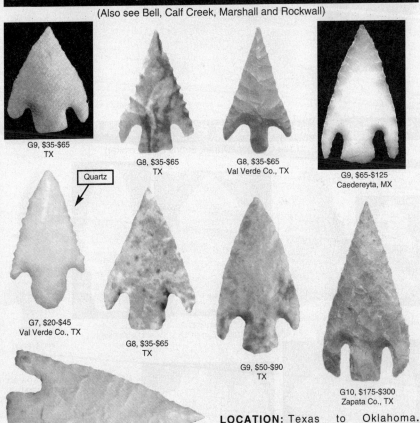

G9, $35-$65
TX

G8, $35-$65
TX

G8, $35-$65
Val Verde Co., TX

G9, $65-$125
Caedereyta, MX

Quartz

G7, $20-$45
Val Verde Co., TX

G8, $35-$65
TX

G9, $50-$90
TX

G10, $175-$300
Zapata Co., TX

G8, $65-$125
Val Verde Co.,
TX

LOCATION: Texas to Oklahoma.
DESCRIPTION: A small size, basal
notched point with convex, straight or
recurved sides. Barbs turn in towards and
usually extend to the base.

SHUMLA (continued)

G8, $250-$400
Austin, TX

G9, $150-$250
N. OK

G6, $60-$100
TX

SINNER - Woodland, 3000 - 2000 B. P.

(Also see Charcos, Duran, Evans and Huffaker)

G3, $1-$3
Lincoln Parrish, LA

G4, $3-$6
LA

G6, $12-$20
Lincoln Parrish, LA

G5, $5-$10
Lincoln Parrish, LA

G5, $15-$25
TX

G6, $12-$20
Lincoln Parrish, LA

G5, $8-$15
Lincoln Parish, LA

LOCATION: Louisiana to Texas. **DESCRIPTION:** A medium size, expanded stemmed point with several barbs occurring above the shoulders. **I.D. KEY:** Barbed edges.

SMITH - Late Archaic, 4000 - 3000 B. P.

(Also see Bell, Castroville, Calf Creek, Little River, San Saba, Shumla)

G8, $125-$200
Comanche Co., TX

G8, $175-$300
Benton Co., AR

SC

LOCATION: Arkansas into Missouri and Illinois. **DESCRIPTION:** A very large size, broad, point with long parallel shoulders and a squared to slightly expanding base. Some examples may appear to be basally notched due to the long barbs.

SPOKESHAVE - Woodland, 3000 -1500 B. P.

(Also see Scraper)

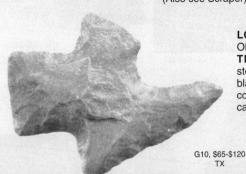

LOCATION: Tennessee, Kentucky, Ohio, Indiana into Texas. **DESCRIPTION:** A medium to large size stemmed tool used for scraping. The blade is asymmetrical with one edge convex or notched and the other concave.

G10, $65-$120
TX

STARR - Mississippian to Historic, 1000 - 250 B. P.

(Also see Maud and Talco)

LOCATION: Texas westward. **DESCRIPTION:** A small size, thin, triangular point with a "V" base concavity. Blade edges can be concave to straight. An eccentric form of Starr is call "New Form" found near the Mexican border. **I.D. KEY:** "V" base.

STARR (continued)

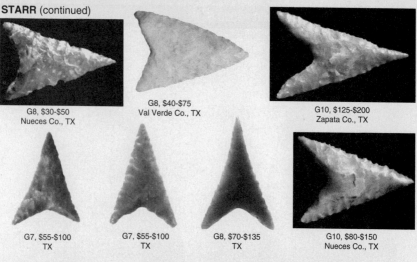

G8, $30-$50
Nueces Co., TX

G8, $40-$75
Val Verde Co., TX

G10, $125-$200
Zapata Co., TX

G7, $55-$100
TX

G7, $55-$100
TX

G8, $70-$135
TX

G10, $80-$150
Nueces Co., TX

STEINER - Mississippian, 1000 - 400 B. P.

(Also see Friley, Scallorn and Sequoyah)

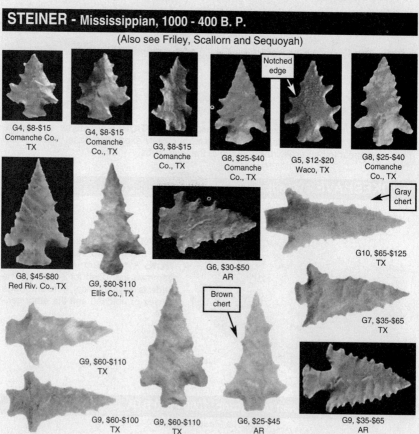

G4, $8-$15
Comanche Co.,
TX

G4, $8-$15
Comanche
Co., TX

G3, $8-$15
Comanche
Co., TX

G8, $25-$40
Comanche
Co., TX

Notched edge

G5, $12-$20
Waco, TX

G8, $25-$40
Comanche
Co., TX

G8, $45-$80
Red Riv. Co., TX

G9, $60-$110
Ellis Co., TX

G6, $30-$50
AR

Gray chert

G10, $65-$125
TX

G7, $35-$65
TX

G9, $60-$110
TX

Brown chert

G9, $60-$100
TX

G9, $60-$110
TX

G6, $25-$45
AR

G9, $35-$65
AR

LOCATION: Mexico, E. Texas into Arkansas. **DESCRIPTION:** A small size, thin, barbed arrow point with strong shoulders. The stem is short and may be horizontal or expanded. **I.D. KEY:** Strong barbs.

STEINER (continued)

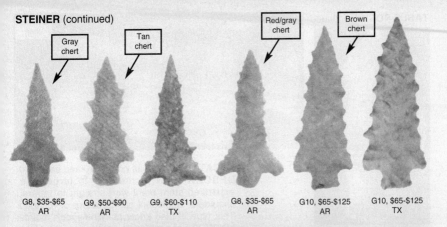

Gray chert

Tan chert

Red/gray chert

Brown chert

G8, $35-$65
AR

G9, $50-$90
AR

G9, $60-$110
TX

G8, $35-$65
AR

G10, $65-$125
AR

G10, $65-$125
TX

SC

STEUBEN - Woodland, 2000 - 1000 B. P.

(Also see Lange, Palmillas and Table Rock)

G4, $4-$8
Saline Co., AR

LOCATION: Arkansas to Illinois.
DESCRIPTION: A medium to large size, narrow, expanded stem point. shoulders can be tapered to straight. The base is straight to convex. This type is very similar to *Bakers Creek* in the Southeast.

G5, $5-$10
Saline Co., AR

G7, $12-$20
AR

G7, $20-$35
Saline Co., AR

TABLE ROCK - Late Archaic, 4000 - 3000 B. P.

(Also see Lange, Matanzas, Motley and Steuben)

G6, $20-$35
AR

Colorful chert

G5, $15-$30, AR

TABLE ROCK (continued)

G5, $12-$20
AR

Colorful chert

G9, $150-$250
AR

LOCATION: Arkansas northward and eastward.
DESCRIPTION: A medium to large size, expanded stem point with straight to tapered shoulders. Shoulders can be sharp or rounded. This type is also know as "Bottleneck" points.
I.D. KEY: Long expanding base.

TALCO - Mississippian to Historic, 800 - 500 B. P.

(Also see Guerrero, Maud and Starr)

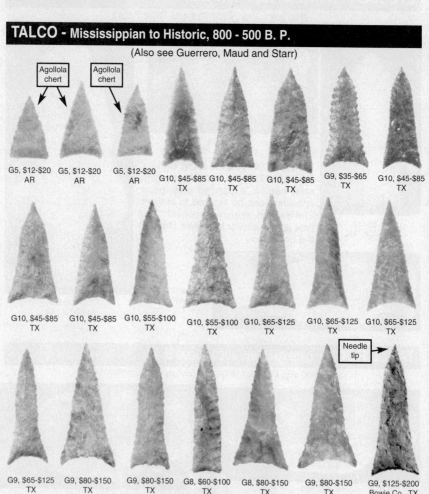

Agollola chert

Agollola chert

Agollola chert

Needle tip

G5, $12-$20
AR

G5, $12-$20
AR

G5, $12-$20
AR

G10, $45-$85
TX

G10, $45-$85
TX

G10, $45-$85
TX

G9, $35-$65
TX

G10, $45-$85
TX

G10, $45-$85
TX

G10, $45-$85
TX

G10, $55-$100
TX

G10, $55-$100
TX

G10, $65-$125
TX

G10, $65-$125
TX

G10, $65-$125
TX

G9, $65-$125
TX

G9, $80-$150
TX

G9, $80-$150
TX

G8, $60-$100
TX

G8, $80-$150
TX

G9, $80-$150
TX

G9, $125-$200
Bowie Co., TX

TALCO (continued)

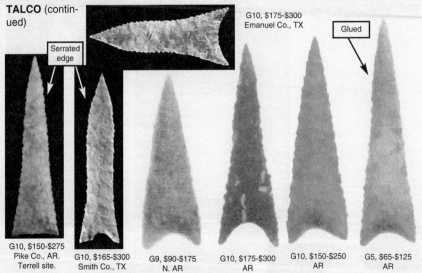

G10, $175-$300
Emanuel Co., TX

Glued

Serrated edge

G10, $150-$275
Pike Co., AR.
Terrell site.

G10, $165-$300
Smith Co., TX

G9, $90-$175
N. AR

G10, $175-$300
AR

G10, $150-$250
AR

G5, $65-$125
AR

LOCATION: Texas to Oklahoma. **DESCRIPTION:** A small to medium size, thin, narrow, triangular arrow point with recurved sides and a concave base. Blade edges are very finely serrated. On classic examples, tips are more angled than *Maud*. Tips and corners are sharp. This type is found on Caddo and related sites. **I.D. KEY:** Angled tip.

TEXAS KIRK   (see Coryell)

TORTUGAS - Middle Archaic to Woodland, 6000 - 1000 B. P.   SC

(Also see Kinney, Early Triangular and Matamoros)

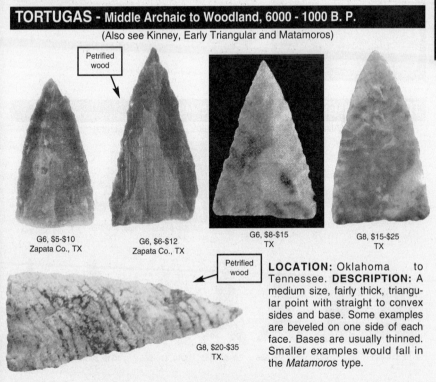

Petrified wood

G6, $5-$10
Zapata Co., TX

G6, $6-$12
Zapata Co., TX

G6, $8-$15
TX

G8, $15-$25
TX

Petrified wood

G8, $20-$35
TX.

LOCATION: Oklahoma to Tennessee. **DESCRIPTION:** A medium size, fairly thick, triangular point with straight to convex sides and base. Some examples are beveled on one side of each face. Bases are usually thinned. Smaller examples would fall in the *Matamoros* type.

TORTUGAS (continued)

G8, $15-$25
TX

G7, $25-$45
TX

G7, $20-$35
TX

G10, $35-$65
TX

G9, $25-$45
TX

TOYAH - Mississippian to Historic, 600 - 400 B. P.

(Also see Garza, Harrell, Huffaker, Morris and Washita)

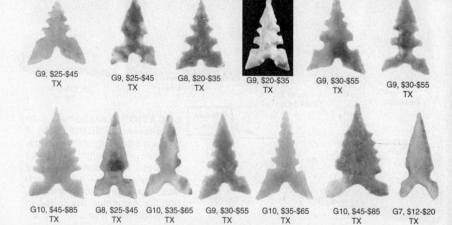

G9, $25-$45
TX

G9, $25-$45
TX

G8, $20-$35
TX

G9, $20-$35
TX

G9, $30-$55
TX

G9, $30-$55
TX

G10, $45-$85
TX

G8, $25-$45
TX

G10, $35-$65
TX

G9, $30-$55
TX

G10, $35-$65
TX

G10, $45-$85
TX

G7, $12-$20
TX

800

TOYAH (continued)

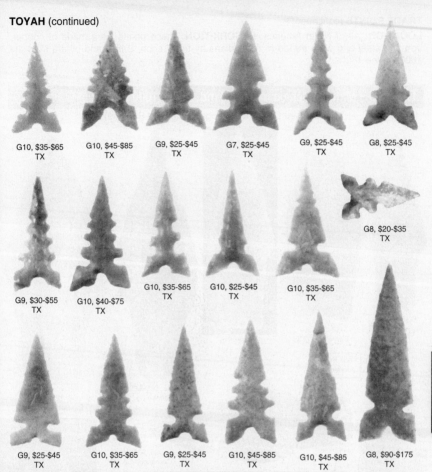

G10, $35-$65
TX

G10, $45-$85
TX

G9, $25-$45
TX

G7, $25-$45
TX

G9, $25-$45
TX

G8, $25-$45
TX

G9, $30-$55
TX

G10, $40-$75
TX

G10, $35-$65
TX

G10, $25-$45
TX

G10, $35-$65
TX

G8, $20-$35
TX

G9, $25-$45
TX

G10, $35-$65
TX

G9, $25-$45
TX

G10, $45-$85
TX

G10, $45-$85
TX

G8, $90-$175
TX

SC

LOCATION: Northern Mexico to Texas. **DESCRIPTION:** A small size, thin, triangular point with expanded barbs and one or more notches on each side and a basal notch. **I.D. KEY:** Has drooping, pointed barbs.

TRADE POINTS - Historic, 400 - 170 B. P.

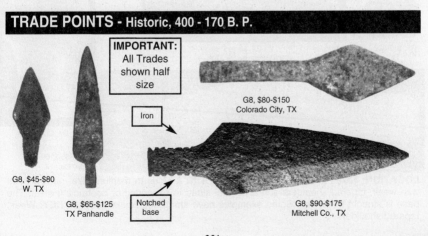

IMPORTANT:
All Trades
shown half
size

Iron

G8, $80-$150
Colorado City, TX

G8, $45-$80
W. TX

G8, $65-$125
TX Panhandle

Notched
base

G8, $90-$175
Mitchell Co., TX

TRADE POINTS (continued)

LOCATION: All of North America. **DESCRIPTION:** These points were made of copper, iron and steel and were traded to the Indians by the French, British and others from the 1600s to the 1800s.

TRAVIS - Middle-Archaic to Woodland, 5500 - 1000 B. P.

(Also see Darl, Gary, Lange, Nolan and Pandale)

G3, $5-$10
Coryell Co., TX

G4, $8-$15
Coryell Co., TX

G4, $85-$15
Austin, TX

Leon River chert

G6, $25-$45
Comanche Co., TX

G6, $25-$45
Big Springs, TX

G6, $22-$40
Comanche Co., TX

G5, $12-$20
TX

G4, $8-$15
Comanche Co., TX

G4, $12-$20
TX

G9, $55-$100
Bell Co., TX

LOCATION: Texas to Oklahoma. **DESCRIPTION:** A small to medium size, narrow point with weak, tapered shoulders and a parallel sided to expanded or contracting stem. The base is straight to convex. Some examples have sharp needle-like tips. **I.D. KEY:** Weak, tapered shoulders.

TRAVIS (continued)

G5, $15-$30
TX

SC

G7, $60-$110
Bell Co., TX

G8, $60-$100
Bell Co., TX

G8, $60-$110
Austin, TX

G7, $40-$70
Travis Co., TX

TRINITY - Late Archaic, 4000 - 2000 B. P.

(Also see Ellis, Godley and Travis)

G4, $5-$10
Comanche Co., TX

G4, $1-$2
Comanche Co., TX

G6, $12-$20
Waco, TX

LOCATION: Texas to Oklahoma. **DESCRIPTION:** A small to medium size point with broad side notches, weak shoulders and a broad convex base which is usually ground.

TURNER - Mississippian, 1000 - 800 B. P.

(Also see Alba, Blevins, Hayes, Homan, Howard, Perdiz and Sequoyah)

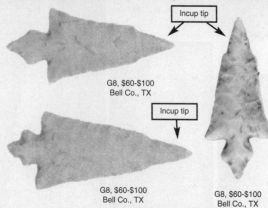

Incup tip

G8, $60-$100
Bell Co., TX

Incup tip

G8, $60-$100
Bell Co., TX

G8, $60-$100
Bell Co., TX

LOCATION: Louisiana to Oklahoma. **DESCRIPTION:** Related to *Hayes* points and is a later variety. A small size, narrow, expanded tang arrow point with a turkeytail base. The tip is inset about 1/4th the distance. Blade edges are usually incurved forming sharp, "squarish" pointed tangs. Base is pointed and can be double notched. Some examples are serrated. Has been found in caches. **I.D. KEY:** Diamond shaped base and flaking style.

UVALDE - Middle Archaic to Woodland, 6000 - 1500 B. P.

(Also see Frio, Hoxie, Langtry, Pedernales, Rice Lobbed and Val Verde)

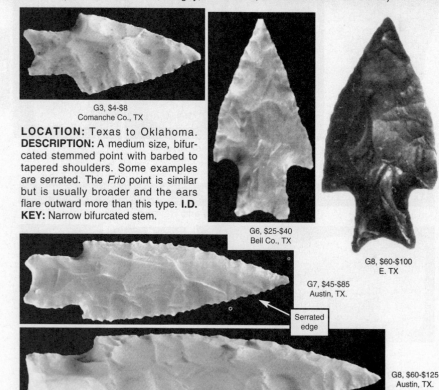

G3, $4-$8
Comanche Co., TX

LOCATION: Texas to Oklahoma. **DESCRIPTION:** A medium size, bifurcated stemmed point with barbed to tapered shoulders. Some examples are serrated. The *Frio* point is similar but is usually broader and the ears flare outward more than this type. **I.D. KEY:** Narrow bifurcated stem.

G6, $25-$40
Bell Co., TX

G7, $45-$85
Austin, TX.

Serrated edge

G8, $60-$100
E. TX

G8, $60-$125
Austin, TX.

804

UVALDE (continued)

G7, $25-$45
Comanche Co., TX

SC

G8, $55-$100
Williamson Co., TX

G8, $55-$100
Comanche Co., TX

G8, $55-$100
Llano Co., TX

G7, $65-$125
TX

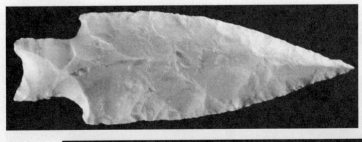

G9, $165-$300
Austin, TX

High quality
example

G9, $250-$400
Austin, TX.

805

Exotic
material

G9, $125-$200
Coryell Co., TX.

G10, $275-$500
Llano Co., TX.

G10, $250-$400
Austin, TX.

VAL VERDE - Middle to Late Archaic, 5000 - 3000 B. P.

(Also see Langtry, Pedernales and Uvalde)

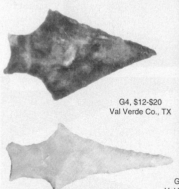

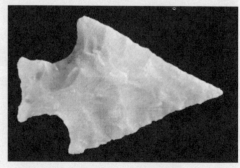

G4, $12-$20
Val Verde Co., TX

G4, $12-$20
Val Verde Co., TX

G6, $35-$65
Comanche Co., TX

VAL VERDE (continued)

LOCATION: Texas. **DESCRIPTION:** A variant of the Langtry point. Medium size point with outward flaring tapered shoulders, an expanding stem and a concave base. On some examples the basal corners form auricles. **I.D. KEY:** Expanding basal ears, strong shoulders.

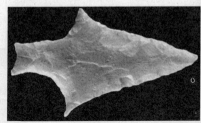

G6, $30-$50
Terrell Co., TX

G9, $65-$125
Val Verde Co., TX

G8, $55-$100
Val Verde Co., TX

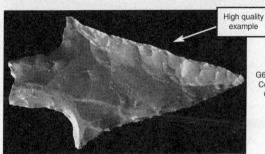

High quality example

G6, $40-$75
Comanche
Co., TX

G9, $125-$225
Val Verde Co., TX

G6, $35-$60
Val Verde
Co., TX

VICTORIA - Early Archaic, 8000 - 6000 B. P.

(Also see Angostura, Early Stemmed Lanceolate, Hell Gap, Rio Grande and Searcy)

G5, $35-$65
TX

G7, $45-$80
TX

807

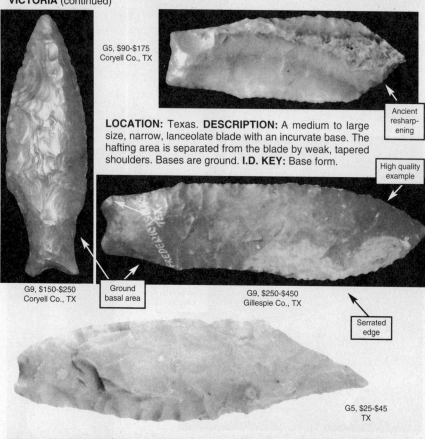

G5, $90-$175
Coryell Co., TX

Ancient resharpening

LOCATION: Texas. **DESCRIPTION:** A medium to large size, narrow, lanceolate blade with an incurvate base. The hafting area is separated from the blade by weak, tapered shoulders. Bases are ground. **I.D. KEY:** Base form.

High quality example

G9, $150-$250
Coryell Co., TX

Ground basal area

G9, $250-$450
Gillespie Co., TX

Serrated edge

G5, $25-$45
TX

WASHITA - Mississippian, 800 - 400 B. P.

(Also see Harrell, Haskell, Keota, Reed, Schustorm and Toyah)

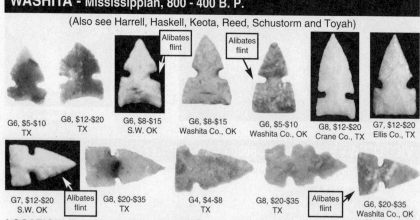

Alibates flint

Alibates flint

G6, $5-$10
TX

G8, $12-$20
TX

G6, $8-$15
S.W. OK

G6, $8-$15
Washita Co., OK

G6, $5-$10
Washita Co., OK

G8, $12-$20
Crane Co., TX

G7, $12-$20
Ellis Co., TX

G7, $12-$20
S.W. OK

Alibates flint

G8, $20-$35
TX

G4, $4-$8
TX

G8, $20-$35
TX

Alibates flint

G6, $20-$35
Washita Co., OK

LOCATION: Texas to Oklahoma. **DESCRIPTION:** A small size, thin, triangular side notched arrow point with a concave to straight base. Basal area is usually large in proportion to the blade size. Similar forms occur in the Southwest and Plains states under different names. Concave base forms are called "Peno." **I.D. KEY:** Small triangle with side notches high up from base.

WASHITA (continued)

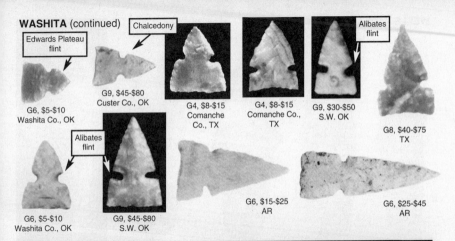

Edwards Plateau flint

Chalcedony

Alibates flint

G6, $5-$10
Washita Co., OK

G9, $45-$80
Custer Co., OK

G4, $8-$15
Comanche Co., TX

G4, $8-$15
Comanche Co., TX

G9, $30-$50
S.W. OK

G8, $40-$75
TX

Alibates flint

G6, $5-$10
Washita Co., OK

G9, $45-$80
S.W. OK

G6, $15-$25
AR

G6, $25-$45
AR

WASHITA-PENO - Mississippian, 800 - 400 B. P.

(Also see Harrell, Keota, Reed and Toyah)

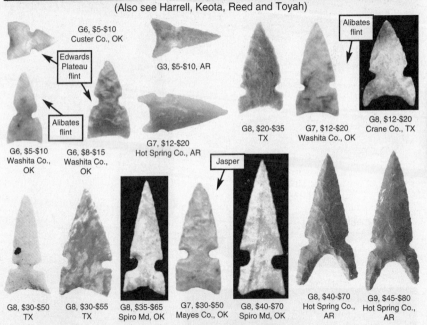

G6, $5-$10
Custer Co., OK

Edwards Plateau flint

G3, $5-$10, AR

Alibates flint

Alibates flint

G8, $20-$35
TX

G7, $12-$20
Washita Co., OK

G8, $12-$20
Crane Co., TX

SC

G6, $5-$10
Washita Co., OK

G6, $8-$15
Washita Co., OK

G7, $12-$20
Hot Spring Co., AR

Jasper

G8, $30-$50
TX

G8, $30-$55
TX

G8, $35-$65
Spiro Md, OK

G7, $30-$50
Mayes Co., OK

G8, $40-$70
Spiro Md, OK

G8, $40-$70
Hot Spring Co., AR

G9, $45-$80
Hot Spring Co., AR

LOCATION: Texas to Oklahoma. **DESCRIPTION:** A variant form with side notches one third to one half the distance up from the base and the base is concave. Basal concavity can be slight to very deep. **I.D. KEY:** Base form and notch placement.

WELLS - Early to Middle Archaic, 8000 - 5000 B. P.

(Also see Adena, Bulverde, Carrolton, Coryell, Dawson & Searcy)

LOCATION: Eastern Texas and Oklahoma. **DESCRIPTION:** A medium to large size, thin, usually serrated point with a long, narrow, contracting to parallel stem that has a rounded to straight base. Shoulders are weak and can be tapered, horizontal or barbed. **I.D. KEY:** Basal form, extended and squared up. Early flaking style.

WELLS (continued)

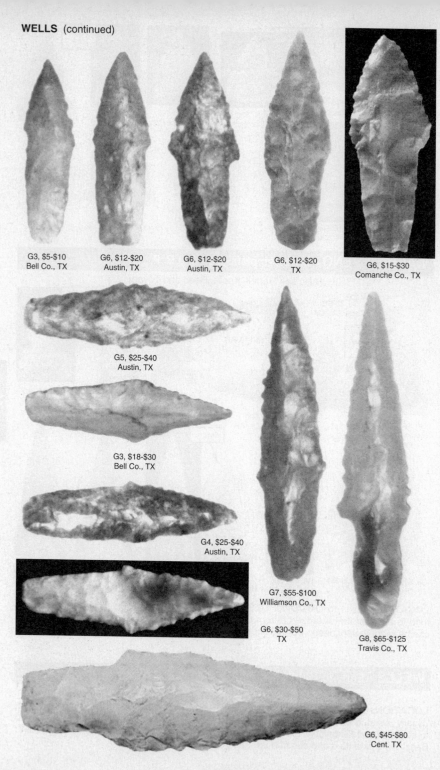

G3, $5-$10
Bell Co., TX

G6, $12-$20
Austin, TX

G6, $12-$20
Austin, TX

G6, $12-$20
TX

G6, $15-$30
Comanche Co., TX

G5, $25-$40
Austin, TX

G3, $18-$30
Bell Co., TX

G4, $25-$40
Austin, TX

G7, $55-$100
Williamson Co., TX

G6, $30-$50
TX

G8, $65-$125
Travis Co., TX

G6, $45-$80
Cent. TX

WHITE RIVER - Middle Archaic to Woodland, 6000 - 1000 B. P.

(Also see Big Sandy and Hickory Ridge)

LOCATION: Arkansas, Missouri. **DESCRIPTION:** A medium to large size, narrow, side notched point with a straight to concave base. Blade edges can be beveled and serrated. Similar to *Graham Cave* points found further north.

G7, $40-$70
N. OK

G8, $150-$250
AR

G7, $60-$100
N. OK

WILLIAMS - Middle Archaic to Woodland, 6000 - 1000 B. P.

(Also see Axtel, Castroville, Marcos, Marshall, Palmillas and Shumla)

G8, $12-$20
TX

G6, $15-$25
Comanche Co., TX

G9, $25-$45
TX

G9, $25-$45
TX

G6, $15-$25
Comanche Co., TX

G8, $40-$70
Belton, TX

LOCATION: Texas to Oklahoma. **DESCRIPTION:** A medium to large size, barbed point with an expanded, rounded base. Resharpened examples have tapered shoulders. **I.D. KEY:** Base form, barbs.

G6, $85-$160
Lampassas, TX

G6, $35-$60
Comanche Co., TX

Tip
nick

G8, $125-$200
Georgetown Co., TX

G9, $250-$400
Travis Co., TX

G7, $175-$300
Williamson Co., TX

G7, $125-$225
TX

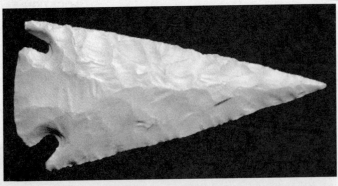

G8, $150-$250
Coryell Co., TX

YARBROUGH - Woodland, 2500 - 1000 B. P.

(Also see Darl, Hoxie, Lange, Travis and Zorra)

G5, $8-$15
Comanche Co., TX

G6, $15-$25
Bell Co., TX

SC

G5, $12-$20
Bell Co., TX

G7, $55-$100
Ellis Co., TX

G7, $60-$110
Bell Co., TX

G6, $50-$90
Comanche Co., TX

YARBROUGH (continued)

LOCATION: Texas to Oklahoma. **DESCRIPTION:** A medium size, narrow point with a long, expanding, rectangular stem that has slightly concave sides. The shoulders are very weak and tapered. The stem edges are usually ground. **I.D. KEY:** Expanding stem.

G6, $8-$15
TX

YOUNG - Mississippian, 1000 - 400 B. P.

(Also see Catan and Clifton)

G1, $.50-$1
Waco, TX

G5, $.50-$1
Comanche Co., TX

G3, $.50-$1
Comanche Co., TX

LOCATION: Texas. **DESCRIPTION:** A small size, crudely chipped, elliptical shaped, usually round base point made from a flake. One side is commonly uniface. **I.D. KEY:** Base form, uniface.

ZELLA - Early Archaic, 8500 - 7500 B. P.

(Also see Agate Basin, Angostura, Lerma and Mahaffey)

G9, $125-$225
TX

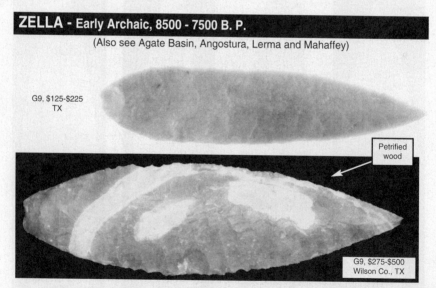

Petrified wood

G9, $275-$500
Wilson Co., TX

LOCATION: Texas. **DESCRIPTION:** A large size, narrow, lanceolate blade with a rounded to small straight base. Bases are ground. Believed to be a form of Angostura.

ZEPHYR - Early Archaic, 9000 - 6000 B. P.

(Formerly Lampasos; also see Darl Stemmed, Darl, Hoxie and Uvalde)

Beveled edge

G5, $5-$10
TX

G7, $30-$50
Austin, TX

G7, $30-$50
Comanche Co, TX

G5, $12-$20
Llano Co., TX

G5, $12-$20
Comanche Co., TX

G8, $70-$135
Comanche Co., TX

SC

G7, $80-$150
Comanche Co., TX

G8, $90-$175
Lampasos Co., TX

G8, $80-$150
Comanche Co., TX

G9, $125-$200
Coryell Co., TX

LOCATION: Texas. **DESCRIPTION:** A medium to large size, narrow, serrated point with square to tapered, barbed shoulders and an eared base. Blade edges are beveled on one side of each face on resharpened forms. Flaking is of high quality. These points were classified with *Darl* in the past. Also known as *Mahomet* locally. **I.D. KEY:** Fishtail base and serrations.

ZORRA - Middle Archaic, 6000 - 4000 B. P.

(Also see Darl, Lange, Nolan and Travis)

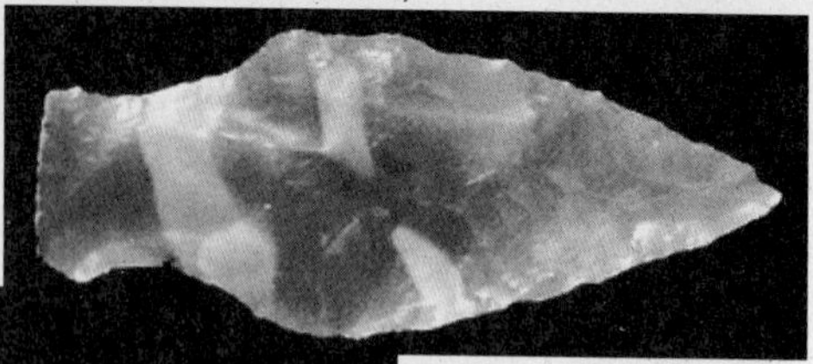

G6, $12-$20
Austin, TX

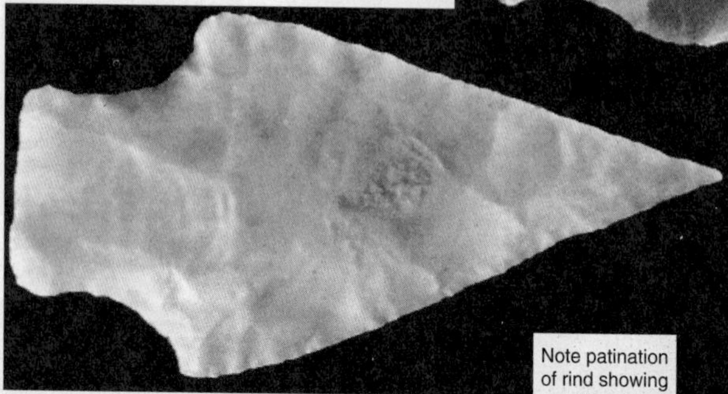

Rootbeer colored flint

G7, $25-$40
Austin, TX

Note patination of rind showing at base

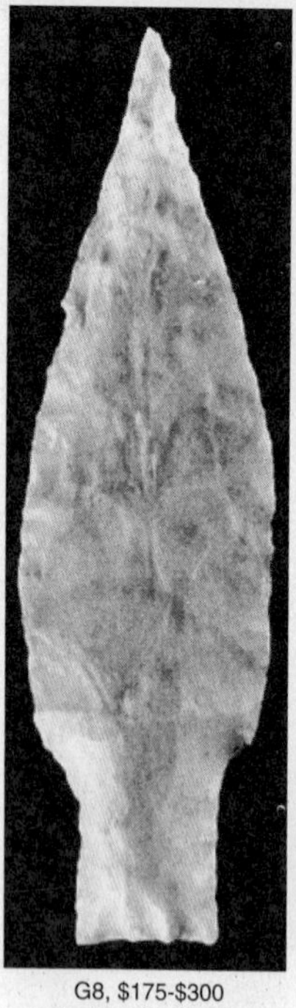

G8, $175-$300
Austin, TX. Classic

G9, $150-$250
Austin Co., TX

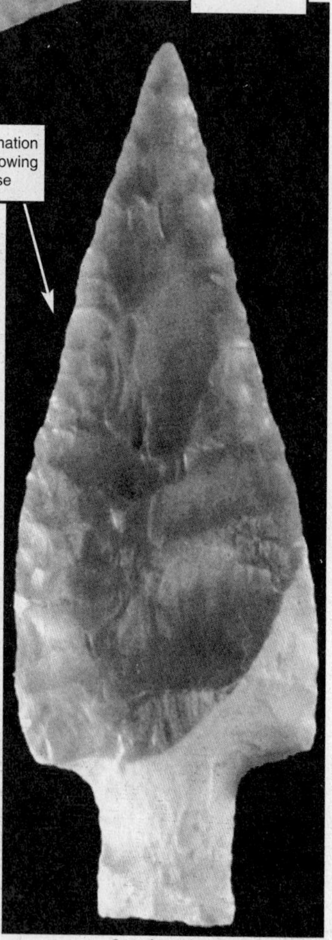

G10, $350-$600
Austin, TX. Excellent quality.

LOCATION: Texas. **DESCRIPTION:** A medium to large size point with tapered shoulders and stem that is usually flat on one face and beveled on both sides of the opposite face. Otherwise identical to *Nolan*. Most have needle tips and good quality flaking. **I.D. KEY:** Base beveling.

NORTHERN CENTRAL SECTION:

This section includes point types from the following states:
Eastern Colorado, Kansas, Illinois, Iowa, Minnesota, Missouri, Nebraska and Wisconsin.

The points in this section are arranged in alphabetical order and are shown **actual size**. All types are listed that were available for photographing. Any missing types will be added to future editions as photographs become available. We are always interested in receiving sharp, black and white or color glossy photos or color slides of your collection. Be sure to include a ruler in the photograph so that proper scale can be determined.

Lithics: Materials employed in the manufacture of point types from this region include: agate, Burlington, chalcedony, chert, conglomerate, crystal, flint, jasper, kaolin, Knife River, hornstone, novaculite, petrified wood, quartzite, silicified sandstone and vein quartz.

Regional Consultant:
Roy Motley

Special Advisors:
Tom Davis, Bill Jackson
Glenn Leesman, Floyd Ritter,
Larry Troman, Brian Wrage

NC

NORTHERN CENTRAL
(Archaeological Periods)

PALEO (14,000 B.P. - 11,000 B.P.)

Beaver Lake	Clovis-St. Louis	Drill	
Clovis	Cumberland	Folsom	
Clovis-Hazel	Cumberland Unfluted	Redstone	

LATE PALEO (12,000 B.P. - 10,000 B.P.)

Gosen	Plainview	Wheeler	
Hi-Lo	Quad		

TRANSITIONAL PALEO (11,000 B.P. - 9,000 B.P.)

Agate Basin	Eden	Howard County	Scottsbluff Type I & 2
Allen	Early Ovoid Knife	Lerma	
Angostura	Greenbrier	Paleo Knife	
Browns Valley	Hell Gap	Pelican	

EARLY ARCHAIC (10,000 B.P. - 7,000 B.P.)

Burroughs	Decatur	Kirk Corner Notched	Rochester
Cache River	Dovetail	Lake Erie	St. Charles
Calf Creek	Fox Valley	Lost Lake	Stilwell
Cobbs Triangular	Graham Cave	Meserve	Tennessee River
Cossatot River	Hardin	Nebo Hill	Thebes
Dalton Breckenridge	Heavy Duty	Neuberger	Turin
Dalton Classic	Hickory Ridge	Osceola	Warrick
Dalton-Hemphill	Hidden Valley	Pike County	
Dalton-Nuckolls	Holland	Pine Tree Corner Notched	
Dalton-Sloan	Johnson	Rice Lobbed	

MIDDLE ARCHAIC (7,000 B.P. - 4,000 B.P.)

Afton	Hemphill	Raddatz	Smith
Epps	Kings	Ramey Knife	Stone Square Stem
Exotic Forms	Matanzas	Red Ochre	
Ferry	Motley	Sedalia	

LATE ARCHAIC (4,000 B.P. - 3,000 B.P.)

Copena Classic	Gary	Merkle	Turkeytail-Fulton
Delhi	Godar	Robinson	Turkeytail-Harrison
Etley	Helton	Square Knife	Turkeytail-Hebron
Evans	Mehlville	Table Rock	Wadlow

WOODLAND (3,000 B.P. - 1,300 B.P.)

Adena	Carter	Jacks Reef Corner Notched	Rice Side-Notched
Adena Blade	Collins	Kampsville	Ross
Adena-Narrow Stem	Cupp	Kramer	Snyders
Adena-Notched Base	Dickson	Lehigh	Steuben
Alba	Gibson	Morse Knife	Waubesa
Apple Creek	Grand	North	
Burkett	Hopewell	Peisker Diamond	

MISSISSIPPIAN (1300 B.P. - 400 B.P.)

Agee	Haskell	Lundy	Washita
Bayogoula	Hayes	Madison	
Cahokia	Homan	Nodena	
Harahey	Huffaker	Scallorn	
Harrell	Kay Blade	Sequoyah	

HISTORIC (450 B.P. - 170 B.P.)

No types listed.

NORTHERN CENTRAL
THUMBNAIL GUIDE SECTION

The following references are provided to aid the collector in easier and quicker identification of point types. All photos are exactly 30% of actual size and are proportional to each other. Each point pictured in this section represents a classic form for the type. When a match is found, go to the alphabetical location of that type for more examples in actual size.

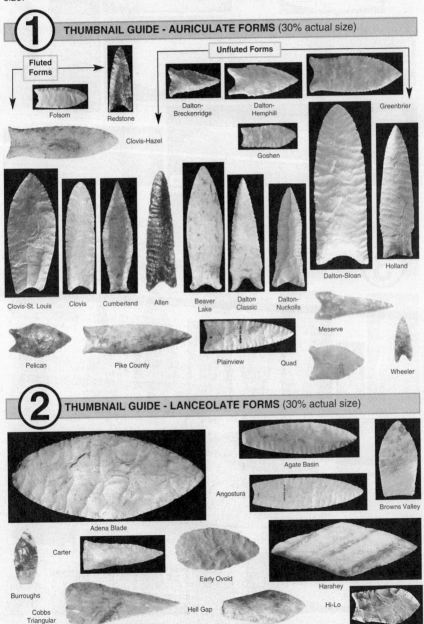

1 THUMBNAIL GUIDE - AURICULATE FORMS (30% actual size)

Fluted Forms

Unfluted Forms

Folsom

Redstone

Dalton-Breckenridge

Dalton-Hemphill

Greenbrier

Clovis-Hazel

Goshen

Clovis-St. Louis

Clovis

Cumberland

Allen

Beaver Lake

Dalton Classic

Dalton-Nuckolls

Dalton-Sloan

Holland

Meserve

Pelican

Pike County

Plainview

Quad

Wheeler

NC

2 THUMBNAIL GUIDE - LANCEOLATE FORMS (30% actual size)

Agate Basin

Angostura

Browns Valley

Adena Blade

Carter

Early Ovoid

Harahey

Burroughs

Cobbs Triangular

Hell Gap

Hi-Lo

THUMBNAIL GUIDE - Lanceolate forms (continued)

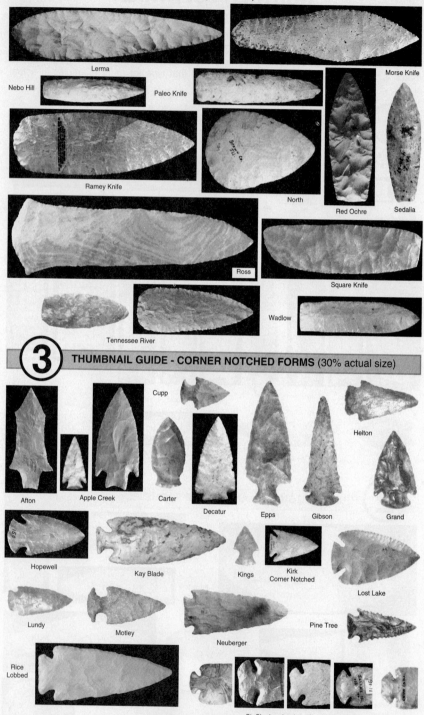

Lerma

Nebo Hill

Paleo Knife

Morse Knife

Ramey Knife

North

Red Ochre

Sedalia

Ross

Square Knife

Tennessee River

Wadlow

③ THUMBNAIL GUIDE - CORNER NOTCHED FORMS (30% actual size)

Cupp

Afton

Apple Creek

Carter

Decatur

Epps

Gibson

Helton

Grand

Hopewell

Kay Blade

Kings

Kirk Corner Notched

Lost Lake

Lundy

Motley

Neuberger

Pine Tree

Rice Lobbed

St. Charles showing different base forms

THUMBNAIL GUIDE - Corner Notched forms (continued)

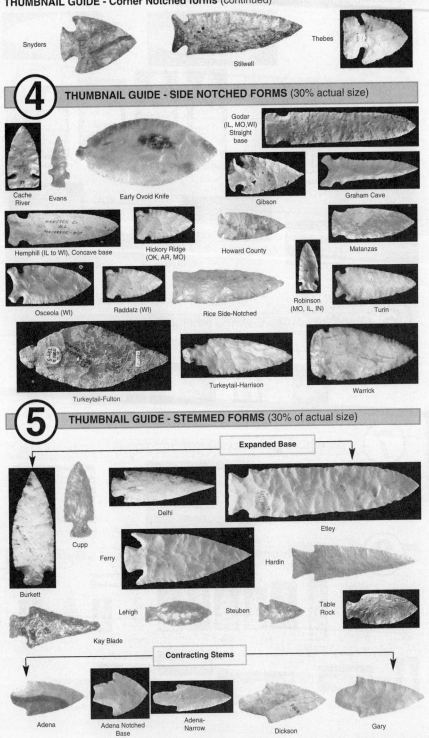

Snyders

Stilwell

Thebes

④ THUMBNAIL GUIDE - SIDE NOTCHED FORMS (30% actual size)

Godar (IL, MO,WI) Straight base

Cache River

Evans

Early Ovoid Knife

Gibson

Graham Cave

Hemphill (IL to WI), Concave base

Hickory Ridge (OK, AR, MO)

Howard County

Matanzas

Osceola (WI)

Raddatz (WI)

Rice Side-Notched

Robinson (MO, IL, IN)

Turin

Turkeytail-Fulton

Turkeytail-Harrison

Warrick

⑤ THUMBNAIL GUIDE - STEMMED FORMS (30% of actual size)

Expanded Base

NC

Delhi

Etley

Cupp

Ferry

Hardin

Burkett

Lehigh

Steuben

Table Rock

Kay Blade

Contracting Stems

Adena

Adena Notched Base

Adena-Narrow

Dickson

Gary

821

THUMBNAIL GUIDE - Stemmed Forms (continued)

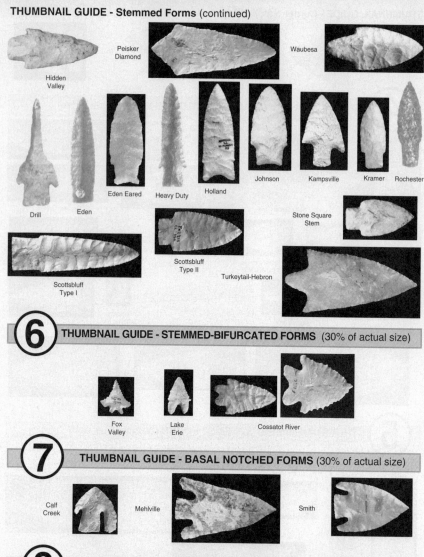

Hidden Valley

Peisker Diamond

Waubesa

Drill

Eden

Eden Eared

Heavy Duty

Holland

Johnson

Kampsville

Kramer

Rochester

Scottsbluff Type I

Scottsbluff Type II

Turkeytail-Hebron

Stone Square Stem

6 THUMBNAIL GUIDE - STEMMED-BIFURCATED FORMS (30% of actual size)

Fox Valley

Lake Erie

Cossatot River

7 THUMBNAIL GUIDE - BASAL NOTCHED FORMS (30% of actual size)

Calf Creek

Mehlville

Smith

8 THUMBNAIL GUIDE - ARROW POINTS (30% of actual size)

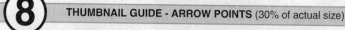

Collins

Agee

Alba

Bayogoula

Cahokia

Harrell

Haskell

Hayes

Homan

Madison

Huffaker

Jacks Reef Corner Notched

Madison-Titterington

Nodena

Scallorn

Sequoyah

Washita

ADENA - Late Archaic to late Woodland, 3000 - 1200 B. P.

(see Burkett, Dickson, Gary, Kramer, Hidden Valley, Rochester and Waubesa)

Blunt tip

G6, $20-$35
MO

G6, $25-$40
S.W. IL

G7, $55-$100
NE

G10, $50-$90
MO

Harrison chert

G9, $90-$175
Ogle Co., IL

NC

LOCATION: Eastern to Southeastern states. **DESCRIPTION:** A medium to large, thin, narrow, triangular blade that is sometimes serrated, and with a medium to long, narrow to broad rounded "beaver tail" stem. Most examples are from average to excellent quality. Base can be ground. **I.D. KEY:** Rounded base, Woodland random flaking.

ADENA BLADE - Late Archaic to Woodland, 3000 - 1200 B. P.

(Also see Lerma, North, Red Ochre & Stenfield)

G6, $50-$90
IL

LOCATION: Midwestern to Eastern states.
DESCRIPTION: A large size, thin, broad, ovate blade with a rounded base and is often found in caches. **I.D. KEY:** Random flaking.

G7, $175-$300
WI

ADENA-DICKSON (See Dickson)

ADENA-NARROW STEM - Late Archaic to Woodland, 3000 - 1200 B. P.

(Also see Adena, Dickson, Rochester and Waubesa)

LOCATION: Eastern to Southeastern states. **DESCRIPTION:** A medium to large, thin, narrow triangular blade that is sometimes serrated, and a medium to long, narrow, rounded stem. Most examples are well made. **I.D. KEY:** Narrow rounded base with more secondary work than ordinary Adena.

ADENA-NARROW STEM
(continued)

Shoulder nick →

G5, $20-$35
IL

G6, $45-$80
Pettis Co., MO

ADENA-NOTCHED BASE - Late Archaic to Woodland, 3000 - 1200 B. P.

G5, $30-$50
MO

LOCATION: Southeast to Midwest.
DESCRIPTION: Identical to Adena, but with a notched or snapped-off concave base. **I.D. KEY:** Basal form different.

G5, $15-$25
MO

NC

ADENA-WAUBESA   (See Waubesa)

AFTON - Middle Archaic to early Woodland, 5000 - 2000 B. P.
(Also see Apple Creek, Ferry and Helton)

G4, $15-$25
MO

AFTON (continued)

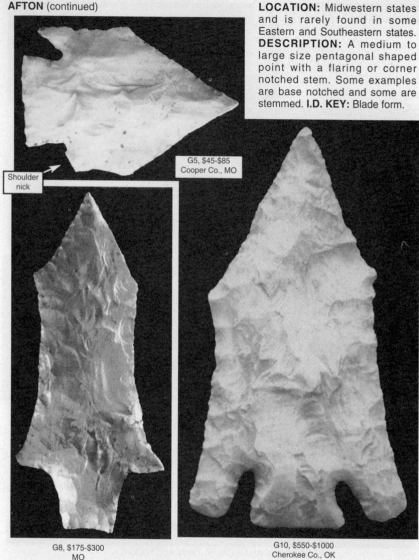

LOCATION: Midwestern states and is rarely found in some Eastern and Southeastern states. **DESCRIPTION:** A medium to large size pentagonal shaped point with a flaring or corner notched stem. Some examples are base notched and some are stemmed. **I.D. KEY:** Blade form.

G5, $45-$85
Cooper Co., MO

Shoulder nick

G8, $175-$300
MO

G10, $550-$1000
Cherokee Co., OK

AGATE BASIN - Transitional Paleo to Early Archaic, 10500 - 8000 B. P.

(Also see Allen, Angostura, Burroughs, Eden, Lerma, Nebo Hill and Sedalia)

G5, $65-$125
MO.

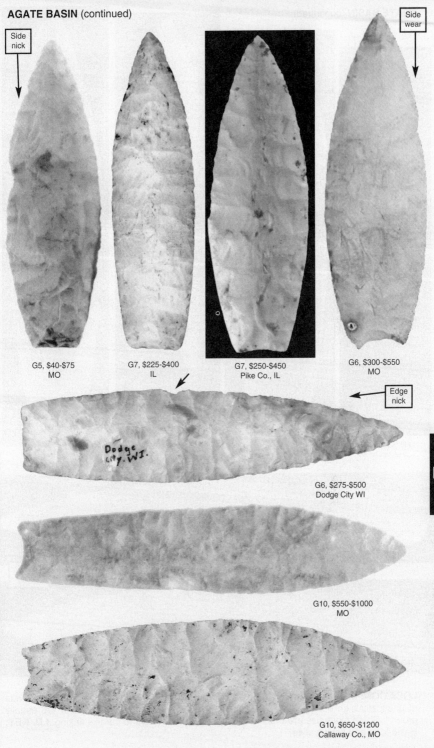

AGATE BASIN (continued)

Side nick

Side wear

G5, $40-$75
MO

G7, $225-$400
IL

G7, $250-$450
Pike Co., IL

G6, $300-$550
MO

Edge nick

Dodge City. WI.

G6, $275-$500
Dodge City WI

NC

G10, $550-$1000
MO

G10, $650-$1200
Callaway Co., MO

827

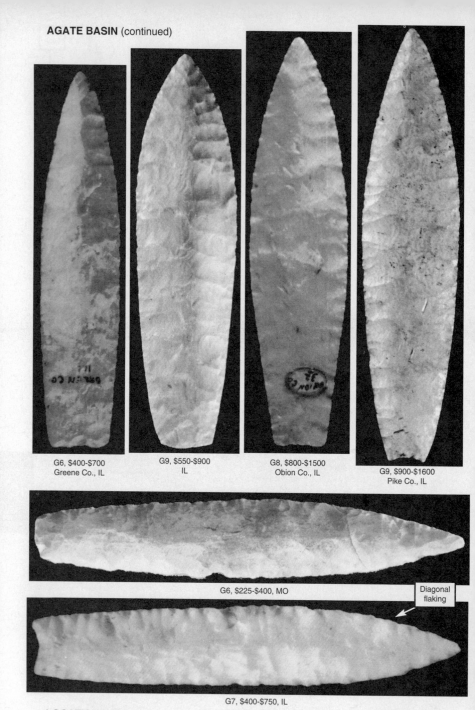

G6, $400-$700
Greene Co., IL

G9, $550-$900
IL

G8, $800-$1500
Obion Co., IL

G9, $900-$1600
Pike Co., IL

G6, $225-$400, MO

Diagonal
flaking

G7, $400-$750, IL

LOCATION: Midwestern states. **DESCRIPTION:** A medium to large size lanceolate blade of unusually high quality. Bases are either convex, concave or straight, and are usually ground. Some examples are median ridged and have random to parallel flaking. **I.D. KEY:** Basal form and flaking style.

Orange/ yellow color

G7, $150-$250
MO

G9, $800-$1500
Jersey Co., IL

G9, $800-$1500
Mahaska Co., IA

G8, $200-$350
MO

NC

G10, $500-$950
Pike Co., IL

G9, $300-$550
IL

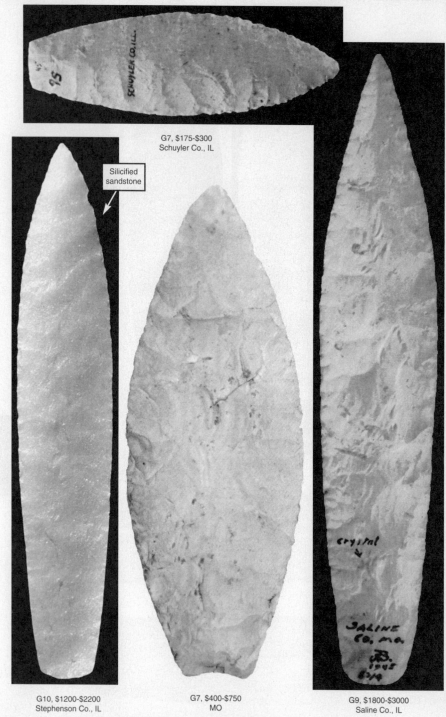

G7, $175-$300
Schuyler Co., IL

Silicified
sandstone

G10, $1200-$2200
Stephenson Co., IL

G7, $400-$750
MO

G9, $1800-$3000
Saline Co., IL

830

AGEE - Mississippian, 1200 - 700 B. P.

(Also see Alba, Hayes, Homan)

LOCATION: Arkansas; rarely into Missouri and Illinois. **DESCRIPTION:** A small to medium size, narrow, expanded barbed, corner notched point. Tips are needle sharp. Some examples are double notched at the base. A rare type **I.D. KEY:** Basal form and barb expansion.

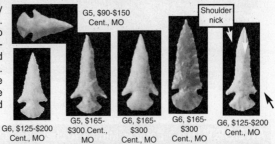

G5, $90-$150 Cent., MO

Shoulder nick

G6, $125-$200 Cent., MO

G5, $165-$300 Cent., MO

G6, $165-$300 Cent., MO

G6, $165-$300 Cent., MO

G6, $125-$200 Cent., MO

ALBA - Woodland to Mississippian, 2000 - 400 B. P.

(Also see Agee, Hayes, Homan and Sequoyah)

G7, $80-$150 IL

LOCATION: Louisiana, Arkansas into Oklahoma; rarely into Illinois. **DESCRIPTION:** A small to medium size, narrow, well made point with prominent tangs, a recurved blade and a bulbous stem. Some examples are serrated. **I.D. KEY:** Rounded base and expanded barbs.

ALLEN - Transitional Paleo to Early Archaic, 10,000 - 7500 B. P.

(Also see Angostura, Browns Valley, Clovis, Goshen and Plainview)

LOCATION: Midwestern states to Canada. **DESCRIPTION:** A medium to large size lanceolate point that has oblique transverse flaking and a concave base. Basal area is ground. **I.D. KEY:** Flaking style and blade form.

G6, $125-$200 Osage Co., OK

G5, $250-$450 Pottowatomie Co., KS

Tip nick

Diagonal parallel flaking

G10, $1800-$3000 W. KS

ALLEN (continued)

Diagonal parallel flaking

Ground basal area

G7, $800-$1500
Riley Co., KS

ANGOSTURA - Early to Middle Archaic, 10,000 - 8000 B. P.

(Also see Agate Basin, Allen, Eden & Wheeler Excurvate)

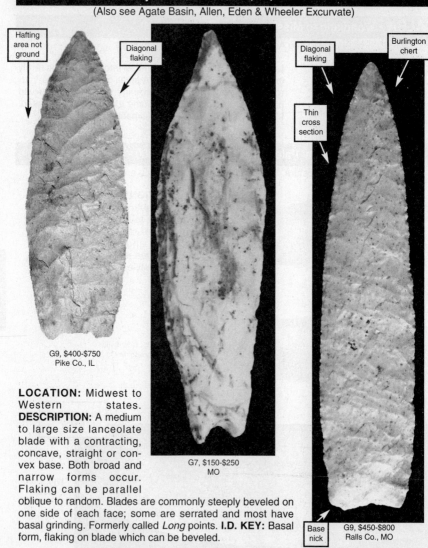

Hafting area not ground

Diagonal flaking

Diagonal flaking

Burlington chert

Thin cross section

G9, $400-$750
Pike Co., IL

G7, $150-$250
MO

Base nick

G9, $450-$800
Ralls Co., MO

LOCATION: Midwest to Western states. **DESCRIPTION:** A medium to large size lanceolate blade with a contracting, concave, straight or convex base. Both broad and narrow forms occur. Flaking can be parallel oblique to random. Blades are commonly steeply beveled on one side of each face; some are serrated and most have basal grinding. Formerly called *Long* points. **I.D. KEY:** Basal form, flaking on blade which can be beveled.

ANGOSTURA (continued)

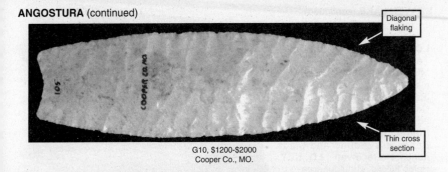

Diagonal flaking

Thin cross section

G10, $1200-$2000
Cooper Co., MO.

APPLE CREEK - Late Woodland, 1700 - 1500 B. P.

(Also see Helton, Jacks Reef, Kirk Corner Notched, Lundy and Pine Tree)

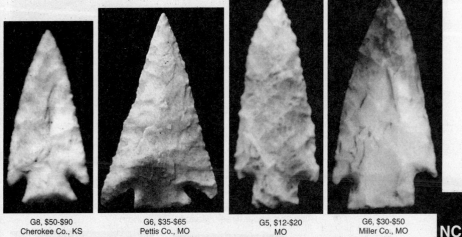

G8, $50-$90
Cherokee Co., KS

G6, $35-$65
Pettis Co., MO

G5, $12-$20
MO

G6, $30-$50
Miller Co., MO

NC

LOCATION: Kansas, Missouri & Illinois. **DESCRIPTION**: A medium to large size, broad, corner notched point with an expanded stem. Barbs are short to moderate. Bases are convex, straight or concave. **I.D. KEY**: Angle of corner notches.

BAYOGOULA - Mississippian, 800 - 400 B. P.

(Also see Cahokia, Madison)

Restored base

G1, $40-$70
Cahokia Mound site, IL

LOCATION: Louisiana. **DESCRIPTION**: A small to medium size, thin, narrow, arrowpoint with tapered shoulders and a short, expanded base that is concave. A Louisiana type that has been found at Cahokia Mound site.

BEAVER LAKE - Paleo, 11,000 - 8000 B. P.

(Also see Clovis, Cumberland, Greenbrier, Pike County and Quad)

833

BEAVER LAKE (continued)

LOCATION: Alabama, Tennessee into Illinois and Missouri. **DESCRIPTION:** A medium to large size lanceolate blade with flaring ears. Contemporaneous and associated with *Cumberland*, but thinner than unfluted *Cumberlands*. Bases are ground and blade edges are recurved. **I.D. KEY:** Paleo flaking, shoulder area.

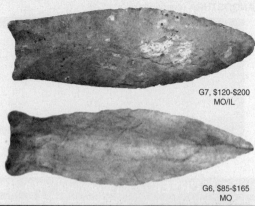

G7, $120-$200
MO/IL

G6, $85-$165
MO

G10, $1500-$2800
MO

BLACK SAND (Now typed as Godar)

BREWERTON CORNER NOTCHED - Mid-late Archaic, 6000 - 4000 B. P.

(Also see Apple Creek, Helton, Kirk, Lundy)

G5, $12-$20
MO

G6, $15-$25
MO

G5, $15-$30
MO

LOCATION: Midwestern states into the Northeast. **DESCRIPTION:** A small size triangular point with faint corner notches and a convex base. Called *Freeheley* in Michigan.

BREWERTON SIDE NOTCHED - Mid-late Archaic, 6000 - 4000 B. P.

(Also see Godar, Graham Cave, Hickory Ridge, Howard County, Raddatz and Robinson)

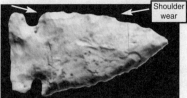

Shoulder wear

LOCATION: Midwestern states into the Northeast. **DESCRIPTION:** A small to medium size, triangular point with weak side notches and a concave to straight base.

G5, $12-$20
MO

BROWNS VALLEY - Transitional Paleo, 10,000 - 8000 B. P.

(Also see Agate Basin, Allen, Angostura, Burroughs, Clovis, Plainview and Sedalia)

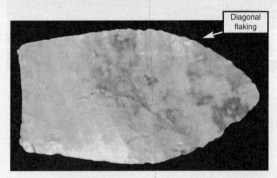

Diagonal flaking

LOCATION: Upper Midwest - ern states. **DESCRIPTION:** A medium to large, thin, lanceolate blade with usually oblique to horizontal transverse flaking and a concave to straight base which can be ground. **I.D. KEY:** Paleo transverse flaking.

G7, $300-$550
Cent. IL. Note oblique parallel
flaking which is characteristic
of the type.

BURKETT - Woodland, 2300 - 1800 B. P.

(Also see Adena, Dickson, Gary)

G7, $65-$125
Stockton Lake, MO

LOCATION: Missouri into Arkansas. **DESCRIPTION:** A medium to large size point with a short rectangular to contracting stem. The base can be straight to rounded. Shoulders can be tapered to barbed.

BURROUGHS - Early Archaic, 8000 - 6000 B. P.

(Also see Agate Basin and Browns Valley

NC

BURROUGHS (continued)
LOCATION: Northern Midwestern states.
DESCRIPTION: A small to medium size, lanceolate point with convex sides and a straight to slightly concave base.

G6, $45-$80
Riley Co., KS

CACHE RIVER - Early to Middle Archaic, 10,000 - 5000 B. P.

(Also see Godar, Graham Cave, Hickory Ridge, Howard County, Raddatz and Robinson)

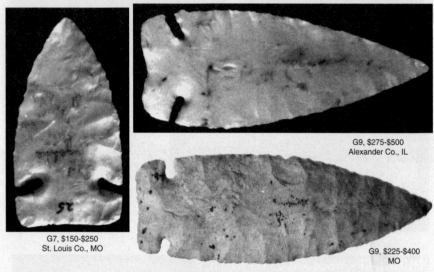

G9, $275-$500
Alexander Co., IL

G7, $150-$250
St. Louis Co., MO

G9, $225-$400
MO

LOCATION: Midwestern states. **DESCRIPTION:** A small to medium size, fairly thin, side-notched, triangular point with a concave base. Could be related to *Big Sandy* points. **I.D. KEY:** Base form, narrow notched & flaking of blade.

CAHOKIA - Mississippian, 1000 - 500 B. P.

(Also see Harrell, Huffaker, Madison and Washita)

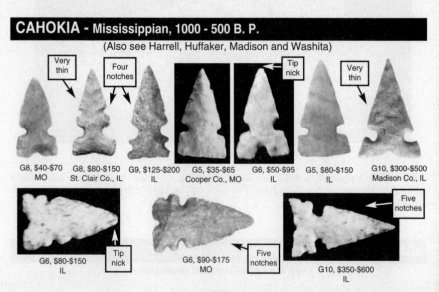

G8, $40-$70
MO

G8, $80-$150
St. Clair Co., IL

G9, $125-$200
IL

G5, $35-$65
Cooper Co., MO

G6, $50-$95
IL

G5, $80-$150
IL

G10, $300-$500
Madison Co., IL

G6, $80-$150
IL

G6, $90-$175
MO

G10, $350-$600
IL

836

CAHOKIA (continued)

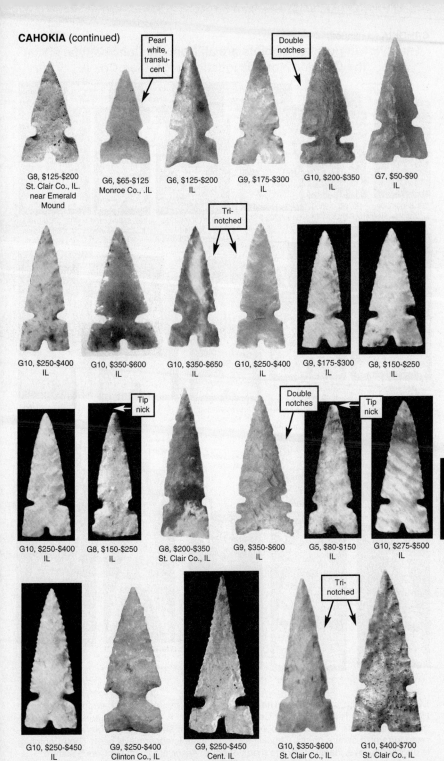

Pearl white, translucent

Double notches

G8, $125-$200
St. Clair Co., IL.
near Emerald Mound

G6, $65-$125
Monroe Co., .IL

G6, $125-$200
IL

G9, $175-$300
IL

G10, $200-$350
IL

G7, $50-$90
IL

Tri-notched

G10, $250-$400
IL

G10, $350-$600
IL

G10, $350-$650
IL

G10, $250-$400
IL

G9, $175-$300
IL

G8, $150-$250
IL

Tip nick

Double notches

Tip nick

NC

G10, $250-$400
IL

G8, $150-$250
IL

G8, $200-$350
St. Clair Co., IL

G9, $350-$600
IL

G5, $80-$150
IL

G10, $275-$500
IL

Tri-notched

G10, $250-$450
IL

G9, $250-$400
Clinton Co., IL

G9, $250-$450
Cent. IL

G10, $350-$600
St. Clair Co., IL

G10, $400-$700
St. Clair Co., IL

CAHOKIA (continued)

The following valuable points are all from the Cahokia type site at the Cahokia Mounds location in St. Clair Co., IL

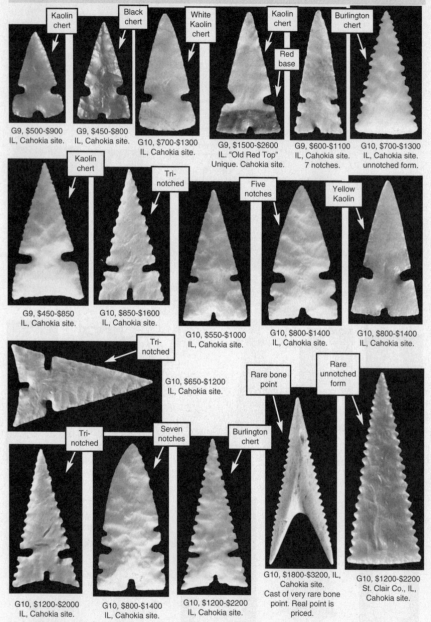

Kaolin chert

G9, $500-$900
IL, Cahokia site.

Black chert

G9, $450-$800
IL, Cahokia site.

White Kaolin chert

G10, $700-$1300
IL, Cahokia site.

Kaolin chert / Red base

G9, $1500-$2600
IL. "Old Red Top"
Unique. Cahokia site.

Kaolin chert

G9, $600-$1100
IL, Cahokia site.
7 notches.

Burlington chert

G10, $700-$1300
IL, Cahokia site.
unnotched form.

Kaolin chert

G9, $450-$850
IL, Cahokia site.

Tri-notched

G10, $850-$1600
IL, Cahokia site.

G10, $550-$1000
IL, Cahokia site.

Five notches

G10, $800-$1400
IL, Cahokia site.

Yellow Kaolin

G10, $800-$1400
IL, Cahokia site.

Tri-notched

G10, $650-$1200
IL, Cahokia site.

Tri-notched

G10, $1200-$2000
IL, Cahokia site.

Seven notches

G10, $800-$1400
IL, Cahokia site.

Burlington chert

G10, $1200-$2200
IL, Cahokia site.

Rare bone point

G10, $1800-$3200, IL,
Cahokia site.
Cast of very rare bone
point. Real point is
priced.

Rare unnotched form

G10, $1200-$2200
St. Clair Co., IL,
Cahokia site.

LOCATION: Midwestern states. The famous Cahokia mounds are located in Illinois close to the Mississippi River in St. Clair Co. **DESCRIPTION:** A small to medium size, thin, triangular point that can have one or more notches on each blade edge. A rare unnotched serrated form also occurs on the Cahokia site. The base is either plain, has a center notch or is deeply concave. Rarely, they are made of bone. Associated with the Caddo culture.

838

CALF CREEK - Early to Middle Archaic, 8000 - 5000 B. P.

(Also see Andice and Bell in Southern Central Section)

Broken shoulder

G3, $80-$200
Cherokee Co., KS

G6, $350-$600
Manhattan, KS

G10, $1500-$2800
Riley Co., KS

LOCATION: Texas into Oklahoma, Arkansas, Kansas and Missouri. The type site is in Searcy Co., Arkansas. **DESCRIPTION:** A medium to large size thin, broad, triangular point with very deep parallel basal notches. Related to the *Andice* and *Bell* points found in Texas. Tangs on first-stage examples extended to the base. Very rare in type area. **I.D. KEY:** Notches almost straight up.

CARTER - (Hopewell) - Woodland, 2500 - 1500 B. P.

(Also see Grand and Snyders)

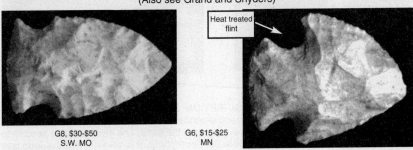

Heat treated flint

G8, $30-$50
S.W. MO

G6, $15-$25
MN

LOCATION: Illinois. **DESCRIPTION:** A medium to large size, narrow, wide corner to side notched point with a convex base. Shoulders are rounded, weak to non-existent. The Blade form has no shoulders and is similar in appearance to *Copena* found in Tennessee and Alabama. Related to the Snyders point.

839

G6, $35-$65
MN

G10, $150-$250
IL

G5, $20-$35
IL

G7, $25-$45
MO

CLOVIS - Early Paleo, 14,000 - 10,000 B. P.

(Also see Allen, Angostura, Browns Valley, Cumberland, Dalton, Folsom and Plainview)

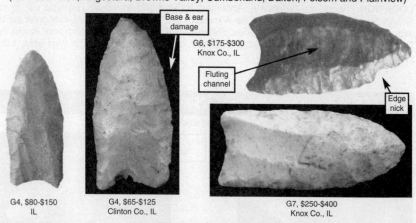

Base & ear
damage

G6, $175-$300
Knox Co., IL

Fluting
channel

Edge
nick

G4, $80-$150
IL

G4, $65-$125
Clinton Co., IL

G7, $250-$400
Knox Co., IL

LOCATION: All of North America. **DESCRIPTION:** A medium to large size, auriculate, fluted, lanceolate point with convex sides and a concave base that is ground. Most examples are fluted on both sides about 1/3 the way up from the base. The flaking can be random to parallel. *Clovis* is the earliest point type in the hemisphere. It is believed that this form was brought here by early man from Siberia or Europe some 14,000 years ago. Current theories place the origin of *Clovis* in the Southeastern U.S. since more examples are found in Florida, Alabama and Tennessee than anywhere else. **I.D. KEY:** Paleo flaking, shoulders, billet or baton fluting instead of indirect style.

CLOVIS (continued)

Flute channel

Side damage

G6, $175-$300
IL

G8, $450-$800
Schuyler Co., IL

G6, $175-$300
MO

G6, $275-$500
IL

G9, $650-$1200
Montgomery Co., MO

G9, $650-$1200
IL

G2, $150-$250
Pope Co., IL

G9, $700-$1250
MO

NC

G9, $1700-$3000
IL

841

CLOVIS (continued)

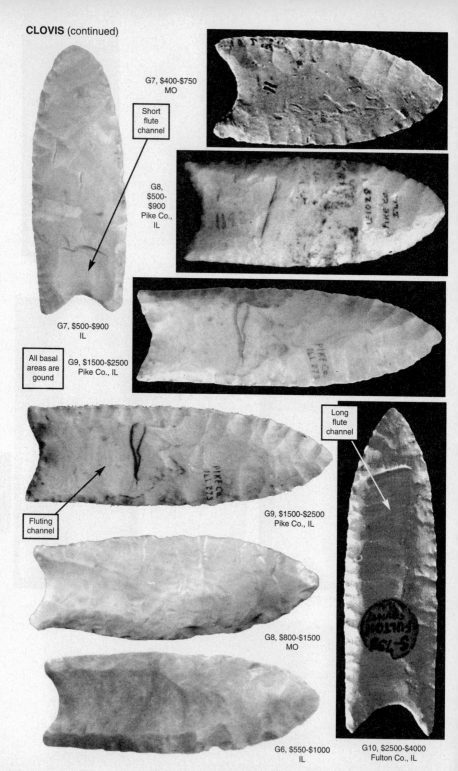

G7, $400-$750
MO

Short flute channel

G8, $500-$900
Pike Co., IL

G7, $500-$900
IL

All basal areas are gound

G9, $1500-$2500
Pike Co., IL

Long flute channel

Fluting channel

G9, $1500-$2500
Pike Co., IL

G8, $800-$1500
MO

G6, $550-$1000
IL

G10, $2500-$4000
Fulton Co., IL

842

CLOVIS (continued)

Broken ear

G7, $800-$1500
KS

G7, $400-$750
Sou. IL

Jasper

NC

G7, $2000-$3500
St. Louis, MO

G9, $3000-$5000
KS

G7, $3500-$6500
Fayette Co., IL

843

CLOVIS-HAZEL - Early Paleo, 14,000 - 10,000 B. P.

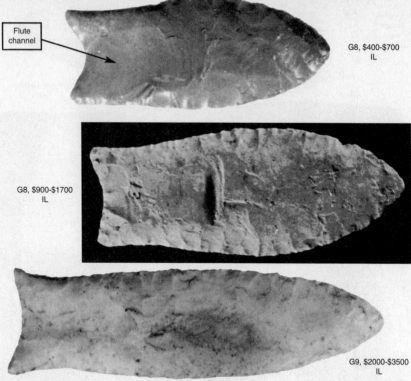

Flute channel

G8, $400-$700
IL

G8, $900-$1700
IL

G9, $2000-$3500
IL

LOCATION: Midwestern states eastward. **DESCRIPTION:** A small to large size auriculate point with recurved blade edges and a fishtailed base that is concave. **I.D. KEY:** Fishtailed base.

CLOVIS-ST. LOUIS - Early Paleo, 14,000 - 10,000 B. P.

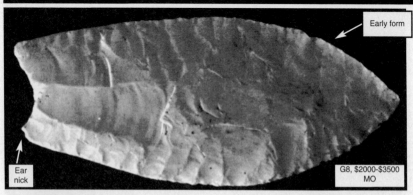

Early form

Ear nick

G8, $2000-$3500
MO

LOCATION: The Dakotas, Wisconsin southward to Arkansas and eastward to Michigan. **DESCRIPTION:** A large size, broad, auriculate, fluted, lanceolate point with convex sides and a concave base that is ground. Most examples are fluted on both sides 1/3 or more up from the base. The flaking can be random to parallel. One of the largest *Clovis* forms. **I.D. KEY:** Size and broadness.

COBBS TRIANGULAR - Early Archaic, 8000 - 5000 B. P.

(Also see Decatur, Dovetail, Lerma and Lost Lake)

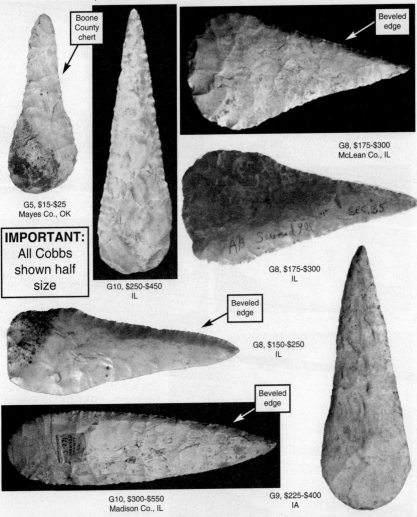

Boone County chert

Beveled edge

G5, $15-$25
Mayes Co., OK

IMPORTANT: All Cobbs shown half size

G10, $250-$450
IL

G8, $175-$300
McLean Co., IL

G8, $175-$300
IL

Beveled edge

G8, $150-$250
IL

Beveled edge

G10, $300-$550
Madison Co., IL

G9, $225-$400
IA

NC

LOCATION: Southeastern states. **DESCRIPTION:** A medium to large size, thin, lanceolate blade with a broad, rounded to square base. One side of each face is usually steeply beveled. These are un-notched preforms for early Archaic beveled types such as *Decatur, Dovetail, Lost Lake,* etc.

COLLINS - Woodland, 1500 - 1200 B. P.

(Also see Haskell, Scallorn)

G8, $35-$65
Cherokee
Co., KS

LOCATION: Arkansas into Kansas. **DESCRIPTION:** A small, narrow arrowpoint with broad side notches. Bases can be straight, to eared to convex.

845

COSSATOT RIVER - Early Archaic, 9500 - 8000 B. P.

(Also see Fox Valley and Lake Erie)

G4, $12-$20
Logan Co., IL

G6, $15-$30
Madison Co., IL

G6, $20-$35
Logan Co., IL

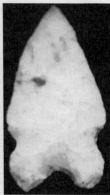

G6, $20-$35
Logan Co., IL

Serrated edge

G9, $65-$125, Logan Co., IL.

G8, $40-$75
Logan Co., IL

Serrated edge

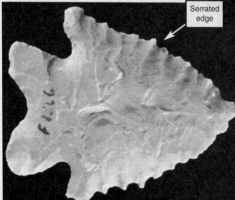

LOCATION: Illinois, Missouri into Oklahoma. **DESCRIPTION:** A medium to large size, thin, usually serrated, widely corner notched point with large round to square ears and a deep notch in the center of the base. Bases are usually ground. **I.D. KEY:** Basal notching, early Archaic flaking.

G9, $125-$200
Adams Co., IL

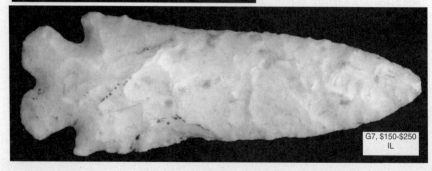

G7, $150-$250
IL

CUMBERLAND - Paleo, 12,000 - 8000 B. P.

(Also see Beaver Lake, Clovis, Dalton and Quad)

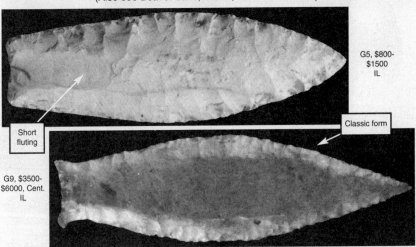

G5, $800-$1500
IL

Classic form

Short fluting

G9, $3500-$6000, Cent. IL

LOCATION: Southeastern states into Illinois. Called *Barnes Cumberland* in the Northeast. **DESCRIPTION:** A medium to large size, lanceolate, eared form that is usually fluted on both faces. The fluting and flaking technique is an advanced form as in *Folsom*, with the flutes usually extending the entire length of the blade. Bases are ground on all examples. An unfluted variant which is thicker than *Beaver Lake* has been found. This point is scarce everywhere and has been reproduced in large numbers. **I.D. KEY:** Paleo flaking, indirect pressure fluted.

CUMBERLAND UNFLUTED - Paleo, 12,000 - 8000 B. P.

(Also see Beaver Lake, Clovis, Pike County and Quad)

NC

DESCRIPTION: Identical to fluted *Cumberland*, but without the fluting. **Very rare** in the type area. Cross section is thicker than *Beaver Lake*.

G10, $3000-$5000
St. Clair Co., IL

CUPP - Late Woodland to Mississippian, 1500 - 600 B. P.

(Also see Epps, Helton, Kay Blade, Lundy, Motley, Snyders, Steuben, Table Rock)

LOCATION: Eastern states. **DESCRIPTION:** A medium to large size, narrow point with wide corner notches, shoulder barbs and a convex base. Similar to *Motley,* but the base stem is shorter and broader. *Epps* has square to tapered shoulders and a straight base, otherwise is identical to *Motley.*

CUPP (continued)

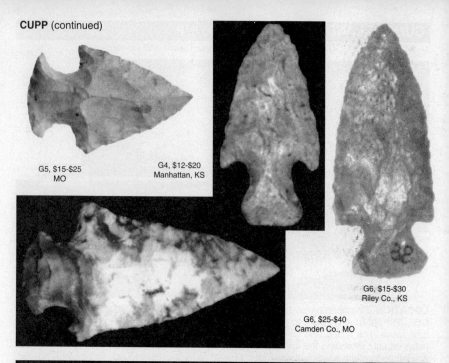

G5, $15-$25
MO

G4, $12-$20
Manhattan, KS

G6, $15-$30
Riley Co., KS

G6, $25-$40
Camden Co., MO

DALTON-BRECKENRIDGE - Early Archaic, 10,00 - 9200 B. P.

(Also see Dalton and Meserve)

LOCATION: Midwestern states, **DESCRIPTION:** A medium to large size, auriculate point with an obvious bevel extending the entire length of the point from tip to base. Similar in form to the *Dalton-Greenbrier*. Basal area is usually ground.

G5, $35-$65
MO

G10, $250-$400
MO/KY

DALTON CLASSIC - Early Archaic, 10,000 - 9200 B. P.

(Also see Beaver Lake, Greenbrier, Meserve, Pelican, Plainview and Quad)

LOCATION: Midwestern to Southeastern states. **DESCRIPTION:** A medium to large size, thin, auriculate, fishtailed point. Many examples are finely serrated and exhibit excellent flaking. Beveling may occur on one side of each face but is usually on the right side. All have basal grinding. This early type spread over most of the Eastern and Midwestern U.S. and strongly influenced many other types to follow.

DALTON CLASSIC (continued)

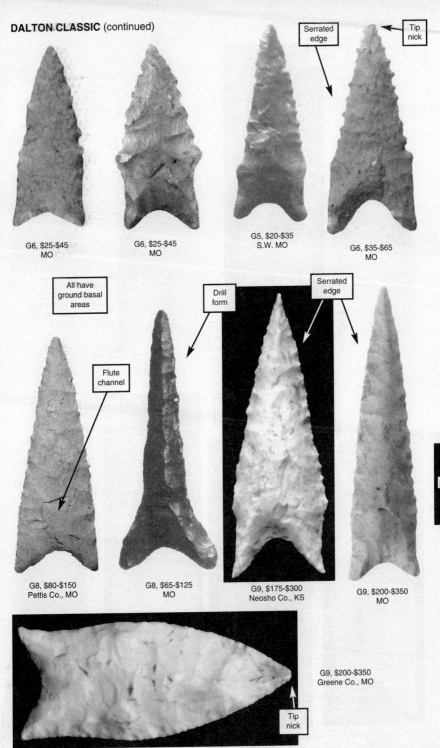

Serrated edge

Tip nick

G6, $25-$45
MO

G6, $25-$45
MO

G5, $20-$35
S.W. MO

G6, $35-$65
MO

All have ground basal areas

Drill form

Serrated edge

Flute channel

G8, $80-$150
Pettis Co., MO

G8, $65-$125
MO

G9, $175-$300
Neosho Co., KS

G9, $200-$350
MO

NC

G9, $200-$350
Greene Co., MO

Tip nick

849

DALTON CLASSIC (continued)

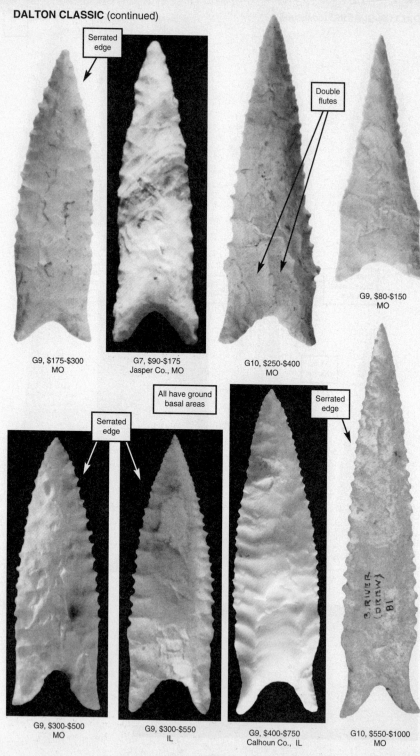

Serrated edge

Double flutes

All have ground basal areas

Serrated edge

Serrated edge

G9, $175-$300
MO

G7, $90-$175
Jasper Co., MO

G10, $250-$400
MO

G9, $80-$150
MO

G9, $300-$500
MO

G9, $300-$550
IL

G9, $400-$750
Calhoun Co., IL

G10, $550-$1000
MO

DALTON CLASSIC (continued)

G9, $1200-$2000
Bond Co., IL

G9, $900-$1600
MO

Diagonal flaking

F.E. MOSER. 1¼ × 3½.
ANGLUM MO.

G10, $2000-$3500
Anglum, MO

G9, $800-$1500
MO

Burlington chert

Diagonal flaking

G8, $1500-$2800
Pettis Co., MO

G9, $500-$900
Cooper Co., MO

IMPORTANT:
Daltons on this
page shown
half size

Flute channel

Wild Horse Creek Rd
Mo. River Bluffs

53.

NC

G10, $1500-$2500
MO

G9, $900-$1600
Pike Co., IL

G9, $1500-$2500
Greene Co., AR

G9, $1700-$3000
MO

G10, $3000-$5000
MO

DALTON-HEMPHILL - Early Archaic, 10,000 - 9200 B. P.

(Also see Holland and Scottsbluff)

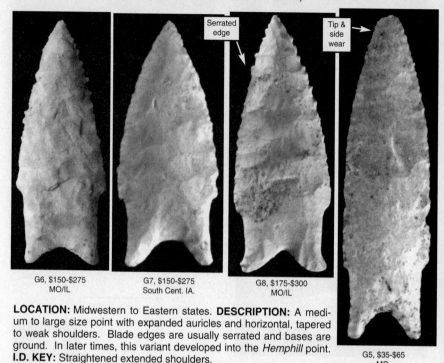

Serrated edge

Tip & side wear

G6, $150-$275
MO/IL

G7, $150-$275
South Cent. IA.

G8, $175-$300
MO/IL

G5, $35-$65
MO.

LOCATION: Midwestern to Eastern states. **DESCRIPTION:** A medium to large size point with expanded auricles and horizontal, tapered to weak shoulders. Blade edges are usually serrated and bases are ground. In later times, this variant developed into the *Hemphill* point. **I.D. KEY:** Straightened extended shoulders.

DALTON-NUCKOLLS - Early Archaic, 10,000 - 9200 B. P.

(Also see Dalton and Holland)

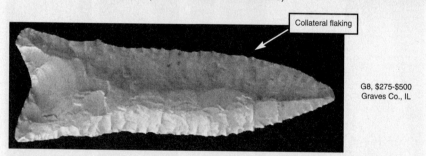

Collateral flaking

G8, $275-$500
Graves Co., IL

LOCATION: Midwestern to Southeastern states. **DESCRIPTION:** A medium to large size variant form, probably occurring from resharpening the *Greenbrier Dalton.* Bases are squared to lobbed to eared, and have a shallow concavity. **I.D. KEY:** Broad base and shoulders, flaking on blade.

DALTON-SLOAN - Early Archaic, 10,000 - 9200 B. P.

(Also see Allen, Angostura, Dalton, Greenbrier and Plainview)

DALTON-SLOAN (continued)

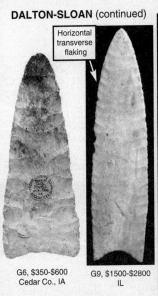

Horizontal transverse flaking

White chert

G6, $350-$600
Cedar Co., IA

G9, $1500-$2800
IL

IMPORTANT:
All Sloans shown half size

G9, $3500-$6500
Warren Co., MO

G6, $800-$1500
Shelby Co., MO

LOCATION: Midwestern states. **DESCRIPTION:** A large size variant of the *Dalton* point. This point is usually serrated, lacking shoulders and has a concave, fishtail base. Flaking is typically of the Dalton parallel style. **I.D. KEY:** No shoulders, serrations, fishtail base.

G10, $4000-$7500
St. Clair Co., IL

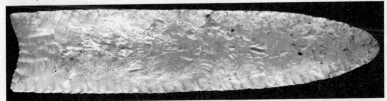

G10+, $5500-$10,000
Bloomfield, MO

NC

DECATUR - Early Archaic, 9000 - 3000 B. P.

(Also see Cobbs Triangular, Hardin, Kirk, Lost Lake and St. Charles)

Tip nick

G4, $35-$65
Fulton Co., IL

LOCATION: Eastern to Midwestern states. **DESCRIPTION:** A small to medium size, serrated, corner notched point that is usually beveled on one side of each face. The base is usually broken off (fractured) by a blow inward from each corner of the stem. Sometimes the sides of the stem and backs of the tangs are also fractured, and in rare cases, the tip may be fractured by a blow on each side directed towards the base. Bases are usually ground and flaking is of high quality. Basal fracturing also occurs in *Dovetail, Kirk, Motley* and *Snyders.*

853

DECATUR (continued)

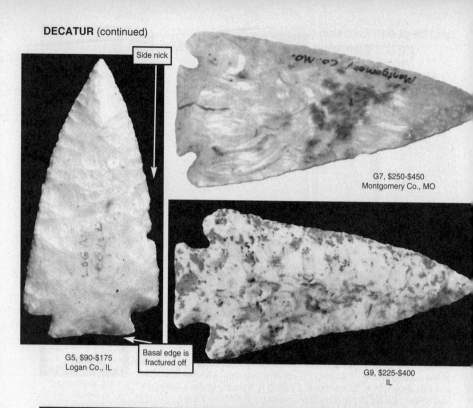

Side nick

Basal edge is fractured off

G7, $250-$450
Montgomery Co., MO

G5, $90-$175
Logan Co., IL

G9, $225-$400
IL

DELHI - Late Archaic, 3500 - 2000 B. P.
(Also see Helton)

G8, $65-$125
Cooper Co., MO

G9, $80-$150
Cooper Co., MO

LOCATION: Louisiana into Missouri. **DESCRIPTION:** A medium to large size, narrow, stemmed point with a long blade and strong, barbed shoulders. The stem can be square but usually expands and the base is straight to slightly convex. **I.D. KEY:** Base form, narrowness of blade.

854

DICKSON - Woodland, 2500 - 1600 B. P.

(Also see Adena, Burkett, Gary, Hidden Valley and Waubesa)

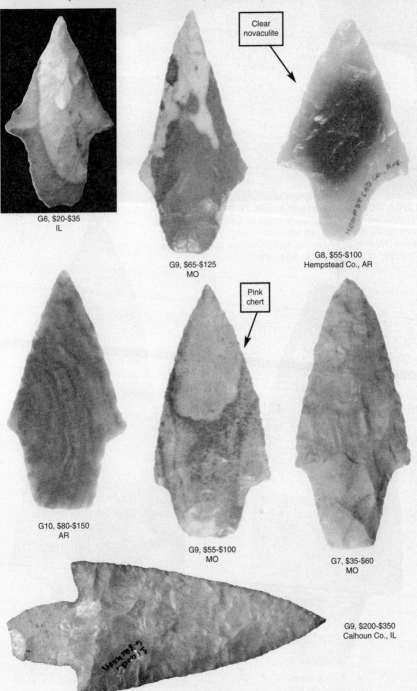

G6, $20-$35
IL

Clear novaculite

G9, $65-$125
MO

G8, $55-$100
Hempstead Co., AR

Pink chert

G10, $80-$150
AR

G9, $55-$100
MO

G7, $35-$60
MO

NC

G9, $200-$350
Calhoun Co., IL

855

G10, $350-$650
IL

LOCATION: Midwestern states. **DESCRIPTION:** Associated with the Hopewell culture. A medium to large size point with tapered shoulders and a contracting stem. High quality flaking and thinness is evident on most examples. **I.D. KEY:** Basal form.

G10 $275-$500
Benton Co., MO

G10, $400-$750
Boone Co., MO

856

DICKSON (continued)

G8, $250-$450
Warren Co., MO

Beveled
edge

NC

G10, $500-$900
Cooper Co., MO

G10, $800-$1500
MO

857

DRILL - Paleo to Historic, 14,000 - 200 B. P.

(Also see Scraper)

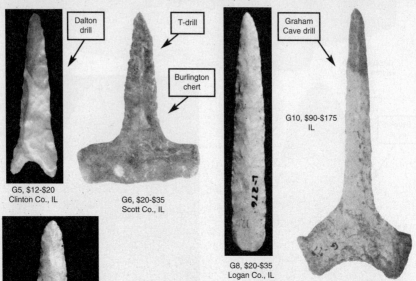

Dalton drill

T-drill

Burlington chert

Graham Cave drill

G10, $90-$175
IL

G5, $12-$20
Clinton Co., IL

G6, $20-$35
Scott Co., IL

G8, $20-$35
Logan Co., IL

LOCATION: Everywhere. **DESCRIPTION:** Although many drills were made from scratch, all point types were made into the drill form. Usually, heavily resharpened and broken points were salvaged and rechipped into drills. These objects were certainly used as drills (evidence of extreme edge wear), but there is speculation that some of these forms may have been used as pins for clothing, ornaments, ear plugs and other uses.

G8, $30-$50
Logan Co., IL

G8, $80-$150
Tazewell Co., IL

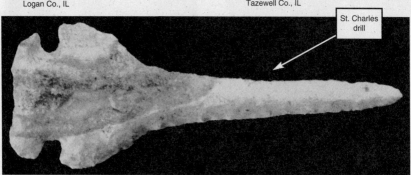

St. Charles drill

G9, $400-$750
IL

EARLY OVOID KNIFE - Trans. Paleo-Early Archaic, 11,000 - 9000 B. P.

(Also see Turkeytail)

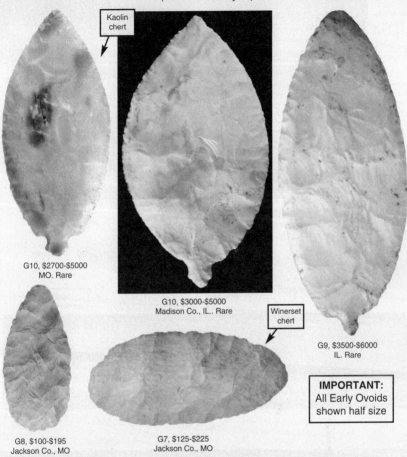

Kaolin chert

G10, $2700-$5000
MO. Rare

G10, $3000-$5000
Madison Co., IL.. Rare

Winerset chert

G9, $3500-$6000
IL. Rare

IMPORTANT:
All Early Ovoids
shown half size

G8, $100-$195
Jackson Co., MO

G7, $125-$225
Jackson Co., MO

NC

LOCATION: Arkansas, Missouri to Wisconsin. **DESCRIPTION:** A medium to large size, broad, thin, flat ovoid knife. Usually occurs as a double pointed blade but examples have been found with a small, notched stem. A very rare type. **I.D. KEY:** Broad blade, small stem to ovoid shape.

EDEN - Early Archaic, 9500 - 7500 B. P.

(Also see Agate Basin, Angostura, Hardin, Holland, Nebo Hill, Scottsbluff)

Collateral flaking

G6, $350-$600
W. MO

LOCATION: Midwestern states. **DESCRIPTION:** A medium to large size, narrow, lanceolate blade with a straight to concave base. Many examples have a median ridge and collateral to oblique parallel flaking. Bases are usually ground. **I.D. KEY:** Weak shoulders.

EDEN (continued)

G6, $650-$1200
N. Cent. MO

Note knobbed base →

Eden Eared form
G5, $550-$1000
Rock Co., WI

Hixton quartzite

Note slight shoulders-sets the type

Collateral flaking

G9, $2500-$4500
NE

Retipped impact fracture

Knife River flint

G8, $3000-$5000
Otoe Co., NE

EPPS - Late Archaic to Woodland, 3500 - 2000 B. P.

(Also see Cupp, Kay Blade and Motley)

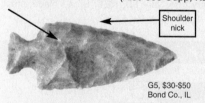

Shoulder nick

G5, $30-$50
Bond Co., IL

LOCATION: Louisiana, Arkansas into Illinois. **DESCRIPTION:** A medium to large broadly corner notched to expanded stemmed point. Base is straight. Shoulders are not as strongly barbed as *Motley* points which also have a convex base.

ETLEY - Late Archaic, 4000 - 2500 B. P.

(Also see Hardin, Mehlville, Smith, Stilwell, Stone Square Stem and Wadlow)

LOCATION: Midwestern states. The Etley site is in Calhoun Co., IL. Many *Wadlow* points were found there which is the preform for this type. **DESCRIPTION:** A large, narrow, blade with an angular point, recurved blade edges, a short, expanded stem and a straight to slightly convex base. Shoulders usually expand but have a tendency to point inward towards the base. **I.D. KEY:** Large size, barbs, narrow blade.

ETLEY (continued)

G6, $35-$65
IL

G8, $65-$125
MO

G6, $30-$50
MO

G6, $40-$75
IL

G6, $35-$65
IL

G8, $150-$250
MO

G8, $150-$250
Cent. IL

IMPORTANT:
All Etleys shown half size

G8 $150-$250
MO

G7 $55-$100
MO

NC

G8, $250-$400
Jersey Co., IL

G8, $200-$350
IL

G9, $275-$500
MO

G9, $275-$500
IL

G9, $350-$600
IL

EVANS - Late Archaic to Woodland, 4000 - 2000 B. P.

(Also see Hickory Ridge, Merkle and Turkeytail)

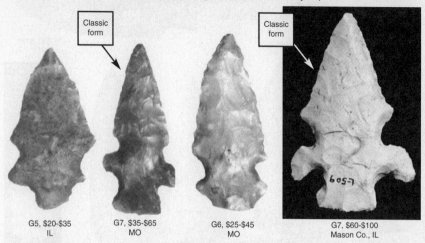

Classic form

Classic form

6057

G5, $20-$35
IL

G7, $35-$65
MO

G6, $25-$45
MO

G7, $60-$100
Mason Co., IL

LOCATION: Midwestern to Southeastern states. **DESCRIPTION:** A medium to large size stemmed point that is notched on each side somewhere between the point and shoulders. A similar form is found in Ohio and called *Ohio Double-Notched.*

EXOTIC FORMS - Archaic-Mississippian, 5000 - 1000 B. P.

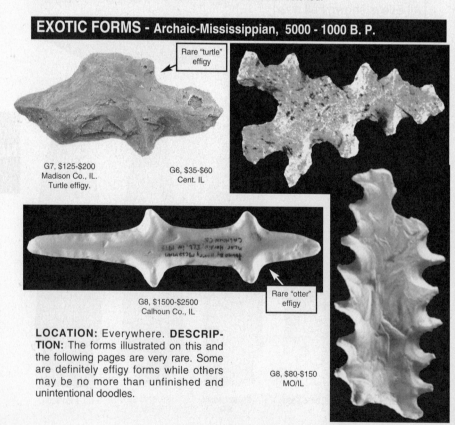

Rare "turtle" effigy

G7, $125-$200
Madison Co., IL.
Turtle effigy.

G6, $35-$60
Cent. IL

G8, $1500-$2500
Calhoun Co., IL

Rare "otter" effigy

LOCATION: Everywhere. **DESCRIPTION:** The forms illustrated on this and the following pages are very rare. Some are definitely effigy forms while others may be no more than unfinished and unintentional doodles.

G8, $80-$150
MO/IL

862

Rare otter
effigy

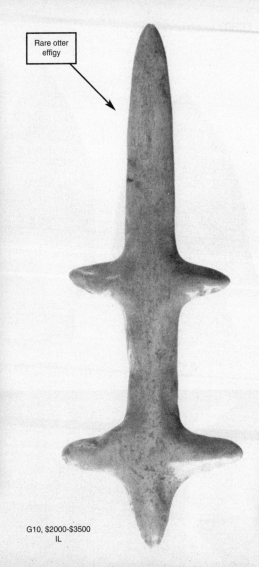

G6, $150-$250
Boone Co., IL

G10, $2000-$3500
IL

NC

FERRY - Middle to late Archaic, 5500 - 4500 B. P.

(Also see Grand, Hardin, Kay Blade, Kirk Corner Notched and Stilwell)

LOCATION: Illinois and Missouri. **DESCRIPTION:** A medium to large size, broad, stemmed point with a bulbous base. The blade is convex to recurved. The shoulders are barbed. **I.D. KEY:** Basal form and barbs.

G5, $15-$25
Madison Co., IL

FERRY (continued)

G6, $20-$35
Sou. IL

G5, $15-$25
MO

G8, $40-$70
Cherokee Co., KS

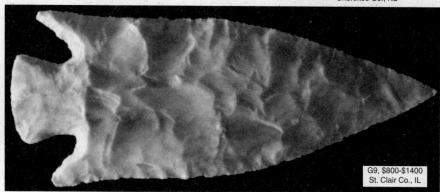

G9, $800-$1400
St. Clair Co., IL

FOLSOM - Paleo, 11,000 - 9000 B. P.
(Also see Clovis, Cumberland and Goshen)

LOCATION: N. Indiana Westward to Texas, northward to the Dakotas and West to Montana. **DESCRIPTION:** A small to medium size, thin, high quality, fluted point with contracted to slightly expanding, pointed auricles and a concave base. Fluting usually extends the entire length of each face. Blade flaking is extremely fine. The hafting area is ground. A very rare type, even in area of highest incidence. Modern reproductions have been made and extreme caution should be exercised in acquiring an original specimen. Often found in association with extinct bison fossil remains. **I.D. KEY:** Thinness and flaking style (Excessive secondary flaking). **NOTE:** A *Folsom* site was recently found on the Tippecanoe River in N. Indiana. *Clovis* and *Beaver Lake* were also found there.

864

FOLSOM (continued)

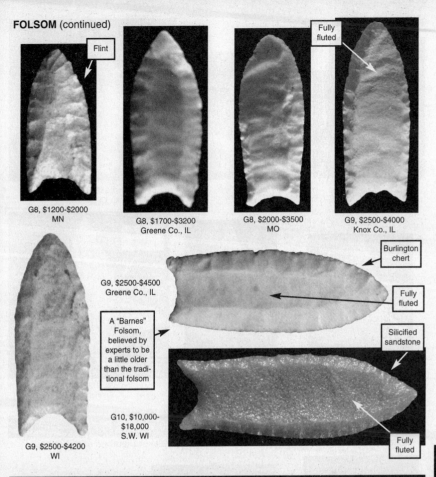

G8, $1200-$2000
MN

G8, $1700-$3200
Greene Co., IL

Flint

G8, $2000-$3500
MO

Fully fluted

G9, $2500-$4000
Knox Co., IL

G9, $2500-$4500
Greene Co., IL

A "Barnes" Folsom, believed by experts to be a little older than the traditional folsom.

Burlington chert

Fully fluted

Silicified sandstone

G10, $10,000-$18,000
S.W. WI

Fully fluted

G9, $2500-$4200
WI

FOX VALLEY - Early to Middle Archaic, 9000 - 4000 B. P.

(Also see Kirk, Lake Erie and Cossatot River)

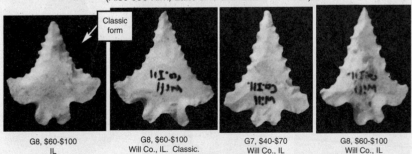

Classic form

G8, $60-$100
IL

G8, $60-$100
Will Co., IL. Classic.

G7, $40-$70
Will Co., IL

G8, $60-$100
Will Co., IL

LOCATION: Midwestern states. **DESCRIPTION:** A small size, triangular point with flaring shoulders and a short bifurcated stem. Shoulders are sometimes clipped winged and have a tendency to turn towards the tip. Blades exhibit early parallel flaking and the edges are usually serrated. An identical point is found in TN, KY to WV to New York known as *Kanawha Stemmed.* **I.D. KEY:** Bifurcated base and barbs.

FOX VALLEY (continued)

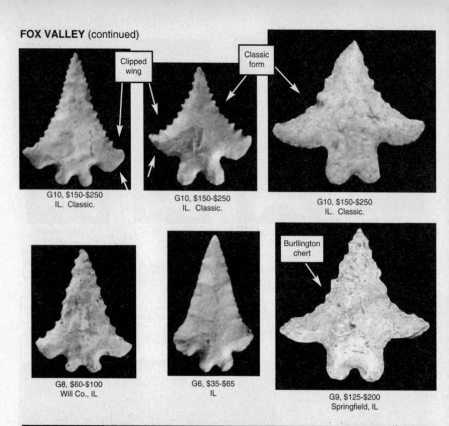

Clipped wing

Classic form

Burllington chert

G10, $150-$250
IL. Classic.

G10, $150-$250
IL. Classic.

G10, $150-$250
IL. Classic.

G8, $60-$100
Will Co., IL

G6, $35-$65
IL

G9, $125-$200
Springfield, IL

GARY - Late Archaic to Early Woodland, 3200 - 300 B. P.

(Also see Adena, Burkett, Dickson, Hidden Valley, Peisker Diamond and Waubesa)

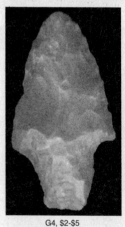

G4, $2-$5
Clinton Co., IL

G5, $8-$15
KS

G7, $25-$45
IL

LOCATION: Midwestern to Southwestern states. **DESCRIPTION:** A medium size, triangular point with a medium to long, contracted, pointed to rounded base. Shoulders are usually tapered. **I.D. KEY:** Similar to *Adena*, but thinned more.

G8, $30-$50
MO

Mozarkite

G9, $125-$200
MO

G10, $250-$450
MO

NC

1024

G8, $80-$150
IL

GIBSON - Mid to late Woodland, 2000 - 1500 B. P.

(Also see Cupp, Dovetail, Motley and St. Charles)

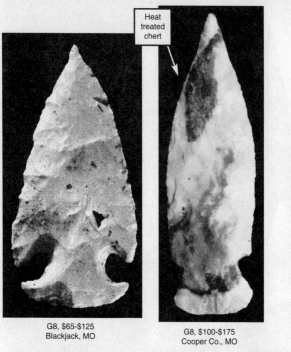

Heat treated chert

G8, $65-$125
Blackjack, MO

G8, $100-$175
Cooper Co., MO

G9, $150-$250
Lee Co., IA

Mozarkite chert

G7, $125-$200
Benton Co., MO

LOCATION: Midwestern to Eastern states. Gibson Mound group (1969), type site in Calhoun Co., IL. **DESCRIPTION:** A medium to large size side to corner notched point with a large, convex base.

GODAR - Late Archaic, 4500 - 3500 B. P.

(Also see Hemphill, Hickory Ridge, Osceola and Raddatz)

LOCATION: Illinois, Missouri into Wisconsin. **DESCRIPTION:** A medium to large size, sturdy, narrow to wide, side-notched point with a straight base and parallel sides. Some examples show parallel flaking. **Note:** *Black Sand* points are now typed as *Godar* points.

Heat treated Burlington

G6, $25-$45
Cooper Co., MO

GODAR (continued)

Heavily resharpened

G8, $80-$150
Cooper Co., MO

G7, $80-$150
Morgan Co., MO

G8, $150-$275
Clinton Co., IL

GOSHEN - Paleo, 11,500 - 10,000 B. P.

(Also see Clovis, Folsom, Midland and Plainview)

G7, $200-$350
S.E. KS

LOCATION: Plains states. **DESCRIPTION:** A small to medium size, very thin, auriculate point with a concave base. Basal corners range from being rounded to pointed. Blade edges are parallel sided to recurved. Basal area is ground. Flaking is oblique to horizontal transverse. A very rare type. **I.D. KEY:** Thinness, auricles

NC

GRAHAM CAVE - Early to Middle Archaic, 9000 - 5000 B. P.

(Also see Godar, Hemphill, Howard County, Osceola and Raddatz)

Broken ear

G3, $80-$150
Washington Co., KS

G5 $40-$75
IL

G10, $250-$450
Morgan Co., MO

G8, $80-$150
IL

LOCATION: Midwestern states. **DESCRIPTION:** A medium to large size, narrow, side-notched point with recurved sides, pointed auricles, and a concave base. Rarely, examples have been found fully fluted. Similar to *White River* points found in Ark. & OK.

G8, $350-$600
St. Clair Co., IL

G8, $275-$500
Peoria, IL

G9, $350-$650
St. Louis, MO

GRAND- Mid-Woodland, 1800 - 1600 B. P.

(Also see Carter, Ferry, Helton, Kirk Corner Notched, Lost Lake, Lundy and Snyders)

G6, $25-$40
Burlington, IL

G5, $15-$25
MO

G10, $65-$125
MO

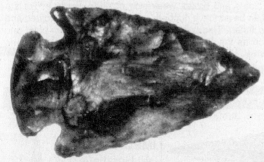

LOCATION: Oklahoma, Kansas. **DESCRIPTION:** A medium sized, broad, corner notched point with barbed shoulders and an expanding, convex base. Basal corners can be sharp. **I.D. KEY:** Width of blade, corner notching.

G8, $65-$125
Riley Co., KS

GREENBRIER - Early Archaic 9500 - 6000 B. P.

(Also see Dalton, Pike County and Pine Tree)

G5, $15-$30
Bond Co., IL

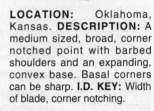

Banded chert

G8, $80-$150
MO/IL

G10, $250-$450
MO

GREENBRIER (continued)

G10, $700-$1200
IL

G8, $400-$750
Adams Co., IL

LOCATION: Southeastern to Midwestern states. **DESCRIPTION:** A medium to large size, auriculate point with tapered shoulders and broad, weak side notches. Blade edges are usually finely serrated. The base can be concave, lobbed, eared, straight or bifurcated and is ground. Early examples can be fluted. This type developed from the *Dalton* point and later evolved into other types such as the *Pine Tree* point. **I.D. KEY:** Heavy grinding in shoulders, good secondary edgework.

HARAHEY - Mississippian, 700 - 350 B. P.

(Also see Lerma and Morse Knife)

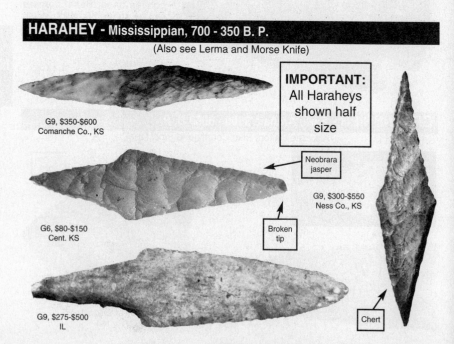

G9, $350-$600
Comanche Co., KS

IMPORTANT: All Haraheys shown half size

Neobrara jasper

G6, $80-$150
Cent. KS

Broken tip

G9, $300-$550
Ness Co., KS

G9, $275-$500
IL

Chert

872

HARAHEY (continued)

LOCATION: Midwestern states to Texas. **DESCRIPTION:** A large size, double pointed knife that is usually beveled on one or all four sides of each face. The cross section is rhomboid. **I.D. KEY:** Rhomboid cross section, two and four beveled form.

HARDIN - Early Archaic, 9000 - 6000 B. P.

(Also see Ferry, Kirk, Lost Lake, St. Charles, Scottsbluff and Stilwell)

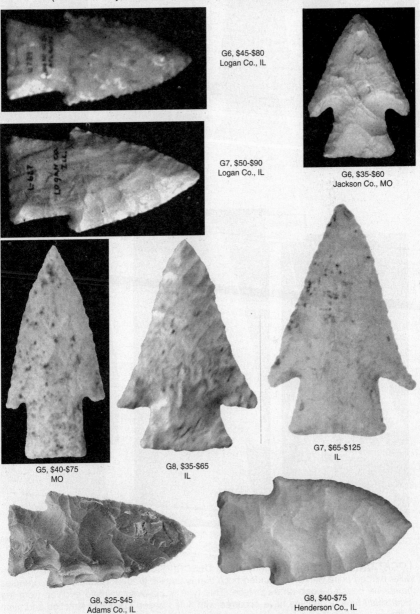

G6, $45-$80
Logan Co., IL

G7, $50-$90
Logan Co., IL

G6, $35-$60
Jackson Co., MO

G5, $40-$75
MO

G8, $35-$65
IL

G7, $65-$125
IL

NC

G8, $25-$45
Adams Co., IL

G8, $40-$75
Henderson Co., IL

873

HARDIN (continued)

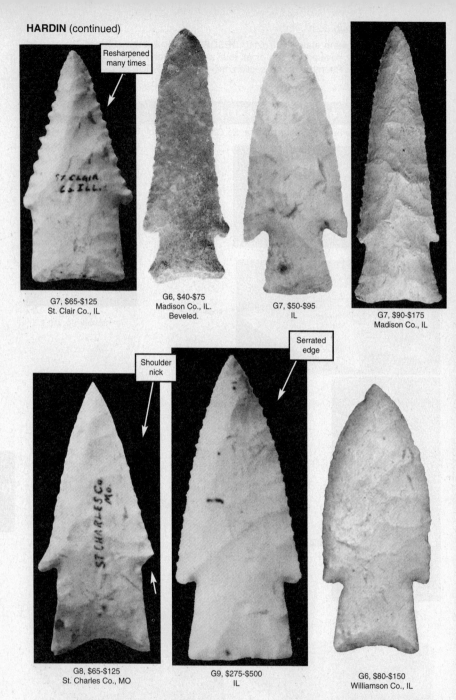

Resharpened many times

G7, $65-$125
St. Clair Co., IL

G6, $40-$75
Madison Co., IL.
Beveled.

G7, $50-$95
IL

G7, $90-$175
Madison Co., IL

Shoulder nick

Serrated edge

G8, $65-$125
St. Charles Co., MO

G9, $275-$500
IL

G6, $80-$150
Williamson Co., IL

LOCATION: Midwestern to Eastern states. **DESCRIPTION:** A large size, well made triangular barbed point with an expanded base that is usually ground. Resharpened examples have one beveled edge on each face. This type is believed to have evolved from the *Scottsbluff* type. Examples have occurred with fluted bases **I.D. KEY:** Notches and stem form.

§74

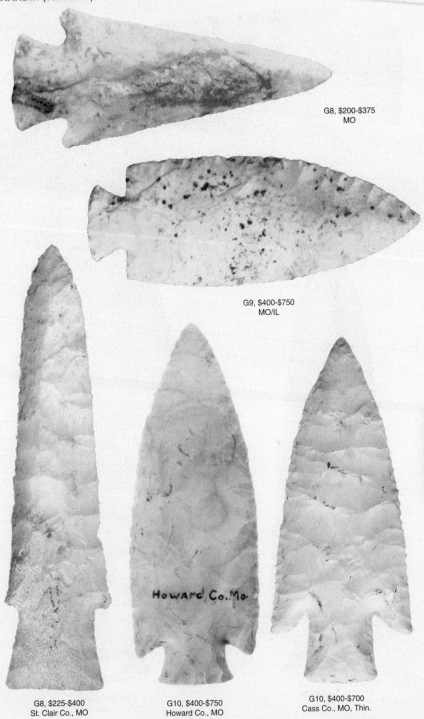

G8, $200-$375
MO

G9, $400-$750
MO/IL

NC

Howard Co. Mo.

G8, $225-$400
St. Clair Co., MO

G10, $400-$750
Howard Co., MO

G10, $400-$700
Cass Co., MO, Thin.

G10, $1200-$2000
MO

G10, $850-$1600
IL

G9, $1500-2500
MO

HARRELL- Mississippian, 900 - 500 B. P.

(Also see Cahokia, Huffaker and Washita)

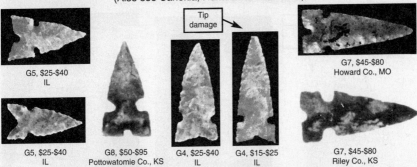

G5, $25-$40
IL

G5, $25-$40
IL

Tip damage

G8, $50-$95
Pottowatomie Co., KS

G4, $25-$40
IL

G4, $15-$25
IL

G7, $45-$80
Howard Co., MO

G7, $45-$80
Riley Co., KS

LOCATION: Midwestern states. **DESCRIPTION:** A small, thin, triangular arrow point with side and basal notches. Basal ears can be pointed. Bases are usually slightly concave with a basal notch. **I.D. KEY:** Triple notching.

HASKELL- Mississippian to Historic, 800 - 600 B. P.

(Also see Bayogoula, Collins and Washita)

G6, $20-$35
Cherokee Co., KS

G7, $65-$45
Cherokee Co., KS

G9, $65-$125
IL

LOCATION: Midwestern states. **DESCRIPTION:** A small, thin, triangular arrow point with upward sloping side notches. The base is concave and on some examples, basal ears can be extreme. **I.D. KEY:** Broad basal ears.

HAYES - Mississippian, 1200 - 600 B. P.

NC

(Also see Alba, Homan and Sequoyah)

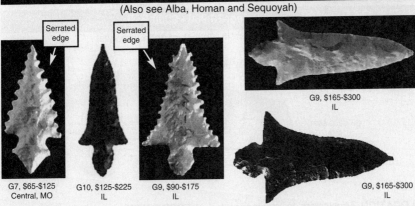

Serrated edge

Serrated edge

G7, $65-$125
Central, MO

G10, $125-$225
IL

G9, $90-$175
IL

G9, $165-$300
IL

G9, $165-$300
IL

LOCATION: Midwestern states. **DESCRIPTION:** A small to medium size, narrow, expanded tang point with a turkeytail base. Blade edges are usually strongly recurved forming sharp pointed tangs. Base is pointed and can be double notched. Some examples are serrated. **I.D. KEY:** Pointed base and flaking style.

877

HEAVY DUTY - Early to Middle Archaic, 7000 - 5000 B. P.

(Also see Rochester, Stone Square Stem)

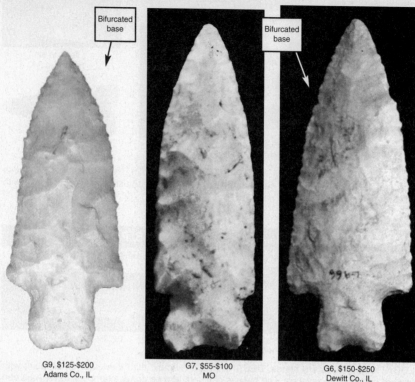

Bifurcated base

Bifurcated base

G9, $125-$200
Adams Co., IL

G7, $55-$100
MO

G6, $150-$250
Dewitt Co., IL

LOCATION: Eastern to Midwestern states. **DESCRIPTION:** A medium to large size, thick, serrated point with a parallel stem and a straight to slightly concave base. **I.D. KEY:** Base, thickness, flaking.

HELL GAP - Transitional Paleo, 10,900 - 9000 B. P.

(Also see Agate Basin, Angostura and Burroughs)

G8, $200-$350
MO

LOCATION: Midwestern to Western states. **DESCRIPTION:** A medium to large size, lanceolate point with a long, contracting stem. The widest part of the blade is above the midsection. The base is straight to slightly concave and the stem edges are usually ground. **I.D. KEY:** Early flaking and base form.

G7, $150-$250
MO

G7, $65-$125
S.E. KS

G7, $55-$100
Adams Co., IL

G9, $350-$600
MO

NC

HELTON - Late Archaic to early Woodland, 4000 - 2500 B. P.

(Also see Apple Creek, Delhi, Kay Blade, Lehigh, Lundy and Motley)

G6, $25-$40
Riley Co., KS

G8, $30-$50
Cherokee Co., KS

LOCATION: Midwestern states.
DESCRIPTION: A medium to large size, broad point with a short, expanding stem. Shoulders are horizontal to barbed, and the base is convex. **I.D. KEY:** Base form.

HELTON (continued)

G8, $30-$50
Cherokee Co., KS

HEMPHILL - Mid to Late Archaic, 7000 - 5000 B. P.

(Also see Godar, Graham Cave, Howard County, Osceola, Raddatz and Turin)

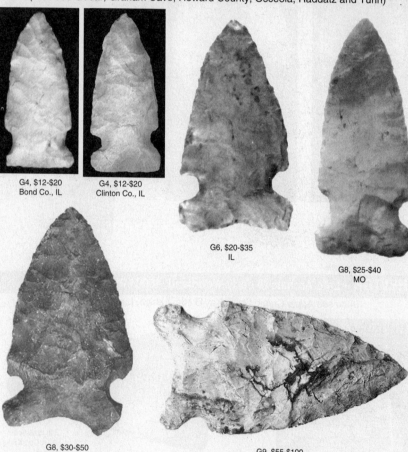

G4, $12-$20
Bond Co., IL

G4, $12-$20
Clinton Co., IL

G6, $20-$35
IL

G8, $25-$40
MO

G8, $30-$50
Madison Co., IL

G9, $55-$100
Cooper Co., MO

LOCATION: Illinois, Missouri into Wisc. Type site-Brown Co., IL. Associated with the Old Copper & Red Ochre culture. **DESCRIPTION:** A medium to large size side-notched point with a concave base and parallel to convex sides. These points are usually thinner and of higher quality than the similar *Osceola* type.

HEMPHILL (continued)

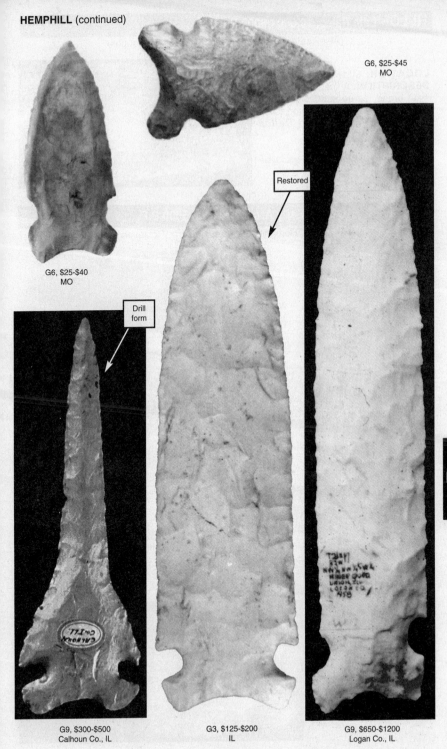

G6, $25-$45
MO

G6, $25-$40
MO

Restored

Drill
form

G9, $300-$500
Calhoun Co., IL

G3, $125-$200
IL

G9, $650-$1200
Logan Co., IL

NC

881

HI-LO - Late Paleo, 10,000 - 8000 B. P.

(Also see Angostura, Browns Valley and Burroughs)

LOCATION: Midwestern states.
DESCRIPTION: A medium to large size, broad, eared, lanceolate point with a concave base. Believed to be related to *Plainview* and *Dalton* points.

G7, $150-$250
MO

HICKORY RIDGE - Early Archaic, 7000 - 5000 B.P.

(Also see Godar, Hemphill, Osceola, Raddatz, Robinson and Turin)

G5, $25-$40
Sedalia, MO

G7, $25-$40
MO

Tang nick

G6, $30-$50
Greene Co., IL

G7, $65-$125
Cent. MO

LOCATION: Oklahoma, Arkansas into Missouri.
DESCRIPTION: A medium to large size side notched point with a straight to slightly concave base

G9, $225-$400
MO

882

HIDDEN VALLEY - Early to mid-Archaic, 8500 - 7000 B. P.

(Also see Adena, Dickson, Gary and Waubesa)

Worn tip

G5, $15-$25
IL

Burlington chert

Ground basal area

Tang ding

G7, $150-$250
Hancock Co., IL

LOCATION: Oklahoma, Missouri, Illinois into Indiana. **DESCRIPTION:** A medium to large size point with square to barbed shoulders and a contracting stem that can be pointed to straight. Flaking is earlier and more parallel than on *Gary* points. Basal areas are ground. Called *Rice Contracted Stemmed* in Missouri.

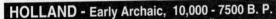

HOLLAND - Early Archaic, 10,000 - 7500 B. P.

(Also see Dalton, Eden, Hardin, Johnson, Pike County and Scottsbluff)

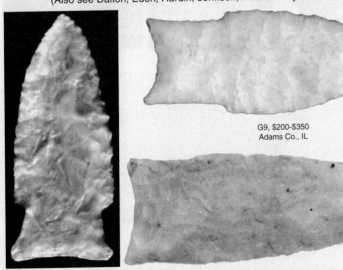

G9, $200-$350
Adams Co., IL

G6, $80-$150
MO

G5, $90-$175
IL

G7, $150-$250
Franklin Co., MO

G8, $350-$600
Adams Co., IL

G6, $200-$350
Pike Co., IL

G10, $550-$1000
MO

G9, $400-$750
Fulton Co., IL

LOCATION: Midwestern states. **DESCRIPTION:** A medium to large size lanceolate blade that is very well made. Shoulders are weak to nonexistent. Bases can be knobbed to auriculate and are usually ground. Some examples have horizontal to oblique transverse flaking. **I.D. KEY:** Weak shoulders, concave base.

HOLLAND (continued)

G7, $275-$500
Anglum, MO

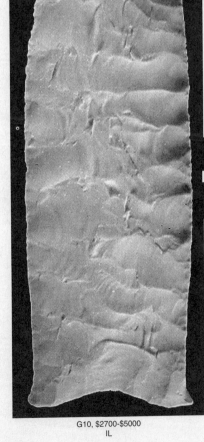

NC

G9, $1500-$2500
MO

G10, $2700-$5000
IL

HOMAN - Mississippian, 1000 - 700 B. P.

(Also see Agee, Alba, Hayes and Sequoyah)

LOCATION: Northwest to Midwestern states. **DESCRIPTION:** A small size expanded barb point with a bulbous stem. Some tips are mucronate or apiculate.

G6, $35-$65
IL

HOPEWELL - Woodland, 2500 - 1500 B. P.

(Also see Carter, Dickson, Gibson, Motley, North, St. Charles, Snyders & Waubesa)

LOCATION: Midwestern to Eastern states. **DESCRIPTION:** A large size, broad, corner notched point that is similar to *Snyders*. Made by the Hopewell culture.

G6, $20-$35
Jackson Co., IL

G8, $90-$165
Cooper Co., MO

G8, $100-$175
Springfield, MO

G8, $65-$125
St. Clair Co., IL, thin.

886

HOPEWELL (continued)

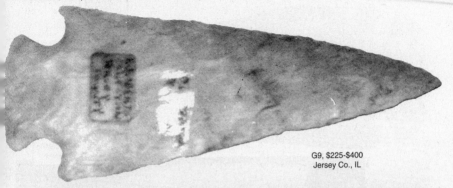

G9, $225-$400
Jersey Co., IL

HOWARD COUNTY - Early Archaic, 7500 - 6500 B. P.
(Also see Cache River, Gibson, Grand, Helton, St. Charles)

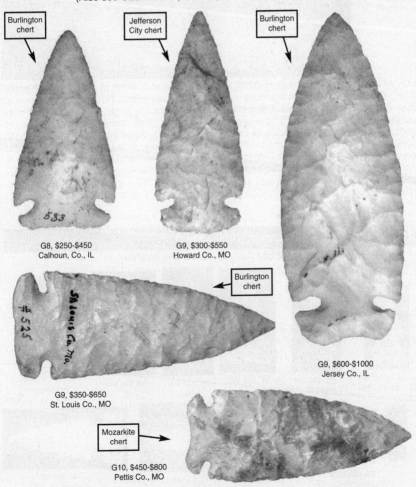

Burlington chert

Jefferson City chert

Burlington chert

Burlington chert

Mozarkite chert

G8, $250-$450
Calhoun, Co., IL

G9, $300-$550
Howard Co., MO

G9, $350-$650
St. Louis Co., MO

G9, $600-$1000
Jersey Co., IL

G10, $450-$800
Pettis Co., MO

NC

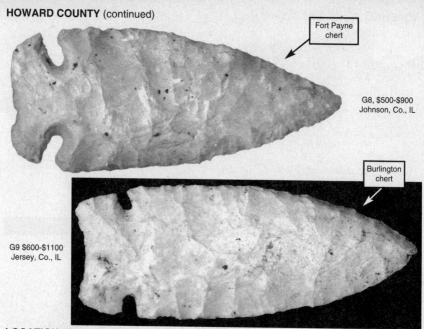

Fort Payne chert

G8, $500-$900
Johnson, Co., IL

Burlington chert

G9 $600-$1100
Jersey, Co., IL

LOCATION: Illinois and Missouri. **DESCRIPTION:** A small to medium size, thin, well-made point. The blade is long and triangular with slightly convex edges. Notches are narrow and fairly low on the sides, entering at a slight diagonally upward angle. The basal edge may range from straight to slightly convex. It has squared basal corners on straight-based points and rounded basal corners on convex-based points. Basal edge has light grinding to none. If grinding is absent, light crushing of the basal edge is noted. A peculiarity of this point is that it has been recognized primarily for its like-new, unused condition with little to no evidence of resharpening, as has been noted on *Cache River* and *Kessel* points. For years this has been an un-named variant of the *Cache River* points. **I.D. KEY:** Lack of basal grinding and resharpening. Can be much larger than *Cache River* or *Kessel* points.

HUFFAKER - Mississippian, 1000 - 500 B. P.

(Also see Cahokia, Evans and Washita)

G8, $40-$75
Cooper Co., MO

G8, $40-$75
Cooper Co., MO

G6, $25-$40
IL

G6, $25-$40
IL

G6, $25-$40
IL

G7, $30-$50
Pottowatomie Co., KS

G8, $65-$125
Pottowatomie Co., KS

G10, $90-$175, Central IL

G9, $50-$80
Cooper Co., MO

HUFFAKER (continued)

LOCATION: Midwestern states. **DESCRIPTION:** A small size triangular point with a straight to concave base and double side notches. Bases can have a single notch.

JACKS REEF CORNER NOTCHED - Late Woodland to Miss., 1500 - 1000 B. P.

(Also see Afton, Apple Creek, Hopewell, Kirk Corner Notched)

G8, $30-$50
Madison Co., IL

G9, $70-$120
Cooper Co., MO

G8, $55-$100
Madison Co., IL

G9, $80-$150
Cooper Co., MO

LOCATION: Midwestern to Eastern states. **DESCRIPTION:** A small to medium size, thin, corner notched point that is well made. The blade is convex to pentagonal. Some examples are widely corner notched and appear to be expanded stem points with barbed shoulders. Rarely, they are basal notched. **I.D. KEY:** Thinness, made by the birdpoint people.

JOHNSON - Early to Middle Archaic, 9000 - 5000 B. P.

(Also see Hidden Valley & Holland)

NC

LOCATION: Mississippi to Kansas. **DESCRIPTION:** A medium size, thick, well made, expanded to contracting stem point with a broad, short, concave base. Bases are usually thinned and grinding appears on some specimens. Shoulders can be slight and are roughly horizontal. **I.D. KEY:** Broad stem that is thinned.

G7, $35-$65
Cherokee Co., KS

KAMPSVILLE - Late Archaic to Woodland, 3000 - 2500 B. P.

(Also see Cupp, Helton, Kings, Kramer, Lundy, Lehigh and Motley)

KAMPSVILLE (continued)

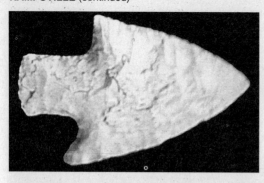

LOCATION: Midwestern states. **DESCRIPTION:** A medium to large size, point with broad corner notches producing a parallel stem and barbed shoulders. Similar to *Buck Creek* found in Kentucky.

G8, $45-$85
Pettis Co., MO

KAY BLADE - Mississippian, 1000 - 600 B. P.

(Also see Cupp, Epps, Helton, Kramer, Lundy, Lehigh and Motley)

G10, $400-$750
Green Co., MO

IMPORTANT:
Kay Blades
shown half size

G7, $150-$300
St. Louis Co., MO

G6, $35-$60
Douglas Co., KS

G9, $80-$150
N.E. OK

LOCATION: Midwestern states. **DESCRIPTION:** A medium to large size point with a long expanding stem and barbed shoulders. Used by the Mississippian, Caddoan people.

KINGS - Middle Archaic to Woodland, 4500 - 2500 B. P.

(Also see Apple Creek, Hopewell, Kampsville, Kirk Corner and Motley)

G7, $20-$35
MO

G5, $15-$25
AR

KINGS (continued)

G5, $15-$25
MO

G10, $65-$125
MO

G8, $40-$75
Cherokee Co., KS

LOCATION: Midwestern states. **DESCRIPTION:** A medium size corner notched point with an expanding stem and barbed shoulders. Barbs and basal corners are sharp. Base can be convex, straight or concave.

KIRK CORNER NOTCHED - Early to Middle Archaic, 9000 - 6000 B. P.

(Also see Apple Creek, Decatur, Lost Lake, Pine Tree, St. Charles & Stilwell)

NC

G6, $25-$45
Cherokee Co., KS

G6, $40-$75
IL

G5, $20-$35
IL

LOCATION: Midwestern to Southeasten states. **DESCRIPTION:** A medium to large size, corner notched point. Blade edges can be convex to recurved and are finely serrated on many examples. The base can be convex, concave, straight or auriculate. Points that are beveled on one side of each face would fall under the *Lost Lake* type. **I.D. KEY:** Secondary edgework.

KIRK CORNER NOTCHED (continued)

G8, $125-$200
IL

Pitkin chert

G9, $250-$450
Scott Co., IL

G4, $25-$40
Cherokee Co., KS

G8, $80-$150
IL

G7, $50-$95
IA

Ground basal area

G7, $125-$200
MO

892

KIRK CORNER NOTCHED (continued)

Edge nick

G7, $65-$125
Cooper Co., MO

Serrated edge

G9, $150-$250
Crawford Co., IL

G7, $125-$200
Cooper Co., MO

G9, $400-$750
Bond Co., IL

NC

Side & tang nick

G8, $225-$400
IL

893

KRAMER - Woodland, 3000 - 2500 B. P.

(Also see Helton, Lehigh, Rochester and Stone Square Stem)

Resharpened several times

G7, $20-$35
Miller Co., MO

G6, $15-$25
Miller Co., MO

G5, $30-$50
Bond Co., IL

G7, $55-$100
MO

G6, $25-$45
Fayette Co., IL

LOCATION: Midwest. **DESCRIPTION:** A medium size, narrow point with weak shoulders that are tapered to horizontal and a long rectangular stem. Stems are usually ground. **I.D. KEY:** Rectangular stem.

LAKE ERIE - Early to Middle Archaic, 9000 - 5000 B. P.

(Also see Cossatot River and Fox Valley)

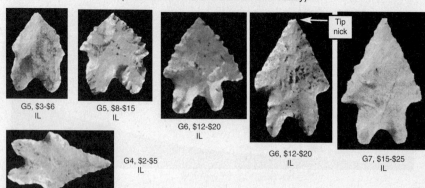

Tip nick

G5, $3-$6
IL

G5, $8-$15
IL

G6, $12-$20
IL

G6, $12-$20
IL

G7, $15-$25
IL

G4, $2-$5
IL

LAKE ERIE (continued)

G8, $35-$65
Randolph Co., IL

G5, $8-$15
IL

G6, $15-$25
IL

LOCATION: Northeastern states. **DESCRIPTION:** A small to medium size, thin, deeply notched or serrated, bifurcated stemmed point. The basal lobes are parallel with a tendency to turn inward and are pointed. The outward sides of the basal lobes are usually fractured from the base towards the tip and can be ground. Similar to *LeCroy* found further south.

LEHIGH - Woodland, 2500 - 1500 B. P.

(Also see Helton, Kay Blade, Kramer, Lundy and Steuben)

LOCATION: Midwest. **DESCRIPTION:** A medium to large size, narrow point with tapered shoulders and a long expanding stem. Bases are straight. **I.D. KEY:** Long expanding stem.

G6, $25-$40
Pottowatomie Co., KS

LERMA - Early to Middle Archaic, 10,000 - 5000 B. P.

(Also see Agate Basin, Burroughs and Sedalia)

NC

G7, $175-$300
MO

IMPORTANT:
All Lermas shown half size

G8, $450-$800
IL

G8, $150-$250
Fulton Co., IL

895

LERMA (continued)

G10, $300-
$550
Cent. MO

shown
half size

LOCATION: Siberia to Alaska, Canada, Mexico, South America and across the U.S.
DESCRIPTION: A large size, narrow, lanceolate blade with a pointed base. Most are fairly thick in cross section but finer examples can be thin. Flaking tends to be collateral.
Basal areas can be ground. Western forms are beveled on one side of each face. Similar
forms have been found in Europe and Africa dating back to 20,000 - 40,000 B.P., but
didn't appear in the U.S. until after the advent of *Clovis*.

LOST LAKE - Early Archaic, 9000 - 6000 B. P.
(Also see Hardin, Kirk Corner Notched, St. Charles and Thebes)

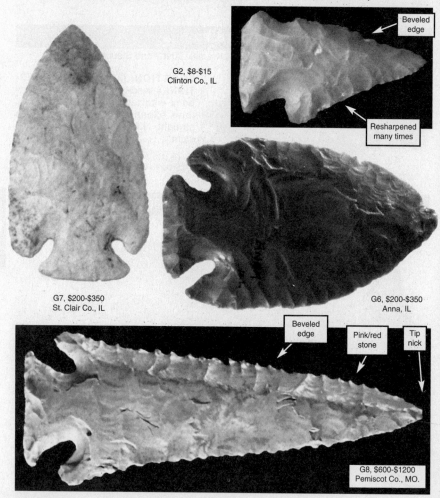

Beveled
edge

G2, $8-$15
Clinton Co., IL

Resharpened
many times

G7, $200-$350
St. Clair Co., IL

G6, $200-$350
Anna, IL

Beveled
edge

Pink/red
stone

Tip
nick

G8, $600-$1200
Pemiscot Co., MO.

LOST LAKE (continued)

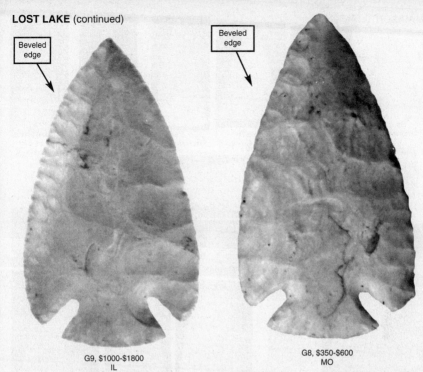

Beveled edge

Beveled edge

G9, $1000-$1800
IL

G8, $350-$600
MO

LOCATION: **DESCRIPTION:** A medium to large size, broad, corner notched point that is beveled on one side of each face. The beveling continues when resharpened and creates a flat rhomboid cross section. Most examples are finely serrated and exhibit high quality flaking and symmetry. **I.D. KEY:** Notching, secondary edgework is always opposite creating at least slight beveling on one side of each face.

LUNDY- Late Caddoan, 800 - 600 B. P.
(Also see Helton, Kay Blade, Lehigh, Motley, Steuben and Table Rock)

NC

LOCATION: Midwestern states. **DESCRIPTION:** A small to medium size, narrow, corner notched point with barbed shoulders and a convex base.

G6, $15-$30
Geary Co., KS

MADISON - Mississippian, 1100 - 200 B. P.
(Also see Cahokia)

G3, $1-$2
MN

G5, $3-$5
MN

G5, $5-$8
Madison Co., IL

G7, $15-$25
Cooper Co., MO

MADISON (continued)

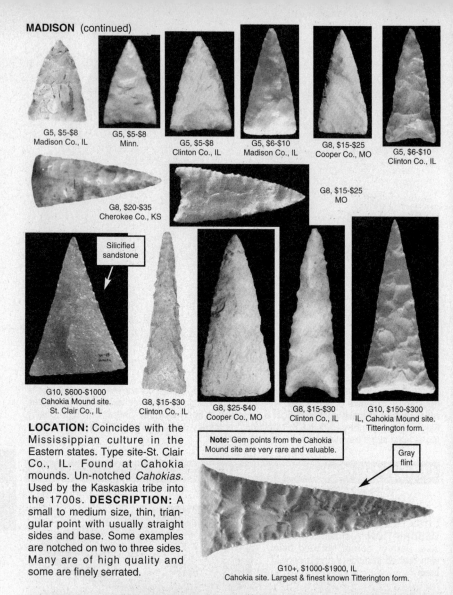

G5, $5-$8
Madison Co., IL

G5, $5-$8
Minn.

G5, $5-$8
Clinton Co., IL

G5, $6-$10
Madison Co., IL

G8, $15-$25
Cooper Co., MO

G5, $6-$10
Clinton Co., IL

G8, $20-$35
Cherokee Co., KS

G8, $15-$25
MO

Silicified
sandstone

G10, $600-$1000
Cahokia Mound site.
St. Clair Co., IL

G8, $15-$30
Clinton Co., IL

G8, $25-$40
Cooper Co., MO

G8, $15-$30
Clinton Co., IL

G10, $150-$300
IL, Cahokia Mound site.
Titterington form.

LOCATION: Coincides with the Mississippian culture in the Eastern states. Type site-St. Clair Co., IL. Found at Cahokia mounds. Un-notched *Cahokias.* Used by the Kaskaskia tribe into the 1700s. **DESCRIPTION:** A small to medium size, thin, triangular point with usually straight sides and base. Some examples are notched on two to three sides. Many are of high quality and some are finely serrated.

Note: Gem points from the Cahokia Mound site are very rare and valuable.

Gray
flint

G10+, $1000-$1900, IL
Cahokia site. Largest & finest known Titterington form.

MATANZAS - Mid-Archaic to Woodland, 4500 - 2500 B. P.

(Also see Carter, Cupp, Hickory Ridge, Kirk Corner Notched)

G4, $2-$5
Fayette Co., IL

G5, $5-$10
Clinton Co., IL

G6, $8-$15
Clinton Co., IL

898

MATANZAS (continued)

G5, $5-$10
Madison Co., IL

G6, $25-$40
IL

G6, $25-$45
Cooper Co., MO

G6, $35-$50
Cass Co., IL

LOCATION: Midwestern states. **DESCRIPTION:** A small to medium size, narrow, side notched point with a concave, convex or straight base.

MEHLVILLE - Late Archaic, 4000 - 3000 B. P.

(Also see Etley and Smith)

G5, $65-$120
Logan Co., IL

LOCATION: Midwestern states. **DESCRIPTION:** A large size, broad, triangular point with expanding shoulders and a squared base. The long barbs give the appearance of basal notching and droop inward on some examples. **I.D. KEY:** Expanding barbs.

G5, $35-$65
AR

MEHLVILLE (continued)

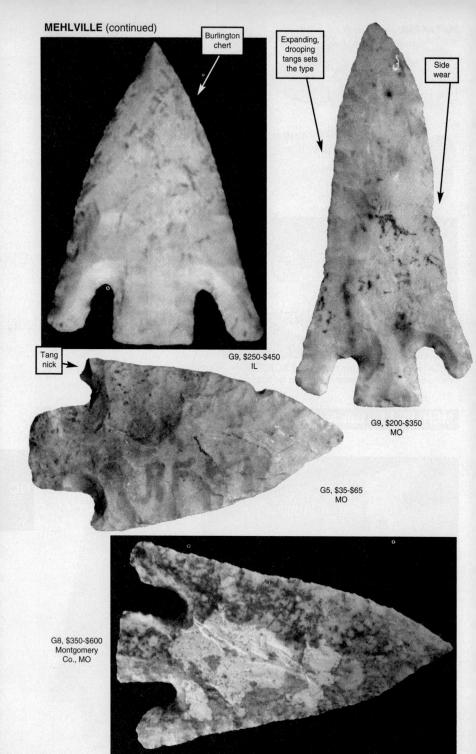

Burlington chert

Expanding, drooping tangs sets the type

Side wear

Tang nick

G9, $250-$450
IL

G9, $200-$350
MO

G5, $35-$65
MO

G8, $350-$600
Montgomery
Co., MO

MERKLE - Late Archaic to Woodland, 4000 - 2000 B. P.

(Also see Evans)

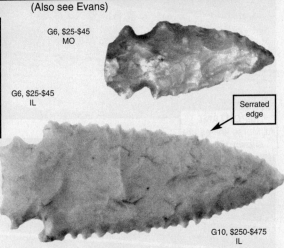

G6, $25-$45
MO

G6, $25-$45
IL

Serrated
edge

LOCATION: Midwestern states. **DESCRIPTION:** A medium to large size point with a short stem and broad side notches and corner notches at the base. Bases are usually straight to convex. **I.D. KEY:** Double notching.

G10, $250-$475
IL

MESERVE - Early Archaic, 9500 - 4000 B. P.

(Also see Dalton, Greenbrier and Plainview)

G8, $150-$250
Manhattan, KS

LOCATION: Midwestern states to Texas and west to Montana. **DESCRIPTION:** A medium size auriculate point with a blade that is beveled on one side of each face. Beveling extends into the basal area. Related to *Dalton* points. **I.D. KEY:** Beveling into the base.

NC

MORSE KNIFE - Woodland, 3000 - 1500 B. P.

(Also see Harahey, Lerma, Ramey Knife and Red Ochre)

G8, $500-$900
Benton Co., MO

IMPORTANT: All Morse knives are shown 1/2 size

G9, $900-$1750
LaSalle Co., IL

LOCATION: Midwestern states. **DESCRIPTION:** A large lanceolate blade with a long contracting stem and a rounded base. The widest part of the blade is towards the tip.

MORSE KNIFE (continued)

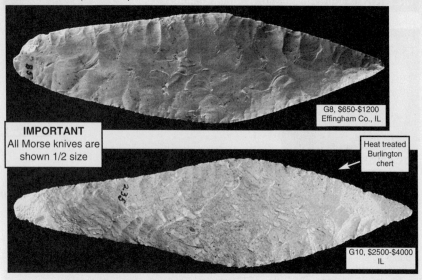

G8, $650-$1200
Effingham Co., IL

IMPORTANT
All Morse knives are
shown 1/2 size

Heat treated
Burlington
chert

G10, $2500-$4000
IL

MOTLEY - Late Archaic-Woodland, 4500 - 2500 B. P.

(Also see Cupp, Epps, Helton, Kay Blade, Lundy, Snyders, Steuben, Table Rock)

G8, $125-$200
Lee Co. IA

G9, $225-$400
Pettis Co., MO

LOCATION: Iowa, Missouri, Illinois, Kentucky into the southeast. **DESCRIPTION:** A medium to large size, expanded stemmed to widely corner notched point with strong barbs. The blade edges and the base are convex to straight. Has been found associated with *Wade* points in caches. Similar to *Epps* found in Louisiana which has a straight base; *Motleys* are more barbed than *Epps.* **I.D. KEY:** Large corner notches.

NEBO HILL - Early Archaic, 7500 - 6000 B. P.

(Also see Agate Basin, Burroughs, Eden, Lerma and Sedalia)

NEBO HILL (continued)

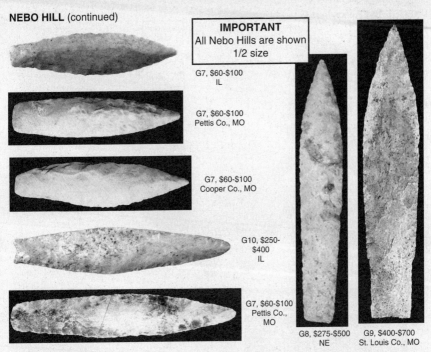

G7, $60-$100
IL

G7, $60-$100
Pettis Co., MO

G7, $60-$100
Cooper Co., MO

G10, $250-
$400
IL

G7, $60-$100
Pettis Co.,
MO

G8, $275-$500
NE

G9, $400-$700
St. Louis Co., MO

LOCATION: Missouri & Kansas. **DESCRIPTION:** A large size, narrow, thick, lanceolate blade with convex sides that gently taper to the base. On some examples, the basal area is determined by the presence of slight shoulders. Collateral flaking does occur on some examples.

NEUBERGER - Early to Mid-Archaic, 9000 - 6000 B. P.

(Also see Kirk Corner Notched and Pine Tree)

NC

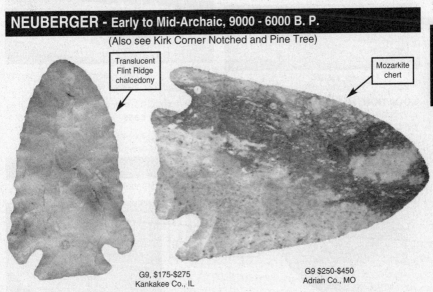

Translucent
Flint Ridge
chalcedony

Mozarkite
chert

G9, $175-$275
Kankakee Co., IL

G9 $250-$450
Adrian Co., MO

LOCATION: Illinois, Indiana and Ohio. **DESCRIPTION:** A medium to large size, broad corner notched point with a short, incurvate base. Some bases are fishtailed. Barbs are strong that turn inward.

NEUBERGER (continued)

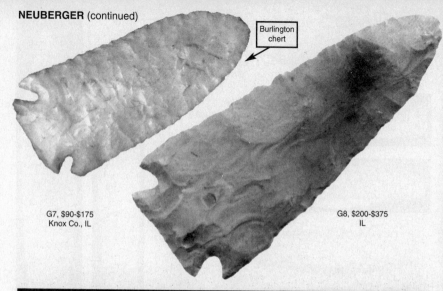

Burlington chert

G7, $90-$175
Knox Co., IL

G8, $200-$375
IL

NODENA - Mississippian to Historic, 600 - 400 B. P.

G7, $30-$50
Pemiscot Co., MO

G7, $30-$50
Washington Co., IL

G7, $35-$60
Pemiscot Co., MO

G7, $40-$75
Pemiscot Co., MO

LOCATION: Midwestern states. **DESCRIPTION:** A small to medium size, narrow, thin elliptical shaped arrow point with a pointed to rounded base. Some examples have oblique, parallel flaking.

NORTH - Woodland, 2200 - 1600 B. P.

(Also see Hopewell, Snyders and Stenfield)

IMPORTANT:
All Norths
shown 1/2 size

G7, $200-$350
Logan Co., IL

G6, $45-$85
MO

904

G9, $400-$750
Osage Co., MO

G8, $80-$150
MO

G7, $275-$500
Calhoun Co., IL

G7, $55-$100
IL

G10, $275-$500
Logan Co., IL

NC

G9, $350-$600
Pike Co., IL

LOCATION: Midwestern to Eastern states.
DESCRIPTION: A large, thin, elliptical, broad, well made blade with a convex base. This type is usually found in caches and is related to the *Snyders* point of the Hopewell culture. Believed to be unnotched *Snyders* points.

IMPORTANT:
All Norths shown 1/2 size

OSCEOLA - Early to Middle Archaic, 7000 - 5000 B. P.

(Also see Cache River, Godar, Graham Cave, Hemphill, Raddatz and Turin)

LOCATION: Wisconsin into Iowa. **DESCRIPTION:** A large size, narrow, side notched point with parallel sides on longer examples and a straight to concave to notched base which could be ground. **I.D. KEY:** Always has early flaking to the middle of the blade.

OSCEOLA (continued)

G8, $65-$125
MO

G8, $250-$450
Keokuk Co., IA

PALEO KNIFE - Transitional Paleo, 10,000 - 8000 B. P.

(Also see Scraper and Square Knife)

G9, $400-$700
Stark Co., IL

IMPORTANT:
All Paleo Knives
shown half size

G6, $150-$250
Pettis Co., MO

Flaked to the
center

LOCATION: All of North America. **DESCRIPTION:** A large size lanceolate blade finished with broad parallel flakes. These are found on Paleo sites and were probably used as knives.

PEISKER DIAMOND - Woodland, 2500 - 2000 B. P.

(Also see Adena and Gary)

PEISKER DIAMOND (continued)

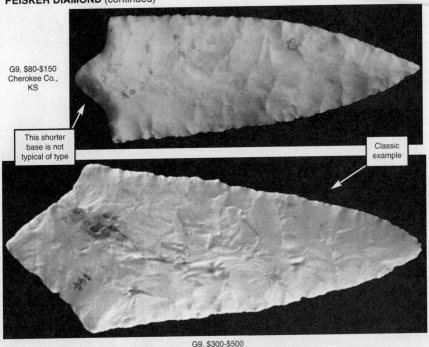

G9, $80-$150
Cherokee Co.,
KS

This shorter
base is not
typical of type

Classic
example

G9, $300-$500
IL

LOCATION: Illinois, Missouri, Kansas into Iowa. **DESCRIPTION:** A large, broad blade with sharp shoulders and a short to moderate contracting base that comes to a point. Blade edges are recurved, convex or straight. Similar in form to the Morrow Mountain point found in the Southeast, but not as old. **I.D.KEY:** Contracted base, pointed base.

PELICAN - Transitional Paleo, 10,000 - 6000 B. P.

NC

(Also see Beaver Lake, Dalton, Greenbrier and Holland)

LOCATION: Louisiana, Texas, Arkansas into Kansas. **DESCRIPTION:** A medium size auriculate point with recurved sides. The base is concave with edge grinding. **I.D. KEY:** Basal contraction.

Ear
restored

G4, $125-$200
Douglas Co., KS

PIKE COUNTY - Early Archaic, 9500 - 7500 B. P.

(Also see Beaver Lake, Dalton, Greenbrier and Holland)

LOCATION: Midwestern states. **DESCRIPTION:** A medium to large size, lanceolate blade with an eared, fishtail base. Basal area is ground. Related to *Dalton*.

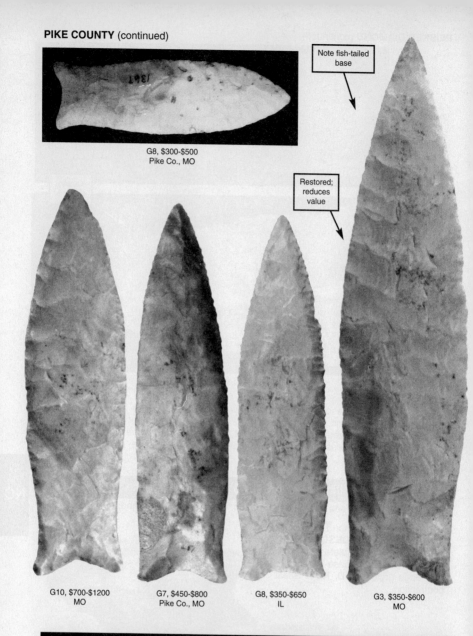

Note fish-tailed base

Restored; reduces value

G8, $300-$500
Pike Co., MO

G10, $700-$1200
MO

G7, $450-$800
Pike Co., MO

G8, $350-$650
IL

G3, $350-$600
MO

PINE TREE CORNER NOTCHED - Early Archaic, 8000 - 5000 B. P.

(Also see Kirk and Lost Lake and Stilwell)

LOCATION: DESCRIPTION: A small to medium size, thin, corner notched point with a concave, convex, straight, bifurcated or auriculate base. Blade edges are usually serrated and flaking is parallel to the center of the blade. The shoulders expand and are barbed. The base is ground. Small examples would fall under the *Palmer* type. **I.D. KEY:** Archaic flaking to the center of each blade.

PINE TREE CORNER NOTCHED (continued)

Needle tip

Serrated edge

G9, $60-$120
Cooper Co., MO

G8, $60-$100
Cooper Co., MO

G9, $250-$450
MO

G8, $125-$200
Morgan Co., MO

Serrated edge

Serrated edge

G8, $165-$300
MO

G8, $80-$150
IL

PLAINVIEW - Late Paleo, 10,000 - 7000 B. P.
(Also see Angostura, Browns Valley, Clovis, Cumberland and Dalton)

NC

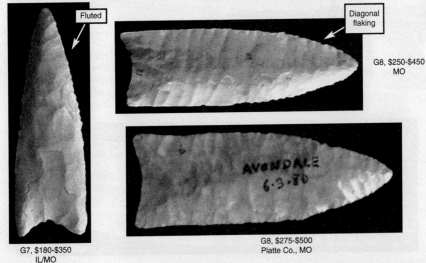

Fluted

Diagonal flaking

G8, $250-$450
MO

AVONDALE
6-3-80

G7, $180-$350
IL/MO

G8, $275-$500
Platte Co., MO

PLAINVIEW (continued)

Fluted

G9, $650-$1200
Cooper Co., MO

G9, $500-$900
Pike Co., IL

Ground basal area

G9, $650-$1200
Adams Co., IL

G9, $500-$900
Johnson Co., KS, Kaw
River. Flint Hills flint.

G9, $300-$500
MO

G8, $600-$1000
Peoria Co., IL

LOCATION: Midwestern states and Canada. **DESCRIPTION:** A medium size, thin, lanceolate point with usually parallel sides and a concave base that is ground. Some examples are thinned or fluted and is believed to be related to the earlier *Clovis* and contemporary *Dalton* type. Flaking is of high quality and can be collateral to oblique transverse.

G9, $1000-$1800
IL

910

G10, $800-$1500
Franklin Co., MO. Ground
half way up, thin.

Diagonal
flaking

G10, $2000-$3500
Cent. IA

G9, $1200-$2000
MO

QUAD - Late Paleo, 10,000 - 6000 B. P.

(Also see Beaver Lake, Clovis, Gosen and Cumberland)

NC

G9, $250-$400
MO

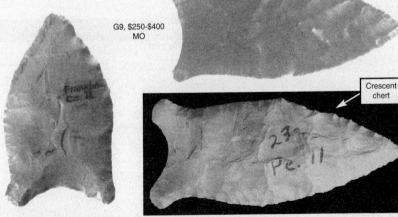

Crescent
chert

G5, $90-$175
Franklin Co., IL

G10, $500-$900
Pettis Co., MO

QUAD (continued)

LOCATION: Southeastern states into Missouri. **DESCRIPTION:** A medium to large size lanceolate point with flaring "squared" auricles and a concave base which is ground. Most examples show basal thinning and some are fluted. Believed to be related to the earlier *Cumberland* point. **I.D. KEY:** Paleo flaking, squarish auricles.

G8, $400-$750
Cape Girardeau Co., MO

RADDATZ - Mid-Archaic to Woodland, 5000 - 2000 B. P.

(Also see Godar, Graham Cave, Hemphill, Hickory Ridge and Osceola)

Flintridge flint

Chert

Flint

G5, $15-$30
MN

Hixton quartzite

G4, $8-$15
WI

G6, $20-$35
WI

G6, $20-$35
WI E-Notch.

LOCATION: Wisconsin & Minnesota. **DESCRIPTION:** A medium size, side notched point with a concave to striaght base. Similar in outline to *Hickory Ridge* points centered in Arkansas.

RAMEY KNIFE- Mid-Archaic, 5000 - 4000 B. P.

(Also see Lerma, Morse Knife and Red Ochre)

IMPORTANT:
Rameys shown half size

G7, $300-$500
Van Buren Co., IA

LOCATION: Midwestern states. **DESCRIPTION:** A large size, broad, lanceolate blade with a rounded base and high quality flaking.

912

RAMEY KNIFE (continued)

IMPORTANT:
Rameys
shown half size

G8, $1600-$3000
Calloway Co., MO

G10, $3000-$5000
Brown Co., IL

G9, $1800-$3500
MO

NC

RED OCHRE - Mid to Late Archaic, 5000 - 3000 B. P.

(Also see Adena Blade, Sedalia and Wadlow)

G5, $25-$40
St. Clair Co., IL
One of a cache.

Shown
half size

LOCATION: Midwestern to Southeastern states. Type site-St. Louis MO. Named by Scully ('51)- Red Ochre Mound in Fulton Co., MO. **DESCRIPTION:** A large, thin, broad blade with a contracting basal area. The base is convex to straight. Very similar to *Wadlow* which has the parallel sides. Possibly related to the *Turkeytail* type.

RED OCHRE (continued)

G8, $80-$150
Sikeston, MO

Burlington chert

G10, $350-$600
St. Clair Co., IL

IMPORTANT: All Red Ochres shown half size

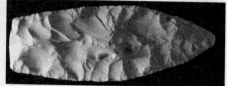

G6, $45-$80
St. Clair Co., IL. One of a cache

REDSTONE - Paleo, 13,000 - 9000 B. P.

(Also see Allen, Angostura, Clovis, Cumberland, Dalton, Folsom & Plainview)

Flute channel

G8, $450-$800
MO

LOCATION: Midwestern to Southeastern states. **DESCRIPTION:** A medium to large size, thin, auriculate, fluted point with convex sides expanding to a wide, deeply concave base. The hafting area is ground. This point is widest at the base. Fluting can extend most of the say down each face. Multiple flutes are usual. **I.D. KEY:** Baton or billet fluted, edgework on the hafting area.

RICE LOBBED - Early Archaic, 9000 - 5000 B. P.

(Also see Grand, Helton and Lundy)

G8, $40-$70
MO

G8, $15-$25
MO

LOCATION: Midwestern to Northeastern states. **DESCRIPTION:** A medium to large size broad point with a straight to lobbed base. Blade edges can be serrated and beveled. The lobbed base variety has a shallow indentation compared to the other bifurcated types. Shoulders are horizontal to tapered and basal corners are rounded.

914

RICE LOBBED (continued)

G8, $25-$45
Clinton Co., IL

G4, $12-$20
Stone Co., MO

RICE SIDE-NOTCHED - Late Woodland, 1600 - 1400 B. P.

(Also see Carter, Lehigh, Mantanzas and Steuben)

G5, $15-$25
MO

LOCATION: Arkansas into Missouri and Kansas. **DESCRIPTION:** A medium to large size, narrow, point with broad side notches to an expanding stem and weak shoulders. The base is straight but can be slightly concave. **I.D. KEY:** Basal form.

G8, $35-$60
Pettis Co., MO

Note "shallow" side notches

G8, $125-$200
Boone Co., MO

NC

ROBINSON - Late Archaic, 4000 - 3000 B. P.

(Also see Cache River, Hickory Ridge and Raddatz)

DESCRIPTION: A small to medium size, narrow, side-notched point with a straight to concave base. **I.D. KEY:** Size, small basal notches.

G8, $60-$100
Cooper Co., MO

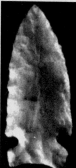

G4, $2-$5
Clinton Co., IL

G6, $12-$20
Clinton Co., IL

G5, $6-$12
Clinton Co., IL

G6, $15-$25
MO

G6, $25-$40
MO

ROCHESTER - Early Archaic, 8000 - 6000 B. P.

(Also see Kramer)

Blunt tip

G5, $20-$35
Marion Co., KS

G6, $35-$50
Pottowatomie Co., KS

G6, $50-$90
Riley Co., KS

LOCATION: Midwestern states. **DESCRIPTION:** A medium to large size, narrow point with weak, tapered shoulders and a long rectangular stem.

ROSS- Woodland, 2500 - 1500 B. P.

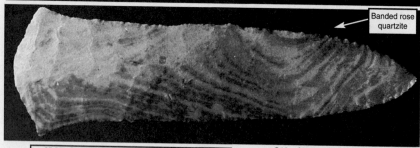

Banded rose quartzite

IMPORTANT: Shown half size

G10+, $12,000-$20,000+
Kent Co., MI. 9-3/4" long

LOCATION: Midwestern to Eastern states. **DESCRIPTION:** A large size ceremonial blade with an expanded, rounded base. Some examples have a contracting "V" shaped base.

ST. CHARLES - Early Archaic, 9500 - 8000 B. P.

(Also see Gibson, Grand, Helton, Kirk Corner Notched and Lost Lake)

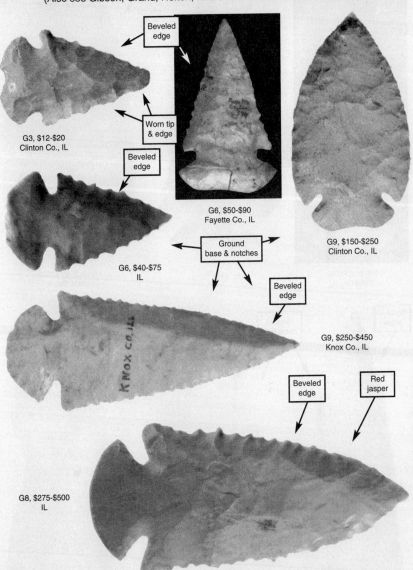

Beveled edge

Worn tip & edge

Beveled edge

G3, $12-$20
Clinton Co., IL

G6, $40-$75
IL

G6, $50-$90
Fayette Co., IL

Ground base & notches

G9, $150-$250
Clinton Co., IL

Beveled edge

G9, $250-$450
Knox Co., IL

Beveled edge

Red jasper

NC

G8, $275-$500
IL

LOCATION: Midwestern to Eastern states. **DESCRIPTION:** Also known as *Dovetail*. A medium to large size, broad, thin, elliptical, corner notched point with a dovetail base. Blade edges are beveled on opposite sides when resharpened. The base is convex and most examples exhibit high quality flaking. There is a rare variant that has the barbs clipped (clipped wing) as in the *Decatur* type. There are many variations on base style from bifurcated to eared, rounded or squared. Base size varies from small to very large. **I.D. KEY:** Dovetailed base.

917

ST. CHARLES (continued)

Beveled edge

Beveled edge

Beveled edge

G8, $150-$250
Bond Co., IL

G8, $150-$250
IL

G10, $550-$1000
Union Co., IL

Beveled edge

Ground basal area

Used as a spokeshave

G7, $200-$350
IL

G8, $225-$400
MO

G3, $40-$75
White Co., IL

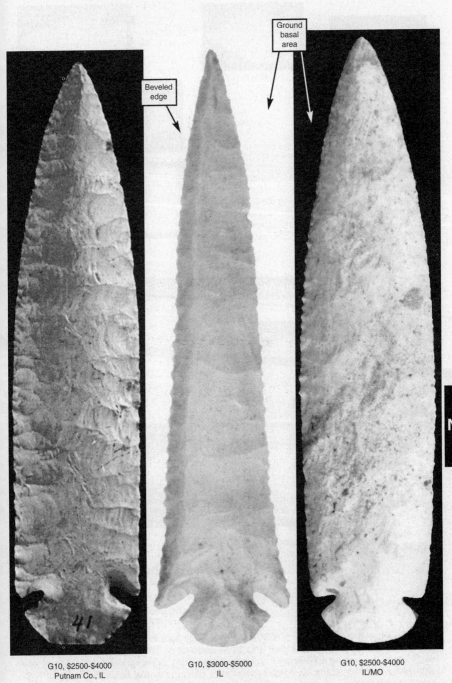

Beveled edge

Ground basal area

NC

G10, $2500-$4000
Putnam Co., IL

G10, $3000-$5000
IL

G10, $2500-$4000
IL/MO

SCALLORN - Woodland to Mississippian, 1300 - 500 B. P.

(Also see Alba, Collins, Haskell, Jacks Reef and Sequoyah)

G3, $2-$5
IL

G6, $25-$40
IL

G8, $50-$80
Cooper Co., MO

G6, $25-$40
Cooper Co., MO

G8, $50-$80
Cooper Co., MO

G8, $50-$95
Cooper Co., MO

LOCATION: Texas, Oklahoma, Arkansas into Missouri. **DESCRIPTION:** A small size, corner notched arrow point with a flaring stem. Bases and bladed edges are straight, concave or convex and many examples are serrated. **I.D. KEY:** Small corner notched point with sharp tangs and tip.

SCOTTSBLUFF I - Early Archaic, 9500 - 7000 B. P.

(Also see Eden, Hardin, Holland and Stone Square Stem)

Oolitic flint

G5, $65-$125
MN

G6, $250-$400
MO

G8, $600-$1200
MO

G8, $300-$550
MO

LOCATION: Midwestern states. **DESCRIPTION:** A medium to large size, broad stemmed point with convex to parallel sides and weak shoulders. The stem is parallel sided to expanding. The hafting area is ground. Made by the Cody Complex people. Contemporary with *Hardins*. Most examples have horizontal to oblique parallel flaking and are of high quality and thinness.

Collateral flaking

G9, $600-$1000
MO

G9, $800-$1500
Pike Co., IL

G7, $250-$450
MO

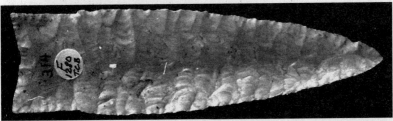

G9, $1300-$2400
N.E. KS

NC

G8, $1200-$2200
MO

G9, $1500-$2800
IL

SCOTTSBLUFF II - Early Archaic, 9500 - 7000 B. P.

(Also see Hardin and Holland)

Diagonal flaking

G5, $80-$150
Moro, IL

G7, $175-$300
MO

G6, $40-$75
Morris Co.,
KS

G9, $600-$1000
Kansas City, MO.

G7, $350-$600
KS

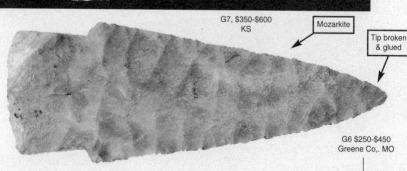

Mozarkite

Tip broken
& glued

G6 $250-$450
Greene Co,. MO

922

SCOTTSBLUFF II (continued)

G8, $800-$1500
Jackson Co., MO

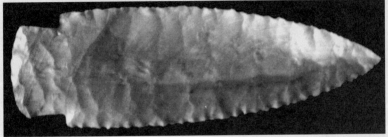

G9, $1600-$3000
Cooper Co., MO

Hixton
quartzite

G8, $2200-$4000
MO

NC

LOCATION: Midwestern states. **DESCRIPTION:** A medium to large size triangular point with shoulders a little stronger than on Type I and a broad parallel sided/expanding stem.

SEDALIA - Mid-Late Archaic, 5000 - 3000 B. P.

(Also see Agate Basin, Burroughs, Lerma, Nebo Hill and Red Ochre)

G5, $25-$40
MO

G5, $15-$30
MO

G6, $65-$125
MO

G7, $80-$150
MO

G7, $90-$175
MO

G6, $40-$75
MO

G9, $200-$350
MO

G9, $250-$400
MO

LOCATION: Midwestern states. **DESCRIPTION:** A medium to large size, narrow, lanceolate blade with straight to convex sides and base. Flaking is usually cruder than in *Agate Basin*. Believed to have evolved from the Nebo Hill type.

G10, $350-$600
MO

NC

G10, $150-$250
MO

G10, $250-$400
Cooper Co., MO

G8, $250-$400
MO

925

G7, $80-$150
IL

G8, $90-$175
Cooper Co., MO

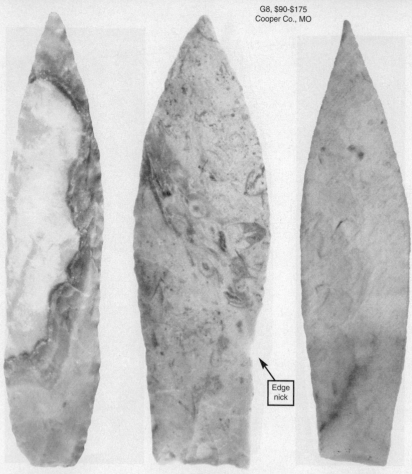

Edge
nick

G10, $250-$450
MO

G7, $40-$75
MO

G7, $165-$300
MO

NC

G9, $175-$300
IL

G10, $550-$1000
MO

G10 $450-$800
Adams Co., IL,
near Lima Lake.

SEQUOYAH - Mississippian, 1000 - 600 B. P.

(Also see Alba, Hayes and Homan)

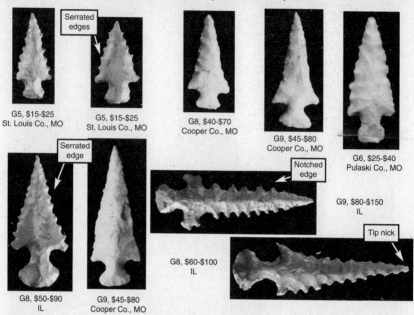

G5, $15-$25
St. Louis Co., MO

Serrated edges

G5, $15-$25
St. Louis Co., MO

G8, $40-$70
Cooper Co., MO

G9, $45-$80
Cooper Co., MO

G6, $25-$40
Pulaski Co., MO

Serrated edge

Notched edge

G9, $80-$150
IL

Tip nick

G8, $60-$100
IL

G8, $50-$90
IL

G9, $45-$80
Cooper Co., MO

LOCATION: IL, OK, AR, MO. **DESCRIPTION:** A small size, thin, narrow point with coarse serrations and an expanded, bulbous stem. Believed to have been made by Caddo and other people. Associated with Mississippian Caddo culture sites. Named after the famous Cherokee chief of the same name. **I.D. KEY:** Bulbous base, coarse serrations.

SMITH - Middle Archaic, 7000 - 4000 B. P.

(Also see Etley and Mehlville)

IMPORTANT:
All Smiths shown half size

G8, $175-$300
Cherokee Co., KS

Resharpened into the shoulder

G5, $65-$125
IL

G9, $350-$600
Advance, MO

G10, $400-$700
Menard Co., IL

G8, $300-$550
Pettis Co., MO

G9, $350-$650
Cooper Co., MO

928

SMITH (continued)

G8, $350-$650
Calloway Co., MO

G10, $400-$700
Cole Co., MO

G9, $400-$700
Lincoln Co., MO

LOCATION: Midwestern states. **DESCRIPTION:** A very large size, broad, point with long parallel shoulders and a squared to slightly expanding base. Some examples may appear to be basally notched due to the long barbs.

| **IMPORTANT:** |
| All Smiths shown half size |

SNYDERS - HOPEWELL - Woodland, 2500 - 1500 B. P.

(Also see Carter, Grand, Helton, Hopewell. North and Steuben)

G3, $8-$15
Bond Co., IL

| **IMPORTANT:** |
| All Snyders points on this page shown actual size |

G5, $40-$75
Cent. IL

NC

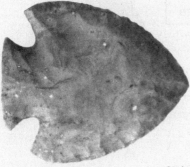

G7, $55-$100
IL

G5, $12-$20
IL

SNYDERS (continued)

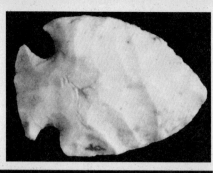

G5, $20-$35
Cherokee Co., KS

G8, $60-$100
IL

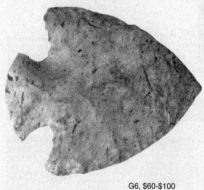

G10, $150-$250
MO

G6, $60-$100
IL

LOCATION: Midwestern to Eastern states. Type site located in Calhoun Co., IL. **DESCRIPTION:** A medium to large size, broad, thin, wide corner notched point of high quality. Blade edges and base are convex. Many examples have intentional fractured bases. Made by the Hopewell culture. This point has been reproduced in recent years. **I.D. KEY:** Size and broad corner notches.

IMPORTANT: All Snyders points on this page shown actual size

G9, $80-$150
IL

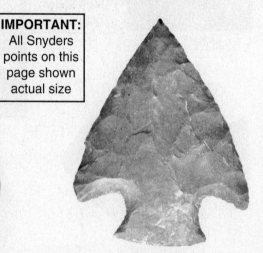

G10, $150-$250
Clinton Co., IL

SNYDERS (continued)

Red/cream chert

Tang nick

G10, $250-$450
IA

G9, $275-$500
Peoria Co., IL

G5, $40-$75
MO

G8, $175-$300
Madison Co., IL

G7, $80-$150
Logan Co., IL

IMPORTANT:
All Snyders
points on this
page shown
half size

Base nick

G6, $150-$250
IL

G6, $65-$125
IL

G6, $175-$300
IL

NC

G10, $350-$600
IL

G9, $275-$500
IA

Banded
hornstone

Edge nick

G6, $80-$150
IL

G7, $350-$600
Lincoln Co., MO

Base nick

G7, $175-$300
Johnson Co., IL

931

SQUARE KNIFE - Late Archaic to Historic, 3500 - 400 B. P.

(Also see Angostura, Red Ochre and Wadlow)

G10, $800-$1500
Douglas Co., KS. Classic. Cache blade.

IMPORTANT: shown half size

G6, $150-$250
Morris Co., KS

LOCATION: Midwestern states. **DESCRIPTION:** A medium to large size squared blade with rounded corners.

G6, $65-$120
Morgan Co., MO

G9, $350-$600
Madison Co., IL

STANFIELD (see Tennessee River)

STEUBEN- Woodland, 2000 - 1000 B. P.

(Also see Carter, Ferry, Hardin, Lehigh, Matanzas, Motley, Rice Side Notched and Table Rock)

G5, $2-$5
Fayette Co., IL

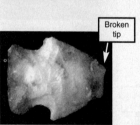

Broken tip

G1, $.25-$.50
Clinton Co., IL

Tangs worn

G5, $1-$3
Clinton Co., IL

G5, $1-$2
Clinton Co., IL

G5, $1-$3
Clinton Co., IL

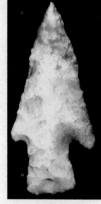

G6, $8-$15
Clinton Co., IL

G6, $30-$50
Custer Co., NB

STEUBEN (continued)

G4, $8-$15
N.E. KS

G4, $8-$15
Washington Co., KS

Base
nick

G6, $8-$15
Madison Co., IL

G6, $15-$25
Washington Co., KS

G6, $25-$45
Washington Co., KS.

G7, $35-$65
Washington Co., KS

LOCATION: Midwestern states. **DESCRIPTION:** A medium to large size, narrow point with tapered to horizontal shoulders and a medium to long expanding stem. The base is straight. Convex base places it under the *Snyder* type. **I.D. KEY:** Long expanded stem.

NC

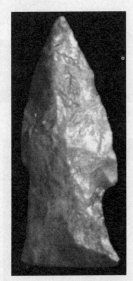

G6, $25-$40
Boone Co., MO

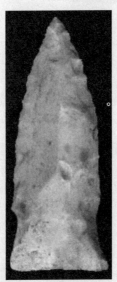

G6, $25-$40
Madison Co., IL

G7, $25-$45
Madison Co., IL

G8, $65-$125
Cooper Co., MO

STILWELL - Early Archaic, 9000 - 7000 B. P.

(Also see Kirk Corner Notched and Pine Tree)

G8, $150-$250
MO

G8, $250-$450
Boone Co., MO

G8, $165-$300
Cherokee Co., KS

G9, $800-$1500
Pike Co., IL

934

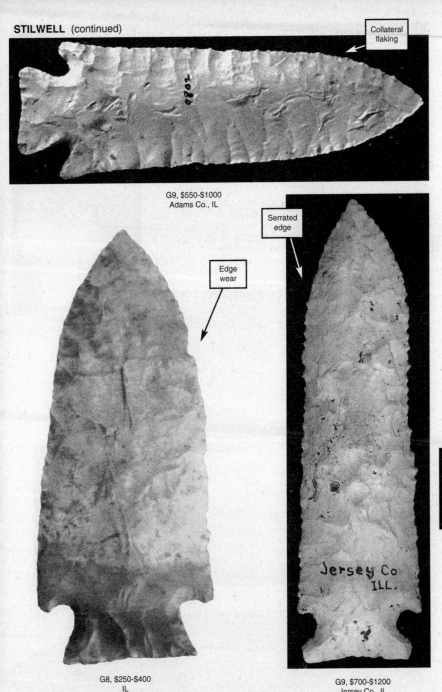

Collateral flaking

G9, $550-$1000
Adams Co., IL

Serrated edge

Edge wear

G8, $250-$400
IL

G9, $700-$1200
Jersey Co., IL

Jersey Co ILL.

NC

LOCATION: Midwestern to Eastern states. **DESCRIPTION:** A medium to large size, corner notched point with usually serrated blade edges. The shoulders are barbed. The base is concave to eared and ground. The blade edges are convex, parallel or recurved. This type may be related to *Kirk*.

935

STONE SQUARE STEM - Middle Archaic, 6000 - 4000 B. P.

(Also see Etley, Heavy Duty, Kramer and Rochester)

G5, $14-$25
Clinton Co., IL

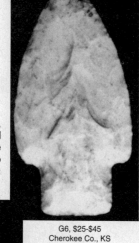

LOCATION: Midwestern states. Type site is in Stone Co., MO. **DESCRIPTION:** A medium to large size, broad stemmed point. Blade edges are convex to recurved. The shoulders are horizontal to barbed and the base is square to slightly expanding with a prominent, short stem. **I.D. KEY:** Short, square stem.

G6, $25-$45
Cherokee Co., KS

G6, $20-$35
Morgan Co., MO

G7, $35-$65
Pettis Co., MO

G7, $90-$175
IL

STONE SQUARE STEM (continued)

G10, $250-$400
Cent. IL

TABLE ROCK - Late Archaic, 4000 - 3000 B. P.
(Also see Kay Blade, Lehigh, Motley and Steuben)

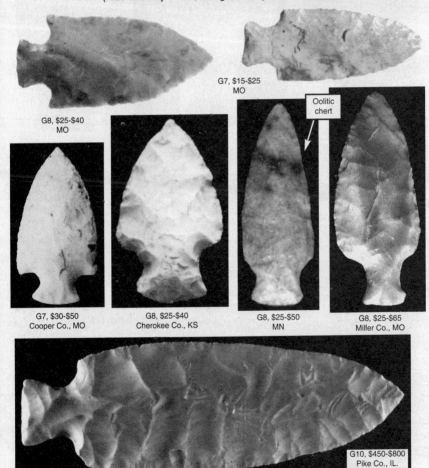

G8, $25-$40
MO

G7, $15-$25
MO

G7, $30-$50
Cooper Co., MO

G8, $25-$40
Cherokee Co., KS

Oolitic chert

G8, $25-$50
MN

G8, $25-$65
Miller Co., MO

NC

G10, $450-$800
Pike Co., IL.

LOCATION: Midwestern to Northeastern states. **DESCRIPTION:** A medium to large size, expanded stem point with straight to tapered shoulders. Shoulders can be sharp or rounded. This type is also known as a "Bottleneck" point.

937

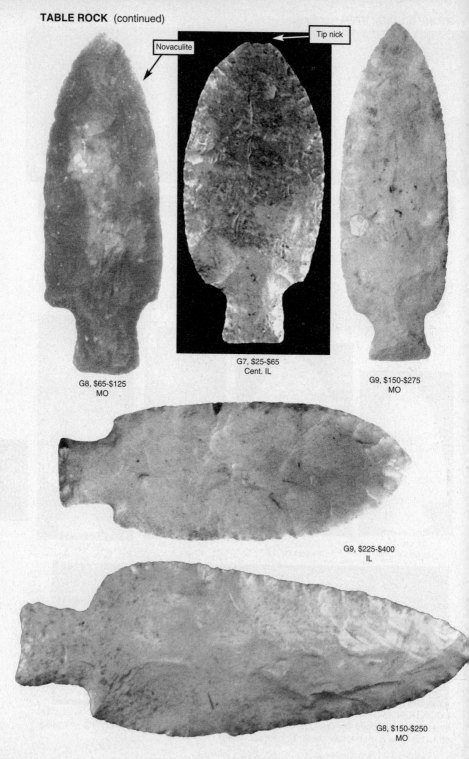

Novaculite

Tip nick

G7, $25-$65
Cent. IL

G8, $65-$125
MO

G9, $150-$275
MO

G9, $225-$400
IL

G8, $150-$250
MO

(Also see Adena Blade, Cobbs Triangular, Kirk, Red Ochre and Stanfield)

G8, $35-$60
Madison Co., IL

G8, $55-$100
Pemiscott Co., MO

Pink jasper

NC

G10, $400-$750
IL

LOCATION: Midwestern to Southeastern states. **DESCRIPTION:** These are unnotched preforms for early Archaic types such as *Kirk, Eva,* etc. and would have the same description as that type without the notches. Bases can be straight, concave or convex. **I.D. KEY:** Archaic style edgework. **NOTE:** This type has been confused with the *Stanfield* point which is a medium size, narrow, thicker point. A beveled edge would place your point under the *Cobbs Triangular* type.

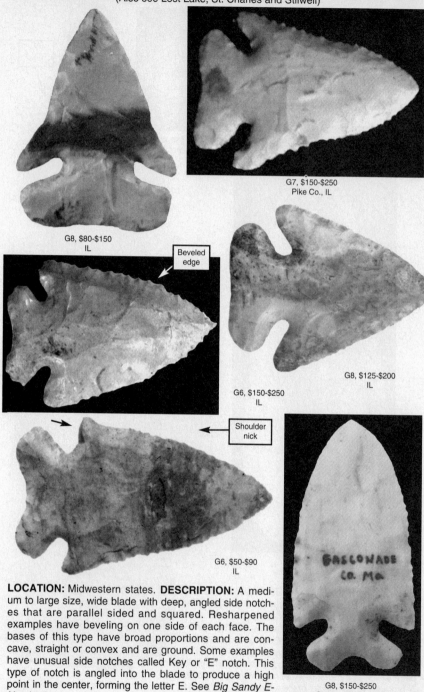

G7, $150-$250
Pike Co., IL

G8, $80-$150
IL

Beveled edge

G6, $150-$250
IL

G8, $125-$200
IL

Shoulder nick

G6, $50-$90
IL

GASCONADE Co. Mo

G8, $150-$250
Gasconade Co., MO

LOCATION: Midwestern states. **DESCRIPTION:** A medium to large size, wide blade with deep, angled side notches that are parallel sided and squared. Resharpened examples have beveling on one side of each face. The bases of this type have broad proportions and are concave, straight or convex and are ground. Some examples have unusual side notches called Key or "E" notch. This type of notch is angled into the blade to produce a high point in the center, forming the letter E. See *Big Sandy E-Notched.*

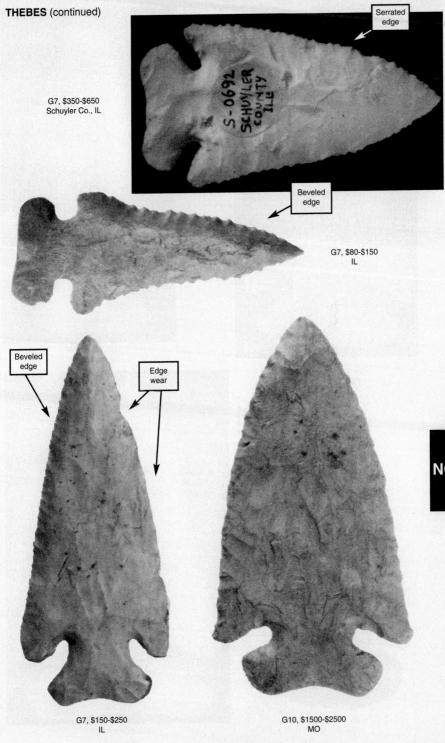

Serrated edge

G7, $350-$650
Schuyler Co., IL

S-0692
SCHUYLER
COUNTY
ILL.

Beveled edge

G7, $80-$150
IL

Beveled edge

Edge wear

NC

G7, $150-$250
IL

G10, $1500-$2500
MO

941

Beveled edge

G7, $225-$400
Pike Co., IL

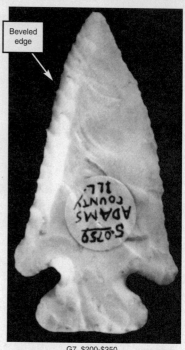

Beveled edge

G7, $200-$350
Pike Co., IL

Resharpened many times

G6, $35-$65
Pike Co., IL

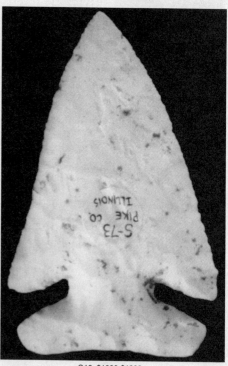

G10, $1000-$1800
Pike Co., IL

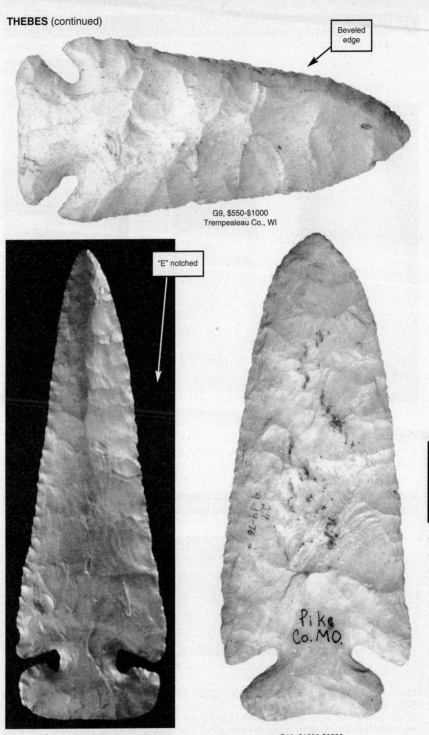

Beveled edge

G9, $550-$1000
Trempealeau Co., WI

"E" notched

Pike
Co. MO.

NC

G9, $1200-$2200
Richland Co., IL

G10, $1200-$2200
Pike Co., IL

TURIN- Early Archaic, 8500 - 7500 B. P.

(Also see Godar, Graham Cave, Hemphill, Hickory Ridge, Osceola, Raddatz and Robinson)

Kankakee chert

G8, $55-$100
Christian Co., IL

G7, $65-$125
Pottowatomie Co., KS

G7, $125-$200
S.E. KS

LOCATION: Illinois, Missouri, Nebraska northward. **DESCRIPTION:** A small to medium size side-notched point with an auriculate base that is concave. Notching occurs close to the base and the shoulders are barbed. Bases are ground. **I.D. KEY:** Eared base.

TURKEYTAIL-FULTON- Late Archaic to Woodland, 4000 - 2500 B. P.

(Also see Early Ovoid Knife)

IMPORTANT:
This Turkeytail
shown half size

One of a large cache

G8, $800-$1400
St. Charles Co., MO

LOCATION: Midwestern to Eastern states. **DESCRIPTION:** A medium to large size, wide, thin, elliptical blade with shallow notches very close to the base. This type is usually found in caches and has been reproduced in recent years. Made by the Adena culture. An earlier form was found in *Benton* caches in Mississippi carbon dated to about 4700 B.P.

TURKEYTAIL-FULTON (continued)

Kaolin flint

One of a large cache

G6, $65-$125
Logan Co., IL

G8, $900-$1600
St. Charles Co., MO

G8, $800-$1400
St. Charles Co., MO

G9, $1500-$2800
Morgan Co., IL

IMPORTANT:
Turkeytails
shown half size

G6, $400-$700
MO. Titterington cache.

NC

G9, $1200-$2000
St. Charles Co.,
MO.
Part of Turkeytail
cache.

TURKEYTAIL-HARRISON - Late Archaic to Woodland, 4000 - 2500 B. P.

LOCATION: Midwestern to Eastern states. **DESCRIPTION:** A medium to large size, narrow, elliptical tapered, horizontal or barbed shoulders, and an elongated, diamond-shaped stem in the form of a turkey's tail. Large examples may have fine pressure flaking on one edge of each face. Made by the Adena culture. Lengths up to 20 inches know.

TURKEYTAIL-HARRISON (continued)

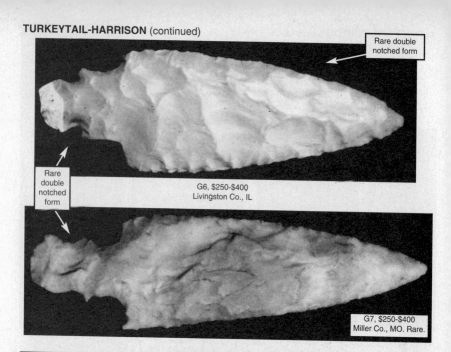

Rare double notched form

Rare double notched form

G6, $250-$400
Livingston Co., IL

G7, $250-$400
Miller Co., MO. Rare.

TURKEYTAIL-HEBRON - Late Archaic to Woodland, 3500 - 2500 B. P.
(Also see Waubesa)

G10, $1500-$2500
Cairo., IL

LOCATION: Around the great lakes region from Wisconsin to New York. **DESCRIPTION:**
A medium to large size blade with barbed shoulders, and a narrow, contracting stem with a
convex base. Made by the *Adena* culture.

WADLOW - Late Archaic, 4000 - 2500 B. P.
(Also see Cobbs Triangular, Etley and Red Ochre)

WADLOW (continued)

G6, $55-$100
IL

G6, $50-$90
MO

G7, $50-$90
IL

IMPORTANT:
All Wadlows
shown half
size

G6, $50-$90
St. Louis Co., MO

G8, $125-$200
IL

G8, $175-$300
IL

G9, $300-$550
Ralls Co., MO

G8, $2500-$4000
Cooper Co., MO

NC

947

G7, $175-$300
IL

G9, $200-$350
IL

G7, $175-$300
MO

LOCATION: Midwestern states. Type site-The Etley site, Calhoun Co., IL. Walter Wadlow first discovered this form in 1939, Jersey Co., IL. **DESCRIPTION:** A large to very large size, broad, parallel sided blade with a straight to convex base. The preform for the *Etley* point.

IMPORTANT:
All Wadlows
shown half size

G9, $350-$600
Cherokee Co., MO

WARRICK - Early Archaic, 9000 - 5000 B. P.
(Also see St. Charles)

G6, $25-$40
Washington Co., KS.

G8, $135-$250
Washington Co., KS.

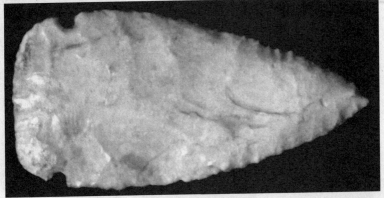

G8, $275-$500
Camden Co., MO

LOCATION: Midwestern states. **DESCRIPTION:** A medium to large size, sturdy, side to corner notched point. Notching is close to the base which is ground. Flaking is of high quality.

WASHITA - Mississippian, 800 - 400 B. P.

(Also see Cahokia and Huffaker)

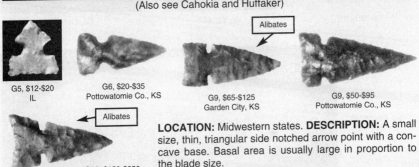

G5, $12-$20
IL

G6, $20-$35
Pottowatomie Co., KS

Alibates

G9, $65-$125
Garden City, KS

G9, $50-$95
Pottowatomie Co., KS

Alibates

G10, $150-$250
Garden City, KS

LOCATION: Midwestern states. **DESCRIPTION:** A small size, thin, triangular side notched arrow point with a concave base. Basal area is usually large in proportion to the blade size.

NC

WAUBESA - Woodland, 2500 - 1500 B. P.

(Also see Adena, Dickson, Gary, Hidden Valley & Turkeytail-Hebron)

G5, $15-$25
Kay Co., OK

LOCATION: Midwestern to Southeastern United States. **DESCRIPTION:** Associated with the Hopewell culture. A medium to large, narrow, thin, well made point with a contracting stem that is rounded or pointed. Some examples exhibit unusually high quality flaking and saw-tooth serrations. Blades are convex to recurved. Shoulders are squared to barbed. **I.D. KEY:** Basal form pointed or near pointed. Good secondary flaking and thin.

Sugar quartz

G9, $65-$125
IL

G5, $25-$50
WI

G8, $125-$200
IL

G9, $160-$300
Sedalia, MO

WHEELER EXCURVATE - Transitional Paleo, 10,000 - 8000 B. P.

(Also see Angostura)

G9, $125-$200
S.W. MO

LOCATION: Southeastern states. Rare in Illinois and Missouri. **DESCRIPTION:** A small to medium size, lanceolate point with a deep concave base that is steeply beveled. Some examples are fluted, others are finely serrated and show excellent quality collateral flaking. Most bases are deeply notched but some examples have a more shallow concavity. Basal grinding is usually absent. The ears on some examples turn inward. Blade edges are excurvate. **I.D. KEY:** Base form and flaking style.

DESERT SOUTHWEST SECTION:

This section includes point types from the following states: Arizona, Colorado, Nevada, New Mexico, Texas, Utah and from Mexico

The points in this section are arranged in alphabetical order and are shown **actual size**. All types are listed that were available for photographing. Any missing types will be added to future editions as photographs become available. We are always interested in receiving sharp, black and white or color glossy photos or color slides of your collection. Be sure to include a ruler in the photograph so that proper scale can be determined.

Lithics: Materials employed in the manufacture of projectile points from this region are: agate, basalt, chalcedony, chert, jasper, obsidian, petrified wood, quartzite, siltstone.

Important sites: Clovis (Paleo), Blackwater Draw, NM. Folsom (Paleo), Folsom NM. Sandia (Paleo), Sandia Cave, NM.

SPECIAL SENIOR ADVISOR:
Ben Stermer

Other advisors:
John Byrd
William J. "Bill" Creighton, William H. "Bill" Dickey
George E. Johnston, Alan L. Phelps,
Art Tatum

In memory of Charles D. Meyer who was instrumental in establishing this section of the guide with his advice, descriptions, and photographs.

SW

DESERT SOUTHWEST POINT TYPES
(Archaeological Periods)

PALEO (14,000 B.P - 8,000 B.P.)

Belen	Folsom	Lake Mohave	Midland
Clovis	Goshen	Lancet	Milnesand
Drill	Graver	Madden Lake	Sandia

EARLY ARCHAIC (11,000 B.P - 5,500 B.P.)

Abasolo	Bat Cave	Eden	Moyote	Scottsbluff
Agate Basin	Bell	Embudo	Northern Side	Scraper
Allen	Circular Uniface	Escobas	Notched	Silver Lake
Angostura	Knife	Firstview	Palmillas	Sudden Series
Archaic Knife	Cody Knife	Golondrina	Pelona	Texcoco
Augustin	Cruciform I	Hell Gap	Perforator	Tortugas
Augustin Snapped	Cruciform II	Jay	Pinto Basin	Uvalde
Base	Darl Stemmed	Lancet	Plainview	Ventana-Amargosa
Bajada	Datil	Marshall	Rio Grande	Zephyr
Baker	Early Leaf	Meserve	Round-Back Knife	Zorra
Barreal	Early Triangular	Mount Albion	San Jose	

MIDDLE ARCHAIC (5,500 B.P - 3,300 B.P.)

Ahumada	Dagger	Gypsum Cave	Refugio
Armijo	Disc	Hanna	San Rafael
Catan	Duncan	Kinney	Squaw Mountain
Chiricahua	Frio	Lerma	Ventana Side
Cortero	Frio Transitional	Manzano	Notched
Crescent	Green River	Neff	

LATE ARCHAIC (3,500 B.P - 2,300 B.P.)

Acatita	Conejo	Gobernadora	Shumla
Amaragosa	Duran	Maljamar	Socorro
Basal Double Tang	Early Stemmed	Martis	Triangular Knife
Carlsbad	Elko Corner Notched	Matamoros	Yavapai
Charcos	Elko Eared	San Pedro	
Cienega	Exotic	Saw	

DESERT TRADITIONS:
TRANSITIONAL (2,300 B.P - 1600 B.P.)

Black Mesa Narrow Neck	Figueroa	Guadalupe	Humboldt

DEVELOPMENTAL (1600 - 700 B.P)

Awatovi Side Notched	Eastgate Split-Stem	Rose Springs Corner	Truxton
Basketmaker	Gatlin Side Notched	Notched	Walnut Canyon Side
Bonito Notched	Gila River Corner Notched	Sacaton	Notched
Bull Creek	Hodges Contracting Stem	Salado	
Chaco Corner Notrched	Hohokam Knife	Salt River Indented Base	
Citrus Side Notched	Mimbre	Santa Cruz	
Cohonina Stemmed	Nawthis	Snaketown	
Convento	Parowan	Snaketown Side Notched	
Deadman's	Point Of Pines Side	Snaketown Triangular	
Dolores	Notched	Soto	
Dry Prong	Pueblo Side Notched	Temporal	

CLASSIC PHASE (700 - 400 B.P)

Aguaje	Cow's Skull	Desert-Sierra	Toyah
Buck Taylor Notched	Del Carmen	Garza	White Mountain Side
Caracara	Desert-Delta	Mescal Knife	Notched
Cottonwood Leaf	Desert-General	San Bruno	
Cottonwood Triangle	Desert-Redding	Sobaipuri	

HISTORIC (400 B.P - Present)

Glass	Trade

DESERT SOUTHWEST
THUMBNAIL GUIDE SECTION

The following references are provided to aid the collector in easier and quicker identification of point types. All photos are exactly 30% of actual size and are proportional to each other. Each point pictured in this section represents a classic form for the type. When a match is found, go to the alphabetical location of that type for more examples in true actual size.

① THUMBNAIL GUIDE - AURICULATE FORMS (30% actual size)

Fluted Forms

Belen

Unfluted Forms

Barreal

Cortero

Goshen

Clovis

Folsom

Allen

Angostura

Bat Cave

Elko Eared

Golondrina

Green River

Humboldt

Meserve

Meserve

Plainview

Midland

Salt Riv. Indented base

San Jose

Sandia III

Sandia IV

Squaw Mountain

② THUMBNAIL GUIDE - LANCEOLATE FORMS (30% actual size)

Cruciform II

Crescent

Circular Uniface Knife

Cruciform I

Drill

Angostura

Catan

Archaic Knife

Abasolo

Agate asin

Disc

Early Leaf

Early Triangular

Hell Gap

Hohokam Knife

SW

Kinney

Lake Mohave

Lancet

Lerma

Matamoros

Mescal Knife

Midland

Milnesand

Pelona

Perforator

Refugio

Round-back Knife

Saw

LANCEOLATE FORMS (continued)

Scraper (Thumb)

Scraper (Turtleback)

Tortugas

Trade

Triangular Knife

Sandia I

③ THUMBNAIL GUIDE - CORNER NOTCHED FORMS (30% actual size)

Amargosa

Dolores

Drill

Exotic

Maljamar

Mount Albion

Rose Springs

Cienega

Elko Corner Notched

Frio

Marshall

Moyote

San Pedro

Scraper (Blunt)

Texcoco

④ THUMBNAIL GUIDE - SIDE NOTCHED FORMS (30% actual size)

Basketmaker

Martis

Frio Transitional

Drill

San Jose

Rose Springs

Black Mesa Narrow Neck

Caracara

Frio

Mimbre

Mount Albion

Northern Side Notched

San Pedro

San Rafael

Scraper

Squaw Mountain

Sudden (Rocker)

Sudden

Texcoco

Ventana Side Notched

⑤ THUMBNAIL GUIDE - STEMMED FORMS (30% of actual size)

Acatita

Ahumada

Augustin

Bajada

Baker

Carlsbad

Charcos

Cody knife

Datil

Dagger

Darl

Early Stemmed

Duran

Eden

Lake Mohave

Augustin Snapped Base

Embudo

Exotic

Escobas

Figueroa

Firstview

Gobernadora

Gypsum Cave

Jay

Maljamar

954

STEMMED FORMS (continued)

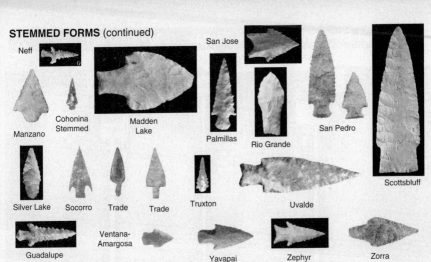

Neff

Manzano

Cohonina Stemmed

Madden Lake

San Jose

Palmillas

Rio Grande

San Pedro

Scottsbluff

Silver Lake

Socorro

Trade

Trade

Truxton

Uvalde

Guadalupe

Ventana-Amargosa

Yavapai

Zephyr

Zorra

---

⑥ THUMBNAIL GUIDE - STEMMED-BIFURCATED FORMS (30% of actual size)

Barreal

Chiricauha

Conejo

Duncan

Eastgate Split Stem

Hanna

San Jose

---

⑦ THUMBNAIL GUIDE - BASAL NOTCHED FORMS (30% of actual size)

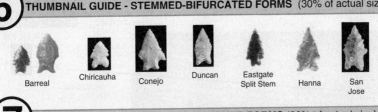

Bell

Basal Double Tang

Moyote

Parowan

Shumla

---

⑧ THUMBNAIL GUIDE - ARROW POINTS (30% of actual size)

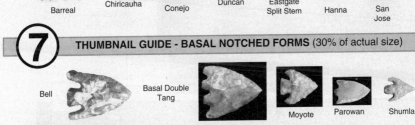

Bonito Notched

Citrus Side Notched

Deadman's

Aguaje

Awatovi Side Notched

Bull Creek

Buck Taylor Notched

Chaco Corner Notched

Convento

Cottonwood Leaf

Cottonwood Triangle

Cow's Skull

Del Carmen

SW

Desert Delta

Desert General

Desert Redding

Desert Sierra

Dry Prong

Garza

Gatlin Side Notched

Gila River Corner Notched

Glass

Hodges Contr. Stem

Mimbre

Nawthis

San Bruno

Point Of Pines Side Notched

Pueblo Side Notched

Rose Springs Corner Notched

Sacaton

Salado

Santa Cruz

Snaketown

Snaketown Side Notched

Snaketown Triangular

Sobaipuri

Soto

Temporal

Toyah

Walnut Canyon Side Notched

White Mountain Side Notched

ABASOLO - Early to Middle Archaic, 7000 - 5000 B. P.

(Also see Catan, Matamoros and Refugio)

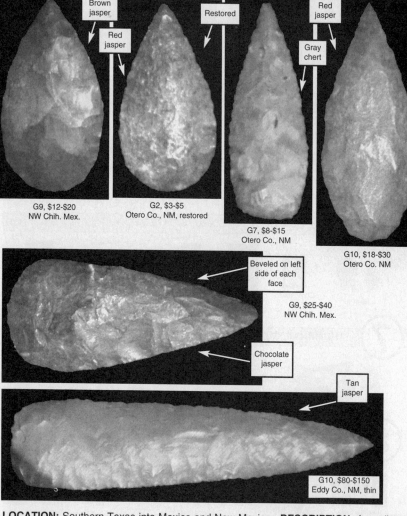

Brown jasper

Red jasper

Restored

Red jasper

Gray chert

G9, $12-$20
NW Chih. Mex.

G2, $3-$5
Otero Co., NM, restored

G7, $8-$15
Otero Co., NM

G10, $18-$30
Otero Co. NM

Beveled on left side of each face

G9, $25-$40
NW Chih. Mex.

Chocolate jasper

Tan jasper

G10, $80-$150
Eddy Co., NM, thin

LOCATION: Southern Texas into Mexico and New Mexico. **DESCRIPTION:** A medium to large size, broad, lanceolate point with a rounded base. The blade can be beveled on one side of each face and the base can be thinned. **I.D. KEY:** Early form of flaking on blade with good secondary edgework and rounded base.

ACATITA - Late Archaic, 3000 - 2600 B.P.

(Also see Augustine, Gobernadora, Gypsum Cave, Manzano, Socorro and Shumla)

LOCATION: Northern Mexico into New Mexico. **DESCRIPTION:** A small to medium sized, thin dart/knife point with with drooping barbs and a pointed to rounded contracting stem. A cross between the *Shumla* and the *Perdiz* point. Formerly known as *Cedral*; given the name *Acatita* by Perino in his Vol. 3. **I.D. KEY:** Barbs and base form.

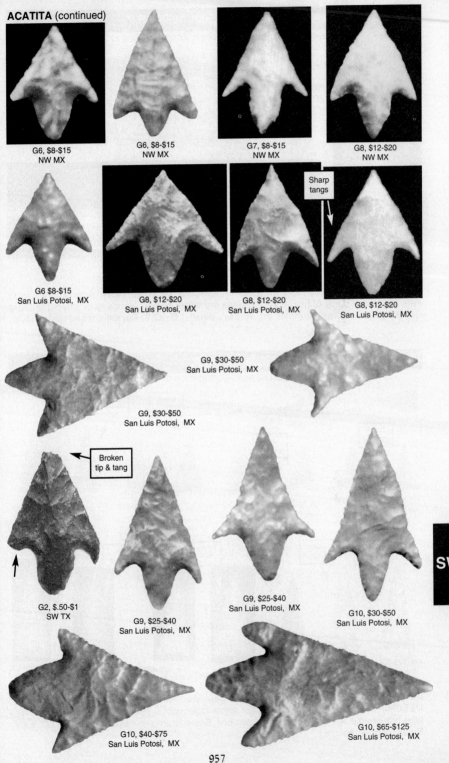

ACATITA (continued)

G6, $8-$15
NW MX

G6, $8-$15
NW MX

G7, $8-$15
NW MX

G8, $12-$20
NW MX

G6 $8-$15
San Luis Potosi, MX

G8, $12-$20
San Luis Potosi, MX

G8, $12-$20
San Luis Potosi, MX

Sharp tangs

G8, $12-$20
San Luis Potosi, MX

G9, $30-$50
San Luis Potosi, MX

G9, $30-$50
San Luis Potosi, MX

Broken tip & tang

G2, $.50-$1
SW TX

G9, $25-$40
San Luis Potosi, MX

G9, $25-$40
San Luis Potosi, MX

G10, $30-$50
San Luis Potosi, MX

SW

G10, $40-$75
San Luis Potosi, MX

G10, $65-$125
San Luis Potosi, MX

957

AGATE BASIN - Early Archaic, 10,500 - 10,000 B.P.

(Also see Allen, Angostura, Archaic Knife, Lerma and Sandia)

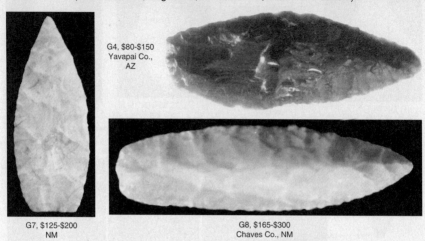

G4, $80-$150
Yavapai Co.,
AZ

G7, $125-$200
NM

G8, $165-$300
Chaves Co., NM

LOCATION: New Mexico eastward to Pennsylvania. **DESCRIPTION:** A medium to large size lanceolate blade of high quality. Bases are either convex, concave or straight and are usually ground. Some examples are median ridged. **I.D. KEY:** Basal form and flaking style.

AGUAJE - Classic Phase, 600 - 550 B.P.

(Also see Bull Creek, Cottonwood and Sobaipuri)

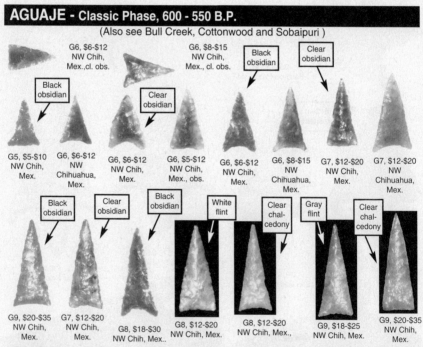

G6, $6-$12
NW Chih,
Mex.,cl. obs.

G6, $8-$15
NW Chih,
Mex., cl. obs.

Black obsidian

Clear obsidian

Black obsidian

Clear obsidian

G5, $5-$10
NW Chih,
Mex.

G6, $6-$12
NW
Chihuahua,
Mex.

G6, $6-$12
NW Chih,
Mex.

G6, $5-$12
NW Chih,
Mex., obs.

G6, $6-$12
NW Chih,
Mex.

G6, $8-$15
NW
Chihuahua,
Mex.

G7, $12-$20
NW Chih,
Mex.

G7, $12-$20
NW
Chihuahua,
Mex.

Black obsidian

Clear obsidian

Black obsidian

White flint

Clear chalcedony

Gray flint

Clear chalcedony

G9, $20-$35
NW Chih,
Mex.

G7, $12-$20
NW Chih,
Mex.

G8, $18-$30
NW Chih, Mex..

G8, $12-$20
NW Chih, Mex.

G8, $12-$20
NW Chih, Mex.,

G9, $18-$25
NW Chih, Mex.

G9, $20-$35
NW Chih,
Mex.

LOCATION: Northwest Chihuahua, MX. into Sou. New Mexico and Far West Texas. **DESCRIPTION:** A small, thin triangular arrow point with a straight to concave base. This type has needle tips and sharp basal corners. Some examples have basal ears. **I.D. KEY:** Small, narrow triangle.

AGUAJE (continued)

Clear obsidian
G8, $20-$35 El Paso Co., TX

Gray flint

Clear obsidian

Gray flint

Clear crystal
G8, $40-$75 NW Chih, Mex.

Gray chert

G8, $20-$35 NW Chih, Mex.

G8, $20-$35 NW Chih, Mex.

G9, $20-$35 NW Chih, Mex.

G10, $25-$40 NW Chih, Mex, white/gray chert

G10, $35-$60 NW Chih, Mex.

AHUMADA - Mid-Late Archaic, 4000 - 2500 B.P.

(Also see Carlsbad, Cienega, Dolores, Guadalupe, Maljamar, Neff and Truxton)

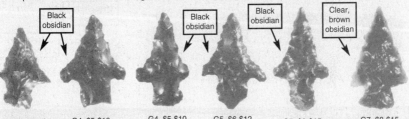

Black obsidian

Black obsidian

Black obsidian

Clear, brown obsidian

G4, $4-$8 NW Chih, Mex.

G4, $5-$10 NW Chih, Mex.

G4, $5-$10 NW Chih, Mex.

G5, $6-$12 NW Chih, Mex.

G7, $8-$15 NW Chih, Mex.

G7, $8-$15 NW Chih, Mex.

Red jasper

Basalt

Black obsidian

Grey chert

G7, $8-$15 NW Chih, Mex.

G4, $5-$10 NW Chih, Mex.

G7, $8-$15 NW Chih, Mex.,

G8, $12-$20 NW Chih, Mex.

G8, $12-$20 NW Chih, Mex.

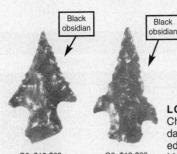

Black obsidian

Black obsidian

G8, $12-$20 NW Chih, Mex.

Gray chert

G8, $12-$20 NW Chih, Mex.

G8, $12-$20 NW Chih, Mex.

SW

LOCATION: Arizona, New Mexico and N.W. Chihuahua, MX. **DESCRIPTION:** A corner notched dart point with a triangular blade; almost always serrated and with an expanding stem. Named "Pindejo" by McNish who reported that most examples are from Villa Ahumada in N.W. Chihuahua, MX. **I.D. KEY:** Fan shaped stem and serrations.

ALLEN - Early Archaic, 10,000 - 9500 B.P.

(Also see Angostura, Clovis, Cortero, Goshen, Humboldt, Meserve, Plainview)

Oblique flaking

Note side notches added by a later culture

Tan flint

G3, $30-$50
El Paso Co., Tx. Hueco Mountains.
Altered by a later culture.

LOCATION: New Mexico to Canada.
DESCRIPTION: A small to medium size lanceolate point that has oblique transverse flaking and a ground concave base. **I.D. KEY:** Flaking style and blade form.

G8, $275-$500
Chaves Co., NM

Note oblique flaking

Restored tip reduces value

G2, $65-$125
NM

AMARGOSA - Middle Archaic, 3000 - 2000 B.P.

(Also see Basketmaker, Cienega, Elko Corner Notched, Figueroa, Mt. Albion, San Pedro)

LOCATION: Southeastern California into W. Arizona and W. Nevada.
DESCRIPTION: A small size, corner notched dart/knife point with a needle tip and sharp tangs. Some examples are serrated. Bases are straight to slightly convex or concave. **I.D. KEY:** Sharp tangs and corners, needle tip.

Serrated edge

G4, $5-$10
Mohave Co., AZ

G8, $15-$25
Pima Co., AZ

ANGOSTURA - Early Archaic, 10,000 - 8000 B.P.

(Also see Agate Basin, Allen, Archaic Knife, Clovis and Humboldt)

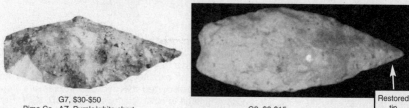

G7, $30-$50
Pima Co., AZ. Purple/white chert.

Restored tip

G2, $8-$15
Otero Co., NM, ground stem sides and base. thick.

960

ANGOSTURA (continued)

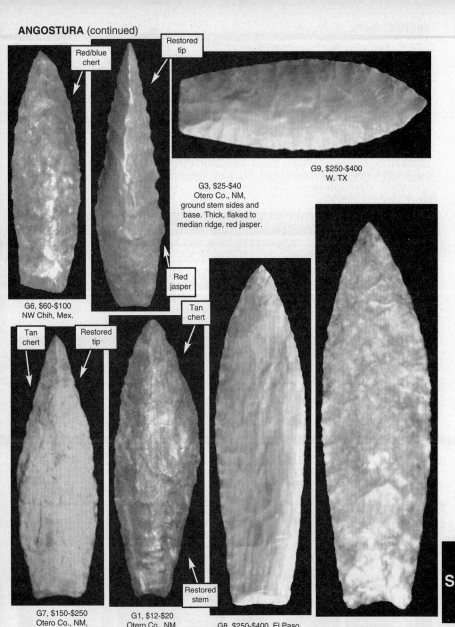

Restored tip

Red/blue chert

G6, $60-$100
NW Chih, Mex.

G3, $25-$40
Otero Co., NM,
ground stem sides and
base. Thick, flaked to
median ridge, red jasper.

G9, $250-$400
W. TX

Red jasper

Tan chert

Tan chert

Restored tip

G7, $150-$250
Otero Co., NM,
ground stem sides and
base. Thin.

G1, $12-$20
Otero Co., NM,
ground stem sides.
Thick

Restored stem

G8, $250-$400, El Paso
Co., TX

G9, $350-$650
Union Co., NM

SW

LOCATION: Southwestern states. **DESCRIPTION:** A medium to large size lanceolate blade of unusually high quality. Bases are either convex, concave or straight and are usually ground. Most examples have oblique transverse flaking. **I.D. KEY:** Basal form and flaking style.

ARCHAIC KNIFE - Early to Mid Archaic, 6000 - 4000 B.P.

(Also see Angostura and Early Triangular)

ARCHAIC KNIFE (continued)

G2, $25-$40
Pima Co., AZ

Broken & glued

Base nick

LOCATION: Arizona into Plains states. **DESCRIPTION:** A medium to large size triangular blade with a concave to straight base. **I.D. KEY:** Large triangle with early flaking.

ARMIJO - Early to Mid Archaic, 3800 - 2800 B.P.

(Also see Meserve, San Jose)

Ground stem & base

G3, $5-$10 NM

LOCATION: Arizona, New Mexico. **DESCRIPTION:** A small size auriculate, serrated point with a ground stem and base that is concave. Related to the earlier *San Jose* type. **I.D. KEY:** Eared base.

AUGUSTIN - Early to Middle Archaic, 7000- 5000 B.P.

(Also see Acatita, Gypsum Cave, Manzano and Santa Cruz)

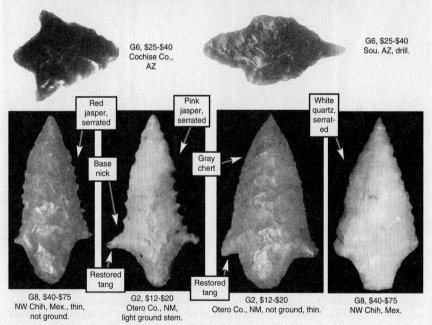

G6, $25-$40
Cochise Co., AZ

G6, $25-$40
Sou. AZ, drill.

Red jasper, serrated

Pink jasper, serrated

White quartz, serrated

Base nick

Gray chert

Restored tang

Restored tang

G8, $40-$75
NW Chih, Mex., thin, not ground.

G2, $12-$20
Otero Co., NM, light ground stem.

G2, $12-$20
Otero Co., NM, not ground, thin.

G8, $40-$75
NW Chih, Mex.

LOCATION: The southern portion of the southwestern states and northern Mexico. **DESCRIPTION:** A small to medium sized dart/knife point with a broad triangular blade and a contracting, rounded to pointed stem and obtuse shoulders. The *Gypsum Cave* point may be a westerly and northerly extension of this point. **I.D. KEY:** Contracting base.

AUGUSTIN (continued)

G6, $35-$65
AZ

Gray chert

G8, $60-$100
Otero Co., NM, ground stem.

White chert, serrated

Restored tang

G2, $12-$20
Otero Co., NM, not ground.

Red jasper, serrated

G9, $90-$175
NW Chih, Mex, ground stem, thin.

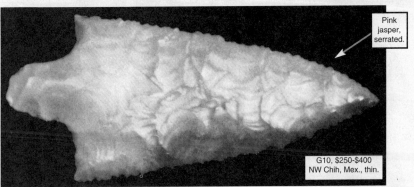

Pink jasper, serrated.

G10, $250-$400
NW Chih, Mex., thin.

AUGUSTIN-SNAPPED BASE - Early to Mid-Archaic, 7000 - 5000 B.P.
(Also see Gypsum Cave)

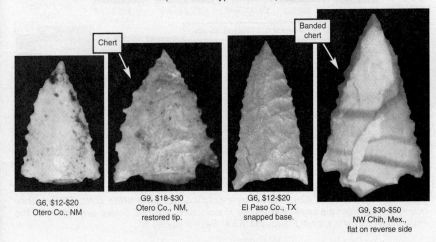

SW

Chert

Banded chert

G6, $12-$20
Otero Co., NM

G9, $18-$30
Otero Co., NM,
restored tip.

G6, $12-$20
El Paso Co., TX
snapped base.

G9, $30-$50
NW Chih, Mex.,
flat on reverse side

963

AUGUSTIN SNAPPED BASE (continued)

G3, $5-$10
El Paso Co., TX

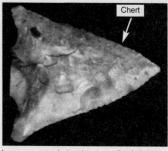

G7, $18-$30
Otero Co., NM,

LOCATION: E. Arizona **DESCRIPTION:** A medium size, serrated, barbed point with a snapped-off base to facilitate hafting. Similar in form to Kirk Snapped Base points found in the southeastern U.S. **I.D. KEY:** Base snapped off.

AWATOVI SIDE NOTCHED - Develop. to Classic Phase, 750 - 600 B.P.

(Also see Buck Taylor Notched, Dell Carmen, Desert Sierra, Pueblo Side, White Mountain)

LOCATION: Arizona, New Mexico, northern Mexico, southern Utah and S.W. Colorado. **DESCRIPTION:** A small size, narrow, triple-notched, triangular arrow point. Side notches occur high up from the base. Part of the *Pueblo Side Notched* cluster and similar to the *Harrell* point of the southern Plains. **I.D. KEY:** Base snapped off.

BAJADA - Late Archaic to Developmental Phase, 6000 - 5000 B.P.

(Also see Conejo, Duncan, Escobas, Hanna, Jay and Rio Grande)

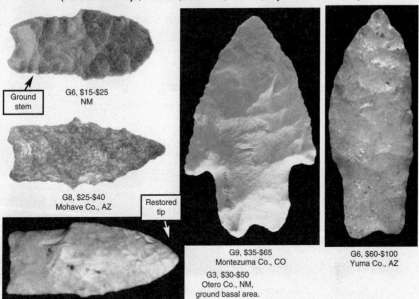

Ground stem

G6, $15-$25
NM

G8, $25-$40
Mohave Co., AZ

Restored tip

G9, $35-$65
Montezuma Co., CO

G3, $30-$50
Otero Co., NM,
ground basal area.

G6, $60-$100
Yuma Co., AZ

LOCATION: Northern Arizona to New Mexico, Sou. Colorado & Utah. **DESCRIPTION:** A medium sized birfurcated, stemmed point with weak shoulders and serrated blade edges. Related to the earlier *Escobas* point. **I.D. KEY:** Long concave stem.

BAKER - Early Archaic, 7500 - 6000 B. P.

(Also see Bajada, Darl, Datil, San Jose, Uvalde and Zephyr)

Side nicks

Needle tip

G4, $4-$8
NM

G4, $4-$8
NM

G9, $25-$45
NM

G8, $15-$25
NM

G7, $8-$15
NM

SW

G7, $8-$15
NM

Tip nick

G8, $15-$25
NM

G5, $4-$8
NM

G7, $12-$20
NM

G9, $18-$30
NM

LOCATION: Western Texas into New Mexico. **DESCRIPTION:** A small to medium size, thin, point with a sharp tip and a bifurcated to concave base. Tangs are sharp and the stem expands. The stem length varies from short to long. Similar to the *Bandy* point found in southern Texas. **I.D. KEY:** Base extended and bifurcated.

BAKER (continued)

G9, $25-$45
NM

G8, $15-$25
NM

G9, $18-$30
NM

G9, $20-$35
NM

G9, $20-$35
NM

G8, $20-$35
NM

G9, $35-$65
NM

G9, $30-$50
NM

Tip nick

G6, $12-$20
NM

G10, $35-$65
NM

Chalcedony

Resharpened many times

G9, $35-$60
NM

G10, $35-$65
NM

G8, $18-$30

G10, $80-$150
NM

BARREAL - Early Archaic, 9000 - 7200 B.P.
(Also see Duncan, Hanna, San Jose, Squaw Mountain)

Black obsidian

Green obsidian

Black ob.

G6, $8-$15
NW Chihuahua, Mex.

G6, $8-$15
NW Chih, Mex, ground basal area

G6, $8-$15
NW Chih, Mex,

G6, $8-$15
NW Chih, Mex, ground, heavy patina.

G7, $12-$20
NW Chih, Mex, ground, heavy patina

NW Chih, Mex, ground basal area, heavy patina

966

BARREAL (continued)

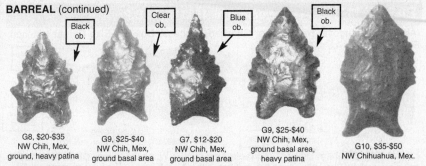

Black ob.

Clear ob.

Blue ob.

Black ob.

Black ob.

G8, $20-$35
NW Chih, Mex,
ground, heavy patina

G9, $25-$40
NW Chih, Mex,
ground basal area

G7, $12-$20
NW Chih, Mex,
ground basal area

G9, $25-$40
NW Chih, Mex,
ground basal area,
heavy patina

G10, $35-$50
NW Chihuahua, Mex.

LOCATION: N.W. Chihuahua, Mexico into southern New Mexico and far west Texas.
DESCRIPTION: A small sized, thin, serrated dart point with projecting ears and a concave base. The stem sides are straight to concave. Basal area is usually ground. Shoulders are weak to non-existent. **I.D. KEY:** Basal form and serrations.

BASAL DOUBLE TANG - Late Archaic, 3500 - 2300 B.P.

(Also see Bell and Parowan)

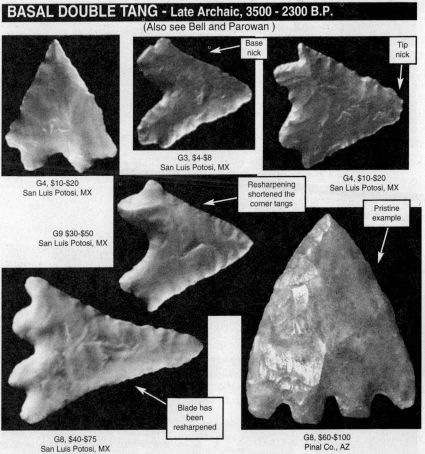

Base nick

Tip nick

G3, $4-$8
San Luis Potosi, MX

G4, $10-$20
San Luis Potosi, MX

G4, $10-$20
San Luis Potosi, MX

Resharpening shortened the corner tangs

Pristine example

G9 $30-$50
San Luis Potosi, MX

Blade has been resharpened

G8, $40-$75
San Luis Potosi, MX

G8, $60-$100
Pinal Co., AZ

SW

LOCATION: Sou. Arizona, New Mexico and northern Mexico. **DESCRIPTION:** A medium sized dart/knife point which is baseally notched, and then with the stem bifurcated. Worn out examples appear as a lanceolate blade with a notched basal edge.. **I.D. KEY:** Triple basal notches.

967

BASKETMAKER - Developmental, 1500 - 1300 B.P.

(Also see Amargosa, Black Mesa, Carlsbad, Cienega, Dolores, Elko Corner Notched, Figueroa, Mount Albion)

G8, $8-$15
Maricopa Co., AZ

Thin

Black basalt

Oblique blaking

G10, $125-$200
Aneth, UT, from a dry cave; knife form.

LOCATION: Southern Utah into northern Arizona & N.W. New Mexico. **DESCRIPTION:** A small to medium size, thin, dart/knife point that is side to corner notched. **I.D. KEY:** Corner notching.

BAT CAVE - Early Archaic, 9000 - 8000 B.P.

(Also see Humboldt)

G4, $10-$20
Yavapai Co., AZ

G6, $35-$60
Yavapai Co., AZ

G5, $15-$30
Yavapai Co., AZ

G5, $15-$30
Yavapai Co., AZ

G6, $25-$45
Cochise Co., AZ

G8, $125-$225
CO

G3, $5-$10
Yavapai Co., AZ

G7, $50-$95
NM

LOCATION: The southwestern states and northern Mexico. **DESCRIPTION:** A small, lanceolate dart/knife with convex blade edges, constricting toward the base to form small, flaring ears. The basal edge is slightly concave and is well thinned. **I.D. KEY:** Waisted appearance and small, flaring ears.

BELEN - Paleo, 10,500 - 8000 B.P.

(Also see Midland, Milnesand)

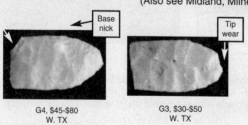

Base nick

Tip wear

G4, $45-$80
W. TX

G3, $30-$50
W. TX

LOCATION: E. New Mexico into W. Texas. **DESCRIPTION:** A small, thin lanceloate point with ground stem sides and a straight to concave base. Similar to *Midland* points but differ in that *Belen* points have one basal ear that is more prominent. **I.D. KEY:** Thinness, prominent single basal ear.

968

BELL - Middle Archaic, 7000 - 5000 B.P.

(Also see Basal Double Tang, Moyote and Parowan)

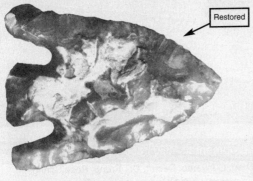

Restored

G3, $80-$150
NW Chihuahua, MX

LOCATION: Cent. Texas into N. Mexico. **DESCRIPTION:** A small to medium size point with medium-deep parallel basal notches, but not as deep as in Andice. Larger examples usually would fall under Andice. Found primarily in Texas. Tangs turn inward at the base. **I.D. KEY:** Shorter tangs and notching.

G6, $250-$400
NW Chihuahua, MX

BLACK MESA NARROW NECK - Trans.-Developmental Phase, 2000 - 1200 B.P.

(Also see Amargosa, Basketmaker, Figueroa and San Pedro)

G6, $15-$25
Chinle, AZ

Broken back

G1, $1-$2
Pima Co., AZ

Mottled blue chert

G8, $30-$50
Big Bend, TX

Basalt

Red/brown jasper

G8, $40-$75
NM

Gray basalt

G10+, $225-$400
Pima Co., AZ

Gray chert

G7, $25-$40
Pima Co., AZ

SW

969

BLACK MESA NARROW NECK (continued)

LOCATION: Sou. California into Arizona and New Mexico. DESCRIPTION: A medium to large deeply corner notched dart point with a narrow neck and an expanding stem. Bases are straight to convex. I.D. KEY: Very narrow neck.

G10, $350-$650
S.E. CA

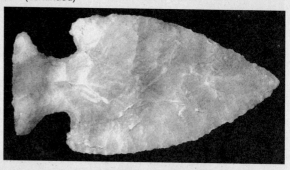

BONITO NOTCHED - Developmental, 1050 - 850 B.P.

(Also see Chaco Corner Notched, Convento, Desert, Dry Prong, Rose Springs)

Obsidian

G9, $30-$50
NM

LOCATION: Arizona, New Mexico, S.W. Colorado, sou. Utah. DESCRIPTION: A small size, narrow, side notched arrow point with a convex base. Some examples are double or triple notched on one side. I.D. KEY: Convex base.

BUCK TAYLOR NOTCHED- Classic to Historic Phase, 600 - 200 B.P.

(Also see Awatovi Side Notched, Desert, Dell Carmen, Walnut Canyon, White Mountain)

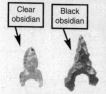

Clear obsidian

Black obsidian

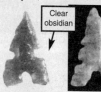

Clear obsidian

G7, $20-$35
Pima Co., AZ.

G6, $8-$15
Maricopa Co., AZ

G5, $8-$15
Mohave Co., AZ

G4, $6-$12
Mohave Co., AZ

G6, $12-$20
Mohave Co., AZ

G6, $18-$30
NW Chihuahua, Mex.

G5, $8-$15
Yavapai Co., AZ

LOCATION: Arizona. DESCRIPTION: A small, triangular, tri-notched arrow point including a deep basal notch. Part of the *Pueblo Side Notched* cluster. Formerly known as *Red Horn*. I.D. KEY: Very narrow neck.

Obsidian

G7, $8-$15
Maricopa Co., AZ

BULL CREEK - Desert Traditions-Developmental Phase, 950 - 700 B.P.

(Also see Aguaje, Cottonwood, Desert, Pueblo Side Notched & Snaketown Triangular)

Chalcedony

G6, $5-$10
Pima Co., AZ

G4, $12-$20
AZ

G7, $30-$55
AZ

G5, $25-$45
AZ

G7, $30-$55
AZ

G10, $50-$90
AZ

G8, $35-$65
AZ

G9, $40-$75
AZ

G10, $65-$125
AZ

BULL CREEK (continued)

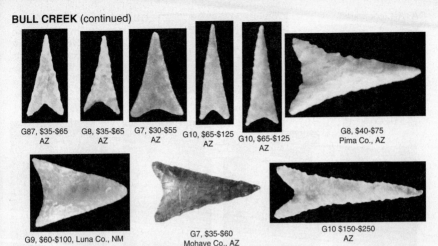

G87, $35-$65
AZ

G8, $35-$65
AZ

G7, $30-$55
AZ

G10, $65-$125
AZ

G10, $65-$125
AZ

G8, $40-$75
Pima Co., AZ

G9, $60-$100, Luna Co., NM

G7, $35-$60
Mohave Co., AZ

G10 $150-$250
AZ

LOCATION: Northern Arizona, southern Utah and northeastern Nevada. **DESCRIPTION:** A long, thin triangular arrow point with a deeply concave basal edge. They are sometimes serrated. Some examples have been shortened by resharpening. **I.D. KEY:** Isosceles triangle shape and concave base.

CARACARA - Mississippian to Historic, 600 - 400 B.P.

(Also see Desert, Hohokam, Martis, Sacaton, Saladom Ventana Side Notched)

G10, $65-$125
NM

LOCATION: Texas into N.W. Chihuahua, MX. **DESCRIPTION:** A small size, thin, side notched arrow point with a straight, concave or convex base. Shoulders can be tapered to horizontal to barbed. Side notches are shallow to deep.

CARLSBAD - Late Archaic-Transitional, 3000 - 1700 B.P.

(Also see Amargosa, Basketmaker, Black Mesa, Cienega, Dolores and Guadalupe)

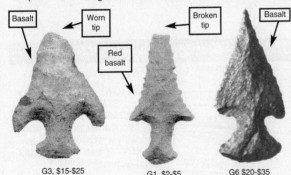

Basalt

Worn tip

Red basalt

Broken tip

Basalt

G3, $15-$25
Pima Co., AZ

G1, $2-$5
Pima Co., AZ

G6 $20-$35
Alamosa, CO

LOCATION: Sou. New Mexico into Mexico and Arizona. **DESCRIPTION:** Part of the *Cienega* cluster. A small size, deep basal to corner notched point and a convex base. Most examples have been resharpened to exhaustion reducing the shoulders significantly. Stem sides are concave and expanding.

SW

CATAN - Late Archaic to Mississippian, 4000 - 300 B. P.

(Also see Abasolo and Matamoros)

CATAN (continued)

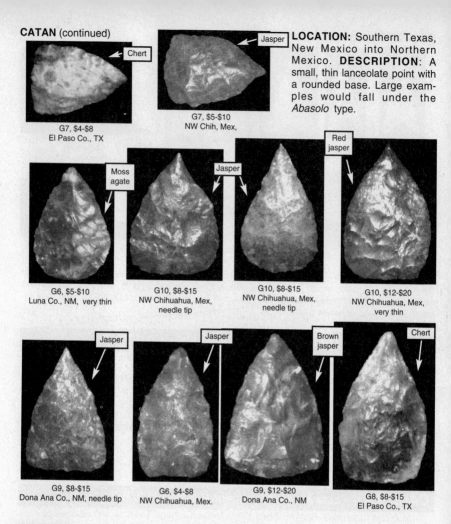

LOCATION: Southern Texas, New Mexico into Northern Mexico. **DESCRIPTION:** A small, thin lanceolate point with a rounded base. Large examples would fall under the *Abasolo* type.

G7, $4-$8
El Paso Co., TX

G7, $5-$10
NW Chih, Mex,

G6, $5-$10
Luna Co., NM, very thin

G10, $8-$15
NW Chihuahua, Mex,
needle tip

G10, $8-$15
NW Chihuahua, Mex,
needle tip

G10, $12-$20
NW Chihuahua, Mex,
very thin

G9, $8-$15
Dona Ana Co., NM, needle tip

G6, $4-$8
NW Chihuahua, Mex.

G9, $12-$20
Dona Ana Co., NM

G8, $8-$15
El Paso Co., TX

CEDRAL (see Acatita)

CHACO CORNER NOTCHED - Developmental, 1250 - 1050 B.P.

(Also see Convento and Rose Springs)

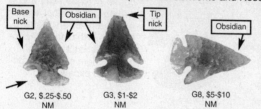

LOCATION: Arizona, New Mexico, S.W. Colorado, sou. Utah. **DESCRIPTION:** A small size, thin, corner notched arrow point with a wide convex base. **I.D. KEY:** Broad convex base, deep notches.

G2, $.25-$.50
NM

G3, $1-$2
NM

G8, $5-$10
NM

CHARCOS - Late Archaic-Trans., 3000 - 2000 B.P.

(Also see Duncan, Frio-Transitional, Hanna, San Jose and Squaw Mountain)

CHARCOS (continued)

LOCATION: N. Mexico into New Mexico, Texas and Colorado. **DESCRIPTION:** A small size, thin, single barbed point with a notch near the opposite shoulder. Stem is rectangular or expanding. **I.D. KEY:** Asymmetrical form. Some are double notched.

G6, $12-$20
Alamosa Co., CO

CHIRICAHUA - Middle Archaic, 5000 - 4000 B.P.

(Also see Duncan, Frio-Transitional, Hanna, San Jose, Squaw Mountain and Ventana Side Notched)

Basalt

G3, $2-$4
Alamosa Co., CO

G3, $2-$4
Cochise Co., AZ

G3, $2-$4
Yavapai Co., AZ

G3, $2-$4
Cochise Co., AZ

G6, $8-$15
Cochise Co., AZ

G5, $6-$12
Cochise Co., AZ

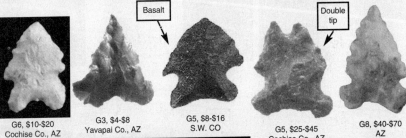

Basalt

Double tip

G6, $10-$20
Cochise Co., AZ

G3, $4-$8
Yavapai Co., AZ

G5, $8-$16
S.W. CO

G5, $25-$45
Cochise Co., AZ

G8, $40-$70
AZ

G8, $40-$70
AZ

G6, $15-$25
Cochise Co., AZ

G9, $40-$70
Cochise Co., AZ

LOCATION: New Mexico, Arizona, southern California and northern Mexico. **DESCRIPTION:** A small to medium sized dart/knife point with side notches and a concave base, producing an eared appearance. **I.D. KEY:** Generally ears are "rounded" in appearance.

CIENEGA - Late Archaic-Transitional, 2800 - 1800 B.P.

(Also see Amargosa, Basketmaker, Black Mesa, Carlsbad, Dolores, Guadalupe and San Pedro)

G7, $15-$25
NM

G6, $12-$20
Mohave Co., AZ

SW

973

CIENEGA (continued)

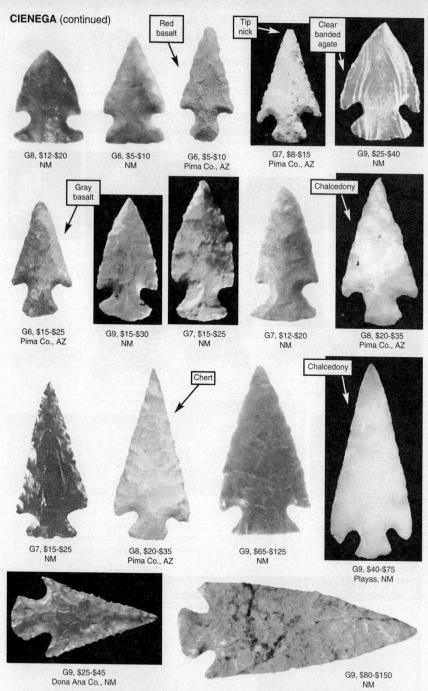

Red basalt

Tip nick

Clear banded agate

G8, $12-$20
NM

G6, $5-$10
NM

G6, $5-$10
Pima Co., AZ

G7, $8-$15
Pima Co., AZ

G9, $25-$40
NM

Gray basalt

Chalcedony

G6, $15-$25
Pima Co., AZ

G9, $15-$30
NM

G7, $15-$25
NM

G7, $12-$20
NM

G8, $20-$35
Pima Co., AZ

Chert

Chalcedony

G7, $15-$25
NM

G8, $20-$35
Pima Co., AZ

G9, $65-$125
NM

G9, $40-$75
Playas, NM

G9, $25-$45
Dona Ana Co., NM

G9, $80-$150
NM

LOCATION: Arizona into New Mexico. **DESCRIPTION:** A small to medium sized dart/knife point with corner notches, shoulder barbs and a convex base, producing an expanded stem. **I.D. KEY:** Narrow stems and broad corner notches. Illustrated points are called *Tularosa Corner Notched* which are part of the Cienega cluster.

974

CIENEGA (continued)

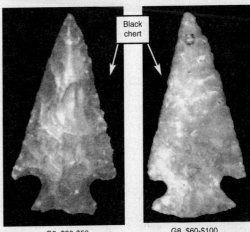

Dark gray banded slate

Black chert

G6, $18-$30
Otero Co., NM

G8, $30-$50
Otero Co., NM

G8, $60-$100
S.W. CO

CIRCULAR UNIFACE KNIFE - Archaic, 6000 - 4000 B.P.
(Also see Disc, Lancet, Scraper)

LOCATION: New Mexico. **DESCRIPTION:**
A medium sized circular knife that is uniface
on one side and steeply flaked on the other
side. **I.D. KEY:** Circular uniface.

G10, $12-$20
NM, knife.

CITRUS SIDE NOTCHED - Develop. to Classic Phase, 800 - 600 B.P.
(Also see Desert, Gatlin Side Notched, Salado)

SW

Tip nick

G7, $30-$50
AZ

G7, $30-$50
AZ

LOCATION: Arizona **DESCRIPTION:** A small size, very thin, triangular, side notched
Hohokam arrow point with a straight to slightly convex base which is the widest part of the
point. Blade edges are concave, tips are long and slender. **I.D. KEY:** Long, needle tips

CLOVIS - Early Paleo, 14,000 - 10,000 B.P.

(Also see Allen, Angostura, Folsom, Golondrina, Goshen, Madden Lake, Meserve and
Sandia)

CLOVIS (continued)

Brown/beige banded chert

Broken base

Gray chert

G8, $200-$350
Eddy Co., NM, ground basal area.

$45-$80
Cochise Co., AZ

G3, $125-$200
Hudspeth Co., TX,
ground basal.

Fluting channel

Tan/gray chert

Fluting channel

G5, $$450-$800
NW Chih, Mex,
flint, ground basal area.
Restored small side piece.

G6, $800-$1500
Lehner site, AZ

Broken tip

G3, $35-$65
NM

G8, $1600-$3000, Curry Co., NM,
Blanco Creek. Colorful chert.

976

CLOVIS (continued)

LOCATION: All of North America. Named after Clovis, New Mexico near where these fluted projectile points were found. **DESCRIPTION:** A medium to large size, auriculate, fluted, lanceolate point with a concave base that is ground. Most examples are fluted on both sides about 1/3 the way up from the base. *Clovis* is the earliest known point type in the hemisphere. The first *Clovis* find associated with Mastodons was in 1979 at Mastodon State Park, Jefferson Co., MO. in the Kimmswick bone bed dated to 12,000 B.P. The origin of Clovis is a mystery as there is no pre-*Clovis* evidence here (crude forms that pre-date Clovis). **I.D. KEY:** Paleo flaking, basal ears, baton or billet fluting instead of indirect style.

CODY KNIFE - Early to Middle Archaic, 8000 - 5000 B. P.

(Also see Base-Tang Knife, Corner Tang, Eden, Mid-Back Tang and Scottsbluff)

G5, $350-$600
Luna Co., NM,
snapped base, not
ground

LOCATION: Northern Plains states. **DESCRIPTION:** A medium to large size asymmetrical blade with one or two shoulders and a medium to short stem. Stem edges are ground on early examples. Made by the Cody complex people who made *Scottsbluff* points. Flaking is similar to the *Scottsbluff* type and some examples were made from *Scottsbluff* points. **I.D. KEY:** Paleo flaking, asymmetrical form.

COHONINA STEMMED - Developmental Phase, 1300 - 900 B.P.

(Also see Rose Springs)

G4, $2-$4
Coconino Co., AZ

G5, $4-$8
Coconino Co., AZ

G6, $8-$15
Coconino Co., AZ

G7, $8-$15
Coconino Co., AZ

LOCATION: Northern Arizona. **DESCRIPTION:** A small size, narrow, stemmed to corner notched point with tapered shoulders and an expanding stem.

CONEJO - Late Archaic, 3500 - 2300 B.P.

(Also see Bell, Duncan)

SW

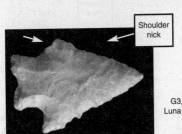

Shoulder
nick

G7, $35-$60
Luna Co., NM

G3, $4-$8
Luna Co., NM

LOCATION: Extreme western Texas and most of New Mexico. **DESCRIPTION:** A corner notched dart/knife with convex blade edges, short barbs and a short, straight stem. The basal edge may be straight or concave.

CONVENTO - Developmental Phase, 950 - 850 B. P.

(Also see Chaco Corner Notched, Rose Springs)

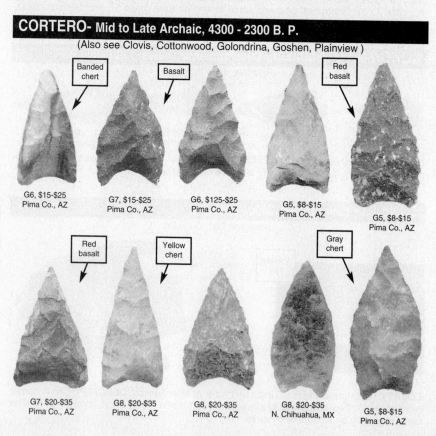

Banded obsidian

Black obsidian

Clear obsidian

Black obsidian

G4, $4-$8

G3, $2-$5 basal notch

G5, $8-$15   G5, $5-$10   G6, $8-$15

G7, $12-$20

G7, $5-$15

G7, $8-$15

All from N.W. Chihuahua, Mexico

Clear obsidian

Clear obsidian

Black obsidian

G7, $8-$15 bl. obs.

G7, $5-$15 NW MX.

Black obsidian

G7, $5-$15

Black obsidian

G8, $12-$20   G8, $12-$20   G8, $12-$20   G7, $5-$20   G7, $12-$20   G8, $15-$25   G8, $15-$25   G9, $20-$35

LOCATION: N.W. Chihuahua, MX into southern New Mexico and far west Texas.
DESCRIPTION: A small, thin, barbed, corner notched arrow point with an expanding stem and a convex base. **I.D. KEY:** Barbs and base form.

CORTERO- Mid to Late Archaic, 4300 - 2300 B. P.

(Also see Clovis, Cottonwood, Golondrina, Goshen, Plainview)

Banded chert

Basalt

Red basalt

G6, $15-$25 Pima Co., AZ

G7, $15-$25 Pima Co., AZ

G6, $125-$25 Pima Co., AZ

G5, $8-$15 Pima Co., AZ

G5, $8-$15 Pima Co., AZ

Red basalt

Yellow chert

Gray chert

G7, $20-$35 Pima Co., AZ

G8, $20-$35 Pima Co., AZ

G8, $20-$35 Pima Co., AZ

G8, $20-$35 N. Chihuahua, MX

G5, $8-$15 Pima Co., AZ

978

CORTERO (continued)

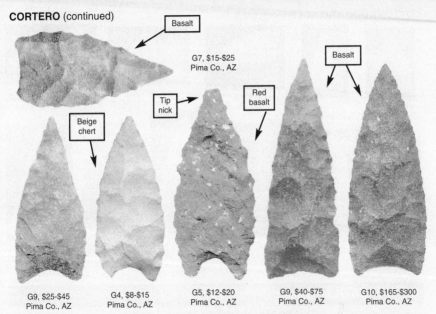

Basalt

G7, $15-$25
Pima Co., AZ

Basalt

Tip nick

Red basalt

Basalt

Beige chert

G9, $25-$45
Pima Co., AZ

G4, $8-$15
Pima Co., AZ

G5, $12-$20
Pima Co., AZ

G9, $40-$75
Pima Co., AZ

G10, $165-$300
Pima Co., AZ

LOCATION: Southern Arizona and S.W. New Mexico. **DESCRIPTION:** A small, fairly thick, triangular point with a concave base. Cross-section is diamond shaped. Bases are not ground. Some examples show pressure flaking along the edges. **I.D. KEY:** Blade form and thickness.

COTTONWOOD LEAF - Desert Traditions-Classic/Historic Phases, 700 - 200 B.P.

(Also see Catan, Datil and Pelona)

G6, $5-$10
Pima Co., AZ

G7, $25-$50
Apache Co., AZ

G2, $.50-$1
Mohave Co., AZ

G8, $30-$50
Pima Co., AZ

G3, $2-$4
Pima Co., AZ

G7, $20-$40
Yavapai Co., AZ

SW

LOCATION: Arizona and westward into California and Nevada. **DESCRIPTION:** A small, thin, leaf shaped arrow point that resembles a long tear-drop. The base is rounded. **I.D. KEY:** Size and blade form.

COTTONWOOD TRIANGLE - Desert Traditions-Classic and Historic Phases, 700 - 200 B.P.

(Also see Aguaje, Bull Creek, Cottonwood Leaf, Desert, Pueblo Side Notched, Sobaipari)

LOCATION: Arizona and westward into California and Nevada. **DESCRIPTION:** A small, thin triangular arrow point with a straight to slightly convex basal edge. **I.D. KEY:** Size and blade form.

COTTONWOOD TRIANGLE (continued)

G6, $8-$15
Cochise Co., AZ

G4, $3-$5
Cochise Co., AZ

G2, $1-$2
Cochise Co., AZ

G6, $10-$20
Cochise Co., AZ

G4, $3-$5
Pima Co., AZ

G2, $1-$2
Pima Co., AZ

G6, $15-$30
Cochise Co., AZ

G6, $15-$30
Mohave Co., AZ

G5, $8-$15
Pima Co., AZ

G6, $15-$30
Coconino Co., AZ

G6, $15-$30
Cochise Co., AZ

COW'S SKULL- Classic Phase, 600 - 550 B. P.

(Also see Del Carmen, Desert, Toyah)

LOCATION: Northwest Chihuahua, Mex.
DESCRIPTION: A small, thin triangular arrow point with a concave base and exaggerated basal ears that are long and swing upwards towards the tip. Shoulders are tapered and the blade is serrated. A very rare form. **I.D. KEY:** Base form.

G6, $15-$30
Yavapai Co., AZ

Black obsidian →

G10, $35-$60
NW Chih, Mex

CRESCENT - Mid-Archaic, 5000 - 4500 B. P.

(Also see Cruciform, Disc, Drill and Lancet)

G8, $18-$30
San Luis Potosi, MX

G7, $18-$30
San Luis Potosi, MX

G8, $25-$40
San Luis Potosi, MX

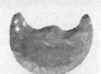

G6, $20-$35
San Luis Potosi, MX

G8, $25-$40
San Luis Potosi, MX

G7, $25-$40
San Luis Potosi, MX

G7, $25-$40
San Luis Potosi, MX

G8, $18-$30
San Luis Potosi, MX

LOCATION: Central Mexico. **DESCRIPTION:** A thin, uniface tool, convex on one side and concave on the opposite side with sharp corners. Long strikes were taken off with delicate pressure flaking. Chalcedony, agates, jaspers, cherts and flints were used. Different than the Crescents from the Northwest which are not uniface. **I.D. KEY:** Crescent form.

CRESCENT (continued)

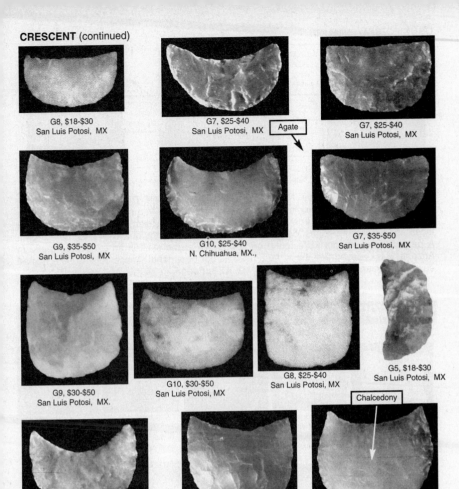

G8, $18-$30
San Luis Potosi, MX

G7, $25-$40
San Luis Potosi, MX

Agate

G7, $25-$40
San Luis Potosi, MX

G9, $35-$50
San Luis Potosi, MX

G10, $25-$40
N. Chihuahua, MX.,

G7, $35-$50
San Luis Potosi, MX

G9, $30-$50
San Luis Potosi, MX.

G10, $30-$50
San Luis Potosi, MX

G8, $25-$40
San Luis Potosi, MX

G5, $18-$30
San Luis Potosi, MX

Chalcedony

G8, $25-$40
San Luis Potosi, MX

G10, $35-$65
Chihuahua, MX

G10, $40-$75
Chihuahua, MX

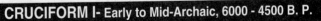

CRUCIFORM I- Early to Mid-Archaic, 6000 - 4500 B. P.

(Also see Disc, Drill, Exotic and Lancet)

SW

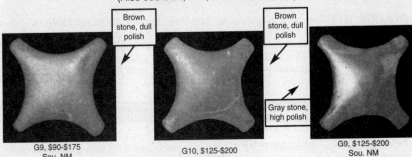

Brown stone, dull polish

Brown stone, dull polish

Gray stone, high polish

G9, $90-$175
Sou. NM

G10, $125-$200
Sou. NM

G9, $125-$200
Sou. NM

CRUCIFORM I (continued)

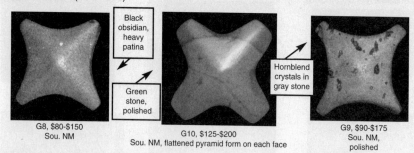

Black obsidian, heavy patina

Green stone, polished

Hornblend crystals in gray stone

G8, $80-$150
Sou. NM

G10, $125-$200
Sou. NM, flattened pyramid form on each face

G9, $90-$175
Sou. NM,
polished

LOCATION: W. Texas, Sou. New Mexico, and Sou. Arizona. **DESCRIPTION:** Occurs in two forms. Type one is a medium sized, four pronged object in a pyramidal form on opposing faces. It is hand tooled from hardstone or flaked from obsidian and then ground on both faces and around the edges. Careful attention was given to the quality of the finished form. A pair of these objects were found on both sides of the skull in an excavated grave in Arizona. It is believed that these were used as ear ornaments. These objects were named due to their resemblance to cruciforms. **I.D. KEY:** Form.

CRUCIFORM II- Late to Transitional, 3000 - 2000 B. P.

(Also see Disc, Drill, Exotic and Lancet)

G3, $40-$75
Lordsberg, NM

G6, $40-$75
Sou. NM,
clear obsidian,
ground, heavy patina

G6, $50-$90
Sou. NM,
clear obsidian,
ground, heavy patina

G6, $50-$90
Sou. NM,
black obsidian,
ground, heavy patina

G8, $55-$100
Sou. NM,
clear obsidian,
ground, heavy patina

 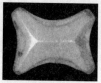 

G9, $55-$100
Sou. NM,
black obsidian, flaked and
not yet ground.

G9 $55-$100
Sou. NM,
black obsidian, ground,
heavy patina

G10, $55-$100
Sou. NM,
clear obsidian, ground,
heavy patina

G10, $55-$100
Sonora, MX, basalt,
ground.

LOCATION: W. Texas, Sou. New Mexico, and Sou. Arizona. **DESCRIPTION:** Occurs in two forms. Type two is a small sized, four pronged object in a slanted roof form on opposing faces. It is flaked from hard stone or black or clear obsidian and then ground on both faces and around the edges. Careful attention was given to the quality of the finished form. These objects' actual use is unknown and were named due to their resemblance to cruciforms. **I.D. KEY:** Form.

DAGGER- Mid-Archaic, 4000 - 2500 B. P.

(Also see Disc, Drill, Early Stemmed and Lancet)

LOCATION: Mexico. **DESCRIPTION:** A large size lanceolate knife with a recurved blade, expanding, tapered tangs and a long contracting stem. Probably hafted to a handle in use. **I.D. KEY:** Size and form.

DAGGER (continued)

Shown half size

G9, $300-$575
MX

DARL STEMMED - Early Archaic, 8000 - 5000 B. P.
(Also see Ahumata, Datil, San Pedro and Ventana Amargosa)

G6, $5-$10
Otero Co., NM

G6, $5-$10
Otero Co., NM

G7, $12-$20
Otero Co., NM

LOCATION: Central Texas into New Mexico and Northern Mexico. **DESCRIPTION:** A medium to large size, narrow point with horizontally barbed shoulders and an expanding to square stem. The blades on most examples are steeply beveled on one side of each face. Flaking is early parallel and is of much higher quality than *Darl*. **I.D. KEY:** Early flaking, straight base.

DATIL - Early Archaic, 7000 - 6000 B. P.
(Also see Cottonwood Leaf, Darl, Embudo, Lerma, Pelona, San Pedro and Truxton)

G5, $15-$30
Cochise Co., AZ

G6, $15-$30
Yavapai Co., AZ

Basalt

Yellow jasper

Basalt

SW

G7, $15-$30
Chihuahua, MX

G7, $25-$40
Yavapai Co., AZ

G8, $25-$40
NW Chihuahua, MX

G4, $5-$10
Yavapai Co., AZ

G6, $15-$30
Navajo Co., AZ

G7, $25-$40
Yavapai Co., AZ

DATIL (continued)

basalt

Banded purple chert

Orange chert

Serrated edge

G5, $15-$25
Pima Co., AZ

G4, $8-$15
Pima Co., AZ

G7, $80-$150
Pima Co., AZ

G5, $8-$15
Pima Co.,
AZ,.trans. point.

G10, $120-$200
Yavapai Co., AZ

LOCATION: The southern portion of the southwestern states. **DESCRIPTION:** A small dart/knife with long, narrow, heavily serrated blade edges. The stem is short and rectangular to rounded. Shoulders are straight to obtuse and are very small to non-existent in relation to the overall size of the point.

DEADMAN'S - Desert Traditions-Developmental Phase, 1600 - 1300 B. P.

(Also see Hodges Contracting Stem, Gila Butte, Perdiz and Rose Springs)

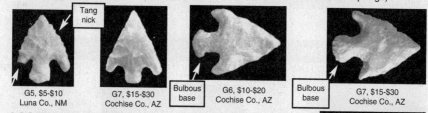

Tang nick

G5, $5-$10
Luna Co., NM

G7, $15-$30
Cochise Co., AZ

Bulbous base

G6, $10-$20
Cochise Co., AZ

Bulbous base

G7, $15-$30
Cochise Co., AZ

LOCATION: Southeastern Arizona, southern New Mexico and western Texas. **DESCRIPTION:** A small arrow point with very deep basal notches creating a long, straight to slightly bulbous stem with a rounded basal edge. The blade is triangular. **I.D. KEY:** Long stem and barbs.

G8, $25-$40
Cochise Co., AZ

DEL CARMEN - Classic Phase, 550 B. P.

(Also see Awatovi Side Notched, Buck Taylor Notched, Desert, Pueblo Side, Soto, Toyah)

G6, $8-$15   G7, $12-$20   G6, $8-$15   G7, $12-$20   G8, $15-$25   G9, $15-$25   G7, $12-$20   G9, $18-$30

All from N.W. Chihuahua, MX

LOCATION: N.W. Chihuahua, Mx. into sou. New Mexico. **DESCRIPTION:** A small, thin, arrow point with an elongated tip, side notches, expanding ears and a concave base. Some examples are double notched. **I.D. KEY:** Barbs always flare out beyond the base.

DEL CARMEN (continued)

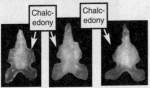

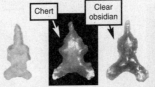

G7, $12-$20   G8, $15-$25   G8, $15-$25   G6, $8-$15   G7, $12-$20   G6, $12-$20   G9, $18-$30   G9, $20-$35

All from N.W. Chihuahua, MX   Otero Co., NM   All from N.W. Chihuahua, MX

DESERT DELTA - Desert Traditions-Classic to Historic, 700 - 200 B. P.

(Also see Pueblo Side Notched, Sacaton, Salado, Tempora, Walnut Canyon)

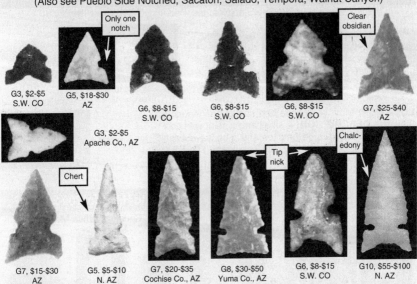

G3, $2-$5
S.W. CO

G5, $18-$30
AZ

G6, $8-$15
S.W. CO

G6, $8-$15
S.W. CO

G6, $8-$15
S.W. CO

G7, $25-$40
AZ

G3, $2-$5
Apache Co., AZ

G7, $15-$30
AZ

G5, $5-$10
N. AZ

G7, $20-$35
Cochise Co., AZ

G8, $30-$50
Yuma Co., AZ

G6, $8-$15
S.W. CO

G10, $55-$100
N. AZ

LOCATION: Most of Arizona and contiguous states to the west. **DESCRIPTION:** A small arrow point with straight blade edges, side notches and a concave, expanding basal edge. **I.D. KEY:** Expanding basal edge..

DESERT GENERAL-Desert Traditions-Classic to Historic,700-200 B. P.

(Also see Pueblo Side Notched, Sacaton and Salado)

SW

G3, $2-$5
Yavapai Co., AZ-
N. of Prescott.

G6, $6-$12
NW Chih,
Mex.

G6, $5-$12
NW Chih,
Mex.

G6, $6-$12
NW Chih,
Mex.

G6, $8-$15.
Yavapai Co., AZ.
N. of Prescott.

G7, $8-$15
NW Chih, Mex

G7, $8-$15
NW Chih, Mex.,

G6, $8-$15
AZ

LOCATION: Most of Arizona and contiguous states to the west. **DESCRIPTION:** A small arrow point with convex blade edges, side notches and a straight to slightly concave basal edge. **I.D. KEY:** Straight to concave base.

985

DESERT GENERAL (continued)

Tip nick ←

G6, $12-$20
S.W. CO

G8, $30-$50
S.W. CO

G6, $12-$20
AZ

G6, $15-$30
Yuma Co., AZ

G7, $18-$30
AZ

G8, $30-$50
Cochise Co., AZ

G9, $35-$60
S.W. CO

DESERT REDDING-Desert Traditions-Classic to Historic, 700-200 B. P.

(Also see Mimbre, Pueblo Side Notched, Sacaton, Salado and Temporal)

G4, $5-$10
NM

G6, $8-$15
NM

G6, $8-$15
AZ.

G5, $6-$10
Pima Co., AZ

G7, $12-$25
Pima Co., AZ

LOCATION: Most of Arizona and contiguous states to the west. **DESCRIPTION:** A small arrow point with convex sides, diagonal side notches and a concave basal edge which is narrower than the shoulders. **I.D. KEY:** Narrow basal edge.

G8, $18-$30
NW Chih, Mex.
chalc.

DESERT SIERRA - Desert Traditions-Classic to Historic, 700-200 B. P.

(Also see Awatovi, Buck Taylor, Notched, Del Carmen, Sacaton, White Mountain)

G4, $2-$5
S.W. CO

G4, $6-$10
NM

G6, $8-$15
S.W. CO

G6, $8-$15
S.W. CO

G6, $8-$15
AZ

G4, $6-$10
Pima Co., AZ

G5, $6-$10
AZ

G6, $12-$20
AZ

G6 $12-$20
AZ

G6, $12-$20
NM

G6, $12-$20
AZ

G6, $8-$15
AZ

G6, $12-$20
S. W. CO

G6, $12-$20
AZ

G6, $12-$20
AZ

G5, $6-$12
Cochise Co., AZ

G7, $15-$30
AZ

LOCATION: Most of Arizona and contiguous states to the west. **DESCRIPTION:** A small arrow point with straight sides, a straight basal edge and a basal notch. **I.D. KEY:** Triangular tri-notched point.

DISC - Mid-Archaic, 5000 - 4500 B.P.

(Also see Crescent, Cruciform and Exotic)

G7, $8-$15   G8, $12-$20   G9, $12-$20   G9, $12-$25   G9, $15-$30

All from San Luis Potosi, MX

LOCATION: Central Mexico. **DESCRIPTION:** A small circular object pressure flaked to an edge on each face. The purpose of these objects is unknown. These were in use about the same time as the *Crescents*. Examples show good patination. **I.D. KEY:** Circular form.

DOLORES - Developmental Phase, 1400 - 1100 B.P.

(Also see Amargosa, Basketmaker, Carlsbad, Cienega, Guadalupe)

LOCATION: Northern Arizona & New Mexico into southern Utah and Colorado. **DESCRIPTION:** A small, barbed arrow point with a medium to long, narrow expanding to parallel stem. Blade edges are concave to recurved. **I.D. KEY:** Barbs and narrow stem.

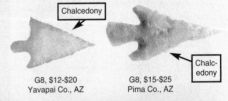

Chalcedony

Chalcedony

G8, $12-$20
Yavapai Co., AZ

G8, $15-$25
Pima Co., AZ

DRILL - Paleo to Historic, 14,000 - 850 B.P.

(Also see Circular Uniface Knife, Lancet and Scraper)

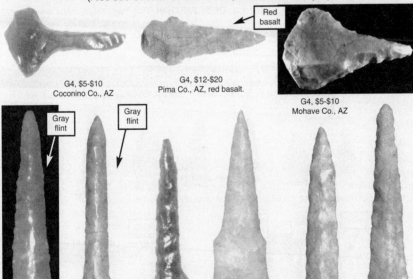

G4, $5-$10
Coconino Co., AZ

G4, $12-$20
Pima Co., AZ, red basalt.

Red basalt

G4, $5-$10
Mohave Co., AZ

Gray flint

Gray flint

G7, $15-$30
NW Chih, Mex.,
gray flint

G8, $18-$35
Otero Co., NM,
gray flint

G7, $15-$30
Coconino Co., AZ

G2, $8-$15
Otero Co., NM, San
Jose drill, ground
basal area. restored.

G8, $18-$35
Van Horn, TX

G8, $30-$50
Sou. NM

SW

987

DRILL (continued)

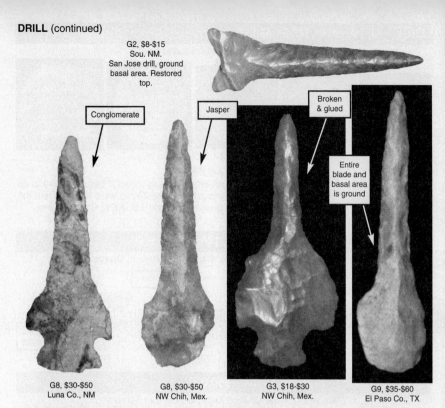

G2, $8-$15
Sou. NM.
San Jose drill, ground
basal area. Restored
top.

Conglomerate

Jasper

Broken
& glued

Entire
blade and
basal area
is ground

G8, $30-$50
Luna Co., NM

G8, $30-$50
NW Chih, Mex.

G3, $18-$30
NW Chih, Mex.

G9, $35-$60
El Paso Co., TX

LOCATION: Throughout North America. **DESCRIPTION:** Although many drills were made from scratch, all point types were made into the drill form. Usually, heavily resharpened and broken points were salvaged and rechipped into drills. **I.D. KEY:** Narrow blade form.

DRY PRONG - Desert Traditions, 1000 - 850 B.P.

(Also see Desert, Mimbre, Pueblo Side Notched, Sacaton and Temporal)

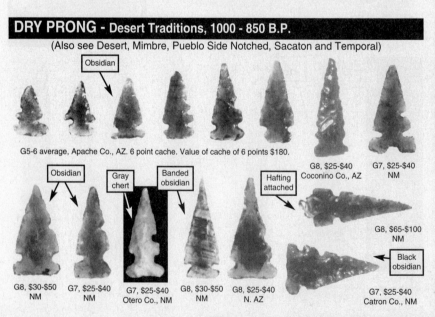

Obsidian

G5-6 average, Apache Co., AZ. 6 point cache. Value of cache of 6 points $180.

Obsidian

Gray
chert

Banded
obsidian

Hafting
attached

G8, $25-$40
Coconino Co., AZ

G7, $25-$40
NM

G8, $65-$100
NM

Black
obsidian

G8, $30-$50
NM

G7, $25-$40
NM

G7, $25-$40
Otero Co., NM

G8, $30-$50
NM

G8, $25-$40
N. AZ

G7, $25-$40
Catron Co., NM

DRY PRONG (continued)

Obsidian → | Basalt →

G8, $35-$50
NM

G7, $25-$40
NW Chihuahua,
Mex., thick

LOCATION: East central Arizona and west central New Mexico. **DESCRIPTION:** A small, narrow triangular arrow point with side notches and one or two additional side notches on one side of the blade. Some examples do not have the extra notch(es) and must be found in association with the extra notch variety to be typed as *Dry Prong* points. **I.D. KEY:** The extra side notch(es).

DUNCAN - Middle to Late Archaic, 4500 - 2850 B. P.

(Also see Bajada, Barreal, Chiricahua, Escobas and Hanna)

Chalcedony | Tip wear

G7, $15-$30
Apache Co., AZ

G8, $25-$40
Yavapai Co., AZ

G8, $25-$40
Pinal Co., AZ

G6, $10-$20
Cochise Co., AZ

G5, $6-$12
Apache Co., AZ

Black basalt

G7, $10-$20
Yavapai Co., AZ

Ground stem sides

G8, $25-$40
NW Chihuahua, Mex.,

Chalcedony

G8, $25-$40
Mohave Co., AZ

LOCATION: Northern Arizona to Canada on the north and to eastern Oklahoma on the east. **DESCRIPTION:** A small to medium sized dart/knife point with a triangular blade and angular shoulders. The stem is straight with a V-shaped notch in the basal edge. Stem edges are usually ground. **I.D. KEY:** Straight stem edges.

DURAN - Late Archaic to Transitional Phase, 3000 - 2000 B. P.

SW

(Also see Guadalupe, Maljamar, Neff and Truxton)

G7, $25-$40
Apache Co., AZ

G6, $20-$35
Apache Co., AZ

G6, $18-$30
Otero Co., NM

LOCATION: Texas into Mexico. **DESCRIPTION:** A small size, narrow, stemmed point with double to multiple notches on each side. Base can be parallel sided to tapered with rounded basal corners. **I.D. KEY:** Double notches, round base.

989

DURAN (continued)

Red jasper

Yellow jasper

Flint

Clear chalcedony

Yellow jasper

G2, $5-$10
NW Chihuahua, Mex., restored tip.

G7, $18-$30
NW Chih, Mex.

G8, $25-$45
NW Chih, Mex.

G6, $25-$40
San Luis Potosi, MX

G6,$25-$40
Otero Co., NM

G8, $30-$50
NW Chih, Mex.

G10, $40-$70
W. TX

G7, $30-$50
Otero Co., NM

G9, $65-$125
NM

G10, $65-$125
Chaves Co., NM

Basalt

G9, $35-$60
NW Chihuahua, Mex.

G10, $150-$250
Chaves Co., NM

EARLY LEAF - Early to Middle Archaic, 8000 - 5000 B. P.

(Also see Early Stemmed, Refugio, Round-back Knife)

IMPORTANT:
All Early Leafs
shown half
size

Black obsidian

G8,$125-$200
MX

LOCATION: Mexico. **DESCRIPTION:** A large size, thin, ovoid blade with a pointed base. Early parallel flaking is evident on many examples.

EARLY LEAF (continued)

> **IMPORTANT:**
> All Early Leafs
> shown half
> size

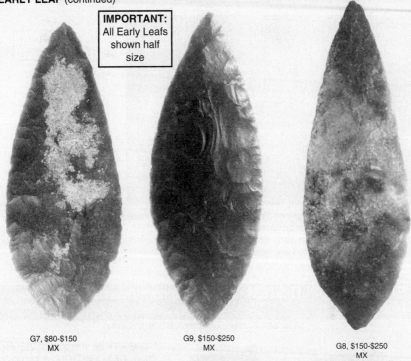

G7, $80-$150
MX

G9, $150-$250
MX

G8, $150-$250
MX

EARLY STEMMED - Late Archaic to Woodland, 3500 - 2300 B. P.

(Also see Augustin, Early Leaf, Escobas)

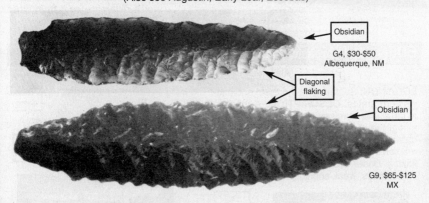

Obsidian

G4, $30-$50
Albequerque, NM

Diagonal
flaking

Obsidian

G9, $65-$125
MX

SW

LOCATION: Mexico. **DESCRIPTION:** A medium size point with sloping shoulders. Stems are straight to contracting to a straight to convex base. Shoulders are weak and sloping. Stem sides are sometimes ground. Flaking is oblique transverse and the cross section is elliptical. **I.D. KEY:** Base form and size.

EARLY TRIANGULAR - Early Archaic, 9000 - 7000 B. P.

(Also see Angostura, Clovis, Kinney, Mescal Knife, Tortugas & Triangular Knife)

EARLY TRIANGULAR (continued)

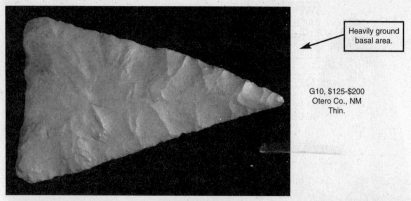

Heavily ground basal area.

G10, $125-$200
Otero Co., NM
Thin.

LOCATION: New Mexico into Texas. **DESCRIPTION:** A medium to large size, broad, thin, trianglular blade that can be serrated. The base is either fluted or has long thinning strikes. Quality is excellent with early oblique transverse and possible right hand beveling when resharpened. Basal areas are ground. **I.D. KEY:** Basal thinning and edgework.

EASTGATE SPLIT-STEM - Desert Traditions-Developmental Phase, 1400 - 1000 B. P.

(Also see Conejo, Duncan, Elko and Hanna)

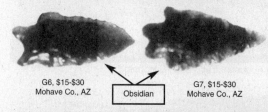

G6, $15-$30
Mohave Co., AZ

Obsidian

G7, $15-$30
Mohave Co., AZ

LOCATION: Arizona to Washington. **DESCRIPTION:** A corner to base notched arrow point with a triangular blade and a straight to slightly expanding stem with a basal notch. **I.D. KEY:** The basal notch differentiates it from other *Eastgate* points.

EDEN - Early Archaic, 9500 - 7500 B. P.

(Also see Firstview and Scottsbluff)

LOCATION: Southwest to northern and midwestern states. **DESCRIPTION:** A medium to large size, narrow, lanceolate blade with a straight to concave base and almost unnoticable shoulders. Many examples have a median ridge and collateral oblique parallel flaking. Bases are usually ground. **I.D. KEY:** Narrowness, weak shoulders.

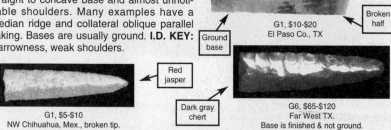

Petrified wood

Broken half

G1, $10-$20
El Paso Co., TX

Ground base

Red jasper

Dark gray chert

G1, $5-$10
NW Chihuahua, Mex., broken tip.

G6, $65-$120
Far West TX.
Base is finished & not ground.

ELKO CORNER NOTCHED - Mid-Archaic to Developmental Phase, 3500 - 1200 B.P.

(Also see Amargosa, Cienega, Eastgate, Mount Albion, San Pedro)

ELKO CORNER NOTCHED (continued)

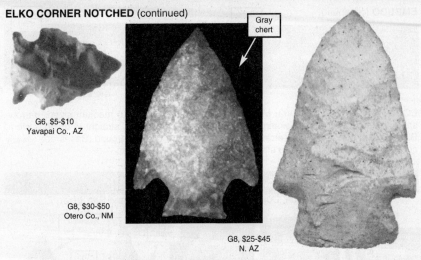

G6, $5-$10
Yavapai Co., AZ

G8, $30-$50
Otero Co., NM

Gray chert

G8, $25-$45
N. AZ

LOCATION: Great Basin into Arizona. **DESCRIPTION:** A small to large size, thin, corner notched dart point with shoulder tangs and a convex, concave or auriculate base. Shoulders and tips are sharp. Some examples exhibit excellent parallel flaking on blade edges. **I.D. KEY:** Corner notches, sharp tangs.

ELKO EARED - Mid-Archaic to Developmental Phase, 3500 - 1200 B.P.

(Also see Eastgate, Hanna and San Jose)

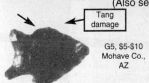

Tang damage

G5, $5-$10
Mohave Co., AZ

LOCATION: Great Basin into Arizona. **DESCRIPTION:** A small to large size, thin, corner notched dart point with shoulder tangs and an eared base. Basal ears are usually exaggerated and corners and tips are sharp. Some examples exhibit excellent parallel flaking on blade edges. **I.D. KEY:** Expanding to drooping ears.

EMBUDO - Early Archaic, 7000 - 6000 B. P.

(Also see Cohonina Stemmed, Datil and Pelona)

Obsidian

Black basalt

Obsidian

Obsidian

Black obsidian

G5, $5-$10   G6, $8-$15   G6, $8-$15   G6, $8-$15   G6, $8-$15   G8, $12-$20   G6, $8-$15

Dark gray basalt

Gray basalt

G7, $18-$30

G8, $25-$40

All from NW Chihuahua, Mexico

EMBUDO (continued)

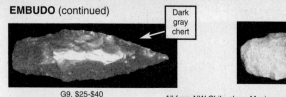

Dark gray chert

G9, $25-$40

All from NW Chihuahua, Mexico

White chert

G10, $30-$50

LOCATION: N.W. Chihuahua, Mex. **DESCRIPTION:** A small to medium sized, narrow, spike dart point with weak, sloping shoulders and a contracting, straight to bulbous stem. Blade edges can have fine serrations. Stem sides are usually ground. Bases are usually convex but can be incurvate to straight. **I.D. KEY:** Spike-like form.

ESCOBAS - Mid-Archaic, 6500 - 5000 B. P.

(Also see Bajada, Duncan, Hanna, Jay, Rio Grande and San Jose)

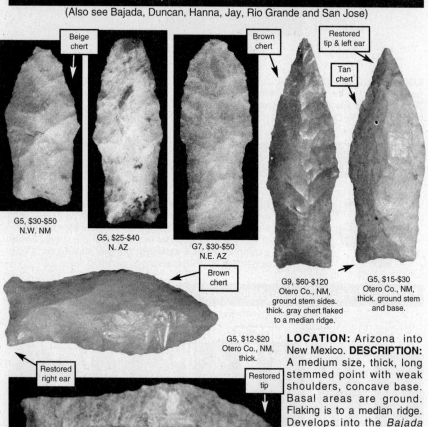

Beige chert

G5, $30-$50
N.W. NM

G5, $25-$40
N. AZ

G7, $30-$50
N.E. AZ

Brown chert

Restored tip & left ear

Tan chert

G9, $60-$120
Otero Co., NM,
ground stem sides.
thick. gray chert flaked
to a median ridge.

G5, $15-$30
Otero Co., NM,
thick. ground stem
and base.

Brown chert

G5, $12-$20
Otero Co., NM,
thick.

Restored right ear

Restored tip

G3, $15-$30
Otero Co., NM, ground stem sides. thick. flaked to a median ridge.

LOCATION: Arizona into New Mexico. **DESCRIPTION:** A medium size, thick, long stemmed point with weak shoulders, concave base. Basal areas are ground. Flaking is to a median ridge. Develops into the *Bajada* point. Related to the earlier *Rio Grande* type. **I.D. KEY:** Long straight stem; concave base

---

EXOTIC - Late Archaic to Developmental Phase, 3000 - 1000 B. P.

(Also see Crescent, Cruciform and Disc)

EXOTIC (continued)

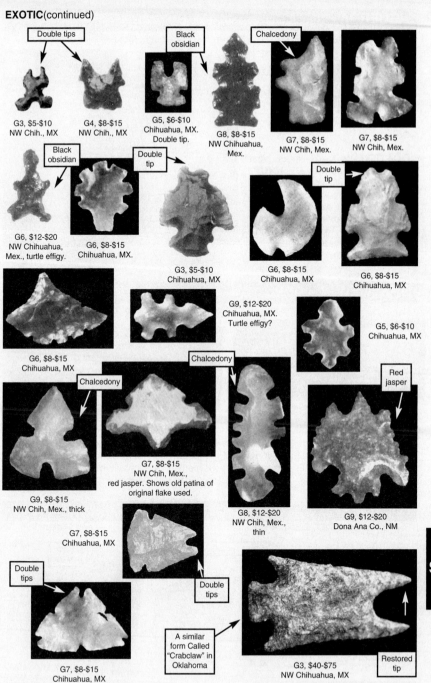

Double tips

G3, $5-$10
NW Chih., MX

G4, $8-$15
NW Chih., MX

Black obsidian

G5, $6-$10
Chihuahua, MX.
Double tip.

G8, $8-$15
NW Chihuahua,
Mex.

Chalcedony

G7, $8-$15
NW Chih, Mex.

G7, $8-$15
NW Chih, Mex.

Black obsidian

Double tip

G6, $12-$20
NW Chihuahua,
Mex., turtle effigy.

G6, $8-$15
Chihuahua, MX.

G3, $5-$10
Chihuahua, MX

Double tip

G6, $8-$15
Chihuahua, MX

G6, $8-$15
Chihuahua, MX

G6, $8-$15
Chihuahua, MX

G9, $12-$20
Chihuahua, MX.
Turtle effigy?

G5, $6-$10
Chihuahua, MX

Chalcedony

Chalcedony

Red jasper

G9, $8-$15
NW Chih, Mex., thick

G7, $8-$15
NW Chih, Mex.,
red jasper. Shows old patina of
original flake used.

G8, $12-$20
NW Chih, Mex.,
thin

G9, $12-$20
Dona Ana Co., NM

G7, $8-$15
Chihuahua, MX

Double tips

Double tips

A similar form Called "Crabclaw" in Oklahoma

Restored tip

G7, $8-$15
Chihuahua, MX

G3, $40-$75
NW Chihuahua, MX

SW

LOCATION: Everywhere. **DESCRIPTION:** Some of the forms illustrated are definitely effigy, some are double tipped points, while others may be no more than unfinished and unintentional doodles.

FIGUEROA - Transitional Phase, 2200 B. P.

(Also see Amargosa, Black Mesa Narrow Neck, Cienega, Mount Albion, San Pedro)

Black basalt

G8, $8-$15
Sou. NM

Gray chert

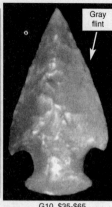

Gray flint

LOCATION: Western Texas, New Mexico and Arizona. **DESCRIPTION:** A dart/knife point with medium-wide side notches, an expanding stem and a convex basal edge. Similar to the *Motley* point found in Louisiana. **I.D. KEY:** Wide side notches, convex base.

G8, $25-$40
Otero Co., NM

G10, $35-$65
Otero Co., NM

FIRSTVIEW - Late Paleo, 8700 - 8050 B. P.

(Also see Eden, Escobas and Scottsbluff)

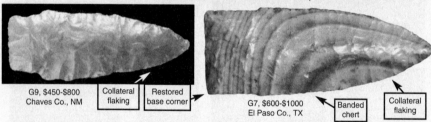

G9, $450-$800
Chaves Co., NM

Collateral flaking

Restored base corner

G7, $600-$1000
El Paso Co., TX

Banded chert

Collateral flaking

LOCATION: Extreme W. Texas into New Mexico and Sou. Colorado. **DESCRIPTION:** A lanceolate point with slightly convex edges, slight shoulders and a rectangular stem. Shoulders are sometimes absent from resharpening. It generally exhibits parallel-transverse flaking. **I.D. KEY:** A diamond shaped cross-section.

FOLSOM - Paleo, 11,000 - 10,000 B. P.

(Also see Allen, Belen, Angostura, Clovis, Goshen, Green River and Midland)

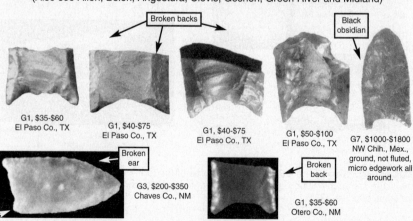

Broken backs

Black obsidian

G1, $35-$60
El Paso Co., TX

G1, $40-$75
El Paso Co., TX

G1, $40-$75
El Paso Co., TX

G1, $50-$100
El Paso Co., TX

G7, $1000-$1800
NW Chih., Mex.,
ground, not fluted,
micro edgework all
around.

Broken ear

G3, $200-$350
Chaves Co., NM

Broken back

G1, $35-$60
Otero Co., NM

FOLSOM (continued)

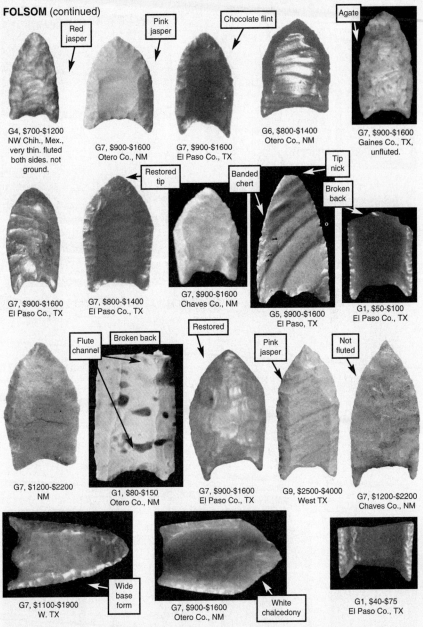

Red jasper

G4, $700-$1200
NW Chih., Mex.,
very thin. fluted
both sides. not
ground.

Pink jasper

G7, $900-$1600
Otero Co., NM

G7, $900-$1600
El Paso Co., TX

Chocolate flint

G6, $800-$1400
Otero Co., NM

Agate

G7, $900-$1600
Gaines Co., TX,
unfluted.

Restored tip

G7, $900-$1600
El Paso Co., TX

G7, $800-$1400
El Paso Co., TX

Banded chert

G7, $900-$1600
Chaves Co., NM

Tip nick

Broken back

G5, $900-$1600
El Paso, TX

G1, $50-$100
El Paso Co., TX

Flute channel

Broken back

G7, $1200-$2200
NM

G1, $80-$150
Otero Co., NM

Restored

G7, $900-$1600
El Paso Co., TX

Pink jasper

G9, $2500-$4000
West TX

Not fluted

G7, $1200-$2200
Chaves Co., NM

Wide base form

G7, $1100-$1900
W. TX

G7, $900-$1600
Otero Co., NM

White chalcedony

G1, $40-$75
El Paso Co., TX

SW

LOCATION: The southwestern states and as far north as Canada and east to northern Indiana. Type site is a bison kill site near Folsom, NM, where 24 fluted *Folsom* points were excavated in 1926-1928. Being the first fluted point named, for years all fluted points were called *Folsom*. **DESCRIPTION:** A very thin, small to medium sized, lanceolate point with convex to parallel edges and a concave basal edge creating sharp ears or basal corners. Most examples are fluted from the basal edge to nearly the tip of the point. They do rarely occur unfluted. Workmanship is very fine and outstanding. Most examples found have worn out tips or were rebased from longer points that broke at the haft. **I.D. KEY:** Micro secondary flaking, pointed auricles.

997

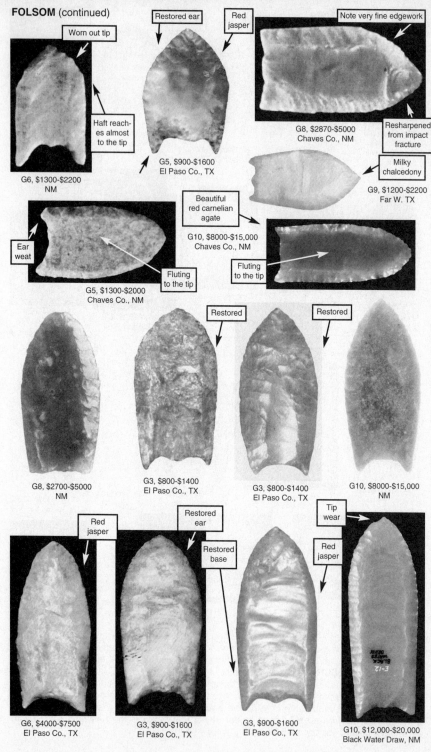

FOLSOM (continued)

Worn out tip

Restored ear

Red jasper

Note very fine edgework

Haft reaches almost to the tip

G6, $1300-$2200
NM

G5, $900-$1600
El Paso Co., TX

G8, $2870-$5000
Chaves Co., NM

Resharpened from impact fracture

Milky chalcedony

G9, $1200-$2200
Far W. TX

Beautiful red carnelian agate

G10, $8000-$15,000
Chaves Co., NM

Ear weat

Fluting to the tip

Fluting to the tip

G5, $1300-$2000
Chaves Co., NM

Restored

Restored

G8, $2700-$5000
NM

G3, $800-$1400
El Paso Co., TX

G3, $800-$1400
El Paso Co., TX

G10, $8000-$15,000
NM

Red jasper

Restored ear

Restored base

Tip wear

Red jasper

G6, $4000-$7500
El Paso Co., TX

G3, $900-$1600
El Paso Co., TX

G3, $900-$1600
El Paso Co., TX

G10, $12,000-$20,000
Black Water Draw, NM

998

FRIO - Early to Middle Archaic, 5000 - 1500 B. P.

(Also see Caracara, Uvalde, Squaw Mountain, Ventana Side Notched)

Clear obsidian

Gray flint

Clear Moss agate

Clear obsidian

G6, $12-$20
NW Chih, Mex.

G8, $18-$30
NW Chih, Mex,
needle tip and tangs,
very thin

G7, $12-$20
NW Chih, Mex,
very thin

G5, $12-$20
NW Chih, Mex.

G8, $18-$30
NW Chih, Mex.,

Black obsidian

Chalcedony

Yellow jasper

White chert

G10, $35-$60
NW Chih, Mex, very thin

G6, $18-$30
NW Chih, Mex, very thin

G7, $18-$30
NW Chih, Mex,
thin

G7, $18-$30
NW Chih, Mex.,

White chert

Red basalt

Agate; pink base, beige tip

G8, $18-$30
NW Chih, Mex.,

G8, $25-$40
NW Chih, Mex.,

Red jasper

G6, $25-$40
NW Chihuahua,
Mex.

G10, $65-$125
NW Chih, Mex,
very thin, ground base

G10, $80-$150
NW Chih, Mex,
pink base, beige tip,
agate, very thin

SW

LOCATION: N.W. Chihuhhua, Mexico into Texas and Oklahoma. **DESCRIPTION:** A small to medium size, side to corner-notched point with a concave to notched base that has squared to rounded ears that flare. Some examples are similar to *Big Sandy Auriculate* forms from Tennessee. **I.D. KEY:** Flaring ears.

FRIO-TRANSITIONAL - Late Archaic to Trans., 3000 - 2000 B. P.

(Also see Barreal, Chiricahua)

FRIO-TRANSITIONAL (continued)

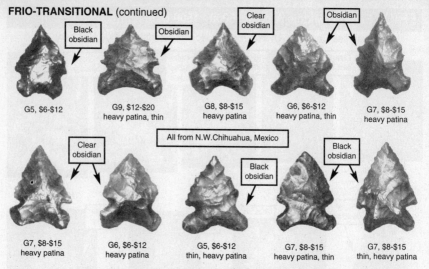

G5, $6-$12

G9, $12-$20
heavy patina, thin

G8, $8-$15
heavy patina

G6, $6-$12
heavy patina, thin

G7, $8-$15
heavy patina

All from N.W.Chihuahua, Mexico

G7, $8-$15
heavy patina

G6, $6-$12
heavy patina

G5, $6-$12
thin, heavy patina

G7, $8-$15
heavy patina, thin

G7, $8-$15
thin, heavy patina

LOCATION: N.W. Chihuahua, Mexico. **DESCRIPTION:** A small size dart point with side notches and an eared base. Serrations and basal grinding occur. Ears are usually rounded. Shoulders are tapered to horizontal and can be sharp. Very similar to the *Chiricahua* point found in Arizona but not as old. **I.D. KEY:** Short stubby point with flaring ears.

GARZA - Desert Traditions-Classic Phase, 500 - 300 B.P.

(Also see Buck Taylor Notched, Snaketown Triangular, Soto and Toyah)

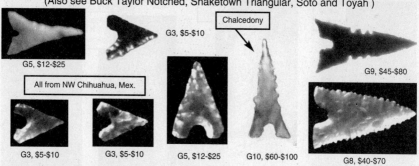

G5, $12-$25

G3, $5-$10

Chalcedony

G9, $45-$80

All from NW Chihuahua, Mex.

G3, $5-$10

G3, $5-$10

G5, $12-$25

G10, $60-$100

G8, $40-$70

LOCATION: NW Chihuahua, Mexico. **DESCRIPTION:** A small, thin, triangular arrow point. Blade edges vary from convex to concave and can be serrated. The basal edge is deeply concave and notched, creating long, thin ears.

GATLIN SIDE NOTCHED Devel. to Classic Phase, 800 - 600 B. P.

(Also see Pueblo Side Notched, Snaketown Triangular)

Tip nick

G5, $35-$65
AZ

Serrated edge

G9, $175-$300
Mohave Co., AZ

GATLIN SIDE NOTCHED (continued)

LOCATION: Sou. California into Arizona. **DESCRIPTION:** A medium size, thin, triangular *Hohokam* arrow point with broad side notches, a long needle tip and a wide base that can be deeply concave. Some examples are serrated. Basal corners are sharp to rounded. **I.D. KEY:** Long needle tip.

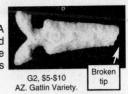

G2, $5-$10
AZ. Gatlin Variety.

Broken tip

GILA BUTTE   (see Hodges Contracting Stem)

GILA RIVER CORNER NOTCHED- Devel. Phase, 1350-1000 B. P.

(Also see Snaketown)

G9, $125-$200
AZ

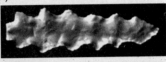

G10, $135-$250
Phoenix, AZ

LOCATION: Arizona. **DESCRIPTION:** A very rare, ceremonial form of *Hohokam* arrow point. The stem is straight to expanded and sometimes concave to bifurcated and has large serrations on both sides of the blade. Some examples are serrated on the lower half of the point. **I.D. KEY:** Narrowness, length, broad serrations.

GLASS- Historic, 400 - 100 B. P.

(Also see Bull Creek, Cottonwood, Sobaipuri and Trade)

Green glass

Green glass

Amber glass

G3, $5-$10
Pima Indian,
Maricopa Co., AZ

G3, $8-$15
Pima Indian,
Maricopa Co., AZ

G6, $20-$25
Pima IIndian,
Maricopa Co., AZ

G6, $20-$25
Pima Indian,
Maricopa Co., AZ

G8, $20-$35
Pima Indian, Maricopa Co., AZ

LOCATION: Historic sites everywhere. **DESCRIPTION:** A small, thin arrow point that can be triangular or side notched fashioned from bottle and telephone insulator glass. Such tribes as Pima, Papago and others utilized glass for this purpose. **I.D. KEY:** Made from glass.

GOBERNADORA - Late Archaic, 3000 B. P.

(Also see Acatita, Augustin, Gypsum Cave and Socorro)

G9, $80-$150
N.W. MX.

G10, $80-$150
N.W. MX.

LOCATION: S.E. Arizona into southern New Mexico and N.E. Mexico. **DESCRIPTION:** A medium sized, thin, dart/knife with inward-sloping tangs and a long contracting turkeytail stem. **I.D. KEY:** Stem form.

GOBERNADORA (continued)

G10, $80-$150
N.W. MX

GOLONDRINA - Transitional Paleo, 9000 - 7000 B. P.

(Also see Angostura, Cortero, Meserve, Midland, Plainview & San Jose)

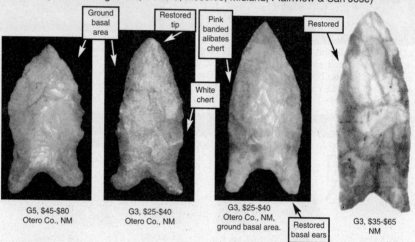

Ground basal area

Restored tip

Pink banded alibates chert

White chert

Restored

G5, $45-$80
Otero Co., NM

G3, $25-$40
Otero Co., NM

G3, $25-$40
Otero Co., NM,
ground basal area.

Restored basal ears

G3, $35-$65
NM

LOCATION: New Mexico, Texas, Arkansas to Oklahoma. **DESCRIPTION:** A medium to large size auriculate unfluted point with rounded ears that flare and a deeply concave base. Basal areas are ground. Believed to be related to Dalton. **I.D. KEY:** Expanded ears, paleo flaking.

GOSHEN - Paleo, 11,500 - 10,000 B. P.

(Also see Clovis, Folsom, Green River, Meserve, Midland, Milnesand)

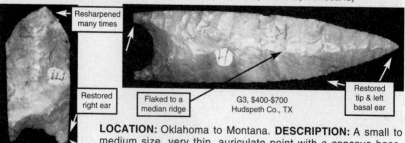

Resharpened many times

Restored right ear

Flaked to a median ridge

G3, $400-$700
Hudspeth Co., TX

Restored tip & left basal ear

G4, $125-$200
El Paso Co., NM

LOCATION: Oklahoma to Montana. **DESCRIPTION:** A small to medium size, very thin, auriculate point with a concave base. Basal corners slope inward and are rounded. Flaking is oblique to horizontal transverse. A rare type. **I.D. KEY:** Thinness, auricles.

GRAVER - Paleo to Archaic, 14,000 - 4000 B. P.

(Also see Drill, Perforator and Scraper)

GRAVER (continued)

Graver tip

G6, $2-$5
Coconino Co., AZ

G6, $4-$8
Coconino Co., AZ

LOCATION: Paleo and Archaic sites everywhere. **DESCRIPTION:** An irregular shaped uniface took with one or more sharp, pointed projections used for puncturing, incising, tattooing, etc. Some examples served a dual purpose for scraping as well. **I.D. KEY:** Stem form.

GREEN RIVER - Mid-Archaic, 4500 - 4200 B. P.

(Also see Allen, Bat Cave, Folsom, Goshen, Humboldt and Midland)

G6, $25-$40
Mohave Co., AZ

G6, $30-$50
Mohave Co., AZ

G4, $8-$15
Mohave Co.,
AZ

G6, $25-$40
Mohave Co.,
AZ

LOCATION: Central Arizona to Wyoming, Colorado, Montana, New Mexico and Nebraska. **DESCRIPTION:** A small size auriculate point with a concave base. Auricles turn inward and are rounded. Similar to *McKean* found further north. **I.D. KEY:** Stem form.

GUADALUPE - Transitional-Developmental., 1900 - 1200 B. P.

(Also see Ahumada, Carlsbad, Cienega, Dolores and Neff)

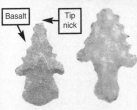

Basalt

Tip nick

G8, $20-$40
Pinal Co., AZ

G4, $8-$15
Pima Co., AZ

G3, $15-$25
Pima Co., AZ

Tang nick

LOCATION: Arizona, New Mexico into N. Mexico. **DESCRIPTION:** A medium size, barbed, corner notched dart/arrow point with an expanding stem. Blades are serrated and bases are straight to convex. Believed to be part of the Livermore cluster. **I.D. KEY:** Wild serrations, expanded stem with corner notches.

G8, $18-$30
Saguache Co., CO

SW

GYPSUM CAVE - Middle Archaic, 5000 - 3300 B. P.

(Also see Augustin, Manzano, Parowan and Santa Cruz)

LOCATION: Northwestern Arizona and into contiguous states to the west and north. Type site is Gypsum Cave, NV. **DESCRIPTION:** A medium sized dart/knife with straight blade edges and a short stem which contracts to a rounded point. The shoulders are obtuse. This point may be a northerly and westwardly extension of the *Augustin* point, though, in general, it seems to have better workmanship. **I.D. KEY:** Stubby stem.

GYPSUM CAVE (continued)

G6, $8-$15
Yavapai Co., AZ

G5, $5-$10
Yavapai Co., AZ

Basalt

G7, $30-$50
Mohave Co., AZ

G7, $20-$35
Pima Co., AZ

G8, $25-$40
Mohave Co., AZ

G6, $18-$30
S.W. TX

G7, $25-$40
Cohonino Co., AZ

Black obsidian

Basalt

G6, $12-$20
Otero Co., NM

G5, $5-$10
Pima Co., AZ

G9, $30-$50
Mexico

G9, $60-$100, Mohave Co., AZ

G8, $45-$80, Mohave Co., AZ

1004

GYPSUM CAVE (continued)

G6, $15-$30
Virgin River, NV

G7, $25-$40
Otero Co., NM

HANNA - Middle to Late Archaic, 4500 - 2850 B. P.
(Also see Barreal, Chiricahua, Duncan and Squaw Mountain)

Basalt

Basalt

Basalt

G4, $8-$15
Yavapai Co., AZ

G4, $8-$15
Yavapai Co., AZ

G4, $8-$15
Yavapai Co., AZ

G5, $15-$30
Yavapai Co., AZ

G4, $8-$15
Yavapai Co., AZ

Basalt

Basalt

Tip nick

G6, $12-$20
S.W. CO

G6, $12-$20
S.W. CO

G6, $18-$30
Mineral Co., CO

G7, $30-$50
Yavapai Co., AZ

G6, $30-$50
Mineral Co., CO

Orange mottled agate

G7, $30-$50
Otero Co., NM

G10, $150-$250
NW Chihuahua, Mex., not ground.

SW

LOCATION: Southwestern states and north as far as Canada and east as far as Nebraska. **DESCRIPTION:** A small dart/knife with obtuse shoulders and an expanding stem which is notched to produce diagonally projecting ears. **I.D. KEY:** Expanding stem.

1005

HANNA (continued)

G6, $30-$50
Santa Fe N.M

Side and tip wear

Black basalt

HARRELL (see Awatovi)

HELL GAP - Late Paleo, 10,900 - 9500 B. P.

(Also see Agate Basin, Angostura, Escobas, Jay, Lake Mohave, Rio Grande)

LOCATION: Colorado northward to the Dakotas and Canada and eastward to Texas. **DESCRIPTION:** A medium size lanceolate point with a long, contracting basal stem and a short, stubby tip. Bases are generally straight and are ground. High quality flaking. **I.D. KEY:** Long stem.

Basalt

G7, $125-$200
S.W., CO

HOHOKAM (see Awatovi Side Notched, Buck Taylor Notched, Citrus Side Notched, Gatlin Side Notched, Gila River Corner Notched, Hodges Contracted Stem, Pueblo Side Notched, Salt River Indented Base, Snaketown Triangular, Sobaipuri, Walnut Canyon Side Notched)

HODGES CONTRACTING STEM - Develop. Phase,1500 - 1300 B. P.

(Also see Gila River, Santa Cruz and Snaketown)

G8, $18-$30
Mohave Co.,
AZ

G6, $5-$10
Mohave Co., AZ

G4, $5-$10
Mohave Co., AZ

G4, $8-$15
Yavapai Co., AZ

G4, $8-$15
Hildago Co., NM

G6, $12-$20
Navajo Co., AZ

White chert

Red basalt

Basalt

White chert

G4, $8-$15
Hildago Co., NM

G7, $12-$20
Tucson, AZ

G7, $25-$40
Mohave Co., AZ

G6, $8-$15
AZ

G8, $15-$25
Pima Co., AZ

G9, $25-$45
Pima Co., AZ

G3, $6-$10
Mohave Co., AZ

LOCATION: Arizona ranging into adjacent parts of contiguous states. **DESCRIPTION:** A small *Hohokam* arrow point with basal notching which creates barbs ranging from shallow to deep. The stem may be pointed or truncated. part of the *Snaketown* cluster. **I.D. KEY:** Basal notches.

HOHOKAM KNIFE - Desert Trad.-Develop. Phase, 1200 - 1000 B. P.

(Also see Abasolo, Archaic Knife)

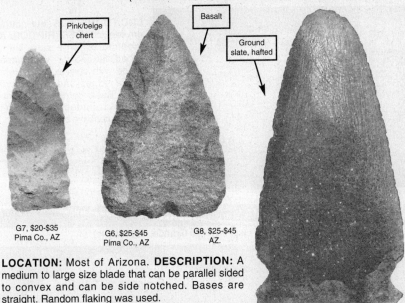

Pink/beige chert

Basalt

Ground slate, hafted

G7, $20-$35
Pima Co., AZ

G6, $25-$45
Pima Co., AZ

G8, $25-$45
AZ.

LOCATION: Most of Arizona. **DESCRIPTION:** A medium to large size blade that can be parallel sided to convex and can be side notched. Bases are straight. Random flaking was used.

HUMBOLDT - Transitional Phase, 2000 - 1500 B. P.

(Also see Allen, Angostura)

Obsidian

G6, $15-$30
Mohave Co., AZ

G7, $40-$70
NM

LOCATION: Great Basin states, esp. Nevada. **DESCRIPTION:** A small to medium size, narrow, lanceolate point with a constricted, concave base. Basal concavity can be slight to extreme. **I.D. KEY:** Base form.

JAY- Early Archaic, 8000 - 6800 B. P.

(Also see Bajada, Hell Gap, Lake Mohave, Rio Grande, Silver Lake)

Basalt

G9, $125-$200
Otero Co., NM, ground stem
sides & base.

LOCATION: Southern Arizona. **DESCRIPTION:** A medium to large size, narrow, long stemmed point with tapered shoulders. The base is convex. Stem sides and base are ground. Similar to the Hell Gap point found further east. **I.D. KEY:** Broad, concave base.

SW

KINNEY - Middle Archaic-Woodland, 5000 - 2000 B. P.

(Also see Early Triangular, Matamoros, Mescal Knife and Tortugas)

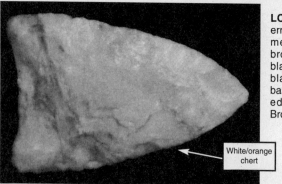

LOCATION: Texas into northern Mexico. **DESCRIPTION:** A medium to large size, thin, broad, lanceolate, well made blade with convex to straight blade edges and a concave base. Basal corners are pointed to rounded. **I.D. KEY:** Broad, concave base.

White/orange chert

G8, $80-$150
NW Chihuahua, Mex., thin

LAKE MOHAVE - Paleo, 13,200 - 10,000 B.P.

(Also see Hell Gap, Jay, Rio Grande, Silver Lake)

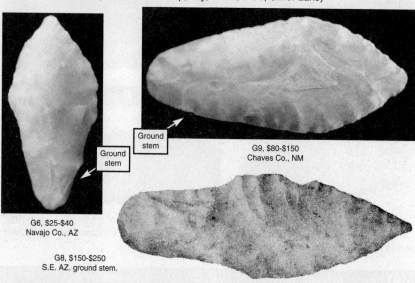

Ground stem

Ground stem

G9, $80-$150
Chaves Co., NM

G6, $25-$40
Navajo Co., AZ

G8, $150-$250
S.E. AZ. ground stem.

LOCATION: Southern California into Arizona and the Great Basin. **DESCRIPTION:** A medium sized, narrow, parallel to contracting stemmed point with weak, tapered to no shoulders. Stem is much longer than the blade. Some experts think these points are worn out *Parman* points. **I.D. KEY:** Long stem, very short blade.

LANCET- All Periods from Paleo to Historic

LOCATION: Over the entire U.S. **DESCRIPTION:** This artifact is also known as a lammeler flake blade and was produced by knocking a flake or spall off a parent stone. Most of the western examples are of obsidian. Perhaps the best known of the type were those made and used by the Hopewell people in the midwest. **I.D. KEY:** Double uniface and the presence, generally, of the parent stone showing on one face.

LANCET (continued)

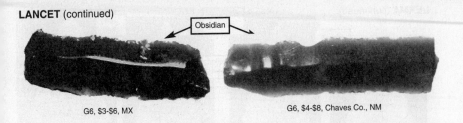

Obsidian

G6, $3-$6, MX

G6, $4-$8, Chaves Co., NM

LERMA - Middle to Late Archaic, 4000 - 1000 B. P.
(Also see Abasolo, Agate Basin, Angostura, Catan, Datil and Pelona)

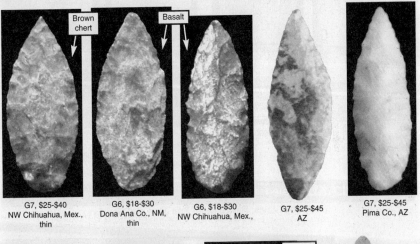

Brown chert

Basalt

G7, $25-$40
NW Chihuahua, Mex.,
thin

G6, $18-$30
Dona Ana Co., NM,
thin

G6, $18-$30
NW Chihuahua, Mex.,

G7, $25-$45
AZ

G7, $25-$45
Pima Co., AZ

Brown chert

Gray flint

Brown basalt

G6, $30-$50
NW Chihuahua, Mex.,
ground stem

G8, $35-$60
Otero Co., NM

G7, $35-$60
Otero Co., NM,
ground base

G8, $60-$100
Otero Co., NM

SW

LOCATION: From central Texas westward through New Mexico, N.W. Chihuahua, Mexico and into eastern Arizona. Examples of *Lerma* points from further east are, most likely, Guilford points. **DESCRIPTION:** A long ovoid with a rounded to somewhat pointed basal edge.

LERMA (continued)

Basalt

Restored tip

Mottled chert

Tan chert

G9, $45-$80
NW Chihuahua, Mex.,
heavy grinding in basal area

G9, $90-$165
Hidalgo Co., NM

G3, 12-$20
NW Chihuahua, Mex., thin.

G9, $60-$100
Otero Co., NM,
ground basal area, thin.

MADDEN LAKE - Paleo, 10,700 B. P.

(Also see Clovis, Rio Grande, San Jose and Sandia)

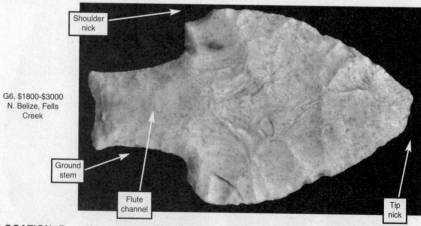

Shoulder nick

G6, $1800-$3000
N. Belize, Fells
Creek

Ground stem

Flute channel

Tip nick

LOCATION: Panama to southern South America. **DESCRIPTION:** A medium to large size, fluted stemmed point with horizontal to tapered shoulders. Bases are fishtailed and ground. **I.D. KEY:** Fishtail stem.

MALJAMAR - Late Archaic, 3500 - 2300 B. P.

(Also see Ahumada, Duran, Mount Albion, Neff, San Jose and Truxton)

MALJAMAR (continued)

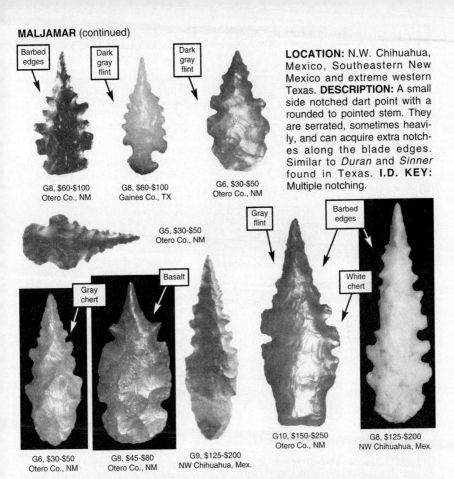

LOCATION: N.W. Chihuahua, Mexico, Southeastern New Mexico and extreme western Texas. **DESCRIPTION:** A small side notched dart point with a rounded to pointed stem. They are serrated, sometimes heavily, and can acquire extra notches along the blade edges. Similar to *Duran* and *Sinner* found in Texas. **I.D. KEY:** Multiple notching.

G8, $60-$100
Otero Co., NM

G8, $60-$100
Gaines Co., TX

G6, $30-$50
Otero Co., NM

G5, $30-$50
Otero Co., NM

G6, $30-$50
Otero Co., NM

G8, $45-$80
Otero Co., NM

G9, $125-$200
NW Chihuahua, Mex.

G10, $150-$250
Otero Co., NM

G8, $125-$200
NW Chihuahua, Mex.

MANZANO - Mid to Late Archaic, 5000 - 3000 B. P.

(Also see Augustin, Gypsum Cave and Santa Cruz)

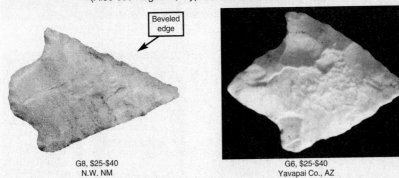

G8, $25-$40
N.W. NM

G6, $25-$40
Yavapai Co., AZ

SW

LOCATION: N.W. New Mexico into Arizona. **DESCRIPTION:** A medium size, broad, triangular point with a short, contracting, rounded stem. Shoulders are prominent and slightly barbed. Opposite edges are beveled. Related to the *Gypsum Cave* type. **I.D. KEY:** Blade beveling, short stem.

MARSHALL - Mid-Archaic to Woodland, 6000 - 2000 B. P.

(Also see Cienega, Elko Corner Notched, Figueroa, Mount Albion)

LOCATION: Western New Mexixo into Texas. **DESCRIPTION:** A medium to large size, broad, high quality, corner to basal notched point with long barbs that turn inward towards the base. Notching is less angled than in *Marcos*. Bases are straight to concave to bifurcated. **I.D. KEY:** Drooping tangs.

G7, $30-$50
Lea Co. NM.
Showing a Marshall
point embedded in an
animal bone

MARTIS- Late Archaic, 3000 - 1500 B. P.

(Also see Northern, San Rafael, Ventana Side Notched)

Clear obsidian

Red jasper

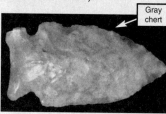

Gray chert

G6, $20-$35
NW Chihuahua, Mex, thick

G6, $18-$30
NW Chihuahua, Mex.

G6, $15-$25
NW Chihuahua, Mex.

LOCATION: W.Arizona into the Great Basin. **DESCRIPTION:** A small to medium size side notched point with a straight to concave base. Shoulders are tapered to horizontal.

MATAMOROS - Late Archaic to Classic Phase, 3000 - 400 B. P.

(Also see Abasolo, Catan, Early Triangular, Mescal Knife and Triangular Knife)

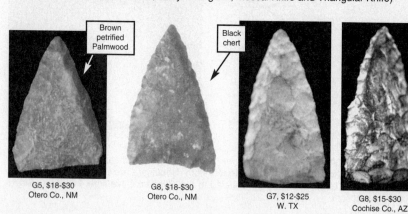

Brown petrified Palmwood

Black chert

G5, $18-$30
Otero Co., NM

G8, $18-$30
Otero Co., NM

G7, $12-$25
W. TX

G8, $15-$30
Cochise Co., AZ

MATAMOROS (continued)

LOCATION: Western Texas into Arizona. **DESCRIPTION:** A small to medium size, broad, triangular point with concave, straight, or convex base. On some examples, beveling occurs on one side of each face as in *Tortugas* points. **I.D. KEY:** Triangular form.

G8, $25-$40
Mohave Co., AZ

Banded red jasper

G10, $35-$60
N.W. Chihuahua, Mex.

MESCAL KNIFE - Desert Traditions-Classic and Historic Phases, 700 B. P. to historic times

(Also see Matamoros, Kinney and Triangular Knife)

LOCATION: Southwestern states. **DESCRIPTION:** A well made triangular blade which was hafted horizontally along one edge.

G9, $120-$200
Yavapai Co., AZ

MESERVE - Early Archaic, 9500 - 8500 B.P.

(Also see Allen, Angostura, Midland and San Jose)

Edges & tip wear

G5, $35-$60
Luna Co., N

G5, $35-$60
Yavapai Co., AZ

Edge wear

G5, $35-$60
Luna Co., NM

G7 $45-$80
Otero Co., NM

Basalt; restored tip

Yellow/tan chert; restored tip

Restored right ear

Petrified wood

G9, $145-$275
CO

G3, $15-$30
Otero Co., NM, ground basal area. Heavy wear and patination.

G3, $12-$20
Otero Co., NM, ground basal area. Heavy wear and patination.

SW

MESERVE (continued)

G9, $250-$425
Apache Co., AZ

LOCATION: Throughout the U.S. from the Rocky Mountains to the Mississippi River.
DESCRIPTION: A member of the *Dalton* Family. Blade edges are straight to slightly concave with a straight to very slightly concave sided stem. They are basally thinned and most examples are beveled and have light serrations on the blade edges. The basal edge is concave. **I.D. KEY:** Squared, concave base.

MIDLAND - Paleo, 10,700 - 10,400 B. P.

(Also see Belen, Folsom, Goshen, Mescal Knife and Milnesand)

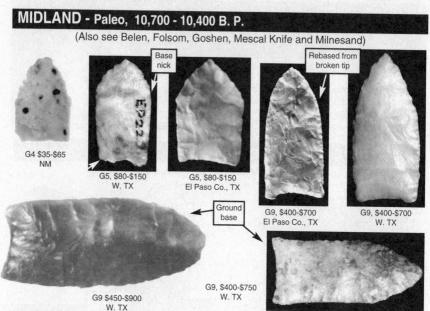

G4 $35-$65
NM

G5, $80-$150
W. TX

Base nick

G5, $80-$150
El Paso Co., TX

Rebased from broken tip

G9, $400-$700
El Paso Co., TX

G9, $400-$700
W. TX

Ground base

G9 $450-$900
W. TX

G9, $400-$750
W. TX

LOCATION: New Mexico northward to Montana, the Dakotas and Minnesota. **DESCRIPTION:** An unfluted *Folsom*. A small to medium size, thin, unfluted lanceolate point with a straight to concave base. Basal thinning is weak and the blades exhibit fine, micro edgework. Bases are ground.

MILNESAND - Transitional Paleo, 11,000 - 8000 B. P.

(Also see Folsom, Goshen and Midland)

Ground basal area

Yellow jasper

G6, $300-$550
Tucumcari, NM

G8, $700-$1100
Chihuahua, MX

MILNESAND (continued)

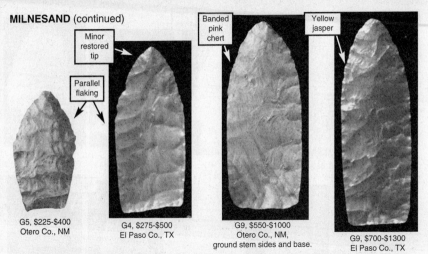

Minor restored tip

Parallel flaking

Banded pink chert

Yellow jasper

G5, $225-$400
Otero Co., NM

G4, $275-$500
El Paso Co., TX

G9, $550-$1000
Otero Co., NM,
ground stem sides and base.

G9, $700-$1300
El Paso Co., TX

LOCATION: Texas, New Mexico northward to Canada. **DESCRIPTION:** Medium size unfluted lanceolate point that becomes thicker and wider towards the tip. The base is basically square and ground. Thicker than *Midland.* A scarce type. **I.D. KEY:** Square base and Paleo parallel flaking.

MIMBRE - Developmental Phase, 800 B. P.

(Also see Del Carmen, Desert, Dry Prong, Nawthis and Sacaton)

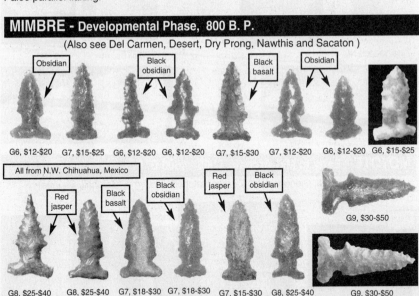

Obsidian

Black obsidian

Black basalt

Obsidian

G6, $12-$20   G7, $15-$25   G6, $12-$20   G6, $12-$20   G7, $15-$30   G7, $12-$20   G6, $12-$20   G6, $15-$25

All from N.W. Chihuahua, Mexico

Red jasper

Black basalt

Black obsidian

Red jasper

Black obsidian

G9, $30-$50

G8, $25-$40   G8, $25-$40   G7, $18-$30   G7, $18-$30   G7, $15-$30   G8, $25-$40   G9, $30-$50

LOCATION: N.W. Chihuahua, Mexico into Sou. New Mexico and far west Texas. **DESCRIPTION:** A small size, narrow, side notched arrow point with a base that flares out wider than the blade. The base is straight to slightly incurvate to excurvate. Blade edges are serrated. **I.D. KEY:** Broad base, wide notches.

MOUNT ALBION - Early to Middle Archaic, 5800 - 5350 B. P.

(Also see Cienega, Elko Corner Notched, Figueroa, Martis and San Pedro)

LOCATION: Northeastern Arizona, southeastern Utah, northern New Mexico and southern Colorado. **DESCRIPTION:** A medium sized dart/knife with small side to corner notches, an expanded stem and convex blade edges. The basal edge is convex. **I.D. KEY:** Large expanded, convex base

MOUNT ALBION (continued)

Tip wear

G8, $15-$25
N. AZ

G8, $20-$35
Hidalgo Co., NM

G5, $8-$15
Cochise Co., AZ

G5, $8-$15
Hidalgo Co., NM

G7, $12-$20
Santa Fe Co., NM

Agate

G8, $30-$55, NM

G5, $8-$15, UT

G7, $25-$45
AZ

G6, $20-$35
Luna Co., NM

G7, $25-$45, NM

G7, $30-$55
AZ

G8, $20-$35
NM

MOYOTE - Early to Mid-Archaic, 7000 - 4500 B. P.

(Also see Bell, Cienega, Elko Corner Notched, Figueroa, Marshall, Shumla)

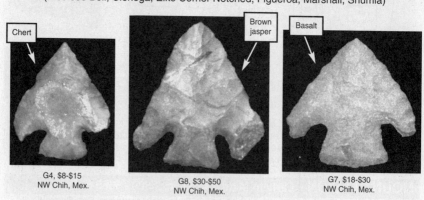

Chert

Brown jasper

Basalt

G4, $8-$15
NW Chih, Mex.

G8, $30-$50
NW Chih, Mex.

G7, $18-$30
NW Chih, Mex.

LOCATION: N.W. Chihuahua, Mex. **DESCRIPTION:** A medium size, thin, broad, corner notched point with an expanding stem. Blade edges can be straight to convex. Base is mostly convex but can be straight. Tangs are broad and squarrish and some examples show a clipped wing on at least one tang. **I.D. KEY:** Broadness and angle of notching.

MOYOTE (continued)

Black obsidian

Pink/gray chert

Brown jasper

G9, $20-$35
NW Chih, Mex.

G3, $8-$15
NW Chih, Mex.

G5, $12-$20
NW Chih, Mex.

Translucent obsidian

Brown/gray banded chert

Brown chalcedony

G9, $40-$70
NW Chih, Mex.

G8, $25-$40
NW Chih, Mex.

G9, $30-$50
NW Chih, Mex., very thin

NAWTHIS- Developmental Phase, 1100 - 700 B.P.

(Also see Buck Taylor Side Notched, Desert, Mimbre and Sacaton)

G8, $15-$30
NM

LOCATION: Northern New Mexico into Colorado. **DESCRIPTION:** A well made, side notched arrow point. It is triangular in shape with deep, narrow notches placed low on the blade. **I.D. KEY:** Low, deep and narrow side notches.

NEFF - Late Archaic, 3500 - 2300 B. P.

(Also see Ahumada, Duran, Escobas, Maljamar and San Jose)

G2, $1-$3
S.W. NM

G27, $1-$3
S.W. NM

G2, $1-$3
SW NM

G2, $1-$3
SW NM

G3, $8-$15
SW NM

G7, $25-$50
SW NM

G7, $40-$70
SW NM

G5, $12-$20
S.W. NM

LOCATION: Eastern New Mexico and western Texas. **DESCRIPTION:** A small to medium sized dart/knife with an expanded stem, drooping shoulders and multiple notches between the shoulders and tip. Another variation similar to *Duran, Sinner* and *Livermore* found in Texas. **I.D. KEY:** Large expanded, convex base.

NEFF (continued)

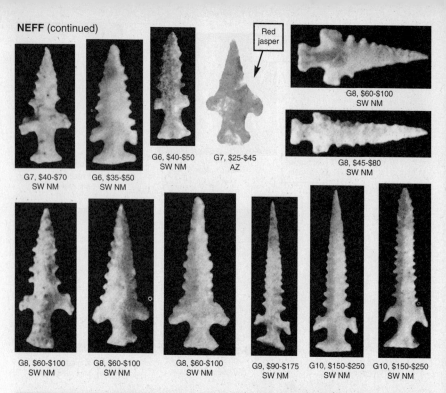

Red jasper

G7, $40-$70
SW NM

G6, $35-$50
SW NM

G6, $40-$50
SW NM

G7, $25-$45
AZ

G8, $60-$100
SW NM

G8, $45-$80
SW NM

G8, $60-$100
SW NM

G8, $60-$100
SW NM

G8, $60-$100
SW NM

G9, $90-$175
SW NM

G10, $150-$250
SW NM

G10, $150-$250
SW NM

NORTHERN SIDE NOTCHED - Paleo to LateArchaic, 9000 - 3000 B. P.

(Also see San Pedro, San Rafael, Sudden, Ventana Side Notched,)

Red jasper

G9, $25-$40
NW Chih, Mex.

LOCATION: Great Basin states into Arizona and N. Mexico. **DESCRIPTION:** A medium to large size, narrow side-notched point with early forms showing basal grinding and parallel flaking. Bases are usually concave to eared. Shoulders are tapered to horizontal. **I.D. KEY:** Broad side notched point.

PALMILLAS - Middle to Late Archaic, 6000 - 3000 B. P.

(Also see Axtel, Godley, Williams, Yavapai)

Banded chert

G10, $150-$250
Otero Co., NM, thin and excellent.

LOCATION: Texas to Oklahoma. **DESCRIPTION:** A small to medium size triangular point with a bulbous stem. Shoulders are prominent and can be horizontal to barbed or weak and tapered. Stems expand and are rounded. **I.D. KEY:** Bulbous stem.

PALMILLAS (continued)

White chalcedony

G5, $8-$15
NW Chihuahua, Mex., serrated.

Red base, clear chalcedony

G4, $8-$15
NW Chihuahua, Mex.

Red jasper

G7, $15-$25
NW Chihuahua, Mex.

Pink jasper

G8, $25-$40
El Paso Co., TX, serrated.

Gray chert

G6, $18-$30
El Paso Co. TX

Banded chert

Milky chalcedony

Gray chert

White chert

agate

G10, $30-$50
Otero Co., NM, thin
& perfect, serrated

G8, $30-$50
Otero Co., NM

G8, $30-$50
NW Chihuahua, Mex.,
thin.

G7, $30-$50
NW Chihuahua, Mex.,
serrated.

G9, $65-$125
NW Cihuahua, Mex.

Beige chert

G9, $55-$100
Otero Co., NM, ground base.

SW

PAROWAN - Desert Traditions-Developmental Phase, 1300 - 800 B. P.

(Also see Augustin, Basal Double Tang, Hodges Contracting and Santa Cruz)

G4, $12-$20
CO

LOCATION: Southern Utah, northern Arizona and into Nevada & Colorado. **DESCRIPTION:** A medium to large triangular arrowpoint with two shallow basal notches creating a short straight to contracting stem. **I.D. KEY:** Stem and barbs are the same length.

PAROWAN (continued)

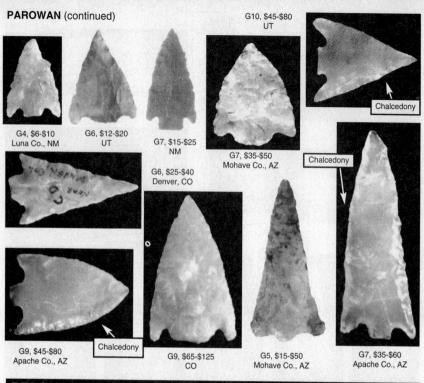

G4, $6-$10
Luna Co., NM

G6, $12-$20
UT

G7, $15-$25
NM

G10, $45-$80
UT

Chalcedony

G7, $35-$50
Mohave Co., AZ

Chalcedony

G6, $25-$40
Denver, CO

Chalcedony

G9, $45-$80
Apache Co., AZ

G9, $65-$125
CO

G5, $15-$50
Mohave Co., AZ

G7, $35-$60
Apache Co., AZ

PELONA - Early to Middle Archaic, 6000 - 4000 B. P.

(Also see Abasolo, Catan, Cottonwood, Datil, Lerma and Refugio)

Used as a graver

Basalt

G7, $15-$30
Cochise Co., AZ

G8, $18-$30
Pima Co., AZ

G5, $5-$10
Pima Co., AZ

Chert

Basalt

Basalt

G7, $15-$25
Pima Co., AZ

G7, $15-$25
Apache Co., AZ

G3, $5-$10
Cochise Co., AZ

G7, $15-$25
Pima Co., AZ

G3, $5-$10
Yavapai Co., AZ

Gray
flint

G7, $12-$20
Dona Ana Co.,
NM

LOCATION: Southern Arizona, southwestern New Mexico and southeastern California.
DESCRIPTION: Ranges from lozenge to ovoid in shape. It may have serrations on the blade, or, less frequently, on the hafting area, or, in most cases, not serrated.

1020

PELONA (continued)

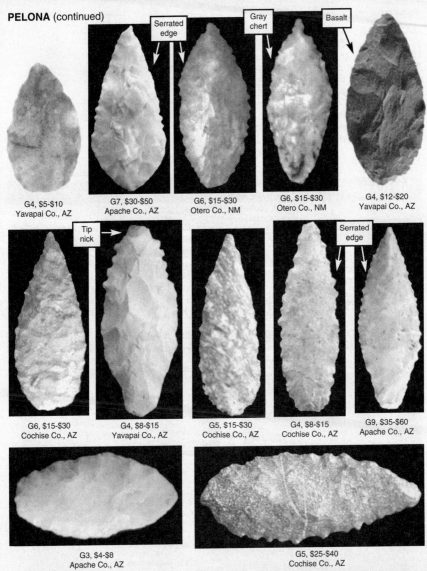

G4, $5-$10
Yavapai Co., AZ

G7, $30-$50
Apache Co., AZ

Serrated edge

Gray chert

G6, $15-$30
Otero Co., NM

Basalt

G6, $15-$30
Otero Co., NM

G4, $12-$20
Yavapai Co., AZ

Tip nick

G6, $15-$30
Cochise Co., AZ

G4, $8-$15
Yavapai Co., AZ

G5, $15-$30
Cochise Co., AZ

G4, $8-$15
Cochise Co., AZ

Serrated edge

G9, $35-$60
Apache Co., AZ

G3, $4-$8
Apache Co., AZ

G5, $25-$40
Cochise Co., AZ

SW

PERFORATOR - Archaic to Historic, 9000 - 400 B. P.

(Also see Drill, Graver and Scraper)

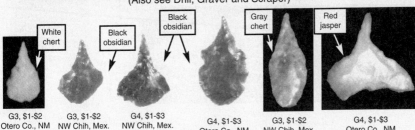

White chert

G3, $1-$2
Otero Co., NM

Black obsidian

G3, $1-$2
NW Chih, Mex.

Black obsidian

G4, $1-$3
NW Chih, Mex.

G4, $1-$3
Otero Co., NM

Gray chert

G3, $1-$2
NW Chih, Mex.

Red jasper

G4, $1-$3
Otero Co., NM

PERFORATOR (continued)

LOCATION: Archaic and Woodland sites everywhere. **DESCRIPTION:** A jabbing projection at the tip would qualify for the type. It is believed that *perforators* were used for tattooing, incising or to punch holes in leather or other materials or objects. Paleo peoples used *Gravers* for the same purpose. All Archaic and Woodland cultures converted their points into this type. Therefore, most point types could occur in this form.

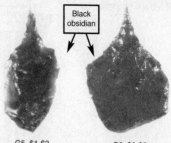

Black obsidian

G5, $1-$3
NW Chih, Mex.

G9, $2-$5
NW Chih, Mex.

PINTO BASIN - Early to Late Archaic, 8000 - 3000 B. P.

(Also see Duncan and Hanna)

G4, $8-$15
Apache Co., AZ

Tip nick

LOCATION: Arizona, New Mexico into E. California, Utah, Nevada, Idaho and Oregon. **DESCRIPTION:** A medium size auriculate point. Shoulders can be tapered, horizontal or barbed. Bases are either deeply bifurcated with parallel to expanding ears or tapered with a concave basal edge. **I.D. KEY:** Bifurcated base.

PLAINVIEW - Late Paleo, 10,000 - 7000 B. P.

(Also see Allen, Angostura, Clovis, Golondrina, Goshen)

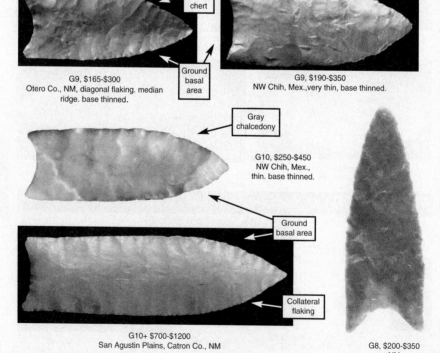

Yellow/white chert

Ground basal area

G9, $165-$300
Otero Co., NM, diagonal flaking. median ridge. base thinned.

G9, $190-$350
NW Chih, Mex.,very thin, base thinned.

Gray chalcedony

G10, $250-$450
NW Chih, Mex., thin. base thinned.

Ground basal area

Collateral flaking

G10+ $700-$1200
San Agustin Plains, Catron Co., NM

G8, $200-$350
NM

PLAINVIEW (continued)

LOCATION: Mexico northward to Canada. **DESCRIPTION:** A medium to large size, thin, lanceolate point with usually parallel sides and a concave base that is ground. Some examples are thinned or fluted and is believed to be related to the earlier *Clovis* and contemporary *Dalton* type. Flaking is of high quality and can be collateral to oblique transverse. **I.D. KEY:** Base form, thinness.

POINT OF PINES SIDE NOTCHED - Dev. Phase, 850 - 700 B. P.

(Also see Pueblo Side notched, Salado, Snaketown Triangular & Walnut Canyon)

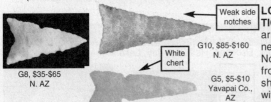

Weak side notches

White chert

G10, $85-$160
N. AZ

G8, $35-$65
N. AZ

G5, $5-$10
Yavapai Co., AZ

LOCATION: Arizona. **DESCRIPTION:** A small size, thin, triangular, arrow point with a concave base, needle tip and weak side notches. Notches occur about half way up from the base. Basal corners are sharp. **I.D. KEY:** Triangular form with weak side notches.

PUEBLO SIDE NOTCHED - Dev. to Classic Phase, 850 - 500 B. P.

(Also see Awatovi Side Notched, Buck Taylor Notched, Desert, Walnut Canyon)

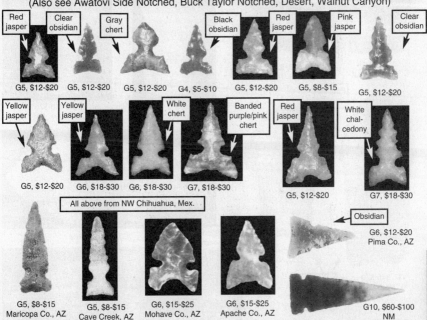

Red jasper — G5, $12-$20

Clear obsidian — G5, $12-$20

Gray chert — G5, $12-$20

G4, $5-$10

Black obsidian

Red jasper — G5, $12-$20

Pink jasper — G5, $8-$15

Clear obsidian — G5, $12-$20

Yellow jasper — G5, $12-$20

Yellow jasper — G6, $18-$30

White chert — G6, $18-$30

Banded purple/pink chert — G7, $18-$30

Red jasper — G5, $12-$20

White chalcedony — G7, $18-$30

All above from NW Chihuahua, Mex.

G5, $8-$15
Maricopa Co., AZ

G5, $8-$15
Cave Creek, AZ

G6, $15-$25
Mohave Co., AZ

G6, $15-$25
Apache Co., AZ

Obsidian — G6, $12-$20
Pima Co., AZ

G10, $60-$100
NM

LOCATION: Sou. California into Arizona, New Mexico and N. Mex. **DESCRIPTION:** A small size, thin, triangular, side notched arrow point with a straight to concave base. Notches can occur one fourth to half way up from the base. Basal corners can be squared to eared. **I.D. KEY:** Triangular form with side notches.

RED HORN (see Buck Taylor Notched and White Mountain Side Notched)

REFUGIO - Middle Archaic, 5000 - 2000 B. P.

(Also see Abasolo, Lerma, Pelona)

SW

REFUGIO (continued)

LOCATION: New Mexico into Texas. **DESCRIPTION:** A medium to large size, narrow, lanceolate blade with a rounded base.

G7, $20-$35
Otero Co., NM

RIO GRANDE - Early Archaic, 7500 - 6000 B. P.

(Also see Agate Basin, Angostura, Escobas, Hell Gap, Jay, Lake Mohave, Madden Lake)

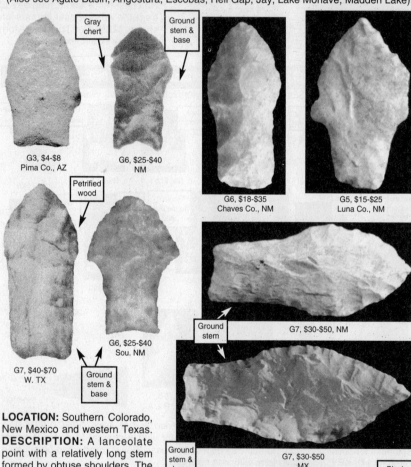

Gray chert

Ground stem & base

G3, $4-$8
Pima Co., AZ

G6, $25-$40
NM

G6, $18-$35
Chaves Co., NM

G5, $15-$25
Luna Co., NM

Petrified wood

G7, $30-$50, NM

Ground stem

G6, $25-$40
Sou. NM

G7, $40-$70
W. TX

Ground stem & base

G7, $30-$50
MX

Ground stem & base

Black obsidian

G7, $35-$70
Sante Fe, NM

LOCATION: Southern Colorado, New Mexico and western Texas. **DESCRIPTION:** A lanceolate point with a relatively long stem formed by obtuse shoulders. The stem contracts slightly and stem edges are ground. Developed from the earlier *Jay* point and related to the later *Escobas* point. **I.D. KEY:** The shoulders are more pronounced then on *Hell Gap* points.

1024

ROSE SPRINGS CORNER NOTCHED - Developmental Phase, 1600 - 700 B. P.

(Also see Chaco Corner Notched, Convento, Bonito and Desert)

G3, $2-$5
Otero Co., NM

G4, $4-$8
Otero Co., NM

G4, $4-$8
Otero Co., NM

G7, $8-$15
NM

G7, $8-$15
NM

G8, $8-$15
NM

Clear obsidian

Black obsidian

Black obsidian

Black obsidian

G7, $12-$25
NM

G7, $15-$25
NM

G7, $15-$30
N.W. AZ, Virgin Riv.

G8, $25-$40
S.W. CO

G7, $25-$40
Dona Ana Co., NM

G8, $20-$35
S.W. CO

Black obsidian

Banded agate

Black obsidian

G7, $20-$35
N.W. AZ, Virgin Riv.

G7, $20-$35
N.W. AZ

G6, $18-$30
NM

G5, $4-$8
NM

G9, $25-$45
NM

G8, $25-$45
NW. AZ

G8, $30-$50
NM

LOCATION: Arizona and New Mexico northward. **DESCRIPTION:** A small size, thin, light weight, corner notched arrow point. Notching is usually wide producing sharp tangs. Base corners are sharp to rounded. **I.D. KEY:** Size, broad corner notches.

ROUND-BACK KNIFE - Arachaic, 8000 - 2300 B. P.

(Also see Agate Basin, Early Leaf, Lerma, Refugio)

G8, $40-$75
NW Chihuahua, Mex.,

SW

LOCATION: Arizona into N.W. Chihuahua, Mexico. **DESCRIPTION:** A large size lanceolate blade with a convex base. Some examples are very thin and well made. **I.D. KEY:** Convex base.

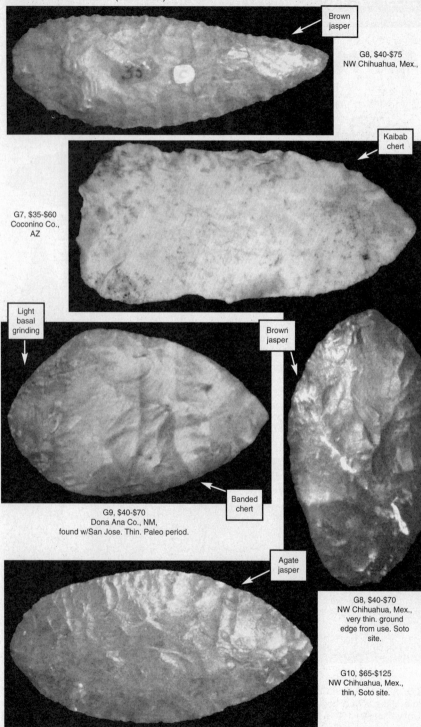

Brown jasper

G8, $40-$75
NW Chihuahua, Mex.,

Kaibab chert

G7, $35-$60
Coconino Co.,
AZ

Light basal grinding

Brown jasper

Banded chert

G9, $40-$70
Dona Ana Co., NM,
found w/San Jose. Thin. Paleo period.

Agate jasper

G8, $40-$70
NW Chihuahua, Mex.,
very thin. ground
edge from use. Soto
site.

G10, $65-$125
NW Chihuahua, Mex.,
thin, Soto site.

SACATON - Desert Traditions-Developmental Phase, 1100 - 900 B. P.

(Also see Desert, Dry Prong, Mimbre and Temporal)

Clear obsidian

G6, $8-$15
Mohave Co., AZ

G8, $25-$40
NM

G8, $25-$40
NM

G7, $15-$30
Apache Co., AZ

LOCATION: Arizona and central and southwestern New Mexico. **DESCRIPTION:** A small, triangular arrow point with relatively large side notches placed close to the basal edge. The base is the widest part of the point and is slightly concave. **I.D. KEY:** Wide base.

SALADO - Developmental-Classic Phase, 850 - 500 B.P.

(Also see Desert, Pueblo Side Notched and Walnut Canyon Side Notched)

G5, $15-$25
N. AZ

G6, $15-$25
Cedar Ridge, AZ

G5, $15-$25
AZ

G6, $20-$35
AZ

G8, $25-$45
AZ

G8, $25-$45
AZ

G8, $25-$45
Cedar Ridge, AZ

G6, $20-$35
N. AZ, chalc.

G8, $25-$45
Cedar Ridge, AZ

G7, $12-$20
Cedar Ridge, AZ

G7, $25-$45
AZ

G9, $35-$65
Cedar Ridge, AZ

G8, $40-$70
AZ

G6, $20-$35
AZ

G6, $20-$35
AZ

G6, $20-$35
AZ

Chalcedony

G7, $15-$30
Cedar Ridge, AZ

G6, $30-$45
AZ

G9, $70-$130
AZ

G9, $80-$150
AZ

G8, $15-$25
AZ

G7, $35-$65
AZ

G10, $125-$200
AZ

SW

G8, $25-$40.
Gila River, AZ.

   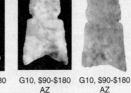  

G10 $80-$150
AZ

G10, $80-$150
AZ

G9, $65-$125
AZ

G10, $90-$180
AZ

G10, $90-$180
AZ

G10, $90-$180
AZ

G10, $90-$180
AZ

1027

SALADO (continued)

LOCATION: Arizona to California. **DESCRIPTION:** A small, thin, arrow point with a straight to concave base and tiny side notches set well up from the base. Related to *Hohokam*. Given this name in Perino #3. Also known as *Pueblo Side Notched*; see Justice, 2002. **I.D. KEY:** Large basal area.

SALT RIVER INDENTED BASE - Developmental, 1150 - 1000 B. P.

(Also see Gila River Corner Notched, Snaketown Side Notched)

Heavily resharpened

G6, $8-$15 Yavapai Co., AZ

G8, $20-$35 Pima Co., AZ

Red basalt

G3, $5-$10 Yavapai Co., AZ

Broken tip

LOCATION: Arizona and New Mexico. **DESCRIPTION:** A medium size, narrow, spike, auriculate Hohokam arrow point with multiple barbs that are larger close to the base. The base is eared and deeply concave. **I.D. KEY:** Exaggerated barbs and auriculate base.

SAN BRUNO- Classic to Historic Phase, 600 - 200 B. P.

(Also see Desert, Gatlin, Gila River, Pueblo Side Notched & Rose Springs, Snaketown)

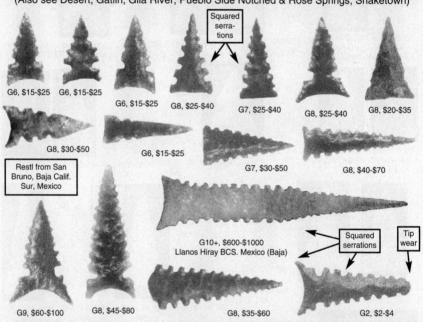

Squared serrations

G6, $15-$25   G6, $15-$25

G6, $15-$25   G8, $25-$40   G7, $25-$40   G8, $25-$40   G8, $20-$35

G8, $30-$50

G6, $15-$25

Restl from San Bruno, Baja Calif. Sur, Mexico

G7, $30-$50

G8, $40-$70

G10+, $600-$1000 Llanos Hiray BCS. Mexico (Baja)

Squared serrations

Tip wear

G9, $60-$100   G8, $45-$80   G8, $35-$60   G2, $2-$4

LOCATION: Bajo Calif. Sur, Mexico. **DESCRIPTION:** A small size, thin, side notched, triangular arrow point with serrated edges and a straight to concave base. Edge barbs are square as in *Stockton* points found further north. **I.D. KEY:** Square serrations.

SAN JOSE - Early Archaic, 9000 - 6000 B. P.

(Also see Armijo, Bajada, Baker, Barreal, Chiricahua, Escobas, Hanna, Maljamar, Meserve, Neff, Snaketown and Uvalde)

LOCATION: Arizona, New Mexico, sou. Utah, Nevada and Colorado. **DESCRIPTION:** A small to medium size dart/knife with wide, shallow side notches creating an auriculate base. The shoulders are obtuse and the blade edges always have relatively large serrations. Stem and base edges are usually ground. Similar to the *Barreal* point of the same age. **I.D. KEY:** Auriculate base.

SAN JOSE (continued)

Ground stem

Serrated edge

G6, $12-$20
Otero Co., NM

G5, $5-$10
Yavapai Co., AZ

G3, $5-$10
NM

G5, $5-$10
Yavapai Co., AZ

G6, $15-$30
Apache Co., AZ

G9, $35-$60
Yavapai Co., AZ

Restored tip

Obsidian

G3, $12-$20
Otero Co., NM,
ground stem, serrated.

G6, $25-$40
Otero Co., NM

G6, $25-$40
NM

G5, $18-$30
Otero Co., NM

G5, $15-$25
Otero Co., NM

Ground stem & base

Obsidian

Ground stem sides

Serrated

G7, $35-$60
Santa Fe Co., NM

G7, $35-$60
Luna Co., NM

G7, $35-$60
NW Chih, Mex.

G7, $35-$60
Otero Co., NM

G5, $12-$20
Otero Co., NM,
ground stem.

Tip nick

Serrated edge

Restored tip

Restored ear

Restored tip

SW

G5, $30-$50
Conejos Co.,
CO

G9, $125-$200
Otero Co., NM,
ground stem, ser-
rated

G2, $8-$15
Otero Co., NM,
ground stem.

G2, $8-$15
Otero Co., NM,
ground stem, agate,
serrated.

G3, $15-$25
Otero Co., NM,
ground stem, ser-
rated, right-hand
bevel.

G3, $15-$25
Otero Co., NM,
ground stem, ser-
rated, right-hand
bevel.

SAN JOSE (continued)

G3, $12-$20
Otero Co., NM,
ground stem, serrated.

G3, $8-$15
Otero Co., NM,
ground basal area.

G10, $125-$200
Otero Co., NM,
ground basal area, thinned
base

G10, $125-$200
Otero Co., NM,
ground basal area,
thinned base.

G3, $12-$20
Otero Co., NM,
ground stem, serrated.

G6, $65-$125
Otero Co., NM

SAN PEDRO - Late Archaic, 2500 - 1800 B. P.

(Also see Black Mesa Narrow Neck, Carlsbad, Cienega, Mount Albion and Yavapai Stemmed)

G5, $8-$15
Cochise Co., AZ

G3, $3-$6
Cochise Co., AZ

G5, $15-$25
Pima Co., AZ

G5, $15-$25
NW Chih, Mex.

G6, $18-$30
NW Chih, Mex.

G1, $1-$2
Pima Co., AZ

G6, $15-$25
Pima Co., AZ,
trans. point.

LOCATION: New Mexico, Arizona and northern Mexico. **DESCRIPTION:** A small to medium sized dart/knife made on a triangular preform and having side notches which begin at the basal corners and range from shallow to as deep as wide. Blade edges may be lightly serrated and the basal edge is straight to slightly convex.

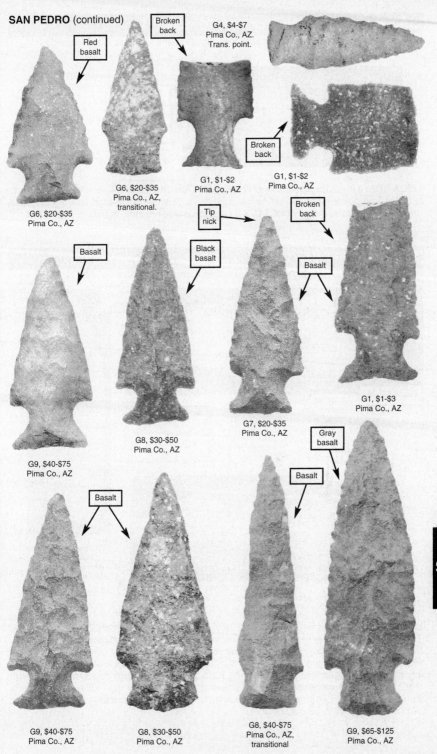

SAN PEDRO (continued)

Red basalt

Broken back

G4, $4-$7
Pima Co., AZ.
Trans. point.

Broken back

G6, $20-$35
Pima Co., AZ,
transitional.

G1, $1-$2
Pima Co., AZ

G1, $1-$2
Pima Co., AZ

G6, $20-$35
Pima Co., AZ

Basalt

Black basalt

Tip nick

Broken back

Basalt

Broken back

G1, $1-$3
Pima Co., AZ

G8, $30-$50
Pima Co., AZ

G7, $20-$35
Pima Co., AZ

G9, $40-$75
Pima Co., AZ

Gray basalt

Basalt

Basalt

G9, $40-$75
Pima Co., AZ

G8, $30-$50
Pima Co., AZ

G8, $40-$75
Pima Co., AZ,
transitional

G9, $65-$125
Pima Co., AZ

SW

1031

SAN RAFAEL - Middle Archaic, 4,400 - 3500 B. P.
(Also see Frio, Martis, Northern Side Notched and Ventana Side Notched)

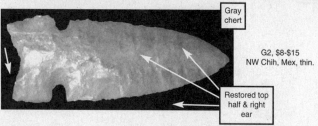

Gray chert

G2, $8-$15
NW Chih, Mex, thin.

Restored top half & right ear

LOCATION: Utah into Arizona and N. Mexico. **DESCRIPTION:** A medium size, broad, side-notched point with a straight to concave base. Notches occur high up from the base and the cross section is very thin. **I.D. KEY:** High-up side notches, thinness.

SANDIA I-III - Paleo, 14,000 - 10,000 B. P.
(Also see Clovis, Folsom and Madden Lake)

Convex base

Base nick

Single shoulder

G9, type I, $500-$1000
Sandia Mtns, NM. (shot from cast of real point from the type site discovered between 1936 and 1940)

IMPORTANT: This type may not exist. Points from the type site may not be authentic. More data needed.

Fluted with single shoulder

G6, type II, $350-$700
Sandia Mtns, NM.
(shot from cast of real point from the type site)

G9, type III, $750-$1500
Sandia Mtns, NM. (shot from cast of real point from the type site)

LOCATION: Type site is Sandia Mtns., New Mexico, south of Albuquerque. **DESCRIPTION:** This point occurs in three forms: The first form is a narrow, elliptical shape with only one shoulder and a rounded base. The second form has a slightly concave base, otherwise it is the same as the first form. The third form has a deeply concave base with drooping auricles. This, as well as the second form, have been found fluted on one or both faces. This type is extremely rare everywhere and may be later than *Clovis*. Another site with datable contex has not yet been found. Originally (questionably?) carbon dated to 20,000 B.P. **I.D. KEY:** Single shoulder.

SANDIA IV - Paleo, 14,000 - 10,000 B. P.

(Also see Clovis and Folsom)

Fluting channel

Ground basal area

G9, $650-$1000
Colfax Co., NM.

LOCATION: Type site is Sandia Mtns., New Mexico, south of Albuquerque. **DESCRIP-TION:** This authenticated point is very thin, single shouldered and fluted on both sides. Percussion flaked with fine pressure flaking. Basal area is ground. The classic *Sandia* form, but is thinner and better made than Sandia I points which lack the fine pressure flaking. **I.D. KEY:** Single shoulder, fine retouch.

SANTA CRUZ -Desert Traditions-Developmental Phase, 1400-600 B. P.

(Also see Augustin, Gypsum Cave, Hodges Contr. Stem, Manzano and Truxton)

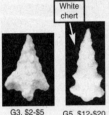     

White chert

G3, $2-$5
Apache Co., AZ

G5, $12-$20
Tucson, AZ

G5 $8-$15
Cochise Co., AZ

G3, $2-$5
Mohave Co., AZ

G7, $25-$40
Apache Co., AZ

G5, $12-$20
Coconino Co., AZ

G5, $8-$15
Apache Co., AZ

LOCATION: Arizona and contiguous parts of adjoining states. **DESCRIPTION:** A small, triangular arrow point with straight to obtuse shoulders and a short, tapering stem. These may prove to be small *Hodges Contracting Stem* points. **I.D. KEY:** Tiny, triangular stem.

SAW - Late Archaic, 3500 - 3000 B. P.

(Also see Drill, Perforator, Scraper)

G5, $2-$5
Otero Co., NM

Beige chert

Quartz

G6, $2-$5
Otero Co., NM

Gray chert

G8, $5-$10
Otero Co., NM

G4, $1-$3
Otero Co., NM

Gray chert

Chert

G7, $4-$8
Hudspeth Co., TX

SW

LOCATION: New Mexico into Texas. **DESCRIPTION:** A small to large size double uniface tool made from a flake with at least on edge with saw-tooth serrations for sawing.

SAW (continued)

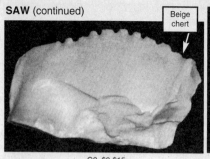

Beige chert

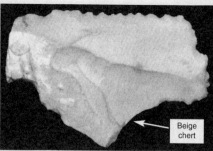

Beige chert

G9, $8-$15
Otero Co., NM

G9, $8-$15
Otero Co., NM

SCOTTSBLUFF II - Early Archaic, 9500 - 8500 B. P.

(Also see Bajada, Eden and Firstview)

IMPORTANT:
Shown half size →

Note parallel flaking

G8, $800-$1500,
Taos, NM

LOCATION: Midwestern states. **DESCRIPTION:** A medium to large size triangular point with shoulders a little stronger than on Type I and a broad parallel sided/expanding stem.

SCRAPER- Archaic, 8000 - 2300 B. P.

(Also see Drill, Lancel and Saw)

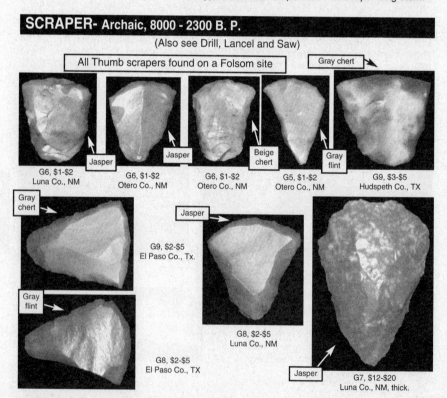

All Thumb scrapers found on a Folsom site

Gray chert

Jasper

Jasper

Beige chert

Gray flint

G6, $1-$2
Luna Co., NM

G6, $1-$2
Otero Co., NM

G6, $1-$2
Otero Co., NM

G5, $1-$2
Otero Co., NM

G9, $3-$5
Hudspeth Co., TX

Gray chert

Gray flint

Jasper

G9, $2-$5
El Paso Co., Tx.

G8, $2-$5
El Paso Co., TX

G8, $2-$5
Luna Co., NM

Jasper

G7, $12-$20
Luna Co., NM, thick.

1034

SCRAPER (continued)

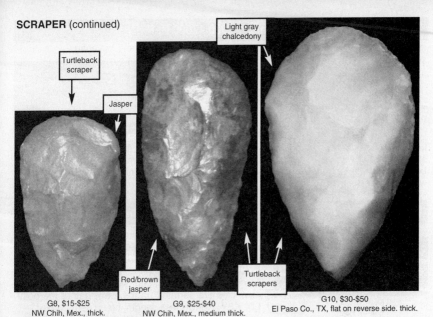

Light gray chalcedony

Turtleback scraper

Jasper

Red/brown jasper

Turtleback scrapers

G8, $15-$25
NW Chih, Mex., thick.

G9, $25-$40
NW Chih, Mex., medium thick.

G10, $30-$50
El Paso Co., TX, flat on reverse side. thick.

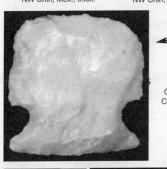

Hafted scraper

G8, $30-$50 ea.
Coconino Co., AZ

LOCATION: All of the United States. **DESCRIPTION:** A small to large size scraping tool either made from spent points or fresh from scratch. Thumb and Turtleback scrapers are uniface with steeply beveled edges. Many were hafted while others were hand-held in use.

G10, $2-$5
N.IW. Chihuahua, MX

G7, $2-$4
N.W. Chihuahua, MX

G8, $2-$4
N.W. Chihuahua, MX

G5, $1-$2
N.IW. Chihuahua, MX

G2, .50-$1
N.W. Chihuahua, MX

SW

SHUMLA - Woodland, 3000 - 1000 B. P.

(Also see Acatita, Marshal, Parowan)

LOCATION: Northern Mexico to Oklahoma. **DESCRIPTION:** A small size, basal notched point with convex, straight or recurved sides. Basal corners can be rounded to sharp. Bases are straight to slightly convex. Barbs turn in towards and usually extend to the base. Related to *Acatita* in Mexico?

G6, $15-$25
San Luis Potosi, MX

SILVER LAKE- Early Archaic, 11,000 - 7000 B. P.

(Also see Early Stemmed, Firstview, Lake Mohave and Yavapai)

G9, $85-$150
Yavapai Co., AZ

G6, $30-$50
NV

LOCATION: Arizona, Nevada to California. **DESCRIPTION:** A medium to large size, stemmed point with weak, tapered shoulders and usually a serrated edge. The stem can be up to half its length. The base is usually rounded and ground. **I.D. KEY:** Long stem, weak shoulders.

SNAKETOWN-Desert Traditions-Developmental Phase, 1200-1050 B. P.

(Also see Gila River, Hodges Contracting Stem and Salt River Indented Base)

G10, $125-$200
Kearny, AZ

Serrated edge

LOCATION: Arizona. **DESCRIPTION:** A very rare, form of *Hohokam* arrow point. The stem is straight to expanded and sometimes concave to bifurcated and has large serrations on both sides of the blade. Some examples are serrated on the lower half of the point. **I.D. KEY:** Narrowness, length, broad serrations.

SNAKETOWN SIDE NOTCHED - Dev.-Classic Phase, 800-600 B. P.

(Also see Bonito Notched, Gatlin, Gila River, Pueblo Side Notched)

G6, $5-$10
Yavapai Co., AZ

G5, $12-$20
Apache Co., AZ

G9, $25-$45
Pima Co., AZ

G6, $15-$30
Apache Co., AZ

LOCATION: Southern California into Arizona and New Mexico. **DESCRIPTION:** A small, serrated, side notched, *Hohokam* triangular arrow point with a concave to straight base. Basal corners are wide and rounded. Notches are broad. **I.D. KEY:** Broad notches.

G9, $35-$50
Yavapai Co., AZ

SNAKETOWN TRIANGULAR-Developmental Phase, 1050-850 B. P.

(Also see Bull Creek, Salt River Indented Base, Sobaipuri, Soto)

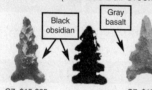

Black obsidian

Gray basalt

White chert

Straight base form

G7, $15-$25
Pima Co., AZ

G7, $15-$25
Pima Co., AZ

G7, $15-$25
Maricopa Co., AZ

G7, $15-$25
Cedar Ridge, AZ

G7, $15-$30
Pima Co., AZ

G6, $8-$15
Yavapai Co., AZ.

G7, $15-$25
Cedar Ridge, AZ

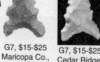

G6, $15-$30
Yavapai Co., AZ

G6, $12-$20
Cochise Co. AZ

G7, $12-$20
AZ

White chert

G7, $15-$25
Cedar Ridge, AZ

SNAKETOWN TRIANGULAR (continued)

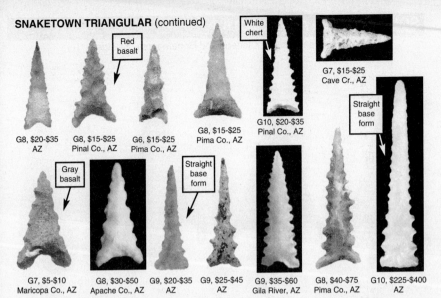

Red basalt

White chert

G7, $15-$25
Cave Cr., AZ

Straight base form

G8, $20-$35
AZ

G8, $15-$25
Pinal Co., AZ

G6, $15-$25
Pima Co., AZ

G8, $15-$25
Pima Co., AZ

G10, $20-$35
Pinal Co., AZ

Gray basalt

Straight base form

G7, $5-$10
Maricopa Co., AZ

G8, $30-$50
Apache Co., AZ

G9, $20-$35
AZ

G9, $25-$45
AZ

G9, $35-$60
Gila River, AZ

G8, $40-$75
Pima Co., AZ

G10, $225-$400
AZ

LOCATION: Southern California into Arizona and New Mexico. **DESCRIPTION:** A small, serrated, triangular *Hohokam* arrow point with a concave to straight base. Made by the Hohokam people. **I.D. KEY:** Wild barbs.

SOBAIPURI - Classic to Historic Phase, 500 - 200 B. P.

(Also see Aguaje, Bull Creek, Cottonwood, Salt River Indented Base, Snaketown

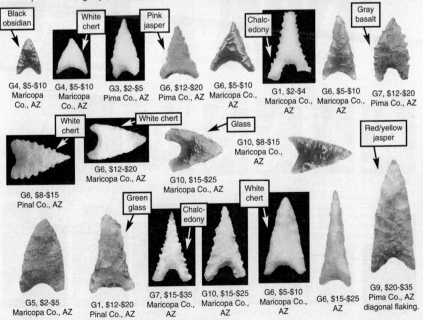

Black obsidian

White chert

Pink jasper

Chalcedony

Gray basalt

G4, $5-$10
Maricopa Co., AZ

G4, $5-$10
Maricopa Co., AZ

G3, $2-$5
Pima Co., AZ

G6, $12-$20
Pima Co., AZ

G6, $5-$10
Maricopa Co., AZ

G1, $2-$4
Maricopa Co., AZ

G6, $5-$10
Maricopa Co., AZ

G7, $12-$20
Pima Co., AZ

White chert

White chert

Glass

Red/yellow jasper

G10, $8-$15
Maricopa Co., AZ

G6, $12-$20
Maricopa Co., AZ

G10, $15-$25
Maricopa Co., AZ

G6, $8-$15
Pinal Co., AZ

Green glass

Chalcedony

White chert

G5, $2-$5
Maricopa Co., AZ

G1, $12-$20
Pinal Co., AZ

G7, $15-$35
Maricopa Co., AZ

G10, $15-$25
Maricopa Co., AZ

G6, $5-$10
Maricopa Co., AZ

G6, $15-$25
AZ

G9, $20-$35
Pima Co., AZ
diagonal flaking.

LOCATION: Southern Arizona, New Mexico and northern Mexico. **DESCRIPTION:** A small triangular, finely serrated, arrow point with convex sides and a deep, concave basal notch. **I.D. KEY:** Small triangular point with serrations.

SW

SOCORRO - Late Archaic, 3000 B. P.

(Also see Acatita, Cienega and Gobernadora, Yavapai)

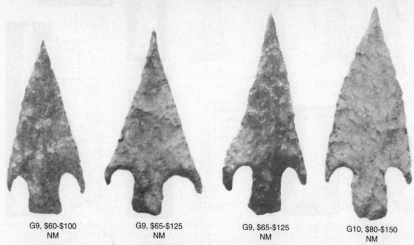

G9, $60-$100
NM

G9, $65-$125
NM

G9, $65-$125
NM

G10, $80-$150
NM

LOCATION: Northern Mexico into New Mexico. **DESCRIPTION:** A medium size dart/knife point with a long needle tip and drooping tangs. Stems are generally long and expanding to slightly contracting with a straight to bulbous base.

SOTO- Classic Phase to Early Historic, 1000-700 B. P.

(Also see Awatovi, Del Carmen, Garza, Pueblo Side Notched and Toyah)

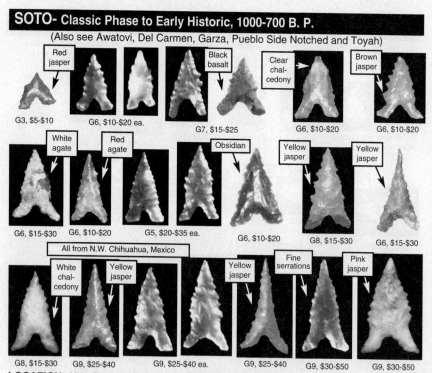

Red jasper

Black basalt

Clear chalcedony

Brown jasper

G3, $5-$10

G6, $10-$20 ea.

G7, $15-$25

G6, $10-$20

G6, $10-$20

White agate

Red agate

Obsidian

Yellow jasper

Yellow jasper

G6, $15-$30

G6, $10-$20

G5, $20-$35 ea.

G6, $10-$20

G8, $15-$30

G6, $15-$30

All from N.W. Chihuahua, Mexico

White chalcedony

Yellow jasper

Yellow jasper

Fine serrations

Pink jasper

G8, $15-$30

G9, $25-$40

G9, $25-$40 ea.

G9, $25-$40

G9, $30-$50

G9, $30-$50

LOCATION: NW Chihuahua Mexico. **DESCRIPTION:** A small, serrated arrow point with expanding ears, weak shoulders and a concave base. Most are made of agate and jasper. Similar to Garza & Toyah. Named by Alan Phelps. **I.D. KEY:** Thinness, drooping ears.

SQUAW MOUNTAIN - Middle Archaic, 5000 - 3000 B. P.

(Also see Barreal, Chiricahua, Hanna, San Jose & Ventana Side Notched)

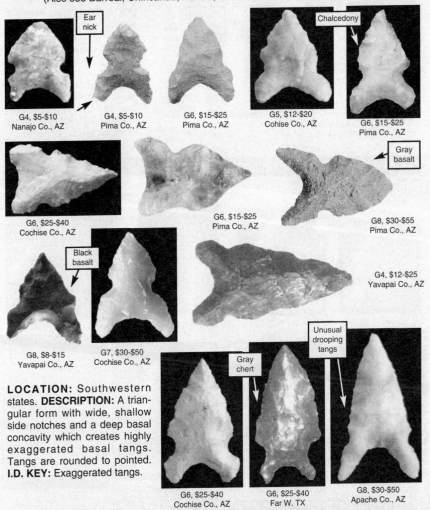

Ear nick

G4, $5-$10
Nanajo Co., AZ

G4, $5-$10
Pima Co., AZ

G6, $15-$25
Pima Co., AZ

Chalcedony

G5, $12-$20
Cohise Co., AZ

G6, $15-$25
Pima Co., AZ

Gray basalt

G6, $25-$40
Cochise Co., AZ

G6, $15-$25
Pima Co., AZ

G8, $30-$55
Pima Co., AZ

Black basalt

G4, $12-$25
Yavapai Co., AZ

G8, $8-$15
Yavapai Co., AZ

G7, $30-$50
Cochise Co., AZ

Unusual drooping tangs

Gray chert

LOCATION: Southwestern states. **DESCRIPTION:** A triangular form with wide, shallow side notches and a deep basal concavity which creates highly exaggerated basal tangs. Tangs are rounded to pointed. **I.D. KEY:** Exaggerated tangs.

G6, $25-$40
Cochise Co., AZ

G6, $25-$40
Far W. TX

G8, $30-$50
Apache Co., AZ

SW

SUDDEN SERIES - Early to Mid Archaic, 6300 - 4180 B. P.

(Also see Northern Side Notch, San Rafael & Ventana Side Notched)

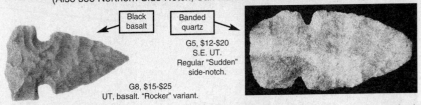

Black basalt

Banded quartz

G5, $12-$20
S.E. UT.
Regular "Sudden" side-notch.

G8, $15-$25
UT, basalt. "Rocker" variant.

LOCATION: Southeast Utah into Arizona. **DESCRIPTION:** A medium size side notched art/knife point that comes in two forms. The regular form has a large basal area and a straight to convex base. The "Rocker" form has a convex base.

TEMPORAL - Desert Traditions-Developmental Phase, 1000 - 800 B. P.

(Also see Bonito Notched, Desert, Dry Prong and Sacaton)

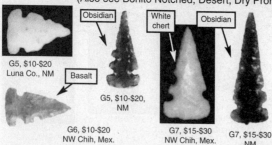

Obsidian

White chert

Obsidian

G5, $10-$20
Luna Co., NM

Basalt

G5, $10-$20,
NM

G6, $10-$20
NW Chih, Mex.

G7, $15-$30
NW Chih, Mex.

G7, $15-$30
NM

LOCATION: New Mexico, Arizona and western Texas. **DESCRIPTION:** A small side notched arrow point with one or two extra notches on one side. It is triangular with straight sides and a convex basal edge. Notches are narrow and deeper than they are wide. **I.D. KEY:** Rounded or rocker like basal edge.

TEXCOCO - Late Archaic, 6000 - 5000 B.P.

(Also see Elko Corner Notched, Mount Albion and San Pedro)

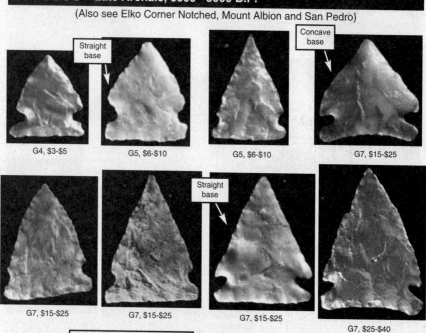

Straight base

Concave base

G4, $3-$5

G5, $6-$10

G5, $6-$10

G7, $15-$25

Straight base

G7, $15-$25

G7, $15-$25

G7, $15-$25

G7, $25-$40

All from San Luis Potosi, Mexico

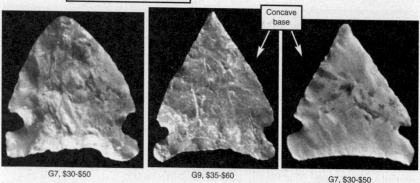

Concave base

G7, $30-$50

G9, $35-$60

G7, $30-$50

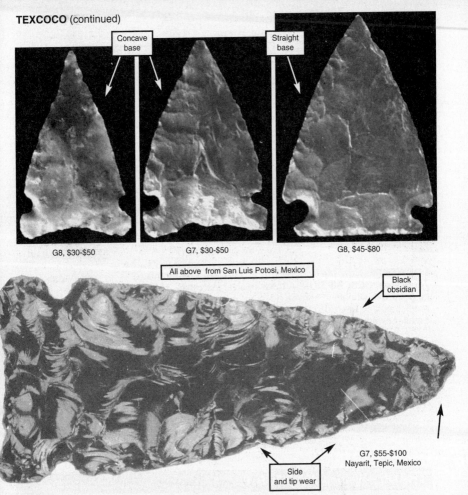

Concave base

Straight base

G8, $30-$50

G7, $30-$50

G8, $45-$80

All above from San Luis Potosi, Mexico

Black obsidian

G7, $55-$100
Nayarit, Tepic, Mexico

Side and tip wear

LOCATION: Central Mexico. **DESCRIPTION:** A triangular, wide based, thin, flat, corner to side notched point. The base is straight to concave. **I.D. KEY:** Width and thinness.

TORTUGAS - Middle Archaic to Woodland, 6000 - 1000 B. P.

(Also see Kinney, Early Triangular, Matamoros, Mescal & Trangular Knife)

SW

White quartz

Chert

Brown chert

G6, $18-$30
N.W. Chih, Mex.

G5, $15-$25
N. AZ

G7, $25-$40
N.W. Chihuahua, Mex.

TORTUGAS (continued)

Gray banded chert

Brown jasper

Black chert

G7, $25-$40
Otero Co., NM., thick.

G9, $40-$70
NW Chihuahua, Mex..

G8, $45-$80
NW Chih, Mex., thick.

LOCATION: New Mexico, Northern Mexico, Oklahoma to Tennessee. **DESCRIPTION:** A medium size, fairly thick, triangular point with straight to convex sides and base. Some examples are beveled on one side of each face. Bases are usually thinned. Smaller examples would fall in the *Matamoros* type.

TOYAH- Desert Traditions-Late Classic Phase, 600 - 400 B. P.

(Also see Awatovi Side Notched, Del Carmen, Desert , Pueblo Side notched and Soto)

G9, $25-$45
W. TX

LOCATION: Western Texas. **DESCRIPTION:** A small triangular arrow point with straight blade edges, side notches, and a concave base which often has a further central notch. Variations of this point may have multiple sets of side notches.

TRADE - Historic, 400 - 170 B. P.

(Also see Glass)

Damaged area

Broken tip

G7, $15-$25
Graham Co., AZ.,
Apache trade item

G8, $15-$25
Pinal Co., AZ.,
Apache

G2, $15-$25
Pinal Co., AZ.,
Apache

G2, $20-$35
Pinal Co., AZ.,
Apache

G8, $20-$35
Cochise Co., AZ

TRADE (continued)

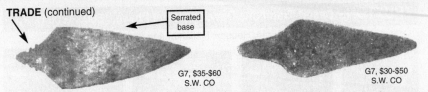

Serrated base

G7, $35-$60
S.W. CO

G7, $30-$50
S.W. CO

LOCATION: All over North America. **DESCRIPTION:** These points were made of copper, iron, and steel and were traded to the Indians by the French, British and others from the 1600s to the 1800s. Examples have been found all over the United States.

TRIANGULAR KNIFE - Late Archaic, 3500 - 2300 B. P.

(Also see Early Triangular, Matamoros and Mescal Knife)

Gray chert

Brown chert

Red chert

G7, $10-$20
Otero Co., NM., thin.

G8, $25-$40
Otero Co., NM., thin.

G7, $25-$40
N.W. Chih, Mex.

Beveled all four edges

Yellow jasper

G9, $40-$70
NW Chih, Mex.,

G8, $35-$60
Otero Co., NM

SW

LOCATION: Northwestern Arizona and, possibly, into adjacent areas of contiguous states. **DESCRIPTION**: A large, asymmetrical to triangular knife form which may have been hafted horizontally. The blade is very thin and flat for its size.

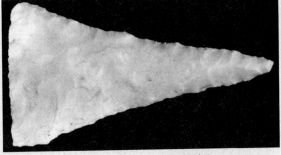

G6, $25-$40
Mohave Co., AZ

TRUXTON - Desert Traditions-Developmental Phase, 1500 - 1000 B. P.

(Also see Duran, Hodges, Maljamar and Santa Cruz)

G4, $6-$12
Mohave Co., AZ

G4, $8-$15
Mohave Co., AZ

G4, $5-$10
Navajo Co., AZ

G6, $25-$40
Mohave Co., AZ

G5, $12-$25
Mohave Co., AZ

G4, $8-$15
Mohave Co., AZ

LOCATION: Northern Arizona and possibly into adjacent states. **DESCRIPTION:** A small arrow point with a short stem, most often with a convex basal edge. The central portion of the blade has multiple notches and the tip of the blade is straight-sided converging to a sharply pointed tip.

TULAROSA CORNER NATCHED (see Cienega)

UVALDE - Middle Archaic to Woodland, 6000 - 1500 B. P.

(Also see Frio, Hanna, San Jose and Zephyr)

G10 $275-$500
Otero Co., NM

LOCATION: Texas to Oklahoma and New Mexico. **DESCRIPTION:** A medium size, bifurcated stemmed point with barbed to tapered shoulders. Some examples are serrated. The *Frio* point is similar but is usually broader and the ears flare outward more than this type. **I.D. KEY:** Narrow bifurcated stem.

VENTANA-AMARGOSA - Early Archaic, 7000 - 5000 B. P.

(Also see Yavapai Stemmed)

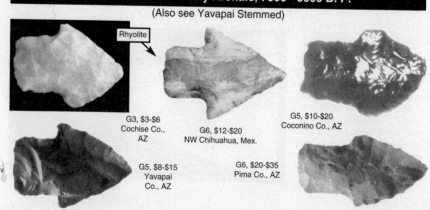

Rhyolite

G3, $3-$6
Cochise Co.,
AZ

G6, $12-$20
NW Chihuahua, Mex.

G5, $10-$20
Coconino Co., AZ

G5, $8-$15
Yavapai
Co., AZ

G6, $20-$35
Pima Co., AZ

VENTANA-AMARGOSA (continued)

G6, $20-$35
Pima Co., AZ

G4, $5-$10
Yavapai Co., AZ

LOCATION: Arizona and contiguous parts of adjacent states. **DESCRIPTION:** A small to medium sized dart/knife with a triangular blade with straight to slightly convex edges and straight to angular shoulders. The stem is parallel sided and rectangular to square. The basal edge is straight to rounded. **I.D. KEY:** A very square appearing stem.

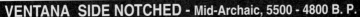

VENTANA SIDE NOTCHED - Mid-Archaic, 5500 - 4800 B. P.

(Also see Basketmaker, Northern Side Notched, San Rafael, Sudden)

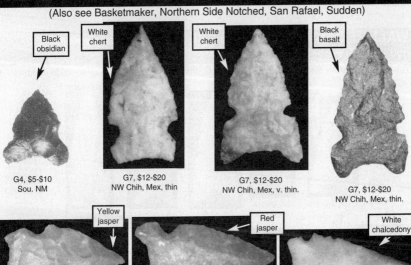

Black obsidian

White chert

White chert

Black basalt

G4, $5-$10
Sou. NM

G7, $12-$20
NW Chih, Mex, thin

G7, $12-$20
NW Chih, Mex, v. thin.

G7, $12-$20
NW Chih, Mex, thin.

Yellow jasper

Red jasper

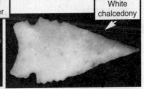

White chalcedony

G6, $8-$15
NW Chuahua, Mex.,
not ground

G8, $15-$25
NW Chihuahua, Mex.,

G10, $60-$100
NW Chihuahua, Mex, translucent, v. thin

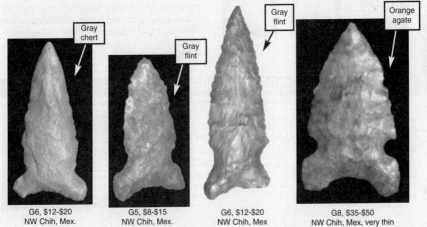

Gray chert

Gray flint

Gray flint

Orange agate

SW

G6, $12-$20
NW Chih, Mex.

G5, $8-$15
NW Chih, Mex.

G6, $12-$20
NW Chih, Mex

G8, $35-$50
NW Chih, Mex, very thin

1045

VENTANA SIDE NOTCHED (continued)

Gray flint

Red basalt

Clear chalcedony

G5, $8-$15
NW Chih, Mex., thick.

G6, $12-$20
NW Chih, Mex.

G8, $25-$45
Pima Co., AZ

LOCATION: Arizona, New Mexico & sou. Utah. **DESCRIPTION:** A small to medium size, side notched dart point. Bases are concave forming drooping ears. Many examples are heavily resharpened with the shoulders almost gone.

WALNUT CANYON SIDE NOTCHED - Dev. to Classic Phase 850 - 700 B. P.

(Also see Awatovi Side Notched, Desert, Gatlin Side Notched, Pueblo Side Notched & Salado)

White chert

G6, $30-$45
AZ

G9, $15-$25
Pima Co., AZ

G6, $8-$15
Pima Co., AZ

G8, $8-$15
Pima Co., AZ

G7, $30-$55
AZ

G10, $125-$200
AZ

G10, $125-$200
AZ

Agate

G8, $40-$70
N. AZ

G6, $30-$45
AZ

G9, $90-$180
Cedar Ridge, AZ

G10, $100-$195
AZ

G10, $125-$225
AZ

LOCATION: Arizona into New Mexico. **DESCRIPTION:** A small, narrow, side notched, triangular *Hohokam* arrow point with a deeply concave base. Notches occur high up from the base below mid-section. Basal corners are rounded to sharp. **I.D. KEY:** Narrowness and large basal area.

WHITE MOUNTAIN SIDE NOTCHED - Classic-Historic, 600 - 200 B. P.

(Also see Del Carmen, Desert and Rose Springs Side Notched)

LOCATION: Most of Arizona, southern New Mexico, S.W. Texas and northern Mexico. **DESCRIPTION:** A small, triangular arrow point with a deep basal notch and multiple side notches, most often with two pairs of side notches but examples with three pairs are not uncommon. Blade edges are generally straight. **I.D. KEY:** Multiple side notches.

G6, $12-$25
Navajo Co., AZ

G8, $25-$50
Navajo Co., AZ

G4, $8-$15
Yavapai Co., AZ

G5, $15-$30
Yavapai Co., AZ

G4, $10-$20
Cochise Co., AZ

Tip nick

Basalt

G3, $5-$10
Yavapai Co., AZ

G5, $15-$30
Yavapai Co., AZ

G6, $20-$35
Pima Co., AZ

G8, $25-$40
Yavapai Co., AZ

G8, $25-$45
Pima Co., AZ

G7, $40-$75
Pima Co., AZ, torque blade.

G3, $50-$10
Yavapai Co., AZ

G6, $25-$40
Yavapai Co., AZ

SW

LOCATION: Arizona and contiguous areas of adjacent states. **DESCRIPTION:** A medium sized dart point with a triangular blade and obtuse to lightly barbed shoulders. The stem is rectangular to slightly tapering or slightly expanding and longer than wide. The basal edge is straight to slightly concave or convex. **I.D. KEY:** Stem longer than wide.

ZEPHYR - Early Archaic, 9000 - 6000 B. P.

(Formerly Lampasos; also see San Jose and Uvalde)

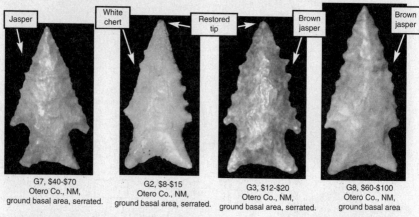

G7, $40-$70
Otero Co., NM,
ground basal area, serrated.

G2, $8-$15
Otero Co., NM,
ground basal area, serrated.

G3, $12-$20
Otero Co., NM,
ground basal area, serrated.

G8, $60-$100
Otero Co., NM,
ground basal area

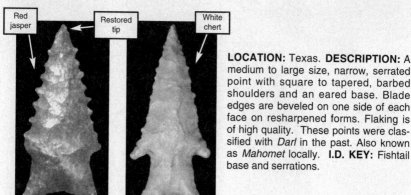

G3, $15-$30
NW Chih, Mex.
red jasper. ground basal
area, serrated.

G9, $80-$150
Otero Co., NM,
ground basal area, serrated.

LOCATION: Texas. **DESCRIPTION:** A medium to large size, narrow, serrated point with square to tapered, barbed shoulders and an eared base. Blade edges are beveled on one side of each face on resharpened forms. Flaking is of high quality. These points were classified with *Darl* in the past. Also known as *Mahomet* locally. **I.D. KEY:** Fishtail base and serrations.

ZORRA - Middle Archaic, 6000 - 4000 B. P.

(See Augustin, Gypsum Cave, Yavapai)

G8, $25-$40
W. TX

LOCATION: Texas. **DESCRIPTION:** A medium to large size point with tapered shoulders and stem that is usually flat on one face and beveled on both sides ot the opposite face. Most have needle tips and good quality flaking. **I.D. KEY:** Base beveling.

NORTHERN HIGH PLAINS SECTION:

This section includes point types from the following states:
Colorado, Idaho, Kansas, Montana, Nebraska, North Dakota,
South Dakota, Utah and Wyoming

The points in this section are arranged in alphabetical order and are shown **actual size**. All types are listed that were available for photographing. Any missing types will be added to future editions as photographs become available. We are always interested in receiving sharp, black and white or color glossy photos or color slides of your collection. Be sure to include a ruler in the photograph so that proper scale can be determined.

Lithics: Materials employed in the manufacture of projectile points from this region are: agate, basalt, chert, Dendritic chert, Flat Top chert, Flint, Knife River flint, obsidian, petrified wood, porcellanite, siltstone, Swan River chert and quartzite.

Regional Consultant:
John Byrd

Special Advisors:
Jerry Cubbuck, John Grenawalt, Jeb Taylor, Greg Truesdell

NP

HUNTING THE BUFFALO JUMPS
By John Byrd

Throughout all of the 14,000 plus years that prehistoric peoples lived in the geographical area now known as Montana, hunting has been the primary subsistence base. The open prairie grass lands and abundant water found in the eastern three quarters of this region provided an ideal habitat for all manner of grazing herd animals. Chief among these were the bison and later the buffalo, both of which were favorite prey for these early hunters.

To a limited degree, mass kills of these herds by coordinated communal hunting techniques were employed from the earliest of times. However, the sheer number of these kill sites dramatically increased around 1,200 to 1,300 years ago. Interestingly enough, this fits the time period when the bow and arrow technology was replacing the atlatl and a number of these kill sites will show evidence of use with both weapon types. The systematic use of this hunting method continued up until the 1600s when horses finally became readily available to the Indian population.

The technique employed was usually very similar from one location to another. Small groups of between 10 and 100 animals were gathered from their grazing areas or intercepted going to or from water. They were then driven or stampeded to the site chosen as the kill area (no small task given the nature of these animals). This actual kill would either be a low cliff 10 to 50 feet high or more frequently a steep bank or low lying depression. In the later cases, a stout corral was built to

Digging in the bone beds of this Montana Buffalo Jump has yielded many fine projectile points.

contain the herd long enough to complete the slaughter. The intent was not necessarily to kill the animals from the drop over a cliff or down a bank, but rather to injure them severely enough that they were easier to kill with the weapons available.

In efficiency, this method of hunting was unsurpassed for many centuries. These sites are usually packed with multiple layers of bone as silent testimony to the sheer volume of animals killed. One such kill site had bone forty feet thick, and it was estimated that over 400,000 buffalo had been slaughtered there. Some of the especially strategic sites were used over thousands of years.

Example of Buffalo Jump located in Montana. Animals were driven over this cliff for slaughter.

Of course, to kill these creatures a vast number of projectiles were used and many of these were either lost, damaged or left behind. Since the 1930s these kill sites have been popular locations for collectors and archaeologists alike. Many hundreds of thousands of projectile points have been found and placed in collections from what have become commonly referred to as "Buffalo Jumps". The highest percentage of these are true arrow points rather than the dart points used by the earlier atlatl. The very small size of these "arrowheads" is surprising to many people when considering the large stature of the animal being hunted. The average length will be between 3/4" and 1 1/4" with examples as small as 1/4" not being uncommon. Specimens that are over 1 1/2" are relatively scarce and very sought after. Many people who do not know the difference refer to these small arrow points as "bird points" which is completely erroneous. It was not the size that made these arrowheads effective on large animals but rather their ability to penetrate into the vital organs.

NORTHERN HIGH PLAINS POINT TYPES
(Archaeological Periods)

PALEO (14,000 B. P. - 8,000 B. P.)

Agate Basin	Clovis-Colby	Lancet	Scraper
Alder Complex	Drill	Mahaffey	
Allen	Folsom	Midland	
Anderson	Goshen	Milnesand	
Browns Valley	Graver	Paleo Knife	
Clovis	Hell Gap	Plainview	

EARLY ARCHAIC (8,000 B. P. - 5,500 B. P.)

Alberta	Dalton	Logan Creek	Rio Grande
Angostura	Eden	Lookingbill	Scottsbluff I & II
Archaic Knife	Firstview	Lovell	Simonsen
Archaic Side Notched	Logan Creek	Meserve	
Archaic Triangle	Hawken	Mount Albion	
Bitterroot	Holland	Plains Knife	
Cody Knife	Hollenberg Stemmed	Pryor Stemmed	

MIDDLE ARCHAIC (5,500 B. P. - 3,300 B. P.)

Base Tang Knife	Green River	McKean	Pinto Basin
Buffalo Gap	Hanna	Mid-Back Tang	Yonkee
Corner Tang	Hanna-Northern	Oxbow	
Duncan	Lerma	Pelican Lake	
Elko	Mallory	Pelican Lake-Harder Variety	

LATE ARCHAIC (3,300 B. P. - 2,300 B. P.)

Exotic Forms	Gary	Plains Side Notched

DESERT TRADITIONS

TRANSITIONAL PHASE (2,300 B. P. - 1,600 B. P.)

Hafted Knife	Samantha Dart

DEVELOPMENTAL PHASE (1,600 B. P. - 700 B. P.)

Avonlea-Carmichael	Glendo Dart	Nanton	Sattler
Avonlea-Classic	Harrell	Paskapoo	Side Knife
Avonlea-Gull Lake	High River	Pekisko	Sonota
Avonlea-Timber Ridge	Hog Back	Pipe Creek	Stott
Besant	Horse Fly	Plains Side Notched	Swift Current
Besant Knife	Huffaker	Plains Triangular	Tompkins
Eastgate	Irvine	Prairie Side Notched	Washita
Emigrant	Lewis	Rose Springs	Washita Northern
Glendo Arrow	Mummy Cave	Samantha-Arrow	

CLASSIC PHASE (700 B. P. - 400 B. P.)

Camel Back	Cottonwood Triangle	Desert Sierra
Cottonwood Leaf	Desert-General	Harahey

HISTORIC PHASE (400 B. P. - Present)

Billings	Bone Point	Cut Bank Jaw Notched	Trade Points

NP

NORTHERN HIGH PLAINS
THUMBNAIL GUIDE SECTION

The following references are provided to aid the collector in easier and quicker identification of point types. All photos are exactly 30% of actual size and are proportional to each other. Each point pictured in this section represents a classic form for the type. When a match is found, go to the alphabetical location of that type for more examples in actual size.

① THUMBNAIL GUIDE - AURICULATE FORMS (30% actual size)

Fluted Forms | Unfluted Forms

Clovis — Clovis Colby — Folsom — Allen — Dalton — Duncan

Goshen — Green River — Hanna — Holland — Lovell — McKean — Midland — Milnesand — Meserve — Oxbow — Plainview

② THUMBNAIL GUIDE - LANCEOLATE FORMS (30% actual size)

Agate Basin — Alder Complex — Anderson — Angostura

Archaic Knife — Archaic Triangle — Browns Valley — Cottonwood Leaf — Cottonwood Triangle — Drill — Graver

Harahey — Lerma — Mahaffey — Paleo Knife

Peisker Diamond — Plains Triangular — Scraper — Side Knife — Side Knife

③ THUMBNAIL GUIDE - CORNER NOTCHED FORMS (30% actual size)

Camel Back — Corner Tang — High River — Mummy Cave — Pelican Lake — Eastgate

Glendo Arrow — Glendo Dart — Hog Back — Mid-BackTang — Pelican Lake-Harder Variety — Pipe Creek — Rose Springs

1052

Archaic Side Notched

Avonlea-Classic

Avonlea-Carmichael

Avonlea-Timber Ridge

Avonlea-Gull Lake

Besant

Besant

Besant

Besant Knife

Billings

Bitterroot

Buffalo Gap

Cut Bank Jaw Notched

Harrell

Huffaker

Desert-General

Desert-Sierra

Desert-General

Desert-Sierra

Emigrant

Hawkens

Irvine

Lancet

Lewis

Logan Creek

Looking Bill

Mallory

Mount Albion

Nanton

Paskapoo

Pekisko

Plains Knife

Plains Side Notched

Prairie Side Notched

Simonsen

Samantha Arrow

Samantha Dart

Sonota

Stott

Swift Current

Washita

Washita-Northern

Yonkee

Alberta

Base Tang Knife

Duncan

Besant

Cody Knife

Eastgate

Eden

Elko

Firstview

Hanna

Hollenberg Stemmed

Pryor Stemmed

Rose Springs

Hanna-Northern

Hell Gap

Pinto Basin

Horse Fly

Rio Grande

Rose Springs

Sattler

Scottsbluff I

Scottsbluff II

Trade

NP

AGATE BASIN - Transitional Paleo to Early Archaic, 10,500 - 8000 B. P.

(Also see Alder Complex, Angostura, Browns Valley, Eden & Mahaffey)

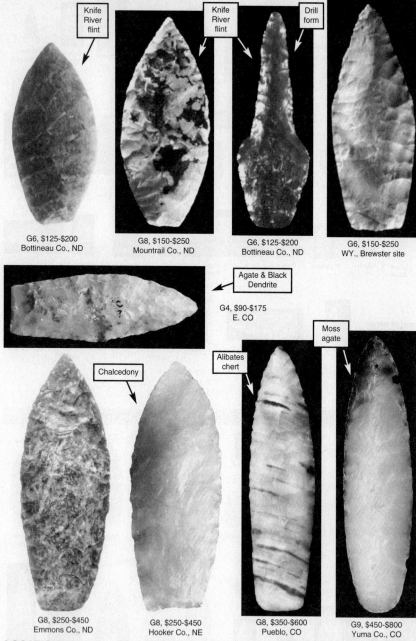

Knife River flint

Knife River flint

Drill form

G6, $125-$200
Bottineau Co., ND

G8, $150-$250
Mountrail Co., ND

G6, $125-$200
Bottineau Co., ND

G6, $150-$250
WY., Brewster site

Agate & Black Dendrite

G4, $90-$175
E. CO

Moss agate

Alibates chert

Chalcedony

G8, $250-$450
Emmons Co., ND

G8, $250-$450
Hooker Co., NE

G8, $350-$600
Pueblo, CO

G9, $450-$800
Yuma Co., CO

LOCATION: Northern states from Pennsylvania to western states. **DESCRIPTION:** A medium to large size lanceolate blade of unusually high quality. Bases are either convex, concave or straight, and are usually ground. Some examples are median ridged and have random to parallel flaking. **I.D. KEY:** Basal form and flaking style.

1054

AGATE BASIN (continued)

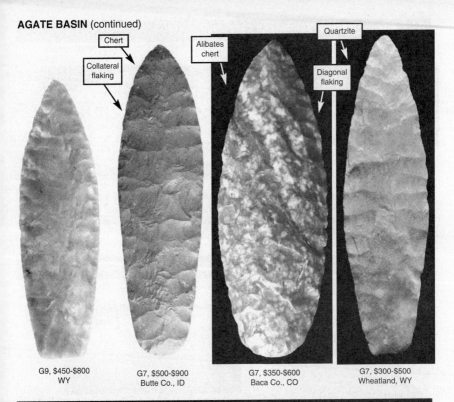

Chert

Collateral flaking

Alibates chert

Quartzite

Diagonal flaking

G9, $450-$800
WY

G7, $500-$900
Butte Co., ID

G7, $350-$600
Baca Co., CO

G7, $300-$500
Wheatland, WY

ALBERTA - Early Archaic, 10,000 - 7000 B. P.

(Also see Cody Knife, Eden, Rio Grande and Scottsbluff)

LOCATION: Northern states from Michigan to Montana and Nevada. **DESCRIPTION:** A medium to large size point with a broad, long parallel stem and weak shoulders. Believed to belong to the Cody Complex and is related to the *Eden* and *Scottsbluff* type. Stems are ground. **I.D. KEY:** Long stem, weak shoulders.

Basalt

G5, $125-$200
WY

Ground base & stem

Basalt

G3, $85-$150
Lewis & Clark Co., MT

G4, $135-$250
E. CO

Tip wear

Brown jasper

G9, $2,500-$4,000
W. NE

Alberta/Eden cross type

NP

1055

ALDER COMPLEX - Paleo, 9500 - 8000 B. P.

(Also see Agate Basin, Browns Valley, Clovis, Dalton, Green River and Lovell)

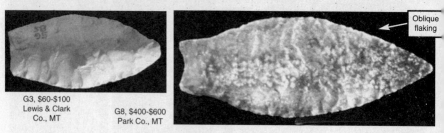

G3, $60-$100
Lewis & Clark
Co., MT

G8, $400-$600
Park Co., MT

Oblique
flaking

LOCATION: Plains states. **DESCRIPTION:** A medium to large size unfluted lanceolate point of high quality with convex sides and a straight to concave base. Flaking is usually the parallel oblique type. Basal areas are ground. **I.D. KEY:** Basal form and flaking style.

ALLEN - Transitional Paleo to Early Archaic, 10,000 - 9500 B. P.

(Also see Alder Complex, Browns Valley, Clovis, Dalton, Goshen, Green River and Lovell)

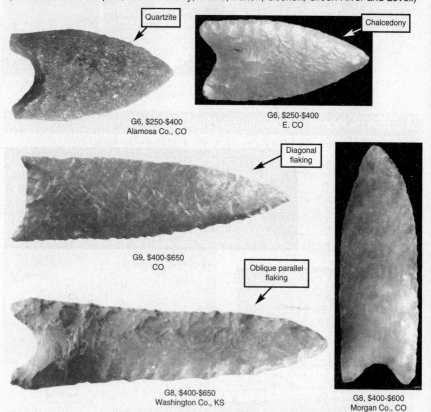

Quartzite

Chalcedony

G6, $250-$400
Alamosa Co., CO

G6, $250-$400
E. CO

Diagonal
flaking

G9, $400-$650
CO

Oblique parallel
flaking

G8, $400-$650
Washington Co., KS

G8, $400-$600
Morgan Co., CO

LOCATION: Plains states. Named after Jimmy Allen of Wyoming. **DESCRIPTION:** A medium to large size lanceolate point that has oblique tranverse flaking and a concave base with usually rounded ears. Basal area is ground. **I.D. KEY:** Basal form and flaking style.

ANDERSON - Early Archaic, 9000 - 7500 B. P.

(Also see Allen, Angostura, Plainview)

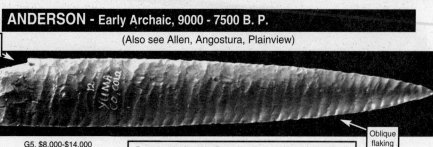

ase
ick

G5, $8,000-$14,000
Yuma Co., CO

Oblique
flaking

Famous point found by Perry Anderson published as 1st Yuma
point; later named Allen or Angostura and recently named
Anderson after its founder.

LOCATION: Colorado into KS, MO & AR. **DESCRIPTION:** Very rare. A long slender lanceolate form exhibiting a uniform profile that is very thin with straight edges; stem edge grinding is short (similar to Cody Complex) and basal grinding is present; pressure flaking is superb and serial, parallel oblique. **Note:** This type was first identified years ago as *Yuma* and later changed to *Allen, Angostura* and other types. Recently it has been determined that this type is unique and different enough to have its own distinct name which has been proposed by Jeb Taylor. Named for Perry Anderson who found the first well known example.

ANGOSTURA - Early Archaic, 9000 - 7500 B. P.

(Also see Alder Complex, Allen, Anderson, Archaic Knife, Browns Valley, Clovis, Dalton and Goshen)

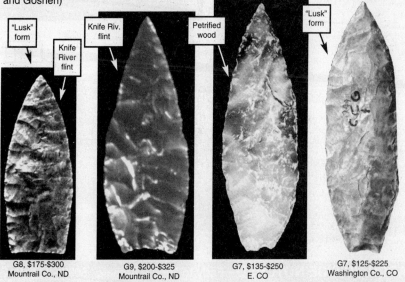

"Lusk"
form

Knife
River
flint

Knife Riv.
flint

Petrified
wood

"Lusk"
form

G8, $175-$300
Mountrail Co., ND

G9, $200-$325
Mountrail Co., ND

G7, $135-$250
E. CO

G7, $125-$225
Washington Co., CO

Side
nicks

G5, $135-$250
Lewis & Clark Co., MT

NP

ANGOSTURA (continued)

G1, $40-$75
E. CO. Chert. Broken.

Nice oblique, parallel flaking

G1, $40-$75
E. CO. Chert. Broken.

LOCATION: Plains states. **DESCRIPTION:** A medium to large size lanceolate blade of unusually high quality. Bases are either convex, concave or straight and are usually ground. Most examples have oblique transverse flaking. **I.D. KEY:** Basal form and flaking style.

ARCHAIC KNIFE - Early to Middle Archaic, 6000 - 4000 B. P.

(Also see Angostura, Harahey, Plains Knife and Plains Triangular)

LOCATION: Plains states. **DESCRIPTION:** A medium to large triangular blade with a concave to straight base. **I.D. KEY:** Large triangle with early flaking.

G5, $12-$20
E. CO

Agate

G10, $180-$300
Costilla Co., CO

ARCHAIC SIDE NOTCHED - Early to Middle Archaic, 6000 - 4000 B. P.

(Also see Besant, Bitterroot and Plains Knife)

G5, $30-$50
E. Co

Translucent

G5, $12-$20
E. CO

LOCATION: Northern Plains states. **DESCRIPTION:** A small to medium size, narrow, side-notched point with early flaking.

ARCHAIC SIDE NOTCHED (continued)

G5, $12-$20
Hooker Co., NE

Knife River flint

G6, $85-$165
Mountrail Co., ND

G7, $60-$100
Lewis & Clark Co., MT

ARCHAIC TRIANGLE - Early to Middle Archaic, 6000 - 4000 B. P.

(Also see Cottonwood and Plains Triangular)

Chalcedony

G6, $8-$15
Custer Co., NE

G6, $12-$20
Lewis & Clark Co., MT

G7, $18-$30
E. CO

LOCATION: Plains states. **DESCRIPTION:** A small size triangular point that shows early flaking. **I.D. KEY:** Triangle with early flaking.

AVONLEA-CARMICHAEL - Developmental, 1300 - 400 B. P.

(Also see High River, Irvine, Lewis, Nanton, Pekisko, Swift Current and Tompkins)

G5, $18-$30
Meagher Co., MT

G5, $25-$40
Cascade Co., MT

G6, $25-$45
Choteau, MT

G6, $25-$45
Cascade Co., MT

G6, $30-$50
Choteau, MT

G6, $35-$60
Choteau, MT

G6, $45-$80
MT

NP

G8, $40-$75
Teton Co., MT

G8, $40-$75
Saco, MT, Milk River.

G8, $40-$75
MT

AVONLEA-CARMICHAEL (continued)

LOCATION: Plains states. **DESCRIPTION:** A small size, very thin, high quality arrow point with shallow side notches close to the base which is concave. The blade is constructed with broad, parallel flakes that extend to the center. Quality is slightly lower than the other forms of this type. Frequently found on Bison kill sites. **I.D. KEY:** Low side notches, very thin.

G8, $50-$90
Teton Co., MT

AVONLEA-CLASSIC - Developmental Phase, 1300 - 400 B. P.

(Also see High River, Irvine, Lewis, Nanton, Pekisko, Swift Current and Tompkins)

G6, $15-$30
Meagher Co., MT

G6, $15-$30
Choteau Co., MT

LOCATION: Plains states. **DESCRIPTION:** A small size, very thin, high quality arrow point with shallow side notches close to the base which is concave. High quality parallel flaking is evident on the blade. Found at Bison kill sites. **I.D. KEY:** Low side notches, very thin.

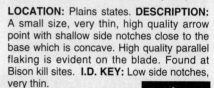

Siltstone

G6, $15-$30
Phillips Co., MT

G6, $15-$30
Meagher Co., MT

G6, $15-$30
Phillips Co., MT

G6, $15-$30
Meagher Co., MT

G8, $30-$50
Cascade Co., MT

G8, $35-$60
Saco, MT, Milk Riv.

G7, $30-$50
Saco, MT, Milk Rv.

G8, $35-$60
Meagher Co., MT

G8, $40-$75
Teton Co., MT

AVONLEA-GULL LAKE - Developmental Phase, 1800 - 400 B. P.

(Also see Besant, High River, Irvine, Lewis, Nanton, Pekisko, Swift Current and Tompkins)

G5, $15-$30
Meagher Co., MT.

G7, $45-$80
Meagher Co., MT.

G7, $45-$80
Phillips Co., MT.

G8, $45-$80
Phillips Co., MT.

G8, $50-$90
Meagher Co., MT.

G8, $50-$90
Cascade Co., MT.

LOCATION: Plains states. **DESCRIPTION:** A small to medium size, thin, high quality point with shallow notches located close to the base. The earliest form for the type. Carefully controlled parallel flaking was used in the construction. Some examples have basal grinding. The earliest forms of this variety were dart points changing into arrow points at a later time. Believed to be related to the *Besant* type. **I.D. KEY:** Basal form and flaking style.

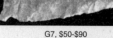
G7, $50-$90
Meagher Co., MT.

AVONLEA-GULL LAKE (continued)

G9, $90-$165
Cascade Co., MT

G9, $65-$125
Meagher Co., MT

G9, $90-$175
Cascade Co., MT.

G10, $100-$180
Cascade Co.,
MT

G10, $125-$200
Meagher Co.,
MT

G10, $200-$350
Meagher Co., MT
Best known example.

AVONLEA-TIMBER RIDGE - Developmental to Historic Phase, 1300 - 400 B. P.

(Also see Besant, High River, Irvine, Nanton, Pekisko, Swift Current and Tompkins)

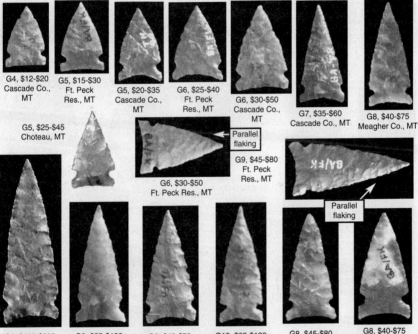

G4, $12-$20
Cascade Co.,
MT

G5, $15-$30
Ft. Peck
Res., MT

G5, $20-$35
Cascade Co.,
MT

G6, $25-$40
Ft. Peck
Res., MT

G6, $30-$50
Cascade Co.,
MT

G7, $35-$60
Cascade Co., MT

G8, $40-$75
Meagher Co., MT

G5, $25-$45
Choteau, MT

G6, $30-$50
Ft. Peck Res., MT

G9, $45-$80
Ft. Peck
Res., MT

G9, $125-$200
Saco, MT

G9, $55-$100
Cascade Co., MT

G8, $40-$70
Ft. Peck Res., MT

G10, $65-$120
Meagher Co., MT

G8, $45-$80
MT

G8, $40-$75
Ft. Peck Res., MT

LOCATION: Northern Plains states. **DESCRIPTION:** A small size, very thin, narrow, arrow point with shallow side notches close to the base. Bases can be straight to concave. Corners of ears are sharper than the other varieties.

NP

BASE TANG KNIFE - Middle Archaic to Transitional Phase, 4000 - 2000 B. P.

(Also see Cody Knife, Corner Tang and Mid-Back Tang)

BASE TANG KNIFE (continued)

G6, $60-$100
E. CO.

G8, $65-$125
N.E. OK

LOCATION: Northern Plains states. **DESCRIPTION:** Two forms. First: A medium to large size shouldered point with a long stem meeting the base at a sharp angle. Second: A large size ovoid double pointed blade with a small, side notched base. **I.D. KEY:** Asymmetrical form.

BESANT - Developmental Phase, 1600 - 1400 B. P.

(Also see Avonlea, Glendo Dart, Pelican Lake and Samantha)

Knife River flint

Quartz

G5, $8-$15
Custer Co., NE

G5, $12-$20
Liberty Co., MT

G4, $8-$15
Liberty Co., MT

G5, $15-$30
Liberty Co., MT

G5, $15-$30
Phillips Co., MT

G5, $12-$20
Zortman, MT

Tip wear

G5, $12-$20
Liberty Co., MT

Quartzite

G6, $35-$60
Zortman, MT

G6, $40-$70
Zortman, MT

G6, $35-$60
Phillips Co., MT

LOCATION: Northern Plains states. **DESCRIPTION:** A small to medium size, high quality corner to side notched dart point. Notches occur close to the base. The base is straight to convex. Believed to be related to the *Avonlea* type and the earlier *Pelican Lake* type. Shoulders are tapered to straight.

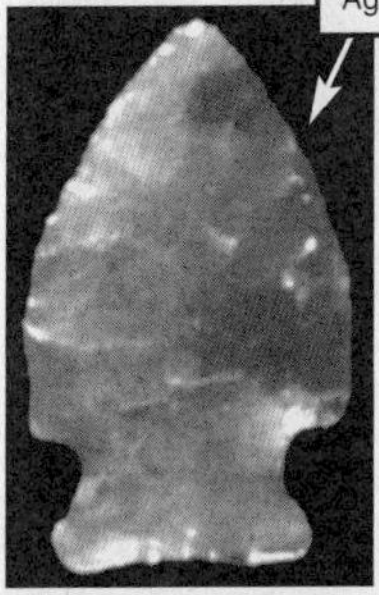

BESANT (continued)

Agate

Knife River flint

G6, $55-$100
Mountrail Co., ND

G8, $90-$175
Harding Co., SD

G6, $50-$80
Zortman, MT

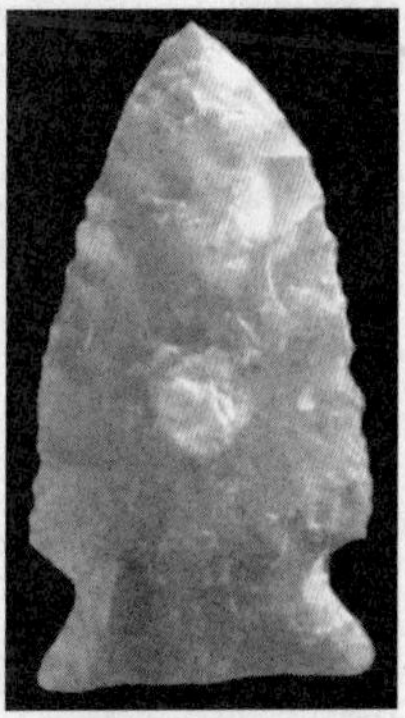

G7, $50-$80
Meagher Co., MT

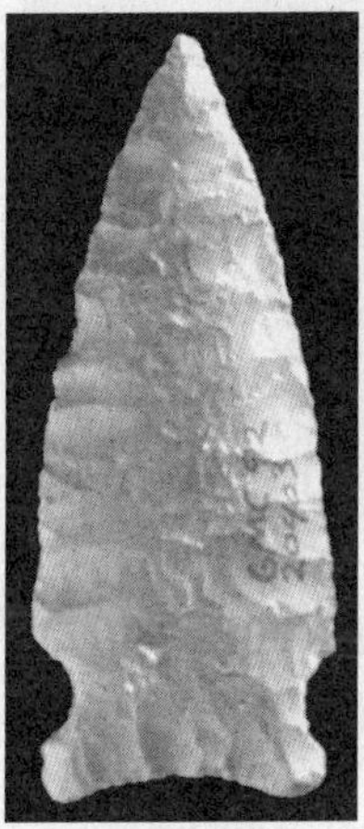

G9 $100-$190
Meagher Co., MT

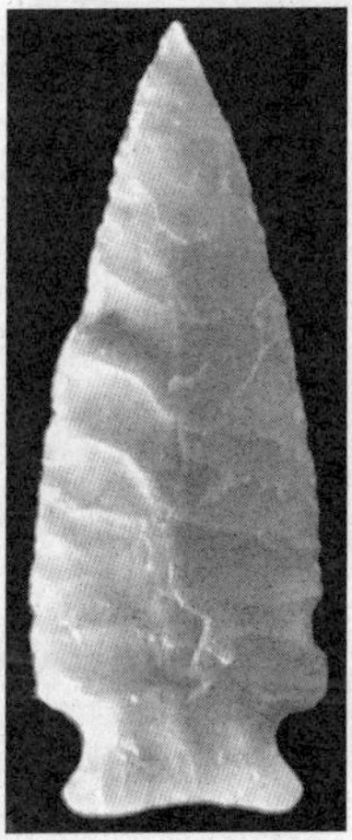

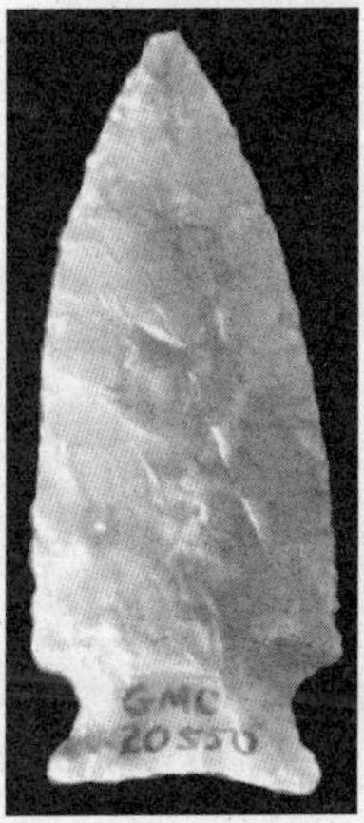

G9, $100-$190
Meagher Co., MT

G8, $90-$175
Meagher Co., MT

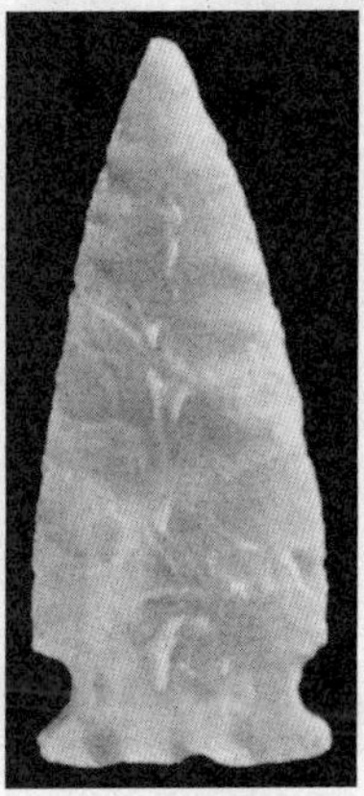

G8, $80-$150
Meagher Co., MT

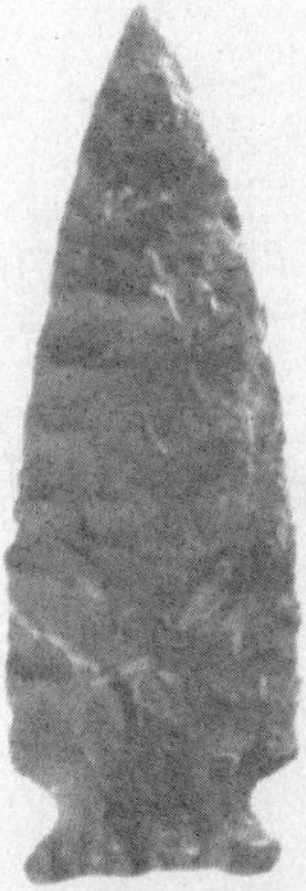

G9, $125-$200
Meagher Co., MT

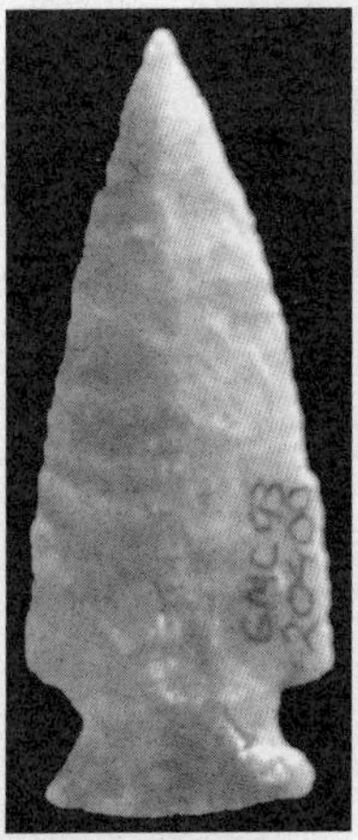

G9, $90-$175
Meagher Co., MT

G8, $80-$150
Cascade Co., MT

G8, $80-$150
Meagher Co., MT

NP

BESANT (continued)

Knife River flint

Best known example

G9, $100-$175
Mountrail Co., ND

Impact fracture

Tip nick

Collateral flaking

Basalt

G9, $85-$150
Meagher Co., MT

G3, $8-$15
Liberty Co., MT

G8, $90-$175
Meagher Co., MT

G10, $300-$425
Meagher Co., MT

BESANT KNIFE - Developmental Phase, 1600 - 1400 B. P.

(Also see Plains Knife)

G7, $150-$275
SD

Agate

LOCATION: Northern Plains states. **DESCRIPTION:** A medium to large size asymmetrical knife with wide corner to side notches. On some examples the blade leans heavily to one side. **I.D.KEY:** Symmetry of blade and notches.

G8, $175-$300
ND

BESANT KNIFE (continued)

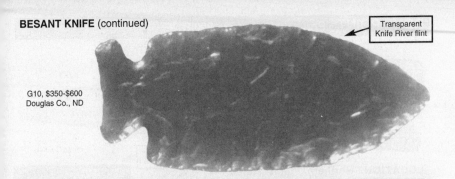

Transparent Knife River flint

G10, $350-$600
Douglas Co., ND

BILLINGS - Historic Phase, 300 - 200 B. P.

(Also see Desert Sierra, Emigrant and Mallory)

G8, $30-$50
Lewis & Clark
Co., MT

G8, $30-$50
Teton Co., MT

G8, $35-$65
Lewis & Clark
Co., MT

G8, $35-$65
Lewis & Clark
Co., MT

G9, $40-$75
Lewis & Clark
Co., MT

G8, $40-$75
Lewis & Clark
Co., MT

Black obsidian

G8, $45-$85
Lewis & Clark Co.,
MT

LOCATION: Northern Plains states. **DESCRIPTION:** A small, thin, tri-notched point with a straight to convex base. Blade edges can be serrated. Basal corners are sharp to pointed. Widest at the base, this point has excellent flaking, usually of the oblique transverse variety. If basal corners are rounded the type would be *Emigrant*.

BITTERROOT - Early to Middle Archaic, 7000 - 5000 B. P.

(Also see Archaic Side Notched, Hawken, Lookingbill and Logan Creek)

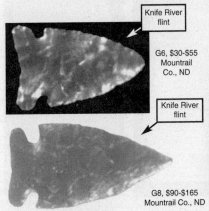

Knife River flint

G6, $30-$55
Mountrail
Co., ND

Knife River flint

G8, $90-$165
Mountrail Co., ND

LOCATION: Northern Plains states. **DESCRIPTION:** A small to medium size, short, broad, side notched point with a concave to convex base. Notches are placed at an angle into each side of the blade. Early Archaic flaking is evident on many examples.

G9, $90-$175
Mountrail Co., ND

Knife River flint

NP

BONE POINT - Proto Historic, 400 - 200 B. P.

(Also see Hafted Knife and Side Knife)

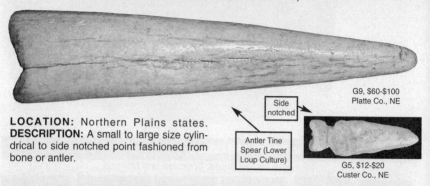

LOCATION: Northern Plains states.
DESCRIPTION: A small to large size cylindrical to side notched point fashioned from bone or antler.

Side notched

Antler Tine Spear (Lower Loup Culture)

G9, $60-$100
Platte Co., NE

G5, $12-$20
Custer Co., NE

BROWNS VALLEY - Transitional Paleo, 10,000 - 8000 B. P.

(Also see Agate Basin, Alder Complex, Allen, Angostura, Goshen and Lovell)

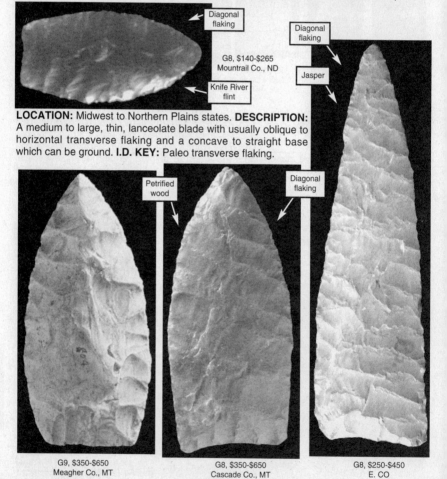

Diagonal flaking

G8, $140-$265
Mountrail Co., ND

Knife River flint

Diagonal flaking

Jasper

LOCATION: Midwest to Northern Plains states. **DESCRIPTION:** A medium to large, thin, lanceolate blade with usually oblique to horizontal transverse flaking and a concave to straight base which can be ground. **I.D. KEY:** Paleo transverse flaking.

Petrified wood

Diagonal flaking

G9, $350-$650
Meagher Co., MT

G8, $350-$650
Cascade Co., MT

G8, $250-$450
E. CO

BUFFALO GAP - Middle Archaic, 5500 - 3500 B. P.

(Also see Bitterroot and Desert Side Notched)

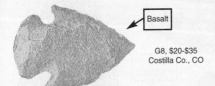

Knife River flint

G6, $25-$40
Mountrail Co., ND

G3, $12-$20
Teton Co., MT

Asymmetrical base

LOCATION: Northern Plains states. **DESCRIPTION:** A medium size, thin, side notched triangular point with a concave base. Basal corners are asymmetrical with one higher than the other, called a "single spur" base. **I.D. KEY:** Asymmetrical basal corners.

CAMEL BACK - Middle Archaic, 700 - 500 B. P.

(Also see Hog Back and Pelican Lake)

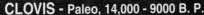

Basalt

G8, $20-$35
Costilla Co., CO

LOCATION: Colorado. **DESCRIPTION:** A small corner notched point with a broad, bulbous base. Larger than *Hog Back*. **I.D. KEY:** Bulbous base.

CLOVIS - Paleo, 14,000 - 9000 B. P.

(Also see Alder Complex, Allen, Angostura, Dalton, Folsom, Goshen and Plainview)

Flute channel

Petrified wood

G5, $175-$225
Pine Ridge, SD,
Bison kill site.

G6, $200-$350
Weld Co., CO

G6, $200-$350
E. CO

Patinated Knife River flint

G7, $1200-$2000
ND

Chert

NP

G7, $200-$350
Cascade Co., MT

G8, $500-$900
Sundance, WY

1067

CLOVIS (continued)

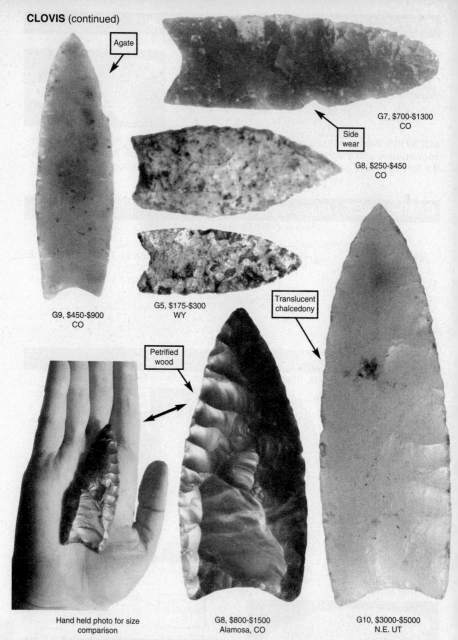

Agate

Side wear

G7, $700-$1300
CO

G8, $250-$450
CO

G9, $450-$900
CO

G5, $175-$300
WY

Translucent chalcedony

Petrified wood

Hand held photo for size comparison

G8, $800-$1500
Alamosa, CO

G10, $3000-$5000
N.E. UT

LOCATION: All of North America. **DESCRIPTION:** A medium to large size, auriculate, fluted, lanceolate point with convex sides and a concave base that is ground. Most examples are fluted on both sides about 1/3 the way up from the base. The flaking can be random to parallel. Clovis is the earliest point type in the hemisphere. It is believed that this form was developed elsewhere and brought here from Russia or Europe 14,000 years ago. There is no evidence of pre-Clovis technology here. The first Clovis find associated with Mastodon was in 1979 at Mastodon State Park, Jefferson Co., MO. in the Kimmswick bone bed carbon dated to 12,000 B.P. **I.D. KEY:** Paleo flaking, shoulders, baton or billet fluting instead of indirect style.

CLOVIS-COLBY - Paleo, 12,700 - 10,000 B. P.

(Also see Alder Complex, Allen, Angostura, Folsom, Goshen, Midland and Plainview)

LOCATION: Northern Plains states.
DESCRIPTION: Rebased *Clovis* points. A later form for the type. A medium to large size, auriculate, fluted, lanceolate point with convex sides and a deep, concave base that is ground. Most examples are fluted on both sides up to about 1/3 the way from the base. The flaking can be random to parallel. Has been found associated with bison and mammoth remains. *Clovis* is the earliest point type in the hemisphere. **I.D. KEY:** Paleo flaking, shoulders, baton or billet fluting instead of indirect style.

G8, $1000-$1800
Colby, WY. Mammoth kill.

Translucent

G9, $3000-$5000
Colby, WY.
Mammoth kill.

Flute channel showing hafting surface wear

Black obsidian

G10, $4500-$8000
N.E. UT, Fenn cache.

CODY KNIFE - Early to Middle Archaic, 8000 - 5000 B. P.

(Also see Base-Tang Knife, Corner Tang, Eden, Mid-Back Tang and Scottsbluff)

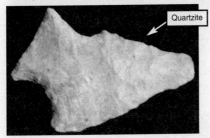

Quartzite

G5, $135-$250
E. CO

LOCATION: Northern Plains states.
DESCRIPTION: A medium to large size asymmetrical blade with one or two shoulders and a medium to short stem. Stem edges are ground on early examples. Made by the Cody complex people who made *Scottsbluff* points. Flaking is similar to the *Scottsbluff* type and some examples were made from *Scottsbluff* points. **I.D. KEY:** Paleo flaking, asymmetrical form.

NP

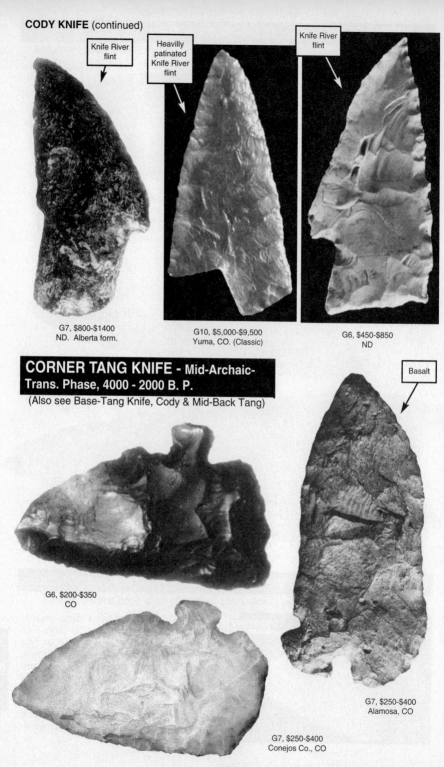

CODY KNIFE (continued)

Knife River flint

Heavilly patinated Knife River flint

Knife River flint

G7, $800-$1400
ND. Alberta form.

G10, $5,000-$9,500
Yuma, CO. (Classic)

G6, $450-$850
ND

CORNER TANG KNIFE - Mid-Archaic-Trans. Phase, 4000 - 2000 B. P.
(Also see Base-Tang Knife, Cody & Mid-Back Tang)

Basalt

G6, $200-$350
CO

G7, $250-$400
Alamosa, CO

G7, $250-$400
Conejos Co., CO

CORNER TANG KNIFE (continued)

LOCATION: Arizona northward. **DESCRIPTION:** A medium to large size knife that is notched at one corner producing a tang for hafting to a handle. Tang knives are rare and have been reproduced in recent years. **I.D. KEY:** Angle of hafting.

COTTONWOOD LEAF - Classic to Historic Phase, 700 - 200 B. P.

(Also see Archaic Triangle and Plains Triangular)

G2, $4-$6 CO

G2, $4-$6 CO

G2, $4-$6 CO

G6, $4-$6 Alamosa CO

Knife River flint

G6, $6-$12, Morton Co., ND

LOCATION: Arizona northward. **DESCRIPTION:** A small to medium size triangular arrow point with a rounded base.

COTTONWOOD TRIANGLE - Classic to Historic Phase, 700 - 200 B. P.

(Also see Archaic Triangle and Plains Triangular)

G2, $2-$4 CO

G2, $4-$6, CO

G4, $5-$9, CO

G3, $6-$10, CO

G2, $4-$6 Lander, WY

G2, $4-$6 CO

LOCATION: Arizona northward. **DESCRIPTION:** A small to medium size triangular arrow point with a straight, slightly convex or concave base. Basal corners tend to be sharp.

CUT BANK JAW-NOTCHED - Historic Phase, 300 - 200 B. P.

(Also see Buffalo Gap, Desert, Emigrant, Paskapoo, Pekisko and Plains Side Notched)

Parallel flaking

Black obsidian

Parallel flaking

G8, $20-$30 Teton Co., MT

G8, $20-$30 Lewis & Clark Co., MT

G8, $30-$45 MT

G9, $40-$75 Teton Co., MT

G9, $35-$60 Teton Co., MT

G9, $60-$100 Teton Co., MT

NP

CUTBANK JAW-NOTCHED (continued)

G4, $8-$15
Custer Co., NE

G5, $12-$20 (Classic)
Cascade Co., MT

G4, $12-$20
Great Falls, MT

G8, $35-$60
Lewis & Clark Co., MT

LOCATION: Northern Plains states. **DESCRIPTION:** A small size, thin, triangular arrow point with deep, narrow side notches that expand towards the center of the blade. Base can be straight to concave. Flaking is of high quality, usually oblique parallel struck from the edge to the center of the blade.

DALTON - Early Archaic, 10,000 - 8000 B. P.

(Also see Alder Complex, Allen, Clovis, Folsom, Goshen and Meserve)

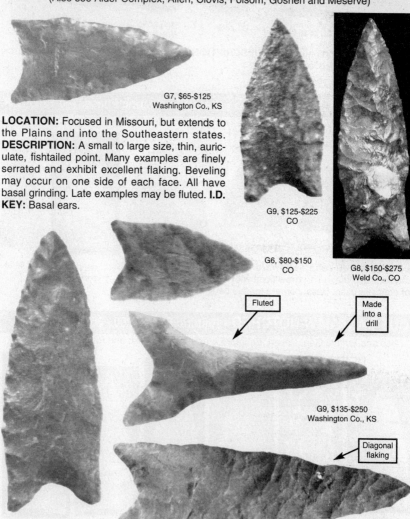

G7, $65-$125
Washington Co., KS

LOCATION: Focused in Missouri, but extends to the Plains and into the Southeastern states. **DESCRIPTION:** A small to large size, thin, auriculate, fishtailed point. Many examples are finely serrated and exhibit excellent flaking. Beveling may occur on one side of each face. All have basal grinding. Late examples may be fluted. **I.D. KEY:** Basal ears.

G9, $125-$225
CO

G6, $80-$150
CO

G8, $150-$275
Weld Co., CO

Fluted

Made into a drill

G9, $135-$250
Washington Co., KS

Diagonal flaking

G8, $185-$350
CO

G7, $185-$350
Nuckols Co., NE

1072

DALTON (continued)

Diagonal flaking

G9, $450-$850
Washington Co., KS

DESERT-GENERAL - Classic to Historic Phase, 700 - 200 B. P.

(Also see Bitterroot, Buffalo Gap, Cold Springs, Emigrant, Irvine, Plains Side Notched and Swift Current)

G9, $12-$20
Bent Co., CO

G9, $12-$20
Bent Co., CO

G9, $12-$20
Crowley Co., CO

G6, $8-$15
Bent Co., CO

G9, $15-$25
Bent Co., CO

G9, $15-$25
Bent Co., CO

G9, $15-$25
Crowley Co., CO

G6, $8-$15
Crowley Co., CO

G7, $8-$15
Alamosa, CO

G8, $12-$20
Bent Co., CO

Peno variety

G8, $12-$20
Bent Co., CO

G5, $8-$15
Alamosa, CO

G8, $20-$35
Bent Co., CO

G8, $12-$20
Crowley Co., CO

G7, $20-$35
Alamosa., CO

G9, $25-$45
Crowley Co., CO

LOCATION: Arizona northward and westward. **DESCRIPTION:** A small, thin, side notched arrow point with a straight, convex or concave base. Blade edges can be serrated. Reported to have been used by the Shoshoni Indians of the Historic period.

DESERT-SIERRA - Classic to Historic Phase, 700 - 200 B. P.

(Also see Billings and Emigrant)

LOCATION: Northern Plains to California to Arizona. **DESCRIPTION:** A small, thin, tri-notched arrow point with a concave to straight base. Blade edges can be serrated.

G9, $12-$20
Bent Co., CO

G8, $20-$35
CO

G10, $35-$65
CO

G10, $35-$65
CO

NP

DRILL - Paleo to Historic Phase, 14,000 - 200 B. P.

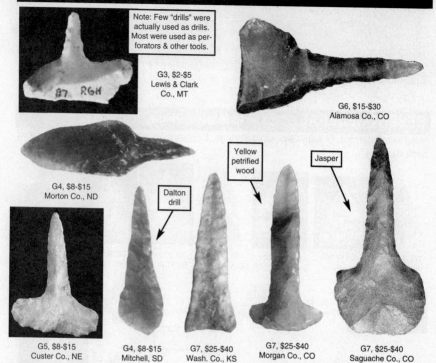

Note: Few "drills" were actually used as drills. Most were used as perforators & other tools.

G3, $2-$5
Lewis & Clark
Co., MT

G6, $15-$30
Alamosa Co., CO

G4, $8-$15
Morton Co., ND

Dalton drill

Yellow petrified wood

Jasper

G5, $8-$15
Custer Co., NE

G4, $8-$15
Mitchell, SD

G7, $25-$40
Wash. Co., KS

G7, $25-$40
Morgan Co., CO

G7, $25-$40
Saguache Co., CO

LOCATION: Throughout North America. **DESCRIPTION:** Although many drills were made from scratch, all point types were made into the drill form. Usually, heavily resharpened and broken points were salvaged and rechipped into drills. **I.D. KEY:** Narrow blade form.

DUNCAN - Middle to Late Archaic, 4500 - 2850 B. P.
(Also see Hanna)

Gem

G4, $20-$35
CO

G5, $8-$15
CO

G4, $8-$15
Sundance, WY

G5, $12-$20
Alamosa Co., CO

G5, $15-$25
Dillon, MT

G4, $12-$20
Pryor Mtns., MT

LOCATION: Northern Arizona to Canada and to eastern Oklahoma. **DESCRIPTION:** A small to medium size dart/knife point with a triangular blade and angular shoulders. The stem is straight with a V-shaped notch in the basal edge. Stem edges are usually ground. **I.D. KEY:** Straight stem edges.

DUNCAN (continued)

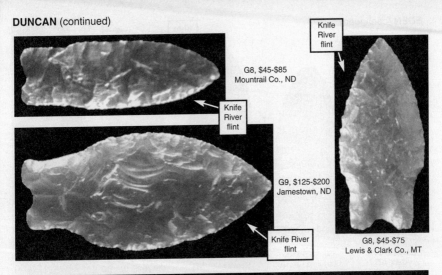

Knife River flint

G8, $45-$85
Mountrail Co., ND

Knife River flint

G9, $125-$200
Jamestown, ND

Knife River flint

Knife River flint

G8, $45-$75
Lewis & Clark Co., MT

EASTGATE - Developmental Phase, 1400 - 1000 B. P.

(Also see Mummy Cave, Pelican Lake and Rose Springs)

G9, $25-$40
Custer Co., NE

G9, $50-$80
Alamosa Co., CO

G5, $8-$15
Alamosa, Co

LOCATION: Great Basin to Northern Plains states. **DESCRIPTION:** A small, thin, tri-angular corner notched arrow point with a short parallel sided to expanding stem. Barbs can be pointed or square.

EDEN - Early Archaic, 9500 - 7500 B. P.

(Also see Agate Basin, Alder Complex, Angostura, Browns Valley, Hollenberg Stemmed and Scottsbluff)

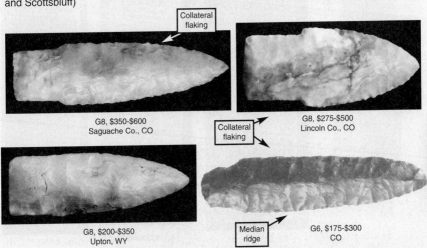

Collateral flaking

G8, $350-$600
Saguache Co., CO

Collateral flaking

G8, $275-$500
Lincoln Co., CO

G8, $200-$350
Upton, WY

Median ridge

G6, $175-$300
CO

NP

EDEN (continued)

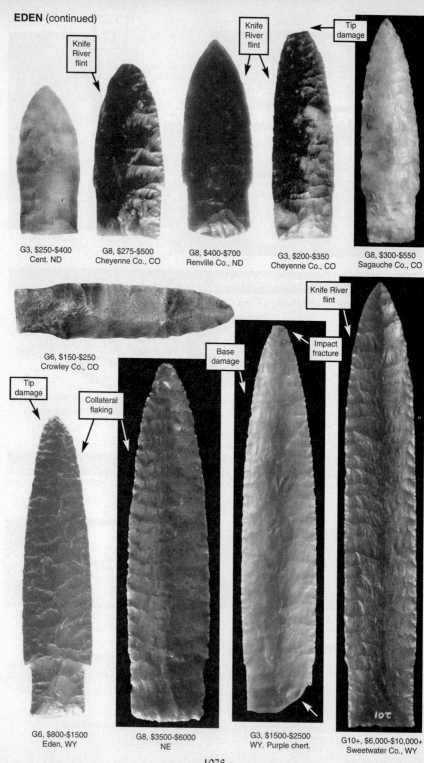

Knife River flint

Knife River flint

Tip damage

G3, $250-$400
Cent. ND

G8, $275-$500
Cheyenne Co., CO

G8, $400-$700
Renville Co., ND

G3, $200-$350
Cheyenne Co., CO

G8, $300-$550
Sagauche Co., CO

G6, $150-$250
Crowley Co., CO

Knife River flint

Base damage

Impact fracture

Tip damage

Collateral flaking

G6, $800-$1500
Eden, WY

G8, $3500-$6000
NE

G3, $1500-$2500
WY. Purple chert.

G10+, $6,000-$10,000+
Sweetwater Co., WY

EDEN (continued)

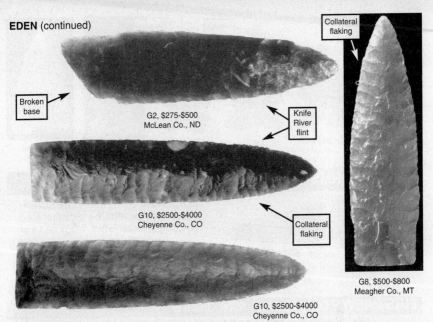

Collateral flaking

Broken base

G2, $275-$500
McLean Co., ND

Knife River flint

Collateral flaking

G10, $2500-$4000
Cheyenne Co., CO

G10, $2500-$4000
Cheyenne Co., CO

G8, $500-$800
Meagher Co., MT

LOCATION: Northern Plains to Midwestern states. **DESCRIPTION:** A medium to large size, narrow, stemmed point with very weak shoulders and a straight to convex base. Basal sides are parallel to slightly expanding. Many examples have a median ridge and collateral to oblique parallel flaking. Bases are usually ground. A Cody Complex point. **I.D. KEY:** Paleo flaking, narrowness.

ELKO - Mid-Archaic to Developmental Phase, 3500 - 2000 B. P.

(Also see Mummy Cave, Pelican Lake and Rose Springs)

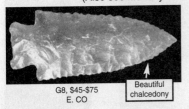

Photo by John Grenawalt

Beautiful chalcedony

G8, $45-$75
E. CO

G8, $25-$40
Sweetwater Co., WY, hand held to show translucency

G7, $15-$25
Weld Co., CO

LOCATION: Primarily Great Basin area. **DESCRIPTION:** A medium to large size, narrow, stemmed to side notched point with convex to straight sides. Bases are parallel to bulbous to expanding. Blade edges are usually serrated. **I.D. KEY:** Narrow blade, short stem.

EMIGRANT - Developmental Phase, 900 - 400 B. P.

NP

(Also see Billings, Bitterroot, Buffalo Gap, Cut Bank, Desert, Plains Side Notched and Swift Current)

LOCATION: Northern Plains states. **DESCRIPTION:** A small size, thin, tri-notched point with rounded basal corners. If basal corners are pointed the type would be Billings. **I.D. KEY:** Rounded basal corners.

EMIGRANT (continued)

Classic form

Obsidian

G7, $25-$40
MT

G8, $30-$50
CO

G8, $35-$65
Meagher Co., MT

G10, $35-$65
Meagher Co., MT

G9, $40-$75
Teton Co., MT

G9, $35-$65
Teton Co., MT

EXOTIC FORMS - Late Archaic to Developmental, 3000 - 1000 B. P.

LOCATION: Everywhere. **DESCRIPTION:** These may be exaggerated notching on other types, effigy forms or may only be no more than unfinished and unintentional doodles.

G3, $5-$8
Alamosa Co., CO

G4, $6-$12
Alamosa Co., CO

FIRSTVIEW - Early Archaic, 8700 - 8000 B. P.

(Also see Alberta, Alder Complex, Cody Knife, Eden and Scottsbluff)

Ground base & stem

Collateral flaking

Ground base & stem

Jasper

Tip has artificial restoration, reduces value

G8, $225-$400
Lincoln Co., CO

G8, $500-$800
Cheyenne Co., CO

G10, $1500-$2500
Rawlins, WY

G7, $275-$500
S.E. MT. Pryor Mtns.
Conglomerate

G10, $1700-$3000
Cheyenne Co., CO

Knife River flint

FIRSTVIEW (continued)

LOCATION: Colorado, Western Texas, New Mexico into Wyoming & Montana. **DESCRIPTION:** A medium to large size lanceolate point with slightly convex blade edges, slight shoulders and a rectangular stem. Shoulders are sometimes absent from resharpening. It generally exhibits parallel-transverse flaking. A variant form of the *Scottsbluff* type made by Cody Complex people. **I.D. KEY:** Weak shoulders, diamond shaped cross-section.

FOLSOM - Paleo, 11,000 - 9000 B. P.

(Also see Alder Complex, Clovis, Goshen, Green River, Midland and Milnesand)

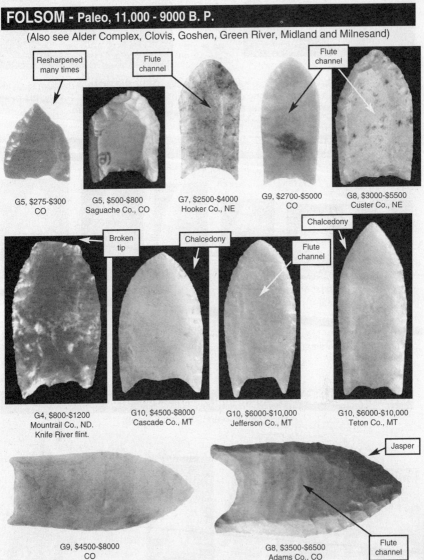

Resharpened many times

Flute channel

Flute channel

G5, $275-$300
CO

G5, $500-$800
Saguache Co., CO

G7, $2500-$4000
Hooker Co., NE

G9, $2700-$5000
CO

G8, $3000-$5500
Custer Co., NE

Broken tip

Chalcedony

Chalcedony

Flute channel

G4, $800-$1200
Mountrail Co., ND.
Knife River flint.

G10, $4500-$8000
Cascade Co., MT

G10, $6000-$10,000
Jefferson Co., MT

G10, $6000-$10,000
Teton Co., MT

Jasper

G9, $4500-$8000
CO

G8, $3500-$6500
Adams Co., CO

Flute channel

NP

LOCATION: Canada to the Southwestern states and to N. Indiana. **DESCRIPTION:** A very thin, small to medium sized lanceolate point with convex edges and a concave basal edge creating sharp ears or basal corners. Most examples are fluted from the basal edge to nearly the tip of the point. Blade flaking is extremely fine. The hafting area is ground. A very rare type. Modern reproductions have been made and extreme caution should be exercised in acquiring an original specimen. Usually found in association with extinct bison fossil remains. **I.D. KEY:** Flaking style (Excessive secondary flaking).

GARY - Late Archaic to Historic, 3200 - 300 B.P.

G6, $5-$10
Custer Co., NB

G6, $5-$10
Custer Co., NB

LOCATION: Oklahoma, Arkansas, Kansas, Nebraska. **DESCRIPTION:** A medium size, triangular point with a medium to long contracted, pointed to rounded stem. Rarely, the base is straight. Shoulders are usually tapered. **I.D. KEY:** Long, contracted stem.

GLENDO ARROW - Developmental Phase, 1500 - 800 B. P.

(Also see Pelican Lake)

Base
nick

| G5, $4-$8 Custer Co., NB | G6, $8-$15 Custer Co., NB | G6, $8-$15 Meagher Co., MT | G8, $20-$35 Meagher Co., MT | G8, $20-$35 Meagher Co., MT | G8, $20-$35 Bent/Crowler Co., CO |

LOCATION: New Mexico into Colorado, Wyoming, southern Idaho and Montana. **DESCRIPTION:** A small size, broad, corner to side notched arrow point with a straight to convex base.

GLENDO DART - Developmental Phase, 1700 - 1200 B. P.

(Also see Pelican Lake and Besant)

Tip
nick

| G5, $5-$10 Custer Co., NB | G3, $2-$5 Meagher Co., MT | G6, $20-$35 El Paso Co., CO | G6, $20-$35 Bent Co., CO | G7, $30-$50 Teller Co., CO |

LOCATION: New Mexico into Colorado, Wyoming, southern Idaho and Montana. **DESCRIPTION:** A medium to large size, broad, corner to side notched dart point with a straight to convex base. Some examples have a concave base producing ears. Believed to be related to the *Besant* point.

G9, $40-$75
Custer Co., NB

GOSHEN - Paleo, 11,500 - 10,000 B. P.

(Also see Alder Complex, Clovis, Folsom, Green River, Midland and Milnesand)

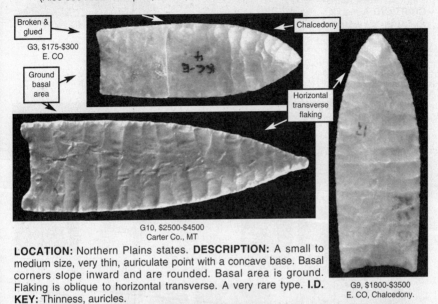

Broken & glued → G3, $175-$300 E. CO

Ground basal area →

Chalcedony

Horizontal transverse flaking

G10, $2500-$4500
Carter Co., MT

G9, $1800-$3500
E. CO, Chalcedony.

LOCATION: Northern Plains states. **DESCRIPTION:** A small to medium size, very thin, auriculate point with a concave base. Basal corners slope inward and are rounded. Basal area is ground. Flaking is oblique to horizontal transverse. A very rare type. **I.D. KEY:** Thinness, auricles.

GRAVER - Paleo to Archaic, 14,000 - 4000 B. P.

(Also see Scraper)

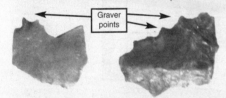

Graver points

LOCATION: Early man sites everywhere. **DESCRIPTION:** An irregular shaped uniface tool with sharp, pointed projections used for puncturing, incising, tattooing, etc.

G6, $5-$10 ea.
Alamosa, CO, Folsom site.

GREEN RIVER - Mid-Archaic, 4500 - 4200 B.P.

(Also see Alder Complex, Clovis, Folsom, Green River, Midland and Milnesand)

LOCATION: Mont., WY, CO, NE, NM & AZ. **DESCRIPTION:** A small, very thin, auriculate point with contracting, almost pointed auricles and a small, deep basal concavity. **I.D. KEY:** Thinness, auricles.

G6, $25-$40
N. UT

G7, $35-$65
Red Desert, WY

G1, $5-$10
Casper, WY.
Broken Back.

G1, $8-$15
Casper, WY,
Tip damage.

HAFTED KNIFE Transitional to Historic Phase - 2300 - 400 B.P.

(Also see Round-End and Square-End Knife)

HAFTEN KNIFE (continued)

LOCATION: Northern Plains states. **DESCRIPTION:** A medium to large size blade hafted into a wooden, antler or bone handle. Usually asphaltum and fiber were used in the hafting process.

IMPORTANT: Hafted Knife shown half size

G8, $450-$800
Custer Co., NE

HANNA - Middle to Late Archaic, 4500 - 2850 B. P.

(Also see Duncan)

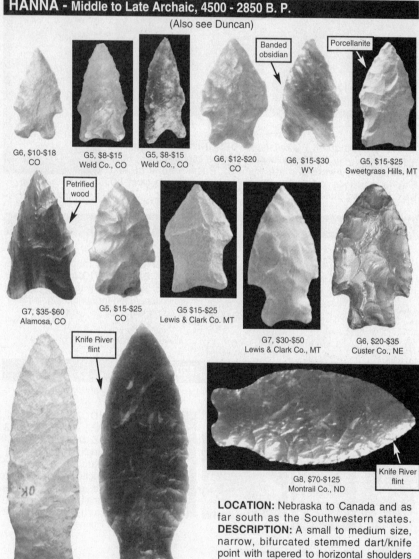

Banded obsidian

Porcellanite

G6, $10-$18
CO

G5, $8-$15
Weld Co., CO

G5, $8-$15
Weld Co., CO

G6, $12-$20
CO

G6, $15-$30
WY

G5, $15-$25
Sweetgrass Hills, MT

Petrified wood

G7, $35-$60
Alamosa, CO

G5, $15-$25
CO

G5 $15-$25
Lewis & Clark Co. MT

G7, $30-$50
Lewis & Clark Co., MT

G6, $20-$35
Custer Co., NE

Knife River flint

G8, $70-$125
Montrail Co., ND

Knife River flint

G7, $45-$80
N. OK

G10, $85-$165
Bottineau Co., ND

LOCATION: Nebraska to Canada and as far south as the Southwestern states. **DESCRIPTION:** A small to medium size, narrow, bifurcated stemmed dart/knife point with tapered to horizontal shoulders and an expanding stem which is notched to produce diagonally projecting rounded "ears". **I.D. KEY:** Expanding stem.

HANNA NORTHERN - Middle to Late Archaic , 4500 - 3000 B. P.

(Also see Duncan)

LOCATION: Northern Plains states to Canada. **DESCRIPTION:** A small to medium size, narrow, long stemmed point with tapered to horizontal shoulders. Stem can be bifurcated.

G6, $30-$50
Alberta, Canada

HARAHEY - Classic Phase, 700 - 350 B. P.

(Also see Archaic Knife)

Beveled on 4 sides

G6, $20-$35
SD

Petrified wood

ALL HARAHEYS SHOWN
HALF SIZE

G5, $125-$250
Prowers Co., CO

G6, $25-$45
SD

G8, $45-$85
SD

G7, $35-$65
SD

Beveled on 4 sides

Quartzite

Beveled on 4 sides

Jasper

Alibates chert

Beveled on 4 sides

G9, $400-$700
Hamilton Co., KS

G8, $150-$250
SD

G10, $250-$450
Elbert Co., CO

G10, $300-$500
Natrona Co., WY

LOCATION: Northern Plains states to Texas to Illinois to Canada. **DESCRIPTION:** A large size, double pointed knife that can be beveled on two to four edges. The cross section is rhomboid. **I.D. KEY:** Rhomboid cross section.

1083

HARRELL- Developmental to Classic Phase, 900 - 500 B. P.

(Also see Billings, Desert and Washita)

G9, $12-$20
Sherman Co., NE

G6, $8-$15
Bismark, ND

G9, $20-$35
Sherman Co., NE

G9, $20-$35
Buffalo Co., NE

G9, $30-$50
Custer Co., NE

LOCATION: Eastern Colorado, Arkansas, Oklahoma, Kansa, Nebraska and Missouri.
DESCRIPTION: A small size, thin, triangular arrow point with side notches and a basal notch. Bases are slightly concave to straight.

HAWKEN - Early to Middle Archaic, 7000 - 5000 B. P.

(Also see Besant, Logan Creek and Lookingbill)

G7, $150-$250
Meagher Co.,
MT

Tip
nick

G5, $60-$100
Custer Co., NE

G7, $120-$200
Teton Co., MT

G8, $275-$500
Meagher Co., MT

LOCATION: Northern Plains state. Type site is in Wyoming.
DESCRIPTION: A small to medium size, narrow point with broad, shallow side notches and an expanding stem. Blade flaking is of high quality and is usually the oblique to horizontal parallel type. Along with *Logan Creek* and *Lookingbill* this is one of the earliest side-notched points of the Plains states. **I.D. KEY:** Broad side notches, expanding base.

HELL GAP - Transitional Paleo, 10,900 - 9000 B. P.

(Also see Agate Basin, Angostura, Browns Valley and Rio Grande)

Alibates
flint

G5, $100-$180
Weld Co., CO

G8, $250-$400
E. CO

HELL GAP (continued)

Jasper

Alibates chert

G9, $400-$700
Custer Co., NE

G7, $185-$300
E. CO

Flattop chalcedony

G5, $65-$125
CO.

G7, $125-$200
Cascade Co., MT

G9, $450-$700
Lincoln Co., CO

Jasper

G10, $600-$1000
E. CO

Basalt

NP

G10, $500-$800
Alamosa Co., CO

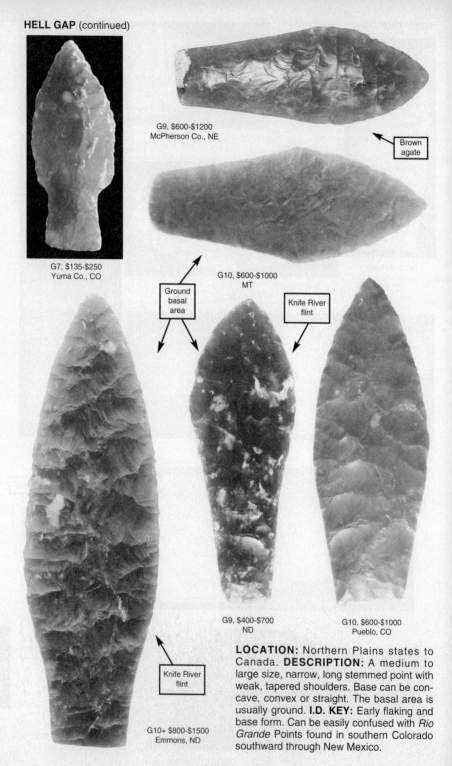

G9, $600-$1200
McPherson Co., NE

Brown agate

G7, $135-$250
Yuma Co., CO

Ground basal area

G10, $600-$1000
MT

Knife River flint

G9, $400-$700
ND

G10, $600-$1000
Pueblo, CO

Knife River flint

G10+ $800-$1500
Emmons, ND

LOCATION: Northern Plains states to Canada. **DESCRIPTION:** A medium to large size, narrow, long stemmed point with weak, tapered shoulders. Base can be concave, convex or straight. The basal area is usually ground. **I.D. KEY:** Early flaking and base form. Can be easily confused with *Rio Grande* Points found in southern Colorado southward through New Mexico.

HIGH RIVER - Developmental Phase, 1300 - 800 B. P.

(Also see Avonlea, Hog Back, Pelican Lake and Samantha)

G4, $4-$7
Chouteau
Co., MT

G4, $6-$10
Meagher Co.,
MT

G4, $4-$7 ea.
Ft. Peck Res.,
MT

G7, $8-$15
Meagher
Co., MT

G7, $8-$15
Lewis & Clark Co., MT

G8, $15-$20
Meagher Co., MT

LOCATION: Northern Plains states to Canada. **DESCRIPTION:** A small, thin, corner notched triangular arrow point with a straight to convex base. Basal grinding is evident on some specimens. **I.D. KEY:** Small corner notched point.

HOG BACK - Developmental Phase, 1300 - 1000 B. P.

(Also see Camel Back, High River, Mummy Cave, Pelican Lake and Samantha)

Tang nick   Obsidian   Agate   Tang nick

G5, $5-$8
S.W. CO

G6, $10-$15
Alamosa Co.,
CO

G6, $12-$20
S.W. CO

G7, $15-$25
CO

G4, $6-$12, CO

G6, $8-$15
CO

G87, $8-$15
Saguache Co., CO

LOCATION: Northern Plains states to Canada. **DESCRIPTION:** A small, thin, corner notched triangular arrow point with barbed shoulders and a convex base. The preform is ovoid and blade edges can be serrated. **I.D. KEY:** Small corner notched point, barbs.

Clear agate

G8, $15-$25
CO

G8, $15-$25
S.W. CO

G10, $50-$85
S.E. MT, Pryor Mountains

HOLLAND - Early Archaic, 9500 - 200 B. P.

(Also see Dalton, Eden, Firstview and Scottsbluff)

G7, $150-$275
Cheyenne Co., CO

Both faces of same
point shown ➡

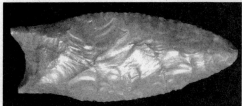

LOCATION: Northern Plains states. **DESCRIPTION:** A medium to large size lanceolate blade with weak to tapered shoulders. Bases can be knobbed to auriculate and are ground. **I.D. KEY:** Weak shoulders, concave base.

NP

HOLLENBERG STEMMED - Early Archaic, 9000 - 7500 B. P.

(Also see Eden and Scottsbluff)

G7, $150-$250
Washington Co., KS

G6, $75-$150
Washington Co., KS

G7, $150-$250
Washington Co., KS

G7, $150-$250
Washington Co., KS

G7, $150-$250
Washington Co., KS

LOCATION: Northern Plains states eastward into Nebraska and Kansas. **DESCRIPTION:** A medium to large size, narrow, stemmed point with tapered shoulders and a straight to convex base. Related to *Eden* and *Eden Eared*. Stem sides are parallel to slightly expanding. Stems are ground.

HORSE FLY - Developmental Phase, 1500 - 1000 B. P.

(Also see High River and Lewis)

G7, $18-$30
E. CO.
Petrified
wood.

LOCATION: Colorado. **DESCRIPTION:** A medium to large size, narrow, stemmed point with a short, expanding stem and a straight to slightly convex base. Shoulders are horizontal to slightly barbed. **I.D. KEY:** Short, expanding stem.

HUFFAKER - Developmental Phase, 1000 - 500 B. P.

(Also see Desert and Washita)

LOCATION: Midwest to Northern Plains states. **DESCRIPTION:** A small size, thin, arrowpoint with a straight to concave base and double side notches. Bases can have a single notch. **I.D. KEY:** Double side notches.

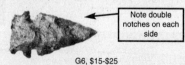

Note double
notches on each
side

G6, $15-$25
Bismark, ND

IRVINE - Developmental Phase, 1400 - 800 B. P.

(Also see Avonlea, Bitterroot, Emigrant, Plains Side Notched and Samantha)

IRVINE (continued)

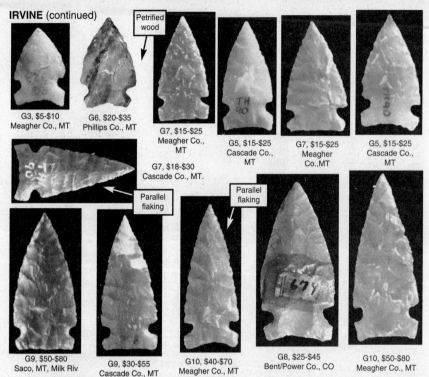

Petrified wood

G3, $5-$10
Meagher Co., MT

G6, $20-$35
Phillips Co., MT

G7, $15-$25
Meagher Co.,
MT

G5, $15-$25
Cascade Co.,
MT

G7, $15-$25
Meagher
Co.,MT

G5, $15-$25
Cascade Co.,
MT

G7, $18-$30
Cascade Co., MT.

Parallel flaking

Parallel flaking

G9, $50-$80
Saco, MT, Milk Riv

G9, $30-$55
Cascade Co., MT

G10, $40-$70
Meagher Co., MT

G8, $25-$45
Bent/Power Co., CO

G10, $50-$80
Meagher Co., MT

LOCATION: Northern Plains states. **DESCRIPTION:** A small size, thin, side notched arrow point with a concave base. The notching is distinct forming squarish basal ears. **I.D. KEY:** Square basal ears.

LANCET - Paleo to Historic Phase, 14,000 - 200 B. P.

(Also see Drill and Scraper)

G7, $8-$12 ea. (All hafted)
Lewis & Clark Co., MT

LOCATION: Everywhere. **DESCRIPTION:** Also known as a lammeler flake blade, it was produced by striking a flake or spall off a parent stone and was used as a knife for cutting. Some examples are notched for hafting. Recent experiments proved that these knives were sharper than a surgeon's scalpel. Similar to *burins* which are fractured at one end to produce a sharp point.

NP

LERMA - Mid-Archaic, 4000 - 3000 B. P.

(Also see Agate Basin, Angostura, Harahey & Mahaffey)

LERMA (continued)

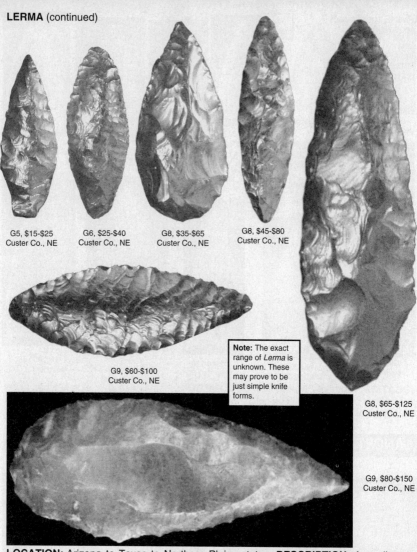

G5, $15-$25
Custer Co., NE

G6, $25-$40
Custer Co., NE

G8, $35-$65
Custer Co., NE

G8, $45-$80
Custer Co., NE

G9, $60-$100
Custer Co., NE

Note: The exact range of *Lerma* is unknown. These may prove to be just simple knife forms.

G8, $65-$125
Custer Co., NE

G9, $80-$150
Custer Co., NE

LOCATION: Arizona to Texas to Northern Plains states. **DESCRIPTION:** A medium to large size lanceolate point with a pointed to rounded base. Beveling can occur on one side of each face. **I.D. KEY:** Lanceolate form.

LEWIS - Developmental to Historic Phase, 1400 - 400 B. P.

(Also see Avonlea, High River, Irvine, Nanton, Paskapoo, Swift Current and Tompkins)

G5, $5-$10
Lewis & Clark Co.,
MT

G6, $12-$20
Phillips Co.,
MT

LOCATION: Midwestern to Northern Plains states. **DESCRIPTION:** A small to medium size, thin, side notched point with a convex to concave base. The width of the base is less than the shoulders and the basal corners are rounded. Some specimens have basal grinding.

LEWIS (continued)

Petrified wood

G6, $12-$20
Phillips Co., MT

G6, $6-$12
Phillips Co., MT

LOGAN CREEK - Early to Middle Archaic, 7000 - 5000 B. P.

(Also see Hawken and Lookingbill)

LOCATION: Midwestern to Northern Plains states. **DESCRIPTION:** A medium to large size, broad side-notched point with a straight, concave or convex base. Along with *Hawkens* and *Lookingbill* , this is one of the earliest side-notched points of the Plains states. Oblique to horizontal blade flaking is evident. **I.D. KEY:** Broad side-notches close to the base, early flaking.

Tip nick

Oblique flaking

Knife River flint

G7, $35-$65
Jefferson Co., NE

G5, $10-$15
Pryor Mtns, MT. Tip nick.

G8, $70-$135
Douglas Co., ND

G9, $150-$265
S.D

G9, $125-$200
N. OK

LOOKINGBILL - Early to Middle Archaic, 7000 - 5000 B. P.

(Also see Archaic Side Notched, Bitterroot and Logan Creek)

Patinated Knife River flint

NP

G7, $15-$25
Tongue Riv., WY

G8, $35-$65
Mountrail Co., ND

G8, $45-$85
Jamestown, ND

LOOKINGBILL (continued)

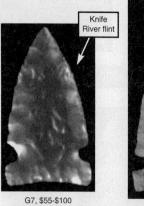

G7, $55-$100
Mountrail Co., ND

G9, $55-$100
Pryor Mtns., S.E. MT

G7, $45-$85
Sweetwater Co., WY

G9, $70-$135
Bottineau Co., ND

G10, $125-$200
Nashua, MT, Tongue River.

LOCATION: Midwestern to Northern Plains states. **DESCRIPTION:** A medium to large size, broad side-notched point with a straight to concave base. Along with *Hawkens* and *Logan Creek* this is one of the earliest side-notched points of the Plains states. **I.D.KEY:** Broad side notches close to the base, parallel flaking.

LOVELL - Early Archaic, 8500 - 8000 B. P.

(Also see Agate Basin, Alder Complex, Clovis, Folsom, Goshen and Green River)

G7, $40-$75
Mountrail Co., ND

G6, $40-$75
Brookings Co., SD

G6, $60-$100
Lewis & Clark Co., MT

G6, $40-$75
Lewis & Clark Co., MT

G5, $150-$250
Lewis & Clark Co., MT

LOCATION: Northern Plains states. **DESCRIPTION:** A small to medium size, narrow, unfluted lanceolate point with a straight to concave base. Blade edges recurve towards the base on most examples. Random to oblique or horizontal parallel flaking occurs. **I.D. KEY:** Form and basal constriction.

LOVELL (continued)

Patinated Knife River flint

G6, $125-$200
Bottineau Co., ND

Ground base

G10, $300-$550
Broadwater Co., MT

G5, $150-$250
WY

MAHAFFEY - Transitional Paleo-Early Archaic, 10,500 - 8000 B. P.

(Also see Agate Basin, Angostura and Lerma)

Petrified wood

G9, $250-$400
Alamosa, CO

LOCATION: Texas, Arkansas, Oklahoma, sou. Colorado. **DESCRIPTION:** A medium size, ovate point with a rounded base. Widest near the tip, the basal area is usually ground. Believed to be related to the *Agate Basin* point. **I.D. KEY:** Blade form.

MALLORY - Middle to Late Archaic, 4000 - 3000 B. P.

(Also see Billings, Bitterroot, Emigrant and Lookingbill)

G7, $35-$55
UT

Jasper

G8, $50-$90
Morgan Co., CO

NP

LOCATION: Northern Plains states. **DESCRIPTION:** A small to medium size, broad, tri-notched to side notched point with a concave base and sharp basal corners. Side notches occur high up from the base. **I.D. KEY:** Size and tri-notching.

MALLORY (continued)

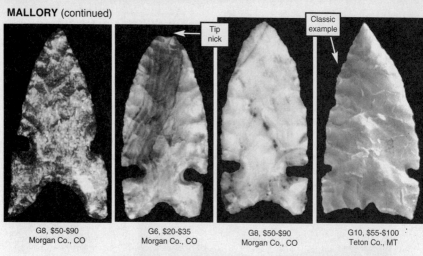

G8, $50-$90
Morgan Co., CO

G6, $20-$35
Morgan Co., CO

Tip nick

G8, $50-$90
Morgan Co., CO

Classic example

G10, $55-$100
Teton Co., MT

MCKEAN - Middle to Late Archaic, 4500 - 2500 B. P.

(Also see Folsom, Goshen, Green River and Lovell)

G5, $8-$15
CO

G5, $12-$20
CO

Jasper

G6, $30-$50
Morgan Co., CO

Pet. wood

Knife River flint

G7, $30-$50
Cheyenne, ND

G8, $40-$75
Weld Co., CO

G6, $30-$50
Morgan Co., CO

G6, $30-$50
Moorcroft, WY

Classic form

G9, $165-$300
Larimer Co., CO

G6, $40-$75
Weld Co., CO

G8, $45-$80
Lewis & Clark Co., MT

Yellow Pet. wood

Parallel flaking

G8, $60-$100
WY

G10, $175-$325
Cascade Co., MT

1094

MCKEAN (continued)

LOCATION: Northern Plains states. Type site is in N.E. Wyoming. **DESCRIPTION:** A small to medium size, narrow, basal notched point. No basal grinding is evident. Similar to the much earlier *Wheeler* points of the Southeast. Basal ears are rounded to pointed. Flaking is more random although earlier examples can have parallel flaking. **I.D. KEY:** Narrow lanceolate with notched base.

MESERVE - Early Archaic, 9500 - 8500 B. P.

(Also see Clovis, Dalton, Folsom, Goshen and Lovell)

G4, $25-$40
Alamosa, CO

G4, $25-$40
Crowley Co., CO

G9, $40-$70
UT

G4, $25-$45
E. CO

G10, $350-$600
E. CO, Alibates.

LOCATION: Throughout the U.S. from the Rocky Mountains to the Mississippi River. **DESCRIPTION:** A member of the *Dalton* family. Blade edges are straight to slightly concave with a straight to very slightly concave sided stem. They are basally thinned and most examples are beveled and have light serrations on the blade edges. Beveling extends to the basal area. **I.D. KEY:** Beveling into base.

MID-BACK TANG - Middle Archaic to Transitional Phase, 4000 - 2000 B. P.

(Also see Base Tang Knife, Cody Knife and Corner Tang)

LOCATION: Midwestern states and Canada. **DESCRIPTION:** A variation fo the corner tang knife with the hafting area occurring near the center of one side of the blade. **I.D. KEY:** Tang in center of blade.

G7, $250-$400
E. CO

NP

1095

MID-BACK TANG (continued)

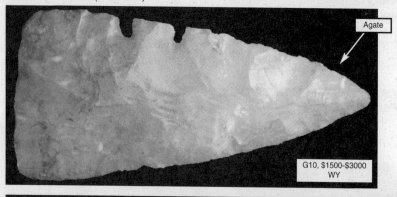

G10, $1500-$3000
WY

MIDLAND - Transitional Paleo, 10,700 - 9000 B. P.

(Also see Alder Complex, Clovis, Folsom, Goshen and Milnesand)

Ground basal area

Obsidian

Knife River flint

Chalcedony

G5, $25-$45
CO

G8, $125-$200
CO

G7, $125-$200
Caribou Co., ID

G6, $125-$200
Mountrail Co., ND

G8, $250-$450
E. CO

Knife River flint

G8, $350-$600
Alamosa Co., CO

Translucent chalcedony

G7, $175-$300
Mountrail Co., ND

G8, $300-$500
Alamosa Co., CO

G10, $600-$1000
S.W. MT, Ruby Valley.

Ground basal area

G9, $400-$700
Mountrail Co., ND

Knife River flint

LOCATION: Texas to the Northern Plains states. **DESCRIPTION:** A small to medium size, very thin, unfluted lanceolate point with the widest part near the tip. Believed to be unfluted *Folsoms*. Bases have a shallow concavity. Basal thinning is weak and the blades exhibit fine micro-edgework. **I.D. KEY:** Form and thinness.

1096

MIDLAND (continued)

G10, $1800-$2800
Dillon, MT

Ground basal area →

Black chert

MILNESAND - Paleo, 11,000 - 9500 B. P.

(Also see Alder Complex and Midland)

Resharpened many times

Yellow jasper

Ground basal area

Obsidian

Alibates chert

Knife River flint

G7, $150-$300
Washington Co, KS

G7, $250-$400
WY

Basal grinding

G7, $275-$450
Mountrail Co., ND

G7, $350-$600
E. CO

G9, $600-$1000
Marshall Co., KS

LOCATION: North Dakota to Colorado to west Texas and eastern New Mexico. **DESCRIPTION:** A lanceolate point with parallel to very slightly convex blade edges. The basal edge is straight and is beveled and ground, as are the stem edges. Thicker than *Midland*. **I.D. KEY:** Thickness and Paleo parallel flaking.

MOUNT ALBION - Early to Middle Archaic, 5800 - 5500 B. P.

(Also see Besant)

G3, $4-$8
Weld Co., CO

G4, $2-$5
CO

G3, $1-$3
CO

LOCATION: Southwestern states to Colorado. **DESCRIPTION:** A small to medium size, narrow, broad side notched point with a convex base. Shoulders are tapered. Basal corners are rounded.

NP

1097

MOUNT ALBION (continued)

G3, $4-$8
Weld Co., CO

G6, $6-$12
Weld Co., CO

G5, $6-$12
Weld Co., CO

G6, $5-$10
CO

G6, $6-$12
E. CO, Alibates.

MUMMY CAVE - Developmental Phase, 1400 - 1200 B. P.
(Also see Hog Back, Pelican Lake and Rose Springs)

Petrified
wood

G10, $70-$125
Weld Co., CO

G10, $80-$150
Sweetwater Co., WY

G10, $40-$70
Casper, WY.

LOCATION: Northern Plains states. **DESCRIPTION:** A small size, thin, corner notched dart point with sharp, pointed tangs and an expanding base. Blade edges can be serrated. **I.D. KEY:** Thinness, sharp tangs, early flaking.

NANTON - Developmental to Historic Phase, 1400 - 300 B. P.
(Also see Avonlea, Cut Bank, Pekisko, Irvine and Swift Current)

   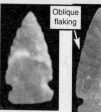 

Knife
Rv. flint

Oblique
flaking

Classic
example

G5, $4-$8
Choteau Co., MT

G6, $6-$12
Phillips Co., MT

G6, $6-$12
Phillips Co., MT

G6, $6-$12
Meagher Co., MT

G8 $15-$25
Meagher Co., MT

G10, $20-$35
Lewis & Clark Co., MT

LOCATION: Northern Plains states. **DESCRIPTION:** A small to medium size, thin, narrow, side-notched point with rounded basal ears. Basal grinding occurs on some examples.

OXBOW - Middle Archaic, 5500 - 5000 B. P.
(Also see Dalton and McKean)

LOCATION: Northern Plains states and Canada. **DESCRIPTION:** A small to medium size, side notched, auriculate point with a concave to bifurcated base that may be ground. Ears are squared to rounded and extend outward or downward from the base. Flaking is random to parallel oblique. **I.D. KEY:** Basal form.

OXBOW (continued)

G7, $20-$35
Weld Co., CO

G7, $20-$35
Cascade, WY

G7, $20-$35
Lewis & Clark Co., MT

G8, $50-$90
Divide Co., ND

Knife River flint

Knife River flint

Tip nick

G7, $45-$85
Jamestown, ND

G7, $20-$35
Divide Co., ND

G7, $35-$60
Mountrail Co., ND

G7, $20-$35
Broadwater Co., MT

G6, $30-$50
Mountrail Co., ND

Classic form

Knife River flint

Knife River flint

G10, $200-$350
Meagher Co., MT

G9, $175-$300
ND

G10, $80-$150
MT

G9, $150-$250
Bottineau Co., ND

Yellow petrified wood

Knife River flint

Knife River flint

G10, $65-$115
Mountrail Co., ND

G7 $40-$75
Mountrail Co., ND

G9, $90-$175
Mountrail Co., ND

NP

OXBOW (continued)

Colorful chert

Knife River flint

Patinated Knife River flint

G10, $150-$275
Bottineau Co., ND

G10, $125-$200
Pollack, SD

G8, $100-$180
Mountrail Co., ND

G10, $250-$400
Bottineau Co., ND

PALEO KNIFE - Transitional Paleo, 10,000 - 8000 B. P.

(Also see Lerma, Side knife)

G9, $65-$125
SD

Petrified wood

G9, $80-$150
Cascade Co., MT

1100

PALEO KNIFE (continued)

LOCATION: Plains states. **DESCRIPTION:** A medium to large size lanceolate blade finished with broad parallel flakes. These are found on Paleo sites and were probably used as knives.

PASKAPOO - Developmental to Classic Phase, 1000 - 400 B. P.

(Also see Cut Bank, Irvine, Nanton, Pekisko and Plains Side Notched)

G8, $10-$18
Lewis & Clark Co.,
MT

G6, $8-$15
Choteau, MT

G4, $4-$8
Teton Co., MT

G3, $2-$5
Custer Co., NE

G6, $8-$15
Lewis & Clark Co., MT

G8, $20-$35
Meagher Co., MT

G10, $25-$45
S.E. MT. Pryor
Mtns.

G8, $20-$35
Meagher Co.,
MT

G8, $20-$35
Lewis & Clark
Co., MT

G8, $15-$25
Ft. Peck Res., MT

G10, $30-$50
Lewis & Clark
Co., MT

G10, $30-$50
Cascade, MT

LOCATION: Northern Plains states. **DESCRIPTION:** A small to medium size, thin arrow point with side-notches that occur higher up from the base than other Plains forms. The base is straight with rounded corners and are usually ground.

PEKISKO - Developmental to Historic Phase, 800 - 400 B. P.

(Also see Buffalo Gap, Cut Bank, Nanton and Paskapoo)

G3, $3-$6
Custer Co., NE

G4, $5-$10
Custer Co., NE

G5, $5-$8
Custer Co., NE

G6, $5-$10
Meagher Co., MT

G8, $8-$15
Custer Co., NE

G7, $12-$20
Custer Co., NE

LOCATION: Northern Plains states. **DESCRIPTION:** A small to medium size, thin, triangular arrow point with v-notches on both sides above the base. Bases are concave to straight and are as wide as the shoulders. **I.D.KEY:** v-notches.

PEKISKO (continued)

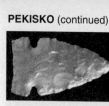

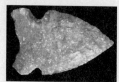

G9, $15-$25
Great Falls, MT

G9, $12-$20
Lewis & Clark Co., MT

G8, $8-$15
Custer Co., NE

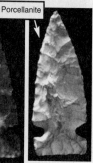

Glued

Porcellanite

G8, $25-$40
Hooker Co., NE

G8, $20-$35
Cascade Co., MT

G8, $20-$35
Great Falls, MT

G8, $15-$25
Custer Co., NE

G5, $15-$25
Teton Co., MT

G10, $30-$50
Cascade Co., MT

PELICAN LAKE - Middle Archaic to Transitional Phase, 3500 - 2200 B. P.
(Also see Camel Back, Desert, Elko, Glendo Arrow, Hog Back and Samantha)

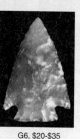

G6, $12-$20
Custer Co., NE

G6, $12-$20
Toole Co., MT

G6, $20-$35
E. CO

G6, $20-$35
Toole Co., MT

G6, $20-$35
Toole Co., MT

Petrified
wood

G8, $20-$35
E. CO

G6, $20-$35
Lewis & Clark Co., MT

G8, $25-$45
Custer Co., N

Hand held view
showing translucency;
photo by John Grenawalt.

LOCATION: Northern Plains states to Canada. **DESCRIPTION:** A small to medium size, thin, corner notched dart point with a straight to convex, expanding base. Tangs are usually pointed. Grinding may occur in notches and around base. Believed to have evolved into the *Samantha Dart* point. **I.D. KEY:** Sharp tangs.

PELICAN LAKE (continued)

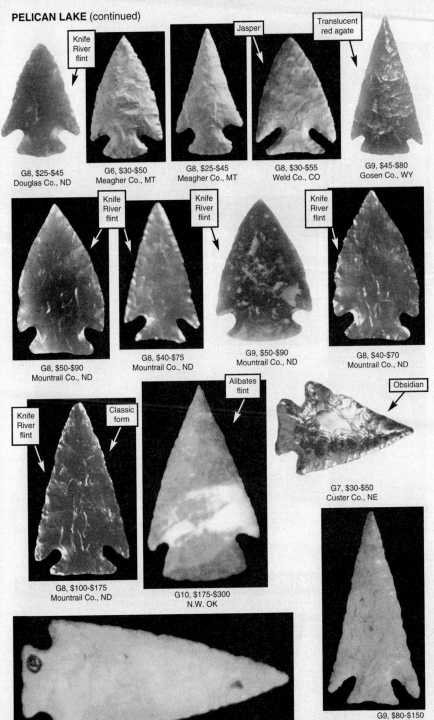

Knife River flint

G8, $25-$45
Douglas Co., ND

G6, $30-$50
Meagher Co., MT

Jasper

Translucent red agate

G8, $25-$45
Meagher Co., MT

G8, $30-$55
Weld Co., CO

G9, $45-$80
Gosen Co., WY

Knife River flint

Knife River flint

Knife River flint

G8, $50-$90
Mountrail Co., ND

G8, $40-$75
Mountrail Co., ND

G9, $50-$90
Mountrail Co., ND

G8, $40-$70
Mountrail Co., ND

Knife River flint

Classic form

Alibates flint

Obsidian

G7, $30-$50
Custer Co., NE

G8, $100-$175
Mountrail Co., ND

G10, $175-$300
N.W. OK

G9 $125-$200
N. OK

G9, $80-$150
N. OK

NP

1103

PELICAN LAKE (continued)

Knife River flint

G10, $80-$150
Casper, WY

G10, $90-$165
Custer Co., NE

G7, $55-$100
N.E. OK

Knife River flint

G10, $125-$200
Emmons Co., ND

G10, $125-$200
Mountrail Co., ND

G10, $125-$200
Bottineau Co., ND

G9, $100-$185
N. OK

G9, $80-$150
N. OK

PELICAN LAKE-HARDER VARIETY - Late Archaic, 3500 - 3000 B. P.
(Also see Base Notched, Mount Albion and Samantha Dart)

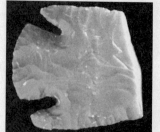

Broken back

G1, $2-$5
Casper, WY

G4, $20-$35
Custer Co., NE

Blunt tip

1104

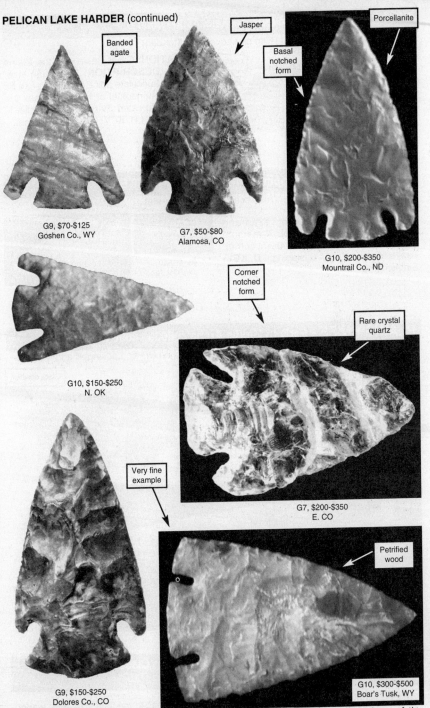

Banded agate

Jasper

Basal notched form

Porcellanite

G9, $70-$125
Goshen Co., WY

G7, $50-$80
Alamosa, CO

G10, $200-$350
Mountrail Co., ND

Corner notched form

Rare crystal quartz

G10, $150-$250
N. OK

G7, $200-$350
E. CO

Very fine example

Petrified wood

G9, $150-$250
Dolores Co., CO

G10, $300-$500
Boar's Tusk, WY

NP

LOCATION: Northern Plains states to Canada. **DESCRIPTION:** The earliest form of the type. A medium size corner to base notched point with a convex base. Tangs are sharp to squared and the base that is usually ground is convex.

PINTO BASIN - Mid to Late Archaic, 4500 - 4000 B. P.

(Also see Lovell and McKean)

LOCATION: Great Basin into the Plains states. **DESCRIPTION:** A medium size, narrow, auriculate point. Shoulders can be tapered, horizontal or barbed. Bases are deeply bifurcated. Ears can be parallel to expanding. **I.D. KEY:** Long pointed ears.

G4, $5-$10
Alamosa, CO

PIPE CREEK - Developmental Phase, 1200 - 1000 B. P.

(Also see Corner Tang Knife)

LOCATION: Colorado into Texas and Tennessee. **DESCRIPTION:** A medium size knife with a notch in one basal corner. Bases can be straight to sloping. **I.D. KEY:** Single corner notch.

G5, $5-$10
Custer Co., NB

G6, $12-$20
Weld Co., CO

PLAINS KNIFE - Early to Middle Archaic, 6000 - 4000 B. P.

(Also see Archaic Knife, Archaic Side, Bitterroot, Logan Creek, Lookingbill and Mallory)

LOCATION: Northern Plains states. **DESCRIPTION:** A medium to large size, triangular, side-notched point with a straight to concave base. Flaking is horizontal transverse. The widest part of the point is at the basal corners. Bases are ground. **I.D. KEY:** Size, wide base.

Black obsidian

G8, $35-$65
Lewis & Clark Co., MT

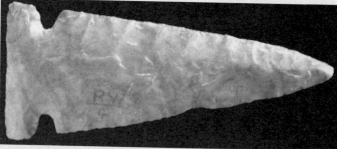

G9, $75-$140
Lewis & Clark
Co., MT

PLAINS SIDE NOTCHED - Developmental to Classic Phase, 1000 - 500 B. P.

LOCATION: Northern Plains states. **DESCRIPTION:** A small to medium size, thin, triangular, side-notched arrow point with a concave base. Notches are narrow and occur high up from the base. Basal corners are usually sharp and blade edges are not serrated. Many have been dug in buffalo kill sites. **I.D. KEY:** Notches.

PLAINS SIDE NOTCHED (continued)

(Also see Bitterroot, Buffalo Gap, Cut Bank, Desert, Nanton, Paskapoo and Pekisko)

G5, $5-$10
Bismark, ND

G6, $5-$10
Sherman Co.,
NE

G6, $5-$10
Sherman Co.,
NE

G6, $5-$10
Choteau Co.,
MT

G7, $8-$15
Bismark, ND

G6, $8-$15
Choteau Co.,
MT

G7, $8-$15
Bismark, ND

G7, $8-$15
Morton Co., ND

G7, $8-$15
Mobridge, SD

G7, $12-$20
Bismark, ND

G7, $12-$20
Bismark, ND

G7, $12-$20
Sherman Co.,
NE

G7, $12-$20
CO

G7, $15-$25
Morton Co., ND

Agate

G5, $12-$20
Morton Co., ND

G9, $20-$35
Sherman Co.,
NE

G7, $12-$20
Cascade Co.,
MT

G7, $12-$20
Morton Co.,
ND

G8, $15-$30
Sherman Co.,
NE

G8, $15-$30
Sherman Co.,
NE

G7, $20-$35
CO

G8, $15-$30
Teton Co., MT

G10, $30-$50
Hooker Co., NE

G8, $25-$45
MT

G8, $25-$45
Teton Co., MT

G8, $25-$45
Teton Co., MT

G8, $25-$45
Teton Co., MT

G7, $20-$35
Hooker Co., NE

G97, $40-$70
Teton Co., MT

NP

G10, $35-$65
MT

G10, $40-$70
Teton Co., MT

1107

PLAINS SIDE NOTCHED (continued)

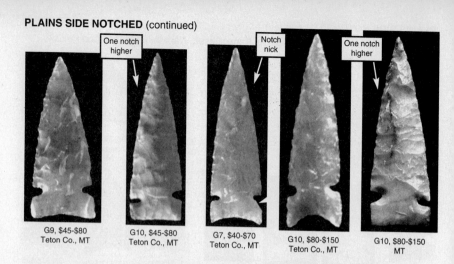

G9, $45-$80
Teton Co., MT

G10, $45-$80
Teton Co., MT

One notch higher

G7, $40-$70
Teton Co., MT

Notch nick

G10, $80-$150
Teton Co., MT

One notch higher

G10, $80-$150
MT

PLAINS TRIANGULAR - Developmental to Classic Phase, 1000 - 500 B. P.

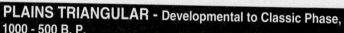

(Also see Archaic Triangle, Cottonwood)

G5, $5-$10
Bent Co., CO

G6, $12-$20
Alamosa Co., CO

G9, $15-$30
Bismarck, ND

G9, $18-$30
Bismarck, ND

G9, $15-$25
Bismarck, ND

G9, $15-$25
Bismarck, ND

Knife River flint

G9, $35-$65
ND

G9, $15-$25
E. CO

Agate

G9, $18-$30
Bismarck, ND

G8, $12-$20
Mobridge, SD

G9, $20-$35
Bismarck, ND

G9, $15-$45
Bismarck, ND

G8, $20-$35 ea.
S.E. MT, Pryor Mtns.

LOCATION: Northern Plains states. **DESCRIPTION:** A small size, thin, triangular arrow point with a straight to concave base and sharp basal ears. **I.D. KEY:** Small triangle

PLAINVIEW - Late Paleo to Early Archaic, 10,000 - 7000 B. P.

(Also see Clovis, Folsom, Goshen, Lovell and Midland)

Flat top Chalcedony

Hand held to show translucency. Photo by John Grenawalt

G7, $145-$275
Kiowa Co., CO

Collateral flaking

Ear nick

Petrified wood

Brown agate

G5, $55-$100
CO

G7, $150-$275
Kiowa Co., CO

G6, $140-$250
CO

G8, $165-$300
E. CO

G7, $350-$600
Elbert Co., CO

Jasper

G9, $1200-$2000
E. CO

Knife River flint

G10, $1500-$2400
ND

NP

LOCATION: Colorado eastward. **DESCRIPTION:** A medium to large size, thin, lanceolate point with usually parallel sides and a concave base that is ground. Some examples are thinned or fluted and are believed to be related to the earlier *Clovis* and contemporary *Dalton* type. Flaking is of high quality and can be collateral to oblique transverse. A cross type between *Clovis* and *Dalton*. **I.D. KEY:** Basal form and parallel flaking.

1109

PLAINVIEW (continued)

G7, $140-$275
E. CO

G7, $400-$750
E. CO

G7, $80-$150
MT

G9, $600-$1000
E. CO

PRAIRIE SIDE NOTCHED - Developmental Phase, 1300 - 800 B. P.

(Also see Irvine, Nanton, Paskapoo, Pekisko and Plains Side Notched)

G5, $6-$10
Mitchell, SD

G5, $7-$12
Mitchell, SD

G5, $12-$20
Phillips Co., MT

G6, $12-$20
Mitchell, SD

G6, $15-$25
Mitchell, SD

G5, $12-$20
Phillips Co., MT

G5, $12-$20
Phillips Co., MT

G6, $12-$20
Lewis & Clark Co., MT

G6, $12-$20
Lewis & Clark Co., MT

G7, $15-$25
Lewis & Clark Co., MT

G7, $20-$35
Lewis & Clark Co., MT

LOCATION: Northern Plains states.
DESCRIPTION: A medium size triangular arrow point with broad side notches. Bases are straight to slightly concave.

PRYOR STEMMED - Early Archaic, 8000 - 7000 B. P.

(Also see Eden eared and Hell Gap)

PRYOR STEMMED (continued)

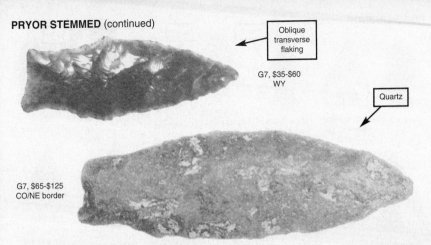

Oblique transverse flaking

G7, $35-$60
WY

Quartz

G7, $65-$125
CO/NE border

LOCATION: Northern Plains states into W. Oregon. **DESCRIPTION:** A medium size, short stemmed point with slight, tapered shoulders, a concave base and rounded basal corners. Flaking is usually oblique transverse. Stems are ground.

RIO GRANDE - Early Archaic, 7500 - 6000 B. P.

(Also see Hell Gap)

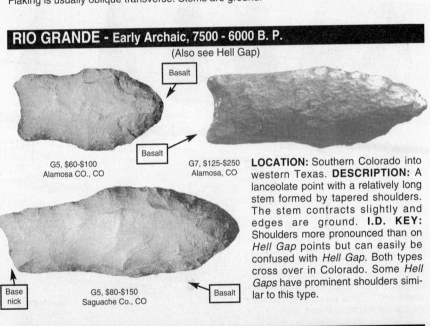

Basalt

Basalt

G5, $60-$100
Alamosa CO., CO

G7, $125-$250
Alamosa, CO

LOCATION: Southern Colorado into western Texas. **DESCRIPTION:** A lanceolate point with a relatively long stem formed by tapered shoulders. The stem contracts slightly and edges are ground. **I.D. KEY:** Shoulders more pronounced than on *Hell Gap* points but can easily be confused with *Hell Gap.* Both types cross over in Colorado. Some *Hell Gaps* have prominent shoulders similar to this type.

Base nick

G5, $80-$150
Saguache Co., CO

Basalt

ROSE SPRINGS - Developmental to Historic Phase, 1600 - 700 B. P.

(Also see Hog Back, Mummy Cave and Pelican Lake)

NP

G8, $8-$15
Custer Co., NE

G7, $8-$15
CO

G9, $15-$25
CO

G8, $12-$20
Saguache
Co., CO

G9, $15-$25
CO

G6, $5-$10
CO

G9, $15-$25
CO

ROSE SPRINGS (continued)

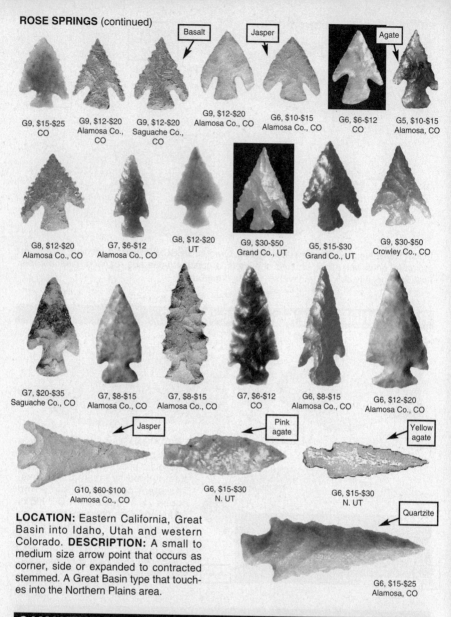

Basalt

Jasper

Agate

G9, $15-$25
CO

G9, $12-$20
Alamosa Co.,
CO

G9, $12-$20
Saguache Co.,
CO

G9, $12-$20
Alamosa Co., CO

G6, $10-$15
Alamosa Co., CO

G6, $6-$12
CO

G5, $10-$15
Alamosa, CO

G8, $12-$20
Alamosa Co., CO

G7, $6-$12
Alamosa Co., CO

G8, $12-$20
UT

G9, $30-$50
Grand Co., UT

G5, $15-$30
Grand Co., UT

G9, $30-$50
Crowley Co., CO

G7, $20-$35
Saguache Co., CO

G7, $8-$15
Alamosa Co., CO

G7, $8-$15
Alamosa Co., CO

G7, $6-$12
CO

G6, $8-$15
Alamosa Co., CO

G6, $12-$20
Alamosa Co., CO

Jasper

Pink agate

Yellow agate

G10, $60-$100
Alamosa Co., CO

G6, $15-$30
N. UT

G6, $15-$30
N. UT

Quartzite

LOCATION: Eastern California, Great Basin into Idaho, Utah and western Colorado. **DESCRIPTION:** A small to medium size arrow point that occurs as corner, side or expanded to contracted stemmed. A Great Basin type that touches into the Northern Plains area.

G6, $15-$25
Alamosa, CO

SAMANTHA-ARROW - Developmental Phase, 1500 - 1200 B. P.
(Also see Avonlea, High River, Lewis and Tompkins)

G3, $2-$5
Tiber Res., MT

G6, $15-$25
Tiber Res., MT

G7, $25-$45
Tiber Res., MT

G6, $18-$30
Tiber Res., MT

1112

SAMANTHA-ARROW (continued)

G6, $20-$35
Tiber Res., MT

G7, $25-$45
Meagher Co., MT

G6, $20-$35
Tiber Res., MT

Yellow agate

Petrified wood

G9, $50-$85
Tiber Res., MT

G10, $125-$200
Lewis & Clark Co., MT

G10, $70-$135
Mountrail Co., ND

G10, $70-$125
Meagher Co., MT

G10, $70-$125
Tiber Res., MT

LOCATION: Canada to the Northern Plains states. **DESCRIPTION:** A small to medium size, narrow, thin, corner to side-notched arrow point. Flaking is random to oblique transverse. Related and developed from the earlier *Samantha Dart* point. Shoulders are tapered and the stem expands to a straight to slightly concave base.

SAMANTHA-DART - Transitional to Developmental Phase, 2200 - 1500 B. P.

(Also see Besant and Pelican Lake)

Gem

G5, $12-$20
CO

G5, $12-$20
CO

G8, $20-$35
CO

G7, $20-$35
CO

G5, $12-$20
Lewis & Clark Co., MT

LOCATION: Canada to the Northern Plains states. **DESCRIPTION:** A medium to large size, corner to side-notched dart point with with horizontal, tapered or slightly barbed shoulders. Believed to have evolved from the *Pelican Lake* type changing into the *Besant* type at a later time.

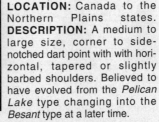

NP

G5, $12-$20
Sundance, WY

G4, $18-$30
Custer Co., NE

G9, $20-$35
CO

SAMANTHA-DART (continued)

G8, $60-$100
Renville Co., ND

Knife River flint

Knife form

G8, $20-$35
CO

G6, $12-$20
Lewis & Clark Co., MT

G8, $20-$35
Zortman, MT

G6, $25-$40
S.E. MT

Knife River flint

G8, $40-$75
Harding Co., SD

G5, $30-$50
Lewis & Clark Co., MT

G7, $35-$65
Lewis & Clark Co., MT

G7, $60-$100
Teton Co., MT

SATTLER - Developmental to Historic Phase, 1400 - 400 B. P.
(Also see Rose Springs)

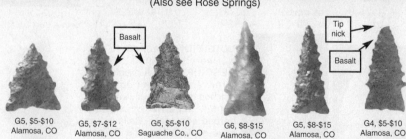

Basalt

Tip nick

Basalt

G5, $5-$10
Alamosa, CO

G5, $7-$12
Alamosa, CO

G5, $5-$10
Saguache Co., CO

G6, $8-$15
Alamosa, CO

G5, $8-$15
Alamosa, CO

G4, $5-$10
Alamosa, CO

LOCATION: Sou. Colorado. **DESCRIPTION:** A small size, thin, serrated arrow point with an expanded base. Base is straight to concave. Tips are sharp.

SATTLER (continued)

Basalt

Basalt

G6, $8-$15
Alamosa, CO

G6, $8-$15
Alamosa, CO

G6, $8-$15
Alamosa, CO

G8, $12-$20
Alamosa, CO

G6, $8-$15
Seguache Co., CO

G8, $15-$25
Alamosa, CO

G8, $12-$20
Costilla Co.,
CO

SCOTTSBLUFF I - Early Archaic, 9500 - 7000 B. P.

(Also see Alberta, Cody Knife, Eden, Firstview, Hell Gap & Hollenberg Stemmed)

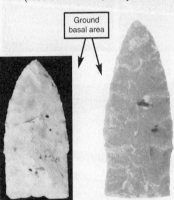

Ground
basal area

Agate

G5, $125-$200
El Paso Co., CO

G6, $225-$400
CO

G7, $165-$300
Broadwater Co., MT

G6, $150-$300
E. CO

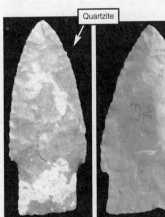

Quartzite

Oblique
transverse
flaking

G8, $250-$450
E. CO

G7, $250-$450
Broadwater Co., MT

G8, $250-$400
Upton, WY

G7, $350-$650
Broadwater Co., MT

NP

1115

SCOTTSBLUFF I (continued)

G9, $275-$500
Crowley Co., CO

G8, $400-$700
Pueblo Co., CO

G9, $400-$700
Eden, WY

Petrified
wood

G8, $400-$750
Lincoln Co., CO

Quartzite

G10, $1400-$2250
E. CO

LOCATION: Midwestern states to Texas and Colorado. **DESCRIPTION:** A medium to large size, broad, stemmed point with parallel to convex sides and weak shoulders. The stem is parallel sided or expands slightly. The base is straight to concave. Made by the Cody complex people. Flaking is of the high quality parallel horizontal to oblique transverse type. Bases are ground. **I.D. KEY:** Broad stem, weak shoulders.

SCOTTSBLUFF II - Early Archaic, 9500 - 7000 B. P.

(Also see Alberta, Cody Knife, Eden and Hell Gap)

G3, $40-$75
E. SD

G5, $125-$200
Phillips Co., MT

1116

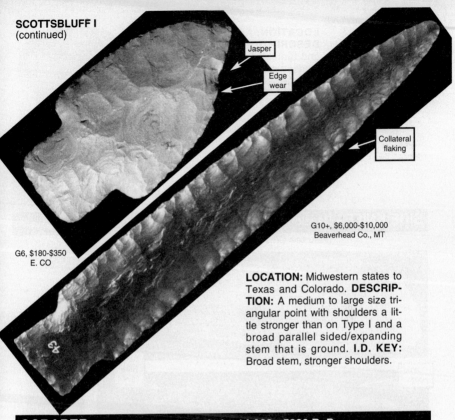

SCOTTSBLUFF I
(continued)

Jasper

Edge wear

Collateral flaking

G10+, $6,000-$10,000
Beaverhead Co., MT

G6, $180-$350
E. CO

LOCATION: Midwestern states to Texas and Colorado. **DESCRIPTION:** A medium to large size triangular point with shoulders a little stronger than on Type I and a broad parallel sided/expanding stem that is ground. **I.D. KEY:** Broad stem, stronger shoulders.

SCRAPER - Paleo to Middle Archaic, 14,000 - 5000 B. P.

(Also see Drill, Hafted Knife, Paleo Knife and Side knife)

15-$25
Park Co., MT

NP

1117

SCRAPER (continued)

G2, $1-$3
Mitchell, SD

Thumb scraper

LOCATION: All early-man sites.
DESCRIPTION: Thumb, duckbill and turtleback forms are small to medium size, thick, ovoid shaped, uniface, scraping tools that are steeply beveled, especially at the broadest end. Side scrapers are long hand-held uniface flakes with beveling on all blade edges of one face. Scraping was done primarily from the sides of these blades. Many of these tools were hafted.

Hafted scraper

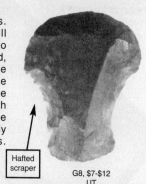

G8, $7-$12
UT

SIDE KNIFE - Develop. to Historic Phase, 1000 - 300 B. P.

(Also see Crescent, Scraper & Square-End Knife)

G6, $20-$35
SD

Cutting edge

Knife River flint

G7, $30-$50
Morton Co., ND

G7, $30-$55
SD

G6, $25-$45
Cascade Co., MT

G6, $20-$35
SD

1118

SIDE KNIFE (continued)

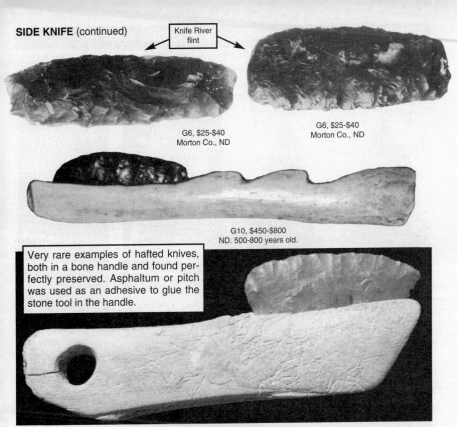

Knife River flint

G6, $25-$40
Morton Co., ND

G6, $25-$40
Morton Co., ND

G10, $450-$800
ND. 500-800 years old.

Very rare examples of hafted knives, both in a bone handle and found perfectly preserved. Asphaltum or pitch was used as an adhesive to glue the stone tool in the handle.

G10, $650-$1000
E. CO. Bone handle, stone blade.

LOCATION: Northern Plains states. **DESCRIPTION:** Side Knives were generally hafted into bison rib-bone handles as illustrated above..Gut and plant fibers were also used when needed to bind the hafting. Also known as *Round-End Knife.*

SIDE NOTCH (See Archaic Side Notch)

SIMONSEN - Early Archaic, 8500 - 7000 B. P.
(Also see Besant and Bitterroot)

G6, $25-$40
Cascade Co., MT

G8, $35-$60
Custer Co., NE

NP

LOCATION: Canada to the Northern Plains states. **DESCRIPTION:** A small to medium size, side-notched point with a concave base. Notching can be shallow to deep. Basal ears can be rounded to squared.

SONOTA - Developmental to Classic Phase, 1000 - 400 B. P.

(Also see Besant and Bitterroot)

Knife River flint

Excellent example

Knife River flint

Knife River flint

G8, $55-$100
Mountrail Co., ND

G10, $150-$250
Bottineau Co., ND

G9, $200-$350
McKenzie Co., ND

G9, $200-$350
McClean Co., ND

LOCATION: Canada to the Northern Plains states. **DESCRIPTION:** A small to medium size, thin, side to corner-notched point with a concave base. Base usually is not as wide as the shoulders.

STOTT - Developmental to Classic Phase, 1300 - 600 B. P.

(Also see Besant, Bitterroot, Nanton, Paskapoo, Pekisko and Tompkins)

G5, $4-$8
Custer Co., NE

G6, $5-$10
Phillips Co., MT

G6, $5-$10
Lewis & Clark Co., MT

G6, $4-$8
Lewis & Clark Co., MT

Tip nick

Moss agate

G5, $4-$8
Meagher Co., MT

G6, $5-$10
Custer Co. NE

G9, $25-$45
Sweetwater Co., WY

Hand held showing translucency. Photo by John Grenawalt.

LOCATION: Canada to the Northern Plains states. **DESCRIPTION:** A small size, v-notched point with a convex base. Size of base is large in proportion the the blade size. **I.D. KEY:** V-notches, large base.

SWIFT CURRENT - Developmental Phase, 1300 - 800 B. P.

(Also see Avonlea, Cut Bank, Irvine and Pekisko)

Petrified wood

Knife River flint

G6, $12-$20
Phillips Co., MT

G6, $15-$25
Phillips Co., MT

G5, $8-$15
Augusta, MT

G6, $12-$20
Saco, MT, Milk Rv.

G6, $15-$30
Phillips Co., MT

G6, $15-$30
Saco, MT, Milk Rv.

From a Buffalo jump kill site

G6, $15-$30
Nelson Res., MT

G7, $15-$30
Lewis & Clark Co., MT

G6, $15-$25
Saco, MT

G7, $15-$30
Cascade Co., MT

G7, $15-$30
Saco, MT, Milk Rv.

G7, $15-$30
Great Falls, MT

G7, $25-$45
Lewis & Clark Co., MT

G8, $25-$40
Great Falls, MT

G8, $30-$50
Saco, MT

Classic form

Variant base form

G7, $25-$45
Lewis & Clark Co., MT

G9, $25-$45
Phillips Co., MT

G8, $30-$55
Lewis & Clark Co., MT

G8, $30-$55
Meagher Co., MT

G8, $25-$45
Lewis & Clark Co., MT

NP

LOCATION: Northern Plains states. **DESCRIPTION:** A small size, thin, side notched arrow point with a concave base. Blade edges can be serrated. Ancient buffalo jump kill sites have been discovered in the Plains states where this type is found. Early man drove the buffalo over cliffs and into corrals for easy killing. **I.D. KEY:** Drooping ears.

TOMPKINS - Developmental Phase, 1200 - 800 B. P.

(Also see Cut Bank, High River, Irvine, Nanton, Pekisko, Paskapoo, Prairie Side Notched and Swift Current)

G6, $4-$8
Phillips Co., MT

G6, $4-$8
Choteau Co., MT

G6, $5-$10
Phillips Co., MT.

Knif. Riv. flint

G6, $4-$8
Phillips Co., MT

LOCATION: Northern Plains states. **DESCRIPTION:** A small size, thin, serrated, side to corner notched arrow point with a concave base. On some examples, one notch is from the corner and the other definitely from the side. Some have basal grinding. Found on ancient Buffalo jump kill sites.

TRADE POINTS - Classic to Historic Phase, 400 - 170 B. P.

These points were made of copper, iron, and steel and were traded to the Indians by the French, British and others from the 1600s to the 1800s. Examples have been found all over the United States. **NOTE:** All points with * were probably blacksmith made trade points.

Copper   Broken tip

G5, $25-$40
Mountrail Co., ND

G5, $25-$40
Custer Co., NE

G5, $25-$40
Custer Co., NE

Copper

G9, $45-$85
Mountrail Co., ND

All above points were probably made by the indians.

G6, $25-$45
Lewis & Clark Co., MT

G6, $35-$65
Custer Co., NE

G6, $25-$40
Lewis & Clark Co., MT

G6, $40-$75
Custer Co., NE

"Little Big Horn" form

*G9, $125-$200
Meagher Co., MT

TRADE POINTS (continued)

"Little Big Horn" form

Lettering adds value

*G7, $60-$100
Custer Co., NE

*G7, $80-$150
Custer Co., NE

*G8, $80-$150
Custer Co., NE

*G10, $150-$275
Cascade Co., MT

*G9, $90-$175
Meagher Co., MT

"Little Big Horn" form

*G10, $175-$300
Cheyenne, MT.
Little Big Horn site. ca. 1850/Iron.

Note: All points with * were probably blacksmith made trade points.

WASHITA - Classic Phase, 800 - 400 B. P.

(Also see Desert and Harrell)

G9, $8-$15   G9, $8-$15   G9, $8-$15   G9, $8-$15   G9, $12-$20   G9, $12-$20   G9, $12-$20

NP

All above from Bent/Crowley Co., CO

LOCATION: Kansas, E. Colorado northward into the Dakotas. **DESCRIPTION:** A small size, thin, side notched arrow point with a concave base and sharp basal corners. Notches usually occur far up from the base. Can be confused with the Desert series.

WASHITA (continued)

G7, $5-$10   G7, $5-$10   G9, $8-$15   G8, $12-$20   G9, $15-$30   G10, $30-$50   G10, $30-$50

All above from Bent/Crowley Co., CO

G6, $5-$10
CO

G10, $35-$60
Hooker Co., KS

G9, $30-$55
Weld Co., CO

WASHITA-NORTHERN - Developmental to Classic Phase, 800 - 400 B. P.

(Also see Desert)

G6, $15-$25
Cascade Co., MT

G6, $15-$25
Cascade Co., MT
Classic form

G6, $15-$25
Lewis & Clark Co., MT

G6, $18-$30
Bismark, ND

G7, $8-$15
ND
Knife River flint

LOCATION: Northern Plains states. **DESCRIPTION:** A small size, thin, triangular side notched arrow point with a concave base. Basal area is usually large in proportion to the blade size. Basal corners are sharp. Notches are narrow.

YONKEE - Middle to Late Archaic, 4500 - 2500 B. P.

(Also see Besant and Bitterroot)

  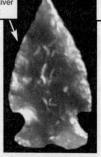 

Knife River flint

Classic form

G6, $25-$40
Custer Co., NE

G6, $20-$35
Moorcroft, WY

G7, $35-$60
Mountrail Co., ND

G7, $40-$75
Lewis & Clark Co., MT

LOCATION: Northern Plains states. **DESCRIPTION:** A medium size, narrow point that is corner or side-notched. The base is concave to bifurcated forming ears. Shoulders are slightly barbed to horizontal. Found in conjunction with McKean points on Bison jump-kill sites. **I.D. KEY:** Lobed ears.

GREAT BASIN WESTWARD SECTION:

This section includes point types from the following states:
Alaska, California, Idaho, Nevada, Oregon, Utah, Washington

The points in this section are arranged in alphabetical order and are shown **actual size**. All types are listed that were available for photographing. Any missing types will be added to future editions as photographs become available. We are always interested in receiving sharp, black and white or color glossy photos or color slides of your collection. Be sure and include a ruler in the photograph so that proper scale can be determined.

Lithics: Materials employed in the manufacture of projectile points from this region are: obsidian, basalt, dacite and ignumbrite with lesser amounts of agate, jasper, chert, chalcedony, Jadeite, Nephrite, opal, petrified wood.

Important sites: Clovis: Borax Lake, N. California, Wenatchee Clovis cache, WA.

Regional Consultants:
John Byrd, Jim Hogue

Special Advisors:
Mark Berreth, John Cockrell, Bill & Donna Jackson,
Randy McNeice, Ben Stermer, Jeb Taylor
Gregory J. Truesdell

GB

GREAT BASIN WESTWARD POINT TYPES
(Archaeological Periods)

PALEO (14,000 B. P. - 8,000 B. P.)

Agate Basin	Cougar Mountain	Haskett	Mesa	Spedis I
Black Rock Concave	Crescent	Kennewick	Paleo Knife	Spedis II
Chindadn	Drill	Lake Mohave	Pieces Esquillees	Sub-Triangular
Chopper	Folsom	Lancet	Scraper	Tulare Lake
Clovis	Graver	Lind Coulee	Silver Lake	Windust

EARLY ARCHAIC (10,500 B. P. - 5,500 B. P.)

Alberta	Cody Complex Knife	Jalama Side Notched	Pryor Stemmed
Atlatl Valley Triangular	Early Eared	Nightfire	Salmon River
Base Tang Knife	Early Leaf	Northern Side Notched	Sierra Stemmed
Bitterroot	Excelsior	Owl Cave	Tulare Lake Bi-Point
Cascade	Firstview	Palisades	Wahmuza
Cascade Knife	Hawken	Parman	Wendover
Cascade Shouldered	Humboldt Basal Notched	Perforator	Wildcat Canyon
Chilcotin Plateau	Humboldt Constricted	Pinto Basin	
Chumash Knife	Base	Pinto Basin Sloping	
Cody Complex	Humboldt Triangular	Shoulder	

MIDDLE ARCHAIC (5,500 B. P. - 3,300 B. P.)

Big Valley Stemmed	Coquille Narrowneck	McKee Uniface	Triangular Knife
Bullhead	Coquille Side Notched	Portage	Triple "T"
Cold Springs	Gatecliff	Rabbit Island	Vandenberg Contracting
Coquille Broadneck	Gold Hill	Rossi Square-Stemmed	Stem
Coquille Knife	McGillivray	Square-End Knife	Willits Side Notched

LATE ARCHAIC (3,500 B. P. - 2,300 B. P.)

Ahsahka	Notched	Martis	Priest Rapids	Tuolumne Notched
Año Nuevo	Elko Eared	Merrybell, Var. I	Quilomene Bar	Whale
Bear	Elko Split-Stem	Merrybell, Var. II	Shaniko Stemmed	
Buchanan Eared	Exotic Forms	Merrybell, Var. III	Sierra Stemmed	
Elko	Harpoon	Need Stemmed	Spedis III	
Elko Corner	Hendricks	Lanceolate	Triangular Knife	

DESERT TRADITIONS:

TRANSITIONAL PHASE (2,300 B. P. - 1,600 B. P.)

Hafted Knife	Sizer	Auriculate
Sauvie's Island Shoulder	Snake River	Three-Piece Fish Spear
Notched	Strong Barbed	Vendetta

DEVELOPMENTAL PHASE (1,600 B. P. - 700 B. P.)

Alkali	Deschutes Knife	Notched	Side Knife
Bear River	Eastgate	Malaga Cove Leaf	Stockton
Bone Arrow	Eastgate Split-Stem	One-Que	Trojan
Bone Pin	Emigrant Springs	Parowan	Uinta
Buck Gulley	Gunther Barbed	Rose Springs Corner	Wallula Gap Rect. Stem
Bull Creek	Gunther Triangular	Notched	Wealth Blade
Calapooya	Hell's Canyon Basal	Rose Springs Side	Wintu
Calapooya Knife	Notched	Notched	Yana
Dagger	Hell's Canyon Corner	Rose Springs Stemmed	

CLASSIC PHASE (700 B. P. - 400 B. P.)

Canalino Triangular	Cottonwood Triangle	Desert Redding	Plateau Pentagonal
Columbia Mule Ear	Deschutes Knife	Desert Sierra	Snow Knife
Columbia Plateau	Desert Delta	Harahey	Whale
Cottonwood Leaf	Desert General	Piquinin	

HISTORIC (400 B. P. - Present)

Ground Stone	Kavik	Nottoway	Snow Knife	Ulu
Ishi	Klickitat	Panoche	Trade Points	

GREAT BASIN WESTWARD
THUMBNAIL GUIDE SECTION

The following references are provided to aid the collector in easier and quicker identification of point types. All photos are exactly 30% of actual size and are proportional to each other. Each point pictured in this section represents a classic form for the type. When a match is found, go to the alphabetical location of that type for more examples in true actual size.

1 THUMBNAIL GUIDE - AURICULATE FORMS (30% actual size)

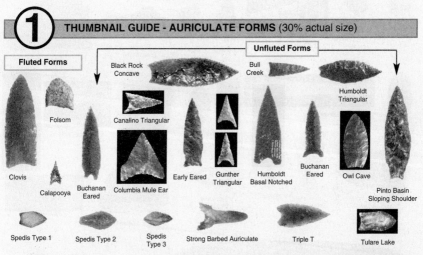

Fluted Forms

Unfluted Forms

Black Rock Concave

Bull Creek

Humboldt Triangular

Folsom

Canalino Triangular

Clovis

Calapooya

Buchanan Eared

Columbia Mule Ear

Early Eared

Gunther Triangular

Humboldt Basal Notched

Buchanan Eared

Owl Cave

Pinto Basin Sloping Shoulder

Spedis Type 1

Spedis Type 2

Spedis Type 3

Strong Barbed Auriculate

Triple T

Tulare Lake

2 THUMBNAIL GUIDE - LANCEOLATE FORMS (30% actual size)

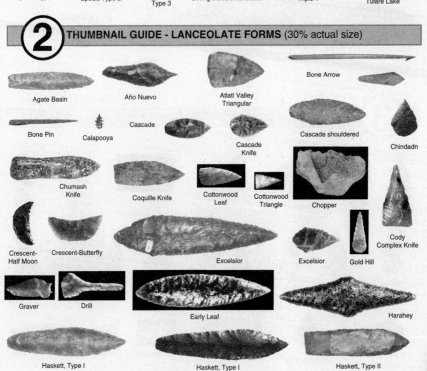

Agate Basin

Año Nuevo

Atlatl Valley Triangular

Bone Arrow

Bone Pin

Calapooya

Cascade

Cascade Knife

Cascade shouldered

Chindadn

Chumash Knife

Coquille Knife

Cottonwood Leaf

Cottonwood Triangle

Chopper

Cody Complex Knife

Crescent-Half Moon

Crescent-Butterfly

Excelsior

Excelsior

Gold Hill

Graver

Drill

Early Leaf

Harahey

Haskett, Type I

Haskett, Type I

Haskett, Type II

GB

LANCEOLATE FORMS (continued)

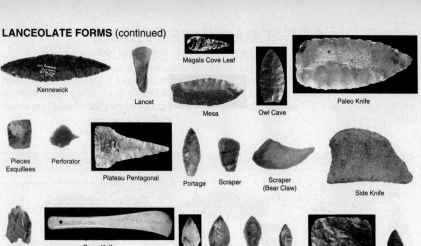

Kennewick

Lancet

Magala Cove Leaf

Mesa

Owl Cave

Paleo Knife

Pieces Esquillees

Perforator

Plateau Pentagonal

Portage

Scraper

Scraper (Bear Claw)

Side Knife

Sizer

Snow Knife

Spedis I

Spedis II

Spedis III

Square Knife

Sub-Triangular

Triangular Knife

Three-Piece Fish Spear

Trojan

Tulare Lake Bi-point

Hafted Ulu

Wahmuza

Wealth Blade

Wildcat Canyon

③ THUMBNAIL GUIDE - CORNER NOTCHED FORMS (30% actual size)

Bullhead

Chilcotin Plateau

Elko Corner Notched

Elko Eared

Elko Eared Double Tip

Exotic, Double Tip

Hell's Canyon Corner Notched

Hendricks

Martis

Merrybell, Var. I

Merrybell 3

Northern

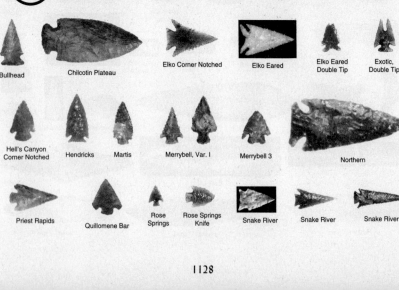

Priest Rapids

Quillomene Bar

Rose Springs

Rose Springs Knife

Snake River

Snake River

Snake River

Ahsahka

Base Tang Knife

Bear River

Bitterroot

Calapooya

Cold Springs

Coquille Side Notched

Desert Delta

Desert General

Desert Redding

Desert Sierra

Hawkens

Ishi

Jalama Side Notched

Merrybell Var. II

Merrybell Var. II

Need Stemmed Lanceolate

Nightfire

Northern (Wolf Ears)

Northern

Panoche

Piquinin

Rose Springs

Tuolumne Notched

San Bruno

Uinta

Wendover

Wintu

BASAL NOTCHED FORM

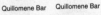

Eastgate

Eastgate Split-Stem

Emigrant Springs

Hell's Canyon

Quillomene Bar

Quillomene Bar

Alberta

Alkali

Bear

Chilcotin Plateau

Big Valley Stemmed

Cody Complex

Calapooya

Calapooya

Columbia Plateau

Columbia Plateau

Columbia Plateau

Columbia Plateau

Cody Knife

Exotic

Dagger

Eastgate

Elko

Firstview

Gunther

Kavik

Klickitat

Lake Mohave

Lind Coulee 1

Lind Coulee 2

Lind Coulee 3

1129

GB

STEMMED FORMS (continued)

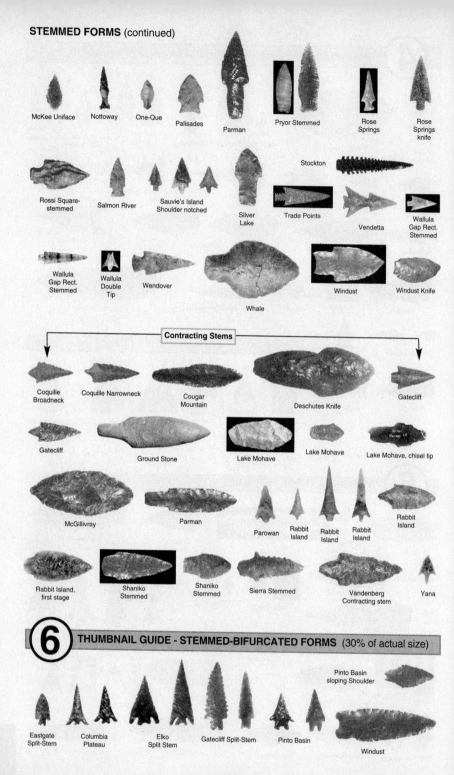

McKee Uniface

Nottoway

One-Que

Palisades

Parman

Pryor Stemmed

Rose Springs

Rose Springs knife

Rossi Square-stemmed

Salmon River

Sauvie's Island Shoulder notched

Silver Lake

Stockton

Trade Points

Vendetta

Wallula Gap Rect. Stemmed

Wallula Gap Rect. Stemmed

Wallula Double Tip

Wendover

Whale

Windust

Windust Knife

Contracting Stems

Coquille Broadneck

Coquille Narrowneck

Cougar Mountain

Deschutes Knife

Gatecliff

Gatecliff

Ground Stone

Lake Mohave

Lake Mohave

Lake Mohave, chisel tip

McGillivray

Parman

Parowan

Rabbit Island

Rabbit Island

Rabbit Island

Rabbit Island

Rabbit Island, first stage

Shaniko Stemmed

Shaniko Stemmed

Sierra Stemmed

Vandenberg Contracting stem

Yana

⑥ THUMBNAIL GUIDE - STEMMED-BIFURCATED FORMS (30% of actual size)

Eastgate Split-Stem

Columbia Plateau

Elko Split Stem

Gatecliff Split-Stem

Pinto Basin

Pinto Basin sloping Shoulder

Windust

AGATE BASIN - Transitional Paleo-Early Archaic, 10,500 - 8000 B. P.

(Also see Cody Complex, Haskett, Mesa and Owl Cave)

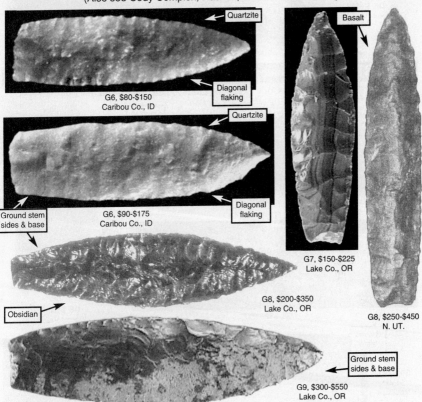

Quartzite

Diagonal flaking

G6, $80-$150
Caribou Co., ID

Quartzite

Diagonal flaking

G6, $90-$175
Caribou Co., ID

Ground stem sides & base

Basalt

G7, $150-$225
Lake Co., OR

G8, $200-$350
Lake Co., OR

G8, $250-$450
N. UT.

Obsidian

Ground stem sides & base

G9, $300-$550
Lake Co., OR

LOCATION: Northern states from Pennsylvania westward into Idaho and Canada. **DESCRIPTION:** A medium to large size lanceolate blade of high quality. Bases are either convex, concave or straight, and stems are usually ground. Some examples are median ridged and have random to parallel flaking. Believed to have evolved from the earlier *Haskett/Lind Coulee* types. **I.D. KEY:** Basal form and flaking style. **NOTE:** The Alaska *Mesa* point is a similar form and has been reportedly dated to 13,700 years B.P., but more data is needed to verify this extreme age.

AHSAHKA - Late Archaic-Classic Phase, 3,000 - 500 B. P.

(Also see Cold Springs, Northern Side Notched & Piqunin)

Agate

G5, $2-$5
Spokane, WA

G5, $2-$5
Spokane, WA

G2, $1-$3
Spokane, WA

G4, $2-$5
Spokane, WA

G4, $2-$5
Spokane, WA

G1, $.50-$1
Snake River, ID

LOCATION: Idaho into Washington. **DESCRIPTION:** A medium size dart point with shallow side notches and a straight to convex base. A descendent of *Hatwai* which is a descendent of *Cold Springs*. **NOTE:** Shallow side notches.

GB

G6, $3-$6
Snake River, ID

G6, $4-$8
Snake River, ID

ALBERTA - Early Archaic, 10,000 - 7000 B. P.

(Also see Cody Complex, Lind Coulee and Parman)

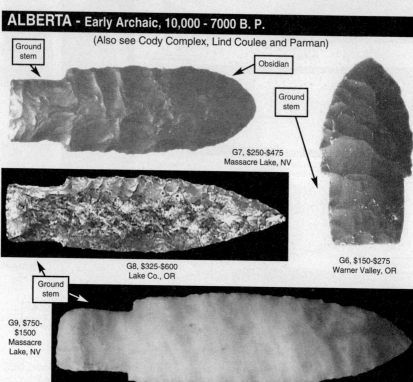

Ground stem

Obsidian

Ground stem

G7, $250-$475
Massacre Lake, NV

G8, $325-$600
Lake Co., OR

G6, $150-$275
Warner Valley, OR

Ground stem

G9, $750-$1500
Massacre Lake, NV

LOCATION: Northern States from Michigan to Montana to Nevada and Oregon.
DESCRIPTION: A medium to large size point with a broad, long parallel stem that is ground and weak shoulders. Developed from the *Lind Coulee* in the Great Basin and later changed into the Cody Complex and is related to the *Eden* and *Scottsbluff* types.
I.D. KEY: Long, broad rectangular stem, weak shoulders.

ALKALI - Developmental to Classic Phase, 1500 - 500 B. P.

(Also see Colonial, Eastgate, Elko and Rose Springs)

Yellow agate

G7, $3-$6
Col. Riv. OR,
Yellow agate

G10, $20-$35
Lake Co., OR

G10, $20-$35
Lake Co., OR

LOCATION: California to Canada. **DESCRIPTION:** A small size, barbed arrow point with a long parallel sided stem. This type was included with *Rose Springs* in early reports.
I.D. KEY: Flaking style and long stem.

ALKALI (continued)

G8, $8-$15
Lake Co., OR

G8, $5-$10
Lake Co., OR

G8, $8-$15
Lake Co., OR

G8, $12-$20
Lake Co., OR

G8, $12-$20
Columbia Riv., OR

G10, $25-$40
Columbia Riv., OR

AÑo NUEVO - Late Archaic 2950 - 2500 B. P.

(Also see Cougar Mountain, Deschutes Knife, Lind Coulee, Parman and Wildcat Canyon)

Apiculate tip

Light rootbeer colored Monterey chert

Apiculate tip

Monterey chert

Dark rootbeer colored Monterey chert

G8, $35-$60
Coasta CA

G6, $25-$40
San Mateo Co., CA

G8, $60-$100
Mendocino Co., CA

Dark rootbeer colored Monterey chert

G9, $65-$125
San Mateo Co., CA

G10, $125-$225
San Mateo Co., CA

LOCATION: Type site is in San Mateo Co., CA. **DESCRIPTION:** A medium to large size point with a long, tapered stem and weak tapered shoulders. The base is convex and stem sides are not ground. The distal end can be apiculate and flaking is random. Thicker than *Cougar Mountain* points. Made almost exclusively of Monterey Chert which is rootbeer colored, similar to Knife River flint from the Dakotas. **I.D. KEY:** Tip style and long stem.

ATLATL VALLEY TRIANGULAR - Early to late Archaic, 7000 - 3500 B. P.

(Also see Chindadn, Cottonwood, Sub-Triangular, Triangular Knife)

GB

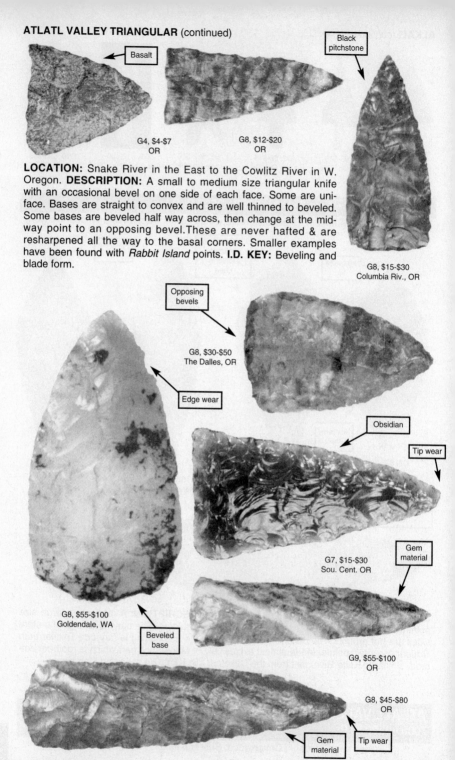

Basalt

Black pitchstone

G4, $4-$7
OR

G8, $12-$20
OR

LOCATION: Snake River in the East to the Cowlitz River in W. Oregon. **DESCRIPTION:** A small to medium size triangular knife with an occasional bevel on one side of each face. Some are uniface. Bases are straight to convex and are well thinned to beveled. Some bases are beveled half way across, then change at the midway point to an opposing bevel. These are never hafted & are resharpened all the way to the basal corners. Smaller examples have been found with *Rabbit Island* points. **I.D. KEY:** Beveling and blade form.

G8, $15-$30
Columbia Riv., OR

Opposing bevels

G8, $30-$50
The Dalles, OR

Edge wear

Obsidian

Tip wear

G8, $55-$100
Goldendale, WA

Beveled base

G7, $15-$30
Sou. Cent. OR

Gem material

G9, $55-$100
OR

G8, $45-$80
OR

Gem material

Tip wear

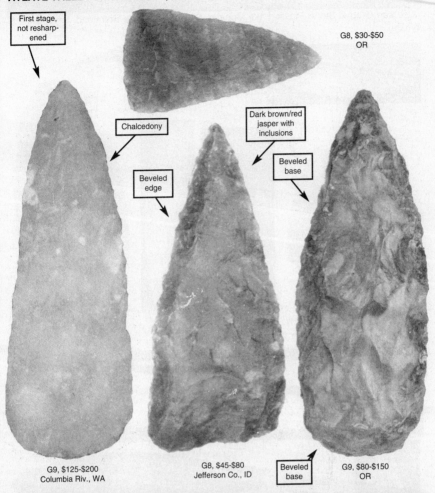

First stage, not resharpened

G8, $30-$50
OR

Chalcedony

Dark brown/red jasper with inclusions

Beveled base

Beveled edge

G9, $125-$200
Columbia Riv., WA

G8, $45-$80
Jefferson Co., ID

Beveled base

G9, $80-$150
OR

BASE TANG KNIFE - Late Archaic-Transitional, 10,000 - 2000 B. P.

(Also see Paleo Knife)

Obsidian

IMPORTANT
This point shown 1/2 actual size

G10, $650-$1200
Modoc Co., CA

LOCATION: California. **DESCRIPTION:** A large size elliptical blade with a very small side notched base. Similar to the Turkeytail point found in the East. **I.D. KEY:** Large, broad blade with side notches close to the base.

GB

BEAR - Late Archaic, 3200 - 1500 B. P.

(Also see Ground Stone, Kavik, Lake Mohave, Parman, Shaniko Stemmed, Silver Lake & Whale)

G4, $5-$10
Point Hope, Alaska

Tip nick

G6, $12-$20
Point Hope, Alaska

Flint

Flint

Flint

G6, $15-$30
High Arctic, Alaska

G6, $12-$20
High Arctic, Alaska

G7, $20-$40
Point Hope, Alaska

G5, $20-$35
Point Hope, Alaska

G4, $5-$10
High Arctic, Alaska

G4, $8-$15
St. Lawrence, Island, Alaska

Collateral flaking to a median ridge

G10, $225-$400
Alaska

G7, $65-$125
Alaska

G6, $75-$140
Alaska

Collateral flaking to a median ridge

G4, $25-$40
Alaska

G9, $125-$200
St. Lawrence Island, Alaska

1136

BEAR (continued)

LOCATION: Alaska. **DESCRIPTION:** A medium to large size, narrow point with a parallel sided, narrow stem. Parallel flaking is common. The stem is moderately long. This type may date back to 5,000-6,000 B.P. **I.D. KEY:** Long, narrow stemmed point.

BEAR RIVER - Developmental to Classic Phase, 1300 - 400 B. P.

(Also see Desert, Emigrant, Rose Spring)

| G6, $5-$10 Gooding Co., ID | G7, $5-$10 OR | G9, $15-$25 Gooding Co., ID | G9, $15-$30 Gooding Co., ID | G10, $30-$50 OR |

LOCATION: Great Basin area. Found in the Fremont area of Utah into SW Idaho. **DESCRIPTION:** A small size, thin, side-notched arrow point with deep notches. The base is large in relation to its overall size. Basal corners are rounded. **I.D. KEY:** Large base, small overall size.

BIG VALLEY STEMMED - Middle Archaic, 4000 - 3500 B. P.

(Also see Alberta, Cody Complex, Lind Coulee, Parman and Silver Lake)

G8, $100-$180
Sou. OR

LOCATION: Northern California into southern Cascade, Oregon. **DESCRIPTION:** A medium to large size, long stemmed point with rounded basal corners. Shoulders are horizontal and bases are straight. **I.D. KEY:** Large stem.

BITTERROOT - Early to middle Archaic, 7500 - 5000 B. P.

(See Ahsahka, Desert, Emigranti, Nightfire, Northern Side Notched & Salmon River)

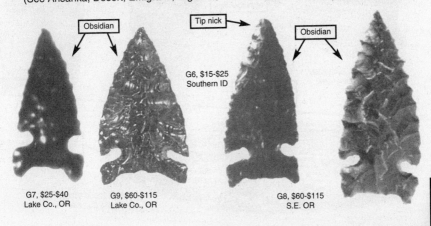

Obsidian

Tip nick

Obsidian

G6, $15-$25
Southern ID

| G7, $25-$40 Lake Co., OR | G9, $60-$115 Lake Co., OR | G8, $60-$115 S.E. OR |

BITTERROOT (continued)

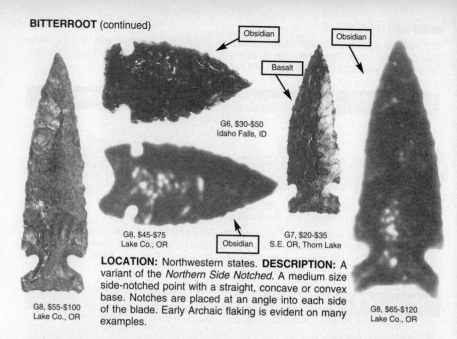

Obsidian

Basalt

Obsidian

G6, $30-$50
Idaho Falls, ID

G8, $45-$75
Lake Co., OR

Obsidian

G7, $20-$35
S.E. OR, Thorn Lake

LOCATION: Northwestern states. **DESCRIPTION:** A variant of the *Northern Side Notched*. A medium size side-notched point with a straight, concave or convex base. Notches are placed at an angle into each side of the blade. Early Archaic flaking is evident on many examples.

G8, $55-$100
Lake Co., OR

G8, $65-$120
Lake Co., OR

BLACK ROCK CONCAVE - Paleo, 11,000 - 10,500 B. P.

(Also see Cascade, Clovis, Folsom, Humboldt, Owl Cave and Tulare Lake)

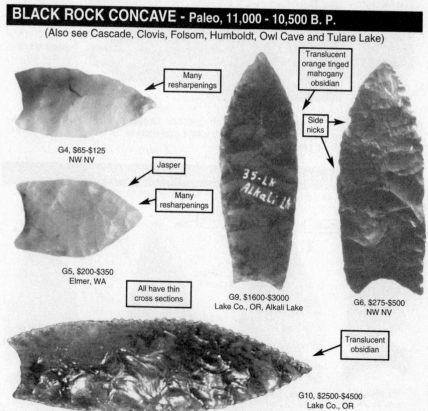

Many
resharpenings

G4, $65-$125
NW NV

Jasper

Many
resharpenings

G5, $200-$350
Elmer, WA

All have thin
cross sections

Translucent
orange tinged
mahogany
obsidian

Side
nicks

35-Lk
Alkali Lk

G9, $1600-$3000
Lake Co., OR, Alkali Lake

G6, $275-$500
NW NV

Translucent
obsidian

G10, $2500-$4500
Lake Co., OR

1138

BLACKROCK CONCAVE (continued)

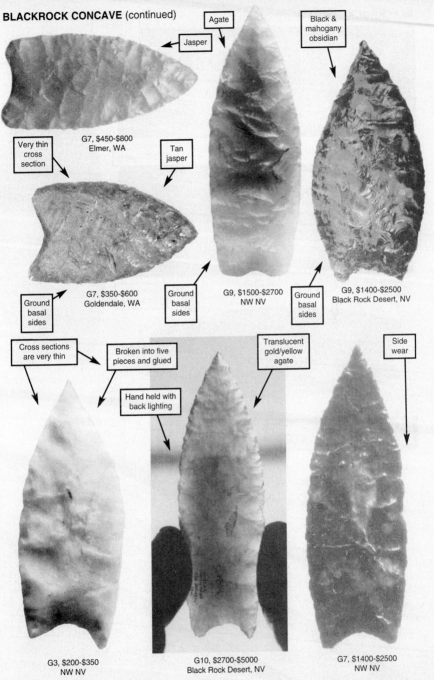

Jasper

Agate

Black & mahogany obsidian

G7, $450-$800
Elmer, WA

Very thin cross section

Tan jasper

Ground basal sides

G7, $350-$600
Goldendale, WA

Ground basal sides

G9, $1500-$2700
NW NV

Ground basal sides

G9, $1400-$2500
Black Rock Desert, NV

Cross sections are very thin

Broken into five pieces and glued

Translucent gold/yellow agate

Side wear

Hand held with back lighting

G3, $200-$350
NW NV

G10, $2700-$5000
Black Rock Desert, NV

G7, $1400-$2500
NW NV

LOCATION: NW Nevada and SE Oregon. An extremely rare type with few complete examples known. **DESCRIPTION:** A medium size, thin, lanceolate point with a concave base. Basal edges are usually ground. Blade flaking is horizontal transverse. Similar in flaking style and form to *Midland* and *Goshen* points and is considered to be the unfluted *Folsom* of the Great Basin. **I.D. KEY:** Micro secondary flaking, ground basal sides.

1139

GB

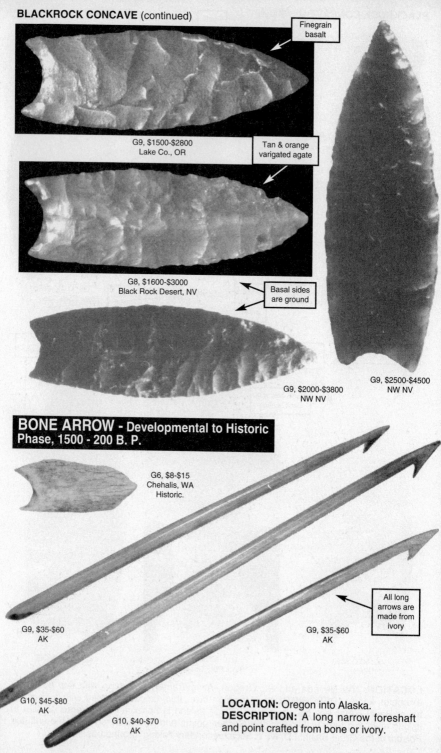

BLACKROCK CONCAVE (continued)

Finegrain basalt

G9, $1500-$2800
Lake Co., OR

Tan & orange
varigated agate

G8, $1600-$3000
Black Rock Desert, NV

Basal sides
are ground

G9, $2000-$3800
NW NV

G9, $2500-$4500
NW NV

BONE ARROW - Developmental to Historic Phase, 1500 - 200 B. P.

G6, $8-$15
Chehalis, WA
Historic.

All long arrows are made from ivory

G9, $35-$60
AK

G9, $35-$60
AK

G10, $45-$80
AK

G10, $40-$70
AK

LOCATION: Oregon into Alaska.
DESCRIPTION: A long narrow foreshaft and point crafted from bone or ivory.

BONE ARROW (continued)

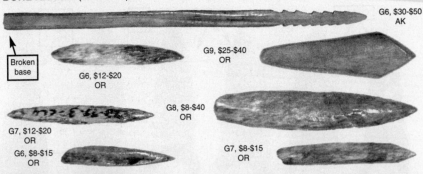

G6, $30-$50
AK

Broken base

G9, $25-$40
OR

G6, $12-$20
OR

G8, $8-$40
OR

G7, $12-$20
OR

G6, $8-$15
OR

G7, $8-$15
OR

BONE PIN - Developmental to Historic Phase, 1500 - 300 B. P.

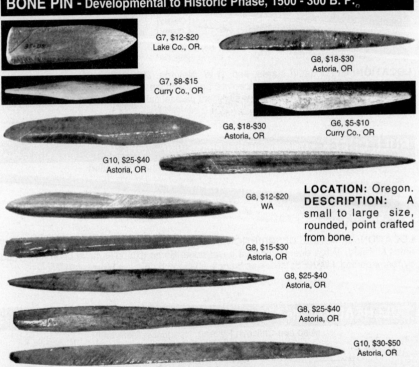

G7, $12-$20
Lake Co., OR.

G8, $18-$30
Astoria, OR

G7, $8-$15
Curry Co., OR

G8, $18-$30
Astoria, OR

G6, $5-$10
Curry Co., OR

G10, $25-$40
Astoria, OR

G8, $12-$20
WA

LOCATION: Oregon.
DESCRIPTION: A small to large size, rounded, point crafted from bone.

G8, $15-$30
Astoria, OR

G8, $25-$40
Astoria, OR

G8, $25-$40
Astoria, OR

G10, $30-$50
Astoria, OR

BUCHANAN EARED - Late Archaic - Developmental, 3000 - 1300 B. P.

(Also see Black Rock Concave, Early Eared, Humboldt and Strong)

G9, $25-$40
Mendocino Co., CA

GB

BUCHANAN EARED (continued)

G6, $15-$25
Owyhee Co., ID

G6, $15-$25
Warner Valley, OR

G8, $25-$40
Warner Valley, OR
Classic.

G6, $25-$40
Lake Co., OR

G6, $20-$40
Warner Valley, OR

G9, $75-$150
Warner Valley, OR

G9, $700-$1200
Malhuer Co., OR

LOCATION: Great Basin states, esp. N.W. Nevada. **DESCRIPTION:** A small to medium size, narrow, lanceolate point with an expanded, eared, concave base. Some examples show excellent parallel flaking. An early form of *Humboldt*.

BULL CREEK - Developmental Phase, 950 - 700 B. P.

(Also see Canalino Triangular & Gunther Triangular)

G9, $25-$40
Mendocino Co., CA

LOCATION: W. Nevada. **DESCRIPTION:** A long, thin triangular arrow point, that is sometimes serrated, with a deeply concave basal edge. Some examples have been shortened by resharpening. **I.D. KEY:** Isosceles triangle shape and concave base.

BULLHEAD - Middle Archaic, 4000 - 3500 B. P.

(Also see Chilcotin Plateau, Hendricks, Merrybell)

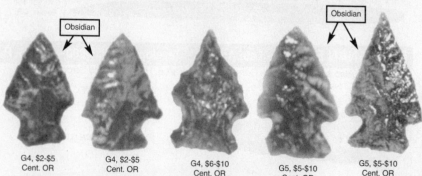

G4, $2-$5
Cent. OR

G4, $2-$5
Cent. OR

G4, $6-$10
Cent. OR

G5, $5-$10
Cent. OR

G5, $5-$10
Cent. OR

BULLHEAD (continued)

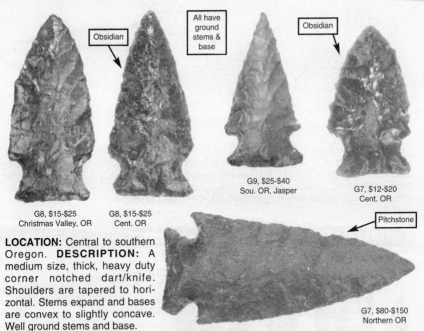

Obsidian

All have ground stems & base

Obsidian

G8, $15-$25
Christmas Valley, OR

G8, $15-$25
Cent. OR

G9, $25-$40
Sou. OR, Jasper

G7, $12-$20
Cent. OR

Pitchstone

G7, $80-$150
Northern OR

LOCATION: Central to southern Oregon. **DESCRIPTION:** A medium size, thick, heavy duty corner notched dart/knife. Shoulders are tapered to horizontal. Stems expand and bases are convex to slightly concave. Well ground stems and base.

CALAPOOYA - Developmental to Historic Phase, 1000 - 200 B. P.

(Also see Columbia Plateau, Gunther, Wallula and Wintu)

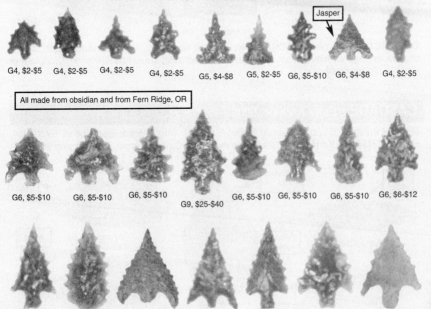

Jasper

G4, $2-$5   G4, $2-$5   G4, $2-$5   G4, $2-$5   G5, $4-$8   G5, $2-$5   G6, $5-$10   G6, $4-$8   G4, $2-$5

All made from obsidian and from Fern Ridge, OR

G6, $5-$10   G6, $5-$10   G6, $5-$10   G9, $25-$40   G6, $5-$10   G6, $5-$10   G6, $5-$10   G6, $6-$12

G8, $12-$20   G8, $12-$20   G9, $25-$40   G8, $25-$40   G9, $25-$40   G9, $25-$40   G9, $15-$30

GB

1143

CALAPOOYA (continued)

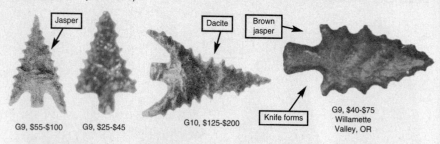

G9, $55-$100   G9, $25-$45   G10, $125-$200   Knife forms   G9, $40-$75 Willamette Valley, OR

Jasper   Dacite   Brown jasper

LOCATION: Willamette Valley, Oregon between the Columbia and Rogue rivers. **DESCRIPTION:** A small size, thin, arrow point that occurs either as stemmed, side notched, triangular and ovate. Most examples are heavily serrated and imitate local styles such as Gunther, Desert, Columbia Plateau, Wallula and other types. The barbed edge variant is locally called a *Fern Leaf* point. **I.D. KEY:** Wild serrations.

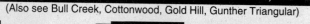

CANALINO TRIANGULAR - Classic to Historic Phase, 700 - 200 B. P.

(Also see Bull Creek, Cottonwood, Gold Hill, Gunther Triangular)

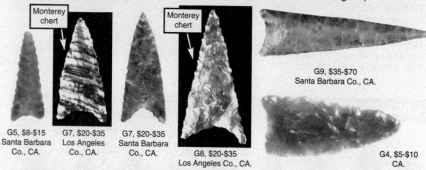

Monterey chert   Monterey chert

G5, $8-$15 Santa Barbara Co., CA.

G7, $20-$35 Los Angeles Co., CA.

G7, $20-$35 Santa Barbara Co., CA.

G8, $20-$35 Los Angeles Co., CA.

G9, $35-$70 Santa Barbara Co., CA.

G4, $5-$10 CA.

LOCATION: California. **DESCRIPTION:** A small size, thin, triangular arrow point with a shallow to deep concave base. Some are serrated. Also known as *Canalino Triangular* or *Coastal Cottonwood*.

CASCADE - Early Archaic, 8000 - 4000 B. P.

(Also see Agate Basin, Cascade Knife, Cascade Shouldered, Early Leaf, Excelsior, Harahey, Haskett, Kennewick, Need Stemmed, Owl Cave, Parman, Portage and Windust)

Red jasper   Burinated tip   Red jasper

G5, $13-$25, OR

Yellow agate   Agate

G7, $15-$30 Lake Co., OR

G7, $15-$30 OR

Jasper

G5, $12-$20 Atlatl Valley, OR

G5, $15-$30 Columbia Riv., OR

1144

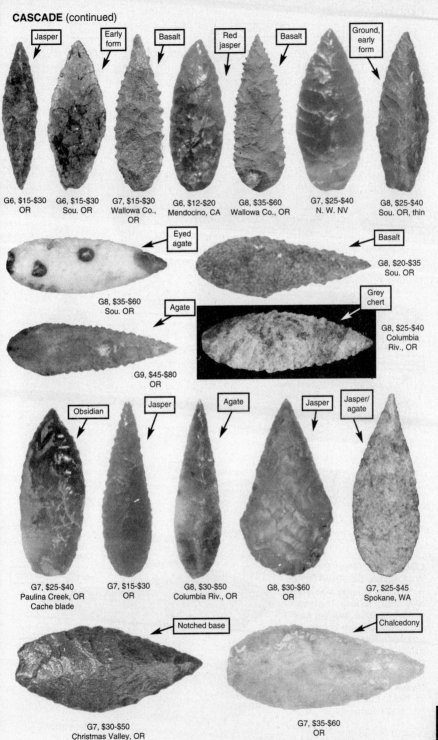

Jasper

Early form

Basalt

Red jasper

Basalt

Ground, early form

G6, $15-$30
OR

G6, $15-$30
Sou. OR

G7, $15-$30
Wallowa Co.,
OR

G6, $12-$20
Mendocino, CA

G8, $35-$60
Wallowa Co., OR

G7, $25-$40
N. W. NV

G8, $25-$40
Sou. OR, thin

Eyed agate

Basalt

G8, $20-$35
Sou. OR

G8, $35-$60
Sou. OR

Agate

Grey chert

G8, $25-$40
Columbia
Riv., OR

G9, $45-$80
OR

Obsidian

Jasper

Agate

Jasper

Jasper/ agate

G7, $25-$40
Paulina Creek, OR
Cache blade

G7, $15-$30
OR

G8, $30-$50
Columbia Riv., OR

G8, $30-$60
OR

G7, $25-$45
Spokane, WA

Notched base

Chalcedony

G7, $30-$50
Christmas Valley, OR

G7, $35-$60
OR

GB

CASCADE (continued)

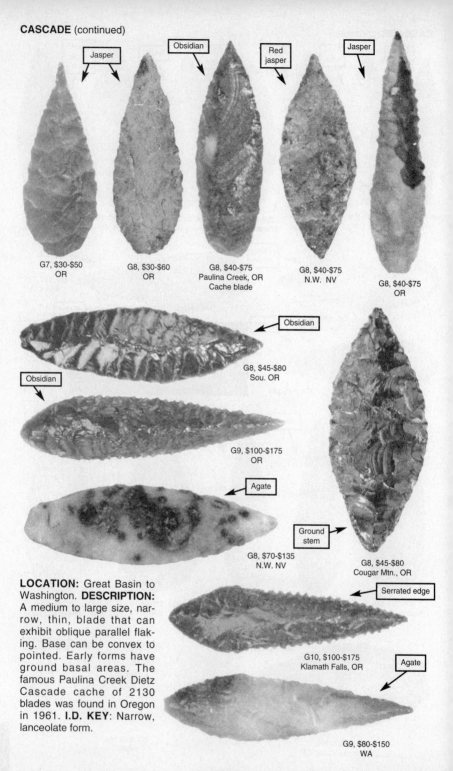

Jasper

Obsidian

Red jasper

Jasper

G7, $30-$50
OR

G8, $30-$60
OR

G8, $40-$75
Paulina Creek, OR
Cache blade

G8, $40-$75
N.W. NV

G8, $40-$75
OR

Obsidian

G8, $45-$80
Sou. OR

Obsidian

G9, $100-$175
OR

Agate

G8, $70-$135
N.W. NV

Ground stem

G8, $45-$80
Cougar Mtn., OR

Serrated edge

G10, $100-$175
Klamath Falls, OR

Agate

G9, $80-$150
WA

LOCATION: Great Basin to Washington. **DESCRIPTION:** A medium to large size, narrow, thin, blade that can exhibit oblique parallel flaking. Base can be convex to pointed. Early forms have ground basal areas. The famous Paulina Creek Dietz Cascade cache of 2130 blades was found in Oregon in 1961. **I.D. KEY:** Narrow, lanceolate form.

CASCADE (continued)

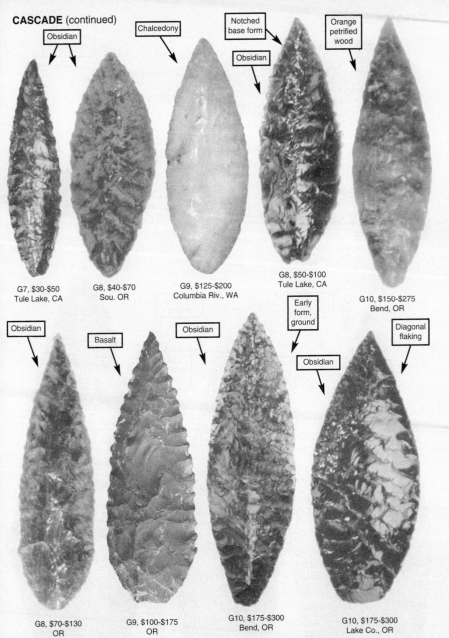

Obsidian

Chalcedony

Notched base form

Obsidian

Orange petrified wood

G7, $30-$50
Tule Lake, CA

G8, $40-$70
Sou. OR

G9, $125-$200
Columbia Riv., WA

G8, $50-$100
Tule Lake, CA

G10, $150-$275
Bend, OR

Obsidian

Basalt

Obsidian

Early form, ground

Obsidian

Diagonal flaking

G8, $70-$130
OR

G9, $100-$175
OR

G10, $175-$300
Bend, OR

G10, $175-$300
Lake Co., OR

NOTE: There is a difference between the *Cascade base-notched* and the *Humboldt* points. The *Humboldt* point usually has a straight more visible hafting area than the *Cascade*. The *Cascade* hafting area tapers to the base, while the *Humboldt* usually expands slightly near the base. Most *Humboldts* have wider base notches than the *Cascades*. The *Cascade* base-notch appears to be a field improvisation while the *Humboldt* notch is preplanned and usually has multiple strokes. While approximately 90% of *Humboldt* stems are ground, less than 10% of the Cascades have ground stems. Completely worn out or damaged specimens could be mistaken for one another.

GB

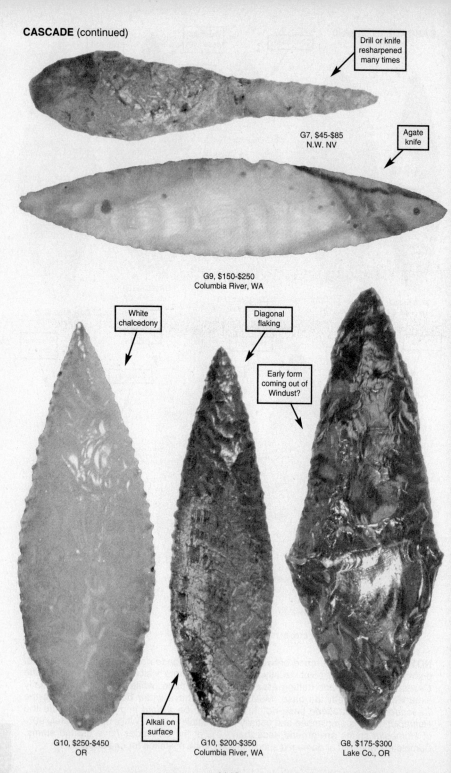

CASCADE (continued)

Drill or knife resharpened many times

G7, $45-$85
N.W. NV

Agate knife

G9, $150-$250
Columbia River, WA

White chalcedony

Diagonal flaking

Early form coming out of Windust?

Alkali on surface

G10, $250-$450
OR

G10, $200-$350
Columbia River, WA

G8, $175-$300
Lake Co., OR

1148

CASCADE (continued)

Obsidian

G9, $30-$50
Paulina Creek, OR. Cache blade

Agate

G7, $20-$35
Lake Co., OR

G9, $30-$50
Paulina Creek, OR
Cache blade

G7, $45-$80
OR

Obsidian

Diagonal flaking

G8 $65-$125
N. W. NV

Obsidian

Clear chalcedony

Gem petrified wood

Faint side notches, transitional point

G9, $80-$150
OR

G8, $80-$150
OR.

G10, $300-$550
Oregon desert.

GB

CASCADE KNIFE - Early Archaic, 8000 - 6000 B. P.

(Also see Cascade Knife, Cascade Shouldered, Early Leaf, Excelsior, Harahey, Haskett, Kennewick, Parman, Shaniko Stemmed and Windust)

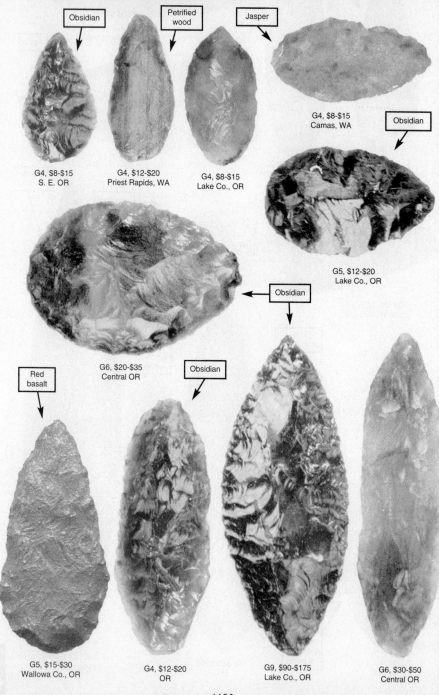

Obsidian

Petrified wood

Jasper

G4, $8-$15
Camas, WA

Obsidian

G4, $8-$15
S. E. OR

G4, $12-$20
Priest Rapids, WA

G4, $8-$15
Lake Co., OR

G5, $12-$20
Lake Co., OR

Obsidian

G6, $20-$35
Central OR

Red basalt

Obsidian

G5, $15-$30
Wallowa Co., OR

G4, $12-$20
OR

G9, $90-$175
Lake Co., OR

G6, $30-$50
Central OR

1150

CASCADE KNIFE (continued)

LOCATION: Great Basin to Washington. **DESCRIPTION:** A medium to large size, broad blade with a rounded base. The distal is rounded to pointed. Broad, wide, flat flakes were taken to thin the blade. Edge alignment and resharpening are short, steeply taken flakes from one or both faces. **I.D. KEY:** Resharpening technique.

Red/black jasper

G4, $8-$15
Atlatl Valley, OR

Very thin, cross section 1/8"

Truncated (bias) tip, chisel tip

One of the finest knives known from Wakemap Mound

Wascolite

G10, $150-$250
Lake Co., OR

G9, $275-$500
Wakemap Mound, OR

GB

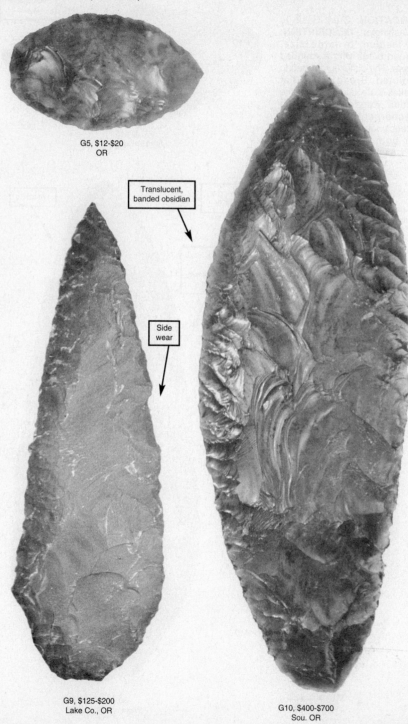

G5, $12-$20
OR

Translucent,
banded obsidian

Side
wear

G9, $125-$200
Lake Co., OR

G10, $400-$700
Sou. OR

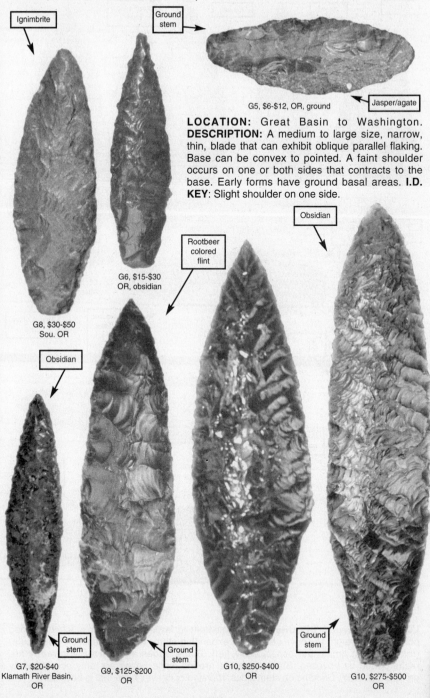

CASCADE SHOULDERED - Early Archaic, 8000 - 6000 B. P.

(Also see Cascade, Cascade Knife, Early Leaf, Excelsior, Harahey, Haskett, Kennewick, Parman, Shaniko Stemmed and Windust)

Ignimbrite

Ground stem

G5, $6-$12, OR, ground

Jasper/agate

LOCATION: Great Basin to Washington. **DESCRIPTION:** A medium to large size, narrow, thin, blade that can exhibit oblique parallel flaking. Base can be convex to pointed. A faint shoulder occurs on one or both sides that contracts to the base. Early forms have ground basal areas. **I.D. KEY**: Slight shoulder on one side.

Obsidian

Rootbeer colored flint

G6, $15-$30
OR, obsidian

G8, $30-$50
Sou. OR

Obsidian

Ground stem

Ground stem

Ground stem

G7, $20-$40
Klamath River Basin,
OR

G9, $125-$200
OR

G10, $250-$400
OR

G10, $275-$500
OR

1153

GB

CHILCOTIN PLATEAU - Early Archaic, 8000 - 5000 B. P.

(See Bullhead, Elko Corner, Hell's Canyon, Northern Side Notched and Snake River)

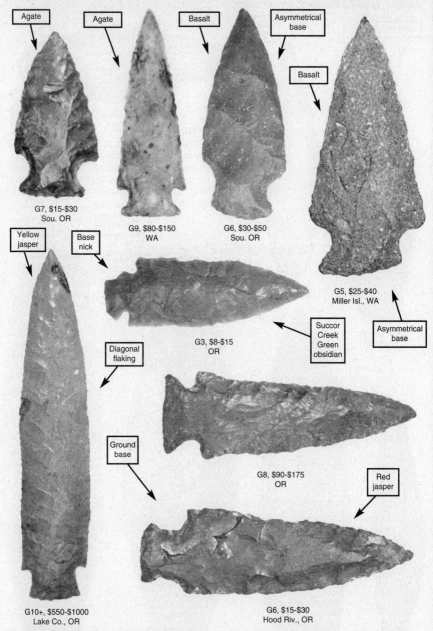

Agate

Agate

Basalt

Asymmetrical base

Basalt

G7, $15-$30
Sou. OR

G9, $80-$150
WA

G6, $30-$50
Sou. OR

Yellow jasper

Base nick

Diagonal flaking

Ground base

Succor Creek Green obsidian

G3, $8-$15
OR

G5, $25-$40
Miller Isl., WA

Asymmetrical base

G8, $90-$175
OR

Red jasper

G10+, $550-$1000
Lake Co., OR

G6, $15-$30
Hood Riv., OR

LOCATION: Oregon. **DESCRIPTION:** A medium to large size, corner notched, barbed point with a straight to convex base and expanding stem. The cross section is lenticular (fairly thick at times, but occasionally flat). Blade edges are convex and rarely are resharpened by beveling. Stem sides are ground while bases are only occassionally ground. **I.D. KEY:** Grinding on stem sides, rounded or convex base that is beveled.

1154

CHILCOTIN PLATEAU (continued)

Jasper

G8, $350-$650
Yakima Co., WA

Agate

Perfect base example, round & beveled

Brown petrified wood

G10, $325-$600
Wakemap Mound, The Dalles, OR

G10+ $800-$1500
OR

Ground notches & base

G10+ $800-$1500
OR

1155

GB

CHINDADN - Paleo, 11,300 - 11,000 B. P.

(Also see Cascade, Clovis, Mesa and Sub-Triangular)

G8, $25-$50
Nenana Valley, AK

LOCATION: Alaska. **DESCRIPTION:** A small size, broad, thin, ovate point made from a flake that has a convex base. Made during the Nenana occupation. **I.D. KEY:** Broad, ovate form.

CHOPPER - Paleo, 14,000 - 10,000 B. P.

(Also see Scraper)

LOCATION: California. **DESCRIPTION:** A medium to large size, thick, early chopping and pounding tool. Most are irregular shaped to oval to circular.

G6, $25-$50 ea.
San Bernadino, CA

Famed Calico site choppers dated to 50,000 B.P. by L.S.B. Leakey, San Bernadino Co., CA.

IMPORTANT: Shown 40% actual size

CHUMASH KNIFE - Early to Middle Archaic, 9000 - 5000 B. P.

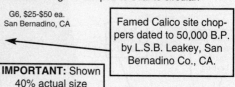

Broken and glued

G2, $100-$200
Santa Barbara
Co., CA

Actual size 7-1/2" long

IMPORTANT:
Both shown
HALF size

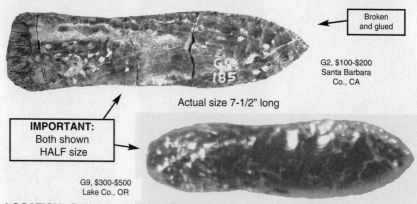

G9, $300-$500
Lake Co., OR

LOCATION: California. **DESCRIPTION:** A large size, lanceolate blade that expands towards the base, hafted and used as a knife. Some examples have tar residue on stem area.

CLOVIS - Paleo, 14,000 - 10,000 B. P.

(Also see Black Rock Concave, Cascade, Folsom, Humboldt, Tulare Lake & Windust)

CLOVIS (continued)

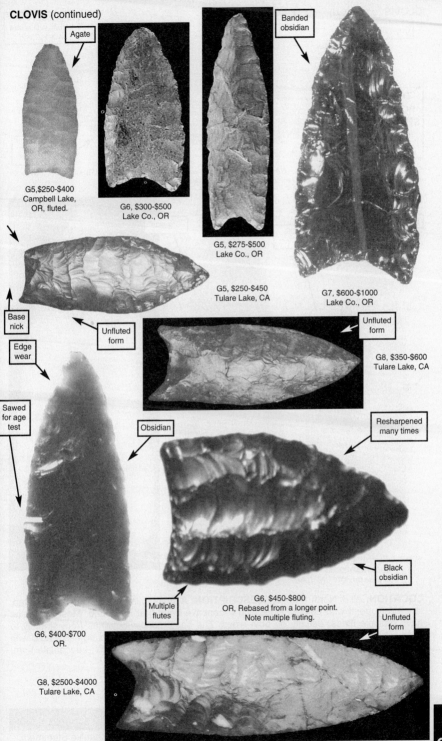

Agate

G5, $250-$400
Campbell Lake,
OR, fluted.

G6, $300-$500
Lake Co., OR

Banded
obsidian

G5, $275-$500
Lake Co., OR

G5, $250-$450
Tulare Lake, CA

G7, $600-$1000
Lake Co., OR

Base
nick

Edge
wear

Unfluted
form

Unfluted
form

G8, $350-$600
Tulare Lake, CA

Sawed
for age
test

Obsidian

Resharpened
many times

Black
obsidian

Multiple
flutes

G6, $450-$800
OR, Rebased from a longer point.
Note multiple fluting.

Unfluted
form

G6, $400-$700
OR.

G8, $2500-$4000
Tulare Lake, CA

GB

1157

CLOVIS (continued)

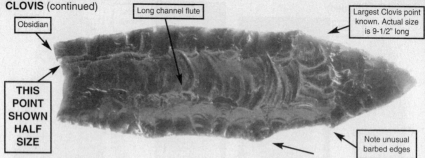

Obsidian

Long channel flute

Largest Clovis point known. Actual size is 9-1/2" long

THIS POINT SHOWN HALF SIZE

Note unusual barbed edges

G10+, $15,000-$25,000, Douglas Co., WA. Obsidian. This point was probably used as a knife. It was found next to an extinct bison trail close to where the Wenatchee Clovis site is located.

CLOVIS (continued)

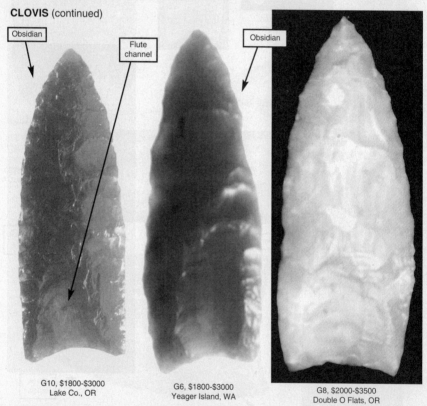

Obsidian

Flute channel

Obsidian

G10, $1800-$3000
Lake Co., OR

G6, $1800-$3000
Yeager Island, WA

G8, $2000-$3500
Double O Flats, OR

LOCATION: All of North America. **DESCRIPTION:** A small to large size, auriculate, fluted, lanceolate point with convex sides and a concave base that is ground. Most examples have multiple flutes, usually on both sides. The basal concavity varies from shallow to deep. The oldest known point in North America. This point has been found associated with extinct mammoth & bison remains in several western states. **I.D. KEY:** Lanceolate form, batan fluting instead of indirect style.

CODY COMPLEX - Early Archaic, 9500 - 7000 B. P.

(Also see Alberta, Cody Knife, Firstview, Lind Coulee, Parman and Shaniko Stemmed)

CODY COMPLEX (continued)

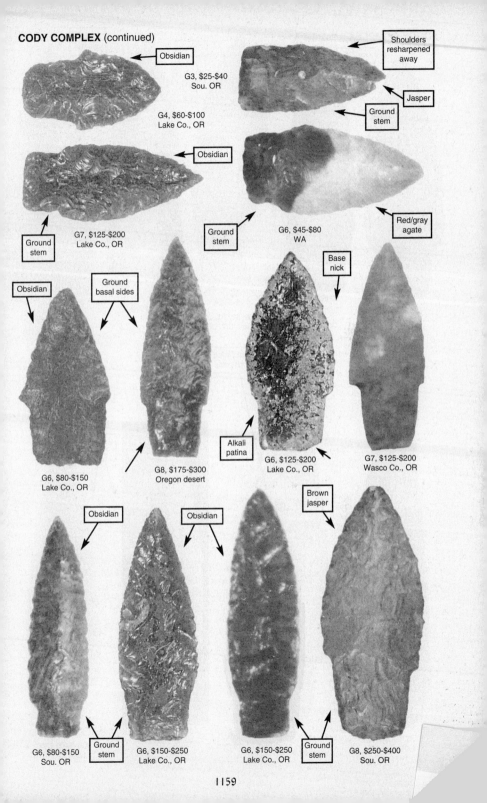

Obsidian

Shoulders resharpened away

Jasper

Ground stem

G3, $25-$40
Sou. OR

G4, $60-$100
Lake Co., OR

Obsidian

Ground stem

Ground stem

G7, $125-$200
Lake Co., OR

G6, $45-$80
WA

Red/gray agate

Obsidian

Ground basal sides

Base nick

Alkali patina

G6, $80-$150
Lake Co., OR

G8, $175-$300
Oregon desert

G6, $125-$200
Lake Co., OR

G7, $125-$200
Wasco Co., OR

Obsidian

Obsidian

Brown jasper

G6, $80-$150
Sou. OR

Ground stem

G6, $150-$250
Lake Co., OR

G6, $150-$250
Lake Co., OR

Ground stem

G8, $250-$400
Sou. OR

CODY COMPLEX (continued)

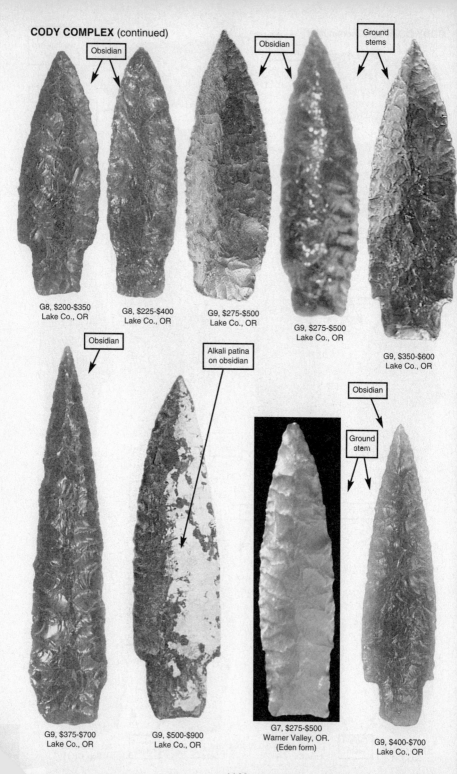

Obsidian

Obsidian

Ground stems

Obsidian

Alkali patina on obsidian

Obsidian

Ground stem

G8, $200-$350
Lake Co., OR

G8, $225-$400
Lake Co., OR

G9, $275-$500
Lake Co., OR

G9, $275-$500
Lake Co., OR

G9, $350-$600
Lake Co., OR

G9, $375-$700
Lake Co., OR

G9, $500-$900
Lake Co., OR

G7, $275-$500
Warner Valley, OR.
(Eden form)

G9, $400-$700
Lake Co., OR

CODY COMPLEX (continued)

G9, $350-$600
Lake Co., OR

Ground stem

Very early Cody coming out of Windust

Ground stem

Ground stem

G10, $400-$1200
Lake Co., OR

Ground stem

G8, $550-$1000
Lake Co., OR

G9, $650-$1200
Lake Co., OR

LOCATION: Western Oregon into Idaho, Nevada and Montana. **DESCRIPTION:** A medium to large size, broad, stemmed point with weak shoulders and a broad parallel sided to expanding stem that is ground. Developed from earlier *Alberta* points. *Cody* points in this area have shorter and longer stems than anywhere else in the country. Flaking is usually the horizontal to oblique style. Chisel tips are known. Type names are *Eden, Firstview* and *Scottsbluff*. **I.D. KEY:** Early flaking, square stem that is ground.

GB

CODY COMPLEX KNIFE - Early Archaic, 9500 - 7000 B. P.

(Also see Cody Complex)

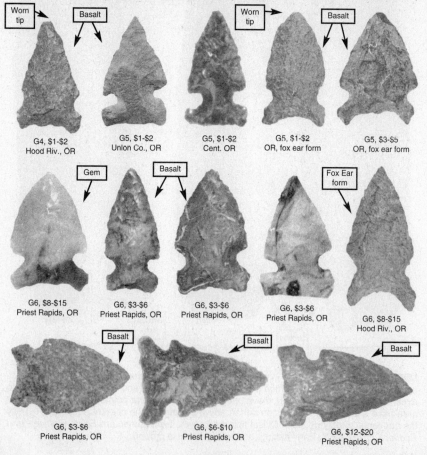

The best example known

Thin cross-section

Dark green chert or cryptocrystalline silicate (ccs) or chrysophase

G10+, $6,000-$10,000
Owyhee Co., ID, Snake River

Ground stem

LOCATION: Western Idaho into Oregon and Washington. **DESCRIPTION:** A medium to large size, well made, triangular knife with a broad base. Resharpened examples have prominent shoulders forming a pentagonal form. The classic blade form has a diagonal slant. **I.D. KEY:** Early flaking, diagonal slant.

COLD SPRINGS - Middle Archaic, 5000 - 4000 B. P.

(Also see Ahsahka, Bitterroot, Jalama Side Notched, Nightfire and Northern Side Notched)

Worn tip

Basalt

Worn tip

Basalt

G4, $1-$2
Hood Riv., OR

G5, $1-$2
Union Co., OR

G5, $1-$2
Cent. OR

G5, $1-$2
OR, fox ear form

G5, $3-$5
OR, fox ear form

Gem

Basalt

Fox Ear form

G6, $8-$15
Priest Rapids, OR

G6, $3-$6
Priest Rapids, OR

G6, $3-$6
Priest Rapids, OR

G6, $3-$6
Priest Rapids, OR

G6, $8-$15
Hood Riv., OR

Basalt

Basalt

Basalt

G6, $3-$6
Priest Rapids, OR

G6, $6-$10
Priest Rapids, OR

G6, $12-$20
Priest Rapids, OR

COLD SPRINGS (continued)

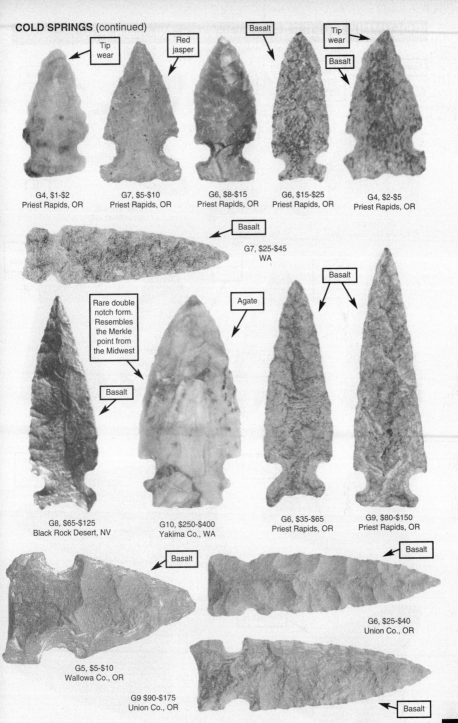

Tip wear

Red jasper

Basalt

Tip wear

Basalt

G4, $1-$2
Priest Rapids, OR

G7, $5-$10
Priest Rapids, OR

G6, $8-$15
Priest Rapids, OR

G6, $15-$25
Priest Rapids, OR

G4, $2-$5
Priest Rapids, OR

Basalt

G7, $25-$45
WA

Rare double notch form. Resembles the Merkle point from the Midwest

Basalt

Agate

Basalt

G8, $65-$125
Black Rock Desert, NV

G10, $250-$400
Yakima Co., WA

G6, $35-$65
Priest Rapids, OR

G9, $80-$150
Priest Rapids, OR

Basalt

Basalt

G5, $5-$10
Wallowa Co., OR

G6, $25-$40
Union Co., OR

G9 $90-$175
Union Co., OR

Basalt

LOCATION: Oregon, Washington & Idaho. **DESCRIPTION:** A small to medium size broadly side-notched point with a straight to concave base. Most are made from Basalt.

1163

GB

COLUMBIA MULE EAR - Classic Phase, 700 - 400 B. P.

(Also see Plateau Pentagonal and Strong)

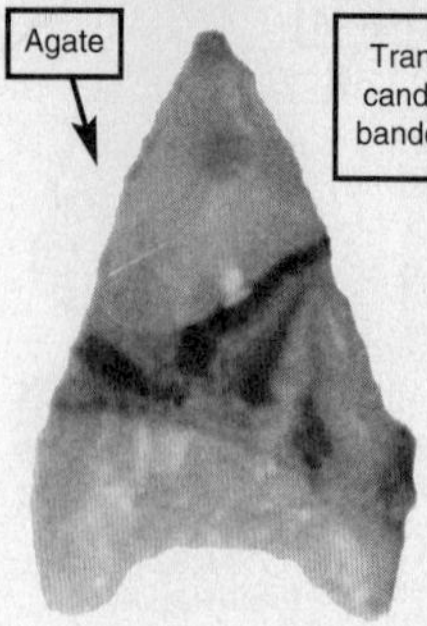

Agate

Translucent candy stripe, banded agate

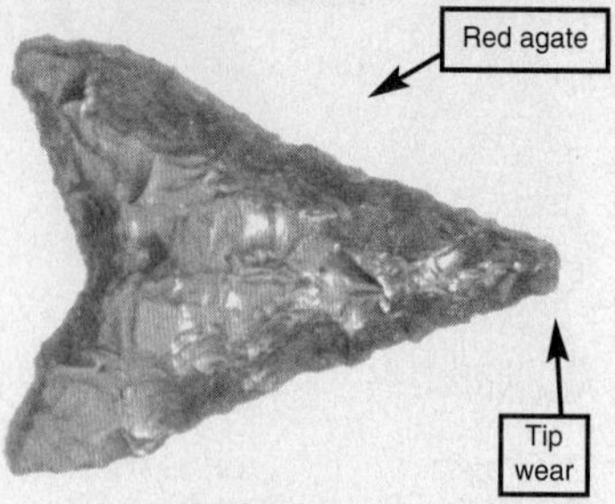

Red agate

Tip wear

G5, $18-$35
Hood River, OR

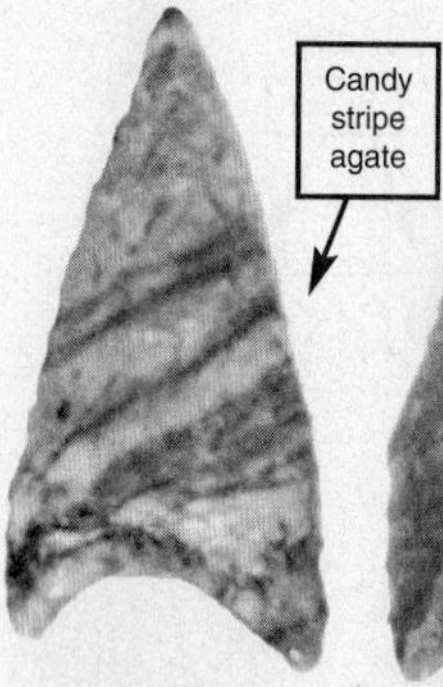

G5, $15-$30
Columbia Riv. Basin, OR

G6, $40-$75
Hood River, OR

Candy stripe agate

Agate

Shallow base type

Gem material

G5, $30-$50
Columbia River Basin, OR

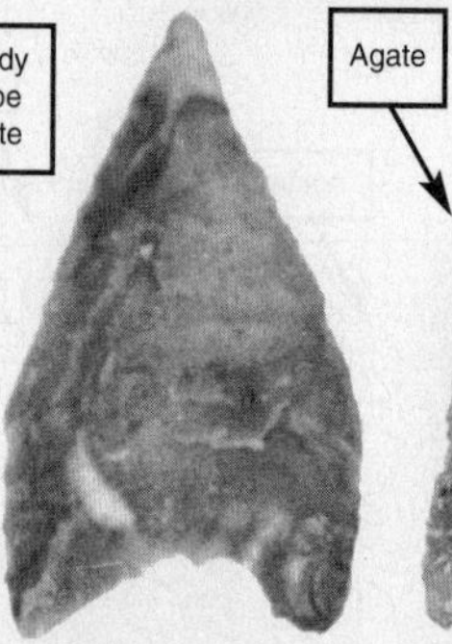

G5, $18-$35
Columbia River Basin, OR

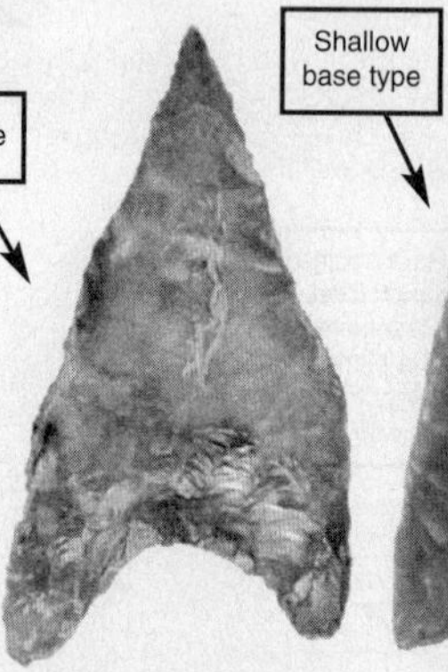

G6, $18-$35
Columbia River Basin, OR

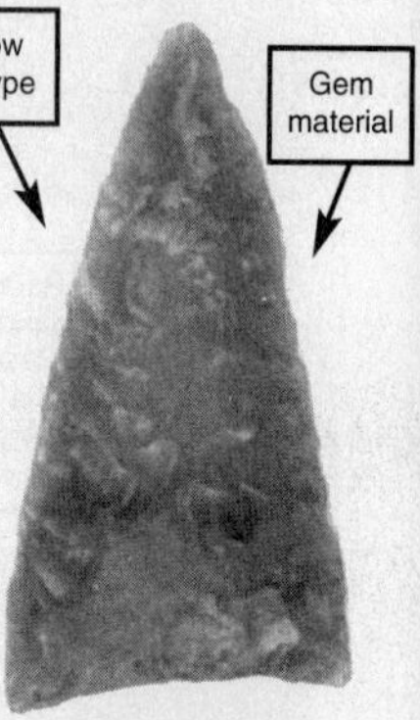

G5, $15-$25
OR

Gray agate

First stage form

G8, $40-$75
Pasco, WA

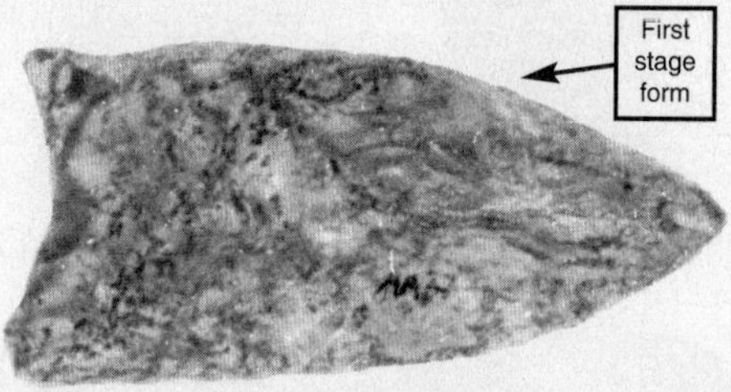

G8, $35-$60
Bonneville Dam, OR

Chalcedony

Gem material

G6, $30-$50
Columbia River Basin, OR

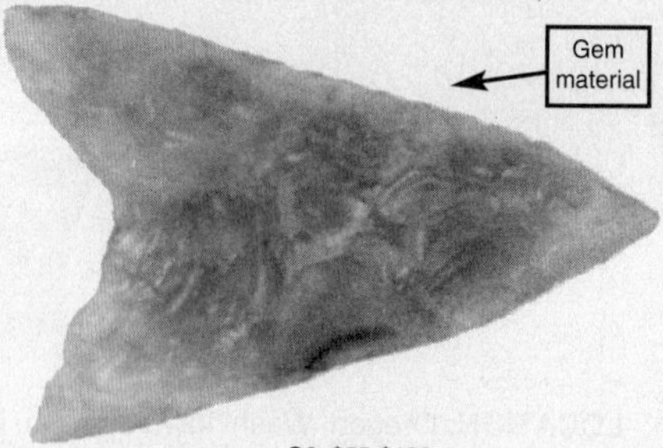

G8, $55-$100
OR

White chalcedony with yellow lines

Agate

Very thin & well-ground base & auricles

G8, $65-$125
WA

G8, $55-$100
Columbia Riv., OR

Red jasper

Resharpened, worn-out specimen

Petrified wood

Ground basal area

G8, $40-$75
WA

G10, $150-$250
Hood River, OR

Obsidian

Gem material

Ground basal area

G9, $150-$250
Umatilla Co., OR

G10, $175-$300
Columbia River Basin, WA

GB

COLUMBIA MULE EAR (continued)

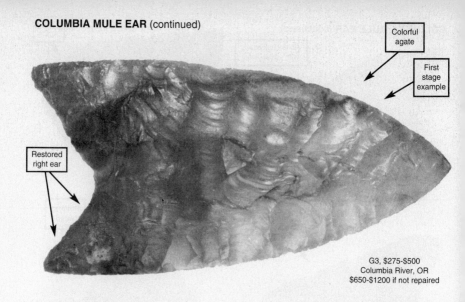

Colorful agate

First stage example

Restored right ear

G3, $275-$500
Columbia River, OR
$650-$1200 if not repaired

LOCATION: Oregon and Washington. **DESCRIPTION:** A small to medium size, well made, triangular knife with a broad base. Resharpened examples have prominent shoulders forming a pentagonal form. Found only along the Columbia River in Washington & Oregon. **I.D. KEY:** Pentagonal form.

COLUMBIA PLATEAU - Classic to Historic Phase, 500 - 200 B. P.

(Also see Eastgate, Gatecliff, Gunther, Rose Springs, Sauvies Island and Wallula)

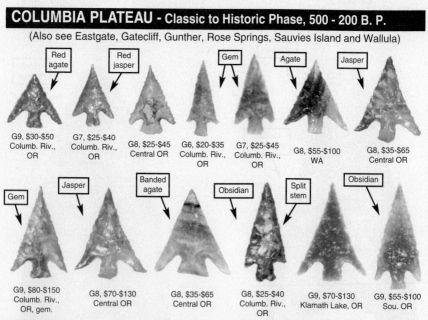

Red agate

Red jasper

Gem

Agate

Jasper

G9, $30-$50
Columb. Riv.,
OR

G7, $25-$40
Columb. Riv.,
OR

G8, $25-$45
Central OR

G6, $20-$35
Columb. Riv.,
OR

G7, $25-$45
Columb. Riv.,
OR

G8, $55-$100
WA

G8, $35-$65
Central OR

Gem

Jasper

Banded agate

Obsidian

Split stem

Obsidian

G9, $80-$150
Columb. Riv.,
OR, gem.

G8, $70-$130
Central OR

G8, $35-$65
Central OR

G8, $25-$40
Columb. Riv.,
OR

G9, $70-$130
Klamath Lake, OR

G9, $55-$100
Sou. OR

LOCATION: Columbia River in Oregon and Washington. **DESCRIPTION:** A small size, thin, triangular arrow point with strong barbs and a short, expanding to parallel sided stem. Shoulder barbs are usually pointed and can extend to the base. Blade edges can be serrated and the base can be bifurcated. Broader tangs than Wallula. Related to the earlier *Snake River* dart points.

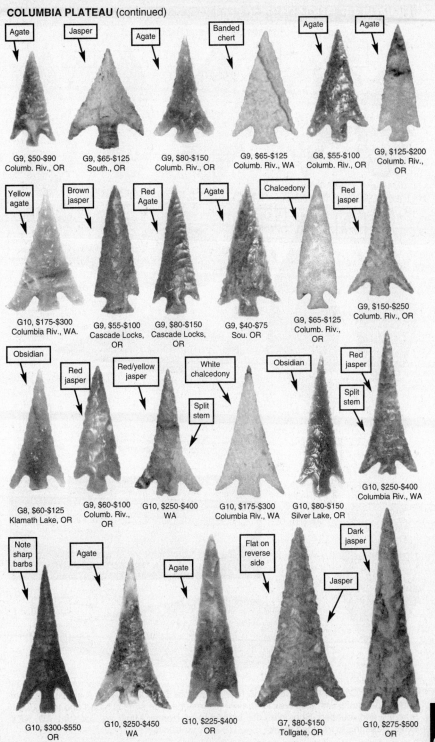

Agate
G9, $50-$90
Columb. Riv., OR

Jasper
G9, $65-$125
South., OR

Agate
G9, $80-$150
Columb. Riv., OR

Banded chert
G9, $65-$125
Columb. Riv., WA

Agate
G8, $55-$100
Columb. Riv., OR

Agate
G9, $125-$200
Columb. Riv., OR

Yellow agate
G10, $175-$300
Columbia Riv., WA.

Brown jasper
G9, $55-$100
Cascade Locks, OR

Red Agate
G9, $80-$150
Cascade Locks, OR

Agate
G9, $40-$75
Sou. OR

Chalcedony
G9, $65-$125
Columb. Riv., OR

Red jasper
G9, $150-$250
Columb. Riv., OR

Obsidian
G8, $60-$125
Klamath Lake, OR

Red jasper
G9, $60-$100
Columb. Riv., OR

Red/yellow jasper
G10, $250-$400
WA

White chalcedony
Split stem
G10, $175-$300
Columbia Riv., WA

Obsidian
G10, $80-$150
Silver Lake, OR

Red jasper
Split stem
G10, $250-$400
Columbia Riv., WA

Note sharp barbs
G10, $300-$550
OR

Agate
G10, $250-$450
WA

Agate
G10, $225-$400
OR

Flat on reverse side
G7, $80-$150
Tollgate, OR

Dark jasper
Jasper
G10, $275-$500
OR

GB

COQUILLE BROADNECK - Mid Archaic-Trans. Phase, 4500 - 2200 B. P.

(Also see Gatecliff and Rabbit Island)

Red jasper

Tip nick

Jasper

G4, $15-$25
Curry Co., OR

G3, $5-$10
Curry Co., OR

G5, $8-$15
Curry Co., OR

G5, $15-$25
Curry Co., OR

G7, $15-$25
Curry Co., OR

Red jasper

Brown jasper

Dark red jasper

G7, $30-$50
Curry Co., OR

Barbed edge

G7, $30-$50
Curry Co., OR

G6, $15-$25
Curry Co., OR

G10, $35-$65
Curry Co., OR

Serrated edge

G9, $60-$100
Coquille Riv., OR

Serrated edge

Serrated edge

G10, $80-$150
Josephine Co.,
OR

Jasper

G9, $60-$100
Coquille Riv., OR

G10, $80-$150
Curry Co., OR

LOCATION: Coos & Curry Co. OR & N.W. California. **DESCRIPTION:** A medium size, triangular dart/knife with a convex to straight blade edge. The stem is broad and triangular to tapering and rounded. Shoulders are barbed to horizontal. Many are serrated. **I.D. KEY:** Broad, tapering to rounded stem.

COQUILLE BROADNECK (continued)

Basalt

Serrated edge

G7, $30-$50
Curry Co., OR

G7, $45-$80
Coquille Riv., OR

G8, $45-$80
Coquille Riv., OR

G8, $45-$80
Coquille Riv., OR

G8, $50-$90
Coquille Riv., OR

COQUILLE KNIFE - Mid-Archaic to Trans. Phase, 4500 - 400 B. P.

(Also see Triangular Knife)

Red jasper

LOCATION: Coos & Curry Co. OR. **DESCRIPTION:** A medium sized lanceolate knife with a straight base. **I.D. KEY:** Medium lanceolate form.

G8, $25-$45
Curry Co., OR

COQUILLE NARROWNECK - Mid-Archaic to Transition Phase 2200 - 400 B. P.

(Also see Gatecliff, Portage and Rabbit Island)

Agate

Jasper

Agate

Quartz

G5, $5-$10
Camas Valley, OR

G5, $5-$10
Camas Valley, OR

G6, $8-$15
S.W. OR

G5, $5-$10
Camas Valley, OR

G5, $8-$15
Camas Valley, OR

G6, $8-$15
S.W. OR

LOCATION: Coos Co. & Curry Co. OR. & N.W. California. **DESCRIPTION:** A medium size, triangular dart/knife wiath a convex to straight blade edge. The stem is narrow and triangular to tapering and rounded. Shoulders are barbed to horizontal. Many are serrated. **I.D. KEY:** Narrow, tapering to rounded stem.

1169

GB

COQUILLE NARROWNECK (continued)

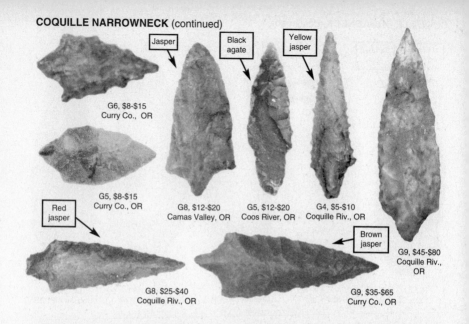

G6, $8-$15
Curry Co., OR

G5, $8-$15
Curry Co., OR

Jasper

Black agate

Yellow jasper

G8, $12-$20
Camas Valley, OR

G5, $12-$20
Coos River, OR

G4, $5-$10
Coquille Riv., OR

Red jasper

Brown jasper

G9, $45-$80
Coquille Riv., OR

G8, $25-$40
Coquille Riv., OR

G9, $35-$65
Curry Co., OR

COQUILLE SIDE NOTCHED - Mid-Archaic to Transition Phase, 4500 - 2200 B. P.

(Also see Cold Springs, Rose Springs Side Notched)

Red jasper

Green chert

Red jasper

Tip nick

Agate

G5, $12-$20
Curry Co., OR

G6, $5-$10
Coos Co., OR

G6, $5-$10
Curry Co., OR

G3, $2-$5
Curry Co., OR

G6, $20-$35
Curry Co., OR

LOCATION: Coos & Curry Co. OR. & N.W. Calif. **DESCRIPTION:** A medium size, triangular dart/knife wiath a convex blade edge and broad side notches. The stem is broad and triangular to tapering and rounded. Shoulders are barbed to tapered. **I.D. KEY:** Broad, side notches.

COTTONWOOD LEAF - Classic to Historic Phase, 700 - 200 B. P.

(Also see Canalino, Cottonwood Triangle, Gold Hill and Trojan)

LOCATION: Great Basin states northward. **DESCRIPTION:** A small size, thin, ovoid point with a convex base. Similar to the *Nodena* type from Arkansas. **I.D. KEY:** Small ovoid form.

COTTONWOOD LEAF (continued)

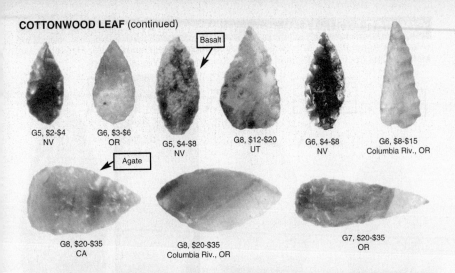

G5, $2-$4
NV

G6, $3-$6
OR

Basalt

G5, $4-$8
NV

G8, $12-$20
UT

G6, $4-$8
NV

G6, $8-$15
Columbia Riv., OR

Agate

G8, $20-$35
CA

G8, $20-$35
Columbia Riv., OR

G7, $20-$35
OR

COTTONWOOD TRIANGLE - Classic to Historic Phase, 700 - 200 B. P.

(Also see Canalino Triangular, Cottonwood Leaf and Desert)

G6, $6-$12
Reno, NV

G6, $8-$15
WA/OR

Obsidian

G6, $8-$15
Tule Lake, CA

Jasper

G6, $6-$10
Bonner Co., ID

G5, $6-$15
Owyhee Co., ID

Agate

G6, $12-$20
Owyhee Co., ID

Green Chert

G8, $35-$60
Rabbit Isle, WA

G8, $15-$25
UT

Banded obsidian

Edge wear

Jasper

G7, $5-$18
OR.

G8, $15-$30
OR

G5, $12-$20
CA

G8, $15-$30
Owyhee Co., ID

G7, $12-$20
CA

G7, $12-$20
CA

LOCATION: Great Basin states northward. **DESCRIPTION:** A small to medium size, thin, triangular point with a straight to concave base. Basal corners are sharp to rounded. The preform for the *Desert* series. **I.D. KEY:** Small triangle form.

1171

GB

COUGAR MOUNTAIN - Paleo, 11,500 - 9000 B. P.

(Also see Agate Basin, Año Nuevo, Cody Complex, Deschutes Knife, Haskett, Lake Mohave, Lind Coulee and Parman, Shaniko Stemmed and Wildcat Canyon)

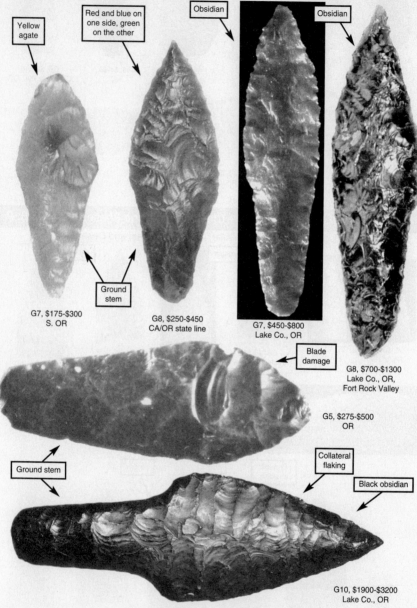

Yellow agate

Red and blue on one side, green on the other

Obsidian

Obsidian

Ground stem

G7, $175-$300
S. OR

G8, $250-$450
CA/OR state line

G7, $450-$800
Lake Co., OR

Blade damage

G8, $700-$1300
Lake Co., OR,
Fort Rock Valley

G5, $275-$500
OR

Ground stem

Collateral flaking

Black obsidian

G10, $1900-$3200
Lake Co., OR

LOCATION: Southern Oregon, N.W. Nevada. **DESCRIPTION:** A large size, long stemmed form with weak tapered shoulders and a convex base. Basal area is ground. Associated with *Haskett* points found on the same sites. Co-existed with *Clovis* and later developed into *Lind Coulee* points. Among the earliest points found at Cougar Mountain Cave in Southern Oregon. Very rare. **I.D. KEY:** Long tapered stem.

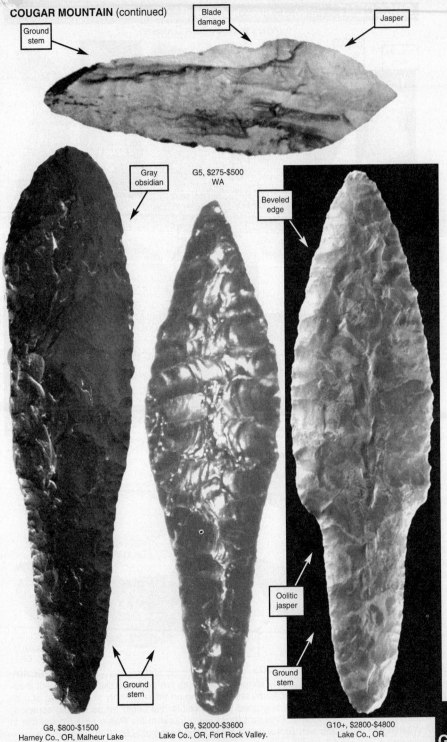

COUGAR MOUNTAIN (continued)

Ground stem

Blade damage

Jasper

Gray obsidian

G5, $275-$500
WA

Beveled edge

Oolitic jasper

Ground stem

Ground stem

G8, $800-$1500
Harney Co., OR, Malheur Lake

G9, $2000-$3600
Lake Co., OR, Fort Rock Valley.

G10+, $2800-$4800
Lake Co., OR

GB

(Also see Black Rock Concave)

Butterfly form

Quarter moon

Half moon

G8, $60-$100
Tulare Lake, CA

G6, $30-$50
Lake Co., OR

G7, $60-$100
Borax Lake, OR

G9, $60-$100
Harney Co., OR

G6, $25-$40
Tulare Lake, CA

G6, $25-$40
OR

G6, $40-$80
Columbia River, OR

Agate

Chalcedony

G7, $80-$150
OR

Butterfly form

G6, $35-$65
OR

G8, $150-$250
Harney Co., OR

G9 $175-$300
OR

Chalcedony

G7, $45-$80
OR

Black obsidian

G8, $125-$200
OR

G7, $60-$115
Black Rock Desert NV

Black obsidian

G8, $150-$250
Harney Co., OR

LOCATION: *Black Rock Concave* sites in N.W. Nevada and southern Oregon. **DESCRIP-TION:** Crescent moon to butterfly shaped, *Crescents* are controversial with different theories as to their use. The earlier forms show grinding on the edge only at the center of both sides as well as one or more burinated tips. Possible use could be as knives, scrapers, transverse points or gravers. Crescent forms were found at the Paleo *Lind Coulee* site in Washington state. and with *Clovis* points in the Fenn cache of N.E. Utah.

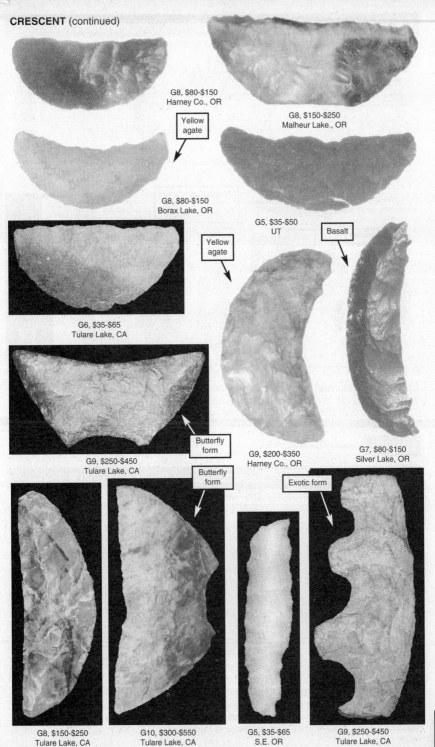

CRESCENT (continued)

G8, $80-$150
Harney Co., OR

G8, $150-$250
Malheur Lake., OR

Yellow agate

G8, $80-$150
Borax Lake, OR

G5, $35-$50
UT

Yellow agate

Basalt

G6, $35-$65
Tulare Lake, CA

Butterfly form

G9, $250-$450
Tulare Lake, CA

G9, $200-$350
Harney Co., OR

G7, $80-$150
Silver Lake, OR

Butterfly form

Exotic form

G8, $150-$250
Tulare Lake, CA

G10, $300-$550
Tulare Lake, CA

G5, $35-$65
S.E. OR

G9, $250-$450
Tulare Lake, CA

1175

GB

DAGGER - Developmental to Classic Phase, 1200 - 400 B. P.

(Also see Klickitat and Nottoway)

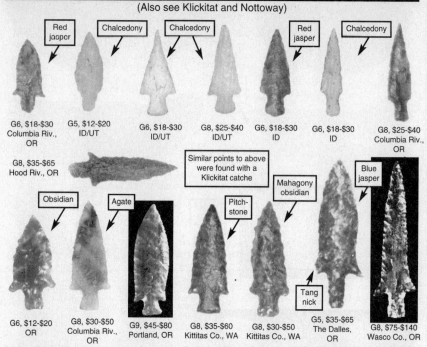

Red jaspor

Chalcedony

Chalcedony

Red jasper

Chalcedony

G6, $18-$30
Columbia Riv.,
OR

G5, $12-$20
ID/UT

G6, $18-$30
ID/UT

G8, $25-$40
ID/UT

G6, $18-$30
ID

G6, $18-$30
ID

G8, $25-$40
Columbia Riv.,
OR

G8, $35-$65
Hood Riv., OR

Similar points to above
were found with a
Klickitat catche

Mahagony
obsidian

Blue
jasper

Obsidian

Agate

Pitch-
stone

Tang
nick

G6, $12-$20
OR

G8, $30-$50
Columbia Riv.,
OR

G9, $45-$80
Portland, OR

G8, $35-$60
Kittitas Co., WA

G8, $30-$50
Kittitas Co., WA

G5, $35-$65
The Dalles,
OR

G8, $75-$140
Wasco Co., OR

LOCATION: Columbia River basin along the Columbia River. **DESCRIPTION:** A small to large size, narrow, thin, barbed point or knife. Bases vary from expanded to contracted. These forms may prove to be various types yet un-named. **I.D. KEY:** Blade form.

DAGGER (see Klickitat)

DESCHUTES KNIFE - Classic to Historic Phase, 500 - 250 B. P.

(Also see Ano Nuevo & Cougar Mountain)

Rootbeer
colored flint

Must have
notch in base

G8, $350-$600
Lake Co., OR

LOCATION: Mid-Columbia River basin in Oregon. **DESCRIPTION:** Very rare. A large size, long stemmed to lanceolate knife with slight to tapered shoulders and a concave base. Length can be 4 to 9". There is edge grinding on the stem. This blade had a wrapped handle and was held as a knife and probably is ceremonial. **I.D. KEY:** Size, basal notch & blade form.

DESERT DELTA - Classic to Historic Phase, 700 - 200 B. P.

(Also see Bitterroot, Cold Spring, Panoche, Piquinin, Uinta)

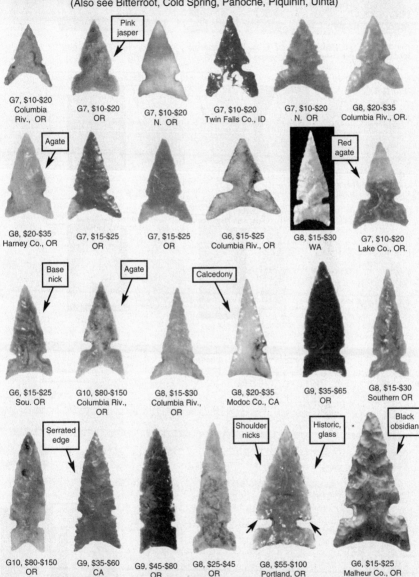

Pink jasper

G7, $10-$20
Columbia
Riv., OR

G7, $10-$20
OR

G7, $10-$20
N. OR

G7, $10-$20
Twin Falls Co., ID

G7, $10-$20
N. OR

G8, $20-$35
Columbia Riv., OR.

Agate

Red agate

G8, $20-$35
Harney Co., OR

G7, $15-$25
OR

G7, $15-$25
OR

G6, $15-$25
Columbia Riv., OR

G8, $15-$30
WA

G7, $10-$20
Lake Co., OR.

Base nick

Agate

Calcedony

G6, $15-$25
Sou. OR

G10, $80-$150
Columbia Riv.,
OR

G8, $15-$30
Columbia Riv.,
OR

G8, $20-$35
Modoc Co., CA

G9, $35-$65
OR

G8, $15-$30
Southern OR

Serrated edge

Shoulder nicks

Historic, glass

Black obsidian

G10, $80-$150
OR

G9, $35-$60
CA

G9, $45-$80
OR

G8, $25-$45
OR

G8, $55-$100
Portland, OR

G6, $15-$25
Malheur Co., OR

LOCATION: Great Basin westward. **DESCRIPTION:** A small, thin, triangular, side notched arrow point with a deeply concave base, straight blade edges and pointed ears. Blade edges can be serrated. **I.D. KEY:** Small triangle, side notched form.

DESERT GENERAL - Classic to Historic Phase, 700 - 200 B. P.

(Also see Bear River, Bitterroot, Cold Spring, Panoche, Piqunin, Uinta & Wintu)

GB

DESERT GENERAL (continued)

Basalt

G4, $2-$4
Gooding Co.,
ID

G7, $10-$20
Gooding Co.,
ID

G4, $2-$5
Owyhee Co.,
ID

G7, $10-$20
OR

Chalce-
dony

G5, $5-$10
Sou. OR

G5, $5-$10
OR

G5, $5-$10
OR

G6, $8-$15
Cent. OR

G7, $10-$20
Owyhee Co.,
ID

G6, $8-$15
OR

Banded
obsidian

G9, $15-$30
OR

Obsidian

Double
notched

G7, $10-$20
OR

G8, $40-$75
WA

G8, $15-$25
N. OR

Serrated

Double
notched

Obsidian

Agate

Red
jasper

G6, $12-$20
NV

G8, $15-$30
Columbia
Riv., WA

G7, $12-$20
Sou. OR

G9, $50-$90
WA

G8, $15-$25
OR

G8, $15-$25
Gooding Co., ID

G8, $15-$25
Chehalis, WA

Clear

Banded
obsidian

Agate

Rare
snowflake
obsidian

G6, $8-$15
Gooding Co., ID

G8 $15-$25
Columbia Riv., WA

G10, $30-$50
OR

G7, $12-$20
Sou. Cent. OR

G9, $15-$30
OR

G9, $30-$50
OR

Clear
agate

Basalt

Double
notched

G10, $50-$90
OR

G8, $12-$20
OR

G8, $15-$25
Columbia Riv., WA

G8, $15-$30
Gooding Co., ID

G8, $15-$25
OR

G10, $80-$150
WA

DESERT GENERAL (continued)

LOCATION: Great Basin westward. **DESCRIPTION:** A small, thin, side notched arrow point with a straight to slightly concave base. Blade edges can be serrated. Similar to the *Reed* point found in Oklahoma. Reported to have been used by the Shoshoni Indians of the Historic period.

DESERT REDDING - Classic to Historic Phase, 700 - 200 B. P.

(Also see Bear River, Bitterroot, Cold Spring, Panoche, Piquinin)

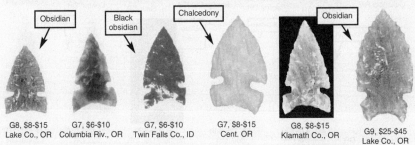

G8, $8-$15
Lake Co., OR

G7, $6-$10
Columbia Riv., OR

G7, $6-$10
Twin Falls Co., ID

G7, $8-$15
Cent. OR

G8, $8-$15
Klamath Co., OR

G9, $25-$45
Lake Co., OR

LOCATION: Great Basin westward. **DESCRIPTION:** A small, thin, side notched arrow point with a concave base. Blade edges curve into the base and can be serrated. Reported to have been used by the Shoshoni Indians of the Historic period.

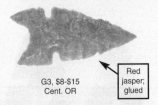

G3, $8-$15
Cent. OR

Red jasper; glued

DESERT - SIERRA VARIETY - Classic to Historic Phase, 700 - 200 B. P.

(Also see Bitterroot, Cold Spring and Panoche)

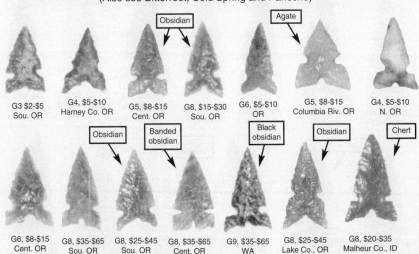

G3 $2-$5
Sou. OR

G4, $5-$10
Harney Co. OR

G5, $8-$15
Cent. OR

G8, $15-$30
Sou. OR

G6, $5-$10
OR

G5, $8-$15
Columbia Riv. OR

G4, $5-$10
N. OR

G6, $8-$15
Cent. OR

G8, $35-$65
Sou. OR

G8, $25-$45
Sou. OR

G8, $35-$65
Cent. OR

G9, $35-$65
WA

G8, $25-$45
Lake Co., OR

G8, $20-$35
Malheur Co., ID

LOCATION: Great Basin westward. **DESCRIPTION:** A small size, thin, triangular side and basal notched arrow point with distinctive basal pointed barbs and a basal notch. **I.D. KEY:** Triple notches, pointed basal corners.

GB

DESERT SIERRA (continued)

Gem

G8, $15-$25
Columbia Riv.,
OR

G9, $15-$30
Central OR

Obsidian

G6, $12-$20
Central OR

G9, $30-$50
Shasta Co., CA

G9, $12-$20
Sou. OR

Obsidian

G6, $12-$20
Central OR

G6, $12-$20
Central OR

Obsidian

G5, $5-$10
Columbia Riv., OR

G7, $15-$30
Central OR

Obsidian

G9, $25-$40
Sou. OR

White chert

G8, $15-$30
Malheur Co., OR

Obsidian

G9, $25-$40
Sou. OR

G9, $25-$40
Central OR

G8, $25-$40
Klamath Co., OR

G7, $25-$40
Twin Falls Co., ID

G9, $35-$65
Sou. OR

Black obsidian

G8, $30-$50
Central OR

G8, $30-$50
Central OR

Obsidian

G8, $30-$50
Columbia Riv.,
WA

G8, $35-$65
Central OR

G8 $35-$65
Lake Co. OR

G9, $35-$65
Sou. OR

G9, $35-$65
Sou. OR

G9, $35-$65
Central OR

Chalcedony

G10, $45-$80
Columbia Riv.,
WA

G9, $35-$65
Sou. OR

Obsidian

G9, $45-$80
Central OR

G10, $65-$125
Central OR

G7, $35-$65
Columbia Riv., WA.

Clear obsidian

G9, $40-$70
Cenral. OR

G7, $30-$50
Central OR

G7, $30-$50
Warner Valley, OR

1180

DOUBLE TIP   (See Elko Eared and Wallula)

DRILL - Paleo to Historic Phase, 14,000 - 200 B. P.

(Also see Graver, Lancet, Perforator and Scraper)

Ground base

Obsidian

Elko Eared drill

Ignimbrite

G3, $2-$4
Lady Island, WA

G4, $2-$5
OR

G6, $25-$40
OR

G6, $8-$15
OR

G6, $8-$15
OR

G4, $4-$8
Sou. OR

Agate

Opaque agate

G6, $12-$20
OR

G9, $30-$50
Columbia Riv., OR

G6, $8-$15
OR

Green Nephrite

Black basalt

G9, $30-$55
Lake Co., OR

G9, $30-$55
Curry Co., OR, Pistol Riv.

Jasper/ agate

Basalt

Rose Springs drill

Cody Complex drill, ground base & sides

G9, $35-$60
OR

G6, $15-$30
Bonner Co., ID

G9, $35-$60
Sou. OR

G9, $50-$90
OR

LOCATION: Everywhere. **DESCRIPTION:** Although many drills were made from scratch, all point types were made into the drill form. Usually, heavily resharpened and broken points were salvaged and rechipped into drills. These objects were certainly used as drills (evidence of extreme edge wear), but there is speculation that some of these forms may have been used as pins for clothing, ornaments, ear plugs and other uses.

GB

DRILL (continued)

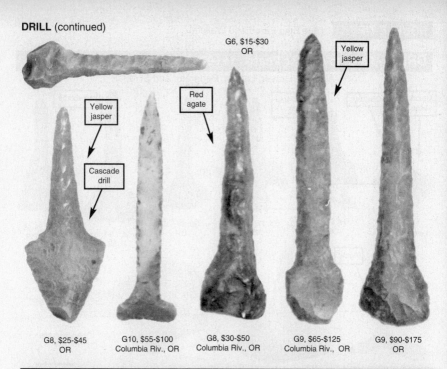

Yellow jasper

Cascade drill

Red agate

Yellow jasper

G6, $15-$30
OR

G8, $25-$45
OR

G10, $55-$100
Columbia Riv., OR

G8, $30-$50
Columbia Riv., OR

G9, $65-$125
Columbia Riv., OR

G9, $90-$175
OR

EARLY EARED - Early to Middle Archaic, 8000 - 5000 B. P.

(Also see Hawken, Humboldt Expanded Base, Pryor Stemmed and Shaniko Stemmed)

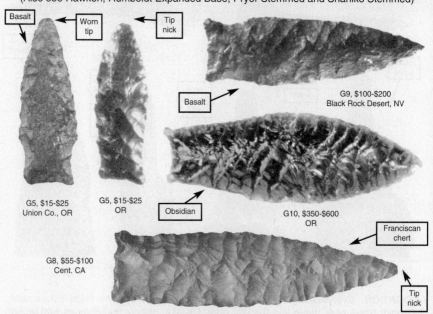

Basalt

Worn tip

Tip nick

Basalt

G9, $100-$200
Black Rock Desert, NV

Obsidian

G10, $350-$600
OR

Franciscan chert

Tip nick

G5, $15-$25
Union Co., OR

G5, $15-$25
OR

G8, $55-$100
Cent. CA

LOCATION: Great Basin westward. **DESCRIPTION:** A medium size, thin, lanceolate point with broad, shallow side notches expanding into rounded ears that may be ground. The base is concave. These haven't been officially named yet.

EARLY EARED (continued)

Tip nick

Obsidian

G7, $25-$45
Lake Co., OR

G9, $250-$400
Nixon, NV

EARLY LEAF - Early to Middle Archaic, 8000 - 5000 B. P.

(Also see Cascade, Excelsior, Kennewick, Shaniko Stemmed and Wildcat Canyon)

Basalt

Diagonal flaking

Ground stem

Diagonal flaking

Diagonal flaking

Side nicks

Obsidian

G6, $25-$45
S.E. OR

G9, $150-$250
Lake Co., OR

G8, $55-$100
S.E. OR

G7, $35-$60
OR

G9, $80-$150
Lake Co.,OR

LOCATION: Great Basin to Washington. **DESCRIPTION:** A medium to large size lanceolate point or blade with a convex, pointed or straight base. Early parallel flaking is evident on many examples. These haven't been officially named yet and could be early *Cascade* forms.

GB

EARLY LEAF (continued)

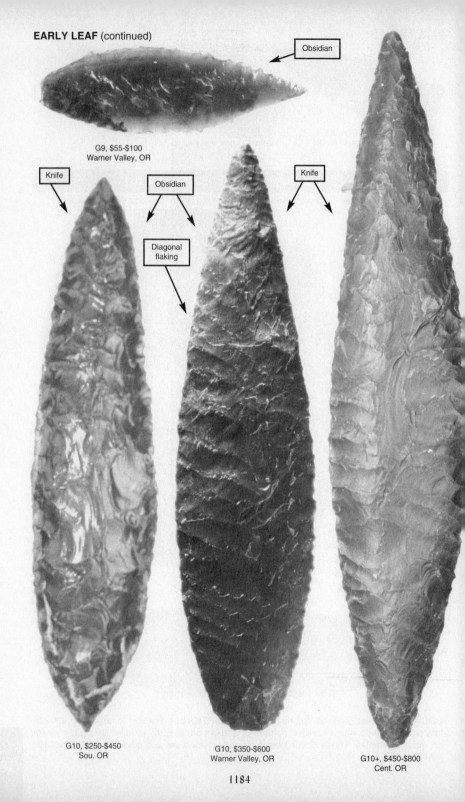

Obsidian

G9, $55-$100
Warner Valley, OR

Knife

Obsidian

Diagonal
flaking

Knife

G10, $250-$450
Sou. OR

G10, $350-$600
Warner Valley, OR

G10+, $450-$800
Cent. OR

EARLY STEMMED-LANCEOLATE (see Shaniko Stemmed)

EASTGATE - Developmental to Classic Phase, 1400 - 400 B. P.

(Also see Columbia Plateau, Eastgate, Elko, Emigrant Springs, Gunther, Rose Springs, Wallula)

Clear obsidian

Chert

Red jasper

Agate

G6, $8-$15
OR

G6, $12-$20
Owyhee Co., ID

G8, $15-$25
OR

G6 $15-$25
OR

G8 $15-$30
OR

G8, $25-$40
Malhuer Co., OR

Obsidian

Obsidian

Banded obsidian

G7, $5-$10
Malhuer Co., OR

G9, $65-$120
Lake Co., OR

G9, $40-$75
Lake Co., OR

G9, $35-$65
Malhuer Co., OR

G6, $15-$30
Humboldt Riv., NV

G6, $25-$40
Humboldt Riv., NV

G6, $15-$30
Humboldt Riv., NV

G8, $30-$50
OR

G6, $35-$60
Washoe Lake, NV

G7, $40-$75
Humboldt Riv., NV

Banded obsidian

Hand held to show translucency

Obsidian

Agate

G8, $35-$60
Bonner Co., ID

G5, $5-$10
CA

Pink chert

G9, $90-$175
Silver Lake, OR

G8, $55-$100
Humboldt Riv., NV

G9, $90-$175
Owens, River, CA, very thin.

LOCATION: Great Basin westward.
DESCRIPTION: A small, thin, triangular corner-notched arrow point with a short parallel sided to expanded stem. Barbs can be pointed or squared and usually extend to base.

1185

GB

EASTGATE (continued)

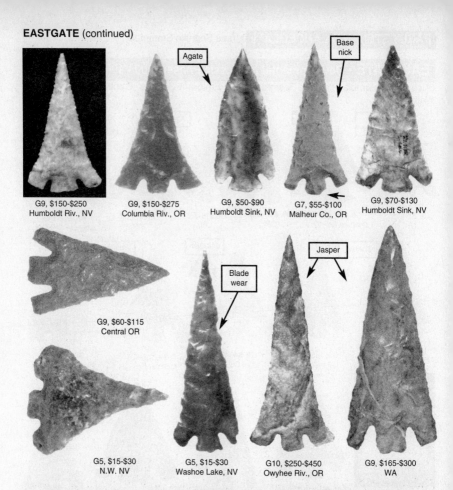

Agate

Base nick

G9, $150-$250
Humboldt Riv., NV

G9, $150-$275
Columbia Riv., OR

G9, $50-$90
Humboldt Sink, NV

G7, $55-$100
Malheur Co., OR

G9, $70-$130
Humboldt Sink, NV

Jasper

Blade wear

G9, $60-$115
Central OR

G5, $15-$30
N.W. NV

G5, $15-$30
Washoe Lake, NV

G10, $250-$450
Owyhee Riv., OR

G9, $165-$300
WA

EASTGATE SPLIT STEM - Developmental to Classic Phase, 1400 - 400 B. P.

(Also see Columbia Plateau, Gunther, Wallula)

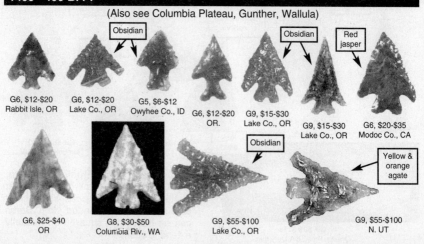

Obsidian

Obsidian

Red jasper

G6, $12-$20
Rabbit Isle, OR

G6, $12-$20
Lake Co., OR

G5, $6-$12
Owyhee Co., ID

G6, $12-$20
OR.

G9, $15-$30
Lake Co., OR

G9, $15-$30
Lake Co., OR

G6, $20-$35
Modoc Co., CA

Obsidian

Yellow & orange agate

G6, $25-$40
OR

G8, $30-$50
Columbia Riv., WA

G9, $55-$100
Lake Co., OR

G9, $55-$100
N. UT

EASTGATE SPLIT STEM (continued)

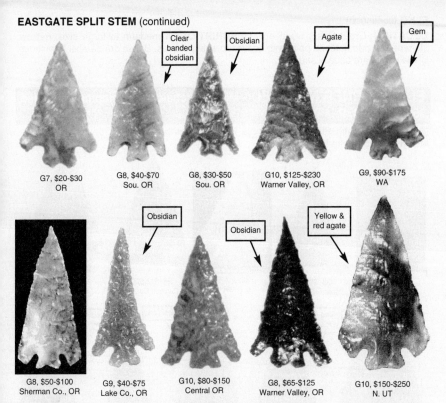

G7, $20-$30
OR

Clear banded obsidian

Obsidian

Agate

Gem

G8, $40-$70
Sou. OR

G8, $30-$50
Sou. OR

G10, $125-$230
Warner Valley, OR

G9, $90-$175
WA

Obsidian

Obsidian

Yellow & red agate

G8, $50-$100
Sherman Co., OR

G9, $40-$75
Lake Co., OR

G10, $80-$150
Central OR

G8, $65-$125
Warner Valley, OR

G10, $150-$250
N. UT

LOCATION: Great Basin westward. **DESCRIPTION:** A small, thin, triangular arrow point with expanding barbs and a small bifurcated base. Blade edges are usually finely serrated.

EDEN (See Cody Complex)

ELKO - Middle Archaic to Developmental Phase, 3500 - 1200 B. P.
(Also see Hell's Canyon, Quillomene Bar and Rose Springs)

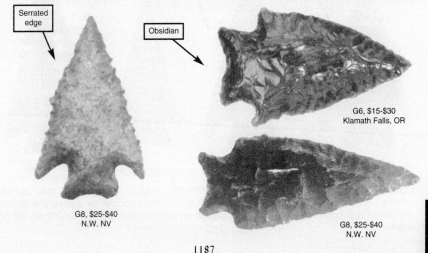

Serrated edge

Obsidian

G6, $15-$30
Klamath Falls, OR

G8, $25-$40
N.W. NV

G8, $25-$40
N.W. NV

1187

GB

ELKO (continued)

LOCATION: Great Basin westward. **DESCRIPTION:** A medium to large size, narrow, stemmed to side notched point with convex to straight sides. Bases are parallel to bulbous. Blade edges are usually serrated.

ELKO CORNER NOTCHED - Middle Archaic to Developmental Phase, 3500 - 1200 B. P.

(Also see Chilcotin Plateau, Columbia Plateau, Eastgate, Hell's Canyon, Hendricks, Merrybell, and Snake River)

G5, $12-$20
OR

G4, $8-$15
Colum. Riv., OR

G6, $15-$30
OR

G5, $12-$20
Owyhee Co., ID

G5, $12-$20
Gooding Co., ID

Red jasper

G9, $70-$135
Warner Valley, OR

G9, $50-$90
Lake Co., OR

Obsidian

G9, $35-$60
Warner Val., OR

Obsidian

G9, $45-$85
Warner Valley, OR

G5, $12-$20
Owyhee Co. ID

Obsidian

G9, $35-$65
Crump Lake, OR

G7, $30-$50
Malheur Co., OR

Basalt

G8, $40-$75
Lake Co., OR

Obsidian

G8, $45-$85
Malheur Co., OR

LOCATION: Great Basin westward. **DESCRIPTION:** A small to large size, thin, corner notched dart point with shoulder tangs and a convex, concave or auriculate base. Shoulders and tips are sharp. Some examples exhibit excellent parallel flaking on blade edges.

ELKO CORNER NOTCHED (continued)

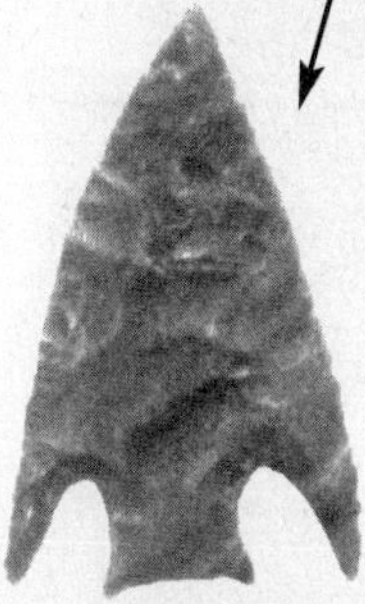
Needle
tangs

G9, $60-$115
N.W. NV

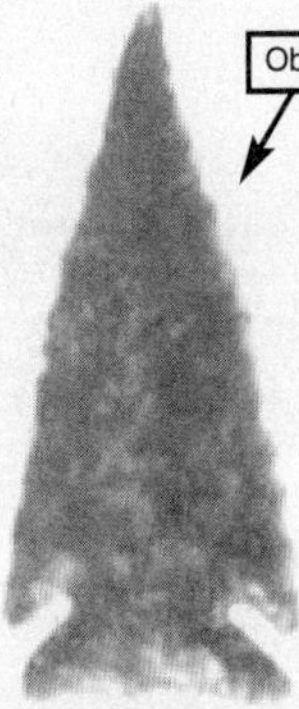
Obsidian

G7, $40-$75
Malheur Co., OR

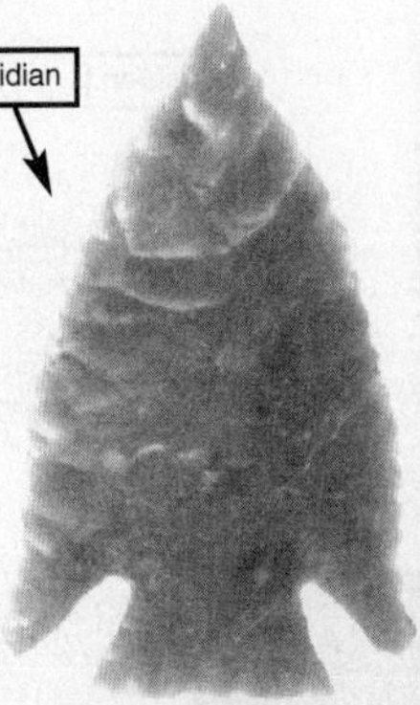

G9, $150-$250
OR

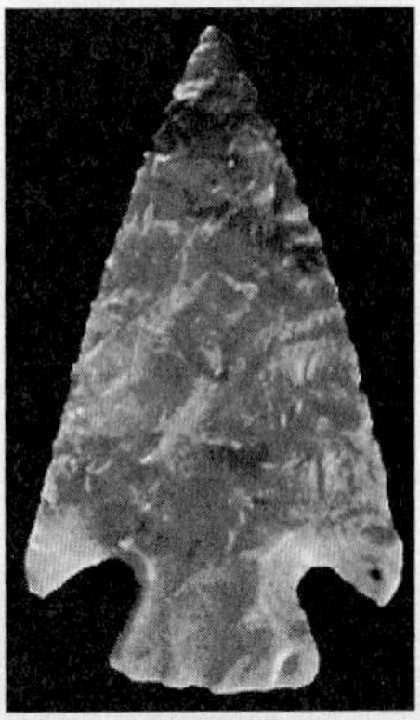

G7, $35-$65
WA./OR

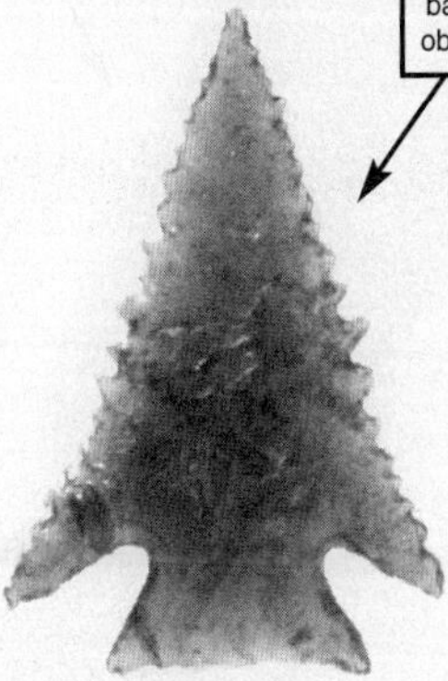
Clear
banded
obsidian

G10, $200-$350
Warner Valley, OR

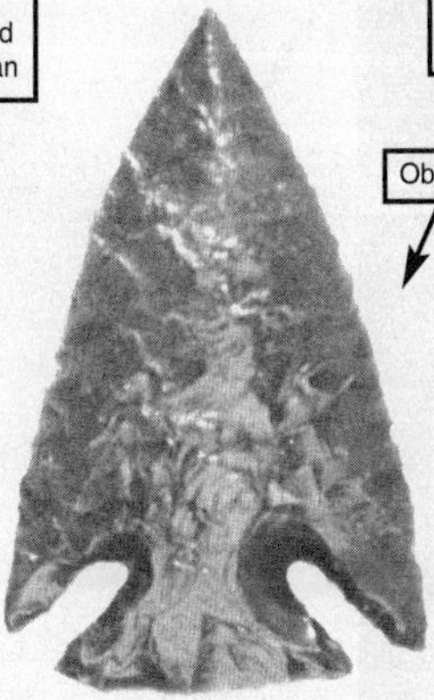
Obsidian

G10, $200-$350
Lake Co., OR

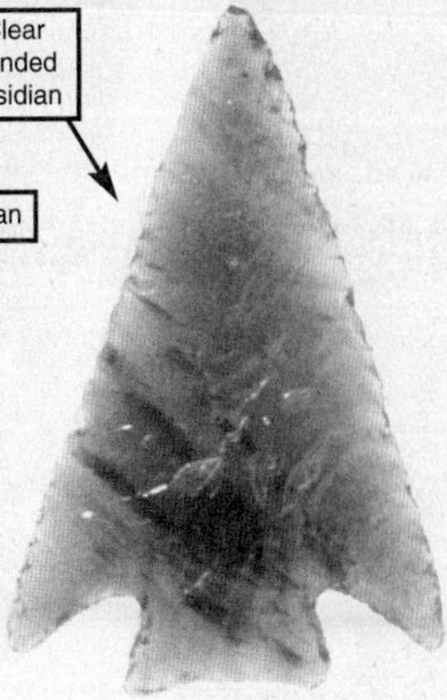
Clear
banded
obsidian

G9, $165-$300
Warner Valley, OR

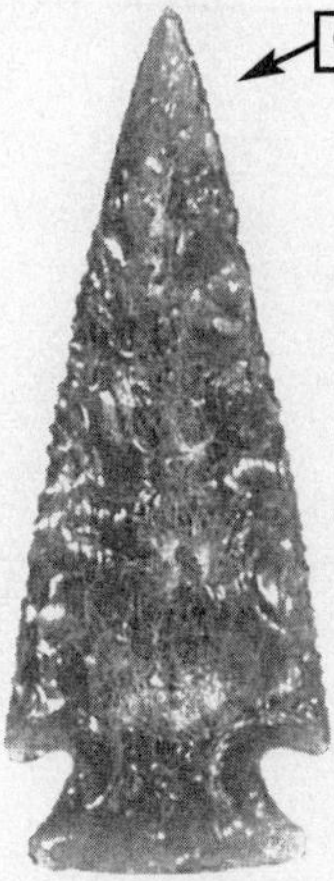
Obsidian

G10, $150-$250
Lake Co., OR

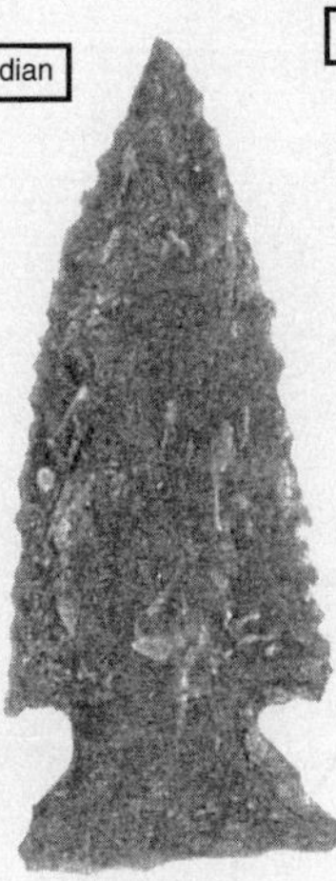

G7, $65-$125
Lake Co., OR

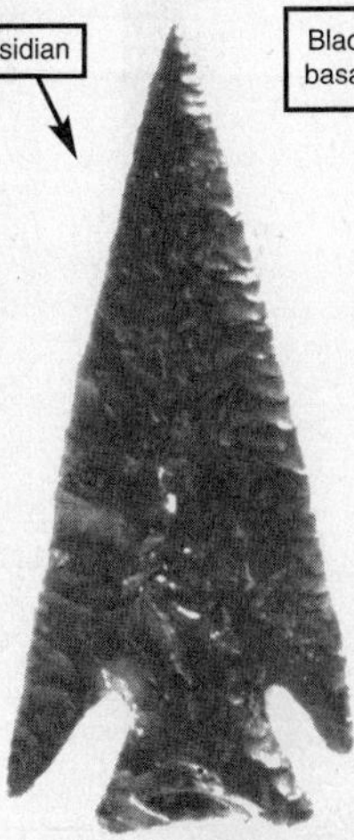
Obsidian

G9, $200-$350
Warner Valley, OR

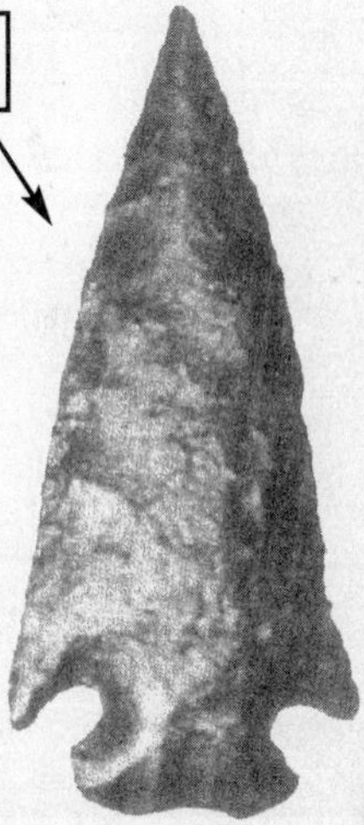
Black
basalt

G9, $125-$225
N. UT

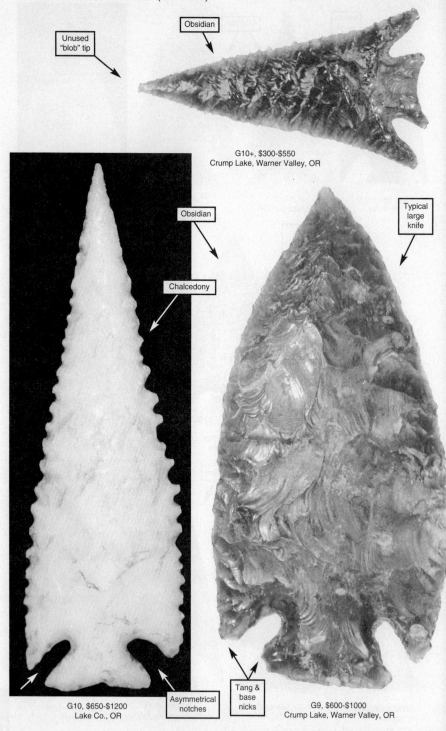

Unused "blob" tip

Obsidian

G10+, $300-$550
Crump Lake, Warner Valley, OR

Obsidian

Chalcedony

Typical large knife

G10, $650-$1200
Lake Co., OR

Asymmetrical notches

Tang & base nicks

G9, $600-$1000
Crump Lake, Warner Valley, OR

(Also see Eastgate, Elko Corner Notched and Merrybell)

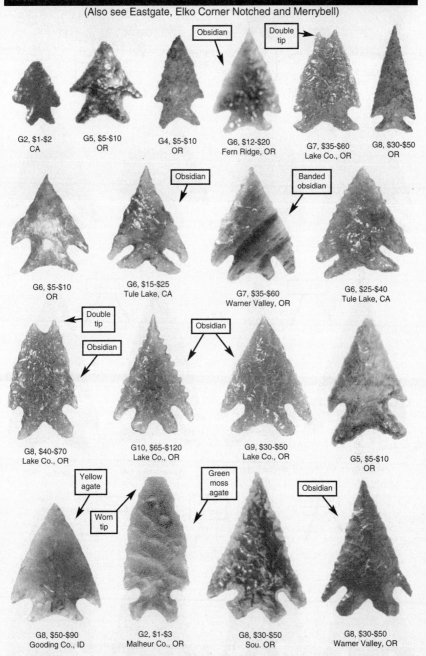

Obsidian

Double tip

G2, $1-$2
CA

G5, $5-$10
OR

G4, $5-$10
OR

G6, $12-$20
Fern Ridge, OR

G7, $35-$60
Lake Co., OR

G8, $30-$50
OR

Obsidian

Banded obsidian

G6, $5-$10
OR

G6, $15-$25
Tule Lake, CA

G7, $35-$60
Warner Valley, OR

G6, $25-$40
Tule Lake, CA

Double tip

Obsidian

Obsidian

G8, $40-$70
Lake Co., OR

G10, $65-$120
Lake Co., OR

G9, $30-$50
Lake Co., OR

G5, $5-$10
OR

Yellow agate

Worn tip

Green moss agate

Obsidian

G8, $50-$90
Gooding Co., ID

G2, $1-$3
Malheur Co., OR

G8, $30-$50
Sou. OR

G8, $30-$50
Warner Valley, OR

LOCATION: Great Basin westward. **DESCRIPTION:** A small to large size corner notched dart point with shoulder tangs and an eared base. Basal ears are usually exaggerated, and corners and tips are sharp. Some examples exhibit excellent parallel flaking on blade edges.

GB

ELKO EARED (continued)

Notched ear

Heat-treated Wascoite

G8, $40-$75
Wasco Co., OR

G8, $70-$125
Lake Co., OR

Black obsidian

Obsidian

G9, $85-$160
Lake Co., OR

G9, $70-$125
OR

G7, $35-$60
Malheur Co., OR

G9, $65-$125
Warner Valley, OR

Obsidian

Obsidian

G9, $55-$100
Modoc Co., CA

G8, $35-$60
Warner Valley, OR

G9, $150-$275
Warner Valley, OR

G7, $30-$50
Lake Co., OR

Obsidian

Black obsidian

Obsidian

G8, $50-$90
Lake Co., OR

G9, $80-$150
Warner Valley, OR

G10, $200-$350
Lake Co., OR

G9, $80-$150
Sou. OR

1192

ELKO EARED (continued)

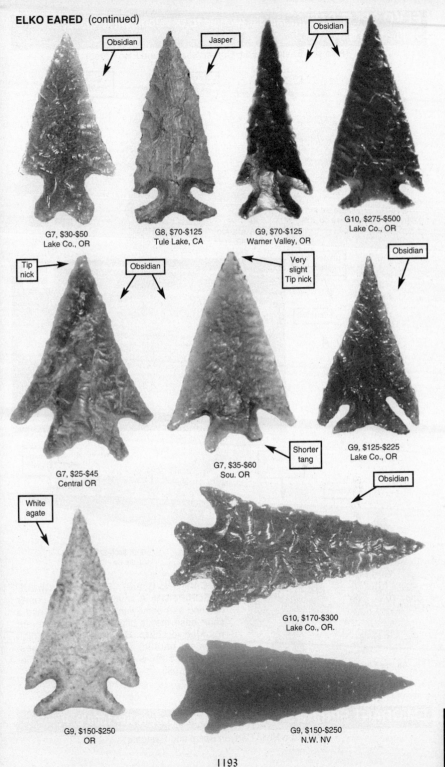

Obsidian

Jasper

Obsidian

G7, $30-$50
Lake Co., OR

G8, $70-$125
Tule Lake, CA

G9, $70-$125
Warner Valley, OR

G10, $275-$500
Lake Co., OR

Tip nick

Obsidian

Very slight Tip nick

Obsidian

G7, $25-$45
Central OR

Shorter tang

G7, $35-$60
Sou. OR

G9, $125-$225
Lake Co., OR

White agate

Obsidian

G10, $170-$300
Lake Co., OR.

G9, $150-$250
OR

G9, $150-$250
N.W. NV

1193

GB

ELKO SPLIT-STEM - Middle Archaic to Developmental Phase, 3500 - 1200 B. P.

(Also see Eastgate, Elko Corner Notched and Elko Eared)

Obsidian

Obsidian

Black obsidian

G5, $8-$15
Warner Valley, OR

G6, $8-$15
Lake Co., OR

G6, $12-$20
Lake Co., OR

G7, $15-$25
Lake Co., OR

G8, $25-$40
NV

Unusual rare base form

Obsidian

Moss agate

G10, $275-$500
Pershing Co., NV

G10, $175-$375
Crump Lake, OR

Black obsidian

Purple agate

Obsidian

G10, $400-$750
Lake Co., OR

G8, $25-$40
OR

G6, $25-$40
Warner Valley, OR.

LOCATION: Great Basin westward. **DESCRIPTION:** A small to large size corner notched dart point with shoulder tangs and a short base that is bifurcated. Shoulders are rounded to sharp. Some examples exhibit excellent parallel flaking on blade edges. Believed to have evolved from the earlier *Gatecliff* point.

EMIGRANT SPRINGS - Developmental Phase, 1200 - 1000 B. P.

(Also see Hells Canyon Basal and Eastgate)

EMIGRANT SPRINGS (continued)

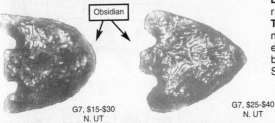

Obsidian

LOCATION: Utah and surrounding area. **DESCRIPTION:** A broad, short basal notched point. Tangs can extend beyond the base. The base is straight to rounded. Shoulders are rounded.

G7, $15-$30
N. UT

G7, $25-$40
N. UT

EXCELSIOR - Late Archaic-Trans. Phase, 3000 - 1700 B. P.

(Also see Cascade, Early Leaf, Kennewick)

Serrated edge

G6, $12-$25
Mendocino Co., CA

Serrated edge

G5, $12-$20
Mendocino Co., CA

Ground stem

G7, $80-$150
CA/OR.

Obsidian

Ground stem

G7, $80-$150
CA/OR

Obsidian

Ground stem

Obsidian

Serrated edge

G10, $200-$350
Marin Co., CA

LOCATION: Northern California and Sou. Oregon. **DESCRIPTION:** A medium to large size, narrow, lanceolate, double pointed blade. Some examples are serrated. Basal areas are usually ground.

GB

EXCELSIOR (continued)

EXOTIC (continued)

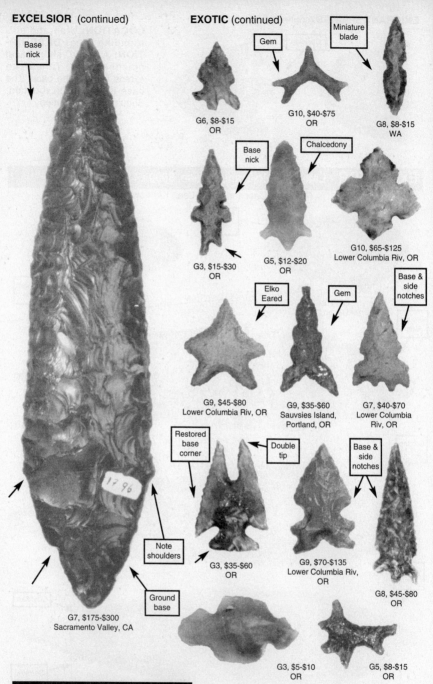

Base nick

G6, $8-$15
OR

Gem

G10, $40-$75
OR

Miniature blade

G8, $8-$15
WA

Base nick

G3, $15-$30
OR

Chalcedony

G5, $12-$20
OR

G10, $65-$125
Lower Columbia Riv, OR

Elko Eared

G9, $45-$80
Lower Columbia Riv, OR

Gem

G9, $35-$60
Sauvsies Island,
Portland, OR

Base & side notches

G7, $40-$70
Lower Columbia
Riv, OR

Restored base corner

Double tip

Base & side notches

Note shoulders

G3, $35-$60
OR

G9, $70-$135
Lower Columbia Riv,
OR

G8, $45-$80
OR

Ground base

G7, $175-$300
Sacramento Valley, CA

G3, $5-$10
OR

G5, $8-$15
OR

EXOTIC FORMS - Late Archaic to Developmental, 3000 - 1000 B. P.

(Also see Stockton & Vendetta)

LOCATION: Everywhere. **DESCRIPTION:** The forms illustrated are rare. Some are definitely effigy forms or exotic point designs while others may be no more than unfinished and unintentional doodles.

EXOTIC (continued)

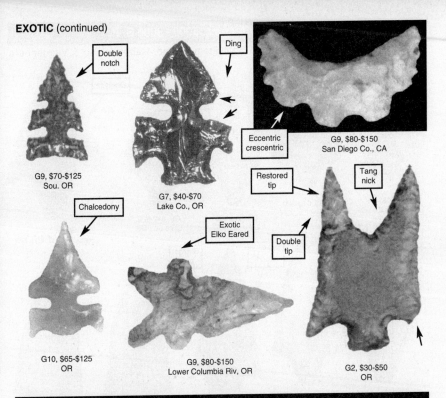

Double notch

G9, $70-$125
Sou. OR

Ding

G7, $40-$70
Lake Co., OR

Eccentric crescentric

G9, $80-$150
San Diego Co., CA

Restored tip

Tang nick

Double tip

Exotic Elko Eared

Chalcedony

G10, $65-$125
OR

G9, $80-$150
Lower Columbia Riv, OR

G2, $30-$50
OR

FIRSTVIEW - Early Archaic, 8700 - 7000 B. P.

(Also see Alberta, Cody Complex)

Obsidian

Ground stem

G7, $250-$425
Massacre Lake, NV

LOCATION: Great Basin into the Plains states. **DESCRIPTION:** A medium to large size lanceolate point with slight shoulders and a rectangular stem that is ground. Shoulders are sometimes absent from resharpening. Most examples exhibit excellent parallel transverse flaking. A variant form of the *Scottsbluff* type made by the Cody Complex people. **I.D. KEY:** Weak shoulders, diamond shaped cross-section.

FOLSOM - Paleo, 11.000 - 9000 B. P.

(Also see Black Rock Concave, Clovis and Humboldt)

Resharpened many times

LOCATION: Canada into Southwestern states and east-ward to N. Indiana. **DESCRIPTION:** A very thin, small to medium sized lanceolate point with convex to straight sides and a convex basal edge creating sharp ears or basal corners. Most examples are fluted from the basal edge to near-ly the tip of the point. Blade flaking is extremely fine and the hafting area is ground. **I.D. KEY:** Thinness and form.

G4, $350-$600
NV

GB

GATECLIFF - Middle to Late Archaic, 5000 - 3000 B. P.

(Also see Coquille, Eastgate, Elko Split-Stem, Pismo, Rabbit Island & Vandenberg Contracting Stem)

Obsidian

Obsidian

Obsidian

G4, $3-$6
Malheur Co., OR

G6, $12-$20
Lake Co., OR

G6, $12-$20
Lake Co., OR

G6, $12-$20
Lake Co., OR

G6, $20-$40
Black Rock Desert, NV

Straight base

Petrified wood

Straight base

G7, $15-$25
Lake Co., OR

G8, $20-$35
Lake Co., OR

G8, $25-$45
OR

G6, $12-$20
S. OR

G8, $20-$35
Lake Co., OR

G8, $20-$35
Lake Co., OR

Oblique flaking

Obsidian

Obsidian

G9, $30-$50
Bend., OR

G8, $20-$35
Lake Co., OR

G8, $25-$45
Lake Co., OR

G9, $65-$125
Klamath Lake, OR

LOCATION: Great Basin westward. **DESCRIPTION:** A medium to large size dart point with horizontal to barbed shoulders and a contracted stem. Bases are straight, rounded or pointed. Blade edges are convex to recurved. Most of the contracting stem points are known as *Gypsum Cave* further south. Parallel, oblique flaking does occur on this type. **I.D. KEY:** Tapered stem.

GATECLIFF SPLIT-STEM - Middle to Late Archaic, 5000 - 3000 B. P.

(Also see Coquille, Eastgate, Elko Split-Stem, Pismo, Rabbit Island & Vandenberg Contracting Stem)

Agate

Basalt

Obsidian

G4, $5-$10
Lakeview, OR

G4, $8-$15
Sou. OR.

G7, $15-$25
Warner Valley, OR

G6, $12-$20
Cent. OR

Base nick

Oblique flaking

G9, $35-$65
Bend, OR

G9, $35-$65
Bend, OR

G8, $55-$100
Tule Lake, CA

Serrated edge

Obsidian

Serrated edge

Oblique flaking

Obsidian

G8, $30-$60
Warner Valley, OR

G9, $65-$125
N.W. NV

G8, $40-$70
Lake Pend Oreill, ID

G9, $100-$200
Warner Valley, OR

LOCATION: Great Basin westward. **DESCRIPTION:** A medium to large size stemmed, bifurcated dart point that is usually serrated with horizontal to barbed shoulders. Believed to have evolved into *Elko* points. The *Gatcliff* usually has a longer stem and a shallowerer base notch than *Pinto Basin* of which it was a part. Parallel, oblique blade flaking does occur. Slightly contracting or expanding is acceptible. **I.D. KEY:** Shallow bifurcated stem.

GB

GOLD HILL - Early Archaic, 4,500 - 2200 B. P.

(Also see Cottonwood Leaf, Malaga Cove Leaf, Portage and Trojan)

G3, $1-$2, Sou. OR

G3, $2-$3, Sou. OR

G5, $3-$6, Sou. OR

G3, $2-$3, Sou. OR

Red/black chert

Red jasper

G5, $3-$6 Sou. OR

G5, $3-$6 Sou. OR

G5, $5-$8 Sou. OR

G7, $8-$15 S.W. OR

G8, $8-$15 S.W. OR

G7, $8-$15 Sou. OR

Agate

Ground base

Not ground

Agate

Lite basal grinding

G9, $15-$30 Camas Valley, OR

G6, $8-$15 Sou. OR

G9, $25-$40 S.W. coast, OR

G9, $25-$40 S.W. coast, OR

G7, $15-$20 S.W. coast, OR

LOCATION: S.W. Oregon and N.W. Calif. **DESCRIPTION:** A descendant of the *Cascade* type. A small to medium size lanceolate dart point with a rounded base. Similar in form to *Malaga Cove Leaf* found in southern California.

GRAVER - Paleo to Archaic, 14,000 - Historic

(Also see Drill, Lancet, Perforator, Scraper & Sizer)

Graver tip

Agate

G6, $8-$15 OR

Paleo

Graver tip

Graver tip

Chalcedony

G6, $8-$15 OR

G6, $12-$20 OR

1200

GRAVER (continued)

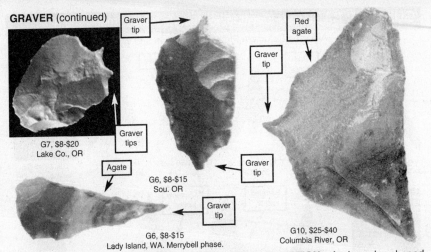

G7, $8-$20
Lake Co., OR

Graver tip

Graver tips

Agate

Graver tip

G6, $8-$15
Lady Island, WA. Merrybell phase.

Graver tip

G6, $8-$15
Sou. OR

Red agate

Graver tip

G10, $25-$40
Columbia River, OR

LOCATION: Paleo and Archaic sites everywhere. **DESCRIPTION:** An irregular shaped uniface tool with sharp, pointed projections used for puncturing, incising, tattooing, etc. Some examples served a dual purpose for scraping as well. Gravers have been found on *Black Rock Concave* sites in the Great Basin.

GROUND STONE - Historic Phase, 300 - 100 B. P.

(Also see Bear, Side Knife, Snow Knife, Ulu and Whale)

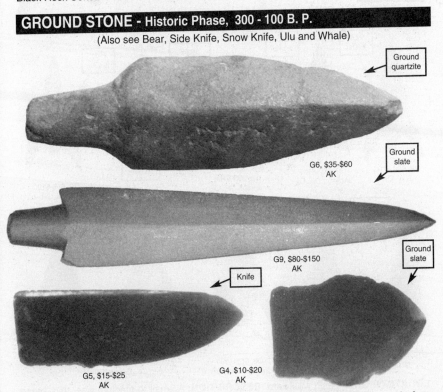

Ground quartzite

G6, $35-$60
AK

Ground slate

G9, $80-$150
AK

Ground slate

Knife

G5, $15-$25
AK

G4, $10-$20
AK

LOCATION: Alaska. **DESCRIPTION:** A medium to large size, stemmed point made from stone. Some examples have a median ridge running along the center of the blade. These points were probably used as knives and harpoons by the Eskimos along the coastal waters.

1201

GB

GUNTHER BARBED - Develop. to Historic Phase, 1000 - 200 B. P.

(Also see Columbia Plateau, Deadman and Wallula)

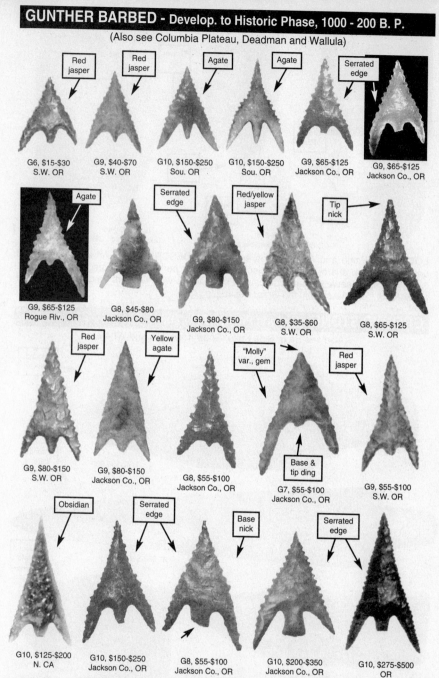

Red jasper

G6, $15-$30
S.W. OR

Red jasper

G9, $40-$70
S.W. OR

Agate

G10, $150-$250
Sou. OR

Agate

G10, $150-$250
Sou. OR

Serrated edge

G9, $65-$125
Jackson Co., OR

Serrated edge

G9, $65-$125
Jackson Co., OR

Agate

G9, $65-$125
Rogue Riv., OR

Serrated edge

G8, $45-$80
Jackson Co., OR

Red/yellow jasper

G9, $80-$150
Jackson Co., OR

G8, $35-$60
S.W. OR

Tip nick

G8, $65-$125
S.W. OR

Red jasper

G9, $80-$150
S.W. OR

Yellow agate

G9, $80-$150
Jackson Co., OR

G8, $55-$100
Jackson Co., OR

"Molly" var., gem

Base & tip ding

G7, $55-$100
Jackson Co., OR

Red jasper

G9, $55-$100
S.W. OR

Obsidian

G10, $125-$200
N. CA

Serrated edge

G10, $150-$250
Jackson Co., OR

G8, $55-$100
Jackson Co., OR

Base nick

G10, $200-$350
Jackson Co., OR

Serrated edge

G10, $275-$500
OR

LOCATION: Great Basin westward. **DESCRIPTION:** A small to medium size, thin, broad, triangular arrow point with long barbs that extend to and beyond the base. The blade sides are straight to concave and the stem is parallel sided to slightly contracting or expanding. These points exhibit high quality flaking. Other local names used for this type are "Camas Valley," "Mad River," "Molalla," "Roger River," and "Shasta."

GUNTHER BARBED (continued)

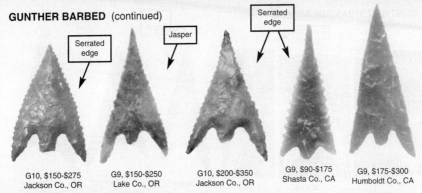

Serrated edge

Jasper

Serrated edge

Serrated edge

G10, $150-$275
Jackson Co., OR

G9, $150-$250
Lake Co., OR

G10, $200-$350
Jackson Co., OR

G9, $90-$175
Shasta Co., CA

G9, $175-$300
Humboldt Co., CA

Below: Gunther Preforms that were discarded after a barb broke or a high-step fracture appeared that couldn't be removed.

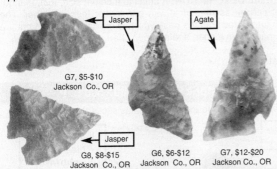

Jasper

Agate

These have been confused as knife forms when they are actually discarded preforms found on Gunther sites in this area.

G7, $5-$10
Jackson Co., OR

Jasper

G8, $8-$15
Jackson Co., OR

G6, $6-$12
Jackson Co., OR

G7, $12-$20
Jackson Co., OR

GUNTHER TRIANGULAR - Developmental to Historic Phase, 1000 - 200 B. P.

(Also see Canalino Triangular and Cottonwood)

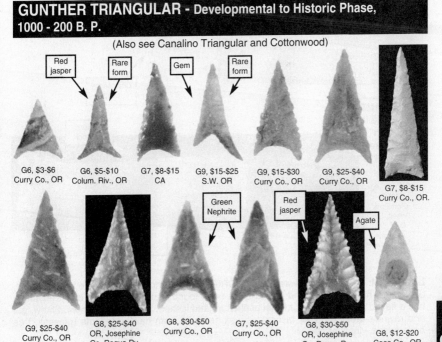

Red jasper

Rare form

Gem

Rare form

G6, $3-$6
Curry Co., OR

G6, $5-$10
Colum. Riv., OR

G7, $8-$15
CA

G9, $15-$25
S.W. OR

G9, $15-$30
Curry Co., OR

G9, $25-$40
Curry Co., OR

G7, $8-$15
Curry Co., OR.

Green Nephrite

Red jasper

Agate

G9, $25-$40
Curry Co., OR

G8, $25-$40
OR, Josephine
Co. Rogue Rv.

G8, $30-$50
Curry Co., OR

G7, $25-$40
Curry Co., OR

G8, $30-$50
OR, Josephine
Co. Rogue Rv.

G8, $12-$20
Coos Co., OR

GB

1203

GUNTHER TRIANGULAR (continued)

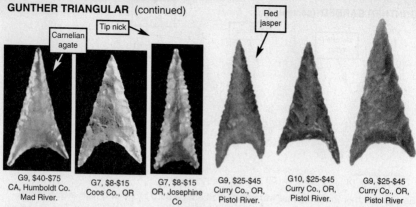

G9, $40-$75
CA, Humboldt Co.
Mad River.

G7, $8-$15
Coos Co., OR

G7, $8-$15
OR, Josephine
Co

G9, $25-$45
Curry Co., OR,
Pistol River.

G10, $25-$45
Curry Co., OR,
Pistol River.

G9, $25-$45
Curry Co., OR,
Pistol River

LOCATION: Great Basin westward. **DESCRIPTION:** A small to medium size, thin, triangular point with basal barbs that can be asymmetrical with one longer than the other. The basal ears have a tendency to turn in towards the base which is concave. Early forms are called U-Back locally. Usually made from jasper, agate, green chert, rarely from obsidian.

GYPSUM CAVE   (see Gatecliff)

HAFTED KNIFE -Transitional-Historic Phase, 2300 - 500 B. P.

(Also see Hafted Knife in Northern High Plains section)

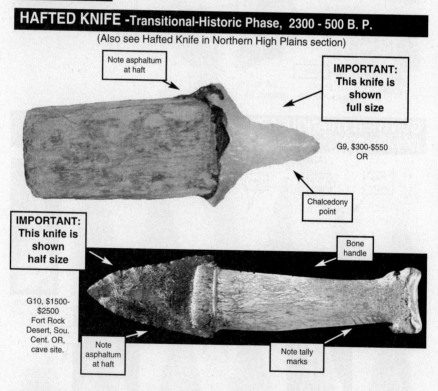

Note asphaltum
at haft

IMPORTANT:
This knife is
shown
full size

G9, $300-$550
OR

Chalcedony
point

IMPORTANT:
This knife is
shown
half size

G10, $1500-
$2500
Fort Rock
Desert, Sou.
Cent. OR,
cave site.

Note
asphaltum
at haft

Bone
handle

Note tally
marks

LOCATION: Great Basin westward. **DESCRIPTION:** Due to the dry climate in this region, completely hafted arrows and knives have been found in dry caves. The above example has a flaked stone blade glued with asphaltum and lashed on the bone handle. Sinew, gut and rawhide were used for lashing as well as fibers from hair and plants (grasses, tree bark, yucca, vines, etc.).

HARAHEY - Classic Phase, 700 - 400 B. P.

(Also see Cascade, Early Leaf, Wahmuza)

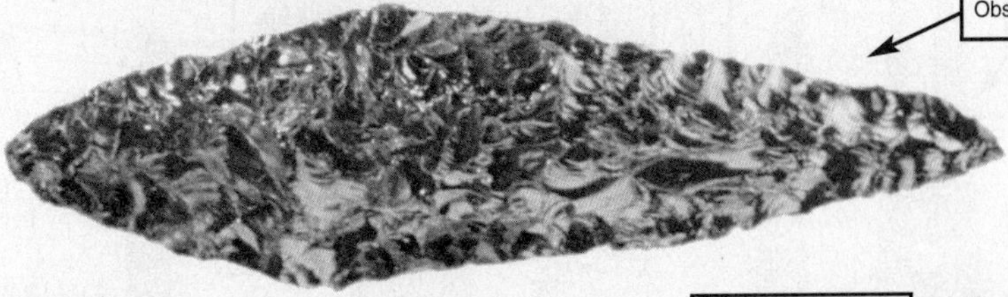
Obsidian

G7, $35-$60
Lake Co., OR

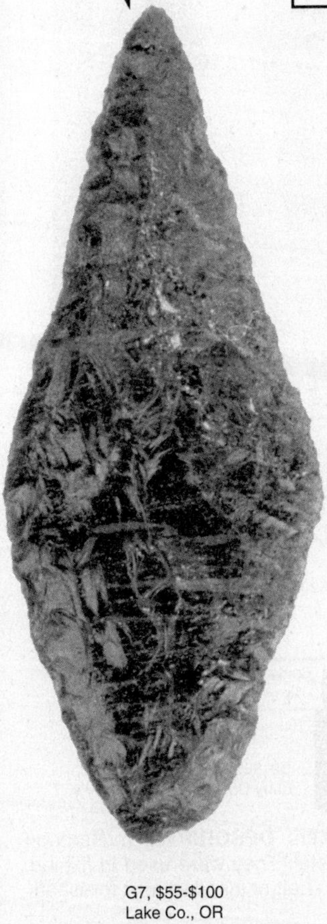
Obsidian

G7, $55-$100
Lake Co., OR

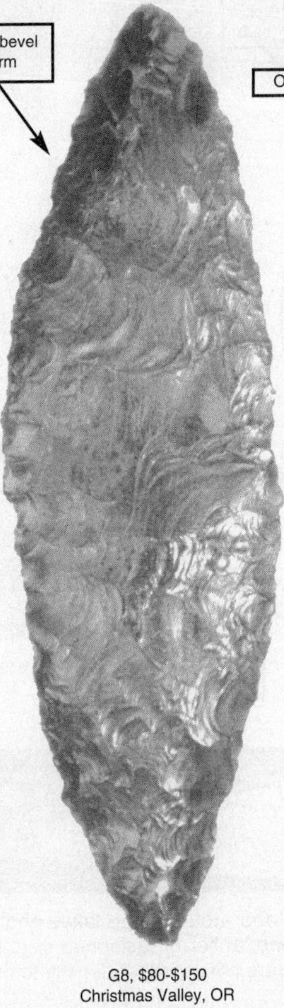
Two-bevel form

G8, $80-$150
Christmas Valley, OR

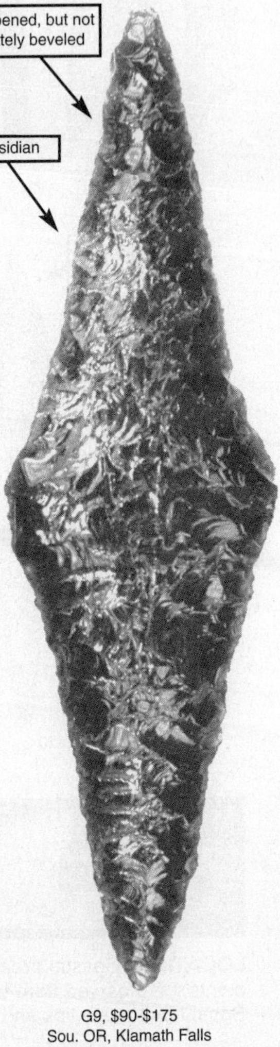
Resharpened, but not alternately beveled
Obsidian

G9, $90-$175
Sou. OR, Klamath Falls

LOCATION: N. California into S. Oregon. **DESCRIPTION:** A large size double pointed knife that is usually beveled on one or all four sides of each face. The cross section is rhomboid. The true skinning knife. **I.D. KEY:** Two and four beveled double pointed form. **NOTE:** This form is also found from Wyoming, Colorado and Texas into Kansas, Illinois, Kentucky, Tennessee and Georgia.

(Also see Three-Piece Fish Spear)

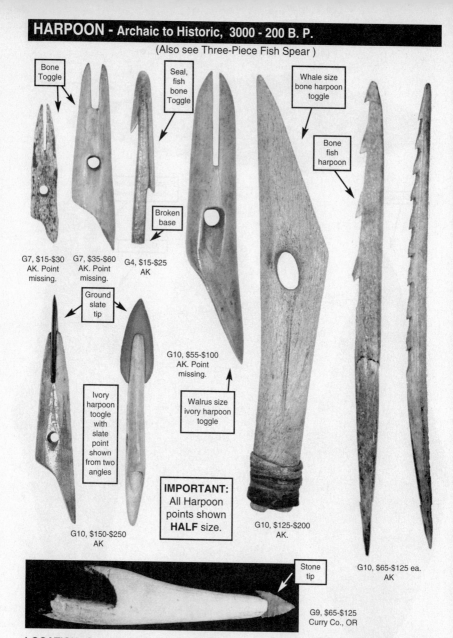

Bone Toggle

Seal, fish bone Toggle

Whale size bone harpoon toggle

Bone fish harpoon

Broken base

G7, $15-$30 AK. Point missing.

G7, $35-$60 AK. Point missing.

G4, $15-$25 AK

Ground slate tip

G10, $55-$100 AK. Point missing.

Walrus size ivory harpoon toggle

Ivory harpoon toogle with slate point shown from two angles

IMPORTANT: All Harpoon points shown **HALF** size.

G10, $150-$250 AK

G10, $125-$200 AK.

Stone tip

G10, $65-$125 ea. AK

G9, $65-$125 Curry Co., OR

LOCATION: Coastal areas and around large lakes and rivers. **DESCRIPTION:** Harpoon points were carved from bone, antler or fashioned from metal. They were used in fishing. Some have stone tips and were hafted either directly to the shaft or inserted as a foreshaft.

HASKETT - Late Paleo, 12,000 - 8000 B. P.

(Also see Agate Basin, Año Nuevo, Cougar Mountain, Cascade, Humboldt, Lake Mojave, Lind Coulee, Owl Cave and Wildcat Canyon)

HASKETT (continued)

Basalt

Type II

Ground stem sides

G8, $350-$650
Sou. OR

This Hasket has attributes of the Haskett (long hafting area) and Lind Coulee (wide stem & randomly thinned blade). The base is Alberta style and could be a cross-type linking Haskett with Alberta.

Type II Haskett

G8, $175-$300
OR

Obsidian

Obsidian

Found in same hole with a large Lind Coulee

Gray obsidian

Obsidian

Type II

Translucent tan chalcedony

Type I

Type I

Type I

Ground stem sides

Ground stem sides

Ground basal area

G7, $400-$750
Lake Co., OR

G7, $500-$900
Warner Valley, OR

G8, $900-$1600
Lake Co., OR, Silver Lake

G8, $800-$1400
Lake Co., OR

1207

GB

HASKETT (continued)

Type I

Black obsidian

Type II Hasket

Red/black gold sheen obsidian

Type II Hasket

Side wear

G9, $1000-$1800 Power Co., ID, black obsidian.

Ground basal area

Type I

G10+, $3000-$5000+ Lake Co., OR

G10+, $4000-$7000+ Humboldt Co., NV

G9, $1200-$2200 Sou. OR

HASKETT (continued)

Yellow jasper

Type I

Diamond cross section

G6, $350-$600
Warner Valley, OR

G7, $700-$1200
Fort Rock, OR

Type II

Ground stem

G7, $800-$1400
Fort Rock, OR

G10+, $3500-$6000+
Harney Co., OR

1209

GB

HASKETT (continued)

LOCATION: Idaho, N.W. Nevada and Southern Oregon. **DESCRIPTION:** A medium to large size, narrow, thick, lanceolate point with parallel flaking and a ground, convex to straight base. It comes in two types: **Type I** expands towards the tip (Could be resharpened **type IIs**). **Type II** is basically parallel sided to excurvate. Co-existing with *Clovis* the *Haskett* point is related to *Cougar Mountain* points found on the same sites. *Haskett /Lind Coulee* points later evolved into *Alberta & Agate Basins*. An extremely rare type with only a few dozen complete examples known. **I.D. KEY:** Early parallel flaking and base form.

HATWAI   (See Ahsahka and Cold Springs)

HAWKEN - Early to Mid-Archaic, 7000 - 5000 B. P.

(Also see Early Eared)

LOCATION: Wyoming westward into eastern Oregon. **DESCRIPTION:** A small to medium size, narrow point with broad, shallow side notches and an expanding stem. Blade flaking is of high quality and can be the oblique to horizontal parallel style. One of the earliest side notched points of the plains states. **I.D. KEY:** Broad side notches, expanding base.

G8, $35-$60, Lake Co., OR

HELL'S CANYON BASAL NOTCHED - Developmental to Historic Phase, 1200 - 200 B. P.

(Also see Eastgate, Elko Corner Notched, Emigrant Springs and Quillomene Bar)

Basalt

G5, $12-$20
OR

G5, $15-$30
N. UT

G6, $30-$50
Umatilla Co., OR

G9, $80-$150
WA/OR

Chalcedony

Obsidian

Black obsidian

G8, $55-$100
Columbia Riv., OR

G8, $50-$90
WA/OR.

G8, $65-$125
Lake Co., OR

LOCATION: Great Basin westward. **DESCRIPTION:** A medium to large size, broad, basal notched point with tangs usually dropping to the base line.

HELL'S CANYON BASAL NOTCHED (continued)

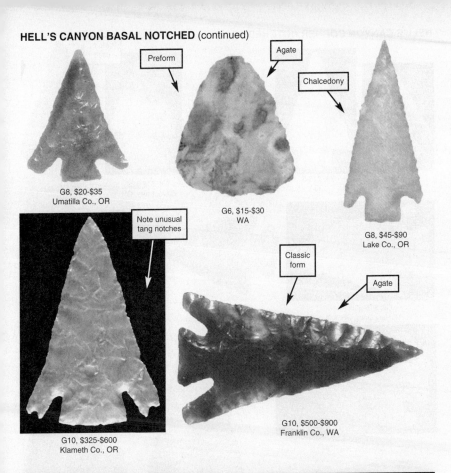

Preform

Agate

Chalcedony

G8, $20-$35
Umatilla Co., OR

Note unusual
tang notches

G6, $15-$30
WA

G8, $45-$90
Lake Co., OR

Classic
form

Agate

G10, $325-$600
Klameth Co., OR

G10, $500-$900
Franklin Co., WA

HELL'S CANYON CORNER NOTCHED - Developmental to Historic, Phase, 1200 - 200 B. P.

(Also see Elko Corner Notched & Quillomene Bar)

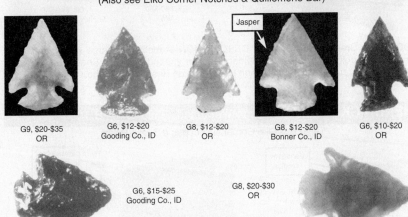

Jasper

G9, $20-$35
OR

G6, $12-$20
Gooding Co., ID

G8, $12-$20
OR

G8, $12-$20
Bonner Co., ID

G6, $10-$20
OR

G6, $15-$25
Gooding Co., ID

G8, $20-$30
OR

GB

HELL'S CANYON CORNER NOTCHED (continued)

G7, $15-$25
OR

G8, $15-$25
OR

G6, $15-$25
OR. Gem.

G6, $15-$25
Silver Lake, OR

Preform,
used

G8, $15-$25
WA

G6, $15-$35
McNary Dam, OR

G5, $20-$35
Gooding Co., ID

G5, $15-$25
OR

Gem

G7, $25-$40
John Day Riv., OR

Agate

Agate

G6, $15-$30
Twin Falls Co., ID

G8, $30-$60
WA

G8, $40-$80
McNary Dam, OR. Agate.

LOCATION: Great Basin westward. **DESCRIPTION:** A medium to large size, broad, corner notched point with barbed shoulders and an expanding stem. Shoulder barbs are rounded. First recognized and found on Hell's Canyon Reservoir in Idaho.

HENDRICKS - Late Archaic to Woodland, 3500 - 1500 B. P.

(Also see Elko Corner Notched and Snake River)

Mahagony
obsidian

G10, $50-$90
Sauvie's Island,
OR

Translucent
rootbeer
chalcedony

Ground
base

G10, $125-$225
Oregon City, OR,
Willamette Valley

HENDRICKS (continued)

Pink jasper

Ground basal area

Jasper

G10, $150-$250
Portland, OR

G9, $65-$125
Portland, OR, Sauvie's Island

G10, $125-$200
Sauvie's Island, OR

Chalcedony

Agate

G9, $80-$150
WA

G10, $200-$350
Willamette Valley, OR

LOCATION: Northern Willamette Valley in Oregon. **DESCRIPTION:** A medium sized corner notched point with fine blade serrations. Basal corners and tangs are sharp. Bases are straight and are usually ground. Similar to the *Snake River* point which mostly have concave bases. **I.D. KEY:** Straight bases and quality.

HUMBOLDT - BASAL NOTCHED - Early to mid-Archaic, 8000 - 5000 B. P.

(Also see Black Rock Concave, Clovis, Pinto Basin)

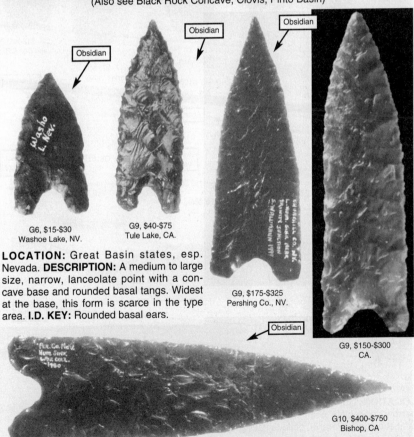

Obsidian

Obsidian

Obsidian

Obsidian

G6, $15-$30
Washoe Lake, NV.

G9, $40-$75
Tule Lake, CA.

LOCATION: Great Basin states, esp. Nevada. **DESCRIPTION:** A medium to large size, narrow, lanceolate point with a concave base and rounded basal tangs. Widest at the base, this form is scarce in the type area. **I.D. KEY:** Rounded basal ears.

G9, $175-$325
Pershing Co., NV.

G9, $150-$300
CA.

Obsidian

G10, $400-$750
Bishop, CA

GB

HUMBOLDT BASAL NOTCHED (continued)

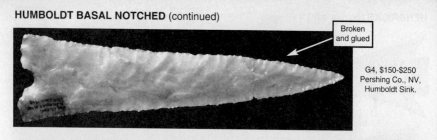

Broken and glued

G4, $150-$250
Pershing Co., NV,
Humboldt Sink.

HUMBOLDT - CONSTRICTED BASE - Early to mid-Archaic, 7000 - 5000 B. P.

(Also see Buchannan Eared, Early Leaf, Pinto Basin and Pryor Stemmed)

Obsidian

Orange chert

Agate

Obsidian

G5, $5-$10
CA

G5, $6-$12
Union Co., OR

G5, $8-$15
Owyhee Co., ID.

G5, $5-$10
Tule Lake, CA

G7, $20-$35
Christmas Valley, OR.

G6, $12-$20
Lake Co., OR

G10, $55-$100
NV

Agate

Obsidian

Ground basal

G6, $12-$20
Sou. OR

Impact fracture

G6, $25-$40
N.W. NV

G8 $35-$65
Mud Lake, NV.

Obsidian

Obsidian

G8 $30-$50
Tule Lake, CA.

Moss agate

G7, $30-$50
Harney Co., OR.

G7, $30-$55
Lake Co., OR

G10, $75-$140
WA

LOCATION: Great Basin states, esp. Nevada. **DESCRIPTION:** A small to medium size, narrow, lanceolate point with a constricted, concave, eared base. Some examples have faint shoulders. Parallel, oblique flaking occurs on many examples.

1214

G8, $55-$100
N.W. NV

Banded obsidian

Obsidian

G7, $25-$40
Cent. OR

Obsidian

Obsidian

Banded obsidian

G9, $125-$200
Klamath Co., OR

G9, $90-$175
Lake Co., OR

G8, $35-$65
Owyhee Co., ID

G9, $125-$200
Warner Valley, OR.

G8, $80-$150
N.W. NV

Obsidian

Diagonal flaking

Obsidian

Obsidian

G10, $225-$400
Sou. OR

G9, $80-$150
Tule Lake, CA

G8, $80-$150
Lake Co., OR

G8, $90-$175
Lake Co., OR

1215

GB

HUMBOLDT EXPANDED BASE (see Buchanan Eared)

HUMBOLDT-TRIANGULAR - Mid-late Archaic, 7000 - 5000 B. P.

(Also see Black Rock Concave, Cascade, Clovis, Early Leaf and Owl Cave)

Chert

G6, $12-$20
Owyhee Co., ID

G5, $12-$20
Mendocino Co., CA

G6, $10-$20
Warner Val., OR.

G8, $30-$50
Owyhee Co., ID

G8 $30-$50
Lake Co., OR

G6, $15-$25
OR

Obsidian

G8 $35-$65
Lake Co., OR

G8 $25-$40
Owyhee Co., ID

Diagonal flaking

Obsidian

Obsidian

G8, $45-$80
Warner Valley, OR.

G8, $65-$125
Warner Valley, OR

G8, $80-$150
Cougar Mtn., OR

G8, $55-$100
Cougar Mtn., OR

1216

HUMBOLDT-TRIANGULAR (continued)

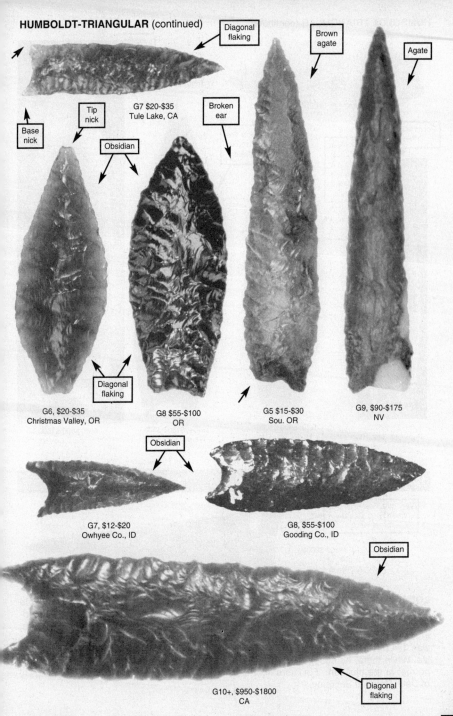

Diagonal flaking

Brown agate

Agate

G7 $20-$35
Tule Lake, CA

Broken ear

Tip nick

Base nick

Obsidian

Diagonal flaking

G6, $20-$35
Christmas Valley, OR

G8 $55-$100
OR

G5 $15-$30
Sou. OR

G9, $90-$175
NV

Obsidian

G7, $12-$20
Owhyee Co., ID

G8, $55-$100
Gooding Co., ID

Obsidian

G10+, $950-$1800
CA

Diagonal flaking

LOCATION: Great Basin states, esp. Nevada. **DESCRIPTION:** A small to medium size, narrow, lanceolate point with a tapered, concave base. Basal concavity can be slight to extreme. Many examples have high quality oblique parallel flaking.

GB

HUMBOLDT TRIANGULAR (continued)

G7, $30-$50
Warner Valley, OR.

Jasper

Possible McKean
in Nevada

Excellent
oblique
flaking &
clear with
black
bands

Note fine
diagonal
flaking

G9, $175-$300
Humboldt Sink, NV

G10, $600-$1000
Modoc Co., CA

G10+, $1800-$3000
Warner Valley, OR

G10, $900-$1600
Humboldt Co., NV

ISHI - Historic Phase, 100 - 80 B.P.

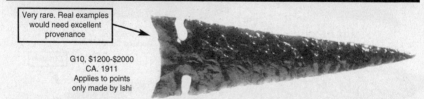

Very rare. Real examples
would need excellent
provenance

G10, $1200-$2000
CA. 1911
Applies to points
only made by Ishi

LOCATION: Northern California. **DESCRIPTION:** A medium size, thin, corner to side notched point with deep notches set close to the base. Bases vary from concave to convex. Ishi, known as the last wild Indian in North America and the last survivor of his tribe, in fear for his life, turned himself in to the local authorities in Oroville, California. The year was 1911. The University of California museum offered him sanctuary for the rest of his life. While there, he knapped arrowpoints which were given to friends and acquaintances he met at the museum. For more information, read "Ishi in Two Worlds", 1963, University of Calif. Press at Berkeley.

JALAMA SIDE NOTCHED - Early to Mid Archaic, 6000 - 4500 B. P.

(Also see Cold Springs, Northern Side Notched)

JALAMA SIDE NOTCHED (continued)

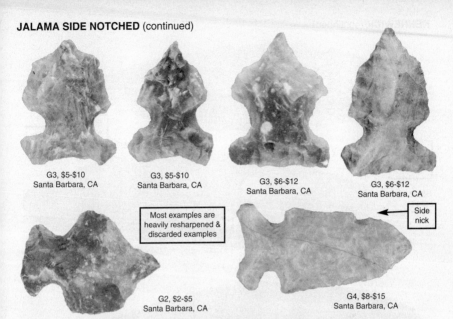

G3, $5-$10
Santa Barbara, CA

G3, $5-$10
Santa Barbara, CA

G3, $6-$12
Santa Barbara, CA

G3, $6-$12
Santa Barbara, CA

Most examples are heavily resharpened & discarded examples

Side nick

G2, $2-$5
Santa Barbara, CA

G4, $8-$15
Santa Barbara, CA

LOCATION: Pacific coast of southern California. **DESCRIPTION:** A medium to large side notched point with straight to concave bases. Notches are close to the base and are deep and broad producing basal ears on some examples. Shoulders are horizontal to tapered. Grinding in the hafting area is rare. **I.D. KEY:** Broad notches, eared base.

KAVIK - Historic Phase, 300 - 200 B.P.

(Also see Bear)

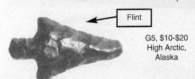

Flint

G5, $10-$20
High Arctic,
Alaska

LOCATION: Alaska. **DESCRIPTION:** A medium size stemmed point with the blade expanding towards the base. Shoulders are horizontal and the stem is narrow and parallel sided. Base is straight to convex. **I.D. KEY:** Base and shoulder form.

KENNEWICK - Paleo, 11,000 - 9000 B.P.

(Also see Cascade, Cougar Mountain, Early Leaf, Lind Coulee, Parman & Windust)

G7, $125-$225
Lake Co., OR, Fort Rock

Ground stem

Black obsidian

G7, $150-$275
Lake Co., OR, Fort Rock

GB

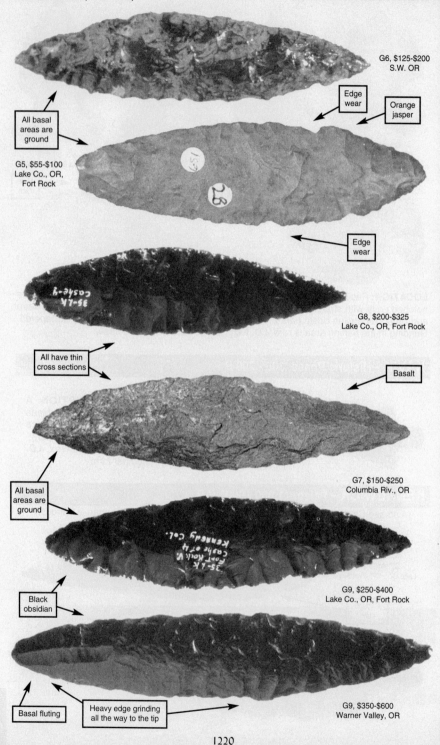

G6, $125-$200
S.W. OR

Edge wear

Orange jasper

All basal areas are ground

G5, $55-$100
Lake Co., OR, Fort Rock

Edge wear

G8, $200-$325
Lake Co., OR, Fort Rock

All have thin cross sections

Basalt

All basal areas are ground

G7, $150-$250
Columbia Riv., OR

Black obsidian

G9, $250-$400
Lake Co., OR, Fort Rock

Basal fluting

Heavy edge grinding all the way to the tip

G9, $350-$600
Warner Valley, OR

KENNEWICK (continued)

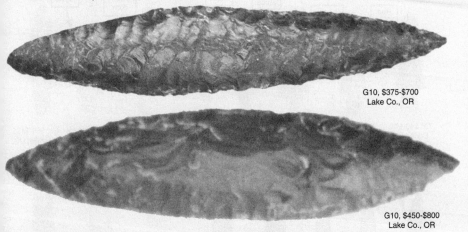

G10, $375-$700
Lake Co., OR

G10, $450-$800
Lake Co., OR

LOCATION: Columbia Plateau in Washington, south into Oregon, Nevada and Utah.
DESCRIPTION: The lanceolate form of *Windust* or *Lind Coulee*. A medium to large size, thin, double pointed lanceolate blade with convex sides. The basal end is usually a little more rounded than the tip. Flaking is to a median ridge with a very thin to medium thin cross-section. Stem sides are heavily ground for hafting. Previously known as *Cascade* bi-point. **I.D. KEY:** Basal grinding and double pointed form. A similar point was found in the hip of "Kennewick Man," a 9300 year old Caucasoid. Named by Jim Hogue and John Cockrell. Similar points were found at the lowest levels in Cougar Mtn. Cave.

KLICKITAT - Historic Phase, 300 - 160 B.P.

(Also see Dagger, Nottoway and One Que)

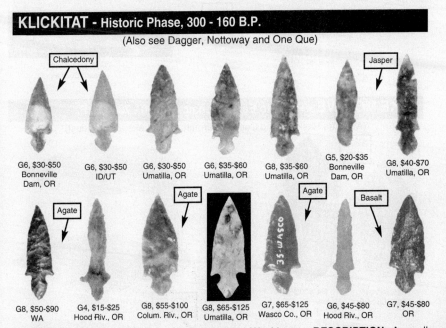

Chalcedony

Jasper

G6, $30-$50
Bonneville
Dam, OR

G6, $30-$50
ID/UT

G6, $30-$50
Umatilla, OR

G6, $35-$60
Umatilla, OR

G8, $35-$60
Umatilla, OR

G5, $20-$35
Bonneville
Dam, OR

G8, $40-$70
Umatilla, OR

Agate

Agate

Basalt

Agate

G8, $50-$90
WA

G4, $15-$25
Hood Riv., OR

G8, $55-$100
Colum. Riv., OR

G8, $65-$125
Umatilla, OR

G7, $65-$125
Wasco Co., OR

G6, $45-$80
Hood Riv., OR

G7, $45-$80
OR

LOCATION: The Columbia River in Oregon and Washington. **DESCRIPTION:** A small size, narrow, thin, lanceolate, barbed arrow point with a usually diamond shaped base. Bases can also be rectangular with horizontal barbs. Some examples have excellent oblique, parallel flaking. Other base forms would fall under the Dagger type.

GB

KLICKITAT (continued)

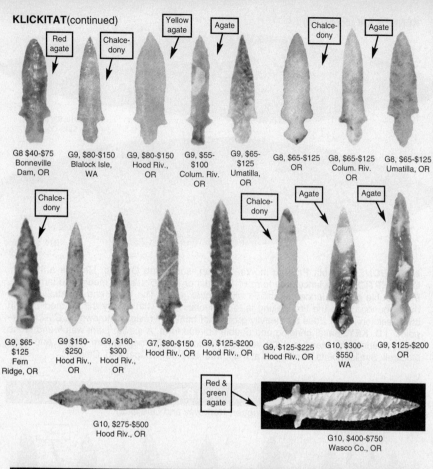

Red agate

Chalcedony

Yellow agate

Agate

Chalcedony

Agate

G8 $40-$75
Bonneville
Dam, OR

G9, $80-$150
Blalock Isle,
WA

G9, $80-$150
Hood Riv.,
OR

G9, $55-
$100
Colum. Riv.
OR

G9, $65-
$125
Umatilla,
OR

G8, $65-$125
OR

G8, $65-$125
Colum. Riv.
OR

G8, $65-$125
Umatilla, OR

Chalcedony

Chalcedony

Agate

Agate

G9, $65-
$125
Fern
Ridge, OR

G9 $150-
$250
Hood Riv.,
OR

G9, $160-
$300
Hood Riv.,
OR

G7, $80-$150
Hood Riv., OR

G9, $125-$200
Hood Riv., OR

G9, $125-$225
Hood Riv., OR

G10, $300-
$550
WA

G9, $125-$200
OR

G10, $275-$500
Hood Riv., OR

Red & green agate

G10, $400-$750
Wasco Co., OR

LAKE MOHAVE - Paleo to Early Archaic, 13,200 - 7000 B. P.

(Also see Haskett, Lind Coulee, Parman, Silver Lake and Windust)

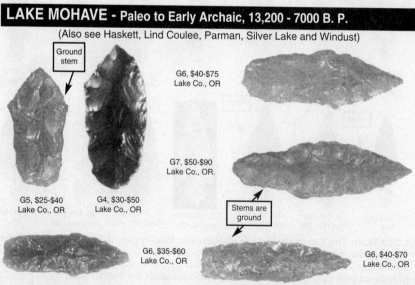

Ground stem

G6, $40-$75
Lake Co., OR

G7, $50-$90
Lake Co., OR.

G5, $25-$40
Lake Co., OR

G4, $30-$50
Lake Co., OR

Stems are ground

G6, $35-$60
Lake Co., OR

G6, $40-$70
Lake Co., OR

LAKE MOHAVE (continued)

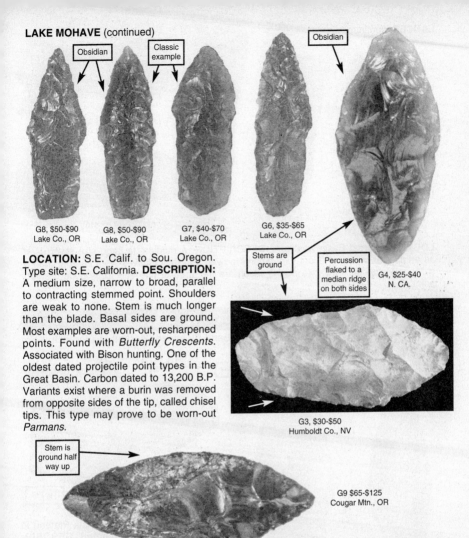

G8, $50-$90
Lake Co., OR

G8, $50-$90
Lake Co., OR

G7, $40-$70
Lake Co., OR

G6, $35-$65
Lake Co., OR

Obsidian

Classic example

Obsidian

Stems are ground

Percussion flaked to a median ridge on both sides

G4, $25-$40
N. CA.

G3, $30-$50
Humboldt Co., NV

Stem is ground half way up

G9 $65-$125
Cougar Mtn., OR

LOCATION: S.E. Calif. to Sou. Oregon. Type site: S.E. California. **DESCRIPTION:** A medium size, narrow to broad, parallel to contracting stemmed point. Shoulders are weak to none. Stem is much longer than the blade. Basal sides are ground. Most examples are worn-out, resharpened points. Found with *Butterfly Crescents*. Associated with Bison hunting. One of the oldest dated projectile point types in the Great Basin. Carbon dated to 13,200 B.P. Variants exist where a burin was removed from opposite sides of the tip, called chisel tips. This type may prove to be worn-out *Parmans*.

LANCET - Paleo to Archaic, 14,000 - 5000 B. P.

(Also see Drill, Graver, Perforator, Paleo Knife and Scraper)

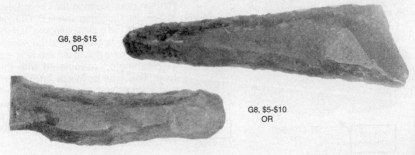

G8, $8-$15
OR

G8, $5-$10
OR

1223

GB

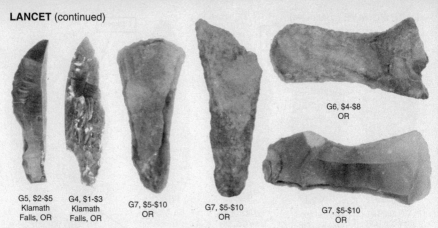

G5, $2-$5
Klamath
Falls, OR

G4, $1-$3
Klamath
Falls, OR

G7, $5-$10
OR

G7, $5-$10
OR

G6, $4-$8
OR

G7, $5-$10
OR

LOCATION: Great Basin westward. **DESCRIPTION:** A medium to large size sliver used as a knife for cutting. Recent experiments proved that these knives were sharper than a surgeon's scalpel. Similar to *Burins* which are fractured at one end to produce a sharp point.

LIND COULEE - Late Paleo, 11,500 - 11,000 B.P.

(Also see Año Nuevo, Cougar Mountain, Early Stemmed, Haskett, Kennewick, Lake Mohave, Parman, Silver Lake and Windust)

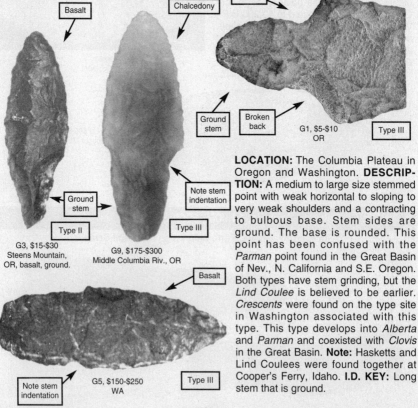

Basalt

Chalcedony

Basalt

Ground stem

Broken back

G1, $5-$10
OR

Type III

Ground stem

Note stem indentation

Type II

Type III

G3, $15-$30
Steens Mountain, OR, basalt, ground.

G9, $175-$300
Middle Columbia Riv., OR

Basalt

Note stem indentation

G5, $150-$250
WA

Type III

LOCATION: The Columbia Plateau in Oregon and Washington. **DESCRIPTION:** A medium to large size stemmed point with weak horizontal to sloping to very weak shoulders and a contracting to bulbous base. Stem sides are ground. The base is rounded. This point has been confused with the *Parman* point found in the Great Basin of Nev., N. California and S.E. Oregon. Both types have stem grinding, but the *Lind Coulee* is believed to be earlier. *Crescents* were found on the type site in Washington associated with this type. This type develops into *Alberta* and *Parman* and coexisted with *Clovis* in the Great Basin. **Note:** Hasketts and Lind Coulees were found together at Cooper's Ferry, Idaho. **I.D. KEY:** Long stem that is ground.

1224

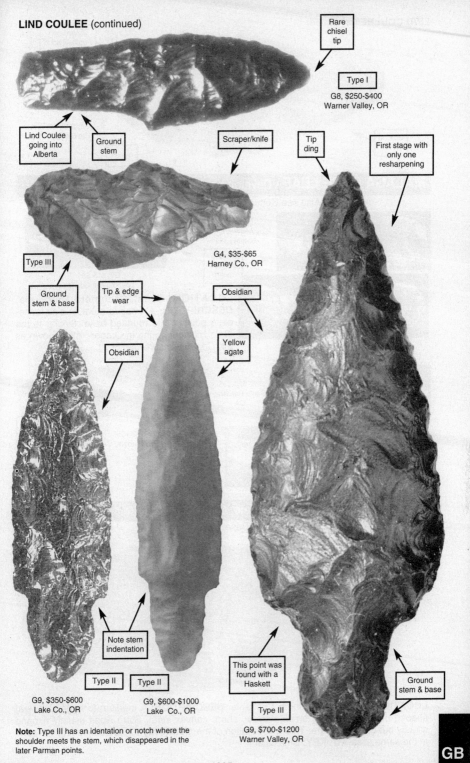

LIND COULEE (continued)

Rare chisel tip

Type I

G8, $250-$400
Warner Valley, OR

Lind Coulee going into Alberta

Ground stem

Scraper/knife

Tip ding

First stage with only one resharpening

Type III

Ground stem & base

Tip & edge wear

Obsidian

Yellow agate

G4, $35-$65
Harney Co., OR

Obsidian

Note stem indentation

This point was found with a Haskett

Ground stem & base

Type II

Type II

Type III

G9, $350-$600
Lake Co., OR

G9, $600-$1000
Lake Co., OR

G9, $700-$1200
Warner Valley, OR

Note: Type III has an identation or notch where the shoulder meets the stem, which disappeared in the later Parman points.

GB

LIND COULEE (continued)

Amber with Petrified wood

Ground stem

G5, $125-$200
The Dalles, WA

Type I

MALAGA COVE LEAF - Developmental Phase, 1500 - 700 B. P.

(Also see Cottonwood, Gold Hill, and Trojan)

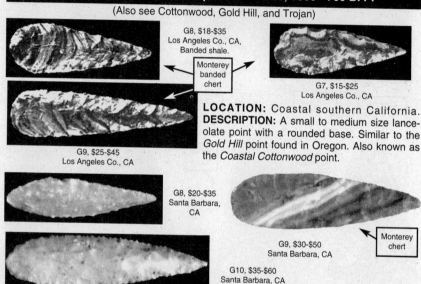

G8, $18-$35
Los Angeles Co., CA,
Banded shale.

Monterey banded chert

G7, $15-$25
Los Angeles Co., CA

G9, $25-$45
Los Angeles Co., CA

LOCATION: Coastal southern California.
DESCRIPTION: A small to medium size lanceolate point with a rounded base. Similar to the *Gold Hill* point found in Oregon. Also known as the *Coastal Cottonwood* point.

G8, $20-$35
Santa Barbara, CA

G9, $30-$50
Santa Barbara, CA

Monterey chert

G10, $35-$60
Santa Barbara, CA

MCGILLIVRAY Mid-Late Archaic, 4500 - 2500 B. P.

(Also see Base Tang, Cascade)

G7, $35-$50
Tule Lake, CA

LOCATION: Central to Northern California. **DESCRIPTION:** A medium to large size, leaf shaped point with a very small, narrow, short, convex stem. Stem sides usually expand slightly but can be square. This is a variation of the *McGillivray Expanded stem* point found in the same area. **I.D. KEY:** Small stem.

1226

MCKEE UNIFACE- Middle Archaic, 5000 - 4000 B. P.

(Also see Cascade, Excelsior and Marybelle, Portage)

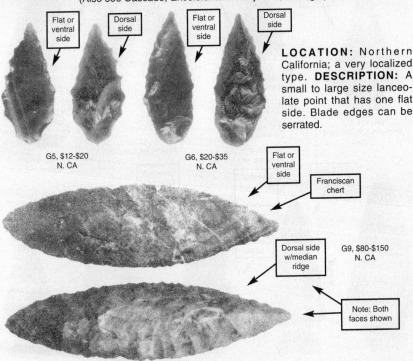

Flat or ventral side

Dorsal side

Flat or ventral side

Dorsal side

LOCATION: Northern California; a very localized type. **DESCRIPTION:** A small to large size lanceolate point that has one flat side. Blade edges can be serrated.

G5, $12-$20
N. CA

G6, $20-$35
N. CA

Flat or ventral side

Franciscan chert

Dorsal side w/median ridge

G9, $80-$150
N. CA

Note: Both faces shown

MARTIS- Late Archaic, 3000 - 1500 B. P.

(Also see Elko Corner Notched and Merrybell)

G6, $15-$25
OR

LOCATION: Western Arizona northward into the Great Basin. **DESCRIPTION:** A medium size corner to side notched point with small tapered to horizontal shoulders.

MERRYBELL, VAR. I - Late Archaic-Trans. Phase, 2500 - 1750 B.P.

(Also see Elko Corner Notched, Martis and Snake River)

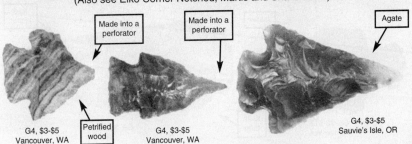

Made into a perforator

Made into a perforator

Agate

G4, $3-$5
Vancouver, WA

Petrified wood

G4, $3-$5
Vancouver, WA

G4, $3-$5
Sauvie's Isle, OR

GB

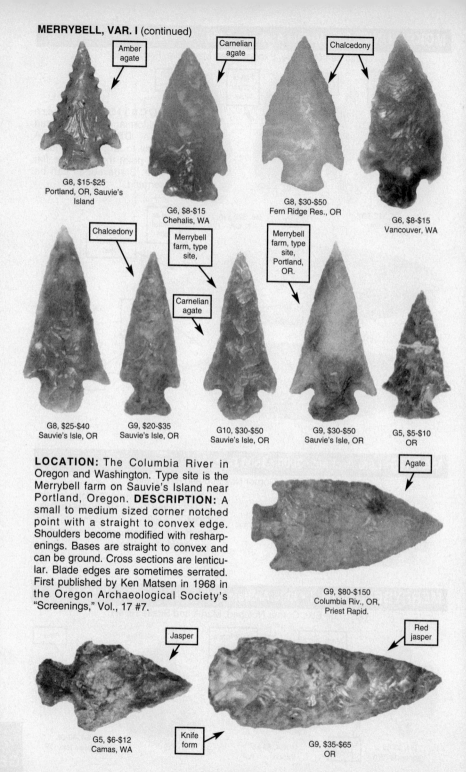

Amber agate

Carnelian agate

Chalcedony

G8, $15-$25
Portland, OR, Sauvie's Island

G6, $8-$15
Chehalis, WA

G8, $30-$50
Fern Ridge Res., OR

G6, $8-$15
Vancouver, WA

Chalcedony

Merrybell farm, type site,

Carnelian agate

Merrybell farm, type site, Portland, OR.

G8, $25-$40
Sauvie's Isle, OR

G9, $20-$35
Sauvie's Isle, OR

G10, $30-$50
Sauvie's Isle, OR

G9, $30-$50
Sauvie's Isle, OR

G5, $5-$10
OR

LOCATION: The Columbia River in Oregon and Washington. Type site is the Merrybell farm on Sauvie's Island near Portland, Oregon. **DESCRIPTION:** A small to medium sized corner notched point with a straight to convex edge. Shoulders become modified with resharpenings. Bases are straight to convex and can be ground. Cross sections are lenticular. Blade edges are sometimes serrated. First published by Ken Matsen in 1968 in the Oregon Archaeological Society's "Screenings," Vol., 17 #7.

Agate

G9, $80-$150
Columbia Riv., OR, Priest Rapid.

Jasper

Red jasper

Knife form

G5, $6-$12
Camas, WA

G9, $35-$65
OR

MERRYBELL, VAR. II - Late Archaic-Trans. Phase, 2500 - 1750 B.P.

(Also see Cold Springs, Uinta and Wendover)

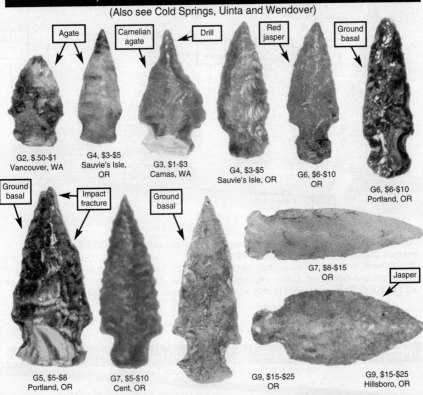

Agate

Carnelian agate

Drill

Red jasper

Ground basal

G2, $.50-$1
Vancouver, WA

G4, $3-$5
Sauvie's Isle, OR

G3, $1-$3
Camas, WA

G4, $3-$5
Sauvie's Isle, OR

G6, $6-$10
OR

G6, $6-$10
Portland, OR

Ground basal

Impact fracture

Ground basal

Jasper

G7, $8-$15
OR

G5, $5-$8
Portland, OR

G7, $5-$10
Cent. OR

G9, $15-$25
OR

G9, $15-$25
Hillsboro, OR

LOCATION: The Columbia River in Oregon and Washington. **DESCRIPTION:** A small widely side-notched point with a convex base. Stem sides and base can be ground. Blade edges are convex to incurvate.

MERRYBELL, VAR. III - Late Archaic-Trans. Phase, 2500 - 1750 B.P.

(Also see Elko Corner Notched, Elko Eared)

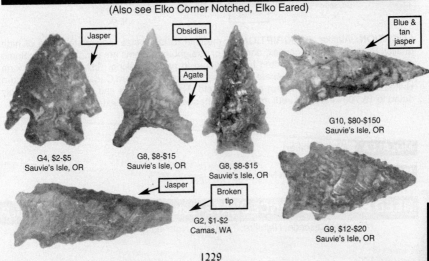

Jasper

Obsidian

Agate

Blue & tan jasper

G10, $80-$150
Sauvie's Isle, OR

G4, $2-$5
Sauvie's Isle, OR

G8, $8-$15
Sauvie's Isle, OR

G8, $8-$15
Sauvie's Isle, OR

Jasper

Broken tip

G2, $1-$2
Camas, WA

G9, $12-$20
Sauvie's Isle, OR

GB

MERRYBELL, VAR. III (continued)

Yellow jasper

Jasper

Jasper

Tang nick

Chalcedony

Broken ear

Tang nick

G8, $30-$50
Sauvie's Isle, OR

Tang nick

G3, $2-$5
Camas, WA

G5, $15-$30
Sauvie's Isle, OR

G2, $2-$5
Camas, WA

LOCATION: The Columbia River in Oregon and Washington. **DESCRIPTION:** A small to medium sized corner notched point with a convex to concave edge. Corner notches are usually wide and start at or slightly above the corner. Bases are concave to notched and almost always smoothed. Cross sections are lenticular. Blade edges are sometimes serrated. **I.D. KEY:** Basal treatment is only significant difference from the type I

MESA - Paleo-Early Archaic, 13,700 B. P.
(Also see Agate Basin and Cody Complex)

G6, $80-$150
N. AK

Collateral flaking.

G7, $175-$300
N. AK

LOCATION: Alaska. **DESCRIPTION:** A medium to large size lanceolate blade of high quality. Bases are either convex, concave or straight, and stems are usually ground. Some examples are median ridged and have random to parallel flaking. **I.D. KEY:** Basal form and flaking style. **Note:** The *Agate Basin* point, found in southern Canada into the western United States, is similar in form but not as old. The *Mesa* point and has been reportedly dated to 13,700 years B.P., but more data is needed to verify this extreme age.

MOLALLA (See Gunther)

MULE EAR (See Columbia Mule Ear)

NEED STEMMED LANCEOLATE- Late Archaic-Dev. , 2500 - 1500 B. P.
(Also see Cascade, Nightfire, Tuolumne Notched & Willits Side Notched)

NEED STEMMED LANCEOLATE (continued)

G7, $15-$30
N. CA

Side notches

LOCATION: Northern California into Sou. Oregon. **DESCRIPTION:** A medium to large size, narrow leaf shaped point with shallow side notches, and random flaking, that is occasionally oblique. Cross sections are varied, flattened to oval to plano-convex. Bases are tapered to round or straight. **I.D. KEY:** Bi-pointed blade with shallow side notches.

NEWBERRY (See Pismo)

NIGHTFIRE- Early to mid-Archaic, 7000 - 4000 B. P.

(Also see Bitterroot, Cold Springs and Need Stemmed Lanceolate, Northern Side Notched & Tuolumne Notched)

Obsidian

G7, $40-$75
Lake Co., OR

G6, $30-$50
Sou. OR

Straight base form

Ignimbrite

G8, $80-$150
Lake Co., OR

G8, $65-$120
OR

G5, $35-$60
OR

Base nick

G7, $25-$40
Sou. OR

Basalt

G8, $65-$120
Lake Co., OR

Obsidian

G6, $150-$250
Christmas Valley, OR

GB

NIGHTFIRE (continued)

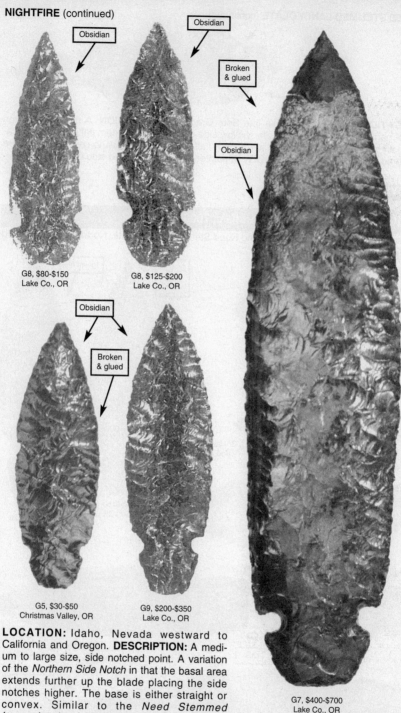

Obsidian

Obsidian

Broken & glued

Obsidian

G8, $80-$150
Lake Co., OR

G8, $125-$200
Lake Co., OR

Obsidian

Broken & glued

G5, $30-$50
Christmas Valley, OR

G9, $200-$350
Lake Co., OR

G7, $400-$700
Lake Co., OR
Not broken would be
worth $3000

LOCATION: Idaho, Nevada westward to California and Oregon. **DESCRIPTION:** A medium to large size, side notched point. A variation of the *Northern Side Notch* in that the basal area extends further up the blade placing the side notches higher. The base is either straight or convex. Similar to the *Need Stemmed Lanceolate* but is earlier and better made **I.D. KEY:** Higher side notches.

NIGHTFIRE (continued)

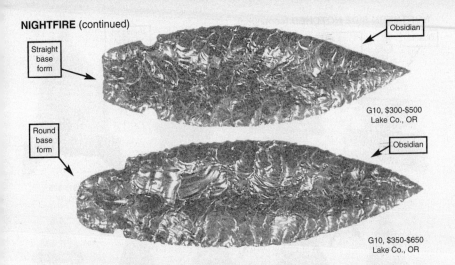

Obsidian

Straight base form

G10, $300-$500
Lake Co., OR

Round base form

Obsidian

G10, $350-$650
Lake Co., OR

NORTHERN SIDE NOTCHED - Paleo to late Archaic, 9000 - 3000 B. P.

(Also see Ahsahka, Bitterroot, Chilcotin Plateau, Cold Springs, Emigrant, Jalama Side Notched, Nightfire & Willits Side Notched)

Pink jasper

Obsidian

Obsidian

G2, $2-$5
Union Co., OR

G6, $5-$10
Union Co., OR

G2, $5-$10
OR

G4, $5-$10
Union Co., OR

G8, $15-$25
OR

Obsidian

G7, $15-$25
NV

G6, $8-$15
OR

G6, $8-$15
Tule Lake, CA

G6, $15-$25
Cent. OR

G8, $25-$45
Lake Co., OR

G8, $30-$50
Lake Co., OR

G8, $30-$50
Lake Co., OR

GB

NORTHERN SIDE NOTCHED (continued)

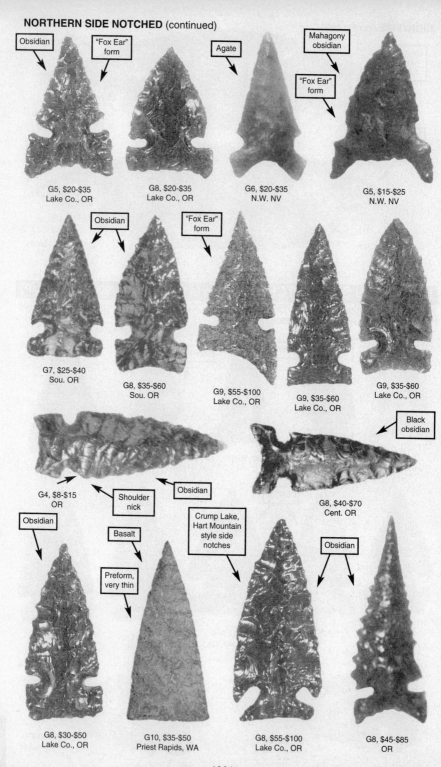

Obsidian

"Fox Ear" form

Agate

Mahagony obsidian

"Fox Ear" form

G5, $20-$35
Lake Co., OR

G8, $20-$35
Lake Co., OR

G6, $20-$35
N.W. NV

G5, $15-$25
N.W. NV

Obsidian

"Fox Ear" form

G7, $25-$40
Sou. OR

G8, $35-$60
Sou. OR

G9, $55-$100
Lake Co., OR

G9, $35-$60
Lake Co., OR

G9, $35-$60
Lake Co., OR

Shoulder nick

Obsidian

Black obsidian

G4, $8-$15
OR

G8, $40-$70
Cent. OR

Obsidian

Basalt

Preform, very thin

Crump Lake, Hart Mountain style side notches

Obsidian

G8, $30-$50
Lake Co., OR

G10, $35-$50
Priest Rapids, WA

G8, $55-$100
Lake Co., OR

G8, $45-$85
OR

1234

NORTHERN SIDE NOTCHED (continued)

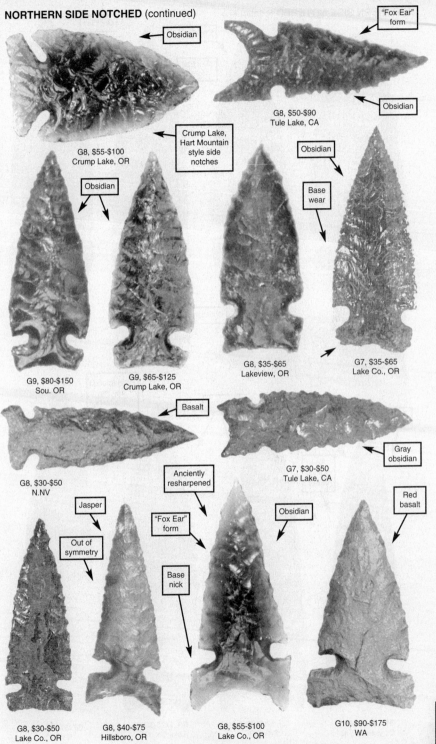

Obsidian

"Fox Ear" form

Obsidian

G8, $50-$90
Tule Lake, CA

Crump Lake, Hart Mountain style side notches

G8, $55-$100
Crump Lake, OR

Obsidian

Base wear

Obsidian

G9, $80-$150
Sou. OR

G9, $65-$125
Crump Lake, OR

G8, $35-$65
Lakeview, OR

G7, $35-$65
Lake Co., OR

Basalt

Gray obsidian

G7, $30-$50
Tule Lake, CA

G8, $30-$50
N.NV

Anciently resharpened

Jasper

Out of symmetry

"Fox Ear" form

Base nick

Obsidian

Red basalt

G8, $30-$50
Lake Co., OR

G8, $40-$75
Hillsboro, OR

G8, $55-$100
Lake Co., OR

G10, $90-$175
WA

GB

NORTHERN SIDE NOTCHED (continued)

Obsidian

"Fox Ear" form

Obsidian

G7, $80-$150
Lake Co., OR

G8, $125-$200
Lake Co., OR

G9, $175-$300
Crump Lake, Warner Valley, OR

G9, $175-$300
Sou. OR

Obsidian

G8, $55-$100
Sou. OR

Very thin

Crump Lake/Hart Mtn. style notches

Fine grained basalt

Obsidian

Resharpened into the shoulders

G10, $450-$800
Owyhee Co., ID

G9, $200-$350
Sou. OR

G9, $175-$300
Lake Co., OR

G7, $150-$250
N.W. NV

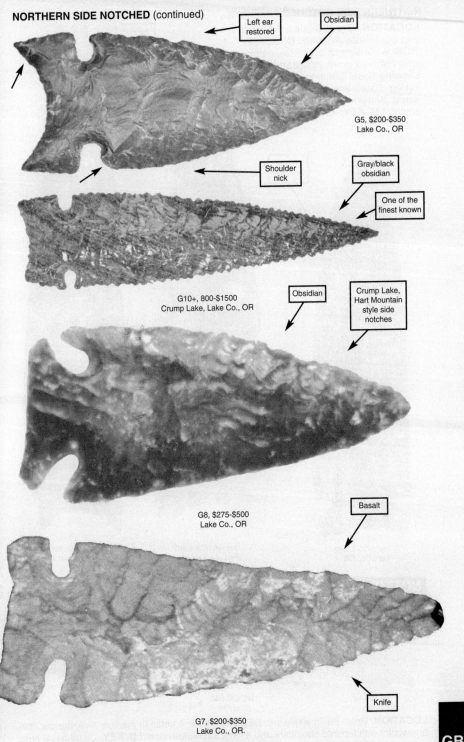

Left ear restored

Obsidian

G5, $200-$350
Lake Co., OR

Shoulder nick

Gray/black obsidian

One of the finest known

G10+, 800-$1500
Crump Lake, Lake Co., OR

Obsidian

Crump Lake, Hart Mountain style side notches

G8, $275-$500
Lake Co., OR

Basalt

Knife

G7, $200-$350
Lake Co., OR.

GB

NORTHERN SIDE NOTCHED (continued)

LOCATION: Great Basin westward and south into Arizona. **DESCRIPTION:** A medium to large size, narrow side-notched point with early forms showing basal grinding and parallel flaking. Bases are usually concave to eared. Shoulders are tapered to horizontal. **I.D. KEY:** Broad side notched point.

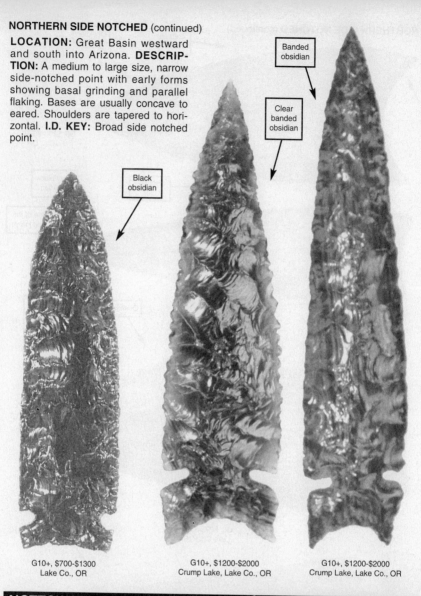

Banded obsidian

Clear banded obsidian

Black obsidian

G10+, $700-$1300
Lake Co., OR

G10+, $1200-$2000
Crump Lake, Lake Co., OR

G10+, $1200-$2000
Crump Lake, Lake Co., OR

NOTTOWAY - Historic Phase, 300 - 160 B. P.

(Also see Merrybell and Rose Springs)

White chalcedony

Red chalcedony

G8, $20-$35
Malheur Co., OR

G8, $20-$35
Sou. OR

G8, $20-$35
OR

LOCATION: Great Basin westward. **DESCRIPTION:** A small to medium size, narrow, thin, arrowpoint with tapered shoulders and a long, expanded base. **I.D. KEY:** Large basal area.

1238

ONE-QUE - Developmental to Historic Phase, 1320 - 1000 B. P.

(Also see Dagger and Klickitat)

G3, $2-$5
Spokane, WA

Chalce-dony

Yellow jasper

Obsidian

Agate

G5, $5-$10
Spokane, WA

G6, $8-$15
Lady Isle, WA
Made from a flake

G9, $8-$15
Sauvie's Isle,
WA

G3, $2-$5
Kalama, WA

G7, $12-$20
OR

G8, $20-$35
Spokane, WA

G8, $25-$40
OR

G7, $15-$25
Sauvie's Isle, Wa

Yellow agate

LOCATION: Lower Columbia River in Oregon.
DESCRIPTION: A small to medium size, arrow point with side notches. The base is diamond shaped, similar to Klikitat but rougher made. **I.D. KEY:** Diamond shaped base.

OWL CAVE - Late Paleo, 9500 - 8000 B. P.

(Also see Cody Complex, Haskett, Humboldt Triangular, Pryor Stemmed, Sub-Triangular)

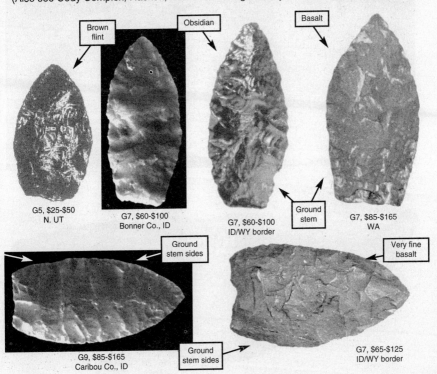

Brown flint

Obsidian

Basalt

G5, $25-$50
N. UT

G7, $60-$100
Bonner Co., ID

G7, $60-$100
ID/WY border

Ground stem

G7, $85-$165
WA

Ground stem sides

G9, $85-$165
Caribou Co., ID

Ground stem sides

Very fine basalt

G7, $65-$125
ID/WY border

LOCATION: Oregon, Nevada, Idaho, Wyoming. The Wasden Site in southern Idaho is the type area. **DESCRIPTION:** A medium size, narrow, lanceolate point with a straight to concave base. Blade edges are convex. Basal sides are ground. Very similar to and can be confused with small **Agate Basin** points. **I.D. KEY:** Basal form and flaking style.

GB

OWL CAVE (continued)

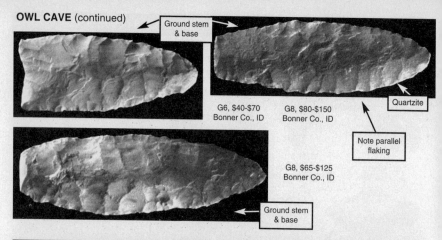

Ground stem & base

Quartzite

Note parallel flaking

G6, $40-$70
Bonner Co., ID

G8, $80-$150
Bonner Co., ID

G8, $65-$125
Bonner Co., ID

Ground stem & base

PALEO KNIFE - Paleo, 10,000 - 8000 B. P.

(Also see Base Tang Knife, Lancet, Scraper, Wildcat Canyon and Windust)

G7, $40-$75
Cortez, CA

G8, $65-$125
OR

LOCATION: Great Basin westward. **DESCRIPTION:** A medium to large size, broad, lanceolate blade with a rounded base. Look for parallel horizontal flaking.

PALISADES - Early to Mid-Archaic, 6000 B. P.

(Also see Merrybell, Salmon River, Snake River)

G7, $12-$20
AK

LOCATION: Alaska. **DESCRIPTION:** Northern extension of the *Snake River* type. A small to medium size dart point with an expanding stem that is concave. Shoulders are horizontal to slightly barbed. Blade edges are convex. Basal corners are pointed to rounded. Notches and stem edges are ground.

PANOCHE - Historic, 300 - 200 B. P.

(Also see Bear River and Desert)

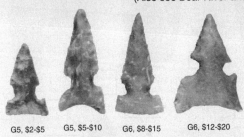

G5, $2-$5   G5, $5-$10   G6, $8-$15   G6, $12-$20

All Monterey Co., CA

LOCATION: Panoche Reservoir in Fresno Co., California. **DESCRIPTION:** A small size, thin side notched arrow point with a straight to concave base. Notches are larger than other *Desert Side Notched* forms.that they are related. Similar to *Salado* found further East.

PARMAN - Early Archaic, 10,500 - 9000 B. P.

(Also see Cougar Mountain, Early Stemmed, Lake Mohave, Lind Coulee & Silver Lake)

Tip nick | Brown basalt | Basalt | Obsidian | Jasper

Ground stem

G3, $5-$10
N. UT

G4, $5-$10
Wallowa Co., OR

G3, $3-$7
N.W. NV

G6, $35-$65
Silver Lake, OR

G6, $40-$70
N. UT

LOCATION: N.W. Nevada and southern Oregon. **DESCRIPTION:** A medium size, medium to long contracted stemmed point with tapered to squared shoulders. The Basal area is rounded to square and is ground on early examples. Flaking is random. Heavily resharpened examples may be the same as *Lake Mohave* points. A very rare type. Occurs in chisel tip along with *Lake Mohave* and *Windust*. Believed to have evolved from the earlier *Lind Coulee*. **I.D. KEY:** Long stem with straight to convex base.

GB

1241

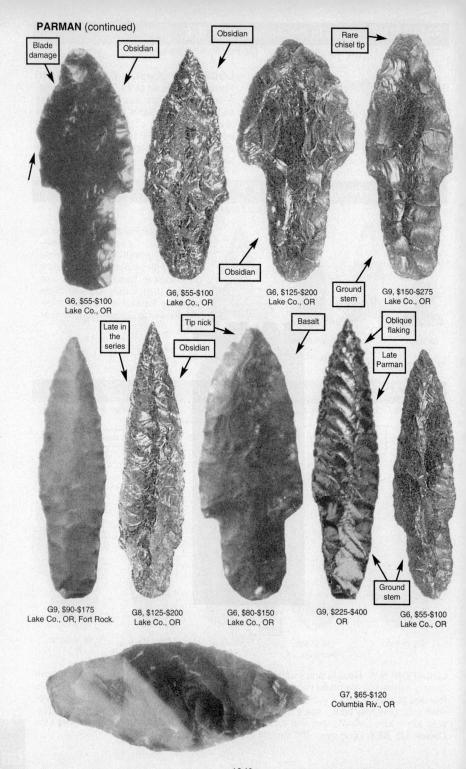

Blade damage

Obsidian

Obsidian

Rare chisel tip

Obsidian

Ground stem

G6, $55-$100
Lake Co., OR

G6, $55-$100
Lake Co., OR

G6, $125-$200
Lake Co., OR

G9, $150-$275
Lake Co., OR

Late in the series

Tip nick

Obsidian

Basalt

Oblique flaking

Late Parman

Ground stem

G9, $90-$175
Lake Co., OR, Fort Rock.

G8, $125-$200
Lake Co., OR

G6, $80-$150
Lake Co., OR

G9, $225-$400
OR

G6, $55-$100
Lake Co., OR

G7, $65-$120
Columbia Riv., OR

PARMAN (continued)

Obsidian

Obsidian

Red agate

Side dings

Ground stem

G9, $250-$450
Lake Co., OR

G8, $200-$350
Christmas Valley, OR

G7, $115-$200
OR

G10, $350-$600
OR

Obsidian

Obsidian

Basalt

Classic form

Ground stem

Ground stem

G8, $250-$450
Lake Co., OR

G8, $175-$300
Lake Co., OR

G8, $200-$350
N. OR

G10, $275-$500
Lake Co., OR

GB

PARMAN (continued)

G9, $350-$600
Lake Co., OR

Rare chisel tip

Ground stem

Moss agate

Stem grinding

Basalt

G9, $250-$450
Lake Co., OR

Very rare first stage form

Very rare first stage form

Black obsidian

Tang nick

Ground stem

Ground stem

G6, $200-$350
OR

G9, $500-$900
Lake Co., OR

G10, $700-$1200
Crump Lake, OR

PAROWAN - Developmental Phase, 1300 - 800 B. P.

(Also see Rabbit Island)

LOCATION: Nevada into Utah southward to Arizona. **DESCRIPTION:** A medium size triangular arrowpoint with two shallow basal notches creating a short, straight to contracting stem. Barbs can reach the base. Bases are straight to rounded. **I.D. KEY:** Basal notches.

PERFORATOR - Archaic to Historic, 9000 - 400 B. P.

(Also see Drill, Graver and Scraper)

Red agate

Brown bottle glass

Historic

Agate

G9, $1-$2
Lady Isle, WA

G4, $.50-$1
OR

G5, $.50-$1
OR

G3, $1-$2
Chehalis, WA

G6, $1-$2
OR

Agate

Jasper

G3, $.50-$1
OR

G5, $1-$3
OR

Black obsidian

Chalcedony

G6, $1-$3
Sonoma Co., CA

G6, $1-$3
OR

G6, $1-$3
OR

G8, $3-$6
Columbia Riv., OR

G7, $3-$6
OR

LOCATION: Archaic and Woodland sites everywhere. **DESCRIPTION:** A jabbing projection at the tip would qualify for the type. It is believed that *perforators* were used for tattooing, incising or to punch holes in leather or other materials or objects. Paleo peoples used Gravers for the same purpose. All Archaic and Woodland cultures converted their points into this type. Therefore, most point types could occur in this form, although many examples were made from scratch. **I.D. KEY:** Long pointed ears; tapered base.

1245

GB

PIECES ESQUILLEES - Paleo to Historic, 10,000 - 400 B. P.

(Also see Drill, Graver and Scraper)

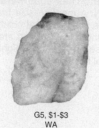

G5, $1-$3
WA

LOCATION: Oregon & Washington **DESCRIPTION:** A splitting wedge. Some in the old world may be 30,000 years old. The bottom cutting edge should be beveled or V shaped. The opposing edge or hammering surface should be flattened or knobbed enough to receive a hammer blow. The larger pieces could be used to split house timbers or planks, or perhaps spear shafts and foreshafts. The smaller pieces could be used to split bone for needles and arrow or small dart points. Look for hammer scars on the edge opposing the "V" or beveled edge. **I.D. KEY:** Wedge form.

Blade edge

Red/brown jasper

Basalt

G6, $2-$5
Vancouver, WA

Hammer strokes

G6, $5-$10
Columbia Riv., OR

PINTO BASIN - Middle to late Archaic, 8000 - 2650 B. P.

(Also see Eastgate Bifurcated, Elko, Gatecliff and Humboldt)

Ancient resharpening

Obsidian

Obsidian

G6, $8-$15
OR

G6, $12-$20
Malheur Co., OR

G6, $15-$25
Columbia Riv., OR

G5, $12-$20
CA

G6, $15-$25
Warner Valley, OR

Obsidian

G8, $25-$40
Warner Valley, OR

G8, $20-$35
Warner Valley, OR

LOCATION: Great Basin states. **DESCRIPTION:** A medium to large sized, narrow, auriculate point. Shoulders can be tapered, horizontal or barbed. Bases are either deeply bifurcated with parallel to expanding ears or tapered with a concave basal edge. The bifurcated form may prove to be *Gatecliff* forms. Most examples show excellent flaking. **I.D. KEY:** Long pointed ears; tapered base.

Obsidian

Obsidian

Mahagony obsidian

G8, $25-$40
Lake Co., OR

G8, $25-$45
Warner Valley, OR

G8, $25-$45
Warner Valley, OR

G6, $20-$35
N.W. NV

Obsidian

Obsidian

G8, $25-$45
Cent. OR

G8, $30-$50
OR

G8, $40-$75
Warner Valley, OR

G8, $35-$60
Warner Valley, OR

Obsidian

G8, $30-$55
Lake Co. OR

Obsidian

Chalcedony

Basalt

G8, $45-$80
Crump Lake, OR

G7, $35-$65
NV

G8, $35-$60
ID

G8, $30-$55
Lake Co. OR

GB

PINTO BASIN (continued)

Obsidian

Obsidian

G8, $25-$45
Lake Co., OR

G8, $40-$75
Lake Co., OR

Obsidian

Ground stem

Jasper

Obsidian

G9, $40-$75
Lake Co., OR

G7 $40-$75
N.W. NV

G8, $55-$100
Lake Co., OR

G8, $55-$100
Lake Co., OR

G10, $175-$300
OR

Obsidian

Clear obsidian

Black obsidian

Obsidian

Ground stem

G10, $80-$150
N.W. NV

G10, $125-$200
OR

G10, $125-$200
CA

G10, $175-$300
Lake Co., OR

G10, $250-$450
Sou. OR

1248

PINTO BASIN SLOPING SHOULDER - Middle to late Archaic
8000 - 3000 B. P.
(Also see Eastgate Bifurcated, Elko, Gatecliff, Humboldt and Windust)

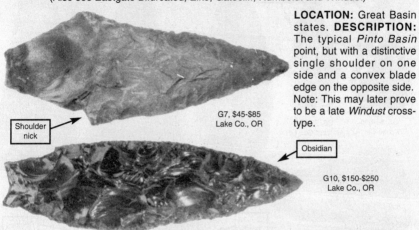

LOCATION: Great Basin states. **DESCRIPTION:** The typical *Pinto Basin* point, but with a distinctive single shoulder on one side and a convex blade edge on the opposite side. Note: This may later prove to be a late *Windust* cross-type.

Shoulder nick

G7, $45-$85
Lake Co., OR

Obsidian

G10, $150-$250
Lake Co., OR

PIQUNIN - Classic Phase to Historic, 700 - 150 B. P.
(Also see Elko Eared, Hatwai and Merrybell)

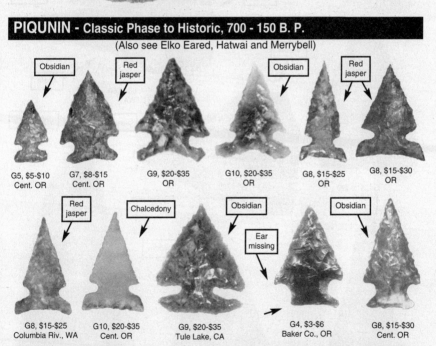

Obsidian

Red jasper

Obsidian

Red jasper

G5, $5-$10
Cent. OR

G7, $8-$15
Cent. OR

G9, $20-$35
OR

G10, $20-$35
OR

G8, $15-$25
OR

G8, $15-$30
OR

Red jasper

Chalcedony

Obsidian

Ear missing

Obsidian

G8, $15-$25
Columbia Riv., WA

G10, $20-$35
Cent. OR

G9, $20-$35
Tule Lake, CA

G4, $3-$6
Baker Co., OR

G8, $15-$30
Cent. OR

LOCATION: Idaho into Oregon and Washington. **DESCRIPTION:** A variant of the *Desert Side Notched*. A small to medium size, side notched point with flaring ears. Shoulders are barbed to tapered.

PISMO (see Rabbit Island)

PLATEAU PENTAGONAL - Classic Phase, 600 - 400 B. P.
(Related to Columbia Mule Ear; see Wahmuza and Wildcat Canyon)

GB

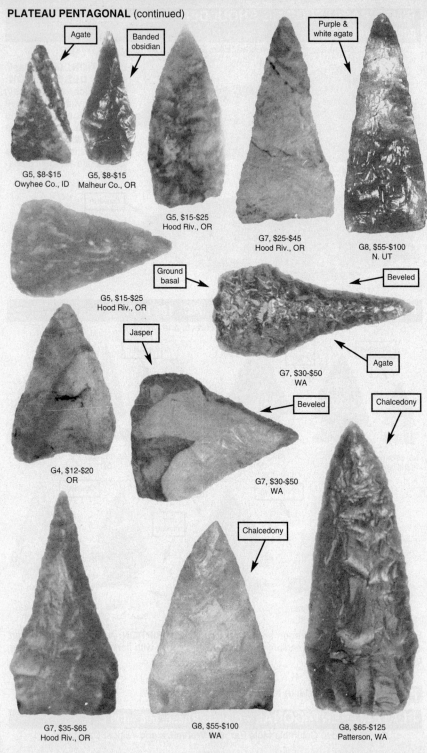

Agate

G5, $8-$15
Owyhee Co., ID

Banded obsidian

G5, $8-$15
Malheur Co., OR

G5, $15-$25
Hood Riv., OR

Purple & white agate

G7, $25-$45
Hood Riv., OR

G8, $55-$100
N. UT

G5, $15-$25
Hood Riv., OR

Ground basal

Beveled

Agate

G7, $30-$50
WA

Jasper

Beveled

G4, $12-$20
OR

G7, $30-$50
WA

Chalcedony

G7, $35-$65
Hood Riv., OR

Chalcedony

G8, $55-$100
WA

G8, $65-$125
Patterson, WA

PLATEAU PENTAGONAL (continued)

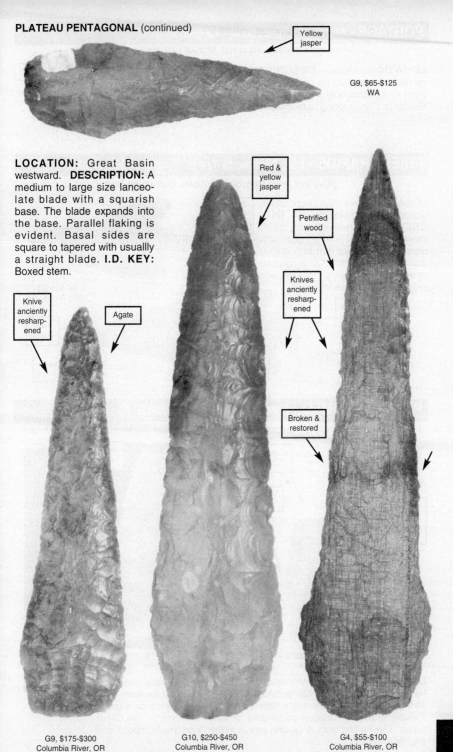

Yellow jasper

G9, $65-$125
WA

LOCATION: Great Basin westward. **DESCRIPTION:** A medium to large size lanceolate blade with a squarish base. The blade expands into the base. Parallel flaking is evident. Basal sides are square to tapered with usuallly a straight blade. **I.D. KEY:** Boxed stem.

Red & yellow jasper

Petrified wood

Knife anciently resharpened

Knives anciently resharpened

Agate

Broken & restored

G9, $175-$300
Columbia River, OR

G10, $250-$450
Columbia River, OR

G4, $55-$100
Columbia River, OR

GB

PORTAGE - Middle Archaic, 5000 - 4000 B. P.

(Also see Cascade, Gold Hill, McKee Uniface and Spedis)

LOCATION: Alaska. **DESCRIPTION:** A medium size lanceolate point with a tapered stem and a straight to slightly rounded base. Similar to *Spedis* found further south.

Gray chert

G9, $20-$35
Alaska

PRIEST RAPIDS - Late Archaic to Trans. Phase, 3000 - 1750 B.P.

(Also see Hells Canyon, Merrybell, Quilomene Bar)

LOCATION: Columbia River basin, Oregon & Priest Rapids, WA. **DESCRIPTION:** A medium size, short stemmed to basal notched point with drooping shoulders that turn inward and a rounded stem that is notched or well-thinned. A very rare type with only a few examples known

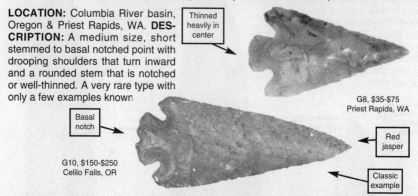

Thinned heavily in center

Basal notch

G8, $35-$75
Priest Rapids, WA

Red jasper

G10, $150-$250
Celilo Falls, OR

Classic example

PRYOR STEMMED - Early Archaic, 8000 - 7000 B. P.

(Also see Cody Complex, Humboldt Constricted, Owl Cave, Parman, Shaniko Stemmed)

G6, $3-$5
Sauvie's Isle, OR

Made into a blunt

Gem

Diagonal flaking

Heavily resharpened with ground stem

Ground stem

Flint

G2, $5-$10
OR

G3, $12-$20
Chehalis, WA

G5, $35-$50
Lake Pend Oreill, ID

G7 $35-$65
Caribou Co., ID

G6, $25-$50
Lake Co., OR

LOCATION: Type area is Montana and Wyoming but identical examples have been found in the Great Basin. **DESCRIPTION:** A medium size, short stemmed point with slight, tapered shoulders and a concave base. Flaking is usually oblique transverse. A very rare type in the Great Basin. The hafting area is ground and is longer than the Humboldt and slightly incurvate.

PRYOR STEMMED (continued)

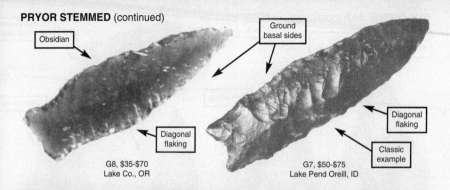

Obsidian

Ground basal sides

Diagonal flaking

Diagonal flaking

Classic example

G8, $35-$70
Lake Co., OR

G7, $50-$75
Lake Pend Oreill, ID

QUILOMENE BAR - Late Archaic to Transitional Phase, 3000 - 2000 B. P.

(Also see Elko Corner Notched & Hell's Canyon)

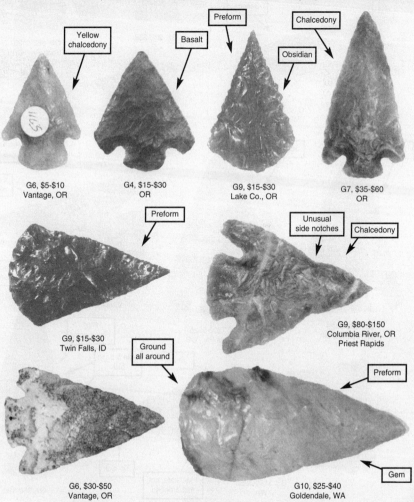

Yellow chalcedony

Basalt

Preform

Obsidian

Chalcedony

G6, $5-$10
Vantage, OR

G4, $15-$30
OR

G9, $15-$30
Lake Co., OR

G7, $35-$60
OR

Preform

Unusual side notches

Chalcedony

G9, $15-$30
Twin Falls, ID

G9, $80-$150
Columbia River, OR
Priest Rapids

Ground all around

Preform

Gem

G6, $30-$50
Vantage, OR

G10, $25-$40
Goldendale, WA

1253

GB

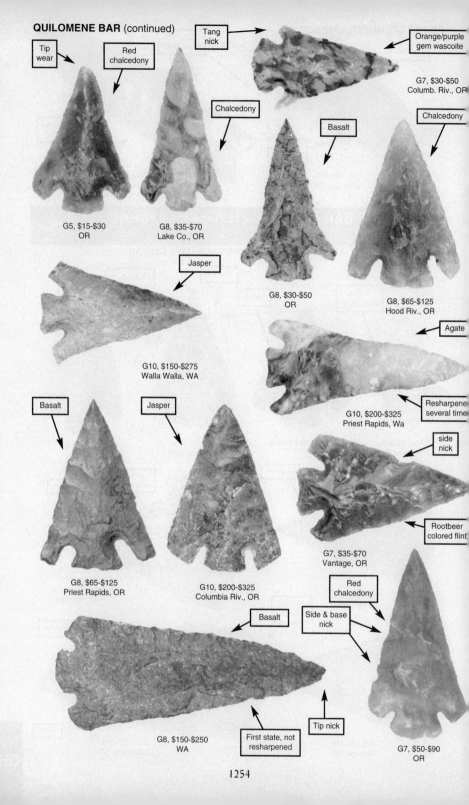

QUILOMENE BAR (continued)

Tip wear

Red chalcedony

Tang nick

Orange/purple gem wascoite

G7, $30-$50
Columb. Riv., OR

Chalcedony

Basalt

Chalcedony

G5, $15-$30
OR

G8, $35-$70
Lake Co., OR

Jasper

G8, $30-$50
OR

G8, $65-$125
Hood Riv., OR

Agate

G10, $150-$275
Walla Walla, WA

Resharpened
several times

G10, $200-$325
Priest Rapids, Wa

side nick

Basalt

Jasper

Rootbeer
colored flint

G7, $35-$70
Vantage, OR

Red
chalcedony

G8, $65-$125
Priest Rapids, OR

G10, $200-$325
Columbia Riv., OR

Side & base
nick

Basalt

First state, not
resharpened

Tip nick

G8, $150-$250
WA

G7, $50-$90
OR

QUILOMENE BAR (continued)

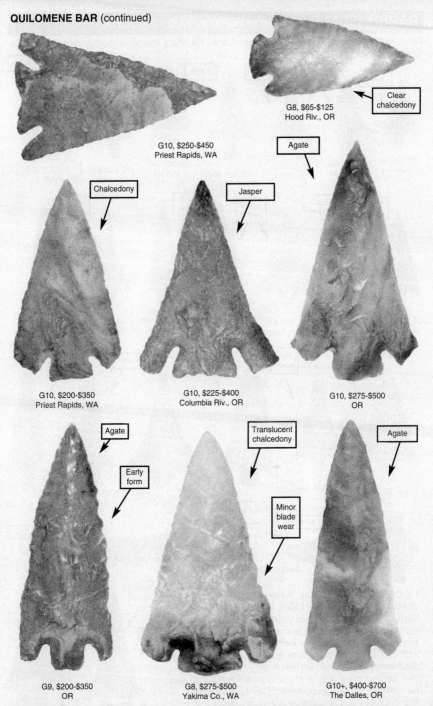

G10, $250-$450
Priest Rapids, WA

Clear chalcedony
G8, $65-$125
Hood Riv., OR

Chalcedony

Jasper

Agate

G10, $200-$350
Priest Rapids, WA

G10, $225-$400
Columbia Riv., OR

G10, $275-$500
OR

Agate
Early form

Translucent chalcedony
Minor blade wear

Agate

G9, $200-$350
OR

G8, $275-$500
Yakima Co., WA

G10+, $400-$700
The Dalles, OR

LOCATION: Columbia River in Oregon and Washington. **DESCRIPTION:** A medium size base to corner notched point. The classic form has a convex base. The stem is straight to expanded.

1255

GB

RABBIT ISLAND - Middle to Historic, 4000 - 200 B. P.

(Also see Coquille, Gatecliff, Gypsum Cave, Sauvie's Island Shoulder Notched, Rose Springs & Yana)

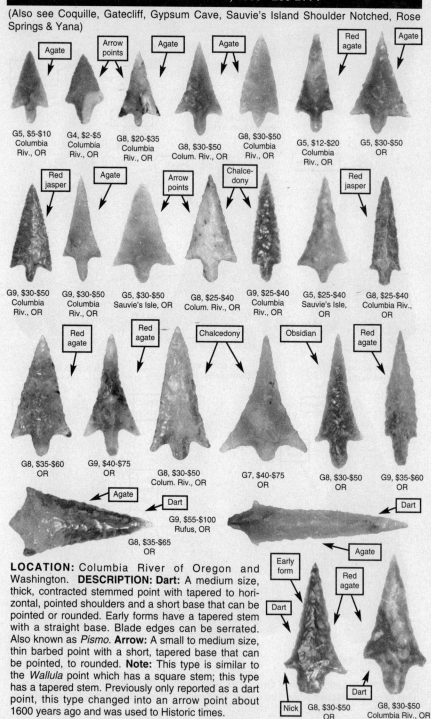

Agate — G5, $5-$10 Columbia Riv., OR

Arrow points — G4, $2-$5 Columbia Riv., OR

Agate — G8, $20-$35 Columbia Riv., OR

Agate — G8, $30-$50 Colum. Riv., OR

Agate — G8, $30-$50 Columbia Riv., OR

Red agate — G5, $12-$20 Columbia Riv., OR

Agate — G5, $30-$50 OR

Red jasper — G9, $30-$50 Columbia Riv., OR

Agate — G9, $30-$50 Columbia Riv., OR

G5, $30-$50 Sauvie's Isle, OR

Arrow points — G8, $25-$40 Colum. Riv., OR

Chalcedony — G9, $25-$40 Columbia Riv., OR

Red jasper — G5, $25-$40 Sauvie's Isle, OR

G8, $25-$40 Columbia Riv., OR

Red agate — G8, $35-$60 OR

Red agate — G9, $40-$75 OR

Chalcedony — G8, $30-$50 Colum. Riv., OR

Obsidian — G7, $40-$75 OR

Red agate — G8, $30-$50 OR

G9, $35-$60 OR

Agate — G8, $35-$65 OR

Dart — G9, $55-$100 Rufus, OR

Dart

Early form — Agate — Red agate — Dart — Nick — G8, $30-$50 OR

Dart — G8, $30-$50 Columbia Riv., OR

LOCATION: Columbia River of Oregon and Washington. **DESCRIPTION: Dart:** A medium size, thick, contracted stemmed point with tapered to horizontal, pointed shoulders and a short base that can be pointed or rounded. Early forms have a tapered stem with a straight base. Blade edges can be serrated. Also known as *Pismo.* **Arrow:** A small to medium size, thin barbed point with a short, tapered base that can be pointed, to rounded. **Note:** This type is similar to the *Wallula* point which has a square stem; this type has a tapered stem. Previously only reported as a dart point, this type changed into an arrow point about 1600 years ago and was used to Historic times.

RABBIT ISLAND (continued)

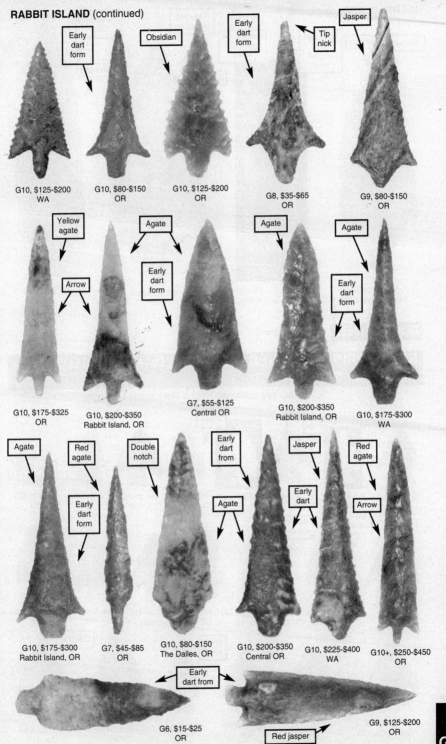

Early dart form

Obsidian

Early dart form

Jasper

Tip nick

G10, $125-$200
WA

G10, $80-$150
OR

G10, $125-$200
OR

G8, $35-$65
OR

G9, $80-$150
OR

Yellow agate

Arrow

Agate

Early dart form

Agate

Agate

Early dart form

G10, $175-$325
OR

G10, $200-$350
Rabbit Island, OR

G7, $55-$125
Central OR

G10, $200-$350
Rabbit Island, OR

G10, $175-$300
WA

Agate

Red agate

Early dart form

Double notch

Early dart from

Agate

Jasper

Early dart

Red agate

Arrow

G10, $175-$300
Rabbit Island, OR

G7, $45-$85
OR

G10, $80-$150
The Dalles, OR

G10, $200-$350
Central OR

G10, $225-$400
WA

G10+, $250-$450
OR

Early dart from

G6, $15-$25
OR

Red jasper

G9, $125-$200
OR

1257

GB

Obsidian
Dart/knife
Early dart form, ground stem
Transparent light green agate
Early first stage form
Dart/knife
Translucent agate
Dart/knife
Obsidian

G7, $15-$30
Sauvie's Island, OR

G10, $125-$200
The Dalles, OR

G9, $65-$125
OR

G7, $55-$100
OR

ROGUE RIVER (See Gunther)

ROSE SPRINGS CORNER NOTCHED - Developmental to Classic Phase, 1600 - 600 B. P.

(Also see Eastgate, Elko & Wendover)

Arrow points
Yellow agate

G7, $12-$20
OR

G7, $12-$20
OR

G7, $12-$20
OR

G8, $15-$30
OR

G7, $15-$30
Col. Riv., OR

G8, $15-$25
OR

G8, $15-$30
OR

G8, $18-$30
OR

Opalite
Banded obsidian
Arrow points

G9, $30-$60
Clearwater Co., ID

G5, $18-$30
Owyhee Co., ID

G8, $18-$30
Owyhee Co., ID

G7, $12-$20
OR

G6, $8-$15
OR

G9, $20-$35
OR

G6, $12-$20
OR

Arrow points
Obsidian

G7, $15-$30
Malheur Co., OR

G7, $15-$30
OR

G9, $30-$45
OR

G7, $12-$20
OR

G8, $15-$30
OR

G8, $25-$45
Sou. OR

ROSE SPRINGS CORNER NOTCHED (continued)

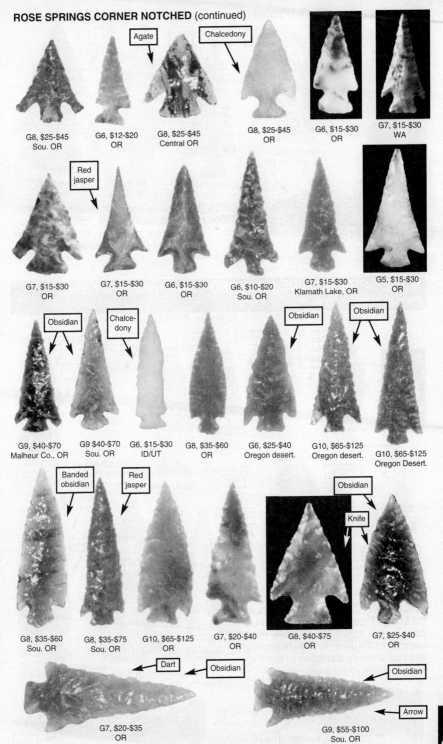

G8, $25-$45
Sou. OR

G6, $12-$20
OR

Agate

G8, $25-$45
Central OR

Chalcedony

G8, $25-$45
OR

G6, $15-$30
OR

G7, $15-$30
WA

Red jasper

G7, $15-$30
OR

G7, $15-$30
OR

G6, $15-$30
OR

G6, $10-$20
Sou. OR

G7, $15-$30
Klamath Lake, OR

G5, $15-$30
OR

Obsidian

Chalce-dony

G9, $40-$70
Malheur Co., OR

G9 $40-$70
Sou. OR

G6, $15-$30
ID/UT

G8, $35-$60
OR

Obsidian

G6, $25-$40
Oregon desert.

Obsidian

G10, $65-$125
Oregon desert.

G10, $65-$125
Oregon Desert.

Banded obsidian

Red jasper

G8, $35-$60
Sou. OR

G8, $35-$75
Sou. OR

G10, $65-$125
OR

G7, $20-$40
OR

Obsidian

Knife

G8, $40-$75
OR

G7, $25-$40
OR

Dart

Obsidian

G7, $20-$35
OR

Obsidian

Arrow

G9, $55-$100
Sou. OR

1259

GB

ROSE SPRINGS CORNER NOTCHED (continued)

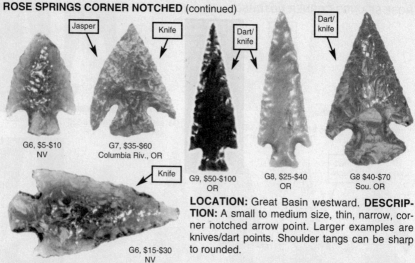

G6, $5-$10
NV

G7, $35-$60
Columbia Riv., OR

Jasper

Knife

Dart/knife

Dart/knife

Knife

G9, $50-$100
OR

G8, $25-$40
OR

G8 $40-$70
Sou. OR

G6, $15-$30
NV

LOCATION: Great Basin westward. **DESCRIPTION:** A small to medium size, thin, narrow, corner notched arrow point. Larger examples are knives/dart points. Shoulder tangs can be sharp to rounded.

ROSE SPRINGS SIDE NOTCHED - Developmental to Classic Phase, 1600 - 600 B. P.

(Also see Coquille, Eastgate, Elko, Nottoway, Piqunin, San Bruno & Wendover)

G5, $5-$10
OR

G7, $8-$15
OR

Red & white agate

G7, $15-$25
OR

Obsidian

Arrow

Chalcedony

Obsidian

Knife

G7, $12-$20
Black Rock
Desert, NV

G9, $35-$60
OR

G9, $25-$45
Columbia Riv., WA

G7, $16-$30
OR

Double Tip

Obsidian

Dart/knife

Knife

Dart/knife

Obsidian

G5, $12-$20
Klamath Falls, OR

G7, $12-$20
Sou. OR

LOCATION: Great Basin westward. **DESCRIPTION:** A small to medium size, narrow, side notched arrow point. Larger examples are dart/knives. Notches are very distinctive in that they are very close to the base.

G7, $16-$30
Columbia Riv., WA

G7, $15-30
OR

G8, $15-$30
Cent. OR

Obsidian

G8, $30-$50
Lake Co., OR.

Knife

G5, $12-$20
CA

Knife

1260

ROSE SPRINGS STEMMED - Developmental to Classic
Phase, 1600 - 600 B. P.

(Also see Calapooya Knife, Colonial, Eastgate, Elko, Nottoway, Wendover)

Agate

Obsidian

Obsidian

Obsidian

G3, $2-$5
Malheur Co., OR

G6, $5-$10
Sou. OR

G6, $5-$10
Malheur Co.OR

G6, $8-$15
OR

G5, $5-$10
Malheur Co.OR

G5, $5-$10
Owyhee Co., ID

G9, $20-$35
Cent. OR

Obsidian

Obsidian

Agate

G4, $5-$10
Malheur Co.,
OR

G8, $18-$30
Malheur Co., OR

G8, $15-$30
Colum. Riv.,
Basin, OR

G8, $15-$30
Klamath
Lake, OR

G8, $15-$30
Mendocino
Co., CA

G7, $12-$20
OR

G6, $12-$20
Malheur
Co., OR

G10, $50-$100
Cent. OR

G9, $30-$55
Warner Valley, OR

Obsidian

G7, $25-$40
Lake Co., OR

Obsidian

G8, $50-$90
Sou. OR

G10, $125-$200
Sou. OR

LOCATION: Great Basin westward.
DESCRIPTION: A small to medium size, narrow, expanded to contracted stemmed arrow point. Larger examples are dart/knives. The base can be incurvate to rounded.

Dart/knife

Early
dart
from

G10+, $200-$350
Lake Co., OR

ROSSI SQUARE-STEMMED - Mid-Archaic-Trans., 4000 - 2000 B. P.

(Also see Shaniko Stemmed)

Monterey
Chert

LOCATION: San Mateo Co., California and surrounding area into central and sou. coastal California. Usually made of Monterey Chert. **DESCRIPTION:** A medium size, square stemmed dart/knife point with horizontal shoulders.

G6, $8-$15
San Mateo Co., CA

Base nick

GB

SALMON RIVER - Early Archaic., 8000 - 5800 B. P.

(Also see Bitterroot, Palisades, Shaniko Stemmed & Wendover)

Basalt

G6, $15-$25
WA

Basalt

G6, $15-$25
WA

G6, $20-$35
S.E. OR

LOCATION: Oregon and Washington state. **DESCRIPTION:** A *Bitterroot* variant. A medium size, narrow, dart point with weak, tapered shoulders, an expanding stem and a straight base. Basal corners are sharp to rounded. Stems can be short to long.

SAUVIE'S ISLAND SHOULDER NOTCHED
- Transitional to Classic Phase., 1750 - 400 B. P.

(Also see Columbia Plateau, Rabbit Island and Wallula)

Agate

Red agate

Agate

Agate

Jasper

G8, $25-$40
Vacouver,
WA

G10, $25-$45
Vancouver,
WA

G8, $35-$60
Portland, OR

G10, $35-$60
Portland, OR

G10, $40-$75
Vancouver,
WA

G10, $40-$75
Vancouver,
WA

G9, $35-$60
Vancouver, WA

Jasper

Double notched

Tan jasper

Agate

Red jasper

Double notched

Red jasper

G10, $55-$100
Portland, OR

G9, $55-$100
Portland, OR

G8, $40-$70
Portland, OR

G10, $40-$70
Vancouver, WA

G10, $55-$100
Vancouver, WA

G9 $55-$100
Vancouver, WA

G9, $55-$100
Portland, OR

Agate

Chalcedony

G9, $40-$70
Vancouver, WA.

Red jasper

Jasper

G9, $50-$90
Vancouver, WA

G10, $125-$225
Portland, OR

G10, $150-$250
Vancouver, WA

LOCATION: Oregon and Washington state. **DESCRIPTION:** A thin, small size, stemmed arrow point with one or both shoulders that contain a notch. These are consistently *Rabbits & Wallula Gaps* with shoulder notches. Shoulders can be tapered to barbed. Bases are straight to convex. Stems are short and are either squared or tapered. Named by Jim Hogue.

SCOTTSBLUFF (See Cody Complex)

SCRAPER- Paleo to Developmental Phase, 14,000 - 1000 B. P.

(Also see Drill, Graver, Lancet, Paleo Knife, Perforator and Sizer)

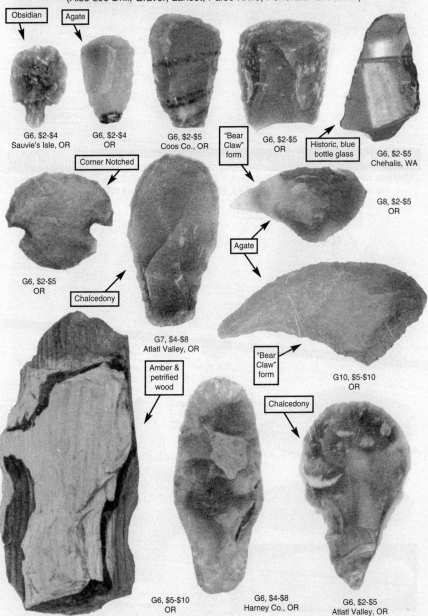

Obsidian

Agate

G6, $2-$4
Sauvie's Isle, OR

G6, $2-$4
OR

G6, $2-$5
Coos Co., OR

"Bear
Claw"
form

G6, $2-$5
OR

Historic, blue
bottle glass

G6, $2-$5
Chehalis, WA

Corner Notched

G8, $2-$5
OR

Agate

G6, $2-$5
OR

Chalcedony

G7, $4-$8
Atlatl Valley, OR

"Bear
Claw"
form

G10, $5-$10
OR

Amber &
petrified
wood

Chalcedony

G6, $5-$10
OR

G6, $4-$8
Harney Co., OR

G6, $2-$5
Atlatl Valley, OR

LOCATION: All early-man sites. **DESCRIPTION:** Thumb, duckbill, claw and turtleback forms are small to medium size, thick, ovoid shaped, uniface, scraping tools that are steeply beveled, especially at the broadest end. Side scrapers are long to oval hand-held uniface flakes with beveling on the edges intended for use. Scraping was done primarily from the sides of these blades. Some of these tools were hafted.

GB

SCRAPER (continued)

G8, $12-$20
Atlatl Valley, OR

Petrified wood

SHANIKO STEMMED - Late Archaic to Woodland, 3500 - 2300 B. P.

(Also see Bear, Cascade, Cody Complex, Lake Mohave, Lind Coulee, Owl Cave, Parman, Pryor Stemmed, Rossi Square-Stemmed, Silver Lake, Whale and Windust)

Chalcedony

Basalt

Agate

Ground stem

G7, $18-$30
WA

G7, $15-$30
OR

G6, $8-$15
Union Co., OR

G7, $25-$45
OR

Pink jasper

G10, $18-$30
WA

Basalt

Ground stem

Dark yel-low/red agate

Ground stem

G5, $12-$20
Columbia Riv.
Basin, OR.

G6, $12-$20
OR

Yellow jasper

G9, $18-$30
Lake Co., OR

G8, $18-$30
Columbia Riv., WA

G9, $55-$100
WA

LOCATION: Mid-Columbia River area in Oregon. **DESCRIPTION:** A medium size point with sloping to slightly barbed shoulders. Stems are straight to contracting to a straight to convex base. Stem sides are sometimes ground and bases can be thinned. Flaking is random and the cross section is flat. Named by A.R. Snyder and J.L. Hogue in April, 2000. Formerly called *Early Stemmed*. **I.D. KEY:** Base form and size.

SHANIKO STEMMED (continued)

G6, $12-$20
Warner Valley, OR

G7, $18-$30
Warner Valley, OR

G7, $18-$30
OR

Obsidian

Obsidian

Ground stem

G9, $65-$125
OR

G5, $15-$20
OR

G8, $55-$100
Jefferson Co., OR

G8, $35-$65
Warner Valley, OR

Well ground stem

Ground stem

Basalt

Agate

G9, $55-$100
OR

G8, $35-$60
Deschutes Co., OR

G9, $40-$75
Columbia Riv., WA

G6, $8-$15
Union Co., OR

GB

1265

SIDE KNIFE - Devlopmental to Historic Phase, 1000 - 300 B. P.

(Also Scraper, Snow Knife, Square-End Knife and Ulu)

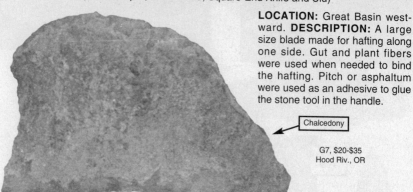

LOCATION: Great Basin westward. **DESCRIPTION:** A large size blade made for hafting along one side. Gut and plant fibers were used when needed to bind the hafting. Pitch or asphaltum were used as an adhesive to glue the stone tool in the handle.

Chalcedony

G7, $20-$35
Hood Riv., OR

SIERRA STEMMED - Early to Late Archaic, 6000 - 3000 B. P.

(Also see Coquille, Rabbit Island & Silver Lake)

G7, $25-$40
Mendocino Co., CA

Serrated edge

G7, $15-$25
Mendocino Co., CA

G6, $12-$20
Mendocino Co., CA

LOCATION: Northern Calif. southward into Arizona. **DESCRIPTION:** A narrow triangular dart point with horizontal barbs and a contracting, rounded stem. Stem edges can be serrated. **I.D. KEY:** base form and size.

SILVER LAKE - Late Paleo to Early Archaic, 11,000 - 7000 B. P.

(Also see Cody Complex, Lake Mohave, Lind Coulee, Parman, Shaniko Stemmed & Sierra Stemmed)

G5, $25-$45
Lake Co., OR

G7, $30-$60
Warner Valley, OR

LOCATION: Sou. California into sou. Oregon. **DESCRIPTION:** A small to medium size, narrow point with slight to moderate tapered to square shoulders and a long, contracting to bulbous stem that is ground. **I.D. KEY:** Long stem, weak shoulders.

SILVER LAKE (continued)

G6, $80-$150
Lake Co., OR

G7, $125-$200
Lake Co., OR

G7, $125-$200
Lake Co., OR

G6, $90-$175
Massacre Lake, NV,
Washoe Co.

G7, $125-$200
Lake Co., OR

G7, $125-$200
N. NV

G8, $135-$250
Warner Valley, OR

SIZER - Transitional to Historic Phase, 2,300 - 200 B. P.

(Also see Graver and Scraper)

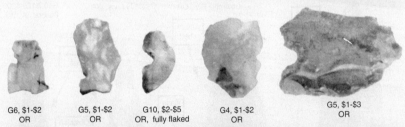

G6, $1-$2
OR

G5, $1-$2
OR

G10, $2-$5
OR, fully flaked

G4, $1-$2
OR

G5, $1-$3
OR

LOCATION: North to central Oregon. **DESCRIPTION:** A small, notched scraper used to make basket material the same size. Spruce or cedar roots vary considerably. A uniform diameter would produce a tighter, higher quality basket. Look for use wear in notch. **I.D. KEY:** Small notch.

SNAKE RIVER - Late Archaic to Developmental Phase, 2000 - 1000 B. P.

(Also see Columbia Plateau, Eastgate, Elko, Hell's Canyon, Hendricks, Merrybell & Wendover)

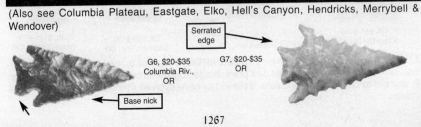

G6, $20-$35
Columbia Riv.,
OR

G7, $20-$35
OR

GB

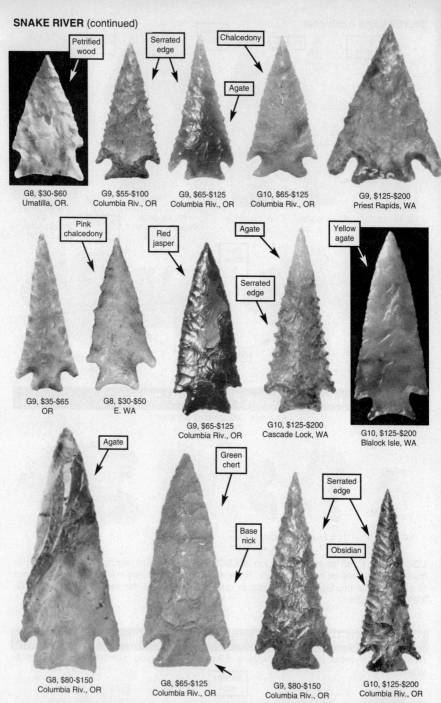

Petrified wood

Serrated edge

Chalcedony

Agate

G8, $30-$60
Umatilla, OR.

G9, $55-$100
Columbia Riv., OR

G9, $65-$125
Columbia Riv., OR

G10, $65-$125
Columbia Riv., OR

G9, $125-$200
Priest Rapids, WA

Pink chalcedony

Red jasper

Agate

Serrated edge

Yellow agate

G9, $35-$65
OR

G8, $30-$50
E. WA

G9, $65-$125
Columbia Riv., OR

G10, $125-$200
Cascade Lock, WA

G10, $125-$200
Blalock Isle, WA

Agate

Green chert

Base nick

Serrated edge

Obsidian

G8, $80-$150
Columbia Riv., OR

G8, $65-$125
Columbia Riv., OR

G9, $80-$150
Columbia Riv., OR

G10, $125-$200
Columbia Riv., OR

LOCATION: Great Basin westward. **DESCRIPTION:** A small to medium size barbed, corner, side or expanded, stemmed dart point. Blade edges can be serrated. Bases are usually straight to concave to auriculate. Believed to have evolved into *Columbia Plateau* arrow points.

SNAKE RIVER (continued)

Chalcedony

Basalt

G10, $175-$300
Columbia Riv., OR

G10, $225-$400
WA

SNOW KNIFE - Historic, 400 - 200 B. P.
(Also see Ground Stone, Side Knife and Ulu)

Ivory

G10, $80-$150
AK

LOCATION: Alaska. **DESCRIPTION:** A medium size knife made of ivory or bone for hafting.

SPEDIS I - Paleo, 10,000 - 8000 B. P.
(Also see Cascade, Gypsum Cave, Haskett, Pismo, Portage and Rabbit Island)

G6, $8-$15
Umatilla, OR

G6, $12-$20
Columbia
Plateau, OR

G6, $12-$20
Umatilla, OR

G5, $8-$15
Umatilla, OR

G7, $15-$25
Morrow Co., OR

G5, $8-$15
Morrow Co., OR

Tan
agate

G6, $15-$30
Umatilla, OR

G7, $12-$20
Morrow Co., OR

G8, $25-$40
WA

G6, $15-$25
Umatilla, OR

G6, $15-$25
Morrow Co. OR

G7, $20-$35
Morrow Co. OR

LOCATION: Oregon and Washington, Columbia River basin. **DESCRIPTION:** A small to medium size, thin, narrow, lanceolate dart/knife point with a distinctive "pumpkin seed" shape. The stems are contracting and have straight to slightly concave sides and are ground. The bases are straight, truncated, diagonally biased or notched and are usually smoothed. Single shoulder examples occur. Usually exotic materials were employed. They are thinned by a combination of percussion and pressure. The cross sections are flattened to lenticular. **I.D. KEY:** "Pumpkin seed" form.

GB

SPEDIS I (continued)

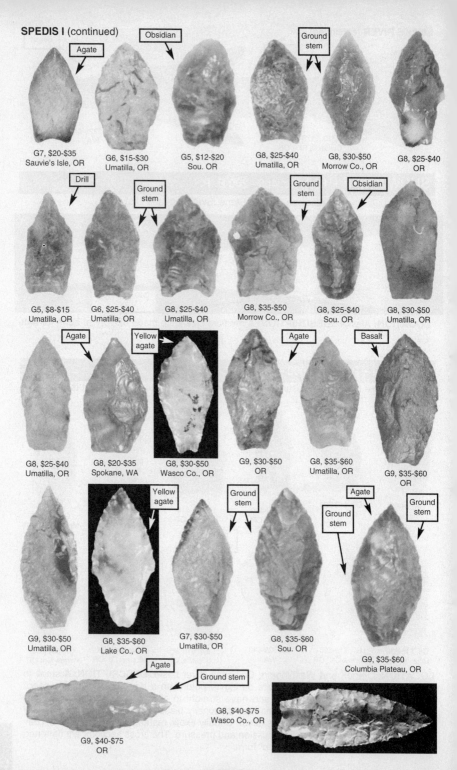

Agate

G7, $20-$35
Sauvie's Isle, OR

Obsidian

G6, $15-$30
Umatilla, OR

G5, $12-$20
Sou. OR

Ground stem

G8, $25-$40
Umatilla, OR

G8, $30-$50
Morrow Co., OR

G8, $25-$40
OR

Drill

G5, $8-$15
Umatilla, OR

Ground stem

G6, $25-$40
Umatilla, OR

G8, $25-$40
Umatilla, OR

Ground stem

G8, $35-$50
Morrow Co., OR

Obsidian

G8, $25-$40
Sou. OR

G8, $30-$50
Umatilla, OR

Agate

G8, $25-$40
Umatilla, OR

Yellow agate

G8, $20-$35
Spokane, WA

G8, $30-$50
Wasco Co., OR

Agate

G9, $30-$50
OR

G8, $35-$60
Umatilla, OR

Basalt

G9, $35-$60
OR

G9, $30-$50
Umatilla, OR

Yellow agate

G8, $35-$60
Lake Co., OR

G7, $30-$50
Umatilla, OR

Ground stem

G8, $35-$60
Sou. OR

Agate

Ground stem

G9, $35-$60
Columbia Plateau, OR

Ground stem

Agate

Ground stem

G9, $40-$75
OR

G8, $40-$75
Wasco Co., OR

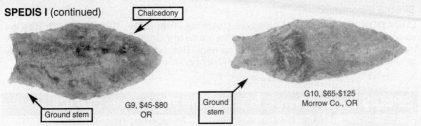

Chalcedony

Ground stem

G9, $45-$80
OR

Ground stem

G10, $65-$125
Morrow Co., OR

SPEDIS II - Paleo, 10,000 - 8000 B. P.

(Also see Cascade, Gypsum Cave, Haskett, Pismo and Rabbit Island)

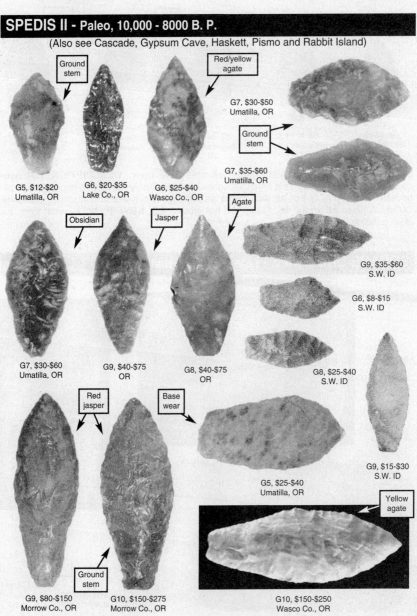

Ground stem

Red/yellow agate

G7, $30-$50
Umatilla, OR

Ground stem

G7, $35-$60
Umatilla, OR

G5, $12-$20
Umatilla, OR

G6, $20-$35
Lake Co., OR

G6, $25-$40
Wasco Co., OR

Agate

Obsidian

Jasper

G9, $35-$60
S.W. ID

G6, $8-$15
S.W. ID

G7, $30-$60
Umatilla, OR

G9, $40-$75
OR

G8, $40-$75
OR

G8, $25-$40
S.W. ID

Red jasper

Base wear

G9, $15-$30
S.W. ID

Yellow agate

G5, $25-$40
Umatilla, OR

Ground stem

G9, $80-$150
Morrow Co., OR

G10, $150-$275
Morrow Co., OR

G10, $150-$250
Wasco Co., OR

GB

SPEDIS II (continued)

LOCATION: Oregon and Washington, Columbia River basin. **DESCRIPTION:** Has the same "pumpkin seed" shaped blade, but the stems are slightly longer. The stem sides contract to a straight base with rounded corners. Both stem sides and base are usually ground. **I.D. KEY:** "Pumpkin seed" form with longer stem.

SPEDIS III - Late Archaic to Transitional Phase, 3000 - 2000 B. P.

(Also see Cascade, Gold Hill, Portage and Trojan)

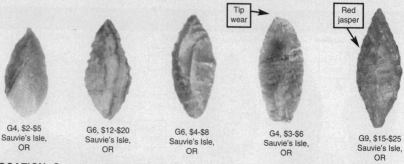

G4, $2-$5
Sauvie's Isle,
OR

G6, $12-$20
Sauvie's Isle,
OR

G6, $4-$8
Sauvie's Isle,
OR

G4, $3-$6
Sauvie's Isle,
OR

G9, $15-$25
Sauvie's Isle,
OR

LOCATION: Oregon and Washington, Columbia River basin. **DESCRIPTION:** This type commonly called "Spedis" is a small Woodland point that only has the "pumpkin seed" silhouette. This point is not as well made as the first two types and qualifies as lower Columbia types #5 and/or #6. Stems are not ground. **I.D. KEY:** "Pumpkin seed" form, no stem grinding.

SQUARE-END KNIFE - Late Archaic to Historic, 3500 - 400 B. P.

(Also see Drill, Scraper, Paleo Knife & Side Knife)

G6, $10-$20
Lake Co., OR,
Christmas
Lake.

White chert

G6, $12-$20
Lake Co., OR

Basalt

G8, $30-$50
Lake Co., OR

SQUARE-END KNIFE (continued)

LOCATION: Great Basin westward. **DESCRIPTION:** A medium to large size squared blade that is beveled on all four sides for cutting. **I.D. KEY:** Squared form.

STOCKTON - Develop. to Historic Phase, 1200 - 200 B. P.

(Also see Exotic and Vendetta)

Unique double notch

G6, $60-$110
Holt, CA

G5, $40-$75
Holt, CA

G7, $80-$150
San Joaquin Co.,
CA

G7, $150-$250
Holt, CA

G8, $200-$375
Holt, CA

Black obsidian

Tip and right ear are broken & glued

G10, $500-$900
Holt, CA

"Squared" notches

Note rare and unique notching

Black obsidian

All are black obsidian

Classic form

G8, $250-$450
Holt, CA

G8, $250-$450
Holt, CA

G9, $275-$550
Holt, CA

G9, $700-$1300
Holt, CA

Restored ear

G6, $500-$900
Holt, CA

Black obsidian

G8, $400-$700
Holt, CA

1273

GB

STOCKTON (continued)

LOCATION: Stockton, California area. Very rare. **DESCRIPTION:** A small to large size, thin, narrow, point that has exaggerated, squared barbs along the blade edges. Believed to have been used for sawing as well as an arrow point. Forms vary from stemmed to auriculate to corner notched. **I.D. KEY:** Deep square barbs.

STRONG BARBED AURICULATE - Late Archaic, 1750 - 700 B. P.

(Also see Columbia Mule Ear, Humboldt and Triple T)

Note: Absolute authentication of this rare type is necessary as modern reproductions may exist.

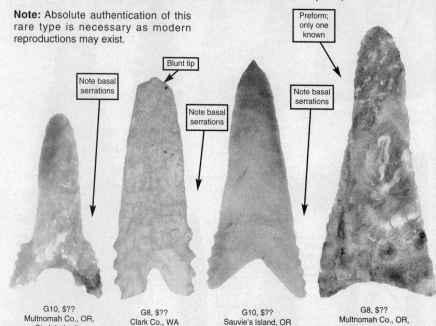

Blunt tip

Preform; only one known

Note basal serrations

Note basal serrations

Note basal serrations

G10, $??
Multnomah Co., OR,
St. John's site

G8, $??
Clark Co., WA

G10, $??
Sauvie's Island, OR

G8, $??
Multnomah Co., OR,
St. John's site.

LOCATION: Sauvie's Island, Oregon and adjacent areas. **DESCRIPTION:** A very rare type with only 11 examples known. A medium size auriculate point with a concave, notched to v-shaped base and an obtuse to apiculate tip. The basal ears are serrated. **I.D. KEY:** Basal ears serrated. **Note:** Unique; none have been sold and value will be determined when sales data becomes available.

SUB-TRIANGULAR - Paleo, 11,300 - 11,000 B. P.

(Also see Black Rock Concave, Cascade, Chindadn and Owl Cave)

G8, $25-$50
Nenana Valley,
south central AK

LOCATION: Alaska. **DESCRIPTION:** A small size, broad, thin, triangular point made from a flake that has a straight to slightly concave base. Made during the Nenana occupation. **I.D. KEY:** Broad triangle.

THREE-PIECE FISH SPEAR- Trans. to Historic Phase, 2300 - 200 B.P.

(Also see Harpoon)

LOCATION: East & west coast into Canada. **DESCRIPTION:** A small size bone point consisting of two flanges and a short center shaft. The flanges comprise the barbs and a portion of the point. The flanges are grooved at one end to fit over the center shaft. They were tied together to form the point. This point was then hafted over a spear shaft. Rarely found complete. **I.D. KEY:** Three-prong form.

THREE PIECE FISH SPEAR (continued)

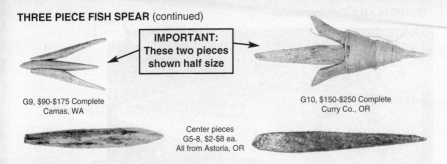

IMPORTANT:
These two pieces
shown half size

G9, $90-$175 Complete
Camas, WA

G10, $150-$250 Complete
Curry Co., OR

Center pieces
G5-8, $2-$8 ea.
All from Astoria, OR

TOGGLE (See Harpoon)

TRADE POINTS - Classic to Historic Phase, 400 - 170 B.P.

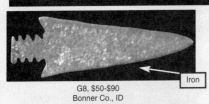

G8, $50-$90
Bonner Co., ID

Iron

LOCATION: These points were made of copper, iron, and steel and were traded to the Indians by the French, British and others from the 1600s to the 1800s. Examples have been found all over the United States. Forms vary from triangular to conical to stemmed.

TRIANGULAR KNIFE- Late Archaic, 3500 B.P.

(Also see Atlatl Valley Triangular and Cascade Knife)

Chalcedony

Obsidian

G8, $55-$100
Silver Lake, OR

Obsidian

Beveled
edge

G6, $20-$35
N.W. NV

G10, $85-$160
Lake Co., OR

LOCATION: Southern Oregon southward to Mexico. **DESCRIPTION:** A large size triangular knife with a straight base. Beveling occurs on resharpened examples.

GB

TRIANGULAR KNIVE (continued)

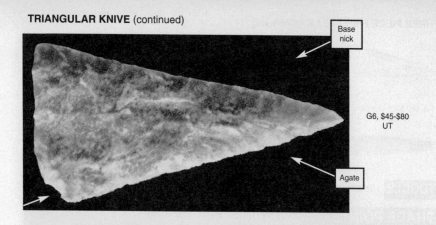

Base nick

G6, $45-$80
UT

Agate

TRIPLE "T" - Middle Archaic, 5500 - 5000 B. P.
(Also see Black Rock Concave, Cascade, Humboldt and Strong)

LOCATION: Great Basin westward. **DESCRIPTION:** A medium size, lanceolate point with rounded basal corners and a concave base. Blade edges curve from point to base. Another variation of the *Humboldt* series.

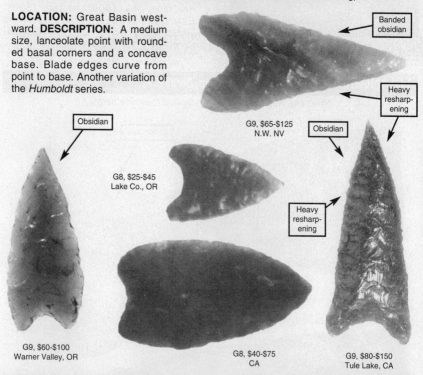

Banded obsidian

Heavy resharpening

Obsidian

G9, $65-$125
N.W. NV

Obsidian

G8, $25-$45
Lake Co., OR

Heavy resharpening

G9, $60-$100
Warner Valley, OR

G8, $40-$75
CA

G9, $80-$150
Tule Lake, CA

TROJAN - Developmental to Classic Phase, 1320 - 300 B. P.
(Also see Cottonwood, Gold Hill, Magala Cove Leaf and Portage)

LOCATION: Lower Columbia River from Portland to Astoria. **DESCRIPTION:** A small, thin, triangular to ovate arrow point. Many are made from flakes with unfinished bases and minimal retouch. Over 2200 were found at the Trojan site. Possible use as tips in bone harpoons for hunting seal and fish.

TROJAN (continued)

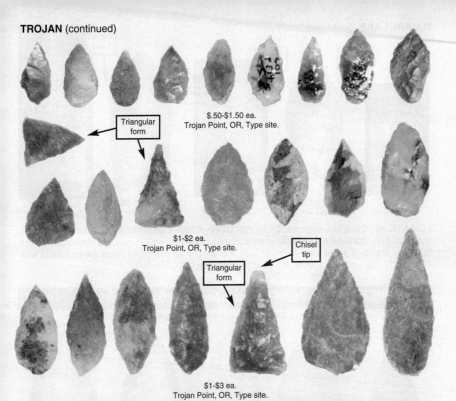

Triangular form

$.50-$1.50 ea.
Trojan Point, OR, Type site.

Triangular form

$1-$2 ea.
Trojan Point, OR, Type site.

Chisel tip

Triangular form

$1-$3 ea.
Trojan Point, OR, Type site.

TUOLUMNE NOTCHED - Late Archaic, 3100 - 2500 B. P.
(Also see Need Stemmed Lanceolate, Nightfire & Willits Side Notched)

Obsidian

G9, $450-$800
Humboldt Bay, CA

LOCATION: Central Northern California. **DESCRIPTION:** A large corner to side notched point with a convex, bulbous base. Some examples have excellent oblique, parallel flaking on the blade faces. Similar to but later than the Nightfire point found further North. **I.D. KEY:** Bulbous base.

TULARE LAKE - Paleo- 12,000 - 10,000 B. P.
(Also see Black Rock Concave, Clovis, Humboldt and Mesa)

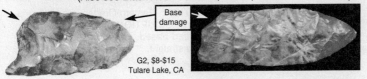

Base damage

G2, $15-$30
Tulare Lake, CA

G2, $8-$15
Tulare Lake, CA

1277

GB

TULARE LAKE (continued)

G5, $125-$200
Tulare Lake, CA

G6, $175-$300
Tulare Lake, CA

G6, $175-$300
Tulare Lake, CA

G6, $175-$300
Tulare Lake, CA

G6, $150-$250
Tulare Lake, CA

LOCATION: Central California. **DESCRIPTION:** A late *Clovis* variant. A small to medium size unfluted, auriculate point with a concave base. Basal area is ground. Some bases are thinned. Basal area is usually over half the length of the point. Has been found with *Crescents* and unfluted *Clovis* points at the Witt site.

TULARE LAKE BI-POINT - Early Archaic 8,000 - 6,000 B. P.

(Also see Cascade, Early Leaf, Excelsior, Kennewick, Wildcat Canyon)

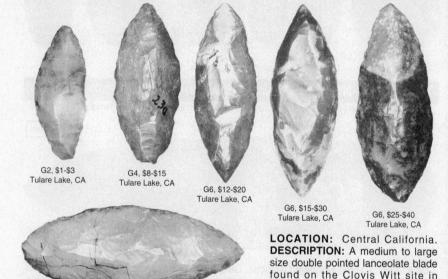

G2, $1-$3
Tulare Lake, CA

G4, $8-$15
Tulare Lake, CA

G6, $12-$20
Tulare Lake, CA

G6, $15-$30
Tulare Lake, CA

G6, $25-$40
Tulare Lake, CA

G8, $35-$60
Tulare Lake, CA

LOCATION: Central California. **DESCRIPTION:** A medium to large size double pointed lanceolate blade found on the Clovis Witt site in California.

UINTA - Developmental Phase, 1,200 - 800 B. P.

(Also see Ahsahka, Bitterroot, Cold Springs, Desert Side-Notched)

G8, $12-$20
Columbia Riv. Basin,
OR

LOCATION: Eastern Oregon into Utah and Idaho. **DESCRIPTION:** A small size, serrated, broad-based, side-notched point. The base is straight.

(Also see Ground Stone, Side Knife and Snow Knife)

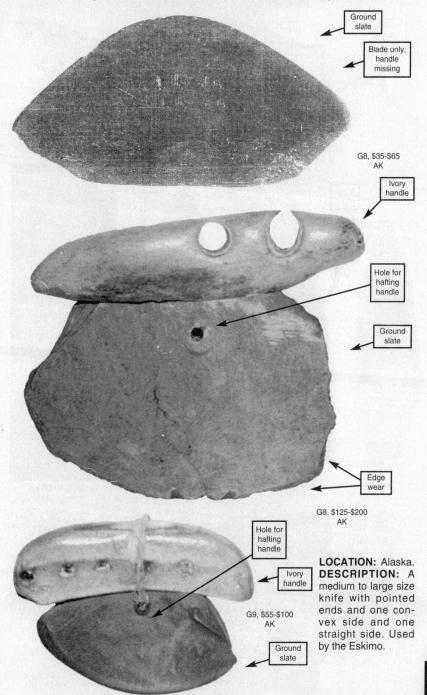

Ground slate

Blade only, handle missing

G8, $35-$65
AK

Ivory handle

Hole for hafting handle

Ground slate

Edge wear

G8, $125-$200
AK

Hole for hafting handle

Ivory handle

G9, $55-$100
AK

Ground slate

LOCATION: Alaska.
DESCRIPTION: A medium to large size knife with pointed ends and one convex side and one straight side. Used by the Eskimo.

GB

VANDENBERG CONTRACTING STEM - Mid Archaic to
Developmental Phase, 5000 - 1500 B. P.

(Also see Gatecliff, Parman and Wahmuza)

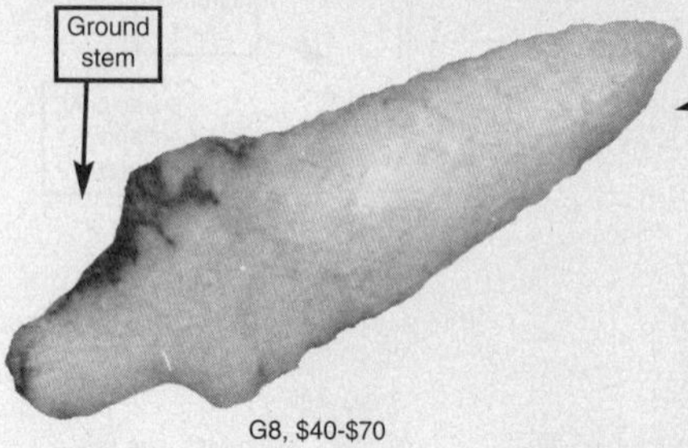

Ground stem

Quartzite

Obsidian

G6, $35-$60
CA

G8, $40-$70
N. CA

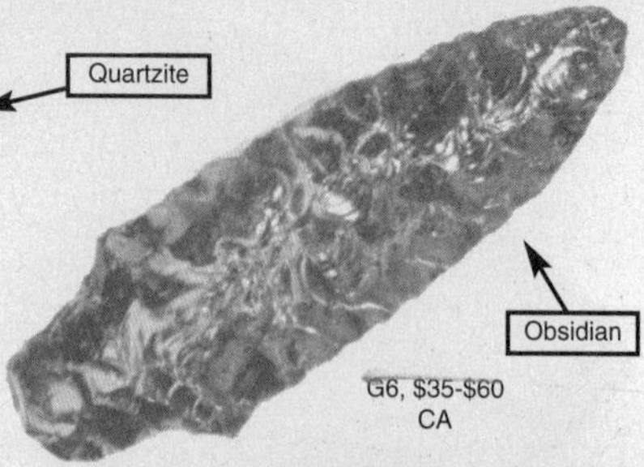

Obsidian

Blade wear

Agate

Moss agate

Ground stem

Blade wear

G7, $50-$90
CA

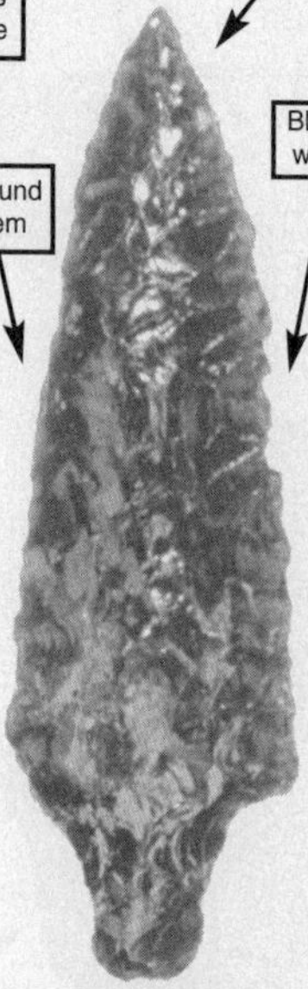

G8, $50-$90
CA

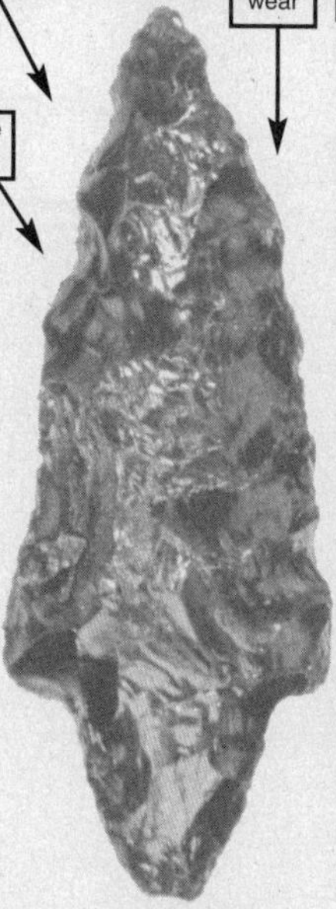

G6, $30-$50
CA

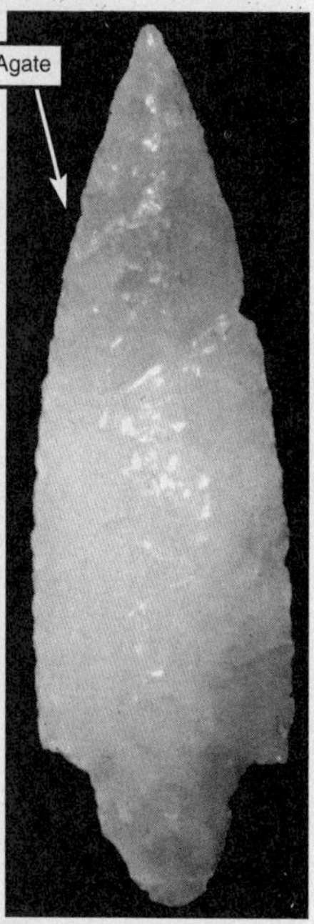

G8, $150-$275
Lake Co., OR

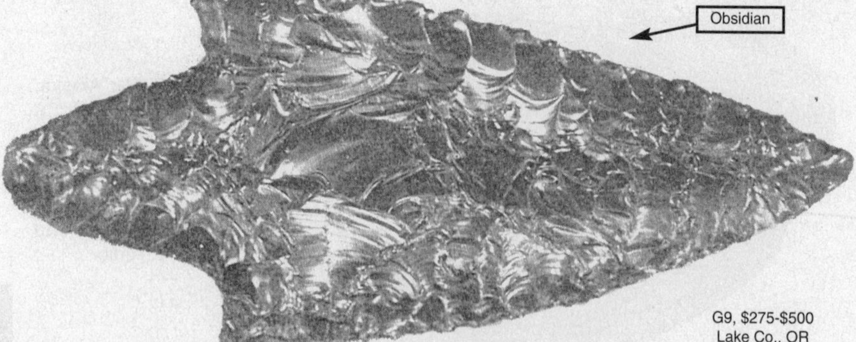

Obsidian

G9, $275-$500
Lake Co., OR

VANDENBERG CONTRACTING STEM (continued)

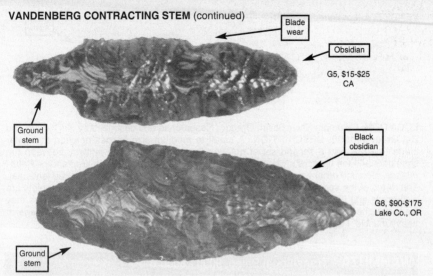

Blade wear

Obsidian

G5, $15-$25
CA

Black obsidian

G8, $90-$175
Lake Co., OR

Ground stem

Ground stem

LOCATION: California, Nevada, Oregon. Named after Vandenberg Air Force base where the type site is located. **DESCRIPTION:** A medium to large size, contracting stemmed point. Shoulders are barbed to contracting. Bases are convex and stems are usually ground. Similar to the *Gypsum Cave* point but much larger and earlier in age.

VENDETTA - Transitional to Classic Phase, 1750 - 200 B. P.

(Also see Dagger and Exotic)

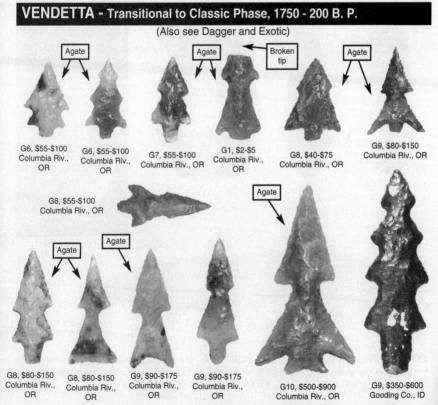

Agate

Agate

Broken tip

Agate

G6, $55-$100
Columbia Riv.,
OR

G6, $55-$100
Columbia Riv.,
OR

G7, $55-$100
Columbia Riv., OR

G1, $2-$5
Columbia Riv.,
OR

G8, $40-$75
Columbia Riv., OR

G9, $80-$150
Columbia Riv., OR

G8, $55-$100
Columbia Riv., OR

Agate

Agate

Agate

G8, $80-$150
Columbia Riv.,
OR

G8, $80-$150
Columbia Riv.,
OR

G9, $90-$175
Columbia Riv.,
OR

G9, $90-$175
Columbia Riv.,
OR

G10, $500-$900
Columbia Riv., OR

G9, $350-$600
Gooding Co., ID

GB

1281

VENDETTA (continued)

G10, $250-$400
Columbia Riv., OR

Agate

Agate

G10, $200-$350
Columbia Riv., OR

LOCATION: Columbia River Basin, Oregon. Researched and described by Jim Hogue and Del Greer in 1998. **DESCRIPTION:** A small to medium size barbed-notched triangular blade that has had a second set of notches flaked into the blade halfway between the shoulders and the tip. This style is usually made on larger sized *Wallula Gap* and/or *Rabbit Islands*, although other types are sometimes used. The cross section is flattened lenticular. The depth of the second set of barbs varies, and triple notches do occur. These points are well made and usually of gem material, and were locally called "*Vendetta*" points as they were designed to snap at the weakened halfway point, on contact with bone, cartilage or heavy muscle. **I.D. KEY:** Double shoulders.

WAHMUZA - Transitional Paleo, 9000 - 8000 B. P.

(Also see Cascade, Owl Cave, Plateau Pentagonal, Vandenberg Contracting Stem & Wildcat Canyon)

Chalcedony

Ground basal sides

G6, $12-$20
OR

G7, $25-$45
Lake Co., OR

G8, $40-$75
OR

G8, $65-$125
Caribou Co., ID

G8, $65-$125
S.E. OR

LOCATION: Great Basin area. **DESCRIPTION:** A medium size lanceolate point with a recurved edge and a long, straight-sided, tapered base that is ground. The basal edge is short and straight to rounded. **I.D. KEY:** Pronounced contracting base.

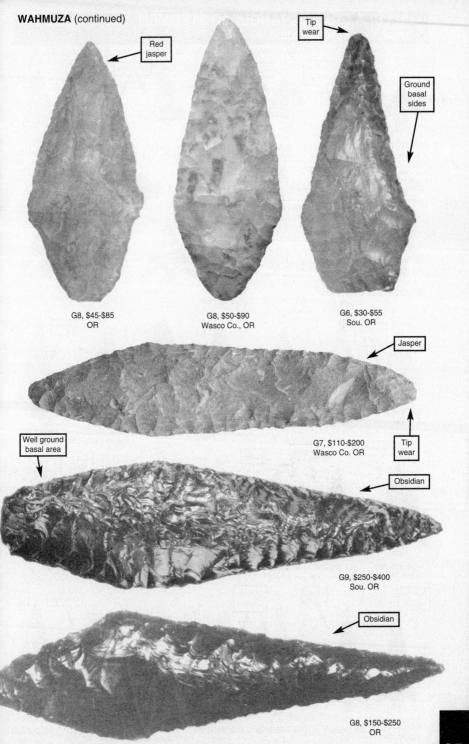

Red jasper

Tip wear

Ground basal sides

G8, $45-$85
OR

G8, $50-$90
Wasco Co., OR

G6, $30-$55
Sou. OR

Jasper

G7, $110-$200
Wasco Co. OR

Tip wear

Well ground basal area

Obsidian

G9, $250-$400
Sou. OR

Obsidian

G8, $150-$250
OR

GB

WALLULA GAP RECTANGULAR STEMMED - Developmental to Historic Phase, 1000 - 200 B. P.

(Also see Columbia Plateau, Eastgate, Rabbit Island, Rose Spring & Sauvie's Island)

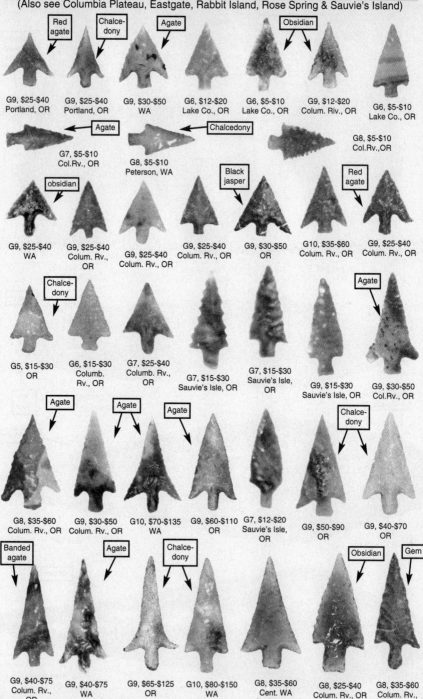

Red agate — G9, $25-$40 Portland, OR

Chalcedony — G9, $25-$40 Portland, OR

Agate — G9, $30-$50 WA

G6, $12-$20 Lake Co., OR

G6, $5-$10 Lake Co., OR

Obsidian — G9, $12-$20 Colum. Riv., OR

G6, $5-$10 Lake Co., OR

Agate — G7, $5-$10 Col.Rv., OR

Chalcedony — G8, $5-$10 Peterson, WA

G8, $5-$10 Col.Rv., OR

obsidian — G9, $25-$40 WA

G9, $25-$40 Colum. Rv., OR

G9, $25-$40 Colum. Rv., OR

G9, $25-$40 Colum. Rv., OR

Black jasper — G9, $30-$50 OR

G10, $35-$60 Colum. Rv., OR

Red agate — G9, $25-$40 Colum. Rv., OR

Chalcedony — G5, $15-$30 OR

G6, $15-$30 Columb. Rv., OR

G7, $25-$40 Columb. Rv., OR

G7, $15-$30 Sauvie's Isle, OR

G7, $15-$30 Sauvie's Isle, OR

G9, $15-$30 Sauvie's Isle, OR

Agate — G9, $30-$50 Col.Rv., OR

Agate — G8, $35-$60 Colum. Rv., OR

Agate — G9, $30-$50 Colum. Rv., OR

Agate — G10, $70-$135 WA

G9, $60-$110 OR

G7, $12-$20 Sauvie's Isle, OR

Chalcedony — G9, $50-$90 OR

G9, $40-$70 OR

Banded agate — G9, $40-$75 Colum. Rv., OR

Agate — G9, $40-$75 WA

Chalcedony — G9, $65-$125 OR

G10, $80-$150 WA

G8, $35-$60 Cent. WA Chalcedony.

Obsidian — G8, $25-$40 Colum. Rv., OR

Gem — G8, $35-$60 Colum. Rv., OR

1284

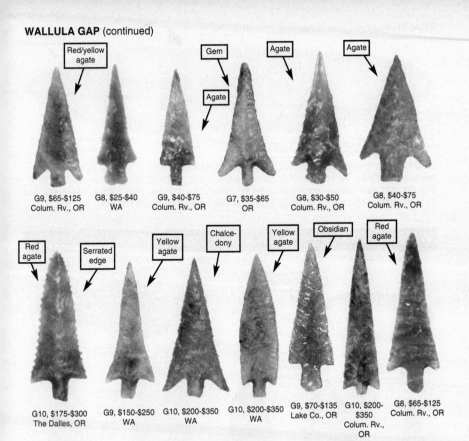

Red/yellow agate

Gem

Agate

Agate

Agate

G9, $65-$125
Colum. Rv., OR

G8, $25-$40
WA

G9, $40-$75
Colum. Rv., OR

G7, $35-$65
OR

G8, $30-$50
Colum. Rv., OR

G8, $40-$75
Colum. Rv., OR

Red agate

Serrated edge

Yellow agate

Chalce-dony

Yellow agate

Obsidian

Red agate

G10, $175-$300
The Dalles, OR

G9, $150-$250
WA

G10, $200-$350
WA

G10, $200-$350
WA

G9, $70-$135
Lake Co., OR

G10, $200-$350
Colum. Rv., OR

G8, $65-$125
Colum. Rv., OR

LOCATION: Columbia River basin of Oregon and Washington. **DESCRIPTION:** A small size, thin, stemmed, arrow point usually with barbs. Blades are more narrow and Barbs are not as prominent as on *Columbia River* points.The stem can be slightly expanding or contracting or bulbous but is usually rectangular. Shoulders barbed to horizontal. Blade edges can be serrated. A contracting stem would place the point in the *Rabbit Island* type.

WEALTH BLADE - Developmental to Present, 1200 B.P. - Present

(Also see Cascade, Early Leaf,)

IMPORTANT: ALL WEALTH BLADES SHOWN HALF SIZE

Basalt

G9, $400-$750
Sou. OR

Obsidian

G9, $500-$950
Sou. OR.

GB

WEALTH BLADE (continued)

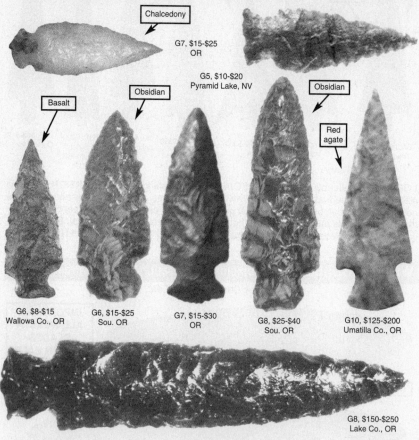

Obsidian

Classic example

Shown half size

Waist area

G9, $800-$1400
Sou. OR

LOCATION: Southern Oregon. **DESCRIPTION:** A large to very large size lanceolate, double pointed blade. Some examples have a waist in the center of the blade to facilitate holding. Recent examples have been used in dance ceremonies. The classic examples are 11"–16" long, well made, generally always waisted. **I.D. KEY:** Extreme size.

WENDOVER - Early to middle Archaic, 7000 - 5000 B. P.

(Also see Bitterroot, Chilcotin Plateau, Eastgate, Merrybell and Rose Springs)

Chalcedony

G7, $15-$25
OR

G5, $10-$20
Pyramid Lake, NV

Obsidian

Basalt

Obsidian

Red agate

G6, $8-$15
Wallowa Co., OR

G6, $15-$25
Sou. OR

G7, $15-$30
OR

G8, $25-$40
Sou. OR

G10, $125-$200
Umatilla Co., OR

G8, $150-$250
Lake Co., OR

LOCATION: Great Basin westward. **DESCRIPTION:** A medium size, narrow, expanded stemmed to side notched dart point with a convex base. Shoulders can be slightly tapered to barbed. Base corners are sharp to rounded. Found on buffalo jump sites in Owyhee Co., ID.

WHALE - Late Archaic, 3000 - 200 B. P.

(Also see Bear and Kavik)

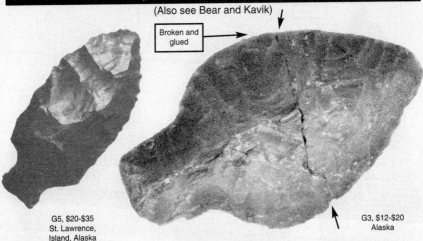

Broken and glued

G5, $20-$35
St. Lawrence,
Island, Alaska

G3, $12-$20
Alaska

LOCATION: Northern Alaska. **DESCRIPTION:** A medium to large size, fairly thick-stemmed point with tapered shoulders and a rectangular stem. Blades are broad compared to stem width. These have been found associated with **Bear** points.

WILDCAT CANYON - Early Archaic, 9000 - 7500 B. P.

(Also see Cascade, Early Leaf, Paleo Knife & Plateau Pentagonal & Wahmuza)

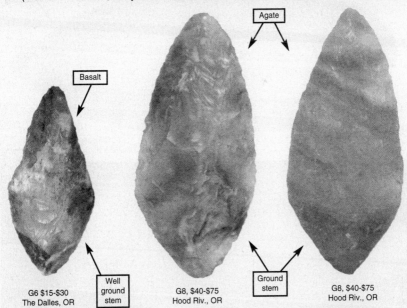

Agate

Basalt

G6 $15-$30
The Dalles, OR

Well ground stem

G8, $40-$75
Hood Riv., OR

Ground stem

G8, $40-$75
Hood Riv., OR

LOCATION: Found in Wildcat Canyon near The Dalles, Oregon. **DESCRIPTION:** A large, broad, lanceolate knife with a convex base. Most basal areas are ground where they were hafted. Blades are usually beveled when resharpened. *Cascades* do not have this beveling.

GB

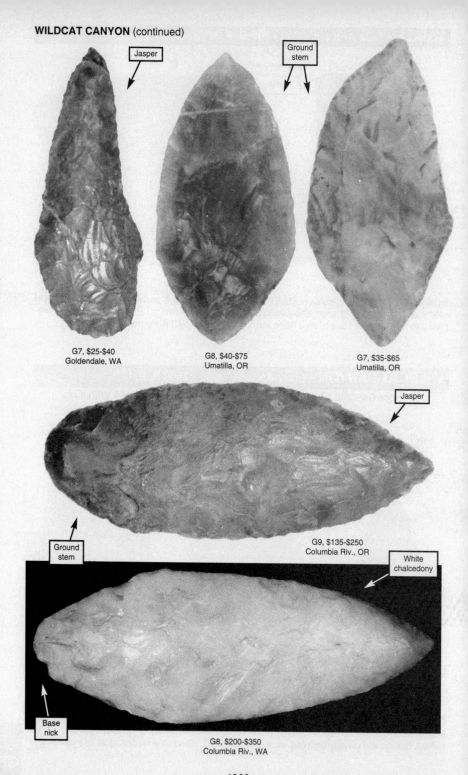

Jasper

Ground stem

G7, $25-$40
Goldendale, WA

G8, $40-$75
Umatilla, OR

G7, $35-$65
Umatilla, OR

Jasper

Ground stem

G9, $135-$250
Columbia Riv., OR

White chalcedony

Base nick

G8, $200-$350
Columbia Riv., WA

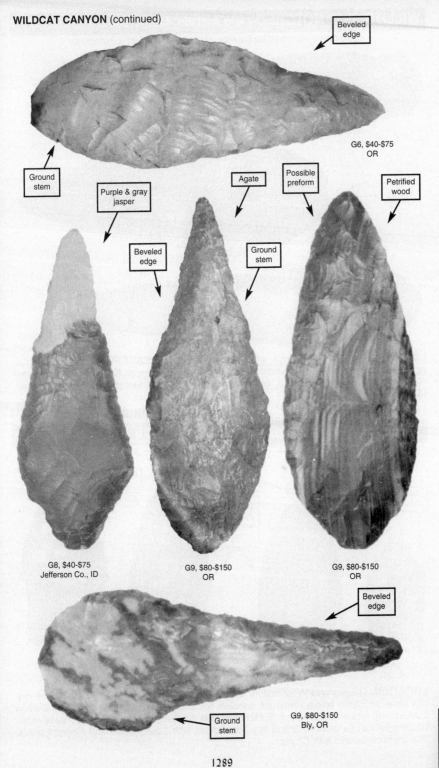

Beveled edge

Ground stem

G6, $40-$75
OR

Purple & gray jasper

Beveled edge

Agate

Ground stem

Possible preform

Petrified wood

G8, $40-$75
Jefferson Co., ID

G9, $80-$150
OR

G9, $80-$150
OR

Beveled edge

Ground stem

G9, $80-$150
Bly, OR

GB

WILLITS SIDE NOTCHED - Mid-Archaic, 4000 - 1500 B. P.

(See Need stemmed lanceolate, Nightfire & Tuolumne Notched)

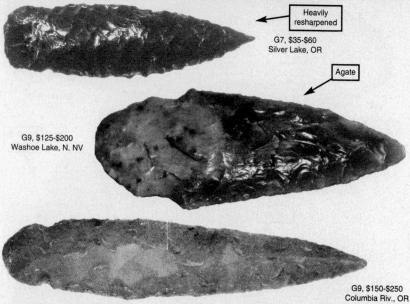

Heavily resharpened

G7, $35-$60
Silver Lake, OR

Agate

G9, $125-$200
Washoe Lake, N. NV

G9, $150-$250
Columbia Riv., OR

LOCATION: Northern California into southern Oregon. **DESCRIPTION:** A medium to large size, narrow, weakly side-notched point with a convex base. Notches usually appear high up from the base creating a large, bulbous stem. Some examples are lightly serrated. **I.D. KEY:** Bulbous stem.

WINDUST - Paleo to Early Archaic, 11,500 - 8000 B. P.

(See Lake Mojave, Lind Coulee, Owl Cave, Parman, Shaniko Stemmed and Silver Lake)

Red jasper

Tip nick

Agate

Bifurcated stem

Basal grinding

Bifurcated stem

Shoulders gone from resharpening

Bifurcated stem

G4, $25-$40
Sou. OR

G3, $25-$40
OR

G6, $55-$100
WA

G6, $55-$100
Lake Co., OR

LOCATION: Oregon and Washington. **DESCRIPTION:** A medium size, broad point that has weak shoulders and a stemmed, concave basal area. Basal concavity can be shallow to deep and rarely can be fluted. Some examples are non-stemmed with a concave base. Basal area can be ground. Chisel tips occur along with *Lake Mojave* and *Parman* points. This point co-existed with *Clovis*.

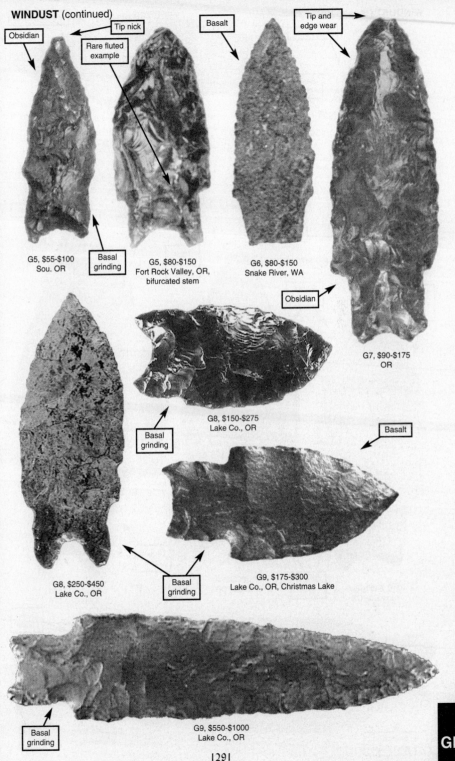

WINDUST (continued)

Obsidian

Tip nick

Rare fluted example

Basalt

Tip and edge wear

G5, $55-$100
Sou. OR

Basal grinding

G5, $80-$150
Fort Rock Valley, OR,
bifurcated stem

G6, $80-$150
Snake River, WA

Obsidian

G7, $90-$175
OR

Basal grinding

G8, $150-$275
Lake Co., OR

Basalt

G8, $250-$450
Lake Co., OR

Basal grinding

G9, $175-$300
Lake Co., OR, Christmas Lake

Basal grinding

G9, $550-$1000
Lake Co., OR

1291

GB

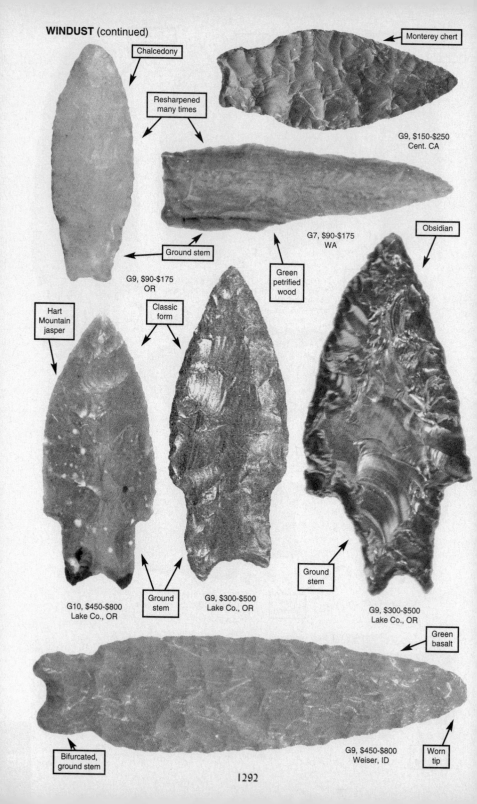

WINDUST (continued)

Monterey chert

Chalcedony

Resharpened many times

G9, $150-$250
Cent. CA

Ground stem

G9, $90-$175
OR

G7, $90-$175
WA

Green petrified wood

Obsidian

Hart Mountain jasper

Classic form

Ground stem

G10, $450-$800
Lake Co., OR

Ground stem

G9, $300-$500
Lake Co., OR

Ground stem

G9, $300-$500
Lake Co., OR

Green basalt

Bifurcated, ground stem

G9, $450-$800
Weiser, ID

Worn tip

1292

WINDUST (continued)

Ground stem

Thinning strikes at base

Andesite

Obsidian

Shoulder wear

G9, $325-$600
S.E. OR. Classic form.

G8, $275-$500
Sou. OR

G9, $250-$400
N.W. NV

WINTU - Developmental to Historic Phase, 1000 - 200 B. P.

(Also see Desert Side Notched and San Bruno)

LOCATION: Central California **DESCRIPTION:** A rare, thin, needle tipped point with unique upward sloping, narrow side notches and a concave base. Usually made of jasper and obsidian.

G10, $150-$250
Redding, CA

YANA - Developmental to Historic Phase, 1500 - 400 B. P.

(Also see Coquille, Gatecliff, Gunther, Rabbit Island and Wallula)

LOCATION: Northern California **DESCRIPTION:** A rare, thin, small to medium size, barbed point with a short to long, narrow, tapered stem. A rare type. Part of the *Gunther* cluster. **I.D. KEY:** Stem form.

G9, $15-$25
Shasta Co., CA,
Redding, CA

G8, $35-$50
Mendocino Co., CA

GB

COLLECTING
OLD WORLD
PREHISTORIC ARTIFACTS

by Duncan Caldwell

This section gives an overview of artifact types from Western Europe, the Sahara & the Sahel from 2.6 million to 3,000 years ago. A few tools from elsewhere appear for comparison.

For the first time, this chapter includes photographic sections illustrating:
- how radically patina can differ from one face of an artifact to the other (& often should),
- various hand-ax grips, showing how a few types were held,
- ground-breaking evidence for Neanderthal hafting of blades into compound tools.
- & unpublished proof of how large Neolithic prestige axes were hafted – in the middle, not at the end.

As in the previous edition, artifacts are presented in chronological, rather than alphabetical order, to give the reader an idea of their evolution. Furthermore, although this chapter contains **all new photographs**, many of the artifacts are again larger than this book, so they can not be presented actual size. Instead, dimensions are given. Also, only superior specimens have been chosen in most cases, because there is not enough space to show the quality range for each type. In addition to sculptural hand-axes – which are the oldest evidence for the birth of aesthetics - I have added 5 works of figurative & abstract prehistoric art (4 of which have never been published) to emphasize the expansion of assemblages with the addition of such artifacts starting roughly 45,000 years ago. Lastly, the multitude of preserved types that arose over a prehistoric period that spanned 2.6 million years as opposed to the Americas' 18,000 is correspondingly bigger, so this section, as opposed to the North American ones, is an overview containing major gaps. All the same, by compiling this chapter with its predecessors in the previous 2 editions of this guide, enthusiasts may start to get a clear idea of the artifacts in the 3 regions.

RULES OF THUMB:
1)   Patinas Usually Differ from One Side to the Other:
The European and African artifacts that follow all have some kind of patina, usually a pronounced one that is different from one face to the other. This is because most prehistoric tools have just 2 main faces & tend to lie on the surface with one side exposed & the other buried both before burial and again before discovery. The part exposed to the air would be slowly adulterated by gamma radiation, lichens and wind weathering, for example, while the face lying against soil might experience silica loss

and the intrusion of lime salts. An artifact's buried face could also acquire a crusty ring of minerals leached out of the surrounding soil that adhered to the artifact by tensile force and longer humidity in its shade. At the very least a stone tool would acquire soil sheen and in cold regions manganese or iron oxide concretions might "grow" from cleavage lines in frost pits. In most cases, each face would undergo several of these changes as its position shifted over hundreds of millenia.

But don't be fooled by almost unpatinated resharpening into thinking that such chipping is inevitably modern or even from a much later date than the rest of the knapping. Long experience in the field has shown that certain flake scars that are as old or nearly as old as the rest may hardly patinate. There could be several overlapping reasons for their relative failure to change color: these facets might exhibit different geometry vis-à-vis the crystalline structure of the material – reducing porosity in their zone: even short exposure to solar radiation, gastric or other body acids, heat from fires, etc. during the tool's use may have predisposed older chipping to patination once the tool was abandoned and buried, but the surface of the latest resharpening might not have been stressed enough before burial to patinate as easily. Finally, it is true that a few tools found in highly preservative stable clay or cave deposits show only soil sheen and fine hydration mists. These account for such a negligible proportion that most collectors should simply avoid collecting Lower & Middle Paleolithic artifacts unless they exhibit intense patination, and, for surface finds, a different one on each side. There are enough fine patinated specimens that you should never have to worry about whether your pieces are authentic.

A) Dark face of an Acheulean cleaver vs. lighter face of same cleaver. Differential patination – the patina on one face is quite different from that on the other. Also see photo 15 in ID section. Gravel pit find.

B) Browner side of a Mousterian Triangular biface vs. its creamier side. Also see ph. 65.

C) More colorful side of a Malian Neolithic flared celt vs. its milky side. Also see ph. 103.

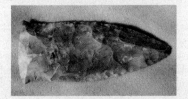 

2) Only suckers look for "perfection":

Don't expect artifacts that are often 100 times older than the oldest American ones to be unchipped. After all, many have undergone glacial periods, surviving long weathering by frost & high winds on plateaus or rolling in tumultuous thawing rivers before being deposited in gravel-beds. In fact, a collector should be comforted by a little breakage, because depending on whether the posterior chips are ancient or modern, they will show a surprising depth & variety of patinas, often on the same piece.

3) Be circumspect about famous origins:

Another point to remember is that a famous origin may increase the value of an artifact, but buyers should be circumspect. For example, in my early days, I purchased hand-axes in an auction held by France's most famous "expert" that he described as having come from the type sites of La Micoque & St. Acheul & as having been in the collection of one the greatest 19th prehistorians, de Mortillet. Later I was invited to examine large collections from those sites that had remained intact since the original excavations. The pieces I had were almost dead ringers for certain specimens from the 2 sites – but not quite. Although they had been chosen shrewdly to fool most prehistorians, the palette of patinas was slightly off, indicating subtly different lithics & geological processes. But I had no proof. Then I got a call. It was the finder of the hand-axes who had sold them directly to the "expert" with full provenance. When he had seen them being sold to me under false pretenses during the "expert's" next auction, the collector had fumed & obtained my name. The field collector pointed out tiny innocuous initials that he had put on the bifaces & provided the key for deciphering them. They were the abbreviations of his sites in the Nievre region, far from the type-sites. I was able to confirm this by checking the rest of the man's collection & even finding identical tools at his sites. Talk about a silver lining.

But I'd learned my lesson. Even if you have just spent $50,000,000 out of an $80 million dollar budget, as one European collector has just done, read up, familiarize yourself with well provenanced collections & take claims from merchants who may be more interested in lucre than prehistory with salt. It is absolutely essential that the seller be honorable and provide a *lifetime* guarantee of authenticity.

Finally, collecting artifacts from a time span over 140 times longer than all of American prehistory combined will begin to reveal the vast iceberg of humanity's past, of which American prehistory is just the peak of the tip. As the collector of Paleolithic artifacts explores that vast new domain, he will discover unending nuances and whole zones of mystery, while developing increasing respect for the prowess of ancestors we can all truly share. To aide new-comers to this passionate field of study, I recommend not only the Handbook of Paleolithic Typology by Debénath and Dibble and Tools of the Old and New Stone Age by Bordaz, but broader books by Susan Allport, The Primal Feast, Juan Luis Arsuaga, The Neanderthal's Necklace, & Jared Diamond, Guns, Germs & Steel.

Lithics: Some of the materials from the 2 continents that this chapter concentrates on are: **For Europe:** Grand Pressigny flint - Indre et Loire & Vienne regions of France; Jablines flint - Seine et Marne; Thanatian flint - Oise & Somme valleys; jadeite, metahornblendite & dolerite - Brittany; Font-Maure jasper, France; Pelite-quartz - W. Alps; Obsidian - Italy, S. France, Greece; Green slate - W. Russia, Baltic states; etc. **For North Africa:** quartzite, flint, siltstone, jasper, etc. **Important sites:** Because the region and time frame are so vast, only a few almost random sites are listed. However, an effort has been made to choose fully provenanced tools from famous sites, which are referred to in the captions. **T.S.** after a site indicates that it is a cultural type-site, although it should be kept in mind that other locations are often type-sites for particular traits and tools.

Prices: Price ranges have been extrapolated from the results of auctions and consultations with dealers from around the world. Conflicting forces have been wreaking havoc on prices over the last 3 years. First is the massive importation of Saharan hand-axes, celts and arrowheads from Morocco south & eastwards to Niger. A few dealers have financed a sweep of those desert countries, where artifacts have been exposed in many places by state-sized blowouts. Due to the poverty & corruption of those nations, some sites that could have provided collectors, museums & the public with an understanding of the artifacts disappeared. Ironically, the very people who have shown their appreciation for the Sahara's artifacts by buying them will be among those who suffer the most because they will never be able to determine the distributions, ages & links of many of their possessions. Perhaps it would have been better for the vestiges to be studied *& then exported with proper provenance* – but such a pragmatic solution is neither politically correct nor commercially expedient.

Other factors driving prices downwards, of course, are the NASDAQ crash & Sept. 11th – both of which reduced collectors' spare cash.

But a huge upward factor has been at work when it comes to specifically French artifacts in the top range. Two collectors reputed to be the first & 5th richest men in France have plunged into the market directly & through a proxy, spending fortunes. The intent of one is reportedly to create a major museum in a renovated industrial site near Paris. Given the closing of Paris's Museum of Man, this may turn out to be a blessing for enthusiasts of prehistory. At least one non-European collector of French material in the same bracket has also bought up almost entire auctions.

So the market has gone haywire in both directions. Although the following prices reflect both the ups & downs, they are largely guided by the more stable environment of galleries & their loyal, knowledgeable clientele. I am grateful to all those collectors & galleries who allowed me to picture their artifacts.

Hand-ax & Mousterian Scraper Grips:

Hand-axes & other Paleolithic bifaces, which superficially resemble hand-axes but may have been hafted, are traditionally grouped by the geometry of their faces. But classifying a tool only on this basis can be misleading because its silhouette may change as the tool is worn, resharpened and used up. Hand-axes that are apparently quite different may just illustrate stages in the reduction sequence of a single true type. It is important to identify those types from their first stage, to determine if methods of reducing tools were also culturally specific, & to emphasize that some types are indeed particular to regions, periods & traditions. The hand-axes & bifaces below are classified not only by their silhouettes, but more importantly by:

- **their contours when seen edge-on.** Such examination reveals that certain hand-held bifaces (hand-axes) have bases that are tipped up relative to the cutting plane. This creates a <u>protective pocket</u> for the user's fingers above the material being cut & is just as intentional a design element as the contours of an artifact's face. So a protective pocket must be considered in classification. Another trait best seen from this perspective is <u>inverse beveling</u> due to the sharpening of one edge of a hand-ax, then flipping the hand-ax on its axis to sharpen the other edge. This results in opposite edges being flaked along opposite faces. Many typologists group such skewed hand-axes in a type, but inversely beveled hand-axes probably just represent advanced stages in reduction sequences.

- **the position of their grips.** True hand-axes have some sort of direct grip – whether it is an ergonomic patch of rough, rounded cortex left along a base or edge or else a *"mi-plat"* – a flat section along the rim that is perpendicular to the tool's plane. Beginners often dismiss the grip's departure from expected symmetry as breakage or an un-finished section. Instead grips testify to the care taken by the earliest toolmakers to achieve comfortable & effective designs. Since a grip's position also remains stable during reduction sequences, it is even more useful for classifying hand-axes than their changing contours.

- **an edge-on analysis of peripheral flaking, retouch, crushing, etc.** If one edge has been straightened with secondary soft-hammer retouch for cutting, whereas the opposite one has only been roughed out with hard hammer flaking or seems to have been *thinned* as opposed to sharpened, the rougher edge may have been prepared for insertion in a slotted grip that rotted away. If there is no direct grip at all – just all-around sharpness that bites into your palm when you press on one edge to cut with another - then a hafting scenario becomes almost inescapable. The use of such rim analysis has led to distinctions between triangular bifaces that appear in this edition *for the first time anywhere*. Other tools which could be differentiated based on the distribution of straightened, thinned, crushed, resharpened, & ground edges have probably been lumped together too because their faces looked so similar that typologists thought the artifacts were the same kind. As a result, the inventiveness & cultural variety of Neanderthals probably continues to be under-estimated even by their champions.

1) Dagger grip hand-axes. These have a long "handle" composed of two facing oblique planes. Thrusting & slashing cuts. Very rare. See ph 18.

2) Oblique cortical grip on a concave crescent hand-ax. The grip is common, the concavity not so. A lateral cut.

3) Side grip. A rocking or sawing cut.

4) Basal pocket grip. The base twists about 30 degrees away from the cutting plane, allowing fingers to be tucked into a safe pocket away from the meat or hide being prepared. Inwards lateral cuts. Aisne.

5) Crescent side-scraper grip. Such a Neanderthal tool may also have been inserted in a slotted handle like an ulu.

6) Inverse beveling seen from tip. The result of resharpening.

Proof of Hafting:

Neanderthal compound tools: The 2 photos show a much reduced Mousterian convergent side-scraper. Its most interesting feature is the thinning of the flat side of the base. This must have been done to turn the base into a peg that could by inserted and glued (with reduced birch sap or rabbit glue for example) into a handle as was the case with the 400,000 + BP flint at Schöningen. The recognition of an artifact's most telling but elusive features is one of an enthusiast's greatest pleasures, but students of prehistory should look forward to contesting their theories.

Neolithic polished axes:

1) The detail of a giant celt from Calvados shows grooves where lashing gradually ground into the ax's edge on either side of a lighter zone where the wooden handle surrounded the blade. See ph. 124

2) A belt of lighter patination around the middle of this ax found in a peat bog shows where the wooden handle survived long enough to impede patination until it had disintegrated.

AFRICAN, ASIAN & EUROPEAN POINT AND TOOL TYPES:

Grouping artifacts into Technological Modes:

Stone Age artifacts are currently grouped as follows:

MODE I: Oldowan. Unifacial or bifacial flaking along a cobble to make a cutting edge or remove flakes for use

MODE II: Acheulean. The first tools of a pre-determined shape not suggested by the block of stone. Working towards a mental template, the maker had to carry out dozens of gestures to achieve his goal, just like an origami master turning a sheet of paper into a swan. A sense of correctness was born – in other words, aesthetics.

MODE III: Levallois/ Mousterian/ Kombewa. The first tools of a standardized & repeated shape struck in succession from a pre-adapted core. The maker had to envision 2 successive phases at once: the core to be shaped & the products to be struck from it once the core was made. This involved planning & first occurred when modern human & Neanderthal ancestors independently reached cranial capacities of about 1,400 cc.

MODE IV: Upper Paleolithic. Blade, antler & bone tools of enormous diversity.

Archeological Periods:

The entire Stone Age fits fairly neatly into the geological **Quaternary Period**, which is currently defined as having begun 2.5 million years ago at the boundary of the Gauss/Matuyama paleomagnetic epochs. The Quaternary consists of 2 epochs: the **PLEISTOCENE** from 2.5 million until 10,000 years ago with its succession of Ice Ages, & the **HOLOCENE** from 10,000 BP till now.

Unlike in the Americas, where "Paleolithic" refers to the period from 18,000 to 8,000 B.P., in the Old World it is split into three sub-sections, each of which is linked to one or more technological Modes. The dates are approximate & shift from region to region since the modes appeared in them at different times:

1) the **Lower Paleolithic** linked to Mode I & Mode II technologies from 2.6 million to roughly 250,000 B.P.,

2) the **Middle Paleolithic** linked to Mode II & Mode III technologies from 250,000 to approximately 45,000 B.P., and

3) the **Upper Paleolithic** linked to Mode IV technologies from 45,000 B.P. to 12,000 B.P.

LOWER PALEOLITHIC (ca. 2,600,000 B.P. - 250,000 B.P.)

CHOPPER AND FLAKE TRADITION (a Mode I technology): At first *Homo habilis* &/or *Homo rudolfensis*, then *Homo ergaster* in Africa & its basic equivalent, *Homo erectus*, in Eurasia - 2.6 - 1.4 million B.P. in Africa, 1.8 million+ BP – 780,000 BP in S. Europe, with much later vestiges in Hungary, E. Asia, etc.

Oldowan I and II industries - Pebble choppers, Bifacial chopping-tools, Inverse choppers; **Clactonian flake tools:** notches, denticulates, becs. **Important sites:** Olduvai Gorge, Tanzania T.S.); Damanisi, Georgia; Longgupo, China (1.8 million); Sangiran, Indonesia; Gran Dolina, Sierra de Atapuerca, Spain (800,000 BP); Tatoui, Romania; Orce, Greece; Clacton-on-Sea, U.K. (T.S.); Vértesszöllös, Hungary; Wimereux, France; etc.

ASIAN CHOPPER/CHOPPING TOOL TRADITION:
Important sites: Choukoutien, Patjitan, etc.

ABBEVILLEAN (Also known as the EARLY ACHEULEAN – the period of the first MODE II Technology. Mode II is defined by tapered bifaces (LCTs), which are commonly called handaxes. Abbevillean ones were made only with direct hard hammer flaking.):
Homo ergaster & *Homo erectus* - 1,600,000 - 780,000 B.P. in Africa/ later in Eurasia)
Abbevillean hand-axes (Africa & Europe) - **Trihedral picks** (Africa) - **Amygdaloid hand-axes, Ficrons. Important sites:** Ubeidiya, Israel; Bose Basin, S. China (app. 803,000 BP), Pingliang, China; Abbeville, France (T.S.); Konso, Ethiopia; Beni Ihklef, Algeria; etc.

MID TO LATE ACHEULEAN: Homo erectus to archaic *Homo sapiens* in Africa & *Homo antecessor* to *Homo heidelbergensis* in Eurasia, etc. - 780,000 - 250,000 B.P.:
NOTES: 1) The MODE II hand-axes of the later Acheulean often show *both* direct hard hammer & secondary soft hammer flaking.

2) The first MODE III technologies such as Levallois & Kombewa flake tools appeared earlier - at around 300,000 BP - in both Africa & Europe than the conventional date for the start of the Middle Paleolithic at 250,000 BP, suggesting that the Middle Paleolithic should be extended backwards.

HAND-AX TYPES: Tihodaine type cleavers (Africa), Tabel Balalt type cleaver (Africa), Kombewa flake cleavers (Africa), Chalossian pic, Lanceolate, Backed bifaces, Cordiform hand-axes, Limandes, Ovates, Discoids, Triangular (late transitional form), Elongated triangular, Fusiform hand-axes, Naviforms, Shark's tooth hand-axes, Pélécyformes, Ogivo-triangulaire, Lagéniformes, Micoquekeile, Etc.

ASSOCIATED TOOLS: Kombewa flakes (Africa), Centripetal Levallois flakes, Levallois point, Levallois blades, Side-scrapers, Wooden spears (Schöningen, Germany - ca. 400,000 B.P.), Hafted knives (Schöningen)
IMPORTANT SITES (Mid-Acheulean - 780,000 - 500,000 B.P.): St. Acheul (T.S.), Soleihac & Artenac France; Petrolona, Greece; Boxgrove, U.K.; Sima de los Huesos, Burgos, Spain; Latamne, Syria; Kudaro, Georgia; Beni Ikhlef, Algeria; etc.
IMPORTANT SITES (Late Acheulean - 500,000 - 250,000 B.P.): Terra Amata & Tautavel, France; Gesher Benot Ya'aqov, Israel (tranchet cleavers); Torralba, Spain; Fontana Ranuccio, Italy; Swanscombe, U.K.; Schöningen & Karlich-Seeufer, Germany; El Ma el Abiod, Algeria; etc.

MIDDLE PALEOLITHIC (ca. 250,000 B.P. - 45,000 B.P.) – Mode III Technologies: Late Homo heidelbergensis to Classic Homo neanderthalensis (after 130,000 BP) in Eurasia, Archaic to Modern Homo sapiens in Africa & Middle East

TRUE MOUSTERIAN INDUSTRIES (EUROPE) First signs at **250,000 BP.** Full flower **170,000 - 45,000 B.P.: 1)** Mousterian in the Acheulean Tradition, **2)** Denticulate Tool Tradition, **3)** Quina Tool Tradition **4)** Ferrassie Mousterian - **"MOUSTEROID" FLAKE TOOL INDUSTRY** (North Africa, Middle East) - **SANGOAN INDUSTRY** (Central Africa) - **ATERIAN INDUSTRY** (N. Africa), etc.
Elongated Mousterian points, Levallois points, Mousterian points (wholly retouched), Soyons points, Tayac points, Emireh points, Bifacial leaf-points - Blattspitzen (Eastern Europe), Aterian points, Raclette side-scrapers (21 types), Limaces, Burins, Cleaver hand-axes, Continuation of Micoquian hand-axes, Small to medium cordiform hand-axes (with direct soft-hammer retouching), Mousterian discs, Convex scrapers, Concave scrapers, Backed knives, First "retouchoirs" for pressure flaking, Levallois blade tools, Wooden spears (Lehringen), Borers, Non-Levallois truncated backed blades, etc.
Important sites: Le Moustier (T.S.), Fontéchevade, La Quina, Combe-Grenal, Laussel, Pech-de-l'Azé, La Chapelle-aux-Saints, Arcy-sur-Cure (France); Spy (Belgium); Monte Circeo (Italy); Neandertal (Germany); Tata, Molodova (Ukraine); High Lodge, Saccopastore, Krapina (Croatia); Mt. Carmel (Israel); Solo (Indonesia); Ain Meterchem, Kalambo Falls (Sangoan) & Charaman (T.S. Zambia), Lupemba (T.S. Congo), Pietersburg (T.S.), Howieson's Port (T.S.) & Klasies River Mouth (S. Africa); etc.
NOTE: According to traditional dating, based on European sites, the last 4 references are Mid Paleolithic, but typologically they anticipate the Upper Paleolithic.

UPPER PALEOLITHIC: Mode IV Technologies (45,000 B.P. - 12,000 B.P.)
ULUZZIAN (late Neanderthals - ITALY - Circa 45,000 - 35,000 B.P.)
Crescents, Backed pionts, Burins, End-scrapers, Flake tools; Bone tools: awls, Conical points, biconical points, Etc. **Important site:** Grotta del Cavallo

CHATELPERRONIAN (late Neanderthals - France - ca. 45,000 - 35,000 B.P.)
Châtelperronian knives, Châtelperronian points, End-scrapers, Truncated pieces, Burins, Incised tooth ornaments, Ivory pendants; Bone tools: awls, ivory pins, digging sticks, tubes, lozenge-shaped points, etc.
Important sites: Châtelperron (T.S.), Grotte du Renne, St.-Césaire, Isturitz, Gargas, Caminade Est, Belvis, Quinçay, etc.

OTHER TRANSITIONAL MID-TO-UPPER PALEOLITHIC CULTURES: SZELETIAN (C. & E. Europe)/ LUPEMBIAN (Africa)

AURIGNACIAN (first European Homo Sapiens sapiens, also known as Cro-Magnons - ca. 40,000 - 28,000 B.P.)
Dufour bladelets, Retouched blades, Strangulated blades, Caminade scraper, Carinated (keeled) scraper, Nosed scraper, Plane, Dihedral burins; Bone tools: Split based atlatl points, etc. **Important sites:** Chauvet, Arcy-sur-Cure, La Ferrassie, Caminade Ouest, Dufour, Baden-Württemberg, Geissenklösterle, Vogelherd, etc.

GRAVETTIAN & PERIGORDIAN (W. Europe), PAVLOVIAN (C. Europe), KOSTIENKI (Ukraine & Russia), ETC. - Homo sapiens 28,000 - 23,000 B.P. - *Despite different names, the cultures of this period shared many features from the Pyrenees to Siberia, with Venus figurines made at Brassempouy in S. France sharing many stylistic aspects with those found at Kostienki, for example, although Kostienki craftsmen had a better understanding of how to align their sculptures with the grain of tusks for durability.*
Noaille gravers, Kostienki shouldered points, Font Robert points, Gravette points, Micro-Gravette points, Pointed median groove bone points, Obliquely truncated blades, Scrapers on large thin flakes, "Batons de Commandment" (wrenches), Dihedral burins, Etc.
Important sites: La Gravette (T.S.), Chateau de Corbiac, Cougnac, Peche Merle, La Font-Robert, La Ferrassie, Laugerie Haute, Tursac, Predmosti, Dolni Vestonice, Avdievo, Kostienki, etc.

SOLUTREAN (France & Spain) & EPI-GRAVETTIAN (Italy, Central & E. Europe): 23,000 - 17,000 B.P.
Early Solutrean unifacial points, Mid-Sol. bifacial laurel leaf points (13 types), late Sol. shouldered points (4 types), Bifacial willow leaf points, Tanged bifacial points (Spain), Bevel based bone points, Backed bladelets, Borers, Bifacial knives, End-scrapers, Various dihedral burins, Laugerie Haute micro-scraper, Carinated scraper, Raclettes, Becs, Eyed needles, etc. **Important sites:** La Solutré (T.S.), Volgu, Lascaux, etc.

MAGDALENIAN (W. Europe), EPI-GRAVETTIAN (Italy, C. & E. Europe), KEBARIAN (Levant), IBEROMAURSIAN (N. Africa), etc. 17,000 - 12,000 B.P.
Teyjat points, dihedral burins, Magdalenian shouldered points, Many new microliths, Backed bladelets, Saw-toothed backed bladelets, End-scrapers, Dual burin-scraper tools, Parrot-beaked burin, Lacan burin, Carinated scraper, Thumb-nail scrapers; Bone & antler tools: Atl-atls, Harpoons (many types), Polished awls, Polished bone chisels, "lissoirs" & spatulas, Pincer tipped "navette" double ended blade grips, Engraved split bone rods, Eyed needles, wrenches, etc. **Important sites:** Gönnersdorf, Altamira, La Madeleine, Marsoulas, Pincevent, Isturitz, Niaux, Castillo, La Vache, Le Portel, Kesslerloch, etc.

MESOLITHIC: MANY DISTINCT CULTURES (end of glacial period - W. Europe: ca. 12,000 - 8,000 B.P. , Middle East: ca. 13,000 - 10,000 B.P.)
Microliths: small blade fragments retouched into geometric shapes (100s of types): Azilian points, Chaville points, Sauveterre points, Tardenois points, Capsian arrowheads, Trapezes (over 13 types), Rouffignac backed knives, Lunates, Triangles (over 11 types), Microburins, Tranchet chisels, Thumb-nail & other scrapers, Azilian Harpoons, Bone fish hooks, bone & antler mattocks, hafted adzes, etc.
Important sites: Mas d'Azil (T.S. - Early Meso.), Milheeze (Federmesser), Ahrensbourg (T.S. - early mid-Meso.), Remouchamps, Sonchamp (T.S.), Sauveterre-la-Lémance (T.S. - late mid-Meso.), Fère-en-Tardenois (T.S. - late Meso.), Shoukba & Jericho (Natufian), Gough's Cave (Creswellian), Horsham, Shippea Hill, Star Carr (Maglemosian); Otwock (Poland - Swiderian); Relilai, El Oued, Medjez (N. Africa); Mureybet (Mesopotamia: Meso. to Neo.)

NEOLITHIC: MANY CULTURES (Europe: ca. 8,000 - 5,000 B.P., Middle East: ca. 11,000 - 6,000 B.P.)

Amouq points (I & II), Byblos points, Temassinine points, Labied points, Bifacial leaf points, Tell Mureybet points; Saharan points (at least 9 families consisting of 103 groups, encompassing many more types), Chisel-ended arrowheads, French flint daggers, Sickle blades, Gouges, Chisels, Antler sleeve shock absorbers for celts, First polished celts, Antler harpoons, Eyed needles, First ceramic pottery outside Jomon (Mesolithic) Japan. **Important sites:** *Europe* --> Stonehenge, Skara Brae (U.K.); Newgrange (Ireland); Barnenez, Carnac, Fort-Harrouard, Gavrinis, Filatosa (France); Michelsberg (T.S.) Belgium, Sittard (Holland); Starcevo, Sesklo, Vinca (T.S.), Butmir (T.S.), Cucuteni (T.S.), Cernavoda (Balkans); Nea Nikomedeia (Greece); *W. Asia* --> Catal Huyuk (T.S.), Hacilar, Mersin (Turkey), Jericho (West Bank), Jarmo, Hassuna, Halaf (T.S.), Jemdet Nasr (Mesopototamia), Khirokitia (Cyprus); Ali Kosh, Tépé Hissar (Iran); Dzejtun, Kelteminar; *N. Africa* --> Merimde, Badari, Fayoum (Egypt); Jaatcha, Tazina, Djerat, Redeyef, Adrar Bous III, etc. *China* --> Yangshao (T.S.)

CHALCOLITHIC & BRONZE AGE (E. Europe & Anatolia 7,500 - 3,000 B.P. / W. Europe: 5,000 - 2,800 B.P.)

NOTE: All but the most prestigious tools (& even some of those) during these periods still tended to be made of stone.

Egyptian fishtail flint knives, Gerzean flint knives, Armorican flint arrowheads, Scandanavian flint daggers based on copper & bronze models, Hardstone shaft-hole battleaxes, First Copper, then Bronze tools: Axes, Adzes, Chisels, Razors, Bronze arrowheads, Etc. **Important sites:** Cambous & Mont Bego (France); Nagada (Egypt); Hagar Qim & Mnajdra (Malta), Su Nuraxi, Sardinia; etc.

Putting The Artifacts Into Perspective

The artifacts shown below were made by a succession of human species with ever-bigger brains, who also had to adapt, in the case of the Neanderthals, to several Ice Ages. The following figures are helpful for situating each artifact in these progressions.

Brain Sizes of Hominids Who Made Stone Tools: Cranial capacity progressed from roughly **500 cc** at the beginning of the Stone Age, 2.6 million years ago, to approximately **1,400 cc** about 150,000 years ago. But it is also important to remember that a species did not necessarily go extinct as soon as a new species had evolved from it, so directly related species overlapped & probably made different types of tools simultaneously. Finally, brains did not expand much until more than 2.5 million years after hominids had become bipedal over 5 million years ago, so the Australopithecines & their descendant, *Homo habilis*, had brains only marginally bigger than a **gorilla's 500 cc** or a **chimp's 410 cc**.

Homo habilis (Africa)	2.3 - 1.5 million BP	**510 cc to 674 cc**.
Homo rudolfensis (Africa)	ca. 2 million BP	**752 cc** (skull KNM-ER 1470).
Homo ergaster (Africa)	1.9 million - 800,000 BP	**804 cc to 900 cc**.
Homo erectus (Eurasia)	1.9 million - to 54,000? BP	**813 cc to 1,225 cc** at start
		1,013 cc to 1,251 cc later on

Javan specimens of *erectus* have more robust crania than African *ergaster* but are otherwise basically the same. The name *ergaster* may be folded back into the older term *erectus*.

Homo antecessor (Europe)	ca. 800,000 BP	**App. 1,000+ cc.**

Possibly the last common ancestor of Neanderthals & our lineage, Homo sapiens

Archaic Homo sapiens (Africa)	400,000 - 250,000 BP	**1,285 cc** (Broken Hill) to
		1,400 cc (Lake Turkana).
Pre-modern Homo sapiens (Africa)	250,000 - 100,000 BP	**1,300 cc** to **1,430 cc**.
Homo heidelbergensis (Europe)	700,000 - 200,000 BP.	App. **1,000** (Steinheim) to

1,390 cc (Sima de los Huesos).

Proto-Homo neanderthalensis (Europe) 250,000 (Ehringsdorf) & 200,000 (Biache-St.-Vaast)

Classic Neanderthals　　　ca. 130,000 – 30,000 BP.　　　Av. **1,450 cc**. Max. **1,750 cc**
　　　　　　　　　　　　　　　　　　　　　　　　　　　　　　(Amud, Israel).

Modern Homo sapiens　　　120,000+ - Present　　　　　Average **1,350 cc**.

The conventional average cranial capacity of modern humans is 100 cc less than the Neanderthal average. But the average Neanderthal weighed over 168 lb. – more than the average for modern humans from any continent. So in relation to their body weight, Neanderthal brains were slightly smaller than ours. It must also be emphasized that cranial capacity by itself is NOT indicative of intelligence. Einstein's brain was twice the size of that of the great 19th century French writer, Anatole France. Because of sexual dimorphism, men have brains about 100 cc larger than a woman's of equal body weight – the same relative difference as in macaque monkeys. This difference is unconnected to cognitive functions. But it may be related to natural selection of males with better spatial orientation. Such males would have been able to mentally map landscapes & rotate images. Mental rotation may have been necessary to produce the first tapered bifaces (also known as LCTs – large cutting tools – which are the defining trait of Mode II technology).

GLACIAL PERIODS & INTER-GLACIALS OF THE PLEISTOCENE:

Glacial periods were first defined both by moraines they left in the Alps & in outwash sediment deposited around the N. Sea. So each period has both an Alpine & Lowland name. The Alpine name appears in ***BOLD ITALICIZED CAPITALS*** & is the most common one for Old World usage. The Lowland name appears next in SIMPLE CAPITALS & the equivalent American name third. Warm to temperate inter-glacial periods, like the one we are in now, were first defined from the lowland deposits & appear between the Glacial Periods. Dates are based on oxygen isotope levels recorded from core samples extracted from ocean floors.

0 – 18,000 BP:	Inter-glacial (Although glaciers generally did not grow after 18,000 BP, fluctuating cold conditions continued until 10,000 BP when tundra animals disappeared from western Europe);		
18,000 – 67,000 BP:	***WÜRM***	= WEICHSEL	= Wisconsin
67,000 – 128,000 BP:	Inter-glacial ***UZNACH***	= EEM	= Sangamon;
128,000 – 180,000 BP:	***RISS***	= SAALE	= Illinoian;
180,000 – 230,000 BP:	Inter-glacial ***HOETTING***	= HOLSTEIN	= Yarmouth;
230,000 – 300,000 BP:	***MINDEL***	= ELSTER	= Kansan;
300,000 – 330,000 BP:	Inter-glacial ***G-M***	= CROMER	= Aftonian;
330,000 – 470,000 BP:	***GUNZ***	= MENAP	= Nebraskan;
470,000 – 540,000 BP:	Inter-glacial ***D-G***	= WAALIAN;	
540,000 – 550,000 BP:	***DONAU II***	= WEYBOURNE;	
550,000 – 585,000 BP:	Inter-glacial	TIGLIAN;	
585,000 – 600,000 BP:	***DONAU I (DANUBE)***;		

600,000 to 2 million BP: Roughly 20 more glacial advances

OLD WORLD TYPOLOGY & PRICE GUIDE

CHOPPERS - Chopper & Flake Tradition: ca. 2,600,000 to 1,400,000 / 100,000 B.P. (depending on region): *Essentially Homo habilis or Homo ergaster through Homo erectus*

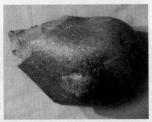

1) 6" Oldowan chopper on split cobble. Taouz, Morocco. 1.4 to 2.2 million BP. Basalt. $900-$1,400 **NOTES:** Large, sculptural, elegant wind gloss & vermicular channeling caused by wind-blown sand in flake scars. If crude or small, from $50.

2) 5 1/2" Ancorian chopper. Portugal. Manganese & bedded sediment patinas. Oldest tool type in Europe – some may be contemporaneous with Dmanisi, Georgia fossils ca. 1.8 million BP but recent stratified dig by Tixier shows evolution of Ancorian choppers towards Ancorian picks from the Mindel-Riss interglacial to the Riss-Wurm interglacial – in other words during the Mid Paleolithic! Quartzite. Large & dramatic. $600 - $900.

3) 3 1/2" Ancorian chopper. Arranches, Portugal. Choppers are Europe's oldest tool type – perhaps contemporaneous with Dmanisi, Georgia fossils, probably closer to mid Paleolithic. Monochromatic patinated quartzite. $290 - $450. Poor specimens from $35.

LOCATION: Africa and Europe as faron north as Hungary. **DESCRIPTION:** A cobble with 2 or more flakes struck from one side. Although choppers & chopping tools (see below) are found throughout the Stone Age, those from early sites are especially sought after as the oldest surviving vestiges of hominid tool-use: **I.D. KEY:** Lower & Middle Paleolithic specimens always patinated.

CHOPPING TOOLS - Chopper & Flake Tradition: ca. 2,600,000 to 1,400,000 / 100,000 B.P. (depending on region): *Essentially Homo habilis or Homo ergaster through Homo erectus*

4) 6" x 5 1/2" pre-Acheulean chopper. Pointes aux Oies, France. Beneath the waves of the English Channel, the tools are in situ in peat underlying a bluff. Over 750,000 BP. Black flint turned calico in flaked area by peat acids. Massive, colorful. Unique site now covered by Nazi surf defenses & bunkers fallen from the eroded bluff & sand diverted to prevent silting of port. $850 - $1,300. Small or crude from $150

5) 6" pre-Acheulean chopper. Pointes aux Oies, France. Over 750,000 BP. Black flint turned calico. Massive, sculptural. $750 - $1,100.

LOCATION: Africa, Europe as far north as Hungary. **DESCRIPTION:** A cobble with flakes struck bifacially from both sides of at least one edge, usually by alternate flaking forming a sinuous cutting edge. **I.D. KEY:** Lower & Middle Paleolithic specimens always patinated

CLACTONIAN TOOLS - European Chopper & Flake Tradition, depending on region: 1,700,000 to 500,000 B.P.: *Homo ergaster to Homo erectus to Homo antecessor*

6) 7" Clactonian denticulated knife. Sainte Adresse, France. Over 500,000 BP. Soil sheen & hydration fogging. Found 200 meters off-shore at low tide in a unique site. Cortical side grip & retouched cutting edge. $600 - $1,000. Small/crude from $50.

I.D. KEY: Thick flakes with percussion bulb & ripples obtained by striking a nodule against a stone anvil. Coarsely retouched with heavy hammer stone.

LOCATION: An industry without bifaces, whose official southwestern limit is Clacton-on-Sea, England, survived in the middle latitudes of Europe as Acheulean hand-axes spread into S. Europe & east into India &, exceptionally, China. The Clactonian tool set consists of choppers, chopping tools, becs (borers), dendiculates, side-scrapers & notches. Fire was known by the tradition's end.

PRIMITIVE "ABBEVILLEAN" HAND-AXES -
Early Acheulean, 1.4 million + B.P. - 780,000 B.P./Later outside Africa: *Homo ergaster to Homo erectus to Homo antecessor*

The oldest tapered idealized artifacts known are large bifaces & trihedral picks that herald the start of Mode II technology. The term LCT (Large Cutting Tool) may be applied to either of them. Both types of hand-axes were made by direct hard-stone percussion & were found with a 1.4 million year old Homo ergaster mandible in Konso, Ethiopia. The oldest datable African specimens were found in the same complex of sites below a level of volcanic tuff dated at 1.6 million BP. The oldest European specimens are more conservatively dated at roughly 650,000 BP.

AFRICAN TYPE:

7) 11" trihedral pick hand-ax. Quartzite. Beni Ikhlef, Algeria. Dated by comparison with dated series at KGA 10 in Konso, Ethiopia: 1.4 million years old. On the unshown ridge side, there is wind luster & desert varnish caused by Metallogenium & Pedomicrobium bacteria absorbing manganese, iron & clay particles as a sun-shield. Leaching crust. The only one this big ever seen with decorative burgundy and beige coloring. $7,500 - $9,000. **NOTES:** If crude, from $50. If plain, from $300.

8) 8" hybrid trihedral pick/Abbevillean ficron hand-ax. Quartzite. Beni Ikhlef, Algeria. Ca. 1.4 million BP. Leaching crust, Aeolian erosion, bacterial patina. Thin tip & one of few in red & beige. $3,500 - $4,500. **NOTES:** If crude, from $50. If plain, from $300.

LOCATION: Africa and S. Europe. **DESCRIPTION:** A core tool resulting from the reduction of a block to a big bifacial or tri-hedral blade flaked by a direct hard hammer. The flaking is relatively short and massive, with the percussion bulbs leaving deep scars that produce an inefficient wavy cutting edge, when viewed in hindsight. **I.D. KEY:** Always heavily patinated. Don't confuse with Mesolithic Asturian picks from Iberia which have globular bases.

AFRICAN MID TO LATE ACHEULEAN HAND-AXES - Lower Paleolithic, ca. 750,000 - 250,000 B.P.: *late Homo erectus*

The discovery that a biface's edges could be straightened by retouching them with a soft hammer made of antler, bone or wood revolutionized bifaces around 750,000 years ago. Not only were the new hand-axes more efficient knives, but their makers could now adapt their silhouettes for specific tasks and, perhaps more importantly, as an expression of their group's particular technological culture. The oldest artifact to have been found expressly deposited with the dead is a hand-axe dropped on top of bodies that had been dragged deep into a Spanish cave before the invention of lamps & pitched into a shaft. Such hand-axes were charged with symbolism & represent another step in the evolution of the mind.

9) 12" lanceolate hand-ax. Quartzite with micro-exfoliation. N. Tchigheti, Mauritania. Wind gloss on 1 side. Huge bifaces appear as early as tri-hedral picks in dated series, but were made in some areas until the end of the Acheulean. Interestingly, smaller tools are nearly absent from the oldest African Acheulean horizon. This elegant giant is 550,000 - 250,000 years old – perhaps older. Huge & perfect. $4,500 - $6,000.

10) 12" lagéniforme (tongue-shaped) hand-ax with concave edges. Quartzite with micro-exfoliation. N. Tchigheti, Mauritania. This huge, perfect & refined specimen is 550,000 - 250,000 B.P. $5,000 - $7,000.

11) 6" ovate hand-ax. Typical of late Acheulean & Middle Stone Age. Fine secondary flaking. Colorful burgundy, orange & tan quartzite. Wind gloss. Beni Ikhlef, Algeria. ca. 350,000 B.P. to 150,000 BP. $680 - $1,100. **NOTE:** Record low prices were set 2 years ago after the NASDAQ crash & Sept. 11th when 2 or 3 wholesale lots of 1,000 crude brown bifaces were sold by N. Africans for about $1 per artifact. The next year the same sellers sold a couple of lots of 1,000 at $15 per hand-ax, but not one was of high quality. Interesting Saharan specimens appear occasionally at the grassroots level for as low as $80 but require a huge investment in traveling, contacts, sorting & frustration.

12) 7 5/8" amygdaloid (almond-shaped) hand-ax. Mid Acheulean. Flint with extreme wind erosion & coloration. Minimal temperature-change cupping. Very thin & rare origin - S. Libya near Chad. Largest seen

from area. Flint hand-axes are far rarer than quartzite ones in private collections of Saharan prehistory. ca. 350,000 B.P. $2,300 - $3,000.

13) 8 1/2" x 5 1/2" cordiform hand-ax. mid-Acheulean. Jasper with differential wind erosion & sheen. Huge & beautiful material sculpturally enhanced by the wind. Finest seen. Traveller guarding his source gave provenance as Mali, but rumor & archeological data suggest the origin is the extreme south of the former Spanish Sahara. ca. 350,000 B.P. $4,500 - $6,000. Small or crude ones $400. Nice ones as low as $800.

EUROPEAN ACHEULEAN HAND-AXES - Lower Paleolithic, ca. 600,000 (possibly much older) - 250,000 B.P.: *Homo erectus, Homo antecessor, Homo heidelbergensis*

14) 6" Tranchet bit cleaver. Eure, France. Found 1880s. ca. 350,000 B.P. **NOTES:** While fairly common in parts of Africa, the cleaver is a rare biface in Europe. Whereas African types are usually made from large Levallois or Kombewa flakes, European examples tend to be core tools – meaning that a block of stone was reduced to make a single tool, not several. $1,100 - $1,500. Crude specimens from $250; NW African granular monochromatic specimens from $70.

FIRST TIME EVER TOOL DISTINCTION:
15) 6 1/4" bifacial bit cleaver. Black flint turned olive & khaki by water table & peat patina. Salginac, Charente, France. $1,400 - $2,000. **NOTE:** Whereas the "bit" on the photoed side of the above cleaver from the Eure is composed of a single flake scar, both sides of this specimen's bit are the result of many separate flake removals. Since this may be the first distinction between the 2 European types, it hasn't been determined whether their distribution in time and space differs.

16) 8 1/2" tongue-shaped (lagéniforme) hand-ax. Bon Secour, Dreux, Eure et Loir, France. Found 1884. Glued along frost crack but complete. Finest & biggest example of this extremely rare type seen. Mid Acheulean. **ID:** The type combines the taper & length of lanceolates with the broad razor tip of a cleaver. $6,600 - $8,000

17) 7 1/2" bevel-ended, elongated cordiform hand-ax with centered 1" diameter hole. Pezou, France. Gray flint turned tan by water table. Late Acheulean. **NOTE:** The largest biface from an assembly – in other words, the specimen which did not undergo as much resharpening and reduction as others – often has a centered feature that none of the re-edged tools ever had: a patch of kaleidoscopic crystals, a fossil or a hole. The biface's shape was not only becoming culturally specific, but was beginning to be used to frame non-functional features. In other words to show off. The ego & a sense of wonderment had been born. $12,000 - $15,000. Without hole, $1,200 - $1,700.

FIRST TIME EVER TOOL ID:
18) 6 1/2" dagger-grip "Micoquian" hand-ax. Boves, next door to Amiens & St. Acheul. Found 1889. Tiny prehistoric tip fracture. For a similar specimen see Overstreet's 6th Edition pg. 32 ph. 13. **ID:** Blade is half of length, very thin, almost flat on one side but still totally bifacial. Oblique grips on both sides together form a dagger grip perfect for thrusting. Most hand-ax grips are better suited for sawing sweeps of the edges. Extremely rare. $3,800 - $5,200

19) 7" oblique grip, amygdaloid hand-ax. Eure et Loir, France. Found 1886. Different patina each side. Unusually thin with finely wrought straight edges. $2,300 - $2,900. Small or crude specimens are much more common & 1/10th of price. This would be the find of a lifetime for a field collector.

20) 6 1/4" crescent hand-ax. Boves next door to Amiens & St. Acheul. Dark gray flint turned white by lime salt substitution for leached-out silica. Found 1883. **ID:** A concave cutting edge opposite a convex edge with an oblique grip. It is difficult to explain such hand-axes as being a step in a reduction sequence since they seem to be specific to certain sites and are exceedingly rare in those assemblages. $1,800 - $2,600. Small cordiforms down to $30 if frost damaged or ugly material, especially in mat brown, NW African quartzite.

NEW TOOL ID:

21) 10" arch-backed naviform hand-ax. Vailly-sur-Aisne, France. Sparkling quartzite with patina & crusts. The American prehistorian and frequent companion of Abbé Breuil, Harper Kelley, reported on similar giant hand-axes from the Aisne in1963. **ID:** Arch-backed hand-axes with an oblique grip on a convex edge opposite a much straighter cutting edge that runs from the tip to the base, have been reported from the Seine northwards through the Aisne, the English Wolvercote assemblage and into central Europe. $3,600 - $4,500. Small & crude bifaces from same valley from $250.

NEW TOOL ID:

22) 8" arched-edge naviform hand-ax. Dark gray flint patinated white by silica loss and lime salt intrusion. For other hand-axes from the same site see François Bordes. **ID:** Whereas the arch-backed naviform has an oblique basal grip along the arched edge, the arched-edge naviform has the grip along the straighter one. On this specimen, the long bulging edge across from the grip works best with a rocking saw motion. True naviforms are double bitted & usually have a lateral grip. $3,900 - $4,900

23) 7" x 5 1/4" proto-triangular hand-ax. Boves next door to St. Acheul. Found 1883. Orange water-table patina over dark gray flint. Big & colorful for this rare type. $4,500 - $5,700

24) 5" shark's tooth lanceolate hand-ax. ID: Straight sides & Basal grip. Boves, next door to St. Acheul from1883 excavation. Tri-color peat patina with fossilized worm burrow in flint. Original label, painterly colors, bold example of rare form. $5,800 - $7,000.

25) 6" basal grip, shark's tooth hand-ax. Aisne, France. Flint with calcite crusting (on reverse) & water table patina. Beautiful but not varied color, no fossil and less history than 24. $2,900 – $3,600

NEW TOOL ID:

26) 9" x 5" monofacial hand-ax. Sparkling but patinated quartzite. Vailly-sur-Aisne. The biggest seen of a rare type often confused with convergent side-scrapers. The flaking is shallow and invasive, on scrapers steeper and scaled. Dramatic contrast of textured cortex and flaking. $7,500 - $9,000

27) 6 1/2" amygdaloid hand-ax. St. Même la Carrière, Charente. Mid-Acheulean. Extremely varied patinas from many processes. The 6 major collections in the area are black holes, sucking local artifacts in & never parting with anything. $3,800 - $5,000

NEW HYPOTHESIS:

28) 7" extremely elongated cordiform biface with hole through it & tip gloss. Bon Secour, Dreux, France. Found 1885. Dark, mat gray flint turned snowy white. All around cutting edge. The blade is so thin, it foreshadows Central European mid to upper paleo leaf points & knives. Late Acheulean to Mid Paleolithic. **HYPOTHESIS:** Although gloss on hand-axes & similar but possibly hafted bifaces may derive from soil mechanics or even the silica particles in corn roots, the author has noticed that gloss usually appears around tips, rather than elsewhere. It is hard to explain a predilection of roots for tips, so cases of tip gloss may be due to their use for digging among the silica in soil - probably for root storage organs & post pits. Hole, artisanal perfection, thinness, & 2 intriguing features. $5,500 - $7,500

NEW TOOL ID:

29) 7" "Micoquian" tri-hedral lanceolate hand-ax. Water table patinas. St. Même la Carrière, Charente. Extreme mastery of shallow flaking makes photoed side flat. Isoceles triangle cross-section. First specimen seen. **ID:** Typical Micoquian hand-axes have slightly concave edges & sharp tips. $4,500 - $5,900

NEW TOOL ID:

30) 9 1/4" "Micoquian" finger-pocket hand-ax with concave edges & lens cross-section. Heavily patinated black flint. Pommiers, Aisne. Tip thin for 2/5ths of tool's length. Seen from the side, the handle goes up at a 35 degree angle from the plane of the cutting edges – creating a sheltered space for the fingers when the knife is used for cutting flesh sideways off hide. See the Grip Demo section for a side view of a similar hand-ax. One of the biggest specimens of a type seen (rarely) from the Seine into central Europe. $7,500 - $9,500

31) 7 1/4" bi-pointed, side-grip limande hand-ax. Chevrière, Oise. Faces patinated differently: the one with cortex black, the other olive. The edge with the most cortex is actually the main cutting side. The only blunt ergonomic surface that could serve as a grip is a small patch of cortex along the opposite edge. Side-grip limande & naviform hand-axes work best with a downwards rocking & sawing motion. Rare sub-type, large size. $2,400 - $2,800

32) 8" naviform hand-ax. Rue des Boves, St. Acheul itself, Somme. Double bit, all around cutting edge, unusually large, type site & super rare type. $5,900 - $7,500

33) 7 1/2" thin amygdaloid/limande hand-ax. Eure, France. Gray flint heavily patinated by 350,000 years beneath the water table. Found 1884. Thin blade & all-around cutting edge. ID: Thinner & more even contours than typical amygdaloids. $3,500 - $4,900

34) 6 1/2" basal grip, ovate hand-ax. Eure et Loir, France. Dark flint turned creamy by lime salts. Photoed side nearly flat, other, which has been attacked by lichen, domed. Huge, rare type, differential patination. $2,300 - $3,200

OTHER EUROPEAN ACHEULEAN TOOLS - Lower Paleolithic, ca. 650,000 (possibly older) - 250,000 B.P.: *Homo erectus, Homo antecessor, Homo heidelbergensis*

35) 5 1/2" Acheulean side-scraper. Oissel, France. See François Bordes for tools from this site. As with most sites mentioned here, this gravel pit disappeared under urban sprawl. Huge early example. $500 - $800. Mousterian side-scrapers from $30.

THE MIDDLE PALEOLITHIC - ca. 250,000 - 45,000 B.P.: *Neanderthals & Archaic Homo sapiens*

AFRICAN MID-PALEOLITHIC TOOLS - ca. 250,000 - 45,000 B.P.: *Advanced Homo erectus variants (Broken Hill Man, Saldana Man) & "Gracile" Neanderthals (in N. Africa) to Archaic Homo sapiens*

36) A: 2" Aterian stemmed scraper. Petrified wood. Wind gloss. S. Algeria. **ID:** A Levallois flake which has been given a stem. One of the first indisputably hafted tools.

B: 2" Aterian stemmed point. Petrified wood. Wind gloss. S. Algeria. **ID:** A Levallois point that has been given a stem. The oldest stemmed point type seen. Late Middle Stone Age into Upper Paleolithic. Particularly fine specimens $150 - $250. But mostly broken & crude Aterian points & scrapers were sold a few years ago by Africans for just $3 a piece in lots of 1,000 - a mind-boggling bargain. Even at $250, the cheapest Paleolithic points available.

37) A 3" & a 3 3/4" T-shaped tool. W. Sahara. Tabular flint with 3 concave "spoke-shave" concavities. Wind gloss & color alteration. Some early prehistorians speculated that the longest spoke represented a bird goddess's beak while the other spokes represented her brows. Still speculating, they could be a culturally specific whittling tool or parts of a thrown snare, similar in conception to bolas. Middle Stone Age. Rare. $450 - $600

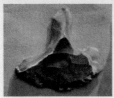

38) 3 1/4" T-shaped tool (or symbol). An extremely unusual specimen for 2 reasons: There are 2 concavities, not 3, & the convex section, although worked, bears significantly darker & older patina. If the narrow spoke had been a stem for hafting, one would expect the convex edge to show preparation for use as a chisel or scraper. Neither is the case. Could it be a zoomorphic or anthropomorphic representation after all? For years, the only one seen on the market. $550 - $800.

39) 3 1/2" mid-Paleolithic drill made of Libyan Glass, an impactite from a meteorite explosion that vitrified dunes at the end of the Acheulean. W. Egypt. Transparent. Extreme wind smoothing & stippling. $1,300 - $1,900. If debitage from $150.

40) 7" ovate biface. Wind patinated quartzite. Erg Titersine, Libya. Middle Stone Age ovates seem to be typical of the Libyan & Egyptian Sahara rather than the Western Sahara. Could they be a guide-artifact to a specific culture? The most colorful and perfect have a shield-like boldness. Travelers have sold some fine specimens for as low as $130! More traditional & reliable markets such as galleries sell from $1,450 to $1,900.

41) 6 1/2" ovate biface. Libyan Desert in Egypt. Quartzite. Intense differential weathering of rock on photoed side. Other side unweathered! This piece lay like a turtle hunkered in the wind for tens of thousands of years. $1,450 - $1,900

42) 8 1/4" "Micoquian" lanceolate hand-ax. Libya. Beige & red quartzite. Leaching crust & aeolized on domed face. Tip unbroken, colorful, & rare type. One of 2 seen in 5 years. **NOTE:** Unlike true Micoquian hand-axes, from SW Europe which are localized late Acheulean to Mousterian transitional artifacts, bifaces with concave edges appeared earlier in Africa. $3,200 - $4,900

FIRST TIME EVER TOOL ID:
43) 8 1/2" fishtail cleaver hand-ax. One of two reported. Akin to both Tabelbala-Tachenghit (type 4) & tihodaine (type 5) cleavers which are common. Quartzite with micro-exfoliation & patina. Late Acheulean to early Middle Stone Age. Mauritania. **ID:** Like

Saharan cleavers illustrated in Overstreet editions 6 & 7, made from a huge flake with bifacial thinning along both edges. But the thinning is a tour-de-force to create a flared bit. Elegance & only 2 reported. $5,800 - $7,000. Most Saharan cleavers from $30 to $800. **NOTE:** Type 4 has an asymmetrically tilted bit, one convex & one concave edge, an oblique base & thinning around the sides & base of the flat bottom. Type 5 has a straight bit, parallel sides, a semi-circular base & is bifacial except at the bit. Acheulean cleavers are also found in Spain, Sicily & the Middle East.

EUROPEAN MOUSTERIAN HAND-AXES, OTHER TOOLS & CORES - Middle Paleolithic, ca. 250,000 - 45,000 B.P.: *Neanderthals*

Only one of the several Mousterian cultures continued to make "hand-axes" with any regularity, the Mousterian in the Acheulean Tradition, as opposed to the Quina tradition, the Denticulate tradition, and others. What follows is a sampling of the most commonly collected types along with a new tool hypothesis & 2 technically precocious burins.

44) 6 1/2" diameter Levallois flake-tool core. From a unique site 500 meters offshore at Ault, Somme. Barnacles on back & peaty patina. This site provided so many flint nodules from a chalk cliff that has now eroded back half a kilometer that pre-Neanderthals often used cores to remove just one tool – instead of dozens as elsewhere. So the cores are among the biggest known. The workmanship is also superb. $2,300 - $2,900 for finest. Small ones from elsewhere from $10.

45) 3 1/2" Quina side-scraper. One of the biggest from the type-site of this Mousterian culture: La Quina, Les Gardes, Charente. Most are half size. Found 1912. Gray chert patinated white. $1,750 - $2,100. If small from $300. If from elsewhere, from $75.

46) 5" Levallois flake convergent side-scraper/crescent knife. Vailly-sur-Aisne. Black flint with soil sheen & water-table patina. Incredible preservation due to the Neanderthals' camp being covered by still waters & precipitating clay. Never tumbled or chipped. Both edges show fine scaling from the base to the tip. Rarer than most hand-ax types. $1,600 - $2,300.

47) 4 1/2" Mousterian convergent side-scraper/leaf-blade knife. Thanatian flint typical of Picardy & the Somme. Calcite caliche on unphotoed side. Bifacial basal thinning – probably for hafting! Soissons, Aisne. Such an elegant tool bears so little resemblance to typical side-scrapers, that it seems reasonable to see it more as a finely contoured, leaf-blade knife. Dibble is correct about the reduction sequence of convergent side-scrapers to Mousterian points in some – but far from all – cases. One would expect to find the reduction sequence in all sites with double-edged side-scrapers. That is NOT the case. One would also expect many more points since they would be end products, jettisoned like cigarette butts. That is not the case either. Highly symmetrical leaf blade & crescent knives are regularly found at a few Middle Paleolithic sites, but unheard of in most others with double side-scrapers. The dismissive reduction sequence theory looks better in a drawing than in the field. Incredibly rare. $1,900 - $2,400

NEW CULTURAL INDICATOR:

48) 4 1/2" Mousterian monoface. Boulogne-la-Grasse, Oise. Water table patina. A cultural indicator for an un-named aspect of the Mousterian – I'd dub it the Oise Mousterian -since it comes from an assemblage with many fine monofaces & few bifaces. Unlike on a convergent side-scraper, the flaking is invasive and not simply scaled around edges. Cortical concavity near base. $2,400 - $3,000. Poor specimens from $70

49) 2 1/2" Mousterian unifacial limace. St. Amand de Coly, Dordogne. Rare & small in true form. Some are probably the end-result of reduction of a doubly convergent side-scraper. But not all of them can be dismissed  so lightly (see below). They are also regional, far more being seen in Dordogne collections than in the Yonne for example. $490 - $840

50) 3 1/2" Mousterian unifacial limace with burin. Cosne, Nievre. Burins are rare in the Mousterian – on a limace, rarer still. $590 - $780

FIRST TIME EVER TOOL ID:

51) 4" Mousterian bifacial crescent limace terminated by burins at both ends. Precociously early but clear burins on an atypical biface. **First ID ever:** will more be noticed now? Lime patinated flint. Senonais, France. Reference specimen. $3,400 - $4,900

52) 2" classic 2nd stage Levallois point. Exceptionally pronounced diagnostic bulge of multi-faceted striking platform. This bulge is known as a "chapeau de gendarme" after 19th C hats worn by policemen. No edgework, since sharp edges did the job. One plow-ding & pseudo-burin tip which might be an impact fracture. ID: Note the triangular negative left by  the removal of an earlier Levallois point from the same core. $450 - $600

53) 3 3/4" Levallois point. Cosne, Nievre. Water table patina plus manganese & iron ion transfer from loess. ID: 2 diagnostic traits – multifaceted striking platform & negative of previous point. A perfect giant. $900 - $1,600 COMMENT: Just as some AmerIndian "points" are too big to have been projectiles, but were hafted knife blades, the thickest & broadest Levallois points were almost certainly used as knives. The word "point" to a prehistorian does NOT identify an artifact's use, but its form.

54) 2 1/4" classic Levallois point with fully retouched edges & chapeau de gendarme. So small & thin it is hard to explain as anything but a projectile point. $1,500 - $2,300 COMMENT: Almost all the Levallois points at some sites (which were probably task-specific) are wafer-thin 1" "microliths" that are simply too small to be knives, but make perfect projectile heads. The variety of Mousterian cultures and/or task-specific sites such as long blade industries found in northern France into Germany is only beginning to be fathomed. Any dismissal of variability, inventiveness and complexity among Neanderthals by researchers who have worked mainly with skeletal material, the minutiae of excavations or statistics should be taken with circumspection due to the experts' lack of access to thousands of alienated amateurs who could extend their range a thousand-fold and tell them which open-air sites are exceptional. Laws & attitudes will have to change before that happens. Although Neanderthals have been dismissed as overly conservative in the past because of our chauvinism as a species, they continue to be under-estimated, partly because of a failure to seek synergies among those who all wish to celebrate and study prehistory.

55) 3" Levallois point. Fully retouched edges & pronounced chapeau de gendarme. **HYPOTHESIS:** The hollow triangle left by the removal of a previous point provides the same kind of hafting possibility within a slot at the end of a shaft as a Clovis's flute. Will a search for resin on Levallois points or even spears preserved in peat or lignite resolve the question? Plow ding but still one of the best seen. Ca. 70,000 BP. Each side has own patina. Photoed side has webbing - other only soil sheen. Cosne-sur-Loire. $850 – 1,550.

56) 2 1/4" first stage Levallois point. Contrary to received wisdom, not all Levallois points have faceted striking platforms. NOT a used-up convergent side-scraper, but a probable projectile point given its small size. Edges already so sharp, there was no need for edge-work & the piece was never resharpened. St. Père, Nievre. $600 - $800

57) 4 1/4" Mousterian point. Basal thinning for possible hafting. Cosne, Nievre. Giant, yet narrow & thin enough to be a spearhead. **COMMENT:** The theory that many Mousterian points are reduced convergent side-scrapers does not preclude the possibility – even probability – that the resulting points found second lives as spearheads. Neanderthals were probably almost as capable of killing two birds with one stone as we are. $2,400 - $2,900

58) 2 3/4" Mousterian point. Minutely & fully flaked edges. Léré, Cher. Almost unfacetted platform. Translucent. $800 - $1,200

59) 3 1/4" Mousterian point. Manzac-sur-Vern., Dordogne. Delicate retouch from base to tip along both sides. A prehistoric "spoke-shave" on one edge, but no damage. Silica dissolved out & lime salts gone in. Probably a knife. $900 - $1,300. If perfectly symmetrical & needle-tipped $2,000 & up. If crude & small $50 & up.

60) 2 3/4" Mousterian in the Acheulean Tradition (MAT) cordiform biface. Max. thickness half inch. Basal thinning for probable hafting. Too small & thin to be a "hand-ax". Narrow examples may even be projectile points related to late Neanderthals' leaf points in central Europe. Colorful $850 - $1,300. If crude & monochrome from $200.

61) 2" MAT biface. Quartz (rare material). Manzac-sur-Vern. $700 - $1,200. See 60.

62) 5" ovate biface. Gray flint turned yellow. Hydration webbing. Upper terrace of Loire, Nievre. The find of a decade of intensive searching. Perfect geometry. $1,900 - $3,000

63) 4 3/4" ovate biface. Bu, Eure et Loir. Completely de-silicified in spots. A geometrical gem. $1,600 - $1,900

64) 5" cordiform biface. Bucey-en-Othe, Aube. The paradigm for cordiforms. All around cutting (or hafting) edge & overall thinness. $2,400 - $3,000

65) 4 1/2" Triangular biface. Nievre, France. Smaller than examples in Overstreet's 6th & 7th editions, but one of 3 finest seen in private hands since then. $3,500 - $5,500
DESCRIPTION: Straight or slightly convex sides, fairly straight base, often sharp, with suggestion of thinning for hafting. After the discovery of a hafted Acheulean flint in a coalmine in Schöningen, Germany, the creation of such complex tools by even the earliest Neanderthals is incontestable. Complete triangular bifaces/hand-axes are especially rare because - (1) of their thinness & consequent delicacy, (2) they were produced during the transition from the Acheulean to Mousterian, and (3) they are the first hand-axes to consistently show tip fractures suggesting impact damage (thus hafting).

FIRST TIME EVER TOOL IDs 66 vs. 67:
66) 5" Triangular point-oriented biface. Base roughly thinned for probable hafting. Catigny, Oise. Reference specimen. $4,000 - $6,000

67) 5 1/2" Triangular base-oriented spatulate biface. The "tip" is roughly knapped for probable hafting, while the base is finely edged for cutting use.   Foissy-sur-Vanne.
HYPOTHESIS: Despite the superficial resemblance of these 2 triangular bifaces, which would have been previously classified as exceptional specimens of Triangular hand-

axes, their identical face-on silhouette may be deceiving. Edge-on examination suggests that Triangulars should be divided into at least 2 separate types: ones whose cortical or roughly thinned bases were hidden in a haft or served as grips, creating a V-shaped knife. And, two, bifaces whose points are crude but whose bases are refined. The points instead of the "bases" of the latter may have been inserted in a haft, creating a spatulate knife like an Inuit ulu. The author awaits micro-traceology analysis to check this hypothesis. Reference specimen $5,000 -$7,000

68) 7 1/2" bifacial naviform leaf-blade. 3 color quartzite – milky, tan & dark gray. Water-table patinas. Aisne, France. So thin & finely knapped, it resembles a gigantic Solutrean laurel leaf knife. Possibly a precursor to SZELETIAN leaf points. This is the finest & most colorful specimen seen for such a late mid-Paleolithic biface. $7,000 - $7,600

THE UPPER PALEOLITHIC ca. 45,000 - 12,000 B.P.: Over-lapping sub-periods/cultures: Châtelperronian [*last Neanderthals*]. *Cro-Magnons*, the name for European Upper Paleolithic modern humans who were as much Homo sapiens as we are, were responsible for <u>all</u> the succeeding cultures: the Aurignacian (ca. 40,000 – 28,000 BP), Gravettian (28,000 – 23,000 BP), Solutrean (23,000 BP – 17,000 BP) & Magdalenian (17,000 – 12,000 BP).

SOME INVENTIONS: MEASURING SYSTEMS, ATL-ATL POINTS, NEEDLES, HARPOONS, BASKETRY & OTHER "WEAVING" TECHNOLOGIES, JEWELRY & ART:
NOTE: *Despite the fact that Upper Paleolithic tools are often much smaller than the preceding ones, they are also much rarer than most of them because:*
• *populations were extremely sparse due to often extreme glacial conditions*
• *the periods were much shorter and*
• *most sites have been off-limits to collectors for 60 or more years.*

CHATELPERRONIAN - ca. 45,000 - 35,000 B.P.
Neanderthals

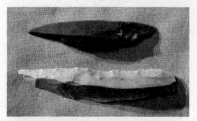

69) A: 4" Châtelperronian point. Palis, Aube – not far from Châtelperronian site at Arcy-sur-Cure. Knapping of back usually from one face. The steeply retouched back on Gravettes is usually from *both* faces. Perhaps the biggest specimen of the rarest point. $18,000 up **NOTE:** The Châtelperronian is one of several Neanderthal cultures that represent a final flourish before they went extinct (except for a few genetic markers they seem to have left in people of European descent). Most prehistorians have a tendency to dismiss the final Neanderthal cultures as desperate attempts to cope with intruding members of our species, Homo sapiens sapiens. There has been much speculation of a deficiency of Neanderthal language, despite their well-developed hyoid bone used to anchor vocal muscles and brains that were larger than ours on average. Supposedly, our species was also far more efficient because of its ability to manipulate symbols and a newly invented blade technology that lent itself to the manufacture of complex compound tools with insertable standardized parts. The problem is that almost all Châtelperronian layers seem to pre-date the Aurignacian ones associated with modern humans.

So the theory *may* be flawed. In fact, Neanderthals may have made jewelry and invented a blade technology *before* our lineage arrived. They may have been just as capable of invention, yet simply had less virulent microbes. Whereas our lineage had recently come out of the tropics' incredible microbial diversity - which the migrants carried within themselves (along with immunities acquired over millenia of epidemics), Neanderthals had developed in cold regions with much lower exposure to microbes. So our ancestors were walking biological bombs infecting Neanderthals directly & indirectly. Neanderthal bands would have become too small to compete in favorable areas. Mortality would have exceeded the birth rate and they would have gone extinct like the Taino before the onslaught of the Conquistadors. In the mean time, our lineage may actually have acquired some behaviors from Neanderthals – as well as vice versa. At the very least, the final Neanderthal flourishes – either independently, or in the face of disease and advancing intruders - proved Neanderthal adaptability once and for all.

B: 3 1/4" Gravette point for comparison. From the type-site: La Gravette, Bayac, Dordogne. Steep retouch along one edge creating a back for insertion & gluing in a slotted shaft. A true projectile point. Ca. 25,000 BP. One of the rarest Paleolithic point types. $4,900 - $6,000

AURIGNACIAN [ca. 40,000 (N. Europe) / 34,000 (SW Europe) - 28,000 B.P.] & LATER UPPER PALEOLITHIC CULTURES: Our species

70) 5 1/2" Aurignacian calibrated antler tine. Blanchard rock shelter, Dordogne. One of the oldest examples of non-functional (in the traditional sense) notation, counting or measurement. Mathematical, musical and linguistic literacy eventually took off from the breakthrough represented by this specimen. Ca. 32,000 BP. Only one this old seen in private hands. Inestimable.

71) 4" Aurignacian blade. Fully retouched edges & tip. Manzac-sur-Vern, Dordogne. A diagnostic tool for the culture along with Dufour backed bladelets & strangled blades. Hyper rare. $1,500 - $2,400. Difficult to ID without retouch – must have convincing provenance. If problematic but authentic from $200.

72) 3 1/4" atypical Gravettian point. Unlike true Gravette points, which have a steeply retouched back, both edges are retouched. Don't underestimate variability within site assemblages. Flint with cave deposits. Found in same Gravettian (Perigordian) level of Combe Capelle by Otto Hauser as supposedly hybridized Neanderthal-Cro-Magnon skeleton destroyed in Berlin during WW II bombing. $4,900 - $5,900

73) 3" Gravettian drill/point. Bayac, Dordogne. Iron ion patina. $1,200 - $1,600

74) 2 5/8" type 1 unifacial Solutrean point. Note stem. Laussel Rock Shelter, Dordogne. Same site as the Paleolithic Laussel "Venus with the Horn". Exceedingly rare as with all upper Paleolithic points; $2,800 - $3,500

75) 4 1/2" type 2, early Solutrean, unifacial point. Vienne, France. This newly identified type has also been identified from a Yonne site. Only one known in private hands. $4,500 - $6,000

76) 2 1/2" Solutrean bifacial lozenge point. Only projectile of this sort seen in private hands. See Philip Smith's Le Solutréen en France for similar specimens. Laugerie Haute shelter, Dordogne. Don't confuse with almost equally rare but thicker lozenge points from Copper Age dolmens. $7,000 - $9,000

A MISSING LINK BETWEEN EUROPE & THE AMERICAS?

77) 3 1/4" Solutrean laurel leaf point with basal grinding like on American Paleo points. This feature has never been reported before on laurel leaves – even in Smith's encyclopedic Le Solutréen en France. Basal grinding was invented independently in several places in the world, but has never been found with so many traits shared with the earliest undisputed American tool kits. Many prehistorians suspect that a small Solutrean band may have succeeded in crossing a continuous land & ice bridge from the Pyrenees area because only American Clovis and SW European Laurel Leaf points share outre-passé flaking & lens-shaped cross sections at about the same time. Except for a single fluted point, which may represent later flux *out of* America, these features are missing at the Asian end of Berengia, where points typically have diamond-shaped cross-sections. Now that Clovis points share *3 features* with European Laurel Leaves, the case for a Solutrean migration is even harder to dismiss.

The Paleolithic population of Europe would have been demographically squeezed by advancing ice towards the peninsular dead-end of SW Europe & out onto its vast exposed continental shelves. But for a short period during the coldest phase of the last Ice Age – which occurred during the Solutrean – those shelves merged with continuous floes, ice-locked islands and other shelves rich in auks, belugas, cod and seals to make a dry passage to the Americas. Such a bridge could only have been negotiated after the invention of weather-tight clothing made possible by the eyed needle: a Solutrean invention. Similarities between the Solutrean tool set and the pre-Clovis assemblage found at Cactus Hill, Dinwiddle County, Virginia lend support to the hypothesis. A genetic marker only reported among American Indians & Basques of the Pyrenees lends further support. Although a Solutrean band may have been the first to arrive, a 9,000 year old Brazilian skeleton with features reminiscent of Micronesians suggests a possible sea voyage around the Pacific rim. NE Asian populations living in 300 mile wide Berengia obviously got through too when the Yukon Corridor opened between the Alaskan and Canadian Ice Shields after the Solutrean. Then around 4,500 BP proto-Eskimos developed technologies to begin their remarkable expansion around the Arctic. Flint patinated with lime salt intrusion & hydration. Carsac, Dordogne. A missing link & reference specimen: Over $20,000. True Solutrean laurel leaves are scarce as hen's teeth in private collections, but poor specimens are seen from $800. Beware of later Clovis preforms & Saharan & Afghani Neolithic leaf points in different flints & patinas masquerading as infinitely rarer Solutrean laurel leaves!

78) 1 1/2" Crystal Solutrean laurel leaf point. Laugerie Haute, Dordogne. Utterly transparent. Much resharpened prehistorically but only crystal one seen outside a dozen in museums. $5,500 - $7,500 Fakes could become a problem.

79) A: 2 1/2" Solutrean shouldered point. Bifacial. Bayac, Dordogne. Tip missing but one of 3 finest seen since last book. $4,900 - $6,000
B: 2 7/8" Solutrean shouldered point. Bourdeilles, Dordogne. Lime & hydration patinas. All bifacial. Tip missing

but superb. May have been meant to break like Folsoms to bleed an animal. $5,000 - $7,000 Beware of fakes in colorful Bergerac flint.
C: 2 1/4" complete Solutrean shouldered point. Descartes, Indre et Loire. Fine bifacial retouch at edges. $5,500 - $7,500 **WARNING:** Fakers often use orange Grand Pressigny flint. American knappers import it to make gunflints. A French family swimming in a river recently discovered fakes with their toes. A forger had put them in the river to acquire soil sheen. Consult an expert.

FOR COMPARISON:
80) 4 1/2" long stemmed & shouldered Taino point. Dominican Republic. Pre-European contact. Although the Sandia site turned out to be a fabrication seeded with real French Solutrean shouldered points, there are genuine non-European shouldered point types. None of them are nearly as old – or probably as rare. $490 - $650

81) 4" Australian Paleo point. Basaltic rock with wind sheen & iron oxide patina. Up to 15,000 BP. $750 - $1,000

82) 3 1/2" Australian Paleo point. Both examples have flat striking platforms, but this specimen with its negative of a previous removal otherwise resembles a Levallois point. $750 - $1,000

83) A: 4 1/2" Solutrean end-scraper. Vezere valley, Dordogne. Steeply retouched sides. 19th C find. Such tools are no longer found because they came from rock shelters that are now protected for future research. $1,600 - $1,900
B: 5 1/2" un-retouched Aurignacian blade. Indisputable provenance. La Rochette, Dordogne. $450 - $600.

84) A: 3 1/4" Gravettian end-scraper & burin in one. Residual red ochre. Double blade tools became common later - during the Magdalenian. Excavated by Hauser from Combe Capelle skeleton's layer. $1,800 - $2,700
B: 3 1/8" Gravettian end-scraper with retouched convex edge. Found by Otto Hauser in same level as the Combe Capelle man. Ex Denis Peyrony collection. $900 - $1,600. Neolithic scrapers from $5 to $900 for unique specimens such as one with inverse flaking along the bottom of blade edges.

85) A & B: Both 2 1/2" Gravettian double burins. Combe Capelle – original Hauser dig. Historical & museological importance: est. $1,900 - $2,500 each. Without provenance from $200.

86) 2 1/2" rose chalcedony Gravettian burin. Combe Capelle – the only one in the assemblage made of this rare material. $4,900 - $5,900

87) 5" stemmed Magdalenian burin. An end-burin with a shouldered stem was also found at Verberie, the nearest controlled dig, suggesting a local type. Only one seen in private hands. Gisors, France. $2,900 - $4,400

88) A: 3 1/2" prehistoric Inuit harpoon. Patinated ivory.
B: 2 5/8" Inuit harpoon. Barbs on both sides. Pre-Contact. Bone with leash hole. *Not one authentic Magdalenian harpoon is known to have appeared on the market* since the last Overstreet edition, so a sampling of prehistoric Inuit specimens is shown. There have been several cases of dealers trying to sell Inuit harpoons as Paleolithic or Mesolithic specimens. Mid-range Inuit harpoons like these are found at $300 - $800 instead of over $15,000 for a fine Paleolithic specimen.
C: 4" prehistoric Inuit harpoon with engraving. Patinated ivory. The finest Old Bering Sea culture harpoons with copious engraving & flint inserts are $5,000 - $11,000

UPPER PALEOLITHIC ART - ca. 34,000 - 12,000 B.P.

89) A delicate engraving of a chamois on bone in its cave breccia. Published upon discovery before WW II but unpublished since. Magdalenian. The depiction of beings & drafting of symbols may have occurred in a scattered & tentative way before the upper Paleolithic but only took hold and became essential behaviors at the dawn of the new era. The oldest evidence for such behaviors comes from S. Africa and consists of geometrical incisions comparable to the calibrated Aurignacian antler tine shown above. No undisputed pieces of Upper Paleolithic art have appeared at auction in over 50 years. Inestimable.

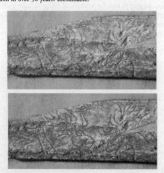

90) Two reindeer meet as a harpoon head approaches from bottom left. Placard rock shelter, France. One of the most remarkable pieces of prehistoric art seen in private hands for 3 reasons: it appears to be a narrative – something rare in the period's art. Two, the meeting deer resemble a famous polychrome scene in the Font-de-Gaume cave. And, three, it supports the hypothesis that the first "harpoons" were used on big game. This theory is based on the concentration of harpoons at sites in dry interiors as opposed to along water. Inestimable.

THE MESOLITHIC, ca. 14,000 – 11,000 B.P. Middle East / 12,000 - 8,000 B.P. (W. Europe) - *Homo sapiens*

SOME INVENTIONS: EARLIEST POTTERY VESSELS (JOMON, JAPAN - 12,000 B.P.); RESOURCE EFFICIENT MICROLITHIC TECHNOLOGIES; ARCHERY; SPREAD OF NARRATIVE ROCK-ART

91) 1 1/4" & 1" Mesolithic bladelet cores. Iran. Site flooded by a reservoir. Such tiny conical cores illustrate the finesse of the period's knappers whose masterpieces are often less than 1 cm. long. $300 - $600, if available

NEOLITHIC - ca. 11,000 - 6,000 B.P. (Middle East) / 8,000 - 5,000 B.P. (W. Europe): *Homo sapiens*

SOME INVENTIONS: AGRICULTURE, CERAMIC VESSELS, URBANISATION

SAHARAN POINTS, AXES & OTHER TOOLS:

92) A: Double-edged denticulate. Mauritania. Mesolithic to Neolithic. Although arrowheads from Niger to Mauritania have swamped the market in the last 4 years, few other tools have appeared – although they can be more interesting conceptually than another pointed arrowhead. Narrower serrated bladelets are also known from the European Magdalenian. Only one seen. $490 - $650
B: A strangled blade. Mauritania. Strangled blades are also one of the key artifacts of the European Aurignacian. $480 - $600

93) Six lunates with steeply retouched crescent backs. Made from blade segments. W. African Mesolithic to Neolithic. The same form occurs in the European Mesolithic – suggesting a link. Mauritanian lunates are extreme varieties of the Transverse razor arrowhead. Arrows have survived in the Sahara's aridity with lunate razors still in position. So, despite preconceptions, NOT all arrowheads are pointed! Ethnographic clues suggest that these were dipped in toxins and used to sever vessels of animals as large as giraffes. The prey would succumb over 2 or 3 days to bleeding & poisoning. Lunates could also be slotted along shafts or curved sickles to create segmented (& easily replaceable) cutting edges. The original, adaptable & light spare part. Usually unseen in collections. $130 - $450. If European & fine, double to triple.

94) 1" & 1 3/8" trapeze arrowheads: wide transverse razor arrowheads with slight stem. Mauritanian Sahara. The bigger one was made from a wafer-thin quartzite blade – the smaller from flint. Only a few dozen seen so far. $390 - $650

95) 7 average N. African Capsian Mesolithic to Neolithic arrowheads PLUS a serrated point from India for comparison. The *Transverse razor point* is similar to S. European ones & is terribly rare in NW Africa. The *barbed & stemmed point* is also found on both sides of the Mediterranean. But the notched base Eiffel Tower points & long tanged points are typical of NW Africa. Eiffel Tower points are never as deeply notched as Fayoum points (see Overstreet 6th Ed. pg. 38 ph. 97) from Egypt. The point in the center is one of the world's more unusual types – an Escutcheon Point described from Bir es-Sof. A bladelet has been steeply retouched to create both stem & tip. These 7 points are probably NOT contemporaries but their distribution may never be studied due to their rapid disappearance from the desert, inaccessibility to westerners and lack of funds. **NOTE:** Capsian (but not transverse) points have flooded the market since the last edition, with Africans selling them in lots of 3,000 for $1 an arrowhead. A famous Californian web site advertises average specimens for $175 - $250. Such prices will give you the pick of the litter from other dealers. Beware of dealers reselling these genuine & wonderful artifacts as Texas bird points and Columbia River gem points. For comparison: 1 1/16" Spiked Xmas tree point from India. Super rare. $500 - $700.

96) Colorful 3/4" & 1" Eiffel Tower points. Aoulef (Tidikelt) types. Capsian. NW Africa. The most colorful of several 1,000. $40 - $80. Small black Eiffels average $15 retail. Finest black ones $25 - $40.

97) 4 excellent Capsian points. All extremely long for NW Africa. **A)** 2" gray *concave base point* was the only one of its type amid 25,000; **B)** The 1 7/8" jasper *Eiffel Tower point* with 3 notches on each side was the finest Eiffel; **C)** the 1 3/4" *translucent quartz Eiffel* stood out for its size & material; Both Eiffels are Aoulef (Tidikelt) types. **D)** the 2 1/8" *stemmed & barbed point* because it was the only one converted into a drill. **NOTE:** To find Capsian points of this caliber you must be there at the right moment to buy thousands. Otherwise, $60 to $140 & the best will appreciate – the rest stagnate.

98) Moroccan points: **LARGEST:** Limace point on flake. Zagoura. Bottom slightly concave. Heavily patinated & wind gloss. $45 – $90
MEDIUM: Bulbous stemmed point. Parallel oblique flaking. Rootbeer flint. S. Morocco. Normally $15 – $30
SMALLEST: Capsian stemmed point. Usually retails for $15 but seen on web for $175 - $250. **NOTE:** The Mesolithic phase of the Capsian culture reached into Spain. But Spanish points do not appear on the market.

99) Fine green jasper points from the "Sudanese" Neolithic Tradition of the S. Sahara & Sahel. Longest is 2 1/16". Light green point is from Niger. All others from Kiffa region, Mauritania. Amazing micro-denticulation on needle point. The workmanship of the S. Sahara, especially in the Teneré Desert, is often more impressive than that of the Capsian Tradition of the NW Sahara. But because of the poverty of the countries in question, the prices at the grassroots are lower. One wholesale buyer even indicated a price of 35 cents per pound in the Sahara for annual shipments totaling 150,000 points! Talk about site depletion! Each pound contained 3 outstanding, fully serrated, rainbow flint specimens according to this source. These 3 would then be sold for $85 to $100 each to 2 top collectors. Other collectors were offered their pick at $25 a point by US dealers. Remainders would be jobbed out to dealers at lower prices. European "runners" who visit Africa have been charging $5 each for purchases of 100 good jasper points & $7 for slightly imperfect, serrated Niger points made of rainbow flint. They will sell transcendent examples for $15 - $25. Only gem-quality will tend to appreciate – despite the amazingly high premium paid by top collectors.

100) 3 above-average Burkina Faso points: Barbed & stemmed point 1 3/4": Leaf point 2": Concave base point 1 5/8". Same price situation as for Mauritanian, Malian or Nigerese points during a brief period of saturation. But the arrowheads are beautiful. Normal retail $15 - $30.

101) 2 1/2" Serrated leaf point. Niger. The best of a common form. A thousand were acquired to acquire 1 this perfect. $85 - $150

102) 2 1/2" serrated point with toothed stem & 2 3/4" spike point with toothed stem. Mali & Niger. The best of their types amid thousands. $85 - $150

103) 2 1/2" serrated V-stemmed point. Niger. Only one of its type in huge collection. $85 - $150

104) 2" serrated, long bulb-stemmed point. Stem or ears usually snapped. Mali & Niger. $70 - $130

105) A) 1 1/2" side-toothed point with a long bulbous stem. Best seen intact. B) 2" white double side-toothed point with in-curving ears. One of the 3 masterpieces from a large collection. $85 - $150 & climbing. C) 1 1/4" double side-toothed quartz point. Rarity. First described by H.J. Hugot (who found 5) in the journal Libyca. $45 - $85. All Mali & Niger.

106) A) 1 7/8" Fan-eared point. One of the few with intact barbs. $75 - $100 B) 1 7/8" Fan-eared point. One barb broken, but best overall shape & color. $80 - $100. Probably rare as Calf Creeks. The best 2 of a huge collection. ID: Long wire-thin ears, often accompanied by bulbous blade. Mali & Niger.

107) 2" double-tiered, serrated, Xmas tree point. Best of only 2 seen from 1,000s of points. The ultimate point from the Sahel. $300 – $600 & climbing fast.

108) 2 1/4" heavy-duty fishtail point. Best of 3 in huge collection. Niger. $100 - $200

109) 2" heavy-duty side-toothed point. Not delicate or elegant, but rare. Niger. $60 - $100

110) 2 1/4" concave base needle point. Niger. Most color & longest intact specimen seen for type. $85 - $180

111) 2 outstanding Egyptian points. Mesolithic to Neolithic. Extremely rare & will remain so due to Egypt's antiquities laws, minefields towards Libya, draconian licensing requirements for desert travel, extreme sand cover, etc. The 3 1/8" Leaf blade is similar in conception to Solutrean laurel leaves but the flint & patina are different. $790 - $1,000.
The flaking of the 1 5/8" stemmed & barbed point is worthy of a jeweler. Impact spall. $850 - $1,300

112) 3 7/8 Mesolithic shouldered point/knife. Fayoum basin. Egypt. One of few ever seen in private hands. Flint with extreme patination & gloss. $1,600 - $2,000

113) Two out-standing Pre-dynastic Egyptian knives:
A: 6 3/4" dagger with parallel flaking. Super thin on flint plaque. Wind gloss & mocha patina. Only 1 seen in 10 years. $5,500 - $8,000
B: 7 3/8" ceremonial, shouldered, crescent knife. Pink to beige flint. Wind gloss & soil sheen. Flat flaking on one side for close "shave". Finest seen in a decade. $6,500 - $9,000

114) 1 1/2" "Blunt" arrowhead. Polished & sculpted walrus molar. Hollowed at one end for shaft. Incisions in head to improve aerodynamics. Prehistoric Inuit. Just as transverse razor arrowheads don't have a point, Blunts don't either. They were used to stun seabirds nesting on inaccessible cliff ledges. The birds would then fall & the hunter would dispatch them. Such enigmatic vestiges show how important it is to think outside the box when interpreting artifacts. Polished molar blunts are rare. $850 - $1,500. Parabolic blunts are common $150 & up.

115) 7 3/4" flared celt. Mali. Rainbow flint. Paler patina on unphotoed side. Flared celts are rare suggesting a ceremonial use. Colorful common celts have flooded the market. A couple of Africans sell lots of 1,000 for as low as 75 cents a celt. But local prices range much higher. Exceptional pieces are culled out locally & sold in the hundreds to thousands of dollars. In the USA, common celts have been selling for as low as $5 wholesale to $250 retail. Exceptional ones like this $1,900 - $2,800.

116) 5" grooved Tenerean Desert ax. Niger. Hard greenstone. Pecked & polished. Only 5 seen on the market in so many years. This part of the Sahara was never wooded, so probably a prestige ax. Beware of unpatinated fakes. $2,900 - $4,000 Bigger & finer more; much less for crude ones.

117) 5" omphalos ax or adze. Heavy crusting & wind erosion. S. Algeria. The central hole is too small for a strong shaft. Could this have been a totemic ax head or an elaborate pectoral ax? Although the celt form is so utilitarian that it occurs around the world, there are fabulous local variants on the polished ax. UNIQUE. $8,900 - $11,000

FOR COMPARISON:
118) 3 1/2" x 3 1/4" Incan T-shaped ax. Lima region, Peru. Another example of a unique local variant on the polished ax theme. French button-poll axes are another instance but only 8 have cropped up in 10 years. This specimen $1,700 - $2,800. If poor stone from $200.

119) 5 3/4" wool carder/needle sharpener/polissoir. Burkina Faso. Neolithic to Iron Age. Used to keep yarn threads separate on their way to the loom. Usually misidentified as a bead polisher. One of only 2 seen of this caliber. $600 - $900. If rough or unsymmetrical from $60.

120) 5 1/4" grinding basin with an abstract design pecked into its domed back. The zigzag may be a snake circling a solar egg, based on more figurative examples. The Saharan Neolithic convention for the sun was a circle or oval amid concentric pecked zones that replicate solar halos caused by suspended dust. 2 hand-held grinding basins bearing this specific design are known. Fewer than 300 portable art objects are known for the culture. $16,000 or more. **WARNING:** NON-portable rock art is being extracted from cliffs in the NW Sahara with diamond saws. Poverty, lack of local appreciation, Islamic traditions against figurative art & unscrupulous dealers have abetted pillaging of immobile petroglyphs which I hope no western dealer or collector would tolerate from his own country. There is no reason to hypocritically encourage the destruction of rock art from elsewhere, regardless of mitigating circumstances. Draw the line & stop the traffic.

EUROPEAN POINTS, AXES & OTHER TOOLS:

121) 2 French Neolithic arrowheads: **A:** 1 1/2" transverse razor arrowhead. Even rarer than Saharan equivalents. Only one seen with steep inverse beveling along sides. Yvelines, France. The razor arrowhead is so unusual on a world scale that its existence on both sides of the Mediterranean attests to cultural flows during the Mesolithic & Neolithic between N. Africa & Europe. Iberian & Saharan rock art from the period is also similar. $350 - $650. If crude from $20.
B: 2" long-stemmed & barbed point. Grand Pressigny, Indre et Loire. The find of a couple of lifetimes in terms of French arrowheads. $1,400 - $2,500. Lesser ones from $80.

122) **EUROPEAN DAGGERS: A:** 6 1/2" Scandinavian semi-fishtail dagger. Natural concavity in handle. Peat patina. Many thousands are known. $2,700 - $3,500 Best specimens over $10,000. Danish fakers place forgeries in tide pools to acquire soil sheen. Beginners should go for peat patina.
B: 7" Grand Pressigny dagger. One of about 300. Pithiviers, Loiret. ID: Made from Neo-Levallois cores called Livres de Beurres (Pounds of Butter), which are almost unique to the Grand Pressigny region. A few similar cores have been found around Bergerac, Dordogne & Spiennes, Belgium. They were used to produce the longest & straightest blades known. The blades were delicately retouched & exported as far as Holland & the Alps for 500 years at the end of the Neolithic. Several were found at the Charavines lake site with wicker & wood handles. Micro-tracelogy shows they were used for harvesting, but most daggers in private collections – including this perfect specimen – were found before WW II in megalithic graves – underlining their ceremonial importance. $6,500 - $8,500

123) EUROPEAN CHISELS: A: 6 1/2" polished chisel. Extremely narrow. One per 1,000 polished axes. The finest specimen seen. Osny, Seine et Oise. $6,800 - $8,000. Most French collections don't have polished chisels. **B:** 7 3/4" knapped Danish chisel. Peat patination. Fine large specimen. Such chisels were included in many individual graves around the S. Baltic. $1,500 - $2,500.

124) Side-view of a 10" polished prestige ax showing differences in color where the ax was hafted & "rope burns" where cordage bit into the stone on either side of the ax handle! Courson, Calvados. Although a few axes have been found in their handles in peat bogs & lake sites, the author does not know of another LARGE ax blade with direct evidence not only of where the handle was placed (not at the poll, but near the middle) but also of how it was lashed. $10,000 - $13,000

125) 9" polished prestige ax with a band of lighter patina around the middle of the ax where the handle survived in peat long enough to show where it had been. Pithiviers, Loiret. Large, perfect, beautiful colors & probably unique. $13,000 - $15,000. Polished axes start from $200.

126) 6" polished pendant ax. One of 2 seen in private hands – both found in dolmens. Le Grand Dolmen, Bagneux, Maine et Loire. Superficially similar to Chinese Neolithic drilled axes which are fairly common. $6,500 - $8,500

127) 10 1/2" Ceremonial flint double pick with bi-conical pecked shaft hole. Heavily patinated. Late Neolithic. Maintenon, Eure et Loir. The only other one known to the author is in the Chartres museum. These two totemic instruments appear to have been modeled on the first copper implements imported from Eastern Europe via the Danube corridor. One of 3 imported copper ax/adzes found in France was discovered in the same area during the 19th century. Over $17,000

128) 8" Bone shaft-hole ax. Perishable material preserved in the Seine & revealed by dredging. Bardouville, Seine Maritime. Not all axes were made of stone. Very rare. $4,500 - $6,000.

129) 3 3/4" chisel in original antler handle. Neolithic. Chalain Lake, Jura. If the grip had not survived, the tiny stone blade might have been mis-identified as a "votive" ax. Amazing preservation of organic material. $4,500 - $5,800

130) 5 1/4" early Neolithic polished ax in antler sleeve. Reconstruction using an ax from Picardy & a sleeve from Chalain Lake. When the first lumberjacks hit trees with axes, they drove their blades into the handles – rapidly splitting them. That is until some genius used antler's shock absorbing plasticity to create a buffer between the ax & wood. He had to make the blade smaller but did not have to replaced the handle as often. $3,900 - $5,000

131) 5 1/8" jadeite ax in original late antler sleeve with blocking panel. From the reference site of Charavines, Isere. The only way to improve this would be to add the original handle, but none with the shaft are known in private hands. $8,500 - $10,000. Near equivalents for half.

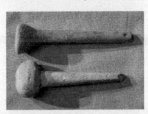

132) 4 1/2" & 4 1/4" chalcolithic (Copper Age) to Bronze Age bone pins for fastening clothing. Influenced by metal pins. Neufchatel Lake, Switzerland. Possibly as old as the Ice Man, Otzi. Only 2 seen. $3,800 - $5,000 each.

FIRST TIME EVER TOOL ID:

133) Two 3" Neolithic seeding spikes. Nezel & Montainville, Yvelines. Often mistaken for small picks. The tip is abraded smooth. Identified by other prehistorians as a knapper's tool for retouching tools, but the abrasion appears to be from repeated poking into soil, not retouching stone. Nothing comparable is found in earlier industries when just as much retouching took place. So these instruments may have been linked to the unique feature of the Neolithic: farming. I believe these spikes were set in the end of canes used to poke seed holes. Quite rare. I have only managed to acquire 5. $450 - $550 Almost identical but functionally different & common picks from $20.

134) 2 3/4" double end-notch harvesting knife. Aulnay-sur-Mauldre, Yvelines. Unifacial with fine edging. Rare tool unique to Europe. Based on several found intact in lakes, a cord was looped around the notches to make a grip. Neolithic. ca. 6,000 B.P. $850 - $1,400. **NOTES:** Exceptional

turtle carapace shape & overall knapping. Lesser examples $250 - $400.

135) 3 1/4" bifacial Neolithic harvesting knife. Vexin, France. Superficially similar to a Solutrean laurel leaf point or Chalcolithic point. But no outre-passé flaking & tips are not terminated. Most importantly, the flaking along the crescent edge is sublime, whereas the flaking along the other edge is rougher since that edge was inserted into a slotted grip. Only example seen. $2,450 - $3,000

136) 3 1/2" Neolithic double end-scraper. Fully worked edges. Two types of scrapers on same tool. Epone, Yvelines. Double end scrapers are more typical of the Magdalenian, but were made from blades, whereas this one is a reduced flake. $450 - $550. Neol. scrapers from $10.

FIRST TIME EVER TOOL ID:
137) 2 1/2" sea urchin fossil hammer-stone. Yvelines, France. Although these ball-like fossils could just as easily have been concussed all around like normal Neolithic hammer-stones, the half dozen seen only show pecking on the crown. Were they ceremonial? Were they used for knapping or crushing pigments? An unpublished sculpture of a sea urchin was found in a dolmen in the area during the 19th C. $900 - $1,700

138) 2 1/2" sea urchin fossil hammer-stone & mano. Jumeauville, Yvelines. The specimen with the most hammered crown. Sides smoothed by grinding grain. All urchin hammers come from one small area. $1,100 - $1,700

139) 5 1/2" grooved copper-mining hammer. Found in one of the earliest copper mines. Cordoub, Spain. Grooved tools are incredibly rare in Europe. Grooved American axes are sometimes sold in Europe as local specimens to unsuspecting collectors. Utterly utilitarian. 1st seen on market. $1,900 - $2,800

140) 5 1/2" decorated bronze hub ax. The arches that appear in relief derive from functional bent-over hafting flanges on an earlier type. Ax caches with dozens of undecorated axes with their bits pointing inwards to form the spokes of a once-glistening solar wheel typically have just one ax like this, set perpendicularly at the center. Dredged at Meung-sur-Loire. Only hub ax with the characteristic 4 bumps between inverted arcs seen outside a book. $11,000 - $13,000. Undecorated specimens from $700

141) 4 3/4" Neolithic bird-headed goddess. Desilicified marble. Thrace. Ca. 7,000 BP. 1st publication. $45,000 - $60,000

142) 4 1/2" Cycladic goddess. Copper or Bronze Age. A faint green deposit circles the neck & torso from a now lost miniature copper necklace. One of the most refined expressions of the female figures that first appeared in the Aurignacian. Original 1912 label on back. $50,000 - $80,000 Fragments & Anatolian violin idols much less.

NOTE: Concerning 78B in Overstreet's 7th Edition, the author has concluded that this unique specimen is probably not a harpoon, but a pendant.

HANNA
4,500 B.P., SD,
Knife River flint

MOTLEY
4,500 B.P., KY

HANNA
4,500 B.P., MX,
agate

WADE
4,500 B.P., KY

MOTLEY
4,500 B.P., OH

KINGS
4,500 B.P., MO

BAKERS CREEK
4,000 B.P., TN

ASHTABULA
4,000 B.P., OH

CASTROVILLE
4,000 B.P., TX

COAHUILA
4,000 B.P., TX

BRADLEY SPIKE
4,000 B.P., AL

COPENA
4,000 B.P., TN,
Dover chert

COPENA
4,000 B.P., TN,
jasper

DESMUKE
4,000 B.P., TX

COPENA
4,000 B.P., TN,
red jasper

LITTLE BEAR CREEK
4,000 B.P., TN

HERNANDO
4,000 B.P., FL

MEADOWOOD
4,000 B.P., KY

MERKLE
4,000 B.P., IL

RABBIT ISLAND
4,000 B.P., OR,
early form, agate

RABBIT ISLAND
4,000 B.P., WA,
agate, early form

RABBIT ISLAND
4,000 B.P., WA,
jasper

RABBIT ISLAND
4,000 B.P., OR,
agate

TURKEYTAIL
4,000 B.P., TN,
drill form

RABBIT ISLAND
4,000 B.P., OR,
agate

RABBIT ISLAND
4,000 B.P., OR,
agate

RABBIT ISLAND
4,000 B.P., OR,
agate

TABLE ROCK
4,000 B.P., MO

TURKEYTAIL
4,000 B.P., MI,
hornstone

ELKO EARED
3,500 B.P., NV,
obsidian

HENDRICKS
3,500 B.P., WA,
agate

HENDRICKS
3,500 B.P., WA,
jasper

ZELLA
4,000 B.P., TX

MALJAMAR
3,500 B.P., TX

NEFF
3,500 B.P., AZ

HENDRICKS
3,500 B.P., WA,
chalcedony

GARY
3,200 B.P., MO,
mozarkite

**SHANIKO
STEMMED**
5,000 B.P., WA,
agate

CHARCOS
3,000 B.P., TX

DURAN
3,000 B.P., TX

DURAN
3,000 B.P., TX

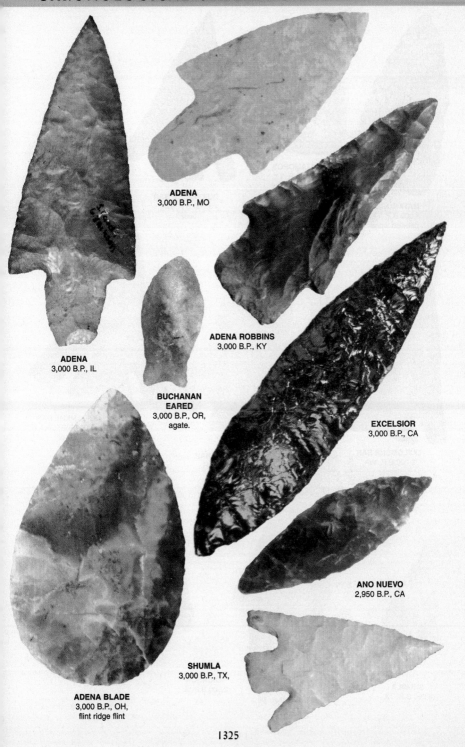

ADENA
3,000 B.P., MO

ADENA
3,000 B.P., IL

ADENA ROBBINS
3,000 B.P., KY

**BUCHANAN
EARED**
3,000 B.P., OR,
agate.

EXCELSIOR
3,000 B.P., CA

ANO NUEVO
2,950 B.P., CA

SHUMLA
3,000 B.P., TX,

ADENA BLADE
3,000 B.P., OH,
flint ridge flint

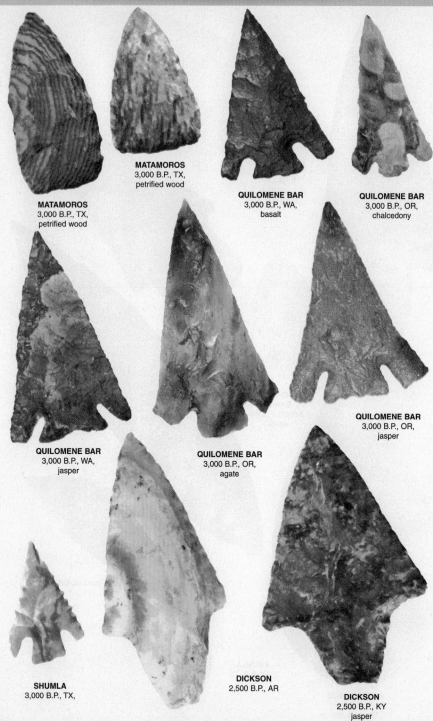

MATAMOROS
3,000 B.P., TX,
petrified wood

MATAMOROS
3,000 B.P., TX,
petrified wood

QUILOMENE BAR
3,000 B.P., WA,
basalt

QUILOMENE BAR
3,000 B.P., OR,
chalcedony

QUILOMENE BAR
3,000 B.P., WA,
jasper

QUILOMENE BAR
3,000 B.P., OR,
agate

QUILOMENE BAR
3,000 B.P., OR,
jasper

SHUMLA
3,000 B.P., TX,

DICKSON
2,500 B.P., AR

DICKSON
2,500 B.P., KY
jasper

HOPEWELL
2,500 B.P., OH,
Flintridge flint

MERRYBELL
2,500 B.P., OR,
jasper

MERRYBELL
2,500 B.P., OR

DICKSON
2,500 B.P., AR,
novaculite

SNYDERS
2,500 B.P., IL

WAUBESA
2,500 B.P., TN

WAUBESA
2,500 B.P., TN
jasper

**BLACK MESA
NARROW NECK**
2,000 B.P., AZ
basalt

**BLACK MESA
NARROW NECK**
2,000 B.P., W. TX

SNAKE RIVER
2,000 B.P., OR,
chalcedony

SNAKE RIVER
2,000 B.P., WA,
serrated edge, agate

SNAKE RIVER
2,000 B.P., WA,
basalt

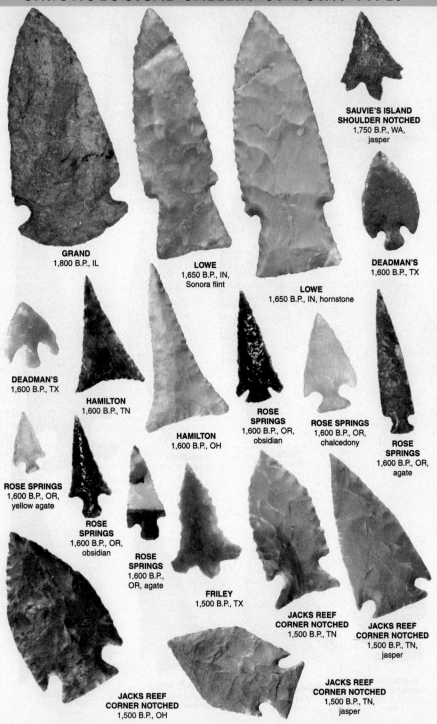

GRAND
1,800 B.P., IL

LOWE
1,650 B.P., IN,
Sonora flint

LOWE
1,650 B.P., IN, hornstone

**SAUVIE'S ISLAND
SHOULDER NOTCHED**
1,750 B.P., WA,
jasper

DEADMAN'S
1,600 B.P., TX

DEADMAN'S
1,600 B.P., TX

HAMILTON
1,600 B.P., TN

HAMILTON
1,600 B.P., OH

**ROSE
SPRINGS**
1,600 B.P., OR,
obsidian

ROSE SPRINGS
1,600 B.P., OR,
chalcedony

**ROSE
SPRINGS**
1,600 B.P., OR,
agate

ROSE SPRINGS
1,600 B.P., OR,
yellow agate

**ROSE
SPRINGS**
1,600 B.P., OR,
obsidian

**ROSE
SPRINGS**
1,600 B.P.,
OR, agate

FRILEY
1,500 B.P., TX

**JACKS REEF
CORNER NOTCHED**
1,500 B.P., TN

**JACKS REEF
CORNER NOTCHED**
1,500 B.P., TN,
jasper

**JACKS REEF
CORNER NOTCHED**
1,500 B.P., OH

**JACKS REEF
CORNER NOTCHED**
1,500 B.P., TN,
jasper

JACKS REEF PENTAGONAL
1,500 B.P., TN

JACKS REEF PENTAGONAL
1,500 B.P., TN

JACKS REEF PENTAGONAL
1,500 B.P., AL

KNIGHT ISLAND
1,500 B.P., TN

JACKS REEF CORNER NOTCHED
1,500 B.P., TN

SALADO
1,500 B.P., AZ, agate

SALADO
1,500 B.P., AZ

SALADO
1,500 B.P., AZ

SALADO
1,500 B.P., AZ

EASTGATE
1,400 B.P., OR, obsidian

KNIGHT ISLAND
1,500 B.P., KY

EASTGATE
1,400 B.P., OR, jasper

EASTGATE
1,400 B.P., OR

EASTGATE
1,400 B.P., CO, agate

EASTGATE
1,400 B.P., TX, obsidian

ONE-QUE
1,320 B.P., WA, agate

ONE-QUE
1,320 B.P., WA, agate

HOG BACK
1,300 B.P., CO, agate

LEVANNA
1,300 B.P., KY, Carter Cave flint

SCALLORN
1,300 B.P., TX

BEAR RIVER
1,300 B.P., ID

AGEE
1,200 B.P., AR,
novaculite

AGEE
1,200 B.P., AR,
novaculite

BONHAM
1,200 B.P., TX

DAGGER
1,200 B.P.,
OR

BONHAM
1,200 B.P., TX

HOHOKAM
1,200 B.P., AZ

HAYES
1,200 B.P., TX

LIVERMORE
1,200 B.P., TX

MADISON
1,100 B.P., OH

**HELL'S CANYON
BASAL NOTCHED**
1,200 B.P., OR

CAHOKIA
1,000 B.P., IL,
jasper

CAHOKIA
1,000 B.P., IL

CALAPOOYA
1,000 B.P., OR,
obsidian

CALAPOOYA
1,000 B.P., OR,
obsidian

CALAPOOYA
1,000 B.P., OR,
jasper

GUNTHER BARBED
1,000 B.P., OR,
agate

GUNTHER BARBED
1,000 B.P., OR,
agate

GUNTHER BARBED
1,000 B.P., OR,
yellow agate

GUNTHER BARBED
1,000 B.P., OR,
obsidian

**GUNTHER
TRIANGULAR**
1,000 B.P., OR,
green chert

CHRONOLOGICAL GALLERY OF POINT TYPES

PERDIZ
1,000 B.P., TX

PERDIZ
1,000 B.P., TX

STARR
1,000 B.P., TX

WALLULA
1,000 B.P., OR,
chalcedony

STEINER
1,000 B.P., TX

WALLULA
1,000 B.P., OR,
agate

WALLULA
1,000 B.P., OR,
agate

WALLULA
1,000 B.P., OR,
agate

WALLULA
1,000 B.P., OR,
agate

WALLULA
1,000 B.P., OR,
agate

WALLULA
1,000 B.P., OR,
agate

BULL CREEK
950 B.P., AZ

TALCO
800 B.P., TX

TALCO
800 B.P., TX

TALCO
800 B.P., TX

WASHITA
800 B.P., TX

TURNER
900 B.P., TX

FORT
ANCIENT
800 B.P., OH

WASHITA
800 B.P., TX

COLUMBIA MULE EAR
700 B.P., OR,
red agate

COLUMBIA MULE EAR
700 B.P., OR,
candy stripe agate

COTTONWOOD
700 B.P., OR,
red agate

CHRONOLOGICAL GALLERY OF POINT TYPES

DESERT SIERRA
700 B.P., OR, obsidian

AGUAJE
600 B.P., MX

PIQUNIN
700 B.P., OR

CARACARA
600 B.P., NM, jasper

CARACARA
600 B.P., TX, chalcedony

CARACARA
600 B.P., TX

DARDANELLE
600 B.P., OK

PLATEAU PENTAGONAL
600 B.P., WA, jasper

TOYAH
600 B.P., TX, jasper

TOYAH
600 B.P., TX, agate

TOYAH
600 B.P., TX, agate

TOYAH
600 B.P., TX

COLUMBIA PLATEAU
500 B.P., OR, agate

COLUMBIA PLATEAU
500 B.P., OR, agate

COLUMBIA PLATEAU
500 B.P., OR, agate

COLUMBIA PLATEAU
500 B.P., OR, agate

COLUMBIA PLATEAU
500 B.P., OR, agate

COLUMBIA PLATEAU
500 B.P., OR, jasper, early form

COLUMBIA PLATEAU
500 B.P., OR, agate

GARZA
500 B.P., TX

GARZA
500 B.P., TX

KLICKITAT
300 B.P., OR

KLICKITAT
300 B.P., OR

KLICKITAT
300 B.P., OR

KLICKITAT
300 B.P., OR

Index of Point Types

1333

Cotaco Preform (2,500) EC
Cotaco-Wright (2,500) EC
Cotaro (4,500) SW
Cottonbridge (6,000) GC
Cottonwood Leaf (700) GB, NP, SW
Cottonwood Triangle (700) GB, NP, SW
Cougar Mountain (11,500) GB
Covington (4,000) SC
Cowhouse Slough (10,000) GC
Cow's Skull (600) SW
Crawford Creek (8,000) EC
Cresap (3,000) EC
Crescent (11,000) GB, NP
Crescent (5,000) SW
Crescent Knife (10,200) SC
Crooked Creek (9,000) NE
Crowfield (11,000) NE
Cruciform I (6,000) SW
Cruciform II (3,000) SW
Culbreath (5,000) GC
Cumberland (12,000) EC, NC
Cumberland Barnes (11,000) NE
Cumberland Unfluted (12,000) NC
Cuney (400) SC
Cupp (1,500) EC, NC, SC
Cut Bank Jaw Notched (300) NP
Cypress Creek (5,000) EC
Cypress Creek (5,500) GC
Dagger (arrow) (1,200) GB
Dagger (large) (4,000) EC
Dallas (4,000) SC
Dalton-Breckenridge (10,000) NC, SC
Dalton Classic (10,000) EC, NC, NE, NP, SC
Dalton-Colbert (10,000) EC, SC
Dalton-Greenbrier (10,000) EC, SC
Dalton-Hemphill (10,000) EC, NC, SC
Dalton-Hempstead (10,000) SC
Dalton-Nansemond (10,000) ES
Dalton-Nuckolls (10,000) EC, NC, NE
Dalton-Sloan (10,000) NC
Damron (8,000) EC
Dardanelle (600) SC
Darl (2,500) SC
Darl Blade (2,500) SC
Darl Stemmed (8,000) SC
Datil (7,000) SW
Dawson (7,000) SC
Deadman's (1,600) SC, SW
Debert (11,000) EC, NE
Decatur (9,000) EC, ES, NC, NE
Decatur Blade (9,000) EC
Del Carmen (550) SW
Delhi (3,500) SC
Deschutes Knife (500) GB
Desert-Delta (700) GB, SW
Desert-General (700) GB, NP, SW
Desert-Redding (700) GB, SW
Desert-Sierra (700) GB, NP, SW
Desert-Stemmed (see Rose Springs)
Desmuke (4,000) SC
Dewart Stemmed (5,000) NE
Dickson (2,500) EC, ES, NC, SC
Disc (5,000) SW
Dismal Swamp (3,500) ES
Dolores (1,400) SW
Double Tip (see Elko,

Pedernales, Samantha)
Dovetail (see St. Charles)
Drill (14,000) EC, ES, GB, GC, NC, NE, NP, SC, SW
Dry Prong (1,000) SW
Drybrook Fishtail (3,500) NE
Duck River Sword (1,100) EC
Duncan (4,500) NP, SW
Duncan's Island (6,000) NE
Duran (3,000) SC
Durant's Bend (1,600) EC, GC
Durst (3,000) EC
Duval (2,000) EC, GC
Early Eared (8,000) GB
Early Leaf (8,000) GB
Early Ovoid Knife (11,000) EC
Early Side Notched (see Archaic --)
Early Stemmed (9,000) SC
Early Stemmed (see Shaniko Stemmed)
Early Stemmed Lanceolate (9,000) GB, SC
Early Triangular (9,000) SC
Eastern Stemmed Lanceolate (9,500) EC
Eastgate (1,400) GB, NP
Eastgate Split Stem (1,400) GB, SW
Ebenezer (2,000) EC
Eccentric (see Exotic)
Ecusta (8,000) EC, ES
Eden (9,500) NC, NP, SW
Edgefield Scraper (10,500) ES, GC
Edgewood (3,000) SC
Edwards (2,000) SC
Elam (4,000) SC
Elk River (8,000) EC
Elko Corner Notched (3,500) GB, SW
Elko Eared (3,500) GB, SW
Elko Snapped Base (3,500) SW
Elko Split Stem (3,500) GB
Ellis (4,000) SC
Elora (6,000) EC, GC
Embudo (7,000) SW
Emigrant (900) NP
Emigrant Springs (1,200) GB
Ensor (4,000) SC
Ensor Split Base (4,000) SC
Epps (3,500) NC, SC
Erb Basal Notched (2,000) NE
Erie Triangle (1,500) NE
Escobas (6,500) SW
Eshback (5,500) NE
Etley (4,000) EC, NC
Eva (8,000) EC
Evans (4,000) EC, NC, SC
Excelsior (3,000) GB
Exotic (5,000) EC, ES, GB, NC, SC
Fairland (3,000) EC, SC
Ferry (5,500) NC
Figueroa (3,000) SC, SW
Firstview (8,700) GB, NP, SC, SW
Fishspear (9,000) EC, ES
Flint Creek (3,500) EC
Flint River (4,000) GC
Flint River Spike (see McWhinney)
Folsom (11,000) EC, GB, NC, NP, SC, SW
Forest Notched (3,000) NE
Fort Ancient (800) EC
Fort Ancient Blade (800) EC

Fountain Creek (9,000) EC, ES
Fox Creek (2,500) ES, NE
Fox Valley (9,000) NC
Frazier (7,000) EC
Frederick (9,000) EC
Frederick (10,000) SC
Fresno (1,200) SC
Friday (4,000) SC
Friley (1,500) SC
Frio (5,000) SC, SW
Frio Transitional (3,000) SW
Frost Island (3,200) NE
Gahagan (4,000) SC
Gar Scale (1,800) SC
Garth Slough (9,000) EC, ES
Garver's Ferry (1,800) NE
Gary (3,200) NC, SC
Garza (500) SC, SW
Gatlin Side Notched (800) SW
Genesee (5,000) NE
Gibson (2,000) EC, NC, SC
Gila Butte (see Hodges Contr. Stem)
Gila River Corner Notched (1,350) SW
Gilchrist (10,000) GC
Glendo Arrow (1,500) NP
Glendo Dart (1,700) NP
Gobernadora (3,000) SW
Godar (4,500) NC, SC
Goddard (1,000) NE
Godley (2,500) SC
Gold Hill (4,500) GB
Golondrina (9,000) EC, SC
Goshen (11,500) NP, SC, SW
Gower (8,000) SC
Graham Cave (9,000) EC, NC, SC
Grand (1,800) NC, SC
Graver (14,000) EC, GB, NE, NP, SC, SW
Green River (4,500) NP, SW
Greenbrier (9,500) EC, NC
Greene (1,700) NE
Greeneville (3,000) EC, ES
Ground Slate (6,000) NE
Ground Stone (300) GB
Guadalupe (1,900) SW
Guerrero (300) SC
Guilford Round Base (6,500) ES, NE
Guilford Stemmed (6,500) ES
Guilford Straight Base (6,500) ES
Guilford Yuma (7,500) ES, NE
Guntersville (700) EC
Gunther Barbed (1,000) GB
Gunther Triangular (1,000) GB
Gypsum Cave (4,500) SW
Gypsy (2,500) ES
Hafted Knife (2,300) GB
Hale (Bascom) (4,000) SC
Halifax (6,000) EC, ES
Hamilton (1,600) EC
Hamilton (8,000) GC
Hamilton Stemmed (3,000) EC
Hanna (4,500) NP, SW
Hanna Northern (4,500) NP
Harahey (700) EC, GB, GC, NC, NP, SC
Hardaway (9,500) EC, ES, GC, NE
Hardaway Blade (9,500) ES
Hardaway Dalton (9,500) EC, ES
Hardaway Palmer (9,500) ES
Hardee Beveled (5,500) GC
Hardin (9,000) EC, ES, GC, NC, SC
Hare Bi-Face (3,000) SC

Harpeth River (9,000) EC
Harpoon (3,000) GB
Harrell (900) NC, SC
Haskell (800) NC, SC
Haskett (12,000) GB
Hatwai (5,000) GB
Haw River (11,000) EC, NE
Hawken (7,000) GB, NP
Hayes (see Turner)
Hayes (1,200) NC, SC
Heavy Duty (7,000) EC, ES, NC
Hell Gap (10,900) NC, NP, SC, SW
Hellgramite (3,000) NE
Hell's Canyon Basal Notched (1,200) GB
Hell's Canyon Corner Notched (1,200) GB
Helton (4,000) NC
Hemphill (7,000) NC, SC
Hendricks (3,500) GB
Hernando (4,000) GC
Hi-Lo (7,000) EC, NC
Hickory Ridge (7,000) NC, SC
Hidden Valley (8,000) NC, SC
High River (1,300) NP
Hillsboro (300) ES
Hillsborough (5,500) GC
Hinds (10,000) EC
Hodges Contracting Stem (1,300) SW
Hog Back (1,300) NP
Hohokam (1,200) SW
Hohokam Knife (1,200) SW
Holcomb (11,000) NE
Holland (10,000) EC, NC, NP, SC
Hollenberg Stemmed (9,500) NP
Holmes (4,000) ES
Homan (1,000) NC, SC
Hoover's Island (6,000) NE
Hopewell (2,500) NC
Hopewell Blade (2,500) NE
Horse Fly (1,500) NP
Howard (700) SC
Howard County (7,500) NC
Hoxie (8,000) SC
Huffaker (1,000) NC, NP, SC
Hughes (1,100) SC
Humboldt (7,000) SW
Humboldt Basal Notched (8,000) GB
Humboldt Constricted Base (7,000) GB, SW
Humboldt Expanded Base (see Buchanan Eared)
Humboldt Triangular (7,000) GB
Intrusive Mound (1,500) EC
Irvine (1,400) NP
Ishi (100) GB
Itcheetucknee (700) GC
Jacks Reef Corner Notched (1,500) EC, ES, NC, NE
Jacks Reef Pentagonal (1,500) EC, NE
Jackson (2,000) GC
Jakie Stemmed (8,000) SC
Jalama (6,000) GB
Jay (8,000) SW
Jeff (10,000) EC
Jetta (8,000) SC
Jim Thorpe (6,000) NE
Johnson (9,000) EC, SC
Jude (9,000) EC, ES
Kampsville (3,000) NC
Kanawha Stemmed (8,200) EC, ES, NE
Kaskaskia (see Trade Points)
Kavik (300) GB

Kay Blade (1,000) NC, SC
Kays (5,000) EC
Keithville (see San Patrice)
Kennewick (11,000) GB
Keota (800) EC, SC
Kerrville Knife (5,000) SC
Kessel (10,000) NE
Kings (4,500) NC, SC
Kinney (5,000) EC
Kirk Corner Notched
    (9,000) EC, ES, GC, NC, NE
Kirk Snapped Base (9,000) EC
Kirk Stemmed (9,000) EC, ES,
    GC, NE
Kirk Stemmed-Bifurcated
    (9,000) EC, ES
Kiski Notched (2,000) NE
Kittatiny (6,000) NE
Klickitat (300) GB
Kline (9,000) NE
Knight Island (1,500) EC, SC
Koens Crispin (4,000) NE
Kramer (3,000) NC
La Jita (7,000) SC
Lackawaxen (6,000) NE
Lafayette (4,000) GC
Lake Erie (9,000) EC, NC, NE
Lake Mohave (13,200) GB, SW
Lamoka (5,500) NE
Lancet (14,000) EC, NP, SW
Lange (6,000) SC
Langtry (5,000) SC
Langtry-Arenosa (5,000) SC
Lecroy (9,000) EC, ES, NE
Ledbetter (6,000) EC
LeFlore Blade (500) SC
Lehigh (2,500) NC
Lehigh (4,000) NE
Leighton (8,000) EC
Leon (1,500) GC
Lerma (4,000) SW
Lerma Pointed (9,000) SC
Lerma Rounded (9,000)
    EC, NC, NP, SC, SW
Levanna (1,300) EC, NE
Levy (5,000) EC
Lewis (1,400) NP
Limestone (5,000) EC
Limeton Bifurcate (9,000) EC
Lind Coullee (11,500) GB
Little Bear Creek (4,000) EC
Little River (4,500) SC
Livermore (1,200) SC
Logan Creek (7,000) NP
Lookingbill (7,000) NP, SW
Lost Lake (9,000) EC, ES, NC, NE
Lott (500) SC
Lovell (8,500) NP
Lowe (1,650) EC
Lozenge (1,000) EC
Lundy (800) NC
Lycoming Co. (6,000) NE
MacCorkle (8,000) EC, NE
Mace (1,100) EC
Madden Lake (10,700) SW
Madison (1,100) EC, ES, NC, NE
Mahaffey (10,500) NP, SC
Malaga Cove Leaf (1,500) GB
Maljamar (3,500) SW
Mallory (4,000) NP
Manker (2,500) NC
Mansion Inn Blade (3,700) NE
Manzano (5,000) SW
Maples (4,500) EC
Marcos (3,500) SC
Marianna (10,000) EC, GC
Marion (7,000) GC
Marshall (6,000) SC, SW
Martindale (8,000) SC

Martis (3,000) GB
Matamoros (3,000) SC, SW
Matanzas(4,500) EC, NC, SC
Maud (800) SC
McGillivray (4,500) GB
McIntire (6,000) EC
McKean (4,500) NP, SC
McKee Uniface (5,000) GB
McWhinney Heavy Stemmed
    (5,000) EC
Meadowood (4,000) EC, NE
Mehlville (4,000) NC
Merkle (4,000) SC, NC
Merom (4,000) EC
Merrimack Stemmed
    (6,000) NE
Merrybelle, Type I (2,500) GB
Merrybelle, Type II (2,500) GB
Merrybelle, Type III (2,500) GB
Mesa (13,700) GB
Mescal Knife (700) SW
Meserve (9,500) EC, NC, NP,
    SC, SW
Mid-Back Tang (4,000) NP, SC
Midland (10,700) NP, SC, SW
Milnesand (11,000) NP, SC, SW
Mimbre (800) SW
Mineral Springs (1,300) SC
Molalla (see Gunther)
Montell (5,000) SC
Montgomery (2,500) EC
Moran (1,200) SC
Morhiss (4,000) SC
Morrill (3,000) SC
Morris (1,200) SC
Morrow Mountain
    (7,000) EC, ES, GC, NE
Morrow Mountain Round
    (7,000) EC
Morrow Mountain Straight
    (7,000) EC, ES
Morse Knife (3,000) EC, NC
Motley (4,500) EC, NC, SC
Mount Albion (5,800) NP, SW
Mount Floyd (see Cohonina
    Stemmed)
Mountain Fork (6,000) EC
Mouse Creek (1,500) EC
Moyote (7,000) SW
Mud Creek (4,000) EC
Mulberry Creek (5,000) EC
Mule Ear (see Columbia
    Mule Ear)
Mummy Cave (1,400) NP
Muncy Bifurcate (8,500) NE
Nanton (1,400) NP
Nawthis (1,100) SW
Nebo Hill (7,500) NC
Need Stemmed Lanceolate
    (2,500) GB
Neff (3,500) SW
Neosho (400) SC
Neuberger (9,000) EC, NC
Neville (7,000) NE
New Market (3,000) EC
Newmanstown (7,000) NE
Newnan (7,000) GC
Newton Falls (7,000), EC
Nightfire (7,000) GB
Nodena (600) EC, NC, SC
Nolan (6,000) SC
Nolichucky (3,000) EC
Normanskill (4,000) NE
North (2,200) EC, NC
Northern Side Notched
    (9,000) GB
Northumberland Fluted Knife
    (12,000) NE
Notchaway (5,000) GC

Nottoway (300) GB
Nova (1,600) EC
Oauchita (3,000) GC, SC
Ocala (2,500) GC
Occaneechee Large Triangle
    (600) ES
Ohio Double Notched
    (3,000) EC
Ohio Lanceolate
    (10,500) EC, NE
O'leno (2,000) GC
Oley (2,200) NE
One-Que (1,320) GB
Orient (4,000) EC, NE
Osceola (7,000) NC
Osceola Greenbrier I
    (9,500) GC
Osceola Greenbrier II
    (9,500) GC
Otter Creek (5,000) ES, NE
Ovates (3,000) NE
Owl Cave (9,500) GB
Oxbow (5,500) NP
Paint Rock Valley (10,000) EC
Paisano (6,000) SC
Paleo Knife (10,000) GB, NC, SC
Palisades (6,000) GB
Palmer (9,000) EC, ES, NE
Palmillas (6,000) SC, SW
Pandale (6,000) SC
Pandora (4,000) SC
Panoche (1,500) GB
Papago (see Sobaipuri)
Parman (10,500) GB
Parowan (1,300) GB, SW
Parallel Lanceolate (9,500) NE
Paskapoo (1,000) NP
Patrick (5,000) EC
Patrick Henry (9,500) ES
Patuxent (4,000) NE
Pedernales (6,000) SC
Pee Dee (1,500) ES
Peisker Diamond (2,500) NC, SC
Pekisko (800) NP
Pelican (10,000) NC, SC
Pelican Lake (3,500) NP
Pelican Lake "Harder" Variety
    (3,500) NP
Pelican Lake "Keaster"
    Variety (see Samantha)
Pelona (6,000) SW
Penn's Creek (9,000) NE
Penn's Creek Bifurcate
    (9,000) NE
Pentagonal knife (6,500)
    EC, NE
Perdiz (1,000) SC
Perforator (9,000) EC, GB,
    SC, SW
Perkiomen (4,000) NE
Pickwick (6,000) EC, ES GC
Pièces Esquillées (10,000) GB
Piedmont Northern Variety
    (6,000) NE
Piedmont Southern Variety
    (see Hoover's Island) NE
Pigeon Creek (2,000) GC
Pike County (10,000) NC, SC
Pine Tree (8,000) EC
Pine Tree Charleston Variety
    (8,000) NE
Pine Tree Corner-Notched
    (8,000) EC, NC
Pinellas (800) GC
Piney Island (6,000) NE
Pinto Basin (8,000) GB, NP, SW
Pinto Basin Sloping Shoulder
    (8,000) GB
Pipe Creek (1,200) EC, NP

Piquinin (700) GB
Piscataway (2,500) NE
Pismo (see Rabbit Island)
Plains Knife (6,000) NP
Plains Side Notched
    (1,000) NP
Plains Triangular (1,000) NP
Plainview (10,000) EC, NC,
    NP, SC, SW
Plateau Pentagonal (6,000) GB
Pogo (2,000) SC
Point Of Pines Side Notched
    (850) SW
Pontchartrain Type I
    (3,400) EC, SC
Pontchartrain Type II
    (3,400) EC
Poplar Island (6,000) NE
Port Maitland (2,500) NE
Portage (5,000) GB
Potts (3,000) ES
Prairie Side Notched (1,300) NP
Priest Rapids (3,000) GB
Pryor Stemmed (8,000) GB
Pueblo Side Notched (850) SW
Putnam (5,000) GC
Quad (10,000) EC, ES, NC
Quillomene Bar (3,000) GB
Rabbit Island (4,000) GB
Raccoon Notched (1,500) NE
Raddatz (5,000) NC, SC
Ramey Knife (5,000) EC, NC
Randolph (2,000) ES, NE
Rankin (4,000) EC
Red Horn (see Buck Taylor)
Red Ochre (3,000) EC, NC
Red River Knife (9,500) SC
Redstone (13,500) EC, ES,
    GC, NC, NE
Reed (1,500) SC
Refugio (4,000) SC
Rheems Creek (4,000) EC
Rice Contracted Stem
    (see Hidden Valley) NC
Rice Lobbed (9,000) EC, NC, SC
Rice Shallow Side-Notched
    (1,600) NC, SC
Rio Grande (7,500) SC, SW
Robinson (4,000) NC
Rochester (8,000) NC
Rocker (see Sudden) SW
Rockwall (1,400) SC
Rodgers Side Hollowed
    (10,000) SC
Rogue River (see Gunther) GB
Rose Springs (1,600) GB, SW
Rose Springs Contracted
    Stem (1,600) SW
Rose Springs Corner Notched
    (1,600) GB, NP, SW
Rose Springs Knife (1,600) GB
Rose Springs Side Notched
    (1,600) GB, SW
Rose Springs Stemmed
    (1,600) GB
Ross (2,500) EC, NC
Ross County (see Clovis)
Rossi Square-Stemmed
    (4,000) GB
Round-Back Knife (8,000) SW
Round-End Knife
    (see Side Knife)
Rowan (9,500) ES
Russell Cave (9,000) EC
St. Albans (8,900) EC, ES, NE
St. Anne (9,000) NE
St. Charles (9,500) EC, NC,
    NE, SC
St. Helena (8,000) EC

St. Tammany (8,000) EC
Sabinal (1,000) SC
Sabine (4,000) SC
Sacaton (1,100) SW
Safety Harbor (800) GC
Salado (1,500) SW (also see Pueblo Side Notched)
Sallisaw (800) SC
Salmon River (8,000) GB
Salt River Indented Base (1,150) SW
Samantha Arrow (1,500) NP
Samantha Dart (2,200) NP
San Bruno (600) GB
San Gabriel (2,000) SC
San Jacinto (6,000) SC
San Jose (9,000) SW
San Patrice-Geneill Var. (10,000) SC
San Patrice-Hope Var. (10,000) SC
San Patrice-Keithville Var. (10,000) SC
San Patrice-St. Johns Var. (10,000) SC
San Pedro (2,500) SW
San Rafael (4,400) SW
San Saba (3,000) SC
Sand Mountain (1,500) EC
Sandhill Stemmed (2,200) NE
Sandia (14,000) SW
Santa Cruz (1,400) SW
Santa Fe (9,500) GC
Sarasota (3,000) GC
Sattler (1,400) NP
Sauvie's Island Shoulder Notched (4,000) GB
Savage Cave (7,000) EC, SC
Savannah River (5,000) EC, ES, GC, NE, SC
Saw (3,500) SW
Scallorn (1,300) NC, SC
Schustorm (1,200) SW
Schuykill (4,000) NE
Scottsbluff I (9,500) NC, NE, NP, SC, SW
Scottsbluff II (9,500) NC, NE, NP, SC, SW
Scraper (14,000) EC, GB, NE, NP, SC, SW
Scraper-Turtleback (10,000) SW
Searcy (7,000) EC, SC
Sedalia (5,000) EC, NC
Seminole (5,000) GC
Sequoyah (1,000) NC, SC
Shaniko Stemmed (3,500) GB
Shark's Tooth (2,000) NE
Shoals Creek (4,000) EC
Shumla (3,000) SC, SW
Side Knife (1,000) GB, NP
Sierra Stemmed (6,000) GB, SW
Silver Lake (11,000) GB, SW

Simonsen (8,500) NP
Simpson (12,000) ES, GC
Simpson-Mustache (12,000) GC
Sinner (3,000) SC
Six Mile Creek (7,500) GC
Sizer (2,300) GB
Smith (7,000) EC, NC
Smithsonia (4,000) EC
Snake Creek (4,000) EC
Snake River (2,000) GB
Snaketown (1,200) SW
Snaketown Side Notched (800) SW
Snaketown Triangular (1,050) SW
Snook Kill (4,000) NE
Snow Knife (400) GB
Snyders (2,500) EC, NC
Snyders (Mackinaw Var.) (2,500) EC, NC
Sobaipuri (500) SW
Socorro (3,000) SW
Sonota (1,000) NP
Soto (1,000) SW
South Prong Creek (5,000) GC
Southhampton (8,000) ES
Spedis I, II (10,000) GB
Spedis III (3,000) GB
Spokeshave (4,000) EC, SC
Square-end Knife (3,500) EC, GB, NC, NP, SC
Squaw Mountain (5,000) SW
Squibnocket Stemmed (4,200) NE
Squibnocket Triangle (4,200) NE
Stanfield (10,000) EC, GC
Stanly (8,000) EC, ES, NE
Stanly Narrow Stem (8,000) ES
Stark (7,000) NE
Starr (1,000) SC
Steiner (1,000) SC
Steuben (2,000) NC, SC
Steubenville (9,000) EC
Stilwell (9,000) EC, NC
Sting Ray Barb (2,500) GC
Stockton (1,200) GB
Stone Square Stem (6,000) NC
Stott (1,300) NP
Strike-a-Lite Type I (9,000) NE
Strike-a-Lite Type II (3,000) NE
Stringtown (9,500) EC, NE
Strong Barbed Auriculate (1,750) GB
Sublet Ferry (4,000) EC
Sub-Triangular (11,300) GB
Sudden Series (6,300) SW
Sumter (7,000) GC
Sun Disc (1,100) EC
Susquehanna Bifurcated (9,000) NE
Susquehanna Broad (3,700) NE

Susquehannock Triangle (1,500) NE
Suwannee (12,000) GC
Swan Lake (3,500) EC
Swatara-Long (5,000) NE
Swift Current (1,300) NP
Sykes (6,000) EC
Table Rock (4,000) EC, NC, SC
Taconic Stemmed (5,000) NE
Talahassee (9,500) GC
Talco (800) SC
Tampa (800) GC
Taunton River Bifurcate (9,000) NE
Taylor (9,000) ES
Taylor Side Notched (9,000) GC
Taylor Stemmed (2,500) GC
Tear Drop (2,000) EC
Temporal (1,000) SW
Tennessee River (9,000) EC, NC
Tennessee Saw (8,000) EC
Tennessee Sword, (see Duck River Sword)
Texcoco (6,000) SW
Thebes (10,000) EC, ES, NC, NE
Thonotosassa (8,000) GC
Three-Piece Fish Spear (2,300) GB
Tock's Island (1,700) NE
Tompkins (1,200) NP
Tortugas (6,000) EC, SC
Toyah (600) SC, SW
Trade Points (400) EC, ES, GB, NE, NP, SC, SW
Travis (5,500) SC
Triangular Knife (3,500) GB, SW
Trinity (4,000) SC
Triple T (5,500) GB, SW
Trojan (1,320) GB
Truxton (1,500) SW
Tulare Lake (12,000) GB
Tulare Lake Bi-point (8,000) GB
Tuolumne Notched (3,100) GB
Turin (8,500) NC
Turkeytail-Fulton (4,000) EC, NC
Turkeytail-Harrison (4,000) EC, NC
Turkeytail-Hebron (4,000) EC, NC
Turkeytail-Tupelo (4,750) EC
Turner (900) SC
Uinta (1,200) GB
Ulu (400) GB
Union Side Notched (11,000) GC
Uvalde (6,000) SC
Uwharrie (1,600) ES
Val Verde (5,000) SC, SW
Valina (2,500) EC
Vandenberg Contracting Stem (5,000) NW
Vendetta (1,750) GB
Ventana-Amorgosa (7,000) SW
Ventana Side Notched (5,500) SW

Vernon (2,800) NE
Vestal Notched (4,500) NE
Victoria (10,000) SC
Virginsville (5,000) NE
Vosburg (5,000) NE
Wacissa (9,000) GC
Wade (4,500) EC
Wading River (4,200) NE
Wadlow (4,000) NC
Wahmuza (9,000) GB
Waller Knife (9,000) ES, GC
Wallula Gap Rectangular Stemmed (1,000) GB
Walnut Canyon Side Notched (850) SW
Wapanucket (6,000) NE
Waratan (3,000) ES, NE
Warito (5,500) EC
Warrick (9,000) EC, NC
Wasco Knife (see Plateau Pentagonal)
Washington (3,000) EC
Washita (800) NC, NP, SC
Washita Northern (800) NP
Washita (Peno) (800)SC
Wateree (3,000) ES
Watts Cave (10,000) EC
Waubesa (2,500) EC, NC
Wayland Notched (3,700) NE
Wealth Blade (1,200) GB
Web Blade (1,500) NE
Weeden Island (2,500) GC
Wells (8,000) SC
Wendover (7,000) GB
Westo (5,000) GB
Whale (3,000) GB
Wheeler Excurvate (10,000) EC, GC, NC
Wheeler Expanded Base (10,000) EC, GC
Wheeler Recurvate (10,000) EC
Wheeler Triangular (10,000) EC
White Mountain Side Notched (600) SW
White River (6,000) SC
White Springs (8,000) EC
Wildcat Canyon (9,000) GB
Will's Cove (3,000) ES
Williams (6,000) SC
Willits Side Notched (4,000) GB
Windust (11,500) GB
Windust Knife (11,500) GB
Wintu (1,000) GB
Yadkin (2,500) EC, ES,
Yadkin Eared (2,500) ES
Yana (1,500) GB
Yarbrough (2,500) SC
Yavapai (3,300) SW
Yonkee (4,500) NP
Young (1,000) SC
Zella (4,000) SC
Zephyr (9,000) SC, SW
Zorra (6,000) SC

Bibliography

Alabama Projectile Point Types, by A. B. Hooper, Ill. Albertville, AL, 1964.
Album of Prehistoric Man, by Tom McGowen, illustrated by Rod Ruth, Rand McNally and Co., Chicago-New York-San Francisco, 1975.
American Indian Almanac, by John Upton Terrell, Thomas Y. Crowell Co., New York, N.Y., 1974.
American Indian Point Types of North Florida, South Alabama and South Georgia, by Son Anderson, 1987.
American Indian Ways of Life, by Thorne Deuel, Illinois State Museum, Springfield, IL, 1968.
Americans Before Columbus, by Elizabeth Chesley Baity. The Viking Press, New York, N.Y., 1951.
America's Beginnings-the Wild Shores, by Loften Snell, National Geographic Society, Washington, D.C., 1974.

America's Fascinating Indian Heritage, The Readers Digest Association, Inc., Pleasantville, N.Y., 1978.
Americans in Search of their Prehistoric Past, by Stuart Struever and Felicia Antonelli, Holter Anchor Press, Doubleday, New York, 1979.
The Arkansas Archeologist, Bulletin, Vol. 19, Univ. of Arkansas, Fayetteville, AR., 1978.
The Ancient Civilizations of Peru, by J. Alden Mason, Penguin Books, Ltd., Middlesex, England, 1968.
The Ancient Kingdoms of the Nile, by Walter A. Fairservis, Jr., N.A.L. Mentor Books, The North American Library, Thomas Y. Crowell Co., New York, N.Y., 1962.
Ancient Native Americans, by Jesse D. Jennings, editor, W.H. Freeman & Co., San Francisco, CA, 1978.
Antiquities of Tennessee, by Gates P. Thurston, The Robert Clarke Co., Cincinnati, OH, 1964.
An Archaeological Survey and Documentary History of the Shattuck Farm, Andover, Mass., (Catherine G. Shattuck Memorial Trust), Mass. Historical Commission, March, 1981.
Archaeology, by Dr. Francis Celoria, Bantam Books, New York, N.Y., 1974.
Archaeology-Middle America (A science program) - U.S.A., Nelson Doubleday, Inc., 1971.
The Archaeology of Essex County, by Gwenn Wells, Essex Life, summer, 1983.
Arrowheads and Projectile Points, by Lar Hothem, Collector Books, Paducah, KY, 1983.
Arrowhead Collectors Handbook, produced by John L. Sydman, Charles Dodds (author), Danville, Iowa, 1963.
Artifacts of North America (Indian and Eskimo), by Charles Miles, Bonanza Books, Crown Publ., Inc., New York, N.Y., 1968.
Beginners Guide to Archaeology, by Louis A. Brennan, Dell Publishing Co., Inc., New York, N.Y., 1973.
The Bog People (Iron-Age Man Preserved), by P.V. Glob, Faber and Faber, London, 1965.
The Book of Indians, by Holling C. Holling, Platt and Munk Co., Inc., New York, N.Y., 1935.
The Chattanooga News-Free Press, Thursday, Nov. 14, 1989, page B5, U.P.I. dateline, Los Angeles, CA article by James Ryan.
Cherokee Indian Removal from the Lower Hiwassee Valley, by Robert C. White, A Resource Intern Report, 1973.
The Cherokees, Past, and Present, by J. Ed Sharpe, Cherokee Publications, Cherokee, NC., 1970.
The Columbia Encyclopedia Edition, Clarke F. Ansley, Columbia University Press, New York, N.Y., 1938.
The Corner-Tang Flint Artifacts of Texas, University of Texas, Bulletin No. 3618, Anthropological Papers, Vol.1., No. 3618, 1936.
Cro-Magnon Man, Emergence of Man Series, by Tom Prideaux, Time-Life Books, New York, N.Y., 1973.
The Crystal Skull, by Richard Garvin, Pocket Books-Simon & Schuster, Inc., New York, N.Y. 1974.
Cypress Creek Villages, by William S. Webb and G. Haag, University of Kentucky, Lexington, KY., 1940.
Death on the Prairie, by Paul I. Wellman, Pyramid Books, Pyramid Publications, Doubleday and Co., Inc. New York, 1947.
Digging into History, by Paul S. Martin, Chicago National History Museum, Chicago, IL., 1963.
Duck River Cache, by Charles K. Peacock, published by T. B. Graham, Chattanooga, TN., 1954.
Early Man, by F. Clark Howell, Time-Life Books, New York, N.Y., 1965.
Early Man East of the Mississippi, by Olaf H. Prufer, Cleveland Museum of Natural History, Cleveland, Ohio, 1960.
Etowah Papers, by Warren K. Moorehead, Phillips Academy, Yale University Press, New Haven, CT. 1932.
Eva-An Archaic Site, by T.M.N. Lewis and Madelin Kneberg Lewis, University of Tennessee Press, Knoxville, TN., 1961.
Field Guide to Point Types of the State of Florida, by Son Anderson and Doug Puckett, 1984.
Field Guide to Point Types (The Tennessee River Basin), by Doug Puckett, Custom Productions (printer), Savannah, TN.,1987.
A Field Guide to Southeastern Point Types, by James W. Cambron, Decatur, AL.
A Field Guide to Stone Artifacts of Texas Indians, by Sue Turner and Thomas R. Hester, 1985, Texas Monthly Press.
Field Identification of Stone Artifacts of the Carolinas, by Russell Peithman and Otto Haas, The Identifacs Co., 1978.
The First American (Emergence of Man), by Robert Claiborne, Time-Life Books, New York, N.Y., 1973.
Flint Blades and Projectile Points of the North American Indian, by Lawrence N. Tully, Collector Books, Paducah, KY, 1986.
Flint Type Bulletin, by Lynn Mungen, curator, Potawatomi Museum, Angola, IN., 1958.
Flint Types of the Continental United States, by D.C. Waldorf and Valerie Waldorf, 1976.
Fluted Points in Lycoming County, Penn., by Gary L. Fogelman and Richard P. Johnston, Fogelman Publ. Co., Turbotville, Pennsylvania.
The Formative Cultures of the Carolina Piedmont, by Joffre Lanning Coe, New Series-Vol. 54, part 5, The American Philosophical Society, 1964.
Fossil Man, by Michael H. Day, Bantam Books, Grosset & Dunlap, Inc., New York, N.Y. 1971.
Frontiers in the Soil, (Archaeology of Georgia), by Roy S. Dickens and James L. McKinley, Frontiers Publ. Co., Atlanta, GA, 1979.
Geological Survey of Alabama, Walter B. Jones, Geologist, University of Alabama, 1948.
The Great Histories-The Conquest of Mexico, The Conquest of Peru, Prescott, edited by Roger Howell, Washington Square Press, Inc., New York, N.Y., 1966.
Guide to the Identification of Certain American Indian Projectile Points, by Robert E. Bell, Oklahoma Anthropological Society, Norman, OK., 1958, 1960, and 1968.
A Guide to the Identification of Florida Projectile Points, by Ripley P. Bullen, Kendall Books, 1975.
A Guide to the Identification of Virginia Projectile Points, by Wm. Jack Hranicky and Floyd Painter, Special Publ. No. 17, Archaeological Society of Virginia, 1989.
Handbook of Alabama Archaeology, by Cambron and Hulse, edited by David L. DeJarnette, Universtiy of Alabama, 1986.
A Handbook of Indian Artifacts from Southern New England, drawings by William S. Fowler, Mass. Archaeological Society.
A History of American Archaeology, by Gorgen R. Willey and J.A. Sabloff, Thomas and Hudson, Great Britain, 1974.
Hiwassee Island, by T.M.N. Lewis and Madeline Kneberg, University of Tenn. Press, Knoxville, TN. 1946.
How to Find and Identify Arrowheads and Other Indian Artifacts (Southeastern United States), by Frank Kenan Barnard, 1983.
A Hypothetical Classification of some of The Flaked Stone Projectiles, Tools and Ceremonials From the Southeastern United States, by Winston H. Baker, Williams Printing Inc., 1225 Furnace Brook Parkway, Quincy, MA, 1995.
In Search of the Maya, by Robert L. Brunhouse, Ballentine Books-Random House, Inc., New York, N.Y., 1974.
The Incredible Incas, by Loren McIntyre, National Geographic Society, Washington, D.C., 1980.
Indian Artifacts, by Virgil U. Russell & Mrs. Russell, Johnson Publ. Co., Boulder, CO., 1962.
Indian Relics and Their Story, by Hugh C. Rogers, Yoes Printing and Lithographing Co., Fort Smith, AR., 1966.
Indian Relics and Their Values, by Allen Brown, Lightner Publishing Co., Chicago, IL., 1942.
Indian Relics Price Guide, by Lynn Munger, published by Potawatomi Museum, Angola, IN., 1961.
Indiana Archaeological Society Yearbook, The Indiana Archaeological Society, 1975-1986.
Indianology, by John Baldwin, Messenger Printing Co., St. Louis, MO. 1974.
Indians and Artists In the Southeast, by Bert W. Bierer, published by the author, State Printing Co., Columbia, SC, 1979.

Indians of the Plains, by Harry L. Shapino, McGraw-Hill Book Co., Inc., New York, NY, 1963.

An Introduction to American Archaeology (Middle & North America), by Gordon R. Willey, Prentice-Hall, Inc. Englewood Cliffs, NJ, 1966.

Ishl-In Two Worlds (The Last Wild Indian in North America), by Theodora Kroeber, Univ. of Calif. Press, Berkeley & Los Angeles 1965.

Journal of Alabama Archaeology, David L. DeJarnette, editor, University of Alabama, 1967.

Man's Rise to Civilization, by Peter Faro, Avon Books, The Hearst Corp., New York, N.Y., 1966.

Massachusetts Archaeological Society, Bulletin of the, by William S. Fowler, Vol. 25, No. 1, Bronson Museum, Attleboro, Mass, Oct., 1963.

The Mighty Aztecs, by Gene S. Stuart, National Geographic Society, Washington, D.C., 1981.

The Mississippian Culture, by Robert Overstreet & Ross Bentley, Preston Printinq, Cleveland, TN, 1967.

The Missouri Archaeologist (The First Ten Years, 1935-1944), The Missouri Archaeological Society, Inc., Columbia, MO, 1975.

The Missouri Archaeologist Edition, Carl H. Chapman, University of Missouri, Columbia MO.

The Mound Builders, by Henry Clyde Shetrone, D. Appleton-Century Co., New York, N.Y., 1941.

Mysteries of the Past, by Lionel Casson, Robert Claibome, Brian Fagan and Walter Karp, American Heritage Publ., Co., Inc., New York, N.Y., 1977.

The Mysterious Maya, by George E. and Gene S. Stuart, National Geographic Society, Washington, D.C., 1983.

The Mystery of Sandia Cave, by Douglas Preston, The New Yorker, June 12, 1995.

National Geographic, National Geographic Society, Numerous issues, Washington, D.C.

The Neanderthals, The Emergence of Man Series, by George Constable, Time-Life Books, New York, N.Y., 1973.

New World Beginnings (Indian Cultures in the Americas), by Olivia Viahos, Fawcett Publ., Inc., Greenwich, CT, 1970.

North American Indian Artifacts, by Lar Hothem, Books Americana, Florence, AL, 1980.

North American Indian Arts, by Andrew Hunter Whiteford, Golden Press-Western Publ. Co. Inc., New York, N.Y., 1970.

North American Indians-Before the Coming of the Europeans, by Phillip Kopper (The Smithsonian Book), Smithsonian Books, Washington, D.C.

Notes In Anthropology, by David L. Dejarnette & Asael T. Hansen, The Florida State University, Tallahassee, FL, 1960.

Paleo Points, Illustrated Chronology of Projectile Points, by G. Bradford, published by the author, Ontario Canada,1975.

The Papago Indians of Arizona, by Ruth Underhill, Ph. D., U.S. Dept. of the Interior, Bureau of Indian Affairs, Washington, D.C.

The Plants, (Life Nature Library), by Frits W. Went, Time-Life Books, New York, N.Y, 1971.

Pocket Guide to Indian Points, Books Americana, Inc., Florence AL, 1978.

Points and Blades of the Coastal Plain, by John Powell, American Systems of the Carolinas, Inc., 1990.

Prehistoric Art, R.E. Grimm, editor, Greater St. Louis Archaeological Society, Wellington Print., St. Louis, MO, 1953.

Prehistoric Artifacts of North America, John F. Berner, editor, The Genuine Indian Relic Society, Inc., Rochester, IN, 1964.

Prehistoric Implements, by Warren K. Moorehead, Publisher, Charley G. Drake, Union City GA, 1968.

Prehistoric Implements, by Warren K. Moorehead, Publisher, Charley G. Drake, American Indian Books, Union City, GA, Amo Press, Inc., New York, NY, 1978.

Projectile Point Types In Virginia and Neighboring Areas, by Wm. Jack Hranicky and Floyd Painter, Special Publ. No. 16, Archaeological Society of Virginia, 1988.

Projectile Point Types of the American Indian, by Robert K. Moore published by Robert K. Moore, Athens AL.

A Projectile Point Typology for Pennsylvania and the Northeast, by Gary L. Fogelman, Fogelman Publ., Co., Turbotville, Pennsylvania, 1988.

Projectile Points of the Tri-Rivers Basin, (Apolachicola, Flint and Chattahoochee), by John D. Sowell & Udo Volker Nowak, Generic Press, Dothan, Alabama, 1990.

The Redskin, Genuine Indian Relic Society, Inc., published by the Society, East St. Louis, IL, 1964.

Relics of Early Man Price Guide, by Philip D. Brewer, Athens, AL, 1988.

Secrist's Simpilfied Identification Guide (Stone Relics of the American Indian), by Clarence W. Secrist, published by the author, Muscatine, Iowa.

Second Preliminary Report: The St. Albans Site, Kanawha County, West Virginia by Bettye J. Broyles. Number 3, West Virginia Geological and Economic Survey, 1971.

Selected Preforms, Points and Knives of the North American Indian, by Gregory Perino, Vol. No. 1, Idabel, OK, 1985.

Selected Preforms, Points and Knives of the North American Indian, by Gregory Perino, Vol. No. 2, Idabel, OK, 1991.

Selected Preforms, Points and Knives of the North American Indian, by Gregory Perino, Vol. No. 3, Idabel, OK, 2002.

Shoop Pennsylvania's Famous Paleo Site, Fogelman Publ., Co., Turbotville, Pennsylvania.

Solving The Riddles of Wetherill Mesa, by Douglas Osborne, Ph. D., National Geographic, Feb. 1964, Washington, D.C.

Southern Indian Studies, by The Archaelogoical Society of N.C., University of North Carolina, Chapel Hill, NC, 1949.

Stone Age Spear and Arrow Points of California and the Great Basin, by Noel D. Justice, Indiana University Press, 2002.

Stone Age Spear and Arrow Points of the Southwestern United States by Noel D. Justice, Indiana University Press, 2002.

Stone Artifacts of the Northwestern Plains, by Louis C. Steege, Northwestern Plains Publ., Co., Colorado Springs, CO.

Stone Implements of the Potomac Chesapeake Province, by J.W. Powell, 15th Annual Report, Bureau of Ethnology, Washington, DC, 1893-1894.

Story In Stone (Flint Types of Central & Southern U.S.), by Valene and D.C. Waldorf, Mound Builder Books, Branson, MO, 1987.

Sun Circles and Human Hands, Emma Lila Fundaburk & Mary Douglas Foreman, editors. Published by the editors, Paragon Press, Montgomery, AL, 1957.

Ten Years of the Tennessee Archaeologist, Selected Subjects, J.B. Graham, Publisher, Chattanooga, TN.

Tennessee Anthropologist, Vol. XIV, No. 2, Fall, 1989, U.T., Knoxville, 1989.

Tennessee Archaeologist, T. M.N. Lewis and Madeline Kneburg, University of Tennessee, Knoxville, TN.

Tennessee Anthropologist, Vol. 14, No. 2, 1989, The Quad Site Revisted, by Charles Faulkner

A Topology and Nomenclature of New York Projectile Points, by William A. Ritchie, Bulletin No. 384, New York State Museum, NY, 1971.

U.S. News and World Report (Weekly News Magazine) article by William F. Amman and Joannie M. Schrof-"Last Empires of the Americas," April 2, 1990 issue, Washington, DC.

The Vail Site (A Paleo Indian Encampment in Maine), by Dr. Richard Michael Gramly, Bulletin of the Buffalo Society of Natural Science, Vol. No. 30, Buffalo, NY, 1982.

Walk with History, Joan L. Franks, editor, Chattanooga Area Historical Assn., Chattanooga, TN, 1976.

Who's Who In Indian Relics, by H.C. Wachtel, publisher, Charley G. Drake, American Indian Books, Union City, GA, 1980.

The World Atlas of Archaeology (The English Edition of "Le Grand Atlas de Parcheologie"), executive editor- James Hughes, U.S. & Canada, G.K. Hall & Co., Boston, Mass, 1985.

World Book Encyclopedia, Field Enterprises, Inc., W.F. Quarrie and Company, Chicago, Ill.,1953.

The World of the American Indian (A volume in the Story of Man Library), National Geographic Society, Jules B. Billard-Editor, Washington, DC, 1989.

INVEST IN THE BEST.

The long-standing leader in high-quality archival supplies,
E. Gerber Supply Products understands why every one of its valued
customers is serious about this deceptively simple sentiment. Why
else would they choose its archival products – the finest
preservation and storage supply products on the market – to keep
their collectibles pristine and resistant to the ravages of age?

The answer is simple:

E. Gerber Supply Products offers serious protection for the serious collector. And its
customers only demand the best. **Shouldn't you?**

Formerly "Snugs"™

Made from 4 mil thick Mylar D®.
Dimensions are width x height plus two-7/8" flaps.

Item#	Size	Description	Price per:	50	200	1000
950R	9 1/2 x 12 1/4	Sheet Music, Large Magazines		31.25	106.00	468.00
1013R	10 x 13	Playboy Magazine (no flaps)		$34.75	$115.00	$504.00
Add Shipping & Handling*				$2.00	$7.00	$22.00

Item#	No Flaps Size	Description	Price per:	10	50	200
1114R	11 1/2 x 14 1/2	Lobby Cards & Photos		$13.50	$55.25	$190.00
1117R	11 1/2 x 17 1/2	Portfolio, Art		16.00	66.00	228.00
1218R	12 1/2 x 18 1/2	Tabloid, Art		18.00	75.50	258.00
1313R	13 x 13	Record		19.25	80.50	288.00
1418R	14 3/4 x 18 1/2	Original Art, Posters		21.50	86.50	300.00
1422R	14 3/4 x 22 3/4	Window Card Poster		28.75	115.25	408.00
1518R	15 1/2 x 18 1/2	Art, Photo, Poster		22.00	90.00	312.00
1524R	15 1/2 x 24 1/2	Newspaper, Poster		30.00	122.50	426.00
1620R	16 1/2 x 20 1/2	Photo, Original Art		27.50	114.00	396.00
1721R	17 1/2 x 21 1/2	Art, Newspaper		28.50	116.50	408.00
1824R	18 1/2 x 24 1/2	Art, Photo, Maps		36.50	150.00	522.00
2136R	21 1/2 x 36 1/2	Maps, Art, Posters		48.00	198.00	696.00
2436R	24 1/2 x 36 1/2	Newspapers, Posters		52.00	212.50	744.00
3626R	36 1/2 x 26 1/2	Maps		60.50	249.50	864.00
2819R	28 3/4 x 19 1/2	Maps, Atlas Pages		47.00	193.25	672.00
2822R	28 3/4 x 22 3/4	Half-Sheet, Poster		49.25	201.50	714.00
4331R	43 x 31	Posters, Maps		84.00	345.50	1,200.00
4836R	48 1/2 x 36 1/2	Newspapers, Maps		106.00	434.50	1,512.00
Add Shipping & Handling*				$5.00	$10.00	$35.00

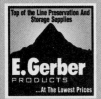

For a complete list of our affordable archival products, please call us toll-free at

1-800-79-MYLAR

from 8:00 a.m. to 5:00 p.m. EST, or mail your request to:
E. Gerber Products ● 1720 Belmont Ave. Suite C
Baltimore, MD 21244 ● Fax: 1-410-944-9363
e-mail: archival@egerber.com

OWENSBORO, KY

The Fall Show will be held in Owensboro at the Executive Inn Rivermont. This show will have over 300 booths with plenty to see, buy, sell, or trade in a 21,000 sq. ft. space!

▶ DATES
August 1st—3rd, 2003
August 6th—8th, 2004
August 5th—7th, 2005
August 4th—6th, 2006
August 3rd—5th, 2007
August 1st—3rd, 2008
July 31st—Aug. 2nd, 2009
August 6th—8th, 2010
August 5th—7th, 2011
August 3rd—5th, 2012
August 2nd—4th, 2013

*Annually on the first Saturday and Sunday in August with a **Sneak Preview** on Friday afternoon.*

▶ ADMISSION IS CHARGED
on Friday, Saturday & Sunday.

▶ LODGING RESERVATIONS
Executive Inn Rivermont
One Executive Blvd.,
Owensboro, KY 42301
1-800-626-1936
for room reservations.
Much lower rates for show attendance.

▶ CERTIFICATES OF AUTHENTICITY
Panel of experts will judge the authenticity of artifacts for a minimal cost. Certificates will be provided.

▶ TABLES
To reserve booth space or for information, contact:
KATHY POHL FINLEY
P.O. Box 93, Cannelton, IN 47520-0093
Phone 812-547-3255
Fax 812-547-2525
E-mail kpohl@psci.net

KP SHOWS, INC.
P.O. Box 93, Cannelton, IN 47520-0093 ◆ 812-547-3255
Fax 812-547-2525 ◆ E-mail kpohl@psci.net

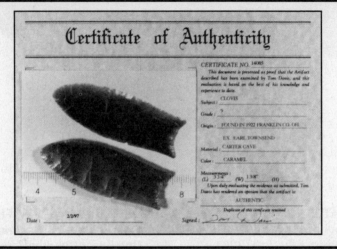